FIFTH EDITION

PHILOSOPHY OF RELIGION

An Anthology

LOUIS P. POJMAN

Late of the United States Military Academy, West Point

MICHAEL REA

University of Notre Dame

THOMSON

WADSWORTH

AUSTRALIA • BRAZIL • CANADA • MEXICO • SINGAPORE
SPAIN • UNITED KINGDOM • UNITED STATES

THOMSON
WADSWORTH

Philosophy Editor: *Worth Hawes*
Assistant Editors: *Barbara Hillaker*
Editorial Assistant: *Patrick Stockstill*
Technology Project Manager: *Julie Aguilar*
Marketing Manager: *Christina Shea*
Marketing Assistant: *Mary Anne Payumo*
Marketing Communications Manager:
  Stacey Purviance
Creative Director: *Rob Hugel*
Executive Art Director: *Maria Epes*

Print Buyer: *Nora Massuda*
Permissions Editor: *Bob Kauser*
Production Service: *Ruth Cottrell*
Text Designer: *Lisa Henry*
Copy Editor: *Ruth Cottrell*
Cover Designer: *Yvo Riezebos Design/Hatty Lee*
Cover Image: *Sunset in Desert. Bill Frymire, Masterfile*
Compositor: *International Typesetting
  and Composition*
Text and Cover Printer: *West Group*

Thomson Higher Education
10 Davis Drive
Belmont, CA 94002-3098
USA

Library of Congress Control Number: 2007923272

ISBN-13: 978-0-495-09504-0
ISBN-10: 0-495-09504-4

Dedicated to the memory of Louis A. and Helen Pojman

CONTENTS

PART TWO

The Argument from Religious Experience   93

PART THREE

The Problem of Evil   143

PART FOUR

The Attributes of God   221

IV.A   Time and Eternity   221

IV.B   God's Omniscience and Human Freedom   245

*An asterisk indicates a more challenging article.

PART EIGHT
Science, Religion, and Evolution   423

VIII.A   Ways of Relating Science and Religion   424

VIII.B   Evolution, Naturalism, and Intelligent Design   443

PART NINE
Religious Pluralism   507

PART TEN

Religion and Ethics

555

PREFACE

I AM GRATEFUL for the opportunity to be involved with this and subsequent editions of the late Louis Pojman's widely used *Philosophy of Religion* anthology. I have received a variety of helpful suggestions for improving and updating the text, and I have tried to incorporate as many of these as I could while still preserving a great deal of what was already here and has been found to work for so many different instructors and students over the nearly fifteen years in which this anthology has been in print.

The most significant changes have been in the section on science and religion. The previous edition focused in this section primarily on the creation-evolution debate and Alvin Plantinga's "evolutionary argument against naturalism." In the present edition, these issues are still discussed; but the emphasis in the section on creation and evolution has been shifted away from so-called "creation-science" toward the "Intelligent Design" movement, which has, of late, received a great deal of attention both in the scholarly literature and in the popular media. I have also added readings by Steven Jay Gould and Pope John Paul II in an effort to round out the discussion of different perspectives on the nature of the relationship between science and religion. Other important additions to the text include Robin Collins's presentation of the "fine-tuning" version of the Argument from Design in the section on arguments for the existence of God, the famous "Rebellion" chapter from Dostoevsky's *The Brothers Karamazov* in the section on the problem of evil, and Robert Adams's "A Modified Divine Command Theory of Ethical Wrongness" in the section on religion and morality.

The same format of general introductions followed by individual classic and contemporary readings has been continued, and the same topics are still treated: traditional arguments for the existence of God, the argument from religious experience, the problem of evil, the attributes of God, miracles and revelation, death and immortality, faith and reason, religion and ethics, and religious pluralism. There are also individual introductions to each reading. More than half of the general introductions and some of the individual introductions have been modified or updated, but here too I have tried to preserve as much as possible of what was already good and useful, making, for the most part, only very modest changes for the sake of clarity or accuracy. More advanced or difficult readings are still marked by an asterisk in the table of contents. These more difficult readings are intended for advanced students and graduate students.

This book has been used successfully in both undergraduate and graduate courses, and Wadsworth has two excellent single-author textbooks that may serve as an accompaniment to this anthology: William Rowe's *Philosophy of Religion: An Introduction* (2nd ed., 1992) and William Wainwright's *Philosophy of Religion* (1988). Naturally, I am also inclined to recommend my own *Introduction to the Philosophy of Religion,* co-authored with Michael Murray and published by Cambridge University Press (2008).

I am grateful to the reviewers who offered advice that led to the various changes in the present edition of the text: Craig Dunca, Ithaca College; Robert Good, Rider University; Michael Henry, St. John's University; Frederik Kaufman, Ithaca College; David McNaughton, Florida State University; Dennis Monokroussos, University of Notre Dame; Ed Mooney, Syracuse University; William Smith, Millersville University; Eric Sotnak, University of Akron; and Jay M. Van Hook, University of Central Florida. I am also grateful to Lee McCracken, my editor at Wadsworth, for helpful advice and support at each of the various stages of this project, and to Ruth Cottrell for her work in producing and copyediting the manuscript. I am especially grateful to Luke Potter, who devoted a great deal of time to helping me to assemble the manuscript and to secure permission to reprint the readings herein, and to Hugh McCann for putting me in touch with Wadsworth, for encouraging me to take on the project, and for encouraging them to work with me.

Following are Professor Pojman's own acknowledgments from the 4th edition, still relevant I assume:

> I would like to express my thanks to all the reviewers who offered me helpful advice in shaping this work: Houston Craighead, Winthrop University; Paul Draper, Florida International University; Robin Harwood, Georgia State University; Bill Lawhead, University of Mississippi; Scott MacDonald, Cornell University; and Barbara A. D. Swyhart, California University of Pennsylvania. I would also like to thank my students at West Point for helping me to discover which essays are especially helpful to college students. Special thanks should be accorded to Erik Aadland, Joshua Conary, Evan Trivette, Abraham Osborn, Michael Robillard, and David Robison.
>
> Kara Kindstrom, my editor at Wadsworth, was most helpful in providing me with advice and reviews. Peter Adams, the philosophy editor for Wadsworth, enthusiastically supported this project at every step. To Ruth Cottrell, who did a marvelous job with production and copyediting, I owe a special debt of gratitude.
>
> Most of all, thanks are due to my wife, Trudy, who, as always, assisted me in producing this book.
>
> This book was and remains dedicated to the memory of my father and mother, one an agnostic, who searched for truth and deeply pondered issues of religion, the other a devout Christian. Among my earliest childhood memories are discussions of questions about religion, a sense of wonder of the agony over the problem of evil, debates over the necessity of religion for morality. All this in the context of love and mutual respect was a patrimony that I would bequeath to those who read and reflect on the essays contained in this work.

As seems only right and natural, I have left the dedication of the volume intact. But I want to close with words of gratitude to those to whom it would be natural for me to dedicate a volume like this—to my friends Darci (Cadis) Bradbury, Megan

(Cadis) Hudzinski, Robert Timm, Tracy Peck, Kevin McClure, Mark Rodriguez, and Marc Bellaart; to my sister, Cheryl Marzano; and to my children, Aaron and Kristina Rea—all of whom in one way or another have influenced my thinking about the issues treated in this book and have inspired me to want to learn how to make those issues more accessible to others.

Michael C. Rea
University of Notre Dame
South Bend, Indiana

INTRODUCTION

RELIGION HAS PLAYED a profound role in human history. Offering a comprehensive explanation of the universe and of our place in it, religion offers us a cosmic map and shows us our place on the map. Through its sacred books, it enables us to find our way through what would otherwise be a labyrinth of chaos and confusion.

Religion helps to legitimize and entrench our social mores, rituals, and values. It offers comfort in sorrow, hope in death, courage in danger, and spiritual joy in the midst of despair. It also helps to give us a sense of dignity and self-worth. "We hold these truths to be self-evident," wrote Thomas Jefferson in the Declaration of Independence, "that all men are created equal, that they are endowed by their Creator with certain inalienable rights, that among these are life, liberty and the pursuit of happiness." The notions of equal worth and dignity were originally religious notions, derived from the idea that humans were created in the image of a benevolent Supreme Being; and these notions become problematic apart from their original religious framework.

The sacred tomes of the religions of the world—the Vedas, the Bhagavad Gita, the Bible, the Koran, the Dhammapada—are literary classics in their own right. In the Western tradition, who has not marveled at the elegance of the Creation story in Genesis 1, or the stories of Joseph's brothers selling him into slavery, Moses leading the children of Israel out of bondage in Egypt, the birth of Jesus, the Sermon on the Mount, or the parable of the good Samaritan?

Religion has inspired millions in every age: Its architecture—from the pyramids to the Parthenon, from the Hindu Juggernaut to the cathedral at Chartres—rises as a triumph of the human hope; its art—from the Muslim mosaics in Grenada to Michelangelo's Sistine Chapel—is without peer; its music—from Hindu chants through Bach's cantata and Handel's *Messiah* to thousands of hymns and spirituals—has lit the hearts in weal and in woe of people throughout history. Every time we date a letter, a check, or a contract, we pay homage to the founder of Christianity, dividing the calendar into BC and AD (anno domini).

Religion holds a power over humanity like nothing else. Saints and martyrs have been created in its crucible, reformations and revolutions have been ignited by its flame, and outcasts and criminals have been catapulted to a higher level of existence by its propulsion. Auschwitz survivor Olga Lengyel writes that almost the only people to keep their dignity in the Nazi concentration camp were people animated by faith—"priests and nuns in the camp [who] proved that they had real strength of character." Religious belief sustains people through times of tremendous suffering; it enables them to overcome life-crippling habits and addictions; and it has motivated some of the most amazing acts of artistic expression, generosity, courage, and self-sacrifice in all human history.

But religion's power and influence are no guarantee of truth. It could be that the impact of religion in human affairs shows only that humans are mythmaking and myth-craving animals. We need a Big Myth to help us make it through the darkness of existence, whether it be a religion, Nazism, Marxism, or astrology. And it could be that humanity will someday "come of age," outgrow religion and stand on its own as an autonomous adult. There is a dark side to religion, too—its bigotry, wars, and intolerance—which should give us pause in evaluating its merits.

Sigmund Freud, in *The Future of an Illusion,* said that religion is an illusion—a belief that we hold because we want it to be true, and which can be neither verified nor refuted. Little children, according to Freud, grow up thinking their parents, often their fathers, are godlike and very powerful. Children stand in reverent awe of this grandeur and look to their fathers for providential support. When they become teens, they realize that their fathers are also mortal and not especially powerful, but they still have this inclination to worship the kind of being that they revered as small children—hence, the projection on the empty skies of a father image, an all-powerful, providential, and morally authoritative object of worship.

Similarly, Karl Marx viewed religion as expressing the misplaced longings of alienated people:

> Religion...is the self-conscious and self-feeling of the man who either has not yet found himself, or else (having found himself) has lost himself once more. But man is not an abstract being....Man is the world of men, the State, society. This State, this society, produces religion, produces a perverted world consciousness, because they are a perverted world....Religion is the sigh of the oppressed creature, the feelings of a heartless world, just as it is the spirit of unspiritual conditions. It is the opium of the *people.*
>
> The people cannot be really happy until it has been deprived of illusory happiness by the abolition of religion. The demand that people should shake itself free of illusion as to its own condition is the demand that it should abandon a condition which needs illusion.*

Are Freud and Marx correct in treating religion as a simple product of wish-fulfillment? And if they are, does that show that religious belief is somehow irrational? Some say yes. Others have suggested that the sorts of longings that, according to Freud and Marx, give rise to religious belief are simply the media by which we are divinely motivated and prepared to seek and enter into a trusting relationship with God. Marxism has been criticized as a mistaken attempt to reduce all human experience to class struggle and economic conditions; and many would argue that Freudianism itself, together with Freud's thesis in *The Future of an Illusion,* is as much

---

*"Introduction to a Critique of the Hegelian Philosophy of Right," in K. Marx and F. Engles, *Collected Works,* Vol. 3 (London: Lawrence & Wishart, 1975).

an illusion as Freud claims religion to be. There is, after all, no real evidence in support of Freud's story about the origin of religious belief; and the *fear* of cosmic authority figures is as real a psychological phenomenon as the longing for cosmic father figures. In the end, however, you will have to decide for yourself the relative merits of these theories.

What is the truth about religion? Which doctrines are true? We want, if possible, to assess the evidence and arguments for and against the claims of the religions we encounter in an impartial, judicious, and open-minded manner. Careful attention to the essays in this text and to the considerations that they raise can help us with this process.

At the heart of the great theistic religions—Judaism, Christianity, and Islam—is the idea that the universe was created by an all-powerful, benevolent, and providential God. Questions connected with the existence of God may be the most important that we can ask and try to answer. If God exists, then it is of the utmost importance that we come to know that fact; and it is also important to learn as much as we can about God and God's plan. Implications follow that affect our understanding of the world and ourselves. If God exists, the world is not accidental, a product of mere chance and necessity, but a home that has been designed for rational and sentient beings, a place of personal purposefulness. We are not alone in our struggle for justice but are working together with one whose plan is to redeem the world from evil. Most importantly, if God exists then there is someone to whom we are ultimately responsive and to whom we owe our absolute devotion and worship. Other implications follow for our self-understanding, the way we ought to live our lives, and our prospects for continued life after death. On the other hand, it may be that a supreme, benevolent being does not exist. If there is no God, this too will affect our lives. We will have to look elsewhere for meaning and purpose; we will be forced to reconsider the grounds of what we take to be our moral obligations; we will enjoy or come to despair in the thought that we are entirely free from the obligation to live in devotion and submission to a cosmic authority figure. Whether there is a God or not will thus make a significant difference in the way we view the universe and in the way we live. And so it seems only rational to do everything we can to find out the truth of the matter.

Many people have lived well without believing in God. Pierre Simon Laplace, when asked about his faith, is reported to have replied, "I have no need of that hypothesis." But the testimony of humankind is against him. Millions have needed and been inspired by the idea of God—so much so that it is tempting to think that if God doesn't exist, the idea of God is one of the greatest and most important inventions to which the human mind has ever given birth. What are all the world's works of literature, art, music, drama, science, and philosophy compared to this simple concept?

To quote Anthony Kenny,

> If there is no God, then God *is* incalculably the greatest single creation of the human imagination. *No* other creation of the imagination has been so fertile of ideas, so great an inspiration to philosophy, to literature, to painting, sculpture, architecture, and drama. Set beside the idea of God, the most original inventions of the mathematicians and the most unforgettable characters in drama are minor products of the imagination: Hamlet and the square root of minus one pale into insignificance by comparison.*

**Faith and Reason* (New York: Columbia University Press, 1983), 59.

The field of philosophy of religion documents the history of humanity's quest for a supreme being. Even if God does not exist, the arguments centering on this quest are interesting in their own right for their ingenuity and subtlety. Arguably, the Judeo-Christian tradition has informed our self-understanding to such a degree that it is imperative for every person who would be well informed to come to grips with the arguments and counterarguments surrounding its claims. Hence, even if one rejects the assertions of religion, it is important to understand what is being rejected and why.

In this work, we examine the major problems in philosophy of religion: whether God exists, the significance of religious and mystical experience, the nature and coherence of the alleged attributes of God, the problem of evil, miracles, survival after death, faith and reason, the possibility that all (or many) religions point to the same truth, and the relations between religion and science and between religion and morality.

We can only hope that the passion and vitality of the debate that has lasted for more than 2,000 years will ignite your hearts and minds in coming to grips with these issues.

Traditional Arguments for the Existence of God

CAN THE EXISTENCE OF GOD be demonstrated or made probable by argument? The debate between those who believe that reason can demonstrate that God exists and those who do not has an ancient lineage, going back to Protagoras (ca. 450 BCE) and Plato (427–347 BCE). The Roman Catholic church has traditionally held that the existence of God is demonstrable by human reason. The strong statement of the First Vatican Council (1870) indicates that human reason is adequate to arrive at a state of knowledge:

> If anyone says that the one and true God, our creator and Lord, cannot be known with certainty with the natural light of human reason by means of the things that have been made: let him be anathema.

Many others, including theists of various denominations, among them Catholics, have denied that human reason is adequate to arrive at knowledge or demonstrate the existence of God.

Arguments for the existence of God divide into two main groups: a priori and a posteriori arguments. An *a priori argument* rests on premises that can be known to be true independently of experience of the world. One need only clearly conceive of the proposition in order to see that it is true. An *a posteriori argument,* on the other hand, is based on premises that can be known only by means of experience of the world (e.g., that there is a world, events have causes, and so forth). In this work we consider one a priori argument for the existence of God and two a posteriori arguments. The a priori argument is the ontological argument. The a posteriori arguments are the cosmological argument and the teleological argument.

The question before us in this part of our work is, What do the arguments for the existence of God establish? Do any of them demonstrate beyond reasonable doubt the existence of a supreme being or deity? Do any of them make it probable (given the evidence at hand) that such a being exists?

I.A THE ONTOLOGICAL ARGUMENT FOR THE EXISTENCE OF GOD

THE ONTOLOGICAL ARGUMENT for the existence of God is the most intriguing of all the arguments for theism. It is one of the most remarkable arguments ever set forth. First devised by St. Anselm (1033–1109), Archbishop of Canterbury in the eleventh century, the argument has continued to puzzle and fascinate philosophers ever since. Let the testimony of the agnostic philosopher Bertrand Russell serve as a typical example here:

> I remember the precise moment, one day in 1894, as I was walking along Trinity Lane [at Cambridge University where Russell was a student], when I saw in a flash (or thought I saw) that the ontological argument is valid. I had gone out to buy a tin of tobacco; on my way back, I suddenly threw it up in the air, and exclaimed as I caught it: "Great Scott, the ontological argument is sound!"*

The argument is important not only because it claims to be an a priori proof for the existence of God but also because it is the primary locus of such philosophical problems as whether existence is a property and whether the notion of necessary existence is intelligible. Furthermore, it has special religious significance because it is the only one of the traditional arguments that clearly concludes to the necessary properties of God, that is, his omnipotence, omniscience, omnibenevolence, and other great-making properties.

Although there are many versions of the ontological argument and many interpretations of some of these, most philosophers agree on the essential form of Anselm's version in the second chapter of his *Proslogion*. Anselm believes that God's existence is absolutely certain. Yet he desires understanding to fulfill his faith. Thus he writes: Therefore, Lord, you who grant understanding to faith, grant that, insofar as you know it is useful for me, I may understand that you exist as we believe you exist, and that you are what we believe you to be. Now we believe that you are something than which nothing greater can be thought. So can it be that no such nature exists, since 'The fool has said in his heart, "There is no God."'?

The argument that follows may be treated as a reductio ad absurdum argument. That is, it begins with a supposition (*S*: suppose that the greatest conceivable being exists in the mind alone) that is contradictory to what one desires to prove. One then goes about showing that (*S*) together with other certain or self-evident assumptions yields a contradiction, which in turn demonstrates that the contradictory of (*S*) must be true: A greatest possible being must exist in reality. You, the reader, can work out the details of the argument.

A monk named Gaunilo, a contemporary of Anselm's, sets forth the first objection to Anselm's argument. Accusing Anselm of pulling rabbits out of hats, he tells the story of a delectable lost island, one that is more excellent than all lands. Since it is better that such a perfect island exist in reality than

---

Autobiography of Bertrand Russell (New York: Little, Brown & Co., 1967).

simply in the mind alone, this Isle of the Blest must necessarily exist. Anselm's reply is that the analogy fails, for unlike the greatest possible being, the greatest possible island can be conceived as not existing. Recently, Alvin Plantinga has clarified Anselm's point. The idea is that some properties have intrinsic maximums and others do not. No matter how wonderful we make the Isle of the Blest, we can conceive of a more wonderful island. The greatness of islands is like the greatness of numbers in this respect. There is no greatest natural number, for no matter how large the number we choose, we can always conceive of one twice as large. On the other hand, the properties of God have intrinsic maximums. For example, perfect knowledge has an intrinsic maximum: For any proposition, an omniscient being knows whether it is true or false.

Our next reading is the critique by Immanuel Kant (1724–1804), who accused the proponent of the argument of defining God into existence. Kant claims that Anselm makes the mistake of treating 'exists' as a first-order predicate like 'blue' or 'great.' When we say that the castle is blue, we are adding a property (viz., blueness) to the idea of a castle, but when we say that the castle exists, we are not adding anything to the concept of a castle. We are saying only that the concept is exemplified or instantiated. In Anselm's argument 'exists' is treated as a first-order predicate, which adds something to the concept of an entity and makes it *greater*. This, according to Kant, is the fatal flaw in the argument.

There are many considerations involved in the ontological argument that are not dealt with in our readings. For a clear discussion of the wider issues involved in this argument, see William Rowe's introductory work, *Philosophy of Religion* (Chapter 3, "The Ontological Argument").

I.A.1   The Ontological Argument

ST. ANSELM

St. Anselm (1033–1109), Abbot of Bec and later Archbishop of Canterbury, is the originator of one of the most intriguing arguments ever devised by the human mind, the ontological argument for the existence of a supremely perfect being. After the short selection from Anselm's *Proslogion,* there follows a brief selection from Gaunilo's reply, *In Behalf of the Fool,* and a counterresponse by Anselm.

[ST. ANSELM'S PRESENTATION]

Therefore, Lord, you who grant understanding to faith, grant that, insofar as you know it is useful for me, I may understand that you exist as we believe you exist, and that you are what we believe you to be. Now we believe that you are something than which nothing greater can

From *Monologion and Proslogion, with the replies of Gaunilo and Anselm,* trans. with introduction and notes by Thomas Williams. (Indianapolis, IN: Hackett Publishing Company, 1996.) © 1996 by Thomas Williams. Used with permission.

be thought. So can it be that no such nature exists, since "The fool has said in his heart, 'There is no God'" (Psalm 14:1; 53:1)? But when this same fool hears me say "something than which nothing greater can be thought," he surely understands what he hears; and what he understands exists in his understanding,[1] even if he does not understand that it exists [in reality]. For it is one thing for an object to exist in the understanding and quite another to understand that the object exists [in reality]. When a painter, for example, thinks out in advance what he is going to paint, he has it in his understanding, but he does not yet understand that it exists, since he has not yet painted it. But once he has painted it, he both has it in his understanding and understands that it exists because he has now painted it. So even the fool must admit that something than which nothing greater can be thought exists at least in his understanding, since he understands this when he hears it, and whatever is understood exists in the understanding. And surely that than which a greater cannot be thought cannot exist only in the understanding. For if it exists only in the understanding, it can be thought to exist in reality as well, which is greater. So if that than which a greater cannot be thought exists only in the understanding, then that than which a greater *cannot* be thought is that than which a greater *can* be thought. But that is clearly impossible. Therefore, there is no doubt that something than which a greater cannot be thought exists both in the understanding and in reality....

This [being] exists so truly that it cannot be thought not to exist. For it is possible to think that something exists that cannot be thought not to exist, and such a being is greater than one that can be thought not to exist. Therefore, if that than which a greater cannot be thought can be thought not to exist, then that than which a greater cannot be thought is *not* that than which a greater cannot be thought; and this is a contradiction. So that than which a greater cannot be thought exists so truly that it cannot be thought not to exist.

And this is you, O Lord our God. You exist so truly, O Lord my God, that you cannot be thought not to exist. And rightly so, for if some mind could think something better than you, a creature would rise above the Creator and sit in judgment upon him, which is completely absurd. Indeed, everything that exists, except for you alone, can be thought not to exist. So you alone among all things have existence most truly, and therefore most greatly. Whatever else exists has existence less truly, and therefore less greatly. So then why did "the fool say in his heart, 'There is no God,'" when it is so evident to the rational mind that you among all beings exist most greatly? Why indeed, except because he is stupid and a fool? ...

But how has he said in his heart what he could not think? Or how could he not think what he said in his heart, since to say in one's heart is the same as to think? But if he really—or rather, *since* he really—thought this, because he said it in his heart, and did not say it in his heart, because he could not think it, there must be more than one way in which something is "said in one's heart" or "thought." In one sense of the word, to think a thing is to think the word that signifies that thing. But in another sense, it is to understand what exactly the thing is. God can be thought not to exist in the first sense, but not at all in the second sense. No one who understands what God is can think that God does not exist, although he may say these words in his heart with no signification at all, or with some peculiar signification. For God is that than which a greater cannot be thought. Whoever understands this properly, understands that this being exists in such a way that he cannot, even in thought, fail to exist. So whoever understands that God exists in this way cannot think that he does not exist.

Thanks be to you, my good Lord, thanks be to you. For what I once believed through your grace, I now understand through your illumination, so that even if I did not want to *believe* that you exist, I could not fail to *understand* that you exist....

[GAUNILO'S CRITICISM]

"For example, there are those who say that somewhere in the ocean is an island, which, because of the difficulty—or rather, impossibility—of finding what does not exist, some call 'the Lost Island'. This island (so the story goes) is more plentifully endowed than even the Isles of the Blessed with an indescribable abundance of all sorts of riches and delights. And because it has neither owner nor inhabitant, it is everywhere superior in its abundant riches to all the other lands that human beings inhabit.

"Suppose someone tells me all this. The story is easily told and involves no difficulty, and so I understand it. But if this person went on to draw a conclusion, and say, You cannot any longer doubt that this island, more excellent than all others on earth, truly exists somewhere in reality. For you do not doubt that this island exists in your understanding, and since it is more excellent to exist not merely in the understanding, but also in reality, this island must also exist in reality. For if it did not, any land that exists in reality would be greater than it. And so this more excellent thing that you have understood would not in fact be more excellent.'–If, I say, he should try to convince me by this argument that I should no longer doubt whether the island truly exists, either I would think he was joking, or I would not know whom I ought to think more foolish: myself, if I grant him his conclusion, or him, if he thinks he has established the existence of that island with any degree of certainty, without first showing that its excellence exists in my understanding as a thing that truly and undoubtedly exists and not in any way like something false or uncertain." . . .

[ST. ANSELM'S REJOINDER]

But, you say, this is just the same as if someone were to claim that it cannot be doubted that a certain island in the ocean, surpassing all other lands in its fertility (which, from the difficulty– or rather, impossibility–of finding what does not exist, is called "the Lost Island"), truly exists in reality, because someone can easily understand it when it is described to him in words. I say quite confidently that if anyone can find for me something existing either in reality or only in thought to which he can apply this inference in my argument, besides that than which a greater cannot be thought, I will find and give to him that Lost Island, never to be lost again. In fact, however, it has already become quite clear that that than which a greater cannot be thought cannot be thought not to exist, since its existence is a matter of such certain truth. For otherwise it would not exist at all.

Finally, if someone says that he thinks it does not exist, I say that when he thinks this, either he is thinking something than which a greater cannot be thought, or he is not. If he is not, then he is not thinking that it does not exist, since he is not thinking it at all. But if he is, he is surely thinking something that cannot be thought not to exist. For if it could be thought not to exist, it could be thought to have a beginning and an end, which is impossible. Therefore, someone who is thinking it, is thinking something that cannot be thought not to exist. And of course someone who is thinking this does not think that that very thing does not exist. Otherwise he would be thinking something that cannot be thought. Therefore, that than which a greater cannot be thought cannot be thought not to exist. . . .

NOTE

1. The word here translated 'understanding' is *'intellectus'*. The text would perhaps read better if I translated it as 'intellect', but this would obscure the fact that it is from the same root as the verb *'intelligere'*, 'to understand'. Some of what Anselm says makes a bit more sense if this fact is constantly borne in mind.

I.A.2   A Critique of the Ontological Argument

IMMANUEL KANT

The German Philosopher Immanuel Kant (1724–1804) in his remarkable work *Critique of Pure Reason* (1781), from which our selection is taken, set forth a highly influential critique of the ontological argument. Essentially, the objection is that "existence is not a predicate," whereas the opposite is assumed to be true in the various forms of the ontological argument. That is, when you say that Mary is my mother, you are noting some property that describes or adds to who Mary is. But when you say, "Mary, my mother, exists," you are not telling us anything new about Mary; you are simply affirming that the concepts in question are exemplified. 'Existence' is a second-order predicate or property, not to be treated as other first-order, normal predicates or properties are.

THE IMPOSSIBILITY OF AN ONTOLOGICAL PROOF OF THE EXISTENCE OF GOD

It is evident from what has been said, that the conception of an absolutely necessary being is a mere idea, the objective reality of which is far from being established by the mere fact that it is a need of reason. On the contrary, this idea serves merely to indicate a certain unattainable perfection, and rather limits the operations than, by the presentation of new objects, extends the sphere of the understanding. But a strange anomaly meets us at the very threshold; for the inference from a given existence in general to an absolutely necessary existence, seems to be correct and unavoidable, while the conditions of the *understanding* refuse to aid us in forming any conception of such a being.

Philosophers have always talked of an absolutely necessary being, and have nevertheless declined to take the trouble of conceiving whether—and how—a being of this nature is even cogitable, not to mention that its existence is actually demonstrable. A verbal definition of the conception is certainly easy enough; it is

something, the non-existence of which is impossible. But does this definition throw any light upon the conditions which render it impossible to cogitate the non-existence of a thing—conditions which we wish to ascertain, that we may discover whether we think anything in the conception of such a being or not? For the mere fact that I throw away, by means of the word *Unconditioned*, all the conditions which the understanding habitually requires in order to regard anything as necessary, is very far from making clear whether by means of the conception of the unconditionally necessary I think of something, or really of nothing at all.

Nay, more, this chance-conception, now become so current, many have endeavored to explain by examples, which seemed to render any inquiries regarding its intelligibility quite needless. Every geometrical proposition—a triangle has three angles—it was said, is absolutely necessary; and thus people talked of an object which lay out of the sphere of our understanding as if it were perfectly plain what the conception of such a being meant.

All the examples adduced have been drawn, without exception, from *judgments*, and not

From Kant's *Critique of Pure Reason*, translated by J. M. D. Meiklejohn (New York: Colonial Press, 1900). Translation revised by Louis Pojman.

from *things*. But the unconditioned necessity of a judgment does not form the absolute necessity of a thing. On the contrary, the absolute necessity of a judgment is only a conditioned necessity of a thing, or of the predicate in a judgment. The proposition above-mentioned, does not enounce that three angles necessarily exist, but, upon condition that a triangle exists, three angles must necessarily exist—in it. And thus this logical necessity has been the source of the greatest delusions. Having formed an *à priori* conception of a thing, the content of which was made to embrace existence, we believed ourselves safe in concluding that, because existence belongs necessarily to the object of the conception (that is, under the condition of my positing this thing as given), the existence of the thing is also posited necessarily, and that it is therefore absolutely necessary—merely because its existence has been cogitated in the conception.

If, in an identical judgment, I annihilate the predicate in thought, and retain the subject, a contradiction is the result; and hence I say, the former belongs necessarily to the latter. But if I suppress both subject and predicate in thought, no contradiction arises; for there *is nothing* at all, and therefore no means of forming a contradiction. To suppose the existence of a triangle and not that of its three angles, is self-contradictory; but to suppose the non-existence of both triangle and angles is perfectly admissible. And so is it with the conception of an absolutely necessary being. Annihilate its existence in thought, and you annihilate the thing itself with all its predicates; how then can there be any room for contradiction? Externally, there is nothing to give rise to a contradiction, for a thing cannot be necessary externally; nor internally, for, by the annihilation or suppression of the thing itself, its internal properties are also annihilated. God is omnipotent—that is a necessary judgment. His omnipotence cannot be denied, if the existence of a Deity is posited—the existence, that is, of an infinite being, the two conceptions being identical. But when you say, *God does not exist,* neither omnipotence nor any other predicate is affirmed; they must all disappear with the subject, and in this judgment there cannot exist the least self-contradiction.

You have thus seen, that when the predicate of a judgment is annihilated in thought along with the subject, no internal contradiction can arise, be the predicate what it may. There is no possibility of evading the conclusion—you find yourselves compelled to declare: There are certain subjects which cannot be annihilated in thought. But this is nothing more than saying: There exist subjects which are absolutely necessary—the very hypothesis which you are called upon to establish. For I find myself unable to form the slightest conception of a thing which, when annihilated in thought with all its predicates, leaves behind a contradiction; and contradiction is the only criterion of impossibility, in the sphere of pure *à priori* conceptions.

Against these general considerations, the justice of which no one can dispute, one argument is adduced, which is regarded as furnishing a satisfactory demonstration from the fact. It is affirmed, that there is one and only one conception, in which the non-being or annihilation of the object is self-contradictory, and this is the conception of an *ens realissimum*.* It possesses, you say, all reality, and you feel yourselves justified in admitting the possibility of such a thing. (This I am willing to grant for the present, although the existence of a conception which is not self-contradictory, is far from being sufficient to prove the possibility of an object.[1]) Now the notion of all reality embraces in it that of existence; the notion of existence lies, therefore, in the conception of this possible thing. If this thing is annihilated in thought, the internal possibility of the thing is also annihilated, which is self-contradictory.

I answer: It is absurd to introduce—under whatever term disguised—into the conception of a thing, which is to be cogitated solely in reference to its possibility, the conception of its existence. If this is admitted, you will have apparently gained the day, but in reality have enounced nothing but a mere tautology. I ask, is the proposition, *this or that thing* (which I am admitting to be possible) exists, an analytical or a synthetical proposition? If the former, there is no addition made to the subject

---

*Latin: "most real being."

of your thought by the affirmation of its existence; but then the conception in your minds is identical with the thing itself, or you have supposed the existence of a thing to be possible, and then inferred its existence from its internal possibility—which is but a miserable tautology. The word *reality* in the conception of the thing, and the word *existence* in the conception of the predicate, will not help you out of the difficulty. For, supposing you were to term all positing of a thing, reality, you have thereby posited the thing with all its predicates in the conception of the subject and assumed its actual existence, and this you merely repeat in the predicate. But if you confess, as every reasonable person must, that every existential proposition is synthetical, how can it be maintained that the predicate of existence cannot be denied without contradiction—a property which is the characteristic of analytical propositions, alone.

I should have a reasonable hope of putting an end forever to this sophistical mode of argumentation, by a strict definition of the conception of existence, did not my own experience teach me that the illusion arising from our confounding a logical with a real predicate (a predicate which aids in the determination of a thing) resists almost all the endeavors of explanation and illustration. *A logical predicate* may be what you please, even the subject may be predicated of itself; for logic pays no regard to the content of a judgment. But the determination of a conception is a predicate, which adds to and enlarges the conception. It must not, therefore, be contained in the conception.

Being is evidently not a real predicate, that is, a conception of something which is added to the conception of some other thing. It is merely the positing of a thing, or of certain determinations in it. Logically, it is merely the copula of a judgment. The proposition, *God is omnipotent,* contains two conceptions, which have a certain object or content; the word *is*, is no additional predicate—it merely indicates the relation of the predicate to the subject. Now, if I take the subject (God) with all its predicates (omnipotence being one), and say, *God is,* or *There is a God,* I add no new predicate to the conception of God, I merely posit or affirm the existence of the subject with all its predicates—

I posit the *object* in relation to my *conception.* The content of both is the same; and there is no addition made to the conception, which expresses merely the possibility of the object, by my cogitating the object—in the expression, it *is*—as absolutely given or existing. Thus the real contains no more than the possible. A hundred real dollars contain no more than a hundred possible dollars. For, as the latter indicate the conception, and the former the object, on the supposition that the content of the former was greater than that of the latter, my conception would not be an expression of the whole object, and would consequently be an inadequate conception of it. But in reckoning my wealth there may be said to be more in a hundred real dollars, than in a hundred possible dollars—that is, in the mere conception of them. For the real object—the dollars—is not analytically contained in my conception, but forms a synthetical addition to my conception (which is merely a determination of my mental state), although this objective reality—this existence—apart from my conception, does not in the least degree increase the aforesaid hundred dollars.

It does not matter which predicates or how many of them we may think a thing possesses, I do not make the least addition to it when we further declare that this thing exists. Otherwise, it would not be the exact same thing that exists, but something more than we had thought in the idea or concept; and hence, we could not say that the exact object of my thought exists. On the contrary, it exists with the same defect with which I have thought it, since otherwise what exists would be something different from what I thought. So when I think of a being as the highest reality, without any imperfection, the question still remains whether or not this being exists. For although, in my idea, nothing may be lacking in the possible real content of a thing in general, something is still lacking in its relation to my mental state; that is, I am ignorant of whether the object is also possible *à posteriori.* It is here we discover the core of our problem. If the question regarded an object of sense merely, it would be impossible for me to confuse the idea of a thing with its existence. For the concept of the object merely enables me to think of it according to universal conditions of experience; while the existence of the object permits me to think of it within the context of actual experience. However, in being connected with the content of experience as a whole, the concept of the object is not enlarged. All that has happened is that our thought has thereby acquired another possible perception. So it is not surprising that, if we attempt to think existence through the pure categories alone, we cannot specify a single mark distinguishing it from mere possibility.

Whatever be the content of our conception of an object, it is necessary to go beyond it, if we wish to predicate existence of an object. In the case of sensuous objects, this is attained by their connection according to empirical laws with some one of my perceptions; but when it comes to objects of pure thought, there is no means whatever of knowing of their existence, since it would have to be known in a completely *à priori* manner. But all our knowledge of existence (be it immediately by perception or by inferences connecting some object with a perception) belongs entirely to the sphere of experience—which is in perfect unity with itself—and although an existence out of this sphere cannot be absolutely declared to be impossible, it is a hypothesis the truth of which we have no means of discovering.

The idea of a supreme being is in many ways a very useful idea; but for the very reason that it is an idea, it is incapable of enlarging our knowledge with regard to the existence of things. It is not even sufficient to instruct us as to the possibility of a being which we do not know to exist. The analytical criterion of possibility, which consists in the absence of contradiction in propositions, cannot be denied it. But the connection of real properties in a thing is a synthesis of the possibility of which an *à priori* judgment cannot be formed, because these realities are not presented to us specifically; and even if this were to happen, a judgment would still be impossible, because the criterion of possibility of synthetical cognitions must be sought for in the world of experience, to which the object of an idea cannot belong. And thus the celebrated Leibniz has utterly failed in his attempt to establish upon *à priori* grounds the possibility of this sublime ideal being.

The celebrated ontological or Cartesian argument for the existence of a Supreme Being is therefore insufficient; and we may as well hope to increase our stock of knowledge by the aid of mere ideas, as the merchant to increase his wealth by adding a few zeros to his bank account.

NOTE

1. A conception is always possible, if it is not self-contradictory. This is the logical criterion of possibility, distinguishing the object of such a conception from *the nihil negativum*. But it may be, notwithstanding, an empty conception, unless the objective reality of this synthesis, by which it is generated, is demonstrated; and a proof of this kind must be based upon principles of possible experience, and not upon the principle of analysis or contradiction. This remark may be serviceable as a warning against concluding, from the possibility of a conception—which is logical, the possibility of a thing—which is real.

I.B THE COSMOLOGICAL ARGUMENT FOR THE EXISTENCE OF GOD

ASKING PEOPLE WHY THEY BELIEVE in God is likely to evoke something like the following response. "Well, things didn't just pop up out of nothing. Someone, a pretty powerful Someone, had to cause the universe to come into existence. You just can't have causes going back forever. God must have made the world. Nothing else makes sense."

All versions of the cosmological argument begin with the a posteriori assumptions that the universe exists and that something outside the universe is required to explain its existence. That is, it is *contingent*, depending on something outside of itself for its existence. That "something else" is logically prior to the birth of the universe. It constitutes the reason for the existence of the universe. Such a being is God.

One version of the cosmological argument is called the "first-cause argument." From the fact that some things are caused, we may reason to the existence of a first cause. The Catholic monk St. Thomas Aquinas (1225–1274) gives a version of this argument in our first reading. His "second way" is based on the idea of causation:

> We find that among sensible things there is an ordering of efficient causes, and yet we do not find—nor is it possible to find—anything that is an efficient cause of its own self. For if something were an efficient cause of itself, then it would be prior to itself—which is impossible.
>
> But it is impossible to go on to infinity among efficient causes. For in every case of ordered efficient causes, the first is a cause of the intermediate and the intermediate is a cause of the last—and this regardless of whether the intermediate is constituted by many causes or by just one. But when a cause is removed, its effect is removed. Therefore, if there were no first among the efficient causes, then neither would there be a last or an intermediate. But if the efficient causes went on to infinity, there would not be a first efficient cause, and so there would not be a last effect or any intermediate efficient causes, either—which is obviously false. Therefore, one must posit some first efficient cause—which everyone calls God.

The general outline, focusing on the second argument, goes something like this:

1. There exist things that are caused.
2. Nothing can be the cause of itself.
3. There cannot be an infinite regress of causes.
4. Therefore, there exists an uncaused first cause.
5. If there is an uncaused first cause, then the uncaused first cause is God.
6. Therefore, God exists.

What can we say of this argument? Certainly the first premise is true—some things have causes. Indeed, we generally believe that every event has a cause that explains why the event happened. The second premise seems correct, for how could something that didn't exist cause anything, let alone its own existence? Note that premise 2 and premise 4 do not contradict one another. There is nothing obviously incoherent about the idea that something or someone existed from eternity and so is uncaused, whereas there is something incoherent about the idea that something nonexistent caused itself to come into being.

One difficulty with the argument is premise 3: There cannot be an infinite regress of causes. Why can't there be such a regress? You might object that there is an infinite regress of numbers, so why can't there be an infinite regress of causes?

One response to this objection is that there is a significant difference between numbers and events and persons. Numbers are just abstract entities, whereas events and persons are concrete, temporal entities, the sorts of things that need to be brought into existence. Numbers exist in all possible worlds. They are eternal, but Napoleon, Mt. Everest, and you are not eternal but need a causal explanation. The child asks, "Mommy, who made me?" and the mother responds, "You came from my womb." The child persists, "Mommy, who made you and your womb?" The mother responds that she came from a fertilized egg in her mother's womb, but the child persists in the query until the mother is forced to admit that she doesn't know the answer or perhaps says, "God made the world and all that is in it." God may be one explanatory hypothesis, answering the question why the world came to be, but the question is, Are there other, equally good explanatory hypotheses? In other words, does the argument from first cause, *even if it is valid,* give us reason to think that *God* is the first cause?

In our second reading, the eighteenth-century philosopher Samuel Clarke sets forth a different version of the cosmological argument, the argument from contingency (Aquinas's third way). Clarke, like Aquinas before him, identifies the independent and necessary being with God. We are dependent, or contingent, beings. Reducing the argument to the bare bones, the argument from contingency is this:

1. Every being that exists is either contingent or necessary.
2. Not every being can be contingent.
3. Therefore, there exists a necessary being upon which the contingent beings depend.
4. A necessary being on which all contingent beings exist is what we mean by *God*.
5. Therefore, God exists.

A necessary being is self-existing, independent, and has the explanation of its existence in itself, whereas contingent beings do not have the reason for their existence in themselves but depend on other beings and, ultimately, depend on a necessary being.

In our third reading, Paul Edwards separates the two versions of the cosmological argument. He argues that the first version commits the fallacy of composition, that of erroneously attributing properties of individuals to the groups they constitute (e.g., each person in the group has a mind, but the group doesn't have a mind), and the second version fails to recognize that the universe may be a brute fact.

Next, William Rowe examines the cosmological argument and especially versions like the argument from contingency based on the *principle of sufficient reason* (PSR)—the thesis that everything must have an explanation to account for it. He points out problems connected with this principle.

In our fifth reading, William Lane Craig and J. P. Moreland defend the *kalām* cosmological argument, an argument first set forth by Arab Islamic scholars, al-Kindi and al-Ghazali, in the Middle Ages.

In our final reading, Paul Draper analyzes the *kalām* argument and claims that, enticing as this argument is, it rests on an equivocation of the idea of "beginning to exist," which undermines its soundness.

I.B.1   The Five Ways

THOMAS AQUINAS

The Dominican monk Thomas Aquinas (1225–1274) is considered by many to be the greatest theologian in Western religion. The five ways of showing the existence of God given in this selection are versions of the cosmological argument. The first way concerns the fact that there is change (or motion) and argues that there must be an Unmoved Mover that originates all change but itself is not moved. The second way is from the idea of causation and argues that there must be a first, uncaused cause to explain the existence of all other causes. The third way is from the idea of contingency. It argues that because there are dependent beings (e.g., humans), there must be an independent or necessary being on whom the dependent beings rely for their subsistence. The fourth way is from excellence, and it argues that because there are degrees of excellence, there must be a perfect being from whence all excellences come. The final way is from the harmony of things. There is a harmony of nature, which calls for an explanation. The only sufficient explanation is that there is a divine designer who planned this harmony.

ARTICLE 3: DOES GOD EXIST?

It seems that God does not exist:

Objection 1: If one of a pair of contraries were infinite, it would totally destroy the other contrary. But by the name 'God' one means a certain infinite good. Therefore, if God existed, there would be nothing evil. But there is evil in the world. Therefore, God does not exist.

Objection 2: What can be accomplished with fewer principles is not done through more principles. But it seems that everything that happens in the world could have been accomplished through other principles, even if God did not exist; for things that are natural are traced back to nature as a principle, whereas things that are purposeful are traced back to human reason or will as a principle. Therefore, there is no need to claim that God exists.

But contrary to this: Exodus 1:14 says under the personage of God, "I am Who am."

I respond: There are five ways to prove that God exists.

The *first* and clearest way is that taken from motion:

It is certain, and obvious to the senses, that in this world some things are moved.

But everything that is moved is moved by another. For nothing is moved except insofar as it is in potentiality with respect to that actuality toward which it is moved, whereas something effects motion insofar as it is in actuality in a relevant respect. After all, to effect motion is just to lead something from potentiality into actuality. But a thing cannot be led from potentiality into actuality except through some being that is in actuality in a relevant respect; for example, something that is hot in actuality—say, a fire—makes a piece of wood, which is hot in potentiality, to be hot in actuality, and it thereby moves and alters the piece of wood. But it is impossible for something to be simultaneously in potentiality and in actuality with respect to same thing; rather, it can be in potentiality and in actuality only with respect to different things. For what is hot in actuality cannot simultaneously be hot in potentiality; rather, it is cold in potentiality. Therefore, it is impossible that something should be both mover and moved in the same way and with respect to the

Printed with the permission of the translator, Alfred J. Freddoso. This translation is being published by Saint Augustine's Press.

same thing, or, in other words, that something should move itself. Therefore, everything that is moved must be moved by another.

If, then, that by which something is moved is itself moved, then it, too, must be moved by another, and that other by still another. But this does not go on to infinity. For if it did, then there would not be any first mover and, as a result, none of the others would effect motion, either. For secondary movers effect motion only because they are being moved by a first mover, just as a stick does not effect motion except because it is being moved by a hand. Therefore, one has to arrive at some first mover that is not being moved by anything. And this is what everyone takes to be God.

The *second* way is based on the notion of an efficient cause:

We find that among sensible things there is an ordering of efficient causes, and yet we do not find—nor is it possible to find—anything that is an efficient cause of its own self. For if something were an efficient cause of itself, then it would be prior to itself—which is impossible.

But it is impossible to go on to infinity among efficient causes. For in every case of ordered efficient causes, the first is a cause of the intermediate and the intermediate is a cause of the last—and this regardless of whether the intermediate is constituted by many causes or by just one. But when a cause is removed, its effect is removed. Therefore, if there were no first among the efficient causes, then neither would there be a last or an intermediate. But if the efficient causes went on to infinity, there would not be a first efficient cause, and so there would not be a last effect or any intermediate efficient causes, either—which is obviously false. Therefore, one must posit some first efficient cause—which everyone calls God.

The *third* way is taken from the possible and the necessary, and it goes like this:

Certain of the things we find in the world are able to exist and able not to exist; for some things are found to be generated and corrupted and, as a result, they are able to exist and able not to exist.

But it is impossible that everything should be like this; for that which is able not to exist is such that at some time it does not exist. Therefore, if everything is such that it is able not to exist, then at some time nothing existed in the world. But if this were true, then nothing would exist even now. For what does not exist begins to exist only through something that does exist; therefore, if there were no beings, then it was impossible that anything should have begun to exist, and so nothing would exist now—which is obviously false. Therefore, not all beings are able to exist [and able not to exist]; rather, it must be that there is something necessary in the world.

Now every necessary being either has a cause of its necessity from outside itself or it does not. But it is impossible to go on to infinity among necessary beings that have a cause of their necessity—in the same way, as was proved above, that it is impossible to go on to infinity among efficient causes. Therefore, one must posit something that is necessary *per se*, which does not have a cause of its necessity from outside itself but is instead a cause of necessity for the other [necessary] things. But this everyone calls God.

The *fourth* way is taken from the gradations that are found in the world:

In the world some things are found to be more and less good, more and less true, more and less noble, etc. But *more* and *less* are predicated of diverse things insofar as they approach in diverse ways that which is maximal in a given respect. For instance, the hotter something is, the closer it approaches that which is maximally hot. Therefore, there is something that is maximally true, maximally good, and maximally noble, and, as a result, is a maximal being; for according to the Philosopher in *Metaphysics* 2, things that are maximally true are maximally beings.

But, as is claimed in the same book, that which is maximal in a given genus is a cause of all the things that belong to that genus; for instance, fire, which is maximally hot, is a cause of all hot things. Therefore, there is something that is a cause for all beings of their *esse*, their goodness, and each of their perfections—and this we call God.

The *fifth* way is taken from the governance of things:

We see that some things lacking cognition, viz., natural bodies, act for the sake of an end. This is apparent from the fact that they always or very frequently act in the same way in order to bring about that which is best, and from this it is clear that it is not by chance, but by design, that they attain the end.

But things lacking cognition tend toward an end only if they are directed by something that has cognition and intelligence, in the way that an arrow is directed by an archer. Therefore, there is something intelligent by which all natural things are ordered to an end—and this we call God.

Reply to objection 1: As Augustine says in the *Enchiridion,* "Since God is maximally good, He would not allow any evil to exist in His works if He were not powerful enough and good enough to draw good even from evil." Therefore, it is part of God's infinite goodness that He should permit evils and elicit goods from them.

Reply to objection 2: Since it is by the direction of a higher agent that nature acts for the sake of a determinate end, those things that are done by nature must also be traced back to God as a first cause. Similarly, even things that are done by design must be traced back to a higher cause and not to human reason and will. For human reason and will are changeable and subject to failure, but, as was shown above, all things that can change and fail must be traced back to a first principle that is unmoved and necessary *per se.*

I.B.2   The Argument from Contingency

SAMUEL CLARKE

Samuel Clarke (1675–1729), an English philosopher and Anglican minister, one of the first to appreciate the work of Isaac Newton, here sets forth a version of the argument from contingency. It is based on the idea that if some beings are dependent, or contingent, there must of necessity be an independent being upon which all other beings are dependent.

There has existed from eternity some one unchangeable and independent being. For since something must needs have been from eternity; as hath been already proved, and is granted on all hands: either there has always existed one unchangeable and *independent* Being, from which all other beings that are or ever were in the universe, have received their original; or else there has been an infinite succession of changeable and *dependent* beings, produced one from another in an endless progression, without any original cause at all: which latter supposition is so very absurd, that tho' all atheism must in its account of most things (as shall be shown hereafter) terminate in it, yet I think very few atheists ever were so weak as openly and directly to defend it. For it is plainly impossible and contradictory to itself. I shall not argue against it from the supposed impossibility of infinite succession, *barely and absolutely considered in itself;* for a reason which shall be mentioned hereafter: but, if we consider such an infinite progression, as *one* entire endless *series of dependent* beings; 'tis plain this whole series of beings can have no cause *from without,* of its existence; because in it are supposed to be included *all things* that are

Reprinted from *A Discourse Concerning Natural Religion* (1705).

or ever were in the universe: and 'tis plain it can have no reason *within itself,* of its existence; because no one being in this infinite succession is supposed to be self-existent or necessary (which is the only ground or reason of existence of any thing, that can be imagined *within the thing itself,* as will presently more fully appear), but every one *dependent* on the foregoing: and where *no part* is necessary, 'tis manifest *the whole* cannot be necessary; absolute necessity of existence, not being an outward, relative, and accidental determination; but an inward and essential property of the nature of the thing which so exists. An infinite succession therefore of merely *dependent beings,* without any original independent cause; is a *series* of beings, that has neither necessity nor cause, nor any reason *at all* of its existence, neither *within itself* nor *from without:* that is, 'tis an express contradiction and impossibility; 'tis a supposing *something to be caused,* (because it's granted in every one of its stages of succession, not to be necessary and from itself); and yet that in the whole it is caused *absolutely by nothing:* Which every man knows is a contradiction to be done *in time;* and because duration in this case makes no difference, 'tis equally a contradiction to suppose it done from eternity: And consequently there must *on the contrary,* of necessity have existed from eternity, *some one* immutable and *independent* Being: Which, what it is, remains in the next place to be inquired.

I.B.3   A Critique of the Cosmological Argument

PAUL EDWARDS

Paul Edwards (1923–2004) was professor of philosophy at Brooklyn College and is the author of several works in philosophy. He was the editor of *The Encyclopedia of Philosophy* (1967). In this article, Edwards distinguishes two versions of the cosmological argument, the causal argument and the argument from contingency, and he argues against both versions. Regarding the first version, he makes an important distinction between a cause *in fieri* (a cause that brought its effect into existence) and a cause *in esse* (a cause that sustains its effect, ensuring its continued existence) and shows how this distinction bears on the argument.

I

The so-called "cosmological proof" is one of the oldest and most popular arguments for the existence of God. It was forcibly criticized by Hume, Kant, and Mill, but it would be inaccurate to consider the argument dead or even moribund. Catholic philosophers, with hardly any exception, appear to believe that it is as solid and conclusive as ever. Thus Father F. C. Copleston confidently championed it in his Third Programme debate with Bertrand Russell, and in America, where Catholic writers are more sanguine, we are told by a Jesuit professor of physics that "the existence of an intelligent being as the First Cause of the universe can be established by *rational scientific inference.*"[1]

I am absolutely convinced [the same writer continues] that any one who would give the same

Reprinted from *The Rationalist Annual,* 1959, edited by Hector Hawton. Reprinted by permission of Paul Edwards. Footnotes edited.

consideration to that proof (the cosmological argument), as outlined for example in William Brosnan's *God and Reason*, as he would give to a line of argumentation found in *Physical Review or the Proceedings of the Royal Society* would be forced to admit that the cogency of this argument for the existence of God far outstrips that which is found in the reasoning which Chadwick uses to prove the existence of the neutron, which today is accepted as certain as any conclusion in the physical sciences.

Mild theists like the late Professor Dawes Hicks and Dr. [A. C.] Ewing, who concede many of Hume's and Kant's criticisms, nevertheless contend that the argument possesses a certain core of truth. In popular discussions it also crops up again and again—for example, when believers address atheists with such questions as "You tell me where the universe came from!" Even philosophers who reject the cosmological proof sometimes embody certain of its confusions in the formulation of their own position. In the light of all this, it may be worth while to undertake a fresh examination of the argument with special attention to the fallacies that were not emphasized by the older critics.

II

The cosmological proof has taken a number of forms, the most important of which are known as the "causal argument" and "the argument from contingency," respectively. In some writers, in Samuel Clarke for example, they are combined, but it is best to keep them apart as far as possible. The causal argument is the second of the "five ways" of Aquinas and roughly proceeds as follows: we find that the things around us come into being as the result of the activity of other things. These causes are themselves the result of the activity of other things. But such a causal series cannot "go back to infinity." Hence there must be a first member, a member which is not itself caused by any preceding member—an uncaused or "first" cause.

It has frequently been pointed out that even if this argument were sound it would not establish the existence of *God*. It would not show that the first cause is all-powerful or all-good or that

it is in any sense personal. Somebody believing in the eternity of atoms, or of matter generally, could quite consistently accept the conclusion. Defenders of the causal argument usually concede this and insist that the argument is not in itself meant to prove the existence of God. Supplementary arguments are required to show that the first cause must have the attributes assigned to the deity. They claim, however, that the argument, if valid, would at least be an important step towards a complete proof of the existence of God.

Does the argument succeed in proving so much as a first cause? This will depend mainly on the soundness of the premise that an infinite series of causes is impossible. Aquinas supports this premise by maintaining that the opposite belief involves a plain absurdity. To suppose that there is an infinite series of causes logically implies that nothing exists now; but we know that plenty of things do exist now; and hence any theory which implies that nothing exists now must be wrong. Let us take some causal series and refer to its members by the letters of the alphabet:

$$A \rightarrow B \ldots W \rightarrow X \rightarrow Y \rightarrow Z$$

Z stands here for something presently existing, e.g. Margaret Truman. Y represents the cause or part of the cause of Z, say Harry Truman. X designates the cause or part of the cause of Y, say Harry Truman's father, etc. Now, Aquinas reasons, whenever we take away the cause, we also take away the effect: if Harry Truman had never lived, Margaret Truman would never have been born. If Harry Truman's father had never lived, Harry Truman and Margaret Truman would never have been born. If A had never existed, none of the subsequent members of the series would have come into existence. But it is precisely A that the believer in the infinite series is "taking away." For in maintaining that the series is infinite he is denying that it has a first member; he is denying that there is such a thing as a first cause; he is in other words denying the existence of A. Since without A, Z could not have existed, his position implies that Z does not exist now; and that is plainly false.

This argument fails to do justice to the supporter of the infinite series of causes. Aquinas has failed to distinguish between the two statements:

1. *A* did not exist, and
2. *A* is not uncaused.

To say that the series is infinite implies (2), but it does not imply (1). The following parallel may be helpful here: Suppose Captain Spaulding had said, "I am the greatest explorer who ever lived," and somebody replied, "No, you are not." This answer would be denying that the Captain possessed the exalted attribute he had claimed for himself, but it would not be denying his existence. It would not be "taking him away." Similarly, the believer in the infinite series is not "taking *A* away." He is taking away the privileged status of *A*; he is taking away its "first causiness." He does not deny the *existence* of *A* or of any particular member of the series. He denies that *A* or anything else *is the first member* of the series. Since he is not taking *A* away, he is not taking *B* away, and thus he is also not taking *X, Y,* or *Z* away. His view, then, does not commit him to the absurdity that nothing exists now, or more specifically, that Margaret Truman does not exist now. It may be noted in this connection that a believer in the infinite series is not necessarily denying the existence of supernatural beings. He is merely committed to denying that such a being, if it exists, is uncaused. He is committed to holding that whatever other impressive attributes a supernatural being might possess, the attribute of being a first cause is not among them.

The causal argument is open to several other objections. Thus, even if otherwise valid, the argument would not prove a *single* first cause. For there does not seem to be any good ground for supposing that the various causal series in the universe ultimately merge. Hence even if it is granted that no series of causes can be infinite the possibility of a plurality of first members has not been ruled out. Nor does the argument establish the *present* existence of the first cause. It does not prove this, since experience clearly shows that an effect may exist long after its cause has been destroyed.

III

Many defenders of the causal argument would contend that at least some of these criticisms rest on a misunderstanding. They would probably go further and contend that the argument was not quite fairly stated in the first place—or at any rate that if it was fair to some of its adherents it was not fair to others. They would in this connection distinguish between two types of causes—what they call "causes *in fieri*" and what they call "causes *in esse*." A cause *in fieri* is a factor which brought or helped to bring an effect into existence. A cause *in esse* is a factor which "sustains" or helps to sustain the effect "in being." The parents of a human being would be an example of a cause *in fieri*. If somebody puts a book in my hand and I keep holding it up, his putting it there would be the cause *in fieri*, and my holding it would be the cause *in esse* of the book's position. To quote Father [G. H.] Joyce:

> If a smith forges a horse-shoe, he is only a cause *in fieri* of the shape given to the iron. That shape persists after his action has ceased. So, too, a builder is a cause *in fieri* of the house which he builds. In both cases the substances employed act as causes *in esse* as regards the continued existence of the effect produced. Iron, in virtue of its natural rigidity, retains in being the shape which it has once received; and similarly, the materials employed in building retain in being the order and arrangement which constitute them into a house.[2]

Using this distinction, the defender of the argument now reasons in the following way. To say that there is an infinite series of causes *in fieri* does not lead to any absurd conclusions. But Aquinas is concerned only with causes *in esse* and an infinite series of *such* causes is impossible. In the words of the contemporary American Thomist, R. P. Phillips:

> Each member of the series of causes possesses being solely by virtue of the actual present operation of a superior cause. . . . Life is dependent, *inter alia*, on a certain atmospheric pressure, this again on the continual operation of physical forces, whose being and operation depends on the position of the earth in the solar system, which itself must endure relatively unchanged, a state of

being which can only be continuously produced by a definite—if unknown—constitution of the material universe. This constitution, however, cannot be its own cause. That a thing should cause itself is impossible: for in order that it may cause it is necessary for it to exist, which it cannot do, on the hypothesis, until it has been caused. So it must *be* in order to cause itself. Thus, not being uncaused nor yet its own cause, it must be caused by another, which produces and preserves it. It is plain, then, that as no member of this series possesses being except in virtue of the actual present operation of a superior cause, if there be no first cause actually operating none of the dependent causes could operate either. We are thus irresistibly led to posit a first efficient cause which, while itself uncaused, shall impart causality to a whole series. . . .

The series of causes which we are considering is not one which stretches back into the past; so that we are not demanding a beginning of the world at some definite moment reckoning back from the present, but an actual cause now operating, to account for the present being of things.[3]

Professor Phillips offers the following parallel to bring out his point:

In a goods train each truck is moved and moves by the action of the one immediately in front of it. If then we suppose the train to be infinite, i.e. that there is no end to it, and so no engine which starts the motion, it is plain that no truck will move. To lengthen it out to infinity will not give it what no member of it possesses of itself, viz. the power of drawing the truck behind it. If then we see any truck in motion we know there must be an end to the series of trucks which gives causality to the whole.[4]

Father Joyce introduces an illustration from Aquinas to explain how the present existence of things may be compatible with an infinite series of causes *in fieri* but not with an infinite series of causes *in esse*.

When a carpenter is at work, the series of efficient causes on which his work depends is necessarily limited. The final effect, e.g. the fastening of a nail is caused by a hammer: the hammer is moved by the arm: and the motion of his arm is determined by the motor-impulses communicated from the nerve centres of the brain. Unless the subordinate causes were limited in number, and were connected with a starting point of motion, the hammer must remain inert; and the nail will never be driven in. If the series be supposed infinite, no work will ever take place. But if there is question of causes on which the work is not essentially dependent, we cannot draw the same conclusion. We may suppose the carpenter to have broken an infinite number of hammers, and as often to have replaced the broken tool by a fresh one. There is nothing in such a supposition which excludes the driving home of the nail.

The supporter of the infinite series of causes, Joyce also remarks, is

. . . asking us to believe that although each link in a suspended chain is prevented from falling simply because it is attached to the one above it, yet if only the chain be long enough, it will, taken as a whole, need no support, but will hang loose in the air suspended from nothing.

This formulation of the causal argument unquestionably circumvents one of the objections mentioned previously. If Y is the cause in esse of an effect, Z, then it must exist as long as Z exists. If the argument were valid in this form it would therefore prove the present and not merely the past existence of a first cause. In this form the argument is, however, less convincing in another respect. To maintain that all "natural" or "phenomenal" objects—things like tables and mountains and human beings—require a cause *in fieri* is not implausible, though even here Mill and others have argued that strictly speaking only *changes* require a causal explanation. It is far from plausible, on the other hand, to claim that all natural objects require a cause *in esse*. It may be granted that the air around us is a cause *in esse* of human life and further that certain gravitational forces are among the causes *in esse* of the air being where it is. But when we come to gravitational forces or, at any rate, to material particles like atoms or electrons it is difficult to see what cause *in esse* they require. To those not already convinced of the need for a supernatural First Cause some of the remarks by Professor Phillips in this connection appear merely dogmatic and question-begging. Most people would grant that such particles as atoms did not cause themselves, since, as Professor Phillips observes, they would in that event have had to exist before they began existing. It is not at all evident, however, that these particles cannot be uncaused. Professor Phillips and all other supporters of the causal argument immediately proceed to claim that there is something else which needs no cause *in esse*. They themselves admit thus, that there is nothing self-evident about the proposition that everything must have a cause *in esse*. Their entire procedure here lends substance to Schopenhauer's gibe that supporters of the cosmological argument treat the law of universal causation like "a hired cab which we dismiss when we have reached our destination."

But waiving this and all similar objections, the restatement of the argument in terms of causes *in esse* in no way avoids the main difficulty which was previously mentioned. A believer in the infinite series would insist that his position was just as much misrepresented now as before. He is no more removing the member of the series which is supposed to be the first cause *in esse* than he was removing the member which had been declared to be the first cause *in fieri*. He is again merely denying a privileged status to it. He is not denying the reality of the cause *in esse* labelled "*A*." He is not even necessarily denying that it possesses supernatural attributes. He is again merely taking away its "first causiness."

The advocates of the causal argument in either form seem to confuse an infinite series with one which is long but finite. If a book, *Z*, is to remain in its position, say 100 miles up in the air, there must be another object, say another book, *Y*, underneath it to serve as its support. If *Y* is to remain where it is, it will need another support, *X*, beneath it. Suppose that this series of supports, one below the other, continues for a long time, but eventually, say after 100,000 members, comes to a first book which is not resting on any other book or indeed on any other support. In that event the whole collection would come crashing down. What we seem to need is a first member of the series, a first support (such as the earth) which does not need another

member as its support, which in other words is "self-supporting."

This is evidently the sort of picture that supporters of the First Cause argument have before their minds when they rule out the possibility of an infinite series. But such a picture is not a fair representation of the theory of the infinite series. A *finite* series of books would indeed come crashing down, since the first or lowest member *would* not have a predecessor on which it could be supported. If the series, however, were infinite this would not be the case. In that event every member *would* have a predecessor to support itself on and there would be no crash. That is to say: a crash can be avoided either by a finite series with a first self-supporting member or by an infinite series. Similarly, the present existence of motion is equally compatible with the theory of a first unmoved mover and with the theory of an infinite series of moving objects; and the present existence of causal activity is compatible with the theory of a first cause *in esse* as much as with the theory of an infinite series of such causes.

The illustrations given by Joyce and Phillips are hardly to the point. It is true that a carpenter would not, *in a finite time-span*, succeed in driving in a nail if he had to carry out an infinite number of movements. For that matter, he would not accomplish this goal in a finite time if he broke an infinite number of hammers. However, to make the illustrations relevant we must suppose that he has infinite time at his disposal. In that case he would succeed in driving in the nail even if he required an infinite number of movements for this purpose. As for the goods train, it may be granted that the trucks do not move unless the train has an engine. But this illustration is totally irrelevant as it stands. A relevant illustration would be that of engines, each moved by the one in front of it. Such a train would move if it were infinite. For every member of this series there would be one in front capable of drawing it along. The advocate of the infinite series of causes does not, as the original illustration suggests, believe in a series whose members are not really causally connected with one another. In the series he believes in every member is genuinely the cause of the one that follows it.

IV

No staunch defender of the cosmological argument would give up at this stage. Even if there were an infinite series of causes *in fieri* or *in esse*, he would contend, this still would not do away with the need for an ultimate, a first cause. As Father Copleston put it in his debate with Bertrand Russell:

> Every object has a phenomenal cause, if you insist on the infinity of the series. But the series of phenomenal causes is an insufficient explanation of the series. Therefore, the series has not a phenomenal cause, but a transcendent cause. . . .
>
> An infinite series of contingent beings will be, to my way of thinking, as unable to cause itself as one contingent being.

The demand to find the cause of the series as a whole rests on the erroneous assumption that the series is something over and above the members of which it is composed. It is tempting to suppose this, at least by implication, because the word "series" is a noun like "dog" or "man." Like the expression "this dog" or "this man" the phrase "this series" is easily taken to designate an individual object. But reflection shows this to be an error. If we have explained the individual members there is nothing additional left to be explained. Supposing I see a group of five Eskimos standing on the corner of Sixth Avenue and 50th Street and I wish to explain why the group came to New York. Investigation reveals the following stories:

- Eskimo No. 1 did not enjoy the extreme cold in the polar region and decided to move to a warmer climate.
- No. 2 is the husband of Eskimo No. 1. He loves her dearly and did not wish to live without her.
- No. 3 is the son of Eskimos 1 and 2. He is too small and too weak to oppose his parents.
- No. 4 saw an advertisement in the *New York Times* for an Eskimo to appear on television.
- No. 5 is a private detective engaged by the Pinkerton Agency to keep an eye on Eskimo No. 4.

Let us assume that we have now explained in the case of each of the five Eskimos why he or she is in New York. Somebody then asks: "All right, but what about the group as a whole; why is *it* in New York?" This would plainly be an absurd question. There is no group over and above the five members, and if we have explained why each of the five members is in New York we have *ipso facto* explained why the group is there. It is just as absurd to ask for the cause of the series as a whole as distinct from asking for the causes of individual members.

V

It is most unlikely that a determined defender of the cosmological line of reasoning would surrender even here. He would probably admit that the series is not a thing over and above its members and that it does not make sense to ask for the cause of the series if the cause of each member has already been found. He would insist, however, that when he asked for the explanation of the entire series, he was not asking for its *cause*. He was really saying that a series, finite or infinite, is not "intelligible" or "explained" if it consists of nothing but "contingent" members. To quote Father Copleston once more:

> What we call the world is intrinsically unintelligible apart from the existence of God. The infinity of the series of events, if such an infinity could be proved, would not be in the slightest degree relevant to the situation. If you add up chocolates, you get chocolates after all, and not a sheep. If you add up chocolates to infinity, you presumably get an infinite number of chocolates. So, if you add up contingent beings to infinity, you still get contingent beings, not a necessary being.

This last quotation is really a summary of the "contingency argument," the other main form of the cosmological proof and the third of the five ways of Aquinas. It may be stated more fully in these words: All around us we perceive contingent beings. This includes all physical objects and also all human minds. In calling them "contingent" we mean that they might not have existed. We mean that the universe can be *conceived* without this or that physical object, without this or that human being, however certain their actual existence may be. These contingent beings we can trace back to other contingent beings—e.g. a human being to his parents. However, since these other beings are also contingent, they do not provide a real or full explanation. The contingent beings we originally wanted explained have not yet become intelligible, since the beings to which they have been traced back are no more necessary than they were. It is just as true of our parents, for example, as it is of ourselves, that they might not have existed. We can then properly explain the contingent beings around us only by tracing them back ultimately to some necessary being, to something which exists necessarily, which has "the reason for its existence within itself." The existence of contingent beings, in other words, implies the existence of a necessary being.

This form of cosmological argument is even more beset with difficulties than the causal variety. In the first place, there is the objection, stated with great force by Kant, that it really commits the same error as the ontological argument in tacitly regarding existence as an attribute or characteristic. To say that there is a necessary being is to say that it would be a self-contradiction to deny its existence. This would mean that at least one existential statement is a necessary truth; and this in turn presupposes that in at least one case existence is contained in a concept. But only a characteristic can be contained in a concept and it has seemed plain to most philosophers since Kant that existence is not a characteristic, that it can hence never be contained in a concept, and that hence no existential statement can ever be a necessary truth. To talk about anything "existing necessarily" is in their view about as sensible as to talk about round squares, and they have concluded that the contingency-argument is quite absurd.

It would lead too far to discuss here the reasons for denying that existence is a characteristic. I will assume that this difficulty can somehow be surmounted and that the expression "necessary being," as is intended by the champions of the contingency-argument, might conceivably apply to something. There remain other objections which are of great weight. I shall try to state these by first quoting again from the debate between Bertrand Russell and Father Copleston:

Russell: . . . it all turns on this question of sufficient reason, and I must say you haven't defined "sufficient reason" in a way that I can understand—what do you mean by sufficient reason? You don't mean cause?

Copleston: Not necessarily. Cause is a kind of sufficient reason. Only contingent being can have a cause. God is his own sufficient reason; and he is not cause of himself. By sufficient reason in the full sense I mean an explanation adequate for the existence of some particular being.

Russell: But when is an explanation adequate? Suppose I am about to make a flame with a match. You may say that the adequate explanation of that is that I rub it on the box.

Copleston: Well for practical purposes—but theoretically, that is only a partial explanation. An adequate explanation must ultimately be a total explanation, to which nothing further can be added.

Russell: Then I can only say that you're looking for something which can't be got, and which one ought not to expect to get.

Copleston: To say that one has not found it is one thing; to say that one should not look for it seems to me rather dogmatic.

Russell: Well, I don't know. I mean, the explanation of one thing is another thing which makes the other thing dependent on yet another, and you have to grasp this sorry scheme of things entire to do what you want, and that we can't do.

Russell's main point here may be expanded in the following way. The contingency-argument rests on a misconception of what an explanation is and does, and similarly on what it is that makes phenomena "intelligible." Or else it involves an obscure and arbitrary redefinition of "explanation," "intelligible," and related terms. Normally, we are satisfied that we have explained a phenomenon if we have found its cause or if we have exhibited some other uniform or near-uniform connection between it and something else. Confining ourselves to the former case, which is probably the most common, we might say that a phenomenon, *Z*, has been explained if it has been traced back to a group of factors, *a*, *b*, *c*, *d*, etc., which are its cause. These factors are the full and real explanation of *Z*, quite regardless of whether they are pleasing or displeasing, admirable or contemptible, necessary or contingent. The explanation would not be adequate only if the factors listed are not really the cause of *Z*. If they are the cause of *Z*, the explanation would be adequate, even though each of the factors is merely a "contingent" being.

Let us suppose that we have been asked to explain why General Eisenhower won the elections of 1952. "He was an extremely popular general," we might answer, "while Stevenson was relatively little known; moreover there was a great deal of resentment over the scandals in the Truman Administration." If somebody complained that this was only a partial explanation we might mention additional antecedents, such as the widespread belief that the Democrats had allowed communist agents to infiltrate the State Department, that Eisenhower was a man with a winning smile, and that unlike Stevenson he had shown the good sense to say one thing on race relations in the North and quite another in the South. Theoretically, we might go further and list the motives of all American voters during the weeks or months preceding the elections. If we could do this we would have explained Eisenhower's victory. We would have made it intelligible. We would "understand" why he won and why Stevenson lost. Perhaps there is a sense in which we might make Eisenhower's victory even more intelligible if we went further back and discussed such matters as the origin of American views on Communism or of racial attitudes in the North and South. However, to explain the outcome of the election in any ordinary sense, loose or strict, it would not be necessary to go back to prehistoric days or to the amoeba or to a first cause, if such a first cause exists. Nor would our explanation be considered in any way defective because each of the factors

mentioned was a "contingent" and not a necessary being. The only thing that matters is whether the factors were really the cause of Eisenhower's election. If they were, then it has been explained although they are contingent beings. If they were not the cause of Eisenhower's victory, we would have failed to explain it even if each of the factors were a necessary being.

If it is granted that, in order to explain a phenomenon or to make it intelligible, we need not bring in a necessary being, then the contingency argument breaks down. For a series, as was already pointed out, is not something over and above its members; and every contingent member of it could in that case be explained by reference to other contingent beings. But I should wish to go further than this and it is evident from Russell's remarks that he would do so also. Even if it were granted, both that the phrase "necessary being" is meaningful and that all explanations are defective unless the phenomena to be explained are traced back to a necessary being, the conclusion would still not have been established. The conclusion follows from this premise together with the additional premise that *there are* explanations of phenomena in the special sense just mentioned. It is this further premise which Russell (and many other philosophers) would question. They do not merely question, as Copleston implies, whether human beings can ever obtain explanations in this sense, but whether they *exist*. To assume without further ado that phenomena have explanations or an explanation in this sense is to beg the very point at issue. The use of the same word "explanation" in two crucially different ways lends the additional premise a plausibility it does not really possess. It may indeed be highly plausible to assert that phenomena have explanations, whether we have found them or not, in the ordinary sense in which this usually means that they have causes. It is then tempting to suppose, because of the use of the same word, that they also have explanations in a sense in which this implies dependence on a necessary being. But this is *a gross non sequitur*.

VI

It is necessary to add a few words about the proper way of formulating the position of those who reject the main premise of the cosmological argument, in either of the forms we have considered. It is sometimes maintained in this connection that in order to reach a "self-existing" entity it is not necessary to go beyond the universe: the universe itself (or "Nature") is "self-existing." And this in turn is sometimes expanded into the statement that while all individual things "within" the universe are caused, the universe itself is uncaused. Statements of this kind are found in Büchner, Bradlaugh, Haeckel, and other free-thinkers of the nineteenth and early twentieth century. Sometimes the assertion that the universe is "self-existing" is elaborated to mean that *it* is the "necessary being." Some eighteenth-century unbelievers, apparently accepting the view that there is a necessary being, asked why Nature or the material universe could not fill the bill as well or better than God.

> "Why," asks one of the characters in Hume's Dialogues, "may not the material universe be the necessarily existent Being? . . . We dare not affirm that we know all the qualities of matter; and for aught we can determine, it may contain some qualities, which, were they known, would make its nonexistence appear as great a contradiction as that twice two is five."

Similar remarks can be found in Holbach and several of the Encyclopedists.

The former of these formulations immediately invites the question why the universe, alone of all "things," is exempted from the universal sway of causation. "The strong point of the cosmological argument," writes Dr. Ewing, "is that after all it does remain incredible that the physical universe should just have happened . . . It calls out for some further explanation of some kind." The latter formulation is exposed to the criticism that there is nothing any more "necessary" about the existence of the universe or Nature as a whole than about any particular thing within the universe.

I hope some of the earlier discussions in this article have made it clear that in rejecting the cosmological argument one is not committed to either of these propositions. If I reject the view that there is a supernatural first cause, I am not thereby committed to the proposition that there is a *natural* first cause, and even less to the proposition that a mysterious "thing" called "the universe" qualifies for this title. I may hold that there is no "universe" over and above individual things of various sorts; and, accepting the causal principle, I may proceed to assert that all these things are caused by other things, and these other things by yet other things, and so on, *ad infinitum*. In this way no arbitrary exception is made to the principle of causation. Similarly, if I reject the assertion that God is a "necessary being," I am not committed to the view that the universe is such an entity. I may hold that it does not make sense to speak of anything as a "necessary being" and that even if there were such a thing as the universe it could not be properly considered a necessary being.

However, in saying that nothing is uncaused or that there is no necessary being, one is not committed to the view that everything, or for that matter anything, is merely a "brute fact." Dr. Ewing laments that "the usual modern philosophical views opposed to theism do not try to give any rational explanation of the world at all, but just take it as a brute fact not to be explained." They thus fail to rationalize the universe. Theism, he concedes, cannot completely rationalize things either since it does not show "how God can be his own cause or how it is that he does not need a cause." Now, if one means by "brute fact" something for which there *exists* no explanation (as distinct from something for which no explanation is in our possession), then the theists have at least one brute fact on their hands, namely God. Those who adopt Büchner's formulation also have one brute fact on their hands, namely "the universe." Only the position I have been supporting dispenses with brute facts altogether. I don't know if this is any special virtue, but the defenders of the cosmological argument seem to think so.

NOTES

1. J. S. O'Connor, "A Scientific Approach to Religion," *The Scientific Monthly* (1940), p. 369; my italics.

2. *The Principles of Natural Theology*, p. 58.
3. *Modern Thomistic Philosophy*, Vol. II, pp. 284–85.
4. Ibid., p. 278.

I.B.4   An Examination of the Cosmological Argument

WILLIAM ROWE

William Rowe (1931–   ) is emeritus professor of philosophy at Purdue University and the author of several works in philosophy of religion, including *Philosophy of Religion: An Introduction* (1978), from which this selection is taken. Rowe begins by distinguishing between a priori and a posteriori arguments and setting the cosmological argument in historical perspective. Next, he divides the argument into two parts: that which seeks to prove the existence of a self-existent being and that which seeks to prove that this self-existent being is the God of theism. He introduces the principle of sufficient reason—"There must be an explanation (a) of the existence of any being and (b) of any positive fact whatever"—and shows its role in the cosmological argument. In the light of this principle, he examines the argument itself and four objections to it.

STATING THE ARGUMENT

Arguments for the existence of God are commonly divided into *a posteriori* arguments and *a priori* arguments. An *a posteriori* argument depends on a principle or premise that can be known only by means of our experience of the world. An *a priori* argument, on the other hand, purports to rest on principles all of which can be known independently of our experience of the world, by just reflecting on and understanding them. Of the three major arguments for the existence of God—the Cosmological, the Teleological, and the Ontological—only the last of these is entirely *a priori*. In the Cosmological Argument one starts from some simple fact about the world, such as that it contains things which are caused to exist by other things. In the Teleological Argument a somewhat more complicated fact about the world serves as a starting point, the fact that the world exhibits order and design. In the Ontological Argument, however, one begins simply with a concept of God.

Before we state the Cosmological Argument itself, we shall consider some rather general points about the argument. Historically, it can be traced to the writings of the Greek philosophers, Plato and Aristotle, but the major developments in the argument took place in the thirteenth and in the eighteenth centuries. In the thirteenth century Aquinas put forth five distinct arguments for the existence of God, and of these, the first three are versions of the Cosmological Argument.[1] In the first of these he started from the fact that there are things in the world undergoing change and reasoned to the conclusion that there must be some ultimate cause of change that is itself unchanging. In the second he started from the fact that there are things in the world that clearly are caused to

---

Reprinted from William Rowe, *Philosophy of Religion* (Wadsworth Publishing Co., 1978), by permission.

exist by other things and reasoned to the conclusion that there must be some ultimate cause of existence whose own existence is itself uncaused. And in the third argument he started from the fact that there are things in the world which need not have existed at all, things which do exist but which we can easily imagine might not, and reasoned to the conclusion that there must be some being that had to be, that exists and could not have failed to exist. Now it might be objected that even if Aquinas' arguments do prove beyond doubt the existence of an unchanging changer, an uncaused cause, and a being that could not have failed to exist, the arguments fail to prove the existence of the theistic God. For the theistic God, as we saw, is supremely good, omnipotent, omniscient, and creator of but separate from and independent of the world. How do we know, for example, that the unchanging changer isn't evil or slightly ignorant? The answer to this objection is that the Cosmological Argument has two parts. In the first part the effort is to prove the existence of a special sort of being, for example, a being that could not have failed to exist, or a being that causes change in other things but is itself unchanging. In the second part of the argument the effort is to prove that the special sort of being whose existence has been established in the first part has, and must have, the features—perfect goodness, omnipotence, omniscience, and so on—which go together to make up the theistic idea of God. What this means, then, is that Aquinas' three arguments are different versions of only the first part of the Cosmological Argument. Indeed, in later sections of his *Summa Theologica* Aquinas undertakes to show that the unchanging changer, the uncaused cause of existence, and the being which had to exist are one and the same being and that this single being has all of the attributes of the theistic God.

We noted above that a second major development in the Cosmological Argument took place in the eighteenth century, a development reflected in the writings of the German philosopher, Gottfried Leibniz (1646–1716), and especially in the writings of the English theologian and philosopher, Samuel Clarke (1675–1729). In 1704 Clarke gave a series of lectures, later published under the title *A Demonstration of the Being and Attributes of God*. These lectures constitute, perhaps, the most complete, forceful, and cogent presentation of the Cosmological Argument we possess. The lectures were read by the major skeptical philosopher of the century, David Hume (1711–1776), and in his brilliant attack on the attempt to justify religion in the court of reason, his *Dialogues Concerning Natural Religion*, Hume advanced several penetrating criticisms of Clarke's arguments, criticisms which have persuaded many philosophers in the modern period to reject the Cosmological Argument. In our study of the argument we shall concentrate our attention largely on its eighteenth-century form and try to assess its strengths and weaknesses in the light of the criticisms which Hume and others have advanced against it.

The first part of the eighteenth-century form of the Cosmological Argument seeks to establish the existence of a self-existent being. The second part of the argument attempts to prove that the self-existent being is the theistic God, that is, has the features which we have noted to be basic elements in the theistic idea of God. We shall consider mainly the first part of the argument, for it is against the first part that philosophers from Hume to Russell have advanced very important objections.

In stating the first part of the Cosmological Argument we shall make use of two important concepts, the concept of a *dependent being* and the concept of a *self-existent being*. By a *dependent being* we mean *a being whose existence is accounted for by the causal activity of other things.* Recalling Anselm's division into the three cases: "explained by another," "explained by nothing," and "explained by itself," it's clear that a dependent being is a being whose existence is explained by another. By a *self-existent being* we mean *a being whose existence is accounted for by its own nature.* This idea . . . is an essential element in the theistic concept of God. Again, in terms of Anselm's three cases, a self-existent being is a being whose existence is explained by itself. Armed with these two concepts, the concept of a dependent being and the concept of a self-existent being, we can now state the first part of the Cosmological Argument.

1. Every being (that exists or ever did exist) is either a dependent being or a self-existent being.
2. Not every being can be a dependent being.

Therefore,

3. There exists a self-existent being.

Deductive Validity

Before we look critically at each of the premises of this argument, we should note that this argument is, to use an expression from the logician's vocabulary, *deductively valid*. To find out whether an argument is deductively valid, we need only ask the question: If its premises were true, would its conclusion have to be true? If the answer is yes, the argument is deductively valid. If the answer is no, the argument is deductively invalid. Notice that the question of the validity of an argument is entirely different from the question of whether its premises are in fact true. The following argument is made up entirely of false statements, but it is deductively valid.

1. Babe Ruth is the President of the United States.
2. The President of the United States is from Indiana.

Therefore,

3. Babe Ruth is from Indiana.

The argument is deductively valid because even though its premises are false, if they were true its conclusion would have to be true. Even God, Aquinas would say, cannot bring it about that the premises of this argument are true and yet its conclusion is false, for God's power extends only to what is possible, and it is an absolute impossibility that Babe Ruth be the President, the President be from Indiana, and yet Babe Ruth not be from Indiana.

The Cosmological Argument (that is, its first part) is a deductively valid argument. If its premises are or were true, its conclusion would have to be true. It's clear from our example about Babe Ruth, however, that the fact that an argument is deductively valid is insufficient to establish the truth of its conclusion. What else is required? Clearly that we know or have rational grounds for believing that the premises are true. If we know that the Cosmological Argument is deductively valid, and can establish that its premises are true, we shall thereby have proved that its conclusion is true. Are, then, the premises of the Cosmological Argument true? To this more difficult question we must now turn.

PSR and the First Premise

At first glance the first premise might appear to be an obvious or even trivial truth. But it is neither obvious nor trivial. And if it appears to be obvious or trivial, we must be confusing the idea of a self-existent being with the idea of a being that is not a dependent being. Clearly, it is true that any being is either a dependent being (explained by other things) or it is not a dependent being (not explained by other things). But what our premise says is that any being is either a dependent being (explained by other things) or it is a self-existent being (explained by itself). Consider again Anselm's three cases.

a. explained by another
b. explained by nothing
c. explained by itself

What our first premise asserts is that each being that exists (or ever did exist) is either of sort *a* or of sort *c*. It denies that any being is of sort *b*. And it is this denial that makes the first premise both significant and controversial. The obvious truth we must not confuse it with is the truth that any being is either of sort *a* or not of sort *a*. While this is true it is neither very significant nor controversial.

Earlier we saw that Anselm accepted as a basic principle that whatever exists has an explanation of its existence. Since this basic principle denies that any thing of sort *b* exists or ever did exist, it's clear that Anselm would believe the first premise of our Cosmological Argument. The eighteenth-century proponents of the argument also were convinced of the truth of the basic principle we attributed to Anselm. And because they were convinced of its truth, they readily accepted the first premise of the Cosmological Argument. But by the eighteenth century, Anselm's basic principle had been more fully elaborated and had received a name, the *Principle of Sufficient Reason*. Since this principle (PSR, as we shall call it) plays such an important role in justifying the premises of the Cosmological Argument, it will help us to consider it for a moment before we continue our enquiry into the truth or falsity of the premises of the Cosmological Argument.

The Principle of Sufficient Reason, as it was expressed by both Leibniz and Samuel Clarke, is a very general principle and is best understood as having two parts. In its first part it is simply a restatement of Anselm's principle that there must be an explanation of the existence of any being whatever. Thus if we come upon a man in a room, PSR implies that there must be an explanation of the fact that that particular man exists. A moment's reflection, however, reveals that there are many facts about the man other than the mere fact that he exists. There is the fact that the man in question is in the room he's in, rather than somewhere else, the fact that he is in good health, and the fact that he is at the moment thinking of Paris, rather than, say, London. Now, the purpose of the second part of PSR is to require an explanation of these facts, as well. We may state PSR, therefore, as the principle that *there must be an explanation (a) of the existence of any being, and (b) of any positive fact whatever*. We are now in a position to study the role this very important principle plays in the Cosmological Argument.

Since the proponent of the Cosmological Argument accepts PSR in both its parts, it is clear that he will appeal to its first part, PSRa, as justification for the first premise of the Cosmological Argument. Of course, we can and should enquire into the deeper question of whether the proponent of the argument is rationally justified in accepting PSR itself. But we shall put this question aside for the moment. What we need to see first is whether he is correct in thinking that *if* PSR is true then both of the premises of the

Cosmological Argument are true. And what we have just seen is that if only the first part of PSR, that is, PSRa, is true, the first premise of the Cosmological Argument will be true. But what of the second premise of the argument? For what reasons does the proponent think that it must be true?

The Second Premise

According to the second premise, not every being that exists can be a dependent being, that is, can have the explanation of its existence in some other being or beings. Presumably, the proponent of the argument thinks there is something fundamentally wrong with the idea that every being that exists is dependent, that each existing being was caused by some other being which in turn was caused by some other being, and so on. But just what does he think is wrong with it? To help us in understanding his thinking, let's simplify things by supposing that there exists only one thing now, A_1, a living thing perhaps, that was brought into existence by something else, A_2, which perished shortly after it brought A_1 into existence. Suppose further that A_2 was brought into existence in similar fashion some time ago by A_3, and A_3 by A_4, and so forth back into the past. Each of these beings is a *dependent* being, it owes its existence to the preceding thing in the series. Now if nothing else ever existed but these beings, then what the second premise says would not be true. For if every being that exists or ever did exist is an A and was produced by a preceding A, then every being that exists or ever did exist would be dependent and, accordingly, premise two of the Cosmological Argument would be false. If the proponent of the Cosmological Argument is correct there must, then, be something wrong with the idea that every being that exists or did exist is an A and that they form a causal series: A_1 caused by A_2, A_2 caused by A_3, A_3 caused by A_4, . . . A_n caused by A_{n+1}. How does the proponent of the Cosmological Argument propose to show us that there is something wrong with this view?

A popular but mistaken idea of how the proponent tries to show that something is wrong with the view, that every being might be dependent, is that he uses the following argument to reject it.

1. There must be a first being to start any causal series.
2. If every being were dependent there would be no *first* being to start the causal series.

Therefore,

3. Not every being can be a dependent being.

Although this argument is deductively valid, and its second premise is true, its first premise overlooks the distinct possibility that a causal series might be *infinite,* with no first member at all. Thus if we go back to our series of *A* beings, where each *A* is dependent, having been produced by the preceding *A* in the causal series, it's clear that if the series existed it would have no first member, for every *A* in the series there would be a preceding *A* which produced it, *ad infinitum.* The first premise of the argument just given assumes that a causal series must stop with a first member somewhere in the distant past. But there seems to be no good reason for making that assumption.

The eighteenth-century proponents of the Cosmological Argument recognized that the causal series of dependent beings could be infinite, without a first member to start the series. They rejected the idea that every being that is or ever was is dependent not because there would then be no first member to the series of dependent beings, but because there would then be no explanation for the fact that there are and have always been dependent beings. To see their reasoning let's return to our simplification of the supposition that the only things that exist or ever did exist are dependent beings. In our simplification of that supposition only one of the dependent beings exists at a time, each one perishing as it produces the next in the series. Perhaps the first thing to note about this supposition is that there is no individual *A* in the causal series of dependent beings whose existence is unexplained—A_1 is explained by A_2, A_2 by A_3, and A_n by A_{n+1}. So the first part of PSR, PSRa, appears to be satisfied. There is no particular

being whose existence lacks an explanation. What, then, is it that lacks an explanation, if every particular *A* in the causal series of dependent beings has an explanation? it is the *series itself* that lacks an explanation, Or, as I've chosen to express it, *the fact that there are and have always been dependent beings.* For suppose we ask why it is that there are and have always been *A*s in existence. It won't do to say that *A*s have always been producing other *A*s—we can't explain why there have always been *A*s by saying there always have been *A*s. Nor, on the supposition that only *A*s have ever existed, can we explain the fact that there have always been *A*s by appealing to something other than an *A*— for no such thing would have existed. Thus the supposition that the only things that exist or ever existed are dependent things leaves us with a fact for which there can be no explanation; namely, the fact that there are and have always been dependent beings.

Questioning the Justification of the Second Premise

Critics of the Cosmological Argument have raised several important objections against the claim that if every being is dependent the series or collection of those beings would have no explanation. Our understanding of the Cosmological Argument, as well as of its strengths and weaknesses, will be deepened by a careful consideration of these criticisms.

The first criticism is that the proponent of the Cosmological Argument makes the mistake of treating the collection or series of dependent beings as though it were itself a dependent being, and, therefore, requires an explanation of its existence. But, so the objection goes, the collection of dependent beings is not itself a dependent being any more than a collection of stamps is itself a stamp.

A second criticism is that the proponent makes the mistake of inferring that because each member of the collection of dependent beings has a cause, the collection itself must have a cause. But, as Bertrand Russell noted, such reasoning is as fallacious as to infer that the human race (that is, the collection of human beings) must have a mother because each member of the collection (each human being) has a mother.

A third criticism is that the proponent of the argument fails to realize that for there to be an explanation of a collection of things is nothing more than for there to be an explanation of each of the things making up the collection. Since in the infinite collection (or series) of dependent beings, each being in the collection does have an explanation—by virtue of having been caused by some preceding member of the collection—the explanation of the collection, so the criticism goes, has already been given. As David Hume remarked, "Did I show you the particular causes of each individual in a collection of twenty particles of matter, I should think it very unreasonable, should you afterwards ask me, what was the cause of the whole twenty. This is sufficiently explained in explaining the cause of the parts."[2]

Finally, even if the proponent of the Cosmological Argument can satisfactorily answer these objections, he must face one last objection to his ingenious attempt to justify premise two of the Cosmological Argument. For someone may agree that if nothing exists but an infinite collection of dependent beings, the infinite collection will have no explanation of its existence, and still refuse to conclude from this that there is something wrong with the idea that every being is a dependent being. Why, he might ask, should we think that everything has to have an explanation? What's wrong with admitting that the fact that there are and have always been dependent beings is a *brute fact*, a fact having no explanation whatever? Why does everything have to have an explanation anyway? We must now see what can be said in response to these several objections.

Responses to Criticism

It is certainly a mistake to think that a collection of stamps is itself a stamp, and very likely a mistake to think that the collection of dependent beings is itself a dependent being. But the mere fact that the proponent of the argument thinks that there must be an explanation not only for

each member of the collection of dependent beings but for the collection itself is not sufficient grounds for concluding that he must view the collection as itself a dependent being. The collection of human beings, for example, is certainly not itself a human being. Admitting this, however, we might still seek an explanation of why there is a collection of human beings, of why there are such things as human beings at all. So the mere fact that an explanation is demanded for the collection of dependent beings is no proof that the person who demands the explanation must be supposing that the collection itself is just another dependent being.

The second criticism attributes to the proponent of the Cosmological Argument the following bit of reasoning.

1. Every member of the collection of dependent beings has a cause or explanation.

Therefore,

2. The collection of dependent beings has a cause or explanation.

As we noted in setting forth this criticism, arguments of this sort are often unreliable. It would be a mistake to conclude that a collection of objects is light in weight simply because each object in the collection is light in weight, for if there were many objects in the collection it might be quite heavy. On the other hand, if we know that each marble weighs more than one ounce, we could infer validly that the collection of marbles weighs more than an ounce. Fortunately, however, we don't need to decide whether the inference from 1 to 2 is valid or invalid. We need not decide this question because the proponent of the Cosmological Argument need not use this inference to establish that there must be an explanation of the collection of dependent beings. He need not use this inference because he has in PSR a principle from which it follows immediately that the collection of dependent beings has a cause or explanation. For according to PSR, every positive fact must have an explanation. If it is a fact that there exists a collection of dependent beings then, according to PSR, that fact too must have an explanation. So it is PSR that the proponent of the Cosmological Argument appeals to in concluding that there must be an explanation of the collection of dependent beings, and not some dubious inference from the premise that each member of the collection has an explanation. It seems, then, that neither of the first two criticisms is strong enough to do any serious damage to the reasoning used to support the second premise of the Cosmological Argument.

The third objection contends that to explain the existence of a collection of things is the same thing as to explain the existence of each of its members. If we consider a collection of dependent beings where each being in the collection is explained by the preceding member which caused it, it's clear that no member of the collection will lack an explanation of its existence. But, so the criticism goes, if we've explained the existence of every member of a collection, we've explained the existence of the collection—there's nothing left over to be explained. This forceful criticism, originally advanced by David Hume, has gained considerable support in the modern period. But the criticism rests on an assumption that the proponent of the Cosmological Argument would not accept. The assumption is that to explain the existence of a collection of things it is *sufficient* to explain the existence of every member in the collection. To see what is wrong with this assumption is to understand the basic issue in the reasoning by which the proponent of the Cosmological Argument seeks to establish that not every being can be a dependent being.

In order for there to be an explanation of the existence of the collection of dependent beings, it's clear that the eighteenth-century proponents would require that the following two conditions be satisfied:

C1. There is an explanation of the existence of each of the members of the collection of dependent beings.
C2. There is an explanation of why there are any dependent beings.

According to the proponents of the Cosmological Argument, if every being that exists or ever did exist is a dependent being—that is, if the whole of reality consists of nothing more than a collection of dependent beings—C1 will be satisfied, but C2 will not be satisfied. And since C2 won't be satisfied, there will be no explanation of the collection of dependent beings. The third criticism, therefore, says in effect that if C1 is satisfied, C2 will be satisfied, and, since in a collection of dependent beings each member will have an explanation in whatever it was that produced it, C1 will be satisfied. So, therefore, C2 will be satisfied and the collection of dependent beings will have an explanation.

Although the issue is a complicated one, I think it is possible to see that the third criticism rests on a mistake: the mistake of thinking that if C1 is satisfied C2 must also be satisfied. The mistake is a natural one to make for it is easy to imagine circumstances in which if C1 is satisfied C2 also will be satisfied. Suppose, for example that the whole of reality includes not just a collection of dependent beings but also a self-existent being. Suppose further that instead of each dependent being having been produced by some other dependent being, every dependent being was produced by the self-existent being. Finally, let us consider both the possibility that the collection of dependent beings is finite in time and has a first member, and the possibility that the collection of dependent beings is infinite in past time, having no first member. Using G for the self-existent being, the first possibility may be diagramed as follows:

G, we shall say, has always existed and always will. We can think of d_1 as some presently existing dependent being, d_2, d_3, and so forth as dependent beings that existed at some time in the past, and d_n as the first dependent being to exist. The second possibility may be portrayed as follows:

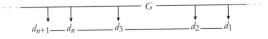

On this diagram there is no first member of the collection of dependent beings. Each member of the infinite collection, however, is explained by reference to the self-existent being *G* which produced it. Now the interesting point about both these cases is that the explanation that has been provided for the members of the collection of dependent beings carries with it, at least in part, an answer to the question of why there are any dependent beings at all. In both cases we may explain why there are dependent beings by pointing out that there exists a self-existent being that has been engaged in producing them. So once we have learned that the existence of each member of the collection of dependent beings has its existence explained by the fact that *G* produced it, we have already learned why there are dependent beings.

Someone might object that we haven't really learned why there are dependent beings until we also learn *why G* has been producing them. But, of course, we could also say that we haven't really explained the existence of a particular dependent being, say *d₃*, until we also learn not just that *G* produced it but *why G* produced it. The point we need to grasp, however, is that once we admit that every dependent being's existence is explained by *G,* we must admit that the fact that there are dependent beings has also been explained. So it is not unnatural that someone should think that to explain the existence of the collection of dependent beings is nothing more than to explain the existence of its members. For, as we've seen, to explain the collection's existence is to explain each member's existence and to explain why there are any dependent beings at all. And in the examples we've considered, in doing the one (explaining why each dependent being exists) we've already done the other (explained why there are any dependent beings at all). We must now see, however, that on the supposition that the whole of reality consists *only* of a collection of dependent beings, to give an explanation of each member's existence is not to provide an explanation of why there are dependent beings.

In the examples we've considered, we have gone outside of the collection of dependent beings in order to explain the members' existence. But if the only beings that exist or ever existed are dependent beings then each dependent being will be explained by some other dependent being, ad infinitum. This does not mean that there will be some particular dependent being whose existence is unaccounted for. Each dependent being has an explanation of its existence; namely, in the dependent being which preceded it and produced it. So C1 is satisfied: there is an explanation of the existence of each member of the collection of dependent beings. Turning to C2, however, we can see that it will not be satisfied. We cannot explain why there are (or have ever been) dependent beings by appealing to all the members of the infinite collection of dependent beings. For if the question to be answered is why there are (or have ever been) any dependent beings at all, we cannot answer that question by noting that there always have been dependent beings, each one accounting for the existence of some other dependent being. Thus on the supposition that every being is dependent, it seems there will be no explanation of why there are dependent beings. C2 will not be satisfied. Therefore, on the supposition that every being is dependent there will be no explanation of the existence of the collection of dependent beings.

The Truth of PSR

We come now to the final criticism of the reasoning supporting the second premise of the Cosmological Argument. According to the criticism, it is admitted that the supposition that every being is dependent implies that there will be a *brute fact* in the universe, a fact, that is, for which there can be no explanation whatever. For there will be no explanation of the fact that dependent beings exist and have always been in existence. It is this brute fact that the proponents of the argument were describing when they pointed out that if every being is dependent, the series or collection of dependent beings would lack an explanation of *its* existence. The final criticism asks what is wrong with admitting that the universe contains such a brute, unintelligible fact.

In asking this question the critic challenges the fundamental principle, PSR, on which the Cosmological Argument rests. For, as we've seen, the first premise of the argument denies that there exists a being whose existence has no explanation. In support of this premise the proponent appeals to the first part of PSR. The second premise of the argument claims that not every being can be dependent. In support of this premise the proponent appeals to the second part of PSR, the part which states that there must be an explanation of any positive fact whatever.

The proponent reasons that if every being were a dependent being, then although the first part of PSR would be satisfied—every being would have an explanation—the second part would be violated; there would be no explanation for the positive fact that there are and have always been dependent beings. For first, since every being is supposed to be dependent, there would be nothing outside of the collection of dependent beings to explain the collection's existence. Second, the fact that each member of the collection has an explanation in some other dependent being is insufficient to explain why there are and have always been dependent beings. And, finally, there is nothing about the collection of dependent beings that would suggest that it is a self-existent collection. Consequently, if every being were dependent, the fact that there are and have always been dependent beings would have no explanation. But this violates the second part of PSR. So the second premise of the Cosmological Argument must be true: Not every being can be a dependent being. This conclusion, however, is no better than the principle, PSR, on which it rests. And it is the point of the final criticism to question the truth of PSR. Why, after all, should we accept the idea that every being and every positive fact must have an explanation? Why, in short, should we believe PSR? These are important questions, and any final judgment of the Cosmological Argument depends on how they are answered.

Most of the theologians and philosophers who accept PSR have tried to defend it in either of two ways. Some have held that PSR is (or can be) known *intuitively* to be true. By this they mean that if we fully understand and reflect on what is said by PSR we can see that it must be true. Now, undoubtedly, there are statements which are known intuitively to be true. "Every triangle has exactly three angles" or "No physical object can be in two different places in space at one and the same time" are examples of statements whose truth we can apprehend just by understanding and reflecting on them. The difficulty with the claim that PSR is intuitively true, however, is that a number of very able philosophers fail to apprehend its truth, and some even claim that the principle is false. It is doubtful, therefore, that many of us, if any, know intuitively that PSR is true.

The second way philosophers and theologians who accept PSR have sought to defend it is by claiming that although it is not known to be true, it is, nevertheless, a presupposition of reason, a basic assumption that rational people make, whether or not they reflect sufficiently to become aware of the assumption. It's probably true that there are some assumptions we all make about our world, assumptions which are so basic that most of us are unaware of them. And, I suppose, it might be true that PSR is such an assumption. What bearing would this view of PSR have on the Cosmological Argument? Perhaps the main point to note is that even if PSR is a presupposition we all share, the premises of the Cosmological Argument could still be false. For PSR itself could still be false. The fact, if it is a fact, that all of us *presuppose* that every existing being and every positive fact has an explanation does not imply that no being exists, and no positive fact obtains, without an explanation. Nature is not bound to satisfy our presuppositions. As the American philosopher William James once remarked in another connection, "In the great boarding house of nature, the cakes and the butter and the syrup seldom come out so even and leave the plates so clear."

Our study of the first part of the Cosmological Argument has led us to the fundamental principle on which its premises rest, the Principle of Sufficient Reason. Since we do not seem to know that PSR is true, we cannot reasonably claim to know that the premises of the

Cosmological Argument are true. They might be true. But unless we do know them to be true they cannot *establish* for us the conclusion that there exists a being that has the explanation of its existence within its own nature. If it were shown, however, that even though we do not *know* that PSR is true we all, nevertheless, *presuppose* PSR to be true, then, whether PSR is true or not, to be consistent we should accept the Cosmological Argument. For, as we've seen, its premises imply its conclusion and its premises do seem to follow from PSR. But no one has succeeded in *showing* that PSR is an assumption that most or all of us share. So our final conclusion must be that although the Cosmological Argument might be a *sound* argument (valid with true premises), it does not provide us with good rational grounds for believing that among

these beings that exist there is one whose existence is accounted for by its own nature. Having come to this conclusion, we may safely put aside the second part of the argument. For even if it succeeded in showing that a self-existent being would have the other attributes of the theistic God, the Cosmological Argument would still not provide us with good rational grounds for belief in God, having failed in its first part to provide us with good rational grounds for believing that there is a self-existent being.

NOTES

1. See St. Thomas Aquinas, *Summa Theologica*, Ila. 2, 3.
2. David Hume, *Dialogues Concerning Natural Religion*, Part IX, ed. H. D. Aiken (New York: Hafner Publishing Company, 1948), pp. 59–60.

I.B.5   The *Kalām* Cosmological Argument

WILLIAM LANE CRAIG AND J. P. MORELAND

William Lane Craig (1949–   ) is a research professor of philosophy at Biola University in Los Angeles. He received his Ph.D. in philosophy from the University of Birmingham (England) and a Th.D. from the University of Munich (Germany). J. P. Moreland (1948–   ) is distinguished professor of philosophy at Biola University. He received his Ph.D. in philosophy from the University of Southern California. Professors Craig and Moreland are the authors of numerous works in philosophy of religion, including *Philosophical Foundations for a Christian Worldview* (2003), from which the following selection is taken. The *kalām* argument is a version of the cosmological argument developed by Arab Islamic scholars, al-Kindi and al-Ghazali, in the Middle Ages. In this article Craig and Moreland develop two versions of the *kalām* argument, both aiming to prove that the universe must have a cause of its existence.

The cosmological argument is a family of arguments that seek to demonstrate the existence of a Sufficient Reason or First Cause of the existence of the cosmos. The roll of the defenders of this argument reads like a *Who's Who* of western

philosophy: Plato, Aristotle, ibn Sina, Al Ghazali, Maimonides, Anselm, Aquinas, Scotus, Descartes, Spinoza, Leibniz and Locke, to name but some. The arguments can be grouped into three basic types: the *kalām* cosmological argument for a First Cause of the beginning of the universe, the Thomist cosmological argument for a sustaining a Ground of Being of the world, and the Leibnizian cosmological argument for a Sufficient Reason why something exists rather than nothing.

The *kalām* cosmological argument derives its name from the Arabic word designating medieval Islamic scholasticism, the intellectual movement largely responsible for developing the argument. It aims to show that the universe had a beginning at some moment in the finite past and, since something cannot come out of nothing, must therefore have a transcendent cause, which brought the universe into being. Classical proponents of the argument sought to demonstrate that the universe began to exist on the basis of philosophical arguments against the existence of an infinite, temporal regress of past events. Contemporary interest in the argument arises largely out of the startling empirical evidence of astrophysical cosmology for a beginning of space and time. Today the controlling paradigm of cosmology is the standard big bang model, according to which the space-time universe originated *ex nihilo* about fifteen billion years ago. Such an origin *ex nihilo* seems to many to cry out for a transcendent cause.

By contrast the Thomist cosmological argument, named for the medieval philosophical theologian Thomas Aquinas, seeks a cause that is first, not in the temporal sense, but in the sense of rank. Aquinas agreed that "if the world and motion have a first beginning, some cause must clearly be posited for this origin of the world and of motion" (*Summa contra gentiles* 1.13.30). But since he did not regard the *kalām* arguments for the past's finitude as demonstrative, he argued for God's existence on the more difficult assumption of the eternity of the world. On Aquinas's Aristotelian-inspired metaphysic, every existing finite thing is composed of essence and existence and is therefore radically contingent. A thing's essence is an individual nature which serves to define what that thing is. Now if an essence is to exist, there must be conjoined with that essence an act of being. This act of being involves a continual bestowal of being, or the thing would be annihilated. Essence is in potentiality to the act of being, and therefore

without the bestowal of being the essence would not exist. For the same reason no substance can actualize itself; for in order to bestow being on itself it would have to be already actual. A pure potentiality cannot actualize itself but requires some external cause. Now although Aquinas argued that there cannot be an infinite regress of causes of being (because in such a series all the causes would be merely instrumental and so no being would be produced, just as no motion would be produced in a watch without a spring even if it had an infinite number of gears) and that therefore there must exist a First Uncaused Cause of being, his actual view was that there can be no intermediate causes of being at all, that any finite substance is sustained in existence immediately by the Ground of Being. This must be a being that is not composed of essence and existence and, hence, requires no sustaining cause. We cannot say that this being's essence includes existence as one of its properties, for existence is not a property, but an act, the instantiating of an essence. Therefore, we must conclude that this being's essence just *is* existence. In a sense, this being has no essence; rather, it is the pure act of being, unconstrained by any essence. It is, as Thomas says, *ipsum esse subsistens,* the act of being itself subsisting. Thomas identifies this being with the God whose name was revealed to Moses as "I am" (Ex 3:14).

The German polymath Gottfried Wilhelm Leibniz, for whom the third form of the argument is named, sought to develop a version of the cosmological argument from contingency without the Aristotelian metaphysical underpinnings of the Thomist argument. In his essay "The Principles of Nature and of Grace, Based on Reason," Leibniz wrote, "The first question which should rightly be asked is this: why is there something rather than nothing?" Leibniz meant this question to be truly universal, not merely to apply to finite things. On the basis of his principle of sufficient reason, as stated in his treatise *The Monadology,* that "no fact can be real or existent, no statement true, unless there be a sufficient reason why it is so and not otherwise," Leibniz held that his question must have an answer. It will not do to say that the universe (or even God) just exists as a brute fact, a simple fact that cannot be explained. There must be an explanation why it exists. He went on to argue that the sufficient reason cannot be found in any individual thing in the universe, nor in the collection of such things which comprise the universe, nor in earlier states of the universe, even if these regress infinitely. Therefore, there must exist an ultramundane being that is metaphysically necessary in its existence, that is to say, its nonexistence is impossible. It is the sufficient reason for its own existence as well as for the existence of every contingent thing.

In evaluating these arguments, let us consider them in reverse order. A simple statement of a Leibnizian cosmological argument runs as follows:

1. Every existing thing has an explanation of its existence, either in the necessity of its own nature or in an external cause.
2. If the universe has an explanation of its existence, that explanation is God.
3. The universe is an existing thing.
4. Therefore the explanation of the existence of the universe is God.

Is this a good argument? One of the principal objections to Leibniz's own formulation of the argument is that the principle of sufficient reason as stated in The *Monadology* seems evidently false. There cannot be an explanation of why there are any contingent states of affairs at all, for if such an explanation is contingent, then it too must have a further explanation, whereas if it is necessary, then the states of affairs explained by it must also be necessary. Some theists have responded to this objection by agreeing that one must ultimately come to some explanatory stopping point that is simply a brute fact, a being whose existence is unexplained. For example, Richard Swinburne claims that in answering the question "Why is there something rather than nothing?" we must finally come to the brute existence of some contingent being. This being will not serve to explain its own existence (and, hence, Leibniz's question goes unanswered), but it will explain the existence of everything else. Swinburne argues that God is the best explanation of why everything other than the brute Ultimate exists because as a unique and infinite being God is simpler than the variegated and finite universe.

But the above formulation of the Leibnizian argument avoids the objection without retreating to the dubious position that God is a contingent being. Premise (1) merely requires any existing *thing* to have an explanation of its existence, either in the necessity of its own nature or in some external cause. This premise is compatible with there being brute *facts* about the world. What it precludes is that there could exist things—substances exemplifying properties—that just exist inexplicably. This principle seems quite plausible, at least more so than its contradictory, which is all that is required for a successful argument. On this analysis, there are two kinds of being: necessary beings, which exist of their own nature and so have no external cause of their existence, and contingent beings, whose existence is accounted for by causal factors outside themselves.

Premise (2) is, in effect, the contrapositive of the typical atheist response to Leibniz that on the atheistic worldview the universe simply exists as a brute contingent thing. Atheists typically assert that, there being no God, it is false that everything has an explanation of its existence, for the universe, in this case, just exists inexplicably. In so saying, the atheist implicitly recognizes that if the universe has an explanation, then God exists as its explanatory ground. Since, as premise (3) states, the universe is obviously an existing thing (especially evident in its very early stages when its density was so extreme), it follows that God exists.

It is open to the atheist to retort that while the universe has an explanation of its existence, that explanation lies not in an external ground but in the necessity of its own nature. In other words, (2) is false; the universe is a metaphysically necessary being. This was the suggestion of David Hume, who demanded, "Why may not the material universe be the necessarily existent being?" Indeed, "How can anything, that exists from eternity, have a cause, since that relation implies a priority in time and a beginning of existence?" (*Dialogues Concerning Natural Religion*, Part 9).

This is an extremely bold suggestion on the part of the atheist. We have, we think we can safely say, a strong intuition of the universe's contingency. A possible world in which no concrete objects exist certainly seems conceivable. We generally trust our modal intuitions on other matters; if we are to do otherwise with respect to the universe's contingency, then atheists need to provide some reason for such skepticism other than their desire to avoid theism. But they have yet to do so.

Still, it would be desirable to have some stronger argument for the universe's contingency than our modal intuitions alone. Could the Thomist cosmological argument help us here? If successful, it would show that the universe is a contingent being causally dependent on a necessary being for its continued existence. The difficulty with appeal to the Thomist argument, however, is that it is very difficult to show that things are, in fact, contingent in the special sense required by the argument. Certainly things are naturally contingent in that their continued existence is dependent on a myriad of factors including particle masses and fundamental forces, temperature, pressure, entropy level and so forth, but this natural contingency does not suffice to establish things' metaphysical contingency in the sense that being must continually be added to their essences lest they be spontaneously annihilated. Indeed, if Thomas's argument does ultimately lead to an absolutely simple being whose essence is existence, then one might well be led to deny that beings are metaphysically composed of essence and existence if the idea of such an absolutely simple being proves to be unintelligible....

But what about the *kalām* cosmological argument? An essential property of a metaphysically necessary and ultimate being is that it be eternal, that is to say, without beginning or end. If the universe is not eternal, then it could not be, as Hume suggested, a metaphysically necessary being. But it is precisely the aim of the *kalām* cosmological argument to show that the universe is not eternal but had a beginning. It would follow that the universe must therefore be contingent in its existence. Not only so, the *kalām* argument shows the universe to be contingent in a very special way: it came into existence out of nothing. The atheist who would answer Leibniz by holding that the existence of the universe is a brute fact, an exception to the principle of sufficient reason, is thus thrust into the very awkward position of maintaining not merely that the universe exists eternally without explanation, but rather that for no reason at all it

magically popped into being out of nothing, a position which might make theism look like a welcome alternative. Thus the *kalām* argument not only constitutes an independent argument for a transcendent Creator but also serves as a valuable supplement to the Leibnizian argument.

The *kalām* cosmological argument may be formulated as follows:

1. Whatever begins to exist has a cause.
2. The universe began to exist.
3. Therefore, the universe has a cause.

Conceptual analysis of what it means to be a cause of the universe then aims to establish some of the theologically significant properties of this being.

Premise (1) seems obviously true—at the least, more so than its negation. It is rooted in the metaphysical intuition that something cannot come into being from nothing. Moreover, this premise is constantly confirmed in our experience. Nevertheless, a number of atheists, in order to avoid the argument's conclusion, have denied the first premise. Sometimes it is said that quantum physics furnishes an exception to premise (1), since on the subatomic level events are said to be uncaused (according to the so-called Copenhagen interpretation). In the same way, certain theories of cosmic origins are interpreted as showing that the whole universe could have sprung into being out of the subatomic vacuum. Thus the universe is said to be the proverbial free lunch.

This objection, however, is based on misunderstandings. In the first place, not all scientists agree that subatomic events are uncaused. A great many physicists today are quite dissatisfied with the Copenhagen interpretation of subatomic physics and are exploring deterministic theories like that of David Bohm. Thus subatomic physics is not a proven exception to premise (1). Second, even on the traditional, indeterministic interpretation, particles do not come into being out of nothing. They arise as spontaneous fluctuations of the energy contained in the subatomic vacuum, which constitutes an indeterministic cause of their origination. Third, the same point can be made about theories of the origin of the universe out of a primordial vacuum. Popular magazine articles touting such theories as getting "something from nothing" simply do not understand that the vacuum is not nothing but rather a sea of fluctuating energy endowed with a rich structure and subject to physical laws. Thus there is no basis for the claim that quantum physics proves that things can begin to exist without a cause, much less that universe could have sprung into being uncaused from literally nothing.

Other critics have said that premise (1) is true only for things *in* the universe, but it is not true *of* the universe itself. But the argument's defender may reply that this objection misconstrues the nature of the premise. Premise (1) does not state merely a physical law like the law of gravity or the laws of thermodynamics, which are valid for things within the universe. Premise (1) is not a physical principle. Rather, premise (1) is a metaphysical principle: being cannot come from nonbeing; something cannot come into existence uncaused from nothing. The principle therefore applies to all of reality, and it is thus metaphysically absurd that the universe should pop into being uncaused out of nothing. This response seems quite reasonable: for on the atheistic view, there was not even the *potentiality* of the universe's existence prior to the big bang, since nothing is prior to the big bang. But then how could the universe become actual if there was not even the potentiality of its existence? It makes much more sense to say that the potentiality of the universe lay in the power of God to create it.

Recently some critics of the *kalm* cosmological argument have denied that in beginning to exist the universe *became actual* or *came into being*. They thereby focus attention on the theory of time underlying the *kalm* argument (see chap. 18). On a static or so-called B-theory of time (according to which all moments of time are equally existent) the universe does not in fact come into being or become actual at the big bang; it just exists tenselessly as a four-dimensional space-time block that is finitely extended in the *earlier than* direction. If time is tenseless, then the critics are right that the universe never really comes into being, and therefore the quest for a cause of its coming into being is misconceived. Although Leibniz's question, "Why is there (tenselessly) something rather than nothing?" should still rightly be asked, there would be no reason to look for a cause of the universe's beginning to exist, since on tenseless theories of time the universe did not truly begin to exist by virtue of its having a first event, any more than a meter stick begins to exist by virtue of its having a first centimeter. In affirming that things which begin to exist need a cause, the proponent of the *kalm* cosmological argument assumes the following understanding of that notion, where x ranges over any entity and t ranges over times, whether instants or moments of nonzero finite duration:

A. x begins to exist at t if and only if x comes into being at t.

B. x comes into being at t if and only if (i) x exists at t, and the actual world includes no state of affairs in which x exists timelessly, (ii) t is either the first time at which x exists or is separated from any $t' < t$ at which x existed by an interval during which x does not exist, and (iii) x's existing at t is a tensed fact.

The key clause in (B) is (iii). By presupposing a dynamic or so-called A-theory of time, according to which temporal becoming is real, the proponent of the *kalm* cosmological argument justifiably assumes that the universe's existing at a first moment of time represents the moment at which the universe came into being. Thus the real issue separating the proponent of the *kalm* cosmological argument and critics of the first premise is the objectivity of tense and temporal becoming.

Premise (2), *The universe began to exist*, has been supported by both deductive philosophical arguments and inductive scientific arguments. The first of four arguments for this premise that we will consider is the argument based on *the impossibility of the existence of an actual infinite*. It may be formulated as follows:

1. An actual infinite cannot exist.
2. An infinite temporal regress of physical events is an actual infinite.
3. Therefore an infinite temporal regress of physical events cannot exist.

In order to assess this argument, it will be helpful to define some terms. By an actual infinite, the argument's defender means any collection having at a time *t* a number of definite and discrete members that is greater than any natural number {0, 1, 2, 3, ... }. This notion is to be contrasted with a **potential infinite,** which is any collection having at any time *t* a number of definite and discrete members that is equal to some natural number but which over time increases endlessly toward infinity as a limit. By *exist* proponents of the argument mean "have extra-mental existence," or "be instantiated in the real world." By a "physical event," they mean any change occurring within the space-time universe. Since any change takes time, there are no instantaneous events. Neither could there be an infinitely slow event, since such an "event" would in reality be a changeless state. Therefore, any event will have a finite, nonzero duration. In order that all the events comprising the temporal regress of past events be of equal duration, one arbitrarily stipulates some event as our standard and, taking as our point of departure the present standard event, we consider any series of such standard events ordered according to the relation *earlier than*. The question is whether this series of events is comprised of an actually infinite number of events or not. If not, then since the universe is not distinct from the series of past physical events, the universe must have had a beginning, in the sense of a first standard event. It is therefore not relevant whether the temporal series had a beginning *point* (a first temporal instant). The question is whether there was in the past an event occupying a nonzero, finite temporal interval that was absolutely first, that is, not preceded by any equal interval.

Premise (1) asserts, then, that an actual infinite cannot exist in the real, spatiotemporal world. It is usually alleged that this sort of argument has been invalidated by Georg Cantor's work on the actual infinite and by subsequent developments in set theory. But this allegation misconstrues the nature of both Cantor's system and modern set theory, for the argument does not in fact contradict a single tenet of either. The reason is this: Cantor's system and set theory are simply a universe of discourse, a mathematical system based on certain adopted axioms and conventions. The argument's defender may hold that while the actual infinite may be a fruitful and

consistent concept within the postulated universe of discourse, it cannot be transposed into the spatiotemporal world, for this would involve counterintuitive absurdities. This can be shown by concrete examples that illustrate the various absurdities that would result if an actual infinite were to be instantiated in the real world.

Take, for example, **Hilbert's Hotel,** a product of the mind of the great German mathematician David Hilbert. As a warm-up, let us first imagine a hotel with a finite number of rooms. Suppose, furthermore, that all the rooms are full. When a new guest arrives asking for a room, the proprietor apologizes, "Sorry, all the rooms are full," and that is the end of the story. But now let us imagine a hotel with an infinite number of rooms and suppose once more that *all the rooms are full*. There is not a single vacant room throughout the entire infinite hotel. Now suppose a new guest shows up, asking for a room. "But of course!" says the proprietor, and he immediately shifts the person in room #1 into room #2, the person in room #2 into room #3, the person in room #3 into room #4 and so on, out to infinity. As a result of these room changes, room #1 now becomes vacant, and the new guest gratefully checks in. But remember, before he arrived, all the rooms were full! Equally curious, according to the mathematicians, there are now no more persons in the hotel than there were before: the number is just infinite. But how can this be? The proprietor just added the new guest's name to the register and gave him his keys—how can there not be one more person in the hotel than before?

But the situation becomes even stranger. For suppose an infinity of new guests show up at the desk, asking for a room. "Of course, of course!" says the proprietor, and he proceeds to shift the person in room #1 into room #2, the person in room #2 into room #4, the person in room #3 into room #6 and so on out to infinity, always putting each former occupant into the room number twice his own. Because any natural number multiplied by two always equals an even number, all the guests wind up in even-numbered rooms. As a result, all the odd-numbered rooms become vacant, and the infinity of new guests is easily accommodated. And yet, before they came, all the rooms were full! And again, strangely enough, the number of guests in the hotel is the same after the infinity of new guests check in as before, even though there were as many new guests as old guests. In fact, the proprietor could repeat this process *infinitely many times,* and yet there would never be one single person more in the hotel than before.

But Hilbert's Hotel is even stranger than the German mathematician made it out to be. For suppose some of the guests start to check out. Suppose the guest in room #1 departs. Is there not now one fewer person in the hotel? Not according to the mathematicians! Suppose the guests in rooms #1, 3, 5,... check out. In this case an infinite number of people have left the hotel, but according to the mathematicians, there are no fewer people in the hotel! In fact, we could have every other guest check out of the hotel and repeat this process infinitely many times, and yet there would never be any fewer people in the hotel. Now suppose the proprietor doesn't like having a half-empty hotel (it looks bad for business). No matter! By shifting occupants as before, but in reverse order, he transforms his half-vacant hotel into one that is jammed to the gills. You might think that by these maneuvers the proprietor could always keep this strange hotel fully occupied. But you would be wrong. For suppose that the persons in rooms #4, 5, 6,... checked out. At a single stroke the hotel would be virtually emptied, the guest register would be reduced to three names, and the infinite would be converted to finitude. And yet it would remain true that the same number of guests checked out this time as when the guests in rooms #1, 3, 5,... checked out! Can anyone believe that such a hotel could exist in reality?

Hilbert's Hotel certainly seems absurd. Since nothing hangs on the illustration's involving a hotel, the argument, if successful, would show in general that it is impossible for an actually infinite number of things to exist in spatiotemporal reality. Students sometimes react to such illustrations as Hilbert's Hotel by saying that we really do not understand the nature of infinity and, hence, these absurdities result. But this attitude is simply mistaken. Infinite set theory is a highly developed

and well-understood branch of mathematics, and these absurdities can be seen to result precisely because we *do* understand the notion of a collection with an actually infinite number of members.

Sometimes it is said that we can find counterexamples to the claim that an actually infinite number of things cannot exist, so that premise (1) must be false. For instance, is not every finite distance capable of being divided into 1/2, 1/4, 1/8,..., on to infinity? Does that not prove that there are in any finite distance an actually infinite number of parts? The defender of the argument may reply that this objection confuses a potential infinite with an actual infinite. He will point out that while you can continue to divide any distance for as long as you want, such a series is merely potentially infinite, in that infinity serves as a limit that you endlessly approach but never reach. If you assume that any distance is *already* composed out of an actually infinite number of parts, then you are begging the question. You are assuming what the objector is supposed to prove, namely that there is a clear counterexample to the claim that an actually infinite number of things cannot exist.

Again, it is worth reiterating that nothing in the argument need be construed as an attempt to undermine the theoretical system bequeathed by Cantor to modern mathematics. Indeed, some of the most eager enthusiasts of the system of transfinite mathematics are only too ready to agree that these theories have no relation to the real world. Thus Hilbert, who exuberantly extolled Cantor's greatness, nevertheless held that the Cantorian paradise exists only in the ideal world invented by the mathematician and is nowhere to be found in reality. The case against the existence of the actual infinite need say nothing about the use of the idea of the infinite in conceptual mathematical systems.

The second premise states that *an infinite temporal regress of events is an actual infinite.* The second premise asserts that if the series or sequence of changes in time is infinite, then these events considered collectively constitute an actual infinite. The point seems obvious enough, for if there has been a sequence composed of an infinite number of events stretching back into the past, then an actually infinite number of events have occurred. If the series of past events were an actual infinite, then all the absurdities attending the real existence of an actual infinite would apply to it.

In summary: if an actual infinite cannot exist in the real, spatiotemporal world and an infinite temporal regress of events is such an actual infinite, we can conclude that an infinite temporal regress of events cannot exist, that is to say, the temporal series of past physical events had a beginning. And this implies the second premise of the original syllogism of the *kalām* cosmological argument.

The second argument against the possibility of an infinite past that we will consider is the argument based on *the impossibility of forming an actual infinite by successive addition*. It may be formulated as follows:

1. The temporal series of physical events is a collection formed by successive addition.
2. A collection formed by successive addition cannot be an actual infinite.
3. Therefore, the temporal series of physical events cannot be an actual infinite.

Here one does not assume that an actual infinite cannot exist. Even if an actual infinite can exist, it is argued that the temporal series of events cannot be such, since an actual infinite cannot be formed by successive addition, as the temporal series of events is.

Premise (1) presupposes once again an A-theory of time. On such a theory the collection of all past events prior to any given event is not a collection whose members all tenselessly coexist. Rather, it is a collection that is instantiated sequentially or successively in time, one event coming to pass on the heels of another. Since temporal becoming is an objective feature of the physical world, the series of past events is not a tenselessly existing continuum, all of whose members are equally real. Rather, the members of the series come to be and pass away one after another.

Premise (2) asserts that a collection formed by successive addition cannot be an actual infinite. Sometimes this is described as the impossibility of traversing the infinite. In order for us to have "arrived" at today, temporal existence has, so to speak, traversed an infinite number of prior events. But before the present event could arrive, the event immediately prior to it would have to arrive, and before that event could arrive, the event immediately prior to it would have to arrive, and so on ad infinitum. No event could ever arrive, since before it could elapse there will always be one more event that had to have happened first. Thus, if the series of past events were beginningless, the present event could not have arrived, which is absurd.

This argument brings to mind Betrand Russell's account of Tristram Shandy, who, in the novel by Sterne, writes his autobiography so slowly that it takes him a whole year to record the events of a single day. Were he mortal, he would never finish, asserts Russell, but if he were immortal, then the entire book could be completed, since to each day there would correspond a year, and both are infinite. Russell's assertion is untenable on an A-theory of time, however, since the future is in reality a potential infinite only. Though he write forever, Tristram Shandy would only get farther and farther behind, so that instead of finishing his autobiography, he will progressively approach a state in which he would be *infinitely* far behind. But he would never reach such a state because the years and hence the days of his life would always be finite in number though indefinitely increasing.

But let us turn the story about: Suppose Tristram Shandy has been writing from eternity past at the rate of one day per year. Should not Tristram Shandy now be infinitely far behind? For if he has lived for an infinite number of years, Tristram Shandy has recorded an equally infinite number of past days. Given the thoroughness of his autobiography, these days are all consecutive days. At any point in the past or present, therefore, Tristram Shandy has recorded a beginningless, infinite series of consecutive days. But now the question inevitably arises: *Which* days are these? Where in the temporal series of events are the days recorded by Tristram Shandy at any given point? The answer can only be that *they are days infinitely distant from the present*. For there is no day on which Tristram Shandy is writing that is finitely distant from the last recorded day.

If Tristram Shandy has been writing for one year's time, then the most recent day he could have recorded is one year ago. But if he has been writing two years, then that same day could not have been recorded by him. For since his intention is to record *consecutive* days of his life, the most recent day he could have recorded is the day immediately after a day at least two years ago. This is because it takes a year to record a day, so that to record two days he must have two years. Similarly, if he has been writing three years, then the most recent day recorded could be no more recent than three years ago plus two days. In fact, the recession into the past of the most recent recordable day can be plotted according to the formula: (present date − *n* years of writing) + (*n* − 1) days. In other words, the longer he has written the further behind he has fallen. But what happens if Tristram Shandy has, *ex hypothesi,* been writing for an infinite number of years? The first day of his autobiography recedes to infinity, that is to say, to a day infinitely distant from the present. Nowhere in the past at a finite distance from the present can we find a recorded day, for by now Tristram Shandy is infinitely far behind. The beginningless, infinite series of days which he has recorded are days which lie at an infinite temporal distance from the present. What therefore follows from the Tristram Shandy story is that an infinite series of past events is absurd, for there is no way to traverse the distance from an infinitely distant event to the present, or, more technically, for an event that was once present to recede to an infinite temporal distance.

But now a deeper absurdity bursts into view. For if the series of past events is an actual infinite, then we may ask, why did Tristram Shandy not finish his autobiography yesterday or the day before, since by then an infinite series of moments had already elapsed? Given that in infinite time he would finish the book, then at any point in the infinite past he should already have finished. No matter how far along the series of past events one regresses, Tristram Shandy would have already completed his autobiography. Therefore, at no point in the infinite series of past events could he be finishing the book. We could never look over Tristram Shandy's shoulder to see if he were now writing the last page. For at any point an actually infinite sequence of events would have transpired and the book would have already been completed. Thus at no time in eternity will we find Tristram Shandy writing, which is absurd, since we supposed him to be writing from eternity. And at no point will he finish the book, which is equally absurd, because for the book to be completed, he must at some point have finished. What the Tristram Shandy story really tells us is that an actually infinite temporal regress is absurd.

Sometimes critics indict this argument as a sleight-of-hand trick like Zeno's paradoxes of motion. Zeno argued that before Achilles could cross the stadium, he would have to cross halfway; but before he could cross halfway, he would have to cross a quarter of the way; but before he could cross a quarter of the way, he would have to cross an eighth of the way, and so on to infinity. It is evident that Achilles could not even move! Therefore, Zeno concluded, motion is impossible. Now even though Zeno's argument is very difficult to refute, nobody really believes that motion is impossible. Even if Achilles must pass through an infinite number of halfway points in order to cross the stadium, somehow he manages to do so! The argument against the impossibility of traversing an infinite past, some critics allege, must commit the same fallacy as Zeno's paradox.

But such an objection fails to reckon with two crucial disanalogies of an infinite past to Zeno's paradoxes: whereas in Zeno's thought experiments the intervals traversed are *potential* and *unequal,* in the case of an infinite past the intervals are *actual* and *equal.* The claim that Achilles must pass through an infinite number of halfway points in order to cross the stadium is question-begging, for it already assumes that the whole interval is a composition of an infinite number of points, whereas Zeno's opponents, like Aristotle, take the line as a whole to be conceptually prior to any divisions which we might make in it. Moreover, Zeno's intervals, being unequal, sum to a merely finite distance, whereas the intervals in an infinite past sum to an infinite distance. Thus his thought experiments are crucially disanalogous to the task of traversing an infinite number of equal, actual intervals to arrive at our present location.

It is frequently objected that this sort of argument illicitly presupposes an infinitely distant starting point in the past and then pronounces it impossible to travel from that point to today. But if the past is infinite, then there would be no starting point whatever, not even an infinitely distant one. Nevertheless, from any given point in the past, there is only a finite distance to the present, which is easily "traversed." But in fact no proponent of the *kalām* argument of whom we are aware has assumed that there was an infinitely distant starting point in the past. (Even the Tristram Shandy paradox does not assert that there was an infinitely distant first day, but merely that there were days infinitely distant in the past.) The fact that there is *no beginning* at all, not even an infinitely distant one, seems only to make the problem worse, not better. To say that the infinite past could have been formed by successive addition is like saying that someone has just succeeded in writing down all the negative numbers, ending at −1. And, we may ask, how is the claim that from any given moment in the past there is only a finite distance to the present even relevant to the issue? The defender of the *kalām* argument could agree to this happily. For the issue is how the *whole* series can be formed, not a finite portion of it. Does the objector think that because every *finite* segment of the series can be formed by successive addition that the whole *infinite* series can be so formed? That is as logically fallacious as saying because every part of an elephant is light in weight, the whole elephant is light in weight. The claim is therefore irrelevant.

In summary: If a collection formed by successive addition cannot be an actual infinite, then since the temporal series of events is a collection formed by successive addition, it follows that the temporal series of past physical events is not beginningless.

The third argument for the universe's beginning advanced by contemporary proponents of the *kalām* cosmological argument is an inductive argument based on the expansion of the universe. In 1917, Albert Einstein made a cosmological application of his newly discovered gravitational theory, the general theory of relativity (GTR). In so doing he assumed that the universe exists in a steady state, with a constant mean mass density and a constant curvature of space. To his chagrin, however, he found that GTR would not permit such a model of the universe unless he introduced into his gravitational field equations a certain "fudge factor" in order to counterbalance the gravitational effect of matter and so ensure a static universe. Unfortunately, Einstein's static universe was balanced on a razor's edge, and the least perturbation would cause the universe either to implode or to expand. By taking this feature of Einstein's model seriously, the Russian mathematician Alexander Friedman and the Belgian astronomer Georges Lemaître were able to formulate independently in the 1920s solutions to the field equations which predicted an expanding universe.

In 1929 the astronomer Edwin Hubble showed that the red-shift in the optical spectra of light from distant galaxies was a common feature of all measured galaxies and was proportional to their distance from us. This red-shift was taken to be a Doppler effect indicative of the recessional motion of the light source in the line of sight. Incredibly, what Hubble had discovered was the isotropic expansion of the universe predicted by Friedman and Lemaître on the basis of Einstein's GTR.

According to the Friedman-Lemaître model, as time proceeds, the distances separating galactic masses become greater. It is important to understand that as a GTR-based theory, the model does not describe the expansion of the material content of the universe into a preexisting, empty space, but rather the expansion of space itself. The ideal particles of the cosmological fluid constituted by the galactic masses are conceived to be at rest with respect to space but to recede progressively from one another as space itself expands or stretches, just as buttons glued to the surface of a balloon would recede from one another as the balloon inflates. As the universe expands, it becomes less and less dense. This has the astonishing implication that as one reverses the expansion and extrapolates back in time, the universe becomes progressively denser until one arrives at a state of "infinite density"[1] at some point in the finite past. This state represents a singularity at which space-time curvature, along with temperature, pressure and density, becomes infinite. It therefore constitutes an edge or boundary to space-time itself. The term "big bang" is thus potentially misleading, since the expansion cannot be visualized from the outside (there being no "outside," just as there is no "before" with respect to the big bang).

The standard big bang model, as the Friedman-Lemaître model came to be called, thus describes a universe that is not eternal in the past but that came into being a finite time ago. Moreover—and this deserves underscoring—the origin it posits is an absolute origin *ex nihilo*. For not only all matter and energy, but space and time themselves come into being at the initial cosmological singularity. There can be no natural, physical cause of the big bang event, since, in Quentin Smith's words, "it belongs analytically to the concept of the cosmological singularity that it is not the effect of prior physical events. The definition of a singularity . . . entails that it is *impossible to extend the spacetime manifold beyond the singularity. . . .* This rules out the idea that the singularity is an effect of some prior natural process."[2] Sir Arthur Eddington, contemplating the beginning of the universe, opined that the expansion of the universe was so preposterous and incredible that "I feel almost an indignation that anyone should believe in it—except myself."[3] He finally felt forced to conclude, "The beginning seems to present insuperable difficulties unless we agree to look on it as frankly supernatural."[4]

Sometimes objectors appeal to scenarios other than the standard model of the expanding universe in an attempt to avert the absolute beginning predicted by the standard model. But while such theories are possible, it has been the overwhelming verdict of the scientific community than none of them is more probable than the big bang theory. The devil is in the details, and once you get down to specifics you find that there is no mathematically consistent model that has been so successful in its predictions or as corroborated by the evidence as the traditional big bang theory. For example, some theories, like the oscillating universe (which expands and recontracts forever) or the chaotic inflationary universe (which continually spawns new universes), do have a potentially infinite future but turn out to have only a finite past. Vacuum fluctuation universe theories (which postulate an eternal vacuum out of which our universe is born) cannot explain why, if the vacuum was eternal, we do not observe an infinitely old universe. The quantum gravity universe theory propounded by the famous physicist Stephen Hawking, if interpreted realistically, still involves an absolute origin of the universe even if the universe does not begin in a so-called singularity, as it does in the standard big bang theory. The recent speculative cyclic ekpyrotic scenario championed by Paul Steinhardt not only leaves unresolved the difficulties facing the old oscillating universe but has also been shown to require a singular beginning in the past. In sum, according to Hawking, "Almost everyone now believes that the universe, and *time itself,* had a beginning at the Big Bang."[5]

The fourth argument for the finitude of the past is also an inductive argument, this time on the basis of the thermodynamic properties of the universe. According to the **second law of thermodynamics,** processes taking place in a closed system always tend toward a state of equilibrium. Now our interest in the law concerns what happens when it is applied to the universe as a whole. The universe is, on a naturalistic view, a gigantic closed system, since it is everything there is and there is nothing outside it. This seems to imply that, given enough time, the universe and all its processes will run down, and the entire universe will come to equilibrium. This is known as the **heat death of the universe.** Once the universe reaches this state, no further change is possible. The universe is dead.

There are two possible types of heat death for the universe. If the universe will eventually recontract, it will die a "hot" death. As it contracts, the stars gain energy, causing them to burn more rapidly so that they finally explode or evaporate. As everything in the universe grows closer together, the black holes begin to gobble up everything around them, and eventually begin themselves to coalesce. In time, all the black holes finally coalesce into one large black hole that is coextensive with the universe, from which the universe will never reemerge.

On the other hand if, as is more likely, the universe will expand forever, then its death will be cold, as the galaxies turn their gas into stars, and the stars burn out. At 10^{30} years the universe will consist of 90% dead stars, 9% supermassive black holes formed by the collapse of galaxies, and 1% atomic matter, mainly hydrogen. Elementary particle physics suggests that thereafter protons will decay into electrons and positrons so that space will be filled with a rarefied gas so thin that the distance between an electron and a positron will be about the size of the present galaxy. Eventually all black holes will completely evaporate and all the matter in the ever-expanding universe will be reduced to a thin gas of elementary particles and radiation. Equilibrium will prevail throughout, and the entire universe will be in its final state, from which no change will occur.

Now the question that needs to be asked is this: if given enough time the universe will reach heat death, then why is it not in a state of heat death now, if it has existed forever, from eternity? If the universe did not begin to exist, then it should now be in a state of equilibrium. Like a ticking clock, it should by now have run down. Since it has not yet run down, this implies, in the words of one baffled scientist, "In some way the universe must have been *wound up.*"[6]

Some people have tried to escape this conclusion by adopting an oscillating model of the universe which never reaches a final state of equilibrium. But even apart from the physical and observational problems plaguing such a model, the thermodynamic properties of this model imply the very beginning of the universe that its proponents sought to avoid. Because entropy increases from cycle to cycle in such a model, it has the effect of generating larger and longer oscillations with each successive cycle. Thus, as one traces the oscillations back in time, they become progressively smaller until one reaches a first and smallest oscillation. Hence, the oscillating model has an infinite future, but only a finite past. In fact, it is estimated on the basis of current entropy levels that the universe cannot have gone through more than 100 previous oscillations.

Even if this difficulty were avoided, a universe oscillating from eternity past would require an infinitely precise tuning of initial conditions in order to last through an infinite number of successive bounces. A universe rebounding from a single, infinitely long contraction is, if entropy increases during the contracting phase, thermodynamically untenable and incompatible with the initial low-entropy condition of our expanding phase. Postulating an entropy decrease during the contracting phase in order to escape this problem would require us to postulate inexplicably special low-entropy conditions at the time of the bounce in the life of an infinitely evolving universe. Such a low-entropy condition at the beginning of the expansion is more plausibly accounted for by the presence of a singularity or some sort of quantum creation event.

So whether one adopts a recontracting model, an ever-expanding model or an oscillating model, thermodynamics suggests that the universe had a beginning. The universe appears to have been created a finite time ago, and its energy was somehow simply put in at the creation as an initial condition.

On the basis of these four arguments for the finitude of the past, the proponent of the *kalām* argument seems to have good grounds for affirming the second premise of the *kalām* cosmological argument: that the universe began to exist. It therefore follows that the universe has a cause. Conceptual analysis enables us to recover a number of striking properties that must be possessed by such an ultramundane being. For as the cause of space and time, this entity must transcend space and time and therefore exist atemporally and nonspatially, at least without the universe. This transcendent cause must therefore be changeless and immaterial, since timelessness entails changelessness, and changelessness implies immateriality. Such a cause must be beginningless and uncaused, at least in the sense of lacking any antecedent causal conditions. Ockham's razor will shave away further causes, since we should not multiply causes beyond necessity. This entity must be unimaginably powerful, since it created the universe without any material cause.

Finally, and most remarkably, such a transcendent cause is plausibly taken to be personal. Three reasons can be given for this conclusion. First, there are two types of causal explanation: scientific explanations in terms of laws and initial conditions and personal explanations in terms of agents and their volitions. A first state of the universe *cannot* have a scientific explanation, since there is nothing before it, and therefore it can be accounted for only in terms of a personal explanation. Second, the personhood of the cause of the universe is implied by its timelessness and immateriality, since the only entities we know of that can possess such properties are either minds or abstract objects, and abstract objects do not stand in causal relations. Therefore, the transcendent cause of the origin of the universe must be of the order of mind. Third, this same conclusion is also implied by the fact that we have in this case the origin of a temporal effect from a timeless cause. If the cause of the origin of the universe were an impersonal set of necessary and sufficient conditions, it would be impossible for the cause to exist without its effect. For if the necessary and sufficient conditions of the effect are timelessly given, then their effect must be given as well. The only way for the cause to be timeless and changeless but for its effect to originate anew a finite time ago is for the cause to be a personal agent who freely chooses to bring about an effect without antecedent determining conditions. Thus we are brought, not merely to a transcendent cause of the universe, but to its Personal Creator. He is, as Leibniz maintained, the Sufficient Reason why anything exists rather than nothing.

NOTES

1. This should not be taken to mean that the density of the universe takes on a value of H_0 but rather that the density of the universe is expressed by a ratio of mass to volume in which the volume is zero; since division by zero is impermissible, the density is said to be infinite in this sense.
2. Quentin Smith, "The Uncaused Beginning of the Universe," in *Theism, Atheism and Big Bang Cosmology*, by William Lane Craig and Quentin Smith (Oxford: Clarendon, 1993), p. 120.
3. Arthur Eddington, *The Expanding Universe* (New York: Macmillan, 1933), p. 124.
4. Ibid., p. 178.
5. Stephen Hawking and Roger Penrose, *The Nature of Space and Time*, The Isaac Newton Institute Series of Lectures (Princeton, N.J.: Princeton University Press, 1996), p. 20.
6. Richard Schlegel, "Time and Thermodynamics," in *The Voices of Time*, ed. J. T. Fraser (London: Penguin, 1948), p. 511.

I.B.6   A Critique of the *Kalām* Cosmological Argument

PAUL DRAPER

Paul Draper is professor of philosophy at Purdue University and the author of several important essays in the philosophy of religion. In this article he analyzes two versions of the *cosmological argument:* the argument from contingency and the *kalām* argument. Draper contends that the argument rests on an equivocation of the phrase "begins to exist" and that this fallacy undermines its force.

Epistemology begins in doubt, ethics in conflict, and metaphysics in wonder.

In a recent book,[1] William Lane Craig offers a philosophical and scientific defense of a very old and very wonderful argument: the *kalām* cosmological argument. Unlike other cosmological arguments, the *kalām* argument bases its conclusion that the universe has a cause of its existence on the premise that the universe began to exist a finite time ago. Craig calls it the "*kalām*" cosmological argument because "*kalām*" is the name of a theological movement within Islam that used reason, including this argument, to defend the Muslim faith against philosophical objections. After being fully developed by Arab thinkers like al-Kindi and al-Ghazali, the argument eventually made its way to the West, where it was rejected by St. Thomas Aquinas and defended by St. Bonaventure.[2] My focus in this paper will be on Craig's philosophical defense of the argument. I will try to show that this defense fails, both because it fails to establish that the universe had a beginning and because it commits the fallacy of equivocation.

Compare the following two cosmological arguments, each of which concludes that the universe has a cause of its existence:

1. Every contingent thing (including things that are infinitely old) has a cause of its existence.
2. The universe is contingent.
3. Therefore, the universe has a cause of its existence.

1. Everything that begins to exist has a cause of its existence.
2. The universe began to exist.
3. Therefore, the universe has a cause of its existence.

The first of these arguments is sometimes called the argument from contingency. It was suggested by Aristotle, clearly formulated by Arabic philosophers like ibn Sina, and later championed in the West by St. Thomas Aquinas. I find it completely unpersuasive. For although the second premise is clearly true (so long as "contingent" means "logically contingent"), I do not find the first premise appealing at all. If something is infinitely old, then it has always existed, and it's hard to see why something that has always existed requires a cause of its existence, even if it is logically possible that it not have existed. (Indeed, it's not even clear that something that has always existed *could* have a cause of its existence.)

The second of these arguments is the *kalām* cosmological argument. This argument avoids the weakness of the argument from contingency by denying that the universe is infinitely old and maintaining that the universe needs a cause, not because it is contingent, but rather because it had a beginning. In other words, it replaces the weak premise that every contingent thing needs a cause of its existence with the compelling premise that everything that begins to exist needs a cause of its existence. Of course, a price must be paid for strengthening the first premise: the second premise—that the universe began to exist—is not by a long shot as unquestionably true as the claim that the universe is contingent.

Craig, however, provides a spirited and plausible defense of this premise. He offers four arguments in support of it, two of which are philosophical (armchair cosmology at its best) and two of which are scientific (but still interesting). Both philosophical arguments depend on a distinction between a potential infinite and an actual infinite. A potential infinite is a series or collection that can increase forever without limit but is always finite (e.g., the set of events that have occurred since the birth of my daughter or the set of completed years after 1000 BCE). An actual infinite is a set of distinct things (real or not) whose number is actually infinite (e.g., the set of natural numbers). The first philosophical argument claims that there can't be an infinite regress of events, because actual infinites cannot exist in reality. According to the second argument, an infinite regress of events is impossible because, even if actual infinites could exist in reality, they could not be formed by successive addition.

The first scientific argument is based on the evidence for the Big Bang theory, which seems to many scientists to support the view that the universe had a beginning. The second scientific argument appeals to the Second Law of Thermodynamics. According to this law, the amount of energy available to do mechanical work always decreases in a closed system. Thus, since the universe as a whole is a closed system with a finite amount of such energy, an infinitely old universe is incompatible with the fact that we have not yet run out of such energy—the universe has not yet reached its "equilibrium end state." Since I'm no scientist, I will focus my attention on Craig's philosophical arguments, beginning with the second one.

As Craig himself points out, his second philosophical argument is very similar to the argument that Immanuel Kant uses to support the thesis of his first antinomy:

> If we assume that the world has no beginning in time, then up to every given moment an eternity has elapsed and there has passed away in the world an infinite series of successive states of things. Now the infinity of a series consists in the fact that it can never be completed through successive synthesis. It thus follows that it is impossible for an infinite world-series to have passed away, and that a beginning of the world is therefore a necessary condition of the world's existence.[3]

Craig formulates the argument as follows:

(i) The temporal series of events is a collection formed by successive addition.
(ii) A collection formed by successive addition cannot be an actual infinite.
(iii) Thus, the temporal series of events cannot be an actual infinite. (from i and ii)
(iv) Therefore, the temporal regress of events is finite. (from iii)[4]

This argument is closely related to Zeno's paradoxes, which depend on the claim that one cannot complete an infinite series of tasks one at a time since that would imply an infinitieth member of the series. As it stands, the argument is unconvincing. For while it is true that one cannot start with a finite collection and then by adding one new member at a time turn it into an infinite collection (no matter how much time one has available), nothing of the sort is required in order for the past to be infinite. For if the temporal regress

of events is infinite, then the universe has never had a finite number of past events. Rather, it has always been the case that the collection of past events is infinite. Thus, if the temporal regress of events is infinite, then the temporal series of events is not an infinite collection formed by successively adding to a finite collection. Rather, it is a collection formed by successively adding to an infinite collection. And surely it is not impossible to form an infinite collection by successively adding to an already infinite collection.

One might object that, if the temporal regress of events is infinite, then there must be some event E separated from the birth of my daughter by an infinite number of intermediate events, in which case the collection containing E and all those intermediate events would have to be an actually infinite collection formed by successively adding to a finite collection of events, namely the collection containing E as its only member. This objection fails because it is simply not true that, if the temporal regress of events is infinite, then there must be two events separated by an infinite number of intermediate events. For consider the set of natural numbers. It is actually infinite, yet every member of it is such that there is a finite number of members between it and its first member.[5]

Craig's first philosophical argument is, I believe, much more promising than his second. It bases its conclusion that the temporal regress of physical events must be finite—there must have been a first physical event—on the premises that an actual infinite cannot exist in reality and an infinite temporal regress of events is an actual infinite.[6] From this and the further claim that a first physical event could not have been preceded by an eternal absolutely quiescent physical universe, the conclusion is drawn that the physical universe had a beginning. The first stage of this argument can be formulated as follows:

a. No set of real things is actually infinite.
b. If there was no first event, then the set of all real events occurring prior to the birth of my daughter is actually infinite.
c. Therefore, there was a first event.

Craig defends premise (a) of this argument by pointing out that the assumption that a set of real things is actually infinite has paradoxical implications.[7] For example, it implies that we could have a library consisting of infinitely many black books (each might be assigned an even number). We could then add infinitely many red books (each might be assigned an odd number) and yet not increase the number of books in the library by a single volume. Indeed, we could add infinitely many different colors of books with infinitely many books of each color (the red books could be assigned rational numbers between 0 and 1, the black books rational numbers between 1 and 2, and so on) and not increase our collection by a single volume.

These paradoxes arise because the following three statements constitute an inconsistent triad:

S1. A set has more members than any of its proper subsets.
S2. If the members of two sets can be placed in one-to-one correspondence, then neither set has more members than the other.
S3. There are actually infinite sets.

For example, since the set of even numbers has one-to-one correspondence with the set of natural numbers and even with the set of rational numbers, S2 implies that one could add infinitely many red books or infinitely many books of each of infinitely many different colors to the library without increasing the size of that library's collection. (One need only make sure that the additions are *denumerably* infinite.) But of course S1 implies that any such addition would increase the size of the collection since the set of even numbers is a proper subset both of the set of natural numbers and of the set of rational numbers. Thus, two intuitively appealing principles together imply a contradiction on the assumption that there can be an actually infinite collection of books. One way to avoid this contradiction is to reject the assumption that there can be an actually infinite collection of books. So the underlying argument in defense of the claim that no collection of real things is actually infinite is simply that, since S1 and S2 are both true of collections of real things, it follows that S3 is not true of

such collections—no collections of real things are actually infinite.

Craig claims that Georg Cantor's theory of transfinite numbers is consistent because it rejects the first member of the triad. But this member is not rejected because it can be proven false about actually infinite sets, nor is the second member accepted because it can be proven that if a one-to-one correspondence between the elements of two actually infinite sets can be established then the sets are equivalent. Rather, equivalent sets are simply defined as sets having one-to-one correspondence. Thus, while Cantor's theory is a consistent mathematical system, there is, according to Craig, no reason to think that it has any interesting ontological implications. In particular, it does not provide any reason to think that S1 is false about actually infinite sets and hence provides no justification for thinking that actual infinites can exist in reality.[8]

Notice that, if Craig is right that past events are real but future events are not, then his argument for a first event does not commit him to the position that there is a last event. For consider the following parallel argument for the conclusion that there will be a last event:

(a) No set of real things is actually infinite.
(b) If there will be no last event, then the set of all real events occurring after the birth of my daughter is actually infinite.
(c) Therefore, there will be a last event.

Since future events are not real, the second premise of this argument is false. If there is no last event, then the set of all real events occurring after the birth of my daughter is merely potentially infinite—not actually infinite. This collection can increase in size indefinitely, but it will always be finite. Past events, on the other hand, are all real. So if there is no first past event, then the set of all real past events is actually infinite, not potentially infinite. Craig concludes that, although there may be no last event, there must be a first event, and hence, since matter cannot exist without events occurring, it follows that the universe has not always existed—it began to exist.

Although this fascinating argument for the second premise of the *kalām* argument may be sound, Craig has not given us adequate reason to believe it is. The problem concerns the inconsistent triad mentioned above. What Craig needs to do is to show that, when it comes to collections of real things, we should reject the third member of the triad instead of S1 or S2. But he has not shown this. S1 and S2 are certainly true for finite collections. But it's far from clear that they are true for all collections. Allow me to explain why.

Consider S1, which says that a set has more members than any of its proper subsets. If "more" means "a greater number," then the claim that S1 is true for actually infinite sets requires us to make sense of claiming that actually infinite sets have a *number* of members. But an actually infinite set doesn't have a natural number of members or a rational number of members or a real number of members, so one such set can't have a greater natural or rational or real number of members than another. Of course, an actually infinite set does have a transfinite number of members. But transfinite numbers are what Cantor defines them to be. And given his definition, it simply isn't true that actually infinite sets have a greater transfinite number of members than all of their proper subsets. We could say that an actually infinite set has a greater "infinite number" of members than all of its proper subsets, but Craig gives us no theory of infinite numbers that would justify that claim.

Of course, Craig might claim that no such theory is necessary, that we don't even need to make use of the word *number* here; for it's just obvious that, in some sense of the word *more,* any set that has every member that another set has and some members it doesn't have has more members than the other set. I agree this is obvious, but in the case of infinite sets, this is obvious only because "more" can just mean "has every member the other set has and some members it doesn't have." If, however, we grant Craig that S1 is true on these grounds, then why accept S2? Why not claim instead that actually infinite collections of real objects are possible, but the fact that two of them have one-to-one correspondence is not a good reason to believe that neither has "more" members than the other? Why, for example, is it more reasonable to believe that actually infinite libraries are impossible than to believe that, although they are possible, one such library can have "more" books than a second despite the fact that the books in the first can be placed in one-to-one correspondence with the books in the second? Craig provides no good answer to these questions. Obviously he cannot all of a sudden appeal to Cantor's theory to justify accepting S2. For that would commit him to rejecting S1. And since, when infinite sets are compared, the word *more* cannot mean what it does when finite sets are compared, the fact that S2 is true for finite sets is not by itself a good reason to believe that it is true for all sets.

So Craig fails to show that S1 and S2 are both true of all collections of real objects, and hence he fails to show that actually infinite collections of real objects are impossible. Therefore, his first philosophical argument, like his second, fails to establish that an infinite regress of events is impossible and so fails to establish that the universe began to exist. This leaves us with Craig's scientific arguments. Since I lack the expertise to evaluate these arguments, let's assume, for the sake of argument, that they succeed and hence that the universe did begin to exist. Must we then conclude that the *kalām* argument succeeds? This would be a profound result. Granted, this argument doesn't get all the way to God's existence. But accepting its conclusion does require rejecting naturalism—since nothing can be a cause of its own existence, a cause outside the natural world would be required.

As wonderful as this conclusion is, I do not believe that Craig's defense of the *kalām* argument justifies accepting it, even assuming that his scientific arguments are sound. This is because Craig commits the fallacy of equivocation. The verb "to begin" has a narrow or strict sense and a broad or loose sense. In the narrow sense, "to begin" means "to begin within time." When used in this way, "x begins to exist" implies that there was a time at which x did not exist and then a later time at which x exists. But "to begin" can also mean "to begin either within or with time." When used in this way, "x begins to exist" does not imply that there was a time at which *x* did not exist, because the past may itself be finite in which case something that begins to exist at the first moment in time is such that there never was a time at which it did not exist—it begins with time rather than within time. Now consider the two premises of the *kalām* argument in the light of this distinction.

The second premise is that the universe began to exist. All of Craig's arguments in favor of this premise, including his scientific ones, would be unsound if one interpreted "began to exist" in the second premise as meaning "began to exist within time." For nothing in these arguments counts against a relational view of time. And on a relational view of time, a first temporal event is simultaneous with a first moment in time. This would mean that, if the temporal series of past events is finite, then the universe began to exist with time. Indeed, if anything, the arguments in favor of the second premise support a beginning with time. For if an infinite regress of events is an actual infinite and for that reason impossible, then it would seem that an infinite past would be an actual infinite and for that reason impossible. Moreover, one of Craig's scientific arguments appeals to an interpretation of the Big Bang Theory according to which time did not exist "before" the big bang. So the most that Craig has established is that the universe began to exist either within or with time.

The first premise is that anything that begins to exist has a cause of its existence. What does "begins to exist" mean here? Craig defends this premise by claiming that it is an "empirical generalisation enjoying the strongest support experience affords."[9] But experience only supports the claim that anything that begins to exist within time has a cause of its existence. For we have no experience whatsoever of things beginning to exist with time.[10] Such things would require timeless causes. And even if it is conceptually possible for a temporal event to have a timeless cause, we certainly have no experience of this. Of course, Craig also claims that premise (1) is intuitively obvious—that it needs no defense at all. But it is far from obvious that a universe that begins to exist with time needs a cause of its existence. Like an infinitely old universe, a universe that begins to exist with time has always existed—for any time t, the universe existed at t. And once again, it's far from obvious that something that has always existed requires a cause for its existence. It's not even clear that such a thing *could* have a cause of its existence.

So in order to be justified in believing both of the premises of the argument—justified, that is, solely on the basis of Craig's defense of those premises—we would need to equivocate on the meaning of "begins to exist." We would need to use this term in the narrow sense in the first premise and in the broad sense in the second premise. But then the conclusion of the argument would not follow from its premises. Thus, Craig commits the fallacy of equivocation.[11]

Do my objections to Craig's defense of the *kalām* argument prove that it is doomed? I don't think so. The argument remains promising. Perhaps, for example, it could be shown that an absolute theory of time is correct, and that such a theory, together with scientific or new philosophical evidence against an infinitely old universe, implies a beginning of the universe within time. Or perhaps it could be shown that the universe began to exist with time and that even something that begins to exist with time requires a cause of its existence. So my conclusion is not that the *kalām* argument should be dismissed. It is just that it has not yet been adequately defended. I still *wonder* whether the argument is a good one.

NOTES

1. William Lane Craig, *The Kalām Cosmological Argument* (New York: Harper & Row Publishers), 1979.
2. For a brief but interesting history of the argument, see Craig, Part I.
3. Immanuel Kant, *Critique of Pure Reason*, trans. Norman Kemp Smith (London: Macmillan & Co., 1929), p. 396. Quoted by Craig on p. 189.
4. Craig, p. 103.
5. Cf. Quentin Smith, "*Infinity and the Past,*" in *Theism, Atheism, and Big Bang Cosmology*, ed. William Lane Craig and Quentin Smith (Oxford: Clarendon Press, 1993), pp. 78–83; Antony Flew, "The Case for God Challenged," in *Does*

God Exist?: The Great Debate, ed. J. P. Moreland and Kai Nielsen (Nashville: Thomas Nelson Publishers, 1990), p. 164; and Keith Parsons, "Is There a Case for Christian Theism?" in *Does God Exist?: The Great Debate*, p. 187.

6. Craig, p. 69.
7. Craig, pp. 82–87.
8. Craig, pp. 94–95.
9. Craig, p. 145. Craig also suggests here that premise (1) could be defended by appealing to an a priori category of causality. Such Kantian maneuvering does not seem very promising in this context. For in order to reconcile it with the realism presupposed by the *kalām* argument, one would need to claim that the causal principle must, as a necessary precondition of thought, hold without exception in the noumenal world!
10. Cf. Quentin Smith, "The Uncaused Beginning of the Universe," in *Theism, Atheism, and Big Bang Cosmology*, p. 123.
11. In "The Caused Beginning of the Universe" (in *Theism, Atheism, and Big Bang Cosmology*) Craig denies that his inference is equivocal on the grounds that "our conviction of the truth of the causal principle is not based upon an inductive survey of existents in space-time, but rather upon the metaphysical intuition that something cannot come out of nothing" (p. 147). Of course, he did appeal to such a survey in his book, but Craig claims that this was just "a last-ditch defence of the principle designed to appeal to the hard-headed empiricist who resists the metaphysical intuition that properly grounds our conviction of the principle" (p. 147, note 13). This response to the charge of equivocation is not at all convincing. For metaphysical intuitions about contingent matters are notoriously unreliable—that's why so many contemporary philosophers are, quite justifiably, "hard-headed empiricists." Further, at the risk of committing the genetic fallacy, it is worth pointing out that it is probably our experience of things beginning to exist within time that causes some of us to have the metaphysical intuition that something cannot come out of nothing.

I.C   THE TELEOLOGICAL ARGUMENT FOR THE EXISTENCE OF GOD

THE TELEOLOGICAL ARGUMENT for the existence of God begins with the premise that the world exhibits intelligent purpose, order, or other marks of design, and it proceeds to the conclusion that there must be or probably is a divine intelligence, a supreme designer, to account for the observed or perceived intelligent purpose or order. Although core ideas of the argument can be found in Plato, in the Bible (Rom. 1), and in Cicero, the most well-known treatment of it is found in William Paley's *Natural Theology* (1802). In his opening chapter, included here as our first selection, he offers his famous "watch" argument, which begins as follows:

> In crossing a heath, suppose I pitched my foot against a stone, and were asked how the stone came to be there, I might possibly answer, that for anything I knew to the contrary, it had lain there for ever; nor would it, perhaps, be very easy to show the absurdity of this answer. But suppose I found a watch upon the ground, and it should be inquired how the watch happened to be in that place, I should hardly think of the answer which I had before given—that, for anything I knew, the watch might have always been there. Yet why should not this answer serve for the watch as well as for the stone? Why is it not as admissible in the second case, as in the first?

Paley argues that just as we infer the existence of an intelligent designer to account for the purpose-revealing watch, we must analogously infer the existence of an intelligent grand designer to account for the purpose-revealing world.

"Every indication of contrivance, every manifestation of design, which existed in the watch, exists in the works of nature; with the difference, on the side of nature, of being greater and more, and that in a degree which exceeds all computation." The skeleton of the argument looks like this:

1. Human artifacts are products of intelligent design (purpose).
2. The works of nature resemble these human artifacts, particularly in having parts that are functionally organized.
3. Therefore, the works of nature are (probably) products of intelligent design (purpose).
4. But these works are vastly more complex and far greater in number than human artifacts.
5. Therefore, there probably is a powerful and vastly intelligent designer who designed the works of nature.

Ironically, Paley's argument was attacked even before Paley had set it down, for David Hume (1711–1776) had long before written his famous *Dialogues Concerning Natural Religion* (published posthumously in 1779), the classic critique of the teleological argument. Paley seems to have been unaware of it. A selection from the *Dialogues* is included as our second reading. In it, the natural theologian, Cleanthes, debates the orthodox believer, Demea, and the skeptic or critic, Philo, who does most of the serious arguing.

Hume, through Philo, attacks the argument from several different angles. He argues first of all that the universe—which might itself be viewed as one of Paley's "works of nature"—is not sufficiently like the productions of human design to support the argument. Philo puts it as follows:

> But can you think, Cleanthes, that your usual phlegm and philosophy have been preserved in so wide a step as you have taken, when you compare to the universe, houses, ships, furniture, machines and from their similarity in some circumstances infer a similarity in their causes? . . . But can a conclusion, with any propriety, be transferred from the parts to the whole? Does not the great disproportion bar all comparison and inferences? From observing the growth of a hair, can we learn anything concerning the generation of a man?

We cannot argue from the parts to the whole. You, the reader, will want to test this judgment with some possible counterexamples.

Philo's second objection is that the analogy from artifact to divine designer fails because you have no other universe with which to compare this one. We would need to make such a comparison in order to decide if it were the kind of universe that was designed or simply the kind that developed on its own. As C. S. Peirce put it, "Universes are not as plentiful as blackberries." Because there is only one of them, we have no standard of comparison by which to judge it. Paley's answer to this would be that if we could find one clear instance of purposefulness in nature (e.g., the eye), it would be sufficient to enable us to conclude that there is probably an intelligent designer. Hume makes several other points against the design argument, which you will want to examine on you own.

A modern objection to the argument, one that was anticipated by Hume, is that based on Darwinian evolution, which has cast doubt upon the notion of teleological explanation altogether. In his *Origin of Species* (1859) Darwin claimed that the process of development from simpler organisms to more complex ones took place gradually over millions of years through an apparently nonpurposeful process of trial and error, of natural selection, and of survival of the fittest. As Julian Huxley put it, the evolutionary process

> results immediately and automatically from the basic property of living matter—that of self-copying, but with occasional errors. Self-copying leads to multiplication and competition; the errors in self-copying are what we call mutations, and mutations will inevitably confer different degrees of biological advantage or disadvantage on their possessors. The consequence will be differential reproduction down the generations—in other words, natural selection.*

As important as Darwin's contribution is in offering us an alternative model of biological development, it doesn't altogether destroy the argument from design. The theist has at least two ways of reviving the argument. First, she can argue that the process of natural selection is the *way* in which a divine designer might work out his purpose for the world, and the inference to the existence of a designer can then still be construed as an inference to the best explanation. Alternatively, she can turn her attention away from biological structures and look for marks of design elsewhere in the universe—as, for example, in the apparent "fine tuning" of the natural laws and physical constants. She might then argue that, regardless of whether a design inference is warranted as an explanation for biological purpose, such an inference is, at any rate, warranted as an explanation for these other features of the universe.

The former strategy is pursued by Richard Swinburne in the third reading in this section: "The Argument from Design," excerpted from the first edition of his *The Existence of God* (2004). The latter strategy is explained by Robin Collins in the fourth and final reading in this section, "A Scientific Argument for the Existence of God."

Swinburne, a modern Cleanthes, rejects all deductive forms of arguments for the existence of God, and in their place he sets a series of inductive arguments: versions of the cosmological argument, the teleological argument, the argument from religious experience, and others. Although none of these alone proves the existence of God or shows it to be more probable than not, each adds to the probability of God's existence. Together they constitute a cumulative case for theism. There is something crying for an explanation: Why does this grand universe exist? Together the arguments for God's existence provide a plausible explanation of the existence of the universe, of why we are here, of why there is anything at all and not just nothing.

Swinburne's arguments are set in terms of confirmation theory. He distinguishes arguments that are "P-inductive" (in which the premises make the conclusion probable) from those that are "C-inductive" (in which the premises confirm the probability of the conclusion or make it more probable than it otherwise would be—although without showing the conclusion to be more probable than not). The cosmological and teleological arguments are, according to Swinburne, good C-inductive arguments. Because there is no counterargument to theism (note that Swinburne

---

Evolution as Process (New York: Harper & Row, 1953), 4.

believes he can successfully meet the argument from evil; see Part III) and because religious experience offers considerable evidential force in favor of theism, the cumulative effect is to significantly increase the probability of theism.

Robin Collins likewise defends the conclusion that theism is more probable on a certain kind of evidence than atheism. In Collins's essay, the evidence in focus is the fact that the laws of nature and fundamental physical constants appear to have been "fine-tuned" so as to make it possible for living organisms to arise. To take just a few examples, Collins notes that if gravity had been stronger or weaker by one part in 10^{40}, or if the neutron were not about 1.001 times the mass of the proton, or if the electromagnetic force had been slightly stronger or weaker, life would have been impossible. In short, the likelihood of the laws and fundamental constants being so well-coordinated as to allow for the possibility of life is staggeringly low; thus, Collins argues, the fact that the laws and constants *are* so well-coordinated constitutes evidence that their values are not the result of chance but rather are due to the creative activity of an intelligent designer.

I.C.1   The Watch and the Watchmaker

WILLIAM PALEY

William Paley (1743–1805), Archdeacon of Carlisle, was a leading evangelical apologist. His most important work is *Natural Theology, or Evidences of the Existence and Attributes of the Deity Collected from the Appearances of Nature* (1802), the first chapter of which is reprinted here. Paley argues that just as we infer the existence of an intelligent designer to explain the presence of a subtle and complex artifact like a watch, so too we must infer the existence of an intelligent Grand Designer to explain the existence of the works of nature, which are far more subtle, complex, and cleverly contrived than any human artifact.

STATEMENT OF THE ARGUMENT

In crossing a heath, suppose I pitched my foot against a stone, and were asked how the stone came to be there, I might possibly answer, that, for anything I knew to the contrary, it had lain there for ever; nor would it, perhaps, be very easy to show the absurdity of this answer. But suppose I found a watch upon the ground, and it should be inquired how the watch happened to be in that place, I should hardly think of the answer which I had given—that, for anything I knew, the watch might have always been there. Yet why should not this answer serve for the watch as well as for the stone? Why is it not as admissible in the second case as in the first? For this reason, and for no other; viz., that, when we come to inspect the watch, we perceive (what we could not discover in the stone) that its several parts are framed and put together for a purpose, e.g. that they are so formed and adjusted as to produce motion, and that motion so regulated as to point out the hour

From William Paley, *Natural Theology, or Evidences of the Existence and Attributes of the Deity Collected from the Appearances of Nature* (1802).

of the day; that, if the different parts had been differently shaped from what they are, if a different size from what they are, or placed after any other manner, or in any other order than that in which they are placed, either no motion at all would have been carried on in the machine, or none which would have answered the use that is now served by it. To reckon up a few of the plainest of these parts, and of their offices, all tending to one result:—We see a cylindrical box containing a coiled elastic spring, which, by its endeavor to relax itself, turns round the box. We next observe a flexible chain (artificially wrought for the sake of flexure) communicating the action of the spring from the box to the fusee. We then find a series of wheels, the teeth of which catch in, and apply to, each other, conducting the motion from the fusee to the balance, and from the balance to the pointer, and, at the same time, by the size and shape of those wheels, so regulating that motion as to terminate in causing an index, by an equable and measured progression, to pass over a given space in a given time. We take notice that the wheels are made of brass, in order to keep them from rust; the springs of steel, no other metal being so elastic; that over the face of the watch there is placed a glass, a material employed in no other part of the work, but in the room of which, if there had been any other than a transparent substance, the hour could not be seen without opening the case. This mechanism being observed, (it requires indeed an examination of the instrument, and perhaps some previous knowledge of the subject, to perceive and understand it; but being once, as we have said, observed and understood,) the inference, we think, is inevitable, that the watch must have had a maker; that there must have existed, at some time, and at some place or other, an artificer or artificers who formed it for the purpose which we find it actually to answer; who comprehended its construction, and designed its use.

I. Nor would it, I apprehend, weaken the conclusion, that we had never seen a watch made; that we had never known an artist capable of making one; that we were altogether incapable of executing such a piece of workmanship ourselves, or of understanding in what manner it was performed; all this being no more than what is true of some exquisite remains of ancient art, of some lost and to the generality of mankind, of the more curious productions of modern manufacture. Does one man in a million know how oval frames are turned? Ignorance of this kind exalts our opinion of the unseen and unknown artist's skill, if he be unseen and unknown, but raises no doubt in our minds of the existence and agency of such an artist, at some former time, and in some place or other. Nor can I perceive that it varies at all the inference, whether the question arise concerning a human agent, or concerning an agent of a different species, or an agent possessing, in some respect, a different nature.

II. Neither, secondly, would it invalidate our conclusion, that the watch sometimes went wrong, or that it seldom went exactly right. The purpose of the machinery, the design, and the designer, might be evident, and, in the case supposed, would be evident, in whatever way we accounted for the irregularity of the movement, or whether we could account for it or not. It is not necessary that a machine be perfect, in order to show with what design it was made; still less necessary, where the only question is, whether it were made with any design at all.

III. Nor, thirdly, would it bring any uncertainty into the argument, if there were a few parts of the watch, concerning which we could not discover, or had not yet discovered, in what manner they conduced to the general effect; or even some parts, concerning which we could not ascertain whether they conduced to that effect in any manner whatever. For, as to the first branch of the case, if by the loss, or disorder, or decay of the parts in question, the movement of the watch were found in fact to be stopped, or disturbed, or retarded, no doubt would remain in our minds as to the utility or intention of these parts, although we should be unable to investigate the manner according to which, or the connection by which, the ultimate effect depended upon their action or assistance; and the more complex is the machine, the more likely is this obscurity to arise. Then, as to the second thing supposed, namely, that there were parts which might be spared without prejudice to the movement of the watch, and that he had proved this by experiment, these superfluous parts, even if we were completely assured that they were such, would not vacate the reasoning which we had instituted concerning other parts. The indication of contrivance remained, with respect to them, nearly as it was before.

IV. Nor, fourthly, would any man in his senses think the existence of the watch, with its various machinery, accounted for, by being told that it was one out of possible combinations of material forms; that whatever he had found in the place where he found the watch, must have contained some internal configuration or other; and that this configuration might be the structure now exhibited, viz., of the works of a watch, as well as a different structure.

V. Nor, fifthly, would it yield his inquiry more satisfaction, to be answered, that there existed in things a principle of order, which had disposed the parts of the watch into their present form and situation. He never knew a watch made by the principle of order; nor can he even form to himself an idea of what is meant by a principle of order, distinct from the intelligence of the watchmaker.

VI. Sixthly, he would be surprised to hear that the mechanism of the watch was no proof of contrivance, only a motive to induce the mind to think so:

VII. And not less surprised to be informed, that the watch in his hand was nothing more than the result of the laws of *metallic* nature. It is a perversion of language to assign any law as the efficient, operative cause of anything. A law presupposes an agent; for it is only the mode according to which an agent proceeds; it implies a power; for it is the order according to which that power acts. Without this agent, without this power, which are both distinct from itself, the *law* does nothing, is nothing. The expression, "the law of metallic nature," may sound strange and harsh to a philosophic ear; but it seems quite as justifiable as some others which are more familiar to him such as "the law of vegetable nature," "the law of animal nature," or, indeed, as "the law of nature" in general, when assigned as the cause of phenomena in exclusion of agency and power, or when it is substituted into the place of these.

VIII. Neither, lastly, would our observer be driven out of his conclusion, or from his confidence in its truth, by being told that he knew nothing at all about the matter. He knows enough for his argument: he knows the utility of the end: he knows the subserviency and adaptation of the means to the end. These points being known, his ignorance of other points, his doubts concerning other points, affect not the certainty of his reasoning. The consciousness of knowing little need not beget a distrust of that which he does know....

APPLICATION OF THE ARGUMENT

Every indication of contrivance, every manifestation of design, which existed in the watch, exists in the works of nature; with the difference, on the side of nature, of being greater and more, and that in a degree which exceeds all computation. I mean that the contrivances of nature surpass the contrivances of art, in the complexity, subtilty, and curiosity of the mechanism; and still more, if possible, do they go beyond them in number and variety; yet in a multitude of cases, are not less evidently mechanical, not less evidently contrivances, not less evidently accommodated to their end, or suited to their office, than are the most perfect productions of human ingenuity.

I.C.2 A Critique of the Design Argument

DAVID HUME

The Scottish empiricist and skeptic David Hume (1711–1776) is one of the most important philosophers who ever lived. Among his most important works are *A Treatise on Human Nature, An Enquiry Concerning Human Understanding,* and *Dialogues Concerning Natural*

Religion (published posthumously in 1979), from which the present selection is taken. The *Dialogues* contain the classic critique of the argument from design. Our reading is from Parts 2 and 5 of this dialogue. Cleanthes, who opens our selection, is a natural theologian, the Paley of his time, who opposes both the orthodox believer, Demea, and the skeptic, Philo. It is Philo who puts forth the major criticisms against the argument from design.

Cleanthes: Look round the world: Contemplate the whole and every part of it: You will find it to be nothing but one great machine, subdivided into an infinite number of lesser machines, which again admit of subdivisions to a degree beyond what human senses and faculties can trace and explain. All these various machines, and even their most minute parts, are adjusted to each other with an accuracy which ravishes into admiration all men who have ever contemplated them. The curious adapting of means to ends, throughout all nature, resembles exactly, though it much exceeds, the productions of human contrivance; of human design, thought, wisdom, and intelligence. Since therefore the effects resemble each other, we are led to infer, by all the rules of analogy, that the causes also resemble, and that the Author of Nature is somewhat similar to the mind of man, though possessed of much larger faculties, proportioned to the grandeur of the work which he has executed. By this argument *a posteriori*, and by this argument alone, do we prove at once the existence of a Deity and his similarity to human mind and intelligence.

Demea: I shall be so free, *Cleanthes,* said *Demea,* as to tell you that from the beginning I could not approve of your conclusion concerning the similarity of the Deity to men; still less can I approve of the mediums by which you endeavor to establish it. What! No demonstration of the Being of God! No abstract arguments! No proofs *a priori!* Are these which have hitherto been so much insisted on by philosophers all fallacy, all sophism? Can we reach no farther in this subject than experience and probability? I will say not that this is betraying the cause of a Deity; but surely, by this affected candor, you give advantages to atheists which they never could obtain by the mere dint of argument and reasoning.

Philo: What I chiefly scruple in this subject, said *Philo,* is not so much that all religious arguments are by *Cleanthes* reduced to experience, as that they appear not to be even the most certain and irrefragable of that inferior kind. That a stone will fall, that fire will burn, that the earth has solidity, we have observed a thousand and a thousand times; and when any new instance of this nature is presented, we draw without hesitation the accustomed inference. The exact similarity of the cases gives us a perfect assurance of a similar event, and a stronger evidence is never desired nor sought after. But wherever you depart, in the least, from the similarity of the cases, you diminish proportionably the evidence; and may at last bring it to a very weak *analogy,* which is confessedly liable to error and uncertainty. After having experienced the circulation of the blood in human creatures, we make no doubt that it takes place in *Titius* and *Maevius;* but from its circulation in frogs and fishes it is only a presumption, though a strong one, from analogy that it takes place in men and other animals. The analogical reasoning is much weaker when we infer the circulation of the sap in vegetables from our experience that the blood circulates in animals; and those who hastily followed that imperfect analogy are found, by more accurate experiments, to have been mistaken.

If we see a house, *Cleanthes,* we conclude, with the greatest certainty, that it had an architect or builder because this is precisely that species of effect which we have experienced to proceed from that species of cause. But surely you will not affirm that the universe bears such a

From David Hume, *Dialogues Concerning Natural Religion* (1779).

resemblance to a house that we can with the same certainty infer a similar cause, or that the analogy is here entire and perfect. The dissimilitude is so striking that the utmost you can here pretend to is a guess, a conjecture, a presumption concerning a similar cause; and how that pretension will be received in the world, I leave you to consider.

Cleanthes: It would surely be very ill received, replied *Cleanthes;* and I should be deservedly blamed and detested did I allow that the proofs of a Deity amounted to no more than a guess or conjecture. But is the whole adjustment of means to ends in a house and in the universe so slight a resemblance? The economy of final causes? The order, proportion, and arrangement of every part? Steps of a stair are plainly contrived that human legs may use them in mounting; and this inference is certain and infallible. Human legs are also contrived for walking and mounting; and this inference, I allow, is not altogether so certain because of the dissimilarity which you remark; but does it, therefore, deserve the name only of presumption or conjecture?

Demea: Good God! cried *Demea,* interrupting him, where are we? Zealous defenders of religion allow that the proofs of a Deity fall short of perfect evidence! And you, *Philo,* on whose assistance I depended in proving the adorable mysteriousness of the Divine Nature, do you assent to all these extravagant opinions of *Cleanthes?* For what other name can I give them? or, why spare my censure when such principles are advanced, supported by such an authority, before so young a man as *Pamphilus?*

Philo: You seem not to apprehend, replied *Philo,* that I argue with *Cleanthes* in his own way, and, by showing him the dangerous consequences of his tenets, hope at last to reduce him to our opinion. But what sticks most with you, I observe, is the representation which *Cleanthes* has made of the argument *a posteriori;* and, finding that that argument is likely to escape your hold and vanish into air, you think it so disguised that you can scarcely believe it to be set in its true light. Now, however much I may dissent, in other respects, from the dangerous principle of *Cleanthes,* I must allow that he has fairly represented that argument, and I shall endeavor so to state the matter to you that you will entertain no further scruples with regard to it.

Were a man to abstract from everything which he knows or has seen, he would be altogether incapable, merely from his own ideas, to determine what kind of scene the universe must be, or to give the preference to one state or situation of things above another. For as nothing which he clearly conceives could be esteemed impossible or implying a contradiction, every chimera of his fancy would be upon an equal footing; nor could he assign any just reason why he adheres to one idea or system, and rejects the others which are equally possible.

Again, after he opens his eyes and contemplates the world as it really is, it would be impossible for him at first to assign the cause of any one event, much less of the whole of things, or of the universe. He might set his fancy a rambling, and she might bring him in an infinite variety of reports and representations. These would all be possible; but, being all equally possible, he would never of himself give a satisfactory account for his preferring one of them to the rest. Experience alone can point out to him the true cause of any phenomenon.

Now, according to this method of reasoning, *Demea,* it follows (and is, indeed, tacitly allowed by *Cleanthes* himself) that order, arrangement, or the adjustment of final causes, is not of itself any proof of design, but only so far as it has been experienced to proceed from that principle. For aught we can know *a priori,* matter may contain the source or spring of order originally within itself, as well as mind does; and there is no more difficulty in conceiving that the several elements, from an internal unknown cause, may fall into the most exquisite arrangement, than to conceive that their ideas, in the great universal mind, from a like internal unknown cause, fall into that arrangement. The equal possibility of both these suppositions is allowed. But, by experience, we find, according to *Cleanthes,* that there is a difference between them. Throw several pieces of steel together, without shape or form; they will never arrange themselves so as to compose a watch. Stone and mortar and wood, without an architect, never erect a house.

But the ideas in a human mind, we see, by an unknown, inexplicable economy, arrange themselves so as to form the plan of a watch or house. Experience, therefore, proves that there is an original principle of order in mind, not in matter. From similar effects we infer similar causes. The adjustment of means to ends is alike in the universe, as in a machine of human contrivance. The causes, therefore, must be resembling.

I was from the beginning scandalized, I must own, with this resemblance which is asserted between the Deity and human creatures, and must conceive it to imply such a degradation of the Supreme Being as no sound theist could endure. With your assistance, therefore, *Demea,* I shall endeavor to defend what you justly call the adorable mysteriousness of the Divine Nature, and shall refute this reasoning of *Cleanthes,* provided he allows that I have made a fair representation of it.

When *Cleanthes* had assented, *Philo,* after a short pause, proceeded in the following manner.

That all inferences, *Cleanthes,* concerning fact are founded on experience, and that all experimental reasonings are founded on the supposition that similar causes prove similar effects, and similar effects similar causes, I shall not at present much dispute with you. But observe, I entreat you, with what extreme caution all just reasoners proceed in the transferring of experiments to similar cases. Unless the cases be exactly similar, they repose no perfect confidence in applying their past observation to any particular phenomenon. Every alteration of circumstances occasions a doubt concerning the event; and it requires new experiments to prove certainly that the new circumstances are of no moment or importance. A change in bulk, situation, arrangement, age, disposition of the air, or surrounding bodies; any of these particulars may be attended with the most unexpected consequences. And unless the objects be quite familiar to us, it is the highest temerity to expect with assurance, after any of these changes, an event similar to that which before fell under our observation. The slow and deliberate steps of philosophers here, if anywhere, are distinguished from the precipitate march of the vulgar, who, hurried on by

the smallest similitude, are incapable of all discernment or consideration.

But can you think, *Cleanthes,* that your usual phlegm and philosophy have been preserved in so wide a step as you have taken when you compared to the universe houses, ships, furniture, machines; and, from their similarity in some circumstances, inferred a similarity in their causes? Thought, design, intelligence, such as we discover in men and other animals, is no more than one of the springs and principles of the universe, as well as heat or cold, attraction or repulsion, and a hundred others which fall under daily observation. It is an active cause by which some particular parts of nature, we find, produce alterations on other parts. But can a conclusion, with any propriety, be transferred from parts to the whole? Does not the great disproportion bar all comparison and inference? From observing the growth of a hair, can we learn anything concerning the generation of a man? Would the manner of a leaf's blowing, even though perfectly known, afford us any instruction concerning the vegetation of a tree?

But allowing that we were to take the *operations* of one part of nature upon another for the foundation of our judgment concerning the *origin* of the whole (which never can be admitted), yet why select so minute, so weak, so bounded a principle as the reason and design of animals is found to be upon this planet? What peculiar privilege has this little agitation of the brain which we call "thought," that we must thus make it the model of the whole universe? Our partiality in our own favor does indeed present it on all occasions, but sound philosophy ought carefully to guard against so natural an illusion.

So far from admitting, continued *Philo,* that the operations of a part can afford us any just conclusion concerning the origin of the whole, I will not allow any one part to form a rule for another part if the latter be very remote from the former, is there any reasonable ground to conclude that the inhabitants of other planets possess thought, intelligence, reason, or anything similar to these faculties in men? When nature has so extremely diversified her manner of operation in this small globe, can we imagine that she incessantly copies herself throughout so immense a universe? And if thought, as we may well suppose, be confined merely to this narrow corner, and has even there so limited a sphere of action, with what propriety can we assign it for the original cause of all things? The narrow view of a peasant who makes his domestic economy the rule for the government of kingdoms is in comparison a pardonable sophism.

But were we ever so much assured that a thought and reason resembling the human were to be found throughout the whole universe, and were its activity elsewhere vastly greater and more commanding than it appears in this globe; yet I cannot see why the operations of a world constituted, arranged, adjusted, can with any propriety be extended to a world which is in its embryo state, and is advancing towards that constitution and arrangement. By observation we know somewhat of the economy, action, and nourishment of a finished animal; but we must transfer with great caution that observation to the growth of a fetus in the womb, and still more to the formation of an animalcule in the loins of its male parent. Nature, we find, even from our limited experience, possesses an infinite number of springs and principles which incessantly discover themselves on every change of her position and situation. And what new and unknown principles would actuate her in so new and unknown a situation as that of the formation of a universe, we cannot, without the utmost temerity, pretend to determine.

A very small part of this great system, during a very short time, is very imperfectly discovered to us; and do we thence pronounce decisively concerning the origin of the whole?

Admirable conclusion! Stone, wood, brick, iron, brass, have not, at this time, in this minute globe of earth, an order or arrangement without human art and contrivance; therefore, the universe could not originally attain its order and arrangement without something similar to human art. But is a part of nature a rule for another part very wide of the former? Is it a rule for the whole? Is a very small part a rule for the universe? Is nature in one situation a certain rule for nature in another situation vastly different from the former?

And can you blame me, *Cleanthes,* if I here imitate the prudent reserve of *Simonides,* who, according to the noted story, being asked by *Hiero, What God was?* desired a day to think of it, and then two days more; and after that manner continually prolonged the term, without ever bringing in his definition or description? Could you even blame me if I had answered, at first, *that I did not know,* and was sensible that this subject lay vastly beyond the reach of my faculties? You might cry out skeptic and raillier, as much as you pleased; but, having found in so many other subjects much more familiar the imperfections and even contradictions of human reason, I never should expect any success from its feeble conjectures in a subject so sublime and so remote from the sphere of our observation. When two species of objects have always been observed to be conjoined together, I can *infer,* by custom, the existence of one wherever I see the existence of the other; and this I call an argument from experience. But how this argument can have place where the objects, as in the present case, are single, individual, without parallel or specific resemblance, may be difficult to explain. And will any man tell me with a serious countenance that an orderly universe must arise from some thought and art like the human because we have experience of it? To ascertain this reasoning it were requisite that we had experience of the origin of worlds; and it is not sufficient, surely, that we have seen ships and cities arise from human art and contrivance. . . .

Philo: But to show you still more inconveniences, continued *Philo,* in your anthropomorphism, please to take a new survey of your principles. *Like effects prove like causes.* This is the experimental argument; and this, you say too, is the sole theological argument. Now it is certain that the liker the effects are which are seen and the liker the causes which are inferred, the stronger is the argument. Every departure on either side diminishes the probability and renders the experiment less conclusive. You cannot doubt of the principle; neither ought you to reject its consequences.

All the new discoveries in astronomy which prove the immense grandeur and magnificence of the works of nature are so many additional arguments for a Deity, according to the true system of theism; but, according to your hypothesis of experimental theism, they become so many objections, by removing the effect still farther from all resemblance to the effects of human art and contrivance. For if *Lucretius,* even following the old system of the world, could exclaim:

> Who is strong enough to rule the sum, who to hold in hand and control the mighty bridle of the unfathomable deep? who to turn about all the heavens at one time, and warm the fruitful worlds with ethereal fires, or to be present in all places and at all times.[1]

If Tully[2] esteemed this reasoning so natural as to put it into the mouth of his Epicurean:

> What power of mental vision enabled your master Plato to descry the vast and elaborate architectural process which, as he makes out, the deity adopted in building the structure of the universe? What method of engineering was employed? What tools and levers and derricks? What agents carried out so vast an understanding? And how were air, fire, water, and earth enabled to obey and execute the will of the architect?

If this argument, I say, had any force in former ages, how much greater must it have at present when the bounds of nature are so infinitely enlarged and such a magnificent scene is opened to us? It is still more unreasonable to form our idea of so unlimited a cause from our experience of the narrow productions of human design and invention.

The discoveries by microscopes, as they open a new universe in miniature, are still objections, according to you; arguments, according to me. The farther we push our researches of this kind, we are still led to infer the universal cause of all to be vastly different from mankind, or from any object of human experience and observation.

And what say you to the discoveries in anatomy, chemistry, botany? . . .

Cleanthes: These surely are no objections, replied *Cleanthes;* they only discover new instances of art and contrivance. It is still the image of mind reflected on us from innumerable objects. *Philo:* Add a mind like the human, said *Philo.* I know of no other, replied *Cleanthes. Philo:* And the liker, the better, insisted *Philo.* To be sure, said *Cleanthes.*

Philo: Now, *Cleanthes,* said *Philo,* with an air of alacrity and triumph, mark the consequences. First, by this method of reasoning you renounce all claim to infinity in any of the attributes of the Deity. For, as the cause ought only to be proportioned to the effect, and the effect, so far as it falls under our cognizance, is not infinite: What pretensions have we, upon your suppositions, to ascribe that attribute to the Divine Being? You will still insist that, by removing him so much from all similarity to human creatures, we give in to the most arbitrary hypothesis, and at the same time weaken all proofs of his existence.

Secondly, you have no reason, on your theory, for ascribing perfection to the Deity, even in his finite capacity; or for supposing him free from every error, mistake, or incoherence, in his undertakings. There are many inexplicable difficulties in the works of Nature which, if we allow a perfect author to be proved *a priori,* are easily solved, and become only seeming difficulties from the narrow capacity of man, who cannot trace infinite relations. But according to your method of reasoning, these difficulties become all real; and, perhaps, will be insisted on as new instances of likeness to human art and contrivance. At least, you must acknowledge that it is impossible for us to tell, from our limited views, whether this system contains any great faults or deserves any considerable praise if compared to other possible and even real systems. Could a peasant, if the *Aeneid* were read to him, pronounce that poem to be absolutely faultless, or even assign to it its proper rank among the productions of human wit, he who had never seen any other production?

But were this world ever so perfect a production, it must still remain uncertain whether all the excellences of the work can justly be ascribed to the workman. If we survey a ship, what an exalted idea must we form of the ingenuity of the carpenter who framed so complicated, useful, and beautiful a machine? And what surprise must we feel when we find him a stupid mechanic who imitated others, and copied an art which, through a long succession of ages, after multiplied trials, mistakes, corrections, deliberations, and controversies, had been gradually improving? Many worlds might have been botched and bungled, throughout an eternity, ere this system was struck out; much labor lost; many fruitless trials made; and a slow but continued improvement carried on during infinite ages in the art of world-making. In such subjects, who can determine where the truth, nay, who can conjecture where the probability lies, amidst a great number of hypotheses which may be proposed, and a still greater which may be imagined?

And what shadow of an argument, continued Philo, can you produce from your hypothesis to prove the unity of the Deity? A great number of men join in building a house or ship, in rearing a city, in framing a commonwealth; why may not several deities combine in contriving and framing a world? This is only so much greater similarity to human affairs. By sharing the work among several, we may so much further limit the attributes of each, and get rid of that extensive power and knowledge which must be supposed in one deity, and which, according to you, can only serve to weaken the proof of his existence. And if such foolish, such vicious creatures as man can yet often unite in framing and executing one plan, how much more those deities or demons, whom we may suppose several degrees more perfect?

To multiply causes without necessity is indeed contrary to true philosophy, but this principle applies not to the present case. Were one deity antecedently proved by your theory who were possessed of every attribute requisite to the production of the universe, it would be needless, I own (though not absurd), to suppose any other deity existent. But while it is still a question whether all these attributes are united in one subject or dispersed among several independent beings; by what phenomena in nature can we pretend to decide the controversy? Where we see a body raised in a scale, we are sure that there is in the opposite scale, however concealed from sight, some counterpoising weight equal to it; but it is still allowed to doubt whether that weight be an aggregate of several distinct bodies or one uniform united mass. And if the weight requisite very much exceeds anything which we have ever seen conjoined in any single body, the former supposition becomes still more probable and natural. An intelligent being of such vast power and capacity as is necessary to produce the universe, or, to speak in the language of ancient philosophy, so prodigious an animal, exceeds all analogy and even comprehension.

But further, *Cleanthes*, men are mortal, and renew their species by generation; and this is common to all living creatures. The two great sexes of male and female, says *Milton*, animate the world. Why must this circumstance, so universal, so essential, be excluded from those numerous and limited deities? Behold, then, the theogony of ancient times brought back upon us.

And why not become a perfect anthropomorphite? Why not assert the deity or deities to be corporeal, and to have eyes, a nose, mouth, ears, etc.? *Epicurus* maintained that no man had ever seen reason but in a human figure; therefore, the gods must have a human figure. And this argument, which is deservedly so much ridiculed by *Cicero*, becomes, according to you, solid and philosophical.

In a word, *Cleanthes,* a man who follows your hypothesis is able, perhaps, to assert or conjecture that the universe sometime arose from something like design: But beyond that position he cannot ascertain one single circumstance, and is left afterwards to fix every point of his theology by the utmost license of fancy and hypothesis. This world, for aught he knows, is very faulty and imperfect, compared to a superior standard; and was only the first rude essay of some infant deity who afterwards abandoned it, ashamed of his lame performance: It is the work only of some dependent, inferior deity, and is the object of derision to his superiors: It is the production of old age and dotage in some superannuated deity; and ever since his death has run on at adventures, from the first impulse and active force which it received from him.... You justly give signs of horror, *Demea,* at these strange suppositions; but these, and a thousand more of the same kind, are *Cleanthes'* suppositions, not mine. From the moment the attributes of the Deity are supposed finite, all these have place. And I cannot, for my part, think that so wild and unsettled a system of theology is, in any respect, preferable to none at all.

Cleanthes: These suppositions I absolutely disown, cried *Cleanthes:* They strike me, however, with no horror, especially when proposed in that rambling way in which they drop from you. On the contrary, they give me pleasure when I see that, by the utmost indulgence of your imagination, you never get rid of the hypothesis of design in the universe, but are obliged at every turn to have recourse to it. To this concession I adhere steadily; and this I regard as a sufficient foundation for religion.

NOTES

1. *On the Nature of Things*, II, 1096–1099 (trans. by W. D. Rouse).
2. Tully was a common name for the Roman lawyer and philosopher, Marcus Tullius Cicero, 106–43 BC.The excerpt is from *The Nature of the Gods*, i, viii, 19 (trans. By H. Rackham).

I.C.3   The Argument from Design

RICHARD SWINBURNE

Richard Swinburne (1934–   ) was, until his retirement, the Nolloth professor of philosophy of religion at Oxford University. He has written extensively in philosophy of religion, and his body of work includes several pieces on the traditional arguments for the existence of God. The following selection is from *The Existence of God* (1979) in which he rejects all deductive forms of arguments for the existence of God but sets in their place a series of inductive arguments. In this selection, he presents an inductive version of the argument from design. His strategy is to show that several of the arguments, although only minimally suggestive when taken in isolation, together make a cumulative case for the truth of theism.

A few notes are crucial to an understanding of Swinburne's essay. First, he contrasts the 'Hempelian account' of scientific explanation with the 'powers-and-liabilities account' of scientific explanation. According to the Hempelian account—named after Carl Hempel—to provide a scientific explanation of an event is (roughly) to show that the occurrence of the event is logically implied by the occurrence of particular circumstances that obtained prior to the event together with facts about the laws of nature. On the other hand, the powers-and-liabilities account says that providing a scientific explanation for an event is a matter of showing that the event's cause had powers to bring about the event that it was liable to exercise under the given circumstances. Second, Hempel thinks that scientific explanations are not the only available explanations for events in the world. There are also what he calls "personal" explanations. Third, Swinburne places a great deal of weight on the notion of simplicity. Other things being equal, if a theory *A* is simpler than a theory *B,* theory *A* is to be preferred. Finally, Swinburne uses Bayes's theorem to sustain his argument: Let h be a theory or hypothesis, let e be the evidential phenomena, and let k be our background knowledge. $P(h/e\&k)$ represents the probability of h being true given the available evidence and our background knowledge. You do not need to understand the intricacies of Bayes's theorem in order to follow Swinburne's reasoning.

I understand by an argument from design one which argues from some general pattern of order in the universe or provision for the needs of conscious beings to a God responsible for these phenomena. An argument from a general pattern of order I shall call a teleological argument. In the definition of 'teleological argument' I emphasize the words 'general pattern'; I shall not count an argument to the existence of God from some particular pattern of order manifested on a unique occasion as a teleological argument.

TWO FORMS OF TELEOLOGICAL ARGUMENT

I begin with the distinction between spatial order and temporal order, between what I shall call regularities of co-presence and regularities of succession. An example of a regularity of co-presence would be a town with all its roads at right angles to each other, or a section of books in a library arranged in alphabetical order of authors. Regularities of succession are simple patterns of behaviour of objects, such as their behaviour in accordance with the laws of nature—for example, Newton's laws.

Many of the striking examples of order in the universe evince an order which is due both to a regularity of co-presence and to a regularity of succession. A working car consists of many parts so adjusted to each other that it follows the instructions of the driver delivered by his pulling and pushing a few levers and buttons and turning a wheel, to take passengers whither he wishes. Its order arises because its parts are so arranged at some instant (regularity of co-presence) that, the laws of nature being as they are (regularity of succession) it brings about the result neatly and efficiently. The order of living animals and plants likewise results from regularities of both types.

Men who marvel at the order of the universe may marvel at either or both of the regularities of co-presence and of succession. The thinkers of the eighteenth century to whom the argument from design appealed so strongly were struck almost exclusively by the regularities of co-presence. They marveled at the order in animals and plants; but since they largely took for granted the regularities of succession, what struck them about the animals and plants, as to a lesser extent about machines made by men, was the subtle and coherent arrangement of their millions of parts. Paley's *Natural Theology* dwells mainly on details of comparative anatomy, on eyes and ears and muscles and bones arranged with minute precision so as to operate with high efficiency, and in the *Dialogues* Hume's Cleanthes produces the same kind of examples: 'Consider, anatomize the eye, survey its structure and contrivance, and tell me from your own feeling, if the idea of a contriver does not immediately flow in upon you with a force like that of sensation.'

The eighteenth-century argument from spatial order seems to go as follows. Animals and plants have the power to reproduce their kind, and so, given the past existence of animals and plants, their present existence is to be expected. But what is vastly surprising is the existence of animals and plants at all. By natural processes they can only come into being through generation. But we know that the world has not been going on for ever, and so the great puzzle is the existence of the first animals and plants in 4004 BC or whenever exactly it was that animals and plants began to exist. Since they could not have come about by natural scientific processes, and since they are very similar to the machines, which certain rational agents, viz. men, make, it is very probable that they were made by a rational agent—only clearly one much more powerful and knowledgeable than men.

In the *Dialogues,* through the mouth of Philo, Hume made some classical objections to the argument in this form, some of which have some force against all forms of the argument; I shall deal with most of these as we come to appropriate places in this chapter. Despite Hume's objections, the argument is, I think, a very plausible one—given its premises. But one of its premises was shown by Darwin and his successors to be clearly false. Complex animals and plants can be produced through generation by less complex animals and plants—species are not eternally distinct; and simple animals and plants can be produced by natural processes from inorganic matter. This discovery led to the virtual disappearance of the argument from design from popular apologetic—mistakenly, I think, since it can easily be reconstructed in a form which does not rely on the premises shown to be false by Darwin. This can be done even for the argument from spatial order.

We can reconstruct the argument from spatial order as follows. We see around us animals and plants, intricate examples of spatial order in the ways which Paley set out, similar to machines of the kind which men make. We know that these animals and plants have evolved by natural processes from inorganic matter. But clearly this evolution can only have taken place, given certain special natural laws. These are first, the chemical laws stating how under certain circumstances inorganic molecules combine to make organic ones, and organic ones combine to make organisms. And secondly, there are the biological laws of evolution stating how organisms have very many offspring, some of which vary in one or more characteristics from their parents, and how some of these characteristics are passed on to most offspring, from which it follows that, given shortage of food and other environmental needs, there will be competition for survival, in which the fittest will survive. Among organisms very well fitted for survival will be organisms of such complex and subtle construction as to allow easy adaptation to a changing environment. These organisms will evince great spatial order. So the laws of nature are such as, under certain circumstances, to give rise to striking examples of spatial order similar to the machines which men make. Nature, that is, is a machine-making machine. In the twentieth century men make not only machines, but machine-making machines. They may therefore naturally infer from nature which produces animals and plants, to a creator of nature similar to men who make machine-making machines.

This reconstructed argument is now immune to having some crucial premises shown false by some biologist of the 1980s. The facts to which its premises appeal are too evident for that—whatever the details, natural laws are clearly such as to produce complex organisms from inorganic matter under certain circumstances. But although this is so, I do not find the argument a very strong one, and this is because of the evident paucity of organisms throughout the universe. The circumstances under which nature behaves as a machine-making machine are rare. For that reason nature does not evince very strongly the character of a machine-making machine and hence the analogies between the products of natural processes on the one hand and machines on the other are not too strong. Perhaps they give a small degree of probability to the hypothesis that a rational agent was responsible for the laws of evolution in some ways similar to the rational agents who make machines, but the probability is no more than that.

I pass on to consider a form of teleological argument which seems to me a much stronger one—the teleological argument from the temporal order of the world. The temporal order of the universe is, to the man who bothers to give it a moment's thought, an overwhelmingly striking fact about it. Regularities of succession are all-pervasive. For simple laws govern almost all successions of events. In books of physics, chemistry, and biology we can learn how almost everything in the world behaves. The laws of their behavior can be set out by relatively simple formulae which men can understand and by means of which they can successfully predict the future. The orderliness of the universe to which I draw attention here is its conformity to formula, to simple, formulable, scientific laws. The orderliness of the universe in this respect is a very striking fact about it. The universe might so naturally have been chaotic, but it is not—it is very orderly.

That the world has this very peculiar characteristic may be challenged in various ways. It may be said of the order which we seem to see in the universe that we impose the order on the world, that it is not there independently of our imposition. Put another way, all that this temporal order amounts to, it might be said, is a coincidence between how things have been so far in the world and the patterns which men can recognize and describe, a coincidence which is itself susceptible of an explanation in terms of natural selection. In fact, however, the temporal order of the world is something deeper than that. The premiss of a good teleological argument is not that so far (within his life or within human history) things have conformed to a pattern which man can recognize and describe. The premiss is rather that things have and will continue to conform to such a pattern however initial conditions vary, however men interfere in the world. If induction is justified, we are justified in supposing that things will continue to behave as they have behaved in the kinds of respect which scientists and ordinary people recognize and describe. I assume that we are justified in believing that the laws of gravity and chemical cohesion will continue to hold tomorrow—that stones will fall, and desks hold together tomorrow as well as today—however initial conditions vary, however men interfere in the world. It may of course be doubted whether philosophers have given a very satisfactory account of what makes such beliefs justified (hence 'the problem of induction'); but I assume the common-sense view that they are justified. So the teleologist's premiss is not just that there has been in nature so far an order which men can recognize and describe; but there has been and will continued to be in nature an order, recognizable and describable by men certainly, but one which exists independently of men. If men are correct in their belief that the order which they see in the world is an order which will hold in the future as in the past, it is clearly not an imposed or

invented order. It is there in nature. For man cannot make nature conform subsequently to an order which he has invented. Only if the order is there in nature is nature's future conformity to be expected.

An objector may now urge that although the order of the universe is an objective matter, nevertheless, unless the universe were an orderly place, men would not be around to comment on the fact. (If there were no natural laws, there would be no regularly functioning organisms, and so no men.) Hence there is nothing surprising in the fact that men find order—they could not possibly find anything else. This conclusion is clearly a little too strong. There would need to be quite a bit of order in and around our bodies if men are to exist and think, but there could be chaos outside the earth, so long as the earth was largely unaffected by that chaos. There is a great deal more order in the world than is necessary for the existence of humans. So men could still be around to comment on the fact even if the world were a much less orderly place than it is. But quite apart from this minor consideration, the argument still fails totally for a reason which can best be brought out by an analogy. Suppose that a madman kidnaps a victim and shuts him in a room with a card-shuffling machine. The machine shuffles ten packs of cards simultaneously and then draws a card from each pack and exhibits simultaneously the ten cards. The kidnapper tells the victim that he will shortly set the machine to work and it will exhibit its first draw, but that unless the draw consists of an ace of hearts from each pack, the machine will simultaneously set off an explosion which will kill the victim, in consequence of which he will not see which cards the machine drew. The machine is then set to work, and to the amazement and relief of the victim the machine exhibits an ace of hearts drawn from each pack. The victim thinks that this extraordinary fact needs an explanation in terms of the machine having been rigged in some way. But the kidnapper, who now reappears, casts doubt on this suggestion. 'It is hardly surprising', he says, 'that the machine draws only aces of hearts. You could not possibly see anything else. For you would not be here to see anything at all, if any other cards had been drawn.' But of course the victim is right and the kidnapper is wrong. There is indeed something extraordinary in need of explanation in ten aces of hearts being drawn. The fact that this peculiar order is a necessary condition of the draw being perceived at all makes what is perceived no less extraordinary and in need of explanation. The teleologist's starting-point is not that we perceive order rather than disorder, but that order rather than disorder is there. Maybe only if order is there can we know what is there, but that makes what is there no less extraordinary and in need of explanation.

So the universe is characterized by vast, all-pervasive temporal order, the conformity of nature to formula, recorded in the scientific laws formulated by men. Now this phenomenon, like the very existence of the world, is clearly something 'too big' to be explained by science. If there is an explanation of the world's order it cannot be a scientific one, and this follows from the nature of scientific explanation. For, in scientific explanation we explain particular phenomena as brought about by prior phenomena in accord with scientific laws; or we explain the operation of scientific laws in terms of more general scientific laws (and perhaps also particular phenomena). Thus we explain the operation of Kepler's laws in terms of the operation of Newton's laws (given the masses, initial velocities, and distances apart of the sun and planets); and we explain the operation of Newton's laws in terms of the operation of Einstein's field equations for space relatively empty of matter. Science thus explains particular phenomena and low-level laws in terms partly of high-level laws. But from the very nature of science it cannot explain the highest-level laws of all; for they are that by which it explains all other phenomena.

At this point we need to rephrase our premisses in terms of the powers-and-liabilities account of science, which we have seen reason for preferring to the Hempelian account. On this account what the all-pervasive temporal order amounts to is the fact that throughout space and time there are physical objects of various kinds, every such object having the powers

and liabilities which are described in laws of nature—e.g. the power of attracting each other physical object in the universe with a force of $\gamma mm^1/r^2$ dynes (where γ is the gravitational constant) the liability always to exercise this power, and the liability to be attracted by each other body in the universe with a force of $\gamma mm^1/r^2$ dynes and so on. From the fact that it has such general powers it follows that an object will have certain more specific powers, given the kind of object that it is. For example, given that it has a mass of 1 gram, it will follow that it has the power of attracting each other body in the universe with a force of $\gamma m^1/r^2$ dynes. This picture allows us to draw attention to one feature of the orderliness of the universe which the other picture makes it easy to ignore. Unlike the feature to which I have drawn attention so far, it is not one of which men have always known; it is one which the atomic theory of chemistry strongly suggested, and the discovery of fundamental particles confirmed. It is this. The physical objects scattered throughout space and time are, or are composed of, particles of a few limited kinds, which we call fundamental particles. Whether the protons and electrons which we suppose to be the fundamental particles are in fact fundamental, or whether they are composed of yet more fundamental particles (e.g. quarks) which are capable of independent existence is not altogether clear—but what does seem clear is that if there are yet more fundamental particles, they too come in a few specific kinds. Nature only has building-blocks of a few kinds. Each particle of a given kind has a few defining properties which determine its behaviour and which are specific to that kind. Thus all electrons have a mass of $1/2 MeV/c^2$, a charge of -1, a spin of $1/2$, etc. All positrons have other properties the same as electrons, but a charge of $+1$. All protons have a mass of $938\ MeV/c^2$, a charge of $+1$, and a spin of $1/2$. And so on. There are innumerably many articles which belong to each of a few kinds, and no particles with characteristics intermediate between those of two kinds. The properties of fundamental kinds, that is, which give specific form to the general powers which all objects have, belong to a small class; and the powers and liabilities of large-scale objects are determined by those of their fundamental components. Particles have constant characteristics over time; they only change their characteristics, or are destroyed or converted into other particles by reason of their own liabilities (e.g. to decay) or the action of other particles acting in virtue of their powers.

Put in these terms then, the orderliness of nature is a matter of the vast uniformity in the powers and liabilities of bodies throughout endless time and space, and also in the paucity of kinds of components of bodies. Over centuries long, long ago and over distances distant in millions of light years from ourselves the same universal orderliness reigns. There are, as we have seen, explanations of only two kinds for phenomena—scientific explanation and personal explanation. Yet, although a scientific explanation can be provided of why the more specific powers and liabilities of bodies hold (e.g. why an electron exerts just the attractive force which it does) in terms of more general powers and liabilities possessed by all bodies (put in Hempelian terms—why a particular natural law holds in terms of more general natural laws), science cannot explain why all bodies do possess the same very general powers and liabilities. It is with this fact that scientific explanation stops. So either the orderliness of nature is where all explanation stops, or we must postulate an agent of great power and knowledge who brings about through his continuous action that bodies have the same very general powers and liabilities (that the most general natural laws operate); and, once again, the simplest such agent to postulate is one of infinite power, knowledge, and freedom, i.e. God. An additional consideration here is that it is clearly vastly simpler to suppose that the existence and the order of the world have the same cause, and the considerations which lead us to postulate a being of infinite power, knowledge, and freedom as the cause of the former reinforce the considerations which lead us to postulate such a cause for the latter.

In the *Dialogues* Hume made the objection—why should we not postulate many gods to give order to the universe, not merely one? 'A great number of men join in building a house or a ship, in rearing a city, in framing a commonwealth, why may not several deities combine in framing a world?' Hume again is aware of the obvious counter-objection to his suggestion. 'To multiply causes without necessity is . . . contrary to true philosophy.' He claims, however, that the counterobjection does not apply here, because (in my terminology) although the supposition that there is one god is a simpler supposition than the supposition that there are many, in postulating many persons to be responsible for the order of the universe we are postulating persons more like to men in power and knowledge—that is we are putting forward a hypothesis which fits in better with our background knowledge of what there is in the world. That may be. But Hume's hypothesis is very complicated—we want to ask about it such questions as why are there just 333 deities (or whatever the number is), why do they have powers of just the strength which they do have, and what moves them to cooperate as closely as obviously they do; questions of a kind which obtrude far less with the far simpler and so less arbitrary theistic hypothesis. Even if Hume were right in supposing that the prior probability of his hypothesis were as great as that of theism (because the fit with background knowledge of the former cancels out the simplicity of the latter) (and I do not myself think that he is right), the hypothesis of theism nevertheless has greater explanatory power than the Humean hypothesis and is for that reason more probable. For theism leads us to expect that we will find throughout nature one pattern of order. But if there were more than one deity responsible for the order of the universe, we would expect to see characteristic marks of the handiwork of different deities in different parts of the universe, just as we see different kinds of workmanship in the different houses of a city. We would expect to find an inverse square of law of gravitation obeyed in one part of the universe, and in another part a law which was just short of being an inverse square law—without the difference being explicable in terms of a more general law. It is enough to draw this absurd conclusion to see how wrong the Humean objection is.

So I shall take as the alternatives—the first, that the temporal order of the world is where explanation stops, and the second, that the temporal order of the world is due to the agency of God; and I shall ignore the less probable possibilities that the order is to be explained as due to the agency of an agent or agents of finite power. The proponent of the teleological argument claims that the order of nature shows an orderer—God.

THE FORCE OF THE SECOND FORM OF TELEOLOGICAL ARGUMENT

The teleological argument, whether from temporal or spatial order, is, I believe, a codification by philosophers of a reaction to the world deeply embedded in the human consciousness. Men see the comprehensibility of the world as evidence of a comprehending creator. The prophet Jeremiah lived in an age in which the existence of a creator-god of some sort was taken for granted. What was at stake was the extent of his goodness, knowledge, and power. Jeremiah argued from the order of the world that he was a powerful and reliable god, that god was God. He argued to the power of the creator from the extent of the creation—'The host of heaven cannot be numbered, neither the sand of the sea measured'; and he argued that its regular behaviour showed the reliability of the creator, and he spoke of the 'covenant of the day and night' whereby they follow each other regularly, and 'the ordinances of heaven and earth',[1] and he used their existence as an argument for the trust-worthiness of the God of Jacob. The argument from temporal order has been with us ever since.

You get the argument from temporal order also in Aquinas's fifth way, which runs as follows:

> The fifth way is based on the guidedness of nature. An orderedness of actions to an end is observed in all bodies obeying natural laws, even when they lack awareness. For their behaviour hardly ever varies, and will practically always turn out well; which shows that they truly tend to a goal, and do not merely hit it by accident. Nothing however that lacks awareness tends to a goal, except under

the direction of someone with awareness and with understanding; the arrow, for example requires an archer. Everything in nature, therefore is directed to its goal by someone with understanding and this we call 'God'.[2]

Aquinas argues that the regular behaviour of each inanimate thing shows that some animate being is directing it (making it move to achieve some purpose, attain some goal); and from that he comes—rather quickly—to the conclusion that one 'being with understanding' is responsible for the behaviour of all inanimate things.

It seems to me fairly clear that no argument from temporal order—whether Aquinas's fifth way or any other argument can be a good deductive argument. For although the premiss is undoubtedly correct—a vast pervasive order characterizes the world—the step from premiss to conclusion is not a valid deductive one. Although the existence of order may be good evidence of a designer, it is surely compatible with the non-existence of one—it is hardly a logically necessary truth that all order is brought about by a person. And although, as I have urged, the supposition that one person is responsible for the orderliness of the world is much simpler and so more probable than the supposition that many persons are, nevertheless, the latter supposition seems logically compatible with the data—so we must turn to the more substantial issue of whether the argument from the temporal order of the world to God is a good inductive argument. We had reached the conclusion that either the vast uniformity in the powers and liabilities of bodies was where explanation stopped, or that God brings this about by his continuous action, through an intention constant over time.

Let us represent by e this conformity of the world to order, and let h be the hypothesis of theism. It is not possible to treat a teleological argument in complete isolation from the cosmological argument. We cannot ask how probable the premiss of the teleological argument makes theism, independently of the premiss of the cosmological argument, for the premiss of the teleological argument entails in part the premiss of the cosmological argument. That there is order of the kind described entails at least that there is a physical universe. So let k be now, not mere tautological evidence, but the existence of a complex physical universe (the premiss of the version of the cosmological argument to which I devoted most attention). Let us ask how much more probable does the orderliness of such a universe make the existence of God than does the mere existence of the universe.

With these fillings, we ask whether $P(h/e\&k) > P(h/k)$ and by how much. As we have seen $P(h/e\&k)$ will exceed $P(h/k)$ if and only if $P(e/h\&k) > P(e/{\sim}h\&k)$. Put in words with our current fillings for h, e, and k, the existence of order in the world confirms the existence of God if and only if the existence of this order in the world is more probable if there is a God than if there is not. We saw in Chapter 6 that where h is the hypothesis that there is a God $P(e/h\&k)$ may exceed $P(e/{\sim}h\&k)$, either because e cannot be explained in any other way and is very unlikely to occur uncaused or because God has character such that he is more likely to bring about e than alternative states. With respect to the cosmological argument, I suggested that its case rested solely on the first consideration. Here I shall suggest that again the first consideration is dominant, but that the second has considerable significance also.

Let us start with the first consideration. e is the vast uniformity in the powers and liabilities possessed by material objects—$P(e/{\sim}h\&k)$ is the probability that there should be that amount of uniformity in a God-less world, that this uniform distribution of the powers of things should be where explanation terminates, that they be further inexplicable. That there should be material bodies is strange enough; but that they should all have such similar powers which they inevitably exercise, seems passing strange. It is strange enough that physical objects should have powers at all—why should they not just be, without being able to make a difference to the world? But that they should all, throughout infinite time and space, have some general powers identical to those of all

other objects (and they all be made of components of very few fundamental kinds, each component of a given kind being identical in all characteristics with each other such component) and yet there be no cause of this at all seems incredible. The universe is complex as we urged, in the last chapter, in that there are so many bodies of different shapes, etc., and now we find an underlying orderliness in the identity of powers and paucity of kinds of components of bodies. Yet this orderliness, if there is no explanation of it in terms of the action of God, is the orderliness of coincidence—the fact that one body has certain powers does not explain the fact that a second body has—not the simplicity of a common underlying explanation. The basic complexity remains in the vast number of different bodies in which the orderliness of identical powers and components is embodied. It is a complexity too striking to occur unexplained. It cries out for explanation in terms of some single common source with the power to produce it. Just as we would seek to explain all the coins of the realm having an identical pattern in terms of their origin from a common mould, or all of many pictures' having a common style in terms of their being painted by the same painter, so too should we seek to explain all physical objects' having the same powers in terms of their deriving them from a common source. On these grounds alone $P(e/h\&k) \gg P(e/k)$, and so $P(h/e\&k) \gg P(h/k)$.[3]

I think, however, that we can go further by bringing in considerations from God's character—we saw in Chapter 6 that God will bring about a state of affairs if it is over all a good thing that he should, he will not bring about a state of affairs if it is over all a bad thing that he should, and that he will only bring about a state of affairs if it is in some way a good thing that he should. Put in terms of reasons—he will always act on overriding reasons and cannot act except for a reason. Now there are two reasons why human beings produce order. One is aesthetic—beauty comes in the patterns of things, such as dances and songs. Some sort of order is a necessary condition of phenomena having beauty; complete chaos is just ugly—although of course not any order is beautiful. The second reason why a human being produces order is that when there is order he or other rational agents can perceive that order and utilize it to achieve ends. If we see that there is a certain pattern of order in phenomena we can then justifiably predict that that order will continue, and that enables us to make predictions about the future on which we can rely. A librarian puts books in an alphabetical order of authors in order that he and users of the library who come to know that the order is there may subsequently be able to find any book in the library very quickly (because, given knowledge of the order, we can predict whereabouts in the library any given book will be).

God has similar reasons for producing an orderly, as opposed to a chaotic universe. In so far as some sort of order is a necessary condition of beauty, and it is a good thing—as it surely is—that the world be beautiful rather than ugly, God has reason for creating an orderly universe. Secondly, I shall argue in Chapter 10 that it is good that God should make finite creatures with the opportunity to grow in knowledge and power. Now if creatures are going consciously to extend their control of the world, they will need to know how to do so. There will need to be some procedures which they can find out, such that if they follow those procedures, certain events will occur. This entails the existence of temporal order. There can only be such procedures if the world is orderly, and, I should add, there can only be such procedures ascertainable by men if the order of the world is such as to be discernible by men. To take a simple example, if hitting things leads to them breaking or penetrating other things, and heating things leads to them melting, men can discover these regularities and utilize them to make artefacts such as houses, tables, and chairs. They can heat iron ore to melt it to make nails, hammers, and axes, and use the latter to break wood into the right shapes to hammer together with nails to make the artefacts. Or, if light and other electro-magnetic radiation behave in

predictable ways comprehensible by men, men can discover those ways and build telescopes and radio and television receivers and transmitters. A world must evince the temporal order exhibited by laws of nature if men are to be able to extrapolate from how things have behaved in the past, to how they will behave in the future, which extrapolation is necessary if men are to have the knowledge of how things will behave in the future, which they must have in order to be able to extend their control over the world. (There would not need to be complete determinism—agents themselves could be exempt from the full rigors of determinism, and there might be violations of natural laws from time to time. But basically the world has to be governed by laws of nature if agents are consciously to extend their control of the world.) If I am right in supposing that God has reason to create finite creatures with the opportunity to grow in knowledge and power, then he has reason to create temporal order. So I suggest that God has at least these two reasons for producing an orderly world. Maybe God has reasons for not making creatures with the opportunity to grow in knowledge and power, and so the second reason for his creating an orderly universe does not apply. But with one possible, and, I shall show, irrelevant qualification, the first surely does. God may choose whether or not to make a physical universe, but if he does, he has reason for making a beautiful and so an orderly one. God has reason, if he does make a physical universe, not to make a chaotic or botched-up one. The only reason of which I can think why God should make the universe in some respects ugly would be to give to creatures the opportunity to discover the aesthetic merits of different states of affairs and through cooperative effort to make the world beautiful for themselves. But then the other argument shows that if they are to be able to exercise such an opportunity the world will need to be orderly in some respects. (There will have to be predictable regularities which creatures may utilize in order to produce beautiful states of affairs.) So, either way, the world will need to be orderly. It rather looks as if God has overriding reason to make an orderly universe if he makes a universe at all. However, as I emphasized, human inquiry into divine reasons is a highly speculative matter. But it is nevertheless one in which men are justified in reaching tentative conclusions. For God is postulated to be an agent like ourselves in having knowledge, power, and freedom, although to an infinitely greater degree than we have. The existence of the analogy legitimizes us in reaching conclusions about his purposes, conclusions which must allow for the quantitative difference, as I have tried to do.

So I suggest that the order of the world is evidence of the existence of God both because its occurrence would be very improbable *a priori* and also because, in virtue of his postulated character, he has very good, apparently overriding, reason for making an orderly universe, if he makes a universe at all. It looks as if $P(e/h\&k)$ equals 1. For both reasons $P(e/h\&k) \gg P(e/\sim h\&k)$ and so $P(h/e\&k) \gg P(h/k)$. I conclude that the teleological argument from temporal order is a good C-inductive argument to the existence of God.[†]

Let us look at the argument from a slightly different angle. It is basically an argument by analogy, an analogy between the order in the natural world (the temporal order codified in laws of nature) and the patterns of order which men often produce (the ordered books on library shelves, or the temporal order in the movements of a dancer or the notes of a song). It argues from similarity between phenomena of two kinds B and $B*$ to similarity between their causes A and $A*$. In view of the similarities between the two kinds of order B and $B*$, the theist postulates a cause ($A*$) in some respects similar to A (men); yet in view of the dissimilarities the theist must postulate a cause in other respects different. All arguments by analogy do and must proceed in this way. They cannot postulate a cause in all respects similar. They postulate a cause who is such that one would expect him to produce phenomena similar to B in the respects in which $B*$ are similar to B and different from B in the respects in which $B*$ are different from B.

All argument from analogy works like this. Thus various properties of light and sound were known in the nineteenth century, among them that both light and sound are reflected, refracted, diffracted, and show interference phenomena. In the case of sound these were known to be due to disturbance of the medium, air, in which it is transmitted. What could one conclude by analogy about the cause of the reflection, etc., of light? One could conclude that the propagation of light was, like the propagation of sound, the propagation of a wave-like disturbance in a medium. But one could not conclude that it was the propagation of a disturbance in the same medium—air, since light passed through space empty of air. Scientists had to postulate a separate medium—aether, the disturbance of which was responsible for the reflection, etc., of light. And not merely does all argument by analogy proceed like this, but all inductive inference can be represented as argument by analogy. For all inductive inference depends on the assumption that in certain respects things continue the same and in other respects they differ. Thus that crude inference from a number of observed swans all having been white to the next swan's being white is an argument by analogy. For it claims that the next swan will be like the observed swans in one respect—color, while being unlike them in other respects.

In our case the similarities between the temporal order which men produce and the temporal order in nature codified in scientific laws mean postulating as cause of the latter a person who acts intentionally. The dissimilarities between the kinds of order include the world-wide extent of the order in nature in comparison with the very narrow range of order which men produce. This means postulating as cause of the former a person of enormous power and knowledge. Now, as we saw in

---

[†]Earlier in the book Swinburne distinguishes a P-inductive argument from a C-inductive argument. A P-inductive argument is one in which the premises make the conclusion probable. A C-inductive argument is one in which the premises *add to the probability of the conclusion (i.e., makes it more probable than it would otherwise be).*

Chapter 2, a person has a body if there is a region of the world under his direct control and if he controls other regions of the world only by controlling the former and by its movements having predictable effects on the outside world. Likewise he learns about the world only by the world having effects on this region. If these conditions are satisfied, the person has a body, and the stated region is that body. But if a person brings about directly the connections between things, including the predictable connections between the bodies of other persons and the world, there is no region of the world, goings-on in which bring about those connections. The person must bring about those connections as a basic action. His control of the world must be immediate, not mediated by a body. So the dissimilarities between the two kinds of order necessarily lead to the postulation of a non-embodied person (rather than an embodied person) as cause of the temporal order in nature.

These considerations should suffice to rebut that persistent criticism of the argument from design which we have heard ever since Hume that, taken seriously, the argument ought to be postulating an embodied god, a giant of a man. 'Why not', wrote Hume, 'become a perfect anthropomorphite? Why not assert the deity or deities to be corporeal, and, to have eyes, a nose, mouth, ears, etc.?' The answer is the simple one that dissimilarities between effects lead the rational man to postulate dissimilarities between causes, and that this procedure is basic to inductive inference.

It is true that the greater the dissimilarities between effects, the weaker is the argument to the existence of a similar cause; and it has been a traditional criticism of the argument from design represented as an argument by analogy that the analogy is weak. The dissimilarities between the natural world and the effects which men produce are indeed striking; but the similarities between these are also, I have been suggesting, striking—in both there is the conformity of phenomena to a simple pattern of order detectable by men. But although the dissimilarities are perhaps sufficiently great to make the argument not a good P-inductive argument, this chapter suggests that it remains a good C-inductive argument. The existence of order in the universe increases significantly the probability that there is a God, even if it does not by itself render it probable.

THE ARGUMENT FROM BEAUTY

We saw that God has reason, apparently overriding reason, for making, not merely any orderly world (which we have been considering so far) but a beautiful world—at any rate to the extent to which it lies outside the control of creatures. (And he has reason too, I would suggest, even in whatever respects the world does lie within the control of creatures, to give them experience of beauty to develop, and perhaps also some ugliness to annihilate.) So God has reason to make a basically beautiful world, although also reason to leave some of the beauty or ugliness of the world within the power of creatures to determine; but he would seem to have overriding reason not to make a basically ugly world beyond the powers of creatures to improve. Hence, if there is a God there is more reason to expect a basically beautiful world than a basically ugly one—by the principles of Chapter 6. *A priori,* however, there is no particular reason for expecting a basically beautiful rather than a basically ugly world. In consequence, if the world is beautiful, that fact would be evidence for God's existence. For, in this case, if we let k be 'there is an orderly physical universe', e be 'there is a beautiful universe', and h be 'there is a God', $P(e/h\&k)$ will be greater than $P(e/k)$; and so by our previous principles the argument from e to h will be another good C-inductive argument.

Few, however, would deny that our universe (apart from its animal and human inhabitants, and aspects subject to their immediate control) has that beauty. Poets and painters and ordinary men down the centuries have long admired the beauty of the orderly procession of the heavenly bodies, the scattering of the galaxies through the heavens (in some ways random, in some ways orderly), and the rocks, sea, and wind interacting on earth, 'The spacious firmament on high, and all the blue aethereal sky', the water lapping against 'the old eternal rocks', and the plants of the jungle and of temperate climates, contrasting with the desert and the Arctic wastes. Who in his senses would deny that here is beauty in abundance? If we confine ourselves to the argument from the beauty of the inanimate and plant worlds, the argument surely works.

NOTES

1. Jer. 33: 20f. and 25f.
2. St. Thomas Aquinas, *Summa Theologiae*, 1 a, 2.3, trans. T. McDermott, OP (London , 1964).
3. '≫' means 'is much greater than', '≪' means 'is much less than'.

I.C.4   A Scientific Argument for the Existence of God

ROBIN COLLINS

Robin Collins (1961–   ) is professor of philosophy at Messiah College, and he has written several articles on the argument from design. The article included here presents a simplified version of an argument that he has developed in much more technical detail elsewhere. He begins by noting that life would have been impossible had certain laws of nature and fundamental physical constants (such as the gravitational constant) been even slightly different. He then argues that since this apparent "fine-tuning" of the laws and constants is significantly more probable on the assumption that the universe was designed to be hospitable for life than on the assumption that it was not designed at all, such apparent fine-tuning counts as evidence in favor of the existence of a designer.

I. INTRODUCTION

The Evidence of Fine-Tuning

Suppose we went on a mission to Mars, and found a domed structure in which everything was set up just right for life to exist. The temperature, for example, was set around 70° F and the humidity was at 50 percent; moreover, there was an oxygen recycling system, an energy gathering system, and a whole system for the production of food. Put simply, the domed structure appeared to be a fully functioning biosphere. What conclusion would we draw from finding this structure? Would we draw the conclusion that it just happened to form by chance? Certainly not. Instead, we would unanimously conclude that it was designed by some intelligent being. Why would we draw this conclusion? Because an intelligent designer appears to be the only plausible explanation for the existence of the structure. That is, the only alternative explanation we can think of—that the structure was formed by some natural process—seems extremely unlikely. Of course, it is *possible* that, for example, through some volcanic eruption various metals and other compounds could have formed, and then separated out in just the right way to produce the "biosphere," but such a scenario strikes us as extraordinarily unlikely, thus making this alternative explanation unbelievable.

From *Reason for the Hope Within*, Michael J. Murray, Ed., © 1999, Wm. B. Eerdmans, Grand Rapids, MI. Used with permission.

The universe is analogous to such a "biosphere," according to recent findings in physics. Almost everything about the basic structure of the universe—for example, the fundamental laws and parameters of physics and the initial distribution of matter and energy—is balanced on a razor's edge for life to occur. As the eminent Princeton physicist Freeman Dyson notes, "There are many . . . lucky accidents in physics. Without such accidents, water could not exist as liquid, chains of carbon atoms could not form complex organic molecules, and hydrogen atoms could not form breakable bridges between molecules"[1]—in short, life as we know it would be impossible.

Scientists call this extraordinary balancing of the parameters of physics and the initial conditions of the universe the "fine-tuning of the cosmos." It has been extensively discussed by philosophers, theologians, and scientists, especially since the early 1970s, with hundreds of articles and dozens of books written on the topic. Today, it is widely regarded as offering by far the most persuasive current argument for the existence of God. For example, theoretical physicist and popular science writer Paul Davies—whose early writings were not particularly sympathetic to theism—claims that with regard to basic structure of the universe, "the impression of design is overwhelming."[2] Similarly, in response to the life-permitting fine-tuning of the nuclear resonances responsible for the oxygen and carbon synthesis in stars, the famous astrophysicist Sir Fred Hoyle declares that

> I do not believe that any scientists who examined the evidence would fail to draw the inference that the laws of nuclear physics have been deliberately designed with regard to the consequences they produce inside stars. If this is so, then my apparently random quirks have become part of a deep-laid scheme. If not then we are back again at a monstrous sequence of accidents.[3]

A few examples of this fine-tuning are listed below:

1. If the initial explosion of the big bang had differed in strength by as little as one part in 10^{60}, the universe would have either quickly collapsed back on itself, or expanded too rapidly for stars to form. In either case, life would be impossible. (As John Jefferson Davis points out, an accuracy of one part in 10^{60} can be compared to firing a bullet at a one-inch target on the other side of the observable universe, twenty billion light years away, and hitting the target.)[4]

2. Calculations indicate that if the strong nuclear force, the force that binds protons and neutrons together in an atom, had been stronger or weaker by as little as five percent, life would be impossible.[5]

3. Calculations by Brandon Carter show that if gravity had been stronger or weaker by one part in 10^{40}, then life-sustaining stars like the sun could not exist. This would most likely make life impossible.[6]

4. If the neutron were not about 1.001 times the mass of the proton, all protons would have decayed into neutrons or all neutrons would have decayed into protons, and thus life would not be possible.[7]

5. If the electromagnetic force were slightly stronger or weaker, life would be impossible, for a variety of different reasons.[8]

Imaginatively, one could think of each instance of fine-tuning as a radio dial: unless all the dials are set exactly right, life would be impossible. Or, one could think of the initial conditions of the universe and the fundamental parameters of physics as a dart board that fills the whole galaxy, and the conditions necessary for life to exist as a small one-foot wide target: unless the dart hits the target, life would be impossible. The fact that the dials are perfectly set, or that the dart has hit the target, strongly suggests that someone set the dials or aimed the dart, for it seems enormously improbable that such a coincidence could have happened by chance.

Although individual calculations of fine-tuning are only approximate and could be in error, the fact that the universe is fine-tuned for life is almost beyond question because of the large number of independent instances of apparent fine-tuning. As philosopher John Leslie has pointed out, "Clues heaped upon clues can constitute weighty evidence despite doubts about each element in the pile."[9] What is controversial, however, is the degree to which the fine-tuning provides evidence for the existence of God. As impressive as the argument from fine-tuning seems to be, atheists have raised several significant objections to it. Consequently, those who are aware of these objections, or have thought of them on their own, often will find the argument unconvincing. This is not only true of atheists, but also many theists. I have known, for instance, both a committed Christian Hollywood filmmaker and a committed Christian biochemist who remained unconvinced because of certain atheist objections to the argument. This is unfortunate, particularly since the fine-tuning argument is probably the most powerful current argument for the existence of God. My goal in this chapter, therefore, is to make the fine-tuning argument as strong as possible. This will involve developing the argument in as objective and rigorous a way as I can, and then answering the major atheist objections to it. Before launching into this, however, I will need to make a preliminary distinction.

A Preliminary Distinction

To develop the fine-tuning argument rigorously, it is useful to distinguish between what I shall call the *atheistic single-universe hypothesis* and the *atheistic many-universes hypothesis*. According to the atheistic single-universe hypothesis, there is only one universe, and it is ultimately an inexplicable, "brute" fact that the universe exists and is fine-tuned. Many atheists, however, advocate another hypothesis, one which attempts to explain how the seemingly improbable fine-tuning of the universe could be the result of chance. We will call this hypothesis the *atheistic many-worlds hypothesis*, or *the atheistic many-universes hypothesis*. According to this hypothesis, there exists what could be imaginatively thought of as a "universe generator" that produces a very large or infinite number of universes, with each universe having a randomly selected set of initial conditions and values for the parameters of physics. Because this generator produces so many universes, just by chance it will eventually produce one that is fine-tuned for intelligent life to occur.

Plan of the Chapter

Below, we will use this distinction between the atheistic single-universe hypothesis and the atheistic many-universes hypothesis to present two separate arguments for theism based on the fine-tuning: one which argues that the fine-tuning provides strong reasons to prefer theism over the atheistic single-universe hypothesis and one which argues that we should prefer theism over the atheistic many-universes hypothesis. We will develop the argument against the atheistic single-universe hypothesis in section II below, referring to it as the *core* argument. Then we will answer objections to this core argument in section III, and finally develop the argument for preferring theism to the atheistic many-universes hypothesis in section IV. An appendix is also included that further elaborates and justifies one of the key premises of the core argument presented in section II.

II. CORE ARGUMENT RIGOROUSLY FORMULATED

General Principle of Reasoning Used

The Principle Explained

We will formulate the fine-tuning argument against the atheistic single-universe hypothesis in terms of what I will call the *prime principle of confirmation*. The prime principle of confirmation is a general principle of reasoning which tells us when some observation counts as evidence in favor of one hypothesis over another. *Simply put, the principle says that whenever we are considering two competing hypotheses, an observation counts as evidence in favor of the hypothesis under which the observation has the highest probability (or is the least improbable).* (Or, put slightly differently, the principle says that whenever we are considering two competing hypotheses, H_1 and H_2, an observation, O, counts as evidence in favor of H_1 over H_2 if O is more probable under H_1 than it is under H_2.) Moreover, the degree to which the evidence counts in favor of one hypothesis over another is proportional to the degree to which the observation is more probable under the one hypothesis than the other.[10] For example, the fine-tuning is much, much more probable under theism than under the atheistic single-universe hypothesis, so it counts as strong evidence for theism over this atheistic hypothesis. In the next major subsection, we will present a more formal and elaborated rendition of the fine-tuning argument in terms of the prime principle. First, however, let's look at a couple of illustrations of the principle and then present some support for it.

Additional Illustrations of the Principle

For our first illustration, suppose that I went hiking in the mountains, and found underneath a certain cliff a group of rocks arranged in a formation that clearly formed the pattern "Welcome to the mountains, Robin Collins." One hypothesis is that, by chance, the rocks just happened to be arranged in that pattern—ultimately, perhaps, because of certain initial conditions of the universe. Suppose the only viable alternative hypothesis is that my brother, who was in the mountains before me, arranged the rocks in this way. Most of us would immediately take the arrangements of rocks to be strong evidence in favor of the "brother" hypothesis over the "chance" hypothesis. Why? Because it strikes us as extremely *improbable* that the rocks would be arranged that way by chance, but *not improbable* at all that my brother would place them in that configuration. Thus, by the prime principle of confirmation we would conclude that the arrangement of rocks strongly supports the "brother" hypothesis over the chance hypothesis.

Or consider another case, that of finding the defendant's fingerprints on the murder weapon. Normally, we would take such a finding as strong evidence that the defendant was guilty. Why? Because we judge that it would be *unlikely* for these fingerprints to be on the murder weapon if the defendant was innocent, but *not unlikely* if the defendant was guilty. That is, we would go through the same sort of reasoning as in the above case.

Support for the Principle

Several things can be said in favor of the prime principle of confirmation. First, many philosophers think that this principle can be derived from what is known as the *probability calculus,* the set of mathematical rules that are typically assumed to govern probability. Second, there does not appear to be any case of recognizably good reasoning that violates this principle. Finally, the principle appears to have a wide range of applicability, undergirding much of our reasoning in science and everyday life, as the examples above illustrate. Indeed, some have even claimed that a slightly more general version of this principle undergirds all scientific reasoning. Because of all these reasons in favor of the principle, we can be very confident in it.

Further Development of Argument

To further develop the core version of the fine-tuning argument, we will summarize the argument by explicitly listing its two premises and its conclusion:

- *Premise 1.* The existence of the fine-tuning is not improbable under theism.
- *Premise 2.* The existence of the fine-tuning is very improbable under the atheistic single-universe hypothesis.
- *Conclusion:* From premises (1) and (2) and the prime principle of confirmation, it follows that the fine-tuning data provide strong evidence to favor the design hypothesis over the atheistic single-universe hypothesis.

At this point, we should pause to note two features of this argument. First, the argument does not say that the fine-tuning evidence proves that the universe was designed, or even that it is likely that the universe was designed. In order to justify these sorts of claims, we would have to look at the full range of evidence both for and against the design hypothesis, something we are not doing in this chapter. Rather, the argument merely concludes that the fine-tuning strongly *supports* theism *over* the atheistic single-universe hypothesis.

In this way, the evidence of the fine-tuning argument is much like fingerprints found on the gun: although they can provide strong evidence that the defendant committed the murder, one could not conclude merely from them alone that the defendant is guilty; one would also have to look at all the other evidence offered. Perhaps, for instance, ten reliable witnesses claimed to see the defendant at a party at the time of the shooting. In this case, the fingerprints would still count as significant evidence of guilt, but this evidence would be counterbalanced by the testimony of the witnesses. Similarly the evidence of fine-tuning strongly supports theism over the atheistic single-universe hypothesis, though it does not itself show that, everything considered, theism is the most plausible explanation of the world. Nonetheless, as I argue in the conclusion of this chapter, the evidence of fine-tuning provides a much stronger and more objective argument for theism (over the atheistic single-universe hypothesis) than the strongest atheistic argument does against theism.

The second feature of the argument we should note is that, given the truth of *the prime principle of confirmation*, the conclusion of the argument follows from the premises. Specifically, if the premises of the argument are true, then we are guaranteed that the conclusion is true: that is, the argument is what philosophers call *valid*. Thus, insofar as we can show that the premises of the argument are true, we will have shown that the conclusion is true. Our next task, therefore, is to attempt to show that the premises are true, or at least that we have strong reasons to believe them.

Support for the Premises

Support for Premise (1)   Premise (1) is easy to support and fairly uncontroversial. One major argument in support of it can be simply stated as follows: *since God is an all good being, and it is good for intelligent, conscious beings to exist, it is not surprising or improbable that God would create a world that could support intelligent life.* Thus, the fine-tuning is not improbable under theism, as premise (1) asserts.

Support for Premise (2)   Upon looking at the data, many people find it very obvious that the fine-tuning is highly improbable under the

atheistic single-universe hypothesis. And it is easy to see why when we think of the fine-tuning in terms of the analogies offered earlier. In the dart board analogy, for example, the initial conditions of the universe and the fundamental parameters of physics are thought of as a dart board that fills the whole galaxy, and the conditions necessary for life to exist as a small one-foot wide target. Accordingly, from this analogy it seems obvious that it would be highly improbable for the fine-tuning to occur under the atheistic single-universe hypothesis—that is, for the dart to hit the target by chance.

Typically, advocates of the fine-tuning argument are satisfied with resting the justification of premise (2), or something like it, on this sort of analogy. Many atheists and theists, however, question the legitimacy of this sort of analogy, and thus find the argument unconvincing. For these people, the appendix to this chapter offers a rigorous and objective justification of premise (2) using standard principles of probabilistic reasoning. Among other things, in the process of rigorously justifying premise (2), we effectively answer the common objection to the fine-tuning argument that because the universe is a unique, unrepeatable event, we cannot meaningfully assign a probability to its being fine-tuned.

III. SOME OBJECTIONS TO CORE VERSION

As powerful as the core version of the fine-tuning argument is, several major objections have been raised to it by both atheists and theists. In this section, we will consider these objections in turn.

Objection 1: More Fundamental Law Objection

One criticism of the fine-tuning argument is that, as far as we know, there could be a more fundamental law under which the parameters of physics *must* have the values they do. Thus, given such a law, it is not improbable that the known parameters of physics fall within the life-permitting range.

Besides being entirely speculative, the problem with postulating such a law is that it simply moves the improbability of the fine-tuning up one level, to that of the postulated physical law itself. Under this hypothesis, what is improbable is that of all the conceivable fundamental physical laws there could be, the universe just happens to have the one that constrains the parameters of physics in a life-permitting way. Thus, trying to explain the fine-tuning by postulating this sort of fundamental law is like trying to explain why the pattern of rocks below a cliff spell "Welcome to the mountains, Robin Collins" by postulating that an earthquake occurred and that all the rocks on the cliff face were arranged in just the right configuration to fall into the pattern in question. Clearly this explanation merely transfers the improbability up one level, since now it seems enormously improbable that of all the possible configurations the rocks could be in on the cliff face, they are in the one which results in the pattern "Welcome to the mountains, Robin Collins."

A similar sort of response can be given to the claim that the fine-tuning is not improbable because it might be *logically necessary* for the parameters of physics to have life-permitting values. That is, according to this claim, the parameters of physics must have life-permitting values in the same way $2 + 2$ must equal 4, or the interior angles of a triangle must add up to 180 degrees in Euclidian geometry. Like the "more fundamental law" proposal above, however, this postulate simply transfers the improbability up one level: of all the laws and parameters of physics that conceivably could have been logically necessary, it seems highly improbable that it would be those that are life-permitting.[11]

Objection 2: Other Forms of Life Objection

Another objection people commonly raise to the fine-tuning argument is that as far as we know, other forms of life could exist even if the parameters of physics were different. So, it is claimed, the fine-tuning argument ends up presupposing that all forms of intelligent life must be like us. The answer to this objection is that most cases of fine-tuning do not make this presupposition. Consider, for instance, the case of the fine-tuning of the strong nuclear force. If it were slightly smaller, no atoms could exist other than hydrogen. Contrary to

what one might see on *Star Trek,* an intelligent life-form cannot be composed merely of hydrogen gas: there is simply not enough stable complexity. So, in general the fine-tuning argument merely presupposes that intelligent life requires some degree of stable, reproducible organized complexity. This is certainly a very reasonable assumption.

Objection 3. Anthropic Principle Objection

According to the weak version of the so-called *anthropic principle,* if the laws of nature were not fine-tuned, we would not be here to comment on the fact. Some have argued, therefore, that the fine-tuning is not really *improbable or surprising* at all under atheism, but simply follows from the fact that we exist. The response to this objection is to simply restate the argument in terms of our existence: our existence as embodied, intelligent beings is extremely unlikely under the atheistic single-universe hypothesis (since our existence requires fine-tuning), but not improbable under theism. Then, we simply apply the prime principle of confirmation to draw the conclusion that *our existence* strongly confirms theism over the atheistic single-universe hypothesis.

To further illustrate this response, consider the following "firing squad" analogy. As John Leslie points out, if fifty sharpshooters all miss me, the response "if they had not missed me I wouldn't be here to consider the fact" is not adequate. Instead, I would naturally conclude that there was some reason why they all missed, such as that they never really intended to kill me. Why would I conclude this? Because my continued existence would be very improbable under the hypothesis that they missed me by chance, but not improbable under the hypothesis that there was some reason why they missed me. Thus, by the prime principle of confirmation, my continued existence strongly confirms the latter hypothesis.[12]

Objection 4: The "Who Designed God?" Objection

Perhaps the most common objection that atheists raise to the argument from design, of which the fine-tuning argument is one instance, is that postulating the existence of God does not solve the problem of design, but merely transfers it up one level. Atheist George Smith, for example, claims that

> If the universe is wonderfully designed, surely God is even more wonderfully designed. He must, therefore, have had a designer even more wonderful than He is. If *God* did not require a designer, then there is no reason why such a relatively less wonderful thing as the universe needed one.[13]

Or, as philosopher J. J. C. Smart states the objection:

> If we postulate God in addition to the created universe we increase the complexity of our hypothesis. We have all the complexity of the universe itself, and we have in addition the at least equal complexity of God. (The designer of an artifact must be at least as complex as the designed artifact).... *If the theist can show the atheist that postulating God actually reduces the complexity of one's total world view, then the atheist should be a theist.*[14]

The first response to the above atheist objection is to point out that the atheist claim that the designer of an artifact must be as complex as the artifact designed is certainly not obvious. But I do believe that their claim has some intuitive plausibility: for example, in the world we experience, organized complexity seems only to be produced by systems that already possess it, such as the human brain/mind, a factory, or an organism's biological parent.

The second, and better, response is to point out that, at most, the atheist objection only works against a version of the design argument that claims that all organized complexity needs an explanation, and that God is the best explanation of the organized complexity found in the world. The version of the argument I presented against the atheistic single-universe hypothesis, however, only required that the fine-tuning be more probable under theism than under the atheistic single-universe hypothesis. But this requirement is still met even if God exhibits tremendous internal complexity, far exceeding that of the universe. Thus, even if we were to grant the atheist assumption that the designer of an artifact must be as complex as the artifact, the fine-tuning would still give us strong reasons to prefer theism over the atheistic single-universe hypothesis.

To illustrate, consider the example of the "biosphere" on Mars presented at the beginning of this paper. As mentioned above, the existence of the biosphere would be much more probable under the hypothesis that intelligent life once visited Mars than under the chance hypothesis. Thus, by the prime principle of confirmation, the existence of such a "biosphere" would constitute strong evidence that intelligent, extraterrestrial life had once been on Mars, even though this alien life would most likely have to be much more complex than the "biosphere" itself.

The final response theists can give to this objection is to show that a supermind such as God would *not* require a high degree of unexplained organized complexity to create the universe. Although I have presented this response elsewhere, presenting it here is beyond the scope of this chapter.

IV. THE ATHEISTIC MANY-UNIVERSES HYPOTHESIS

The Atheistic Many-Universes Hypothesis Explained

In response to the theistic explanation of fine-tuning of the cosmos, many atheists have offered an alternative explanation, what I will call the atheistic many-universes hypothesis. (In the literature it is more commonly referred to as the *many-worlds hypothesis,* though I believe this name is somewhat misleading.) According to this hypothesis, there are a very large—perhaps infinite—number of universes, with the fundamental parameters of physics varying from universe to universe.[15] Of course, in the vast majority of these universes the parameters of physics would not have life-permitting values. Nonetheless, in a small proportion of universes they would, and consequently it is no longer improbable that universes such as ours exist that are fine-tuned for life to occur.

Advocates of this hypothesis offer various types of models for where these universes came from. We will present what are probably the two most popular and plausible, the so-called *vacuum fluctuation* models and the *oscillating big bang* models. According to the vacuum fluctuation models, our universe, along with these other universes, were generated by quantum fluctuations in a preexisting superspace.[16] Imaginatively, one can think of this preexisting superspace as an infinitely extending ocean full of soap, and each universe generated out of this superspace as a soap bubble which spontaneously forms on the ocean.

The other model, the oscillating big bang model, is a version of the big bang theory. According to the big bang theory, the universe came into existence in an "explosion" (that is, a "bang") somewhere between ten and fifteen billion years ago. According to the *oscillating* big bang theory, our universe will eventually collapse back in on itself (what is called the "big crunch") and then from that "big crunch" will arise another "big bang," forming a new universe, which will in turn itself collapse, and so on. According to those who use this model to attempt to explain the fine-tuning, during every cycle, the parameters of physics and the initial conditions of the universe are reset at random. Since this process of collapse, explosion, collapse, and explosion has been going on for all eternity, eventually a fine-tuned universe will occur, indeed infinitely many of them.

In the next section, we will list several reasons for rejecting the atheistic many-universes hypothesis.

Reasons for Rejecting the Atheistic Many-Universes Hypothesis

First Reason

The first reason for rejecting the atheistic many-universes hypothesis, and preferring the theistic hypothesis, is the following general rule: *everything else being equal, we should prefer hypotheses for which we have independent evidence or that are natural extrapolations from what we already know.* Let's first illustrate and support this principle, and then apply it to the case of the fine-tuning.

Most of us take the existence of dinosaur bones to count as very strong evidence that dinosaurs existed in the past. But suppose a dinosaur skeptic claimed that she could explain the bones by postulating a "dinosaur-bone-producing-field" that simply materialized the bones out of thin air. Moreover, suppose further that, to avoid objections such as that there are no known physical laws that would allow for such a mechanism, the dinosaur skeptic simply postulated that we have not yet discovered these laws or detected these fields. Surely, none of us would let this skeptical hypothesis deter us from inferring the existence of dinosaurs. Why? Because although no one has directly observed dinosaurs, we do have experience of other animals leaving behind fossilized remains, and thus the dinosaur explanation is a *natural extrapolation* from our common experience. In contrast, to explain the dinosaur bones, the dinosaur skeptic has invented a set of physical laws, and a set of mechanisms that are *not* a natural extrapolation from anything we know or experience.

In the case of the fine-tuning, we already know that minds often produce fine-tuned devices, such as Swiss watches. Postulating God—a supermind—as the explanation of the fine-tuning, therefore, is a natural extrapolation from what we already observe minds to do. In contrast, it is difficult to see how the atheistic many-universes hypothesis could be considered a natural extrapolation from what we observe. Moreover, unlike the atheistic many-universes hypothesis, we have some experiential evidence for the existence of God, namely religious experience. Thus, by the above principle, we should prefer the theistic explanation of the fine-tuning over the atheistic many-universes explanation, everything else being equal.

Second Reason

A second reason for rejecting the atheistic many-universes hypothesis is that the "many-universes generator" seems like it would need to be designed. For instance, in all current worked-out proposals for what this "universe generator" could be—such as the oscillating big bang and the vacuum fluctuation models explained above—the "generator" itself is governed by a complex set of physical laws that allow it to produce the universes. It stands to reason, therefore, that if these laws were slightly different the generator probably would not be able to produce any universes that could sustain life. After all, even my bread machine has to be made just right in order to work properly, and it only produces loaves of bread, not universes! Or consider a device as simple as a mousetrap: it requires that all the parts, such as the spring and hammer, be arranged just right in order to function. It is doubtful, therefore, whether the atheistic many-universe theory can entirely eliminate the problem of design the atheist faces; rather, at least to some extent, it seems simply to move the problem of design up one level.[17]

Third Reason

A third reason for rejecting the atheistic many-universes hypothesis is that the universe generator must not only select the parameters of physics at random, but must actually randomly create or select the very laws of physics themselves. This makes this hypothesis seem even more far-fetched since it is difficult to see what possible physical mechanism could select or create laws.

The reason the "many-universes generator" must randomly select the laws of physics is that, just as the right values for the parameters of physics are needed for life to occur, the right set of laws is also needed. If, for instance, certain laws of physics were missing, life would be impossible. For example, without the law of inertia, which guarantees that particles do not shoot off at high speeds, life would probably not be possible.[18] Another example is the law of gravity: if masses did not attract each other, there would be no planets or stars, and once again it seems that life would be impossible. Yet another example is the *Pauli Exclusion Principle,* the principle of quantum mechanics that says that no two fermions—such as electrons or protons—can share the same quantum state. As prominent Princeton physicist Freeman Dyson points out,[19] without this principle all electrons would collapse into the nucleus and thus atoms would be impossible.

Fourth Reason

The fourth reason for rejecting the atheistic many-universes hypothesis is that it cannot explain other features of the universe that seem to exhibit apparent design, whereas theism can. For example, many physicists, such as Albert Einstein, have observed that the basic laws of physics exhibit an extraordinary degree of beauty, elegance, harmony, and ingenuity. Nobel prize-winning physicist Steven Weinberg, for instance, devotes a whole chapter of his book *Dreams of a Final Theory*[20] explaining how the criteria of beauty and elegance are commonly used to guide physicists in formulating the right laws. Indeed, one of the most prominent theoretical physicists of this century, Paul Dirac, went so far as to claim that "it is more important to have beauty in one's equations than to have them fit experiment."[21]

Now such beauty, elegance, and ingenuity make sense if the universe was designed by God. Under the atheistic many-universes hypothesis, however, there is no reason to expect the fundamental laws to be elegant or beautiful. As theoretical physicist Paul Davies writes, "If nature is so 'clever' as to exploit mechanisms that amaze us with their ingenuity, is that not persuasive evidence for the existence of intelligent design behind the universe? If the world's finest minds can unravel only with difficulty the deeper workings of nature, how could it be supposed that those workings are merely a mindless accident, a product of blind chance?"[22]

Final Reason

This brings us to the final reason for rejecting the atheistic many-universes hypothesis, which may be the most difficult to grasp: namely, neither the atheistic many-universes hypothesis (nor the atheistic single-universe hypothesis) can at present adequately account for the improbable initial arrangement of matter in the universe required by the second law of thermodynamics. To see this, note that according to the second law of thermodynamics, the entropy of the universe is constantly increasing. The standard way of understanding this entropy increase is to say that the universe is going from a state of order to disorder. We observe this entropy increase all the time around us: things, such as a child's bedroom, that start out highly organized tend to "decay" and become disorganized unless something or someone intervenes to stop it.

Now, for purposes of illustration, we could think of the universe as a scrabble-board that initially starts out in a highly ordered state in which all the letters are arranged to form words, but which keeps getting randomly shaken. Slowly, the board, like the universe, moves from a state of order to disorder. The problem for the atheist is to explain how the universe could have started out in a highly ordered state, since it is extraordinarily improbable for such states to occur by chance.[23] If, for example, one were to dump a bunch of letters at random on a scrabble-board, it would be very unlikely for most of them to form into words. At best, we would expect groups of letters to form into words in a few places on the board.

Now our question is, Could the atheistic many-universes hypothesis explain the high degree of initial order of our universe by claiming that given enough universes, eventually one will arise that is ordered and in which intelligent life occurs, and so it is no surprise that we find ourselves in an ordered universe? The problem with this explanation is that it is overwhelmingly more likely for local patches of order to form in one or two places than for the whole universe to be ordered, just as it is over-whelmingly more likely for a few letters on the scrabble-board randomly to form words than for all the letters throughout the board randomly to form words. Thus, the overwhelming majority of universes in which intelligent life occurs will be ones in which the intelligent life will be surrounded by a small patch of order necessary for its existence, but in which the rest of the universe is disordered. Consequently, even under the atheistic many-universes hypothesis, it would still be enormously improbable for intelligent

beings to find themselves in a universe such as ours which is highly ordered throughout.[24]

Conclusion

Even though the above criticisms do not definitively refute the atheistic many-universes hypothesis, they do show that it has some severe disadvantages relative to theism. This means that if atheists adopt the atheistic many-universes hypothesis to defend their position, then atheism has become much less plausible than it used to be. Modifying a turn of phrase coined by philosopher Fred Dretske: these are inflationary times, and the cost of atheism has just gone up.

V. OVERALL CONCLUSION

In the above sections I showed there are good, objective reasons for claiming that the fine-tuning provides strong evidence for theism. I first presented an argument for thinking that the fine-tuning provides strong evidence for preferring theism over the atheistic single-universe hypothesis, and then presented a variety of different reasons for rejecting the atheistic many-universes hypothesis as an explanation of the fine-tuning. In order to help one appreciate the strength of the arguments presented, I would like to end by comparing the strength of the *core* version of the argument from the fine-tuning to what is widely regarded as the strongest atheist argument against theism, the argument from evil.[25]

Typically, the atheist argument against God based on evil takes a similar form to the core version of the fine-tuning argument. Essentially, the atheist argues that the existence of the kinds of evil we find in the world is very improbable under theism, but not improbable under atheism. Thus, by the prime principle of confirmation, they conclude that the existence of evil provides strong reasons for preferring atheism over theism.

What makes this argument weak in comparison to the core version of the fine-tuning argument is that, unlike in the case of the fine-tuning, the atheist does not have a significant objective basis for claiming that the existence of the kinds of evil we find in the world is highly improbable under theism. In fact, their judgment that it is improbable seems largely to rest on a mistake in reasoning. To see this, note that in order to show that it is improbable, atheists would have to show that it is *unlikely* that the types of evils we find in the world are necessary for any morally good, greater purpose, since if they are, then it is clearly not at all unlikely that an all good, all powerful being would create a world in which those evils are allowed to occur. But how could atheists show this without first surveying all possible morally good purposes such a being might have, something they have clearly not done? *Consequently, it seems, at most the atheist could argue that since no one has come up with any adequate purpose yet, it is unlikely that there is such a purpose.* This argument, how-ever, is very weak, as I will now show.

The first problem with this atheist argu-ment is that it assumes that the various expla-nations people have offered for why an all good God would create evil—such as the free will theodicy—ultimately fail. But even if we grant that these theodicies fail, the argument is still very weak. To see why, consider an anal-ogy. Suppose someone tells me that there is a rattlesnake in my garden, and I examine a por-tion of the garden and do not find the snake. I would only be justified in concluding that there was probably no snake in the garden if either: i) I had searched at least half the garden; or ii) I had good reason to believe that if the snake were in the garden, it would likely be in the portion of the garden that I examined. If, for instance, I were randomly to pick some small segment of the garden to search and did not find the snake, I would be unjustified in con-cluding from my search that there was probably no snake in the garden. Similarly, if I were blindfolded and did not have any idea of how large the garden was (e.g., whether it was ten square feet or several square miles), I would be unjustified in concluding that it was unlikely that there was a rattlesnake in the garden, even if I had searched for hours with my rattlesnake-detecting dogs. Why? Because I would not have any idea of what percentage of the garden I had searched.

As with the garden example, we have no idea of how large the realm is of possible greater purposes for evil that an all good, omnipotent being could have. Hence we do not know what proportion of this realm we have actually searched. Indeed, considering the finitude of our own minds, we have good reason to believe that we have so far only searched a small proportion, and we do not have significant reason to believe that all the purposes God might have for allowing evil would be in the proportion we searched. Thus, we have little objective basis for saying that the existence of the types of evil we find in the world is highly improbable under theism.

From the above discussion, therefore, it is clear that the relevant probability estimates in the case of the fine-tuning are much more secure than those estimates in the probabilistic version of the atheist's argument from evil, since unlike the latter, we can provide a fairly rigorous, objec-tive basis for them based on actual calculations of the relative range of life-permitting values for the parameters of physics. (See the appendix to this chapter for a rigorous derivation of the probabil-ity of the fine-tuning under the atheistic single-universe hypothesis.) *Thus, I conclude, the core argument for preferring theism over the probabil-istic version of the atheistic single-universe hypoth-esis is much stronger than the atheist argument from evil.*[26]

APPENDIX

In this appendix, I offer a rigorous support for premise (2) of the main argument: that is, the claim that the fine-tuning is very improbable under the atheistic single-universe hypothesis. Sup-port for premise (2) will involve three major subsec-tions. The first subsection will be devoted to explicating the fine-tuning of gravity since we will often use this to illustrate our arguments. Then, in our second subsection, we will show how the improbability of the fine-tuning under the atheistic single-universe hypothesis can be derived from a commonly used, objective prin-ciple of probabilistic reasoning called the *prin-ciple of indifference*. Finally, in our third subsection, we will explicate what it could mean to say that the fine-tuning is improbable given that the universe is a unique, unrepeatable event as assumed by the atheistic single-universe hypothesis. The appendix will in effect answer the common atheist objection that theists can neither *justify* the claim that the fine-tuning is improbable under the atheistic single-universe hypothesis, nor can they provide an account of what it could possibly *mean* to say that the fine-tuning is improbable.

i. The Example of Gravity

The force of gravity is determined by Newton's law $F = Gm_1m_2/r^2$. Here G is what is known as the *gravitational constant,* and is basically a number that determines the force of gravity in any given circumstance. For instance, the gravitational attraction between the moon and the earth is given by first multiplying the mass of the moon (m_1) times the mass of the earth (m_2), and then dividing by the distance between them squared (r^2). Finally, one multiplies this result by the number G to obtain the total force. Clearly the force is directly proportional to G: for example, if G were to double, the force between the moon and the earth would double.

In the previous section, we reported that some calculations indicate that the force of gravity must be fine-tuned to one part in 10^{40} in order for life to occur. What does such fine-tuning mean? To understand it, imagine a radio dial, going from 0 to $2G_0$, where G_0 represents the current value of the gravitational constant. Moreover, imagine the dial being broken up into 10^{40}—that is, ten thousand, billion, billion, billion, billion—evenly spaced tick marks. To claim that the strength of gravity must be fine-tuned to one part in 10^{40} is simply to claim that, in order for life to exist, the constant of gravity cannot vary by even one tick mark along the dial from its current value of G_0.

ii. The Principle of Indifference

In the following subsections, we will use the *principle of indifference* to justify the assertion that the fine-tuning is highly improbable under the atheistic single-universe hypothesis.

a. The Principle Stated

Applied to cases in which there is a finite number of alternatives, the principle of indifference can be formulated as the claim that we should assign the same probability to what are called *equipossible alternatives,* where two or more alternatives are said to be equipossible if we have no reason to prefer one of the alternatives over any of the others. (In another version of the principle, alternatives that are relevantly symmetrical are considered equipossible and hence the ones that should be assigned equal probability.) For instance, in the case of a standard two-sided coin, we have no more reason to think that the coin will land on heads than that it will land on tails, and so we assign them each an equal probability. Since the total probability must add up to one, this means that the coin has a 0.5 chance of landing on heads and a 0.5 chance of landing on tails. Similarly, in the case of a standard six-sided die, we have no more reason to think that it will land on one number, say a 6, than any of the other numbers, such as a 4. Thus, the principle of indifference tells us to assign each possible way of landing an equal probability—namely $1/6$.

The above explication of the principle applies only when there are a finite number of alternatives, for example six sides on a die. In the case of the fine-tuning, however, the alternatives are not finite but form a continuous magnitude. The value of G, for instance, conceivably could have been any number between 0 and infinity. Now, continuous magnitudes are usually thought of in terms of ranges, areas, or volumes depending on whether or not we are considering one, two, three, or more dimensions. For example, the amount of water in an 8 oz. glass could fall anywhere within the *range* 0 oz. to 8 oz., such as 6.012345645 oz. Or, the exact position that a dart hits a dart board can fall anywhere within the *area* of the dart board. With some qualifications to be discussed below, the principle of indifference becomes in the continuous case the principle that *when we have no reason to prefer any one value of a parameter over another, we should assign equal probabilities to equal ranges, areas, or volumes.* So, for instance, suppose one aimlessly throws a dart at a dart board. Assuming the dart hits the board, what is the probability it will hit within the bull's eye? Since the dart is thrown aimlessly, we have no more reason to believe it will hit one part of the dart board than any other part. The principle of indifference, therefore, tells us that the probability of its hitting the bull's eye is the same as the probability of hitting any other part of the dart board of equal area. This means that the probability of its hitting the bull's eye is simply the ratio of the area of the bull's eye to the rest of the dart board. So, for instance, if the bull's eye forms only 5 percent of the total area of the board, then the probability of its hitting the bull's eye will be 5 percent.

b. Application to Fine-Tuning

In the case of the fine-tuning, we have no more reason to think that the parameters of physics will fall within the life-permitting range than within any other range, given the atheistic single-universe hypothesis. Thus according to the principle of indifference, equal ranges of these parameters should be assigned equal probabilities. As in the case of the dart board mentioned in the last section, this means that the probability of the parameters of physics falling within the life-permitting range under the atheistic single-universe hypothesis is simply the ratio of the range of life-permitting values (the "area of the bull's eye") to the total *relevant* range of possible values (the "relevant area of the dart board").

Now physicists can make rough estimates of the range of *life-permitting* values for the parameters of physics, as discussed above in the case of gravity, for instance. But what is the "total *relevant* range of possible values"? At first one might think that this range is infinite, since the values of the parameters could conceivably be anything. This, however, is not correct, for although the possible range of values could be infinite, for most of these values we have no way of estimating whether they are life-permitting or not. We do not truly know, for example, what would happen if gravity

were 10^{60} times stronger than its current value: as far as we know, a new form of matter might come into existence that could sustain life. Thus, as far as we know, there could be other life-permitting ranges far removed from the actual values that the parameters have. Consequently, all we can say is that the life-permitting range is very, very small *relative* to the limited range of values for which we can make estimates, a range that we will hereafter refer to as the *"illuminated"* range.

Fortunately, however, this limitation does not affect the overall argument. The reason is that, based on the principle of indifference, we can still say that it is very improbable for the values for the parameters of physics to have fallen in the life-permitting range *instead* of some other part of the "illuminated" range.[27] And this *improbability* is all that is actually needed for our main argument to work. To see this, consider an analogy. Suppose a dart landed on the bull's eye at the center of a huge dart board. Further, suppose that this bull's eye is surrounded by a very large empty, bull's-eye-free, area. Even if there were many other bull's eyes on the dart board, we would still take the fact that the dart landed on the bull's eye instead of some other part of the large empty area surrounding the bull's eye as strong evidence that it was aimed. Why? Because we would reason that *given that the dart landed in the empty area,* it was very improbable for it to land in the bull's eye by chance but not improbable if it were aimed. Thus, by the prime principle of confirmation, we could conclude that the dart landing on the bull's eye strongly confirms the hypothesis that it was aimed over the chance hypothesis.

c. The Principle Qualified

Those who are familiar with the principle of indifference, and mathematics, will recognize that one important qualification needs to be made to the above account of how to apply the principle of indifference. (Those who are not mathematically adept might want to skip this and perhaps the next paragraph.) To understand the qualification, note that the ratio of ranges used in calculating the probability is dependent on how one parameterizes, or writes, the physical laws. For example, suppose for the sake of illustration that the range of life-permitting values for the gravitational constant is 0 to G_0, and the "illuminated" range of possible values for G is 0 to $2G_0$. Then, the ratio of life-permitting values to the range of "illuminated" possible values for the gravitational constant will be ½. Suppose, however, that one writes the law of gravity in the mathematically equivalent form of $F = \sqrt{U} m_1 m_2/r^2$ instead of $F = G m_1 m_2/r^2$, where $U = G^2$. (In this way of writing Newton's law, U becomes the new gravitational constant.) This means that $U_0 = G_0^2$, where U_0, *like* G_0, represents the actual value of U in our universe. Then, the range of life-permitting values would be 0 to U_0, and the "illuminated" range of possible values would be 0 to $4U_0$ on the U scale (which is equivalent to 0 to $2G_0$ on the G scale). Hence, calculating the ratio of life-permitting values using the U scale instead of G scale yields a ratio of ¼ instead of ½. Indeed, for almost any ratio one chooses—such as one in which the life-permitting range is about the same size as the "illuminated" range—there exist mathematically equivalent forms of Newton's law that will yield that ratio. So, why choose the standard way of writing Newton's law to calculate the ratio instead of one in which the fine-tuning is not improbable at all?

The answer to this question is to require that the proportion used in calculating the probability be between *real* physical ranges, areas, or volumes, not merely mathematical representations of them. That is, the proportion given by the scale used in one's representation must directly correspond to the proportions actually existing in physical reality. As an illustration, consider how we might calculate the probability that a meteorite will fall in New York state instead of somewhere else in the northern, contiguous United States. One way of doing this is to take a standard map of the northern, contiguous United States, measure the area covered by New York on the map (say 2 square inches) and divide it by the total area of the map (say 30 square inches). If we were to do this, we would get approximately the right answer because the proportions on a standard map directly correspond

to the actual proportions of land areas in the United States.[28] On the other hand, suppose we had a map made by some lover of the east coast in which, because of the scale used, the east coast took up half the map. If we used the proportions of areas as represented by this map we would get the wrong answer since the scale used would not correspond to real proportions of land areas. Applied to the fine-tuning, this means that our calculations of these proportions must be done using parameters that directly correspond to physical quantities in order to yield valid probabilities. In the case of gravity, for instance, the gravitational constant G directly corresponds to the force between two unit masses a unit distance apart, whereas U does not. (Instead, U corresponds to the square of the force.) Thus, G is the correct parameter to use in calculating the probability.[29]

d. Support for Principle

Finally, although the principle of indifference has been criticized on various grounds, several powerful reasons can be offered for its soundness if it is restricted in the ways explained in the last subsection. First, it has an extraordinarily wide range of applicability. As Roy Weatherford notes in his book, *Philosophical Foundations of Probability Theory,* "an astonishing number of extremely complex problems in probability theory have been solved, and usefully so, by calculations based entirely on the assumption of equiprobable alternatives [that is, the principle of indifference]."[30] Second, at least for the discrete case, the principle can be given a significant theoretical grounding in information theory, being derivable from Shannon's important and well-known measure of *information,* or *negative entropy.*[31] Finally, in certain everyday cases the principle of indifference seems the only justification we have for assigning probability. To illustrate, suppose that in the last ten minutes a factory produced the first fifty-sided die ever produced. Further suppose that every side of the die is (macroscopically) perfectly symmetrical with every other side, except for there being different numbers printed on each side. (The die we are imagining is like a fair six-sided die except that it has fifty sides instead of six.) Now, we all immediately know that upon being rolled the probability of the die coming up on any given side is one in fifty. Yet, we do not know this directly from experience with fifty-sided dice, since by hypothesis no one has yet rolled such dice to determine the relative frequency with which they come up on each side. Rather, it seems our only justification for assigning this probability is the principle of indifference: that is, given that every side of the die is relevantly macroscopically symmetrical with every other side, we have no reason to believe that the die will land on one side over any other side, and thus we assign them all an equal probability of one in fifty.[32]

iii. The Meaning of Probability

In the last section we used the principle of indifference to rigorously justify the claim that the fine-tuning is highly improbable under the atheistic single-universe hypothesis. We did not explain, however, what it could *mean* to say that it is improbable, especially given that the universe is a unique, unrepeatable event. To address this issue, we shall now show how the probability invoked in the fine-tuning argument can be straightforwardly understood either as what could be called *classical probability* or as what is known as *epistemic probability*.

Classical Probability

The *classical conception of probability* defines probability in terms of the ratio of number of "favorable cases" to the total number of equipossible cases.[33] Thus, for instance, to say the probability of a die coming up "4" is one out of six is simply to say that the number of ways a die could come up "4" is one-sixth the number of equipossible ways it could come up. Extending this definition to the continuous case, classical probability can be defined in terms of the relevant ratio of ranges, areas, or volumes over which the principle of indifference applies. Thus, under this extended definition, to say that the probability of the parameters of physics falling into the life-permitting value is very improbable simply *means* that the ratio of life-permitting values

to the range of possible values is very, very small. Finally, notice that this definition of probability implies the principle of indifference, and thus we can be certain that the principle of indifference holds for classical probability.

Epistemic Probability

Epistemic probability is a widely recognized type of probability that applies to claims, statements, and hypotheses—that is, what philosophers call propositions.[34] (A proposition is any claim, assertion, statement, or hypothesis about the world.) Roughly, the epistemic probability of a proposition can be thought of as the degree of credence—that is, degree of confidence or belief—we rationally should have in the proposition. Put differently, epistemic probability is a measure of our rational degree of belief under a condition of ignorance concerning whether a proposition is true or false. For example, when one says that the special theory of relativity is probably true, one is making a statement of epistemic probability. After all, the theory is actually either true or false. But, we do not know for sure whether it is true or false, so we say it is probably true to indicate that we should put more confidence in its being true than in its being false. It is also commonly argued that the probability of a coin toss is best understood as a case of epistemic probability. Since the side the coin will land on is determined by the laws of physics, it is argued that our assignment of probability is simply a measure of our rational expectations concerning which side the coin will land on.

Besides epistemic probability sumpliciter, philosophers also speak of what is known as the *conditional* epistemic probability of one proposition on another. The conditional epistemic probability of a proposition R on another proposition S—written as $P(R/S)$—can be defined as the degree to which the proposition S of itself should rationally lead us to expect that R is true. For example, there is a high conditional probability that it will rain today on the hypothesis that the weatherman has predicted a 100 percent chance of rain, whereas there is a low conditional probability that it will rain today on the hypothesis that the weatherman has predicted only a 2 percent chance of rain. That is, the hypothesis that the weatherman has predicted a 100 percent chance of rain today should strongly lead us to expect that it will rain, whereas the hypothesis that the weatherman has predicted a 2 percent chance should lead us to expect that it will not rain. Under the epistemic conception of probability, therefore, the statement that *the fine-tuning of the Cosmos is very improbable under the atheistic single-universe hypothesis* makes perfect sense: it is to be understood as making a statement about the degree to which the atheistic single-universe hypothesis would or should, *of itself*, rationally lead us to expect the cosmic fine-tuning.[35]

Conclusion

The above discussion shows that we have at least two ways of understanding improbability invoked in our main argument: as classical probability or epistemic probability. This undercuts the common atheist objection that it is meaningless to speak of the probability of the fine-tuning under the atheistic single-universe hypothesis since under this hypothesis the universe is not a repeatable event.

NOTES

1. Freeman Dyson, *Disturbing the Universe* (New York: Harper and Row, 1979), 251.

2. Paul Davies, *The Cosmic Blueprint: New Discoveries in Nature's Creative Ability to Order the Universe* (New York: Simon and Schuster, 1988), 203.

3. Fred Hoyle, in *Religion and the Scientists* (1959); quoted in *The Anthropic Cosmological Principle*, ed. John Barrow and Frank Tipler (Oxford: Oxford University Press, 1986), 22.

4. See Paul Davies, *The Accidental Universe* (Cambridge: Cambridge University Press, 1982), 90–91. John Jefferson Davis, "The Design Argument, Cosmic 'Fine-tuning,' and the Anthropic Principle," *The International Journal of Philosophy of Religion* 22 (1987): 140.

5. John Leslie, *Universes* (New York: Routledge, 1989), 4, 35; *Anthropic Cosmological Principle*, 322.

6. Paul Davies, *Superforce: The Search for a Grand Unified Theory of Nature* (New York: Simon and Schuster, 1984), 242.

7. Leslie, *Universes*, 39–40.

8. John Leslie, "How to Draw Conclusion from a Fine-Tuned Cosmos," in *Physics, Philosophy and Theology: A Common Quest for Understanding*, ed. Robert Russell et al. (Vatican City State: Vatican Observatory Press, 1988), 299.

9. Leslie, "How to Draw Conclusions," 300.

10. For those familiar with the probability calculus, a precise statement of the degree to which evidence counts in favor of one hypothesis over another can be given in terms of the odds form of Bayes's Theorem: that is, $P(H_1/E)/P(H_2/E) = [P(H_1/P(H_2)] \times [P(E/H_1)/(E/H_2)]$. The general version of the principle stated here, however, does not require the applicability or truth of Bayes's Theorem.

11. Those with some training in probability theory will want to note that the kind of probability invoked here is what philosophers call *epistemic probability*, which is a measure of the rational degree of belief we should have in a proposition (see appendix, subsection iii). Since our rational degree of belief in a necessary truth can be less than 1, we can sensibly speak of it being improbable for a given law of nature to exist necessarily. For example, we can speak of an unproven mathematical hypothesis—such as Goldbach's conjecture that every even number greater than 6 is the sum of two odd primes—as being probably true or probably false given our current evidence, even though all mathematical hypotheses are either necessarily true or necessarily false.

12. Leslie, "How to Draw Conclusion," 304.

13. George Smith, "The Case Against God," reprinted in *An Anthology of Atheism and Rationalism,* ed. Gordon Stein (Buffalo: Prometheus Press, 1980), 56.

14. J. J. C. Smart, "Laws of Nature and Cosmic Coincidence," *The Philosophical Quarterly* 35 (July 1985): 275–76, italics added.

15. I define a "universe" as any region of space-time that is disconnected from other regions in such a way that the parameters of physics in that region could differ significantly from the other regions.

16. Quentin Smith, "World Ensemble Explanations," *Pacific Philosophical Quarterly* 67 (1986): 82.

17. Moreover, the advocate of the atheistic many-universes hypothesis could not avoid this problem by hypothesizing that the many universes always existed as "brute fact" without being produced by a universe generator. This would simply add to the problem: it would not only

leave unexplained the fine-tuning or our own universe, but would leave unexplained the existence of these other universes.

18. Leslie, *Universes*, 59.

19. Dyson, *Disturbing the Universe*, 251.

20. Chapter 6, "Beautiful Theories."

21. Paul Dirac, "The Evolution of the Physicist's Picture of Nature," *Scientific American* (May 1963): 47.

22. Davies, *Superforce*, 235–36.

23. This connection between order and probability, and the second law of thermodynamics in general, is given a precise formulation in a branch of fundamental physics called *statistical mechanics*, according to which a state of high order represents a very improbable state, and a state of disorder represents a highly probable state.

24. See Lawrence Sklar, *Physics and Chance: Philosophical Issues in the Foundation of Statistical Mechanics* (Cambridge: Cambridge University Press, 1993), chapter 8, for a review of the nontheistic explanations for the ordered arrangement of the universe and the severe difficulties they face.

25. A more thorough discussion of the atheist argument from evil is presented in Daniel Howard-Snyder's chapter (pp. 76–115), and a discussion of other atheistic arguments is given in John O'Leary-Hawthorn's chapter (pp. 116–34).

26. This work was made possible in part by a Discovery Institute grant for the fiscal year 1997–1998.

27. In the language of probability theory, this sort of probability is known as a conditional probability. In the case of G, calculations indicate that this conditional probability of the fine-tuning would be less than 10^{-40} since the life-permitting range is less than 10^{-40} of the range 0 to $2G_0$, the latter range being certainly smaller than the total "illuminated" range for G.

28. I say "approximately right" because in this case the principle of indifference only applies to strips of land that are the same distance from the equator. The reason for this is that only strips of land equidistant from the equator are truly symmetrical with regard to the motion of the earth. Since the northern, contiguous United States are all about the same distance from the equator, equal land areas should be assigned approximately equal probabilities.

29. This solution will not always work since, as the well-known Bertrand Paradoxes illustrate (e.g., see Roy Weatherford, *Foundations of Probability Theory* [Boston: Routledge and Kegan Paul,

1982], 56), sometimes there are two equally good and conflicting parameters that directly correspond to a physical quantity and to which the principle of indifference applies. In these cases, at best we can say that the probability is somewhere between that given by the two conflicting parameters. This problem, however, typically does not seem to arise for most cases of fine-tuning. Also, it should be noted that the principle of indifference applies best to *classical* or *epistemic* probability, not other kinds of probability such as *relative frequency*. (See subsection iii below.)

30. Weatherford, *Probability Theory*, 35.

31. Sklar, *Physics and Chance*, 191; Bas van Fraassen, *Laws and Symmetry* (Oxford: Oxford University Press, 1989), 345.

32. Of course, one could claim that our experience with items such as coins and dice teaches us that whenever two alternatives are macroscopically symmetrical, we should assign them an equal probability, unless we have a particular reason not to. All this claim implies, however, is that we have experiential justification for the principle of indifference, and thus it does not take away from our main point that in certain practical situations we must rely on the principle of indifference to justify our assignment of probability.

33. See Weatherford, *Probability Theory*, ch. 2.

34. For an in-depth discussion of epistemic probability, see Richard Swinburne, *An Introduction to Confirmation Theory* (London: Methuen, 1973); Ian Hacking, *The Emergence of Probability: A Philosophical Study of Early Ideas About Probability, Induction and Statistical Inference* (Cambridge: Cambridge University Press, 1975); and Alvin Plantinga, *Warrant and Proper Function* (Oxford: Oxford University Press, 1993), chapters 8 and 9.

35. It should be noted here that this rational degree of expectation should not be confused with the degree to which one should expect the parameters of physics to fall within the life-permitting range if one believed the atheistic single-universe hypothesis. For even those who believe in this atheistic hypothesis should expect the parameters of physics to be life-permitting since this follows from the fact that we are alive. Rather, the conditional epistemic probability in this case is the degree to which the atheistic single-universe hypothesis *of itself* should lead us to expect parameters of physics to be life-permitting. This means that in assessing the conditional epistemic probability in this and other similar cases, one

must exclude contributions to our expectations arising from other information we have, such as that we are alive. In the case at hand, one way of doing this is by means of the following sort of thought experiment. Imagine a disembodied being with mental capacities and a knowledge of physics comparable to that of the most intelligent physicists alive today, except that the being does not know whether the parameters of physics are within the life-permitting range. Further, suppose that this disembodied being believed in the atheistic single-universe hypothesis. Then, the degree that being should rationally expect the parameters of physics to be life-permitting will be equal to our conditional epistemic probability, since its expectation is solely a result of its belief in the atheistic single-universe hypothesis, not other factors such as its awareness of its own existence.

PART TWO

The Argument from Religious Experience

There was not a mere consciousness of something there, but fused in the central happiness of it, a startling awareness of some ineffable good. Not vague either; not like the emotional effect of some poem, or scene, or blossom, or music, but the sure knowledge of the close presence of a sort of mighty person, and after it went, the memory persisted as the one perception of reality. Everything else might be a dream, but not that.

(AN ANONYMOUS MYSTIC cited by WILLIAM JAMES
in *Varieties of Religious Experience, 1902.*)

THE HEART OF RELIGION is and always has been experiential. Encounters with the supernatural, a transcendent dimension, the Wholly Other are at the base of every great religion. Abraham hears a Voice calling him to leave his family in Haran and venture out into a broad unknown, thus becoming the father of Israel. Abraham's grandson Jacob wrestles all night with an angel and is transformed, gaining the name "Israel," "prince of God." While tending his father-in-law's flock, Moses has a vision of "I am that I am" (Yahweh) in the burning bush and is ordered to deliver Israel out of slavery into a land flowing with milk and honey. Isaiah has a vision of the Lord "high and exalted, and the train of his robe filled the temple" of heaven. In the New Testament, John, James, and Peter behold Jesus gloriously transformed on the Mount of Transfiguration and are themselves transformed by the experience. After the death of Jesus, Saul is traveling to Damascus to persecute Christians, when he is met by a blazing light and hears a Voice, asking him why he is persecuting the Lord. Changing his name to Paul, he becomes the leader of the Christian missionary movement. The Hindu experiences the Atman (soul) as the Brahman (God), "That art Thou," or beholds the glories of Krishna. The Advaitian Hindu merges with the One, as a drop of water merges with the vast ocean. The Buddhist merges with Nirvana or beholds a vision of the Buddha. Allah reveals his holy word, the Koran, to Mohammed. Joan of Arc hears voices calling on her to save her people, and Joseph Smith has a vision of the Angel Moroni, calling him to do a new work for God.

Saints, mystics, prophets, ascetics, and common believers throughout recorded history have undergone esoteric experiences that are hard to explain but impossible to dismiss as mere nonsense. Common features appear to link these otherwise disparate experiences to one another, resulting in a common testimony to some sort of

Otherness, a *consensus mysticum*. Rudolf Otto characterizes the religious (or "numinal" spiritual) dimension in all these experiences as the "mysterium tremendum et fascinans." Religion is an unfathomable mystery: *tremendum* ("to be trembled at"), awe-inspiring, and *fascinans* ("fascinating"), magnetic. To use a description from Søren Kierkegaard, religious experience is a "sympathetic antipathy and an antipathetic sympathy" before a deep unknown. Like looking into an abyss, it both repulses and strangely attracts.

What, then, is the problem with religious experience? If your friend says that she hears a pleasant tune, and you listen and say, "Yes, I hear it now too," there is no problem; but if you listen carefully and don't hear it, you might well wonder whether your friend is really hearing sounds or only imagines that she is. Perhaps you could bring in others to check out the matter. If they agree with your friend, well and good; but if they agree with you and don't hear the sounds, then there is a problem. Perhaps you could bring in an audiometer to measure the decibels in the room. If the meter confirms your friend's report, then it is simply a case of her having better hearing than you and the rest of the witnesses; but if the meter doesn't register at all, then, assuming that it is in working order, we would have good evidence that she is only imagining the sounds. Perhaps she needs to change her claim, saying instead, "Well, I *seem* to be hearing a pleasant tune."

One problem is that religious experience is typically private. You might have the sense of God forgiving you or of an angel speaking to you while your friend, in the same room with you, neither hears, nor sees, nor feels anything unusual. You might be praying and suddenly feel transported by grace and sense the unity of all reality while your friend sitting next to you simply wonders at the strange expression on your face and asks if something is wrong. Perhaps your brain is experiencing an altered chemical or electrical state.

Yet, as noted above, religious experiences of various varieties have been reported by numerous people, from dairymaids like Joan of Arc to mystics like Teresa of Avila and St. John of the Cross. They cannot simply be dismissed without serious analysis.

There are two levels of problem here: (1) To what degree, if any, is the subject of a religious experience justified in inferring from the psychological experience (the subjective aspect) to the existence of what seems to be the object of the experience (the objective aspect)? (2) To what degree, if any, does the cumulative witness of those undergoing religious experience justify the claim that there is a God or transcendent reality?

Traditionally, the argument from religious experience has not been one of the "proofs" for God's existence. At best, it has confirmed and made existential what the proofs conveyed with icy logic. Some philosophers, such as C. D. Broad (1887–1971), as well as contemporary philosophers such as Richard Swinburne and Gary Gutting, believe that the common experience of mystics is *strong justification* or evidence for all of us for the existence of God. Others, such as William James (1842–1910), believe that religious experience is sufficient evidence for the subject himself or herself for the existence of a divine reality, but does not have this evidential force for the nonexperiencer. That is, religious experience grants us only *weak justification*. Religious skeptics, like Walter Stace (1886–1967) and Wallace Matson, doubt this claim and argue that a subjective experience by itself never warrants making an existential claim (of an object existing outside oneself). It is a fallacy to infer from an apparent psychological experience of X to the reality of X.

There are two main traditions regarding religious experience. One, which we can call *mystical*, posits the unity of all reality or the unity of the subject with its object (the mystic is absorbed in God, becomes one with God, etc.). The second type of religious experience can be called simply *religious experience* in order to distinguish it from the mystical. It does not conflate the subject with the object but is a numinal experience wherein the believer (or subject) experiences the presence of God or an angel or Christ or the Holy Spirit, either speaking or appearing to the experient, or forgiving him or her. While in prayer, believers often experience a sense of the presence of God or the Holy Spirit.

Now, there are many psychological explanations of religious experience that cast doubt on its evidential value. One of the most famous is the Freudian interpretation set forth in our third reading. Sigmund Freud (1856–1939) said that it was the result of the projection of the father image within oneself. The progression goes like this. When you were a child, you looked upon your father as a powerful hero who could do everything, meet all your needs, and overcome whatever obstacles hindered your way. When you grew older, you sadly realized that your father was fallible and finite. But you still had a longing for a benevolent, all-powerful father. So, subconsciously you projected your need for that long lost parent onto the empty heavens and invented a god for yourself. Because this is a common phenomenon, all of us who have successfully "projected daddy onto the big sky" go to church, synagogue, mosque, temple, or whatever and worship the illusion on our favorite holy day. But it is a myth. The sky is empty, and the sooner we realize it, the better for everyone.

This is but one among many naturalistic explanations of religious experience and religion in general. That is, it is a theory that aims to explain religious phenomena without appeal to supernatural entities. It is not a disproof of God's existence, simply an hypothesis. Even if it is true psychologically that we have inner longings for some sort of cosmic parental figure, and even if it is true that such longing is part of the explanation for our tendency to form religious beliefs, those facts by themselves don't show that there is no such being as God.

We begin with four selections of religious experience from four different traditions, the Jewish, the Christian, the Hindu, and the Buddhist.

Our first full reading (the second reading) is an excerpt from William James's classic study *The Varieties of Religious Experience* (1902). In this selection, James describes mystical experience, which he considers to be the deepest kind of religious experience. It is something that transcends our ordinary, sensory experience and that cannot be described in terms of our normal concepts and language. It is 'ineffable experience.' The subject realizes that the experience "defies expression, that no adequate report of its content can be given in words," James writes. "It follows from this that its quality must be directly experienced; it cannot be imparted or transferred to others." And yet it contains a 'noetic quality,' a content. It purports to convey truth about the nature of reality, namely, that there is a unity of all things and that that unity is spiritual, not material. It is antinaturalistic, pantheistic, and optimistic. Further, mystical states are *transient*—that is, they cannot be sustained for long—and they are *passive*—that is, the mystic is acted upon by divine deliverance. We may prepare ourselves for the experience, but it is not something that we do; it is something that happens to us.

James is cautious about what can be deduced from mystical experience. Although mystical states are and ought to be absolutely authoritative for the individuals to whom they come, "no authority emanates from them which should make it a duty for those who stand outside of them to accept their revelations uncritically." But their value for us, James argues, is that they show us a valid alternative to the "nonmystical rationalistic consciousness, based on understanding and the senses alone. They open up the possibility of other orders of truth, in which, so far as anything in us vitally responds to them, we may freely continue to have faith."

Our third selection, from Freud's *Future of an Illusion*, has already been discussed.

Our fourth selection is C. D. Broad's important article, "The Argument from Religious Experience" (1953), in which he considers the extent to which we can reason from religious experience to the existence of God. Broad likens the religious sense to an ear for music. There are a few people on the negative end who are spiritually tone deaf and a few on the positive end who are the founders of religions, the Bachs and Beethovens. In between are the ordinary followers of religion, who are like the average musical listeners, and above them are the saints, who are likened to those with a very fine ear for music.

The chief difference is that religion, unlike music, says something about the nature of reality. Is what it says true? And does religious experience lend any support to the truth claims of religion? Is religious experience *veridical*? Are the claims about "the nature of reality which are an integral part of the experience true or probable"? Broad considers the argument from mystical agreement, which goes as follows:

1. There is an enormous unanimity among the mystics concerning the spiritual nature of reality.
2. When there is such unanimity among observers as to what they believe themselves to be experiencing, it is reasonable to conclude that their experiences are veridical (unless we have good reason to believe that they are deluded).
3. There are no positive reasons for thinking that mystical experiences are delusory.
4. Therefore it is reasonable to believe that mystical experiences are veridical.

He notes that one might object to this argument on the grounds that there is some reason for thinking that mystics might be neuropathic or sexually repressed. But he argues that even if these charges are true, it doesn't follow that the relevant experiences are delusory. Regarding the charge of neuropathology, he urges that "one might need to be slightly 'cracked' in order to have some peep-holes into the super-sensible world." With regard to sexual abnormality, it could simply be the case that no one who was "incapable of strong sexual desires and emotions could have anything worth calling religious experience."

His own guarded judgment is that, given what we know about the origins of religious belief and emotions, there is no reason to think that religious experience is "specially likely to be delusive or misdirected." On the other hand, the evidence suggests that the concepts and beliefs of even the best religions are "extremely inadequate to the facts which they express; that they are highly confused and are mixed up with a great deal of positive error and sheer nonsense; and that, if the human race goes on and continues to have religious experiences and to reflect on them, they will be altered and improved almost out of recognition."

In the fifth essay Louis Pojman distinguishes between a strong and a weak justification for religious belief. A strong justification would make it rationally obligatory for everyone to believe in the conclusion of an argument. A weak justification would provide rational support only for those who had an "of-God" experience (or already accepted the worldview that made such experiences likely). Pojman argues against philosophers, such as Gary Gutting, who believe that they have provided a strong justification for religious belief, showing that the best one can offer is a weak justification. At the end of his essay, he raises the question of why religious experience does not yield ways of checking the accuracy of its content or predictions that would confirm it.

In the last reading in this part, "Religious Experience and Religious Belief," William Alston argues that religious experience can provide grounds for religious belief. Comparing the epistemology of Christian religious experience with the epistemology of perceptual experience, Alston shows that although perceptual practices include more stringent requirements than religious practices, there are good reasons why the two should be different. Whereas the criteria for valid perceptual experiences include verifiability and predictability, God's being wholly other may preclude those criteria from applying to religious experience.

II.1   Selections of Mystical Experiences

AN OLD TESTAMENT SELECTION: THE CALL OF ISAIAH

In the year of King Uzziah's death I saw the Lord seated on a throne, high and exalted, and the skirt of his robe filled the temple. About him were attendant seraphim, and each had six wings; one pair covered his face and one pair his feet, and one pair was spread in flight. They were calling ceaselessly to one another,

> *Holy, holy, holy is the Lord of Hosts:*
> *the whole earth is full of his glory.*

And, as each one called, the threshold shook to its foundations, while the house was filled with smoke. Then I cried,

> *Woe is me! I am lost,*
> *for I am a man of unclean lips*
> *and I dwell among a people of unclean lips;*
> *yet with these eyes I have seen the King, the*
>   LORD *of Hosts.*

Then one of the seraphim flew to me carrying in his hand a glowing coal which he had taken from the altar with a pair of tongs. He touched my mouth with it and said,

> *See, this has touched your lips;*
> *your iniquity is removed,*
> *and your sin is wiped away.*

Then I heard the Lord saying, Whom shall I send? Who will go for me? And I answered, Here am I; send me. He said, Go and tell this people:

> *You may listen and listen, but you will not*
>   *understand.*
> *You may look and look again, but you will*
>   *never know.*
> *This people's wits are dulled,*
>   *their ears are deafened and their eyes*
>   *blinded, so that they cannot see with their*
>   *eyes nor listen with their ears nor under-*
>   *stand with their wits, so that they may turn*
>   *and be healed.*

ISAIAH, Chapter 6, *New English Bible*

THE CHRISTIAN MYSTIC, ST. TERESA OF AVILA

One day when I was at prayer . . . I saw Christ at my side—or, to put it better, I was conscious of Him, for I saw nothing with the eyes of the body or the eyes of the soul (the imagination). He seemed quite close to me and I saw that it was He. As I thought, He was speaking to me. Being completely ignorant that such visions were possible, I was very much afraid at first, and could do nothing but weep, though as soon as He spoke His first word of assurance to me, I regained my usual calm, and became cheerful and free from fear. All the time Jesus Christ seemed to be at my side, but as this was not an imaginary vision I could not see in what form. But I most clearly felt that He was all the time on my right, and was a witness of everything that I was doing . . . if I say that I do not see Him with the eyes of the body or the eyes of the soul, because this is no imaginary vision, how then can I know and affirm that he is beside me with greater certainty than if I saw Him? If one says that one is like a person in the dark who cannot see someone though he is beside him, or that one is like somebody who is blind, it is not right. There is some similarity here, but not much, because a person in the dark can perceive with the other senses, or hear his neighbor speak or move, or can touch him. Here this is not so, nor is there any feeling of darkness. On the contrary, He appears to the soul by a knowledge brighter than the sun. I do not mean that any sun is seen, or any brightness, but there is a light which, though unseen, illuminates the understanding.

J. M. COHEN, trans. *The Life of St. Teresa of Avila*,
London: Penguin, 1957

A HINDU EXAMPLE

The Ego has disappeared. I have realized my identity with Brahman and so all my desires have melted away. I have arisen above my ignorance and my knowledge of this seeming universe. What is this joy I feel? Who shall measure it? I know nothing but joy, limitless, unbounded! The treasure I have found there cannot be described in words. The mind cannot conceive of it. My mind fell like a hailstone into that vast expanse of Brahman's ocean. Touching one drop of it, I melted away and became one with Brahman. Where is this universe? Who took it away? Has it merged into something else? A while ago, I beheld it—now it exists no longer. Is there anything apart or distinct from Brahman? Now, finally and clearly, I know that I am the Atman [the soul identified with Brahman], whose nature is eternal joy. I see nothing, I hear nothing, I know nothing that is separate from me.

SWAMI PRABHAVANDANDA, trans. *Shankara's Crest Jewel of Discrimination*, New York: Mentor Books, 1970

A BUDDHIST MEDITATION

Of one who has entered the first trance the voice has ceased; of one who has entered the second trance reasoning and reflection have ceased; of one who has entered the third trance joy has ceased; of one who has entered the fourth trance the inspiration and expiration have ceased; of one who has entered the realm of the infinity of space the perception of form has ceased; of one who has entered the realm of the infinity of consciousness the perception of the realm of the infinity of space has ceased; of one who has entered the realm of nothingness the perception of the realm of the infinity of consciousness has ceased.

HENRY WARREN, ed. SAMYUTTA-NIKAYA, in *Buddhism in Translation*, New York: Atheneum, 1973

II.2   Mysticism

WILLIAM JAMES

William James (1842–1910), American philosopher and psychologist, was one of the most influential thinkers of his time. He taught at Harvard University and is considered, along

From William James, *The Varieties of Religious Experience* (New York: Longman, Green & Co., 1902). Some footnotes deleted.

with C. S. Peirce, one of the fathers of pragmatism. *The Varieties of Religious Experience* (1902) is his classic study of religious experience. In this selection James describes mystical experience, which he considers to be the deepest kind of religious experience. It is something that transcends our ordinary, sensory experience and that cannot be described in terms of our normal concepts and language.

Over and over again in these lectures I have raised points and left them open and unfinished until we should have come to the subject of Mysticism. Some of you, I fear, may have smiled as you noted my reiterated postponements. But now the hour has come when mysticism must be faced in good earnest, and those broken threads wound up together. One may say truly, I think, that personal religious experience has its root and centre in mystical states of consciousness; so for us, who in these lectures are treating personal experience as the exclusive subject of our study, such states of consciousness ought to form the vital chapter from which the other chapters get their light. Whether my treatment of mystical states will shed more light or darkness, I do not know, for my own constitution shuts me out from their enjoyment almost entirely, and I can speak of them only at second hand. But though forced to look upon the subject so externally, I will be as objective and receptive as I can; and I think I shall at least succeed in convincing you of the reality of the states in question, and of the paramount importance of their function.

First of all, then, I ask, What does the expression "mystical states of consciousness" mean? How do we part off mystical states from other states?

The words "mysticism" and "mystical" are often used as terms of mere reproach, to throw at any opinion which we regard as vague and vast and sentimental, and without a base in either facts or logic. For some writers a "mystic" is any person who believes in thought-transference, or spirit-return. Employed in this way the word has little value: there are too many less ambiguous synonyms. So, to keep it useful by restricting it, I will do what I did in the case of the word "religion," and simply propose to you four marks which, when an experience has them,

may justify us in calling it mystical for the purpose of the present lectures. In this way we shall save verbal disputation, and the recriminations that generally go therewith.

1. *Ineffability.*—The handiest of the marks by which I classify a state of mind as mystical is negative. The subject of it immediately says that it defies expression, that no adequate report of its contents can be given in words. It follows from this that its quality must be directly experienced; it cannot be imparted or transferred to others. In this peculiarity mystical states are more like states of feeling than like states of intellect. No one can make clear to another who has never had a certain feeling, in what the quality or worth of it consists. One must have musical ears to know the value of a symphony; one must have been in love one's self to understand a lover's state of mind. Lacking the heart or ear, we cannot interpret the musician or the lover justly, and are even likely to consider him weak-minded or absurd. The mystic finds that most of us accord to his experiences an equally incompetent treatment.

2. *Noetic quality.*—Although so similar to states of feeling, mystical states seem to those who experience them to be also states of knowledge. They are states of insight into depths of truth unplumbed by the discursive intellect. They are illuminations, revelations, full of significance and importance, all inarticulate though they remain; and as a rule they carry with them a curious sense of authority for aftertime.

These two characters will entitle any state to be called mystical, in the sense in which I use the word. Two other qualities are less sharply marked, but are usually found. These are:—

3. *Transiency.*—Mystical states cannot be sustained for long. Except in rare instances, half an hour, or at most an hour or two, seems to

be the limit beyond which they fade into the light of common day. Often, when faded, their quality can but imperfectly be reproduced in memory; but when they recur it is recognized; and from one recurrence to another it is susceptible of continuous development in what is felt as inner richness and importance.

4. *Passivity.*—Although the oncoming of mystical states may be facilitated by preliminary voluntary operations, as by fixing the attention, or going through certain bodily performances, or in other ways which manuals of mysticism prescribe; yet when the characteristic sort of consciousness once has set in, the mystic feels as if his own will were in abeyance, and indeed sometimes as if he were grasped and held by a superior power. This latter peculiarity connects mystical states with certain definite phenomena of secondary or alternative personality, such as prophetic speech, automatic writing, or the mediumistic trance. When these latter conditions are well pronounced, however, there may be no recollection whatever of the phenomenon, and it may have no significance for the subject's usual inner life, to which, as it were, it makes a mere interruption. Mystical states, strictly so-called, are never merely interruptive. Some memory of their content always remains, and a profound sense of their importance. They modify the inner life of the subject between the times of their recurrence. Sharp divisions in this region are, however, difficult to make, and we find all sorts of gradations and mixtures.

These four characteristics are sufficient to mark out a group of states of consciousness peculiar enough to deserve a special name and to call for careful study. Let it then be called the mystical group.

Our next step should be to gain acquaintance with some typical examples. Professional mystics at the height of their development have often elaborately organized experiences and a philosophy based thereupon. But you remember what I said in my first lecture: phenomena are best understood when placed within their series, studied in their germ and in their over-ripe decay, and compared with their exaggerated and degenerated kindred. The range of mystical experience is very wide, much too wide for us to cover in the time at our disposal. Yet the method of serial study is so essential for interpretation that if we really wish to reach conclusions we must use it. I will begin, therefore, with phenomena which claim no special religious significance, and end with those of which the religious pretensions are extreme.

The simplest rudiment of mystical experience would seem to be that deepened sense of the significance of a maxim or formula which occasionally sweeps over one. "I've heard that said all my life," we exclaim, "but I never realized its full meaning until now." "When a fellow-monk," said Luther, "one day repeated the words of the Creed: 'I believe in the forgiveness of sins,' I saw the Scripture in an entirely new light; and straightway I felt as if I were born anew. It was as if I had found the door of paradise thrown wide open." This sense of deeper significance is not confined to rational propositions. Single words, and conjunctions of words, effects of light on land and sea, odors and musical sounds, all bring it when the mind is tuned aright. Most of us can remember the strangely moving power of passages in certain poems read when we were young, irrational doorways as they were through which the mystery of fact, the wildness and the pang of life, stole into our hearts and thrilled them. The words have now perhaps become mere polished surfaces for us; but lyric poetry and music are alive and significant only in proportion as they fetch these vague vistas of a life continuous with our own, beckoning and inviting, yet ever eluding our pursuit. We are alive or dead to the eternal inner message of the arts according as we have kept or lost this mystical susceptibility. . . .

. . . .

[An] incommunicableness of the transport is the keynote of all mysticism. Mystical truth exists for the individual who has the transport, but for no one else. In this, as I have said, it resembles the knowledge given to us in sensations more than that given by conceptual thought. Thought, with its remoteness and abstractness, has often enough in the history of philosophy been contrasted unfavorably with sensation. It is a commonplace of metaphysics that God's knowledge cannot be discursive but must be intuitive, that is, must be constructed more after the pattern of what in ourselves is called immediate feeling, than after that of proposition and judgment. But *our* immediate feelings have no content but what the five senses supply; and we have seen and shall see again that mystics may emphatically deny that the senses play any part in the very highest type of knowledge which their transports yield.

In the Christian church there have always been mystics. Although many of them have been viewed with suspicion, some have gained favor in the eyes of the authorities. The experiences of these have been treated as precedents, and a codified system of mystical theology has been based upon them, in which everything legitimate finds its place. The basis of the system is "orison" or meditation, the methodical elevation of the soul towards God. Through the practice of orison the higher levels of mystical experience may be attained. It is odd that Protestantism, especially evangelical Protestantism, should seemingly have abandoned everything methodical in this line. Apart from what prayer may lead to, Protestant mystical experience appears to have been almost exclusively sporadic. It has been left to our mind-curers to reintroduce methodical meditation into our religious life.

The first thing to be aimed at in orison is the mind's detachment from outer sensations for these interfere with its concentration upon ideal things. Such manuals as Saint Ignatius's *Spiritual Exercises* recommend the disciple to expel sensation by a graduated series of efforts to imagine holy scenes. The acme of this kind of discipline would be a semi-hallucinatory mono-ideism—an imaginary figure of Christ, for example, coming fully to occupy the mind. Sensorial images of this sort, whether literal or symbolic, play an enormous part in mysticism. But in certain cases imagery may fall away entirely, and in the very highest raptures it tends to do so. The state of consciousness becomes then insusceptible of any verbal description. Mystical teachers are unanimous as to this. Saint John of the Cross, for

instance, one of the best of them, thus describes the condition called the "union of love," which, he says, is reached by "dark contemplation." In this the Deity compensates the soul, but in such a hidden way that the soul—

finds no terms, no means, no comparison whereby to render the sublimity of the wisdom and the delicacy of the spiritual feeling with which she is filled....We receive this mystical knowledge of God clothed in none of the kinds of images, in none of the sensible representations, which our mind makes use of in other circumstances. Accordingly in this knowledge, since the senses and the imagination are not employed, we get neither form nor impression, nor can we give any account or furnish any likeness, although the mysterious and sweet-tasting wisdom comes home so clearly to the inmost parts of our soul. Fancy a man seeing a certain kind of thing for the first time in his life. He can understand it, use and enjoy it, but he cannot apply a name to it, nor communicate any idea of it, even though all the while it be a mere thing of sense. How much greater will be his powerlessness when it goes beyond the senses! This is the peculiarity of the divine language. The more infused, intimate, spiritual, and supersensible it is, the more does it exceed the senses, both inner and outer, and impose silence upon them.

... The soul then feels as if placed in a vast and profound solitude, to which no created thing has access, in an immense and boundless desert, desert the more delicious the more solitary it is. There, in this abyss of wisdom, the soul grows by what it drinks in from the wellsprings of the comprehension of love,... and recognizes, however sublime and learned may be the terms we employ, how utterly vile, insignificant, and improper they are, when we seek to discourse of divine things by their means.

I cannot pretend to detail to you the sundry stages of the Christian mystical life. Our time would not suffice, for one thing; and moreover, I confess that the subdivisions and names which we find in the Catholic books seem to me to represent nothing objectively distinct. So many men, so many minds; I imagine that these experiences can be as infinitely varied as are the idiosyncrasies of individuals.

The cognitive aspects of them, their value in the way of revelation, is what we are directly concerned with, and it is easy to show by citation how strong an impression they leave of being revelations of new depths of truth. Saint Teresa is the expert of experts in describing such conditions, so I will turn immediately to what she says of one of the highest of them, the "orison of union."

> In the orison of union (says Saint Teresa) the soul is fully awake as regards God, but wholly asleep as regards things of this world and in respect of herself. During the short time the union lasts, she is as it were deprived of every feeling, and even if she would, she could not think of any single thing. Thus she needs to employ no artifice in order to arrest the use of her understanding: it remains so stricken with inactivity that she neither knows what she loves, nor in what manner she loves, nor what she wills. In short, she is utterly dead to the things of the world and lives solely in God.... I do not even know whether in this state she has enough life left to breathe. It seems to me she has not; or at least that if she does breathe, she is unaware of it. Her intellect would fain understand something of what is going on within her, but it has so little force now that it can act in no way whatsoever. So a person who falls into a deep faint appears as if dead....
>
> Thus does God, when he raises a soul to union with himself, suspend the natural action of all her faculties. She neither sees, hears, nor understands, so long as she is united with God. But this time is always short, and it seems even shorter than it is. God establishes himself in the interior of this soul in such a way, that when she returns to herself, it is wholly impossible for her to doubt that she has been in God, and God in her. This truth remains so strongly impressed on her that, even though many years should pass without the condition returning, she can neither forget the favor she received, nor doubt of its reality. If you, nevertheless, ask how it is possible that the soul can see and understand that she has been in God, since during the union she has neither sight nor understanding, I reply that she does not see it then, but that she sees it clearly later, after she has returned to herself, not by any vision, but by a certitude which abides with her and which God alone can give her. I knew a person who was ignorant of the truth that God's mode of being in everything must be either by presence, by power, or by essence, but who, after having received the grace of which I am speaking, believed this truth in the most unshakable manner. So much so that, having consulted a half-learned man who was as ignorant on this point as she had been before she was enlightened, when he replied that God is in us only by "grace," she disbelieved his reply, so sure she was of the true answer; and when she came to ask wiser doctors, they confirmed her in her belief, which much consoled her....
>
> But how, you will repeat, *can* one have such certainty in respect to what one does not see? This question, I am powerless to answer. These are secrets of God's omnipotence which it does not appertain to me to penetrate. All that I know is that I tell the truth; and I shall never believe that any soul who does not possess this certainty has ever been really united to God.

The kinds of truth communicable in mystical ways, whether these be sensible or supersensible, are various. Some of them relate to this world— visions of the future, the reading of hearts, the sudden understanding of texts, the knowledge of distant events, for example; but the most important revelations are theological or metaphysical.

> Saint Ignatius confessed one day to Father Laynez that a single hour of meditation at Manresa had taught him more truths about heavenly things than all the teachings of all the doctors put together could have taught him.... One day in orison, on the steps of the choir of the Dominican church, he saw in a distinct manner the plan of divine wisdom in the creation of the world. On another occasion, during a procession, his spirit was ravished in God, and it was given him to contemplate, in a form and images fitted to the weak understanding of a dweller on the earth, the deep mystery of the holy Trinity. This last vision flooded his heart with such sweetness, that the mere memory of it in after times made him shed abundant tears.

Similarly with Saint Teresa.

> One day, being in orison (she writes), it was granted me to perceive in one instant how all things are seen and contained in God. I did not perceive them in their proper form, and nevertheless the view I had of them was of a sovereign clearness, and has remained vividly impressed upon my soul. It is one of the most signal of all

the graces which the Lord has granted me.... The view was so subtle and delicate that the understanding cannot grasp it.

She goes on to tell how it was as if the Deity were an enormous and sovereignly limpid diamond, in which all our actions were contained in such a way their full sinfulness appeared evident as never before. On another day, she relates, while she was reciting the Athanasian Creed—

> Our Lord made me comprehend in what way it is that one God can be in three persons. He made me see it so clearly that I remained as extremely surprised as I was comforted,... and now, when I think of the holy Trinity, or hear It spoken of, I understand how the three adorable Persons form only one God and I experience an unspeakable happiness.

On still another occasion it was given to Saint Teresa to see and understand in what wise the Mother of God had been assumed into her place in Heaven.

The deliciousness of some of these states seems to be beyond anything known in ordinary consciousness. It evidently involves organic sensibilities, for it is spoken of as something too extreme to be borne, and as verging on bodily pain. But it is too subtle and piercing a delight for ordinary words to denote. God's touches, the wounds of his spear, references to ebriety and to nuptial union have to figure in the phraseology by which it is shadowed forth. Intellect and senses both swoon away in these highest states of ecstasy. "If our understanding comprehends," says Saint Teresa, "it is in a mode which remains unknown to it, and it can understand nothing of what it comprehends. For my own part, I do not believe that it does comprehend, because, as I said, it does not understand itself to do so. I confess that it is all a mystery in which I am lost." In the condition called *raptus* or ravishment by theologians, breathing and circulation are so depressed that it is a question among the doctors whether the soul be or be not temporarily dissevered from the body. One must read Saint Teresa's descriptions and the very exact distinctions which she makes, to persuade one's self that one is dealing, not with imaginary experiences, but with

phenomena which, however rare, follow perfectly definite psychological types.

To the medical mind these ecstasies signify nothing but suggested and imitated hypnoid states, on an intellectual basis of superstition, and a corporeal one of degeneration and hysteria. Undoubtedly these pathological conditions have existed in many and possibly in all the cases, but that fact tells us nothing about the value for knowledge of the consciousness which they induce. To pass a spiritual judgment upon these states, we must not content ourselves with superficial medical talk, but inquire into their fruits for life.

Their fruits appear to have been various. Stupefaction, for one thing, seems not to have been altogether absent as a result. You may remember the helplessness in the kitchen and schoolroom of poor Margaret Mary Alacoque. Many other ecstatics would have perished but for the care taken of them by admiring followers. The "other-worldliness" encouraged by the mystical consciousness makes this over-abstraction from practical life peculiarly liable to befall mystics in whom the character is naturally passive and the intellect feeble; but in natively strong minds and characters we find quite opposite results. The great Spanish mystics, who carried the habit of ecstasy as far as it has often carried, appear for the most part to have shown indomitable spirit and energy, and all the more so for the trances in which they indulged.

Saint Ignatius was a mystic, but his mysticism made him assuredly one of the most powerfully practical human engines that ever lived. Saint John of the Cross, writing of the intuitions and "touches" by which God reaches the substance of the soul, tells us that—

> They enrich it marvelously. A single one of them may be sufficient to abolish at a stroke certain imperfections of which the soul during its whole life had vainly tried to rid itself, and to leave it adorned with virtues and loaded with supernatural gifts. A single one of these intoxicating consolations may reward it for all the labors undergone in its life—even were they numberless. Invested with an invincible courage, filled with an impassioned desire to suffer for its God, the soul then

is seized with a strange torment—that of not being allowed to suffer enough.

Saint Teresa is as emphatic, and much more detailed. You may perhaps remember a passage I quoted from her in my first lecture. There are many similar pages in her autobiography. Where in literature is a more evidently veracious account of the formation of a new centre of spiritual energy, than is given in her description of the effects of certain ecstasies which in departing leave the soul upon a higher level of emotional excitement?

Often, infirm and wrought upon with dreadful pains before the ecstasy, the soul emerges from it full of health and admirably disposed for action...as if God had willed that the body itself, already obedient to the soul's desires, should share in the soul's happiness....The soul after such a favor is animated with a degree of courage so great that if at that moment its body should be torn to pieces for the cause of God, it would feel nothing but the liveliest comfort. Then it is that promises and heroic resolutions spring up in profusion in us, soaring desires, horror of the world, and the clear perception of our proper nothingness....What empire is comparable to that of a soul who, from this sublime summit to which God has raised her, sees all the things of earth beneath her feet, and is captivated by no one of them? How ashamed she is of her former attachments! How amazed at her blindness! What lively pity she feels for those whom she recognizes still shrouded in the darkness!... She groans at having ever been sensitive to points of honor, at the illusion that made her ever see as honor what the world calls by that name. Now she sees in this name nothing more than an immense lie of which the world remains a victim. She discovers, in the new light from above, that in genuine honor there is nothing spurious, that to be faithful to this honor is to give our respect to what deserves to be respected really, and to consider as nothing, or as less than nothing, whatsoever perishes and is not agreeable to God....She laughs when she sees grave persons, persons of orison, caring for points of honor for which she now feels profoundest contempt. It is suitable to the dignity of their rank to act thus, they pretend, and it makes them more useful to others. But she knows that in despising the dignity of their rank for the pure love of God they would do more good in a single day than they would effect in ten years by preserving it....She laughs at herself that there should ever have been a time in her life when she made any case of money, when she ever desired it....Oh! if human beings might only agree together to regard it as so much useless mud, what harmony would then reign in the world! With what friendship we would all treat each other if our interest in honor and in money could but disappear from earth! For my own part, I feel as if it would be a remedy for all our ills.

Mystical conditions may, therefore, render the soul more energetic in the lines which their inspiration favors. But this could be reckoned an advantage only in case the inspiration were a true one. If the inspiration were erroneous, the energy would be all the more mistaken and misbegotten. So we stand once more before the problem of truth which confronted us at the end of the lectures on saintliness. You will remember that we turned to mysticism precisely to get some light on truth. Do mystical states establish the truth of those theological affections in which the saintly life has its root?

In spite of their repudiation of articulate self-description, mystical states in general assert a pretty distinct theoretic drift. It is possible to give the outcome of the majority of them in terms that point in definite philosophical directions. One of these directions is optimism, and the other is monism. We pass into mystical states from out of ordinary consciousness as from a less into a more, as from a smallness into a vastness, and at the same time as from an unrest to a rest. We feel them as reconciling, unifying states. They appeal to the yes-function more than to the no-function in us. In them the unlimited absorbs the limits and peacefully closes the account. Their very denial of every adjective you may propose as applicable to the ultimate truth—He, the Self, the Atman, is to be described by "No! no!": only, say the Upanishads—though it seems on the surface to be a no-function, is a denial made on behalf of a deeper yes. Whoso calls the Absolute anything in particular, or says that it is *this,* seems implicitly to shut it off from being *that*— it is as if he lessened it. So we deny the "this," negating the negation which it seems to us to imply, in the interests of the higher affirmative attitude by which we are possessed. The fountain-head of Christian mysticism is Dionysius the Areopagite. He describes the absolute truth by negatives exclusively.

> The cause of all things is neither soul nor intellect; nor has it imagination, opinion, or reason, or intelligence; nor is it reason or intelligence; nor is it spoken or thought. It is neither number, nor order, nor magnitude, nor littleness, nor equality, nor inequality, nor similarity, nor dissimilarity. It neither stands, nor moves, nor rests....It is neither essence, nor eternity, nor time. Even intellectual contact does not belong to it. It is neither science nor truth. It is not even royalty or wisdom; not one; not unity; not divinity or goodness; nor even spirit as we know it (etc., *ad libitum*).

But these qualifications are denied by Dionysius, not because the truth falls short of them, but because it so infinitely excels them. It is above them. It is *super*-lucent, *super*-splendent, *super*-essential, *super*-sublime, *super* everything that can be named. Like Hegel in his logic, mystics journey towards the positive pole of truth only by the "Methode der Absoluten Negativität."

Thus comes the paradoxical expressions that so abound in mystical writings. As when Eckhart tells of the still desert of the Godhead, "where never was seen difference, neither Father, Son, nor Holy Ghost, where there is no one at home, yet where the spark of the soul is more at peace than in itself." As when Boehme writes of the Primal Love, that "it may fitly be compared to Nothing, for it is deeper than any Thing, and is as nothing with respect to all things, forasmuch as it is not comprehensible by any of them. And because it is nothing respectively, it is therefore free from all things, and is that only good, which a man cannot express or utter what it is, there being nothing to which it may be compared, to express it by." Or as when Angelus Silesius sings:—

> [*God is pure Nothing. Neither Now*
> *nor Here affects Him.*
> *But the more you grasp him,*
> *the more He disappears*"] (Ed. trans.)

To this dialectical use, by the intellect, of negation as a mode of passage towards a higher kind of affirmation, there is correlated the subtlest of moral counterparts in the sphere of the personal will. Since denial of the finite self and its wants, since asceticism of some sort, is found in religious experience to be the only doorway to the larger and more blessed life, this moral mystery intertwines and combines with the intellectual mystery in all mystical writings.

> Love (continues Boehme) [is Nothing, for] when thou art gone forth wholly from the Creature and from that which is visible, and art become Nothing to all that is Nature and Creature, then thou art in that eternal One, which is God himself, and then thou shalt feel within thee the highest virtue of Love....The treasure of treasures for the soul is where she goeth out of the Somewhat into that Nothing out of which all things may be made. The soul here saith, *I have nothing*, for I am utterly stripped and naked; *I can do nothing*, for I have no manner of power, but am as water poured out; *I am nothing*, for all that I am is no more than an image of Being, and only God is to me I AM; and so, sitting down in my own Nothingness, I give glory to the eternal Being, and *will nothing* of myself, that so God may will all in me, being unto me my God and all things.

In Paul's language, I live, yet not I, but Christ liveth in me. Only when I become as nothing can God enter in and no difference between his life and mine remain outstanding.

This overcoming of all the usual barriers between the individual and the Absolute is the great mystic achievement. In mystic states we both become one with the Absolute and we become aware of our oneness. This is the everlasting and triumphant mystical tradition, hardly altered by differences of clime or creed. In Hinduism, in Neoplatonism, in Sufism, in Christian mysticism, in Whitmanism, we find the same recurring note, so that there is about mystical utterances an eternal unanimity which ought to make a critic stop and think, and which brings it about that the mystical classics have, as has been said, neither birthday nor native land. Perpetually telling of the unity of man with God, their speech antedates languages, and they do not grow old.

"That are Thou!" says the Upanishads, and the Vedantists add: "Not a part, nor a mode of That, but identically That, that absolute Spirit of the World." "As pure water poured into pure water remains the same, thus, O Gautama, is the Self of a thinker who knows. Water in water, fire in fire, ether in ether, no one can distinguish them: likewise a man whose mind has entered into the self." "Everyman," says the Sufi Gulshan-Râz, "whose heart is no longer shaken by any doubts, knows with certainty that there is no being save only One.... In his divine majesty the me, and we, the thou, are not found, for in the One there can be no distinction. Every being who is annulled and entirely separated from himself, hears resound outside of him this voice and this echo: *I am God*: he has an eternal way of existing, and is no longer subject to death." In the vision of God, says Plotinus, "what sees is not our reason, but something prior and superior to our reason.... He who thus sees does not properly see, does not distinguish or imagine two things. He changes, he ceases to be himself, preserves nothing of himself. Absorbed in God, he makes but one with him, like a Centre of a circle coinciding with another centre." "Here," writes Suso, "the spirit dies, and yet is all alive in the marvels of the Godhead... and is lost in the stillness of the glorious dazzling obscurity and of the naked simple unity. It is in this modeless *where* that the highest bliss is to be found." ["I am as great as God,"] sings Angelus Silesius again, ["He is as small as I. He cannot be above me, nor I under Him."] (Ed. trans.)

In mystical literature such self-contradictory phrases as "dazzling obscurity," "whispering silence," "teeming desert," are continually met with. They prove that not conceptual speech, but music rather, is the element through which we are best spoken to by mystical truth. Many mystical scriptures are indeed little more than musical compositions.

> He who would hear the voice of Nada, "the Soundless Sound," and comprehend it, he has to learn the nature of Dhâranâ....When to himself his form appears unreal, as do on waking all the forms he sees in dreams; when he has ceased to hear the many, he may discern the ONE—the inner sound which kills the outer....For

then the soul will hear, and will remember. And then to the inner ear will speak THE VOICE OF THE SILENCE...And now thy *Self* is lost in SELF, *thyself* unto THYSELF, merged in that SELF from which thou first didst radiate....Behold! thou hast become the Light, thou hast become the Sound, thou art thy Master and thy God. Thou art THYSELF the object of thy search: the VOICE unbroken, that resounds throughout eternities, exempt from change, from sin exempt, the seven sounds in one, the VOICE OF THE SILENCE. *Om tat Sat.*

These words, if they do not awaken laughter as you receive them, probably stir chords within you which music and language touch in common. Music gives us ontological messages which non-musical criticism is unable to contradict, though it may laugh at our foolishness in minding them. There is a verge of the mind which these things haunt; and whispers therefrom mingle with the operations of our understanding, even as the waters of the infinite ocean send their waves to break among the pebbles that lie upon our shores.

> *Here begins the sea that ends not till the*
> *   world's end. Where we stand,*
> *Could we know the next high sea-mark set*
> *   beyond these waves that gleam,*
> *We should know what never man hath known,*
> *   nor eye of man hath scanned.*
>
> ...
>
> *Ah, but here man's heart leaps, yearning*
> *   towards the gloom with venturous glee,*
> *From the shore that hath no shore beyond it,*
> *   set in all the sea.*

That doctrine, for example, that eternity is timeless, that our "immortality," if we live in the eternal, is not so much future as already now and here, which we find so often expressed to-day in certain philosophical circles, finds its support in a "hear, hear!" or an "amen," which floats up from that mysteriously deeper level. We recognize the passwords to the mystical region as we hear them, but we cannot use them ourselves; it alone has the keeping of "the password primeval."

I have now sketched with extreme brevity and insufficiency, but as fairly as I am able in the time allowed, the general traits of the mystic range of consciousness. *It is on the whole pantheistic and optimistic, or at least the opposite of pessimistic. It is anti-naturalistic, and harmonizes best with twice-bornness and so-called other-worldly states of mind.*

My next task is to inquire whether we can invoke it as authoritative. Does it furnish any *warrant for the truth* of the twice-bornness and super-naturality and pantheism which it favors? I must give my answer to this question as concisely as I can.

In brief my answer is this—and I will divide it into three parts:—

1. Mystical states, when well developed, usually are, and have the right to be, absolutely authoritative over the individuals to whom they come.
2. No authority emanates from them which should make it a duty for those who stand outside of them to accept their revelations uncritically.
3. They break down the authority of the non-mystical or rationalistic consciousness, based upon the understanding and the senses alone. They show it to be only one kind of consciousness. They open out the possibility of other orders of truth, in which, so far as anything in us vitally responds to them, we may freely continue to have faith.

I will take up these points one by one.

1. As a matter of psychological fact, mystical states of a well-pronounced and emphatic sort are usually authoritative over those who have them. They have been "there," and know. It is vain for rationalism to grumble about this. If the mystical truth that comes to a man proves to be a force that he can live by, what mandate have we of the majority to order him to live in another way? We can throw him into a prison or a madhouse, but we cannot change his mind—we commonly attach it only the more stubbornly to its beliefs. It mocks our utmost efforts, as a matter of fact, and in point of logic it absolutely escapes our jurisdiction. Our own more "rational" beliefs are based on evidence exactly similar in nature to that which mystics quote for theirs. Our senses, namely, have assured us of certain states of fact; but mystical experiences are as direct perceptions of fact for those who have them as any sensations ever were for us. The records show that even though the five senses be in abeyance in them, they are absolutely sensational in their epistemological quality, if I may be pardoned the barbarous expression—that is, they are face to face presentations of what seems immediately to exist.

The mystic is, in short, *invulnerable*, and must be left, whether we relish it or not, in undisturbed enjoyment of his creed. Faith, says Tolstoy, is that by which men live. And faith-state and mystic state are practically convertible terms.

2. But I now proceed to add that mystics have no right to claim that we ought to accept the deliverance of their peculiar experiences, if we are ourselves outsiders and feel no private call thereto. The utmost they can ever ask of us in this life is to admit that they establish a presumption. They form a consensus and have an unequivocal outcome; and it would be odd, mystics might say, if such a unanimous type of experience should prove to be altogether wrong. At bottom, however, this would only be an appeal to numbers, like the appeal of rationalism the other way; and the appeal to numbers has no logical force. If we acknowledge it, it is for "suggestive," not for logical reasons: we follow the majority because to do so suits our life.

But even this presumption from the unanimity of mystics is far from being strong. In characterizing mystic states as pantheistic, optimistic, etc., I am afraid I over-simplified the truth. I did so for expository reasons, and to keep the closer to the classic mystical tradition. The classic religious mysticism, it now must be confessed, is only a "privileged case." It is an *extract*, kept true to type by the selection of the fittest specimens and their preservation in "schools." It is carved out from a much larger mass; and if we take the larger mass as seriously as religious mysticism has historically taken itself, we find that the supposed unanimity largely disappears. To begin with, even religious mysticism itself, the kind that accumulates traditions and makes schools, is much less unanimous than I have allowed. It has been both ascetic and antinomianly self-indulgent within the Christian church. It is dualistic in Sankhya, and monistic in Vedanta philosophy. I called it pantheistic; but the great Spanish mystics are anything but pantheists. They are with few exceptions non-metaphysical minds, for whom "the category of personality" is absolute. The "union" of man with God is for them much more like an occasional miracle than like an original identity. How different again, apart from the happiness common to all, is the mysticism of Walt Whitman, Edward Carpenter, Richard Jefferies, and other naturalistic pantheists, from the more distinctively Christian sort. The fact is that the mystical feeling of enlargement, union, and emancipation has no specific intellectual content whatever of its own. It is capable of forming matrimonial alliances with material furnished by the most diverse philosophies and theologies, provided only they can find a place in their framework for its peculiar emotional mood. We have no right, therefore, to invoke its prestige as distinctively in favor of any special belief, such as that in absolute idealism, or in the absolute monistic identity, or in the absolute goodness, of the world. It is only relatively in favor of all these things—it passes out of common human consciousness in the direction in which they lie.

So much for religious mysticism proper. But more remains to be told, for religious mysticism is only one half of mysticism. The other half has no accumulated traditions except those which the textbooks on insanity supply. Open any one of these and you will find abundant cases in which "mystical ideas" are cited as characteristic symptoms of enfeebled or deluded states of mind. In delusional insanity, paranoia, as they sometimes call it, we may have a *diabolical* mysticism, a sort of religious mysticism turned upside down. The same sense of ineffable importance in the smallest events, the same texts and words coming with new meanings, the same voices and visions and leadings and missions, the same controlling by extraneous powers; only this time

the emotion is pessimistic: instead of consolations we have desolations; the meanings are dreadful; and the powers are enemies to life. It is evident from the point of view of their psychological mechanism, the classic mysticism and these lower mysticisms spring from the same mental level, from that great subliminal or transmarginal region of which science is beginning to admit the existence, but of which so little is really known. That region contains every kind of matter: "seraph and snake" abide there side by side. To come from thence is no infallible credential. What comes must be sifted and tested, and run the gauntlet of confrontation with the total context of experience, just like what comes from the outer world of sense. Its value must be ascertained by empirical methods, so long as we are not mystics ourselves.

Once more, then, I repeat that non-mystics are under no obligation to acknowledge in mystical states a superior authority conferred on them by their intrinsic nature.

3. Yet, I repeat once more, the existence of mystical states absolutely overthrows the pretension of non-mystical states to be the sole and ultimate dictators of what we may believe. As a rule, mystical states merely add a supersensuous meaning to the ordinary outward data of consciousness. They are excitements like the emotions of love or ambition, gifts to our spirit by means of which facts already objectively before us fall into a new expressiveness and make a new connection with our active life. They do not contradict these facts as such, or deny anything that our senses have immediately seized. It is the rationalistic critic rather who plays the part of denier in the controversy, and his denials have no strength, for there never can be a state of facts to which new meaning may not truthfully be added, provided the mind ascend to a more enveloping point of view. It must always remain an open question whether mystical states may not possibly be such superior points of view, windows through which the mind looks out upon a more extensive and inclusive world. The difference of the views seen from the different mystical windows need not prevent us from entertaining this supposition. The wider world

would in that case prove to have a mixed constitution like that of this world, that is all. It would have its celestial and its infernal regions, its tempting and its saving moments, its valid experiences and its counterfeit ones, just as our world has them; but it would be a wider world all the same. We should have to use its experiences by selecting and subordinating and substituting just as is our custom in this ordinary naturalistic world; we should be liable to error just as we are now; yet the counting in of that wider world of meanings, and the serious dealing with it, might, in spite of all the perplexity, be indispensable stages in our approach to the final fullness of the truth.

In this shape, I think, we have to leave the subject. Mystical states indeed wield no authority due simply to their being mystical states. But the higher ones among them point in directions to which the religious sentiments even of non-mystical men incline. They tell of the supremacy of the ideal, of vastness, of union, of safety, and of rest. They offer us *hypotheses*, hypotheses which we may voluntarily ignore, but which as thinkers we cannot possibly upset. The supernaturalism and optimism to which they would persuade us may, interpreted in one way or another, be after all the truest of insights into the meaning of this life.

"Oh, the little more, and how much it is; and the little less, and what worlds away!" It may be that possibility and permission of this sort are all that our religious consciousness requires to live on. In my last lecture I shall have to try to persuade you that this is the case. Meanwhile, however, I am sure that for many of my readers this diet is too slender. If supernaturalism and inner union with the divine are true, you think, then not so much permission, as compulsion to believe, ought to be found. Philosophy has always professed to prove religious truth by coercive argument; and the construction of philosophies of this kind has always been one favorite function of the religious life, if we use this term in the large historic sense. But religious philosophy is an enormous subject, and in my next lecture I can only give that brief glance at it which my limits will allow.

CONCLUSIONS ON RELIGIOUS EXPERIENCE

Let us agree, then, that Religion, occupying herself with personal destinies and keeping thus in contact with the only absolute realities which we know, must necessarily play an eternal part in human history. The next thing to decide is what she reveals about those destinies, or whether indeed she reveals anything distinct enough to be considered a general message to mankind. We have done as you see, with our preliminaries, and our final summing up can now begin....

Both thought and feeling are determinants of conduct, and the same conduct may be determined either by feeling or by thought. When we survey the whole field of religion, we find a great variety in the thoughts that have prevailed there; but the feelings on the one hand and the conduct on the other are almost always the same, for Stoic, Christian, and Buddhist saints are practically indistinguishable in their lives. The theories which Religion generates, being thus variable, are secondary; and if you wish to grasp her essence, you must look to the feelings and the conduct as being the more constant elements. It is between these two elements that the short circuit exists on which she carries on her principal business, while the ideas and symbols and other institutions form loop-lines which may be perfections and improvements, and may even some day all be united into one harmonious system, but which are not to be regarded as organs with an indispensable function, necessary at all times for religious life to go on. This seems to me the first conclusion which we are entitled to draw from the phenomena we have passed in review.

The next step is to characterize the feelings. To what psychological order do they belong?

The resultant outcome of them is in any case what Kant calls 'sthenic' affection, an excitement of the cheerful, expansive, 'dynamogenic' order which, like any tonic, freshens our vital powers. In almost every lecture, but especially in the lectures on Conversion and on Saintliness, we have seen how this emotion overcomes temperamental melancholy and imparts endurance to the Subject, or a zest, or a meaning, or an enchantment and glory to the common objects of life. The name of 'faith state,' by which Professor Leuba designates it, is a good one. It is a biological as well as a psychological condition, and Tolstoy is absolutely accurate in classing faith among the forces *by which men live.* The total absence of it, anhedonia, means collapse.

The faith-state may hold a very minimum of intellectual content. We saw examples of this in those sudden raptures of the divine presence, or in such mystical seizures as Dr. Bucke described. It may be a mere vague enthusiasm, half spiritual, half vital, a courage, and a feeling that great and wondrous things are in the air.

When, however, a positive intellectual content is associated with a faith-state, it gets invincibly stamped in upon belief, and this explains the passionate loyalty of religious persons everywhere to the minutest details of their so widely differing creeds. Taking creeds and faith-state together, as forming 'religions,' and treating these as purely subjective phenomena, without regard to the question of their 'truth,' we are obliged, on account of their extraordinary influence upon action and endurance, to class them amongst the most important biological functions of mankind. Their stimulant and anaesthetic effect is so great that Professor Leuba, in a recent article, goes so far as to say that so long as men can use their God, they care very little who he is, or even whether he is at all. "The truth of the matter can be put," says Leuba, "in this way: *God is not known, he is not understood; he is used*—sometimes as meat-purveyor, sometimes as moral support, sometimes as friend, sometimes as an object of love. If he proves himself useful, the religious consciousness asks for no more than that. Does God really exist? How does he exist? What is he? are so many irrelevant questions. Not God, but life, more life, a larger, richer, more satisfying life is, in the last analysis, the end of religion. The love of life, at any and every level of development, is the religious impulse."

At this purely subjective rating, therefore, Religion must be considered vindicated in a certain way from the attacks of her critics. It would seem that she cannot be a mere anachronism and survival, but must exert a permanent function, whether she be with or without intellectual content, and whether, if she have any, it be true or false.

We must next pass beyond the point of view of merely subjective utility, and make inquiry into the intellectual content itself.

First, is there, under all the discrepancies of the creeds, a common nucleus to which they bear their testimony unanimously?

And second, ought we to consider the testimony true?

I will take up the first question first, and answer it immediately in the affirmative. The warring gods and formulas of the various religions do indeed cancel each other, but there is a certain uniform deliverance in which religions all appear to meet. It consists of two parts:—

1. An uneasiness; and
2. Its solution.

1. The uneasiness, reduced to its simplest terms, is a sense that there is *something wrong about us* as we naturally stand.
2. The solution is a sense that *we are saved from the wrongness* by making proper connection with the higher powers.

In those more developed minds, which alone we are studying, the wrongness takes a moral character, and the salvation takes a mystical tinge. I think we shall keep well within the limits of what is common to all such minds if we formulate the essence of their religious experience in terms like these:—

The individual, so far as he suffers from his wrongness and criticises it, is to that extent consciously beyond it, and in at least possible touch with something higher, if anything higher exist. Along with the wrong part there is thus a better part of him, even though it may be but a most helpless germ. With which part he should identify his real being is by no means obvious at this stage; but when stage 2 (the stage of solution or salvation) arrives, the man identifies his real being with the germinal higher part of himself; and does so in the following way. *He becomes conscious that this higher part is conterminous and continuous with a* MORE *of the same quality, which is operative in the universe outside of him, and which he can keep in working touch with, and in a fashion get on board of and save himself when all his lower being has gone to pieces in the wreck.*

It seems to me that all the phenomena are accurately describable in these very simple general terms. They allow for the divided self and the struggle; they involve the change of personal centre and the surrender of the lower self; they express the appearance of exteriority of the helping power and yet account for our sense of union with it; and they fully justify our feelings of security and joy. There is probably no autobiographic document, among all those which I have quoted, to which the description will not well apply. One need only add such specific details as will adapt it to various theologies and various personal temperaments, and one will then have the various experiences reconstructed in their individual forms.

So far, however, as this analysis goes, the experiences are only psychological phenomena. They possess, it is true, enormous biological worth. Spiritual strength really increases in the subject when he has them, a new life opens for him, and they seem to him a place of conflux where the forces of two universes meet; and yet this may be nothing but his subjective way of feeling things, a mood of his own fancy, in spite of the effects produced. I now turn to my second question: What is the objective 'truth' of their content?

The part of the content concerning which the question of truth most pertinently arises is that 'MORE of the same quality' with which our own higher self appears in the experience to come into harmonious working relation. Is such a 'more' merely our own notion, or does it really exist? If so, in what shape does it exist? Does it act, as well as exist? And in what form should we conceive of that 'union' with it of which religious geniuses are so convinced?

It is in answering these questions that the various theologies perform their theoretic work, and that their divergencies most come to light. They all agree that the 'more' really exists; though some of them hold it to exist in the shape of a personal god or gods, while others are satisfied to conceive it as a stream of ideal tendency embedded in the eternal structure of the world. They all agree, moreover, that it acts as well as exists, and that something really is effected for the better when you throw your life into its hands. It is when they treat of the experience of 'union' with it that their speculative differences appear most clearly. Over this point pantheism and theism, nature and second birth, works and grace and karma, immortality and reincarnation, rationalism and mysticism, carry on inveterate disputes.

At the end of my lecture on Philosophy I held out the notion that an impartial science of religions might sift out from the midst of their discrepancies a common body of doctrine which she might also formulate in terms to which physical science need not object. This, I said, she might adopt as her own reconciling hypothesis, and recommend it for general belief. I also said that in my last lecture I should have to try my own hand at framing such an hypothesis.

The time has now come for this attempt. Who says 'hypothesis' renounces the ambition to be coercive in his arguments. The most I can do is, accordingly, to offer something that may fit the facts so easily that your scientific logic will find no plausible pretext for vetoing your impulse to welcome it as true.

The 'more,' as we called it, and the meaning of our 'union' with it, form the nucleus of our inquiry. Into what definite description can these words be translated, and for what definite facts do they stand? It would never do for us to place ourselves offhand at the position of a particular theology, the Christian theology, for example, and proceed immediately to define the 'more' as Jehovah, and the 'union' as his imputation to us of the righteousness of Christ. That would be unfair to other religions, and from our present standpoint at least, would be an over-belief.

We must begin by using less particularized terms; and, since one of the duties of the science of religions is to keep religion in connection with the rest of science, we shall do well to seek first of all a way of describing the 'more,' which psychologists may also recognize as real. The *sub-conscious self* is nowadays a well-accredited psychological entity; and I believe that in it we have exactly the mediating term required. Apart from all religious considerations, there is actually and literally more life in our total soul than we are at any time aware of. The exploration of the transmarginal field has hardly yet been seriously undertaken, but what Mr. Myers said in 1892 in his essay on the Subliminal Consciousness is as true as when it was first written: "Each of us is in reality an abiding psychical entity far more extensive than he knows—an individuality which can never express itself completely through any corporeal manifestation. The Self manifests through the organism; but there is always some part of the Self unmanifested; and always, as it seems, some power of organic expression in abeyance or reserve." Much of the content of this larger background against which our conscious being stands out in relief is insignificant. Imperfect memories, silly jingles, inhibitive timidities, 'dissolutive' phenomena of various sorts, as Myers calls them, enter into it for a large part. But in it many of the performances of genius seem also to have their origin; and in our study of conversion, of mystical experiences, and of prayer, we have seen how striking a part invasions from this region play in the religious life.

Let me then propose, as an hypothesis, that whatever it may be on its *farther* side, the 'more' with which in religious experience we feel ourselves connected is on its *hither* side the subconscious continuation of our conscious life. Starting thus with a recognized psychological fact as our basis, we seem to preserve a contact with 'science' which the ordinary theologian lacks. At the same time the theologian's contention that the religious man is moved by an external power is vindicated, for it is one of the peculiarities of invasions from the subconscious region to take on objective appearances, and to suggest to the Subject an external control. In the religious life the control is felt as 'higher'; but since on our hypothesis it is primarily the higher faculties of our own hidden mind which are controlling, the sense of union with the power beyond us is a sense of something, not merely apparently, but literally true.

This doorway into the subject seems to me the best one for a science of religions, for it mediates between a number of different points of view. Yet it is only a doorway, and difficulties present themselves as soon as we step through it, and ask how far our transmarginal consciousness carries us if we follow it on its remoter side. Here the over-beliefs begin: here mysticism and the conversion-rapture and Vedantism and transcendental idealism bring in their monistic interpretations and tell us that the finite self rejoins the absolute self, for it was always one with God and identical with the soul of the world. Here the prophets of all the different religions come with their visions, voices, raptures, and other openings, supposed by each to authenticate his own peculiar faith.

Those of us who are not personally favored with such specific revelations must stand outside of them altogether and, for the present at least, decide that, since they corroborate incompatible theological doctrines, they neutralize one another and leave no fixed result. If we follow any one of them, or if we follow philosophical theory and embrace monistic pantheism on non-mystical grounds, we do so in the exercise of our individual freedom, and build out our religion in the way most congruous with our personal susceptibilities. Among these susceptibilities intellectual ones play a decisive part. Although the religious question is primarily a question of life, of living or not living in the higher union which opens itself to us as a gift, yet the spiritual excitement in which the gift appears a real one will often fail to be aroused in an individual until certain particular intellectual beliefs or ideas which, as we say, come home to him, are touched. These ideas will thus be essential to that individual's religion;—which is as much as to say that over-beliefs in various directions are absolutely indispensable, and that we should treat them with tenderness and tolerance so long as they are not intolerant themselves. As I have elsewhere written, the most interesting and valuable things about a man are usually his over-beliefs.

Disregarding the over-beliefs, and confining ourselves to what is common and generic, we have in *the fact that the conscious person is continuous with a wider self through which saving experiences come*, a positive content of religious experience which, it seems to me, *is literally and objectively true as far as it goes.* If I now proceed to state my own hypothesis about the farther limits of this extension of our personality, I shall be offering my own over-belief—though I know it will appear a sorry under-belief to some of you—for which I can only bespeak the same indulgence which in a converse case I should accord to yours.

The further limits of our being plunge, it seems to me, into an altogether other dimension of existence from the sensible and merely 'understandable' world. Name it the mystical region, or the supernatural region, whichever you choose. So far as our ideal impulses originate in this region (and most of them do originate in it, for we find them possessing us in a way for which we cannot articulately account), we belong to it in a more intimate sense than that in which we belong to the visible world, for we belong in the most intimate sense wherever our ideals belong. Yet the unseen region in question is not merely ideal, for it produces effects in this world. When we commune with it, work is actually done upon our finite personality, for we are turned into new men, and consequences in the way of conduct follow in the natural world upon our regenerative change. But that which produces effects within another reality must be termed a reality itself, so I feel as if we had no philosophic excuse for calling the unseen or mystical world unreal.

God is the natural appellation, for us Christians at least, for the supreme reality, so I will call this higher part of the universe by the name of God. We and God have business with each other; and in opening ourselves to his influence our deepest destiny is fulfilled. The universe, at those parts of it which our personal being constitutes, takes a turn genuinely for the worse or for the better in proportion as each one of us fulfills or evades God's demands. As far as this goes I probably have you with me, for I only translate into schematic language what I may call the instinctive belief of mankind: God is real since he produces real effects.

The real effects in question, so far as I have as yet admitted them, are exerted on the personal centres of energy of the various subjects, but the spontaneous faith of most of the subjects is that they embrace a wider sphere than this. Most religious men believe (or 'know,' if they be mystical) that not only they themselves, but the whole universe of beings to whom the God is present, are secure in his parental hands. There is a sense, a dimension, they are sure, in which we are *all* saved, in spite of the gates of hell and all adverse terrestrial appearances. God's existence is the guarantee of an ideal order that shall be permanently preserved. This world may indeed, as science assures us, some day burn up or freeze; but if it is part of his order, the old ideals are sure to be brought elsewhere to fruition, so that where God is, tragedy is only provisional and partial, and shipwreck and dissolution are not the absolutely final things. Only when this further step of faith concerning God is taken, and remote objective consequences are predicted, does religion, as it seems to me, get wholly free from the first immediate subjective experience, and bring a *real hypothesis* into play. A good hypothesis in science must have other properties than those of the phenomenon it is immediately invoked to explain, otherwise it is not prolific enough. God, meaning only what enters into the religious man's experience of union, falls short of being an hypothesis of this more useful order. He needs to enter into wider cosmic relations in order to justify the subject's absolute confidence and peace.

That the God with whom, starting from the hither side of our own extra-marginal self, we come at its remoter margin into commerce should be the absolute world-ruler, is of course a very considerable over-belief. Over-belief as it is, though, it is an article of almost every one's religion. Most of us pretend in some way to prop it up upon our philosophy, but the philosophy itself is really propped upon this faith. What is this but to say that Religion, in her fullest exercise of function, is not a mere illumination of facts already elsewhere given, not a mere passion, like love, which views things in a rosier light. It is indeed that, as we have seen abundantly. But it is something more, namely, a postulator of new *facts* as well. The world interpreted religiously is not the materialistic world over again, with an altered expression; it must have, over and above the altered expression, a *natural constitution* different at some point from that which a materialistic world would have. It must be such that different events can be expected in it, different conduct must be required.

This thoroughly 'pragmatic' view of religion has usually been taken as a matter of course by common men. They have interpolated divine miracles into the field of nature, they have built a heaven out beyond the grave. It is only transcendentalist metaphysicians who think that, without adding any concrete details to Nature, or subtracting any, but by simply calling it the expression of absolute spirit, you make it more divine just as it stands. I believe the pragmatic way of taking religion to be the deeper way. It gives it body as well as soul, it makes it claim, as everything real must claim, some characteristic realm of fact as its very own. What the more characteristically divine facts are, apart from the actual inflow of energy in the faith-state and the prayer-state, I know not. But the over-belief on which I am ready to make my personal venture is that they exist. The whole drift of my education goes to persuade me that the world of our present consciousness is only one out of many worlds of consciousness that exist, and that those other worlds must contain experiences which have a meaning for our life also; and that although in the main their experiences and those of this world keep discrete, yet the two become continuous at certain points, and higher energies filter in. By being faithful in my poor measure to this over-belief, I seem to myself to keep more sane and true. I *can*, of course, put myself into the sectarian scientist's attitude, and imagine vividly that the world of sensations and of scientific laws and objects may be all. But whenever I do this, I hear that inward monitor of which W. K. Clifford once wrote, whispering the word 'bosh!' Humbug is humbug, even though it bear the scientific name, and the total expression of human experience, as I view it objectively, invincibly urges me beyond the narrow 'scientific' bounds. Assuredly, the real world is of a different temperament,—more intricately built than physical science allows. So my objective and my subjective conscience both hold me to the over-belief which I express. Who knows whether the faithfulness of individuals here below to their own poor over-beliefs may not actually help God in turn to be more effectively faithful to his own greater tasks? ...

II.3 The Future of an Illusion

SIGMUND FREUD

Sigmund Freud (1856–1939), an Austrian psychologist, is considered the father of psychoanalysis. His works include *Beyond the Pleasure Principle, Civilization and Its Discontents,* and *The Complete Introductory Lectures on Psychoanalysis.* Our selection is from *The Future of an Illusion* (1927), in which Freud argues that religion is a projection of the father image onto the heavens. It is an "Infantile neurosis" that is in need of a cure so that the individual can become a healthy, mature adult. When we are children, the father fulfills our needs, protecting us from danger, attributing value to our being, and providing food and shelter. He seems omnipotent, omniscient, and omnibenevolent. When we grow up, we become aware of the fallibility and vulnerability of our fathers but the need for protection remains.

Reprinted from Sigmund Freud, *The Future of an Illusion,* trans. James Strachey (W. W. Norton Publishing Co., 1961) by permission of the publisher. Translation © 1961 by James Strachey, renewed by Alex Strachey.

So humanity has created the idea of a Divine Father to take the place of the human father. This is why we have religious experiences. They are the unconscious internalizations of our primordial need for relief from the insecurity and tragedy of existence.

In what does the peculiar value of religious ideas lie?

We have spoken of the hostility to civilization which is produced by the pressure that civilization exercises, the renunciations of instinct which it demands. If one imagines its prohibitions lifted—if, then, one may take any woman one pleases as a sexual object, if one may without hesitation kill one's rival for her love or anyone else who stands in one's way, if, too, one can carry off any of the other man's belongings without asking leave—how splendid, what a string of satisfactions one's life would be! True, one soon comes across the first difficulty: everyone else has exactly the same wishes as I have and will treat me with no more consideration than I treat him. And so in reality only one person could be made unrestrictedly happy by such a removal of the restrictions of civilization, and he would be a tyrant, a dictator, who had seized all the means to power. And even he would have every reason to wish that the others would observe at least one cultural commandment: 'thou shalt not kill.'

But how ungrateful, how short-sighted after all, to strive for the abolition of civilization! What would then remain would be a state of nature, and that would be far harder to bear. It is true that nature would not demand any restrictions of instinct from us, she would let us do as we liked; but she has her own particularly effective method of restricting us. She destroys us—coldly, cruelly, relentlessly, as it seems to us, and possibly through the very things that occasioned our satisfaction. It was precisely because of these dangers with which nature threatens us that we came together and created civilization, which is also, among other things, intended to make our communal life possible. For the principal task of civilization, its actual *raison d'être*, is to defend us against nature.

We all know that in many ways civilization does this fairly well already, and clearly as time goes on it will do it much better. But no one is under the illusion that nature has already been vanquished; and few dare hope that she will ever be entirely subjected to man. There are the elements, which seem to mock at all human control: the earth, which quakes and is torn apart and buries all human life and its works; water, which deluges and drowns everything in a turmoil; storms, which blow everything before them; there are diseases, which we have only recently recognized as attacks by other organisms; and finally there is the painful riddle of death, against which no medicine has yet been found, nor probably will be. With these forces nature rises up against us, majestic, cruel and inexorable; she brings to our mind once more our weakness and helplessness, which we thought to escape through the work of civilization. One of the few gratifying and exalting impressions which mankind can offer is when, in the face of an elemental catastrophe, it forgets the discordancies of its civilization and all its internal difficulties and animosities, and recalls the great common task of preserving itself against the superior power of nature.

For the individual, too, life is hard to bear, just as it is for mankind in general. The civilization in which he participates imposes some amount of privation on him, and other men bring him a measure of suffering, either in spite of the precepts of his civilization or because of its imperfections. To this are added the injuries which untamed nature—he calls it Fate—inflicts on him. One might suppose that this condition of things would result in a permanent state of anxious expectation in him and a severe injury to his natural narcissism. We know already how the individual reacts to the injuries which civilization and other men inflict on him: he develops a corresponding degree of resistance to the regulations of civilization and of hostility to it. But how does he defend himself against the superior powers of nature, of Fate, which threaten him as they threaten all the rest?

Civilization relieves him of this task; it performs it in the same way for all alike; and it is noteworthy that in this almost all civilizations act alike. Civilization does not call a halt in the task of defending man against nature, it merely pursues it by other means. The task is a manifold one. Man's self-regard, seriously menaced, calls for consolation; life and the universe must be robbed of their terrors; moreover his curiosity, moved, it is true, by the strongest practical interest, demands an answer.

A great deal is already gained with the first step: the humanization of nature. Impersonal forces and destinies cannot be approached; they remain eternally remote. But if the elements have passions that rage as they do in our own souls, if death itself is not something spontaneous but the violent act of an evil Will, if everywhere in nature there are Beings around us of a kind that we know in our own society, then we can breathe freely, can feel at home in the uncanny and can deal by psychical means with our senseless anxiety. We are still defenceless, perhaps, but we are no longer helplessly paralysed; we can at least react. Perhaps, indeed, we are not even defenceless. We can apply the same methods against these violent supermen outside that we employ in our own society; we can try to adjure them, to appease them, to bribe them, and, by so influencing them, we may rob them of a part of their power. A replacement like this of natural science by psychology not only provides immediate relief, but also points the way to a further mastering of the situation.

For this situation is nothing new. It has an infantile prototype, of which it is in fact only the continuation. For once before one has found oneself in a similar state of helplessness: as a small child, in relation to one's parents. One had reason to fear them, and especially one's father; and yet one was sure of his protection against the dangers one knew. Thus it was natural to assimilate the two situations. Here, too, wishing played its part, as it does in dream-life. The sleeper may be seized with a presentiment of death, which threatens to place him in the grave. But the dream-work knows how to select a condition that will turn even that dreaded event into a wish-fulfilment: the dreamer sees himself in an ancient Etruscan grave which he has climbed down into, happy to find his archaeological interests satisfied.[1] In the same way, a man makes the forces of nature not simply into persons with whom he can associate as he would with his equals—that would not do justice to the overpowering impression which those forces make on him—but he gives them the character of a father. He turns them into gods, following in this, as I have tried to show, not only an infantile prototype but a phylogenetic one.[2]

In the course of time the first observations were made of regularity and conformity to law in natural phenomena, and with this the forces of nature lost their human traits. But man's helplessness remains and along with it his longing for his father, and the gods. The gods retain their threefold task: they must exorcize the terrors of nature, they must reconcile men to the cruelty of Fate, particularly as it is shown in death, and they must compensate them for the sufferings and privations which a civilized life in common has imposed on them.

But within these functions there is a gradual displacement of accent. It was observed that the phenomena of nature developed automatically according to internal necessities. Without doubt the gods were the lords of nature; they had arranged it to be as it was and now they could leave it to itself. Only occasionally, in what are known as miracles, did they intervene in its course, as though to make it plain that they had relinquished nothing of their original sphere of power. As regards the apportioning of destinies, an unpleasant suspicion persisted that the perplexity and helplessness of the human race could not be remedied. It was here that the gods were most apt to fail. If they themselves created Fate, then their counsels must be deemed inscrutable. The notion dawned on the most gifted people of antiquity that Moira [Fate] stood above the gods and that the gods themselves had their own destinies. And the more autonomous nature became and the more the gods withdrew from it, the more earnestly were all expectations directed to the third function of the gods—the more did morality become their true domain. It now became the task of the gods to even out the defects and evils of civilization, to attend to the sufferings which men inflict on one another in their life together and to watch over the fulfilment of the precepts of civilization, which men obey so imperfectly. Those precepts themselves were credited with a divine origin; they were elevated beyond human society and were extended to nature and the universe.

And thus a store of ideas is created, born from man's need to make his helplessness tolerable and built up from the material of memories of the helplessness of his own childhood and the childhood of the human race. It can clearly be seen that the possession of these ideas protects him in two directions—against the dangers of nature and Fate, and against the injuries that threaten him from human society itself. Here is the gist of the matter. Life in this world serves a higher purpose; no doubt it is not easy to guess what that purpose is, but it certainly signifies a perfecting of man's nature. It is probably the spiritual part of man, the soul, which in the course of time has so slowly and unwillingly detached itself from the body, that is the object of this elevation and exaltation. Everything that happens in this world is an expression of the intentions of an intelligence superior to us, which in the end, though its ways and byways are difficult to follow, orders everything for the best—that is, to make it enjoyable for us. Over each one of us there watches a benevolent Providence which is only seemingly stern and which will not suffer us to become a plaything of the overmighty and pitiless forces of nature. Death itself is not extinction, is not a return to inorganic lifelessness, but the beginning of a new kind of existence which lies on the path of development to something higher. And, looking in the other direction, this view announces that the same moral laws which our civilizations have set up govern the whole universe as well, except that they are maintained by a supreme court of justice with incomparably more power and consistency. In the end all good is rewarded and all evil punished, if not actually in this form of life then in the later existences that begin after death. In this way all the terrors, the sufferings and the hardships of life

are destined to be obliterated. Life after death, which continues life on earth just as the invisible part of the spectrum joins on to the visible part, brings us all the perfection that we may perhaps have missed here. And the superior wisdom which directs this course of things, the infinite goodness that expresses itself in it, the justice that achieves its aim in it—these are the attributes of the divine beings who also created us and the world as a whole, or rather, of the one divine being into which, in our civilization, all the gods of antiquity have been condensed. The people which first succeeded in thus concentrating the divine attributes was not a little proud of the advance. It had laid open to view the father who had all along been hidden behind every divine figure as its nucleus. Fundamentally this was a return to the historical beginnings of the idea of God. Now that God was a single person, man's relations to him could recover the intimacy and intensity of the child's relation to his father. But if one had done so much for one's father, one wanted to have a reward, or at least to be his only beloved child, his Chosen People. . . .

I THINK we have prepared the way sufficiently for an answer to both these questions. It will be found if we turn our attention to the psychical origin of religious ideas. These, which are given out as teachings, are not precipitates of experience or end-results of thinking: they are illusions, fulfilments of the oldest, strongest and most urgent wishes of mankind. The secret of their strength lies in the strength of those wishes. As we already know, the terrifying impression of helplessness in childhood aroused the need for protection—for protection through love—which was provided by the father; and the recognition that this helplessness lasts throughout life made it necessary to cling to the existence of a father, but this time a more powerful one. Thus the benevolent rule of a divine Providence allays our fear of the dangers of life; the establishment of a moral world-order ensures the fulfilment of the demands of justice, which have so often remained unfulfilled in human civilization; and the prolongation of earthly existence in a future life provides the local and temporal framework in which these wish-fulfilments shall take place. Answers to the riddles that tempt the curiosity of man, such as how the universe began or what the relation is between body and mind, are developed in conformity with the underlying assumptions of this system. It is an enormous relief to the individual psyche if the conflicts of its childhood arising from the father-complex—conflicts which it has never wholly overcome—are removed from it and brought to a solution which is universally accepted.

When I say that these things are all illusions, I must define the meaning of the word. An illusion is not the same thing as an error; nor is it necessarily an error. Aristotle's belief that vermin are developed out of dung (a belief to which ignorant people still cling) was an error; so was the belief of a former generation of doctors that *tabes dorsalis* is the result of sexual excess. It would be incorrect to call these errors illusions. On the other hand, it was an illusion of Columbus's that he had discovered a new sea-route to the Indies. The part played by his wish in this error is very clear. One may describe as an illusion the assertion made by certain nationalists that the Indo-Germanic race is the only one capable of civilization; or the belief, which was only destroyed by psychoanalysis, that children are creatures without sexuality. What is characteristic of illusions is that they are derived from human wishes. In this respect they come near to psychiatric delusions. But they differ from them, too, apart from the more complicated structure of delusions. In the case of delusions, we emphasize as essential their being in contradiction with reality. Illusions need not necessarily be false—that is to say, unrealizable or in contradiction to reality. For instance, a middle-class girl may have the illusion that a prince will come and marry her. This is possible; and a few such cases have occurred. That the Messiah will come and found a golden age is much less likely. Whether one classifies this belief as an illusion or as something analogous to a delusion will depend on one's personal attitude. Examples of illusions which have proved true are not easy to find, but the illusion of the alchemists that all metals can be turned into gold might be one of them. The wish to have a great deal of gold, as much gold as possible, has, it is true, been a good deal damped by our present-day knowledge of the determinants of wealth, but

chemistry no longer regards the transmutation of metals into gold as impossible. Thus we call a belief an illusion when a wish-fulfilment is a prominent factor in its motivation, and in doing so we disregard its relations to reality, just as the illusion itself sets no store by verification.

Having thus taken our bearings, let us return once more to the question of religious doctrines. We can now repeat that all of them are illusions and insusceptible of proof. No one can be compelled to think them true, to believe in them. Some of them are so improbable, so incompatible with everything we have laboriously discovered about the reality of the world, that we may compare them—if we pay proper regard to the psychological differences—to delusions. Of the reality value of most of them we cannot judge; just as they cannot be proved, so they cannot be refuted. We still know too little to make a critical approach to them. The riddles of the universe reveal themselves only slowly to our investigation; there are many questions to which science to-day can give no answer. But scientific work is the only road which can lead us to a knowledge of reality outside ourselves. It is once again merely an illusion to expect anything from intuition and introspection; they can give us nothing but particulars about our own mental life, which are hard to interpret, never any information about the questions which religious doctrine finds it so easy to answer. It would be insolent to let one's own arbitrary will step into the breach and, according to one's personal estimate, declare this or that part of the religious system to be less or more acceptable. Such questions are too momentous for that; they might be called too sacred.

At this point one must expect to meet with an objection. 'Well then, if even obdurate sceptics admit that the assertions of religion cannot be refuted by reason, why should I not believe in them, since they have so much on their side—tradition, the agreement of mankind, and all the consolations they offer?' Why not, indeed? Just as no one can be forced to believe, so no one can be forced to disbelieve. But do not let us be satisfied with deceiving ourselves that arguments like these take us along the road of correct thinking. If ever there was a case of a lame excuse we have it here. Ignorance is ignorance; no right to believe anything can be derived from it. In other matters no sensible person will behave so irresponsibly or rest content with such feeble grounds for his opinions and for the line he takes. It is only in the highest and most sacred things that he allows himself to do so. In reality these are only attempts at pretending to oneself or to other people that one is still firmly attached to religion, when one has long since cut oneself loose from it. Where questions of religion are concerned, people are guilty of every possible sort of dishonesty and intellectual misdemeanour. Philosophers stretch the meaning of words until they retain scarcely anything of their original sense. They give the name of 'God' to some vague abstraction which they have created for themselves; having done so they can pose before all the world as deists, as believers in God, and they can even boast that they have recognized a higher, purer concept of God, notwithstanding that their God is now nothing more than an insubstantial shadow and no longer the mighty personality of religious doctrines. Critics persist in describing as 'deeply religious' anyone who admits to a sense of man's insignificance or impotence in the face of the universe, although what constitutes the essence of the religious attitude is not this feeling but only the next step after it, the reaction to it which seeks a remedy for it. The man who goes no further, but humbly acquiesces in the small part which human beings play

in the great world—such a man is, on the contrary, irreligious in the truest sense of the word.

To assess the truth-value of religious doctrines does not lie within the scope of the present enquiry. It is enough for us that we have recognized them as being, in their psychological nature, illusions. But we do not have to conceal the fact that this discovery also strongly influences our attitude to the question which must appear to many to be the most important of all. We know approximately at what periods and by what kind of men religious doctrines were created. If in addition we discover the motives which led to this, our attitude to the problem of religion will undergo a marked displacement. We shall tell ourselves that it would be very nice if there were a God who created the world and was a benevolent Providence, and if there were a moral order in the universe and an after-life; but it is a very striking fact that all this is exactly as we are bound to wish it to be. And it would be more remarkable still if our wretched, ignorant and downtrodden ancestors had succeeded in solving all these difficult riddles of the universe.

NOTES
1. This was an actual dream of Freud's reported in Chapter VI (G) of *The Interpretation of Dreams* (1900a), Standard Ed., 5, 454–5.]
2. [See Section 6 of the fourth essay in *Totem and Taboo* (1912–13), Standard Ed., 13, 146ff.]

II.4   The Argument from Religious Experience

C. D. BROAD

C. D. Broad (1887–1971) was a professor of philosophy at Cambridge University who wrote prolifically on philosophy of mind, philosophy of religion, and psychical research. In his article "The Argument from Religious Experience" (1953), Broad critically evaluates the suggestion that the phenomenon of religious experience provides evidence for the existence of God.

Reprinted from C. D. Broad, *Religion, Philosophy and Psychical Research* (London: Routledge & Kegan Paul PLC, 1930).

I shall confine myself in this article to specifically religious experience and the argument for the existence of God which has been based on it.

This argument differs in the following important respect from the other two empirical types of argument. The Argument from Design and the arguments from ethical premises start from facts which are common to every one. But some people seem to be almost wholly devoid of any specifically religious experience; and among those who have it the differences of kind and degree are enormous. Founders of religions and saints, e.g., often claim to have been in direct contact with God, to have seen and spoken with Him, and so on. An ordinary religious man would certainly not make any such claim, though he might say that he had had experiences which assured him of the existence and presence of God. So the first thing that we have to notice is that capacity for religious experience is in certain respects like an ear for music. There are a few people who are unable to recognize and distinguish the simplest tune. But they are in a minority, like the people who have absolutely no kind of religious experience. Most people have some light appreciation of music. But the differences of degree in this respect are enormous, and those who have not much gift for music have to take the statements of accomplished musicians very largely on trust. Let us, then, compare tone-deaf persons to those who have no recognizable religious experience at all; the ordinary followers of a religion to men who have some taste for music but can neither appreciate the more difficult kinds nor compose; highly religious men and saints to persons with an exceptionally fine ear for music who may yet be unable to compose it; and the founders of religions to great musical composers, such as Bach and Beethoven.

This analogy is, of course, incomplete in certain important respects. Religious experience raises three problems, which are different though closely interconnected. (i) What is the *psychological analysis* of religious experience? Does it contain factors which are present also in certain experiences which are not religious? Does it

contain any factor which never occurs in any other kind of experience? If it contains no such factor, but is a blend of elements each of which can occur separately or in non-religious experiences, its psychological peculiarity must consist in the characteristic way in which these elements are blended in it. Can this peculiar structural feature of religious experience be indicated and described? (ii) *What are the genetic and causal conditions* of the existence of religious experience? Can we trace the origin and development of the disposition to have religious experiences (*a*) in the human race, and (*b*) in each individual? Granted that the disposition is present in nearly all individuals at the present time, can we discover and state the variable conditions which call it into activity on certain occasions and leave it in abeyance on others? (iii) Part of the content of religious experience is alleged knowledge or well-founded belief about the nature of reality, e.g., that we are dependent on a being who loves us and whom we ought to worship, that values are somehow conserved in spite of the chances and changes of the material world at the mercy of which they seem *prima facie* to be, and so on. Therefore there is a third problem. Granted that religious experience exists, that it has such-and-such a history and conditions, that it seems vitally important to those who have it, and that it produces all kinds of effects which would not otherwise happen, is it *veridical*? Are the claims to knowledge or well-founded belief about the nature of reality, which are an integral part of the experience, *true or probable*? Now, in the case of musical experience, there are analogies to the psychological problem and to the genetic or causal problem, but there is no analogy to the epistemological problem of validity. For, so far as I am aware, no part of the content of musical experience is alleged knowledge about the nature of reality; and therefore no question of its being veridical or delusive can arise.

Since both musical experience and religious experience certainly exist, any theory of the universe which was incompatible with their existence would be false, and any theory which failed to show the connexion between their existence and the other facts about reality would be inadequate. So far the two kinds of experience are in exactly the same position. But a theory which answers to the condition that it allows of the existence of religious experience and indicates the *connexion* between its existence and other facts about reality may leave the question as to its *validity* quite unanswered. Or, alternatively it may throw grave doubt on its cognitive claims, or else it may tend to support them. Suppose, e.g., that it could be shown that religious experience contains no elements which are not factors in other kinds of experience. Suppose further it could be shown that this particular combination of factors tends to originate and to be activated only under certain conditions which are known to be very commonly productive of false beliefs held with strong conviction. Then a satisfactory answer to the questions of psychological analysis and causal antecedents would have tended to answer the epistemological question of validity in the negative. On the other hand, it might be that the only theory which would satisfactorily account for the origin of the religious disposition and for the occurrence of actual religious experiences under certain conditions was a theory which allowed some of the cognitive claims made by religious experience to be true or probable. Thus the three problems, though entirely distinct from each other, may be very closely connected; and it is the existence of the third problem in connexion with religious experience which puts it, for the present purpose, in a different category from musical experience.

In spite of this essential difference the analogy is not to be despised, for it brings out at least one important point. If a man who had no ear for music were to give himself airs on that account, and were to talk [disdainfully] about those who can appreciate music and think it highly important, we should regard him, not as an advanced thinker, but as a self-satisfied Philistine. And, then if he did not do this but only propounded theories about the nature and causation of musical experience, we might think it reasonable to feel very doubtful whether his theories would be adequate or correct. In the same way, when persons without religious experience regard themselves as being *on that ground* superior to those who have it, their attitude must be treated as merely silly and offensive. Similarly, any theories about religious experience constructed by persons who have little or none of their own should be regarded with grave suspicion. (For that reason it would be unwise to attach very much weight to anything that the present writer may say on this subject.)

On the other hand, we must remember that the possession of a great capacity for religious experience, like the possession of a great capacity for musical appreciation and composition, is no guarantee of high general intelligence. A man may be a saint or a magnificent musician and yet have very little common sense, very little power of accurate introspection or of seeing causal connexions, and scarcely any capacity for logical criticism. He may also be almost as ignorant about other aspects of reality as the non-musical or non-religious man is about musical or religious experience. If such a man starts to theorize about music or religion, his theories may be quite as absurd, though in a different way, as those made by persons who are devoid of musical or religious experience. Fortunately it happens that some religious mystics of a high order have been extremely good at introspecting and describing their own experiences. And some highly religious persons have had very great critical and philosophical abilities. St. Teresa is an example of the first, and St. Thomas Aquinas of the second.

Now I think it must be admitted that, if we compare and contrast the statements made by religious mystics of various times, races, and religions, we find a common nucleus combined with very great differences of detail. Of course the interpretations which they have put on their experiences are much more varied than the experiences themselves. It is obvious that the interpretations will depend in a large measure on the traditional religious beliefs in which various mystics have been brought up. I think that such traditions probably act in two different ways.

(i) The tradition no doubt affects the theoretical interpretation of experiences which would have taken place even if the mystic had been brought up in a different tradition. A feeling of unity with the rest of the universe will be interpreted very differently by a Christian who has been brought up to believe in a personal God and by a Hindu mystic who has been trained in a quite different metaphysical tradition.

(ii) The traditional beliefs, on the other hand, probably determine many of the details of the experience itself. A Roman Catholic mystic may have visions of the Virgin and the saints, whilst a Protestant mystic pretty certainly will not.

Thus the relations between the experiences and the traditional beliefs are highly complex. Presumably the outlines of the belief are determined by the experience. Then the details of the belief are fixed for a certain place and period by the special peculiarities of the experiences had by the founder of a certain religion. These beliefs then become traditional in that religion. Thenceforth they in part determine the details of the experiences had by subsequent mystics of that religion, and still more do they determine the interpretations which these mystics will put upon their experiences. Therefore, when a set of religious beliefs has once been established, it no doubt tends to produce experiences which can plausibly be taken as evidence for it. If it is a tradition in a certain religion that one can communicate with saints, mystics of that religion will seem to see and to talk with saints in their mystical visions; and this fact will betaken as further evidence for the belief that one can communicate with saints.

Much the same double process of causation takes place in sense-perception. On the one hand, the beliefs and expectations which we have at any moment largely determine what *interpretation* we shall put on a certain sensation which we should in any case have had then. On the other hand, our beliefs and expectations do to some extent determine and modify some of the sensible characteristics of the *sensa themselves*. When I am thinking only of diagrams a certain visual stimulus may produce a sensation of a sensibly flat sensum; but a precisely similar stimulus may produce a sensation of a sensibly solid sensum when I am thinking of solid objects.

Such explanations, however, plainly do not account for the first origin of religious beliefs, or for the features which are common to the religious experiences of persons of widely different times, races, and traditions.

Now, when we find that there are certain experiences which, though never very frequent in a high degree of intensity, have happened in a high degree among a few men at all times and places; and when we find that, in spite of differences in detail which we can explain, they involve certain fundamental conditions which are common and peculiar to them; two alternatives are open to us. (i) We may suppose that these men are in contact with an aspect of reality which is not revealed to ordinary persons in their everyday experience. And we may suppose that the characteristics which they agree in ascribing to reality on the basis of these experiences probably do belong to it. Or (ii) we may suppose that they are all subject to a delusion from which other men are free. In order to illustrate these alternatives it will be useful to consider three partly analogous cases, two of which are real and the third imaginary.

(*a*) Most of the detailed facts which biologists tells us about the minute structure and changes in cells can be perceived only by persons who have had a long training in the use of the microscope. In this case we believe that the agreement among trained microscopists really does correspond to facts which untrained persons cannot perceive. (*b*) Persons of all races who habitually drink alcohol to excess eventually have perceptual experiences in which they seem to themselves to see snakes or rats crawling about their rooms or beds. In this case we believe that this agreement among drunkards is merely a uniform hallucination. (*c*) Let us now imagine a race of beings who can walk about and touch things but cannot see. Suppose that eventually a few of them developed the power of sight. All that they might tell their still blind friends about colour would be wholly unintelligible to and unverifiable by the latter. But they would also be able to tell their blind friends a great deal about what the latter would feel if they were to walk in certain directions. These statements would be verified. This would not, of course, *prove* to the blind ones that the unintelligible statements about colour correspond to certain aspects of the world which they cannot perceive. But it would show that the seeing persons had a source of additional information about matters which the blind ones could understand and test for themselves. It would not be unreasonable then for the blind ones to believe that probably the seeing ones are also able to perceive other aspects of reality which they are describing correctly when they make their unintelligible statements containing colour-names. The question then is whether it is reasonable to regard the agreement between the experiences of religious mystics as more like the agreement among trained microscopists about the minute structure of cells, or as more like the agreement among habitual drunkards about the infestation of their rooms by pink rats or snakes, or as more like the agreement about colours which the seeing men would express in their statements to the blind men.

Why do we commonly believe that habitual excess of alcohol is a cause of a uniform delusion and not a source of additional information? The main reason is as follows. The things which drunkards claim to perceive are not fundamentally different in kind from the things that other people perceive. We have all seen rats and snakes, though the rats have generally been grey or brown and not pink. Moreover the drunkard claims that the rats and snakes which he sees are literally present in his room and on his bed, in the same sense in which his bed is in his room and his quilt is on his bed. Now we may fairly argue as follows. Since these are the sort of things which we could see if they were there, the fact that we cannot see them makes it highly probable that they are not there. Again, we know what kinds of perceptible effect would generally follow from the presence in a room of such things as rats or snakes. We should expect fox-terriers or mongooses to show traces of excitement, cheese to be nibbled, corn to disappear from bins, and so on. We find that no such effects are observed in the

bedrooms of persons suffering from *delirium tremens*. It therefore seems reasonable to conclude that the agreement among drunkards is a sign, not of a revelation, but of a delusion.

Now the assertions in which religious mystics agree are not such that they conflict with what we can perceive with our senses. They are about the structure and organization of the world as a whole and about the relations of men to the rest of it. And they have so little in common with the facts of daily life that there is not much chance of direct collision. I think that there is only one important point on which there is conflict. Nearly all mystics seem to be agreed that time and change and unchanging duration are unreal or extremely superficial, whilst these seem to plain men to be the most fundamental features of the world. But we must admit, on the one hand, that these temporal characteristics present very great philosophical difficulties and puzzles when we reflect upon them. On the other hand, we may well suppose that the mystic finds it impossible to state clearly in ordinary language what it is that he experiences about the facts which underlie the appearance of time and change and duration. Therefore it is not difficult to allow that what we experience as the temporal aspect of reality corresponds in some sense to certain facts, and yet that these facts appear to us in so distorted a form in our ordinary experience that a person who sees them more accurately and directly might refuse to apply temporal names to them.

Let us next consider why we feel fairly certain that the agreement among trained microscopists about the minute structure of cells expresses an objective fact, although we cannot get similar experiences. One reason is that we have learned enough, from simpler cases of visual perception, about the laws of optics to know that the arrangement of lenses in a microscope is such that it will reveal minute structure, which is otherwise invisible, and will not simply create optical delusions. Another reason is that we know of other cases in which trained persons can detect things which untrained people will overlook, and that in many cases the existence of these things can be verified by indirect methods.

Probably most of us have experienced such results of training in our own lives.

Now religious experience is not in nearly such a strong position as this. We do not know much about the laws which govern its occurrence and determine its variations. No doubt there are certain standard methods of training and meditation which tend to produce mystical experiences. These have been elaborated to some extent by certain Western mystics and to a very much greater extent by Eastern Yogis. But I do not think that we can see here, as we can in the case of microscopes and the training which is required to make the best use of them, any conclusive reason why these methods should produce veridical rather than delusive experiences. Uniform methods of training and meditation would be likely to produce more or less similar experiences, whether these experiences were largely veridical or wholly delusive.

Is there any analogy between the facts about religious experience and the fable about the blind men some of whom gained the power of sight? It might be said that many ideals of conduct and ways of life, which we can all recognize now to be good and useful, have been introduced into human history by the founders of religions. These persons have made actual ethical discoveries which others can afterwards recognize to be true. It might be said that this is at least roughly analogous to the case of the seeing men telling the still blind men of facts which the latter could and did verify for themselves. And it might be said that this makes it reasonable for us to attach some weight to what founders of religions tell us about things which we cannot understand or verify for ourselves; just as it would have been reasonable for the blind men to attach some weight to the unintelligible statements which the seeing men made to them about colours.

I think that this argument deserves a certain amount of respect, though I should find it hard to estimate how much weight to attach to it. I should be inclined to sum up as follows. When there is a nucleus of agreement between the experiences of men in different places, times, and traditions, and when they all tend to put much the same kind of interpretation on the cognitive content of these experiences, it is reasonable to ascribe this agreement to their all being in contact with a certain objective aspect of reality *unless* there be some positive reason to think otherwise. The practical postulate which we go upon everywhere else is to treat cognitive claims as veridical unless there be some positive reason to think them delusive. This, after all, is our only guarantee for believing that ordinary sense-perception is veridical. We cannot *prove* that what people agree in perceiving really exists independently of them; but we do always assume that ordinary waking sense-perception is veridical unless we can produce some positive ground for thinking that it is delusive in any given case. I think it would be inconsistent to treat the experiences of religious mystics on different principles. So far as they agree they should be provisionally accepted as veridical unless there be some positive ground for thinking that they are not. So the next question is whether there is any positive ground for holding that they are delusive.

There are two circumstances which have been commonly held to cast doubt on the cognitive claims of religious and mystical experience. (i) It is alleged that founders of religions and saints have nearly always had certain neuropathic symptoms or certain bodily weaknesses, and that these would be likely to produce delusions. Even if we accept the premises, I do not think that this is a very strong argument. (*a*) It is equally true that many founders of religions and saints have exhibited great endurance and great power of organization and business capacity which would have made them extremely successful and competent in secular affairs. There are very few offices in the cabinet or in the highest branches of the civil service which St. Thomas Aquinas could not have held with conspicuous success. I do not, of course, regard this as a positive reason *for* accepting the metaphysical doctrines which saints and founders of religions have based on their experiences; but it is relevant as a *rebuttal* of the argument which we are considering. (*b*) Probably very few people of extreme genius in science or art are perfectly normal mentally or physically, and some of them are very crazy and eccentric indeed. Therefore it would be rather surprising if persons of religious genius were completely normal, whether their experiences be veridical or delusive. (*c*) Suppose, for the sake of argument, that there is an aspect of the world which remains altogether outside the ken of ordinary persons in their daily life. Then it seems very likely that some degree of mental and physical abnormality would be a necessary condition for getting sufficiently loosened from the objects of ordinary sense perception to come into cognitive contact with this aspect of reality. Therefore the fact that those persons who claim to have this peculiar kind of cognition generally exhibit certain mental and physical abnormalities is rather what might be anticipated if their claims were true. One might need to be slightly 'cracked' in order to have some peep-holes into the supersensible world. (*d*) If mystical experience were veridical, it seems quite likely that it would *produce* abnormalities of behaviour in those who had it strongly. Let us suppose, for the sake of argument, that those who have religious experience are in frequent contact with an aspect of reality of which most men get only rare and faint glimpses. Then such persons are, as it were, living in two worlds, while the ordinary man is living in only one of them. Or, again, they might be compared to a man who has to conduct his life with one ordinary eye and another of a telescopic kind. Their behaviour may be appropriate to the aspect of reality which they alone perceive and think all-important; but, for that very reason, it may be inappropriate to those other aspects of reality which are all that most men perceive or judge to be important and on which all our social institutions and conventions are built.

(ii) A second reason which is commonly alleged for doubt about the claims of religious experience is the following. It is said that such experience always originates from and remains mixed with certain other factors, e.g., sexual emotion, which are such that experiences and beliefs that arise from them are very likely to be delusive. I think that there are a good many confusions on this point, and it will be worth while to begin by indicating some of them.

When people say that B 'originated from' A, they are liable to confuse at least three different kinds of connexion between A and B. (i) It might be that A is a necessary but insufficient condition of the existence of B. (ii) It might be that A is a necessary and sufficient condition of the existence of B. Or (iii) it might be that B simply is A in a more complex and disguised form. Now, when there is in fact evidence only for the first kind of connexion, people are very liable to jump to the conclusion that there is the third kind of connexion. It may well be the case, e.g., that no one who was incapable of strong sexual desires and emotions could have anything worth calling religious experience. But it is plain that the possession of a strong capacity for sexual experience is not a *sufficient* condition of having a religious experience; for we know that the former quite often exists in persons who show hardly any trace of the latter. But, even if it could be shown that a strong capacity for sexual desire and emotion is *both* necessary and sufficient to produce religious experience, it would not follow that the latter is just the former in disguise. In the first place, it is not at all easy to discover the exact meaning of this metaphorical phrase when it is applied to psychological topics. And, if we make use of physical analogies, we are not much helped. A mixture of oxygen and hydrogen in presence of a spark is necessary and sufficient to produce water accompanied by an explosion. But water accompanied by an explosion is not a mixture of oxygen and hydrogen and a spark 'in a disguised form,' whatever that may mean.

Now I think that the present rather vaguely formulated objection to the validity of the claims of religious experience might be stated somewhat as follows. 'In the individual, religious experience originates from, and always remains mixed with, sexual desires and emotions. The other generative factor of it is the religious tradition of the society in which he lives, the teachings of his parents, nurses, schoolmasters, etc. In the race religious experience originated from a mixture of false beliefs about nature and man, irrational fears, sexual and other impulses, and so on. Thus the religious tradition arose from beliefs which we now recognize to have been false and from emotions which we now recognize to have been irrelevant and misleading. It is now drilled into children by those who are in authority over them at a time of life when they are intellectually and emotionally at much the same stage as the primitive savages among whom it originated. It is, therefore, readily accepted, and it determines beliefs and emotional dispositions which persist long after the child has grown up and acquired more adequate knowledge of nature and of himself.'

Persons who use this argument might admit that it does not definitely *prove* that religious beliefs are false and groundless. False beliefs and irrational fears in our remote ancestors *might* conceivably be the origin of true beliefs and of an appropriate feeling of awe and reverence in ourselves. And, if sexual desires and emotions be an essential condition and constituent of religious experience, the experience *may* nevertheless be veridical in important respects. We might merely have to rewrite one of the beatitudes and say 'Blessed are the *impure* in heart, for they shall see God.' But, although it is logically possible that such causes should produce such effects, it would be said that they are most unlikely to do so. They seem much more likely to produce false beliefs and misplaced emotions.

It is plain that this argument has considerable plausibility. But it is worth while to remember that modern science has almost as humble an ancestry as contemporary religion. If the primitive witch-smeller is the spiritual progenitor of the Archbishop of Canterbury, the primitive rain-maker is equally the spiritual progenitor of the Cavendish Professor of Physics. There has obviously been a gradual refinement and purification of religious beliefs and concepts in the course of history, just as there has been in the beliefs and concepts of science. Certain persons of religious genius, such as some of the Hebrew prophets and the founders of Christianity and of Buddhism, do seem to have introduced new ethico-religious concepts and beliefs which

have won wide acceptance, just as certain men of scientific genius, such as Galileo, Newton, and Einstein, have done in the sphere of science. It seems somewhat arbitrary to count this process as a continual approximation to true knowledge of the material aspect of the world in the case of science, and to refuse to regard it as at all similar in the case of religion. Lastly, we must remember that all of us have accepted the current common-sense and scientific view of the material world on the authority of our parents, nurses, masters, and companions at a time when we had neither the power nor the inclination to criticize it. And most of us accept, without even understanding, the more recondite doctrines of contemporary physics simply on the authority of those whom we have been taught to regard as experts.

On the whole, then, I do not think that what we know of the conditions under which religious beliefs and emotions have arisen in the life of the individual and the race makes it reasonable to think that they are *specially* likely to be delusive or misdirected. At any rate any argument which starts from that basis and claims to reach such a conclusion will need to be very carefully handled if its destructive effects are to be confined within the range contemplated by its users. It is reasonable to think that the concepts and beliefs of even the most perfect religions known to us are extremely inadequate to the facts which they express; that they are highly confused and are mixed up with a great deal of positive error and sheer nonsense; and that, if the human race goes on and continues to have religious experiences and to reflect on them, they will be altered and improved almost out of recognition. But all this could be said, *mutatis mutandis,* of scientific concepts and theories. The claim of any particular religion or sect to have complete or final truth on these subjects seems to me to be too ridiculous to be worth a moment's consideration. But the opposite extreme of holding that the whole religious experience of mankind is a gigantic system of pure delusion seems to me to be almost (though not quite) as far-fetched.

II.5   A Critique of the Argument from Religious Experience

LOUIS P. POJMAN

Louis Pojman (1935–2005), the original editor of this anthology, was professor of philosophy at the United States Military Academy, West Point, New York. In this article he analyzes religious experience, distinguishing between a strong and a weak justification for religious belief based on religious experience: A strong justification would make it rationally obligatory for everyone to believe in the conclusion of an argument. A weak justification would provide rational support only for those who had had an "of-God" experience (or already accepted the worldview that made such experiences likely). Pojman argues that only the weak version is plausible. Furthermore, the fact that religious experience fails in not being confirmable in the way perceptual experience is makes it highly problematic even for those who have had religious experiences.

The Ego has disappeared. I have realized my identity with Brahman and so all my desires have melted away. I have arisen above my ignorance and my knowledge of this seeming universe. What is this joy I feel? Who shall measure it? I know nothing but joy, limitless, unbounded! The treasure I have found there cannot be described in words. The mind cannot conceive of it. My mind fell like a hailstone into that vast expanse of Brahman's ocean. Touching one drop of it, I melted away and became one with Brahman. Where is this universe? Who took it away? Has it merged into something else? A while ago, I beheld it—now it exists no longer. Is there anything apart or distinct from Brahman? Now, finally and clearly, I know that I am the Atman [the soul identified with Brahman], whose nature is eternal joy. I see nothing, I hear nothing, I know nothing that is separate from me.[1]

ENCOUNTERS WITH GOD

The heart of religion is and always has been experiential. Encounters with the supernatural, a transcendent dimension, the Wholly Other are at the base of every great religion. Abraham hears a Voice that calls him to leave his family in Haran and venture out into a broad unknown, thus becoming the father of Israel. Abraham's grandson, Jacob, wrestles all night with an angel and is transformed, gaining the name "Israel, prince of God." While tending his father-in-law's flock, Moses is appeared to by "I am that I am" (Yahweh) in the burning bush and ordered to deliver Israel out of slavery into a land flowing with milk and honey. Isaiah has a vision of the Lord "high and exalted, and the train of his robe filled the temple" of heaven. In the New Testament, John, James, and Peter behold Jesus gloriously transformed on the Mount of Transfiguration and are themselves transformed by the experience. After the death of Jesus, Saul is traveling to Damascus to persecute Christians, when he is met by a blazing light and hears a Voice, asking him why he is persecuting the Lord.[2] Changing his name to Paul, he becomes the leader of the Christian missionary movement. The Hindu experiences the Atman (soul) as the Brahman (God), "That art Thou," or beholds the glories of Krishna. The Advaitian Hindu

Reprinted from *Philosophy: The Pursuit of Wisdom* (Wadsworth Publishing Co., 2001). Copyright © 2001 Louis P. Pojman.

merges with the One, as a drop of water merges with the vast ocean. The Buddhist merges with Nirvana or beholds a vision of the Buddha.[3] Allah reveals his holy word, the Koran, to Mohammed. Joan of Arc hears voices calling on her to save her people, and Joseph Smith has a vision of the angel Moroni calling him to do a new work for God.

Saints, mystics, prophets, ascetics, and common believers—of every creed, of every race, in every land, and throughout recorded history—have undergone esoteric experiences that are hard to explain but impossible to dismiss as mere nonsense. Common features appear to link these otherwise disparate experiences to one another, resulting in a common testimony to this Otherness, a *consensus mysticum*. Rudolf Otto characterizes the religious (or "numinal" spiritual) dimension in all of these experiences as the "mysterium tremendum et fascinans."[4] Religion is an unfathomable mystery, *tremendum* ("to be trembled at"), awe-inspiring, *fascinans* ("fascinating"), and magnetic. To use a description from Søren Kierkegaard, religious experience is a "sympathetic antipathy and an antipathetic sympathy" before a deep unknown.[5] Like looking into an abyss, it both repulses and strangely attracts.

AN ANALYSIS OF RELIGIOUS EXPERIENCE

What, then, is the problem with religious experience? If I say that I hear a pleasant tune, and you listen and say, "Yes, I hear it now too," we have no problem; but if you listen carefully and don't hear it, you might well wonder whether I am really hearing sounds or only imagining that I am. Perhaps we could bring in others to check out the matter. If they agree with me, well and good; but if they agree with you and don't hear the sounds, then we have a problem. Perhaps, we could bring in an audiometer to measure the decibels in the room. If the meter confirms my report, then it is simply a case of my having better hearing than you and the rest of the witnesses; but if the meter doesn't register at all, assuming that it is in working order, we would then have good evidence

that I am only imagining the sounds. Perhaps, I need to change my claim and say, "Well, I seem to be hearing a pleasant tune."

One problem is that religious experience is typically private. You have the sense of God forgiving you or an angel speaking to you, but I, who am in the same room with you, neither hear, nor see, nor feel anything unusual. You are praying and suddenly feel transported by grace and sense the unity of all reality. I, who am sitting next to you, wonder at the strange expression on your face and ask you if something is wrong. Perhaps your brain is experiencing an altered chemical or electrical state?

Yet, religious experiences of various types have been reported by numerous people, from dairymaids like Joan of Arc to mystics like Teresa of Avila and St. John of the Cross. They cannot be simply dismissed without serious analysis.

There are two levels of problem here: (1) To what degree, if any, is the subject of a religious experience justified in inferring from the psychological experience (the subjective aspect) to the existential or ontological reality of that which is the object of the experience (the objective aspect)? (2) To what degree, if any, does the cumulative witness of those undergoing religious experience justify the claim that there is a God or transcendent reality?

Traditionally, the argument from religious experience has not been one of the "proofs" for God's existence. At best, it has confirmed and made existential what the proofs conveyed with icy logic. Some philosophers, such as C. D. Broad (1887–1971), as well as contemporary philosophers, such as Richard Swinburne and Gary Gutting, believe that the common experience of mystics is *strong justification* or evidence for all of us for the existence of God.[6] Others, such as William James (1842–1910), believe that religious experience is sufficient evidence for the subject himself or herself for the existence of a divine reality, but only constitutes a possibility for the nonexperiencer. That is, religious experience grants us only *weak justification*. Religious skeptics, like Walter Stace (1886–1967) and Bertrand Russell (1872–1970), doubt this and argue that a subjective experience by itself is never a sufficient warrant for making an existential claim (of an object existing outside oneself). It is a fallacy to go from the psychological experience of *X* to the reality of *X*.

There are two main traditions regarding religious experience. One, which we can call *mystical*, posits the unity of all reality or the unity of the subject with its object (the mystic is absorbed in God, becomes one with God, etc.). The second type of religious experience can be called simply *religious experience* in order to distinguish it from the mystical. It does not conflate the subject with the object but is a numinal experience wherein the believer (or subject) experiences the presence of God or an angel or Christ or the Holy Spirit, either speaking to or appearing to the experient or forgiving him or her. While in prayer, believers often experience a sense of the presence of God or the Holy Spirit.

Many psychological explanations of religious experience cast doubt on its validity. One of the most famous is the Freudian interpretation. Sigmund Freud said that it was the result of the projection of the father image within oneself. The progression goes like this. When you were a child, you looked upon your father as a powerful hero who could do everything, meet all your needs, and overcome the normal obstacles that hindered your way at every step. When you grew older, you sadly realized that your father was fallible and very finite, indeed, but you still had the need of the benevolent, all-powerful father. So, subconsciously you projected your need for that long-lost parent onto the empty heavens and invented a god for yourself. Because this is a common phenomena, all of us who have successfully "projected daddy onto the big sky" go to church or synagogue or mosque or whatever and worship the illusion on our favorite holy day. But it is a myth. The sky is empty, and the sooner we realize it, the better for everyone.

This is one explanation of religious experience and religion in general. It is not a disproof of God's existence, simply an hypothesis. Even if it is psychologically true that we tend to think of God like a powerful and loving parent, it could still be the case that the parental relationship is

God's way of teaching us about himself—by analogy.

In his classic on the subject, *Varieties of Religious Experience* (1902), James describes what he considers the deepest kind of religious experience, mystical experience, a type of experience that transcends our ordinary, sensory experience and that cannot be described in terms of our normal concepts and language. It is "ineffable experience." The experient realizes that the experience "defies expression, that no adequate report of its content can be given in words. It follows from this that its quality must be directly experienced; it cannot be imparted or transferred to others."[7] And yet it contains a noetic quality, a content. It purports to convey truth about the nature of reality, namely, that there is a unity of all things and that unity is spiritual, not material. It is antinaturalistic, pantheistic, and optimistic. Two other characteristics are predicated to this state. Mystical states are *transient*—that is, they cannot be sustained for long—and they are *passive*—that is, the mystic is acted upon by divine deliverance, grace. We can prepare ourselves for the experience, but it is something that happens to us, not something that we do.

James is cautious about what can be deduced from mystic experience. Although mystic states are and ought to be absolutely authoritative over the individuals to whom they come, "no authority emanates from them which should make it a duty for those who stand outside of them to accept their revelations uncritically." But their value is that they provide us a valid alternative to the "non-mystical rationalistic consciousness, based on understanding and the senses alone. They open up the possibility of other orders of truth, in which, so far as anything in us vitally responds to them, we may freely continue to have faith."

Broad goes even further than James. In his book *Religion, Philosophy, and Psychical Research* (1930), he likens the religious sense to an ear for music. There are a few people on the negative end who are spiritually tone deaf and a few on the positive end who are the founders of religion, the Bachs and Beethovens. In between are the ordinary followers of religion, who are like the average musical listener, and above them are the saints, who are likened to those with a very fine ear for music.

The chief difference is that religion, unlike music, says something about the nature of reality. Is what it says true? Does religious experience lend any support to the truth claims of religion? Is religious experience "veridical," and are the claims about "the nature of reality which are an integral part of the experience, true or probable?" Broad considers the argument from mystical agreement:

1. There is an enormous unanimity among the mystics concerning the spiritual nature of reality.
2. When there is such unanimity among observers as to what they take themselves to be experiencing, it is reasonable to conclude that their experiences are veridical (unless we have good reason to believe that they are deluded).
3. There are no positive reasons for thinking that mystical experiences are delusive.
4. ∴ It is reasonable to believe that mystical experiences are veridical.

Premise 3 is weak, for there is evidence that mystics are neuropathic or sexually repressed. Broad considers these charges, admits some plausibility in them, but suggests that they are not conclusive. Regarding the charge of neuropathology, he urges that "one might need to be slightly 'cracked' in order to have some peep-holes into the super-sensible world"; with regard to sexual abnormality, it could simply be the case that no one who was "incapable of strong sexual desires and emotions could have anything worth calling religious experience."

His own guarded judgment is that, given what we know about the origins of religious belief and emotions, there is no reason to think that religious experience is "specially likely to be delusive or misdirected," so that religious experience can be said to offer us strong justification for a transcendent reality.

Gutting develops Broad's strong-justification thesis further, arguing that religious experience "establishes the existence of a good and powerful being concerned about us, and [this] justifies a central core of religious belief."[8] On this basis, he argues that the essential validity of religion is vindicated. However, like Broad, he finds that this sort of justified belief "falls far short of the claims of traditional religions and that detailed religious accounts are nearly as suspect as nonreligious accounts. The heart of true religious belief is a realization that we have *access* to God but only minimal reliable *accounts* of his nature and relation to us." Gutting develops three criteria that veridical religious experiences must meet: They must be repeatable, be experienced by many in many diverse climes and cultures, and issue forth in morally better lives.

But in arguing for the strong-justification thesis, Gutting seems to me to have gone too far. A strong justification makes it rationally obligatory for everyone to believe in the conclusion of an argument, in this case, that God exists. A weak justification only provides rational support for those who have an "of-God" experience (or already accept the worldview that made such experiences likely). Gutting believes that he has given a strong justification for religious belief, sufficient to establish the existence of God, but there are reasons to suppose that the argument from religious experience offers, at best, only weak justification.

A CRITIQUE OF THE STRONG-JUSTIFICATION THESIS

Three criticisms of the strong thesis are the following:

1. Religious experience is too amorphous and disparate for us to generalize from in the way Gutting would have us do. That is, there are many varieties of religious experiences, which seem mutually contradictory or vague, so that it is not clear whether we can give the proper criteria necessary to select "of-God" experiences as veridical or having privileged status.
2. Justification of belief in the veridicality of religious experience is circular, so that the

belief in it will rest on premises that are not self-evident to everyone. In effect, all assessment of the veridicality of such experience depends on background beliefs.

3. When taken seriously as a candidate for veridical experience, religious experience has the liability of not being confirmed in the same way that perceptual experience is. That is, although religious experience may sometimes be veridical, it cannot be checked like ordinary perceptual experience, nor can we make predictions on account of it. This indicates that it cannot be used as an argument for the existence of God in the way that Gutting uses it.

Let us look closer at these counterarguments.

Religious Experience Is Amorphous and Varied

Religious experience is amorphous and too varied to yield a conclusion with regard to the existence of God. Consider the various types of religious experiences, most of which can be documented in the literature:

1. S senses himself absorbed into the One, wherein the subject-object distinction ceases to hold.
2. One senses the unity of all things and that she is nothing at all.
3. The Buddhist monk who is an atheist senses the presence of the living Buddha.
4. One senses the presence of God, the Father of our Lord Jesus Christ.
5. The Virgin Mary appears to S (in a dream).
6. The Lord Jesus appears to Paul on the road one afternoon, though no one else realizes it but him.
7. One senses the presence of Satan, convincing him that Satan is the highest reality.
8. Achilles is appeared to by the goddess Athene, whom he believes to be descended from Zeus's head. She promises that he will win the battle on the morrow.
9. Allah appears to S and tells him to purify the land by executing all infidels (e.g., Jews and

Christians) whose false worship corrupts the land.
10. A guilt-ridden woman senses the presence of her long-deceased father, assuring her that he has forgiven her of her neglect of him while he was aging and dying.
11. A mother senses the presence of the spirit of the river, telling her to throw back her deformed infant because it belongs to the river and not to her.
12. One senses the presence of the Trinity and understands how it could be that the three persons are one God, but he cannot tell others.
13. One senses the presence of the demiurge who has created the universe but makes no pretense to be omnipotent or omnibenevolent.
14. An atheist senses a deep infinite gratitude for the life of his son without in the least believing that a god exists (George Nakhnikian's personal example).
15. An atheist has a deep sense of nothingness in which she is absolutely convinced that the universe has manifested itself to her as a deep void.

The problem for those who would strongly justify the practice of religious experience—that is, show that we are rationally obligated to believe the content of the experience—is to differentiate the valid interpretations from the invalid. Which of these experiences are valid? That is, do any of these guarantee the truth of the propositions contained in the experience? For the believer or experient, each is valid for him or her, but why should the nonexperient accept any of these reports? And why should the experient continue to believe the content of the report himself after it is over and after he notes that there are other possible interpretations of it or that others have had mutually contradictory experiences? It would seem that they cancel each other out. Note the disparity of different types of "nonphysical" or religious experiences in the preceding list. There is not even any consensus that there is one supreme being, who is benevolent. Experiences 1 through 3 do not involve a divine being at all. Contrary to what

Gutting says about the virtual universality of god experiences, the branches of Buddhism and Hinduism (in experiencing Nirvana) have religious experiences without experiencing a god. Furthermore, experience 7 supposes that the supreme being is evil, and experience 13 denies omnibenevolence. Experiences 14 and 15 have all the self-authenticating certainty of a religious experience but involve a conviction that no God exists. Do we understand how to distinguish genuine religious experiences from "spiritually" secular ones like experience 14? Why should we believe that the testimony of "of-God" experients is veridical, but not the other types (e.g., 1–3, 7–9, 11, 13, and 15) that are inconsistent with it? The very private nature of religious experience should preclude our being hasty in inferring from the psychological state to the reality of the object of the experience.

Gutting recognizes the diversity of religious experiences but fails to realize how troublesome this is for his thesis. He tries to find a core in these experiences to the effect that there is a "good and powerful non-human being who cares about us."[9] Gutting admits that we can't derive very much from "of-God" experiences, only that there is a being who is more powerful than us, very powerful and very good. But even if his argument were to show this, would it be sufficient as a definition of "God"? What would be the difference between this and experience 13, Plato's finite demiurge, or experience 10, the guilt-ridden woman's sense of her father, who presumably was both mentally and physically more powerful than she? (He was Arthur Conan Doyle, a genius and pugilist.) How would this show that there is a God, whom we should worship? How would this differ from ancestor worship or polytheism? Or a visitor from outer space? All of these could be "powerful, good, nonhuman, and caring for us." Why should we prefer the "of God" experiences to the "of-a-supreme-devil" experiences? Gutting rejects the notion of self-authentication as the guarantee for the veridicality of these religious experiences,[10] but if this is so, how does the experient tell the difference between the nonhuman being who cares for her and one who only

pretends to care? And how does one reidentify the being who has appeared to him in a nonsensory form?

Religious Experience Is Circular

Justification of belief in religious experience is circular, so that the belief in it will rest on premises that are not self-evident to everyone. If I am right about the difficulties in singling out "of-God" experiences from other deeply felt experiences, it would seem that we can only justify belief in the content of religious experience through circular reasoning, by setting forth hypothetical assumptions that we then take as constraints on the experience itself. For example, we suppose that God's ways are mysterious and beyond finding out, and so we are ready to accept our fellow believer's testimony of a deep "of-God" experience. A polytheist in East Africa already believes that the hippopotamus-god appears to women with deformed children in dreams, asking for them back and so credits his wife with a veridical experience when she reports that she has had such an encounter in a dream.

It would seem, then, that whether or not our interpretations of religious experience are justified depends on our background beliefs and expectations. Our beliefs appear to form a network, or web, in which all our beliefs are variously linked and supported by other beliefs. Some beliefs (call them "core beliefs"—e.g., my belief that 2 + 2 = 4 or that there are other minds or that I am not now dreaming) are more centrally located and interconnected than other beliefs. If our core beliefs fall, our entire noetic structure is greatly affected, whereas some beliefs are only loosely connected to our noetic structure (e.g., my belief that the Dodgers will win the pennant this year or that it is better to have an IBM PC computer than a Macintosh). Similarly, religious people and nonreligious people often differ by having fundamentally different propositions at or near the center of their noetic structure. The religious person already is predisposed to have theistic-type religious experiences, whereas the nonreligious person is not usually so disposed (in the literature, Christians have visions of Jesus; Hindus, of Krishna; Buddhists, of Buddha; ancient Greeks, of Athene and Apollo; etc.). If you had been brought up in a Hindu culture, wouldn't you be more likely to have Hindu religious experiences than a Christian type? Would there be enough in common for you to decide that both really converged to a common truth?

All experiencing takes place within the framework of a worldview. Certain features of the worldview may gradually or suddenly change in importance, thus producing a different total picture, but there is no such thing as neutral evaluation of the evidence. As we have noted, what we see depends to some degree on our background beliefs and expectations. The farmer, real estate dealer, and the artist looking at the same field do not see the same field. Neither do the religious person and the atheist see the same thing when evaluating other people's religious experience.

It might be supposed that we could agree on some criteria of assessment in order to arrive at the best explanatory theory regarding religious experience, and there are, of course, competing explanations. There are Freudian, Marxian, and naturalist accounts that, suitably revised, seem to be as internally coherent as the sophisticated theist account. For one account to win our allegiance, it would be necessary for that account to win out over all others. To do this, we would have to agree on the criteria to be met by explanatory accounts. But it could turn out that there are competing criteria, so that theory A would fulfill criteria 1 and 2 better than theories B and C; but B would fulfill criteria 3 and 4 better than the others, whereas C might have the best overall record without fulfilling any of the criteria best of all. It could be a close second in all of them. At this point, it looks like the very formulation and preference of the criteria of assessment depend on the explanatory account that one already embraces. The theist may single out *self-authentication* of the "of-God" experience, but why should that convince the atheist who suspects that criterion in the first place? It

seems that there is no unambiguous, noncircular consensus of a hierarchy of criteria.

Gutting is confident of a core content that would be experienced (1) repeatedly, (2) by many, and (3) in such a way that these will be led to live better moral lives.[11] But why should this convince a naturalist who already has a coherent explanation of this phenomena? Plato's "noble lie" (a lie that is useful to achieve social harmony) presumably would have had the same effect, but it still is a lie. Even if we took a survey and discovered that the "of-God" experiences were common to all people, what would that in itself prove? We might still have grounds to doubt its veridicality. As Richard Gale notes, mere unanimity or agreement among observers is not a sufficient condition for the truth of what is experienced:

> Everybody who presses his finger on his eyeball will see double, everybody who stands at a certain spot in the desert will see a mirage, etc. The true criterion for objectivity is the Kantian one: An experience is objective if its contents can be placed in a spatiotemporal order with other experiences in accordance with scientific laws.[12]

Gale may go too far in limiting objectivity to that which is accessible to scientific laws, but his negative comments about unanimity are apposite.

Let me illustrate this point in another way. Suppose Timothy Leary had devised a psychogenic pill that had this result: Everyone taking it had a "deep religious experience" exactly similar to that described by the Western theistic mystics. Would this be good evidence for the existence of God? Perhaps some would be justified in believing it to be. We could predict the kinds of religious experience atheists would have upon taking the pill. But suppose, further, that upon taking *two* of the same pills, everyone had a deep religious experience common only to a remote primitive tribe: sensing the presence of a pantheon of gods, one being a three-headed hippopotamus who created the lakes and rivers of the world but didn't care a bit about people. The fact that there was complete agreement about what was experienced in these states hardly *by itself* can count for strong evidence for the truth of the existential claims of the experience. It would be likely that theists took the experience to be veridical until they had a double dosage, and it would be likely that the tribes people believed the double dosage to be veridical until they took a single dosage. Doesn't this indicate that it is our accepted background beliefs that predispose us to accept or reject that which fits or doesn't fit into our worldview?

Religious Experience Cannot Be Confirmed

When taken seriously as candidates of veridical experience, religious experience fails in not being confirmed in the same way that perceptual experience is. There is, however, one criterion of assessment that stands out very impressively in the minds of all rational people (indeed, it is one of the criteria of rationality itself) but that is unduly ignored by proponents of the argument from religious experience, like Gutting. It is the Achilles' heel (if anything is) of those who would place too much weight on religious experience as *evidence* for the content of religion. This is the complex criterion of *checkability–predictability* (I link them purposefully). The chemist who says that Avogadro's law holds (i.e., equal volumes of different gases at the same temperature and pressure contain an equal number of molecules) predicts exactly to what degree the inclusion of certain gases will increase the overall weight of a gaseous compound. Similarly, if, under normal circumstances, we heat water to 100°C, we can predict that it will boil. If you doubt my observation, check it out yourself. After suitable experiment, we see these propositions confirmed in such a way as to leave little room for doubt in our minds about their truth. After studying some chemistry, we see that they play a role in a wider network of beliefs that are mutually supportive. The perceptual beliefs force themselves on us.

This notion of predictability can be applied to social hypotheses as well. For instance, an orthodox Marxist states that if his theory is true, capitalism will begin to collapse in industrialized countries. If it doesn't, we begin to doubt Marxism. Of course, the Marxist may begin to revise her theory and bring in *ad hoc* hypotheses to explain why what was expected didn't occur, but the more ad hoc hypotheses she has to bring to bear in order to explain why the general thesis isn't happening, the weaker the hypothesis itself becomes. We come to believe many important propositions through experiment, either our own or those of others whom we take as authoritative (for the moment at least). With regard to authority, the presumption is that we could check out the propositions in question if we had time or need to do so.

How do we confirm the truth of religious experience? Does it make any predictions that we could test now in order to say, "Look and see, the fact that X occurs shows that the content of the religious experience is veridical"? How do we check on other people's religious experiences, especially if they purport to be nonsensory perceptions?

The checkability factor is weak in Gutting's account. He claims that we have a duty to believe simply on the report of others, not on the basis of our own experience or any special predictions that the experient would be able to make. But, if the Bible is to be believed, this wasn't always the case, nor should it be today. We read in 1 Kings 18 that to convince the Israelites that Yahweh, and not Baal, was worthy of being worshipped, Elijah challenged the priests of Baal to a contest. He proposed that they prepare a bullock and call on Baal to set fire to it. Then he would do the same with Yahweh. The priests failed, but Elijah succeeded. Convincing evidence! Similarly, at the end of Mark, we read of Jesus telling his disciples that "signs shall follow them that believe; in my name shall they cast out devils; they shall speak with new tongues; they shall take up serpents; and if they drink any deadly thing, it shall not hurt them; they shall lay hands on the sick, and they shall recover" (Mark 16:17, 18). Some believers doubt whether this text is authentic, and others seek to explain it away (e.g., "Jesus only meant his apostles and was referring to the apostolic age"), but if a religion is true, we might well expect some outward confirmation of it, such as we find in Elijah's actions at Mt. Carmel or in Jesus' miracles. The fact that religious experience isn't testable and doesn't yield any nontrivial predictions surely makes it less reliable than perceptual experience.

Not only doesn't religious experience usually generate predictions that are confirmed, but it sometimes yields false predictions. An example is an incident that happened to me as a student in an evangelical Christian college. A group of students believed that the Bible is the inerrant Word of God and cannot contain an untruth. Now the Gospel of Matthew 18:19 records Jesus as saying that "if two of you shall agree on earth as touching anything that they shall ask, it shall be done for them of my Father which is in heaven," and Matthew 17:20 tells of faith being able to move mountains: "Nothing shall be impossible for you." Verses in Mark confirm this, adding that God will answer our prayer if we pray in faith and do not doubt. So, one night several believers prayed through the entire night for the healing of a student who was dying of cancer. They prayed for her in childlike faith, believing that God would heal her. As morning broke, they felt the presence of God among them, telling them that their prayer had been answered. As they left rejoicing and were walking out of the room, they received the news that the woman had just died.

It is interesting to note that none of the participants lost faith in God over this incident. Some merely dismissed it as one of the mysteries of God's ways, others concluded that the Bible wasn't to be taken literally, and still others concluded that they hadn't prayed hard enough or with enough faith. But as far as the argument for the veridicality of the content of religion is concerned, this has to be taken as part of the total data. How it weighs against empirically successful prayers or times when the content of the experience was confirmed, I have no idea, and I think Gutting hasn't either. But unless we do, it is hard to see how the argument from religious

experience could be used as strong evidence for the existence of God *to anyone else except those who had the experiences.* As James concludes about mystical states (one form of religious experience), whereas those having the experience have a right to believe in their content, "no authority emanates from them which should make it a duty for those who stand outside of them to accept their revelations uncritically."

Let me close with an illustration of what might be a publicly verifiable experience of God, one that would be analogous to the kind of perceptual experience by which we check scientific hypotheses. What if tomorrow morning (8 AM CST) there were a loud trumpet call and all over North America people heard a voice speak out, saying, "I am the Lord, your God, speaking. I have a message for you all. I am deeply saddened by the violence and lack of concern you have for one another. I am calling upon all nations to put aside nuclear weapons. This same message is being delivered to all other nations of Earth at different times today. I want you to know that I will take all means necessary to prevent a nuclear war and punish those nations who persist on the mad course on which they are now embarked. I love each one of you. A few signs will confirm this message. Later today, while speaking to Israel and the Arab states, I will cause an island, which is intended as a homeland for the Palestinians, to appear west of Lebanon in the Mediterranean. I will also cause the Sahara desert to become fruitful in order to provide food for the starving people in that area. But I will have you know that I will not intervene often in your affairs. Imaking this exception simply because it is an emergency situation."

Imagine that all over the world the same message is conveyed during the next twenty-four hours and the predictions fulfilled. Would your religious faith be strengthened by such an event? The question is, Why don't religious experiences like this happen? If there is a God, why does he seem to hide from us? Why doesn't God give us more evidence? I leave this question for you to reflect on.

SUMMARY

Religious experience is at the core of the religious life. Throughout the ages, in virtually every culture, people have reported deeply religious, even mystical, experiences that have confirmed their beliefs and added meaning to their lives. Yet problems surround the phenomena: There are discrepancies between accounts, they tend to be amorphous and varied, and they seldom are verified.

NOTES

1. Shankara's *Crest Jewel of Discrimination*, trans. Swami Prabhavandanda (New York: Mentor Books, 1970), 103–104.

2. "Now as he journeyed, Saul approached Damascus, and suddenly a light from heaven flashed about him. And he fell to the ground and heard a voice saying to him, 'Saul, Saul, why do you persecute me?' And he said, 'Who are you, Lord?' And he said, 'I am Jesus whom you are persecuting; but rise and enter the city, and you will be told what you are to do.' The men traveling with him stood speechless, hearing the voice but seeing no one. Saul arose from the ground; and when his eyes were opened, he could see nothing; so they led him into Damascus" (Acts 9).

3. Here is an illustration of Buddhist meditation:

> Of one who has entered the first trance the voice has ceased; of one who has entered the second trance reasoning and reflection have ceased; of one who has entered the third trance joy has ceased; of one who has entered the fourth trance the inspiration and expiration have ceased; of one who has entered the realm of the infinity of space the perception of form has ceased; of one who has entered the realm of the infinity of consciousness the perception of

the realm of the infinity of space has ceased; of one who has entered the realm of nothingness the perception of the realm of the infinity of consciousness has ceased. [*Samyutta-Nikaya* 36:115, in *Buddhism in Translation*, ed. Henry C. Warren (New York: Atheneum, 1973), 384.]

4. Rudolf Otto, *The Idea of the Holy* (Oxford: Oxford University Press, 1958).

5. Søren Kierkegaard, *The Concept of Dread* (Princeton, NJ: Princeton University Press, 1939).

6. C. D. Broad, *Religion, Philosophy, and Psychical Research* (London: Routledge & Kegan Paul, 1930); Richard Swinburne, *The Existence of God* (Oxford: Clarendon Press, 1979); and Gary Gutting, *Religious Belief and Religious Skepticism* (Notre Dame, IN: University of Notre Dame Press, 1982).

7. James, op. cit., 371. Here is another testimony reported by James:

> I remember the night, and almost the very spot on the hilltop, where my soul opened out, as it were, into the Infinite, and there was a rushing together of the two worlds, the inner and the outer. I stood alone with Him who had made me, and all the beauty of the world, and love, and sorrow, and even temptation. I did not seek Him, but felt the perfect unison of my spirit with His. The darkness held a presence that was all the more felt because it was not seen. I could not any more have doubted that He was there than that I was. I felt myself to be, if possible, the less real of the two. (p. 67)

8. Gutting, op. cit.

9. Ibid., 113.

10. Ibid., 145.

11. Ibid., 152.

12. Richard Gale, "Mysticism and Philosophy," *Journal of Philosophy* (1960).

II.6   Religious Experience and Religious Belief

WILLIAM P. ALSTON

In the last reading in this part, "Religious Experience and Religious Belief," William Alston (1921–   ), emeritus professor of philosophy at Syracuse University and one of the leading figures in the fields of epistemology and philosophy of religion throughout the past forty years, argues that religious experience can provide grounds for religious belief. Do not be intimidated by Alston's use of symbols; they are simply a convenient shorthand. For example, one of Alston's central theses is as follows: "CP will be J_{nw} for S provided S has no significant reason for regarding it as unreliable." Parsed out, this reads, "Christian practices are justified in the weak, normative sense for a person (S = subject) provided that the person has no significant reason for regarding that practice as unreliable."

I

Can religious experience provide any ground or basis for religious belief? Can it serve to justify religious belief, or make it rational? This paper will differ from many others in the literature by virtue of looking at this question in the light of basic epistemological issues. Throughout we will be comparing the epistemology of religious experience with the epistemology of sense experience.

We must distinguish between experience directly, and indirectly, justifying a belief. It indirectly justifies belief B_1 when it justifies some other beliefs, which in turn justify B_1. Thus I have learned indirectly from experience that Beaujolais wine is fruity, because I have learned from experience that this, that, and the other bottle of Beaujolais is fruity, and these propositions support the generalization. Experience will directly justify a belief when the justification does not go through other beliefs in this way. Thus, if I am justified, just by virtue of having the visual experiences I am now having, in taking what I am experiencing to be a typewriter situated directly in front of me, then the belief that there is a typewriter directly in front of me is directly justified by that experience.

We find claims to both direct and indirect justification of religious beliefs by religious experience. Where someone believes that her new way of relating herself to the world after her conversion is to be explained by the Holy Spirit imparting supernatural graces to her, she supposes her belief *that the Holy Spirit imparts graces to her* to be indirectly justified by her experience. What she directly learns from experience is that she sees and reacts to things differently; this is then taken as a reason for supposing that the

Holy Spirit is imparting graces to her. When, on the other hand, someone takes himself to be experiencing the presence of God, he thinks that his experience justifies him in supposing that God is *what* he is experiencing. Thus, he supposes himself to be directly justified by his experience in believing God to be present to him.

In this paper I will confine myself to the question of whether religious experience can provide direct justification for religious belief. This has implications for the class of experiences we shall be considering. In the widest sense 'religious experience' ranges over any experiences one has in connection with one's religious life, including any joys, fears, or longings one has in a religious context. But here I am concerned with experiences that could be taken to *directly* justify religious beliefs, i.e. experiences that give rise to a religious belief and that the subject takes to involve a direct awareness of what the religious belief is about. To further focus the discussion, let's confine ourselves to beliefs to the effect that God, as conceived in theistic religions, is doing something that is directed to the subject of the experience—that God is speaking to him, strengthening him, enlightening him, giving him courage, guiding him, sustaining him in being, or just being present to him. Call these "M-beliefs" ('M' for 'manifestation').

Note that our question concerns what might be termed a general "epistemic practice," the accepting of M-beliefs on the basis of experience, rather than some particular belief of that sort. I hold that practices, or habits, of belief formation are the primary subject of justification and that

---

Reprinted by permission of the author and of the editor of *NOÛS*, Vol. 16 (1982):3–12. Footnotes deleted.

particular beliefs are justified only by issuing from a practice (or the activation of a habit) that is justified. The following discussion of concepts of justification will provide grounds for that judgment.

Whether M-beliefs can be directly justified by experience depends, *inter alia*, on what it is to be justified in a belief. So let us take a look at that.

First, the justification about which we are asking is an "epistemic" rather than a "moral" or "prudential" justification. Suppose one should hold that the practice in question is justified because it makes us feel good. Even if this is true in a sense, it has no bearing on epistemic justification. But why not? What makes a justification *epistemic*? Epistemic justification, as the name implies, has something to do with knowledge, or, more broadly, with the aim at attaining truth and avoiding falsity. At a first approximation, I am justified in believing that p when, from the point of view of that aim, there is something O.K., all right, to be approved, about that fact that I believe that p. But when we come to spell this out further, we find that a fundamental distinction must be drawn between two different ways of being in an epistemically commendable position.

On the one hand there is what we may call a "normative" concept of epistemic justification (J_n), "normative" because it has to do with how we stand *vis-a-vis* norms that specify our intellectual obligations, obligations that attach to one *qua* cognitive subject, *qua* truth-seeker. Stated most generally, J_n consists in one's not having violated one's intellectual obligations. We have to say "not having violated" rather than "having fulfilled" because in all normative spheres, *being justified* is a negative status; it amounts to one's behavior not being in violation of the norms. If belief is under direct voluntary control, we may think of intellectual obligations as attaching directly to believing. Thus one might be obliged to refrain from believing in the absence of adequate evidence. But if, as it seems to me, belief is not, in general, under voluntary control, obligations cannot attach directly to believing. However, I do have voluntary control over moves that can influence a particular belief formation, e.g., looking for more evidence, and moves that can affect my general belief-forming habits or tendencies,

e.g., training myself to be more critical of testimony. If we think of intellectual obligations as attaching to activities that are designed to influence belief formation, we may say that a certain epistemic practice is normatively justified provided it is not the case that the practitioner would not have engaged in it had he satisfied intellectual obligations to engage in activities designed to inhibit it. In other words, the practice is justified if and only if the practitioner did not fail to satisfy an obligation to inhibit it.

However epistemologists also frequently use the term 'justified' in such a way that it has to do not with how the subject stands *vis-a-vis* obligations, but rather with the strength of her epistemic position in believing that p, with how likely it is that a belief of that sort acquired or held in that way is true. To say that a practice is justified in this, as I shall say, "evaluative" sense (J_e), is to say that beliefs acquired in accordance with that practice, in the sorts of circumstances in which human beings typically find themselves, are generally true. Thus we might say that a practice is J_e if and only if it is reliable.

One further complication in the notion of J_n remains to be canvassed. What is our highest reasonable aspiration for being J_n in accepting a belief on the basis of experience? Being J_n no matter what else is the case? A brief consideration of sense perception would suggest a negative answer. I may be justified in believing that there is a tree in front of me by virtue of the fact that I am currently having a certain kind of sense experience, but this will be true only in "favorable circumstances." If I am confronted with a complicated arrangement of mirrors, I may not be justified in believing that there is an oak tree in front of me, even though it looks for all the world as if there is. Again, it may look for all the world as if water is running uphill, but the general improbability of this greatly diminishes the justification the corresponding belief receives from that experience.

What this shows is that the justification provided by one's experience is only defeasibly so. It is inherently liable to be overridden, diminished, or cancelled by stronger considerations to the contrary. Thus the justification of beliefs about the physical environment that is provided by sense experience is a defeasible or, as we might say, *prima facie* justification. By virtue of having the experience, the subject is in a position such that she will be adequately justified in the belief *unless* there are strong enough reasons to the contrary.

It would seem that direct experiential justification for *M*-beliefs, is also, at most, *prima facie*. Beliefs about the nature and ways of God are often used to override *M*-beliefs, particularly beliefs concerning communications from God. If I report that God told me to kill all phenomenologists, fellow Christians will, no doubt, dismiss the report on the grounds that God would not give me any such injunction as that. I shall take it that both sensory experience and religious experience provide, at most, *prima facie* justification.

One implication of this stand is that a particular experiential epistemic practice will have to include some way of identifying defeaters. Different theistic religions, even different branches of the same religion, will differ in this regard, e.g., with respect to what sacred books, what traditions, what doctrines are taken to provide defeaters. We also find difference of this kind in perceptual practice. For example, with the progress of science new defeaters are added to the repertoire. Epistemic practices can, of course, be individuated with varying degrees of detail. To fix our thoughts with regard to the central problem of this paper let's think of a "Christian epistemic practice" (*CP*) that takes its defeaters from the Bible, the classic creeds, and certain elements of tradition. There will be differences between subsegments of the community of practitioners so defined, but there will be enough commonality to make it a useful construct. My foil to *CP*, the practice of forming beliefs about the physical environment on the basis of sense-experience, I shall call "perceptual practice" (*PP*).

Actually it will prove most convenient to think of each of our practices as involving not only the formation of beliefs on the basis of experience, but also the retention of these beliefs in memory, the formation of rationally self-evident beliefs, and various kinds of reasoning on the basis of all this. *CP* will be the richer complex, since it will include the formation of perceptual beliefs in the usual way, while *PP* will not be thought of as including the distinctive experiential practice of *CP*.

One final preliminary note. J_n is relative to a particular person's situation. If practice P_1 is quite unreliable, I may still be J_n in engaging in it either because I have no way of realizing its unreliability or because I am unable to disengage myself: while you, suffering from neither of these disabilities, are not J_n. When we ask whether a given practice is J_n, we shall be thinking about some normal, reasonably well informed contemporary member of our society.

II

Let's make use of all this in tackling the question as to whether one can be justified in *CP* and in *PP*. Beginning with J_n, we will first have to determine more precisely what one's intellectual obligations are *vis-a-vis* epistemic practices. Since our basic cognitive aim is to come into possession of as much truth as possible and to avoid false beliefs, it would seem that one's basic intellectual obligation vis-a-vis practices of belief formation would be to do what one can (or, at least, do as much as could reasonably be expected of one) to see to it that these practices are as *reliable* as possible. But this still leaves us with an option between a stronger and a weaker view as to this obligation. According to the stronger demand one is obliged to refrain (or try to refrain) from engaging in a practice unless one has adequate reasons for supposing it to be reliable. In the absence of sufficient reasons for considering the practice reliable, it is not justified. Practices are guilty until proved innocent. While on the more latitudinarian view one is justified in engaging in a practice provided one does not have sufficient reasons for regarding it to be unreliable. Practices are innocent until proved guilty. Let's take J_{ns} as an abbreviation for 'justified in the normative sense on the stronger requirement,' and 'J_{nw}' as an abbreviation for 'justified in the normative sense on the weaker requirement.'

Now consider whether Mr. Everyman is J_{nw} in engaging in *PP*. It would seem so. Except for those who, like Parmenides and Bradley, have argued that there are ineradicable inconsistencies in the conceptual scheme involved in PP, philosophers have not supposed that we can show that sense perception is not a reliable guide to our immediate surroundings. Sceptics about PP have generally confined themselves to arguing that we can't show that perception is reliable; i.e., they have argued that PP is not J_{ns}. I shall assume without further ado that PP is J_{nw}.

J_{ns} and J_e can be considered together. Although a practice may actually be reliable without my having adequate reasons for supposing so, and vice versa, still in considering whether a given practice is reliable, we will be seeking to determine whether there are adequate reasons for supposing it reliable, that is whether Everyman *could* be possessed of such reasons. And if we hold, as we shall, that there are no such reasons, the question of whether they are possessed by one or another subject does not arise.

I believe that there are no adequate noncircular reasons for the reliability of PP but I will not be able to argue that point here. If I had a general argument I would unveil it, but, so far as I can see, this thesis is susceptible only of inductive support, by unmasking each pretender in turn. And since this issue has been in the forefront of the Western philosophical consciousness for several centuries, there have been many pretenders. I do not have time even for criticism of a few representative samples. Instead I will simply assume that PP is not J_{ns}, and then consider what bearing this widely shared view has on the epistemic status of CP.

If J_{nw} is the most we can have for perceptual practice, then if CP is also J_{nw} it will be in at least as strong an epistemic position as the former. (I shall assume without argument that CP can no more be noncircularly shown to be reliable than can PP.) And CP will be J_{nw} for S, provided S has no significant reasons for regarding it as unreliable. Are there any such reasons? What might they be? Well, for one thing, the practice might yield a system that is ineradicably internally inconsistent. (I am not speaking of isolated and remediable inconsistencies that continually pop up in every area of thought and experience.) For another, it might yield results that come

into ineradicable conflict with the results of other practices to which we are more firmly committed. Perhaps some fundamentalist Christians are engaged in an epistemic practice that can be ruled out on such grounds as these. But I shall take it as obvious that one can objectify certain stretches of one's experience, or indeed the whole of one's experience, in Christian terms without running into such difficulties.

III

One may grant everything I have said up to this point and still feel reluctant to allow that CP is J_{nw}. CP does differ from PP in important ways, and it may be thought that some of these differences will affect their relative epistemic status. The following features of PP, which it does not share with CP, have been thought to have this kind of bearing.

1. Within PP there are standard ways of checking the accuracy of any particular perceptual belief.
2. By engaging in PP we can discover regularities in the behavior of the objects putatively observed, and on this basis we can, to a certain extent, effectively predict the course of events.
3. Capacity for PP, and practice of it, is found universally among normal adult human beings.
4. All normal adult human beings, whatever their culture, use basically the same conceptual scheme in objectifying their sense experience.

If CP includes PP as a proper part, as I ruled on above, how can it lack these features? What I mean is that there is no analogue of these features for that distinctive part of CP by virtue of which it goes beyond PP. The extra element of CP does not enable us to discover extra regularities, e.g., in the behavior of God, or increase our predictive powers. M-beliefs are not subject to interpersonal check in the same way as perceptual beliefs. The practice of forming M-beliefs on the basis of experience is not engaged in by all normal adults. And so on.

Before coming to grips with the alleged epistemic bearing of these differences, I want to make two preliminary points. (1) We have to engage in *PP* to determine that this practice has features 1.–4., and that *CP* lacks them. Apart from observation, we have no way of knowing that, e.g., while all cultures agree in their way of cognizing the physical environment they differ in their ways of cognizing the divine, or that *PP* puts us in a position to predict while *CP* doesn't. It might be thought that this is loading the dice in favor of my opponent. If we are to use *PP*, rather than some neutral source, to determine what features it has, shouldn't the same courtesy of self-assessment be accorded *CP*? Why should it be judged on the basis of what we learn about it from another practice, while that other practice is allowed to grade itself? To be sure, this is a serious issue only if answers to these questions are forthcoming from *CP* that differ from those we arrive at by engaging in PP. Fortunately, I can avoid getting involved in these issues by ruling that what I am interested in here is how *CP* looks from the standpoint of *PP*. The person I am primarily concerned to address is one who, like all the rest of us, engages in *PP*, and who, like all of us except for a few outlandish philosophers, regards it as justified. My aim is to show this person that, on his own grounds, *CP* enjoys basically the same epistemic status as *PP*. Hence it is consonant with my purposes to allow *PP* to determine the facts of the matter with respect to both practices. (2) I could quibble over whether the contrast is as sharp as is alleged. Questions can be raised about both sides of the putative divide. On the *PP* side, is it really true that all cultures have objectified sense experience in the same way? Many anthropologists have thought not. And what about the idea that all normal adult human beings engage in the same perceptual practice? Aren't we loading the dice by taking participation in what we regard as standard perceptual practice as our basic criterion for normality? On the *CP* side, is it really the case that this practice reveals no regularities to us, or only that they are very different from regularities in the physical world? What about the point that God is faithful to His promises? Or that the pure in heart will

see God? However, I believe that when all legitimate quibbles have been duly registered there will still be very significant differences between the two practices in these respects. So rather than contesting the factual allegations, I will concentrate on the *de jure* issue as to what bearing these differences have on epistemic status.

How could the lack of 1.–4. prevent *CP* from being J_{nw}? Only by providing an adequate ground for a judgment of unreliability. And why suppose that? Of course, the lack of these features implies that we lack certain reasons we might conceivably have had for regarding *CP* as reliable. If we could ascertain that *PP* has those features, without using *PP* to do so, that would provide us with strong reasons for judging *PP* to be reliable. And the parallel possibility is lacking for *CP*. This shows that we cannot have certain reasons for taking *CP* to be reliable, but it doesn't follow that we have reasons for unreliability. That would follow only if we could also premise that a practice is reliable only if (as well as if) it has 1.–4. And why suppose that?

My position is that it is a kind of parochialism that makes the lack of 1.–4. appear to be token untrustworthiness. The reality *CP* claims to put us in touch with is conceived to be vastly different from the physical environment. Why should the sorts of procedures required to put us in effective cognitive touch with this reality not be equally different? Why suppose that the distinctive features of *PP* set an appropriate standard for the cognitive approach to God? I shall sketch out a possible state of affairs in which *CP* is quite trustworthy while lacking 1.–4., and then suggest that we have no reason to suppose that this state of affairs does not obtain.

Suppose, then, that

(A) God is too different from created beings, too "wholly other," for us to be able to grasp any regularities in His behavior.

Suppose further that

(B) for the same reason we can only attain the faintest, sketchiest, and most insecure grasp of what God is like.

Finally, suppose that

(C) God has decreed that a human being will be aware of His presence in any clear and unmistakable fashion only when certain special and difficult conditions are satisfied.

If all this is the case, then it is the reverse of surprising that CP should lack 1.–4., even if it does involve a genuine experience of God. It would lack 1.–2. because of (A). It is quite understandable that it should lack 4. because of (B). If our cognitive powers are not fitted to frame an adequate conception of God, it is not at all surprising that there should be wide variation in attempts to do so. This is what typically happens in science when investigators are grappling with a phenomenon no one really understands. A variety of models, analogues, metaphors, hypotheses, hunches are propounded, and it is impossible to secure universal agreement. 3. is missing because of (C). If very difficult conditions are set it is not surprising that few are chosen. Now it is compatible with (A)–(C) that

(D) religious experience should, in general, constitute a genuine awareness of the divine.

and that

(E) although any particular articulation of such an experience might be mistaken to a greater or lesser extent, indeed even though all such articulations might miss the mark to some extent, still such judgments will, for the most part, contain some measure of truth; they, or many of them, will constitute a useful approximation of the truth;

and that

(F) God's designs contain provision for correction and refinement, for increasing the accuracy of the beliefs derived from religious experience. Perhaps as one grows in the spiritual life one's spiritual sight becomes more accurate and more discriminating; perhaps some special revelation is vouchsafed under certain conditions; and there are many other conceivable possibilities.

If something like all this were the case then CP would be trustworthy even though it lacks features 1.–4. This is a conceivable way in which CP would constitute a road to the truth, while differing from PP in respects 1.–4. Therefore unless we have adequate reason for supposing that no such combination of circumstances obtains, we are not warranted in taking the lack of 1.–4. to be an adequate reason for a judgment of untrustworthiness.

Moreover it is not just that A.–C. constitute a bare possibility. In the practice of CP we seem to learn that this is the way things are. As for (A) and (B) it is the common teaching of all the higher religions that God is of a radically different order of being from finite substances and, therefore, that we cannot expect to attain the grasp of His nature and His doings that we have of worldly objects. As for (C), it is a basic theme in Christianity, and in other religions as well, that one finds God within one's experience, to any considerable degree, only as one progresses in the spiritual life. God is not available for voyeurs. Awareness of God, and understanding of His nature and His will for us, is not a purely cognitive achievement; it requires the involvement of the whole person; it takes a practical commitment and a practice of the life of the spirit, as well as the exercise of cognitive faculties.

Of course these results that we are using to defend CP are derived from that same practice. But in view of the fact that the favorable features of PP, 1.–4., are themselves ascertained by engaging in PP, our opponent is hardly in a position to fault us on this score. However I have not forgotten that I announced it as my aim to show that even one who engaged only in PP should recognize that CP is J_{nw}. For this purpose, I ignore what we learn in CP and revert to the point that my opponent has no basis for ruling out the conjoint state of affairs A.–F., hence has no basis for taking the lack of 1.–4. to show CP to be untrustworthy, and hence has no reason for denying that CP is J_{nw}.

I conclude that CP has basically the same epistemic status as PP and that no one who subscribes to the latter is in any position to cavil at the former.

The Problem of Evil

Is he willing to prevent evil, but not able? then he is impotent. Is he able, but not willing? then he is malevolent. Is he both able and willing? whence then is evil?

EPICURUS (341–270 BCE)

WE HAVE BEEN LOOKING at arguments in favor of God's existence. The agnostic and atheist usually base their case on the *absence* of evidence for God's existence. But they do have at least one arrow in their quiver, an argument for disbelief. It is the problem of evil. With it, the "atheologian" (one who argues against the existence of God) hopes either to neutralize any positive evidence for God's existence, based on whatever in the traditional arguments survives their criticism, or to demonstrate that it is unreasonable to believe in God.

The problem of evil arises from the apparent tension between the divine attributes of omnipotence, omniscience, and omnibenevolence on the one hand and the existence of evil on the other. The Judeo-Christian tradition has affirmed each of the following propositions:

1. God is all-powerful.
2. God is all-knowing.
3. God is perfectly good.
4. Evil exists.

But if he is perfectly good, it seems that he would not want evil to exist; and since he is omniscient, it seems that he must know what potentials for evil lurk in the world and what evils will arise apart from his intervention. And being omnipotent, he surely could prevent any evil that he knows about and wants to prevent. So, then, why does our world contain so much evil? Indeed, why does it contain any evil at all? It seems that if God is as the Judeo-Christian tradition says that he is, the co-existence of God and evil should be impossible—i.e., the existence of God logically precludes the existence of evil, and vice versa.

Generally, Western thought has distinguished between two types of evil: moral and natural. 'Moral evil' covers all those bad things for which creatures are morally responsible. 'Natural evil' or 'surd evil' includes those terrible events that occur in nature of their own accord, such as hurricanes, tornadoes, earthquakes, volcanic eruptions, natural diseases, and so on, that cause suffering to humans and animals. However, some defenses of theism affirm that all evil is essentially moral evil, with the devil brought in as the cause of natural evil.

The main defense of theism in response to the problem of evil is the free will defense, going back as far as St. Augustine (354–430) and receiving modern treatment in the work of John Hick, Alvin Plantinga, and Richard Swinburne. The free will defense maintains that premises 1–4 are not inconsistent with one another since (a) it is logically impossible for God to create free creatures and guarantee that they will never do evil, and (b) for all we know, freedom might be a great enough good that God is justified in permitting evil in order to make room for freedom.

Those developing the free will defense typically assume a libertarian view of freedom. That is, they assume that humans are free to choose between good and evil acts, and that freedom is inconsistent with determinism. This view is opposed to determinism as well as to compatibilism (a view that tries to reconcile freedom of action with determinism). It is widely believed that if either compatibilism or determinism is true, the free will defense will not be effective against the argument from evil. This matter is well treated in Chapter 9 of J. L. Mackie's *The Miracle of Theism*.

Proponents of the free will defense claim that all moral evil derives from creatures' freedom of will. But how does the theist account for natural evil? There are two different ways. The first one, suggested by Alvin Plantinga (see the Part III Bibliography), is to attribute natural evil, such as disease and tornadoes, to the work of the devil and his angels. The second way, favored by Swinburne, argues that natural evil is part and parcel of the nature of things, resulting from the combination of deterministic physical laws that are necessary for consistent action and the responsibility given to humans to exercise their freedom.

One further distinction is necessary to work through this problem: the distinction between *defense* and *theodicy*. A theodicy is a theory whose aim is to explain why God in fact permits evil; a defense is simply a demonstration of consistency—an effort to show that there is no formal contradiction in premises 1–4 mentioned earlier. The difference is that one can offer a defense without believing the details, and so without really having a *theory* about why God permits evil. For example: You are told that the defendant's fingerprints were found on the gun, and security cameras in an outside room place him at the scene of the crime within five minutes of when the crime took place. If (as is unlikely) your goal is simply to show that the evidence is logically consistent with the defendant's innocence, you might say, "Well, for all we know, he walked in, saw the crime being committed, went over and handled the gun right afterward, and then departed without calling the police." You probably wouldn't believe this story, and you might even go on to qualify it by saying something like, "Of course, I really doubt that that's what happened, but my point is just that it's *possible*." But that doesn't matter if your goal is simply to demonstrate consistency. This explanation is analogous to a defense. If, on the other hand, you tried to offer a theory explaining the evidence in a way consistent with the defendant's innocence—perhaps, say, a story, complete with suspects, motives and opportunities, according to which the defendant was framed, and which you were proposing for us actually to believe—you would be giving something analogous to a theodicy.

Let us now outline the main points of the readings that follow. The first three readings are classic formulations of opposite positions. In the first reading, "The Argument from Evil," David Hume argues through his persona Philo that the existence of God is called into doubt not just by the mere existence of evil, but by the enormous amount of evil in the world. It is arguable that there is actually more evil than good in the world, and it is hard to reconcile this fact with the existence of an all-powerful, omnibenevolent deity. In the second reading, "Theodicy: A Defense of Theism," Gottfried Leibniz (1646–1716) argues that the fact of evil in no way refutes theism, and he answers the kinds of objections raised by Hume. He contends that God permitted evil to exist in order to bring about greater good and that Adam's fall was a *felix culpa* ("happy sin") because it led to the incarnation of the Son of God, raising humanity to an ultimately higher destiny. Leibniz argues that although God can foresee the future, humans are still free since they can still act voluntarily. Finally, in the third reading—the famous "Rebellion" chapter from Dostoevsky's *The Brothers Karamazov*—we find a poignant response to the Leibnizian idea that God is justified in permitting evil in order to bring about greater goods. The troubled Ivan Karamazov angrily describes cases of horrendous suffering on the part of children and then challenges his religious brother Alyosha to say whether, if *he* were the architect of the universe, he could bring himself to permit such suffering in order to bring about global happiness. The expected answer is "No" and that is precisely the answer that Alyosha sadly gives.

Next we come to contemporary formulations. Our fourth reading, John Hick's "Evil and Soul-Making," is an example of a theodicy argument that is based on the free will defense. Theodicies can be of two different types, depending on how they justify the ways of God in the face of evil. The Augustinian position is that God created humans without sin and set them in a sinless, paradisical world. However, humanity fell into sin through the misuse of free will. God's grace will save some of us, but others will perish everlastingly. In this division God's goodness is manifested, for his mercy redeems some and his justice is served on the rest. But there is another theory of theodicy, stemming from Irenaeus (120–202), in the tradition of the Greek Church. The Irenaean tradition views Adam not as a free agent rebelling against God but as more akin to a very small child. The fall is humanity's first faulty step in the direction of freedom. God is still working with humanity in order to bring it from undeveloped life (*bios*) to a state of self-realization in divine love, spiritual life (*zoe*). This life is viewed as the "vale of soul-making." Spiritual development requires obstacles and the opportunity to fail as well as to succeed. Hick declares that those who are opposed to the challenge that our freedom grants us are looking for a hedonistic paradise in which every desire is gratified and we are treated by God as pet animals rather than autonomous agents. On the other hand, those who accept the challenge of freedom consider themselves to be coworkers with God in bringing forth the kingdom of God.

In the fifth reading, "A Critique of Hick's Theodicy," Edward H. Madden and Peter H. Hare attack Hick's theory. They ask whether the amount of evil in the world is necessary for soul-making and accuse Hick of three fallacies, called "all or nothing," "it could be worse," and "slippery slope." The *all-or-nothing* fallacy involves the idea that what we have is desirable because not having it at all would be far worse. "The erroneous assumption," write Madden and Hare, "is that we must have this thing either in its present form and amount or not at all. But it is often the case that only *some* amount of the thing in *some* form is necessary to the achievement of a desirable end." Hick concedes that there is an appalling amount of evil in the world but insists that the alternative is for humans to be mere puppets or pets. We may object to this set of extreme alternatives because we can easily imagine intermediate states where there is still great good but much less evil. Taking away Auschwitz or the Gulag Archipelago doesn't seem to leave the world any worse off.

The *it-could-be-worse* fallacy claims that "something is not really bad because it will be followed by all manner of desirable things." Such a claim overlooks the fact that things could also be better. Hick seems to ignore the fact that although it is true that we can imagine the world's being a worse place than it is, we can also imagine it to be a far better place. The question is, Why hasn't God created this far better place?

The *slippery-slope* fallacy states that if God once started eliminating evil from the world, he could not stop short of a perfect world. This notion overlooks the fact that humanity could be shown by God why a certain proportion of good to evil is ideal.

In our sixth essay, J. L. Mackie presses for the conclusion that the existence of an omnipotent, omniscient, perfectly good being—and so the existence of the God of the Judeo-Christian tradition—is logically inconsistent with the existence of evil. A perfectly good being, Mackie contends, always eliminates evil as far as it can; and an omnipotent and omniscient being, he argues, can eliminate evil entirely. He considers the response that the value of creating a world with free creatures might justify God in permitting the existence of evil. But he argues that, since it is not *impossible* for there to be a world in which free creatures always do what is right, God must have been able to create such a world. And so, since a world in which free creatures always do what is right is clearly better than one in which free creatures sometimes do what is wrong, the appeal to freedom fails to solve the problem.

In the seventh essay, Alvin Plantinga argues that Mackie is wrong in thinking that the existence of evil is inconsistent with the existence of God, and he also argues that Mackie is wrong in thinking that every *possible* world is *creatable*. Unlike Leibniz and Hick, Plantinga is offering merely a defense rather than a theodicy. Central to Plantinga's defense are the following three ideas: (a) a perfectly good being might have morally sufficient reason to permit evil, (b) the value of free will might provide such a morally sufficient reason if it's impossible for God to guarantee that a world containing free creatures would be free from evil, and (c) for all we know, it *is* impossible for God to guarantee that a world containing free creatures would be free from evil. In defense of (c), Plantinga invokes the hypothesis of *transworld depravity*. Roughly, to suffer from transworld depravity is to be such that, no matter what total creative act God had performed, you would freely have done something wrong. According to Plantinga, for all we know everyone in the actual world suffers from transworld depravity. If that's so, then no matter what creative act God had performed, if he had created just those creatures who in fact exist, the world would have contained moral evil. Thus, though there are *possible* worlds in which everyone freely does what is right, those worlds are not *creatable*. They are not creatable because, in effect, free creatures *cooperate* with God in determining what sort of world will exist; and (given the hypothesis of transworld depravity) no matter what God had done, his creatures would not have cooperated in such a way as to keep the world free from evil.

In our eighth reading, William Rowe argues that while Plantinga is correct in arguing that the deductive argument from evil against the existence of God fails, an inductive argument from evil succeeds.

In the final reading, Paul Draper argues that a cumulative case against theism can be made by combining the problem of evil with a naturalistic explanation for human existence based on evolution. We now turn to our readings.

III.1   The Argument from Evil

DAVID HUME

A short biographical sketch of David Hume precedes selection I.C.2. In the present selection, Hume argues through his persona Philo that not merely the fact of evil, but the enormous amount of evil makes it dubious that a deity exists. It is arguable that there is actually more evil than good in the world, so it is hard to see how one can reconcile the existence of evil with the existence of an all-powerful, omnibenevolent deity.

PART X

It is my opinion, I own, replied Demea, that each man feels, in a manner, the truth of religion within his own breast, and, from a consciousness of his imbecility and misery rather than from any reasoning, is led to seek protection from that Being on whom he and all nature is dependent. So anxious or so tedious are even the best scenes of life that futurity is still the object of all our hopes and fears. We incessantly look forward and endeavour, by prayers, adoration, and sacrifice, to appease those unknown powers whom we find, by experience, so able to afflict and oppress us. Wretched creatures that we are! What resource for us amidst the innumerable ills of life did not religion suggest some methods of atonement, and appease those terrors with which we are incessantly agitated and tormented?

I am indeed persuaded, said Philo, that the best and indeed the only method of bringing everyone to a due sense of religion is by just representations of the misery and wickedness of men. And for that purpose a talent of eloquence and strong imagery is more requisite than that of reasoning and argument. For is it necessary to prove what everyone feels within himself? It is only necessary to make us feel it, if possible, more intimately and sensibly.

The people, indeed, replied Demea, are sufficiently convinced of this great and melancholy truth. The miseries of life, the unhappiness of man, the general corruptions of our nature, the unsatisfactory enjoyment of pleasures, riches, honours—these phrases have become almost proverbial in all languages. And who can doubt of what all men declare from their own immediate feeling and experience?

In this point, said Philo, the learned are perfectly agreed with the vulgar; and in all letters, *sacred* and *profane*, the topic of human misery has been insisted on with the most pathetic eloquence that sorrow and melancholy could inspire. The poets, who speak from sentiment, without a system, and whose testimony has therefore the more authority, abound in images of this nature. From Homer down to Dr. Young, the whole inspired tribe have ever been sensible that no other representation of things would suit the feeling and observation of each individual.

As to authorities, replied Demea, you need not seek them. Look round this library of Cleanthes. I shall venture to affirm that, except

Reprinted from David Hume, *Dialogues Concerning Natural Religion* (1779); London: Longmans Green, 1878.

authors of particular sciences, such as chemistry or botany, who have no occasion to treat of human life, there is scarce one of those innumerable writers from whom the sense of human misery has not, in some passage or other, extorted a complaint and confession of it. At least, the chance is entirely on that side; and no one author has ever, so far as I can recollect, been so extravagant as to deny it.

There you must excuse me, said Philo: Leibniz has denied it, and is perhaps the first[1] who ventured upon so bold and paradoxical an opinion; at least, the first who made it essential to his philosophical system.

And by being the first, replied Demea, might he not have been sensible of his error? For is this a subject in which philosophers can propose to make discoveries especially in so late an age? And can any man hope by a simple denial (for the subject scarcely admits of reasoning) to bear down the united testimony of mankind, founded on sense and consciousness?

And why should man, added he, pretend to an exemption from the lot of all other animals? The whole earth, believe me, Philo, is cursed and polluted. A perpetual war is kindled amongst all living creatures. Necessity, hunger, want stimulate the strong and courageous; fear, anxiety, terror agitate the weak and infirm. The first entrance into life gives anguish to the new-born infant and to its wretched parent; weakness, impotence, distress attend each stage of that life, and it is, at last, finished in agony and horror.

Observe, too, says Philo, the curious artifices of nature in order to embitter the life of every living being. The stronger prey upon the weaker and keep them in perpetual terror and anxiety. The weaker, too, in their turn, often prey upon the stronger, and vex and molest them without relaxation. Consider that innumerable race of insects, which either are bred on the body of each animal or, flying about, infix their stings in him. These insects have others still less than themselves which torment them. And thus on each hand, before and behind, above and below, every animal is surrounded with enemies which incessantly seek his misery and destruction.

Man alone, said Demea, seems to be, in part, an exception to this rule. For by combination in society he can easily master lions, tigers, and bears, whose greater strength and agility naturally enable them to prey upon him.

On the contrary, it is here chiefly, cried Philo, that the uniform and equal maxims of nature are most apparent. Man, it is true, can, by combination, surmount all his real enemies and become master of the whole animal creation; but does he not immediately raise up to himself *imaginary* enemies, the demons of his fancy, who haunt him with superstitious terrors and blast every enjoyment of life? His pleasure, as he imagines, becomes in their eyes a crime; his food and repose give them umbrage and offence; his very sleep and dreams furnish new materials to anxious fear; and even death, his refuge from every other ill, presents only the dread of endless and innumerable woes. Nor does the wolf molest more the timid flock than superstition does the anxious breast of wretched mortals.

Besides, consider, Demea: This very society by which we surmount those wild beasts, our natural enemies, what new enemies does it not raise to us? What woe and misery does it not occasion? Man is the greatest enemy of man. Oppression, injustice, contempt, contumely, violence, sedition, war, calumny, treachery, fraud—by these they mutually torment each other, and they would soon dissolve that society which they had formed were it not for the dread of still greater ills which must attend their separation.

But though these external insults, said Demea, from animals, from men, from all the elements, which assault us form a frightful catalogue of woes, they are nothing in comparison of those which arise within ourselves, from the distempered condition of our mind and body. How many lie under the lingering torment of diseases? Hear the pathetic enumeration of the great poet.

Intestine stone and ulcer, colic-pangs,
Demoniac frenzy, moping melancholy,
And moon-struck madness, pining atrophy,
Marasmus, and wide-wasting pestilence.
Dire was the tossing, deep the groans:
Despair

Tended the sick, busiest from couch to couch.
And over them triumphant Death *his dart*
Shook: but delay'd to strike, though oft
*   invok'd*
With vows, as their chief good and final
*   hope.*[2]

The disorders of the mind, continued Demea, though more secret, are not perhaps less dismal and vexatious. Remorse, shame, anguish, rage, disappointment, anxiety, fear, dejection, despair— who has ever passed through life without cruel inroads from these tormentors? How many have scarcely ever felt any better sensations? Labour and poverty, so abhorred by everyone, are the certain lot of the far greater number; and those few privileged persons who enjoy ease and opulence never reach contentment or true felicity. All the goods of life united would not make a very happy man, but all the ills united would make a wretch indeed; and any one of them almost (and who can be free from every one?), nay, often the absence of one good (and who can possess all?) is sufficient to render life ineligible.

Were a stranger to drop on a sudden into this world, I would show him, as a specimen of its ills, an hospital full of diseases, a prison crowded with malefactors and debtors, a field of battle strewed with carcases, a fleet foundering in the ocean, a nation languishing under tyranny, famine, or pestilence. To turn the gay side of life to him and give him a notion of its pleasures—whither should I conduct him? To a ball, to an opera, to court? He might justly think that I was only showing him a diversity of distress and sorrow.

There is no evading such striking instances, said Philo, but by apologies which still further aggravate the charge. Why have all men, I ask, in all ages, complained incessantly of the miseries of life?...They have no just reason, says one: these complaints proceed only from their discontented, repining, anxious disposition....And can there possibly, I reply, be a more certain foundation of misery than such a wretched temper?

But if they were really as unhappy as they pretend, says my antagonist, why do they remain in life?...

Not satisfied with life, afraid of death—

this is the secret chain, say I, that holds us. We are terrified, not bribed to the continuance of our existence.

It is only a false delicacy, he may insist, which a few refined spirits indulge, and which has spread these complaints among the whole race of mankind....And what is this delicacy, I ask, which you blame? Is it anything but a greater sensibility to all the pleasures and pains of life? And if the man of a delicate, refined temper, by being so much more alive than the rest of the world, is only so much more unhappy, what judgment must we form in general of human life?

Let men remain at rest, says our adversary, and they will be easy. They are willing artificers of their own misery....No! reply I: an anxious langour follows their repose; disappointment, vexation, trouble, their activity and ambition.

I can observe something like what you mention in some others, replied Cleanthes, but I confess I feel little or nothing of it in myself, and hope that it is not so common as you represent it.

If you feel not human misery yourself, cried Demea, I congratulate you on so happy a singularity. Others, seemingly the most prosperous, have not been ashamed to vent their complaints in the most melancholy strains. Let us attend to the great, the fortunate emperor, Charles V, when, tired with human grandeur, he resigned all his extensive dominions into the hands of his son. In the last harangue which he made on that memorable occasion, he publicly avowed *that the greatest prosperities which he had ever enjoyed had been mixed with so many adversities that he might truly say he had never enjoyed any satisfaction or contentment.* But did the retired life in which he sought for shelter afford him any greater happiness? If we may credit his son's account, his repentance commenced the very day of his resignation.

Cicero's fortune, from small beginnings, rose to the greatest lustre and renown; yet what pathetic complaints of the ills of life do his familiar letters, as well as philosophical discourses, contain? And suitably to his own experience, he introduces Cato, the great, the fortunate Cato protesting in his old age that had he a new life in his offer he would reject the present.

Ask yourself, ask any of your acquaintance, whether they would live over again the last ten or twenty years of their life. No! but the next twenty, they say, will be better:

And from the dregs of life, hope to receive
What the first sprightly running could not
give.[3]

Thus, at last, they find (such is the greatness of human misery, it reconciles even contradictions) that they complain at once of the shortness of life and of its vanity and sorrow.

And is it possible, Cleanthes, said Philo, that after all these reflections, and infinitely more which might be suggested, you can still persevere in your anthropomorphism, and assert the moral attributes of the Deity, his justice, benevolence, mercy, and rectitude, to be of the same nature with these virtues in human creatures? His power, we allow, is infinite; whatever he wills is executed; but neither man nor any other animal is happy; therefore, he does not will their happiness. His wisdom is infinite; he is never mistaken in choosing the means to any end; but the course of nature tends not to human or animal felicity; therefore, it is not established for that purpose. Through the whole compass of human knowledge there are no inferences more certain and infallible than these. In what respect, then, do his benevolence and mercy resemble the benevolence and mercy of men?

Epicurus' old questions are yet unanswered.

Is he willing to prevent evil, but not able? then is he impotent. Is he able, but not willing? then is he malevolent. Is he both able and willing? whence then is evil?

You ascribe, Cleanthes, (and I believe justly) a purpose and intention to nature. But what, I beseech you, is the object of that curious artifice and machinery which she has displayed in all animals—the preservation alone of individuals, and propagation of the species? It seems enough for her purpose, if such a rank be barely upheld in the universe, without any care or concern for the happiness of the members that compose it.

No resource for this purpose: no machinery in order merely to give pleasure or ease; no fund of pure joy and contentment; no indulgence without some want or necessity accompanying it. At least, the few phenomena of this nature are overbalanced by opposite phenomena of still greater importance.

Our sense of music, harmony, and indeed beauty of all kinds, gives satisfaction, without being absolutely necessary to the preservation and propagation of the species. But what racking pains, on the other hand, arise from gouts, gravels, megrims, toothaches, rheumatisms, where the injury to the animal machinery is either small or incurable? Mirth, laughter, play, frolic seem gratuitous satisfactions which have no further tendency; spleen, melancholy, discontent, superstition are pains of the same nature. How then does the Divine benevolence display itself, in the sense of you anthropomorphites? None but we mystics, as you were pleased to call us, can account for this strange mixture of phenomena, by deriving it from attributes infinitely perfect but incomprehensible.

And have you, at last, said Cleanthes smiling, betrayed your intentions, Philo? Your long agreement with Demea did indeed a little surprise me, but I find you were all the while erecting a concealed battery against me. And I must confess that you have now fallen upon a subject worthy of your noble spirit of opposition and controversy. If you can make out the present point, and prove mankind to be unhappy or corrupted, there is an end at once of all religion. For to what purpose establish the natural attributes of the Deity, while the moral are still doubtful and uncertain?

You take umbrage very easily, replied Demea, at opinions the most innocent and the most generally received, even amongst the religious and devout themselves; and nothing can be more surprising than to find a topic like this—concerning the wickedness and misery of man—charged with no less than atheism and profaneness. Have not all pious divines and preachers who have indulged their rhetoric on so fertile a subject, have they not easily, I say, given a solution of any difficulties which may attend it? This world is but a point in comparison of the universe; this life but a moment in comparison of eternity. The present evil phenomena, therefore, are rectified in other regions, and in some future period of existence. And the eyes of men, being then opened to larger views of things, see the whole connection of general laws, and trace, with adoration, the benevolence and rectitude of the Deity through all the mazes and intricacies of his providence.

No! replied Cleanthes, no! These arbitrary suppositions can never be admitted, contrary to matter of fact, visible and uncontroverted. Whence can any cause be known but from its known effects? Whence can any hypothesis be proved but from the apparent phenomena? To establish one hypothesis upon another is building entirely in the air; and the utmost we ever attain by these conjectures and fictions is to ascertain the bare possibility of our opinion, but never can we, upon such terms, establish its reality.

The only method of supporting Divine benevolence—and it is what I willingly embrace—is to deny absolutely the misery and wickedness of man. Your representations are exaggerated; your melancholy views mostly fictitious; your inferences contrary to fact and experience. Health is more common than sickness; pleasure than pain; happiness than misery. And for one vexation which we meet with, we attain, upon computation, a hundred enjoyments.

Admitting your position, replied Philo, which yet is extremely doubtful, you must at the same time allow that, if pain be less frequent than pleasure, it is infinitely more violent and durable. One hour of it is often able to outweigh a day, a week, a month of our common insipid enjoyments; and how many days, weeks, and months are passed by several in the most acute torments? Pleasure, scarcely in one instance, is ever able to reach ecstasy and rapture; and in no one instance can it continue for any time at its highest pitch and altitude. The spirits evaporate, the nerves relax, the fabric is disordered, and the enjoyment quickly degenerates into fatigue and uneasiness. But pain often, good God, how often! rises to torture and agony; and the longer it continues, it becomes still more genuine agony and torture. Patience is

exhausted, courage languishes, melancholy seizes us, and nothing terminates our misery but the removal of its cause or another event which is the sole cure of all evil, but which, from our natural folly, we regard with still greater horror and consternation.

But not to insist upon these topics, continued Philo, though most obvious, certain, and important, I must use the freedom to admonish you, Cleanthes, that you have put the controversy upon a most dangerous issue, and are unawares introducing a total scepticism into the most essential articles of natural and revealed theology. What! no method of fixing a just foundation for religion unless we allow the happiness of human life, and maintain a continued existence even in this world, with all our present pains, infirmities, vexations, and follies, to be eligible and desirable! But this is contrary to everyone's feeling and experience; it is contrary to an authority so established as nothing can subvert. No decisive proofs can ever be produced against this authority; nor is it possible for you to compute, estimate, and compare all the pains and all the pleasures in the lives of all men and of all animals; and thus, by your resting the whole system of religion on a point which, from its very nature, must forever be uncertain, you tacitly confess that that system is equally uncertain.

But allowing you what never will be believed, at least, what you never possibly can prove, that animal or, at least, human happiness in this life exceeds its misery, you have yet done nothing; for this is not, by any means, what we expect from infinite power, infinite wisdom, and infinite goodness. Why is there any misery at all in the world? Not by chance, surely. From some cause then. Is it from the intention of the Deity? But he is perfectly benevolent. Is it contrary to his intention? But he is almighty. Nothing can shake the solidity of this reasoning, so short, so clear, so decisive, except we assert that these subjects exceed all human capacity, and that our common measures of truth and falsehood are not applicable to them—a topic which I have all along insisted on, but which you have, from the beginning, rejected with scorn and indignation.

But I will be contented to retire still from this intrenchment, for I deny that you can ever force me in it. I will allow that pain or misery in man is *compatible* with infinite power and goodness in the Deity, even in your sense of these attributes: what are you advanced by all these concessions? A mere possible compatibility is not sufficient. You must prove these pure, unmixed, and uncontrollable attributes from the present mixed and confused phenomena, and from these alone. A hopeful undertaking! Were the phenomena ever so pure and unmixed, yet, being finite, they would be insufficient for that purpose. How much more, where they are also so jarring and discordant!

Here, Cleanthes, I find myself at ease in my argument. Here I triumph. Formerly, when we argued concerning the natural attributes of intelligence and design, I needed all my sceptical and metaphysical subtilty to elude your grasp. In many views of the universe and of its parts, particularly the latter, the beauty and fitness of final causes strike us with such irresistible force that all objections appear (what I believe they really are) mere cavils and sophisms; nor can we then imagine how it was ever possible for us to repose any weight on them. But there is no view of human life or of the condition of mankind from which, without the greatest violence, we can infer the moral attributes or learn that infinite benevolence, conjoined with infinite power and infinite wisdom, which we must discover by the eyes of faith alone. It is your turn now to tug the labouring oar, and to support your philosophical subtilties against the dictates of plain reason and experience.

NOTES

1. That sentiment had been maintained by Dr. King and some few others before Leibniz, though by none of so great fame as that German philosopher.
2. Milton: *Paradise Lost*, Bk. XI.
3. John Dryden, *Aureng-Zebe*, Act IV, sc. 1.

III.2   Theodicy: A Defense of Theism

GOTTFRIED LEIBNIZ

Gottfried Wilhelm Leibniz (1646–1716) was a German idealist who tried to set forth a thoroughgoing theodicy, a justification of the ways of God. In this selection he argues that the fact of evil in no way refutes theism, and he answers the kinds of objections raised by Hume. He contends that God permitted evil to exist in order to bring about greater good and that Adam's fall was a *felix culpa* (a "happy sin") because it led to the incarnation of the Son of God, raising humanity to an ultimately higher destiny. He argues that although God can foresee the future, humans are still free in that they act voluntarily.

Some intelligent persons have desired that this supplement be made [to the Theodicy], and I have the more readily yielded to their wishes as in this way I have an opportunity again to remove certain difficulties and to make some observations which were not sufficiently emphasized in the work itself.

I. *Objection.* Whoever does not choose the best is lacking in power, or in knowledge, or in goodness.

God did not choose the best in creating this world.

Therefore, God has been lacking in power, or in knowledge, or in goodness.

Reprinted from Gottfried Leibniz, *The Theodicy: Abridgement of the Argument Reduced to Syllogistic Form* (1710).

Answer. I deny the minor, that is, the second premise of this syllogism; and our opponent proves it by this.

Prosyllogism. Whoever makes things in which there is evil, which could have been made without any evil, or the making of which could have been omitted, does not choose the best.

God has made a world in which there is evil; a world, I say, which could have been made without any evil, or the making of which could have been omitted altogether.

Therefore, God has not chosen the best.

Answer. I grant the minor of this prosyllogism; for it must be confessed that there is evil in this world which God has made, and that it was possible to make a world without evil, or even not to create a world at all, for its creation has depended on the free will of God; but I deny the major, that is, the first of the two premises of the prosyllogism, and I might content myself with simply demanding its proof; but in order to make the matter clearer, I have wished to justify this denial by showing that the best plan is not always that which seeks to avoid evil, since it may happen that *the evil is accompanied by a greater good.* For example, a general of an army will prefer a great victory with a slight wound to a condition without wound and without victory. We have proved this more fully in the large work by making it clear, by instances taken from mathematics and elsewhere, that an imperfection in the part may be required for a greater perfection in the whole. In this I have followed the opinion of St. Augustine, who has said a hundred times, that God has permitted evil in order to bring about good, that is, a greater good; and that of Thomas Aquinas (in libr. II. sent. dist. 32, qu. I, art. 1), that the permitting of evil tends to the good of the universe. I have shown that the ancients called Adam's fall *felix culpa*, a happy sin, because it had been retrieved with immense advantage by the incarnation of the Son of God, who has given to the universe something nobler than anything that ever would have been among creatures except for it. For the sake of a clearer understanding, I have added, following many good authors, that it was in accordance with order and the general

good that God allowed to certain creatures the opportunity of exercising their liberty, even when he foresaw that they would turn to evil, but which he could so well rectify; because it was not fitting that, in order to hinder sin, God should always act in an extraordinary manner. To overthrow this objection, therefore, it is sufficient to show that a world with evil might be better than a world without evil; but I have gone even farther, in the work, and have even proved that this universe must be in reality better than every other possible universe.

II. Objection. If there is more evil than good in intelligent creatures, then there is more evil than good in the whole work of God.

Now, there is more evil than good in intelligent creatures.

Therefore, there is more evil than good in the whole work of God.

Answer. I deny the major and the minor of this conditional syllogism. As to the major, I do not admit it at all, because this pretended deduction from a part to the whole, from intelligent creatures to all creatures, supposes tacitly and without proof that creatures destitute of reason cannot enter into comparison nor into account with those which possess it. But why may it not be that the surplus of good in the non-intelligent creatures which fill the world, compensates for, and even incomparably surpasses, the surplus of evil in the rational creatures? It is true that the value of the latter is greater; but, in compensation, the others are beyond comparison the more numerous, and it may be that the proportion of number and quantity surpasses that of value and of quality.

As to the minor, that is no more to be admitted; that is, it is not at all to be admitted that there is more evil than good in the intelligent creatures. There is no need even of granting that there is more evil than good in the human race, because it is possible, and in fact very probable, that the glory and the perfection of the blessed are incomparably greater than the misery and the imperfection of the damned, and that here the excellence of the total good in the smaller number exceeds the total evil in the greater number. The blessed approach the Divinity, by means of a Divine Mediator, as near as may suit these creatures, and make such progress in good as is impossible for the damned to make in evil, approach as nearly as they may to the nature of demons. God is infinite, and the devil is limited; the good may and does go to infinity, while evil has its bounds. It is therefore possible, and is credible, that in the comparison of the blessed and the damned, the contrary of that which I have said might happen in the comparison of intelligent and non-intelligent creatures, takes place; namely, it is possible that in the comparison of the happy and the unhappy, the proportion of degree exceeds that of number, and that in the comparison of intelligent and non-intelligent creatures, the proportion of number is greater than that of value. I have the right to suppose that a thing is possible so long as its impossibility is not proved; and indeed that which I have here advanced is more than a supposition.

But in the second place, if I should admit that there is more evil than good in the human race, I have still good grounds for not admitting that there is more evil than good in all intelligent creatures. For there is an inconceivable number of genii, and perhaps of other rational creatures. And an opponent could not prove that in all the City of God, composed as well of genii as of rational animals without number and of an infinity of kinds, evil exceeds good. And although in order to answer an objection, there is no need of proving that a thing is, when its mere possibility suffices; yet, in this work, I have not omitted to show that it is a consequence of the supreme perfection of the Sovereign of the universe, that the kingdom of God is the most perfect of all possible states or governments, and that consequently the little evil there is, is required for the consummation of the immense good which is found there.

III. *Objection.* If it is always impossible not to sin, it is always unjust to punish.

Now, it is always impossible not to sin; or, in other words, every sin is necessary.

Therefore, it is always unjust to punish.

The minor of this is proved thus:

1. *Prosyllogism.* All that is predetermined is necessary.

Every event is predetermined.

Therefore, every event (and consequently sin also) is necessary.

Again this second minor is proved thus:

2. *Prosyllogism.* That which is future, that which is foreseen, that which is involved in the causes, is predetermined.

Every event is such.

Therefore, every event is predetermined.

Answer. I admit in a certain sense the conclusion of the second prosyllogism, which is the minor of the first; but I shall deny the major of the first prosyllogism, namely, that every thing predetermined is necessary; understanding by the *necessity* of sinning, for example, or by the impossibility of not sinning, or of not performing any action, the necessity with which we are here concerned, that is, that which is essential and absolute, and which destroys the morality of an action and the justice of punishments. For if anyone understood another necessity or impossibility, namely, a necessity which should be only moral, or which was only hypothetical (as will be explained shortly); it is clear that I should deny the major of the objection itself. I might content myself with this answer and demand the proof of the proposition denied; but I have again desired to explain my procedure in this work, in order to better elucidate the matter and to throw more light on the whole subject, by explaining the necessity which ought to be rejected and the determination which must take place. That *necessity* which is contrary to morality and which ought to be rejected. and which would render punishment unjust, is an insurmountable necessity which would make all opposition useless, even if we should wish with all our heart to avoid the necessary action, and should make all possible efforts to that end. Now, it is manifest that this is not applicable to voluntary actions, because we would not perform them if we did not choose to. Also their prevision and predetermination are not absolute, but presuppose the will: if it is certain that we shall perform them, it is not less certain that we shall choose to perform them. These voluntary actions and their consequences will not take place no matter what we do or whether we wish them or not; but, *through* that which we shall do and through that which we shall wish to do, which leads to them. And this is involved in prevision and in predetermination, and even constitutes their ground. And the necessity of such an event is called conditional or hypothetical, or the necessity of consequence, because it supposes the will, and the other *requisites*; whereas the necessity which destroys morality and renders punishment unjust and reward useless, exists in things which will be whatever we may do or whatever we may wish to do, and, in a word, is in that which is essential; and this is what is called an absolute necessity. Thus it is to no purpose, as regards what is absolutely necessary, to make prohibitions or commands, to propose penalties or prizes, to praise or to blame; it will be none the less. On the other hand, in voluntary actions and in that which depends upon them, precepts armed with power to punish and to recompense are very often of use and are included in the order of causes which make an action exist. And it is for this reason that not only cares and labors but also prayers are useful; God having had these prayers in view before he regulated things and having had that consideration for them which was proper. This is why the precept which says *ora et labora* (pray and work), holds altogether good; and not only those who (under the vain pretext of the necessity of events) pretend that the care which business demands may be neglected, but also those who reason against prayer, fall into what the ancients even then called the *lazy sophism*. Thus the predetermination of events by causes is just what contributes to morality instead of destroying it, and causes incline the will, without compelling it. This is why the *determination* in question is not a necessitation—it is certain (to him who knows all) that the effect will follow this inclination; but this effect does not follow by a necessary consequence, that is, one the contrary of which implies contradiction. It is also by an internal inclination such as this that the will is determined, without there being any necessity. Suppose that one has the greatest passion in the world (a great thirst, for example), you will admit to me that the soul can find some reason for resisting it, if it were only that of showing

its power. Thus, although one may never be in a perfect indifference of equilibrium and there may be always a preponderance of inclination for the side taken, it, nevertheless, never renders the resolution taken absolutely necessary.

IV. *Objection.* Whoever can prevent the sin of another and does not do so, but rather contributes to it although he is well informed of it, is accessory to it.

God can prevent the sin of intelligent creatures; but he does not do so, and rather contributes to it by his concurrence and by the opportunities which he brings about, although he has a perfect knowledge of it.

Hence, etc.

Answer. I deny the major of this syllogism. For it is possible that one could prevent sin, but ought not, because he could not do it without himself committing a sin, or (when God is in question) without performing an unreasonable action. Examples have been given and the application to God himself has been made. It is possible also that we contribute to evil and that sometimes we even open the road to it, in doing things which we are obliged to do; and, when we do our duty or (in speaking of God) when, after thorough consideration, we do that which reason demands, we are not responsible for the results, even when we foresee them. We do not desire these evils; but we are willing to permit them for the sake of a greater good which we cannot reasonably help preferring to other considerations. And this is a *consequent* will, which results from *antecedent* wills by which we will the good. I know that some persons, in speaking of the antecedent and consequent will of God, have understood by the *antecedent* that which wills that all men should be saved; and by the consequent, that which wills, in consequence of persistent sin, that some should be damned. But these are merely illustrations of a more general idea, and it may be said for the same reason that God, by his antecedent will, wills that men should not sin; and by his consequent or final and decreeing will (that which is always followed by its effect), he wills to permit them to sin, this permission being the result of superior reasons. And we have the right to say in general that the antecedent will of God tends to the production of good and the prevention of evil, each taken in itself and as if alone (*particulariter et secundum quid*, Thom. I, qu. 19, art. 6), according to the measure of the degree of each good and each evil; but that the divine consequent or final or total will tends toward the production of as many goods as may be put together, the combination of which becomes in this way determined, and includes also the permission of some evils and the exclusion of some goods, as the best possible plan for the universe demands. Arminius, in his *Antiperkinsus*, has very well explained that the will of God may be called consequent, not only in relation to the action of the creature considered beforehand in the divine understanding, but also in relation to other anterior divine acts of will. But this consideration of the passage cited from Thomas Aquinas, and that from Scotus (I. dist. 46, qu. XI), is enough to show that they make this distinction as I have done here. Nevertheless, if anyone objects to this use of terms let him substitute *deliberating* will, in place of antecedent, and final or decreeing will, in place of consequent. For I do not wish to dispute over words.

V. Objection. Whoever produces all that is real in a thing, is its cause.

God produces all that is real in sin.

Hence, God is the cause of sin.

Answer. I might content myself with denying the major or the minor, since the term real admits of interpretations which would render these propositions false. But in order to explain more clearly, I will make a distinction. *Real* signifies either that which is positive only, or, it includes also privative beings: in the first case, I deny the major and admit the minor; in the second case, I do the contrary. I might have limited myself to this, but I have chosen to proceed still farther and give the reason for this distinction. I have been very glad therefore to draw attention to the fact that every reality purely positive or absolute is a perfection; and that imperfection comes from limitation, that is, from the privative: for to limit is to refuse progress, or the greatest possible progress. Now God is the cause of all perfections and consequently of all realities considered as purely positive. But limitations or privations result from the original imperfection of creatures, which limits their receptivity. And it is with them as with a loaded vessel, which the river causes to move more or less slowly according to the weight which it carries: thus its speed depends upon the river, but the retardation which limits this speed comes from the load. Thus in the *Theodicy*, we have shown how the creature, in causing sin, is a defective cause; how errors and evil inclinations are born of privation; and how privation is accidentally efficient; and I have justified the opinion of St. Augustine (lib. I, ad Simpl. qu. 2) who explains, for example, how God makes the soul obdurate, not by giving it something evil, but because the effect of his good impression is limited by the soul's resistance and by the circumstances which contribute to this resistance, so that he does not give it all the good which would overcome its evil. *Nec* (inquit) *ab illo erogatur aliquid quo homo fit deterior, sed tantum quo fit melior non erogatur.* But if God had wished to do more, he would have had to make either other natures for creatures or other miracles to change their natures, things which the best plan could not admit. It is as if the current of the river must be more rapid than its fall admitted or that the boats should be loaded more lightly, if it were necessary to make them move more quickly. And the original limitation or imperfection of creatures requires that even the best plan of the universe could not receive more good, and could not be exempt from certain evils, which, however, are to result in a greater good. There are certain disorders in the parts which marvelously enhance the beauty of the whole; just as certain dissonances, when properly used, render harmony more beautiful. But this depends on what has already been said in answer to the first objection.

VI. Objection. Whoever punishes those who have done as well as it was in their power to do, is unjust.

God does so.

Hence, etc.

Answer. I deny the minor of this argument. And I believe that God always gives sufficient aid and grace to those who have a good will, that is, to those who do not reject this grace by new sin. Thus, I do not admit the damnation of infants who have died without baptism or outside of the church; nor the damnation of adults who have acted according to the light which God has given them. And I believe that if *any one has followed the light which has been given him*, he will undoubtedly receive greater light when he has need of it, as the late M. Hulseman, a profound and celebrated theologian at Leipzig, has somewhere remarked; and if such a man has failed to receive it during his lifetime he will at least receive it when at the point of death.

VII. *Objection.* Whoever gives only to some, and not to all, the means which produces in them effectively a good will and salutary final faith, has not sufficient goodness.

God does this.

Hence, etc.

Answer. I deny the major of this. It is true that God could overcome the greatest resistance of the human heart; and does it, too, sometimes, either by internal grace, or by external circumstances which have a great effect on souls; but he does not always do this. Whence comes this distinction? it may be asked, and why does his goodness seem limited? It is because, as I have already said in answering the first objection, it would not have been in order always to act in an extraordinary manner, and to reverse the connection of things. The reasons of this connection, by means of which one is placed in more favorable circumstances than another, are hidden in the depths of the wisdom of God; they depend upon the universal harmony. The best plan of the universe, which God could not fail to choose, made it so. We judge from the event itself; since God has made it, it was not possible to do better. Far from being true that this conduct is contrary to goodness, it is supreme goodness which led him to it. This objection with its solution might have been drawn from what was said in regard to the first objection; but it seemed useful to touch upon it separately.

VIII. *Objection.* Whoever cannot fail to choose the best, is not free.

God cannot fail to choose the best.

Hence, God is not free.

Answer. I deny the major of this argument; it is rather true liberty, and the most perfect, to be able to use one's free will for the best, and to always exercise this power, without ever being turned aside either by external force or by internal passions, the first of which causes slavery of the body, the second, slavery of the soul. There is nothing less servile, and nothing more in accordance with the highest degree of freedom, than to be always led toward the good, and always by one's own inclination, without any constraint and without any displeasure. And to object therefore that God had need of external things, is only a sophism. He created them freely; but having proposed to himself an end, which is to exercise his goodness, wisdom has determined him to choose the means best fitted to attain this end. To call this a need, is to take that term in an unusual sense which frees it from all imperfection, just as when we speak of the wrath of God.

Seneca has somewhere said that God commanded but once but that he obeys always, because he obeys laws which he willed to prescribe to himself: *semel jussit, semper paret.* But he might better have said that God always commands and that he is always obeyed; for in willing, he always follows the inclination of his own nature, and all other things always follow his will. And as this will is always the same, it cannot be said that he obeys only that will which he formerly had. Nevertheless, although his will is always infallible and always tends toward the best, the evil, or the lesser good, which he rejects, does not cease to be possible in itself; otherwise the necessity of the good would be geometrical (so to speak), or metaphysical, and altogether absolute; the contingency of things would be destroyed, and there would be no choice. But this sort of necessity, which does not destroy the possibility of the contrary, has this name only by analogy; it becomes effective, not by the pure essence of things, but by that which is outside of them, above them, namely, by the will of God. This necessity is called moral, because, to the sage, *necessity* and *what ought to be* are equivalent things; and when it always has its effect, as it really has in the perfect sage, that is, in God, it may be said that it is a happy necessity. The nearer creatures approach to it, the nearer they approach to perfect happiness. Also this kind of necessity is not that which we try to avoid and which destroys morality, rewards and praise. For that which it brings, does not happen whatever we may do or will, but because we will it so. And a will to which it is natural to choose well, merits praise so much the more; also it carries its reward with it, which is sovereign happiness. And as this constitution of the divine nature gives entire satisfaction to him who possesses it, it is also the best and the most desirable for the creatures who are all dependent on God. If the will of God did not have for a rule the principle of the best, it would either tend toward evil, which would be the worst; or it would be in some way indifferent to good and to evil, and would be guided by chance: but a will which would allow itself always to act by chance, would not be worth more for the government of the universe than the fortuitous concourse of atoms, without there being any divinity therein. And even if God should abandon himself to chance only in some cases and in a certain way (as he would do, if he did not always work entirely for the best and if he were capable of preferring a lesser work to a greater, that is, an evil to a good, since that which prevents a greater good is an evil), he would be imperfect, as well as the object of his choice; he would not merit entire confidence; he would act without reason in such a case, and the government of the universe would be like certain games, equally divided between reason and chance. All this proves that this objection which is made against the choice of the best, perverts the notions of the free and of the necessary, and represents to us the best even as evil: which is either malicious or ridiculous.

III.3   Rebellion

FYODOR DOSTOEVSKY

Fyodor Dostoevsky (1821–1881) was one of the greatest and most influential Russian novelists. He is the author of *Crime and Punishment, Notes from the Underground, The Gambler,* and *The Brothers Karamazov,* from which the present selection is taken. In this chapter, Ivan Karamazov challenges the idea that some greater good might justify the horrendous suffering of even one small child, much less the vast amounts of such suffering that our world has so far seen.

"I must admit one thing to you," Ivan began. "I could never understand how one can love one's neighbors. It's just one's neighbors, to my mind, that one can't love, though one might love those at a distance. I once read somewhere of 'John the Merciful,' a saint, that when a hungry, frozen beggar came to him, and asked him to warm him up, he took him into his bed, held him in his arms, and began breathing into his mouth, which was putrid and loathsome from some awful disease. I am convinced that he did that from the laceration of falsity, for the sake of the love imposed by duty, as a penance laid on him. For anyone to love a man, he must be hidden, for as soon as he shows his face, love is gone."

"Father Zosima has talked of that more than once," observed Alyosha; "he, too, said that the face of a man often hinders many people not practised in love, from loving him. But yet there's a great deal of love in mankind, and almost Christ-like love. I know that myself, Ivan."

"Well, I know nothing of it so far, and can't understand it, and the innumerable mass of mankind are with me there. The question is, whether that's due to men's bad qualities or whether it's inherent in their nature. To my thinking, Christ-like love for men is a miracle impossible on earth. He was God. But we are not gods. Suppose I, for instance, suffer intensely. Another can never know how much I suffer, because he is another and not I. And what's more, a man is rarely ready to admit another's suffering (as though it were a distinction). Why won't he admit it, do you think? Because I smell unpleasant, because I have a stupid face, because I once trod on his foot. Besides there is suffering and suffering; degrading, humiliating suffering such as humbles me—hunger, for instance—my benefactor will perhaps allow me; but when you come to higher suffering—for an idea, for instance—he will very rarely admit that, perhaps because my face strikes him not at all as what he fancies a man should have who suffers for an idea. And so he deprives me instantly of his favor, and not at all from badness of heart. Beggars, especially general beggars, ought never to show themselves, but to ask for charity through the newspapers. One can love one's neighbors in the abstract, or even at a distance, but at close quarters it's almost impossible. If it were as on the stage, in the ballet, where if beggars come in, they wear silken rags and tattered lace and beg for alms dancing gracefully, then one might like looking at them. But even then we would not love them. But enough of that. I simply wanted to show you my point of view. I meant to speak of the suffering of mankind generally, but we had better confine ourselves to the sufferings of the children. That reduces the scope of my argument to a tenth of what it would be. Still we'd better keep to the children, though it does weaken my case. But, in the first place, children can be loved even at close quarters, even when they are dirty, even when they are ugly (I fancy, though, children never are ugly). The second reason why I won't speak of grown-up people is that, besides being disgusting and unworthy of love, they have retribution—they've eaten the apple and know good and evil, and they have become 'like God.' They go on eating it still. But the children haven't eaten anything, and are so far innocent. Are you fond of children, Alyosha? I know you are, and you will understand why I prefer to speak of them. If they, too, suffer horribly on earth, they must suffer for their fathers, they must be punished for their fathers, who have eaten the apple; but that reasoning is of the other world and is incomprehensible for the heart of man here on earth. The innocent must not suffer for another's sins, and especially such innocents! You may be surprised at me, Alyosha, but I am awfully fond of children, too. And observe, cruel people, the violent, the rapacious, the Karamazovs are sometimes very fond of children. Children while they are quite little—up to seven, for instance—are so remote from grown-up people; they are different creatures, as it were, of a different species. I knew a criminal in prison who had, in the course of his career as a burglar, murdered whole families, including several children. But when he was in prison, he had a strange affection for them. He spent all his time at his window, watching the children playing in the prison yard. He trained one little boy to come up to his window and made great friends with him. . . . You don't know why I am telling you all this, Alyosha? My head aches and I am sad."

"You speak with a strange air," observed Alyosha uneasily, "as though you were not quite yourself."

"By the way, a Bulgarian I met lately in Moscow," Ivan went on, seeming not to hear his brother's words, "told me about the crimes committed by Turks and Circassians in all parts of Bulgaria through fear of a general rising of the Slavs. They burn villages, murder, rape women and children, they nail their prisoners to the fences by the ears, leave them so till morning, and in the morning they hang them—all sorts of things you can't imagine. People talk sometimes of bestial cruelty, but that's a great injustice and insult to the beast; a beast can never be so cruel as a man, so artistically cruel. The tiger only tears and gnaws, that's all he can do. He would never think of nailing people by the ears, even if he were able to do it. These Turks took a pleasure in torturing children, too; cutting the unborn child from the mother's womb, and tossing babies up in the air and catching them on the points of their bayonets before their mother's eyes. Doing it before the mother's eyes was what gave zest to the amusement. Here is another scene that I thought very interesting. Imagine a trembling mother with her baby in her arms, a circle of invading Turks around her. They've planned a diversion; they pet the baby, laugh to make it laugh. They succeed, the baby laughs. At that moment a Turk points a pistol four inches from the baby's face. The baby laughs with glee, holds out its little hands to the pistol, and he pulls the trigger in the baby's face and blows out its brains. Artistic, wasn't it? By the way, Turks are particularly fond of sweet things, they say."

"Brother, what are you driving at?" asked Alyosha.

"I think if the devil doesn't exist, but man has created him, he has created him in his own image and likeness."

"Just as he did God, then?" observed Alyosha.

"It's wonderful how you can turn words, as Polonius says in *Hamlet*," laughed Ivan. "You turn my words against me. Well, I am glad. Yours must be a fine God, if man created Him in His image and likeness. You asked just now what I was driving at. You see, I am fond of collecting certain little facts, and, would you believe, I even copy anecdotes of a certain sort from newspapers and stories, and I've already got a fine collection. The Turks, of course, have gone into it, but they are foreigners. I have specimens from home that are even better than the Turks. You know we prefer beating—rods and scourges—that's our national institution. Nailing ears is unthinkable for us, for we are, after all, Europeans. But the rod and the scourge we have always with us and they cannot be taken from us. Abroad now they scarcely do any beating. Perhaps manners are more humane, or laws have been passed, so that they don't dare to flog men now. But they make up for it in another way just as national as ours. And so national that it would be practically impossible among us, though I believe we are being inoculated with it, since the religious movement began in our aristocracy. I have a charming pamphlet,

translated from the French, describing how, quite recently, five years ago, a murderer, Richard, was executed—a young man, of twenty-three, I believe, who repented and was converted to the Christian faith at the very scaffold. This Richard was an illegitimate child who was *given* as a child of six by his parents to some shepherds on the Swiss mountains. They brought him up to work for them. He grew up like a little wild beast among them. The shepherds taught him nothing, and scarcely fed or clothed him, but sent him out at age seven to herd the flock in cold and wet, and no one hesitated or scrupled to treat him so. Quite the contrary, they thought they had every right, for Richard had been given to them as a chattel, and they did not even see the necessity of feeding him. Richard himself describes how in those years, like the Prodigal Son in the Gospel, he longed to eat of the mash given to the pigs, which were fattened for sale. But they wouldn't even give him that, and beat him when he stole from the pigs. And that was how he spent all his childhood and his youth, till he grew up and was strong enough to go away and be a thief. The savage began to earn his living as a day laborer in Geneva. He drank what he earned, he lived like a monster, and finished by killing and robbing an old man. He was caught, tried, and condemned to death. They are not sentimentalists there. And in prison he was immediately surrounded by pastors, members of Christian brotherhoods, philanthropic ladies, and the like. They taught him to read and write in prison, and expounded the Gospel to him. They exhorted him, worked upon him, drummed at him incessantly, till at last he solemnly confessed his crime. He was converted. He wrote to the court himself that he was a monster, but that in the end God had vouchsafed him light and shown grace. All Geneva was in excitement about him—all philanthropic and religious Geneva. All the aristocratic and well-bred society of the town rushed to the prison, kissed Richard and embraced him; 'You are our brother, you have found grace.' And Richard does nothing but weep with emotion, 'Yes, I've found grace! All my youth and childhood I was glad of pigs' food, but now even I have found grace. I am dying in the Lord.' 'Yes, Richard, die in the Lord; you have shed blood and must die in the Lord. Though it's not your fault that you knew not the Lord, when you coveted the pig's food and were beaten for stealing it (which was very wrong of you, for stealing is forbidden); but you've shed blood and you must die.' And on the last day, Richard, perfectly limp, did nothing but cry and repeat every minute "This is my happiest day. I am going to the Lord.' 'Yes,' cry the pastors and the judges and philanthropic ladies. 'This is the happiest day of your life, for you are going to the Lord!' They all walk or drive to the scaffold in procession behind the prison van. At the scaffold they call to Richard: 'Die, brother, die in the Lord, for even thou hast found grace!' And so, covered with his brothers' kisses, Richard is dragged on to the scaffold, and led to the guillotine. And they chopped off his head in brotherly fashion, because he had found grace. Yes, that's characteristic. That pamphlet is translated into Russian by some Russian philanthropists of aristocratic rank and evangelical aspirations, and has been distributed gratis for the enlightenment of the people. The case of Richard is interesting because it's national. Though to us it's absurd to cut off a man's head, because he has become our brother and has found grace, yet we have our own speciality, which is all but worse. Our historical pastime is the direct satisfaction of inflicting pain. There are lines in Nekrasov describing how a peasant lashes a horse on the eyes, 'on its meek eyes,' everyone must have seen it. It's peculiarly Russian. He describes how a feeble little nag had foundered under too heavy a load and cannot move. The peasant beats it, beats it savagely, beats it at last not knowing what he is doing in the intoxication of cruelty, thrashes it mercilessly over and over again. 'However weak you are, you must pull, if you die for it.' The nag strains, and then he begins lashing the poor defenseless creature on its weeping, on its 'meek eyes.' The frantic beast tugs and draws the load, trembling all over, gasping for breath, moving sideways, with a sort of unnatural spasmodic action—it's awful in Nekrasov. But that's only a horse, and God

has given horses to be beaten. So the Tatars have taught us, and they left us the knout as a remembrance of it. But men, too, can be beaten. A well-educated, cultured gentleman and his wife beat their own child with a birch rod; a girl of seven. I have an exact account of it. The papa was glad that the birch was covered with twigs. 'It stings more,' said he, and so he began stinging his daughter. I know for a fact there are people who at every blow are worked up to sensuality, to literal sensuality, which increases progressively at every blow they inflict. They beat for a minute, for five minutes, for ten minutes, more often and more savagely. The child screams. At last the child cannot scream, it gasps, 'Daddy! daddy!' By some diabolical unseemly chance the case was brought into court. A lawyer is engaged. The Russian people have long called a lawyer 'a conscience for hire.' The lawyer protests in his client's defense. 'It's such a simple thing,' he says, 'an everyday domestic event. A father corrects his child. To our shame be it said, it is brought into court.' The jury, convinced by him, gives a favorable verdict. The public roars with delight that the torturer is acquitted. Ah, pity I wasn't there! I would have proposed to raise a subscription in his honor! . . . Charming pictures.

"But I've still better things about children. I've collected a great, great deal about Russian children, Alyosha. There was a little girl of five who was hated by her father and mother, 'most worthy and respectable people, of good education and breeding.' You see, I must repeat again, it is a peculiar characteristic of many people, this love of torturing children, and children only. To all other types of humanity these torturers behave mildly and benevolently, like cultivated and humane Europeans; but they are very fond of tormenting children, even fond of children themselves in that sense. It's just their defenselessness that tempts the tormentor, just the angelic confidence of the child who has no refuge and no appeal, that sets his vile blood on fire. In every man, of course, a beast lies hidden—the beast of rage, the beast of lustful heat at the screams of the tortured victim, the beast of lawlessness let off the chain, the beast of diseases that follow on vice, gout, kidney disease, and so on.

"This poor girl of five was subjected to every possible torture by those cultivated parents. They beat her, thrashed her, kicked her for no reason till her body was one bruise. Then, they went to greater refinements of cruelty—shut her up all night in the cold and frost in a privy, and because she didn't ask to be taken up at night (as though a child of five sleeping its angelic, sound sleep could be trained to wake and ask), they smeared her face and made her eat that excrement, and it was her mother, her mother did this. And that mother could sleep, hearing the poor child's groans locked up in that vile place! Can you understand why a little creature, who can't even understand what's done to her, should beat her little aching heart with her tiny fist in that vile place, in the dark and the cold, and weep her sanguine meek, unresentful tears to dear, kind God to protect her? Do you understand that infamy, my friend and my brother, my pious and humble novice? Do you understand why this rigmarole must be and is permitted? Without it, I am told, man could not have existed on earth, for he could not have known good and evil. Why should he know that diabolical good and evil when it costs so much? Why, the whole world of knowledge is not worth that child's prayer to 'dear, kind God'! I say nothing of the sufferings of grown-up people, they have eaten the apple, damn them, and the devil take them all! But these little ones! I am making you suffer, Alyoshka, you are not yourself. I'll leave off if you like."

"Never mind, I want to suffer too," muttered Alyosha.

"One picture, only one more, because it's so curious, so characteristic, and I have only just read it in some collection of Russian antiquities in the *Archive*, or the *Past*. I've forgotten the name. I must look it up. It was in the darkest days of serfdom at the beginning of the century, and long live the Liberator of the People! There was in those days a general of aristocratic connections, the owner of great estates, one of those men—somewhat exceptional, I believe, even

then—who, retiring from the service into a life of leisure, are convinced that they've earned the power of life and death over their subjects. There were such men then. So our general, settled on his property of two thousand souls, lives in pomp, and domineers over his poor neighbors as though they were dependents and buffoons. He has kennels of hundreds of hounds and nearly a hundred dog-boys—all mounted, and in uniform. One day a serf boy, a little child of eight, threw a stone in play and hurt the paw of the general's favorite hound. 'Why is my favorite dog lame?' He is told that the boy threw a stone that hurt the dog's paw. 'So you did it.' The general looked the child up and down 'Take him.' He was taken—taken from his mother and kept shut up all night. Early that morning the general comes out in full pomp, mounts his horse with the hounds, his dependents, dog-boys, and the huntsmen, all mounted around him. The servants are summoned for their edification, and in front of them all stands the mother of the child. The child is brought from the lockup. It's a gloomy cold, foggy autumn day, a capital day for hunting. The general orders the child to be undressed; the child is stripped naked. He shivers, numb with terror, not daring to cry.... 'Make him run,' commands the general. 'Run! run!' shout the dog-boys. The boy runs.... 'At him!' yells the general, and he sets the whole pack of hounds on the child. The hounds catch him, and tear him to pieces before his mother's eyes!... I believe the general was afterwards declared incapable of administering his estates. Well—what did he deserve? To be shot? To be shot for the satisfaction of our moral feelings? Speak, Alyoshka!"

"To be shot," murmured Alyosha, lifting his eyes to Ivan with a pale, twisted smile.

"Bravo!" shouted Ivan delighted. "If even you say so, it means...You're a pretty monk! So there is a little devil sitting in your heart, Alyoshka Karamazov!"

"What I said was absurd, but—"

"That's just the point, that 'but'!" cried Ivan. "Let me tell you, novice, that the absurd is only too necessary on earth. The world stands on absurdities, and perhaps nothing would have come to pass in it without them. We know what we know!"

"What do you know?"

"I understand nothing," Ivan went on, as though in delirium. "I don't want to understand anything now. I want to stick to the fact. I made up my mind long ago not to understand. If I try to understand anything, I shall be false to the fact and I have determined to stick to the fact."

"Why are you trying me?" Alyosha cried out with a bitter outburst. "Will you say what you mean at last?"

"Of course, I will; that's what I've been leading up to. You are dear to me, I don't want to let you go, and I won't give you up to your Zosima."

Ivan for a minute was silent, his face became all at once very sad.

"Listen! I took the case of children only to make my case clearer. Of the other tears of humanity with which the earth is soaked from its crust to its center, I will say nothing. I have narrowed my subject on purpose. I am a bug, and I recognize in all humility that I cannot understand why the world is arranged as it is. Men are themselves to blame, I suppose; they were given paradise, they wanted freedom, and stole fire from heaven, though they knew they would become unhappy, so there is no need to pity them. With my pitiful, earthly, Euclidean understanding, all I know is that there is suffering and that there are none guilty; that cause follows effect, simply and directly; that everything flows and finds its level—but that's only Euclidean nonsense, I know that, and I can't consent to live by it! What comfort is it to me that there are none guilty and that cause follows effect simply and directly, and that I know it—I must have retribution, or I will destroy myself. And not retribution in some remote infinite time and space, but here on earth, and that I could see myself. I have believed in it. I want to see it, and if I am dead by then, let me rise again, for if it all happens without me, it will be too unfair. Surely I haven't suffered, simply that I, my crimes and my sufferings, may manure the soil of the future harmony for somebody else. I want to see with my own eyes the

hind lie down with the lion and the victim rise up and embrace his murderer. I want to be there when everyone suddenly understands what it has all been for. All the religions of the world are built on this longing, and I am a believer. But then there are the children, and what am I to do about them? That's a question I can't answer. For the hundredth time I repeat, there are numbers of questions, but I've only taken the children, because in their case what I mean is so unanswerably clear. Listen! If all must suffer to pay for the eternal harmony, what have children to do with it, tell me, please? It's beyond all comprehension why they should suffer, and why they should pay for the harmony. Why should they, too, furnish material to enrich the soil for the harmony of the future? I understand solidarity in sin among men. I understand solidarity in retribution, too; but there can be no such solidarity in sin with children. And if it is really true that they must share responsibility for all their fathers' crimes, such a truth is not of this world and is beyond my comprehension. Some jester will say, perhaps, that the child would have grown up and have sinned, but you see he didn't grow up, he was torn to pieces by the dogs, at eight years old. Oh, Alyosha, I am not blaspheming! I understand, of course, what an upheaval of the universe it will be, when everything in heaven and earth blends in one hymn of praise and everything that lives and has lived cries aloud: 'Thou art just, O'Lord, for Thy ways are revealed.' When the mother embraces the fiend who threw her child to the dogs, and all three cry aloud with tears, 'Thou art just, O Lord!' then, of course, the crown of knowledge will be reached and all will be made clear. But what pulls me up here is that I can't accept that harmony. And while I am on earth, I make haste to take my own measures. You see, Alyosha, perhaps it really may happen that if I live to that moment, or rise again to see it, I, too, perhaps, may cry aloud with the rest, looking at the mother embracing the child's torturer, 'Thou art just, O Lord!' but I don't want to cry aloud then. While there is still time, I hasten to protect myself and so I renounce the higher harmony altogether. It's not worth the tears of that one tortured child who beat itself on the breast with its little fist and prayed in its stinking outhouse, with its unexpiated tears to 'dear, kind God'! It's not worth it, because those tears are unatoned for. They must be atoned for, or there can be no harmony. But how? How are you going to atone for them? Is it possible? By their being avenged? But what do I care for avenging them? What do I care for a hell for oppressors? What good can hell do, since those children have already been tortured? And what becomes of harmony, if there is hell? I want to forgive. I want to embrace. I don't want more suffering. And if the sufferings of children go to swell the sum of sufferings which was necessary to pay for truth, then I protest that the truth is not worth such a price. I don't want the mother to embrace the oppressor who threw her son to the dogs! She dare not forgive him! Let her forgive him for herself, if she will, let her forgive the torturer for the immeasurable suffering of her mother's heart. But the sufferings of her tortured child she has no right to forgive; she dare not forgive the torturer, even if the child were to forgive him! And if that is so, if they dare not forgive, what becomes of harmony? Is there in the whole world a being who would have the right to forgive and could forgive? I don't want harmony. From love for humanity I don't want it. I would rather be left with the unavenged suffering. I would rather remain with my unavenged suffering and unsatisfied indignation, *even if I were wrong*. Besides, too high a price is asked for harmony; it's beyond our means to pay so much to enter on it. And so I hasten to give back my entrance ticket, and if I am an honest man I am bound to give it back as soon as possible. And that I am doing. It's not God that I don't accept, Alyosha, only I most respectfully return Him the ticket."

"That's rebellion," murmured Alyosha, looking down.

"Rebellion? I am sorry you call it that," said Ivan earnestly. "One can hardly live in rebellion, and I want to live. Tell me yourself, I challenge you—answer. Imagine that you are creating a fabric of human destiny with the object of making men happy in the end, giving them peace and rest at last, but that it was essential and inevitable to torture to death only one tiny creature—that little child beating its breast with its fist, for instance—and to found that edifice on its unavenged tears, would you consent to be the architect on those conditions? Tell me, and tell the truth."

"No, I wouldn't consent," said Alyosha softly.

"And can you admit the idea that men for whom you are building it would agree to accept their happiness on the foundation of the unexpiated blood of a little victim? And accepting it would remain happy forever?"

"No, I can't admit it. Brother," said Alyosha suddenly, with flashing eyes, "you said just now, is there a being in the whole world who would have the right to forgive and could forgive? But there is a Being and He can forgive everything, all *and for all*, because He gave His innocent blood for all and everything. You have forgotten Him, and on Him is built the edifice, and it is to Him they cry aloud. 'Thou art just, O Lord, for Thy ways are revealed!'"

"Ah! the One without sin and his blood! No, I have not forgotten Him; on the contrary I've been wondering all the time how it was you did not bring Him in before, for usually all arguments on your side put Him in the foreground. Do you know, Alyosha—don't laugh! I composed a poem about a year ago. If you can waste another ten minutes on me, I'll tell it to you."

"You wrote a poem?"

"Oh, no, I didn't write it," laughed Ivan, "and I've never written two lines of poetry in my life. But I composed up this poem in prose and I remembered it. I was carried away when I composed it. You will be my first reader—that is, listener. Why should an author forego even one listener?" smiled Ivan. "Shall I tell it to you?"

"I am all attention," said Alyosha. . . .

III.4   Evil and Soul-Making

JOHN HICK

John Hick (1922–   ) was for many years professor of theology at the University of Birmingham in England and, until his retirement, was professor of philosophy at Claremont Graduate School. His book *Evil and the God of Love* (1966), from which the following selection is taken, is considered one of the most thorough treatises on the problem of evil. "Evil and Soul-Making" is an example of a theodicy argument that is based on the free will defense. Theodicies can be of two differing types depending on how they justify the ways of God in the face of evil. The Augustinian position is that God created humans without sin and set them in a sinless, paradisical world. However, humanity fell into sin through the misuse of free will. God's grace will save some of us, but others will perish everlastingly. The second type of theodicy stems from the thinking of Irenaeus (120–202), of the Greek Church. The Irenaean tradition views Adam not as a free agent rebelling against God but as more akin to a small child. The fall is humanity's first faulty step in the direction of freedom. God is still working with humanity in order to bring it from undeveloped life (bios) to a state of self-realization in divine love, spiritual life (zoe). This life is viewed as the "vale of soul-making." Hick favors this version and develops it in this reading.

Fortunately there is another and better way. As well as the "majority report" of the Augustinian tradition, which has dominated Western Christendom, both Catholic and Protestant, since the time of Augustine himself, there is the "minority report" of the Irenaean tradition. This latter is both older and newer than the other, for it goes back to Sr. Irenaeus and others of the early Hellenistic Fathers of the Church in the two centuries prior to St. Augustine, and it has flourished again in more developed forms during the last hundred years.

Instead of regarding man as having been created by God in a finished state, as a finitely perfect being fulfilling the divine intention for our human level of existence, and then falling disastrously away from this, the minority report sees man as still in process of creation. Irenaeus himself expressed the point in terms of the (exegetically dubious) distinction between the "image" and the "likeness" of God referred to in Genesis i.26: "Then God said, Let us make man in our image, after our likeness." His view was that man as a personal and moral being already exists in the image, but has not yet been formed into the finite likeness of God. By this "likeness" Irenaeus means something more than personal existence as such; he means a certain valuable quality of personal life which reflects finitely the divine life. This represents the perfecting of man, the fulfillment of God's purpose for humanity, the "bringing of many sons to glory," the creating of "children of God" who are "fellow heirs with Christ" of his glory.

And so man, created as a personal being in the image of God, is only the raw material for a further and more difficult stage of God's creative work. This is the leading of men as relatively free and autonomous persons, through their own dealings with life in the world in which He has placed them, towards that quality of personal existence that is the finite likeness of God. The features of this likeness are revealed in the person of Christ, and the process of man's creation into it is the work of the Holy Spirit. In St. Paul's words, "And we all, with unveiled faces, beholding the glory of the Lord, are being changed into his likeness (εἰκών) from one degree of glory to another; for this comes from the Lord who is the Spirit";[1] or again, "For God knew his own before ever they were, and also ordained that they should be shaped to the likeness (εἰκών) of his Son."[2] In Johannine terms, the movement from the image to the likeness is a transition from one level of existence, that of animal life (*Bios*), to another and higher level, that of eternal life (*Zoe*), which includes but transcends the first. And the fall of man was seen by Irenaeus as a failure within the second phase of this creative process, a failure that has multiplied the perils and complicated the route of the journey in which God is seeking to lead mankind.

In the light of modern anthropological knowledge some form of two-stage conception of the creation of man has become an almost unavoidable Christian tenet. At the very least we must acknowledge as two distinguishable stages the fashioning of *homo sapiens* as a product of the long evolutionary process, and his sudden or gradual spiritualization as a child of God. But we may well extend the first stage to include the development of man as a rational and responsible person capable of personal relationship with the personal Infinite who has created him. This first stage of the creative process was, to our anthropomorphic imaginations, easy for divine omnipotence. By an exercise of creative power God caused the physical universe to exist, and in the course of countless ages to bring forth within it organic life, and finally to produce out of organic life personal life; and when man had thus emerged out of the evolution of the forms of organic life, a creature had been made who has the possibility of existing in conscious fellowship with God. But the second stage of the creative process is of a different kind altogether. It cannot be performed by omnipotent power as such. For personal life is essentially free and self-directing. It cannot be perfected by divine fiat, but only through the uncompelled responses and willing co-operation of human individuals in their actions and reactions in the world in which God

has placed them. Men may eventually become the perfected persons whom the New Testament calls "children of God," but they cannot be created ready-made as this.

The value-judgment that is implicitly being invoked here is that one who has attained to goodness by meeting and eventually mastering temptations, and thus by rightly making responsible choices in concrete situations, is good in a richer and more valuable sense than would be one created *ab initio* in a state either of innocence or of virtue. In the former case, which is that of the actual moral achievements of mankind, the individual's goodness has within it the strength of temptation overcome, a stability based upon an accumulation of right choices, and a positive and responsible character that comes from the investment of costly personal effort. I suggest, then, that it is an ethically reasonable judgment, even though in the nature of the case not one that is capable of demonstrative proof, that human goodness slowly built up through personal histories of moral effort has a value in the eyes of the Creator which justifies even the long travail of the soul-making process.

The picture with which we are working is thus developmental and teleological. Man is in process of becoming the perfected being whom God is seeking to create. However, this is not taking place—it is important to add—by a natural and inevitable evolution, but through a hazardous adventure in individual freedom. Because this is a pilgrimage within the life of each individual, rather than a racial evolution, the progressive fulfillment of God's purpose does not entail any corresponding progressive improvement in the moral state of the world. There is no doubt a development in man's ethical situation from generation to generation through the building of individual choices into public institutions, but this involves an accumulation of evil as well as of good. It is thus probable that human life was lived on much the same moral plane two thousand years ago or four thousand years ago as it is today. But nevertheless during this period uncounted millions of souls have been through the experience of earthly life, and God's purpose has gradually moved towards its fulfillment within each one of them, rather than within a human aggregate composed of different units in different generations.

If, then, God's aim in making the world is "the bringing of many sons to glory," that aim will naturally determine the kind of world that He has created. Antitheistic writers almost invariably assume a conception of the divine purpose which is contrary to the Christian conception. They assume that the purpose of a loving God must be to create a hedonistic paradise; and therefore to the extent that the world is other than this, it proves to them that God is either not loving enough or not powerful enough to create such a world. They think of God's relation to the earth on the model of a human being building a cage for a pet animal to dwell in. If he is humane he will naturally make his pet's quarters as pleasant and healthful as he can. Any respect in which the cage falls short of the veterinarian's ideal, and contains possibilities of accident or disease, is evidence of either limited benevolence or limited means, or both. Those who use the problem of evil as an argument against belief in God almost invariably think of the world in this kind of way. David Hume, for example, speaks of an architect who is trying to plan a house that is to be as comfortable and convenient as possible. If we find that "the windows, doors, fires, passages, stairs, and the whole economy of the building were the source of noise, confusion, fatigue, darkness, and the extremes of heat and cold" we should have no hesitation in blaming the architect. It would be in vain for him to prove that if this or that defect were corrected greater ills would result: "still you would assert in general, that, if the architect had had skill and good intentions, he might have formed such a plan of the whole, and might have adjusted the parts in such a manner, as would have remedied all or most of these inconveniences."[3]

But if we are right in supposing that God's purpose for man is to lead him from human *Bios*, or the biological life of man, to that quality of *Zoe*, or the personal life of eternal worth, which we see in Christ, then the question that we have to ask is not, Is this the kind of world that an all-powerful and infinitely loving being would create as an environment for his human pets? or, Is the architecture of the world the most pleasant and convenient possible? The question that we have to ask is rather, Is this the kind of world that God might make as an environment in which moral beings may be fashioned, through their own free insights and responses, into "children of God"?

Such critics as Hume are confusing what heaven ought to be, as an environment for perfected finite beings, with what this world ought to be, as an environment for beings who are in process of becoming perfected. For if our general conception of God's purpose is correct the world is not intended to be a paradise, but rather the scene of a history in which human personality may be formed towards the pattern of Christ. Men are not to be thought of on the analogy of animal pets, whose life is to be made as agreeable as possible, but rather on the analogy of human children, who are to grow to adulthood in an environment whose primary and overriding purpose is not immediate pleasure but the realizing of the most valuable potentialities of human personality.

Needless to say, this characterization of God as the heavenly Father is not a merely random illustration but an analogy that lies at the heart of the Christian faith. Jesus treated the likeness between the attitude of God to man, and the attitude of human parents at their best towards their children, as providing the most adequate way for us to think about God. And so it is altogether relevant to a Christian understanding of this world to ask, How does the best parental love express itself in its influence upon the environment in which children are to grow up? I think it is clear that a parent who loves his children, and wants them to become the best human beings that they are capable of becoming, does not treat pleasure as the sole and supreme value. Certainly we seek pleasure for our children, and take great delight in obtaining it for them; but we do not desire for them unalloyed pleasure at the expense of their growth in such even greater values as moral integrity, unselfishness, compassion, courage, humour, reverence for the truth, and perhaps above all the capacity for love. We do not act on the premise that pleasure is the supreme end of life; and if the development of these other values sometimes clashes with the provision of pleasure, then we are willing to have our children miss a certain amount of this, rather than fail to come to possess and to be possessed by the finer and more precious qualities that are possible to the human personality. A child brought up on the principle that the only or the supreme value is pleasure would not be likely to become an ethically mature adult or an attractive or happy personality. And to most parents it seems more important to try to foster quality and strength of character in their children than to fill their lives at all times with the utmost possible degree of pleasure. If, then, there is any true analogy between God's purpose for his human creatures, and the purpose of loving and wise parents for their children, we have to recognize that the presence of pleasure and the absence of pain cannot be the supreme and overriding end for which the world exists. Rather, this world must be a place of soul-making. And its value is to be judged, not primarily by the quantity of pleasure and pain occurring in it at any particular moment, but by its fitness for its primary purpose, the purpose of soul-making.

In all this we have been speaking about the nature of the world considered simply as the God given environment of man's life. For it is mainly in this connection that the world has been regarded in Irenaean and in Protestant thought. But such a way of thinking involves a danger of anthropocentrism from which the Augustinian and Catholic tradition has generally been protected by its sense of the relative insignificance of man within the totality of the created universe. Man was dwarfed within the medieval worldview by the innumerable hosts of angels and archangels above him—unfallen rational natures which rejoice in the immediate presence of God, reflecting His glory in the untarnished mirror of their worship. However, this higher creation has in our modern world lost its hold upon the imagination. Its place has been taken, as the minimizer of men, by the immensities of outer space and by the material universe's unlimited complexity transcending our present knowledge. As the spiritual environment envisaged by Western man has shrunk, his physical horizons have correspondingly expanded. Where the human creature was formerly seen as an insignificant appendage to the angelic world, he is now seen as an equally insignificant organic excrescence, enjoying a fleeting moment of consciousness on the surface of one of the planets of a minor star. Thus the truth that was symbolized for former ages by the existence of the angelic hosts is today impressed upon us by the vastness of the physical universe, countering the egoism of our species by making us feel that this immense prodigality of existence can hardly all exist for the sake of man—though, on the other hand, the very realization that it is not all for the sake of man may itself be salutary and beneficial to man!

However, instead of opposing man and nature as rival objects of God's interest, we should perhaps rather stress man's solidarity as an embodied being with the whole natural order in which he is embedded. For man is organic to the world; all his acts and thoughts and imaginations are conditioned by space and time; and in abstraction from nature he would cease to be human. We may, then, say that the beauties and sublimities and powers, the microscopic intricacies and macroscopic vastnesses, the wonders and the terrors of the natural world and of the life that pulses through it, are willed and valued by their Maker in a creative act that embraces man together with nature. By means of matter and living flesh God both builds a path and weaves a veil between Himself and the creature made in His image. Nature thus has permanent significance; for God has set man in a creaturely environment, and the final fulfilment of our nature in relation to God will accordingly take the form of an embodied life within "a new heaven and a new earth." And as in the present age man moves slowly towards that fulfillment through the pilgrimage of his earthly life, so also "the whole creation" is "groaning in travail," waiting for the time when it will be "set free from its bondage to decay."

And yet however fully we thus acknowledge the permanent significance and value of the natural order, we must still insist upon man's special character as a personal creature made in the image of God; and our theodicy must still centre upon the soul-making process that we believe to be taking place within human life.

This, then, is the starting-point from which we propose to try to relate the realities of sin and suffering to the perfect love of an omnipotent Creator. And as will become increasingly apparent, a theodicy that starts in this way must be eschatological in its ultimate bearings. That is to say, instead of looking to the past for its clue to the mystery of evil, it looks to the future, and indeed to that ultimate future to which only faith can look. Given the conception of a divine intention working in and through human time towards a fulfilment that lies in its completeness beyond human time, our theodicy must find the meaning of evil in the part that it is made to play in the eventual outworking of that purpose; and must find the justification of the whole process in the magnitude of the good to which it leads. The good that outshines all ill is not a paradise long since lost but a kingdom which is yet to come in its full glory and permanence.

NOTES

1. II Corinthians iii. 18.
2. Romans viii. 29. Other New Testament passages expressing a view of man as undergoing a process of spiritual growth within God's purpose are: Ephesians ii. 21, iii. 16; Colossians ii. 19; I John iii. 2; II Corinthians iv. 16.
3. *Dialogues Concerning Natural Religion*, pt. xi. Kemp-Smith's ed. (Oxford: Clarendon Press, 1935), p. 251.

III.5 A Critique of Hick's Theodicy

EDWARD H. MADDEN AND PETER H. HARE

Edward H. Madden (1925–   ) and Peter H. Hare (1935–   ) are emeritus professors of philosophy at the State University of New York at Buffalo. In this selection, they attack Hick's theory. They ask whether the amount of evil in the world is necessary for soul-making and accuse Hick of three fallacies, called "all or nothing," "it could be worse," and "slippery slope."

The intellectual honesty of John Hick is impressive. Unlike the majority of Christian apologists he does not try to find safety in the number of solutions but instead searchingly criticizes and disowns many of the favorite solutions. He concludes, nevertheless, the apologetics reduced to fighting trim is all the more effective. He believes that a sophisticated combination of the character-building and free-will solutions will serve. They show evil to serve God's purpose of "soul-making."

Earlier we pointed out the difficulties involved in the usual formulations of the character-building and free-will solutions. We shall consider here how successful Hick is in avoiding these difficulties.

According to Hick,

man, created as a personal being in the image of God, is only the raw material for a further and more difficult stage of God's creative work. This is the leading of men as relatively free and

Reprinted from Edward H. Madden and Peter H. Hare, *Evil and the Concept of God* (1968), 83–90, 102–103. Courtesy of Charles C. Thomas, Publisher, Springfield, Illinois. Footnotes deleted.

autonomous persons through their own dealings with life in the world in which he has placed them, towards that quality of personal existence that is the finite likeness of God.

The basic trouble, he says, with antitheistic writers is that "they assume that the purpose of a loving God must be to create a hedonistic paradise." He concedes that evil is not serving any, even remote, hedonistic end, but insists that it is serving the end of the development of moral personalities in loving relation to God. It is logically impossible to do this either by the forcing them to love him or by forcing them always to act rightly. A creature *forced* to love would not be genuinely loving and a creature *forced* to do the right would not be a moral personality. Only through freedom, suffering, and initial remoteness from God ("epistemic distance") can the sort of person God is looking for come about.

Before we discuss in detail the difficulties involved in Hick's position we will briefly describe three informal fallacies Hick adroitly uses in his solution. They are all fallacies which have been used in one form or another throughout the history of Christian apologetics, and we have had occasion to mention them in our discussion of other writers in the previous chapter. However, it will be convenient in discussing Hick's skillful and elaborate use of them to describe and label clearly these arguments: "All or nothing," "It could be worse," and "slippery slope."

All or nothing. This is the claim that something is desirable because its complete loss would be far worse than the evil its presence now causes. The erroneous assumption is that we must have this thing either in its present form and amount or not at all. But it is often the case that only some amount of the thing in *some* form is necessary to the achievement of a desirable end.

It could be worse. This is the claim that something is not really bad because it will be followed by all manner of desirable things. The erroneous assumption here is that showing that having these later desirable things is a great boon also shows that the original evil is a necessary and not gratuitous one. Actually it only

shows that the situation would be still worse if the desirable things did not follow. To show that it could be worse does not show that it could not be better.

Slippery slope. This is the claim that if God once started eliminating evils of this world he would have no place to stop short of a "perfect" world in which only robots and not men were possible. The erroneous assumption is that God would have no criterion to indicate where on the slippery slope to stop and no ability to implement it effectively. The same argument is used in human affairs and the answer is equally clear. "Once we venture, as we sometimes must, on a dangerous course which may lead to our salvation in a particular situation but which may also be the beginning of our path to perdition, the only answer we can give to the question 'Where will you stop?' is 'Wherever our intelligence tells us to stop!'"

Hick's use of the free-will solution is an example of the "all or nothing" fallacy. He concedes that there is an appalling amount of moral evil in the world but insists that it would be logically impossible for God to achieve his purpose of soul-making by creating puppets who always acted rightly. This is a position we have criticized elsewhere and we must show here how the same criticism applies to Hick.

Hick says that the difficulty with criticisms of the free-will solution has been that they suppose God would have done better to create man as a "pet animal" in a cage, "as pleasant and healthful" as possible. Undeniably critics of the free-will solution have often made this mistake, but it is a mistake easily avoided. We are prepared to grant that a better world would not have been created by making men as pet animals. However, the damaging question is whether God had only two alternatives: to create men with the unfortunate moral inclinations they have at present or to create men as pet animals. There are clearly other alternatives. There are, after all, many different ways for a parent to guide his child's moral growth while respecting his freedom.

Perhaps an analogy will be helpful. God, as Hick views him, might be described as headmaster to a vast progressive school where the absolute freedom of the students is sacred. He does not want to force any children to read textbooks because, he feels, that will only produce students who are more motivated by fear of punishment than by love of knowledge for its own sake. Every student must be left to educate himself as much as possible. However, it is quite unconvincing to argue that because rigid regulation has horrible consequences, almost no regulation is ideal—there are dangers in either extreme. And it is just as much of a mistake to argue that because the possibility of God's creation of men as pet animals is ghastly to contemplate. God's creation of men with the sort of freedom they have now is the best possible choice.

One of Hick's more unfortunate uses of the "all or nothing" argument appears in his justification of man's "initial epistemic distance" from God. He suggests that God has deliberately refrained from giving much knowledge of himself to men for fear that it would jeopardize the development of "authentic fiduciary attitudes" in men. God is fearful (in our analogy) that "spoon-feeding" his creatures will prevent them from developing genuine intellectual curiosity. Because he thinks that constant and thorough spoon-feeding will ruin their intellects, he advocates contact between schoolboy and teacher only once a year.

But we are being too kind in our analogy. God does not even think it wise to deliver a matriculation address to each student. Almost all students must be content with meager historical records of a matriculation address in the distant past and a hope of a commencement speech in the future. It is no wonder there have been student riots. The countless generations before Christ were especially destitute of faculty-student contact. And even now the vast amount of humanity in non-Christian parts of the world find it difficult to be admitted to the soul-making school at all.

Sometimes Hick feels the weakness of the "all or nothing" argument and accordingly shifts to the "it could be worse" strategy. "Christian theodicy must point forward to that final blessedness, and claim that this infinite future good will render worth while all the pain and travail and wickedness that has occurred on the way to it." To be sure, we should be grateful to God for

not tormenting us for an eternity, but the question remains of why he is torturing us at all. However, this strategy is beside the point. Hick must still show us how all the suffering in this world is the most efficient way of achieving God's goal. Merely to assure the student who is threatening riot that in his old age he will somehow come to regard the indignities of his student days as rather unimportant is not to explain why those indignities must be visited upon him at all.

Although Hick does not himself feel confident that in the Kingdom of God all men will completely forget their earthly sufferings, he suggests that, if such a loss of memory were to occur, it would help solve the problem of evil. However, we can concede complete heavenly amnesia and this concession does not move us any closer to a solution. If a man were to torture his wife, and afterwards somehow to remove completely the memory of the torture from her mind so that she returned to her earlier love of him, this would certainly be better than retaining the painful memory, but it still would not explain the necessity of torturing her in the first place.

Hick, however, candidly admits to a feeling that neither of the two strategies discussed above is completely effective in the last analysis and realizes that he must face "excessive or dysteleologicaly suffering." Consequently he moves on to the "slippery slope" argument.

> Unless God eliminated all evils whatsoever there would always be relatively outstanding ones of which it would be said that He should have secretly prevented them. If, for example, divine providence had eliminated Hitler in his infancy, we might now point instead to Mussolini.... - There would be nowhere to stop, short of divinely arranged paradise in which human freedom would be narrowly circumscribed.

He claims, in other words, that there would be no way of eliminating some evils without removing all of them with the effect of returning us to the "all or nothing" situation.

This argument fails because the erroneous assumption is made that in the process of removing evils God would not be able precisely to calculate the effect of each removal and stop at exactly the point at which soul-making was most efficiently achieved. Presumably at that point men would still suffer and complain about their suffering, but it would be possible to offer them an explanation of the necessity of this amount of suffering as a means to the end of soul-making. In the analogy we used earlier, no matter how much is done to increase faculty-student contact there will still be some student complaints, but presumably it is possible to reach a point at which such students can be shown how the present amount of faculty-student contact is precisely the right amount to maximize creative intellectual activity.

Hick even comes to admit that this third strategy is no more effective than the first two. He appears to be like a man flourishing toy weapons before an assailant, knowing that in the last analysis they cannot be effective, but hoping that the assailant will be scared off before he comes close enough to see that they are not genuine weapons. In the last analysis he must appeal to mystery. "I do not now have an alternative theory to offer that would explain in any rational or ethical way why men suffer as they do. The only appeal left is to mystery."

Hick's use of mystery is not the usual appeal to mystical experience or commitment so often made by theists. He suggests that mystery, too, contributes to soul-making. Here again he uses the "all or nothing" argument and asks us to imagine a world which contained no unjust, excessive, or apparently unnecessary misery, a world in which suffering could always be seen to be either punishment justly deserved or a part of moral training.

> In such a world human misery would not evoke deep personal sympathy or call forth organized relief and sacrificial help or service. For it is presupposed in these compassionate reactions both that the suffering is not deserved and that it is *bad* for the sufferer.

There are at least three ways of criticizing this strategy:

(a) It is quite possible to feel intense compassion for someone even though his suffering is understood to be an unavoidable means to an end, desirable both to the sufferer and to oneself. A husband may feel convinced that his wife's labor pains are a necessary means to a highly desirable end and at the same time feel great compassion. One can even feel compassion for the pain suffered by a criminal being punished in a way that one thinks is deserved.

(b) Even if some undeserved and unnecessary suffering is necessary to make possible compassion, it is obvious that a minute percentage of the present unnecessary suffering would do the job adequately.

(c) One must remember that while unjust suffering may increase compassion, it also creates massive resentment. This resentment often causes individuals indiscriminately to lash out at the world. The benefits of compassion are probably more than offset by the damage done by resentment.

However, Hick thinks that there is still one last justification for unjust suffering. He asks us to consider what would happen if all unjust suffering were eliminated. In such a world reward would be the predictable result of virtue and punishment the predictable outcome of wickedness. But in such a world doing right simply for its own sake—what Kant called the good will—would be impossible "for whilst the possibility of the good will by no means precludes that right action shall in fact eventually lead to happiness, and wrong action to misery, it does preclude this happening so certainly, instantly, and manifestly that virtue cannot be separate in experience and thought from its reward, or vice from its punishment."

This solution, itself a sign that the end is near at hand, can be rejected with confidence for the following reasons.

(a) This effort to solve the problem of evil does not do justice to the good sense God presumably would have were he to exist. God would certainly have sense enough to administer rewards and punishments in view of *motives* and not simply in view of what an agent does. It would already be an unjust response if God rewarded an agent for doing what is objectively right on prudential grounds alone.

(b) This effort misfires psychologically as well as theologically. If God usually rewarded men when they sincerely performed an act solely because it was right, this could only have a beneficial effect on human morality. If a parent regularly rewards the child who performs a good act only because he thinks it right more than he rewards a child performing the same act only to curry favor with the parent, this can only tend to reinforce the tendency to act virtuously.

(c) Even if completely regular rewarding of right behavior would tend to undermine the good will, there is still every reason to believe that an enormous amount of the present unjust punishment could be eliminated without jeopardizing the possibility of acting from a sense of duty. The "all-or-nothing" fallacy is omnipresent in theistic arguments and its presence here at the end, after it had been supposedly rejected, comes as no surprise.

III.6   Evil and Omnipotence

J. L. MACKIE

John L. Mackie (1917–1981) was born in Australia and taught at Oxford University until his death. He made important contributions to the fields of metaphysics, epistemology, ethics, and philosophy of religion. Among his works are *The Cement of the Universe* (1974), *Ethics: Inventing Right and Wrong* (1977), and *The Miracle of Theism* (1982). In this essay, Mackie argues that the argument from evil demonstrates the incoherence of theism. If there is a God who is all-powerful and completely good, he will be able and willing to eliminate all evil in the world. But there is evil, so no God exists.

The traditional arguments for the existence of God have been fairly thoroughly criticised by philosophers. But the theologian can, if he wishes, accept this criticism. He can admit that no rational proof of God's existence is possible. And he can still retain all that is essential to his position, by holding that God's existence is known in some other, non-rational way. I think, however, that a more telling criticism can be made by way of the traditional problem of evil. Here it can be shown, not that religious beliefs lack rational support, but that they are positively irrational, that the several parts of the essential theological doctrine are inconsistent with one another, so that the theologian can maintain his position as a whole only by a much more extreme rejection of reason than in the former case. He must now be prepared to believe, not merely what cannot be proved, but what can be *disproved* from other beliefs that he also holds.

The problem of evil, in the sense in which I shall be using the phrase, is a problem only for someone who believes that there is a God who is both omnipotent and wholly good. And it is a logical problem, the problem of clarifying and reconciling a number of beliefs: it is not a scientific problem that might be solved by further observations, or a practical problem that might be solved by a decision or an action. These points are obvious; I mention them only because they are sometimes ignored by theologians, who sometimes parry a statement of the problem with such remarks as "Well, can you solve the problem yourself?" or "This is a mystery which may be revealed to us later" or "Evil is something to be faced and overcome, not to be merely discussed."

In its simplest form the problem is this: God is omnipotent; God is wholly good; and yet evil exists. There seems to be some contradiction

From *Mind*, Vol. LXIV, No. 254 (1955). Reprinted by permission of Oxford University Press.

between these three propositions, so that if any two of them were true the third would be false. But at the same time all three are essential parts of most theological positions: the theologian, it seems, at once *must* adhere and *cannot consistently* adhere to all three. (The problem does not arise only for theists, but I shall discuss it in the form in which it presents itself for ordinary theism.)

However, the contradiction does not arise immediately; to show it we need some additional premises, or perhaps some quasi-logical rules connecting the terms 'good,' 'evil,' and 'omnipotent.' These additional principles are that good is opposed to evil, in such a way that a good thing always eliminates evil as far as it can, and that there are no limits to what an omnipotent thing can do. From these it follows that a good omnipotent thing eliminates evil completely, and then the propositions that a good omnipotent thing exists, and that evil exists, are incompatible.

A. ADEQUATE SOLUTIONS

Now once the problem is fully stated it is clear that it can be solved, in the sense that the problem will not arise if one gives up at least one of the propositions that constitute it. If you are prepared to say that God is not wholly good, or not quite omnipotent, or that evil does not exist, or that good is not opposed to the kind of evil that exists, or that there are limits to what an omnipotent thing can do, then the problem of evil will not arise for you.

There are, then, quite a number of adequate solutions of the problem of evil, and some of these have been adopted, or almost adopted, by various thinkers. For example, a few have been prepared to deny God's omnipotence, and rather more have been prepared to keep the term 'omnipotence' but severely to restrict its meaning, recording quite a number of things that an omnipotent being cannot do. Some have said that evil is an illusion, perhaps because they held that the whole world of temporal, changing things is an illusion, and that what we call evil belongs only to this world, or perhaps because

they held that although temporal things are much as we see them, those that we call evil are not really evil. Some have said that what we call evil is merely the privation of good, that evil in a positive sense, evil that would really be opposed to good, does not exist. Many have agreed with Pope that disorder is harmony not understood, and that partial evil is universal good. Whether any of these views is true is, of course, another question. But each of them gives an adequate solution of the problem of evil in the sense that if you accept it this problem does not arise for you, though you may, of course, have *other* problems to face.

But often enough these adequate solutions are only *almost* adopted. The thinkers who restrict God's power, but keep the term 'omnipotence,' may reasonably be suspected of thinking, in other contexts, that his power is really unlimited. Those who say that evil is an illusion may also be thinking, inconsistently, that this illusion is itself an evil. Those who say that "evil" is merely privation of good may also be thinking, inconsistently, that privation of good is an evil. (The fallacy here is akin to some forms of the "naturalistic fallacy" in ethics, where some think, for example, that "good" is just what contributes to evolutionary progress, and that evolutionary progress is itself good.) If Pope meant what he said in the first line of his couplet, that "disorder" is only harmony not understood, the "partial evil" of the second line must, for consistency, mean "that which, taken in isolation, falsely appears to be evil," but it would more naturally mean "that which, in isolation, really is evil." The second line, in fact, hesitates between two views, that "partial evil" isn't really evil, since only the universal quality is real, and that "partial evil" is really an evil, but only a little one.

In addition, therefore, to adequate solutions, we must recognise unsatisfactorily inconsistent solutions, in which there is only a half-hearted or temporary rejection of one of the propositions which together constitute the problem. In these, one of the constituent propositions is explicitly rejected, but it is covertly re-asserted or assumed elsewhere in the system.

B. FALLACIOUS SOLUTIONS

Besides these half-hearted solutions, which explicitly reject but implicitly assert one of the constituent propositions, there are definitely fallacious solutions which explicitly maintain all the constituent propositions, but implicitly reject at least one of them in the course of the argument that explains away the problem of evil.

There are, in fact, many so-called solutions which purport to remove the contradiction without abandoning any of its constituent propositions. These must be fallacious as we can see from the very statement of the problem, but it is not so easy to see in each case precisely where the fallacy lies. I suggest that in all cases the fallacy has the general form suggested above: in order to solve the problem one (or perhaps more) of its constituent propositions is given up, but in such a way that it appears to have been retained, and can therefore be asserted without qualification in other contexts. Sometimes there is a further complication: the supposed solution moves to and fro between, say, two of the constituent propositions, at one point asserting the first of these but covertly abandoning the second, at another point asserting the second but covertly abandoning the first. These fallacious solutions often turn upon some equivocation with the words 'good' and 'evil,' or upon some vagueness about the way in which good and evil are opposed to one another, or about how much is meant by 'omnipotence.' I propose to examine some of these so-called solutions, and to exhibit their fallacies in detail. Incidentally, I shall also be considering whether an adequate solution could be reached by a minor modification of one or more of the constituent propositions, which would, however, still satisfy all the essential requirements of ordinary theism.

(1) "Good cannot exist without evil" or "Evil is necessary as a counterpart to good."

It is sometimes suggested that evil is necessary as a counterpart to good, that if there were no evil there could be no good either, and that this solves the problem of evil. It is true that it points to an answer to the question "Why should there be evil?" But it does so only by qualifying some of the propositions that constitute the problem.

First, it sets a limit to what God can do, saying that God *cannot* create good without simultaneously creating evil, and this means either that God is not omnipotent or that there are *some* limits to what an omnipotent thing can do. It may be replied that these limits are always presupposed, that omnipotence has never meant the power to do what is logically impossible, and on the present view the existence of good without evil would be a logical impossibility. This interpretation of omnipotence may, indeed, be accepted as a modification of our original account which does not reject anything that is essential to theism, and I shall in general assume it in the subsequent discussion. It is, perhaps, the most common theistic view, but I think that some theists at least have maintained that God can do what is logically impossible. Many theists, at any rate, have held that logic itself is created or laid down by God, that logic is the way in which God arbitrarily chooses to think. (This is, of course, parallel to the ethical view that morally right actions are those which God arbitrarily chooses to command, and the two views encounter similar difficulties.) And this account of logic is clearly inconsistent with the view that God is bound by logical necessities—unless it is possible for an omnipotent being to bind himself, an issue which we shall consider later, when we come to the Paradox of Omnipotence. This solution of the problem of evil cannot, therefore, be consistently adopted along with the view that logic is itself created by God.

But, secondly, this solution denies that evil is opposed to good in our original sense. If good and evil are counterparts, a good thing will not "eliminate evil as far as it can." Indeed, this view suggests that good and evil are not strictly qualities of things at all. Perhaps the suggestion is that good and evil are related in much the same way as great and small. Certainly, when the term 'great' is used relatively as a condensation of 'greater than so-and-so,' and 'small' is used correspondingly, greatness and smallness are counterparts and cannot exist without each other. But in this sense greatness is not a quality, not an intrinsic feature of anything; and it would be absurd to think of a movement in favour of greatness and against smallness in this sense. Such a movement would be self-defeating, since relative greatness can be promoted only by a simultaneous promotion of relative smallness. I feel sure that no theists would be content to regard God's goodness as analogous to this—as if what he supports were not the *good* but the *better*, and if he had the paradoxical aim that all things should be better than other things.

This point is obscured by the fact that 'great' and 'small' seem to have an absolute as well as a relative sense. I cannot discuss here whether there is absolute magnitude or not, but if there is, there could be an absolute sense for 'great,' it could mean of at least a certain size, and it would make sense to speak of all things getting bigger, of a universe that was expanding all over, and therefore it would make sense to speak of promoting greatness. But in *this* sense great and small are not logically necessary counterparts: either quality could exist without the other. There would be no logical impossibility in everything's being small or in everything's being great.

Neither in the absolute nor in the relative sense, then, of 'great' and 'small' do these terms provide an analogy of the sort that would be needed to support this solution of the problem of evil. In neither case are greatness and smallness *both* necessary counterparts *and* mutually opposed forces or possible objects for support and attack.

It may be replied that good and evil are necessary counterparts in the same way as any quality and its logical opposite: redness can occur, it is suggested, only if non-redness also occurs. But unless evil is merely the privation of good, they are not logical opposites, and some further argument would be needed to show that they are counterparts in the same way as genuine logical opposites. Let us assume that this could be given. There is still doubt of the correctness of the metaphysical principle that a quality must have a real opposite: I suggest that it is not really impossible that everything should be, say, red, that the truth is merely that if everything were

red we should not notice redness, and so we should have no word 'red'; we observe and give names to qualities only if they have real opposites. If so, the principle that a term must have an opposite would belong only to our language or to our thought, and would not be an ontological principle, and correspondingly, the rule that good cannot exist without evil would not state a logical necessity of a sort that God would just have to put up with. God might have made everything good, though *we* should not have noticed it if he had.

But, finally, even if we concede that this is an ontological principle, it will provide a solution for the problem of evil only if one is prepared to say, "Evil exists, but only just enough evil to serve as the counterpart of good." I doubt whether any theist will accept this. After all, the ontological requirement that non-redness should occur would be satisfied even if all the universe, except for a minute speck, were red, and, if there were a corresponding requirement for evil as a counterpart to good, a minute dose of evil would presumably do. But theists are not usually willing to say, in all contexts, that all the evil that occurs is a minute and necessary dose.

(2) "Evil is necessary as a means to good."

It is sometimes suggested that evil is necessary for good not as a counterpart but as a means. In its simple form this has little plausibility as a solution of the problem of evil, since it obviously implies a severe restriction of God's power. It would be a *causal* law that you cannot have a certain end without a certain means, so that if God has to introduce evil as a means to good, he must be subject to at least some causal laws. This certainly conflicts with what a theist normally means by omnipotence. This view of God as limited by causal laws also conflicts with the view that causal laws are themselves made by God, which is more widely held than the corresponding view about the laws of logic. This conflict would, indeed, be resolved if it were possible for an omnipotent being to bind himself, and this possibility has still to be considered. Unless a favourable answer can be given to this question, the suggestion that evil is necessary as a means to good solves the problem of evil only by denying one of its constituent propositions, either that God is omnipotent or that 'omnipotent' means what it says.

(3) "The universe is better with some evil in it than it could be if there were no evil."

Much more important is a solution which at first seems to be a mere variant of the previous one, that evil may contribute to the goodness of a whole in which it is found, so that the universe as a whole is better as it is, with some evil in it, than it would be if there were no evil. This solution may be developed in either of two ways. It may be supported by an aesthetic analogy, by the fact that contrasts heighten beauty, that in a musical work, for example, there may occur discords which somehow add to the beauty of the work as a whole. Alternatively, it may be worked out in connection with the notion of progress, that the best possible organization of the universe will not be static, but progressive, that the gradual overcoming of evil by good is really a finer thing than would be the eternal unchallenged supremacy of good.

In either case, this solution usually starts from the assumption that the evil whose existence gives rise to the problem of evil is primarily what is called physical evil, that is to say, pain. In Hume's rather half-hearted presentation of the problem of evil, the evils that he stresses are pain and disease, and those who reply to him argue that the existence of pain and disease makes possible the existence of sympathy, benevolence, heroism, and the gradually successful struggle of doctors and reformers to overcome these evils. In fact, theists often seize the opportunity to accuse those who stress the problem of evil of taking a low, materialistic view of good and evil, equating these with pleasure and pain, and of ignoring the more spiritual goods which can arise in the struggle against evils.

But let us see exactly what is being done here. Let us call pain and misery 'first order evil' or 'evil (1).' What contrasts with this, namely, pleasure and happiness, will be called 'first order good' or 'good (1).' Distinct from this is 'second order good' or 'good (2)' which somehow emerges in a complex situation in which evil (1) is a necessary component—logically not merely causally, necessary. (Exactly *how* it emerges does not matter: in the crudest version of this solution good (2) is simply the heightening of happiness by the contrast with misery, in other versions it includes sympathy with suffering, heroism in facing danger, and the gradual decrease of first order evil and increase of first order good.) It is also being assumed that second order good is more important than first order good or evil, in particular that it more than outweighs the first order evil it involves.

Now this is a particularly subtle attempt to solve the problem of evil. It defends God's goodness and omnipotence on the ground that (on a sufficiently long view) this is the best of all logically possible worlds, because it includes the important second order goods, and yet it admits that real evils, namely first order evils, exist. But does it still hold that good and evil are opposed? Not, clearly, in the sense that we set out originally: good does not tend to eliminate evil in general. Instead, we have a modified, a more complex pattern. First order good (*e.g.* happiness) *contrasts with* first order evil (*e.g.* misery): these two are opposed in a fairly mechanical way; some second order goods (*e.g.* benevolence) try to maximize first order good and minimize first order evil; but God's goodness is not this, it is rather the will to maximize *second* order good. We might, therefore, call God's goodness an example of a third order goodness, or good (3). While this account is different from our original one, it might well be held to be an improvement on it, to give a more accurate description of the way in which good is opposed to evil, and to be consistent with the essential theist position.

There might, however, be several objections to this solution.

First, some might argue that such qualities as benevolence—and *a fortiori* the third order goodness which promotes benevolence—have a merely derivative value, that they are not higher sorts of good, but merely means to good (1), that is, to happiness, so that it would be absurd for God to keep misery in existence in order to make possible the virtues of benevolence, heroism, etc. The theist who adopts the present solution must, of course, deny this, but he can do so with some plausibility, so I should not press this objection.

Secondly, it follows from this solution that God is not in our sense benevolent or sympathetic: he is not concerned to minimize evil (1), but only to promote good (2); and this might be a disturbing conclusion for some theists.

But, thirdly, the fatal objection is this. Our analysis shows clearly the possibility of the existence of a *second* order evil, an evil (2) contrasting with good (2) as evil (1) contrasts with good (1). This would include malevolence, cruelty, callousness, cowardice, and states in which good (1) is decreasing and evil (1) increasing. And just as good (2) is held to be the important kind of good, the kind that God is concerned to promote, so evil (2) will, by analogy, be the important kind of evil, the kind which God, if he were wholly good and omnipotent, would eliminate. And yet evil (2) plainly exists, and indeed most theists (in other contexts) stress its existence more than that of evil (1). We should, therefore, state the problem of evil in terms of second order evil, and against this form of the problem the present solution is useless.

An attempt might be made to use this solution again, at a higher level, to explain the occurrence of evil (2); indeed the next main solution that we shall examine does just this, with the help of some new notions. Without any fresh notions, such a solution would have little plausibility: for example, we could hardly say that the really important good was a good (3), such as the increase of benevolence in proportion to cruelty, which logically required for its occurrence the occurrence of some second order evil. But even if evil (2) could be explained in this way, it is fairly clear that there would be third order evils contrasting with this third order good: and we should be well on the way to an infinite regress, where the solution of a problem of evil, stated in terms of evil (*n*), indicated the existence of an evil (*n* + 1), and a further problem to be solved.

(4) "Evil is due to human free will."

Perhaps the most important proposed solution of the problem of evil is that evil is not to be ascribed to God at all, but to the independent actions of human beings, supposed to have been endowed by God with freedom of the will. This solution may be combined with the preceding one: first order evil (*e.g.* pain) may be justified as a logically necessary component in second order good (*e.g.* sympathy) while second order evil (*e.g.* cruely) is not *justified*, but is so ascribed to human beings that God cannot be held responsible for it. This combination evades my third criticism of the preceding solution.

The free will solution also involves the preceding solution at a higher level. To explain why a wholly good God gave men free will although it would lead to some important evils, it must be argued that it is better on the whole that men should act freely, and sometimes err, than that they should be innocent automata, acting rightly in a wholly determined way. Freedom that is to say, is now treated as a third order good, and as being more valuable than second order goods (such as sympathy and heroism) would be if they were deterministically produced, and it is being assumed that second order evils, such as cruelty, are logically necessary accompaniments of freedom, just as pain is a logically necessary precondition of sympathy.

I think that this solution is unsatisfactory primarily because of the incoherence of the notion of freedom of the will: but I cannot discuss this topic adequately here, although some of my criticisms will touch upon it.

First I should query the assumption that second order evils are logically necessary accompaniments of freedom. I should ask this: if God has made men such that in their free choices they sometimes prefer what is good and sometimes what is evil, why could he not have made men such that they always freely choose the good? If there is no logical impossibility in a man's freely choosing the good on one, or on several, occasions, there cannot be a logical impossibility in his freely choosing the good on every occasion. God was not, then, faced with a choice between making innocent automata and making beings who, in acting freely, would sometimes go wrong: there was open to him the obviously better possibility of making beings who would act freely but always go right. Clearly, his failure to avail himself of this possibility is inconsistent with his being both omnipotent and wholly good.

If it is replied that this objection is absurd, that the making of some wrong choices is logically necessary for freedom, it would seem that 'freedom' must here mean complete randomness or indeterminacy, including randomness with regard to the alternatives good and evil, in other words that men's choices and consequent actions can be "free" only if they are not determined by their characters. Only on this assumption can God escape the responsibility for men's actions; for if he made them as they are, but did not determine their wrong choices, this can only be because the wrong choices are not determined by men as they are. But then if freedom is randomness, how can it be a characteristic of *will*? And, still more, how can it be the most important good? What value or merit would there be in free choices if these were random actions which were not determined by the nature of the agent?

I conclude that to make this solution plausible two different senses of 'freedom' must be confused, one sense which will justify the view that freedom is a third order good, more valuable than other goods would be without it, and another sense, sheer randomness, to prevent us from ascribing to God a decision to make men such that they sometimes go wrong when he might have made them such that they would always freely go right.

This criticism is sufficient to dispose of this solution. But besides this there is a fundamental difficulty in the notion of an omnipotent God creating men with free will, for if men's wills are really free this must mean that even God cannot control them, that is, that God is no longer omnipotent. It may be objected that God's gift of freedom to men does not mean that he *cannot* control their wills, but that he always *refrains* from controlling their wills. But why, we may ask, should God refrain from controlling evil wills? Why should he not leave men free to will rightly, but intervene when he sees them beginning to will wrongly? If God could do this, but

does not, and if he is wholly good, the only explanation could be that even a wrong free act of will is not really evil, that its freedom is a value which outweighs its wrongness, so that there would be a loss of value if God took away the wrongness and the freedom together. But this is utterly opposed to what theists say about sin in other contexts. The present solution of the problem of evil, then, can be maintained only in the form that God has made men so free that he *cannot* control their wills.

This leads us to what I call the Paradox of Omnipotence: can an omnipotent being make things which he cannot subsequently control? Or, what is practically equivalent to this, can an omnipotent being make rules which then bind himself? (These are practically equivalent because any such rules could be regarded as setting certain things beyond his control, and *vice versa*.) The second of these formulations is relevant to the suggestions that we have already met, that an omnipotent God creates the rules of logic or causal laws, and is then bound by them.

It is clear that this is a paradox: the questions cannot be answered satisfactorily either in the affirmative or in the negative. If we answer "Yes," it follows that if God actually makes things which he cannot control, or makes rules which bind himself, he is not omnipotent once he has made them: there are then things which he cannot do. But if we answer "No," we are immediately asserting that there are things which he cannot do, that is to say that he is already not omnipotent.

It cannot be replied that the question which sets this paradox is not a proper question. It would make perfectly good sense to say that a human mechanic has made a machine which he cannot control: if there is any difficulty about the question it lies in the notion of omnipotence itself.

This, incidentally, shows that although we have approached this paradox from the free will theory, it is equally a problem for a theological determinist. No one thinks that machines have free will, yet they may well be beyond the control of their makers. The determinist might reply that anyone who makes anything determines its ways of acting, and so determines its subsequent behaviour: even the human mechanic does this by his *choice* of materials and structure for his machine, though he does not know all about either of these: the mechanic thus determines, though he may not foresee, his machine's actions. And since God is omniscient, and since his creation of things is total, he both determines and foresees the ways in which his creatures will act. We may grant this, but it is beside the point. The question is not whether God *originally* determined the future actions of his creatures, but whether he can *subsequently* control their actions, or whether he was able in his original creation to put things beyond his subsequent control. Even on determinist principles the answers "Yes" and "No" are equally irreconcilable with God's omnipotence.

Before suggesting a solution of this paradox, I would point out that there is a parallel Paradox of Sovereignty. Can a legal sovereign make a law restricting its own future legislative power? For example, could the British parliament make a law forbidding any future parliament to socialise banking, and also forbidding the future repeal of this law itself? Or could the British parliament, which was legally sovereign in Australia in, say, 1899, pass a valid law, or series of laws, which made it no longer sovereign in 1933? Again, neither the affirmative nor the negative answer is really satisfactory. If we were to answer "Yes," we should be admitting the validity of a law which, if it were actually made, would mean that parliament was no longer sovereign. If we were to answer "No," we should be admitting that there is a law, not logically absurd, which parliament cannot validly make, that is, that parliament is not now a legal sovereign. This paradox can be solved in the following way. We should distinguish between first order laws, that is laws governing the actions of individuals and bodies other than the legislature, and second order laws, that is laws about laws, laws governing the actions of the legislature itself. Correspondingly, we should distinguish two orders of sovereignty, first order sovereignty (sovereignty (1)) which is unlimited authority to make first order laws, and second order sovereignty (sovereignty (2)) which is unlimited authority to make second order laws. If we say that parliament is sovereign

we might mean that any parliament at any time has sovereignty (1), or we might mean that parliament has both sovereignty (1) and sovereignty (2) at present, but we cannot without contradiction mean both that the present parliament has sovereignty (2) and that every parliament at every time has sovereignty (1), for if the present parliament has sovereignty (2) it may use it to take away the sovereignty (1) of later parliaments. What the paradox shows is that we cannot ascribe to any continuing institution legal sovereignty in an inclusive sense.

The analogy between omnipotence and sovereignty shows that the paradox of omnipotence can be solved in a similar way. We must distinguish between first order omnipotence (omnipotence (1)), that is unlimited power to act, and second order omnipotence (omnipotence (2)), that is unlimited power to determine what powers to act things shall have. Then we could consistently say that God all the time has omnipotence (1), but if so no beings at any time have powers to act independently of God. Or we could say that God at one time had omnipotence (2), and used it to assign independent powers to act to certain things, so that God thereafter did not have omnipotence (1). But what the paradox shows is that we cannot consistently ascribe to any continuing being omnipotence in an inclusive sense.

An alternative solution of this paradox would be simply to deny that God is a continuing being, that any times can be assigned to his actions at all. But on this assumption (which also has difficulties of its own) no meaning can be given to the assertion that God made men with wills so free that he could not control them. The paradox of omnipotence can be avoided by putting God outside time, but the free will solution of the problem of evil cannot be saved in this way, and equally it remains impossible to hold that an omnipotent God *binds himself* by causal or logical laws.

CONCLUSION

Of the proposed solutions of the problem of evil which we have examined, none has stood up to criticism. There may be other solutions which require examination, but this study strongly suggests that there is no valid solution of the problem which does not modify at least one of the constituent propositions in a way which would seriously affect the essential core of the theistic position.

Quite apart from the problem of evil, the paradox of omnipotence has shown that God's omnipotence must in any case be restricted in one way or another, that unqualified omnipotence cannot be ascribed to any being that continues through time. And if God and his actions are not in time, can omnipotence, or power of any sort, be meaningfully ascribed to him?

III.7   The Free Will Defense

ALVIN PLANTINGA

Alvin Plantinga is professor of philosophy at the University of Notre Dame and is one of the most important figures in the fields of metaphysics, epistemology, and the philosophy of religion. His works include *God and Other Minds* (1957), *The Nature of Necessity* (1974), and *God, Freedom, and Evil* (1974) from which this selection is taken. Plantinga argues that Mackie and other atheologians (those who argue against the existence of God) are mistaken in thinking that the existence of evil is inconsistent with the existence of a perfectly good and powerful God.

2. DOES THE THEIST CONTRADICT HIMSELF?

In a widely discussed piece entitled "Evil and Omnipotence" John Mackie makes this claim:

> I think, however, that a more telling criticism can be made by way of the traditional problem of evil. Here it can be shown, not that religious beliefs lack rational support, but that they are positively irrational, that the several parts of the essential theological doctrine are *inconsistent* with one another. . . . [1]

Is Mackie right? Does the theist contradict himself? But we must ask a prior question: just what is being claimed here? That theistic belief contains an inconsistency or contradiction, of course. But what, exactly, is an inconsistency or contradiction? There are several kinds. An *explicit* contradiction is a *proposition* of a certain sort—a conjunctive proposition, one conjunct of which is the denial or negation of the other conjunct. For example:

Paul is a good tennis player, and it's false that Paul is a good tennis player.

(People seldom assert explicit contradictions.) Is Mackie charging the theist with accepting such a contradiction? Presumably not; what he says is

> In its simplest form the problem is this: God is omnipotent; God is wholly good; yet evil exists. There seems to be some contradiction between these three propositions, so that if any two of them were true the third would be false. But at the same time all three are essential parts of most theological positions; the theologian, it seems, at once *must* adhere and *cannot consistently* adhere to all three.

According to Mackie, then, the theist accepts a group or set of three propositions; this set is inconsistent. Its members, of course, are

(1) God is omnipotent
(2) God is wholly good

From *God, Freedom, and Evil* by Alvin Plantinga (Harper & Row, 1974). Reprinted by permission of the author. Footnotes edited.

and

(3) Evil exists.

Call this set *A*; the claim is that *A* is an inconsistent set. But what is it for a *set* to be inconsistent or contradictory? Following our definition of an explicit contradiction, we might say that a set of propositions is explicitly contradictory if one of the members is the denial or negation of another member. But then, of course, it is evident that the set we are discussing is not explicitly contradictory; the denials of (1), (2), and (3), respectively, are

(1′) God is not omnipotent (or it's false that
    God is omnipotent)
(2′) God is not wholly good

and

(3′) There is no evil

none of which is in set *A*.

Of course many sets are pretty clearly contradictory, in an important way, but not explicitly contradictory. For example, set *B*:

(4) If all men are mortal, then Socrates is mortal
(5) All men are mortal
(6) Socrates is not mortal.

This set is not explicitly contradictory; yet surely *some* significant sense of that term applies to it. What is important here is that by using only the rules of ordinary logic—the laws of propositional logic and quantification theory found in any introductory text on the subject—we can deduce an explicit contradiction from the set. Or to put it differently, we can use the laws of logic to deduce a proposition from the set, which proposition, when added to the set, yields a new set that is explicitly contradictory. For by using the law *modus ponens* (if *p*, then *q*; *p*; therefore *q*) we can deduce

(7) Socrates is mortal

from (4) and (5). The result of adding (7) to *B* is the set {(4), (5), (6), (7)}. This set, of course, is explicitly contradictory in that (6) is the denial of (7). We might say that any set which shares

this characteristic with set *B* is *formally* contradictory. So a formally contradictory set is one from whose members an explicit contradiction can be deduced by the laws of logic. Is Mackie claiming that set *A* is formally contradictory?

If he is, he's wrong. No laws of logic permit us to deduce the denial of one of the propositions in *A* from the other members. Set *A* isn't formally contradictory either.

But there is still another way in which a set of propositions can be contradictory or inconsistent. Consider set *C*, whose members are

(8) George is older than Paul
(9) Paul is older than Nick

and

(10) George is not older than Nick.

This set is neither explicitly nor formally contradictory; we can't, just by using the laws of logic, deduce the denial of any of these propositions from the others. And yet there is a good sense in which it is inconsistent or contradictory. For clearly it is *not possible* that its three members all be true. It is *necessarily true* that

(11) If George is older than Paul, and Paul is
    older than Nick, then George is older
    than Nick.

And if we add (11) to set *C*, we get a set that is formally contradictory; (8), (9), and (11) yield, by the laws of ordinary logic, the denial of (10).

I said that (11) is *necessarily true*; but what does *that* mean? Of course we might say that a proposition is necessarily true if it is impossible that it be false, or if its negation is not possibly true. This would be to explain necessity in terms of possibility. Chances are, however, that anyone who does not know what necessity is, will be equally at a loss about possibility; the explanation is not likely to be very successful. Perhaps all we can do by way of explanation is to give some examples and hope for the best. In the first place many propositions can be established by the laws of logic alone—for example,

(12) If all men are mortal and Socrates is a
    man, then Socrates is mortal.

Such propositions are truths of logic; and all of them are necessary in the sense of question. But truths of arithmetic and mathematics generally are also necessarily true. Still further, there is a host of propositions that are neither truths of logic nor truths of mathematics but are nonetheless necessarily true; (11) would be an example, as well as

(13) Nobody is taller than himself
(14) Red is a color
(15) No numbers are persons
(16) No prime number is a prime minister

and

(17) Bachelors are unmarried.

So here we have an important kind of necessity—let's call it "broadly logical necessity." Of course there is a correlative kind of *possibility*: a proposition *p* is possibly true (in the broadly logical sense) just in case its negation or denial is not necessarily true (in that same broadly logical sense). This sense of necessity and possibility must be distinguished from another that we may call *causal* or *natural* necessity and possibility. Consider

(18) Henry Kissinger has swum the Atlantic.

Although this proposition has an implausible ring, it is not necessarily false in the broadly logical sense (and its denial is not necessarily true in that sense). But there is a good sense in which it is impossible: it is *causally* or *naturally* impossible. Human beings, unlike dolphins, just don't have the physical equipment demanded for this feat. Unlike Superman, furthermore, the rest of us are incapable of leaping tall buildings at a single bound or (without auxiliary power of some kind) traveling faster than a speeding bullet. These things are *impossible* for us—but not *logically* impossible, even in the broad sense.

So there are several senses of necessity and possibility here. There are a number of propositions, furthermore, of which it's difficult to say whether they are or aren't possible in the broadly logical sense; some of these are subjects of philosophical controversy. Is it possible, for example, for a person never to be conscious during his entire existence? Is it possible for a (human) person to exist *disembodied*? If that's possible, is it possible that there be a person who *at no time at all* during his entire existence has a body? Is it possible to see without eyes? These are propositions about whose possibility in that broadly logical sense there is disagreement and dispute.

Now return to set *C*. . . . What is characteristic of it is the fact that the conjunction of its members—the proposition expressed by the result of putting "and's" between (8), (9), and (10)—is necessarily false. Or we might put it like this: what characterizes set *C* is the fact that we can get a formally contradictory set by adding a necessarily true proposition—namely (11). Suppose we say that a set is *implicitly contradictory* if it resembles *C* in this respect. That is, a set *S* of propositions is implicitly contradictory if there is a necessary proposition *p* such that the result of adding *p* to *S* is a formally contradictory set. Another way to put it: *S* is implicitly contradictory if there is some necessarily true proposition *p* such that by using just the laws of ordinary logic, we can deduce an explicit contradiction from *p* together with the members of *S*. And when Mackie says that set *A* is contradictory, we may properly take him, I think, as holding that it is implicitly contradictory in the explained sense. As he puts it:

> However, the contradiction does not arise immediately; to show it we need some additional premises, or perhaps some quasi-logical rules connecting the terms "good" and "evil" and "omnipotent." These additional principles are that good is opposed to evil, in such a way that a good thing always eliminates evil as far as it can, and that there are no limits to what an omnipotent thing can do. From these it follows that a good omnipotent thing eliminates evil completely, and then the propositions that a good omnipotent thing exists, and that evil exists, are incompatible.[2]

Here Mackie refers to "additional premises"; he also calls them "additional principles" and "quasilogical rules"; he says we need them to show the contradiction. What he means, I think, is that to get a formally contradictory set we must add some more propositions to set *A*; and if we aim to show that set *A* is implicitly contradictory, these propositions must be necessary truths—"quasi-logical rules" as Mackie calls them. The two additional principles he suggests are

(19) A good thing always eliminates evil as far as it can

and

(20) There are no limits to what an omnipotent being can do.

And, of course, if Mackie means to show that set *A* is implicitly contradictory, then he must hold that (19) and (20) are not merely *true* but *necessarily true*.

But, are they? What about (20) first? What does it mean to say that a being is omnipotent? That he is *all-powerful*, or *almighty*, presumably. But are there no limits at all to the power of such a being? Could he create square circles, for example, or married bachelors? Most theologians and theistic philosophers who hold that God is omnipotent, do not hold that He can create round squares or bring it about that He both exists and does not exist. These theologians and philosophers may hold that there are no *nonlogical* limits to what an omnipotent being can do, but they concede that not even an omnipotent being can bring about logically impossible states of affairs or cause necessarily false propositions to be true. Some theists, on the other hand—Martin Luther and Descartes, perhaps—have apparently thought that God's power is unlimited even by the laws of logic. For these theists the question whether set *A* is contradictory will not be of much interest. As theists they believe (1) and (2), and they also, presumably, believe (3). But they remain undisturbed by the claim that (1), (2), and (3) are jointly inconsistent—because, as they say, God can do what is logically impossible. Hence He can bring it about that the members of set *A* are all true, even if that set is contradictory (concentrating very intensely upon this suggestion is likely to make you dizzy). So the theist who thinks that the power of God isn't *limited at all*, not even by the laws of logic, will be unimpressed by Mackie's argument and won't find any difficulty in the contradiction set *A* is alleged to contain. This view is not very popular, however, and for good reason; it is quite incoherent. What the theist typically means when he says that God is omnipotent is not that there are *no* limits to God's power, but at most that there are no nonlogical limits to what He can do; and given this qualification, it is perhaps initially plausible to suppose that (20) is necessarily true.

But what about (19), the proposition that every good thing eliminates every evil state of affairs that it can eliminate? Is that necessarily true? Is it true at all? Suppose, first of all, that your friend Paul unwisely goes for a drive on a wintry day and runs out of gas on a deserted road. The temperature dips to −10°, and a miserably cold wind comes up. You are sitting comfortably at home (twenty-five miles from Paul) roasting chestnuts in a roaring blaze. Your car is in the garage; in the trunk there is the full five-gallon can of gasoline you always keep for emergencies. Paul's discomfort and danger are certainly an evil, and one which you could eliminate. You don't do so. But presumably you don't thereby forfeit your claim to being a "good thing"—you simply didn't know of Paul's plight. And so (19) does not appear to be necessary. It says that every good thing has a certain property—the property of eliminating every evil that it can. And if the case I described is possible—a good person's failing through ignorance to eliminate a certain evil he can eliminate—then (19) is by no means necessarily true.

But perhaps Mackie could sensibly claim that if you *didn't know* about Paul's plight, then in fact you were not, at the time in question, able to eliminate the evil in question; and perhaps he'd be right. In any event he could revise (19) to take into account the kind of case I mentioned:

(19a) Every good thing always eliminates every evil that *it knows about* and can eliminate.

{(1), (2), (3), (20), (19a)}, you'll notice is not a formally contradictory set—to get a formal contradiction we must add a proposition specifying that God *knows about* every evil state of affairs. But most theists do believe that God is omniscient or all-knowing; so if this new set—the set that results when we add to set *A* the proposition that God is omniscient—is implicitly contradictory then Mackie should be satisfied and the theist confounded. (And, henceforth, set *A* will be the old set *A* together with the proposition that God is omniscient.)

But is (19a) necessary? Hardly. Suppose you know that Paul is marooned as in the previous example, and you also know another friend is similarly marooned fifty miles in the opposite direction. Suppose, furthermore, that while you can rescue one or the other, you simply can't rescue both. Then each of the two evils is such that it is within your power to eliminate it; and you know about them both. But you can't eliminate *both*; and you don't forfeit your claim to being a good person by eliminating only one—it wasn't within your power to do more. So the fact that you don't doesn't mean that you are not a good person. Therefore (19a) is false; it is not a necessary truth or even a truth that every good thing eliminates every evil it knows about and can eliminate.

We can see the same thing another way. You've been rock climbing. Still something of a novice, you've acquired a few cuts and bruises by inelegantly using your knees rather than your feet. One of these bruises is fairly painful. You mention it to a physician friend, who predicts the pain will leave of its own accord in a day or two. Meanwhile, he says, there's nothing he can do, short of amputating your leg above the knee, to remove the pain. Now the pain in your knee is an evil state of affairs. All else being equal, it would be better if you had no such pain. And it is within the power of your friend to eliminate this evil state of affairs. Does his failure to do so mean that he is not a good person? Of course not; for he could eliminate this evil state of affairs only by bringing about another, much worse evil. And so it is once again evident that (19a) is false. It is entirely possible that a good person fail to eliminate an evil state of affairs that he knows about and can eliminate. This would take place, if, as in the present example, he couldn't eliminate the evil without bringing about a *greater* evil.

A slightly different kind of case shows the same thing. A really impressive good state of affairs *G* will outweigh a trivial *E*—that is, the conjunctive state of affairs *G* and *E* is itself a good state of affairs. And surely a good person would not be obligated to eliminate a given evil if he could do so only by eliminating a good that outweighed it. Therefore (19a) is not necessarily true; it can't be used to show that set *A* is implicitly contradictory.

These difficulties might suggest another revision of (19); we might try

(19b) A good being eliminates every evil *E* that it knows about and that it can eliminate without either bringing about a greater evil or eliminating a good state of affairs that outweighs *E*.

Is this necessarily true? It takes care of the second of the two difficulties afflicting (19a) but leaves the first untouched. We can see this as follows. First, suppose we say that a being *properly eliminates* an evil state of affairs if it eliminates that evil without either eliminating an outweighing good or bringing about a greater evil. It is then obviously possible that a person find himself in a situation where he could properly eliminate an evil *E* and could also properly eliminate another evil *E'*, but couldn't properly eliminate them *both*. You're rock climbing again, this time on the dreaded north face of the Grand Teton. You and your party come upon Curt and Bob, two mountaineers stranded 125 feet apart on the face. They untied to reach their cigarettes and then carelessly dropped the rope while lighting up. A violent, dangerous thunderstorm is approaching. You have time to rescue one of the stranded climbers and retreat before the storm hits; if you rescue both, however, you and your party and the two climbers will be caught on the face during the thunderstorm, which will very likely destroy your entire party. In this case you can eliminate one evil (Curt's being stranded on the face) without causing more evil or eliminating a greater good; and you are also able to properly eliminate the other evil (Bob's being thus stranded). But you can't properly eliminate them *both*. And so the fact that you don't rescue Curt, say, even though you could have, doesn't show that you aren't a good person. Here, then, each of the evils is such that you can properly eliminate it; but you can't properly eliminate them both, and hence can't be blamed for failing to eliminate one of them.

So neither (19a) nor (19b) is necessarily true. You may be tempted to reply that the sort of counterexamples offered—examples where someone is able to eliminate an evil A and also able to eliminate a different evil B, but unable to eliminate them both—are irrelevant to the case of a being who, like God, is both omnipotent and omniscient. That is, you may think that if an omnipotent and omniscient being is able to eliminate each of two evils, it follows that he can eliminate them *both*. Perhaps this is so; but it is not strictly to the point. The fact is the counterexamples show that (19a) and (19b) are not necessarily true and hence can't be used to show that set A is implicitly inconsistent. What the reply does suggest is that perhaps the atheologian will have more success if he works the properties of omniscience and omnipotence into (19). Perhaps he could say something like

(19c) An omnipotent and omniscient good being eliminates every evil that it can properly eliminate.

And suppose, for purposes of argument, we concede the necessary truth of (19c). Will it serve Mackie's purposes? Not obviously. For we don't get a set that is formally contradictory by adding (20) and (19c) to set A. This set (call it A') contains the following six members:

(1)   God is omnipotent
(2)   God is wholly good
(2′)   God is omniscient
(3)   Evil exists
(19c) An omnipotent and omniscient good being eliminates every evil that it can properly eliminate

and

(20) There are no nonlogical limits to what an omnipotent being can do.

Now if A' were formally contradictory, then from any five of its members we could deduce the denial of the sixth by the laws of ordinary logic.

That is, any five would *formally entail* the denial of the sixth. So if A' were formally inconsistent, the denial of (3) would be formally entailed by the remaining five. That is, (1), (2), (2′), (19c), and (20) would formally entail

(3′) There is no evil.

But they don't; what they formally entail is not that there is no evil *at all* but only that

(3″) There is no evil that God can properly eliminate.

So (19c) doesn't really help either—not because it is not necessarily true but because its addition [with (20)] to set A does not yield a formally contradictory set.

Obviously, what the atheologian must add to get a formally contradictory set is

(21) If God is omniscient and omnipotent, then he can properly eliminate every evil state of affairs.

Suppose we agree that the set consisting in A plus (19c), (20), and (21) is formally contradictory. So if (19c), (20), and (21) are all necessarily true, then set A is implicitly contradictory. We've already conceded that (19c) and (20) are indeed necessary. So we must take a look at (21). Is this proposition necessarily true?

No. To see this let us ask the following question. Under what conditions would an omnipotent being be unable to eliminate a certain evil E without eliminating an outweighing good? Well, suppose that E is *included in* some good state of affairs that outweighs it. That is, suppose there is some good state of affairs G so related to E that it is impossible that G obtain or be actual and E fail to obtain. (Another way to put this: a state of affairs S includes S′ if the conjunctive state of affairs S *but not* S′ is impossible, or if it is necessary that S′ obtains if S does.) Now suppose that some good state of affairs G includes an evil state of affairs E that it outweighs. Then not even an omnipotent being could eliminate E without eliminating G. But are there any cases where a good state of affairs includes, in this sense, an evil that it outweighs?[3] Indeed there are such states of affairs. To take an artificial example, let's suppose that E is Paul's suffering from a minor abrasion and G is your being deliriously happy. The conjunctive state of affairs, G *and* E—the state of affairs that obtains if and only if both G and E obtain—is then a good state of affairs: it is better, all else being equal, that you be intensely happy and Paul suffer a mildly annoying abrasion than that this state of affairs not obtain. So G *and* E is a good state of affairs. And clearly G *and* E includes E: obviously it is necessarily true that if you are deliriously happy and Paul is suffering from an abrasion, then Paul is suffering from an abrasion.

But perhaps you think this example trivial, tricky, slippery, and irrelevant. If so, take heart; other examples abound. Certain kinds of values, certain familiar kinds of good states of affairs, can't exist apart from evil of some sort. For example, there are people who display a sort of creative moral heroism in the face of suffering and adversity—a heroism that inspires others and creates a good situation out of a bad one. In a situation like this the evil, of course, remains evil; but the total state of affairs—someone's bearing pain magnificently, for example—may be good. If it is, then the good present must outweigh the evil; otherwise the total situation would not be *good*. But, of course, it is not possible that such a good state of affairs obtain unless some evil also obtain. It is a necessary truth that if someone bears pain magnificently, then someone is in pain.

The conclusion to be drawn, therefore, is that (21) is not necessarily true. And our discussion thus far shows at the very least that it is no easy matter to find necessarily true propositions that yield a formally contradictory set when added to set A.[4] One wonders, therefore, why the many atheologians who confidently assert that this set is contradictory make no attempt whatever to *show* that it is. For the most part they are content just to *assert* that there is a contradiction here. Even Mackie, who sees that some "additional premises" or "quasi-logical rules" are needed, makes scarcely a beginning towards finding some additional premises that are necessarily true and that together with the members of set A formally entail an explicit contradiction.

3. CAN WE SHOW THAT THERE IS NO INCONSISTENCY HERE?

To summarize our conclusions so far: although many atheologians claim that the theist is involved in contradiction when he asserts the members of set A, this set, obviously, is neither *explicitly nor formally* contradictory; the claim, presumably, must be that it is *implicitly* contradictory. To make good this claim the atheologian must find some necessarily true proposition p (it could be a conjunction of several propositions) such that the addition of p to set A yields a set that is formally contradictory. No atheologian has produced even a plausible candidate for this role, and it certainly is not easy to see what such a proposition might be. Now we might think we should simply declare set A implicitly consistent on the principle that a proposition (or set) is to be presumed consistent or possible until proven otherwise. This course, however, leads to trouble. The same principle would impel us to declare the atheologian's claim—that set A is *in*consistent—possible or consistent. But the claim that a given set of propositions is implicitly contradictory, is itself either necessarily true or necessarily false; so if such a claim is *possible*, it is not necessarily false and is, therefore, true (in fact, necessarily true). If we followed the suggested principle, therefore, we should be obliged to declare set A implicitly consistent (since it hasn't been shown to be otherwise), but we should have to say the same thing about the atheologian's claim, since we haven't shown *that* claim to be inconsistent or impossible. The atheologian's claim, furthermore, is necessarily true if it is possible. Accordingly, if we accept the above principle, we shall have to declare set A both implicitly consistent and implicitly inconsistent. So all we can say at this point is that set A has not been shown to be implicitly inconsistent.

Can we go any further? One way to go on would be to try to *show* that set A is implicitly consistent or possible in the broadly logical sense. But what is involved in showing such a thing? Although there are various ways to approach this matter, they all resemble one another in an important respect. They all amount to this: to show that a set *S* is consistent you think of a *possible state of affairs* (it needn't *actually obtain*) which is such that if it were actual, then all of the members of *S* would be true. This procedure is sometimes called *giving a model of S*. For example, you might construct an axiom set and then show that it is consistent by giving a model of it; this is how it was shown that the denial of Euclid's parallel postulate is formally consistent with the rest of his postulates.

There are various special cases of this procedure to fit special circumstances. Suppose, for example, you have a pair of propositions *p* and *q* and wish to show them consistent. And suppose we say that a proposition *p*1 entails a proposition *p*2 if it is impossible that *p*1 be true and *p*2 false— if the conjunctive proposition *p*1 and not *p*2 is necessarily false. Then one way to show that *p* is consistent with *q* is to find some proposition *r* whose conjunction with *p* is both possible, in the broadly logical sense, and entails *q*. A rude and unlettered behaviorist, for example, might hold that thinking is really nothing but movements of the larynx; he might go on to hold that

P Jones did not move his larynx after April 30

is inconsistent (in the broadly logical sense) with

Q Jones did some thinking during May.

By way of rebuttal, we might point out that *P* appears to be consistent with

R While convalescing from an April 30 laryngotomy, Jones whiled away the idle hours by writing (in May) a splendid paper on Kant's *Critique of Pure Reason.*

So the conjunction of *P* and *R* appears to be consistent; but obviously it also entails *Q* (you can't write even a passable paper on Kant's *Critique of Pure Reason* without doing some thinking); so *P* and *Q* are consistent.

We can see that this is a special case of the procedure I mentioned above as follows. This proposition *R* is consistent with *P*; so the proposition *P and R* is possible, describes a possible state of affairs. But *P and R* entails *Q*; hence if *P and R* were true, *Q* would also be true, and hence both *P* and *Q* would be true. So this is

really a case of producing a possible state of affairs such that, if it were actual, all the members of the set in question (in this case the pair set of *P* and *Q*) would be true.

How does this apply to the case before us? As follows, let us conjoin propositions (1), (2), and (2′) and henceforth call the result (1):

(1) God is omniscient, omnipotent, and wholly good.

The problem, then, is to show that (1) and (3) (evil exists) are consistent. This could be done, as we've seen, by finding a proposition *r* that is consistent with (1) and such that (1) and (*r*) together entail (3). One proposition that might do the trick is

(22) God creates a world containing evil and has a good reason for doing so.

If (22) is consistent with (1), then it follows that (1) and (3) (and hence set *A*) are consistent. Accordingly, one thing some theists have tried is to show that (22) and (1) are consistent.

One can attempt this in at least two ways. On the one hand, we could try to apply the same method again. Conceive of a possible state of affairs such that, if it obtained, an omnipotent, omniscient, and wholly good God would have a good reason for permitting evil. On the other, someone might try to specify *what God's reason is* for permitting evil and try to show, if it is not obvious, that it is a good reason. St. Augustine, for example, one of the greatest and most influential philosopher-theologians of the Christian Church, writes as follows:

> . . . some people see with perfect truth that a creature is better if, while possessing free will, it remains always fixed upon God and never sins; then, reflecting on men's sins, they are grieved, not because they continue to sin, but because they were created. They say: He should have made us such that we never willed to sin, but always to enjoy the unchangeable truth.
>
> They should not lament or be angry. God has not compelled men to sin just because He created them and gave them the power to choose between sinning and not sinning. There are angels who have never sinned and never will sin.

Such is the generosity of God's goodness that He has not refrained from creating even that creature which He foreknew would not only sin, but remain in the will to sin. As a runaway horse is better than a stone which does not run away because it lacks self-movement and sense perception, so the creature is more excellent which sins by free will than that which does not sin only because it has no free will.[5]

In broadest terms Augustine claims that God could create a better, more perfect universe by permitting evil than He could by refusing to do so:

Neither the sins nor the misery are necessary to the perfection of the universe, but souls as such are necessary, which have the power to sin if they so will, and become miserable if they sin. If misery persisted after their sins had been abolished, or if there were misery before there were sins, then it might be right to say that the order and government of the universe were at fault. Again, if there were sins but no consequent misery, that order is equally dishonored by lack of equity.[6]

Augustine tries to tell us *what God's reason is* for permitting evil. At bottom, he says, it's that God can create a more perfect universe by permitting evil. A really top-notch universe requires the existence of free, rational, and moral agents; and some of the free creatures He created went wrong. But the universe with the free creatures it contains and the evil they commit is better than it would have been had it contained neither the free creatures nor this evil. Such an attempt to specify God's reason for permitting evil is what I earlier called a *theodicy;* in the words of John Milton it is an attempt to "justify the ways of God to man," to show that God is just in permitting evil. Augustine's kind of theodicy might be called a Free Will Theodicy, since the idea of rational creatures with free will plays such a prominent role in it.

A theodicist, then, attempts to tell us why God permits evil. Quite distinct from a Free Will Theodicy is what I shall call a Free Will Defense. Here the aim is not to say what God's reason *is*, but at most what God's reason *might possibly be*. We could put the difference like this. The Free Will Theodicist and Free Will Defender

are both trying to show that (1) is consistent with (22), and of course if so, then set *A* is consistent. The Free Will Theodicist tries to do this by finding some proposition *r* which in conjunction with (1) entails (22); he claims, furthermore, that this proposition is true, not just consistent with (1). He tries to tell us what God's reason for permitting evil *really is.* The Free Will Defender, on the other hand, though he also tries to find a proposition *r* that is consistent with (1) and in conjunction with it entails (22), does *not* claim to know or even believe that *r* is true. And here, of course, he is perfectly within his rights. His aim is to show that (1) is consistent with (22); all he need do then is find an *r* that is consistent with (1) and such that (1) and (*r*) entail (22); whether *r* is true is quite beside the point.

So there is a significant difference between a Free Will Theodicy and a Free Will Defense. The latter is sufficient (if successful) to show that set *A* is consistent; in a way a Free Will Theodicy goes beyond what is required. On the other hand, a theodicy would be much more satisfying, if possible to achieve. No doubt the theist would rather know what God's reason is for permitting evil than simply that it's possible that He has a good one. But in the present context (that of investigating the consistency of set A), the latter is all that's needed. Neither a defense or a theodicy, of course, gives any hint to what God's reason for some *specific* evil—the death or suffering of someone close to you, for example—might be. And there is still another function[7]—a sort of pastoral function—in the neighborhood that neither serves. Confronted with evil in his own life or suddenly coming to realize more clearly than before the *extent* and *magnitude* of evil, a believer in God may undergo a crisis of faith. He may be tempted to follow the advice of Job's "friends"; he may be tempted to "curse God and die." Neither a Free Will Defense nor a Free Will Theodicy is designed to be of much help or comfort to one suffering from such a storm in the soul (although in a specific case, of course, one or the other could prove useful). Neither is to be thought of first of all as a means of pastoral counseling. Probably neither will enable someone to find peace with himself and with God in the face of the evil the world contains. But then, of course, neither is intended for that purpose.

4. THE FREE WILL DEFENSE

In what follows I shall focus attention upon the Free Will Defense. I shall examine it more closely, state it more exactly, and consider objections to it; and I shall argue that in the end it is successful. Earlier we saw that among good states of affairs there are some that not even God can bring about without bringing about evil: those goods, namely, that *entail* or *include* evil states of affairs. The Free Will Defense can be looked upon as an effort to show that there may be a very different kind of good that God can't bring about without permitting evil. These are good states of affairs that don't include evil; they do not entail the existence of any evil whatever; nonetheless God Himself can't bring them about without permitting evil.

So how does the Free Will Defense work? And what does the Free Will Defender mean when he says that people are or may be free? What is relevant to the Free Will Defense is the idea of *being free with respect to an action*. If a person is free with respect to a given action, then he is free to perform that action and free to refrain from performing it; no antecedent conditions and/or causal laws determine that he will perform the action, or that he won't. It is within his power, at the time in question, to take or perform the action and within his power to refrain from it. Freedom so conceived is not to be confused with unpredictability. You might be able to predict what you will do in a given situation even if you are free, in that situation, to do something else. If I know you well, I may be able to predict what action you will take in response to a certain set of conditions; it does not follow that you are not free with respect to that action. Secondly, I shall say that an action is *morally significant*, for a given person, if it would be wrong for him to perform the action but right to refrain or vice versa. Keeping a promise, for example, would ordinarily be morally significant for a person,

as would refusing induction into the army. On the other hand, having Cheerios for breakfast (instead of Wheaties) would not normally be morally significant. Further, suppose we say that a person is *significantly free*, on a given occasion, if he is then free with respect to a morally significant action. And finally we must distinguish between *moral evil* and *natural evil*. The former is evil that results from free human activity; natural evil is any other kind of evil.[8]

Given these definitions and distinctions, we can make a preliminary statement of the Free Will Defense as follows. A world containing creatures who are significantly free (and freely perform more good than evil actions) is more valuable, all else being equal, than a world containing no free creatures at all. Now God can create free creatures, but He can't *cause* or *determine* them to do only what is right. For if He does so, then they aren't significantly free after all; they do not do what is right *freely*. To create creatures capable of *moral good*, therefore, He must create creatures capable of moral evil; and He can't give these creatures the freedom to perform evil and at the same time prevent them from doing so. As it turned out, sadly enough, some of the free creatures God created went wrong in the exercise of their freedom; this is the source of moral evil. The fact that free creatures sometimes go wrong, however, counts neither against God's omnipotence nor against His goodness; for He could have forestalled the occurrence of moral evil only by removing the possibility of moral good.

I said earlier that the Free Will Defender tries to find a proposition that is consistent with

(1) God is omniscient, omnipotent, and wholly good

and together with (1) entails that there is evil. According to the Free Will Defense, we must find this proposition somewhere in the above story. The heart of the Free Will Defense is the claim that it is *possible* that God could not have created a universe containing moral good (or as much moral good as this world contains) without creating one that also contained moral evil. And if so, then it is possible that God has a good reason for creating a world containing evil.

Now this defense has met with several kinds of objections. For example, some philosophers say that *causal determinism* and *freedom*, contrary to what we might have thought, are not really incompatible.[9] But if so, then God could have created free creatures who were free, and free to do what is wrong, but nevertheless were causally determined to do only what is right. Thus He could have created creatures who were free to do what was wrong, while nevertheless preventing them from ever performing any wrong actions—simply by seeing to it that they were causally determined to do only what is right. Of course this contradicts the Free Will Defense, according to which there is inconsistency in supposing that God determines free creatures to do only what is right. But is it really possible that all of a person's actions are causally determined while some of them are free? How could that be so? According to one version of the doctrine in question, to say that George acts freely on a given occasion is to say only this: *if George had chosen to do otherwise, he would have done otherwise.* Now George's action *A* is causally determined if some event *E*—some event beyond his control—has already occurred, where the state of affairs consisting in *E*'s occurrence conjoined with George's *refraining* from performing *A*, is a causally impossible state of affairs. Then one can consistently hold both that all of a man's actions are causally determined and that some of them are free in the above sense. For suppose that all of a man's actions are causally determined and that he *couldn't*, on any occasion, have made any choice or performed any action different from the ones he did make and perform. It could still be true that if he *had* chosen to do otherwise, he would have done otherwise. Granted, he couldn't have chosen to do otherwise; but this is consistent with saying that *if* he had, things would have gone differently.

This objection to the Free Will Defense seems utterly implausible. One might as well claim that being in jail doesn't really limit one's freedom on the grounds that if one were *not* in jail, he'd be free to come and go as he pleased. So I shall say no more about this objection here.[10]

A second objection is more formidable. In essence it goes like this. Surely it is possible to do only what is right, even if one is free to do wrong. It is *possible*, in that broadly logical sense, that there would be a world containing free creatures who always do what is right. There is certainly no *contradiction* or *inconsistency* in this idea. But God is omnipotent; his power has no nonlogical limitations. So if it's possible that there be a world containing creatures who are free to do what is wrong but never in fact do so, then it follows that an omnipotent God could create such a world. If so, however, the Free Will Defense must be mistaken in its insistence upon the possibility that God is omnipotent but unable to create a world containing moral good without permitting moral evil.). J. L. Mackie...states this objection:

> If God has made men such that in their free choices they sometimes prefer what is good and sometimes what is evil, why could he not have made men such that they always freely choose the good? If there is no logical impossibility in a man's freely choosing the good on one, or on several occasions, there cannot be a logical impossibility in his freely choosing the good on every occasion. God was not, then, faced with a choice between making innocent automata and making beings who, in acting freely, would sometimes go wrong; there was open to him the obviously better possibility of making beings who would act freely but always go right. Clearly, his failure to avail himself of this possibility is inconsistent with his being both omnipotent and wholly good.[11]

Now what, exactly, is Mackie's point here? This. According to the Free Will Defense, it is possible both that God is omnipotent and that He was unable to create a world containing moral good without creating one containing moral evil. But, replies Mackie, this limitation on His power to create is inconsistent with God's omnipotence. For surely it's *possible* that there be a world containing perfectly virtuous persons—persons who are significantly free but always do what is right. Surely there are *possible worlds* that contain moral good but no moral evil. But God, if He is omnipotent, can create any possible world He chooses. So it is *not* possible, contrary to the Free Will Defense, both that God is omnipotent and that He could create a world containing moral good only by creating one containing moral evil. If He is omnipotent, the only limitations of His power are *logical* limitations; in which case there are no possible worlds He could not have created.

This is a subtle and important point. According to the great German philosopher G. W. Leibniz, *this* world, the actual world, must be the best of all possible worlds. His reasoning goes as follows. Before God created anything at all, He was confronted with an enormous range of choices; He could create or bring into actuality any of the myriads of different possible worlds. Being perfectly good, He must have chosen to create the best world He could; being omnipotent, He was able to create any possible world He pleased. He must, therefore, have chosen the best of all possible worlds; and hence *this* world, the one He did create, must be the best possible. Now Mackie, of course, agrees with Leibniz that God, if omnipotent, could have created any world He pleased and would have created the best world he could. But while Leibniz draws the conclusion that this world, despite appearances, must be the best possible, Mackie concludes instead that there is no omnipotent, wholly good God. For, he says, it is obvious enough that this present world is not the best of all possible worlds.

The Free Will Defender disagrees with both Leibniz and Mackie. In the first place, he might say, what is the reason for supposing that there is such a thing as the best of all possible worlds? No matter how marvelous a world is—containing no matter how many persons enjoying unalloyed bliss—isn't it possible that there be an even better world containing even more persons enjoying even more unalloyed bliss? But what is really characteristic and central to the Free Will Defense is the claim that God, though omnipotent, could not have actualized just any possible world He pleased.

5. WAS IT WITHIN GOD'S POWER TO CREATE ANY POSSIBLE WORLD HE PLEASED?

This is indeed the crucial question for the Free Will Defense. If we wish to discuss it with insight and authority, we shall have to look into the idea of *possible worlds*. And a sensible first question is this: what sort of thing is a possible world? The basic idea is that a possible world is *a way things could have been;* it is a *state of affairs* of some kind. Earlier we spoke of states of affairs, in particular of good and evil states of affairs. Suppose we look at this idea in more detail. What sort of thing is a state of affairs? The following would be examples:

> Nixon's having won the 1972 election
> 7 + 5's being equal to 12
> All men's being mortal

and

> Gary, Indiana's, having a really nasty pollution problem.

These are *actual* states of affairs: states of affairs that do in fact obtain. And corresponding to each such actual state of affairs there is a true proposition—in the above cases, the corresponding propositions would be *Nixon won the 1972 presidential election, 7 + 5 is equal to 12, all men are mortal,* and *Gary, Indiana, has a really nasty pollution problem.* A proposition p corresponds to a state of affairs s, in this sense, if it is impossible that p be true and s fail to obtain and impossible that s obtain and p fail to be true.

But just as there are false propositions, so there are states of affairs that do *not* obtain or are *not* actual. *Kissinger's having swum the Atlantic* and *Hubert Horatio Humphrey's having run a mile in four minutes* would be examples. Some states of affairs that do not obtain are impossible: e.g., *Hubert's having drawn a square circle, 7 + 5's being equal to 75,* and *Agnew's having a brother who was an only child.* The propositions corresponding to these states of affairs, of course, are necessarily false. So there are states of affairs that *obtain* or are *actual* and also states of affairs that don't obtain. Among the latter some are *impossible* and others are possible. And a possible world is a possible state of affairs. Of course not every possible state of affairs is a possible world; *Hubert's having run a mile in four minutes* is a possible state of affairs but not a possible world. No doubt it is an *element* of many possible worlds, but it isn't itself inclusive enough to be one. To be a possible world, a state of affairs must be very large—so large as to be *complete* or *maximal.*

To get at this idea of completeness we need a couple of definitions. As we have already seen...a state of affairs A *includes* a state of affairs B if it is not possible that A obtain and B not obtain or if the conjunctive state of affairs A but not B—the state of affairs that obtains if and only if A obtains and B does not—is not possible. For example, *Jim Whittaker's being the first American to climb Mt. Everest includes Jim Whittaker's being an American.* It also includes *Mt. Everest's being climbed, something's being climbed, no American's having climbed Everest before Whittaker did*, and the like. *Inclusion* among states of affairs is like *entailment* among propositions; and where a state of affairs A includes a state of affairs B, the proposition corresponding to A entails the one corresponding to B. Accordingly, *Jim Whittaker is the first American to climb Everest* entails *Mt. Everest has been climbed, something has been climbed*, and *no American climbed Everest before Whittaker did*. Now suppose we say further that a state of affairs A *precludes* a state of affairs B if it is not possible that *both* obtain, or if the conjunctive state of affairs A and B is impossible. Thus *Whittaker's being the first American to climb Mt. Everest* precludes *Luther Jerstad's being the first American to climb Everest*, as well as *Whittaker's never having climbed any mountains.* If A precludes B, than A's corresponding proposition entails the denial of the one corresponding to B. Still further, let's say that the *complement* of a state of affairs is the state of affairs that obtains just in case A does not obtain. [Or we might say that the complement (call it $\bar{A}$) of A is the state of affairs corresponding to the *denial* or *negation* of the proposition corresponding to A.] Given these definitions, we can say

what it is for a state of affairs to be *complete*: A is a complete state of affairs if and only if for every state of affairs B, either A *includes* B or A *precludes* B. (We could express the same thing by saying that if A is a complete state of affairs, then for every state of affairs B, either A includes B or A includes $\bar{B}$ the complement of B.) And now we are able to say what a possible world is: a possible world is any possible state of affairs that is complete. If A is a possible world, then it says something about everything; every state of affairs S is either included in or precluded by it.

Corresponding to each possible world W, furthermore, there is a set of propositions that I'll call the book on W. A proposition is in the book on W just in case the state of affairs to which it corresponds is included in W. Or we might express it like this. Suppose we say that a proposition P *is true in a world W* if and only if *P would have been true if W had been actual*—if and only if, that is, it is not possible that W be actual and P be false. Then the book on W is the set of propositions true in W. Like possible worlds, books are *complete;* if B is a book, then for any proposition P, either P or the denial of P will be a member of B. A book is a *maximal consistent set* of propositions; it is so large that the addition of another proposition to it always yields an explicitly inconsistent set.

Of course, for each possible world there is exactly one book corresponding to it (that is, for a given world W there is just one book B such that each member of B is true in M; and for each book there is just one world to which it corresponds). So every world has its book.

It should be obvious that exactly one possible world is actual. At *least* one must be, since the set of true propositions is a maximal consistent set and hence a book. But then it corresponds to a possible world, and the possible world corresponding to this set of propositions (since it's the set of *true* propositions) will be actual. On the other hand there is at *most* one actual world. For suppose there were two: W and W'. These worlds cannot include all the very same states of affairs; if they did, they would be the very same world. So there must be at least one state of affairs S such that W includes S and W' does not. But a possible world is maximal; W', therefore, includes the complement $\bar{S}$ of S. So if both W and W' were actual, as we have supposed, then both S and $\bar{S}$ would be actual—which is impossible. So there can't be more than one possible world that is actual.

Leibniz pointed out that a proposition p is necessary if it is true in every possible world. We may add that p is possible if it is true in one world and impossible if true in none. Furthermore, p *entails* q if there is no possible world in which p is true and q is false, and p *is consistent with* q if there is at least one world in which both p and q are true.

A further feature of possible worlds is that people (and other things) exist in them. Each of us exists in the actual world, obviously; but a person also exists in many worlds distinct from the actual world. It would be a mistake, of course, to think of all of these worlds as somehow "going on" at the same time, with the same person reduplicated through these worlds and actually existing in a lot of different ways. This is not what is meant by saying that the same person exists in different possible worlds. What is meant, instead, is this: a person Paul exists in each of those possible worlds W which is such that, if W *had been actual*, Paul would have existed—actually existed. Suppose Paul had been an inch taller than he is, or a better tennis player. Then the world that does in fact obtain would not have been actual; some other world—W', let's say—would have obtained instead. If W' had been actual, Paul would have existed; so Paul exists in W'. (Of course there are still other possible worlds in which Paul does not exist—worlds, for example, in which there are no people at all.) Accordingly, when we say that Paul exists in a world W, what we mean is that Paul *would have* existed had W been actual. Or we could put it like this: Paul exists in each world W that includes the state of affairs consisting in Paul's existence. We can put this still more simply by saying that Paul exists in those worlds whose books contain the proposition *Paul exists*.

But isn't there a problem here? *Many* people are named "Paul": Paul the apostle, Paul J. Zwier,

John Paul Jones, and many other famous Pauls. So who goes with "Paul exists"? Which Paul? The answer has to do with the fact that books contain *propositions*—not sentences. They contain the sort of thing sentences are used to express and assert. And the same sentence—"Aristotle is wise," for example—can be used to express many different propositions. When Plato used it, he asserted a proposition predicating wisdom of his famous pupil; when Jackie Onassis uses it, she asserts a proposition predicating wisdom of her wealthy husband. These are distinct propositions (we might even think they differ in truth value); but they are expressed by the same sentence. Normally (but not always) we don't have much trouble determining which of the several propositions expressed by a given sentence is relevant in the context at hand. So in this case a given person, Paul, exists in a world W if and only if W' book contains the proposition that says that *he*—that particular person—exists. The fact that the sentence we use to express this proposition can also be used to express *other* propositions is not relevant.

After this excursion into the nature of books and worlds we can return to our question. Could God have created just any world He chose? Before addressing the question, however, we must note that God does not, strictly speaking, *create* any possible worlds or states of affairs at all. What He creates are the heavens and the earth and all that they contain. But He has not created states of affairs. There are, for example, the state of affairs consisting in God's existence and the state of affairs consisting in His nonexistence. That is, there is such a thing as the state of affairs consisting in the existence of God, and there is also such a thing as the state of affairs consisting in the nonexistence of God, just as there are the two propositions *God exists* and *God does not exist*. The theist believes that the first state of affairs is actual and the first proposition true, the atheist believes that the second state of affairs is actual and the second proposition true. But, of course, both propositions *exist*, even though just one is true. Similarly, there are two states of affairs here, just one of which is actual. So both states of affairs *exist*, but only one *obtains*. And God has not created either one of them since there never was a time at which either did not exist. Nor has he created the state of affairs consisting in the earth's existence; there was a time when *the earth* did not exist, but none when the state of affairs consisting in the earth's existence didn't exist. Indeed, God did not bring into existence any states of affairs at all. What He did was to perform actions of a certain sort—creating the heavens and the earth, for example—which resulted in the *actuality* of certain states of affairs. God *actualizes* states of affairs. He actualizes the possible world that does in fact obtain; He does not create it. And while He has created Socrates, He did not create the state of affairs consisting in Socrates' existence.[12]

Bearing this in mind, let's finally return to our question. Is the atheologian right in holding that if God is omnipotent, then he could have actualized or created any possible world He pleased? Not obviously. First, we must ask ourselves whether God is a *necessary* or a *contingent* being. A necessary being is one that exists in every possible world—one that would have existed no matter which possible world had been actual; a contingent being exists only in some possible worlds. Now if God is not a necessary being (and many, perhaps most, theists think that He is not), then clearly enough there will be many possible worlds He could not have actualized—all those, for example, in which He does not exist. Clearly, God could not have created a world in which He doesn't even exist.

So, if God is a contingent being then there are many possible worlds beyond His power to create. But this is really irrelevant to our present concerns. For perhaps the atheologian can maintain his case if he revises his claim to avoid this difficulty; perhaps he will say something like this: if God is omnipotent, then He could have actualized any of these possible worlds *in which He exists.* So if He exists and is omnipotent, He could have actualized (contrary to the Free Will Defense) any of those possible worlds in which He exists and in which there exist free creatures who do no wrong. He could have actualized worlds containing moral good but no moral evil. Is this correct?

Let's begin with a trivial example. You and Paul have just returned from an Australian hunting expedition: your quarry was the elusive double-waffled cassowary. Paul captured an aardvark, mistaking it for a cassowary. The creature's disarming ways have won it a place in Paul's heart; he is deeply attached to it. Upon your return to the States you offer Paul $500 for his aardvark, only to be rudely turned down. Later you ask yourself, "What would he have done if I'd offered him $700?" Now what is it, exactly, that you are asking? What you're really asking in a way is whether, under a *specific set of conditions*, Paul would have sold it. These conditions include your having offered him $700 rather than $500 for the aardvark, everything else being as much as possible like the conditions that did in fact obtain. Let S' be this set of conditions or state of affairs. S' includes the state of affairs consisting in your offering Paul $700 (instead of the $500 you did offer him); of course it does not include his *accepting* your offer, and it does not include his *rejecting* it; for the rest, the conditions it includes are just like the ones that did obtain in the actual world. So, for example, S' includes Paul's being free to accept the offer and free to refrain; and if in fact the going rate for an aardvark was $650, then S' includes the state of affairs consisting in the going rate's being $650. So we might put your question by asking which of the following conditionals is true:

(23) If the state of affairs S' had obtained, Paul would have accepted the offer
(24) If the state of affairs S' had obtained, Paul would not have accepted the offer.

It seems clear that at least one of these conditionals is true, but naturally they can't both be; so exactly one is.

Now since S' includes neither Paul's accepting the offer not his rejecting it, the antecedent of (23) and (24) does not entail the consequent of either. That is,

(25) S' obtains

does not entail either

(26) Paul accepts the offer

or

(27) Paul does not accept the offer.

So there are possible worlds in which both (25) and (26) are true, and other possible worlds in which both (25) and (27) are true.

We are now in a position to grasp an important fact. Either (23) or (24) is in fact true; and either way there are possible worlds God could not have actualized. Suppose, first of all, that (23) is true. Then it was beyond the power of God to create a world in which (1) Paul is free to sell his aardvark and free to refrain, and in which the other states of affairs included in S' obtain, and (2) Paul does not sell. That is, it was beyond His power to create a world in which (25) and (27) are both true. There is at least one possible world like this, but God, despite His omnipotence, could not have brought about its actuality. For let W be such a world. To actualize W, God must bring it about that Paul is free with respect to this action, and that the other states of affairs included in S' obtain. But (23), as we are supposing, is true; so if God had actualized S' and left Paul *free* with respect to this action, he would have sold: in which case W would not have been actual. If, on the other hand, God had *brought it about* that Paul didn't sell or had *caused him* to refrain from selling, then Paul would not have been free with respect to this action; then S' would not have been actual (since S' includes Paul's being free with respect to it), and W would not have been actual since W includes S'.

Of course if it is (24) rather than (23) that is true, then another class of worlds was beyond God's power to actualize—those, namely, in which S' obtains and Paul *sells* his aardvark. These are the worlds in which both (25) and (26) are true. But either (23) or (24) is true. Therefore, there are possible worlds God could not have actualized. If we consider whether or not God could have created a world in which, let's say, both (25) and (26) are true, we see that the answer depends upon a peculiar kind of fact; it depends upon what Paul would have freely chosen to do in a certain situation. So there are any number of possible worlds such that it is partly up to Paul whether God can create them.[13]

That was a past tense example. Perhaps it would be useful to consider a future tense case, since this might seem to correspond more closely to God's situation in choosing a possible world to actualize. At some time t in the near future Maurice will be free with respect to some insignificant action—having freeze-dried oatmeal for breakfast, let's say. That is, at time t Maurice will be free to have oatmeal but also free to take something else—shredded wheat, perhaps. Next, suppose we consider S', a state of affairs that is included in the actual world and includes Maurice's being free with respect to taking oatmeal at time t. That is, S' includes Maurice's being free at time t to take oatmeal and free to reject it. S' does not include Maurice's taking oatmeal, however; nor does it include his rejecting it. For the rest S' is as much as possible like the actual world. In particular there are many conditions that do in fact hold at time t and are *relevant* to his choice—such conditions, for example, as the fact that he hasn't had oatmeal lately, that his wife will be annoyed if he rejects it, and the like; and S' includes each of these conditions. Now God no doubt knows what Maurice will do at time t, if S obtains; He knows which action Maurice would freely perform if S were to be actual. That is, God knows that one of the following conditionals is true:

(28) If S' were to obtain, Maurice will freely take the oatmeal

or

(29) If S' were to obtain, Maurice will freely reject it.

We may not know which of these is true, and Maurice himself may not know; but presumably God does.

So either God knows that (28) is true, or else He knows that (29) is. Let's suppose it is (28). Then there is a possible world that God, though omnipotent, cannot create. For consider a possible world W' that shares S' with the actual world (which for ease of reference I'll name "Kronos") and in which Maurice does not take oatmeal. (We know there is such a world, since S' does not include Maurice's taking the oatmeal.) S' obtains in W' just as it does in Kronos. Indeed, everything in W' is just as it is in Kronos up to time t. But whereas in Kronos Maurice takes oatmeal at time t, in W' he does not. Now W' is a perfectly possible world; but it is not within God's power to create it or bring about its actuality. For to do so He must actualize S'. But (28) is in fact true. So if God actualizes S' (as He must to create W') and leaves Maurice free with respect to the action in question, then he will take the oatmeal; and then, of course, W' will not be actual. If, on the other hand, God causes Maurice to *refrain* from taking the oatmeal, then he is not *free* to take it. That means, once again, that W' is not actual; for in W' Maurice is free to take the oatmeal (even if he doesn't do so). So if (28) is true, then this world W' is one that God can't actualize, it is not within His power to actualize it even though He is omnipotent and it is a possible world.

Of course, if it is (29) that is true, we get a similar result; then too there are possible worlds that God can't actualize. These would be worlds which share S' with Kronos and in which Maurice *does* take oatmeal. But either (28) or (29) is true; so either way there is a possible world that God can't create. If we consider a world in which S' obtains and in which Maurice freely chooses oatmeal at time t, we see that whether or not it is within God's power to actualize it depends upon what Maurice would do if he were free in a certain situation. Accordingly, there are any number of possible worlds such that it is partly up to Maurice whether or not God can actualize them. It is, of course, up to God whether or not to create Maurice and also up to God whether or not to make him free with respect to the action of taking oatmeal at time t. (God could, if He chose, cause him to succumb to the dreaded *equine obsession*, a condition shared by some people and most horses, whose victims find it *psychologically impossible* to refuse oats or oat products.) But if He creates Maurice and creates him free with respect to this action, then whether or not he actually performs the action is up to Maurice—not God.[14]

Now we can return to the Free Will Defense and the problem of evil. The Free Will Defender, you recall, insists on the possibility that it is not within God's power to create a world containing moral good without creating one containing moral evil. His atheological opponent—Mackie, for example—agrees with Leibniz in insisting that *if* (as the theist holds) God is omnipotent, then it *follows* that He could have created any possible world He pleased. We now see that this contention—call it "Leibniz' Lapse"—is a mistake. The atheologian is right in holding that there are many possible worlds containing moral good but no moral evil; his mistake lies in endorsing Leibniz' Lapse. So one of his premises—that God, if omnipotent, could have actualized just any world He pleased—is false.

6. COULD GOD HAVE CREATED A WORLD CONTAINING MORAL GOOD BUT NO MORAL EVIL?

Now suppose we recapitulate the logic of the situation. The Free Will Defender claims that the following is possible:

(30) God is omnipotent, and it was not within His power to create a world containing moral good but no moral evil.

By way of retort the atheologian insists that there are possible worlds containing moral good but no moral evil. He adds that an omnipotent being could have actualized any possible world he chose. So if God is omnipotent, it follows that He could have actualized a world containing moral good but no moral evil, hence (30), contrary to the Free Will Defender's claim, is not possible. What we have seen so far is that his second premise—Leibniz' Lapse—is false.

Of course, this does not settle the issue in the Free Will Defender's favor. Leibniz' Lapse (appropriately enough for a lapse) is false; but this doesn't show that (30) is possible. To show this latter we must demonstrate the possibility that among the worlds God could not have actualized are all the worlds containing moral good but no moral evil. How can we approach this question?

Instead of choosing oatmeal for breakfast or selling an aardvark, suppose we think about a morally significant action such as taking a bribe. Curley Smith, the mayor of Boston, is opposed to the proposed freeway route; it would require destruction of the Old North Church along with some other antiquated and structurally unsound buildings. L. B. Smedes, the director of highways, asks him whether he'd drop his opposition for $1 million. "Of course," he replies. "Would you do it for $2?" asks Smedes. "What do you take me for?" comes the indignant reply. "That's already established," smirks Smedes; "all that remains is to nail down your price." Smedes then offers him a bribe of $35,000; unwilling to break with the fine old traditions of Bay State politics, Curley accepts. Smedes then spends a sleepless night wondering whether he could have bought Curley for $20,000.

Now suppose we assume that Curley was free with respect to the action of taking the bribe—free to take it and free to refuse. And suppose, furthermore, that he would have taken it. That is, let us suppose that

(31) If Smedes had offered Curley a bribe of $20,000, he would have accepted it.

If (31) is true, then there is a state of affairs S' that (1) includes Curley's being offered a bribe of $20,000; (2) does not include either his accepting the bribe or his rejecting it; and (3) is otherwise as much as possible like the actual world. Just to make sure S' includes every relevant circumstance, let us suppose that it is a *maximal world segment*. That is, add to S' any state of affairs compatible with but not included in it, and the result will be an entire possible world. We could think of it roughly like this: S' is included in at least one world W in which Curley takes the bribe and in at least one world W' in which he rejects it. If S' is a maximal world segment, then S' is what remains of W when *Curley's taking the bribe* is deleted; it is also what remains of W' when *Curley's rejecting the bribe* is detected. More exactly, if S' is a maximal world segment, then every possible state of affairs that includes S', but isn't included by S', is a possible world. So if (31) is true, then there is a maximal world segment S' that (1) includes Curley's being offered a bribe of $20,000; (2) does not include either his accepting the bribe or his rejecting it; (3) is otherwise as much as possible like the actual world—in particular, it includes Curley's being free with respect to the bribe; and (4) is such that if it were actual then Curley would have taken the bribe. That is

(32) if S' were actual, Curley would have accepted the bribe is true.

Now, of course, there is at least one possible world W' in which S' is actual and Curley does not take the bribe. But God could not have created W'; to do so, He would have been obliged to actualize S', leaving Curley free with respect to the action of taking the bribe. But under these conditions Curley, as (32) assures us, would have accepted the bribe, so that the world thus created would not have been S'.

Curley, as we see, is not above a bit of Watergating. But there may be worse to come. Of course, there are possible worlds in which he is significantly free (i.e., free with respect to a morally significant action) and never does what is wrong. But the sad truth about Curley may be this. Consider W', any of these worlds: in W' Curley is significantly free, so in W' there are some actions that are morally significant for him and with respect to which he is free. But at least one of these actions—call it A—has the following peculiar property. There is a maximal world segment S' that obtains in W' and is such that (1) S' includes Curley's being free *re A* but neither his performing A nor his refraining from A; (2) S' is otherwise as much as possible like W' and (3) if S' had been actual, Curley would have gone wrong with respect to A.[15] (Notice that this third condition holds in fact, in the actual world; it does not hold in that world W'.)

This means, of course, that God could not have actualized W'. For to do so He'd have been obliged to bring it about that S' is actual; but then Curley would go wrong with respect to A. Since in W' he always does what is right, the world thus actualized would not be W'. On the other hand, if God *causes* Curley to go right with respect to A or *brings it about* that he does so, then Curley isn't free with respect to A; and so once more it isn't W' that is actual.

Accordingly God cannot create W'. But W' was just any of the worlds in which Curley is significantly free but always does only what is right. It therefore follows that it was not within God's power to create a world in which Curley produces moral good but no moral evil. Every world God can actualize is such that if Curley is significantly free in it, he takes at least one wrong action.

Obviously Curley is in serious trouble. I shall call the malady from which he suffers transworld depravity. (I leave as homework the problem of comparing transworld depravity with what Calvinists call "total depravity.") By way of explicit definition:

(33) A person *P suffers from transworld depravity* if and only if the following holds: for every world W such that P is significantly free in W and P does only what is right in W, therevis an action A and a maximal world segment S' such that
(1) S' includes A's being morally significant for P
(2) S' includes P's being free with respect to A
(3) S' is included in W and includes neither P's performing A nor P's refraining from performing A

and

(4) If S' were actual, P would go wrong with respect to A.

(In thinking about this definition, remember that (4) is to be true in fact, in the actual world—not in that world W.)

What is important about the idea of transworld depravity is that if a person suffers from it, then it wasn't within God's power to actualize any world in which that person is significantly free but does no wrong—that is, a world in which he produces moral good but no moral evil.

We have been here considering a crucial contention of the Free Will Defender: the contention, namely, that

(30) God is omnipotent, and it was not within His power to create a world containing moral good but no moral evil.

How is transworld depravity relevant to this? As follows. Obviously it is possible that there be persons who suffer from transworld depravity. More generally, it is possible that *everybody* suffers from it. And if this possibility were actual, then God, though omnipotent, could not have created any of the possible worlds containing just the persons who do in fact exist, and containing moral good but no moral evil. For to do so He'd have to create persons who were significantly free (otherwise there would be no moral good) but suffered from transworld depravity. Such persons go wrong with respect to at least one action in any world God could have actualized and in which they are free with respect to morally significant actions; so the price for creating a world in which they produce moral good is creating one in which they also produce moral evil.

NOTES

1. John Mackie, "Evil and Omnipotence," in *The Philosophy of Religion*, ed. Basil Mitchell (London Oxford University Press:, 1971), p. 92. [See previous reading.]
2. Ibid., p. 93. [*Philosophy of Religion: Selected Readings, Second Edition*, p. 224.]
3. More simply, the question is really just whether any good state of affairs includes an evil; a little reflection reveals that no good state of affairs can include an evil that it does not outweigh.
4. In Plantinga, *God and Other Minds* (Ithaca, N.Y.: Cornell University Press, 1967), chap. 5, I explore further the project of finding such propositions.
5. *The Problem of Free Choice*, Vol. 22 of *Ancient Christian Writers* (Westminster, Md.: The Newman Press, 1955), bk. 2, pp. 14–15.
6. Ibid., bk. 3, p. 9.
7. I am indebted to Henry Schuurman (in conversation) for helpful discussion of the difference between this pastoral function and those served by a theodicy or a defense.
8. This distinction is not very precise (how, exactly, are we to construe "results from"?), but perhaps it will serve our present purposes.
9. See, for example, A. Flew, "Divine Omnipotence and Human Freedom," in *New Essays in Philosophical Theology*, eds. A. Flew and A. MacIntyre (London SCM:, 1955), pp. 150–53.
10. For further discussion of it see Plantinga, *God and Other Minds*, pp. 132–35.
11. Mackie, in *The Philosophy of Religion*, pp. 100–101.

12. Strict accuracy demands, therefore, that we speak of God as actualizing rather than creating possible worlds. I shall continue to use both locutions, thus sacrificing accuracy to familiarity. For more about possible worlds see my book *The Nature of Necessity* (Oxford The Clarendon Press:, 1974), chaps. 4–8.

13. For a fuller statement of this argument see Plantinga, *The Nature of Necessity*, chap. 9, secs. 4–6.

14. For a more complete and more exact statement of this argument see Plantinga, *The Nature of Necessity*, chap. 9, secs. 4–6.

15. A person goes wrong with respect to an action if he either wrongfully performs it or wrongfully fails to perform it.

III.8   The Inductive Argument from Evil against the Existence of God

WILLIAM ROWE

A short biographical sketch of William Rowe appears before selection I.B.4. In the present selection, Rowe argues that an inductive or probabilistic version of the argument from evil justifies atheism. He concedes that deductive arguments against the existence of God on the basis of evil, such as J. L. Mackie uses (Reading III.6), do not succeed. Nevertheless, he says it is reasonable to believe that there is no God. In the last part of his essay Rowe defines his position as "friendly atheism" since he admits that a theist may be justified in rejecting the probabilistic argument from evil.

This paper is concerned with three interrelated questions. The first is: Is there an argument for atheism based on the existence of evil that may rationally justify someone in being an atheist? To this first question I give an affirmative answer and try to support that answer by setting forth a strong argument for atheism based on the existence of evil.[1] The second question is: How can the theist best defend his position against the argument for atheism based on the existence of evil? In response to this question I try to describe what may be an adequate rational defense for theism against any argument for atheism based on the existence of evil. The final question is: What position should the informed atheist take concerning the rationality of theistic belief? Three different answers an atheist may give to this question serve to distinguish three varieties of atheism: unfriendly atheism, indifferent atheism, and friendly atheism. In the final part of

the paper I discuss and defend the position of friendly atheism.

Before we consider the argument from evil, we need to distinguish a narrow and a broad sense of the terms 'theist,' 'atheist,' and 'agnostic.' By a 'theist' in the narrow sense I mean someone who believes in the existence of an omnipotent, omniscient, eternal, supremely good being who created the world. By a 'theist' in the broad sense I mean someone who believes in the existence of some sort of divine being or divine reality. To be a theist in the narrow sense is also to be a theist in the broad sense, but one may be a theist in the broad sense—as was Paul Tillich—without believing that there is a supremely good, omnipotent, omniscient, eternal being who created the world. Similar distinctions must be made between a narrow and a broad sense of the terms 'atheist' and 'agnostic.' To be an atheist in the broad

Reprinted from "The Problem of Evil and Some Varieties of Atheism," *American Philosophical Quarterly* 16 (1979) by permission. Footnotes edited.

sense is to deny the existence of any sort of divine being or divine reality. Tillich was not an atheist in the broad sense. But he was an atheist in the narrow sense, for he denied that there exists a divine being that is all-knowing, all-powerful and perfectly good. In this paper I will be using the terms 'theism,' 'theist,' 'atheism,' 'atheist,' 'agnosticism,' and 'agnostic' in the narrow sense, not in the broad sense.

I

In developing the argument for atheism based on the existence of evil, it will be useful to focus on some particular evil that our world contains in considerable abundance. Intense human and animal suffering, for example, occurs daily and in great plenitude in our world. Such intense suffering is a clear case of evil. Of course, if the intense suffering leads to some greater good, a good we could not have obtained without undergoing the suffering in question, we might conclude that the suffering is justified, but it remains an evil nevertheless. For we must not confuse the intense suffering in and of itself with the good things to which it sometimes leads or of which it may be a necessary part. Intense human or animal suffering is in itself bad, an evil, even though it may sometimes be justified by virtue of being a part of, or leading to, some good which is unobtainable without it. What is evil in itself may sometimes be good as a means because it leads to something that is good in itself. In such a case, while remaining an evil in itself, the intense human or animal suffering is, nevertheless, an evil which someone might be morally justified in permitting.

Taking human and animal suffering as a clear instance of evil which occurs with great frequency in our world, the argument for atheism based on evil can be stated as follows:

1. There exist instances of intense suffering which an omnipotent, omniscient being could have prevented without thereby losing some greater good or permitting some evil equally bad or worse.[2]
2. An omniscient, wholly good being would prevent the occurrence of any intense

suffering it could, unless it could not do so without thereby losing some greater good or permitting some evil equally bad or worse.
3. There does not exist an omnipotent, omniscient, wholly good being.

What are we to say about this argument for atheism, an argument based on the profusion of one sort of evil in our world? The argument is valid; therefore, if we have rotational grounds for accepting its premises, to that extent we have rational grounds for accepting atheism. Do we, however, have rational grounds for accepting the premises of this argument?

Let's begin with the second premise. Let s be an instance of intense human or animal suffering which an omniscient, wholly good being could prevent. We will also suppose that things are such that s will occur unless prevented by the omniscient, wholly good (OG) being. We might be interested in determining what would be a sufficient condition of OG failing to prevent s. But, for our purpose here, we need only try to state a necessary condition for OG failing to prevent s. That condition, so it seems to me, is this:

Either

(i) there is some greater good, G, such that G is obtainable by OG only if OG permits s,

or

(ii) there is some greater good, G, such that G is obtainable by OG only if OG permits either s or some evil equally bad or worse,

or

(iii) s_1 is such that it is preventable by OG only if OG permits some evil equally bad or worse.

It is important to recognize that (iii) is not included in (i). For losing a good greater than s is not the same as permitting an evil greater than s. And this because the *absence* of a good state of affairs need not itself be an evil state of affairs. It is also important to recognize that s might be such that it is preventable by OG *without* losing G (so condition (i) is not satisfied) but also such that if OG did prevent it, G would be lost unless OG permitted some evil equal to or worse than *s*. If this were so, it does not seem correct to require that *OG* prevent *s*. Thus, condition (ii) takes into account an important possibility not encompassed in condition (i).

Is it true that if an omniscient, wholly good being permits the occurrence of some intense suffering it could have prevented, then either (i) or (ii) or (iii) obtains? It seems to me that it is true. But if it is true then so is premise (2) of the argument for atheism. For that premise merely states in more compact form what we have suggested must be true if an omniscient, wholly good being fails to prevent some intense suffering it could prevent. Premise (2) says that an omniscient, wholly good being would prevent the occurrence of any intense suffering it could, unless it could not do so without thereby losing some greater good or permitting some evil equally bad or worse. This premise (or something not too distant from it) is, I think, held in common by many atheists and nontheists. Of course, there may be disagreement about whether something is good, and whether, if it is good, one would be morally justified in permitting some intense suffering to occur in order to obtain it. Someone might hold, for example, that no good is great enough to justify permitting an innocent child to suffer terribly. Again, someone might hold that the mere fact that a given good outweighs some suffering and would be lost if the suffering were prevented, is not a morally sufficient reason for permitting the suffering. But to hold either of these views is not to deny (2). For (2) claims only that *if* an omniscient, wholly good being permits intense suffering *then* either there is some greater good that would have been lost, or some equally bad or worse evil that would have occurred, had the intense suffering been prevented. (2) does not purport to describe what might be a *sufficient* condition for an omniscient, wholly good being to permit intense suffering, only what is a *necessary* condition. So stated, (2) seems to express a belief that accords with our basic moral principles, principles shared by both theists and nontheists. If we are to fault the argument for atheism, therefore, it seems we must find some fault with its first premise.

Suppose in some distant forest lightning strikes a dead tree, resulting in a forest fire. In the fire a fawn is trapped, horribly burned, and lies in terrible agony for several days before death relieves its suffering. So far as we can see, the fawn's intense suffering is pointless. For there does not appear to be any greater good such that the prevention of the fawn's suffering would require either the loss of that good or the occurrence of an evil equally bad or worse. Nor does there seem to be any equally bad or worse evil so connected to the fawn's suffering that it would have had to occur had the fawn's suffering been prevented. Could an omnipotent, omniscient being have prevented the fawn's apparently pointless suffering? The answer is obvious, as even the theist will insist. An omnipotent, omniscient being could have easily prevented the fawn from being horribly burned, or, given the burning, could have spared the fawn the intense suffering by quickly ending its life, rather than allowing the fawn to lie in terrible agony for several days. Since the fawn's intense suffering was preventable and, so far as we can see, pointless, doesn't it appear that premise (1) of the argument is true, that there do exist instances of intense suffering which an omnipotent, omniscient being could have prevented without thereby losing some greater good or permitting some evil equally bad or worse?

It must be acknowledged that the case of the fawn's apparently pointless suffering does not prove that (1) is true. For even though we cannot see how the fawn's suffering is required to obtain some greater good (or to prevent some equally bad or worse evil), it hardly follows that it is not so required. After all, we are often surprised by how things we thought to be unconnected turn out to be intimately connected. Perhaps, for all we know, there is some familiar good outweighing the fawn's suffering to which that suffering is connected in a way we do not see. Furthermore, there may well be unfamiliar goods, goods we haven't dreamed of, to which the fawn's suffering is inextricably connected. Indeed, it would seem to require something like omniscience on our part before we could lay claim to *knowing* that there is no greater good connected to the fawn's suffering in such a manner than an omnipotent, omniscient being could not have achieved that good without permitting that suffering or some evil equally bad or worse. So the case of the fawn's suffering surely does not enable us to *establish* the truth of (1).

The truth is that we are not in a position to prove that (1) is true. We cannot know with certainty that instances of suffering of the sort described in (1) do occur in our world. But it is one thing to *know* or *prove* that (1) is true and quite another thing to have *rational grounds* for believing (1) to be true. We are often in the position where in the light of our experience and knowledge it is rational to believe that a certain statement is true, even though we are not in a position to prove or to know with certainty that the statement is true. In the light of our past experience and knowledge it is, for example, very reasonable to believe that neither Goldwater nor McGovern will ever be elected President, but we are scarcely in the position of knowing with certainty that neither will ever be elected President. So, too, with (1), although we cannot know with certainty that it is true, it perhaps can be rationally supported, shown to be a rational belief.

Consider again the case of the fawn's suffering. Is it reasonable to believe that there is some greater good so intimately connected to that suffering that even an omnipotent, omniscient being could not have obtained that good without permitting that suffering or some evil at least as bad? It certainly does not appear reasonable to believe this. Nor does it seem reasonable to believe that there is some evil at least as bad as the fawn's suffering such that an omnipotent being simply could not have prevented it without permitting the fawn's suffering. But even if it should somehow be reasonable to believe either of these things of the fawn's suffering, we must then ask whether it is reasonable to believe either of these things of *all* the instances of seemingly pointless human and animal suffering that occur daily in our world. And surely the answer to this more general question must be no. It seems quite unlikely that all the instances of intense suffering occurring daily in our world are intimately related to the occurrence of greater goods or

the prevention of evils at least as bad; and even more unlikely, should they somehow all be so related, that an omnipotent, omniscient being could not have achieved at least some of those goods (or prevented some of those evils) without permitting the instances of intense suffering that are supposedly related to them. In the light of our experience and knowledge of the variety and scale of human and animal suffering in our world, the idea that none of this suffering could have been prevented by an omnipotent being without thereby losing a greater good or permitting an evil at least as bad seems an extraordinary absurd idea, quite beyond our belief. It seems then that although we cannot prove that (1) is true, it is, nevertheless, altogether *reasonable* to believe that (1) is true, that (1) is a *rational* belief.

Returning now to our argument for atheism, we've seen that the second premise expresses a basic belief common to many theists and nontheists. We've also seen that our experience and knowledge of the variety and profusion of suffering in our world provides *rational support* for the first premise. Seeing that the conclusion, 'There does not exist an omnipotent, omniscient, wholly good being' follows from these two premises, it does seem that we have *rational support* for atheism, that it is reasonable for us to believe that the theistic God does not exist.

II

Can theism be rationally defended against the argument for atheism we have just examined? If it can, how might the theist best respond to that argument? Since the argument from (1) and (2) to (3) is valid, and since the theist, no less than the nontheist, is more than likely committed to (2), it's clear that the theist can reject this atheistic argument only by rejecting its first premise, the premise that states that there are instances of intense suffering which an omnipotent, omniscient being could have prevented without thereby losing some greater good or permitting some evil equally bad or worse. How, then, can the theist best respond to this premise and the considerations advanced in its support?

There are basically three responses a theist can make. First, he might argue not that (1) is false or probably false, but only that the reasoning given in support of it is in some way *defective*. He may do this either by arguing that the reasons given in support of (1) are *in themselves* insufficient to justify accepting (1), or by arguing that there are other things we know which, when taken in conjunction with these reasons, do not justify us in accepting (1). I suppose some theists would be content with this rather modest response to the basic argument for atheism. But given the validity of the basic argument and the theist's likely acceptance of (2), he is thereby committed to the view that (1) is false, not just that we have no good reasons for accepting (1) as true. The second two responses are aimed at showing that it is reasonable to believe that (1) is false. Since the theist is committed to this view, I shall focus the discussion on these two attempts, attempts which we can distinguish as 'the direct attack' and 'the indirect attack.'

By a direct attack, I mean an attempt to reject (1) by pointing out goods, for example, to which suffering may well be connected, goods which an omnipotent, omniscient being could not achieve without permitting suffering. It is doubtful, however, that the direct attack can succeed. The theist may point out that some suffering leads to moral and spiritual development impossible without suffering. But it's reasonably clear that suffering often occurs in a degree far beyond what is required for character development. The theist may say that some suffering results from free choices of human beings and might be preventable only by preventing some measure of human freedom. But, again, it's clear that much intense suffering occurs not as a result of human free choices. The general difficulty with this direct attack on premise (1) is twofold. First, it cannot succeed; for the theist does not know what greater goods might be served, or evils prevented, by each instance of intense human or animal suffering. Second, the theist's own religious tradition usually maintains that in this life it is not given to us to know God's purpose in allowing particular instances of suffering. Hence, the direct attack against premise

(1) cannot succeed and violates basic beliefs associated with theism.

The best procedure for the theist to follow in rejecting premise (1) is the indirect procedure. This procedure I shall call 'the G. E. Moore shift', so-called in honor of the twentieth century philosopher, G. E. Moore, who used it to great effect in dealing with the arguments of the skeptics. Skeptical philosophers such as David Hume have advanced ingenious arguments to prove that no one can know of the existence of any material object. The premises of their arguments employ plausible principles, principles which many philosophers have tried to reject directly, but only with questionable success. Moore's procedure was altogether different. Instead of arguing directly against the premises of the skeptic's arguments, he simply noted that the premises implied, for example, that he (Moore) did not know of the existence of a pencil. Moore then proceeded indirectly against the skeptic's premises by arguing:

> I do know that this pencil exists.
> If the skeptic's principles are correct I cannot know of the existence of this pencil.
>
> ∴ The skeptic's principles (at least one) must be incorrect.

Moore then noted that his argument is just as valid as the skeptic's, that both of their arguments contain the premise 'If the skeptic's principles are correct Moore cannot know of the existence of this pencil,' and concluded that the only way to choose between the two arguments (Moore's and the skeptic's) is by deciding which of the first premises it is more rational to believe—Moore's premise 'I do know that this pencil exists' or the skeptic's premise asserting that his skeptical principles are correct. Moore concluded that his own first premise was the more rational of the two.

Before we see how the theist may apply the G. E. Moore shift to the basic argument of atheism, we should note the general strategy of the shift. We're given an argument: p, q, therefore, r. Instead of arguing directly against p, another argument is constructed not-r, q, therefore, not-p—which begins with the denial of the conclusion of the first argument, keeps its second premise, and ends with the denial of the first premise as its conclusion. Compare, for example, these two:

I. p II. not-r

$\dfrac{q}{r}$ $\dfrac{q}{\text{not-}p}$

It is a truth of logic that if I is valid II must be valid as well. Since the arguments are the same so far as the second premise is concerned, any choice between them must concern their respective first premises. To argue against the first premise (p) by constructing the counter argument II is to employ the G. E. Moore shift.

Applying the G. E. Moore shift against the first premise of the basic argument for atheism, the theist can argue as follows:

not-3. There exists an omnipotent, omniscient, wholly good being.
2. An omniscient, wholly good being would prevent the occurrence of any intense suffering it could, unless it could not do so without thereby losing some greater good or permitting some evil equally bad or worse.

therefore,

not-1. It is not the case that there exist instances of intense suffering which an omnipotent, omniscient being could have prevented without thereby losing some greater good or permitting some evil equally bad or worse.

We now have two arguments: the basic argument for atheism from (1) and (2) to (3), and the theist's best response, the argument from (not-3) and (2) to (not-1). What the theist then says about (1) is that he has rational grounds for believing in the existence of the theistic God (not-3), accepts (2) as true, and sees that (not-1) follows from (not-3) and (2). He concludes, therefore, that he has rational grounds for rejecting (1). Having rational grounds for rejecting (1), the theist concludes that the basic argument for atheism is mistaken.

III

We've had a look at a forceful argument for atheism and what seems to be the theist's best response to that argument. If one is persuaded by the argument for atheism, as I find myself to be, how might one best view the position of the theist? Of course, he will view the theist as having a false belief, just as the theist will view the atheist as having a false belief. But what position should the atheist take concerning the *rationality* of the theist's belief? There are three major positions an atheist might take, positions which we may think of as some varieties of atheism. First, the atheist may believe that no one is rationally justified in believing that the theistic God exists. Let us call this position 'unfriendly atheism'. Second, the atheist may hold no belief concerning whether any theist is or isn't rationally justified in believing that the theistic God exists. Let us call this view 'indifferent atheism'. Finally, the atheist may believe that some theists are rationally justified in believing that the theistic God exists. This view we shall call 'friendly atheism'. In this final part of the paper I propose to discuss and defend the position of friendly atheism.

If no one can be rationally justified in believing a false proposition then friendly atheism is a paradoxical, if not incoherent position. But surely the truth of a belief is not a necessary condition of someone's being rationally justified in having that belief. So in holding that someone is rationally justified in believing that the theistic God exists, the friendly atheist is not committed to thinking that the theist has a true belief. What he is committed to is that the theist has rational grounds for his belief, a belief the atheist rejects and is convinced he is rationally justified in rejecting. But is this possible? Can someone, like our friendly atheist, hold a belief, be convinced that he is rationally justified in holding that belief, and yet believe that someone else is equally justified in believing the opposite? Surely this is possible. Suppose your friends see you off on a flight to Hawaii. Hours after take-off they learn that your plane has gone down at sea. After a twenty-four hour search, no survivors have been found. Under these circumstances they are rationally justified in believing that you have perished. But it is hardly rational for you to believe this, as you bob up and down in your life vest, wondering why the search planes have failed to spot you. Indeed, to amuse yourself while awaiting your fate, you might very well reflect on the fact that your friends are rationally justified in believing that you are now dead, a proposition you disbelieve and are rationally justified in disbelieving. So, too, perhaps an atheist may be rationally justified in his atheistic belief and yet hold that some theists are rationally justified in believing just the opposite of what he believes.

What sort of grounds might a theist have for believing that God exists? Well, he might endeavor to justify his belief by appealing to one or more of the traditional arguments: Ontological, Cosmological, Teleological, Moral, etc. Second, he might appeal to certain aspects of religious experience, perhaps even his own religious experience. Third, he might try to justify theism as a plausible theory in terms of which we can account for a variety of phenomena. Although an atheist must hold that the theistic God does not exist, can he not also believe, and be justified in so believing, that some of these 'justifications of theism' do actually rationally justify some theists in their belief that there exists a supremely good, omnipotent, omniscient being? It seems to me that he can.

If we think of the long history of theistic belief and the special situations in which people are sometimes placed, it is perhaps as absurd to think that no one was ever rationally justified in believing that the theistic God exists as it is to think that no one was ever justified in believing that human beings would never walk on the moon. But in suggesting that friendly atheism is preferable to unfriendly atheism, I don't mean to rest the case on what some human beings might reasonably have believed in the eleventh or thirteenth century. The more interesting question is whether some people in modern society, people who are aware of the usual grounds for belief and disbelief and are acquainted to some degree with modern science, are yet rationally justified in accepting theism. Friendly atheism is a significant position only if it answers this question in the affirmative.

It is not difficult for an atheist to be friendly when he has reason to believe that the theist could not reasonably be expected to be acquainted with the grounds for disbelief that he (the atheist) possesses. For then the atheist may take the view that some theists are rationally justified in holding to theism, but would not be so were they to be acquainted with the grounds for disbelief—those grounds being sufficient to tip the scale in favor of atheism when balanced against the reasons the theist has in support of his belief.

Friendly atheism becomes paradoxical, however, when the atheist contemplates believing that the theist has all the grounds for atheism that he, the atheist, has, and yet is rationally justified in maintaining his theistic belief. But even so excessively friendly a view as this perhaps can be held by the atheist if he also has some reason to think that the grounds for theism are not as telling as the theist is justified in taking them to be.

In this paper I've presented what I take to be a strong argument for atheism, pointed out what I think is the theist's best response to that argument, distinguished three positions an atheist might take concerning the rationality of theistic belief, and made some remarks in defense of the position called 'friendly atheism'. I'm aware that the central points of the paper are not likely to be warmly received by many philosophers. Philosophers who are atheists tend to be tough minded—holding that there are no good reasons for supposing that theism is true. And theists tend either to reject the view that the existence of evil provides rational grounds for atheism or to hold that religious belief has nothing to do with reason and evidence at all. But such is the way of philosophy.

NOTES

1. Some philosophers have contended that the existence of evil is *logically inconsistent* with the existence of the theistic God. No one, I think, has succeeded in establishing such an extravagant claim. Indeed, granted incompatibilism, there is a fairly compelling argument for the view that the existence of evil is logically consistent with the existence of the theistic God. (For a lucid

statement of this argument see Alvin Plantinga, *God, Freedom, and Evil* (New York, 1974), 29–59.) There remains, however, what we may call the *evidential* form—as opposed to the *logical* form—of the problem of evil; the view that the variety and profusion of evil in our world, although perhaps not logically inconsistent with the existence of the theistic God, provides, nevertheless, *rational support* for atheism. In this paper I shall be concerned solely with the evidential form of the problem, the form of the problem which, I think, presents a rather severe difficulty for theism. William L. Rowe, 'The Problem of Evil and Some Varieties of Atheism', first published in *American Philosophical Quarterly*, 16 (1979), pp. 335–41. Used with permission.

2. If there is some good, G, greater than any evil, (1) will be false for the trivial reason that no matter what evil, E, we pick the conjunctive good state of affairs consisting of G and E will outweigh E and be such that an omnipotent being could not obtain it without permitting E. (See Alvin Plantinga, *God and Other Minds* (Ithaca, 1967), 167.) To avoid this objection we may insert 'unreplaceable' into our premises (1) and (2) between 'some' and 'greater'. If E isn't required for G, and G is better than G plus E, then the good conjunctive state of affairs composed of G and E would be replaceable by the greater good of G alone. For the sake of simplicity, however, I will ignore this complication both in the formulation and discussion of premises (1) and (2).

III.9   Evolution and the Problem of Evil

PAUL DRAPER

A short biographical sketch of Paul Draper appears before selection I.B.6. In the present article, Draper notes that traditionally the problem of evil has been, with few exceptions, the only atheological argument against the existence of God. He argues that the naturalistic account of evolution can provide a cogent alternative to theism and that by combining that with the problem of evil, one can begin to build a cumulative case against theism.

I. INTRODUCTION

Naturalism and theism are powerful and popular worldviews. They suggest very different conceptions of the nature of human beings, our relationship to the world, and our future. Though I hope that theism is true, I believe that it faces a number of evidential problems, problems that prevent my hope from becoming belief. In this paper I will examine two of those problems: evolution and evil. I will use certain known facts about the origin of complex life and the pattern of pain and pleasure in the world to construct a powerful *prima facie* case against theism.

By "theism" I mean the hypothesis[1] that God is the creator of the physical universe. I take the word "God" to be a title that, by definition, can be borne only by a perfect supernatural person. To claim that God is a "person" is to claim that God performs actions and has beliefs and purposes. "Supernatural" persons are not natural—they are neither a part nor a product of the physical universe—and yet they can affect natural objects. A "perfect" person is, among other things, perfect in power (omnipotent), perfect in knowledge (omniscient), and perfect in moral goodness (morally perfect). While some have dismissed this conception of God as religiously insignificant, I am convinced that, for millions of Jews, Christians, and Muslims, factual belief in a perfect supernatural person is essential for making sense of their forms of worship. By "naturalism" I mean the hypothesis that the physical universe is a "closed system" in the sense that nothing that is neither a part nor a product of it can affect it. So naturalism entails the nonexistence of all supernatural beings, including the theistic God.

Arguments against theism can be divided into two main types. *Logical* arguments attempt to show that theism is either self-contradictory or logically inconsistent with some known fact. *Evidential* arguments attempt to show that certain known facts that are (at least so far as we can tell) consistent with theism nevertheless provide evidence against it.[2] The arguments in this paper will be evidential. I will show that certain known facts support the hypothesis of naturalism over the hypothesis of theism because we have considerably more reason to expect them to obtain on the assumption that naturalism is true than on the assumption that theism is true. This is a threat to theism because naturalism and theism are alternative hypotheses—they cannot both be true. Thus, if (after considering all of the evidence) naturalism turns out to be more probable than theism, then theism is probably false.

II. EVOLUTION

Ever since the publication of Darwin's *On the Origin of Species*, countless theologians, philosophers, and scientists have pointed out that evolution could be the means by which God has chosen to create human beings and the rest of the living world. This is thought to show that, while the truth of evolution does refute the biblical story of creation as told in the book of Genesis, it in no way threatens the more general belief that the universe was created by God. In other words, it provides no reason to doubt theism. The plausibility of this argument is reflected by the fact that many scientists are both evolutionists and theists. Commenting on this fact, Stephen Jay Gould says:

> Unless at least half my colleagues are dunces, there can be—on the most raw and direct empirical grounds—no conflict between science and religion. I know hundreds of scientists who share a conviction about the fact of evolution, and teach

it in the same way. Among these people I note an entire spectrum of religious attitudes—from devout daily prayer and worship to resolute atheism. Either there's no correlation between religious belief and confidence in evolution—or else half these people are fools.[3]

What Gould neglects to mention is that many well-educated people, including many of Gould's colleagues on the irreligious end of the spectrum, reject theism precisely because they believe in evolution. For example, William B. Provine, a leading historian of science, maintains that those who retain their religious beliefs while accepting evolution "have to check [their] brains at the church-house door."[4]

So who is correct? Is it compatibilists like Gould and the liberal preacher Henry Ward Beecher, who claimed in 1885 that evolution "will change theology, but only to bring out the simple temple of God in clearer and more beautiful lines and proportions"[5]? Or is it incompatibilists like Provine and the fundamentalist preacher William Jennings Bryan, who once defined "theistic evolution" as "an anesthetic which deadens the patient's pain while atheism removes his religion"[6]? My own position, as my introductory remarks suggest, lies somewhere between the view that theistic evolution is a happy marriage and the view that it must end in divorce. I agree with the compatibilists that theism and evolution are logically consistent. What I disagree with is the compatibilist's inference from no inconsistency to no conflict. For while consistency implies that the truth of evolution does not disprove theism—that there is no good *logical* argument from evolution against theism just as there is no good logical argument from evil against theism—it does not imply that the truth of evolution is no evidence at all against theism. My position is that evolution is evidence favoring naturalism over theism. There is, in other words, a good *evidential* argument from evolution against theism.

By "evolution," I mean the conjunction of two theses. The first, which I will call "the genealogical thesis," asserts that evolution did in fact occur—complex life did evolve from relatively simple life. Specifically, it is the view that all multicellular organisms and all (relatively) complex unicellular organisms on earth (both present and past) are the (more or less) gradually modified descendents of a small number of relatively simple unicellular organisms. The second thesis, which I will call "the genetic thesis," addresses the issue of how evolution occurred. It states that all evolutionary change in populations of complex organisms either is or is the result of trans-generational genetic change (or, to be more precise, trans-generational change in nucleic acids). It is important to distinguish this claim about the mechanisms by which evolution takes place from the much more specific claim that natural selection operating on random genetic mutation is the principal mechanism driving evolutionary change (or the principal mechanism driving the evolutionary change that results in increased complexity). Let's call this more specific claim "Darwinism" and its conjunction with evolution "Darwinian evolution."

Many evolutionary arguments against theism appeal to Darwinian evolution rather than just to evolution. I believe that such arguments overestimate the strength of the evidence for Darwinism. Darwinism may be highly probable on the assumption that naturalism is true. But it is far less probable on the assumption that theism is true, because on theism it is a real possibility that God has guided evolution by directly causing various genetic changes to occur. Thus, any argument against theism that is based on the truth of Darwinism is at best question-begging. This is why my argument appeals only to evolution rather than to Darwinian evolution. It is my belief (which I won't defend here) that the evidence for evolution, unlike the evidence for Darwinian evolution, is overwhelming—so overwhelming that evolution can legitimately be taken as fact rather than mere theory for the purpose of arguing against theism.

The specific claim I wish to defend is the following:

Antecedently, evolution is much more probable on the assumption that naturalism is true than on the assumption that theism is true.

By "antecedently" I mean "independent of the observations and testimony that together constitute the primary evidence upon which what we know about evolution, as well as the connection between pain and pleasure and reproductive success, is based." Thus, I intend to abstract from our information about selective breeding and other changes within populations of animals, as well as what we know about the geographical distribution of living things, homologies, the fossil record, genetic and biochemical evidence, imperfect adaptations, and vestigial organs. The additional abstraction concerning pain and pleasure is necessary because eventually I will combine my argument concerning evolution with an argument concerning the systematic connection between pain and pleasure and reproductive success. The claim will be made that evolution and this connection are, taken together, antecedently much more likely on naturalism than on theism. One last point. No other abstraction from what we know is intended. For example, I do not intend to abstract from our knowledge that complex life of various forms exists nor from our knowledge that this life has not always existed. It is an interesting and difficult question whether these facts are evidence favoring theism over naturalism, but that issue is beyond the scope of this paper.

Let "T," "N," and "E" stand for theism, naturalism and evolution, let "Pr(p)" stand for the antecedent probability of p being true, and let "Pr(p/q)" stand for the antecedent probability of p being true on the assumption that q is true. Finally, let ">!"stand for "is much greater than." The claim I wish to defend can now be restated as follows:

$$Pr(E/N) >! Pr(E/T)$$

My strategy for proving this claim requires one more symbol and one more definition. Let "S" stand for special creationism, by which I mean the statement that some relatively complex living things did not descend from relatively simple single-celled organisms but rather were independently created by a supernatural person. (The use of the word "independently" here signifies not just that the creation in question violates genealogical continuity, but also that it involves the direct intervention of the deity in the natural order.) Since evolution entails that special creationism is false, some basic theorems of the probability calculus give us:

$$\Pr(E/N) >! \Pr(E/T) \text{ if and only if } \Pr(\sim S/N) \times$$
$$\Pr(E/\sim S\&N) >! \Pr(\sim S/T) \times \Pr(E/\sim S\&T)^7$$

My strategy for establishing that $\Pr(E/N) >! \Pr(E/T)$ will be to show both that $\Pr(\sim S/N) >! \Pr(\sim S/T)$ and that $\Pr(E/\sim S\&N) >! \Pr(E/\sim S\&T)$. In other words, I will show both that special creationism is antecedently much more likely to be false on naturalism than on theism and that, even on the assumption that special creationism is false, evolution is still antecedently at least as likely to be true on naturalism as it is on theism.

Since naturalism entails that no supernatural beings exist, it entails that special creationism is false. Thus, the falsity of special creationism is antecedently certain on naturalism: $\Pr(\sim S/N) = 1$. But on theism special creationism might, for all we know antecedently, be true: $\Pr(\sim S/T) < 1$. Thus, the falsity of special creationism is antecedently more probable on naturalism than on theism, which implies that the falsity of special creationism is some evidence favoring naturalism over theism—it raises the ratio of the probability of naturalism to the probability of theism. But how strong is this evidence? Is the falsity of special creationism *much* more probable on naturalism than on theism? I will show that ~S is at least twice as probable antecedently on naturalism as it is on theism, which implies that it at least doubles the ratio of the probability of naturalism to the probability of theism.[8] Since $\Pr(\sim S/N) = 1$, my task is to show that $\Pr(\sim S/T) \leq 1/2$, which is to say that $\Pr(S/T) \geq 1/2$—that, independent of the evidence for evolution, special creationism is at least as likely as not on the assumption that theism is true. To defend this claim, I will first evaluate some antecedent reasons for believing that God, assuming he exists, did not create any complex living things independently. Then I will show that we have a very strong antecedent

reason for believing that God, assuming he exists, did specially create.

At first glance, it seems that the evidence for evolution is the only strong reason theists have for believing that God is not a special creator (which is to say that we don't have any strong *antecedent* reasons for believing this). After all, for all we know antecedently, God might have chosen to create in a variety of different ways. For example, while he might have created life in a way consistent with genealogical continuity, he might also have created each species independently. Or he might have created certain basic types independently, allowing for evolutionary change, including change resulting in new species, within these types. Or he might have independently created only a few species or even only a single species, humans perhaps. Antecedently—that is, independent of the evidence for evolution—it appears we have no reason at all to think that an omnipotent, omniscient, and morally perfect creator would prefer evolution or any other "naturalistic" approach to one of these forms of special creation.

Some theists, however, are quite confident on purely *a priori* grounds that God is not a special creator. According to Diogenes Allen and Howard J. Van Till, for example, special creationism was implausible even before the evidence for evolution was discovered, because it is an implication of God's "rationality" or his status as creator rather than as "member of the universe" that God "creates a universe with members that are coherently connected."[9] This coherence precludes God's intervening in the natural order and hence precludes any sort of special creation, including the creation of those first simple life forms from which all subsequent life has evolved. Thus, according to these theists, the only sort of explanations of natural phenomena that theistic scientists should look for are ones that are consistent with naturalism. In short, these theists are committed methodological naturalists.

I don't find these arguments at all convincing. What possible justification could be given for thinking that if God were the immediate cause of a natural event that would reduce God's status from creator to "member of the universe"? Also, what does God's rationality have to do with this? Perhaps the idea is that, just as a perfectly rational car manufacturer would produce a car that never needed its gas tank filled or its air filter replaced, a perfectly rational creator would make a universe that ran on its own. But such a car would be preferable because filling up with gas or replacing parts has a cost in terms of time, energy, and so on. An omnipotent and omniscient creator wouldn't have such worries. In general, what counts as a rational or perfect or defective universe depends on the creator's goals. What goal or plan of God would be better served by a universe in which God never intervenes? Of course, human freedom may place limitations on the amount and type of God's interventions. But it doesn't rule out special creation. For all we know, God may have some goal that is furthered by the laws of nature we have, but those laws are such that they will not by themselves produce the sort of complex life God wants. If this were the case, then God would independently create that life. Surely such intervention in the course of nature would not conflict with God's status as creator or with his rationality. Nor would it imply that the universe is in some way defective or inferior to universes in which God never intervenes.

Another theist who holds that we have antecedent reasons for believing that God would not perform any special creative acts is the philosopher Ernan McMullin. In response to Alvin Plantinga's defense of special creationism, McMullin says that "from the theological and philosophical standpoints, such intervention is, if anything, antecedently *improbable*."[10] McMullin claims that "the eloquent texts of *Genesis, Job, Isaiah,* and *Psalms*" support his position, because "The Creator whose powers are gradually revealed in these texts is omnipotent and all-wise, far beyond the reach of human reckoning. His Providence extends to all His creatures; they are all part of His single plan, only a fragment of which we know, and that darkly."[11] But how this is supposed to support his position is never explained. It seems to do the opposite, since any claim to know that God would never intervene in the natural order will be difficult to justify if we are as

much in the dark about God's plans as these texts suggest.[12]

Incidentally, I find it interesting that, when confronted with arguments against theism based on the idea that it is antecedently unlikely that God would permit heinous evil, theistic philosophers are quick to suggest that, since God is omniscient, humans are not in a position to make such a judgment. Yet, if we are to believe Allen and Van Till (McMullin has his doubts), then humans are in a position to judge that it is antecedently unlikely that God would create any life forms independently! Personally, I find the claim that the torturing of innocent children is antecedently improbable on theism vastly more plausible than the claim that special creationism is antecedently improbable on theism.

The problem with the theistic objections to special creationism considered so far is that they all involve *a priori* theological or philosophical speculation, the direction of which is influenced far too much by the conclusion desired.[13] Indeed, these attempts to make special creation seem incompatible with theism are no more objective and no more plausible than William B. Provine's attempt to make evolution seem incompatible with theism. While Allen, Van Till, and McMullin claim that God would never intervene in nature to create life, Provine claims that the idea of a God who "works through the laws of nature" is "worthless" and "equivalent to atheism."[14] How convenient!

A more serious attempt to show that special creationism is antecedently unlikely on theism is a posteriori in nature. We know by past experience that God, if he exists, has at least latent deistic tendencies. Teleology was, after all, eliminated from the physical sciences well before Darwin wrote *On the Origin of Species.* And even independent of the evidence for evolution there is considerable evidence that various biological processes work quite well without divine intervention. In general, even independent of the evidence on which evolution is based, the history of science is a history of success for naturalistic explanations and failure for supernaturalistic ones. Thus, we have a good antecedent *a posteriori* reason to believe that, assuming theism is true, God does not intervene in nature.

I believe that the past success of naturalistic science does provide some reason for theists to believe that God is not a special creator. But it is easy to overestimate the strength of this reason, especially for intellectual theists who must admit to living in a "post-mythological" era or else risk being held personally responsible for the plight of Galileo. But putting scientific propaganda aside, it is important to remember how little we actually know about the causal history of the universe! Were it not for the evidence for evolution, our sample of successful naturalistic explanations seems to me to be much too small to justify great confidence in the claim that, *assuming God exists*, God is not a special creator. Of course, it is worth mentioning that, if I am underestimating how successful the search for naturalistic explanations has been, then theists hardly escape unscathed. For if the search for such explanations has been so successful that any supernaturalistic explanation of a natural phenomenon is implausible even on the assumption that theism is true, then that would be powerful evidence against theism. For such extraordinary success would be antecedently much more likely on naturalism—which entails that all supernaturalistic explanations are false—than it would on theism.

More to the point, however, I believe theists have a very strong antecedent reason for believing that God did create at least some complex life independently. For the division between conscious and nonconscious life is enormously significant if theism is true. Theism implies an extreme metaphysical dualism—a mind existed prior to the physical world and was responsible for its existence. Thus, on the assumption that theism is true, it is antecedently likely that minds are fundamentally nonphysical entities and hence that conscious life is fundamentally different from nonconscious life. But this in turn makes it likely that conscious living things are not just the genetically modified descendents of nonconscious living things—that conscious life was created independently. And since special creationism is defined as the position that at least some complex life was created independently, it follows that, on

the assumption that theism is true, it is antecedently likely that special creationism is true.

The dualism inherent in theism may explain why so many theists were drawn to the idea of special creationism before (and in many cases even after) the evidence for evolution was discovered. For this dualism supports a dualistic view of human nature—a view that must have made the idea that we are the effect of altering the nucleic acids of single-celled organisms seem ludicrous. Offspring don't have to be identical to their parents, but surely genetic change can't result in fundamental metaphysical lines being crossed! Thus, even if we know by past experience that God, assuming he exists, generally doesn't intervene in nature, the sort of metaphysics presupposed by theism makes it antecedently likely that God did intervene in the physical world in order to create a mental world within it. So it's hardly surprising that, before Darwin, many theists were special creationists. They had a good reason and we have a good *antecedent* reason to believe that God, assuming he or she exists, performed at least one special creative act. Thus, $Pr(S/T) \geq 1/2$. And this implies that the falsity of special creationism is at least twice as probable antecedently on naturalism as it is on theism: $Pr(\sim S/N) \geq 2 \times Pr(\sim S/T)$.

Recall that, in order to show that $Pr(E/N) >! Pr(E/T)$, it is sufficient to show first that $Pr(\sim S/N) >! Pr(\sim S/T)$ and second that $Pr(E/\sim S\&N) \geq Pr(E/\sim S\&T)$. I have completed the first of these two tasks. Turning to the second, we are now assuming that special creationism is false and asking how likely evolution is on naturalism and on theism. Of course, naturalism entails that special creationism is false, so the denial of special creationism conjoined with naturalism ($\sim S\&N$) just is naturalism (N). I will call the denial of special creationism conjoined with theism ($\sim S\&T$) "regular theism." So my task is to show that evolution is antecedently at least as probable on naturalism as it is on regular theism.

It is important to recognize that the probabilities in question are to be assessed relative to the background knowledge that various complex life forms do exist. Thus, the issue is not whether complex life together with the evolutionary mechanisms that produce it are more surprising on theism or on naturalism. (Again, whether or not there is a good anthropic design argument supporting theism is beyond the scope of this paper.) Given that complex life exists, what makes evolution so likely on naturalism is the lack of plausible naturalistic alternatives to evolution. On naturalism, it is antecedently much more likely that all complex organisms descended from a small number of relatively simple organisms than that complex life descended from a large number of relatively simple single-celled organisms all of which arose independently from nonliving matter or that complex life arose directly from nonliving matter. Furthermore, given the genealogical thesis, it is antecedently likely on naturalism that all evolutionary change in complex life is or results from one basic sort of change like genetic change. On regular theism, alternatives to evolution are somewhat more likely, simply because there is less reason to assume that the complex must arise from the simple. When one starts with omnipotence and omniscience, so much is possible!

Even if the regular theist grants that these considerations favor naturalism, she might counter that it has never been proven that naturalistic evolution is biologically possible. Perhaps evolution could not have produced complex life without supernatural assistance. For example, it might be argued that, without some intelligent being guiding genetic change, such magnificent ordered systems as the human eye would never have evolved. The stronger the evidence for this, the lower the antecedent probability of evolution on naturalism. I do not believe, however, that the evidence for this is very strong. Admittedly, no one can describe in detail exactly how the eye or any other complex organic system could have come about without supernatural assistance. And it's hard to see how anyone could prove that evolution could produce complex life in a naturalistic universe. But neither has anyone provided good reason for thinking that it couldn't either. (Some special creationists have tried, but their arguments are very weak.[15]) This is not to say that there are no real difficulties for naturalistic evolution. (For example, it's notoriously difficult to explain how sexual reproduction evolved.) It's just to say that no one has given a good reason to believe that naturalistic solutions to these problems will not be found. Indeed, the fact that plausible solutions have been found to some of these problems (e.g., the problem of altruistic behavior) gives the naturalist reason for optimism. So any advantage that the problems faced by naturalistic evolution give to regular theism is more than offset by the considerations favoring naturalism mentioned above. All things considered, then, the modest conclusion that evolution is at least as probable antecedently on naturalism as it is on regular theism is justified. Therefore, since the falsity of special creationism is antecedently much more probable on naturalism than on theism, it follows for the reasons explained earlier that evolution is antecedently much more probable on naturalism than on theism.

III. PAIN AND PLEASURE

It is true by definition that a morally perfect God would permit an instance of pain only if he or she had a morally sufficient reason to do so. (By "pain" I mean any suffering, physical or mental.) Thus, the "logical" problem of pain is the problem of whether or not God's being both omnipotent and omniscient is logically compatible with God's having a morally sufficient reason to permit all of the suffering in the world. No one has been able to demonstrate an incompatibility because not even an omnipotent being can do the logically impossible and it might, for all we know or can prove, be logically impossible to bring about certain important goods without at least risking the existence of the suffering we find in our world. So demonstrative logical arguments from pain have been unsuccessful. And nondemonstrative or probabilistic logical arguments from pain have been challenged on the grounds that they involve questionable inductive generalizations, questionable inferences from there being no *known* morally sufficient reasons for an omnipotent and omniscient being to permit certain instances of suffering to their probably being no such morally sufficient reasons. But these discussions of the logical problem of pain leave unsettled the issue of whether or not the suffering in our world is evidence against theism or evidence favoring naturalism over theism. In other words, the failure of logical arguments from evil, including probabilistic ones, does not preclude a successful evidential argument from evil.

I do not, however, wish to consider suffering in isolation. Instead, I will address the issue of whether the pattern of both pain and pleasure in the world is evidence favoring naturalism over theism. The more common strategy of focusing only on evil, indeed only on a few particularly heinous evils, has its advantages. I choose not to pursue this strategy because the theist might counter such an argument by pointing out a few particularly glorious goods and plausibly claiming that they are equally strong evidence favoring theism over naturalism. So my argument will be based on both pain and pleasure. There may, of course, be other intrinsic evils and intrinsic goods besides pain and pleasure, but the issue of whether or not there are, and whether or not, if there are, their existence is evidence against theism, will not be addressed in this paper.

There are many facts about pain and pleasure that might provide the resources for an evidential argument against theism. Because I wish to explore how our knowledge of evolution affects the problem of evil, I will focus on the fact that much of the pain and pleasure we find in the world is systematically connected (in a variety of often complex ways) to reproductive success. For example, it is no accident that we find a warm fire on a cold night pleasurable and lying naked in a snowbank painful. Maintaining a constant body temperature increases our chances of (temporary) survival and thereby increases our chances of reproducing. Of course, the connections are not all this obvious or this direct. For example, children enjoy playing, which promotes the development of various physical, social, and intellectual skills, which in turn increases children's chances of surviving and reproducing. Even less obviously and less directly, adults find play pleasurable (though typically not as much as children do), which may or may not promote reproductive success, but which results from our capacity to enjoy play as children, which, as we have seen, does promote reproductive success. I could give countless other examples, but the connection between pain and pleasure and reproductive success and the systematic nature of that connection is so striking that additional examples aren't really needed. Instead, I will now turn to the task of showing that, antecedently, this connection is much more probable on evolutionary naturalism than it is on evolutionary theism. I will offer a two-part argument for this position, and then reply to two objections.

The first part of my argument appeals to natural selection. I suggested earlier that Darwinism is much more likely to be true if evolutionary naturalism is true than if evolutionary theism is true. Allow me to explain why. Darwinism is likely on evolutionary naturalism both because it explains the increase in the complexity of life over time better than other naturalistic mechanisms and, most importantly for our purposes, it solves an explanatory problem for naturalism: the problem of explaining teleological or "means–end" order in organic systems. Since evolutionary theism can explain teleological order in terms of God's conscious purposes, it wouldn't be at all surprising on theism if the principal mechanisms driving evolution themselves displayed teleological order—if, for example, organisms had built-in mechanisms that would produce precisely those genetic changes needed to solve a problem arising because of some environmental change. (Such mechanisms would have made William Paley a happy evolutionist!) On naturalism, natural selection is just the sort of process one would expect to drive evolution: a simple "blind" process that can explain the extremely complex teleological order in the living world without itself displaying such order. Notice also that, contrary to popular belief, natural selection does not generally promote the good of individual animals. Variations that result in reproductive success will be favored, regardless of the other consequences—good or bad—of the variation. For example, if walking upright gave our distant ancestors a reproductive advantage (e.g., by allowing them to carry tools while they walked), then this trait was selected despite the foot, back, heart, and numerous other ailments that resulted from it. Further, natural selection requires competition for scarce resources and thus entails that many living things will not flourish. So the claim that natural selection is the principal mechanism driving evolutionary change is much more probable on evolutionary naturalism than on evolutionary theism.

Of course, if natural selection is the principal mechanism driving evolution, then it is likely on evolutionary naturalism that it played a significant role in the evolution of pain and pleasure and so it is likely on evolutionary naturalism that pain and pleasure will, like anything produced by natural selection, be systematically connected to reproductive success. Thus, the fact that natural selection is antecedently much more likely to have governed the evolution of pain and pleasure if evolutionary naturalism is true than if evolutionary theism is true supports my position that the systematic connection between reproductive success and the pain and pleasure we find in the world is antecedently much more likely on evolutionary naturalism than on evolutionary theism.

This position is further supported by our antecedent knowledge that many other parts of organic systems are systematically connected to reproductive success. This gives us much more reason to believe that pain and pleasure will also be so connected if we assume that evolutionary naturalism is true than if we assume that evolutionary theism is true. To see why, consider the inductive inference from a sample consisting of other physical and mental parts of organic systems that are systematically connected to reproductive success to the conclusion that pain and pleasure are also systematically connected to reproductive success. Although a good number of parts of organic systems lack such a connection, this inference is potentially quite strong given the suitability of pain and pleasure for promoting reproductive success. But the assumption that evolutionary theism is true undermines this inference, while the assumption that evolutionary naturalism is true does not. To see why, notice that this inference is an inductive inference from a sample to another member of a population, and the strength of any such inference depends on how much reason one has to believe that this other member is relevantly different from the members of the sample. Now pain and pleasure are strikingly different from other parts of organic systems in one way: They have a specific sort of moral significance that other parts lack. (Other parts of organic systems may have moral significance, but not of the same sort.) But is this a relevant difference? We have much more reason to believe it is on the assumption that evolutionary theism is true than on the assumption that evolutionary naturalism is true. For the biological goal of reproductive success does not provide an omnipotent omniscient creator with a morally sufficient reason for permitting humans and animals to suffer in the ways they do or for limiting their pleasure to the sorts and amounts we find. Thus, on evolutionary theism, pain and pleasure would be systematically connected to the biological goal of reproductive success only if this goal and some unknown justifying moral goal happened to coincide in such a way that each could be simultaneously satisfied. Such a coincidence is (to say the least) antecedently far from certain. So on the assumption that evolutionary theism is true, the inference to the conclusion that pain and pleasure are systematically connected to reproductive success from the premise that other parts of organic systems are so connected is very weak. This inference is much stronger on the assumption that evolutionary naturalism is true because evolutionary naturalism entails nothing that would undermine the inference—on evolutionary naturalism the moral significance of pain and pleasure provides no antecedent reason at all to doubt that they will resemble other parts of organic systems by being systematically connected to reproductive success. Therefore, our antecedent knowledge that pain and pleasure have a certain sort of moral significance adds further support to my position that the systematic connection between pain and pleasure and reproductive success is antecedently much more probable on evolutionary naturalism than on evolutionary theism.

One might object that my argument ignores the many instances of pain and pleasure that are, so far as we can tell, disconnected from the biological goal of reproductive success. For example, some aesthetic pleasures seem to have at most a very remote connection to reproductive success. But neither the existence of such pain and pleasure, nor the fact that, in general, such pain and pleasure is more common in animals that are psychologically complex, is at all surprising on evolutionary naturalism. For the greater the complexity of a system, the more likely that some of its characteristics will be epiphenomenal. Also, much biologically gratuitous pain and pleasure is pathological—it results from the failure of an organic system to function properly. And the existence of this sort of pain and pleasure is also unsurprising on evolutionary naturalism. So on evolutionary naturalism, what we know about biologically gratuitous pain and pleasure is not surprising, while on evolutionary theism, the excess pleasure is perhaps to be expected, but this advantage is offset by the limited amount of such pleasure, by the existence of biologically gratuitous pain, and by the fact that a significant amount of biologically gratuitous pleasure and pain is pathological.

One might also object that theodicies undermine my argument; for theodicies make certain facts about pain antecedently more likely than they would otherwise be. The problem with existing theodicies, however, is that they explain certain facts at the price of making others even more mysterious. That is, they make certain facts more likely only by making others less likely. For example, if one of God's reasons for permitting pain is to punish sinners, then why do the innocent suffer as much as the guilty? Or, if we assume that God wants to use pain to build moral character, then pain (and pleasure) that is demoralizing becomes even more surprising. If, instead of focusing on a few isolated cases, one looks at the overall pattern of pain and pleasure in the world, one cannot help but be struck by its apparent moral randomness. Pain and pleasure do not systematically promote justice or moral virtue. Nor are moral agents treated all that differently from nonmoral agents. Nonhuman animals suffer in many of the ways humans suffer (the more similar the animal, the more similar the suffering), despite the fact that such suffering cannot play a moral role in their lives, since they are not moral agents.

All of these facts, which might be summed up by saying that pain and pleasure do not systematically promote any discernible moral ends, are exactly what one would expect on evolutionary naturalism. For on evolutionary naturalism, the causes of good and evil are morally indifferent. Thus, on the assumption that evolutionary naturalism is true, it would be surprising in the extreme if pain and pleasure appeared to be anything but morally random. But a discernible moral pattern would be less surprising on theism even if, given the cognitive distance between humans and an omniscient being, it should not be expected. Notice that I am not claiming that the apparent moral randomness of pain and pleasure is antecedently unlikely on evolutionary theism. I'm just claiming that it is antecedently less likely on evolutionary theism than on evolutionary naturalism. And it seems to me that this is obvious. But that means that this apparent randomness adds to the evidence favoring evolutionary naturalism over evolutionary theism. It may not add a lot, but it certainly offsets any advantage evolutionary theism has as a result of the moral roles that pain and pleasure admittedly do play in human lives.

IV. CONCLUSION

I have argued both that evolution is antecedently much more probable on naturalism than on theism and that the systematic connection between pain, as well as pleasure, and reproductive success is antecedently much more probable on evolutionary naturalism than on evolutionary theism. This entails that the conjunction of evolution and the statement that pain and pleasure are systematically connected to reproductive success is antecedently very much more probable on naturalism than on theism. And since neither the truth nor falsity of naturalism or theism is certain, it follows that this conjunction substantially raises the ratio of the probability of naturalism to the probability of theism. Of course, if naturalism were far less plausible than theism (or if it were compatible with theism), then this sort of evidence would be worthless. But naturalism is a very serious alternative to theism. Neither evolution nor anything about pain and pleasure is built into it in an *ad hoc* way. (It is not as if I were claiming, for example, that *evolution* is antecedently more probable on *evolutionary* naturalism than on theism.) Also, naturalism doesn't deny the existence of all nonnatural beings—it only denies the existence of supernatural beings. And surely this is no less plausible than asserting the existence of a very specific sort of supernatural being. So naturalism is at least as plausible as theism.

Therefore, it follows from my arguments concerning evil and evolution that, other evidence held equal, naturalism is very much more probable than theism. And since naturalism and theism are alternative hypotheses—they cannot both be true—this implies that, other evidence held equal, it is highly likely that theism is false. So the evidence discussed in this paper provides a powerful *prima facie* case against theism. To put it another way, if one looks only at the evidence discussed here—evolution, the ability of natural selection to explain complex biological order without purpose, the systematic connection between pain and pleasure and reproductive success, and the apparent moral randomness of pain and pleasure—then Hume's words ring true: "The whole presents nothing but the idea of a blind nature, impregnated by a great vivifying principle, and pouring forth from her lap, without discernment or parental care, her maimed and abortive children."[16,17]

APPENDIX

My argument in this paper is based on the following two theorems of the probability calculus:

A: $\dfrac{\Pr(N/E\&P)}{\Pr(T/E\&P)} = \dfrac{\Pr(N)}{\Pr(T)} \times \dfrac{\Pr(E\&P/N)}{\Pr(E\&P/T)}$

B: $\dfrac{\Pr(E\&P/N)}{\Pr(E\&P/T)} = \dfrac{\Pr(E/N)}{\Pr(E/T)} \times \dfrac{\Pr(P/E\&N)}{\Pr(P/E\&T)}$

In using these two equations, I assume that neither naturalism nor theism is certainly true or certainly false.

$\Pr(N/E\&P)$ is the antecedent probability of naturalism given the conjunction of evolution and the statement (P) that pain and pleasure are systematically connected to reproductive success. In other words, it is the probability of naturalism, all things considered. (I assume here that the "given E&P" puts back everything of significance that the "antecedent" takes out.) Similarly, $\Pr(T/E\&P)$ is the probability of theism, all things considered. So the left side of equation A is the ratio of the probability of naturalism to the probability of theism. If this ratio is greater than 1, then naturalism is more probable than theism and hence theism is probably false.

Now consider the right side of equation A. The main purpose of my paper was to evaluate the second ratio here: The ratio of the antecedent probability of evolution conjoined with P given naturalism to the antecedent probability of this conjunction given theism. This ratio was evaluated using equation B. The first of the two ratios on the right side of B is the ratio of the antecedent probability of evolution given naturalism to the antecedent probability of evolution given theism. And the second is the ratio of the antecedent probability of P given evolutionary naturalism to the antecedent probability of P given evolutionary theism. I argued that each of these two ratios is much greater than 1. From this it follows (using equation B) that the ratio of $\Pr(E\&P/N)$ to $\Pr(E\&P/T)$ is very much greater than 1.

Now look at the first ratio on the right side of equation A. $\Pr(N)$ is the antecedent probability of naturalism. In other words, it is the probability of naturalism independent of our knowledge of E&P. And $\Pr(T)$ is the probability of theism independent of our knowledge of E&P. So the first ratio on the right side of equation *A* depends on the plausibility of naturalism and theism as well as on other evidence (propositional or nonpropositional) for and against naturalism and theism (e.g., the existence of life on earth, the success of science, religious experiences, immorality, etc.). I argued very briefly that considerations of plausibility do not give us any reason to believe that this ratio is less than one. But I did not, of course, evaluate all of the other relevant evidence for and against theism and naturalism. So I did not come to any conclusion about this first ratio. This is why my case against theism is a *prima facie* one. I am entitled to conclude only that, other evidence held equal, the ratio on the left side of equation A is very much greater than 1. And this implies that, other evidence held equal, it is highly probable that theism is false.

The following summarizes my argument:

(1) Evolution is antecedently much more probable on the assumption that naturalism is true than on the assumption that theism is true [i.e., $Pr(E/N) >! Pr(E/T)$].

(2) The statement that pain and pleasure are systematically connected to reproductive success is antecedently much more probable on the assumption that evolutionary naturalism is true than on the assumption that evolutionary theism is true [i.e., $Pr(P/E\&N) >! Pr(P/E\&T)$].

(3) Therefore, evolution conjoined with this statement about pain and pleasure is antecedently very much more probable on the assumption that naturalism is true than on the assumption that theism is true [i.e., $Pr(E\&P/N) >!! Pr(E\&P/T)$]. (From 1 and 2)

(4) Naturalism is at least as plausible as theism [i.e., other evidence held equal, $Pr(N) \geq Pr(T)$].

(5) Therefore, other evidence held equal, naturalism is very much more probable than theism [i.e., other evidence held equal, $Pr(N/E\&P) >!! Pr(T/E\&P)$]. (From 3 and 4)

(6) Naturalism entails that theism is false.

(7) Therefore, other evidence held equal, it is highly probable that theism is false [i.e., other evidence held equal, $Pr(T/E\&P) <!! 1/2$. (From 5 and 6)

NOTES

1. By "hypothesis" I mean a statement that is neither certainly true nor certainly false.

2. It is worth noting that, although "probabilistic" arguments from evil are usually classified as evidential, many such arguments are logical—they attempt to show that theism is probably inconsistent with some known fact about evil.

3. "Darwinism Defined: The Difference Between Fact and Theory," *Discover*, Jan. 1987, p. 70.

4. Quoted in James Rachels, *Created from Animals: The Moral Implications of Darwinism* (Oxford University Press, 1990), p. 100.

5. Quoted in Phillip E. Johnson, *Darwin on Trial* (InterVarsity Press, 1993), p. 126.

6. "The Two Revelations," in Gail Kennedy, *Evolution and Religion* (D. C. Heath and Company, 1957), p. 20. Also quoted on p. xiv.

7. Quoted in Kennedy, p. xiv.

8. Proof: Since *E* entails *S*, *E* is logically equivalent to ~S&E. Thus, since it is a theorem of the probability calculus that logically equivalent statements are equally probable, it follows that $Pr(E/N) >! Pr(E/T)$ if and only if $Pr(\sim S\&E/N) >! Pr(\sim S\&E/T)$. But it is also a theorem of the probability calculus that $Pr(p\&q/r) = Pr(p/r) \times Pr(q/p\&r)$. Therefore, $Pr(E/N) >! Pr(E/T)$ if and only if $Pr(\sim S/N) \times Pr(E/\sim S\&N) >! Pr(\sim S/T) Pr(E/\sim S\&T)$.

9. Of course, whether this strong evidence is also significant depends on what the ratio of the probability of naturalism to the probability of theism is prior to considering the fact that special creationism is false. If it is extremely high or low, then the falsity of special creationism will not be significant evidence favoring naturalism. If, on the other hand, the other evidence is nearly balanced and both hypotheses are plausible, then this evidence will be significant. For example, if theism starts out twice as probable as naturalism, then the two hypotheses will end up being equally probable.

10. Diogenes Allen, *Christian Belief in a Postmodern World* (Westminster: John Knox Press, 1989), p. 59. Quoted with approval in Howard J. Van Till, "When Faith and Reason Cooperate," *Christian Scholar's Review* 21.1 (1991), p. 43.

11. "Plantinga's Defense of Special Creation," *Christian Scholar's Review* 21.1 (1991), p. 74. Plantinga refers to McMullin's position as "semideism." McMullin complains that this terminology is loaded, yet he describes his own position as believing in "the integrity of the natural order." It would seem then that Christians have a dilemma. No good Christian wants to be called a "deist," but no good Christian would want to deny that God's creation has "integrity"!

12. Ibid., p. 75.

13. For additional criticisms of the positions of Van Till and McMullin, see Alvin Plantinga, "Evolution, Neutrality, and Antecedent Probability: A Reply to Van Till and McMullin," *Christian Scholar's Review* 21.1 (1991), pp. 80–109.

13. Cf. Plantinga, p. 100.

14. Review of "Trial and Error: The American Controversy over Creation and Evolution," *Academe* 73.1 (1987), 50–52. Quoted in McMullin, p. 58.

15. For an excellent defense of evolution against special creationist objections, see Philip Kitcher, *Abusing Science: The Case Against Creationism* (Cambridge, Massachusetts: The MIT Press, 1982).

16. *Dialogues Concerning Natural Religion*, ed. Norman Kemp Smith (Macmillan Publishing Co., 1947), p. 211.

17. I am grateful to Kai Draper, Daniel Howard Snyder, James Keller, George Mavrodes, Wes Morriston, William L. Rowe, Michael Tooley, and Stephen J. Wykstra for helpful comments on earlier versions of this paper.

PART FOUR

The Attributes of God

IN THE JUDEO-CHRISTIAN TRADITION God is viewed as having attributes that set him apart from other beings as supreme. Traditionally, some of these attributes have been omnibenevolence (being perfectly good), timelessness (eternity), immutability (changelessness), omnipotence (being all-powerful), and omniscience (being all-knowing). From time to time each of these attributes has been challenged, and some philosophers and theologians have suggested that there are problems with all of them. The problem of evil casts doubt primarily on benevolence and omnipotence. The notion of timeless eternity gives rise to questions about divine agency and about God's relationship to and interaction with his temporal creation. The notion of immutability seems inconsistent with the biblical idea that God can become angry or pleased by what we do, that he loves us and forgives us, and that he acts in the world, often in response to things that we do. The notion of omnipotence gives rise to such puzzles as whether God can create a stone heavier than he can lift and whether he can sin; and the notion of omniscience raises difficult questions about how human beings could possibly be free if God infallibly knows everything that we will ever do before we are even born.

In the last few decades, the assault on these attributes has come from within the theistic community as well as from without. Process theologians, such as Charles Hartshorne, have denied all but the first attribute, omnibenevolence, arguing that the other four are holdovers from ancient Greek philosophy and are not found in the Bible at all. For them, God need not be all-powerful and all-knowing in order to be the Creator of the Universe and our loving savior; and since God, like other persons, grows in wisdom and insight, he must be able to change and, consequently, be in time rather than timeless. On the other hand, all of the preceding attributes have had their defenders. In this part of our work we examine the three most controversial of God's attributes—his eternity, his omniscience, and his omnipotence.

IV.A   TIME AND ETERNITY

Thy years do not come and go; while these years of ours do come and go, in order that they all may come. All Thy years stand together (and in one nonextended instant), for they stand still, nor are those going away cut off by those coming, for they do not pass away, but these years of ours shall all be when they are all no more. Thy years are but one day, and Thy day is not a daily recurrent, but today. Thy present day does not give place to tomorrow nor, indeed, does it take the place of yesterday. Thy present day is eternity. *

ALL THEISTS AGREE THAT GOD EXISTS as an eternal being. The question is how to interpret this notion. Does God's eternality put him outside of time, or may he still be inside? That is, is his eternity *timeless* or does it have *temporal duration* (sometimes such words as *everlasting* or *temporally eternal* or *sempiternal indicate* the second position)? The notion of the eternal as timeless first appears in Parmenides' poem "The Way to Truth," in which he says of the One, "It neither was at any time nor will be since it is now all at once a single whole." Parmenides and his disciple, Zeno, denied the reality of time. The concept of the eternal was further developed by Plato in the *Timaeus*, in which it is glorified as infinitely superior to the temporal. The *Timaeus* deeply influenced the early Church, and through Augustine and Boethius the doctrine of eternity (as timelessness) made its way into Christian thought, becoming the dominant position in mainstream Christianity. In the Middle Ages and the Reformation period it was embraced by Anselm, Aquinas, Luther, Calvin, and the vast majority of theologians, but challenged by Duns Scotus and William of Ockham. In recent times Anthony Kenny, Nelson Pike, and Nicholas Wolterstorff, among others, have argued that the notion of timelessness is unbiblical and incoherent and should be replaced with the notion of everlastingness.

In our readings, Hugh McCann defends the traditional timeless notion of God's eternity, while Stephen T. Davis argues that the notion of *temporal eternality* should be substituted for the timeless notion. In the first reading, Davis sets forth the contrasting ideas of "timeless eternity" and "temporal eternity." The former posits a God who is outside time and lacks both temporal location and extension. All events are simultaneously present to God. Temporal eternity, on the other hand, posits a God who has both temporal location and extension. Davis offers three arguments in favor of temporal eternity: (1) The concept of God's creative activity makes far more sense if we accept the notion that he exists in time. For if God creates a given temporal thing, his act of creation itself must be temporal. (2) A timeless being cannot be the personal, caring, involved God of the Bible. (3) The idea that God's timeless eternity is somehow simultaneous with this-worldly events seems to result in absurd consequences. For if events in 3021 BCE are no earlier than the events of 1986 for God, then time must be illusory. But there is no good reason to deem time illusory. Hence the notion of timeless eternity seems incoherent. Davis answers several objections to his view, concluding that the concept of temporal eternity is more coherent than the notion of timeless eternity.

In his contribution, "The God Beyond Time," McCann argues just the opposite. He examines objections to the atemporal notion of eternity and tries to answer them, beginning with Davis's first argument, that the concept of God's creative *activity* makes far more sense if we accept the notion that he exists in time. McCann argues that although things may be said to be brought about at some *time*, this does

---

*St. Augustine, *Confessions*, bk. II, chap. 13, translated by V. J. Bourke, in *The Fathers of the Church* (New York: Catholic University of America Press, 1953), 342f.

not entail that God must *exist at some time* in order to bring them about. He contends that it is coherent to talk about temporal differences from our point of view but not from God's. Hence, the idea of timelessness is coherent. The whole of Creation is one eternal fiat. Furthermore, McCann argues, the notion of an atemporal God makes better sense of God's sovereignty and omniscience without creating problems for human freedom.

IV.A.1   Temporal Eternity

STEPHEN T. DAVIS

Stephen T. Davis is professor of philosophy at Claremont McKenna College. He is the author of several books and numerous articles in the philosophy of religion. Among his works are *Christian Philosophical Theology* (2006) and *The Debate about the Bible: Inerrancy versus Infallibility* (1977). In the present article, he defends the view that God is temporally eternal against the classical view that God is atemporal.

One divine property that we will deal with early in the book is God's eternality. It will be best if we discuss it here because one's opinion on this subject is likely to affect opinions one has about several other divine properties, especially omnipotence, omniscience and immutability. Thus we must now raise the thorny question of God's relation to time.

It is part of the Judeo-Christian tradition that God is eternal.

Lord, thou has been our dwelling place in all generations.
Before the mountains were brought forth, or ever thou hadst formed the earth and the world, from everlasting to everlasting thou art God.
Thou turnest man back to the dust, and sayeth, 'Turn back, O children of man!'
For a thousand years in thy sight are but as yesterday when it is past, or as a watch in the night. (Ps. 90:1–4)

Of old thou didst lay the foundation of the earth, and the heavens are the work of thy hands.
They will perish, but thou dost endure; they will all wear out like a garment.
Thou changest them like raiment, and they pass away; but thou art the same and thy years have no end. (Ps. 102:25–7)
I am the Alpha and the Omega, the first and the last, the beginning and the end. (Rev. 22:13)

But what does it mean to say that God is eternal? Jews and Christians agree that God's eternality entails that he has always existed and always will exist, that he has no beginning and no end. But from this central point there are two routes that might be taken. One is to say that God is *timelessly eternal* and the other is to say that he is *temporally eternal*.

Let us first consider the view that God is timelessly eternal or 'outside of time.' There are

---

Reprinted from Stephen T. Davis, *Logic and the Nature of God* (Grand Rapids, Mich.: Eerdmans. 1983), by permission of the author. Copyright © Stephen T. Davis. Footnotes edited.

a variety of reasons a Christian might be tempted by this thesis. One might be to emphasize God's transcendence over his creation as much as possible. Another might be to reconcile divine foreknowledge and human freedom. (Boethius and others have argued that human beings can be free despite God's knowledge of what they will do in their future because God's knowledge is timeless.) Another might be to retain consistency with other things one says about God, for example that he is immutable. (And it certainly does seem true that a timeless being—to be defined below—must be immutable.)

Whatever the reasons, a variety of Christian theologians and philosophers have claimed that God is timeless. For example, Anselm graphically depicts God's relation to time as follows:

> Thou wast not, then, yesterday, nor wilt thou be tomorrow; but yesterday and today and tomorrow thou art; or, rather, neither yesterday; nor today nor tomorrow thou art; but, simply, thou art, outside all time. For yesterday and today and tomorrow have no existence, except in time; but thou, although nothing exists without thee nevertheless dost not exist in space or time, but all things exist in thee.[1]

That God is timeless was also claimed by Augustine and Boethius before Anselm, and was also held after him, notably by Aquinas and Schleiermacher. In a famous definition, Boethius called eternity 'the complete possession all at once of illimitable life'; it is a kind of 'now that stands still.' (Notice that Boethius is using 'eternal' as a synonym for 'timeless,' which I am not.) Since God is eternal, he lives in what might be called an 'everlasting present'; he has an infinity of movable time—past, present and future—all at once everlastingly present to him. Boethius is perhaps most clear on this point when he speaks of divine foreknowledge:

> Wherefore since . . . God hath always an everlasting and present state, his knowledge also surpassing all motions of time, remaineth in the simplicity of his presence, and comprehending the infinite spaces of that which is past and to come, considereth all things in his simple knowledge, as though they

were now in doing. So that, if thou wilt weigh his foreknowledge with which he discerneth all things, thou wilt more rightly esteem it to be the knowledge of a never fading instant than a foreknowledge as of a thing to come.[2]

Following Boethius, Aquinas stressed that for God there is no past, present and future, and no before and after, that all is 'simultaneously whole' for him.[3]

These statements are not easy to understand. What precisely is meant by the term 'timeless' or 'timeless being'? Following Nelson Pike, let us say that a given being is timeless if and only if it:

(1) lacks temporal location

and

(2) lacks temporal extension.[4]

A being lacks temporal location if it does not make sense to say of it, for example, that it existed before the French Revolution or that it will exist on Jimmy Carter's seventieth birthday. Thus, if God is timeless, statements like these cannot meaningfully be made about him. A being lacks temporal extension if it has no duration, i.e. if it makes no sense to say of it, for example, that it has lived for eighty years or that it was alive during the entire period of the Truman administration.

It is not easy to feel that one has fully grasped the notion of a timeless being. Perhaps this is in part because it is difficult to see precisely what criteria (1) and (2) imply. Very possibly they imply another characteristic of a timeless being, one which is also difficult to state and explicate precisely:

(3) Temporal terms have no significant application to him.

What is a 'temporal term'? Without wishing to suggest that my list is exhaustive, let me stipulate that a temporal term is one like those included in the following list: 'past,' 'present,' 'future,' 'before,' 'after,' and other similar terms like 'simultaneous,' 'always,' 'later,' 'next year,' 'forever,' 'at 6:00 P.M.,' etc. Now there appears to be a sense in which temporal terms cannot meaningfully be predicated of a being that lacks temporal location and temporal extension. Neither the timeless being itself, nor its properties, actions or relations with other beings can be significantly modified by temporal terms. Thus if God is a timeless being, the following sentences are either meaningless or necessarily false:

- God existed before Moses.
- God's power will soon triumph over evil.
- Last week God wrought a miracle.
- God will always be wiser than human beings.

Does this imply that time as we understand it is unreal, a kind of illusion? If the timeless being in question is God, the ultimate reality of the universe, the creator of the heavens and the earth, one might well push the argument in this way: if from God's point of view there is no past, present and future, and no before and after, then—it might well be argued—there is no ultimately real past, present and future, and no ultimately real relationship of before and after. Thus time as we experience it is unreal.

But the argument need not be pushed in this direction. Even if God is a timeless being, it can be argued that time is real and that our temporal distinctions are apt just because God created time (for us to live 'in'). Perhaps an analogy from space will help. Just because God is spaceless (he has no spatial location or extension) no one wants to say that space is unreal. It is just that God does not exist in space as we do. Similarly, he does not exist 'in' time, but time is still real, both for us and for God. Well then—one might want to ask at this point—if God is timeless is it or is it not meaningful to say that 'God existed before Moses' or that 'God will always be wiser than human beings'? The answer is that it depends on who you are: for us these statements are meaningful and true; for God they are meaningless or at least necessarily false.

Is the doctrine of divine timelessness coherent? I do not know. I suspect it is possible for a philosopher to lay out a concept of divine timelessness which I am unable to refute, i.e. prove incoherent. I will discuss one such attempt later in this chapter. However, throughout this book, for reasons I will presently explain, I do not propose to assume that God is timeless. In fact, I plan to make and argue for the assumption that God is 'temporally eternal.' In my view, this is a far simpler procedure, with far fewer theological dangers, as I will explain. For the fact is that every notion of divine timelessness with which I am familiar is subject to difficulties which, at the very least, seem serious.

I will argue against the doctrine of divine timelessness on two counts: first, that a timeless being cannot be the Christian God; and second, that the notion of a timeless being is probably incoherent. The first point has been convincingly argued by both Nelson Pike and Richard Swinburne.[5] I will not mention all of the traditional attributes of God they claim timelessness rules out; I will instead concentrate on just two: the claim that God is the creator of the universe, and the claim that God is a personal being who acts in human history, speaking, punishing, warning, forgiving, etc. Both notions are obviously crucial to Christianity; if timelessness really does rule them out this will constitute a very good reason for a Christian to reject the doctrine.

Notice the following argument:

(5) God creates x.
(6) x first exists at T.
(7) Therefore, God creates x at T.

If this argument is valid, it seems to rule out the possibility of a timeless God creating anything at all, the universe or anything in it, for 'x' here is a variable ranging over anything at all about which it is logically possible that it be created. The reason the argument rules out the doctrine that God is creator is that (7) cannot be true if God lacks temporal location. For we saw earlier that no temporal term like 'at T' can meaningfully be applied to a being or to the actions of a being that lacks temporal location and temporal extension. God is not the creator Christians have traditionally believed in if he is not the creator of things like me and the eucalyptus tree outside my office. But no timeless being can be the creator of such things since they came into existence at various points in time. Thus timelessness is inconsistent with the Christian view of God as creator.

But cannot God, so to speak, timelessly create something temporal? Aquinas, at least, argued that he can. God may create something at a certain point in time (say, create me in the year 1940), but it does not follow from this, Aquinas would say, that God's act of creating occurred at that point in time (or indeed at any point in time); his creating may well be based on changeless and eternal aspects of his will. Thus Aquinas says:

> God's act of understanding and willing is, necessarily, His act of making. Now, an effect follows from the intellect and the will according to the determination of the intellect and the command of the will. Moreover, just as the intellect determines every other condition of the thing made, so does it prescribe the time of its making; for art determines not only that this thing is to be such and such, but that it is to be at this particular time, even as a physician determines that a dose of medicine is to be drunk at such a particular time. So that, if his act of will were of itself sufficient to produce the effect, the effect would follow anew from his previous decision, without any new action on his part. Nothing, therefore, prevents our saying that God's action existed from all eternity, whereas its effect was not present from eternity, but existed at that time when, from all eternity, He ordained it.[6]

Thus—so Aquinas would say—(5) and (6) in the above argument do not entail (7) after all.

Is Aquinas correct? It depends on what he means by 'eternity' in the above lines. If he means temporal eternity I believe he is correct. It may well be true that God can, so to speak, 'from all eternity create x at T.' I have no wish to deny this, at any rate. A temporally eternal being apparently can eternally (that is, at all points in time) will that a given temporal being come to exist at a certain point in time. Of course, this case is not precisely parallel to the case of Aquinas's physician at a given point in time willing that a dosage be taken at a later point in time. But nevertheless, as concerns temporal eternality, Aquinas appears to be correct: as it stands, the (5)–(7) argument is invalid.

But Aquinas's argument, which in my opinion successfully applies to temporally eternal things, does not apply to timeless things. (Notice that the physician in his example is not timeless.) Even if it is true that I was created in 1940 not because of a choice God made in 1940 (or at some other time) but because of a temporally eternal divine choice, this does not make the choice *timeless* in the sense of lacking temporal location and extension. Temporally eternal things certainly do have temporal extention. It would still make sense and quite possibly be true to say, 'God willed in 1940 that Davis exist' (although it would also be meaningful and perhaps equally true to make the same statement with 3469 B.C. or A.D. 2610 or any other date substituted for 1940). Equally, if all God's decisions and actions are temporally eternal they are *simultaneous* with each other; and statements like 'x's desire to create a and x's decision to do b are simultaneous' cannot, as we saw, meaningfully be made about a timeless being.[7] This too is to apply a temporal term—'simultaneous'—to it.

Of course, nothing prevents a defender of timelessness from simply insisting that an action (e.g. the causing of something to exist) can be timeless and the effect (e.g. its coming into existence) temporal. Such a person can ask why the temporality of the effect requires that the cause be temporal. But to anticipate a point I will make in more detail later, the answer to this is that we have on hand no acceptable concept of atemporal causation, i.e. of what it is for a timeless cause to produce a temporal effect. Surely, as Nelson Pike argues, in all the cases of causation with which we are familiar, a temporal relationship obtains between an action and its effect. We are in no position to deny that this need always be the case unless we are armed with a usable concept of atemporal causation, which we are not.

Let us return to the argument mentioned above:

(5) God creates x.
(6) x first exists at T.
(7) Therefore, God creates x at T.

What we need to notice is that (7) is ambiguous between (7a) and (7b):

(7a) God, at T, creates x.
(7b) God creates x, and x first exists at T.

Now (7a) clearly cannot be true of God if God is timeless—a being that performs some action at a certain point in time is temporal. So (7b) is the interpretation of (7) that will be preferred by the defender of divine timelessness. Notice that (7b) is simply the conjunction of (5) and (6), and accordingly is indeed entailed by (5) and (6). But can (7b) be true of God if God is timeless? Only if we have available a usable concept of atemporal causation, which, as I say, we do not have. Therefore, we are within our rights in concluding that (5) and (6) entail that God is temporal, i.e. that a timeless being cannot be the creator of the universe.

Accordingly, it is not clear how a timelessly eternal being can be the creator of this temporal universe. If God creates a given temporal thing, then God's act of creation is itself temporal (though it may be temporally eternal). If God is timelessly eternal in the sense defined earlier, he cannot create temporal things.

Second, a timeless being cannot be the personal, caring, involved God we read about in the Bible. The God of the Bible is, above all, a God who cares deeply about what happens in history and who acts to bring about his will. He makes plans. He responds to what human beings, do, e.g. their evil deeds or their acts of repentance. He seems to have temporal location and extension. The Bible does not hesitate to speak of God's years and days (see Psalm 102:24, 27; Hebrews 1:12). And God seems to act in temporal sequences— first he rescues the children of Israel from Egypt and later he gives them the Law; first he sends his son to be born of a virgin and later he raises him from the dead. These are generalizations meant to be understood as covering the whole Bible rather than specific passages; nevertheless here are two texts where such points seem to be made:

> If you obey the commandments of the Lord your God . . . by loving the Lord your God, by walking in his ways, and by keeping his commandments and his statutes and his ordinances, then you shall live and multiply, and the Lord your God will bless you. . . . But if your heart turns away, and you will not hear, but are drawn away to worship other gods and serve them, I declare to you this day, that you shall perish. (Deut. 30:16–18)

> In many and various ways God spoke of old to our fathers by the prophets; but in these last days he has spoken to us by a Son. (Heb. 1:1–2)

But the obvious problem here is to understand how a timeless being can plan or anticipate or remember or respond or punish or warn or forgive. All such acts seem undeniably temporal.[8] To make plans is to formulate intentions about the future. To anticipate is to look forward to what is future. To remember is to have beliefs or knowledge about what is past. To respond is to be affected by events that have occurred in the past. To punish is to cause someone to suffer because of something done in the past. To warn is to caution someone about dangers that might lie in the future. To forgive someone is to restore a past relationship that was damaged by an offense.

On both counts, then, it is difficult to see how a timeless being can be the God in which Christians have traditionally believed. It does not seem that there is any clear sense in which a timeless being can be the creator of the universe or a being who acts in time.

The other and perhaps more important argument against divine timelessness is that both the notion of a timeless being per se and the notion of a timeless being who is also omniscient are probably incoherent. The incoherence of the notion per se can be seen by considering carefully the Boethius-Anselm-Aquinas claim that for God all times are simultaneously present. Events occurring at 3021 B.C., at 1982, and at A.D. 7643, they want to say, are all 'simultaneously present' to God. If this just means that at any point in time God knows in full and complete detail what happens at any other point in time, I can (and do) accept it. But it clearly means something different and much stronger than this, and in this stronger sense (whatever precisely it comes to) the claim does not seem possibly true.[9]

That is, if the doctrine of timelessness requires us to say that the years 3021 B.C. and A.D. 7643 are simultaneous, then the doctrine is false, for the two are not simultaneous. They may of course be simultaneous in some sense if time is illusory. But since I see no good reason to affirm that time is illusory and every reason to deny that it is illusory, I am within my rights in insisting that the two indicated years are not simultaneous and that the doctrine of divine timelessness is accordingly probably false.

Suppose an event that occurred yesterday is the cause of an event that will occur tomorrow, e.g. suppose your having thrown a banana peel on the pavement yesterday will cause me to trip and break a bone tomorrow. How can the throwing of the banana peel and the breaking of the bone be simultaneous? Surely if the first caused the second the first must be temporally prior to the second; and if so, they are not simultaneous. (Perhaps some causes are simultaneous with their effects, but not causes of events of this sort.)

But the following objection might be raised: 'Any argument for the conclusion that timeless beings cannot exist must be mistaken for the simple reason that timeless beings do exist.' It has been seriously suggested, for example, that numbers are timeless beings. Thus William Kneale says:

> An assertion such as 'There is a prime number between five and ten' can never be countered sensibly by the remark 'You are out of date: things have altered recently.' And this is the reason why the entities discussed in mathematics can properly be said to have a timeless existence. To say only that they have a sempiternal or omnitemporal existence (i.e., an existence at all times) would be unsatisfactory because this way of talking might suggest that it is at least conceivable that they should at some time cease to exist, and that is an absurdity we want to exclude.[10]

Is the number seven, for example, timeless? I do not think so. (I agree that it is eternal and that it would be absurd to suggest that it might not exist; it is, in short, a sort of 'necessary being.') But if the number seven is not just eternal but timeless, then on our earlier definition of

'timeless,' the following statements cannot meaningfully be made:

- The number seven existed on 27 July 1883.
- The number seven was greater than the number six during the whole of the Punic wars.
- The number seven existed yesterday and will exist tomorrow.

But the number seven is not a timeless being; all three of these sentences, in my opinion, are not only meaningful but true. (The fact that the first might be taken by someone to suggest that the number seven might not exist at some time other than 27 July 1883 is only an interesting psychological fact about the person who misreads it in this way. The statement implies nothing of the sort.)

But defenders of divine timelessness can raise an objection to this argument that their notion is incoherent. They can say something like this:

> Of course talk about 'eternal present,' 'simultaneously whole,' etc. seems incoherent to us. This is because such talk is at best a stumbling way of understanding a mystery—the mystery of God's transcendence over time—that we cannot really understand. Statements like 'my nineteenth birthday occurred before my twentieth' only seem indubitable to us because, unlike God, our minds are limited. If we had God's intellectual prowess, if we understood temporal reality as he does, we would see that this statement is false or inadequate or misleading. We would then see time correctly.

There may be some sense in which the claims being made here are true. I will not deny them, at any rate. . . . God's consciousness of time may indeed so far transcend ours that the best way we have of expressing it is by making apparently incoherent statements. But whether or not these claims are true, I am quite sure that we have no good reason to believe them. Like it or not, we are stuck with these limited minds of ours; if we want to be rational we have no choice but to reject what we judge to be incoherent. It may be true, in some sense, that some statements we presently consider true (like 'my nineteenth birthday occurred before my twentieth') are really false or inadequate or misleading when understood in some way which we cannot now understand. But it is irrational for us now to affirm that this is true....

We have been discussing the notion of timelessness as an attempt to understand the Christian tradition that God is eternal. It can now be seen why I find the notion inadequate and why I much prefer the other alternative, which is to say that God is temporally eternal. Let us say that a temporally eternal being is (1) eternal in the sense that there never was or will be a moment when it does not exist, (2) temporal in the sense that it has both temporal location and temporal extension, and (3) temporal in the sense that the distinctions among past, present and future, and between before and after, can meaningfully be applied to it. If God is such a temporally eternal being, there are still several ways of understanding his relation to time.

Perhaps the simplest way is to say that time has always existed alongside God. This is difficult to state coherently—'Time has always existed' reduces to the tautology 'There is no moment of time in which time does not exist.' Perhaps it is better to state this view as the simple claim that time is not a contingent, created thing like the universe.

A second possibility is espoused by Augustine. He says that time was created by God, exists, and then will cease to exist. Before the creation of the universe and after the universe ceases to exist there exists not time but timeless eternity. Thus God has control over time—he created it and can presumably destroy it whenever he wants. While this view has some attractions—time or at least our consciousness of it does seem in some sense dependent on the existence of mutable things—a possible problem is that the notion of timeless eternity before the creation of the universe and after it ceases to exist may be just as difficult to understand as the doctrine of timeless eternity itself. This problem may well be solvable, however. In timeless eternity there will presumably be no appearance of temporal succession, i.e. of events occurring before or after each other, which is at least one of the fundamental problems connected with regarding God as timeless at the same time that we live in a world of apparent temporal succession.

A third possibility was suggested by the eighth century church father John of Damascus. Time has always existed, John appears to say, yet is only measurable when things like the sun and moon exist. Thus before the creation there existed non-measurable time, and after the end of the heavens and the earth non-measurable time will again exist. Measurable time is what exists from the point of creation of the world to the point of its destruction.

Since it is probably the simplest, and since I see no danger in it for Christianity (as I will argue below), I will adopt the first alternative: time was not created; it necessarily exists (like numbers); it depends for its existence on nothing else. Time, perhaps, is an eternal aspect of God's nature rather than a reality independent of God. But the point is that God, on this view, is a temporal being. Past, present and future are real to him; he has simultaneity and succession in his states, acts and knowledge. He knows statements like 'Today is 24 April' and 'My nineteenth birthday occurred before my twentieth.' He has temporal location. It makes good sense to say: 'God exists today' and 'God was omniscient on Napoleon's birthday.' And he has temporal extension. It makes good sense to say 'God existed during the entire period of the Punic wars' and to ask, 'How long has God existed?' The answer to the latter is: forever.

The three main motives for the theory of timeless eternity, I suggested, were to reconcile human freedom and divine foreknowledge, to retain consistency with other things one says about God, and to exalt God's transcendence as much as possible. As to the first, I believe foreknowledge and freedom can be reconciled without appealing to any doctrine of timelessness.... As to the second, I do not believe that anything I say about God in this book (or indeed anything said about God in the Bible) logically requires that he be timeless. And as to the third, I feel no need to exalt God's transcendence in every possible way. What Christians must do, I believe, is emphasize God's transcendence over his creation in the ways that scripture does and in ways that seem essential to Christian theism. And I do not believe that the Bible teaches, implies or presupposes that God is timeless. Nor do I feel any theological or philosophical need to embrace timelessness.

Nor is there any reason to doubt that a temporal God who is 'in' time just as we are is everything the Judeo-Christian God is traditionally supposed to be. He can still be an eternal being, i.e. a being without beginning or end. He can still be the creator of the universe. He can still be immutable in the sense of remaining ever true to his promises and purposes and eternally retaining his essential nature. (But he cannot be immutable in other stronger senses.) He can still have complete knowledge of all past, present and future events. (If he 'transcends time', it is only in the sense that he has this power—a power no other being has.) He can still be the loving, omnipotent redeemer Christians worship.

Some might still wish to object to this as follows: 'Surely God must be free of all temporal limitations if he is truly God. But a temporal God is not so free. Thus God must be timeless.' The answer to this is that a temporally eternally God such as I have described is free of certain temporal limitations, e.g. he is free of our inability to remember things that happened hundreds of years ago. Furthermore, not even a timelessly eternal God is free of all temporal limitations, for he is actually unable to experience 'before' or 'after.' His nature limits him; he is unable to experience such things, for if he did experience them he would be temporal. There is temporal limitation whichever view we take. It appears that however we look at it, the doctrine of divine temporal eternity is greatly preferable to timeless eternity. So it is the former that I will embrace.

NOTES

1. Anselm, *St Anselm: Basic Writings* (LaSalle, Illinois: Open Court Publishing Company, 1958) p. 25.
2. Boethius, *The Theological Treatises and the Consolation of Philosophy* (Loeb Classical Library, London: William Heinemann, 1918) pp. 403–5; cf. also pp. 21–3, 401–5.
3. *The Summa Theologica of St. Thomas Aquinas* (London: Burns, Oates and Washbourne, 1920) Pt. I, Q. X, Arts. 2 and 4.
4. These points are taken from Nelson Pike's *God and Timelessness* (New York: Schocken Books, 1970), p. 7. Pike's work is an outstanding study of this subject and has influenced me at several points.
5. Ibid., pp. 97–118, 125–8; Richard Swinburne, *The Coherence of Theism* (Oxford University Press, 1977) pp. 221–2.
6. Thomas Aquinas, *Summa Contra Gentiles*, trans A. C. Pegis (Notre Dame, Indiana: University of Notre Dame Press, 1975) II, 35.
7. This has been argued by Nicholas Woltersdorff in his 'God Everlasting.' See *God and the Good*, ed. Clifton J. Orlebeke and Lewis B. Smedes (Grand Rapids, Michigan: William B. Eerdmans, 1975) pp. 181–203.
8. See Pike, *God and Timelessness*, pp. 128–9; Swinburne, *The Coherence of Theism*, pp. 220–1.
9. See Swinburne, *The Coherence of Theism*, pp. 220–1.
10. William Kneale, 'Time and Eternity in Theology,' *Proceedings of the Aristotelian Society*, vol. 61 (1961) p. 98.

IV.A.2 The God Beyond Time

HUGH J. MCCANN

Hugh J. McCann is emeritus professor of philosophy at Texas A&M University and works primarily in the areas of metaphysics, philosophy of action, and philosophy of religion. In this essay, he opposes the position of the last essay (Stephen Davis's "Temporal Eternity") and defends the classical doctrine that God is atemporal.

This essay was commissioned for the first edition of this anthology. This is a revised version.

By both tradition and common agreement, God is supposed to be eternal. But the agreement is today more apparent than real, for there is profound conflict over how this claim is to be understood. Traditional theologians, for the most part, took it to mean that God is completely outside of time, and is in fact the Creator of it. Only such a God, they reasoned, could justly be called the Creator of heaven and earth, could have full knowledge of what for us is the future, and could have the sovereignty and immutability appropriate to the divine essence. More recently, however, all of this has come into dispute. It is argued that only a God who is in time could create anything at all, and that only a temporal God could be the loving father Scripture describes, who periodically intervenes in nature and history for our sake. Furthermore, a timeless God's knowledge would be woefully inadequate: Being outside of time, he would be unable to know what is true now, and hence unable to know *any* tensed proposition, not just certain ones about the future. Hence, it is claimed, God's eternity must be understood as *sempiternity*. He is an everlasting God, one who always was and will be, but who is otherwise subject to temporal passage just like you and me. Such a God may not match the ideal of eternalists, but he has as much sovereignty as a God can have, and knows all that a God can know. And if he is not unchanging in knowledge and action, he can still be unchanging in character and temperament.

In what follows I want to defend the first of the above conceptions. I shall argue that there is no reason to think a timelessly eternal God cannot create, or act so as to alter the course of events in the world, and that only a timeless creator can exercise rational and complete sovereignty over creation. As for knowledge, I will claim it is, if anything, a timebound God whose knowledge of tensed propositions must be limited, whereas a timeless God's knowledge of them is complete. I want to begin by getting clear on the two notions of eternity at stake in the dispute, and giving some reasons why God was traditionally understood as timelessly eternal.

I. SEMPITERNITY VERSUS TIMELESSNESS

The more familiar of these two concepts is that of sempiternity or everlastingness. Under this conception God is a temporally persistent or enduring entity just like you and me.[1] He is located within time, and subject to the restrictions of tense and temporal passage. So like us, he has a history and a future; he remembers and anticipates, presumably observes the course of the universe, and acts at his pleasure to produce change in the world he has created. The difference is that God's career extends through all of time, which on this sort of view is usually taken to be without beginning or end. He always was, is now, and always will be. On this conception of eternity, it makes sense to say of God that he always knew you would be reading this sentence at this moment, that he knows now that you are doing so, and that he will always know hereafter that you did. In short, but for its being unbounded at either end, the life and experience of an everlasting God need not in principle be much different from yours and mine.

The conception of God as timelessly eternal is less familiar, and radically different. On this view God, unlike you and I, is not located within time, and tense and related temporal conceptions have no application to him whatever. Strictly speaking, therefore, it is false to say of God that he ever has existed, that he exists now, or that he ever will exist. At best, such claims are a clumsy way of indicating what we who are within time can always truthfully *assert*. And that is simply this: that God exists—where the verb, though in the grammatical present, signifies nothing of temporal presentness, but rather a reality that stands completely outside of time, untouched by becoming or transition of any kind. God exists timelessly on this account, and his life and experience, while they may concern the world of change, are themselves unchanging. So it would also be wrong to say God ever has known or will know about your reading this or any other sentence. Yet, it would be true that he knows, timelessly, that you are reading this sentence—even, if he is omniscient, that you are reading it now. God knows this, and everything else as well, in a single, timeless act of awareness that encompasses all of heaven and earth, in its complete history. His action as Creator is from the same vantage point. There is no time at which he creates the universe, for time itself is an aspect of the world of change and that is what God creates. In a single *fiat* he produces the entire universe, in all of its history, all of it with equal directness and absolute control. This does not prevent its being the case that from our perspective within time, not everything does, or even could, occur at once. But that is tensed talk, which does not apply to God. From his perspective, the production of all that, as we would say, ever was or will be, occurs in a single, unified act, in timeless eternity.

Timeless eternity is, to say the least, not familiar to us, and the conception of it is not easy to grasp. One may wonder, therefore, how it gained ascendancy in accounts of God's nature. Scripture, it is fair to say, leans heavily in the opposite direction. The God of the Bible creates the world over a six-day period, and then desists from his labors on the seventh (Gen. 1:1–2:2). At intervals, he speaks to Moses and the prophets, and he intervenes repeatedly in his people's history to save them from disaster. Above all, he is portrayed as *reacting* to the behavior of humankind; he adjusts his behavior to our own, as when he desists from his plan to destroy Nineveh (Jon. 3:10). Obviously, this is not a God who is remote from the world. His involvement in it is deep, and his actions as a loving father are attuned to the needs of each situation.

There is no denying that such an interactive God is more easily understood as temporal. As always with the reading of Scripture, however, one must be cautious, for too much literalism leads straight into trouble. Indeed, the very first phrase of the entire Bible tells us that the God about to be described as creating the world in six days did so "in the beginning." How could this be if time had no beginning? Furthermore, this same God is presented as a spatial being: as having a head, hands and feet, as dwelling in cities and tabernacles, as moving from place to place. If it is fair to take this kind of talk as metaphorical,

then surely passages that portray God as temporal can in principle be so taken as well. Finally, the Bible contains clear hints of a much more sophisticated conception. The name God gives himself from the burning bush, "I am" (Exod. 3:14), becomes entirely unimpressive when taken to mean only that he existed at that moment. Or consider the sudden shift to the grammatical present in such passages as, "Before the mountains were born, or thou didst give birth to the earth and the world, even from everlasting to everlasting, thou art God" (Ps. 90:2), or, "I say to you, before Abraham was born, I am" (John 8:58). It is not unreasonable to think passages like this aim at an atemporal conception. Finally, despite his seeming change of mind about the Ninevites, the Bible is at points fairly decisive in claiming that in God there is no change, not even a shadow of it (Mal. 3:6, James 1:17).

This kind of conflict is familiar. It has been said that the Bible is a book not of theology but of life, and so cannot be expected to offer a unified and seamlessly consistent theory of the divine nature. That is the work of philosophers and theologians, who have usually aimed at an account that respects the rigors of metaphysics as well as the content of faith. And from a metaphysical perspective, it is not surprising that some theories would call for a timeless God. The view that ultimate reality is timeless is as old as Parmenides, and its association with theories of the divine nature was probably inevitable. But there are reasons for the alliance. Both in Scripture and in cosmological proofs for the existence of God, he is portrayed as the Creator of everything but himself and as ruling the universe with complete power and authority. But if God is in time, his sovereignty is restricted: There is something other than himself that he did not create—namely, time itself—and his experience and action are made subject to the limitations of opportunity. Better, then, if possible, to have a God who in creating the world creates time, but whose own being lies beyond it. A second consideration, of which we will see more below, has to do with human freedom. If it is true that God gives us wills that escape the reach of causal determination, then to treat him as temporal is to threaten his omniscience. How could he know today what I will do tomorrow if I have not yet decided? A timelessly eternal God, by contrast, should be able to know as much about tomorrow as he does about today: everything, presumably.

But perhaps the deepest running argument for a timelessly eternal God is that the divine essence, as well as we are able to understand it, seems incompatible with any sort of change. A thing changes either by coming to have a characteristic it previously lacked, or by losing a characteristic it previously had. Thus an apple might change colors by ceasing to be green and becoming red; or it may fall to the earth, thereby exchanging its position at the end of a branch for one on the ground. Now the characteristics with respect to which a thing changes must be accidental rather than essential ones, at least if the thing is to continue existing, for the essential properties of a thing are by definition characteristics without which it cannot continue in being. An apple may change its color or position, but it cannot cease to be colored or positioned at all and remain in existence, for color and position are essential to apples. The same considerations apply to God. If he is to undergo change without ceasing to be, it must be by gaining or losing accidental features. Perhaps he comes to have a thought he previously did not, or to act in a new way. It turns out, however, that unlike created beings, God cannot have accidental features.

The reason for this is that if God does have accidental properties, his authority over the universe has to be limited. It is fair to demand that any accidental properties God has will have a sufficient explanation. Otherwise, his having them would be arbitrary and not in accordance with the concept of a perfect being. But unfortunately, the explanation for the presence of an accidental property in a thing can never arise entirely from the thing's own nature. If it did, the property would be entailed by the entity's essence, and so be essential rather than accidental. But if it is essential, then it is not a property with respect to which the thing could change after all. So the accidental properties of a thing must always be explained at least in part from without: The color of the apple will depend in part on its

environment, and its location will hinge on the forces to which it is subject. And the same applies to God. If his thought and activity change from time to time, there will have to be an explanation, and the explanation will have to invoke things other than the divine nature. Perhaps what he is thinking will be explained by the events of the moment, or his activity by the opportunity they present. But whatever the explanation is, it will have to invoke something extrinsic to the divine nature, and it cannot do so without introducing dependence and passivity into God. His experience will depend on the stage of world history, and he will have to await his chances to redirect it. For traditional theology at least, that is not what one expects of the Sovereign Lord of heaven and earth.

A perfectly sovereign God cannot, then, have accidental properties; and of course a being that cannot even have accidental properties cannot change with respect to them. On the traditional conception, therefore, God must be completely immutable, completely beyond the reach of becoming. It does not even make sense to put him in time, since he would then have shifting relations of simultaneity with the events of the world, which is not possible. It is unlikely, however, that proponents of the temporal conception of eternity would be persuaded by this argument. For one thing, they may have misgivings about the very idea of there being timelessly eternal entities and states of affairs. Secondly, they might claim the conception of the divine nature called for by atemporalists is simply too demanding. Perhaps it *is* wrong, strictly speaking, to think of there being any change in a being whose essence is to be, and who enjoys complete sovereignty over the world. But, the temporalist might point out, the fact is that we do this with God all the time: we speak of him as learning about things as they occur, and as causing different events at different times. And although we may try to observe protocol by insisting that all of God's knowledge and activity occurs in a single, eternal act, it is not clear that this advances our understanding very much. Indeed, the temporalist may go further. He may argue that causation and knowing, or at least some knowing, are in themselves *intrinsically* temporal operations, so that if we apply these concepts to God at all, we must conceive of him as a temporal being. I want to address these concerns in order, beginning with the one about there being timelessly eternal things.

II. ATEMPORAL STATES OF AFFAIRS

A number of reasons might be given for doubting that there is a realm of timeless entities or timeless facts about them. Some are based on misunderstandings. It may be thought, for example, that if for God there is no time, then time must somehow be unreal—an illusion, perhaps, that accompanies our own creaturely perceptions, but not a genuine aspect of the real world. And it might well be argued that this is too much to swallow; time is too central, too inexpungible from our experience to be plausibly considered an illusion. There is no reason, however, why defenders of timeless eternity need be committed to such a view. After all, no one takes the fact that God is not a spatial entity to imply that space is an illusion, so why take such a position with respect to time? Furthermore, atemporalism is not committed to the view that for God there is no time. It holds, to be precise, that God is not *in* time, that his life and experience transcend change and temporal passage. It does not follow from this that time is unreal or even that God is unfamiliar with it. Indeed, if he is both omniscient and the Creator of time, precisely the opposite would have to be the case. The only restriction is that his activity and awareness must not involve change, even though the world that is their object does. It may, of course, be argued that this is not possible, and we shall shortly be examining such arguments. But the important thing to see at this point is that an argument is needed; it is in no way obvious that the atemporalist position here is untenable.

A second reason for doubting that there are timeless states of affairs stems from the way in which defenders of timeless eternity have been prone to express their view. Boethius described timeless eternity as "the complete possession, all at once, of illimitable life," and held that the God who possesses this life comprehends "the infinite spaces of that which is past and to come...as though they were now in doing."[2] Following this precedent, it is not uncommon for timeless eternity to be described in terms that are at least partly temporal rather than timeless. God's experience is held to be of an "eternal present," for example, or we may be told that in eternity all of the world's history is "simultaneously present" to God. As a stepping stone to understanding timeless eternity such language is probably to be expected, and it is useful in some ways. It conveys the point that God's experience of the world is single and unchanging, that it involves no serial presentation of events or alteration of content. It also suggests something else to which the defender of timeless eternity should be committed: that the *content* of God's experience of the world includes its temporal features, that he is aware of things in their temporality as well as in all other aspects of their being.

But to say that all of history is eternally or *simultaneously* *present* to God leads to implications that are not intended, and that we should not accept. It suggests, first, that besides having temporal content, God's act of experiencing the world is itself a temporal thing, that it occurs in a kind of unchanging present moment, notwithstanding the fact that it is supposed to be completely outside time. This in itself is a contradiction, to which defenders of timeless eternity need not be committed. A lot more contradictions threaten if we add that God's experience must be of all of history, which now must be conceived as *simultaneously* present to God. This makes all of history present "at once" to God's now retemporalized act of awareness, and the effect is that all of history must be held to be simultaneous. So we would have to say that the American Civil War is simultaneous with the Protestant Reformation, that yesterday's events are simultaneous with tomorrow's, etc.[3] Obviously, however, these things are false.

One way of dealing with these problems is to seek to define notions of presentness and simultaneity that would be appropriate to the timeless order and would not carry unacceptable implications.[4] But I think it is better, at least for present purposes, simply to drop the idea that history is "present" to God, in any sense other than being given to him timelessly in experience or awareness. This is not to say the events of which God is aware are not temporal, but it is to say his awareness of them is not. God creates and is aware of all of history neither simultaneously nor at different times, but eternally. His activity as Creator and Knower is unified and unchanging, but it does not occur at any present moment, not even a supposed eternal one. It simply is. To proceed in this way deprives us of some handy ways for describing timeless eternity, but it also forces us to describe the realities it involves in ways that do not threaten immediate contradiction.[5]

But are there any timeless realities? After all, the sempiternalist might urge, apart from its supposed indispensability for describing how things are with God, we would have no need of the notion of timeless reality at all. Nothing in our earthly experience, it seems, is usefully described in terms of timelessness; and since heavenly experience is not now available to us, it may well be that the timeless realities eternalists suppose pertain to it are not really there, but instead are just figments of our inability to comprehend. To this atemporalists have replied that we are in fact familiar with timeless entities, namely, those of the conceptual and mathematical realms. Such entities as propositions and numbers, they have held, are incapable of intrinsic change, and truths about them represent timelessly eternal states of affairs. Consider the fact that the number 2 is even. This, obviously, is not something we expect to change, for we do not view the number 2 as capable of change. And when we say that 2 is even, we mean to assert more than just a fact we take to hold at that particular moment. That 2 is incapable of change, according to the atemporalist, makes the number 2 as timeless a reality as any. And the fact that it is even, along with all other mathematical and conceptual facts, counts as a timelessly eternal state of affairs.[6]

The temporalist rejoinder here is that this view of things goes too far. Granted, mathematical entities and facts do not change. But, it is insisted, all this means is that these are sempiternal, or everlasting, realities, not that they are atemporal. And while "2 is even" does have import beyond the present moment, it need not be taken as reporting a timeless fact. Instead, it can be taken as *omnitemporal*—that is, as speaking about all times. We can understand "2 is even" as saying that 2 always was even, is even now, and always will be even. To do this is to understand 2 as sempiternal rather than timeless, and it accommodates the unchanging character of the fact that 2 is even. What need is there to go further than this, and commit ourselves to an ontology of timeless states of affairs? And of course the same applies to truths about Euclidean triangles, trigonometric functions, or any other conceptual entity you like. In short, there is just no need to invoke the concept of timeless eternity to deal with conceptual realities. Any entity we might view as timelessly eternal can equally well be treated as sempiternal, and any statement we might think describes something timeless can be effectively replaced with one that is omnitemporal—which describes unchanging, but nevertheless temporal, realities.

Unfortunately, however, the replacement does not always work—a fact that emerges when we consider how the sempiternalist would have to formulate the very issues over which the he and the atemporalist disagree. Presumably, the sempiternalist would endorse the following two statements:

(a) There are no timelessly eternal states of affairs.
(b) There is no timelessly eternal God.

The atemporalist, by contrast, would be expected to reject (a) and (b), since he holds that there *are* timelessly eternal facts and a timeless God. But in fact the atemporalist *cannot* reject (a) and (b), if they are understood in the way sempiternalists must understand them—that is, as meaning:

(c) There never have been, are not now, and never will be any timelessly eternal states of affairs.
(d) There never has been, is not now, and never will be a timelessly eternal God.

On the contrary, defenders of timeless eternity must agree with (c) and (d), since they deny that temporal existence pertains to any timeless entity, God or otherwise. But then (c) and (d) cannot express what (a) and (b) mean. In order to capture what the disagreement is about, (a) and (b) have to be taken as atemporal statements, and cannot be replaced by omnitemporal ones. The only way the sempiternalist can express his disagreement with the atemporalist, then, is to accept the idea of there being timeless states of affairs, at least of a negative variety. And once that is done the notion of timeless states of affairs can no longer be considered suspect.

Indeed, it is a mistake to think it is even permissible to treat entities like numbers, propositions, and the like—that is, entities that are incapable of intrinsic change—as temporal. It is tempting to think of time as a matter of there being some cosmic clock "out there," beyond any specific type of change, but nevertheless ticking away inexorably the destiny of anything we can find an expression to refer to. But there is no such thing, and if there were, it would have nothing to do with the temporality of the world as we know it. In that world, things are not made subject to change by being temporal; rather, they are made temporal by being subject to change. It makes sense to treat atoms, or the heavens, or you and me as temporal beings because all of these things are subject to intrinsic changes, and because some of these changes can be used to measure others. Outside of this, the idea of becoming loses its empirical hold, and with it goes any useful notion of time.

Once this is realized, it becomes pointless to treat entities not subject to change as temporal—especially if, as we have just seen, timeless states of affairs have to be accepted anyway. Nothing about abstract entities can usefully be held to be simultaneous with anything in the world of becoming. There is nothing about any supposed career of the number 2, for example, that we are justified in claiming to be simultaneous with my writing this sentence. To be sure, relations between the number and other things can come to be and pass away, as when I think about the number during my writing. But as far as the number 2 is concerned this is only a relational, not an intrinsic change. The intrinsic change is only in

me: I begin to have a thought, and later cease to have it. And, of course, that change could occur whether 2 is in time or not. Only if there are intrinsic changes in the number itself would it be correct to say 2 undergoes an alteration simultaneous with my writing this sentence or with any other genuine event. There are, however, no such changes. Hence, there is nothing about the number 2 that is simultaneous with anything that goes on in the world of genuine becoming. But if this is so, what justification could there be for claiming 2 is an entity "in time"? None, I submit, short of a conception of time that borders on outright mythology. And if that is correct, then 2 and all other abstract entities are eternal, and intrinsic facts about them must be counted as timelessly eternal states of affairs. Does it follow, as Stephen Davis has complained, that we can no longer meaningfully assert, say, that the number 7 was greater than the number 6 during the whole of the Punic Wars?[7] Of course not. Such statements are perfectly meaningful, just as it is meaningful to assert that the interior angles of a triangle total 360 degrees. It is just that they are false: numbers, and triangles, are simply not that sort of thing.

III. ETERNITY AND CREATION

The God of tradition is causally involved with the universe in what appear to be two ways. First, he is responsible for its existence. Popular accounts of this are usually quasi-deistic: God is held to have created the universe "in the beginning," in a series of phases, and then ceased activity. Thus, the universe had a beginning in time and presumably has since continued to exist on its own. But even if it is denied that the universe had a beginning in time, standard theology still makes God responsible for its existence. He must, it is claimed, have been responsible for the existence of the historical whole, since even the existence of a sempiternal universe demands an explanation. God's second causal role is as a worker of wonders. Periodically, he intervenes in history's course to produce unusual and sometimes titanic events for the sake of our well-being. Now both as Creator and as Providential Intervener, God causes specific events to occur at specific times. And it may be argued that no one can cause an event to occur at a given time without being active at that time. So if the parting of the Red Sea occurred in, say, 1500 B.C., then God would have to have been active in 1500 B.C. to cause it, and similarly for any other change he produces. If this is true, then a God who is not in time cannot create or cause anything.[8]

Why should it be, however, that in order to produce a change which occurs at *t*, the agent of the change must be active at *t*? One possibility is that causation itself is an intrinsically temporal concept, signifying an operation that must occur in time. This appears to be the position of Stephen Davis, who holds that God's activity as Creator can only be understood to occur in time, on the ground that we do not have what he calls a "usable concept of atemporal causation."[9] In fact, however, causation is not an intrinsically temporal concept at all. It could not possibly be, for one simple reason: Causation is not a process. When a cue ball strikes an object ball, thereby causing it to accelerate, there is not, between the impact and the acceleration, a third event tucked in, which is the former's causing the latter. Indeed, if there were such an event we would most likely have to invent a second sort of causation to explain its relation to the other two. But as things are there is no need, for causation is not in itself a kind of change. Rather, it signifies a relation of explanation, wherein one thing is held to account for the occurrence of another. There is nothing intrinsically either temporal or atemporal about the notion of explanation, hence to know that a causal relation exists tells us nothing whatever about whether the cause is operative in time or outside it.

If the concept of causation, taken by itself, is neutral on the issue of temporality, then whether a particular causal operation is temporal or not has to depend on how the effect is produced, and whether the agent must change in order to produce it. And where our own activity as agents is concerned, that certainly is necessary. It is worth noting here that we do not require human agents to be active at the very moment an effect is produced. There can be wide temporal gaps—as when by planting bulbs in my garden in the fall, I cause it to have daffodils in the spring. But such gaps are permissible only when my activity as agent occurs before the effect in question, and is connected to it by a continuous process. The reason for this is important: When we, as agents, cause changes in the world beyond ourselves, we have to do so indirectly, by taking advantage of natural processes that begin in us. Natural processes are, of course, temporal, and they do not permit gaps between cause and effect. So for me to cause changes in this way, there has to be a continuous natural process that begins with some doing of mine, and issues in the effect. The process need not, of course, be lengthy: When I ring a doorbell, it is so brief that my activity of pressing the button may well overlap with the sound it causes. Always, however, I have to be active at or before the time of the effect to which my action leads when I produce effects in this way.

Now, of course, it cannot be that every effect I produce as an agent is produced indirectly. If it were, each means I employ would require another, and I would never get anything done. So the doing on my part that initiates a sequence of natural change must be a *direct* product of my agency. This is a controversial topic, but we can see that at least two things would have to be true of such an activity. First, whatever makes it a manifestation of my agency would have to be intrinsic to it.[10] I would have to be active *in* the doing, rather than producing it by some further means, or by some fictitious process of "causing." Second, if this activity is supposed to initiate a process by which I produce further changes, then it is going to have to be found *in me*, since I do not have the capacity to affect the external world directly. But, of course, I am a being in time, and what that means is that even when my agency is directly exercised, I am going to have to be active in time for the exercise to occur. That is, I am going to have to change. As to what the fundamental activity through which I effect changes in the world is, that is part of the controversy. The most plausible candidate is probably my willing the sorts of physical exertion by which I perform voluntary bodily movements. And obviously, willing involves change. I cannot will all of my movements at once, and if I could, it would accomplish nothing. Rather, I must engage in the appropriate exertion at the appropriate time, taking advantage of the opportunities the world presents as they arise. And the same would be true no matter what events we took as direct manifestations of human agency. We would have to change in their production, and so could give rise to them only by being active in time.

We have good reasons for thinking, then, that where human agency is concerned, one can produce an effect at t only by being active at or before t. But do such reasons apply to God? The answer is that they do not. Obviously, God cannot create the world by exploiting any natural process, for there are no natural processes independent of the very world he creates. Moreover, it would be a violation of God's sovereignty to suppose his creative power was limited by available means or in any way hostage to principles external to it. Rather, God's creative activity must be viewed as direct: The results he produces are *ex nihilo*. They are not the outgrowth of changes in anything else or of any manufacturing process, but instead are direct manifestations of his agency. Yet, unlike direct manifestations of human agency, the results of God's creative activity are not changes in him. Rather, the world whose being is owing to God exists as a being in its own right. It cannot be identified with God; for although its existence requires an explanation his does not. And unlike God, who is simple and immaterial, the world is a material entity, composed of parts. It turns out, then, that the reasons why a human agent can produce a change at t only by acting at or before t do not apply to God. Creation cannot involve the exploitation of natural processes, and although the results produced through it are in time, they are not modifications of God.

Are there any other reasons for thinking a being who produces a temporal result must be acting in time? I can think of none, and if that is correct, then there is no reason to suppose a timelessly eternal God is precluded from being the Creator of heaven and earth. Such a being could create the entire universe in a single, unchanging, timeless act. Moreover, in the single act of creating the universe, he would be responsible for its entire existence, through all of its history. It is important to recognize this, for a lot of our tendency to believe that God, as agent, has to be temporal is owing to the fact that, from our position within the bounds of time, God often seems to be more involved in some events than in others. This is reinforced by the biblical story of Creation, which seems to make God directly responsible only for the first existence of things, and by popular conceptions of miracles as involving God occasionally bestirring himself to alter the course of history. Now, in fact, there is nothing about being timelessly eternal that would prevent God from being more directly involved in some of history than the rest. Nevertheless, this model of God's involvement in the universe is adequate neither to the needs of creation nor to divine providence. On the first point, God cannot just cause the world to exist "at t." Indeed, if the atemporalist view is correct, then independent of God's creating the world of change, there is no "t" at which he could cause it to exist. Furthermore, we have no reason to suppose a world that requires a God to create it could somehow keep itself existing once it appears, nor can we imagine any mechanism it might use to do so. On the contrary, God must sustain the world in existence: He must be just as responsible for its surviving another instant as he is for it being here at all. Second, as for providence, a perfectly loving father, one who knows the fall of every sparrow, has to be fully and intimately involved in each aspect of the world's career. This does not prevent there being extraordinary events. If the concept of a miracle requires that there be events that are discontinuous with others as far as natural explanations go, well and good. But we should not let that lead us to believe the occurrence of the others is somehow less a manifestation of God's power. Were it not for his creative activity, nothing would be going on at all, and the most mundane events fall as much within the purview of providence as the most spectacular. Even from our own, timebound perspective, then, God's creative involvement and concern

HUGH J. MCCANN • The God Beyond Time

with the world must be understood as complete and all-embracing. And this should help us to see that the Creator of heaven and earth can after all be timelessly eternal.[11]

But he cannot be temporally eternal, for several reasons. First, if, contrary to what is suggested above, there really is an absolute time "out there," uncreated by God but restrictive of his behavior, then God is not the Creator of heaven and earth, and that is that. There is a pervasive aspect of the universe he has not put there. And if we try to fix this by making him the Creator of time after all, then we give up the claim that God is essentially temporal. God could not create time unless his own being transcends it, and his act of creating it could not be temporal. Second, if time exists independently of the world then God would have had to decide when to produce the world, when to begin his activity as Creator. But what reason could there have been for creating it at one time rather than another? Nor can we avoid this problem by making the created world everlasting too, for even then God would have had to decide whether to have things occur at the times they do, or to move everything forward or backward by, say, twenty-four hours. Again, however, there could not possibly be a reason for such a choice. This is not to say, of course, that God might not have plunged ahead. After all, he might have had good reason for creating a universe at sometime or other, rather than never doing so. All the same, a God who creates in this way could not be fully rational. He would have justification for creating the world, but not for creating it "at *t*."[12]

But the strongest reason for rejecting a temporal creator is what this notion does to God's sovereignty. An all-powerful God should be not just the producer of the universe but its complete master, the absolute ruler of everything that is not himself. To make him subject to the limitations of time flies in the face of this conception. Once launched on the enterprise of creation, at least, such a creator must busy himself with whatever tasks are at hand. If he has goals to achieve by his action, then like us he must await his opportunities, which are now limited by the stern taskmaster of becoming. And like us, his experience of his creation must be hemmed in by time: limited, in the case of the past, to memories that, however vivid, must be of events that can never be retrieved; limited, in the case of the future, to anticipations each of whose fulfillment takes literally forever to come, only to vanish like smoke. Such a God may be the master of much, but of time he is a slave. And that is a high price to pay for accepting the groundless supposition that only a temporal being can produce temporal effects.

IV. ETERNITY AND OMNISCIENCE

An omniscient God should know of every true proposition that it is true, and of every false proposition that it is false. And it is probably fair to say that when it comes to omniscience, proponents of timeless eternity have traditionally thought they had the upper hand. Suppose John mows his lawn next Saturday. If so then it would have been correct to assert now that he will. That is, the statement "John will mow his lawn next Saturday" is true. But suppose also that John's action is free, in the sense that until he decides one way or the other, there are no conditions in place that determine which way he will act. If so, then it does not appear that a temporal being could *know*, prior to the event, what John will do. One could, of course, make a lucky guess: I might venture a prediction that John will mow his lawn next Saturday, believe it is true, and turn out to be right. But it does not follow that I *knew* what John would do; my prediction, though correct, appears to have lacked sufficient grounds.

Needless to say, the same argument applies to God if he is temporal. If the behavior of rational agents is free in the sense described—and it is often claimed that moral responsibility requires this—then no conditions obtain in advance that would enable God to predict such behavior with certainty. It seems the only way he could avoid mistakes would be by an incredible series of lucky guesses or by simply not entertaining beliefs about future free actions. In neither case would he be omniscient. So unless another way can be found for

God to know about future free actions, defenders of temporal eternity must make do with a restricted notion of divine omniscience. Contrast this with the situation of a timelessly eternal God. Such a God does not know about events either before or after their occurrence, or even simultaneously with it. Rather, he knows them timelessly, in a single act of awareness whose content comprises all of history. But then free actions on our part impose no deficit of knowledge on him. A timeless God cannot be in the dark about what for us is the future, since he is directly aware of all of it. He knows, therefore, about John's mowing his lawn next Saturday because he is eternally aware of that very action. And, of course, this does not compromise John's freedom, any more than it would if next Saturday had already arrived, and you and I were watching him mow his lawn.[13]

Initially, then, it would appear defenders of timeless eternity are able to offer a more robust and satisfying account of divine omniscience. Recently, however, sempiternalists have mounted a counterattack, claiming that in fact the limitations on God's omniscience are far worse if he is timelessly eternal than if he is temporal. For suppose in fact John is mowing his lawn right now, and that I report his activity to you by asserting:

(e) John is mowing his lawn.

It would be a mistake to interpret (e) as reporting some timeless state of affairs. That is, (e) says more than that there is (timelessly) some act of lawn mowing on John's part, or even that such an act is (timelessly) located at the point in history which happens to be today. These readings fail to respect the tense of (e), which does not reduce to any timeless reality. Rather, the full force of (e) is that John's act of mowing his lawn is occurring *now*, that it is actually *present*. The situation with the other tenses is similar: If I predict John will mow his lawn again next Saturday, I am saying that act will occur after the present; and if I say he mowed it last Saturday, I am saying the act in question occurred before the present.

Always, then, tensed statements are indexed to a certain temporal location *as present*. But then, it may be argued, knowing which tensed statements are true requires knowing what the present moment is. And, it is claimed, that is something a timelessly eternal God cannot know. Being outside of time, he cannot, as we would say, know what time it is. That is, he cannot know which moment in time is the present one, and hence cannot know which ones are past and which future. But then it must be that a timelessly eternal God cannot know *any* tensed proposition. He cannot know what John will do next week, what he is doing now, or what he has ever done, and the same for any other tensed state of affairs. Not an enviable position for a supposedly omniscient God, and a far worse one than simply being unable to tell about John's future free actions.[14]

A hint that there is something wrong here can be gotten from the fact that an exactly analogous argument could have been given for propositions that are spatially indexed.[15] Suppose I assert that it is raining *here*. My assertion has to mean more than that there is a rainstorm, or that rain is falling outside my study. Neither of the latter statements respects the element of perspective the word "here" introduces, an element that does not reduce to other spatial relations. And surely if God is omniscient and it is raining here, he must know that. Yet no one argues on these grounds that God must be located in space or in any way subject to its limitations. So some sort of mistake appears to have been made. But to have a hint that something is wrong and to be able to say what it is are two different things, and the sources of the present error are not easy to locate. One possible source can, I think, be dismissed pretty quickly. It cannot be the case that when I assert (e), I am in part asserting something about myself—such as that I am in the same temporal location as John's act of lawn mowing, or that I am experiencing that act now. Any temptation to think this is the problem can be overcome simply by realizing that if in fact (e) is true—if John is now mowing his lawn—then this would have been true even if I had never lived. That would be impossible if (e) contained information about me, since it would then be rendered incorrect simply by my failing to exist. Tensed propositions involve a perspective on the world of change, just as spatially indexed propositions involve one on space; but they say nothing about anyone occupying that perspective.

But if this is not the source of the error, then what is? Here is one way in which it can begin: It might be thought that tensed propositions change their truth value, depending on whether the events they report are actually occurring. One might think, for example, that proposition (e) was false before John began mowing his lawn, is true only while he mows it, and thereafter will become false again. And one might think that only a God in time could detect changing truth values. Now, in fact, this last claim is in no way obvious. Atemporalists might well insist that here as elsewhere, there is no reason to think awareness of change requires a changing awareness, and that a God outside of time could be as much aware of truth value changes as of any others. But there is a more fundamental error here, for the fact is that tensed propositions do not change in truth value. What misleads us about this, I think, is a belief that when we employ the same *sentence* assertively on different occasions, we must be asserting the same proposition—so that if twenty-four hours ago I had also uttered the sentence "John is mowing his lawn" assertively, I would then have been asserting exactly the same proposition—namely, (e)—that I assert using the sentence now. But that is mistaken. We might express (e) more carefully as:

John is (this moment) mowing his lawn.

This is to be distinguished from the proposition I would have asserted had I said yesterday that John was mowing his lawn. For even if I had used exactly the same words, the phrase "this moment" would yesterday have referred to a different time. This means the proposition I would have asserted yesterday—let us call it (f)—would have been indexed to a different

"now," and that gives the two propositions different truth conditions. What happened yesterday is decisive for the truth of (f) but irrelevant to that of (e); and what happens today has everything to do with the truth of (e) and nothing to do with that of (f). In short, (e) and (f) count as entirely different pieces of information, and so are different propositions.

This is borne out by our attitudes when we make tensed statements. If I had asserted yesterday that John was mowing his lawn, I would have meant he was mowing it *then*. Were I wrong, I would not have claimed vindication when he began mowing it today, holding that what I said yesterday had now become true. Rather, I need to make a new statement, (e), to cover the present case. Or, suppose John also mowed his lawn two weeks ago, and that I said so at the time. When, upon seeing him mowing it today, I assert (e), you would not accuse me of repeating myself, of stating the same fact I asserted two weeks ago. That fact was an entirely different one. The situation is similar with other tenses. If today I assert that Lincoln will be assassinated, I am not saying something that used to be true. Rather, my statement is false: Lincoln is not going to be assassinated; he already was. If, on the other hand, I report that Lincoln was assassinated, I am not asserting a proposition that used to be false. My assertion is true, because it is indexed to the present, and only what holds from the perspective of the present counts for its truth or falsity.

Each time I use a tensed sentence to make an assertion, then, I am asserting a *different* proposition, even if the sentences are indistinguishable.[16] Each proposition is tied to the perspective of a particular temporal moment, and different conditions determine its truth or falsity. With this in mind, consider again the idea that propositions can change truth values. It is, of course, a suspect idea from the outset. Propositions are abstract entities, which we have seen are incapable of intrinsic change. And propositions that describe timeless states of affairs, like "2 is even," could not change truth values anyway. The state of affairs they describe will either obtain (timelessly) or not, and that is the end of the matter. So change in truth value would have to be confined to tensed propositions, and it would have to be owing to some change outside the proposition itself. But now it turns out that tensed propositions depend for their truth only on what obtains from the perspective in time to which they are indexed. It follows that tensed propositions cannot change in truth value either. Their truth conditions are defined by a perspective that is localized to a single instant. And any conditions thus defined must simply either be satisfied or not. They cannot change within the bounds of a single point in time, and nothing that occurs at any other time matters. How could it? If when I assert (e) my statement does not even concern yesterday or tomorrow, how could conditions yesterday or tomorrow have anything to do with its truth? Obviously, they could not. So even tensed propositions do not change truth values. Indeed, for all that is capable of "happening" to the truth or falsity of a proposition, there is no good reason even for taking the predicates "is true" and "is false" to be tensed predicates. On the contrary, there is every reason to think the truth or falsity of propositions, even tensed ones, is in itself a timelessly eternal state of affairs, one that is not even capable of change.

Where does this leave us on the issue of whether a God beyond time can know tensed propositions? If the above argument is correct, the truth or falsity of a tensed proposition is not an elusive thing at all. It is, rather, a timeless and unchanging state of affairs, just like the truth or falsity of a statement in mathematics. But then surely it should not be a difficult assignment for a timeless God to know a tensed proposition. What would be required, presumably, is the same thing such knowledge requires in our own case—namely, direct experience of the world of change. We have seen no reason to deny such experience to a timeless God, who traditionally has been held to have direct and unchanging awareness of the entire sweep of history. So it looks like God can know tensed propositions after all. Yet it might be thought that something is still missing. What of the point about what time it is? If tensed

propositions are indexed to times, wouldn't God have to know what time it is in order to know that it is (e) rather than, say, (f) that actually describes what John is presently doing? And doesn't this require more than simply having John's action presented to him in awareness? Wouldn't God also have to know that, as opposed to all the other stages of history of which he is aware, the one in which John's act is embedded is the one that is really going on right now? And how could he know this further fact from outside of time?

The answer is that there is no such fact to be known, for there is never anything to "what time it is" beyond the events whose simultaneous occurrence constitutes any given stage of the world's history. The belief that there is more arises from a pervasive but misleading way of representing our experience of change, which underlies the above objection. It begins with our analogizing time to space: We think of the events that make up the world's history as being lined up "out there" in order of their occurrence, rather like a row of barges floating on a river. Then, to account for the fact that our experience is a changing one, we put the river in motion. We think of time itself as flowing past us, sweeping along with it a history all of which is equally real, but only some of which is present. The question what time it "really" is is then just the question, What part of history is really before us? But the question is bogus, as is this picture of temporal transition. It may be useful for some purposes to analogize time to space. But once I do, I have used time up. There is no second time to accommodate or measure any supposed flow of the first or of the events within it. Yet a second time is precisely what we demand if we insist that the truth of statement (e) requires, in addition to the event of John mowing his lawn, a further event of the mowing being present. There is no such event, and the demand for it is just one more manifestation of the myth that there is a time "out there," independent of change. The truth is quite the opposite: The presence of John's mowing his lawn is to be found in the event itself. When it is not present, it does not exist at all. As for the elusive sense of "passage" that characterizes our experience of the world, it is simply a manifestation of the fact that we belong to that world: that our experience of it is not just an experience of change but also a changing experience. Admittedly, this is a difficult thing to describe, and in trying to do so we may feel almost compelled to fall back on the idea of time as a kind of quasi-space that we traverse in living out our lives. But that is a deception. Becoming is a reality; but it consists neither in our marching through time nor in time marching past us.

There is, perhaps, more that could be said about temporal transition and our awareness of it. But the above considerations are enough to show that it is not a matter of an additional change that accrues to events which are somehow already there. Rather, temporal transition lies in the phenomenon of change itself, in the fact that there are entities that undergo alteration of their characteristics. Because this is so, to be aware of the temporal features of events cannot require any more than that one be aware of the events themselves. It is a mistake, therefore, to think that in order to know which tensed proposition describes John's behavior God must, in addition to being directly aware of that behavior, know that it is "really" happening. There is no other way to be directly aware of an event than to be aware of it as really happening. The most we could require in addition is that God know the *setting* of John's behavior: which events are simultaneous with it, which come before, and which after. This, presumably, would be necessary in order to know the other tensed propositions that hold from the perspective of that setting. And to be sure, a timeless God cannot learn about relations of before and after in the way we do, by experiencing different events seriatim. But there is no more reason to think a God beyond time must be ignorant of the distribution of events within it than there is to think a God outside space cannot know the relative positions of physical objects. If he is timelessly aware of all events, then surely he is aware of how they are positioned with respect to each other.

If this is correct, then the God who is beyond time knows all there is to know about what time it is. More important, he knows each and every tensed proposition that is true, from each and every temporal perspective the entire history of the universe has to offer. Furthermore, his position in this respect is far superior to that of a temporal God. For consider again proposition (f), which we said was the proposition I would have asserted yesterday had I then claimed "John is mowing his lawn." And let us suppose (f) is (timelessly, of course) true. John, we may imagine, has a large lawn that takes two days to mow. Now we seem to have a pretty clear idea what proposition (f) is; and certainly we can know *that* (f) is true, since we can know John was mowing his lawn yesterday. Yet it may be questioned whether I could ever *assert* (f) from my present temporal vantage point. It looks as though I am confined in my assertions of tensed propositions to those which are temporally indexed to the point in time at which the assertion is made. If that is so, then even though I can always know that (f) is true, the time is forever gone when (f) could have been a *vehicle* of knowledge for me. As a temporal being, I can only grasp the world from one temporal perspective at a time, and that has to be reflected in the way my knowledge is formulated. In a way, then, I lack access to (f), even though I know it is true. And of course the same limitation would apply to a temporal God. It may not be a serious limitation in terms of the usual definition of omniscience, for it does not prevent him from knowing of each true proposition *that* it is true, and of each false one that it is false. Nevertheless, it reflects the confinement we place upon God when we make him temporally eternal. He, like us, can only see things a certain way. And if that means there are other ways which are closed to him, the result can only be a limitation on his knowing.

V. CONCLUSION

The case for thinking God is timelessly eternal is, then, far stronger than the case for thinking he is temporal. Timeless eternity is more in keeping with God's nature as traditionally defined, and there is no persuasive reason to think it impairs either his creative power or his ability to know. Admittedly, it is the more difficult conception. To say that God can produce and comprehend the universe in all its history in a single timeless act is to attribute to him powers far beyond our own. And even if the attribution is justified, we have far less feel for what it would be like to be such a God than we do for the God of sempiternalism, who is by contrast rather comforting. His experience and abilities are very like our own, even if vastly greater, and we may find it far easier to see in a temporal God the loving father of religious tradition. Nevertheless, I think the timeless conception is to be preferred. The acceptability of a theory of God's nature cannot, after all, be a function of its anthropomorphism. Rather, we must try to understand God's nature in terms that maximize his perfection, both in himself and in his hegemony over creation. Where eternity is concerned, I think it is the timeless conception that does that. And although the task may be more difficult, there is no real reason for pessimism about finding in such a God the personal traits traditionally ascribed to him. It may be that all we need is a higher conception of those as well, a conception commensurate with a God whose ways are as far above our own as the heavens are above the earth.[17]

NOTES

1. The terminology of *enduring* or *persistence* is to be preferred over that which treats God as temporally "extended." The latter suggests God is spread out in time as a physical object is in space, which is an unacceptable analogy. One consequence of it is that just as a physical object cannot exist in its entirety at a single spatial point, so God would be unable to exist at any point in time. But then he could not exist now or at any other time, which is precisely the opposite of what defenders of sempiternity wish to claim.

2. Boethius, *The Consolation of Philosophy*, Bk. V, sec. 6.

3. Cf. Richard Swinburne, *The Coherence of Theism* (New York: Oxford University Press, 1977), pp. 220–21.

4. For this approach, see Eleonore Stump and Norman Kretzmann, "Eternity," *The Journal of Philosophy* 78 (1981): 429–58.

5. For further discussion see Paul Helm, *Eternal God* (New York: Oxford University Press, 1988), chap. 2.

6. William Kneale, "Time and Eternity in Theology," *Proceedings of the Aristotelian Society* 61 (1960–61): 87–108.

7. Stephen T. Davis, *Logic and the Nature of God* (Grand Rapids, Mich.: Eerdmans, 1983). [Reprinted in this anthology. See previous reading.]

8. Arguments of this kind are given by Stephen Davis, op. cit., Nelson Pike, *God and Timelessness* (New York: Schocken Books, 1970), pp. 104–107; and Swinburne, op. cit., p. 221.

9. Stephen Davis, *Logic and the Nature of God*, op. cit.

10. This assumes that human agency does not reduce to a causal relation between passive states like desire and biological events such as the motion of a limb. I have defended this claim in a number of places. See, for example, "Intrinsic Intentionality," *Theory and Decision* 20 (1986): 247–73.

11. These themes are further elaborated by Jonathan Kvanvig and myself in "Divine Conservation and the Persistence of the World," in *Divine and Human Action*, ed. T. V. Morris (Ithaca, N.Y.: Cornell University Press, 1988), pp. 13–19; and in "The Occasionalist Proselytizer: A Modified Catechism," in *Philosophical Perspectives* 5 (1991), ed. J. E. Tomberlin (Atascadero, Calif.: Ridgeview Publishing Company), pp. 587–615.

12. This argument stems from Leibniz. *The Leibniz-Clarke Correspondence*, ed., H. G. Alexander (New York: Barnes & Noble, 1956), pp. 26–27.

13. The problem of divine foreknowledge and human freedom is a difficult one, and recent discussions of it have become complicated indeed. For an excellent summary see John Martin Fischer, "Recent Work on God and Freedom," *American Philosophical Quarterly* 29 (1992): 91–109.

14. Arguments like this stem from A. N. Prior, "The Formalities of Omniscience," *Philosophy* 37 (1962): 114–29. See also Norman Kretzmann, "Omniscience and Immutability," *The Journal of Philosophy* 63 (1966): 409–21.

15. Helm, op. cit., pp. 43–44.

16. Similar treatments of tensed sentences can be found in Richard Swinburne, "Tensed Facts,"

American Philosophical Quarterly 27 (1990): 117–30; and in E. J. Lowe, "The Indexical Fallacy in McTaggart's Proof of the Unreality of Time," *Mind* 96 (1987):62–70.

17. I am grateful to my colleague Jonathan Kvanvig, and to Philip Quinn, Eleonore Stump, and Louis Pojman for helpful discussions of earlier versions of this paper.

IV.B   GOD'S OMNISCIENCE AND HUMAN FREEDOM

THE SECOND ATTRIBUTE WE CONSIDER HERE is God's omniscience. To say that God is omniscient is just to say that he knows everything. More exactly: An omniscient being knows every truth and, furthermore, does not have any false beliefs. Assuming that what it is to know something is the same for God as it is for human beings, to say that God is omniscient is to say, at the very least, that God believes every truth and is warranted in believing every truth (where *warrant* is just whatever it is that makes the difference between true belief and knowledge).

Certain questions immediately arise from the notion of omniscience. For example, much of our descriptive or propositional knowledge depends on knowledge by acquaintance, experiential knowledge. But experiential knowledge is particular to the individual experiencer. You cannot experience your friend's taste of chocolate ice cream or feel her headache, so how can God be said to know our experiences if they are ours? Does he experience our pain when he looks within us? And if so, is his experience of our pain exactly similar to ours? Does he experience our pain when he looks within us? And if so, is his experience of our pain exactly similar to ours? Does he need to take on a body to experience the *kinds* of feelings that we experience?

We leave you to wrestle with these questions; the issue we want to focus on in this section is the problem of freedom and divine foreknowledge. Suppose God now believes that you will go to your early morning class tomorrow. Are you free to stay in bed until noon? Apparently not. For God believes only true propositions, and nobody can change the past. So when tomorrow comes, you can't do anything that would make it the case that God held a false belief today, nor can you do anything to change the fact that God believed (truly) that you would go to class tomorrow. So—it seems—you cannot do anything other than go to class tomorrow, in which case you are not free with respect to that action.

One strategy for responding to this problem is to note that there is no reason to think that God's *knowledge* of our actions is in any way a *cause* of our actions. Indeed, it seems reasonable to think that the order of explanation is the other way around—God's knowledge of what we will do depends upon what we in fact do; not vice versa. This is the classical position on freedom and omniscience, defended by both Boethius and, in our first reading, St. Augustine.

In defending the strategy just described, it is tempting to point to cases of human foreknowledge as illustrations. So, for example, you go to the supermarket and give the cashier more money than your order costs. Given your past experience at supermarkets, don't you have very good evidence about what she will do next? Don't you have very good reason to believe that she will give you change, and that she will not do things like pocket your money and run away, or empty the contents of her register into your shopping cart, or call the police to have you arrested? And assuming your beliefs turn out to be true, won't we say that you knew that she would give you change rather than do any of those other things? It seems that we would. But, of course, your beliefs about her future actions do not cause her to give you your change. She is free to do any of those other things. And likewise, we might think, in the cases where God knows what she (or we) will do.

However, other philosophers have objected to comparing human knowledge with God's. After all, the cashier at the supermarket can falsify your beliefs. She can pocket your money and run, or call the police, or do any of a variety of other things that contravene your expectations. But neither she nor anyone else can falsify God's beliefs because God, unlike you, cannot possibly be wrong. He is *essentially* omniscient—that is, it is a necessary truth that God, if he exists, believes all and only true propositions. And, some argue, it is precisely this fact, together with the unchangeability of the past, that renders the problem intractable.

This is essentially the position of Nelson Pike in the second of our readings. In effect, Pike argues as follows. Suppose:

1. God exists at t and believes at t that the cashier will give you change at t_1, and it is in her power to refrain from giving you change at t_1.

If 1 is true, then there seem to be only three possibilites:

2. The cashier could have brought it about at t_1 that one of God's beliefs at t was false.
3. The cashier could have brought it about at t_1 that God did not believe at t that she would give you change.
4. The cashier had the power to do something that would have brought about that any person who believed before t_1 that she would give you change at t_1 held a false belief and hence was not God. That is to say, she could have brought it about that God has never existed.

Since 2–4 seem impossible, Pike concludes that an examination of the implications of God's essential omniscience shows that it is incompatible with human freedom. Either we must understand God's omniscience differently, or God is not omniscient, or humans are not free.

In our third reading Alvin Plantinga responds to Pike's position, arguing that there really is no incompatibility between divine omniscience and human freedom. Essentially, he argues that all of options 2–4 can be suitably accommodated to the traditional view of God's omniscience and human freedom. For example, 2 can be read as follows:

2a. It was in the cashier's power at t_1 to do something such that if she had done it, then a belief that God held at t would have been false.

But 2a is not at all paradoxical and does not imply that it was within your power to do something that would have *caused* God to hold a false belief. Plantinga carries out a similar strategy with regard to 3 and 4, which you will want to examine carefully.

IV.B.1 Divine Foreknowledge and Human Free Will

ST. AUGUSTINE

St. Augustine (354–430) was Bishop of Hippo in North Africa and one of the greatest thinkers in the history of the Christian Church. Among his most well-known works are *The City of God, Confessions, On Christian Doctrine,* and *On the Trinity.* In the present selection he argues that God's foreknowledge of human actions does not necessitate those actions. Specifically, human sin was not committed because God knew that it would happen, but God knew that it would happen because he knows how humans will choose. We enter the dialogue with a question by Augustine's disciple, Evodius.

Evodius: . . . Since these things are true, I very much wonder how God can have foreknowledge of everything in the future, and yet we do not sin by necessity. It would be an irreligious and completely insane attack on God's foreknowledge to say that something could happen otherwise than as God foreknew. So suppose that God foreknew that the first human being was going to sin. Anyone who admits, as I do, that God foreknows everything in the future will have to grant me that. Now I won't say that God would not have made him—for God made him good, and no sin of his can harm God, who not only made him good but showed His own goodness by creating him, as He also shows His justice by punishing him and His mercy by redeeming him—but I will say this: *since God foreknew that he was going to sin, his sin necessarily had to happen. How, then, is the will free when such inescapable necessity is found in it?*

Augustine: . . . Surely this is the problem that is disturbing and puzzling you. How is it that these two propositions are not contradictory and inconsistent: (1) God has foreknowledge of everything in the future; and (2) We sin by the will, not by necessity? For, you say, if God foreknows that someone is going to sin, then it is

necessary that he sin. But if it is necessary, the will has no choice about whether to sin; there is an inescapable and fixed necessity. And so you fear that this argument forces us into one of two positions: either we draw the heretical conclusion that God does not foreknow everything in the future; or, if we cannot accept this conclusion, we must admit that sin happens by necessity and not by will. Isn't that what is bothering you?

Evodius: That's it exactly.

Augustine: So you think that anything that God foreknows happens by necessity and not by will.

Evodius: Precisely.

Augustine: Now pay close attention. Look inside yourself for a little while, and tell me, if you can, what sort of will you are going to have tomorrow: a will to do right or a will to sin?

Evodius: I don't know.

Augustine: Do you think that God doesn't know either?

Evodius: Not at all—God certainly does know.

Augustine: Well then, if God knows what you are going to will tomorrow, and foresees the future wills of every human being, both

From *On the Free Choice of the Will,* trans. with introduction and notes by Thomas Williams (Indianapolis, IN: Hackett Publishing Company, 1933). © 1993 by Thomas Williams. Used with permission.

those who exist now and those who will exist in the future, he surely foresees how he is going to treat the just and the irreligious.

Evodius: Clearly, if I say that God foreknows all of my actions, I can much more confidently say that he foreknows his own actions and foresees with absolute certainty what he is going to do.

Augustine: Then aren't you worried that someone might object that God himself will act out of necessity rather than by his will in everything that he is going to do? After all, you said that whatever God foreknows happens by necessity, not by will.

Evodius: When I said that, I was thinking only of what happens in his creation and not of what happens within himself. For those things do not come into being; they are eternal.

Augustine: So God does nothing in his creation.

Evodius: He has already established, once for all, the ways in which the universe that he created is to be governed; he does not administer anything by a new act of will.

Augustine: Doesn't he make anyone happy?

Evodius: Of course he does.

Augustine: And he does this when that person is made happy.

Evodius: Right.

Augustine: Then suppose, for example, that you are going to be happy a year from now. That means that a year from now God is going to make you happy.

Evodius: That's right too.

Augustine: And God knows today what he is going to do a year from now.

Evodius: He has always foreknown this, so I admit that he foreknows it now, if indeed it is really going to happen.

Augustine: Then surely you are not God's creature, or else your happiness does not take place in you.

Evodius: But I am God's creature, and my happiness does take place in me.

Augustine: Then the happiness that God gives you takes place by necessity and not by will.

Evodius: His will *is* my necessity.

Augustine: And so you will be happy against your will.

Evodius: If I had the power to be happy I would be happy right now. Even now I will to be happy, but I'm not, since it is God who makes me happy. I cannot do it for myself.

Augustine: How clearly the truth speaks through you! You could not help thinking that the only thing that is within our power is that which we do when we will it. Therefore, nothing is so much within our power as the will itself, for it is near at hand the very moment that we will. So we can rightly say, "We grow old by necessity, not by will"; or "We become feeble by necessity, not by will"; or "We die by necessity, not by will," and other such things. But who would be crazy enough to say "We do not will by the will"? Therefore, although God foreknows what we are going to will in the future, it does not follow that we do not will by the will.

When you said that you cannot make yourself happy, you said it as if I had denied it. Not at all; I am merely saying that when you do become happy, it will be in accordance with your will, not against your will. Simply because God foreknows your future happiness—and nothing can happen except as God foreknows it, since otherwise it would not be foreknowledge—it does not follow that you will be happy against your will. That would be completely absurd and far from the truth. So God's foreknowledge, which is certain even today of your future happiness, does not take away your will for happiness once you have begun to be happy; and in the same way, your blameworthy will (if indeed you are going to have such a will) does not cease to be a will simply because God foreknows that you are going to have it.

Just notice how imperceptive someone would have to be to argue thus: "If God has foreknown my future will, it is necessary that I will what he has foreknown, since nothing can happen otherwise than as he has foreknown it. But if it is necessary, then one must concede that I will it by necessity and not by will." What extraordinary foolishness! If God foreknew a future will that turned out not to be a will at all, things would indeed happen otherwise than as God foreknew them. And I will overlook this objector's equally monstrous statement that "it is necessary that I will," for by assuming necessity he tries to abolish will. For if his willing is necessary, how does he will, since there is no will?

Suppose he expressed it in another way and said that, since his willing is necessary, his will is not in his own power. This would run up against the same problem that you had when I asked whether you were going to be happy against your will. You replied that you would already be happy if you had the power; you said that you have the will but not the power. I answered that the truth had spoken through you. For we can deny that something is in our power only if it is not present even when we will it; but if we will, and yet the will remains absent, then we are not really willing at all. Now if it is impossible for us not to will when we are willing, then the will is present to those who will; and if something is present when we will it, then it is in our power. So our will would not be a will if it were not in our power. And since it is in our power, we are free with respect to it. But we are not free with respect to anything that we do not have in our power, and anything that we have cannot be nothing.

Thus, we believe both that God has foreknowledge of everything in the future and that nonetheless we will whatever we will. Since God foreknows our will, the very will that he foreknows will be what comes about. Therefore, it will be a will, since it is a will that he foreknows. And it could not be a will unless it were in our power. Therefore, he also foreknows this power. It follows, then, that his foreknowledge does not take away my power; in fact, it is all the more certain that I will have that power, since he whose foreknowledge never errs foreknows that I will have it.

Evodius: I agree now that it is necessary that whatever God has foreknown will happen, and that he foreknows our sins in such a way that our wills remain free and are within our power...

IV.B.2   God's Foreknowledge and Human Free Will Are Incompatible

NELSON PIKE

Nelson Pike (1930–   ) is emeritus professor of philosophy at the University of California at Irvine and is one of the leading figures in the philosophy of religion. In this article he argues that given commonly held theological assumptions about God's nature, no human action is free.

In Part V, Section III of his *Consolatio Philosophiae*, Boethius entertained (though he later rejected) the claim that if God is omniscient, no human action is voluntary. This claim seems intuitively false. Surely, given only a doctrine describing God's *knowledge*, nothing about the voluntary status of human actions will follow. Perhaps such a conclusion would follow from a doctrine of divine omnipotence or divine providence, but what connection could there be between the claim that God is *omniscient* and the claim that human actions are determined?

Reprinted from Nelson Pike, "Divine Omniscience and Voluntary Action," *The Philosophical Review* 74 (January 1965).

Yet Boethius thought he saw a problem here. He thought that if one collected together just the right assumptions and principles regarding God's knowledge, one could derive the conclusion that if God exists, no human action is voluntary. Of course, Boethius did not think that all the assumptions and principles required to reach this conclusion are true (quite the contrary), but he thought it important to draw attention to them nonetheless. If a theologian is to construct a doctrine of God's knowledge which does not commit him to determinism, he must first understand that there is a way of thinking about God's knowledge which would so commit him.

In this paper, I shall argue that although his claim has a sharp counterintuitive ring, Boethius was right in thinking that there is a selection from among the various doctrines and principles clustering about the notions of knowledge, omniscience, and God which, when brought together, demand the conclusion that if God exists, no human action is voluntary. Boethius, I think, did not succeed in making explicit all of the ingredients in the problem. His suspicions were sound, but his discussion was incomplete. His argument needs to be developed. This is the task I shall undertake in the pages to follow. I should like to make clear at the outset that my purpose in re-arguing this thesis is not to show that determinism is true, nor to show that God does not exist, nor to show that either determinism is true or God does not exist. Following Boethius, I shall not claim that the items needed to generate the problem are either philosophically or theologically adequate. I want to concentrate attention on the implications of a certain set of assumptions. Whether the assumptions are themselves acceptable is a question I shall not consider.

I

A. Many philosophers have held that if a statement of the form "*A* knows *X*" is true, then "*A* believes *X*" is true and "*X*" is true. As a first assumption, I shall take this partial analysis of "*A* knows *X*" to be correct. And I shall suppose that since this analysis holds for all knowledge claims, it will hold when speaking of God's knowledge. "God knows *X*" entails "God believes *X*" and "'*X*' is true."

Secondly, Boethius said that with respect to the matter of knowledge, God "cannot in anything be mistaken."[1] I shall understand this doctrine as follows. Omniscient beings hold no false beliefs. Part of what is meant when we say that a person is omniscient is that the person in question believes nothing that is false. But, further, it is part of the "essence" of God to be omniscient. This is to say that any person who is not omniscient could not be the person we usually mean to be referring to when using the name "God." To put this last point a little differently: if the person we usually mean to be referring to when using the name "God" were suddenly to lose the quality of omniscience (suppose, for example, He came to believe something false), the resulting person would no longer be God. Although we might call this second person "God" (I might call my cat "God"), the absence of the quality of omniscience would be sufficient to guarantee that the person referred to was not the same as the person formerly called by that name. From this last doctrine it follows that the statement "if a given person is God, that person is omniscient" is an a priori truth. From this we may conclude that the statement "If a given person is God, that person holds no false beliefs" is also an a priori truth. It would be conceptually impossible for God to hold a false belief. "'*X* is true" follows from "God believes *X*. "These are all ways of expressing the same principle—the principle expressed by Boethius in the formula "God cannot in anything be mistaken."

A second principle usually associated with the notion of divine omniscience has to do with the scope or range of God's intellectual gaze. To say that a being is omniscient is to say that he knows everything. "Everything" in this statement is usually taken to cover future, as well as present and past, events and circumstances. In fact, God is usually said to have had foreknowledge of everything that has ever happened. With respect to anything that was, is, or will be the case, God knew, *from eternity*, that it would be the case.

The doctrine of God's knowing everything from eternity is very obscure. One particularly difficult question concerning this doctrine is whether it entails that with respect to everything that was, is, or will be the case, God knew *in advance* that it would be the case. In some traditional theological texts, we are told that God is *eternal* in the sense that He exists "outside of time," that is, in the sense that He bears no temporal relations to the events or circumstances of the natural world.[2] In a theology of this sort, God could not be said to have known that a given natural event was going to happen before it happened. If God knew that a given natural event was going to occur *before* it occurred, at least one of God's cognitions would then have occurred before some natural event. This, surely, would violate the idea that God bears no temporal relations to natural events.[3] On the other hand, in a considerable number of theological sources, we are told that God *has always* existed—that He existed long *before* the occurrence of any natural event. In a theology of this sort, to say that God is eternal is not to say that God exists "outside of time" (bears no temporal relations to natural events), it is to say, instead, God has existed (and will continue to exist) at each moment.[4] The doctrine of omniscience which goes with this second understanding of the notion of eternity is one in which it is affirmed that God *has always* known that what was going to happen in the natural world. John Calvin wrote as follows:

> When we attribute foreknowledge to God, we mean that all things have ever been and perpetually remain before, his eyes, so that to his knowledge nothing is future or past, but all things are present; and present in such manner, that he does not merely conceive of them from ideas formed in his mind, as things remembered by us appear to our minds, but really he holds and sees them as if (*tanquam*) actually placed before him.[5]

All things are "present" to God in the sense that He "sees" them as if (*tanquam*) they were actually before Him. Further, with respect to any given natural event, not only is that event "present" to God in the sense indicated, it has *ever been and has perpetually remained* "present" to Him in that sense. This latter is the point of

special interest. Whatever one thinks of the idea that God "sees" things as if "actually placed before him," Calvin would appear to be committed to the idea that God has *always known* what was going to happen in the natural world. Choose an event (E) and a time (T_2) at which E occurred. For any time (T_1) prior to T_2 (say, five thousand, six hundred, or eighty years prior to T_2), God knew at T_1 that E would occur at T_2. It will follow from this doctrine, of course, that with respect to any human action, God knew well in advance of its performance that the action would be performed. Calvin says, "when God created man, He foresaw what would happen concerning him." He adds, "little more than five thousand years have elapsed since the creation of the world."[6] Calvin seems to have thought that God foresaw the outcome of every human action well over five thousand years ago.

In the discussion to follow, I shall work only with this second interpretation of God's knowing everything *from eternity*. I shall assume that if a person is omniscient, that person has always known what was going to happen in the natural world—and, in particular, has always known what human actions were going to be performed. Thus, as above, assuming that the attribute of omniscience is part of the "essence" of God, the statement "For any natural event (including human actions), if a given person is God, that person would always have known that that event was going to occur at the time it occurred" must be treated as an a priori truth. This is just another way of stating a point admirably put by St. Augustine when he said: "For to confess that God exists and at the same time to deny that He has foreknowledge of future things is the most manifest folly.... One who is not prescient of all future things is not God."[7]

B. Last Saturday afternoon, Jones mowed his lawn. Assuming that God exists and is (essentially) omniscient in the sense outlined above, it follows that (let us say) eighty years prior to last Saturday afternoon, God knew (and thus believed) that Jones would mow his lawn at that time. But from this it follows, I think, that at the time of action (last Saturday afternoon) Jones was not able—that is, it was not *within Jones's power*—to refrain from mowing his lawn.[8] If at the time of action, Jones had been able to refrain from mowing his lawn, then (the most obvious conclusion would seem to be) at the time of action, Jones was able to do something which would have brought it about that God held a false belief eighty years earlier. But God cannot in anything be mistaken. It is not possible that some belief of His was false. Thus, last Saturday afternoon, Jones was not able to do something which would have brought it about that God held a false belief eighty years ago. To suppose that it was would be to suppose that, at the time of action, Jones was able to do something having a conceptually incoherent description, namely something that would have brought it about that one of God's beliefs was false. Hence, given that God believed eighty years ago that Jones would mow his lawn on Saturday, if we are to assign Jones the power on Saturday to refrain from mowing his lawn, this power must not be described as the power to do something that would have rendered one of God's beliefs false. How then should we describe it vis-à-vis God and His belief? So far as I can see, there are only two other alternatives. First, we might try describing it as the power to do something that would have brought it about that God believed otherwise than He did eighty years ago; or, secondly, we might try describing it as the power to do something that would have brought it about that God (who, by hypothesis, existed eighty years earlier) did not exist eighty years earlier— that is, as the power to do something that would have brought it about that any person who believed eighty years ago that Jones would mow his lawn on Saturday (one of whom was, by hypothesis, God) held a false belief, and thus was not God. But again, neither of these latter can be accepted. Last Saturday afternoon, Jones was not able to do something that would have brought it about that God believed otherwise than He did eighty years ago. Even if we suppose (as was suggested by Calvin) that eighty years ago God knew Jones would mow his lawn on Saturday in the sense that He "saw" Jones mowing his lawn as if this action were occurring before Him, the fact remains that God knew (and thus believed) eighty years prior

to Saturday that Jones would mow his lawn. And if God held such a belief eighty years prior to Saturday, Jones did not have the power on Saturday to do something that would have made it the case that God did not hold this belief eighty years earlier. No action performed at a given time can alter the fact that a given person held a certain belief at a time prior to the time in question. This last seems to be an a priori truth. For similar reasons, the last of the above alternatives must also be rejected. On the assumption that God existed eighty years prior to Saturday, Jones on Saturday was not able to do something that would have brought it about that God did not exist eighty years prior to that time. No action performed at a given time can alter the fact that a certain person existed at a time prior to the time in question. This, too, seems to me to be an a priori truth. But if these observations are correct, then, given that Jones mowed his lawn on Saturday, and given that God exists and is (essentially) omniscient, it seems to follow that at the time of action, Jones did not have the power to refrain from mowing his lawn. The upshot of these reflections would appear to be that Jones's mowing his lawn last Saturday cannot be counted as a voluntary action. Although I do not have an analysis of what it is for action to be *voluntary*, it seems to me that a situation in which it would be wrong to assign Jones the *ability* or *power* to do *other* than he did would be a situation in which it would also be wrong to speak of his action as voluntary. As a general remark, if God exists and is (essentially) omniscient in the sense specified above, no human action is voluntary.[9]

As the argument just presented is somewhat complex, perhaps the following schematic representation of it will be of some use.

1. "God existed at T_1" entails "If Jones did X at T_2, God believed at T_1 that Jones would do X at T_2."
2. "God believes X" entails "X is true."
3. It is not within one's power at a given time to do something having a description that is logically contradictory.
4. It is not within one's power at a given time to do something that would bring it about that someone who held a certain belief at a

time prior to the time in question did not hold that belief at the time prior to the time in question.

5. It is not within one's power at a given time to do something that would bring it about that a person who existed at an earlier time did not exist at that earlier time.

6. If God existed at T_1 and if God believed at T_1 that Jones would do X at T_2, then if it was within Jones's power at T_2 to refrain from doing X, then (1) it was within Jones's power at T_2 to do something that would have brought it about that God held a false belief at T_1, or (2) it was within Jones's power at T_2 to do something which would have brought it about that God did not hold the belief He held at T_1, or (3) it was within Jones's power at T_2 to do something that would have brought it about that any person who believed at T_1 that Jones would do X at T_2 (one of whom was, by hypothesis, God) held a false belief and thus was not God— that is, that God (who by hypothesis existed at T_1) did not exist at T_1.

7. Alternative 1 in the consequent of item 6 is false (from 2 and 3).

8. Alternative 2 in the consequent of item 6 is false (from 4).

9. Alternative 3 in the consequent of item 6 is false (from 5).

10. Therefore, if God existed at T_1 and if God believed at T_1 that Jones would do X at T_2, then it was not within Jones's power at T_2 to refrain from doing X (from 6 through 9).

11. Therefore, if God existed at T_1, and if Jones did X at T_2, it was not within Jones's power at T_2 to refrain from doing X (from 1 and 10).

In this argument, items 1 and 2 make explicit the doctrine of God's (essential) omniscience with which I am working. Items 3, 4, and 5 express what I take to be part of the logic of the concept of ability or power as it applies to human beings. Item 6 is offered as an analytic truth. If one assigns Jones the power to refrain from doing X at T_2 (given that God believed at T_1 that he would do X at T_2), so far as I can see, one would have to describe this power in one of the three ways listed

in the consequent of item 6. I do not know how to argue that these are the only alternatives, but I have been unable to find another. Item 11, when generalized for all agents and actions, and when taken together with what seems to me to be a minimal condition for the application of "voluntary action," yields the conclusion that if God exists (and is essentially omniscient in the way I have described) no human action is voluntary.

C. It is important to notice that the argument given in the preceding paragraphs avoids use of two concepts that are often prominent in discussions of determinism.

In the first place, the argument makes no mention of the *causes* of Jones's action. Say (for example, with St. Thomas)[10] that God's foreknowledge of Jones's action was, itself, the cause of the action (though I am really not sure what this means). Say, instead, that natural events or circumstances caused Jones to act. Even say that Jones's action had no cause at all. The argument outlined above remains unaffected. If eighty years prior to Saturday, God believed that Jones would mow his lawn at that time, it was not within Jones's power at the time of action to refrain from mowing his lawn. The reasoning that justifies this assertion makes no mention of a causal series preceding Jones's action.

Secondly, consider the following line of thinking. Suppose Jones mowed his lawn last Saturday. It was then *true* eighty years ago that Jones would mow his lawn at that time. Hence, on Saturday, Jones was not able to refrain from mowing his lawn. To suppose that he was would be to suppose that he was able on Saturday to do something that would have made false a proposition that was *already true* eighty years earlier. This general kind of argument for determinism is usually associated with Leibniz, although it was anticipated in Chapter IX of Aristotle's *De Interpretatione*. It has been used since, with some modification, in Richard Taylor's article, "Fatalism."[11] This argument, like the one I have offered above, makes no use of the notion of causation. It turns, instead, on the notion of its being *true eighty years ago* that Jones would mow his lawn on Saturday.

I must confess that I share the misgivings of those contemporary philosophers who have wondered what (if any) sense can be attached to a statement of the form "it was true at T_1 that E would occur at T_2."[12] Does this statement mean that had someone believed, guessed, or asserted at T_1 that E would occur at T_2, he would have been right?[13] (I shall have something to say about this form of determinism later in this paper.) Perhaps it means that at T_1 there was sufficient evidence upon which to predict that E would occur at T_2.[14] Maybe it means neither of these. Maybe it means nothing at all.[15] The argument presented above presupposes that it makes straightforward sense to suppose that God (or just anyone) held a true belief eighty years prior to Saturday. But this is not to suppose that *what* God believed *was true eighty years prior to Saturday*. Whether (or in what sense) it was true eighty years ago that Jones would mow his lawn on Saturday is a question I shall not discuss. As far as I can see, the argument in which I am interested requires nothing in the way of a decision on this issue.

II

I now want to consider three comments on the problem of divine foreknowledge which seem to be instructively incorrect.

A. Leibniz analyzed the problem as follows:

> They say that what is foreseen cannot fail to exist and they say so truly; but it follows not that what is foreseen is necessary. For necessary truth is that whereof the contrary is impossible or implies a contradiction. Now the truth which states that I shall write tomorrow is not of that nature, it is not necessary. Yet, supposing that God foresees it, it is necessary that it come to pass, that is, the consequence is necessary, namely that it exist, since it has been foreseen; for God is infallible. This is what is termed a *hypothetical necessity*. But our concern is not this necessity; it is an abso*lute* necessity that is required, to be able to say that an action is necessary, that it is not contingent, that it is not the effect of free choice.[16]

The statement "God believed at T_1 that Jones would do X at T_2" (where the interval between T_1 and T_2 is, for example, eighty years) does not entail "'Jones did X at T_2' is necessary." Leibniz is surely right about this. All that will follow from the first of these statements concerning "Jones did X at T_2" is that the latter is true, not that it is necessarily true. But this observation has no real bearing on the issue at hand. The following passage from St. Augustine's formulation of the problem may help to make this point clear.

> Your trouble is this. You wonder how it can be that these two propositions are not contradictory and incompatible, namely that God has foreknowledge of all future events, and that we sin voluntarily and not by necessity. For if, you say, God foreknows that a man will sin, he must necessarily sin. But if there is necessity there is no voluntary choice of sinning, but rather fixed and unavoidable necessity.[17]

In this passage, the term "necessity" (or the phrase "by necessity") is not used to express a modal-logical concept. The term "necessity" is here used in contrast with the term "voluntary," not (as in Leibniz) in contrast with the term "contingent." If one's action is necessary (or by necessity), this is to say that one's action is not voluntary. Augustine says that if God has foreknowledge of human actions, the actions are necessary. But the form of this conditional is "P implies Q," not "P implies $N(Q)$." "Q" in the consequent of this conditional is the claim that human actions are not voluntary—that is, the one is not able, or does not have the power, to do other than he does.

Perhaps I can make this point clearer by reformulating the original problem in such a way as to make explicit the modal operators working within it. Let it be *contingently* true that Jones did X at T_2. Since God holds a belief about the outcome of each human action well in advance of its performance, it is then *contingently true* that God believed at T_1 that Jones would do X at T_2. But it follows from this that it is *contingently* true that at T_2 Jones was not able to refrain from doing X. Had he been (contingently) able to refrain from doing X at T_2, then either he was (contingently) able to do something at T_2 that would have brought it about that God held a false belief at T_1, or he was (contingently) able to do something at T_2 that would have brought it about that God believed otherwise than He did at T_1, or he was (contingently) able to do something at T_2 that would have brought it about that God did not exist at T_1. None of these latter is an acceptable alternative.

B. In *Concordia Liberi Arbitrii*, Luis de Molina wrote as follows:

> It was not that since He foreknew what would happen from those things which depend on the created will that it would happen; but, on the contrary, it was because such things would happen through the freedom of the will, that He foreknew it; and that He would foreknow the opposite if the opposite was to happen.[18]

Remarks similar to this one can be found in a great many traditional and contemporary theological texts. In fact, Molina assures us that the view expressed in this passage has always been "above controversy"—a matter of "common opinion" and "unanimous consent"—not only among the Church fathers, but also, as he says, "among all catholic men."

One claim made in the above passage seems to me to be truly "above controversy." With respect to any given action foreknown by God, God would have foreknown the opposite if the opposite was to happen. If we assume the notion of omniscience outlined in the first section of this paper, and if we agree that omniscience is part of the "essence" of God, this statement is a conceptual truth. I doubt if anyone would be inclined to dispute it. Also involved in this passage, however, is at least the suggestion of a doctrine that cannot be taken as an item of "common opinion" among *all* catholic men. Molina says it is not because God foreknows what He foreknows that men act as they do: it is because men act as they do that God foreknows what He foreknows. Some theologians have rejected this claim. It seems to entail that men's actions determine God's cognitions. And this latter, I think, has been taken by some theologians to be a violation of the notion of God as self-sufficient and incapable of being affected by events of the natural world.[19] But I shall not develop this point further. Where the

view put forward in the above passage seems to me to go wrong in an interesting and important way is in Molina's claim that God can have foreknowledge of things that will happen "through the freedom of the will." It is this claim that I here want to examine with care.

What exactly are we saying when we say that God can know in advance what will happen *through the freedom of the will*? I think that what Molina has in mind is this. God can know in advance that a given man is going to choose to perform a certain action sometime in the future. With respect to the case of Jones mowing his lawn, God knew at T_1 that Jones would *freely* decide to mow his lawn at T_2. Not only did God know at T_1 that Jones would mow his lawn at T_2. He also knew at T_1 that this action would be performed freely. In the words of Emil Brunner, "God knows that which will take place in freedom in the future as something which happens in freedom."[20] What God knew at T_1 is that Jones would *freely* mow his lawn at T_2.

I think that this doctrine is incoherent. If God knew (and thus believed) at T_1 that Jones would do X at T_2,[21] I think it follows that Jones was not able to do other than X at T_2 (for reasons already given). Thus, if God knew (and thus believed) at T_1 that Jones would do X at T_2, it would follow that Jones did X at T_2, but not freely. It does not seem to be possible that God could have believed at T_1 that Jones would freely do X at T_2. If God believed at T_1 that Jones would do X at T_2, Jones's action at T_2 was not free; and if God also believed at T_1 that Jones would freely act at T_2, it follows that God held a false belief at T_1—which is absurd.

C. Frederich Schleiermacher commented on the problem of divine foreknowledge as follows:

> In the same way, we estimate the intimacy between two persons by the foreknowledge one has of the actions of the other, without supposing that in either case, the one or the other's freedom is thereby endangered. So even the divine foreknowledge cannot endanger freedom.[22]

St. Augustine made this same point in *De Libero Arbitrio*. He said:

> Unless I am mistaken, you would not directly compel the man to sin, though you knew beforehand that he was going to sin. Nor does your prescience in itself compel him to sin even though he was certainly going to sin, as we must assume if you have real prescience. So there is no contradiction here. Simply you know beforehand what another is going to do with his own will. Similarly God compels no man to sin, though he sees beforehand those who are going to sin by their own will.[23]

If we suppose (with Schleiermacher and Augustine) that the case of an intimate friend having foreknowledge of another's action has the same implications for determinism as the case of God's foreknowledge of human actions, I can imagine two positions which might then be taken. First, one might hold (with Schleiermacher and Augustine) that God's foreknowledge of human actions cannot entail determinism—since it is clear that an intimate friend can have foreknowledge of another's voluntary actions. Or, secondly, one might hold that an intimate friend cannot have foreknowledge of another's voluntary actions—since it is clear that God cannot have foreknowledge of such actions. This second position could take either of two forms. One might hold that since an intimate friend *can* have foreknowledge of another's actions, the actions in question cannot be voluntary. Or, alternatively, one might hold that since the other's actions *are* voluntary, the intimate friend cannot have foreknowledge of them.[24] But what I propose to argue in the remaining pages of this paper is that Schleiermacher and Augustine were mistaken in supposing that the case of an intimate friend having foreknowledge of other's actions has the same implications for determinism as the case of God's foreknowledge of human actions. What I want to suggest is that the argument I used above to show that God cannot have foreknowledge of voluntary actions cannot be used to show that an intimate friend cannot have foreknowledge of another's actions. Even if one holds that an intimate friend *can* have foreknowledge of another's voluntary actions, one ought not to think that the case is the same when dealing with the problem of divine foreknowledge.

Let Smith be an ordinary man and an intimate friend of Jones. Now, let us start by supposing that Smith believed at T_1 that Jones would do X at T_2. We make no assumption concerning the truth or falsity of Smith's belief, but assume only that Smith held it. Given only this much, there appears to be no difficulty in supposing that at T_2 Jones was able to do X and that at T_2 Jones was able to do not-X. So far as the above description of the case is concerned, it might well have been within Jones's power at T_2 to do something (namely, X) which would have brought it about that Smith held a true belief at T_1, and it might well have been within Jones's power at T_2 to do something (namely, not-X) which would have brought it about that Smith held a false belief at T_1. So much seems apparent.

Now let us suppose Smith *knew* at T_1 that Jones would do X at T_2. This is to suppose that Smith correctly believed (with evidence) at T_1 that Jones would do X at T_2. It follows, to be sure, that Jones did X at T_2. But now let us inquire about what Jones was *able* to do at T_2. I submit that there is nothing in the description of this case that requires the conclusion that it was not within Jones's power at T_2 to refrain from doing X. By hypothesis, the belief held by Smith at T_1 was true. Thus, by hypothesis, Jones did X at T_2. But even if we assume that the belief held by Smith at T_1 was *in fact* true, we can add that the belief held by Smith at T_1 *might* have turned out to be false.[25] Thus, even if we say that Jones *in fact* did X at T_2, we can add that Jones *might not* have done X at T_2— meaning by this that it was within Jones's power at T_2 to refrain from doing X. Smith held a true belief which might have turned out to be false, and, correspondingly, Jones performed an action which he was able to refrain from performing. Given that Smith correctly believed at T_1 that Jones would do X at T_2, we can still assign Jones the *power* at T_2 to refrain from doing X. All we need add is that the power in question is one which Jones *did not exercise*.

These last reflections have no application, however, when dealing with God's foreknowledge. Assume that God (being essentially omniscient) existed at T_1, and assume that He believed at T_1 that Jones would do X at T_2. It follows, again, that Jones did X at T_2. God's beliefs are true. But now, as above, let us inquire into what Jones was *able* to do at T_2. We cannot claim now, as in the Smith case, that the belief held by God at T_1 was *in fact* true but *might* have turned out to be false. No sense of "might have" has application here. It is a conceptual truth that God's beliefs are true. Thus, we cannot claim, as in the Smith case, that Jones *in fact* acted in accordance with God's beliefs but had the *ability* to refrain from so doing. The ability to refrain from acting in accordance with one of God's beliefs would be the ability to do something that would bring it about that one of God's beliefs was false. And no one could have an ability of this description. Thus, in the case of God's foreknowledge of Jones's action at T_2, if we are to assign Jones the ability at T_2 to refrain from doing X, we must understand this ability in some way other than the way we understood it when dealing with Smith's foreknowledge. In this case, either we must say that it was the ability at T_2 to bring it about that God believed otherwise than He did at T_1; or we must say that it was the ability at T_2 to bring it about that any person who believed at T_1 that Jones would do X at T_2 (one of whom was, by hypothesis, God) held a false belief and thus was not God. But, as pointed out earlier, neither of these last alternatives can be accepted.

The important thing to be learned from the study of Smith's foreknowledge of Jones's action is that the problem of divine foreknowledge has as one of its pillars the claim the truth is *analytically* connected with God's *beliefs*. No problem of determinism arises when dealing with human knowledge of future actions. This is because truth is not analytically connected with human belief even when (as in the case of human knowledge) truth is contingently conjoined to belief. If we suppose that Smith knows at T_1 that Jones will do X at T_2, what we are supposing is that Smith believes at T_1 that Jones will do X at T_2

and (as an additional, contingent, fact) that the belief in question is true. Thus having supposed that Smith knows at T_1 that Jones will do X at T_2, when we turn to a consideration of the situation of T_2 we can infer (1) that Jones *will* do X at T_2 (since Smith's belief is true), and (2) that Jones does not have the power at T_2 to do something that would bring it about that Jones did not *believe* as he did at T_1. But paradoxical though it may seem (and it seems paradoxical only at first sight), Jones can have the power at T_2 to do something that would bring it about that Smith did not have *knowledge* at T_1. This is simply to say that Jones can have the *power* at T_2 to do something that would bring it about that the belief held by Smith at T_1 (which was, in fact, true) was (instead) false. We are required only to add that since Smith's belief was in fact true (that is, was knowledge) Jones *did not* (in fact) *exercise* that power. But when we turn to a consideration of God's foreknowledge of Jones's action at T_2 the elbowroom between belief and truth disappears and, with it, the possibility of assigning Jones even the *power* of doing other than he does at T_2. We begin by supposing that God *knows* at T_1 that Jones will do X at T_2. As above, this is to suppose that God believes at T_1 that Jones will do X at T_2, and it is to suppose that this belief is true. But it is *not* an additional, contingent fact that the belief held by God is true. "God believes X" entails "X is true." Thus, having supposed that God knows (and thus believes) at T_1 that Jones will do X at T_2, we can infer (1) that Jones *will do* X at T_2 (since God's belief is true); (2) that Jones does not have the power at T_2 to do something that would bring it about that God did not hold the belief He held at T_1, and (3) that Jones does not have the power at T_2 to do something that would bring it about that the belief held by God at T_1 was false. This last is what we could *not* infer when truth and belief were only factually connected—as in the case of Smith's knowledge. To be sure, "Smith knows at T_1 that Jones will do X at T_2" and "God knows at T_1 that Jones will do X at T_2" both entail "Jones will do X at T_2" ("A knows X" entails "X is true"). But this similarity between "Smith knows X" and "God knows X" is not a point of any special interest in the present discussion. As Schleiermacher and Augustine rightly insisted (and as we discovered in our study of Smith's foreknowledge) the mere fact that someone knows in advance how another will act in the future is not enough to yield a problem of the sort we have been discussing. We begin to get a glimmer of the knot involved in the problem of divine foreknowledge when we shift attention away from the *similarities* between "Smith knows X" and "God knows X" (in particular, that they both entail "'X' is true") and concentrate instead on the logical *differences* which obtain between Smith's knowledge and God's knowledge. We get to the difference which makes the difference when, after analyzing the notion of knowledge as true belief (supported by evidence) we discover the radically dissimilar relations between truth and belief in the two cases. When truth is only factually connected with belief (as in Smith's knowledge) one can have the power (though, by hypothesis, one will not exercise it) to do something that would make the belief false. But when truth is analytically connected with belief (as in God's belief) no one can have the power to do something which would render the belief false.

To conclude: I have assumed that any statement of form "A knows X" entails a statement of the form "A believes X" as well as a statement of the form "'X' is true." I have then supposed (as an analytic truth) that if a given person is omniscient, that person (1) holds no false beliefs, and (2) holds beliefs about the outcome of human actions in advance of their performance. In addition, I have assumed that the statement "if a given person is God that person is omniscient" is an a priori statement. (This last I have labeled the doctrine of God's essential omniscience.) Given these items (plus some premises concerning what is and what is not within one's power), I have argued that if God exists, it is not within one's power to do other than he does. I have inferred from this that if God exists, no human action is voluntary.

As emphasized earlier, I do not want to claim that the assumptions underpinning the argument are acceptable. In fact, it seems to me that a theologian interested in claiming both that God is omniscient and that men have free will could deny any one (or more) of them. For example, a theologian might deny that a statement of the form "A knows X" entails a statement of the form "A believes X" (some contemporary philosophers have denied this) or, alternatively, he might claim that this entailment holds in the case of human knowledge but fails in the case of God's knowledge. This latter would be to claim that when knowledge is attributed to God, the term "knowledge" bears a sense other than the one it has when knowledge is attributed to human beings. Then again, a theologian might object to the analysis of "omniscience" with which I have been working. Although I doubt if any Christian theologian would allow that an omniscient being could believe something false, he might claim that a given person could be omniscient although he did not hold beliefs about the outcome of human actions *in advance* of their performance. (This latter is the way Boethius escaped the problem.) Still again, a theologian might deny the doctrine of God's essential omniscience. He might admit that if a given person is God that person is omniscient, but he might deny that this statement formulates an a priori truth. This would be to say that although God is omniscient, He is not *essentially* omniscient. So far as I can see, within the conceptual framework of theology employing any one of these adjustments, the problem of divine foreknowledge outlined in this paper could not be formulated. There thus appears to be a rather wide range of alternatives open to the theologian at this point. It would be a mistake to think that commitment to determinism is an unavoidable implication of the Christian concept of divine omniscience.

But having arrived at this understanding, the importance of the preceding deliberations ought not to be overlooked. There is a pitfall in the doctrine of divine omniscience. That knowing involves believing (truly) is surely a tempting philosophical view (witness the many contemporary philosophers who have affirmed it). And the idea that God's attributes (including omniscience) are essentially connected to His nature, together with the idea that an omniscient being would hold no false beliefs and would hold beliefs about the outcome of human actions in advance of their performance, might be taken by some theologians as obvious candidates for inclusion in a finished Christian theology. Yet the theologian must approach these items critically. If they are embraced together, then if one affirms the existence of God, one is committed to the view that no human action is voluntary.

NOTES

1. *Consolatio Philosophiae*, Bk. V, sec. 3, par. 6.
2. This position is particularly well formulated in St. Anselm's *Proslogium*, ch. xix and *Monologium*, chs. xxixxii; and in Frederich Schleiermacher's *The Christian Faith*, Pt. 1, sec. 2, par. 51. It is also explicit in Boethius, op. cit., secs. 4–6, and in St. Thomas' *Summa Theologica*, Pt. 1, Q.10.
3. This point is explicit in Boethius, op. cit., secs. 4–6.
4. This position is particularly well expressed in William Paley's *Natural Theology*, ch. xxiv. It is also involved in John Calvin's discussion of predestination, *Institutes of the Christian Religion*, Bk. III, ch. xxi; and in some formulations of the first cause argument for existence of God, e.g., John Locke's *Essay Concerning Human Understanding*, Bk. IV, ch. x.
5. *Institutes of the Christian Religion*, Bk. III, ch. xxi; this passage trans. by John Allen (Philadelphia, 1813), II, 145.
6. Ibid., p. 144.
7. City of God, Bk. V, sec. 9.
8. The notion of someone being *able* to do something and the notion of something being within one's power are essentially the same. Traditional formulations of the problem of divine foreknowledge (e.g., those of Boethius and Augustine) made use of the notion of what is (and what is not) *within one's power*. But the problem is the same when framed in terms of what one is (and one is not) *able* to do. Thus, I shall treat the statements "Jones was able to do X," "Jones had the ability to do X," and "It was within Jones's power to do X" as equivalent. Richard Taylor, in "I Can," *Philosophical Review*, LXIX (1960), 78–89, has argued that the notion of ability or power involved in these last three statements is incapable of philosophical analysis. Be this as it may, I shall not here attempt such an analysis. In what follows I shall, however, be careful to affirm only those statements about what is (or is not) within one's power that would have to be preserved on any analysis of this notion having even the most distant claim to adequacy.

9. In Bk. II, ch. xxi, secs. 8–11 of the *Essay*, John Locke says that an agent is not *free* with respect to a given action (i.e., that an action is done "under necessity") when it is not within the agent's power to do otherwise. Locke allows a special kind of case, however, in which an action may be *voluntary* though done under necessity. If a man chooses to do something without knowing that it is not within his power to do otherwise (e.g., if a man chooses to stay in a room without knowing that the *room* is locked), his action may be voluntary though he is not free to forbear it. If Locke is right in this (and I shall not argue the point one way or the other), replace "voluntary" with (let us say) "free" in the above paragraph and throughout the remainder of this paper.
10. *Summa Theologica*, Pt. 1, Q. 14, a. 8.
11. *Philosophical Review*, LXXI (1962), 56–66. Taylor argues that if an event E fails to occur at T_2, then at T_1 it was true that E would fail to occur at T_2. Thus, at T_1, a necessary condition of anyone's performing an action sufficient for the occurrence of E at T_2 is missing. Thus at T_1, no one could have the power to perform an action that would be sufficient for the occurrence of E at T_2. Hence, no one has the power at T_1 to do something sufficient for the occurrence of an event at T_2 that is not going to happen. The parallel between this argument and the one recited above can be seen very clearly if one reformulates Taylor's argument, pushing back the time at which it was true that E would not occur at T_2.
12. For a helpful discussion of difficulties involved here, see Rogers Albritton's "Present Truth and Future Contingency," a reply to Richard Taylor's "The Problem of Future Contingency," both in the *Philosophical Review*, LXVI (1957), 1–28.
13. Gilbert Ryle interprets it this way. See "It Was to Be," *Dilemmas* (Cambridge , 1954).
14. Richard Gale suggests this interpretation in "Endorsing Predictions," *Philosophical Review*, LXX (1961), 378–385.
15. This view is held by John Turk Saunders in "Sea Fight Tomorrow?" *Philosophical Review*, LXVII (1958), 367–378.
16. *Theodicée*, Pt. 1, sec. 37. This passage trans. by E. M. Huggard (New Haven, 1952), p. 144.

17. *De Libero Arbitrio,* Bk. III. This passage trans. by J. H. S. Burleigh, *Augustine's Earlier Writings* (Philadelphia, 1955).

18. This passage trans. by John Mourant, *Readings in the Philosophy of Religion* (New York, 1954), p. 426.

19. Cf. Boethius' *Consolatio,* Bk. V, sec. 3, par. 2.

20. *The Christian Doctrine of God,* trans. by Olive Wyon (Philadelphia, 1964), p. 262.

21. Note: no comment here about freely doing *X*.

22. *The Christian Faith,* Pt. 1, sec. 2, par. 55. This passage trans. by W. R. Matthew (Edinburgh, 1928), p. 228.

23. Loc. cit.

24. This last seems to be the position defended by Richard Taylor in "Deliberation and Foreknowledge," *American Philosophical Quarterly,* 1 (1964).

25. The phrase "might have" as it occurs in this sentence does not express mere *logical* possibility. I am not sure how to analyze the notion of possibility involved here, but I think it is roughly the same notion as is involved when we say, "Jones might have been killed in the accident (had it not been for the fact that at the last minute he decided not to go)."

IV.B.3 God's Foreknowledge and Human Free Will Are Compatible

ALVIN PLANTINGA

A biography of Alvin Plantinga appears before reading III.7. In this article, Plantinga appeals to the notion of possible worlds in order to show that Pike's logic misfires and that there really is no incompatibility between divine foreknowledge and human free will.

The last argument I wish to discuss is perhaps only mildly atheological. This is the claim that God's omniscience is incompatible with *human freedom.* Many people are inclined to think that if God is omniscient, then human beings are never free. Why? Because the idea that God is omniscient implies that at any given time God knows not only what *has* taken place and what is taking place, but also what *will* take place. He knows the future as well as the past. But now suppose He knows that Paul will perform some trivial action tomorrow—having an orange for lunch, let's say. If God knows in advance that Paul will have an orange for lunch tomorrow, then it must be the case that he'll have an orange tomorrow; and if it *must* be the case that Paul will have an orange tomorrow, then it isn't possible that Paul will *refrain* from so doing—in which case he won't be free to refrain, and

hence won't be free with respect to the action of taking the orange. So if God knows in advance that a person will perform a certain action A, then that person isn't free with respect to that action. But if God is omniscient, then for any person and any action he performs, God knew in advance that he'd perform that action. So if God is omniscient, no one ever performs any free actions.

This argument may initially sound plausible, but the fact is it is based upon confusion. The central portion can be stated as follows:

(49) If God knows in advance that *X* will do *A*, then it must be the case that *X* will do *A*

and

(50) If it must be the case that *X* will do *A*, then *X* is not free to refrain from *A*.

Reprinted from Alvin Plantinga, *God, Freedom and Evil* (New York: Harper & Row, 1974), 66–72, by permission of the author.

From (49) and (50) it follows that if God knows in advance that someone will take a certain action, then that person isn't free with respect to that action. But (49) bears further inspection. Why should we think it's *true*? Because, we shall be told, if God knows that X will do A, it *logically follows* that X will do A: it's necessary that if God knows that p, then p is true. But this defense of (49) suggests that the latter is *ambiguous*; it may mean either

(49a) Necessarily, if God knows in advance that X will do A, then indeed X will do A

or

(49b) If God knows in advance that X will do A, then it is necessary that X will do A.

The atheological argument requires the truth of (49b); but the above defense of (49) supports only (49a), not (49b). It is indeed necessarily true that if God (or anyone else) knows that a proposition P is true, then P is true; but it simply doesn't follow that if God knows P, then P is necessarily true. *If I know that Henry is a bachelor, then Henry is a bachelor* is a necessary truth; it does not follow that if I know that Henry is a bachelor, then it is necessarily true that he is. I know that Henry is a bachelor: what follows is only that *Henry is married* is false; it doesn't follow that it is necessarily false.

So the claim that divine omniscience is incompatible with human freedom seems to be based upon confusion. Nelson Pike has suggested[1] an interesting revision of this old claim: he holds, not that human freedom is incompatible with God's being omniscient, but with God's being *essentially* omniscient. Recall . . . that an object X has a property P essentially if X has P in every world in which X exists—if, that is, it is impossible that X should have existed but lacked P. Now many theologians and philosophers have held that at least some of God's important properties are essential to him in this sense. It is plausible to hold, for example, that God is essentially omnipotent. Things could have gone differently in various ways; but if there had been no omnipotent being, then God would not have existed. *He* couldn't have been powerless or limited in power. But the same may

be said for God's *omniscience*. If God is omniscient, then He is unlimited in knowledge; He knows every true proposition and believes none that are false. If He is *essentially* omniscient, furthermore, then He not only *is not* limited in knowledge; He *couldn't* have been. There is no possible world in which He exists but fails to know some truth or believes some falsehood. And Pike's claim is that this belief—the belief that God is essentially omnipotent—is inconsistent with human freedom.

To argue his case Pike considers the case of Jones who mowed his lawn at T_2—last Saturday, let's say. Now suppose that God is essentially omniscient. Then at any earlier time T_1—80 years ago, for example—God believed that Jones would mow his lawn at T_2. Since He is *essentially* omniscient, furthermore, it isn't possible that God falsely believes something; hence His having believed at T_1 that Jones would mow his lawn at T_2 entails that Jones does indeed mow his lawn at T_2. Pike's argument (in his own words) then goes as follows:

1. "God existed at T_1" entails "if Jones did X at T_2, God believed at T_1 that Jones would do X at T_2."
2. "God believes X" entails "X is true."
3. It is not within one's power at a given time to do something having a description that is logically contradictory.
4. It is not within one's power at a given time to do something that would bring it about that someone who held a certain belief at a time prior to the time in question did not hold that belief at the time prior to the time in question.
5. It is not within one's power at a given time to do something that would bring it about that a person who existed at an earlier time did not exist at that earlier time.
6. If God existed at T_1 and if God believed at T_1 that Jones would do X at T_2, then if it was within Jones' power at T_2 to refrain from doing X, then (1) it was within Jones' power at T_2 to do something that would have brought it about that God held a false belief at T_1, or (2) it was within Jones' power at T_2 to do something which would have

brought it about that God did not hold the belief He held at T_1, or (3) it was within Jones' power at T_2 to do something that would have brought it about that any person who believed at T_1 that Jones would do X at T_2 (one of whom was, by hypothesis, God) held a false belief and thus was not God—that is, that God (who by hypothesis existed at T_1) did not exist at T_1.

7. Alternative 1 in the consequent of item 6 is false (from 2 and 3).

8. Alternative 2 in the consequent of item 6 is false (from 4).

9. Alternative 3 in the consequent of item 6 is false (from 5).

10. Therefore, if God existed at T_1 and if God believed at T_1 that Jones would do X at T_2, then it was not within Jones' power at T_2 to refrain from doing X (from 1 and 10).[2]

What about this argument? The first two premises simply make explicit part of what is involved in the idea that God is essentially omniscient; so there is no quarreling with them. Premises 3–5 also seem correct. But that complicated premise (6) warrants a closer look. What exactly does it say? I think we can understand Pike here as follows. Consider

(51) God existed at T_1, and God believed at T_1 that Jones would do X at T_2, and it was within Jones' power to refrain from doing X at T_2.

What Pike means to say, I believe, is that either (51) entails

(52) It was within Jones' power at T_2 to do something that would have brought it about that God held a false belief at T_1

or (51) entails

(53) It was with Jones' power at T_2 to do something that would have brought it about that God did not hold the belief He did hold at T_1

or it entails

(54) It was within Jones' power at T_2 to do something that would have brought it about

that anyone who believed at T_1 that Jones would do X at T_2 (one of whom was by hypothesis God) held a false belief and thus was not God—that is, that God (who by hypothesis existed at T_1) did not exist at T_1.

[The remainder of Pike's reasoning consists in arguing that each of (52), (53), and (54) is necessarily false, if God is essentially omniscient; hence (51) is necessarily false, if God is essentially omniscient, which means that God's being essentially omniscient is incompatible with human freedom.] Now suppose we look at these one at a time. Does (51) entail (52)? No. (52) says that it was within Jones' power to do something—namely, refrain from doing X—such that if he had done that thing, then God *would* have held a false belief at T_1. But this does not follow from (51). If Jones had refrained from X, then a proposition that God *did in fact* believe would have been false; but if Jones had refrained from X at T_2, then God (since He is omniscient) *would not have believed at T_1 that Jones will do X at T_2*. What follows from (51) is not (52) but only (52′):

(52′) It was within Jones' power to do something such that if he had done it, then a belief that God *did hold* at T_1 *would have been* false.

But (52′) is not at all paradoxical and in particular does not imply that it was within Jones' power to do something that would have brought it about that God held a false belief.

Perhaps we can see this more clearly if we look at it from the vantage point of possible worlds. We are told by (51) both that in the actual world God believes that Jones does X at T_2 and also that it is within Jones' power to *refrain* from doing X at T_2. Now consider any world W in which Jones *does* refrain from doing X. In *that* world, a belief that God holds in the actual world—in Kronos—is false. That is, if W had been actual, then a belief that God *does in fact* hold would have been false. But it does not follow that in W God holds a false belief. For it doesn't follow that if W had been actual, God would have believed that Jones would do X at T_2. Indeed, if God is essentially omniscient (omniscient in every world in which He exists) what follows is that in W God did not believe at T_1 that Jones will do X at T_2; He believed instead that Jones will *refrain* from X. So (51) by no means implies that it was within Jones' power to bring it about that God held a false belief at T_1.

What about

(53) It was within Jones' power at T_2 to do something that would have brought it about that God did not hold the belief He did hold at T_1?

Here the first problem is one of understanding. How are we to take this proposition? One way is this. What (53) says is that it was within Jones' power, at T_2, to do something such that if he had done it, then at T_1 God would have held a certain belief and also not held that belief. That is, (53) so understood attributes to Jones the power to bring about a contradictory state of affairs [call this interpretation (53a)]. (53a) is obviously and resoundingly false; but there is no reason whatever to think that (51) entails it. What (51) entails is rather

(53b) It was within Jones' power at T_2 to do something such that if he had done it, then God would not have held a belief that in fact he did hold.

This follows from (51) but is perfectly innocent. For suppose again that (51) is true, and consider a world W in which Jones refrains from doing X. If God is essentially omniscient, then in this world W He is omniscient and hence does not believe at T_1 that Jones will do X at T_2. So what follows from (51) is the harmless assertion that it was within Jones' power to do something such that if he had done it, then God would not have held a belief that in fact (in the actual world) He did hold. But by no stretch of the imagination does it follow that if Jones had done it, then it would have been true that God *did* hold a belief He didn't hold. Taken one way (53) is obviously false but not a consequence of (51); taken the other it is a consequence of (51) but by no means obviously false.

(54) fares no better. What it says is that it was within Jones' power at T2 to do something such that if he had done it, then God would not have been omniscient and thus would not have been God. But this simply doesn't follow from (51). The latter does, of course, entail

(54′) It was within Jones' power to do something such that if he'd done it, then anyone who believed at T_1 that Jones would do X at T_2 would have held a false belief.

For suppose again that (51) is in fact true, and now consider one of those worlds W in which Jones refrains from doing X. In that world

(55) Anyone who believed at T_1 that Jones will do X at T_2 held a false belief

is true. That is, if W had been actual, (55) would have been true. But again in W God does not believe that Jones will do X at T_2; (55) is true in W but isn't relevant to God there. If Jones had refrained from X, then (55) would have been true. It does not follow that God would not have been omniscient; for in those worlds in which Jones does not do X at T_2, God does not believe at T_1 that He does.

Perhaps the following is a possible source of confusion here. If God is *essentially* omniscient, then He is omniscient in every possible world in which He exists. Accordingly there is no possible world in which He holds a false belief. Now consider any belief that God does in fact hold. It might be tempting to suppose that if He is essentially omniscient, then He holds that belief in every world in which He exists. But of course this doesn't follow. It is not essential to Him to hold the beliefs He does hold; what is essential to Him is the quite different property of holding only true beliefs. So if a belief is true in Kronos but false in some world W, then in Kronos God holds that belief and in W He does not.

Much more should be said about Pike's piece, and there remain many fascinating details. I shall leave them to you, however. And by way of concluding our study of natural atheology:

none of the arguments we've examined has prospects for success; all are unacceptable. There are arguments we haven't considered, of course; but so far the indicated conclusion is that natural atheology doesn't work.

NOTES

1. Nelson Pike, "Divine Omniscience and Voluntary Action," *Philosophical Review* 74 (January 1965): 27.
2. Ibid., pp. 33–34.

IV.C   GOD'S OMNIPOTENCE

OMNIPOTENCE HAS TRADITIONALLY BEEN SEEN AS one of God's attributes, for if God is a being possessing all perfections, surely he must possess omnipotence as a significant perfection. But what exactly is omnipotence? Is it the ability to do just anything at all? Some philosophers, following Descartes, hold that it is and that it even includes the ability to violate logical truths. However, the implications of this view seem catastrophic for any intelligent talk of God (since all rational discussion presupposes the laws of logic). If we do not presuppose that the laws of logic apply to God, we might just as well say that God does and does not exist at the same time, for a contradiction fails to describe any state of affairs at all. Hence, the overwhelming majority of philosophers and theologians, at least since Aquinas, have not seen the ability to do the logically impossible as being among the perfections of God. Following their lead, we may roughly define omnipotence as the ability to do whatever is not logically impossible. God can create a universe, but he cannot square a circle.

Still, there are problems with this definition. On the surface, at least, it does not seem contradictory to say that God could make a stone heavier than he could lift or that he could sin if he wanted to (though his being perfectly good keeps him from exercising this power). Consider the paradox of the stone, as formulated by Wade Savage:*

1. Either x can create a stone that x cannot lift, or x cannot create a stone that x cannot lift.
2. If x can create a stone that x cannot lift, then, necessarily, there is at least one task that x cannot perform (namely, lift the stone in question).
3. If x cannot create a stone that x cannot lift, then, necessarily, there is at least one act that x cannot perform (namely, create the stone in question).
4. Hence, there is at least one task that x cannot perform.
5. If x is an omnipotent being, then x can perform any task.
6. Therefore, x is not omnipotent.

Since x could be any being whatsoever, the paradox apparently proves that the notion of omnipotence is incoherent.

---

*"The Paradox of Stone," *The Philosophical Review* 76 (1967), 75f.

In our readings, George Mavrodes argues that since God is *essentially* omnipotent, the act of creating a stone heavier than he can lift is a logical impossibility. Thus, he cannot do it; but, since omnipotence requires only the ability to do the logically possible, the fact that he cannot do it does not count against his omnipotence. This solution has been criticized by Wade Savage as a case of question-begging, supposing as it does that the statement "God is omnipotent" is necessarily true. A second line of thought is taken by Harry Frankfurt, who argues that if God is able to do one impossible thing, make a stone heavier than he can lift, he can also do a second impossible thing and lift that stone. So the paradox of the stone does not show that the notion of omnipotence is incoherent. Other philosophers have developed still further responses to this puzzle.

Similar to the paradox of the stone but more crucial to our idea of God is the question of whether God's omnipotence gives him the power to sin. Again, Aquinas and many medieval theologians argue that such power would be pseudopower—in fact, impotence. Others, following William of Ockham, have argued that God necessarily cannot sin because sin is defined as simply being that which is opposed to God's will and God cannot oppose his own will at one and the same time. (This view presupposes a divine command theory of morality, which we examine in Part X.) Still others argue that an omniscient and perfectly free being cannot sin because sin necessarily involves a failure in reason or freedom.

IV.C.1   Is God's Power Limited?

ST. THOMAS AQUINAS

Thomas Aquinas (1225–1274), one of the greatest theologians in the Western tradition, argues that although it is difficult to explain what God's omnipotence is, it requires only the ability to do those things that are logically possible. Because God possesses all perfections and sinning is an imperfection, the ability to sin is not part of his omnipotence.

We proceed thus to the Third Article:

Objection 1. It seems that God is not omnipotent. For movement and passiveness belong to everything. But this is impossible for God, since He is immovable, as was said above. Therefore He is not omnipotent.

Obj. 2. Further, sin is an act of some kind. But God cannot sin, nor *deny Himself*, as it is said *2 Tim.* ii. 13. Therefore He is not omnipotent.

Obj. 3. Further, it is said of God that He manifests His omnipotence *especially by sparing and having mercy*. Therefore the greatest act possible to the divine power is to spare and have mercy. There are things much greater, however, than sparing and having mercy; for example, to create another world, and the like. Therefore God is not omnipotent.

Obj. 4. Further, upon the text, *God hath made foolish the wisdom of this world* (*I Cor.* i. 20), the

From *Summa Theologica*, part 1 in *The Basic Writings of St. Thomas Aquinas*, vol. 1, edited by Anton C. Pegis (New York: Random House, 1945), 262–64, by permission of the Anton Pegis Estate.

Gloss says: *God hath made the wisdom of this world foolish* by showing those things to be possible which it judges to be impossible. Whence it seems that nothing is to be judged possible or impossible in reference to inferior causes, as the wisdom of this world judges them; but in reference to the divine power. If God, then were omnipotent, all things would be possible; nothing, therefore, impossible. But if we take away the impossible, then we destroy also the necessary; for what necessarily exists cannot possibly not exist. Therefore, there would be nothing at all that is necessary in things if God were omnipotent. But this is an impossibility. Therefore God is not omnipotent.

On the contrary, It is said: *No word shall be impossible with God* (*Luke* i:37).

I answer that, All confess that God is omnipotent; but it seems difficult to explain in what His omnipotence precisely consists. For there may be a doubt as to the precise meaning of the word "all" when we say that God can do all things. If, however, we consider the matter aright, since power is said in reference to possible things, this phrase, *God can do all things*, is rightly understood to mean that God can do all things that are possible; and for this reason He is said to be omnipotent. Now according to the Philosopher a thing is said to be possible in two ways. First, in relation to some power; thus whatever is subject to human power is said to be possible to man. Now God cannot be said to be omnipotent through being able to do all things that are possible to created nature; for the divine power extends farther than that. If, however, we were to say that God is omnipotent because He can do all things that are possible to His power, there would be a vicious circle in explaining the nature of His power. For this would be saying nothing else but that God is omnipotent because He can do all that He is able to do.

It remains, therefore, that God is called omnipotent because he can do all things that are possible absolutely; which is the second way of saying a thing is possible. For a thing is said to be possible or impossible absolutely, according to the relation in which the very terms stand to one another: possible, if the predicate is not incompatible with the subject, as that Socrates sits; and absolutely impossible when the predicate is altogether incompatible with the subject, as, for instance, that a man is an ass.

It must, however, be remembered that since every agent produces an effect like itself, to each active power there corresponds a thing possible as its proper object according to the nature of that act on which its active power is founded; for instance, the power of giving warmth is related, as to its proper object, to the being capable of being warmed. The divine being, however, upon which the nature of power in God is founded, is infinite; it is not limited to any class of being, but possesses within itself the perfection of all being. Whence, whatsoever has or can have the nature of being is numbered among the absolute possibles, in respect of which God is called omnipotent.

Now nothing is opposed to the notion of being except non-being. Therefore, that which at the same time implies being and non-being is repugnant to the notion of an absolute possible, which is subject to the divine omnipotence. For such cannot come under the divine omnipotence; not indeed because of any defect in the power of God, but because it has not the nature of a feasible or possible thing. Therefore, everything that does not imply a contradiction in terms is numbered among those possibles in respect of which God is called omnipotent; whereas whatever implies contradiction does not come within the scope of divine omnipotence, because it cannot have the aspect of possibility. Hence it is more appropriate to say that such things cannot be done, than that God cannot do them. Nor is this contrary to the word of the angel, saying: *No word shall be impossible with God* (*Luke* i. 37). For whatever implies a contradiction cannot be a word, because no intellect can possibly conceive such a thing.

Reply Obj. **1.** God is said to be omnipotent in respect to active power, not to passive power, as was shown above. Whence the fact that He is immovable or impassible is not repugnant to His omnipotence.

Reply Obj. **2.** To sin is to fall short of a perfect action; hence to be able to sin is to be able to fall short in action, which is repugnant to omnipotence. Therefore it is that God cannot sin, because of His omnipotence. Now it is true that the Philosopher says that *God can deliberately do what is evil.* But this must be understood either on a condition, the antecedent of which is impossible—as, for instance, if we were to say that God can do evil things if He will. For there is no reason why a conditional proposition should not be true, though both the antecedent and consequent are impossible: as if one were to say: *If man is an ass, he has four feet.* Or he may be understood to mean that God can do some things which now seem to be evil: which, however, if He did them, would then be good. Or he is, perhaps, speaking after the common manner of the pagans, who thought that men became gods, like Jupiter or Mercury.

Reply Obj. **3.** God's omnipotence is particularly shown in sharing and having mercy, because in this it is made manifest that God has supreme power, namely, that He freely forgives sins. For it is not for one who is bound by laws of a superior to forgive sins of his own free choice. Or, it is thus shown because by sparing and having mercy upon men, He leads them to the participation of an infinite good; which is the ultimate effect of the divine power. Or it is thus shown because, as was said above, the effect of the divine mercy is the foundation of all the divine works. For nothing is due anyone, except because of something already given him gratuitously by God. In this way the divine omnipotence is particularly made manifest, because to it pertains the first foundation of all good things.

Reply Obj. **4.** The absolute possible is not so called in reference either to higher causes, or to inferior causes, but in reference to itself. But that which is called possible in reference to some power is named possible in reference to its proximate cause. Hence those things which it belongs to God alone to do immediately—as, for example, to create, to justify, and the like—are said to be possible in reference to a higher cause. Those things, however, which are such as to be done by inferior causes, are said to be possible in reference to those inferior causes. For it is according to the condition of the proximate cause that the effect has contingency or necessity, as was shown above. Thus it is that the wisdom of the world is deemed foolish, because what is impossible to nature it judges to be impossible to God. So it is clear that the omnipotence of God does not take away from things their impossibility and necessity.

IV.C.2 Some Puzzles Concerning Omnipotence

GEORGE MAVRODES

George Mavrodes (1926–   ) is emeritus professor of philosophy at the University of Michigan. In this reading he applies the Thomistic view of God's omnipotence to the paradox of the stone (previous selection), arguing that, since creating a stone too heavy for God to lift involves doing something that is logically impossible, God's inability to do this doesn't count against his omnipotence.

Reprinted from *The Philosophical Review* 72 (1963), 221–23.

The doctrine of God's omnipotence appears to claim that God can do anything. Consequently, there have been attempts to refute the doctrine by giving examples of things which God cannot do; for example, He cannot draw a square circle.

Responding to objections of this type, St. Thomas pointed out that "anything" should be here construed to refer only to objects, actions, or states of affairs whose descriptions are not self-contradictory.[1] For it is only such things whose nonexistence might plausibly be attributed to a lack of power in some agent. My failure to draw a circle on the exam may indicate my lack of geometrical skill, but my failure to draw a square circle does not indicate any such lack. Therefore, the fact that it is false (or perhaps meaningless) to say that God could draw one does no damage to the doctrine of His omnipotence.

A more involved problem, however, is posed by this type of question: can God create a stone too heavy for Him to lift? This appears to be stronger than the first problem, for it poses a dilemma. If we say that God can create a stone, then it seems that there might be such a stone. And if there might be a stone too heavy for Him to lift, then He is evidently not omnipotent. But if we deny that God can create such a stone, we seem to have given up His omnipotence already. Both answers lead us to the same conclusion.

Further, this problem does not seem obviously open to St. Thomas' solution. The form "x is able to draw a square circle" seems plainly to involve a contradiction, while "x is able to make a thing too heavy for x to lift" does not. For it may easily be true that I am able to make a boat too heavy for me to lift. So why should it not be possible for God to make a stone too heavy for Him to lift?

Despite this apparent difference, this second puzzle *is* open to essentially the same answer as the first. The dilemma fails because it consists of asking whether God can do a self-contradictory thing. And the reply that He cannot does no damage to the doctrine of omnipotence.

The specious nature of the problem may be seen in this way. God is either omnipotent or not.[2] Let us assume first that He is not. In that case the phrase "a stone too heavy for God to lift" may not be self-contradictory. And then, of course, if we assert either that God is able or that He is not able to create such a stone, we may conclude that He is not omnipotent. But this is no more than the assumption with which we began, meeting us again after our roundabout journey. If this were all that the dilemma could establish it would be trivial. To be significant it must derive this same conclusion *from the assumption that God is omnipotent;* that is, it must show that the assumption of the omnipotence of God leads to a *reductio.* But does it?

On the assumption that God is omnipotent, the phrase "a stone too heavy for God to lift" becomes self-contradictory. For it becomes "a stone which cannot be lifted by Him whose power is sufficient for lifting anything." But the "thing" described by a self-contradictory phrase is absolutely impossible and hence has nothing to do with the doctrine of omnipotence. Not being an object of power at all, its failure to exist cannot be the result of some lack in the power of God. And, interestingly, it is the very omnipotence of God which makes the existence of such a stone absolutely impossible, while it is the fact that I am finite in power which makes it possible for me to make a boat too heavy for me to lift.

But suppose that some die-hard objector takes the bit in his teeth and denies that the phrase "a stone too heavy for God to lift" is self-contradictory, even on the assumption that God is omnipotent. In other words, he contends that the description "a stone too heavy for an omnipotent God to lift" is self-coherent and therefore describes an absolutely possible object. Must I then attempt to prove the contradiction which I assume above as intuitively obvious? Not necessarily. Let me reply simply that if the objector is right in this contention, then the answer to the original question is "Yes, God can create such a stone." It may seem that this reply will force us into the original dilemma. But it does not. For now the objector can draw no damaging conclusion from this answer. And the reason is that he has just now contended that such a stone is compatible with the omnipotence of God. Therefore, from the possibility of God's creating such a stone it cannot be concluded that God is not omnipotent. The objector cannot have it both ways. The conclusion which he himself wishes to draw from an affirmative answer to the original question is itself the required proof that the descriptive phrase which appears there is self-contradictory. And "it is more appropriate to say that such things cannot be done, than that God cannot do them."[3]

The specious nature of this problem may also be seen in a somewhat different way.[4] Suppose that some theologian is convinced by this dilemma that he must give up the doctrine of omnipotence. But he resolves to give up as little as possible, just enough to meet the argument. One way he can do so is by retaining the infinite power of God with regard to lifting, while placing a restriction on the sort of stone He is able to create. The only restriction required here, however, is that God must not be able to create a stone too heavy for Him to lift. Beyond that the dilemma has not even suggested any necessary restriction. Our theologian has, in effect, answered the original question in the negative; and he now regretfully supposes that this has required him to give up the full doctrine of omnipotence. He is now retaining what he supposes to be the more modest remnants which he has salvaged from that doctrine.

We must ask, however, what it is which he has in fact given up. Is it the unlimited power of God to create stones? No doubt. But what stone is it which God is now precluded from creating? The stone too heavy for Him to lift, of course. But we must remember that nothing in the argument required the theologian to admit any limit on God's power with regard to the lifting of stones. He still holds that to be unlimited. And if God's power to lift is infinite, then His power to create may run to infinity also without outstripping that first power. The supposed limitation turns out to be no limitation at all, since it is specified only by reference to another power which is itself infinite. Our theologian need have no regrets, for he has given up nothing. The doctrine of the power of God remains just what it was before.

Nothing I have said above, of course, goes to prove that God is, in fact, omnipotent. All I have intended to show is that certain arguments intended to prove that He is not omnipotent fail. They fail because they propose, as tests of God's power, putative tasks whose descriptions are self-contradictory. Such pseudo-tasks, not falling within the realm of possibility, are not objects of power at all. Hence the fact that they cannot be performed implies no limit on the power of God, and hence no defect in the doctrine of omnipotence.

NOTES

1. St. Thomas Aquinas, *Summa Theologiae*, Ia, q. 25, a. 3.
2. I assume, of course, the existence of God, since that is not being brought in question here.
3. St. Thomas, *loc. cit.*.
4. But this method rests finally on the same logical relations as the preceding one.

IV.C.3 The Logic of Omnipotence

HARRY G. FRANKFURT

Harry Frankfurt (1929–   ) is emeritus professor of philosophy at Princeton University and the author of many important works in philosophy, including an influential study of René Descartes. In this essay he argues that even if Mavrodes' solution to the paradox of the stone (previous selection) is incorrect, the critic of omnipotence is not helped. For if God can do the impossible and create a stone heavier than he can lift, he can also do another impossible thing and lift that stone.

From *The Philosophical Review* 73 (1964).

George Mavrodes has recently presented an analysis designed to show that, despite some appearances to the contrary, a certain well-known puzzle actually raises no serious difficulties in the notion of divine omnipotence.[1] The puzzle suggests a test of God's power—can He create a stone too heavy for Him to lift?—which, it seems, cannot fail to reveal that His power is limited. For He must, it would appear, either show His limitations by being unable to create such a stone or by being unable to lift it once He had created it.

In dealing with this puzzle, Mavrodes points out that it involves the setting of a task whose description is self-contradictory—the task of creating a stone too heavy for an omnipotent being to lift. He calls such tasks "pseudo-tasks" and he says of them: "Such pseudo-tasks, not falling within the realm of possibility, are not objects of power at all. Hence the fact that they cannot be performed implies no limit on the power of God, and hence no defect in the doctrine of omnipotence."[2] Thus his way of dealing with the puzzle relies upon the principle that an omnipotent being need not be supposed capable of performing tasks whose descriptions are self-contradictory.

Now this principle is one which Mavrodes apparently regards as self-evident, since he offers no support for it whatever except some references which indicate that it was also accepted by Saint Thomas Aquinas. I do not wish to suggest that the principle is false. Indeed, for all I know it may even be self-evident. But it happens to be a principle which has been rejected by some important philosophers.[3] Accordingly, it might be preferable to have an analysis of the puzzle in question which does not require the use of this principle. And in fact, such an analysis is easy to provide.

Suppose, then, that God's omnipotence enables Him to do even what is logically impossible and that He actually creates a stone too heavy for Him to lift. The critic of the notion of divine omnipotence is quite mistaken if he thinks that this supposition plays into his hands. What the critic wishes to claim, of course, is that when God has created a stone which He cannot lift He is then faced with a task beyond His ability and is therefore seen to be limited in power. But this claim is not justified.

For why should God not be able to perform the task in question? To be sure, it is a task—the task of lifting a stone which He cannot lift—whose description is self-contradictory. But if God is supposed capable of performing one task whose description is self-contradictory—that of creating the problematic stone in the first place—why should He not be supposed capable of performing another—that of lifting the stone? After all, is there any greater trick in performing two logically impossible tasks than there is in performing one?

If an omnipotent being can do what is logically impossible, then He can not only create situations which He cannot handle but also, since He is not bound by the limits of consistency, He can handle situations which He cannot handle.

NOTES

1. George Mavrodes, "Some Puzzles Concerning Omnipotence," *The Philosophical Review* 72 (1963), 221–23.
2. *Ibid.*, p. 223.
3. Descartes, for instance, who in fact thought it blasphemous to maintain that God can do only what can be described in a logically coherent way: "The truths of mathematics . . . were established by God and entirely depend on Him, as much as do all the rest of His creatures. Actually, it would be to speak of God as a Jupiter or Saturn and to subject Him to the Styx and to the Fates, to say that these truths are independent of Him. . . . You will be told that if God established these truths He would be able to change them, as a king does his laws; to which it is necessary to reply that this is correct. . . . In general we can be quite certain that God can do whatever we are able to understand, but not that He cannot do what we are unable to understand. For it would be presumptuous to think that our imagination extends as far as His power" (letter to Mersenne, 15 April 1630). "God was as free to make it false that all the radii of a circle are equal as to refrain from creating the world" (letter to Mersenne, 27 May 1630). "I would not even dare to say that God cannot arrange that a mountain should exist without a valley, or that one and two should not make three; but I only say that

He has given me a mind of such a nature that I cannot conceive a mountain without a valley or a sum of one and two which would not be three, and so on, and that such things imply contradictions in my conception" (letter to Arnauld, 29 July 1648). "As for the difficulty in conceiving how it was a matter of freedom and indifference to God to make it true that the three angles of a triangle should equal two right angles, or generally that contradictions should not be able to be together, one can easily remove it by considering that the power of God can have no limit.... God cannot have been determined to make it true that contradictions cannot be together, and consequently He could have been determined to make it true that contradictions cannot be together, and consequently he could have done the contrary" (letter to Mesland, 2 May 1644).

Miracles and Revelation

WHAT ARE MIRACLES, and are they possible? Should miracles necessarily be defined as violations of the laws of nature? The idea that miracles are natural law violations has been disputed on the basis of the contention that in the Bible, which is the witness to the most significant alleged miracles in the Judeo-Christian tradition, there is no concept of nature as a closed system of law. For the biblical writers, miracles signify simply an "extraordinary coincidence of a beneficial nature."[1] This view is proposed by R. F. Holland in his article "The Miraculous," in which the following story is illustrative:

> A child riding his toy motor-car strays on to an unguarded railway crossing near his house and a wheel of his car gets stuck down the side of one of the rails. An express train is due to pass with the signals in its favour and a curve in the track makes it impossible for the driver to stop his train in time to avoid any obstruction he might encounter on the crossing. The mother coming out of the house to look for her child sees him on the crossing and hears the train approaching. She runs forward shouting and waving. The little boy remains seated in his car looking downward engrossed in the task of pedaling it free. The brakes of the train are applied and it comes to rest a few feet from the child. The mother thanks God for the miracle; which she never ceases to think of as such, although, as she in due course learns, there was nothing supernatural about the manner in which the brakes of the train came to be applied. The driver had fainted, for a reason that had nothing to do with the presence of the child on the line, and the brakes were applied automatically as his hand ceased to exert pressure on the control lever. He fainted on this particular afternoon because his blood pressure had risen after an exceptionally heavy lunch during which he had quarreled with a colleague, and the change in blood pressure caused a clot of blood to be dislodged and circulate. He fainted at the time when he did on the afternoon in question because this was the time at which the coagulation in his blood stream reached the brain.[2]

Is this a miracle, or not? It is if we define miracles in Fuller's biblical sense. It is not if we define them as violations of laws of nature. We can certainly understand the woman's feeling on the matter, and perhaps in some mysterious way God had 'allowed' nature to run its course so that the little boy would be saved. Perhaps we need not be overly exclusionary but say that if there is a God, each sense is valid: the *weaker* sense of an extraordinary coincidence and the *stronger* sense of a violation of the laws of nature. Nonetheless, what is philosophically interesting as well as controversial with regard to miracles is the stronger sense, that of a violation of the laws of nature by a divine force. It is this sense of miracles that we consider in this part of our work.

The most celebrated article ever written on miracles is by David Hume. In section 10 of *An Enquiry Concerning Human Understanding* he set forth an argument against belief in miracles that provoked a lively response in his day and has continued to be the subject of vigorous dispute up to the present day. Let us analyze it briefly.

Hume begins his attack on miracles by appealing to the biases of his Scottish Presbyterian readers. He tells of a marvelous proof that Dr. Tillotson has devised against the Roman Catholic doctrine of transubstantiation, the doctrine that the body and blood of Christ are present in Holy Communion. Tillotson argues that because the evidence of the senses is of the highest rank and because it is evident that it must diminish in passing through the original witnesses to their disciples, the doctrine of transubstantiation is always contrary to the rules of reasoning and opposed to our sense experience. Thus:

1. Our evidence for the truth of transubstantiation is weaker than the sensory evidence we have against it. (Even for the apostles this was the case, and their testimony must diminish in authority in passing from them to their disciples.)
2. We are never warranted in believing a proposition on the basis of weaker evidence when stronger evidence supports the denial of that proposition.
3. Therefore, we are not warranted in believing in transubstantiation. (Even if the doctrine of transubstantiation were clearly revealed in the Scriptures, it would be against the rule of reason to give our assent to it.)

No doubt Hume's Protestant readers were delighted with such a sound refutation of the doctrine of transubstantiation. But the mischievous Hume now turns the knife on his readers. A wise person always proportions one's belief to the evidence, he goes on. One has an enormous amount of evidence for the laws of nature, so that any testimony to the contrary is to be seriously doubted. Although miracles, as violations of the laws of nature, are not logically impossible, we are never justified in believing in one. The skeleton of the argument contained in the reading goes something like this:

1. One ought to proportion one's belief to the evidence.
2. Experience is generally better evidence than testimony (if for no other reason than that valid testimony is based on another's sense experience).
3. Therefore, when there is a conflict between experience and testimony, one ought to believe according to experience.
4. Miracles are contrary to experience. That is, experience testifies strongly to the fact that miracles never occur, laws of nature are never violated.
5. Therefore, we are never justified in believing in miracles, but we are justified in believing in the naturalness of all events.

Because we have enormous evidence in favor of the uniformity of nature, every miracle report must be weighed against that preponderance and be found wanting. But what if we believe that we personally have beheld a miracle? Aren't we in that case justified in believing that a miracle has occurred? No, for given the principle of induction (that every time we pursue an event *far enough*, we discover it to have a natural cause), we are still not justified in believing the event to be a miracle. Rather we ought to look further (*far enough*) until we discover the natural cause. The only exception to this rule (or "proof" against miracles) would be if it would be even more miraculous for a miracle not to have occurred: "That no testimony is sufficient to establish a miracle, unless the testimony be of such a kind, that its falsehood would be more marvelous, than the fact, which it endeavors to establish; and even in that case there is a mutual destruction of argument, and the superior only gives us an assurance suitable to that degree of force, which remains, after deducting the inferior." The best we can hope for is an agnostic standoff in the matter.

But the criteria that would have to be fulfilled would be that (1) a sufficient number of witnesses of (2) good sense and education and (3) integrity and reputation would have to testify to (4) a public performance of the incident. Hume offers several putative examples of such cases and argues that the criteria are really not fulfilled in any of them.

In our second reading, Peter van Inwagen attacks Hume's argument. Hume's argument, as we have seen, rests in part on the idea that miracles are the sorts of things that run significantly contrary to our experience. But, van Inwagen argues, it's hard to see what this idea really amounts to. Thus, he writes:

> It is very hard indeed to find a sense in which experience testifies in any direct or immediate sense that events of some sort never happen—or in which stories of events of some sort are contrary to experience. If direct, immediate experience testifies to anything (truly or falsely) its testimony seems to be essentially "positive": it testifies that events of certain sorts *do* happen.

Failing to find any other sense of 'contrary to experience' that could drive Hume's argument, van Inwagen concludes that Hume's argument is a failure.

Our third reading is "Miracles and Testimony" by the late J. L. Mackie of Oxford University, a man who loved Hume and exemplified his thought. In this revised Humean account of miracles, Mackie argues that the evidence for miracles will never in practice be very great. The argument is epistemological, not ontological. That is, whereas miracles may be logically possible (and may indeed have occurred), we are never justified in believing in one. The concept of a miracle is a coherent one; but, Mackie argues, the *double* burden of showing both that the event took place *and* that it violated the laws of nature will be extremely hard to lift, for "whatever tends to show that it would have been a violation of natural law tends for that very reason to make it most unlikely that it actually happened." Correspondingly, the deniers of miracles have two strategies of defense. They may argue that the event took place but wasn't a violation of a law of nature (the event simply followed an unknown law of nature); or they can admit that if the event had happened, it would indeed have been a violation of a law of nature, but for that reason, "there is a very strong presumption against its having happened, which it is most unlikely that any testimony will be able to outweigh."

In our fourth reading, however, Richard Swinburne argues that, as a matter of fact, there is fairly strong evidence in support of the occurrence of at least one miracle—namely, the resurrection of Jesus. Swinburne notes several problems with Hume's argument, the most significant of which (on his view) is Hume's failure to attend to the way in which "background assumptions" help to determine what is and is not reasonable for us to believe. If it is unlikely, given your background assumptions, that there is a God or any other being who could work miracles, then it will be harder for you reasonably to believe that a miracle has occurred. But if, on the other hand, your background evidence makes it likely that there is a God who could work miracles, and if you have reason, furthermore, to think that this God would have good reason to work some particular miracle for which you have testimonial and other historical evidence, then it might well be very reasonable for you to believe that such a miracle has occurred. According to Swinburne, such is the case with the resurrection of Jesus.

Finally, in "Hyperspace and Christianity," Hud Hudson challenges the familiar objection that belief in miracles "conflicts with our modern worldview" by arguing that belief in hyperspace—a view that comports quite well with our modern scientific worldview—helps us to see how a wide variety of Biblical miracles could have occurred.

NOTES

1. R. H. Fuller *Interpreting the Miracle* (London, 1968), 8.
2. *American Philosophical Quarterly*, 2 (1965).

V.1   Against Miracles

DAVID HUME

A short biographical sketch of David Hume precedes selection I.C.2. The following selection argues that we are virtually never justified in believing that a miracle has occurred.

PART I.

There is, in Dr. Tillotson's writings, an argument against the *real presence*, which is as concise, and elegant, and strong as any argument can possibly be supposed against a doctrine, so little worthy of a serious refutation. It is acknowledged on all hands, says that learned prelate, that the authority, either of the scripture or of tradition, is founded merely in the testimony of the apostles, who were eye-witnesses to those miracles of our Saviour, by which he proved his divine mission. Our evidence, then, for the truth of the *Christian* religion is less than the evidence for the truth of our senses; because, even in the first authors of our religion, it was no greater; and it is evident it must diminish in passing from them to their disciples; nor can any one rest such confidence in their testimony, as in the immediate object of his senses. But a weaker evidence can never destroy a stronger; and therefore, were the doctrine of the real presence ever so clearly revealed in scripture, it were directly contrary to the rules of just reasoning to give our assent to it. It contradicts sense, though both the scripture and tradition, on which it is supposed to be built, carry not such evidence with them as sense; when they are considered merely as external evidences, and are not brought home to every one's breast, by the immediate operation of the Holy Spirit.

Nothing is so convenient as a decisive argument of this kind, which must at least *silence* the

Reprinted from David Hume, *An Enquiry Concerning Human Understanding* (Oxford: Oxford Univ. Press, 1748). Footnotes edited.

most arrogant bigotry and superstition, and free us from their impertinent solicitations. I flatter myself, that I have discovered an argument of a like nature, which, if just, will, with the wise and learned, be an everlasting check to all kinds of superstitious delusion, and consequently, will be useful as long as the world endures. For so long, I presume, will the accounts of miracles and prodigies be found in all history, sacred and profane.

Though experience be our only guide in reasoning concerning matters of fact; it must be acknowledged, that this guide is not altogether infallible, but in some cases is apt to lead us into errors. One, who in our climate, should expect better weather in any week of June than in one of December, would reason justly, and conformably to experience; but it is certain, that he may happen, in the event, to find himself mistaken. However, we may observe, that, in such a case, he would have no cause to complain of experience; because it commonly informs us beforehand of the uncertainty, by that contrariety of events, which we may learn from a diligent observation. All effects follow not with like certainty from their supposed causes. Some events are found, in all countries and all ages, to have been constantly conjoined together: Others are found to have been more variable, and sometimes to disappoint our expectations; so that, in our reasonings concerning matter of fact, there are all imaginable degrees of assurance, from the highest certainty to the lowest species of moral evidence.

A wise man, therefore, proportions his belief to the evidence. In such conclusions as are founded on an infallible experience, he expects the event with the last degree of assurance, and regards his past experience as a full *proof* of the future existence of that event. In other cases, he proceeds with more caution: He weighs the opposite experiments: He considers which side is supported by the greater number of experiments: to that side he inclines, with doubt and hesitation; and when at last he fixes his judgement, the evidence exceeds not what we properly call *probability*. All probability, then, supposes an opposition of experiments and observations, where the one side is found to overbalance the other, and to produce a degree of evidence,

proportioned to the superiority. A hundred instances or experiments on one side, and fifty on another, afford a doubtful expectation of any event; though a hundred uniform experiments, with only one that is contradictory, reasonably beget a pretty strong degree of assurance. In all cases, we must balance the opposite experiments, where they are opposite, and deduct the smaller number from the greater, in order to know the exact force of the superior evidence.

To apply these principles to a particular instance; we may observe, that there is no species of reasoning more common, more useful, and even necessary to human life, than that which is derived from the testimony of men, and the reports of eye-witnesses and spectators. This species of reasoning, perhaps, one may deny to be founded on the relation of cause and effect. I shall not dispute about a word. It will be sufficient to observe that our assurance in any argument of this kind is derived from no other principle than our observation of the veracity of human testimony, and of the usual conformity of facts to the reports of witnesses. It being a general maxim, that no objects have any discoverable connexion together, and that all the inferences, which we can draw from one to another, are founded merely on our experience of their constant and regular conjunction; it is evident, that we ought not to make an exception to this maxim in favour of human testimony, whose connexion with any event seems, in itself, as little necessary as any other. Were not the memory tenacious to a certain degree; had not men commonly an inclination to truth and a principle of probity; were they not sensible to shame, when detected in a falsehood: Were not these, I say, discovered by *experience* to be qualities, inherent in human nature, we should never repose the least confidence in human testimony. A man delirious, or noted for falsehood and villany, has no manner of authority with us.

And as the evidence, derived from witnesses and human testimony, is founded on past experience, so it varies with the experience, and is regarded either as a *proof* or a *probability,* according to the conjunction between any particular kind of report and any kind of object has been found to be constant or variable. There are a number of circumstances to be taken into consideration in all judgements of this kind; and the ultimate standard, by which we determine all disputes, that may arise concerning them, is always derived from experience and observation. Where this experience is not entirely uniform on any side, it is attended with an unavoidable contrariety in our judgements, and with the same opposition and mutual destruction of argument as in every other kind of evidence. We frequently hesitate concerning the reports of others. We balance the opposite circumstances, which cause any doubt or uncertainty; and when we discover a superiority on any side, we incline to it; but still with a diminution of assurance, in proportion to the force of its antagonist.

This contrariety of evidence, in the present case, may be derived from several different causes; from the opposition of contrary testimony; from the character or number of the witnesses; from the manner of their delivering their testimony; or from the union of all these circumstances. We entertain a suspicion concerning any matter of fact, when the witnesses contradict each other; when they are but few, or of a doubtful character; when they have an interest in what they affirm; when they deliver their testimony with hesitation, or on the contrary, with too violent asseverations. There are many other particulars of the same kind, which may diminish or destroy the force of any argument, derived from human testimony.

Suppose, for instance, that the fact, which the testimony endeavors to establish, partakes of the extraordinary and the marvelous; in that case, the evidence, resulting from the testimony, admits of a diminution, greater or less, in proportion as the fact is more or less unusual. The reason why we place any credit in witnesses and historians, is not derived from any *connexion*, which we perceive *a priori*, between testimony and reality, but because we are accustomed to find a conformity between them. But when the fact attested is such a one as has seldom fallen under our observation, here is a contest of two opposite experiences; of which the one destroys the other, as far as its force goes, and the superior can only operate on the mind by the force, which remains. The very same principle of experience, which gives us a certain degree of assurance in the testimony of witnesses, gives us also, in this case, another degree of assurance against the fact, which they endeavour to establish; from which contradiction there necessarily arises a counterpoise, and mutual destruction of belief and authority.

I should not believe such a story were it told me by Cato, was a proverbial saying in Rome, even during the lifetime of that philosophical patriot. The incredibility of a fact, it was allowed, might invalidate so great an authority.

The Indian prince, who refused to believe the first relations concerning the effects of frost, reasoned justly; and it naturally required very strong testimony to engage his assent to facts, that arose from a state of nature, with which he was unacquainted, and which bore so little analogy to those events, of which we had had constant and uniform experience. Though they were not contrary to his experience, they were not conformable to it.

But in order to increase the probability against the testimony of witnesses, let us suppose, that the fact, which they affirm, instead of being only marvelous, is really miraculous; and suppose also, that the testimony considered apart and in itself, amounts to an entire proof; in that case, there is proof against proof, of which the strongest must prevail, but still with a diminution of its force, in proportion to that of its antagonist.

A miracle is a violation of the laws of nature; and as a firm and unalterable experience has established these laws, the proof against a miracle, from the very nature of the fact, is as entire as any argument from experience can possibly be imagined. Why is it more than probable, that all men must die; that lead cannot, of itself, remain suspended in the air; that fire consumes wood, and is extinguished by water; unless it be, that these events are found agreeable to the laws of nature, and there is required a violation of these laws, or in other words, a miracle to prevent them? Nothing is esteemed a miracle, if it ever happen in the common course of nature. It is no miracle that a man, seemingly in good health, should die on a sudden:

because such a kind of death, though more unusual than any other, has yet been frequently observed to happen. But it is a miracle, that a dead man should come to life; because that has never been observed in any age or country. There must, therefore, be a uniform experience against every miraculous event, otherwise the event would not merit that appellation. And as a uniform experience amounts to a proof, there is here a direct and full *proof,* from the nature of the fact, against the existence of any miracle; nor can such a proof be destroyed, or the miracle rendered credible, but by an opposite proof, which is superior.[1]

The plain consequence is (and it is a general maxim worthy of our attention), 'That no testimony is sufficient to establish a miracle, unless the testimony be of such a kind, that its falsehood would be more miraculous, than the fact, which it endeavours to establish; and even in that case there is a mutual destruction of arguments, and the superior only gives us an assurance suitable to that degree of force, which remains, after deducting the inferior.' When anyone tells me, that he saw a dead man restored to life, I immediately consider with myself, whether it be more probable, that this person should either deceive or be deceived, or that the fact, which he relates, should really have happened. I weigh the one miracle against the other; and according to the superiority, which I discover, I pronounce my decision, and always reject the greater miracle. If the falsehood of his testimony would be more miraculous, than the event which he relates; then, and not till then, can he pretend to command my belief or opinion.

PART II.

In the foregoing reasoning we have supposed, that the testimony, upon which a miracle is founded, may possibly amount to an entire proof, and that the falsehood of that testimony would be a real prodigy: But it is easy to show, that we have been a great deal too liberal in our concession, and that there never was a miraculous event established on so full an evidence.

For *first,* there is not to be found, in all history, any miracle attested by a sufficient number

of men, of such unquestioned good-sense, education, and learning, as to secure us against all delusion in themselves; of such undoubted integrity, as to place them beyond all suspicion of any design to deceive others; of such credit and reputation in the eyes of mankind, as to have a great deal to lose in case of their being detected in any falsehood; and at the same time, attesting facts performed in such a public manner and in so celebrated a part of the world, as to render the detection unavoidable. All which circumstances are requisite to give us a full assurance in the testimony of men.

Secondly. We may observe in human nature a principle which, if strictly examined, will be found to diminish extremely the assurance, which we might, from human testimony, have, in any kind of prodigy. The maxim, by which we commonly conduct ourselves in our reasonings, is, that the objects, of which we have no experience, resemble those, of which we have; that what we have found to be most usual is always most probable; and that where there is an opposition of arguments, we ought to give the preference to such as are founded on the greatest number of past observations. But though, in proceeding by this rule, we readily reject any fact which is unusual and incredible in an ordinary degree; yet in advancing farther, the mind observes not always the same rule; but when anything is affirmed utterly absurd and miraculous, it rather the more readily admits of such a fact, upon account of that very circumstance, which ought to destroy all its authority. The passion of *surprise* and *wonder,* arising from miracles, being an agreeable emotion, gives a sensible tendency towards the belief of those events, from which it is derived. And this goes so far, that even those who cannot enjoy this pleasure immediately, nor can believe those miraculous events, of which they are informed, yet love to partake of the satisfaction at second-hand or by rebound, and place a pride and delight in exciting the admiration of others.

With what greediness are the miraculous accounts of travellers received, their descriptions of sea and land monsters, their relations of wonderful adventures, strange men, and uncouth manners? But if the spirit of religion join itself to the love of wonder, there is an end of common sense; and human testimony, in these circumstances, loses all pretensions to authority. A religionist may be an enthusiast, and imagine he sees what has no reality: he may know his narrative to be false, and yet persevere in it, with the best intensions in the world, for the sake of promoting so holy a cause: or even where this delusion has not place, vanity, excited by so strong a temptation, operates on him more powerfully than on the rest of mankind in any other circumstances; and self-interest with equal force. His auditors may not have, and commonly have not, sufficient judgement to canvass his evidence: what judgment they have, they renounce by principle, in these sublime and mysterious subjects: or if they were ever so willing to employ it, passion and a heated imagination disturb the regularity of its operations. Their credulity increases his impudence: and his impudence overpowers their credulity.

Eloquence, when at its highest pitch, leaves little room for reason or reflection; but addressing itself entirely to the fancy or the affections, captivates the willing hearers, and subdues their understanding. Happily, this pitch it seldom attains. But what a Tully or a Demosthenes could scarcely effect over a Roman or Athenian audience, every *Capuchin*, every itinerant or stationary teacher can perform over the generality of mankind, and in a higher degree, by touching such gross and vulgar passions.

The many instances of forged miracles, and prophecies, and supernatural events, which, in all ages, have either been detected by contrary evidence, or which detect themselves by their absurdity, prove sufficiently the strong propensity of mankind to the extraordinary and the marvellous, and ought reasonably to beget a suspicion against all relations of this kind. This is our natural way of thinking, even with regard to the most common and most credible events. For instance: There is no kind of report which rises so easily, and spreads so quickly, especially in country places and provincial towns, as those concerning marriages; insomuch that two young persons of equal condition never see each other twice, but the whole neighborhood immediately join them

together. The pleasure of telling a piece of news so interesting, of propagating it, and of being the first reporters of it, spreads the intelligence. And this is so well known, that no man of sense gives attention to these reports, till he find them confirmed by some greater evidence. Do not the same passions, and others still stronger, incline the generality of mankind to believe and report, with the greatest vehemence and assurance, all religious miracles.

Thirdly. It forms a strong presumption against all supernatural and miraculous relations, that they are observed chiefly to abound among ignorant and barbarous nations; or if a civilized people has ever given admission to any of them, that people will be found to have received them from ignorant and barbarous ancestors, who transmitted them with that inviolable sanction and authority, which always attend received opinions. When we peruse the first histories of all nations, we are apt to imagine ourselves transported into some new world; where the whole frame of nature is disjointed, and every element performs its operations in a different manner, from what it does at present. Battles, revolutions, pestilence, famine and death, are never the effect of those natural causes, which we experience. Prodigies, omens, oracles, judgements, quite obscure the few natural events, that are intermingled with them. But as the former grow thinner every page, in proportion as we advance nearer the enlightened ages, we soon learn, that there is nothing mysterious or supernatural in the case, but that all proceeds from the usual propensity of mankind towards the marvellous, and that, though this inclination may at intervals receive a check from sense and learning, it can never be thoroughly extirpated from human nature.

It is strange, a judicious reader is apt to say, upon the perusal of these wonderful historians, *that such prodigious events never happen in our days.* But it is nothing strange, I hope, that men should lie in all ages. You must surely have seen instances enough of that frailty. You have yourself heard many such marvellous relations started, which, being treated with scorn by all the wise and judicious, have at last been abandoned even by the vulgar. Be assured, that those renowned lies, which have spread the flourished to such a monstrous height, arose from like beginnings; but being sown in a more proper soil, shot up at last into prodigies almost equal to those which they relate. . . .

I may add as a *fourth* reason, which diminishes the authority of prodigies, that there is no testimony for any, even those which have not been expressly detected, that is not opposed by an infinite number of witnesses; so that not only the miracle destroys the credit of testimony, but the testimony destroys itself. To make this the better understood, let us consider, that, in matters of religion, whatever is different is contrary; and that it is impossible the religions of ancient Rome, of Turkey, of Siam, and of China should, all of them, be established on any solid foundation. Every miracle, therefore, pretended to have been wrought in any of these religions (and all of them abound in miracles), as its direct scope is to establish the particular system to which it is attributed; so has it the same force, though more indirectly, to overthrow every other system. In destroying a rival system, it likewise destroys the credit of those miracles, on which that system was established; so that all the prodigies of different religions are to be regarded as contrary facts, and the evidences of these prodigies, whether weak or strong, as opposite to each other. According to this method of reasoning, when we believe any miracle of Mahomet or his successors, we have for our warrant the testimony of a few barbarous Arabians: And on the other hand, we are to regard the authority of Titus Livius, Plutarch, Tacitus, and, in short, of all the authors and witnesses, Grecian, Chinese, and Roman Catholic, who have related any miracle in their particular religion; I say, we are to regard their testimony in the same light as if they had mentioned that Mahometan miracle, and had in express terms contradicted it, with the same certainty as they have for the miracle they relate. This argument may appear over subtile and refined; but is not in reality different from the reasoning of a judge, who supposes, that the credit of two witnesses, maintaining a crime against any one, is destroyed by the testimony of two others, who affirm him to have been two hundred leagues distant, at the same instant when the crime is said to have been committed. . . .

There is also a memorable story related by Cardinal de Retz, which may well deserve our consideration. When that intriguing politician fled into Spain, to avoid the persecution of his enemies, he passed through Saragossa, the capital of Arragon, where he was shown, in the cathedral, a man, who had served seven years as a door-keeper, and was well known to every body in town, that had ever paid his devotions at that church. He had been seen, for so long a time, wanting a leg; but recovered that limb by the rubbing of holy oil upon the stump; and the cardinal assures us that he saw him with two legs. This miracle was vouched by all the canons of the church; and the whole company in town were appealed to for a confirmation of the fact; whom the cardinal found, by their zealous devotion, to be thorough believers of the miracle. Here the relater was also contemporary to the supposed prodigy, of an incredulous and libertine character, as well as of great genius; the miracle of so *singular* a nature as could scarcely admit of a counterfeit, and the witnesses very numerous, and all of them, in a manner, spectators of the fact, to which they gave their testimony. And what adds mightily to the force of the evidence, and may double our surprise on this occasion, is, that the cardinal himself, who relates the story, seems not to give any credit to it, and consequently cannot be suspected of any concurrence in the holy fraud. He considered justly, that it was not requisite, in order to reject a fact of this nature, to be able accurately to disprove the testimony, and to trace its falsehood, through all the circumstances of knavery and credulity which produced it. He knew, that, as this was commonly altogether impossible at any small distance of time and place; so was it extremely difficult, even where one was immediately present by reason of the bigotry, ignorance, cunning, and roguery of a great part of mankind. He therefore concluded, like a just reasoner, that such an evidence carried falsehood upon the very face of it, and that a miracle, supported by any human testimony, was more properly a subject of derision than of argument.

There surely never was a greater number of miracles ascribed to one person, than those, which were lately said to have been wrought in France upon the tomb of Abbe Paris, the famous Jansenist, with whose sanctity the people were so long deluded. The curing of the sick, giving hearing to the deaf, and sight to the blind, were everywhere talked of as the usual effects of that holy sepulchre. But what is more extraordinary; many of the miracles were immediately proved upon the spot, before judges of unquestioned integrity, attested by witnesses of credit and distinction, in a learned age, and on the most eminent theatre that is now in the world. Nor is this all: a relation of them was published and dispersed every where; nor were the *Jesuits*, though a learned body, supported by the civil magistrate, and determined enemies to those opinions, in whose favour the miracles were said to have been wrought, ever able distinctly to refute or detect them. Where shall we find such a number of circumstances, agreeing to the corroboration of one fact? And what have we to oppose to such a cloud of witnesses, but the absolute impossibility or miraculous nature of the events, which they relate? And this surely, in the eyes of all reasonable people, will alone be regarded as a sufficient refutation.

Is the consequence just, because some human testimony has the utmost force and authority in some cases, when it relates the battle of Philippi or Pharsalia for instance; that therefore all kinds of testimony must, in all cases, have equal force and authority? Suppose that the Caesarean and Pompeian factions had, each of them, claimed the victory in these battles, and that the historians of each party had uniformly ascribed the advantage to their own side; how could mankind, at this distance, have been able to determine between them? The contrariety is equally strong between the miracles related by Herodotus or Plutarch, and those delivered by Mariana, Bede, or any monkish historian.

The wise lend a very academic faith to every report which favours the passion of the reporter; whether it magnifies his country, his family, or himself, or in any other way strikes in with his natural inclinations and propensities. But what greater temptation than to appear a missionary, a prophet, an ambassador from heaven? Who would not encounter many dangers and difficulties, in order to attain so sublime a character? Or if, by the help of vanity and a heated imagination, a man has first made a convert of himself, and entered seriously into the delusion; who ever scruples to make use of pious frauds, in support of so holy and meritorious a cause?

The smallest spark may here kindle into the greatest flame; because the materials are always prepared for it. The *avidum genus auricularum*, the gazing populace, receive greedily, without examination, whatever sooths superstition, and promotes wonder.

How many stories of this nature have, in all ages, been detected and exploded in their infancy? How many more have been celebrated for a time, and have afterwards sunk into neglect and oblivion? Where such reports, therefore, fly about, the solution of the phenomenon is obvious; and we judge in conformity to regular experience and observation, when we account for it by the known and natural principles of credulity and delusion. And shall we, rather than have a recourse to so natural a solution, allow of a miraculous violation of the most established laws of nature?

I need not mention the difficulty of detecting a falsehood in any private or even public history, at the place, where it is said to happen; much more when the scene is removed to ever so small a distance. Even a court of judicature, with all the authority, accuracy, and judgement, which they can employ, find themselves often at a loss to distinguish between truth and falsehood in the most recent actions. But the matter never comes to any issue, if trusted to the common method of altercations and debate and flying rumours; especially when men's passions have taken part on either side.

In the infancy of new religions, the wise and learned commonly esteem the matter too inconsiderable to deserve their attention or regard. And when afterwards they would willingly detect the cheat, in order to undeceive the deluded multitude, the season is now past, and the records and witnesses, which might clear up the matter, have perished beyond recovery.

No means of detection remain, but those which must be drawn from the very testimony itself of the reporters: and these, though always sufficient with the judicious and knowing, are commonly too fine to fall under the comprehension of the vulgar.

Upon the whole, then, it appears, that no testimony for any kind of miracle has ever amounted to a probability, much less to a proof; and that, even supposing it amounted to a proof, it would be opposed by another proof; derived from the very nature of the fact, which it would endeavour to establish. It is experience only, which gives authority to human testimony; and it is the same experience, which assures us of the laws of nature. When, therefore, these two kinds of experience are contrary, we have nothing to do but subtract the one from the other, and embrace an opinion, either on one side or the other, with that assurance which arises from the remainder. But according to the principle here explained, this subtraction, with regard to all popular religions, amounts to an entire annihilation; and therefore we may establish it as a maxim, that no human testimony can have such force as to prove a miracle, and make it a just foundation for any such system of religion.

I beg the limitations here made may be remarked, when I say, that a miracle can never be proved, so as to be the foundation of a system of religion. For I own, that otherwise, there may possibly be miracles, or violations of the usual course of nature, of such a kind as to admit of proof from human testimony; though, perhaps, it will be impossible to find any such in all the records of history. Thus, suppose, all authors, in all languages, agree, that, from the first of January 1600, there was a total darkness over the whole earth for eight days: suppose that the tradition of this extraordinary event is still strong and lively among the people: that all travellers, who return from foreign countries, bring us accounts of the same tradition, without the least variation or contradiction: it is evident, that our present philosophers, instead of doubting the fact, ought to receive it as certain, and ought to search for the causes whence it might be derived. The decay, corruption, and dissolution of nature, is an event rendered probable by so many analogies, that any phenomenon, which seems to have a tendency towards that catastrophe, comes within the reach of human testimony, if that testimony be very extensive and uniform.

But suppose, that all the historians who treat of England, should agree, that, on the first of January 1600, Queen Elizabeth died; that both before and after her death she was seen by her physicians and the whole court, as is usual with persons of her rank; that her successor was acknowledged and proclaimed by the parliament; and that, after being interred a month, she again appeared, resumed the throne, and governed England for three years: I must confess that I should be surprised at the concurrence of so many odd circumstances, but should not have the least inclination to believe so miraculous an event. I should not doubt of her pretended death, and of those other public circumstances that followed it: I should only assert it to have been pretended, and that it neither was, nor possibly could be real. You would in vain object to me the difficulty, and almost impossibility of deceiving the world in an affair of such consequence; the wisdom and solid judgement of that renowned queen; with the little or no advantage which she could reap from so poor an artifice: All this might astonish me; but I would still reply, that the knavery and folly of men are such common phenomena, that I should rather believe the most extraordinary events to arise from their concurrence, than admit of so signal a violation of the laws of nature.

But should this miracle be ascribed to any new system of religion; men, in all ages, have been so much imposed on by ridiculous stories of that kind, that this very circumstance would be a full proof of a cheat, and sufficient, with all men of sense, not only to make them reject the fact, but even reject it without farther examination. Though the Being to whom the miracle is ascribed, be, in this case, Almighty, it does not, upon that account, become a whit more probable; since it is impossible for us to know the attributes or actions of such a Being, otherwise than from the experience which we have of his productions, in the usual course of nature. This still reduces us to past observation, and obliges us to compare the instances of the violation of truth in the testimony of men, with those of the violation of the laws of nature by miracles, in order to judge which of them is most likely and probable. As the violations of truth are more common in the testimony concerning religious miracles, than in that concerning any other matter of fact; this must diminish very much the authority of the former testimony, and make us form a general resolution, never to lend any attention to it, with whatever specious pretence it may be covered.

Lord Bacon seems to have embraced the same principles of reasoning. 'We ought,' says he, 'to make a collection or particular history of all monsters and prodigious births or productions, and in a word of every thing new, rare, and extraordinary in nature. But this must be done with the most severe scrutiny, lest we depart from truth. Above all, every relation must be considered as suspicious, which depends in any degree upon religion, as the prodigies of Livy: And no less so, every thing that is to be found in the writers of natural magic or alchemy, or such authors, who seem, all of them, to have an unconquerable appetite for falsehood and fable.'

I am the better pleased with the method of reasoning here delivered, as I think it may serve to confound those dangerous friends or disguised enemies to the *Christian Religion*, who have undertaken to defend it by the principles of human reason. Our most holy religion is founded on *Faith*, not on reason; and it is a sure method of exposing it to put it to such a trial as it is, by no means, fitted to endure. To make this more evident, let us examine those miracles, related in scripture; and not to lose ourselves in too wide a field, let us confine ourselves to such as we find in the *Pentateuch*, whichwe shall examine, according to the principles of those pretended Christians, not as the word or testimony of God himself, but as the production of a mere human writer and historian. Here then we are first to consider a book, presented to us by a barbarous and ignorant people, written in an age when they were still more barbarous, and in all probability long after the facts which it relates, corroborated by no concurring testimony, and

resembling those fabulous accounts, which every nation gives of its origin. Upon reading this book, we find it full of prodigies and miracles. It gives an account of a state of the world and of human nature entirely different from the present: Of our fall from that state: Of the age of man, extended to near a thousand years: Of the destruction of the world by a deluge: Of the arbitrary choice of one people, as the favorites of heaven; and that people the countrymen of the author: Of their deliverance from bondage by prodigies the most astonishing imaginable: I desire any one to lay his hand upon his heart, and after a serious consideration declare, whether he thinks that the falsehood of such a book, supported by such a testimony, would be more extraordinary and miraculous than all the miracles it relates; which is, however, necessary to make it be received, according to the measures of probability above established.

What we have said of miracles may be applied, without any variation, to prophecies; and indeed, all prophecies are real miracles, and as such only, can be admitted as proofs of any revelation. If it did not exceed the capacity of human nature to foretell future events, it would be absurd to employ any prophecy as an argument for a divine mission or authority from heaven. So that, upon the whole, we may conclude, that the *Christian Religion* not only was at first attended with miracles, but even at this day cannot be believed by any reasonable person without one. Mere reason is insufficient to convince us of its veracity: And whoever is moved by *Faith* to assent to it, is conscious of a continued miracle in his own person, which subverts all the principles of his understanding, and gives him a determination to believe what is most contrary to custom and experience.

NOTE

1. Sometimes an event may not, *in itself*, seem to be contrary to the laws of nature, and yet, if it were real, it might, by reason of some circumstances, be denominated a miracle; because, in *fact* it is contrary to these laws. Thus if a person, claiming a divine authority, should command a sick person to be well, a healthful man to fall down dead, the

clouds to pour rain, the winds to blow, in short, should order many natural events, which immediately follow upon his command; these might justly be esteemed miracles, because they are really, in this case, contrary to the laws of nature. For if any suspicion remain, that the event and command concurred by accident, there is no miracle and no transgression of the laws of nature. If this suspicion be removed, there is evidently a miracle, and a transgression of these laws; because nothing can be more contrary to nature than that the voice or command of a man should have such an influence. A miracle may be accurately defined, a *transgression of a law of nature by a particular volition of the Deity, or by the interposition of some invisible agent*. A miracle may either be discoverable by men or not. This alters not its nature and essence. The raising of a house or ship into the air is a visible miracle. The raising of a feather, when the wind wants ever so little of a force requisite for that purpose, is as real a miracle, though not so sensible with regard to us.

V.2   Of 'Of Miracles'

PETER VAN INWAGEN

Peter van Inwagen is professor of philosophy at the University of Notre Dame and is one of the leading figures in contemporary metaphysics and philosophy of religion. In this article, he attacks Hume's argument against miracles. Hume's argument rests in part on the idea that miracles are the sorts of things that run significantly contrary to our experience. But, according to van Inwagen, there is no clear sense in which experience rules out events of any particular sort. Failing to find any other sense of 'contrary to experience' that could drive Hume's argument, van Inwagen concludes that the argument is a failure.

In the first and briefer part of this essay, my concerns are ontological. I shall explain what a miracle *is* (or would be if there were any). In the second part, my concerns are epistemological: I shall discuss and attempt to refute Hume's argument for the conclusion that it is unreasonable to believe any historical report that would count as a report of a miracle.

THE ONTOLOGY OF MIRACLES

The account of "miracles" that I shall present here is a summary of the account I presented in "The Place of Chance in a World Sustained by God."[1] (It is, I believe, entirely consistent with Hume's "official" definition of 'miracle': "a transgression of a law of nature by a particular volition of the Deity, or by the interposition of some invisible agent." And, I believe, it will not weaken Hume's argument for the conclusion that it would be unreasonable to accept any report of an alleged "miracle" if, in evaluating his argument, we understand the word in the sense I supply in the present section.)

Let us suppose that the physical world is made up of certain fundamental building blocks or units, certain tiny physical things without proper parts. I shall call them elementary particles. Elementary particles are sorted into kinds by their causal powers (e.g., rest mass and charge). It will simplify my account of miracles if I make the assumption (false, of course, at least in our present state of knowledge) that there is only one type of elementary particle. Each particle is continuously sustained in existence by God: At each instant, he supplies it with existence and the causal powers it then has. The motions over the interval t_1–t_2 of the particles that compose the world are determined (insofar as they are determined) entirely by their distribution at t_1 and the causal powers they have at each instant in t_1–t_2. (Here we make a second simplifying assumption: that the propagation of causal influence is instantaneous.)

God always, *or almost always,* supplies each particle with the same causal powers. But he may, *very rarely,* supply *just a few* particles—"just a few" in comparison with the number of all the particles there are—with different causal powers from the powers they normally have. If he momentarily supplies some of the particles in a certain small region of space with powers different from their normal powers, the particles in that region will follow trajectories different from the trajectories they would have followed if he had continued to supply them with their normal powers. Here is a preliminary definition of 'miracle': The early stages of any such "divergence" constitute a miracle. (The later stages of a divergence will be classified as "consequences of a miracle" and not "parts of a miracle.")

Now a qualification and refinement of this definition. A proposition will be called a law of nature in a possible world x if it is a contingent proposition that is true in every world y in which particles *always* have the causal powers that they *always or almost always* have in x. If some particles in the world x do sometimes have "unusual" powers, some of the propositions that are laws in x may be false propositions in x. (If x is a deterministic world, this must be so.) If a proposition p is both a law of nature in x and false in x, it will be said to be violated in x; it will be violated by the behavior of those particles that (owing to their or their neighbors' unusual causal powers) follow trajectories inconsistent with the truth of p.

If a world is indeterministic, some events that are miracles according to our preliminary definition may not involve violations of laws. If the laws of a world allow A to be followed either by B or by C, and if God temporarily changes the causal powers of certain particles in such a way as to determine that A be followed by B, the consequent occurrence of B will be a miracle by our preliminary definition but will not be a violation of the laws of the world in which it occurs. In "The Place of Chance in a World Sustained by God," my topic was Providence, and it suited my purposes to have a definition of 'miracle' that had this feature. In the present essay, however, I wish to conform my usage (more or less) to Hume's. I shall, therefore, understand 'miracle' to imply 'violation of the laws of nature.' God performs a miracle, then, if he momentarily supplies certain particles with unusual causal powers and the consequent divergence of the trajectories of those (and no doubt some other) particles from the courses they would have followed is a violation of the laws of nature. (Of course, a violation of one law will in most cases be a violation of many, since if two propositions are laws, so is their conjunction.) The miracle is the early stages of the divergence.

HUME'S ARGUMENT

In this section, I shall present and attempt to refute the central argument of "Of Miracles."[2] More exactly, the argument I shall present and attempt to refute is my own reconstruction of the central argument of "Of Miracles." I believe that there are, in Hume's presentation of his argument, certain infelicities that arise from his imprecise use of terminology, and my reconstruction is designed to remove them. To subject one's reconstruction of a philosopher's argument to criticisms of one's own devising is a somewhat dubious procedure, and it is dubious on two grounds: First, one's "improvements" may be ones that the author of the original argument would reject, and, worse, they may introduce defects into the argument that were not present in the original. I think, however, that the points I shall make against the reconstructed argument would apply to the original even if Hume would have emphatically rejected my modifications of his argument and even if these modifications introduced errors that were not present in the original.

What, exactly, is the conclusion of the central argument of "Of Miracles"? It is a commonplace that Hume's conclusion is not ontological: He does not claim to show that there are no miracles. His conclusion is epistemological. But it is not that one should not believe that there are miracles. It is not so general as that. It has to do with the attitude one should take toward any (supposed, putative) report of a miracle one might encounter. It is something like this: If one hears a report of a miracle, one should not believe it (or one should believe it only in very special circumstances, circumstances so special that no one has in fact ever been in them). But this formulation of Hume's conclusion raises two important questions. First, what counts as a "report of a miracle"? Secondly, does "one should not believe it" mean "one should reject it" or "one should refrain from accepting it"—or perhaps some third thing?

Let us say that a report of a miracle (or a miracle-report) is any narrative, presented as historical or factual, such that (a) it does not follow logically from that narrative that a miracle has occurred, and (b) if the narrative were true, the only reasonable conclusion would be that at least one of the events it recounted was a miracle.[3] The following story

> Jill was about to cross Sixth Avenue in New York when, all in an instant, she was miraculously translated to Sydney,

does not satisfy the terms of this definition, since it follows logically from the story that a miracle has occurred.[4] Here, by way of contrast, are two stories that—whatever other features they may have—do not logically entail that a miracle has occurred:

> Jill was about to cross Sixth Avenue in New York when, without any sensation of motion, she suddenly found herself in Sydney.[5]

> And when he got into the boat his disciples followed him. And behold there arose a great storm on the sea, so that the boat was being swamped by the waves; but he was asleep. And they went and woke him, saying, "Save us, Lord, for we are perishing." And he said to them, "Why are you afraid, O men of little faith?" Then he rose and he rebuked the wind and the sea, and there was a great calm. And the men marveled, saying, "What manner of man is this that even the wind and the wave obey him?" (Matt. 8:23–27).[6]

Whether either of these two stories satisfies condition (b) in our definition of 'miracle-report'—and thereby qualifies as a miracle-report—is an epistemological question: Given that the story was true, would the only reasonable conclusion be that one of the events recounted in the story was a miracle?[7] It would be possible to argue, some no doubt have argued, that one should never believe of any story (unless it logically entails the occurrence of a miracle) that if that story is true, some of the events it recounts were miracles. One should rather believe (the argument might continue) that if the story is true, there is *some* explanation of the events it relates that is consistent with the laws of nature and this explanation is the correct explanation. (It is not hard to provide gestures at such explanations. Take the story of the stilling of the storm. This story could be embedded in a logically consistent science fiction novel according to which Christianity was "founded" by extraterrestrial beings as an adjunct to a project involving the manipulation of human history; it might be that, in the novel, all the "miracles" related in the New Testament actually happened—at least as far as appearances went—but were the products of an advanced technology rather than true miracles.)

I shall not attempt to answer the (intrinsically very interesting) question whether there in fact are any stories that satisfy the terms of the above definition of 'miracle-report,' for the cogency of Hume's argument does not depend on what the right answer to this question is. His conclusion is that one should react in a certain way to any miracle-report one encounters, and his reasoning can be evaluated independently of the question whether anyone ever does encounter any miracle-reports.

But what *does* Hume say about how one should react to a miracle-report? Is his position simply that one should *not* believe the report, or is it that one should *disbelieve* (not believe *and* believe the denial of) the report—or is it some third thing? I do not think that Hume is clear or entirely consistent about the matter, but I believe that the best way to state his conclusion is this: One should *dismiss* any miracle-report one encounters. The concept of dismissal may be spelled out as follows: One dismisses a report—an allegedly historical narrative—if one either disbelieves it or (does not believe it and) assigns it a very low probability.[8] (How low? Well, let's say very low—a probability of the sort that we describe in ordinary speech by phrases like 'of insignificant probability' and 'no real possibility.')

We shall need one more definition before we turn to Hume's argument for this conclusion. Let us say that a proposition is a *contravention of one's experience* (for short, a contravention) if the truth of that proposition is contrary to one's experience.[9] ("Contravention"—this may be true of "miracle-report" as well—is obviously a person-and-time-relative concept: A proposition may be a contravention of one person's experience and not of another's—or a proposition may be a contravention of a person's experience at one time and not at another. I shall, however, generally speak of contraventions and miracle-reports *sans phrase* and leave it to the reader to fill in the necessary qualifications about person-and-time relativity. And I shall speak of various propositions as "contrary to experience" without bothering to specify whose experience they are contrary to.) Contraventions, moreover, come in "sizes": p is a larger or greater contravention than q if, although q is contrary to experience, p is "even more contrary to experience" than q.[10] (At this point it should be evident, if it was not already, that I am presenting a reconstruction of Hume's argument, for Hume speaks of "greater" and "lesser" *miracles,* and he employs no term that corresponds to my "contravention.") If I tell my friends that on a recent trip from Boston to Los Angeles my 1973 Cadillac averaged sixty miles to the gallon, what I tell them will no doubt be a contravention. If Calvin tells his mother that the jammy handprints on the new sofa were put there not by himself but by an evil Calvin doppelgänger constructed by beings from Arcturus, that will also be a contravention, and perhaps there is some intuitive sense in which it is a larger contravention than the one I have asserted. An *historical narrative* will be called a contravention if its propositional content is a contravention.

I will now present Hume's argument, or my reconstruction of it. The argument has three premises, two epistemological premises and one "historical" premise. The first epistemological premise is:

E1. Any miracle-report must necessarily be a contravention and, in fact, a very *large* contravention.[11] (If a story is a miracle-report for some audience, it will also be a contravention for that audience. If a story is not a contravention, it will not qualify as a miracle-report. Suppose, for example, that we hear the story of Jill's sudden translation from New York to Sydney. It may or may not be reasonable for us to classify this as a miracle-report, but if the proposition that people sometimes find themselves suddenly on the other side of the earth is not contrary to experience, a necessary condition for classifying the story as a miracle-report will be absent. There are, moreover, stories that are contraventions but not large enough contraventions to qualify as miracle-reports. If I am told that Sally, who was hitherto entirely ignorant of French, spoke perfect French after spending three months in France, that story would be a contravention but no doubt not one that is large enough to qualify as a miracle-report. And how large a contravention must a miracle report be? One way to answer this question would be to specify some story that is a large enough contravention by just about anyone's reckoning to be a miracle-report and say, "At least as large as that." I think that the following story will do for this purpose: Let us suppose that we have heard a report of a shaman in Peru who has, it is alleged, restored several incontestably long-dead people to life. Suppose we are willing to agree that this story is "more contrary to experience" than the story of Sally's remarkably quick mastery of French. Then, according to the criterion I have proposed, the story of Sally is not a large enough contravention to be a miracle-report.

We should note that it does not follow from the proposed criterion that just any story that is as large a contravention as the "shaman" story *is* a miracle-report. Indeed, it does not follow from anything we have said that the "shaman" story itself is a miracle-report. And if someone maintained that Calvin's story of the origin of the jammy handprints was as large a contravention as the "shaman" story, despite the fact that Calvin's story was not a miracle-report and the "shaman" story was, that person would have said nothing inconsistent with the proposed criterion. Let us say that any contravention that is at least as large as the "shaman" story is *very large*.)

The second epistemological premise requires a little stage-setting. Let us say that two narratives are (historically) independent if neither is derived from the other. Two narratives will be said to support each other if they are independent and "tell the same story"—(purport to) describe events that are the same or at least very similar. ("Similarity" is to include the elements "cast of characters" and "place and time.") Hume's second epistemological premise is

E2. One should dismiss any very large contravention one encounters unless one knows that one of the following two conditions holds:

(a) if the very large contravention is unhistorical—if it is not a reasonably accurate description of events that actually happened—its existence is itself a contravention and a larger contravention than its truth would be

(b) it is one of two or more mutually supporting narratives such that if they are unhistorical, their (collective) existence is a contravention and a larger contravention than their truth (i.e., the truth of their common propositional content) would be.

(Suppose that X tells me that Jimmy Carter is a tool of malign extraterrestrial beings. And suppose no one else has told me that. X's statement is a very large contravention[12] and should therefore be dismissed—unless X's telling me falsely that Carter is a tool of malign extraterrestrial beings is a contravention and a larger contravention than his being a tool of malign extraterrestrial beings would be. Or suppose that shortly after X has told me that Carter is a tool of malign extraterrestrial beings, Y tells me the same thing. And suppose I am somehow satisfied that X's statement and Y's statement are historically independent. I should dismiss what they have told me—unless the existence of two independent

false allegations that Carter is a tool of malign extraterrestrial beings is a contravention and a larger contravention than his being a tool of malign extraterrestrial beings would be.)

Here, finally, is Hume's "historical" premise:

H. Although it may be possible to imagine a miracle-report that satisfies one or the other of the conditions set out in E2, no miracle-report known to history satisfies either; indeed, all known narratives that anyone might be inclined to classify as miracle-reports (such as the Gospel story of the stilling of the storm) fall far short of satisfying either of them.

I will make a few remarks about E2 and H and then proceed to argue against E1. I shall, in discussing Hume's views, write as if he were familiar with the vocabulary and distinctions of the present essay. I believe that this anachronism could be eliminated from my argument, although only at the cost of a great deal of circumlocution.

Hume wrote in an era when photography and sound recordings had not yet been invented—in an era when almost the only evidence as to what had occurred in the past was human testimony. No doubt if he were writing today, he would want to emend E2 to take account of "nontestimonial" evidence about the past. But any such emendation of E2 would affect no point of principle, and the question of its proper formulation need not detain us.

It is evident that Hume believed that clause (a) in E2 could not possibly be satisfied, for (such is human credulity and epistemic frailty) the proposition that a given person has made a false statement about the past could not possibly be a "very large" contravention. Hume's position was, therefore, that the only possibility of a case in which a very large contravention should not be dismissed would be of this sort: It was one of two or more historically independent contraventions with essentially the same propositional content. It is, however, unclear whether Hume thought that even a very large number of mutually supporting false statements about the past could constitute a "very large" contravention. In introducing the important "eight-day darkness" example ("Thus, suppose, all authors, in all languages, agree, that, from the first of January 1600, there was a total darkness over the whole earth for eight days. . . . "), he says, "For I own, that otherwise [i.e., if we imagine testimony much more extensive and uniform than the testimony to the supposed miracles foundational to Christianity and its rivals], there may possibly be miracles, or violations of the usual course of nature, of such a kind as to admit of proof from human testimony, though, perhaps, it will be impossible to find any such in all the records of history." Although Hume uses the word 'miracle' here, he goes on to say that although philosophers of his own day, if they had available to them the testimony he imagines, ought to grant the historicity of the eight-day darkness (in fact, they should "receive it as certain"), they should proceed to "search for the causes whence it might be derived"—and hence they should presumably *not* regard the darkness as a miracle as the term is "accurately defined" ("A transgression of a law of nature by a particular volition of the Deity, or by the interposition of some invisible agent") but only in the loose and much weaker sense he has supplied: as a violation of the usual course of nature. He then argues that various (unspecified) analogies with known events suggest that a universal eight-day darkness "comes within the reach of human testimony, if that testimony be very extensive and uniform." And this statement implies that other imaginable events might not come within the reach of any testimony, however extensive and uniform. This argument is immediately followed by an example of such an imaginable event: the death and "resurrection" of Elizabeth I. It seems likely, therefore, that Hume would maintain that no imaginable human testimony could be such that its falsity would be what we are calling a very large contravention. And from this and our two epistemological premises, it follows that any imaginable miracle-report should be dismissed.

Even if I have not interpreted Hume correctly, however, even if, in his view, there are imaginable miracle-reports that should not be *dismissed*, it does not follow from this that any imaginable miracle-report should be *accepted*. (I do not believe that the story of King Alfred and the cakes is false—that is, I do not assent to the proposition that the story of King Alfred and the cakes is false. And I do not think that the probability of this story's being true is so low as to be insignificant. I therefore do not *dismiss* the story of Alfred and the cakes. But I certainly do not assent to the proposition that the story is *true*—and, in fact, I think it's very unlikely to be true.) And I think that it would certainly be Hume's position that none should be: Whether or not every imaginable miracle-report should be dismissed, no imaginable miracle-report should be accepted. No imaginable miracle-report should be accepted because a miracle-report, no matter what testimony might support it, is a very large contravention, and no testimonial evidence in favor of a very large contravention could be so good as to make it worthy of belief—even if it were possible for there to be testimonial evidence good enough to lead the judicious reasoner not to dismiss it. (In the most favorable possible case, there would be, as Hume says, "a mutual destruction of arguments.") And, of course, if we leave the realm of the merely imaginable and turn to the actual and historical, it is clear—this is the import of our "historical" premise—that Hume believes that all actual miracle-reports should be dismissed.[13]

Is Hume's argument, as I have reconstructed it, cogent? I think not. My defense of this judgment begins with an examination of E1, the premise that any miracle-report must be a very large contravention. That is, for any story about the past one might hear, one should refuse to make the following judgment about it:

> If that story is true, then some of the events it relates involve violations of the laws of nature,

unless one is also willing to make the following judgment:

> That story is contrary to my experience—and *as* contrary to my experience as the "shaman" story.

In order to evaluate this premise, we must turn to a question we have so far glossed over. What is it for a story to be "contrary to one's experience"? Hume generally writes as if the following were true: A story is contrary to one's experience if that story involves something's having the property F and the property G and one has observed many things having the property F and has observed that all of them had the complement of G. For example, on this account, a story about a man's returning from the dead is contrary to my experience owing simply to the fact that I have known of a very large number of people who have died and all of them have the property "not having returned from the dead." But this account of what it is for a story to be contrary to one's experience is useless for Hume's purposes, since it will classify far too many stories as contrary to one's experience. Suppose for example, that I know of many visits that Tom has made to his mother over the past ten years; it is all but inevitable that if I hear a detailed account of his latest visit to her, this account will ascribe to this visit some property that all of the others lacked. And this will be true even if we do not "count" the *date* of the latest visit as a relevant property. It may, for example, be that the story I have been told of his latest visit includes the information that he arrived on her doorstep at 3:21 P.M. and that the comprehensive diary I have for some reason kept of his earlier visits reveals that on all the other occasions on which he has visited her he arrived at some other time. No doubt we could play a lengthy game of "counterexample and revision" with the above account of what it is for a story to be contrary to experience. But I do not know of any way of "improving" this account that will enable it to avoid consequences like the following: The first reports of someone's making a solo flight across the Atlantic or running a four-minute mile or reaching the summit of Mount Everest were contrary to the experience of those who heard them.

But might Hume not reply that these consequences are acceptable? Might he not argue that such reports would indeed be a *bit* contrary to the experience of those who heard them? Might he not go on to say, "But it would be *more* contrary to the experience of those who heard them if all the reports of these events were false, and that is why it was proper for those who heard the reports to believe them"? Perhaps so. But how, then, are we to understand the relevant notion of *degree* of contrariety? If I hear on Monday that Lindbergh has flown across the Atlantic without a copilot and on

Tuesday that a rival has flown across the Atlantic without an aircraft, on what basis am I to judge that the second story is more contrary to my experience (is a larger contravention) than the first? My experience tells me that all previous transatlantic flights have involved an aircraft of some sort, but it also tells me that all previous transatlantic flights have involved two or more pilots. There simply do not seem to be any materials in the "property-complement" account of a story's being contrary to experience from which to construct an account of the concept of one story's being "more contrary to experience" than another is.

Let us consider an actual example (at least I believe it to be actual, although, unfortunately, I no longer remember where I heard or read it) of someone's applying the "property-complement" account of this concept. Thomas Jefferson was once told that in a museum in Cambridge (Massachusetts) there was exhibited a stone that had fallen from the sky. Jefferson declined to believe this story on the ground that although he had never known a stone to fall from the sky, he had often known a Yankee parson—the staff of Harvard College in those days comprised Congregational ministers—to prevaricate. (He had observed the sky on many occasions, and on each of those occasions, it had the property "not being the source of a falling stone"; he had observed many Yankee parsons making assertions, and on many of these occasions, the assertions had the property "being a lie." He concluded that stones falling from the sky were contrary to his experience and lying Yankee parsons were not.) Now even if Jefferson's statement about his experience of the New England clergy was something of an exaggeration, he was no doubt telling the truth when he said he had never known a stone to fall from the sky. But there were many, many things he had "never known" that he wouldn't have been disinclined to believe reports of, even reports from Yankee parsons. If he thought the story unlikely on the basis of his experience, it cannot have been simply because such a thing had never happened in his experience. If the story was indeed "contrary to his experience," it cannot have been simply because events of the type related in the story were not included in the totality of his experience to date. This observation might lead us to conclude that the "property-complement" account of an event's being contrary to experience must be replaced by some other account.

Was there *any* sense in which the story Jefferson was told was contrary to his experience? Well, suppose that Jefferson had fallen asleep like Rip van Winkle and had slept till the existence and nature of meteors was common knowledge. Suppose that, on awakening, he was given an encyclopedia article on the subject to read and had afterward received the testimony of several eminent (Virginian) astronomers that what the article said was true. Would he have been in a position to complain that his eighteenth-century experience was misleading—that it had somehow "told" him that stones never fell from the sky when stones in fact sometimes *do* fall from the sky? Certainly not. No doubt Descartes was wrong in holding that the testimony of experience was never false, but it does not seem to have testified falsely to Jefferson on this point. Experience may have testified to some persons at some points in history that the earth is at the center of the universe or that maggots are spontaneously generated in dung, but it had never testified to anyone that stones do not fall from the sky (or, for most people, that they do—not "directly," not otherwise than via the testimony of other people; for most people, "direct" experience has had nothing to say about whether stones fall from the sky). Although experience may have testified that if stones ever fall from the sky, their doing so is a very uncommon event, it has not testified that stones never fall from the sky.

It is very hard indeed to find a sense in which experience testifies in any direct or immediate sense that events of some sort never happen—or in which stories of events of some sort are contrary to experience. If direct, immediate experience testifies to anything (truly or falsely) its testimony seems to be essentially "positive": It testifies that events of certain sorts *do* happen. One might of course point out that it is *reasonable* to *believe* of events of various sorts that events of those sorts never happen, and that the

reasonableness of such beliefs must ultimately be based on experience. Having made this observation, one might propose an account of what it is for a story to be "contrary to experience" that is based on what it is reasonable to believe. It would go something like this: A story is contrary to one's experience if that story involves the occurrence of events of sorts such that given one's experience at the time one hears the story, it is reasonable for one to believe that events of those sorts never happen—or perhaps that it is highly improbable that such events ever happen (or, more simply, a story is contrary to one's experience if, given one's experience at the time one hears the story, it is reasonable for one to believe that the story is false or is highly improbable). And one might go on to spell out the concept "more contrary to one's experience" in terms of its being more unreasonable to believe one proposition than another. (One might say that *p* is more contrary to one's experience than *q* just in the case that although what it is reasonable to believe, on the basis of one's experience, is that *p* and *q* are both false, one should also believe that if one or the other of them is, after all, true, it is *q*. Thus, or so I would judge, Calvin's story about the handprints on the sofa is "more contrary to experience" than my story about the mileage my Cadillac got, and the "shaman" story is "more contrary to experience" than the story of Sally's quick mastery of French.)

I think, however, that it is reasonably clear that this is not what Hume means by "contrary to experience" and "more contrary to experience." Whatever he means by these phrases and the related phrases he uses, he means something much more concrete, much more immediate than this. For Hume, if one judges that a story of a man's rising from the dead is "contrary to one's experience," the experience that the story is contrary to is one's experience of the dead's staying dead, not the totality of one's experience of the world to date. But at least in my view, what it is now *reasonable for me to believe* about men's rising from the dead must be based on pretty nearly the whole of my experience to date (e.g., those experiences that are relevant to the truth or falsity of the principles of thermodynamics and the truth or falsity of judgments about the historical reliability of the New Testament and the authority of the Church). In any case, if this is what "contrary to experience" and "more contrary to experience" mean, there seems to me to be no very compelling reason for anyone to accept E1.

It may be reasonable to believe that if the Matthean story of the stilling of the storm is historical, then a miracle, a violation of the laws of nature, occurred. I certainly think that this would be the reasonable conclusion to draw from the truth of the story. But I do not think that this story is, by the terms of the definition we are considering, at least as contrary to experience as the "shaman" story is. In fact, I think that the Matthean story is *true* (and, of course, I think I am being reasonable in thinking that it is true), and I think that anyone who heard and believed the "shaman" story and whose experience of the world was otherwise like mine would be very unreasonable indeed. I am not trying to convince you, the reader, that these epistemological judgments are correct. I am saying only that nowhere in "Of Miracles" do I find any reason to suppose they are not correct. Hume's argument, after all, is of this general form: *Because* certain propositions are contrary to experience—*very* contrary to experience—it is unreasonable to accept them. And it is, to say the least, very hard to see how an argument of this form could be cogent if 'contrary to experience' *means* 'unreasonable to believe.'

I can think of no other plausible sense that can be given to the phrase 'contrary to experience.' I conclude, provisionally, that Hume's argument is a failure, owing to the fact that there is no sense that can be given to 'contrary to experience' such that E1 is compelling when 'contrary to experience' is interpreted in that sense. It should be noted that I do not claim to have shown that anyone is ever justified in believing a miracle-report. Indeed, I do not even claim to have addressed this question. It is perfectly consistent with everything I have said to suppose that anyone who believed any story that could conceivably count as a miracle-report (such as the Matthean story of the stilling of the storm) would be wholly unreasonable. I claim to have shown only that the argument of "Of Miracles" (as I understand the argument) does not establish either this conclusion or any other negative conclusion about the reasonableness of accepting miracle-reports.

NOTES

1. Included in Thomas V. Morris, ed., *Divine and Human Action: Essays in the Metaphysics of Theism* (Ithaca, N.Y.: Cornell University Press, 1988), pp. 211–235. Reprinted in Peter van Inwagen, *God, Knowledge, and Mystery: Essays in Philosophical Theology* (Ithaca, N.Y.: Cornell University Press, 1995), pp. 42–65.

2. "Of Miracles" is section X of *An Enquiry Concerning Human Understanding*. There are numerous editions of the *Enquiry*. I have used the Open Court edition (La Salle, Ill.: 1907 and 1966), which, according to the publisher's preface is "an unannotated reprint . . . made from the second volume of the posthumous edition of 1777." No editor is given on the title page, but the preface notes that the editing was done by one Thomas J. McCormack. Because there are numerous editions of the *Enquiry* (and, of course, "Of Miracles" appears in whole or in part in scores of anthologies) and because "Of Miracles" is very short, I have not provided page citations for the very few direct quotations I have made.

3. The idea behind (b) is as follows. If two people consider the narrative, and one of them says, "If that story is true, at least one of the events it recounts was a miracle," and the other says, "Even if that story is true in every detail, there is some purely natural explanation for every event it recounts," the first speaker is being reasonable and the second unreasonable. Note that if the second speaker is indeed unreasonable, he nevertheless does not contradict himself, since by (a) it does not follow logically from the story that a miracle has occurred.

4. The purpose of clause (a) of the definition is to rule out of consideration as "miracle-reports" narratives that would satisfy clause (b) *only* because the narrative logically entailed that a miracle had occurred. Here are two examples of such narratives: "Last week Sally witnessed a miracle" and "A feather rose when the resultant of all the natural forces acting on it fell short by an insensible amount of the force requisite for that purpose."

5. It does not follow from our definition of 'miracle-report' that if a miracle-report is true, the people

whose deeds and experiences are related in that report should believe that they have witnessed or been involved in a miracle. Consider the story of Jill's translation to Sydney (the second version, the version in which the translation is not described as miraculous). Suppose that we who hear the story should conclude that if the story is true, it recounts a miracle. (It follows from this supposition that the story is a miracle-report.) And suppose that the story *is* true. It does not follow that *Jill* should conclude from her experience that a miracle has happened. We know that if the story is true, Jill was translated instantaneously to Sydney. But it is not evident that Jill knows (or that she will presently come to know) that she has been translated instantaneously to Sydney—or even that it would be reasonable for her to believe that she has been. Perhaps she should believe that she is still in New York but dreaming or mad or that she was never in New York in the first place.

6. To continue the theme of the previous note: It may or may not be true that we should believe that if the events related in this story really happened, at least one of them was a miracle. But if this is what we should believe, it does not follow that if these events really happened, those who witnessed them should have regarded at least one of them as a miracle. For one thing, it is extremely doubtful whether anyone in the first century A.D. possessed the concept expressed by the modern word 'miracle.'

7. It will simplify the statement of our argument if in applying this definition we assume that 'miracle' and 'violation of a law of nature' are interchangeable. The equation of 'miracle' and 'violation' would be objectionable if my purpose were to defend the thesis that it was sometimes reasonable to believe that a miracle had occurred. This would be objectionable because it might be reasonable to believe that an event of type X had occurred and reasonable to believe that the occurrence of an event of type X required the violation of a law of nature, but *not* reasonable to believe that the "transgression of a law of nature" required by the occurrence of X was a consequence of a "particular volition of the Deity." My purpose, however, is to show that Hume's argument does not establish its conclusion, and not that this conclusion is false. And Hume's conclusion is (roughly) that it is unreasonable to believe any report of an event that would require a violation of a law— *whatever* the reason for that violation might be.

8. In my view, the two disjuncts of the definiens are independent: One can disbelieve something without assigning it a low probability (if in no other way, by assigning it no probability at all), and one can assign something a low probability without disbelieving it. A lot of people will want to say that these contentions represent a confused picture of the relation between belief and probability (I am thinking primarily of those who think that belief comes in degrees and that probabilities are measures of these degrees, a conception of the nature of belief and its relation to probability that I reject), but since nothing of substance in this essay turns on the thesis that the two disjuncts of the definiens are independent, I shall not defend it.

9. We shall later discuss the possible meanings of the phrase 'contrary to one's experience.' For the moment, let us simply assume that we understand this phrase.

10. As we did with the phrase 'contrary to experience,' let us for the present simply assume that we understand the phrase 'even more contrary to experience.' We shall later try to decide what it might mean.

11. As our examples show, not all contraventions are miracle-reports. Hume calls the stories that we are calling miracle-reports "miraculous." Contraventions that do not qualify as miraculous he calls "extraordinary" or "prodigies" or "marvelous."

12. Or so I shall assume for the sake of the example. Anyone who would deny this—that is, anyone who would regard the shaman story as a greater contravention than Carter's being a tool of malign extraterrestrial beings—may change the example.

13. Even the "memorable story related by Cardinal de Retz" and the accounts of those miracles "which were lately said to have been wrought in France upon the tomb of Abbe Paris...." "And what have we [Hume asks after telling these two stories] to oppose to such a cloud of witnesses, but the absolute impossibility or miraculous nature of the events, which they relate." It is, incidentally, very hard to reconcile Hume's description of the testimony recorded in these two stories with a statement he had made a few pages before:

> For... there is not to be found in all history, any miracle attested by a sufficient number of men, of such unquestioned good-sense, education, and learning, as to secure us against all delusion in themselves; of such undoubted integrity, as to place them beyond all suspicion of any design to deceive others; of such credit and reputation

in the eyes of mankind, as to have a great deal to lose in case of their being detected in any falsehood; and at the same time, attesting facts performed in such a public manner and in so celebrated a part of the world, as to render the detection unavoidable....

I suspect that what Hume means is that we cannot imagine evidence that would establish the persons who have reported some event as so reliable that it is logically impossible for that evidence to exist and those persons to have given a false report.

V.3   Miracles and Testimony

J. L. MACKIE

A biographical sketch of J. L. Mackie appears before selection III.6. In the present article he argues that the evidence for miracles will never in practice be very great. The argument is epistemological, not ontological.

(A) INTRODUCTION

Traditional theism, as defined in the Introduction, does not explicitly include any contrast between the natural and the supernatural. Yet there is a familiar, if vague and undeveloped, notion of the natural world in contrast with which the theistic doctrines stand out as asserting a supernatural reality. The question whether and how there can be evidence for what, if real, would be supernatural is therefore one of central significance. Besides, explicit assertions about supernatural occurrences, about miracles or divine interventions which have disrupted the natural course of events, are common in nearly all religions: alleged miracles are often cited to validate religious claims. Christianity, for example, has its share of these. In the life of Christ we have the virgin birth, the turning of water into wine, Christ's walking on the water, his healing of the sick, his raising of Lazarus from the dead, and, of course, the resurrection. The Roman Catholic church will not recognize anyone as a saint unless it is convinced that at least two miracles have been performed by the supposed saint, either in his or her life or after death.

The usual purpose of stories about miracles is to establish the authority of the particular figures who perform them or are associated with them, but of course these stories, with their intended interpretation, presuppose such more general religious doctrines as that of the existence of a god. We can, therefore, recognize, as one of the supports of traditional theism, an argument from miracles: that is, an argument whose main premiss is that such and such remarkable events have occurred, and whose conclusion is that a god of the traditional sort both exists and intervenes, from time to time, in the ordinary world....

[Here follows a brief exposition of Hume's essay "Of Miracles".]

(B) HUME'S ARGUMENT-DISCUSSION

What Hume has been expounding are the principles for the rational acceptance of testimony, the rules that ought to govern our believing or not believing what we are told. But the rules that govern people's actual acceptance of testimony are very different. We are fairly good at detecting dishonesty, insincerity, and lack of conviction, and we readily reject what we are told by someone who betrays these defects. But we are strongly inclined simply to accept, without question, statements that are obviously assured and sincere. As Hume would say, a firm association of ideas links someone else's saying, with honest conviction, that *p*, and its being the case that *p*, and we pass automatically from the perception of the one to belief in the other. Or, as he might also have said, there is an intellectual sympathy by which we tend automatically to share what we find to be someone else's belief, analogous to sympathy in the original sense, the tendency to share what we see to be someone else's feelings. And in general this is a useful tendency. People's beliefs about ordinary matters are right, or nearly right, more often than they are wildly wrong, so that intellectual sympathy enables fairly correct information to be passed on more smoothly than it could be if we were habitually cautious and constantly checked testimony against the principles for its rational acceptance. But what is thus generally useful can sometimes be misleading, and miracle reports are a special case where we need to restrain our instinctive acceptance of honest statements, and go back to the basic rational principles which determine whether a statement is really reliable or not. Even where we are cautious, and hesitate to accept what we are told—for example by a witness in a legal case—we often do not go beyond the question 'How intrinsically reliable is this witness?', or, in detail, 'Does he seem to be honest? Does he have a motive for misleading us? Is he the sort of person who might tell plausible lies? Or is he the sort of person who, in the circumstances, might have made a mistake?' If we are satisfied on all these scores, we are inclined to believe what the witness says, without weighing very seriously the question 'How intrinsically improbable is what he has told us?' But, as Hume insists, this further question is highly relevant. His general approach to the problem of when to accept testimony is certainly sound.

Hume's case against miracles is an epistemological argument: it does not try to show that miracles never do happen or never could happen, but only that we never have good reasons for believing that they have happened. It must be clearly distinguished from the suggestion that the very concept of a miracle is incoherent. That suggestion might be spelled out as follows. A miracle is, by definition, a violation of a law of nature, and a law of nature is, by definition, a regularity—or the statement of a regularity—about what happens, about the way the world works; consequently, if some event actually occurs, no regularity which its occurrence infringes (or, no regularity-statement which it falsifies) can really be a law of nature; so this event, however unusual or surprising, cannot after all be a miracle. The two definitions together entail that whatever happens is not a miracle, that is, that miracles never happen. This, be it noted, is not Hume's argument. If it were correct, it would make Hume's argument unnecessary. Before we discuss Hume's case, then, we should consider whether there is a coherent concept of a miracle which would not thus rule out the occurrence of miracles *a priori*.

If miracles are to serve their traditional function of giving spectacular support to religious claims—whether general theistic claims, or the authority of some specific religion or some particular sect or individual teacher—the concept must not be so weakened that anything at all unusual or remarkable counts as a miracle. We must keep in the definition the notion of a violation of natural law. But then, if it is to be even possible that a miracle should occur, we must modify the definition given above of a law of nature. What we want to do is to contrast the order of nature with a possible divine or supernatural intervention. The laws of nature, we must say, describe the ways in which the world—including, of course, human beings—works when left to itself, when not interfered with. A miracle occurs when the world is not left to itself, when something distinct from the natural order as a whole intrudes into it.

This notion of ways in which the world works is coherent and by no means obscure. We know how to discover causal laws, relying on a principle of the uniformity of the course of nature—essentially the assumption that there are some laws to be found—in conjunction with suitable observations and experiments, typically varieties of controlled experiment whose underlying logic is that of Mill's 'method of difference.' Within the laws so established, we can further mark off basic laws of working from derived laws which hold only in a particular context or contingently upon the way in which something is put together. It will be a derived law that a particular clock, or clocks of a particular sort, run at such a speed, and this will hold only in certain conditions of temperature, and so on; but this law will be derived from more basic ones which describe the regular behaviour of certain kinds of material, in view of the way in which the clock is put together, and these more basic laws of materials may in turn be derived from yet more basic laws about sub-atomic particles, in view of the ways in which those materials are made up of such particles. In so far as we advance towards a knowledge of such a system of basic and derived laws, we are acquiring an understanding of ways in which the world works. As well as what we should ordinarily call causal laws, which typically concern interactions, there are similar laws with regard to the ways in which certain kinds of things simply persist through time, and certain sorts of continuous process just go on. These too, and in particular the more basic laws of these sorts, help to constitute the ways in which the world works. Thus there are several kinds of basic 'laws of working.' For our present purpose, however, it is not essential that we should even be approaching an understanding of how the world works; it is enough that we have the concept of such basic laws of working, that we know in principle what it would be to discover them. Once we have this concept, we have moved beyond the definition of laws of nature merely as (statements of) what always happens. We can see how, using this concept and using the assumption that there are some such basic laws of working to be found, we can hope to determine what the actual laws of working are by reference to a restricted range of experiments and observations. This opens up the possibility that we might determine that something *is* a basic law of working of natural objects, and yet also, independently, find that it was occasionally

violated. An occasional violation does not in itself necessarily overthrow the independently established conclusion that this is a law of working.

Equally, there is no obscurity in the notion of intervention. Even in the natural world we have a clear understanding of how there can be for a time a closed system, in which everything that happens results from factors within that system in accordance with its laws of working, but how then something may intrude from outside it, bringing about changes that the system would not have produced of its own accord, so that things go on after this intrusion differently from how they would have gone on if the system had remained closed. All we need do, then, is to regard the whole natural world as being, for most of the time, such a closed system; we can then think of a supernatural intervention as something that intrudes into that system from outside the natural world as a whole.

If the laws by which the natural world works are deterministic, then the notion of a violation of them is quite clear-cut: such a violation would be an event which, given that the world was a closed system working in accordance with these laws, and given some actual earlier complete state of the world, simply could not have happened at all. Its occurrence would then be clear proof that either the supposed laws were not the real laws of working, or the earlier state was not as it was supposed to have been, or else the system was not closed after all. But if the basic laws of working are statistical or probabilistic, the notion of a violation of them is less precise. If something happens which, given those statistical laws and some earlier complete state of the world, is extremely improbable—in the sense of physical probability: that is, something such that there is a strong propensity or tendency for it not to happen—we still cannot say firmly that the laws have been violated: laws of this sort explicitly allow that what is extremely improbable may occasionally come about. Indeed it is highly probable (both physically and epistemically) that some events, each of which is very improbable, will occur at rare intervals. If tosses of a coin were governed by a statistical law that gave a 50 per cent propensity to heads at each toss, a continuous run of ten heads would be a highly improbable occurrence; but it would be highly probable that there would be some such runs in a sequence of a million tosses. Nevertheless, we can still use the contrast between the way of working of the natural world as a whole, considered as a normally closed system, and an intervention or intrusion into it. This contrast does not disappear or become unintelligible merely because we lack decisive tests for its application. We can still define a miracle as an event which would not have happened in the course of nature, and which came about only through a supernatural intrusion. The difficulty is merely that we cannot now say with certainty, simply by reference to the relevant laws and some antecedent situation, that a certain event would not have happened in the course of nature, and therefore must be such an intrusion. But we may still be able to say that it is very probable this is now an epistemic probability—that it would not have happened naturally, and so is likely to be such an intrusion. For if the laws made it physically improbable that it would come about, this tends to make it epistemically improbable that it did come about through those laws, if there is any other way in which it could have come about and which is not equally improbable or more improbable. In practice the difficulty mentioned is not much of an extra difficulty. For even where we believe there to be deterministic laws and an earlier situation which together would have made an occurrence actually impossible in the course of nature, it is from our point of view at best epistemically very probable, not certain, that those are the laws and that that was the relevant antecedent situation.

Consequently, whether the laws of nature are deterministic or statistical, we can give a coherent definition of a miracle as a supernatural intrusion into the normally closed system that works in accordance with those laws, and in either case we can identify conceivable occurrences, and alleged occurrences, which if they were to occur, or have occurred, could be believed with high probability, though not known with certainty, to satisfy that definition.

However, the full concept of a miracle requires that the intrusion should be purposive,

that it should fulfill the intention of a god or other supernatural being. This connection cannot be sustained by any ordinary causal theory; it presupposes a power to fulfil intentions directly, without physical means, which is highly dubious; so this requirement for a miracle will be particularly hard to confirm. On the other hand it is worth noting that successful prophecy could be regarded as a form of miracle for which there could in principle be good evidence. If someone is reliably recorded as having prophesied at t_1 an event at t_2 which could not be predicted at t_1 on any natural grounds, and the event occurs at t_2, then at any later time t_3 we can assess the evidence for the claims both that the prophecy was made at t_1 and that its accuracy cannot be explained either causally (for example, on the ground that it brought about its own fulfilment) or as accidental, and hence that it was probably miraculous.

There is, then, a coherent concept of miracles. Their possibility is not ruled out *a priori*, by definition. So we must consider whether Hume's argument shows that we never have good reason for believing that any have occurred.

Hume's general principle for the evaluation of testimony, that we have to weigh the unlikelihood of the event reported against the unlikelihood that the witness is mistaken or dishonest, is substantially correct. It is a corollary of the still more general principle of accepting whatever hypothesis gives the best overall explanation of all the available and relevant evidence. But some riders are necessary. First, the likelihood or unlikelihood, the epistemic probability or improbability, is always relative to some body of information, and may change if additional information comes in. Consequently, any specific decision in accordance with Hume's principle must be provisional. Secondly, it is one thing to decide which of the rival hypotheses in the field at any time should be provisionally accepted in the light of the evidence then available; but it is quite another to estimate the weight of this evidence, to say how well supported this favoured hypothesis is, and whether it is likely that its claims will be undermined either by additional information or by the suggesting of further alternative hypotheses. What is clearly the best-supported view of some matter at the moment may still be very insecure, and quite likely to be overthrown by some further considerations. For example, if a public opinion poll is the only evidence we have about the result of a coming election, this evidence may point, perhaps decisively, to one result rather than another; yet if the poll has reached only a small sample of the electorate, or if it was taken some time before the voting day, it will not be very reliable. There is a dimension of reliability over and above that of epistemic probability relative to the available evidence. Thirdly, Hume's description of what gives support to a prediction, or in general to a judgement about an unobserved case that would fall under some generalization, is very unsatisfactory. He seems to say that if *all* so far observed *A*s have been *B*s, then this amounts to a 'proof' that some unobserved *A* will be (or is, or was) a *B,* whereas if some observed *A*s have been *B*s, but some have not, there is only a 'probability' that an unobserved *A* will be a *B* (pp. 110–12). This mixes up the reasoning to a generalization with the reasoning *from* a generalization to a particular case. It is true that the premises 'All *A*s are *B*s' and 'This is an *A*' constitute a proof of the conclusion 'This is a *B,*' whereas the premises '*x* per cent of *A*s are *B*s' and 'This is an *A*' yield—if there is no other relevant information—a probability of *x* per cent that this is a *B*: they *probabilify* the conclusion to this degree, or, as we can say, the probability of the conclusion 'This is a *B*' relative to that evidence is *x* per cent. But the inductive argument from the observation 'All so far observed *A*s have been *B*s' to the generalization 'All *A*s are *B*s' is far from secure, and it would be most misleading to call this a proof, and therefore misleading also to describe as a proof the whole line of inference from 'All so far observed *A*s have been *B*s' to the conclusion 'This as yet unobserved *A* is a *B*.' Similarly, the inductive argument from '*x* per cent of observed *A*s have been *B*s' to the statistical generalization '*x* per cent of *A*s are *B*s' is far from secure, so that we cannot say that '*x* percent of observed *A*s have been *B*s' even probabilifies to the degree *x* per cent the conclusion 'This as yet unobserved *A* is a *B*.' A good deal of other information and background

knowledge is needed, in either case, before the generalization, whether universal or statistical, is at all well supported, and hence before the stage is properly set for either proof or probabilification about an as yet unobserved *A*. It is harder than Hume allows here to arrive at well-supported generalizations of either sort about how the world works.

These various qualifications together entail that what has been widely and reasonably thought to be a law of nature may not be one, perhaps in ways that are highly relevant to some supposed miracles. Our present understanding of psychosomatic illness, for example, shows that it is not contrary to the laws of nature that someone who for years has seemed, to himself as well as to others, to be paralysed should rapidly regain the use of his limbs. On the other hand, we can still be pretty confident that it is contrary to the laws of nature that a human being whose heart has stopped beating for forty-eight hours in ordinary circumstances—that is, without any special life-support systems—should come back to life, or that what is literally water should without addition or replacement turn into what is literally good-quality wine.

However, any problems there may be about establishing laws of nature are neutral between the parties to the present debate, Hume's followers and those who believe in miracles; for both these parties need the notion of a well-established law of nature. The miracle advocate needs it in order to be able to say that the alleged occurrence is a miracle, a violation of natural law by supernatural intervention, no less than Hume needs it for his argument against believing that this event has actually taken place.

It is therefore not enough for the defender of a miracle to cast doubt (as he well might) on the certainty of our knowledge of the law of nature that seems to have been violated. For he must himself say that this *is* a law of nature: otherwise the reported event will not be miraculous. That is, he must in effect *concede* to Hume that the antecedent improbability of this event is as high as it could be, hence that, apart from the testimony, we have the strongest possible grounds for believing that the alleged event did not occur. This event must, by the miracle advocate's own admission, be contrary to a genuine, not merely a supposed, law of nature, and therefore maximally improbable. It is this maximal improbability that the weight of the testimony would have to overcome.

One further improvement is needed in Hume's theory of testimony. It is well known that the agreement of two (or more) *independent* witnesses constitutes very powerful evidence. Two independent witnesses are more than twice as good as each of them on his own. The reason for this is plain. If just one witness says that *p*, one explanation of this would be that it was the case that *p* and that he has observed this, remembered it, and is now making an honest report; but there are many alternative explanations, for example that he observed something else which he mistook for its being that *p*, or is misremembering what he observed, or is telling a lie. But if two witnesses who can be shown to be quite independent of one another both say that *p*, while again one explanation is that each of them has observed this and remembered it and is reporting honestly, the alternative explanations are not now so easy. They face the question 'How has there come about this *agreement* in their reports, if it was not the case that *p*? How have the witnesses managed to misobserve to the same effect, or to misremember in the same way, or to hit upon the same lie?' It is difficult for even a single liar to keep on telling a *consistent* false story; it is much harder for two or more liars to do so. Of course if there is any collusion between the witnesses, or if either has been influenced, directly or indirectly, by the other, or if both stories have a common source, this question is easily answered. That is why the independence of the witnesses is so important. This principle of the improbability of coincident error has two vital bearings upon the problem of miracles. On the one hand, it means that a certain sort of testimony can be more powerful evidence than Hume's discussion would suggest. On the other, it means that where we seem to have a plurality of reports, it is essential to check carefully whether they really are independent of one another; the difficulty of meeting this requirement would be an important

supplement to the points made in Part II of Hume's essay. Not only in remote and barbarous times, but also in recent ones, we are usually justified in suspecting that what look like distinct reports of a remarkable occurrence arise from different strands of a single tradition between which there has already been communication.

We can now put together the various parts of our argument. Where there is some plausible testimony about the occurrence of what would appear to be a miracle, those who accept this as a miracle have the double burden of showing both that the event took place and that it violated the laws of nature. But it will be very hard to sustain this double burden. For whatever tends to show that it would have been a violation of natural law tends for that very reason to make it most unlikely that it actually happened. Correspondingly, those who deny the occurrence of a miracle have two alternative lines of defense. One is to say that the event may have occurred, but in accordance with the laws of nature. Perhaps there were unknown circumstances that made it possible; or perhaps what were thought to be the relevant laws of nature are not strictly laws; there may be as yet unknown kinds of natural causation through which this event might have come about. The other is to say that this event would indeed have violated natural law, but that for this very reason there is a very strong presumption against its having happened, which it is most unlikely that any testimony will be able to outweigh. Usually one of these defences will be stronger than the other. For many supposedly miraculous cures, the former will be quite a likely sort of explanation, but for such feats as the bringing back to life of those who are really dead the latter will be more likely. But the *fork*, the disjunction of these two sorts of explanation, is as a whole a very powerful reply to any claim that a miracle has been performed.

However, we should distinguish two different contexts in which an alleged miracle might be discussed. One possible context would be where the parties in debate already both accept some general theistic doctrines, and the point at issue is whether a miracle has occurred which would enhance the authority of a specific sect or teacher. In this context supernatural intervention, though *prima facie* unlikely on any particular occasion, is, generally speaking, on the cards: it is not altogether outside the range of reasonable expectation for these parties. Since they agree that there is an omnipotent deity, or at any rate one or more powerful supernatural beings, they cannot find it absurd to suppose that such a being will occasionally interfere with the course of nature, and this *may* be one of these occasions. For example, if one were already a theist and a Christian, it would not be unreasonable to weigh seriously the evidence of alleged miracles as some indication whether the Jansenists or the Jesuits enjoyed more of the favour of the Almighty. But it is a very different matter if the context is that of fundamental debate about the truth of theism itself. Here one party to the debate is initially at least agnostic, and does not yet concede that there is a supernatural power at all. From this point of view the intrinsic improbability of a genuine miracle, as defined above, is very great, and one or other of the alternative explanations in our fork will always be much more likely—that is, either that the alleged event is not miraculous, or that it did not occur, that the testimony is faulty in some way.

This entails that it is pretty well impossible that reported miracles should provide a worthwhile argument for theism addressed to those who are initially inclined to atheism or even to agnosticism. Such reports can form no significant part of what, following Aquinas, we might call a *Summa contra Gentiles*, or what, following Descartes, we could describe as being addressed to infidels. Not only are such reports unable to carry any rational conviction on their own, but also they are unable even to contribute independently to the kind of accumulation or battery of arguments referred to in the Introduction. To this extent Hume is right, despite the inaccuracies we have found in his statement of the case.

One further point may be worth making. Occurrences are sometimes claimed to be literally, and not merely metaphorically, miracles, that is, to be genuine supernatural interventions into the natural order, which are not even *prima facie* violations of natural law, but at

most rather unusual and unexpected, but very welcome. Thus the combination of weather conditions which facilitated the escape of the British army from Dunkirk in 1940, making the Luftwaffe less than usually effective but making it easy for ships of all sizes to cross the Channel, is sometimes called a miracle. However, even if we accepted theism, and could plausibly assume that a benevolent deity would have favoured the British rather than the Germans in 1940, this explanation would still be far less probable than that which treats it as a mere meteorological coincidence: such weather conditions can occur in the ordinary course of events. Here, even in the context of a debate among those who already accept theistic doctrines, the interpretation of the event as a miracle is much weaker than the rival natural explanation. *A fortiori*, instances of this sort are utterly without force in the context of fundamental debate about theism itself.

There is, however, a possibility which Hume's argument seems to ignore—though, as we shall see, he did not completely ignore it. The argument has been directed against the acceptance of miracles on testimony; but what, it may be objected, if one is not reduced to reliance on testimony, but has observed a miracle for oneself? Surprisingly, perhaps, this possibility does not make very much difference. The first of the above-mentioned lines of defence is still available; maybe the unexpected event that one has oneself observed did indeed occur, but in accordance with the laws of nature. Either the relevant circumstances or the operative laws were not what one has supposed them to be. But at least a part of the other line of defence is also available. Though one is not now relying literally on another witness or other witnesses, we speak not inappropriately of the evidence of our senses, and what one takes to be an observation of one's own is open to questions of the same sort as is the report of some other person. I may have misobserved what took place, as anyone knows who has even been fooled by a conjurer or 'magician,' and, though this is somewhat less likely, I may be misremembering or deceiving myself after an interval of time. And of course the corroboration of one or more independent witnesses would bring in again the testimony of others which it was the point of this objection to do without. Nevertheless, anyone who is fortunate enough to have carefully observed and carefully recorded, for himself, an apparently miraculous occurrence is no doubt rationally justified in taking it very seriously; but even here it will be in order to entertain the possibility of an alternative natural explanation.

As I said, Hume does not completely ignore this possibility. The Christian religion, he says, cannot at this day be believed by any reasonable person without a miracle. 'Mere reason is insufficient to convince us of its veracity: And whoever is moved by *Faith* to assent to it, is conscious of a continued miracle in his own person, which subverts all the principles of his understanding . . .' (p. 131). But of course this is only a joke. What the believer is conscious of in his own person, though it may be a mode of thinking that goes against 'custom and experience,' and so is contrary to the ordinary rational principles of the understanding is not, as an occurrence, a violation of natural law. Rather it is all too easy to explain immediately by the automatic communication of beliefs between persons and the familiar psychological processes of wish fulfillment, and ultimately by what Hume himself was later to call 'the natural history of religion.'

V.4   Evidence for the Resurrection

RICHARD SWINBURNE

A biographical sketch of Richard Swinburne precedes selection I.C.3. In the following article, Swinburne defends the conclusion that there is fairly strong evidence in support of the occurrence of at least one miracle: the resurrection of Jesus. In the course of defending this conclusion, he provides a critical assessment of Hume's argument against miracles.

In assessing what happened on some particular occasion in the past, we have to take into account both detailed historical evidence and general background evidence. The detailed historical evidence may be of three kinds: our own personal (apparent) memories, the testimony of witnesses, and physical traces. The general background evidence will be evidence of what normally happens. This may be free-standing (some generalization about cases similar to that under investigation, confirmed solely by observing such cases) or a consequence of some deeper theory, confirmed by observations over a wide range of cases, some of them rather unlike the case under investigation.

Let me illustrate with a detective example. A detective investigating a safe robbery may himself have a relevant memory. By a 'memory' I mean what should be called, more strictly, an 'apparent personal memory,' one which seems to the subject to be a genuine memory of having done something or having perceived something. The detective may have thought that he saw Jones robbing the safe. More likely, there may be other witnesses who report that they saw Jones robbing the safe. And there will often be physical traces—fingerprints on the safe or money stashed away in Jones's garage. The detective's own apparent memories or the testimony of witnesses may, more likely, be not of seeing the safe being robbed but of other events which in turn provide evidence of who robbed the safe.

That memories and testimony are to be trusted—that is, that they make it probable that what they report occurred—in the absence of counter-evidence, are a priori principles. You might think that memory is to be trusted only if independently confirmed. But what could confirm a memory except another memory, or some generalization about how the world works, itself confirmed by memories of it working on various occasions? You might say that no one memory is to be trusted until confirmed by another. But think how little knowledge we would have if we really thought thus. A memory would only be trustworthy if we simultaneously had another memory (for example, of what someone else said that he saw) confirming the first memory. We don't think that, and we must draw the consequences of our secular thinking: that memory as such, all memory, is to be trusted in the absence of positive counter-evidence that is untrustworthy—for example, that it concerns an occasion on which the subject was drunk, or concerns a matter on which he tends to misobserve, or that there is strong independent evidence that what the subject reports did not happen. That positive counter-evidence will come ultimately from other memories (or the testimony of others—see below) which clash with the given memory and are stronger or more numerous.

The principle of testimony, that we should believe what others tell us that they have done or perceived—in the absence of counter-evidence—is also a priori. Clearly most of our beliefs about the world are based on what others claim to have perceived—beliefs about geography and history and science and everything else beyond immediate experience are thus based. We do not normally check that informants are reliable witnesses before accepting their reports. And we *could* not do so because we form our beliefs about what they are saying, the meaning of the claims which they are making, on the assumption that other people normally tell the truth. We can see this by considering how an anthropologist comes to learn the language of a native tribe. He listens to what the natives say, and observes correlations between what they say and how things are; for example he finds that on the day before a festival natives often say '*p*' but that they do not say '*p*' at any other time. If he takes this as evidence that '*p*' means 'there will be a festival tomorrow,' he must already be assuming that normally natives tell the truth. What applies to the anthropologist applies to a child learning his first language or additions to it. When people point to a colour and say "This is green,' the child believes that 'green' is the name of that colour—because he has already made (implicitly) the assumption that people normally tell the truth. The assumption itself cannot be tested—because if it is up for test whether people normally tell the truth, then we would have to see whether there are correlations between the propositions people utter and how things are—yet we should not know what proposition they were uttering (that is, what they meant by their sentence) unless we had already made the assumption up for test.

But again there can be positive evidence that certain witnesses, or witnesses positioned in certain circumstances, or a particular testimony by a particular witness, are unreliable. But the evidence will have force only on the assumption that most other witnesses are trustworthy. We can show that Smith is an utterly untrustworthy witness on certain matters only if we can trust the combined testimony of other witnesses about what happened. Conjoint testimony can defeat single testimony.

That physical traces are evidence of this or that is, however, an a posteriori matter. That fingerprints of the same pattern as those of Jones are (strong) evidence that Jones put his fingers where the prints are, follows from the theory that fingers leave prints uniquely characteristic of their owner, established in the last century on the basis of a very wide range of evidence. This evidence itself is available to us by the testimony (written or oral) of those who have studied it. That a particular piece of physical evidence, *a*, shows what it does, *b*, is something to be established inductively (that is, as something entailed or rendered probable by a theory which is itself rendered probable by other pieces of evidence). We need to show that *a* would probably not have occurred unless *b* occurred; and that will be so only if *a* would probably not have occurred unless *b*, or a cause of *b*, had caused *a*. And to show that, you need a theory of what causes what. Such a theory is to be accepted in so far as it is a simple theory rendering probable the occurrence of many observed data which there would otherwise be no reason to expect.

The observed data in the fingerprint example are a very large random sample of 'fingerprints' (identified as such by their shape), many of which have been seen being caused by fingers (and none of which can be attributed with any significant probability to any cause other than fingers), each fingerprint uniquely correlating one to one with the fingers of a different human being. The theory of unique fingerprints is a simple theory leading us to expect these observations which we would not otherwise expect, and has the consequence that Jones's fingerprint is evidence of Jones having put his fingers where the fingerprint is found. But this connection is established a posteriori on the basis of trusting what witnesses say about their observations of the large random sample.

Apparent memories, testimony, and physical traces will often be evidence of certain other things, which in turn are evidence of the matter of interest to us—say, that Jones robbed the safe. Here the above pattern of inductive inference will again be evident. Two witnesses may report that Jones was in the neighbourhood of the robbery at the time it was committed; another one may report that a little later Jones boasted about having won the Lottery, and had a lot of money to spend (and Lottery officials witness that he did not win the Lottery). The traces may include fingerprints on the safe and the discovery of much of the stolen money in a garage of which he possessed the key. And so on. A theory immediately suggests itself which leads us to expect all these data, when the combination of all the data together would be otherwise unexpected—namely, that Jones robbed the safe. And the theory is a simple one—that one person caused all these effects. Another theory which would also lead us to expect the data with equal probability would be that the fingerprints were planted by Smith, the goods stolen by Robinson, who dropped them, and Brown picked them up and hid them in the garage of which, coincidentally, Jones had the key; and so on, to deal with the other data. But the latter theory is not supported by the data, because it is complicated—and the former theory is simple.

All the detailed 'historical' data considered so far are causal evidence in the sense that the event reported by our hypothesis, if true, would (in part) have caused those data (or would have been caused by a cause of those data). Thus if Jones had robbed the safe, he would have caused the fingerprints to be on the safe. But now background evidence enters in. The background evidence is not, in the sense delineated, causal evidence, but evidence from a wide area supporting a theory or theories about what normally happens. It shows how likely it is on other grounds that an event of the kind alleged could have occurred. In our example it will include evidence of Jones's behaviour on other occasions, supporting a theory of his character, from which it would follow that he is or is not the sort of person who normally robs safes.

All these kinds of evidence are relevant to determining whether some historical event occurred, and need to be weighed against each other; and the most interesting clashes of evidence, for our purposes, occur when detailed historical evidence points to something which background evidence suggests is most unlikely to have occurred. Consider the sixteenth-century Danish astronomer Tycho Brahe making observations of comets and measuring their angular distance from various stars at different hours of the night. The background evidence in the form of all that had ever been observed in the heavens, and especially the movements of the sun and moon and planets relative to Earth and relative to the 'fixed stars,' supported the Aristotelio–Ptolemaic astronomy which held that the heavenly regions beyond the moon were occupied by crystalline spheres in which there were no changes, and which carried sun, moon, and planets around the Earth. Now it followed from Tycho's observations that comets changed their apparent positions relative to the stars and planets during the year in such a way that if they existed in the heavenly regions, and the Aristotelio–Ptolemaic theory were true, they would be passing through the crystalline spheres—which would of course be impossible. But if comets are sublunary phenomena, they should show a diurnal parallax: that is, as the Earth (or the outer heavenly sphere of the stars) rotates daily, they should change their position during the course of the night relative to the background of the stars. Tycho Brahe in the sixteenth century had very accurate apparatus by which he could have detected any diurnal parallax. He observed the absence of such a parallax. The detailed historical observations supported the theory that any given comet was a body moving far beyond the moon's orbit.[1] In the situation of a clash between the historical evidence and the theory supported by background evidence, it must be the case either that the background theory is false or that the historical evidence is misleading. In any such clash, we must weigh the two types of evidence against each other, and it may not always be clear where the balance lies, although often it may. In the example which I have just discussed it was of course the background theory which was at fault, and eventually (whether or not that was evident at the time) it became evident that the balance of evidence was against the background theory.

In his discussion of miracles, Hume was concerned with just such a clash. He understood by a miracle 'a transgression of a law of nature by a particular volition of the Deity, or by the interposition of some invisible agent.'[2] Here we are concerned with a situation where the background evidence supports a theory, not just about what normally happens (most of the time, on the whole) and so is not all that powerful as evidence of what happened on the given occasion, but rather with a situation where the background evidence powerfully supports a theory about what laws of nature make (almost) inevitable. I write 'almost,' for if we are to have a coherent notion of a 'transgression' or 'violation' of a law of nature, we cannot understand a law of nature as a law determining what inevitably happens. For in that case there could not be a 'violation' of a law of nature, since a 'violation' implies an event contrary to what follows from the operation of a law. An event contrary to what is predicted by a purported law would only show the purported law to be no real law. If a purported law of gravity rules out levitation, and a levitation occurs, then the purported law can be no true law. To make the notion of a violation coherent, we must amend our understanding of 'law of nature' along such lines as the following. We

should understand by a law of nature a principle which determines what often happens, and by a fundamental law a principle which determines what happens, when what happens is determined by law at all. Derivative laws (such as Kepler's laws of planetary motion) determine what happens in certain regions for certain periods of time, subject to non-interference by other laws or powers beyond law. Derivative laws are consequences of fundamental laws, which operate always and everywhere and without exceptions (no other law prevents their operation)—when what happens is determined by law. A violation of a law of nature is then to be understood as an event contrary to the predictions of a fundamental law of nature (or very improbable given that law). Such laws thus determine what happens (either of physical necessity or, if they are indeterminate laws, with physical probability) inevitably—in so far as laws operate at all. But they may be violated by something which has the power to set aside the principles governing the natural behaviour of things. An understanding of a law of nature of this qualified kind is not merely compatible with anything scientists wish to claim, but, more than that, is required, once you allow the possibility of laws of nature (for example, those of quantum theory) which determine what happens only with physical probability, and not necessity, and so you allow the possible occurrence of the physically improbable.

Hume would, I think, have been satisfied with such an amended understanding of a law of nature, because he did not wish to rule out the notion of a miracle as logically impossible. What he did claim was in effect (to fill out his words a little) that to be justified in claiming some generalization to be a fundamental law of nature, we need to show that it operates without exception in a wide range of cases. That evidence will be evidence that it holds in the case in question. If the historical evidence suggests that some event occurred contrary to a fundamental law, we have at best a standoff: we cannot say what happened, certainly not with enough certainty to provide 'a just foundation for any . . . system of religion.'[3] And the normal situation, Hume considers, is that the background evidence, in the form of evidence of the universal conformity to the purported law in many different areas investigated, will outweigh the historical evidence, and so show that what happened accorded with a law of nature, and so was no miracle.

Hume's discussion suffers from one minor deficiency, one medium-sized deficiency, and one major one. The minor one is that the only kind of historical evidence of which he takes account is testimony. He doesn't consider what someone who thinks that he himself has seen a miracle ought to believe. Nor does he consider the possibility of physical traces—for example, X-rays of the internal state of someone before and after a purported healing (whose status as X-rays taken at the time and of the patient is evidenced by many witnesses and much theory). But the addition of these important kinds of historical evidence would not affect the shape of Hume's argument. Far more important is the point that Hume seems to regard the situation as static. We have a certain number of witnesses, and their testimony has a certain limited force against the background evidence, and that's that. But that need not be the situation at all. Evidence can mount up both for the background theory and for the reliability of the detailed historical evidence. Evidence could mount up not merely that people do not pass from the kind of state recorded by the earlier X-ray to the kind of state recorded by the later one, but that it is contrary to some well-established biochemical theory they should. Evidence could also mount in favour of a healing having occurred. True, there could not be an indefinite increase in the number of physical traces and witnesses in favour of a healing; but what could mount up indefinitely is evidence in favour of the reliability of X-rays of the kind in question (and of the reliability of the witnesses who testified to their status). Evidence could mount up that X-ray pictures are, interpreted in a certain way, never misleading, and hence that the two pictures show how things were. And evidence could mount up that certain witnesses or certain kinds of witnesses (for example, those testifying to events of great importance to them, where affirming the event could lead to their execution) are reliable. And when the evidence on both sides

does mount up, the situation—given the logical possibility of miracles—would be not a stand-off, but evidence both that the purported law is a law and that there has been a unique exception to its operation.

But Hume's worst mistake was to suppose that the only relevant background theory to be established from wider experience was a scientific theory about what are the laws of nature. But any theory showing whether laws of nature are ultimate or whether they depend on something higher for their operation is crucially relevant. If there is no God, then the laws of nature are the ultimate determinants of what happens. But if there is a God, then whether and for how long and under what circumstances laws of nature operate depend on God. Any evidence that there is a God, and, in particular, evidence that there is a God of a kind who might be expected to intervene occasionally in the natural order will be evidence leading us to expect occasional violations of laws of nature. And any evidence that God might be expected to intervene in a certain way will be evidence supporting historical evidence that he has done so. To take a human analogy, suppose we have background evidence supporting a theory about some human person that he behaves normally in highly regular ways—Kant, say, going for a walk at totally predictable times through the streets of Königsberg (so that citizens could set their watches by his walk). Then suppose that there is historical evidence of many witnesses that on one day his walk was half an hour late, and other witnesses reported that he delayed because he visited a sick friend first. We might at this point have a stand-off. But suppose that we have other evidence strongly supporting a theory that Kant was a compassionate friend; then we might expect him to change his otherwise inflexible habits to respond to a friend's sickness. The total background evidence supports the historical evidence that on the occasion in question the regularity was broken.

So what of the core physical element of the resurrection understood in the traditional sense: of Jesus being dead for thirty-six hours, coming to life again in his crucified body (in which he then had superhuman powers—for example, to appear and disappear)? Of course, the resurrection is traditionally supposed to have a cosmic significance which goes infinitely far beyond this core physical element. The Jesus who died and is risen is Jesus Christ, Messiah and the Word of God, the second Person of the Trinity. His resurrection constitutes God the Father's acceptance of the sacrifice of Christ on the cross for the sins of the world, and the initiation of a process of redeeming humanity and nature in respects both physical and spiritual. But the resurrection has this cosmic significance, it is traditionally supposed, only because of its physical core. The Word of God is risen from the dead only because the human Jesus is risen from the dead (only *qua* human can the Word rise); a human can only be resurrected fully if he is resurrected in an embodied state (for although, I believe, we can exist without bodies, bodies make for the fullness of human existence—such is the traditional Christian and Jewish view), and although he could have risen in an embodied state with a totally new body, resurrection of a changed old body would manifest 'resurrection,' as opposed to mere coming to life again, most eminently. The Father accepts the sacrifice of Christ by bringing to life what has been sacrificed; thereby he proclaims that suffering and death have been overcome. To initiate the redemption of humanity and of the natural order, he needs to bring to life a previously damaged body, not only a soul. And he gives his signature of approval to the teaching and sacrifice of Christ by doing an act which God alone can do—of interfering in the operation of the natural laws by which he controls the universe. For the coming to life again of a body dead for thirty-six hours is undoubtedly a violation of natural laws, and if brought about by an agent, requires God's action. The core physical element in the resurrection of Jesus has for these reasons been supposed to be a very important element in the Christian tradition. So what detailed historical evidence is there for the physical core?

There are no apparent memories of having seen it happen, and no currently available physical traces. But there is the testimony of witnesses—of an indirect character. There is the testimony of witnesses (the writers of the various books of the New Testament) to the testimony of other witnesses. It looks as though St Paul, St Luke,

and the rest purport to tell us what they have been told, both by witnesses who purported to see the tomb empty and by witnesses who purported to have met the risen Jesus. (There are those who deny that the main New Testament writers claim to report the testimony of direct witnesses of the resurrection events; but time requires me to leave that issue to others. It certainly does look initially as if that is their claim, and so I shall assume.) Let us call the New Testament writers the indirect witnesses, and their informants the direct witnesses. The principles of credulity and testimony require us to believe the indirect witnesses, and so in turn the direct witnesses. No doubt the testimony of one witness about what another witness claimed to have happened is not as strong evidence about what happened as is more direct testimony; but any diminution of trustworthiness by indirectness is compensated by quantity. In this case there are several indirect witnesses, and two at least of them claim to have heard their news from more than one direct witness.[4] In such circumstances positive counter-evidence is needed for not believing the news. The most obvious such counter-evidence of a historical kind in this case is discrepancy in the detailed testimony: and there is certainly some of that. (For a small example, consider the clash between Luke 24: 50, which implies that the ascension occurred on the same day as the resurrection, and Acts 1: 3, which states that it occurred forty days later.) Discrepancies in the details require explaining by the witnesses being deceitful, bad observers, careless reporters, or people whose testimony is not intended to be taken in a fully literal sense; and any such explanation casts some measure of doubt on other details of their testimony, and to some extent (dependent on the kind of explanation given) on the whole testimony. But evidence can only fail to render a hypothesis probable if it renders probable instead the disjunction of all alternative hypotheses. And if none of these has any great probability, the original hypothesis must retain its overall probability—which is only a more careful and precise way of putting Sherlock Holmes's famous remark: 'When you have eliminated the impossible, whatever remains, *however improbable*, must be the truth.'[5]

Alternative hypotheses will need to explain both why false testimony was given and also the absence of any positive testimony in their own favour—for example, testimony of having seen the dead body of Jesus after the first Easter Day.[6] But they may have evidence best explained by them, including, perhaps, the absence of certain evidence which one would expect if the traditional account is correct—for example, the failure of St Mark's Gospel to proceed beyond 16: 8. However, when all that is taken account of, I can only say that alternative hypotheses have always seemed to me to give far less satisfactory accounts of the historical evidence than does the traditional account—in the sense of leading us to expect the evidence we find with much smaller probabilities. Those who think that the total evidence is against the traditional account do so because they think the background evidence makes a resurrection very improbable. There is, in my view, so much testimony to the main outlines of the traditional account that if this event was of a kind which we might expect to happen, one licensed by our overall background theory, we would have no problem whatever in accepting the main point of that testimony. If it were testimony to Jesus having woken from sleep, rather than to Jesus having risen from the dead, there would be no problem (despite the discrepancies of detail) in accepting it.

The problem arises because the (physical core of) resurrection is supposed to be contrary to laws of nature—and, as I suggested earlier, rightly so. Although we are far from clear about what are the laws of biology and their consequences, in comparison with our clarity about some of the consequences of the laws of physics, it seems to me pretty clear that resurrection of the traditional kind is ruled out by the laws of biology very well established by a whole range of background evidence. So if the laws of nature are the ultimate determinants of what happens, there is at least a stand-off, and maybe not even that. True, we could multiply evidence about the reliability of the witnesses or kinds of witnesses with whom we are concerned. The witnesses include some

whose life was in danger if they testified to the resurrection and (plausibly) some whose religious upbringing would not have led them to expect that a crucified rabbi would rise again. And if the evidence became immensely strong that people of that kind could never have testified to the resurrection unless they believed it to have occurred after having checked the matter out thoroughly, then maybe the detailed historical evidence would be so strong, despite the fact that such a resurrection would have been a violation of natural laws, that Jesus had risen that the balance of probability would favour the latter, which would then constitute a miracle.

I am, of course, not an expert on the New Testament, but my own limited acquaintance with it suggests that that is not our situation. There is a significant balance of detailed historical evidence in favour of the resurrection, but it is not strong enough to equal the very strong force of the background evidence—if the latter is construed only as evidence of what are the laws of nature. But in my view that is not the right way to construe the background evidence. My belief is that there is a lot of evidence for the existence of God—a being essentially omnipotent, omniscient, and perfectly free. This evidence is the evidence of the existence of a complex physical universe, the (almost invariable) conformity of material bodies to natural laws, the evolution of animals and humans (souls connected to bodies), the providential ordering of the world in various ways, and the widespread phenomenon of religious experience (in the form of people seeming to be aware of the presence of God). In my view these phenomena are best explained by the causal agency of a God (with the properties stated), and hence provide good inductive evidence for his existence; they make it more probable than not. I have argued this case at length elsewhere,[7] and cannot do so here. But suppose that I am right. It would then follow that the laws of nature depend for their operation from moment to moment on God, who, in virtue of his omnipotence, can suspend them as and when he chooses. But what reason would he have for doing so?

In general, God has good reason to conserve the laws of nature. For by so doing he creates a beautiful universe, a dance of moving material bodies; and only by doing so can he give to us embodied creatures power over nature and power to learn how to extend our powers. For embodiedness involves having under our control the chunk of matter which is our body, and being able to influence the world only by moving it. But only if there are regular laws governing how material bodies behave, which we can come to know, can we come to know which bodily movements to make to produce which results. Only regularities in the behaviour of air will enable me to communicate with you by sound, and only regularities in the behaviour of bricks will enable me to construct a building. And by studying such regularities we can learn to extend the range of our powers—by learning the laws of electromagnetism, we can learn to communicate with distant persons by radio, and so on.

In any household, secure rules give control to those under them. If children know that if they do this, they will be punished, and if they do that, they will be rewarded, that gives them control over their future—which a parent who acted on whim would prevent them from having. But a parent whose every interaction with his children was governed by rules and who never yielded to a plea to bend a rule would cease to be a loving person with whom the child interacted. And the same would be true of a God who never responded to prayer by acting in non-rule-governed ways or by breaking his own rules. Despite all the advantages of the predictable, God would wish to interact with his children—and that means doing things at their request which he would not otherwise do, and responding in non-automatic ways to what they have done—very occasionally. And he would want to show them things directly, not only through a book of nature which he had written in advance.

All this provides reason for God responding to the particular requests and needs of individuals in ways which manifest his presence only to them. But it also provides reason for God to respond to a common need of the human race. There are, I suggest, a number of reasons for God to intervene in a big way in human history and show that he has done so, some of them being reasons for intervening by himself becoming incarnate as a human. The first reason is to make available an atonement for human sin. When humans have badly abused the good life which he has given them, and so wronged him and each other, God will naturally seek to do something about it. He will want us to take our sin seriously, not just ignore it; and so he will want us to make reparation. But we have corrupted each other, and have no serious commitment to making reparation at all, let alone the means wherewith to make it; for we owe so much to God anyway in gratitude for all the good life he has given us. So just as a human parent may provide a child who cannot pay for the damage he has caused with the means to make reparation, so God may provide for humans a human life which they can offer back to him as the life they ought to have led—a human life, which being the life of God, was not the life of one created voluntarily by God who would owe a great debt to God anyway. So God has the reason of providing atonement to intervene personally in the course of human history by becoming incarnate as a human and living so generously as to be prepared to be killed for his teaching (a not unlikely consequence of totally honest and challenging teaching in many a society). But if we are to join in offering a sacrifice, we have to know which sacrifice to offer, for many human lives which might seem to be holy on the outside may not be. God needs not merely to accept the sacrifice, but to show us that he has done so. You accept an offer by taking it over, using it, and making it fruitful. What more obvious way of doing this than by bringing to life the human killed for living a holy life?

Other reasons for God to become incarnate are to identify with us by sharing the hardships of life needed for our perfection, to show us what a good thing humanity is, and that he regards us as friends and not as servants. Also, we need teaching. Reason may show us with some degree of probability that there is a God, and it may teach us some basic moral truths. But we need to know so much more in order to live and worship in the right way. The teaching will need to include teaching that a certain human life was the life of God incarnate; for if we are ignorant that God has become incarnate, we cannot utilize the benefits of divine incarnation. The teaching will need to be handed on to new generations and cultures, and so, whether in oral or written form, it will need to be entrusted to a community, a church, which can interpret it.[8] But how are we to know that a church's teaching about a certain human being is the teaching of God about God incarnate? God must authenticate it, put his signature on the original teaching and the community which resulted from it. Only God who keeps the laws of nature operative can set them aside, and if they are set aside in such a way as to vindicate the life and teaching of a human whose outer life was holy, and forward the teaching of a church which teaches that the incarnate one was God, that indeed is God's signature. So God has abundant reason to intervene in human history to cause a human being to rise from the dead—not just any human, but a human who had lived (outwardly) a certain sort of sacrificial life and proclaimed deep and plausibly true news from God and was killed for doing so.

Now if there is a God of the kind which, in my view, arguments from the vast range of natural phenomena mentioned strongly support, that God, being omnipotent, has, as I mentioned earlier, the power to bring about anything coherently describable, including a resurrection of the cited kind. God is an intentional agent; he performs actions because he has a reason for doing them—that is, he believes that they serve some good. We too do actions because we believe that they serve some good. But we humans are subject to desires, inclinations which lead us to do actions less than the best. If we were freed from those inclinations, nothing but reason would motivate us to act; we would therefore always act for what we believed the best, or equal best. God, as a perfectly free being, is subject to no desires of the stated kind; he will act for what he believes to be the best or equal best, and, being omniscient, will have true beliefs about what is the best or equal best. It may be, however, that there is no best or equal best; that God often has

an infinite range of mutually incompatible actions open to him at any time, each better than some other, but no best. In that case God will do a good action (that is, one in favour of doing which there is a balance of reasons), but not the best. I have sketched a case for supposing that among the good actions open to him are to effect an incarnation leading to a likely death followed by a resurrection, and so for supposing that his goodness would lead him to bring about a resurrection. It is always possible that at every time some other incompatible action would always be as good or better. But at any rate my arguments indicate that a resurrection is the sort of thing which there is significant probability that a God might bring about.

I have not argued here my case for the existence of God; nor have I done more than sketch the case for supposing that if there is a God, he might well be expected to intervene in recorded and historically evidenceable human history in this sort of way. My main point is that we need that sort of background theory well supported by evidence if our evidence overall is to give a significant overall probability to the resurrection. Given that theory, we still require detailed historical evidence of a prophet who lived a holy life, proclaimed that he was the chosen of God and was offering his life for the sins of the world, and proclaimed that he was God himself—or at any rate that his church proclaimed this to be the implication of his teaching. But we don't require too much detailed historical evidence, in view of the background evidence that such an event might well be expected, in order to make it probable that the event occurred, and so rational to believe that it did.

If such a background theory as I have described were much less well supported, or a rival theory (for example, that there is no God and that the laws of nature are ultimate) were well supported, then we would need much more detailed historical evidence in favour of the resurrection to make our belief in it rational. New Testament scholars sometimes boast that they enquire into their subject-matter without introducing any theological presuppositions. If they mean that they investigate without taking into account any background theory, then they misdescribe their enterprise. This simply can't be done. An infinite number of theories are such that they lead you to expect the historical evidence with equal probability—be they theories of invisible visitors from outer space or of the powers of sacred mushrooms. No scholar could decide between these theories on mere historical evidence alone; he must take into account wider evidence (including a priori considerations of simplicity) for supposing such theories to be true or false. What is worrying is that New Testament scholars seem to think that they can do without background theories. But if a theological theory (that there is a God who has certain properties) is well established, that must be taken into account. And even if we could reach some conclusion without taking into account 95 per cent of the relevant evidence (which includes the existence of a universe, its conformity to scientific laws, etc.), we would be highly irrational if we tried to do so. Knowledge is a web, and when some event—if it occurred—would have cosmic significance, the threads of the web stretch to the ends of the cosmos.

I should make clear that in saying that we have evidence supporting a certain background theory, I do not mean that the Jews of the first century AD, or even highly secularized humans today, do in fact expect a sacrificing Messiah, or even could normally be expected to expect such a Messiah, if they had not been familiar with the Christian tradition. I mean that evidence for the existence of God (of a certain kind) is publicly available and supports that theory (by objective criteria of evidential support), and that this theory of the divine nature has the implications which I have drawn out about what we might expect to find in history. But we humans may be too stupid or sinful to see the strength of the evidential support or the implications of the theory until familiarity with the Christian tradition draws this whole line of reasoning to our attention. Yet the fact that it needs a causal stimulus to make us aware of the force of certain evidence does not cast any doubt on the strength of that evidence. Inspector Lestrade and the bumbling police of Victorian Scotland Yard often saw everything which Sherlock Holmes saw. But they could not see its inductive implications,

what it made probable. It needed Sherlock Holmes to suggest a theory to account for the data; and once they heard his theory, then they came to see that the background evidence and historical evidence supported that theory. But the evidential relations were there, whether or not they saw them. We may need the Christian tradition of the divine nature and of what a being with that nature might be expected to do (for example, as worked out in St Athanasius' *De Incarnatione* and St Anselm's *Cur Deus Homo*)—that is, an available theory—before we can see that the evidence supports that theory well. But it does support it very well, and the detailed historical evidence for the resurrection also gives it a modest amount of support. The other participants in this conference will assess the latter amount of support in far more detail and with far more competence than I can. But as one with a mere amateur's interest in New Testament scholarship, I can only say that my own belief is that the historical evidence is quite strong enough, given the background evidence, to make it considerably more probable than not that Jesus Christ rose from the dead on the first Easter Day.

APPENDIX: SUNDAY

I wish to illustrate my account of how evidence for the resurrection should be assessed by bringing into the picture some detailed historical evidence which is very seldom mentioned in this connection.[9] This is the evidence that there was a universal early Christian custom of celebrating the Eucharist on a Sunday, which is in turn to be explained most simply by a very early belief (within much less than a decade of the crucifixion) of many of the original Christian community, including the eleven, that Christ had risen on a particular day. This, in its turn, could only be explained in a simple way by the fact that particular witnesses remembered (apparently) that they had seen either the empty tomb or the risen Jesus on the first Easter Day. I add this further detailed historical evidence to the evidence more normally adduced in this connection as data showing that these were indeed the apparent memories of many of the original community, including the eleven, about events which had happened a very short time beforehand, and thus to be believed in the absence of counter-evidence.

Acts 20: 7 is from one of the 'we' passages in Acts, and so probably reflects the author's participation in the events that occurred. It records for a 'first day of the week' the breaking of bread—κλᾶν ἄρτον was the expression used by St Paul (I Cor.) and the Synoptists for what Jesus did at the Last Supper,[10] and was always used later as a description of the common Christian meal which included the Eucharist. I Corinthians 16: 1–2 suggests that the first day had an important place in the Christian calendar, and Revelation I: 10 suggests that the 'Lord's day' (ἡ κυριακὴ ἡμέρα) has central theological significance.[11] The Sunday Eucharist was not a custom merely of Pauline churches. All references in early literature to when the Eucharist was celebrated refer to a weekly Sunday celebration—see the *Didache* (n. 14) and Justin's *First Apology* (nn. 65–7). Eusebius records of one of the two groups of Ebionites (a Jewish Christian sect who separated from mainstream Christianity in the reign of Trajan) that they 'celebrate the Lord's days very much like us in commemoration of his resurrection.'[12] A group so dedicated to Jewish discipline would not have preserved the custom of Sunday worship if they had regarded it as of non-Palestinian origin. Christians left Jerusalem to found Christian churches in many other parts of the Near East within the first Christian decade. They carried with them not merely a body of doctrine, but a practice of worship. If the practice of celebrating the Eucharist on Sunday had arisen subsequently to the foundation of these churches, one would expect to find some in which the Eucharist was celebrated on some other day (for example, on the day of the original Last Supper—probably a Thursday, and certainly not a Sunday, or annually rather than weekly). No such are known. There is no plausible origin of the sacredness of Sunday from outside Christianity.[13] There is only one simple explanation: the Eucharist was celebrated on a Sunday from the first years of Christianity because Christians believed that the central Christian event of the resurrection occurred on a Sunday. Yet such early practice would have included that of some of the eleven themselves, and so could only go

with a belief of theirs that they had seen either the empty tomb or the risen Jesus on the first Easter Day. This practice gives powerful support to the New Testament witness to the latter.

But a further interesting question then arises: who in those very early days decided that the Eucharist was to be celebrated on a Sunday? One obvious explanation is that some very early gathering of apostles decided, in view of what they believed to have happened on a Sunday, that Sunday would be the most appropriate day on which to hold regular worship in the form in which Jesus instituted it at the Last Supper. But we find no hint in the New Testament of such a decision being taken,[14] analogous to the reported decisions of the apostles about the conditions under which Gentiles were to be admitted to the Church.

The New Testament contains quite a number of hints in favour of a different answer to the 'who decided?' question. A number of the resurrection appearances of Jesus to disciples together are associated with a meal at which Jesus presided or was present (on particular occasions—Mark 16: 14; Luke 24: 30, 35; 24: 43; John 21: 13—and in general—Acts 10: 41).[15] The descriptions of these occasions have associated with them the Eucharistic phrases which St Paul and St Luke recorded in their accounts of the institution in I Corinthians II and Luke 22—Luke 24: 30 and 35 speak of Jesus 'breaking bread' and being 'known' in the 'breaking of the bread.' Luke 24: 43 speaks of Jesus 'taking' (λαβών—see I Cor. II: 23) the fish; John 21: 13 speaks of Jesus 'taking' the bread and 'giving' (δίδωσιν—see Luke 22: 19) it to his disciples, and 'in a like way' (ὁμοίως—see Luke 22: 20, ὡσαύτως) the fish. Although only the additional chapter of the Fourth Gospel mentions a meal, the author of the main body of the Fourth Gospel was unwilling to record the Eucharistic details of the Last Supper, although the wealth of Eucharistic references earlier in the Gospel shows his clear knowledge of them.[16] (St John's unwillingness[17] to record the details of the original Last Supper may be attributed to various reasons, including his awareness that his Christian readers would already know the details of the rite by heart, his desire that non-Christians should not be given details which would allow them to parody the sacred rite (*disciplina arcani*), and consequently his preference for telling a story which showed the 'true meaning' of the Eucharist.) Hence it is not to be expected that he would mention a Sunday meal of Eucharistic character explicitly. But note that the two appearances which St John records, to the disciples as a group, are both Sunday appearances.

St Matthew's account of post-resurrection events, of course, does not include even the hint of a meal, but there is some reason to think that even he was aware of a post-resurrection Eucharist. The three Synoptic Gospels and I Corinthians contain accounts of the institution at the Last Supper in words so similar to each other that it is reasonable to suppose that they were used at subsequent celebrations. The three Gospels all include among the words of Jesus that he will not 'drink again of the fruit of the vine until that day when [he] drinks it anew' in the kingdom of God. These words would not have been preserved as part of Eucharistic celebration unless some common meaning or other was attached to them by the Christian communities which used them. Now the Lucan tradition mentioned earlier records that Jesus did eat and drink (Acts 10: 41) with the disciples after the resurrection (and I have given reasons for thinking of such meals as Eucharists). Hence Luke must have thought of those as occasions when Jesus drank again of the fruit of the vine.[18] So the post-resurrection meals must be what the phrase 'anew in the kingdom of God' was seen by St Luke as referring to. And plausibly, therefore, St Matthew also saw his similar phrase as referring to a post-resurrection meal (and, since the 'vow of abstinence' was made in a Eucharistic context, to a Eucharist). All this suggests an explanation of the universality of the tradition of Sunday celebration—not merely in the belief that Jesus rose on a Sunday, but in the belief of the apostles that they had joined with Jesus in post-resurrection Eucharists which he commanded them to continue on Sundays.[19] By previous arguments, these memory beliefs must be taken as true—especially in virtue of the fact that they are the beliefs of many about what happened on a public occasion—in the absence of strong counter-evidence.

A further important piece of evidence that the source of the tradition is Jesus himself is that St Paul lists instructions on how to celebrate the Eucharist as among the things which he 'received from the Lord' (I Cor. II: 23)—that is, as part of a body of central teaching believed (*c.* 55) to have come via an oral tradition from the mouth of Jesus himself.[20] It would be very odd if such detailed instructions came with no hint as to when the Eucharist should be celebrated. What detailed instructions as to how to celebrate a rite were ever laid down or handed on without some indication of when the rite should be performed? Yet there is no record in the accounts of the Last Supper of such an instruction being given then. And if Jesus had given that instruction only at the Last Supper, that would only have made sense to the disciples if he had also told them that he would rise again on Sunday—and in that case they would certainly have checked out the tomb on that day and not have celebrated on a Sunday unless they had found it empty. But if the instruction did come from the mouth of Jesus himself, I suggest that a post-resurrection instruction is more plausible.

So there is some reason to suppose that the universal custom of Sunday Eucharist derives from the post-resurrection practice and command of Jesus himself, and thereby contributes further evidence of the resurrection. But whichever detailed account of the early origin of the Sunday Eucharist be accepted, it constitutes one further piece of evidence either that witnesses found the tomb empty on the first Easter Sunday, or that witnesses believed that they had seen and probably eaten and drunk with Jesus on or shortly after that day, and hence is further evidence for the resurrection itself.

NOTES

1. For this story, see e.g. S. Sambursky, *The Physical World of the Greeks* (London: Routledge and Kegan Paul, 1956), 218–20; and T. S. Kuhn, *The Copernican Revolution* (New York: Random House, 1957), 206–9.

2. D. Hume, *An Enquiry Concerning Human Understanding*, 1777 edn., ed. L. A. Selby-Bigge, 2nd edn. (Oxford: Clarendon, 1902), 115n. I.

3. D. Hume, *An Enquiry Concerning Human Understanding*, 127.

4. See Luke 1: 2 and Gal. 1: 18–19.

5. A. C. Doyle, *The Sign of Four, The Complete Sherlock Holmes*, 1 (Garden City, NY: Doubleday, 1930), III.

6. A. C. Doyle, 'Silver Blaze,' in *The Memoirs of Sherlock Holmes* (London: George Newnes, 1894), 24:

   'Is there any other point to which you would wish to draw my attention?'
   'To the curious incident of the dog in the night-time.'
   'The dog did nothing in the night-time.'
   'That was the curious incident,' remarked Sherlock Holmes.

7. Richard Swinburne, *The Existence of God* (Oxford: Clarendon, 1979).

8. For a fuller justification of the claims that God has reasons of these various kinds to intervene in human history, especially by himself becoming incarnate, and a further consideration of what kind of evidence additional to a resurrection would show that he had done so, see my *Responsibility and Atonement* (Oxford: Clarendon, 1989), ch. 10; *Revelation* (Oxford: Clarendon, 1992), pt. ii; and *The Christian God* (Oxford: Clarendon, 1994), 216–23. These passages include some argument for supposing that we might expect such an incarnation only once in human history.

9. Much of this appendix consists in rearranging the evidence assembled in W. Rordorf's *Sunday* (London: SCM, 1968), ch. 4, on the origin of the Christian Sunday, into the form of evidence for the resurrection. I am most grateful to Christopher Rowland for his valuable criticism of an earlier draft of this appendix. Note that I am not concerned with the issue of when or why Sunday became the Christian Sabbath, only with the origin of the custom of celebrating the Eucharist on Sunday.

10. The other uses of κλᾶν ἄρτον in the NT (e.g. Acts 2: 46) are also all plausibly taken as referring to a Eucharist, with the exception of Acts 27: 35.

11. For argument that the 'Lord's day' is Sunday, and not Easter Day, see R. J. Bauckham, 'The Lord's Day,' in D. A. Carson (ed.), *From Sabbath to Lord's Day* (Grand Rapids, Mich.: Zondervan, 1982), 230–2.

12. Eusebius, *Ecclesiastical History*, III. 27.

13. See Rordorf, *Sunday*, 180–93.

14. Mark 16: 9; the opening verse of the new ending of St Mark's Gospel sees this phrase as capturing a central part of the Christian message.

15. O. Cullmann (*Essays on the Lord's Supper* (London: Lutterworth, 1958), 11–12) understands Acts 1: 4 as speaking of Jesus 'being assembled together' with his apostles, συναλιζόμενος, as 'taking salt' with them, and so referring to a meal.

16. e.g. John 6: 51b, 'The bread which I will give is my flesh for the life of the world,' surely alludes to the Eucharistic words.

17. John 13: 2.

18. The vast majority of commentators interpret Jesus as vowing to abstain from the fruit of the vine until some final, more distant establishment of his kingdom. But whatever Jesus may have meant by his words, it is hard to suppose that St Luke could have so understood them unless he also supposed that no wine was drunk by Jesus on any of the occasions when Jesus ate and drank after his resurrection. But it is not plausible to claim that St Luke did suppose that—wine was an ordinary enough drink, and was above all to be drunk on an occasion of a new meal with old friends; further, I have given some reason to suppose that he thought of some of these meals as Eucharists.

19. It is true that if there had been one formal Eucharist at which all eleven disciples were present on the first Easter evening, most of the Gospels would inevitably have mentioned it. (See the objection in Bauckham, 'The Lord's Day,' 235.) But that is reason only for supposing that the first post-resurrection Eucharists did not involve all the disciples, and were occasions somewhat unexpected for their participants—both points made in the Gospels (e.g. John explicitly mentions the absence of Thomas on the evening of Easter Sunday).

20. The suggestion that St Paul understood 'received from the Lord' as describing the contents of a private vision is not plausible; there would have been no universal detailed conformity of Christian communities to Eucharistic practice without that practice having roots earlier and stronger than a Pauline vision. That what were received were in effect instructions for subsequent celebration is made clear by v. 26.

V.5   Hyperspace and Christianity

HUD HUDSON

Hud Hudson is professor of philosophy at Western Washington University and works primarily in the areas of metaphysics and the history of modern philosophy. He is the author of *A Materialist Metaphysics of the Human Person* (2001) and *The Metaphysics of Hyperspace* (2005), from which the final reading in this section is taken. In this selection, Hudson argues that, contrary to a fairly widespread and familiar allegation, belief in a wide variety of biblical miracles is fully consistent with our modern scientific worldview.

that ye, being rooted and grounded in love, May be able to comprehend with all saints what is the breadth, and length, and depth, and height; And to know the love of Christ.

Ephesians 3: 17–19, KJV

1. THE AIM OF THESE REFLECTIONS

Every once in a while one encounters a particularly aggressive brand of atheism that mistakes some amorphous thing called "our modern worldview" for an invulnerable fortress, sets up residence there, and then launches volleys from the apparent safety of its walls against various Christian doctrines and themes. Some of these offensives are sophisticated and challenging, some are not, and some appear to be more sophisticated and challenging than they are.[1] I aim to disarm certain kinds of criticism that I believe fall into this third camp. Here is the central form of the kind of argument I wish to target.

Recipe for the rejection of Christian belief that p
1. Christians believe that *p*.
2. *p* is inconsistent with our modern worldview.
3. If a proposition is inconsistent with our modern worldview, then we have justifying reasons to believe that the proposition is false.

4. Hence, we have justifying reasons to believe that Christian belief that *p* is false.

A note on the premises. Premise (1) is ambiguous: it may be read (i) 'Christians (*qua* Christians) believe that *p*' or (ii) 'Christians (as a group) believe that *p*.' On reading (i) the idea is that belief that *p* is partially constitutive of being Christian—that one cannot qualify as Christian without it. (For what it's worth, on that interpretation I suspect that there are remarkably few substitutions for '*p*' that generate truths. But I'm not at all interested here in entering the debate on the minimal belief conditions for being Christian, and I shall set this interpretation aside). On reading (ii) the idea is that whether or not belief that *p* is partially constitutive of being Christian, *p* is—as a matter of fact—held by Christians. (Of course, if 'held by Christians' means held by *all* Christians, then once again there will be precious few substitutions for '*p*' that will generate truths, and most of those that do will be mundane and not connected to traditional Christian doctrines, attitudes, and practices in very significant ways. I suspect, however, that 'held by Christians' is better taken to mean that it is held by a sizeable number (if not a majority) of Christians, that it has the force of some recognizable tradition behind it, and that it has clear and direct relations to well-established

Christian doctrines, attitudes, and practices.[2]) Even without settling on the elusive referent of 'our modern worldview' (which has obvious bearing on the appropriateness of classifying the reasons as justifying), premise (3) is very contentious indeed. I would have thought that the disturbingly frequent pieces in *The New York Times* containing some version of the sentence, "Well, it's time to rewrite the textbooks, since after the last half-century of confident but mistaken consensus, the scientists at one of our leading universities have finally discovered the real story about...," would have inspired a bit more modesty than I have witnessed when watching premise (3) pressed into service. I do not, however, wish to quarrel with the extension of 'our modern worldview' or take issue with what I take to be its cavalier and overworked invocation. Rather, I'll let premise (3) slide and instead direct my critical remarks at a variety of instances of premise (2). Accordingly, one of my two primary aims in this chapter is to undermine a handful of popular representatives of the recipe for the rejection of Christian belief that *p* that I suspect have been far more influential than they deserve.

My other primary aim in this chapter is to transform at least some of these efforts to discredit certain fashionable anti-Christian arguments into positive reasons for Christians to take the hypothesis of hyperspace seriously. In other words, I will suggest that not only does the Christian have something to say in response to certain accusations of having beliefs inconsistent with our modern worldview, but, depending on the available alternatives, that those responses may also provide reasonable grounds for endorsing the hypothesis of hyperspace by way of inference to the best explanation.

2. A BRIEF REMARK ON HEAVEN AND HELL

A respectable number of Christian theists will tell you that they believe in Heaven, and a respectable (but perhaps somewhat smaller) number will tell you that they also believe in Hell. The primary

reason for the difference in number concerns moral problems endangering the hypothesis of Hell that do not have counterparts (or else have less pressing counterparts) to threaten the hypothesis of Heaven. I am here interested in a nonmoral issue, however. Consider this brief quiz: are 'Heaven' and 'Hell' referring expressions? If no—stop; you are finished with the quiz. If yes—do they refer? If no—stop; you are finished with the quiz. If yes—what is the ontological category of their referents?

Christians who get to the third question in this quiz are liable to give very different answers, among which you will find (i) special regions (i.e., special places or perhaps special places at particular times); (ii) a plurality of substances and events that occupy special regions; (iii) certain events or states of affairs—namely, the instantiations of certain states of mind; and (iv) certain events or states of affairs—namely, the instantiations of certain relations between minds. We are all familiar with the standard image of living out our days poised between Heaven (some sacred and distant place "up there") and Hell (some dreaded and distant place "down there"), where wonderful and terrible events transpire—whether now or in a day soon to come. We are likewise familiar with the occasional practice of using an expression indiscriminately to refer both to a region and to its occupants, as with the terms 'the universe' or 'the Arctic Circle.' These remarks, then, illustrate options (i) and (ii) above—both of which, we might note, are committed to there being genuine regions that themselves serve as the referents of the expressions or else as the receptacles for the referents of the expressions. Options (iii) and (iv) can appear to circumvent any commitment to the alleged special regions, by contrast. On options (iii) and (iv), the only straightforward commitment is to minds—and to the extent that one is willing to go idealist or dualist about creaturely persons, this carries an additional commitment only to times.

While I take something like option (i) or (ii) to be the traditional notion, it is common to hear option (iii) or (iv) brought in as a replacement conception designed to avoid pesky questions about just *where* these distant and curious regions are to be found, just how many miles they are from New York, and whether the right space-ship might take us on a visit to Heaven or might be launched on a rescue mission to Hell. Instead, the idea is that (for instance) Hell is a state of mind involving a kind of nonspatial separation from God—option (iii)—or (for instance) Heaven is a relation through which some minds enjoy a beatific vision or a mystical union with God—option (iv). And once again, if these persons are disembodied minds, the relevant states and relations may be instantiated now and forevermore without being instantiated at some particular place. Enough introduction; I have first a minor problem, then an observation, and finally a suggestion to explore.

A minor problem: I take human persons to be material objects. There are (I believe) excellent reasons to do so, both on philosophical grounds and also (perhaps surprisingly) on the grounds that such a metaphysics best conforms to the beliefs, attitudes, and practices that I take to be constitutive of Christianity....Accordingly, I reject the idealist or dualist strategy above that would avoid all commitment to special places. On the metaphysics that I think is required by options (iii) and (iv), the straightforward commitment to human minds doubles as a commitment to certain material objects—and to the extent that one endorses the occupancy account of material objects (as I do), this carries an additional commitment to places, as well. Moreover, given the Christian doctrine of the general resurrection and its very heavy emphasis on an embodied afterlife for human persons, whether or not human bodies are absent from the world to come makes little difference to the need for locations for those equipped with glorious and imperishable bodies to be so embodied (see Bynum 1995 and my 2001*a*: ch. 7). Perhaps it is worth noting, however, that even if a commitment to places were to be thus reestablished, the pesky questions above can still be sidestepped, for there is no requirement that the places in question have current mysterious locations, or are removed at some unfathomable distance, or are unfamiliar in any way—just that they be capable of housing bodies that are enjoying certain distinctive states or bodies that are joined in special relations with one another.

An observation: The attractiveness of demoting Heaven and Hell from their traditional conceptions as places to a mere manner of referring to states or relations depends (I suspect) in large part on painting the new conception as an acceptable enough substitute and as a way to avoid the embarrassment that can be elicited when the incredulous atheist asks why we don't converse with the blessed when our hot-air balloons take us into the clouds, why we don't spy any harp-players when jetting from the East to the West coast, and why the Hubble telescope has yet to photograph any pearly gates. Or, more seriously, when she asks just what sort of miraculous transport is supposed to carry the saved on an intergalactic voyage to their new and eternal home. These inquiries can seem especially awkward in a setting where the received opinion is that the large-scale structure of our universe is very well understood and in which we have fairly impressive access to a rather sizeable local chunk of it. No longer are we inclined to think it compelling to say that, for all anyone knows, the kingdom of Heaven sits proudly in the sky just beyond the reach of our perceptual faculties, or that the tormented suffer in Hell somewhere in the depths below our feet. In fact, retreating from such pointed questions has generated a rather deflationary conception of Heaven in contemporary Christianity. It is easy to feel, though, that we have lost sight of something magnificent when our poor and paltry modern substitute is held up and compared to St Augustine's vision of a realm in which we shall be lovingly reunited with one another clothed in new and glorified bodies, or to the blissful and brilliant kingdom of light championed by medieval scholasticism, or to the Elysian Fields likeness of the Renaissance conception, or to the unbounded opportunities for social interaction and celebration with the saints in the models from the eighteenth and nineteenth centuries.

Yet, despite the discomfiture of it all, participation in the direction-laden talk of Heaven and Hell is very easy to fall into and remarkably well entrenched. The presupposition of location can be found *everywhere*—from speculative ange-lology and demonology to both Old and New Testaments, to the creeds, to the pulpit, to conversations at the dinner table. Angels fall from, and ministers climb Jacob's ladder to Heaven, the rich man looks at Abraham and Lazarus across the great chasm that separates Paradise from Hell, and The Apostles' Creed reports Christ himself descending into Hell. I do not mean to suggest that these well-known traditions and scriptural passages cannot be glossed without commitment to Heaven and Hell as genuine locations, but I do mean to bring to the reader's mind the first few entries on an impressive list of examples of the common presumption of Heaven and Hell as places.

A suggestion: As I see it, there is no pressing need to capitulate or to attempt to avoid embarrassment by replacing the tradition of regarding Heaven and Hell as genuine locations with confused and apologetic talk of states and relations.[3] Where are these curious regions to be found, and how many miles are they from New York? Perhaps they are arbitrarily close both to New York and to the spot on which you are currently standing in the directions ana and kata; compare a two-space of milk-slices and honey-slices that could be hovering just millimeters above Flatland. Why don't we take a spaceship for a blissful vacation in Heaven or on a bold and daring rescue mission to Hell? Perhaps because our modes of transportation are confined to the directions of our three-space prison; whereas we can travel up, down, left, right, forth, and back, no spaceship can take us ana or kata. Why does no astronaut glimpse the host of Heaven when orbiting the Earth, and why does no rig-worker drill into the bowels of Hell when searching for oil? Perhaps because those simply aren't the directions that can take you to those sacred and terrible locations.

One can, of course, happily embrace the deflationary view if it seems best in the end. Significantly, though, the Christian can grant without a fuss the standard pronouncements of our modern worldview regarding the structure and inhabitants of our local corner of the galaxy, and he can even concede that certain traditional locations for Heaven and Hell are thereby forfeit,

while still maintaining that Heaven and Hell are real places with genuine inhabitants (without being ridiculously small, unimaginably far away, or invisible realms magically co-located with the perceptible inhabitants of our everyday world). In fact, given the infinite opportunities for diversity in different subregions of hyperspace, even the most extravagant conceptions of the populations, environments, and hierarchies of Heaven and Hell could be back on the table for discussion, without fear of refutation from what our modern worldview has to say about our own little corner of our own three-space prison.

On an autobiographical note, I do not maintain the receptacle view of Heaven and Hell to be absolutely non-negotiable (but I am a bit hesitant about that). For the impressive number that do, I think that this might appear an attractive argument from Christianity to hyperspace. I will say, however, that I think it is pleasantly suggestive and one of a number of intriguing considerations that together begin to construct a case worthy of consideration. Here's another.

3. A BRIEF REMARK ON THE GARDEN OF EDEN

In the parting paragraph of his beautifully written and absorbing history of the Garden of Eden in myth and tradition, Jean Delumeau writes: "there is no possible way of reconciling, on the one hand, what science tells us about the origin of the human race and, on the other, the earthly paradise of our holy cards and the position given to our first parents by Western theology" [*History of Paradise: The Garden of Eden in Myth and Tradition*, trans. Matthew O'Connell (New York: Continuum, 1995) p. 233]. And a little earlier

> the tragic theology of Western Christendom can be explained only by an exaggerated view of the beauties of the garden of Eden and the unparalleled advantages that God has granted to our first parents. But our age is now compelled to agree with Teilhard de Chardin that there is 'not the least trace on the horizon, not the smallest scar, to mark the ruins of a golden age or our cutting off from a better world.' (1995: 230)

Delumeau's 'there is no possible way of reconciling' is, of course, too strong, and Chardin's 'not the least trace' may be a correct enough estimation of the absence of revealing remains in our own three-space but could be a bit premature as a final verdict prior to examining horizons ana and kata. But first some history.

The modern inclination to regard tales of the Garden of Eden (i.e., Paradise, not Heaven) as charming and quaint allegory (and, one might add, to ridicule non-figurative interpretations) has early roots in prominent figures in the history of Christianity. Philo (in the first century), Origen (in the third century), and St Ephrem and St Gregory of Nyssa (both in the fourth century) all advocated a nonliteral interpretation of the story of the garden, its tree of life, its stunning variety of flora and fauna, and its remarkably well-behaved wildlife. Equally prominent early literalists can be found, however, with St Theophilus of Antioch (in the second century), St Irenaeus and St Hippolytus (both in the third century), and Bishop Epiphanius (in the fourth century) all arguing for the claims that Paradise was beneath the Heavens, its garden, trees, and rivers all material created things, and its genuine location eastward in Eden a historical reality.[4]

Throughout much of Christian history, its leading figures have tended toward realist over figurative readings of the garden passages in Genesis. Undoubtedly, much of this consensus can be traced to the qualified endorsement of Augustine and the heavy endorsement of Aquinas, with the bishop of Hippo and the Angelic Doctor both fully acknowledging the spiritual meaning of the story while firmly insisting on the materiality of the tree of life and on the corporeality of the rivers watering a spatially located garden. Notwithstanding such champions, traditional reasons for finding realism attractive have always been controversial. Nevertheless, they have been compelling to many. The justifications range from applying widely accepted principles about what factual lessons may be appropriately drawn from the different forms of narrative found in Scripture, to arguments to the [then] best explanations of the origin of species, to providing a temporary home for Enoch and Elijah—notable for being taken out of this world prior to their deaths (joined perhaps by the saints and martyrs), to furnishing a way for Christ to keep his promise to the good thief without thereby requiring a doctrine of immediate judgment and resurrection, to make a truth-teller out of Paul and his tale of a third heaven in 2 Corinthians, to reconcile various claims in Revelation with what was already well known about the world's inhabitants and laws, to serving as a place of rest without decay for the bodies of the departed (or at least certain of their parts) to lie in wait for the day of judgment and, hopefully, resurrection.

While running unopposed, as it were, generations of devoted, extravagant proponents of a historical Eden wrote flowery passages on the characteristics of the garden and fought bitter arguments about the spatio-temporal location of Paradise, passages and arguments that frequently contain *considerably* more detail than the available evidence might have warranted.[5] Despite these intricate and fascinating battles over geography and chronology, a commonly shared presumption among the combatants was that, wherever Eden was located, the sin of our predecessors had rendered it inaccessible to us—its paths now barred by a flaming sword and cherubim charged with making its entrance impassable to all flesh. Interestingly, it was also supposedly protected from non-living trespassers, such as the rising waters of the alleged great flood of Genesis, which supposedly covered the Earth, yet could not destroy the garden on the often invoked grounds that its position was "too high" to be reached. Whether or not one has the slightest sympathy with the flood story, the widespread conviction that the location of the garden was somewhere near but removed from the Earth (in some direction or other which could not be traversed merely by rising from its surface) dovetails nicely with the suggestions that will appear below. Of course, agreement on the impassability doctrine would lead to a conviction that a certain kind of resolution to the dispute on location was simply unattainable—with cherubim on patrol, it's not as if the winning theory simply awaited verification by expedition.

Inevitably, however, the wild exuberance of the Middle Ages and the remarkable ingenuity of its realist representatives gave way to a sobering this-worldly orientation in the eighteenth century and to apologetic and more scientifically informed Christians who, feeling the pressure of the worldview of the times, were willing and even eager to retreat to a symbolic reading of the garden of Genesis. Unsurprisingly, a primary catalyst for this turn of mind in the history of Christian thought was buried in the fossil beds and in what they appeared to say about the age of the Earth, the absence of a great deluge, and the origin of species. Nonliteralism has prevailed.

Today any talk of a historical garden is quite likely to be met with a mixture of pity and condescension at best and with open and unreserved hostility at worst. For what it's worth, I suspect that such widespread contempt (which far outstrips the less common contempt for Christianity in general) depends in no small part on conflating a minimal thesis of a historical Garden of Eden—a privileged and sacred place that plays a unique role in the divine plan—with a number of other theses with which it has been historically entwined. Nonetheless, the claim that there was (and perhaps still is) a spatially located paradisiacal garden is radically distinct from the decisively refuted young Earth hypothesis, the seriously dubious tales of a worldwide flood, the unbiblical yet popular tradition that our forebears possessed preternatural gifts, the somewhat more plausible denial of evolutionary theory, and the doctrine of original sin and the Fall.[6] Moreover, minimal realism about the Garden is likewise separable from the fine details of the biblical narrative that purports to tell of a pair of historical individuals, of the naming of the animals, of an outdoor surgery, of the conversing with a snake, of the eating of forbidden fruit, of a sewing party, and of the expulsion from the Garden for transgressing its laws. Just to be clear, I do separate minimal realism about the Garden from this host of other hypotheses; in particular, I take the Adam and Eve story (in almost all of its details) to be mythical, although insofar as I believe the construction and preservation of that myth to have been conducted under the influence of the Holy Spirit, I take it to have special significance and to touch on topics of significance to all human persons (near and far, past and future). While admiring memorable devices such as talking snakes and luscious yet forbidden fruits, I take the primary function of the myth to be to document the occurrence of a historical event involving our ancestors—namely, their falling away from God and their separating themselves and their descendants from the divine presence by a path we cannot retrace by our own power. Whether this Fall was embodied in some special individual or pair of individuals, whether it was accompanied by a loss of preternatural gifts, whether it marked a sudden change in the biology or genetics of its participants, or in the environment in which they lived and died, or in the laws that governed that environment—are all questions on which I am more or less skeptical.

But whether there was (and perhaps still is) a Garden of Eden—a privileged and sacred *place* that plays a unique (and perhaps ongoing) role in the divine plan—is a question for whose affirmative answer I can work up much more sympathy. There are, of course, many many different ways to speculate (with wild abandon even) about how the hypothesis of hyperspace can make way for the Garden. In fact, it takes very little creative reading of the many centuries of discussion of the characteristics of the Garden (informed by the hypothesis of hyperspace) to generate several satisfying "fits," especially when viewed against the variety of historical reasons speaking in favor of realism that were introduced above. I leave such entertaining speculations to the interested reader, who might begin by considering, for instance, questions regarding how the salient landmarks of the Garden could be spatially related to uncontested historical locations (e.g., earthly rivers that allegedly have their headwaters in Paradise), how it might be both spatially proximate, yet altogether unenterable without divine or angelic assistance, how the bodies of the dead might be so easily transported there to await resurrection, and how it might be ringed by fire barring all flesh without the least trace of haze to serve as a smoking gun revealing its presence. Or, to focus on a historically perplexing example, consider a mighty stumbling block for the Renaissance pastime of rediscovering the location of the Garden on Earth: given the assumptions then in play, the

Garden must have been *magnificently* large in order to house the stunning variety of beasts and plants and water enough to supply four major rivers (cf. Delumeau *ibid.*: 172–4). In hyperspace, however, a garden can be as big as you please, as close as you want, and furnished in the most extravagant of ways.

Once again, on an autobiographical note, I do not maintain a minimal realism about the Garden to be absolutely non-negotiable. Again, though, for the minority that do, I would think that this might appear an attractive argument from Christianity to hyperspace. But, as before, I will say that I think it is pleasantly suggestive and one of a number of intriguing considerations that together begin to construct a case worthy of consideration. Here's another.

4. A BRIEF REMARK ON ANGELS AND DEMONS

As a self-professed non-expert, I marvel at the confidence and level of fine detail in the literature on angelology and demonology. To an outsider, this scholarly pursuit—of advancing beyond the meticulously discussed biblical texts (and apocrypha), sifting through the hundreds of redoubtable and uneven authorities found in apocalyptic, kabbalistic, Talmudic, Gnostic, patristic, and Merkabah texts and lore, and properly evaluating the influence of world literature, music, art, and a wealth of diverse and multi-layered rituals on our traditional beliefs and attitudes regarding angels and demons—seems a staggeringly difficult task.[7] Fortunately, though, I do not have to take sides on just which sources properly identify genuine angels and demons and on just which texts or customs properly reveal their activities. Instead, I will simply take up the far less daunting chore of rehearsing some of the commonly ascribed accomplishments of the angels:

> Angels perform a multiplicity of duties and tasks. Preeminently they serve God...They also carry out missions from God to man. But many serve man directly as guardians, counselors, guides, judges, interpreters, cooks, comforters, dragomen, matchmakers, and gravediggers. They are responsive to invocations when such invocations are properly formulated and the conditions are propitious. In occult lore angels are conjured up not only to help an invocant strengthen his faith, heal his afflictions, find lost articles, increase his worldly goods, and procure offspring, but also to circumvent and destroy an enemy. There are instances where an angel or troop of angels turned the tide of battle, abated storms, conveyed saints to Heaven, brought down plagues, fed hermits, helped plowmen, converted heathens. An angel multiplied the seed of Hagar, protected Lot, caused the destruction of Sodom, hardened Pharaoh's heart, rescued Daniel from the lions' den and Peter from prison. (G. Davidson *ibid*: p. xvii)

That's a representative list. For the purposes of the discussion below, let us note that the alleged doings of the demons are similar enough (although unsurprisingly rather less admirable) as to not require separate cataloguing.

One overwhelmingly striking feature of the entries here is the presumption of embodiment and the attribution of causal control over many of the familiar material objects in our everyday world. Hence the challenge: *if* these marvelous entities are really gallivanting about impregnating women, wrestling men, and conveying various messages to frightened young girls—or (better yet) *if* they are paired up with us one-one, vigilantly hovering ever so near, guarding their charges, and watching our every move...then why don't the majority of us see and hear them? At least once in a while? Presumably even the most radiant and beautifully embodied things have definite shapes and locations. Just where is this vast horde of do-gooders camped? How do they travel to their appointed destinations with such apparently law-breaking speed and ease? With all that heavy lifting to do, how on earth do they continually manage to avoid reflecting light or making noises that would expose their hiding places?

As you no doubt anticipate from the preceding two sections, answers to these pointed questions are available from the plentiful resources of hyperspace. There are, of course, serious and troubling worries (both moral and metaphysical) about the existence and status of angels and demons that are worth confronting. There are, of course, serious and troubling questions about the authority (or lack thereof) of texts and traditions reporting their whereabouts and assignments that are also worth confronting. There are, of course, the impatient and contemptuous stares that the mere mention of angels and demons provokes in many educated folk in the twenty-first century. Still, these controversies need not, perhaps, be fueled by worries about literal locations or apparent hiddenness. Angels and demons, should they exist, can be embodied with perfectly determinate shapes and sizes, and they can be endowed with familiar causal powers to manipulate the material objects in our everyday environments, and they can be thoroughly subject to detection even by perceptual faculties as crude and insensitive as ours. Yet they can accomplish their merciful or awesome or sinister feats (as the case may be) while avoiding exposure—simply by carefully exploiting the opportunities afforded by movement in hyperspace.

One final time then, on an autobiographical note, I do not maintain this multi-dimensional route of escape from the pressing questions on the location and mysterious hiddenness of angels and demons to be absolutely non-negotiable. However, I do think that this might ground an argument from Christianity to hyperspace attractive to the sizeable group of Christians who profess belief in angels, demons, and their interactions with each other, the world, and ourselves. But, as before I say that I think it is pleasantly suggestive and one of a number of intriguing considerations that together begin to construct a case worthy of consideration.

5. NEW TESTAMENT MIRACLES

The four gospels of the New Testament tell a series of powerful and moving stories. Belief in the literal occurrence of many of the events relayed in these narratives is often taken to be partly constitutive of being Christian and to be at the very core of Christianity. I have neither the expertise nor the confidence to comment with much authority or at any great length on the passages and traditions which make an appearance below. (In fact, it takes only a brief

trip to a modestly equipped library to teach the novice how frightfully much there is to learn on these topics and to replace any rash intention of making confident pronouncements with the less ambitious hope of advancing tentative hypotheses.) Nevertheless, I have selected three significant moments from the gospels that I would like to discuss in the hopes of paying off a promissory note offered in section 1 above.

As mentioned earlier, I'm not at all interested in entering the debate on the minimal belief conditions for being Christian, but I do think that the case to be made for the centrality to Christianity of the alleged events discussed below is considerably stronger than is, say, the case for a historical Garden of Eden. Consequently, I suspect that a respectably large number of Christians take a straightforwardly literal line on the reporting of these alleged events. But this widespread literalism is precisely the source of a number of deeply influential instances of the recipe for rejection of Christian belief that p (i.e., of instances of the argument form that was the subject of a brief introduction in section 1 above). Since every one of the alleged events in question is frequently criticized as being at irreconcilable odds with our modern worldview, these beliefs are exactly the sort of target that certain fashionable arguments are so often thought to strike with lethal force. Once again, however, it seems to me that not only does the Christian have a way to block the charge of inconsistency with our modern worldview, but also that the very same responses that restore consistency may (depending on the available alternatives) provide reasonable grounds for endorsing the hypothesis of hyperspace by way of inference to the best explanation.

The Virgin Birth

The virgin birth of Jesus Christ is a view very widely endorsed by the councils and creeds and the early church fathers. There are, of course, a variety of interpretations of this traditional view. Perhaps the weakest of these takes as its point of departure the Annunciation (in Luke 1: 26–8), in which Mary acknowledges her virginity to the angel Gabriel, but the account does not take a stand on her virginity beyond the beginning of her pregnancy. At the other end of the spectrum, perhaps the strongest of the interpretations maintains that Mary remained a virgin throughout her life. One central point of agreement, however, is that whereas Mary played a biological role (and a voluntary role) in bringing Jesus into the world (e.g., in supplying biological material for the body of Jesus and nutrition during his stages of prenatal development), tradition declares that Jesus was conceived by the Holy Spirit (as opposed to any human father). These details suffice as background for the objection.

The objection: no one can become pregnant in this fashion, and talk of such a supernatural origin is nothing more than a transparent thievery from pagan mythology. Every child knows that you can't put an object in a closed box without opening its lid or penetrating one of its surfaces, and Christians are in some serious trouble if their only way to explain Mary's pregnancy without threatening her virginity is to maintain that objects suddenly appear out of thin air in her womb or else pass into (and out of) her body without disrupting the integrity of its natural barriers.

A response: first, a quibble. Even if our modern worldview generally frowns upon fanciful tales of material things popping into existence out of thin air and of objects mysteriously moving through walls without disrupting the integrity of their surfaces, it is perhaps an exaggeration to insist that it is *inconsistent* with these events. Indeed, popular presentations of theoretical physics routinely make a grand show of announcing how surprising today's fashionable theories have (at long last) discovered the material world to be, and talk of discontinuous jumps or of objects doing something very much like materializing out of thin air serve as centerpieces in these explanations. But set that aside.

Consider a closed box in Flatland (it's just a square with an unbroken perimeter and an empty interior). You can't put a Flatland object in the box without opening its lid or penetrating one of its surfaces—unless, that is, you don't confine your movements to the two-dimensional space in which the square is found. With access to three dimensions, it's an easy matter to

astonish the simple folk of Flatland by taking an object up, then moving it above the interior of the square, and finally moving it back down so that it rests safely in the square's interior. When the scientists of Flatland inspect the perimeter, they will find that the square's natural barriers are undisturbed and that the lid has remained locked throughout the process. There are, of course, other hypotheses available to the denizens of Flatland. Perhaps the object passes through the surface of the square without doing violence to it in the manner of two material objects that can co-locate without sharing parts and without causally affecting one another in the process. Or perhaps the object underwent a discontinuous jump of location. The relevant point is not that a movement through three-space is the only available way to generate the outcome, but rather, that it is one available way that doesn't require the inhabitants of Flatland to take a stand on the physics of discontinuous motion or on the metaphysics of co-location or on anything at all bound up with their modern worldview.

Similarly, then, with access to four dimensions, even if the Holy Spirit (like Mary) had to make a material contribution to the conception of Jesus, it is an easy matter to take the relevant material object ana, then move it over the interior of Mary's womb, and finally move it back kata so that it rests safely in the womb's interior, without disturbing any natural barriers in the process. Once again, however, perhaps the conception of Jesus by the Holy Spirit required only the presence of material in Mary's womb (or certain changes in material already there) which did not have an empirical causal history extending outside her body. Or perhaps some material object was the subject of divinely directed discontinuous motion from outside to inside Mary's body. Or perhaps material penetrated Mary's body without loss of integrity to its surfaces by way of co-location. As before, though, the point is not that a movement through four-space is the only available way to generate the outcome, but rather that it is one available way not subject to immediate refutation by appeal to our modern worldview.

Three Miracles of Jesus: Water into Wine, the Feeding of the 5,000, Walking on Water

The gospels tell of a number of miracles allegedly performed by Jesus. Several of these alleged miracles have come under heavy fire, and those that profess them under heavy ridicule. I would like to develop some thoughts concerning New Testament miracles by focusing on three that often provoke especially harsh responses: (i) changing water into wine at the wedding atCana (John 2: 1–11) (ii) the feeding the 5,000 with five loaves and two fishes (Matt. 14: 13–21; Mark 6: 32–44; Luke 9: 10–17; John 6: 1–14) and (iii) walking on water in the Sea of Galilee (Matt. 14: 22–33; Mark 6: 45–52; John 6: 15–21). The stories are so familiar that they need no retelling, as is also the case with regard to the most common objections confronting them. How, then, can the hypothesis of hyperspace be of service here?

With respect to the miracle of changing water into wine, allegedly, although the stone jars were filled with water, they poured wine. So where did the water go? Here are some rather intriguing hypotheses. First option: the water went nowhere at all, for a single substance was inside the jars throughout, which was first water and then wine. This option has its share of physical difficulties (e.g., the unpromising view that being water is a phase-form of a kind of stuff which has among its other potential phase-forms being wine). Second option: the water went nowhere at all, for whereas the water remained, the right ingredients were added to and properly mixed with the water already present to produce wine when poured. This option has its share of physical difficulties as well (even though one tradition of commentary of Jesus as magician speculates on the chemicals allegedly residing in the bottom of the jars which would return any gift of water with something approximating a rather poor-quality wine). Third option: the water stayed right where it was (i.e., confined to the partitions of the jar containing only water), and then the jars were emptied of wine (which was carefully hidden away in the other partitions of the jar all

along). This would surely be an amusing party trick, but one supposes rather easily exposed and (given the circumstances of the wedding) rather hard to set the stage for at the outset. Fourth option: the water disappeared from the jars entirely, and was very quickly replaced with wine, which completely filled the cavity thereby vacated. Of course, the natural response to the fourth option is that it offends against our modern worldview; more than a hundred gallons of water doesn't up and vanish from six stone jars so quickly (or at least not without them getting smashed and other things getting noticeably wet), and despite how nice it would be if it were otherwise, wine doesn't cooperatively appear and fill our empty containers from the inside out. Moreover, this natural response is a perfectly sensible response. Suppose, however, that the water is displaced ana, and that the wine is poured into the jars from wineskins lying kata. Then, although nothing in our own three-space gets wet, a hundred gallons or more may well be bathing some garden just inches away, and although no visible container empties its contents into the waiting jars, wineskins arbitrarily close to the cavities of the jars fill them to the brim without ever leaving their own locations outside our three-space. And all this transpires with no dry chemicals hidden within, or multiple partitions secreted away in, the jars.

With respect to the feeding of the 5,000, allegedly five loaves and two fishes fed a multitude (with several basketfuls left over). Where did the food come from? Well, presumably the pattern is becoming clear. Without magic or creation *ex nihilo*, a nearly empty basket can come to contain a previously undetected fish (which travels ana into the basket) and loaf (which travels kata into the basket). And provided that the nearby spaces are well stocked, the basket can prove hard to empty should it acquire its contents in this fashion.

With respect to Jesus' walking on water on the Sea of Galilee, allegedly Jesus walked on water over a considerable distance to reach his disciples, who were rowing a boat in the middle of the Sea in the middle of a storm in the middle of the night.

Objection: No he didn't.

A response: Let your thoughts drift once again to Flatland. Suppose that the polygons residing there are bound by something like gravity to the perimeters of enormous circles—their planets, so to speak. To pass one another, they have to either jump over or tunnel under one another. Moreover, the interior of these circles is occupied by analogues of soil and water (i.e., a kind of substance on which they can rest and move and another kind of substance in which they will sink towards the center-point of the circle and perish). Now one of these planets has the following feature: Flatland soil is found on all points of its perimeter with the exception of a small arc which features Flatland water (i.e., if the circle were a clock, only the region from 12:00 to 1:00 would be Flatland water, while the remainder would be Flatland soil). Any polygon wanting to travel from the point located at 11:59 to the point located at 1:01 either has a long journey ahead of him or else had better build a bridge. Bridges aren't impossible here. Dig up a skinny curved rock in the Flatland soil, keep it in front of you, stand it upright, let it fall across the Flatland water, and then scamper across to the other side. Of course, a proper bridge like that has to come from somewhere, has to have enough length to span the relevant gap, and has to be locatable by the Flatlanders on the other side of the arc awaiting your arrival, since it is extended in the space in which they reside. Finally, suppose that there just don't happen to be any rocks on this planet large enough to do the trick. Not all is lost, however, for with the assistance of a good-natured three-spacer a perfectly good bridge can be had; this benefactor need only take some two-dimensional object out of Flatland, turn it sideways, and reinsert it so that it extends above and below Flatland at right angles. The agreeable object will, of course, still intersect Flatland, but with only one of its one-dimensional cross-sections. Provided this cross-section is more like Flatland soil than Flatland water, that's all you need to bridge the gap. Curiously enough, even if the resulting bridge were merely a proper part of a much larger object, it might nevertheless be very hard for the

Flatlanders on the other side of the gap to detect it, since (after all) it intersects the space in which they reside only on a curve. In fact, it would be natural enough to believe that a Flatlander approaching on this bridge was walking on Flatland water.

The relevant application should be straightforward enough. Take some well-chosen three-dimensional object (either from somewhere in our own three-space or from some neighboring three-space), turn it sideways (so to speak), reinsert it so that it intersects our three-space with only one of its two-dimensional cross-sections, position that cross-section so that it spans the Sea of Galilee, and then (provided that the cross-section is more like soil than water) permit a three-spacer to walk across the bridge. Finally, when the structure has served its purpose, simply withdraw the original object and restore it to its original location—no remnants of the temporary bridge need remain. Curiously enough, even if this bridge is merely a proper part of even a monstrously big object, it may nevertheless be very hard for the three-spacers in the middle of the Sea in the middle of a storm in the middle of the night to detect it, since (after all) it intersects the space in which they reside only on a plane. In fact, it would be natural enough to believe that anyone traversing this bridge was walking on water.[8]

Intriguingly, several of the other allegedly physically impossible events recorded in the New Testament are susceptible to similar candidate explanations that take some detour or other through hyperspace. Perhaps the discussion initiated here can serve as a model for the interested reader to explore the extent to which many of the miracles attributed to Jesus can be defended when subjected to the all too familiar kinds of critique rehearsed above.

The Resurrection of Jesus and the Ascension

One of the most central claims in all Christianity is that, after his suffering, death, and entombment, Jesus Christ rose from the dead and appeared to friends and disciples a number of times before his ascension (Matt. 28; Mark 16; Luke 24; John 20). So central is this that a surprising number of Christians seem willing to let the entire case for their faith rest upon this one foundation.

Philosophical, scientific, and religious questions, objections, and replies concerning the possibility and mechanics of the resurrection of Jesus, its relation to the doctrine of the general resurrection, and its alleged role in our salvation and redemption are legion. Here, however, I am concerned with only a rather small corner of that complex debate.

One might suppose (as I do) that Jesus was embodied throughout the period between his death and ascension. Or one might suppose (as, I suspect, do most of those who are sympathetic to the doctrine at all) that Jesus was separated from his body at death and later reunited with his body before appearing to the women and his disciples. In either case, the body which is Jesus' body (either by identity or in virtue of its past- and future-oriented properties) was somewhere or other throughout the period between his death and ascension.[9] Or, if his body was not somewhere or other, then at least the parts that composed it at its death were still in relative proximity to one another, and those "particles arranged corpse-wise" were jointly somewhere or other throughout the period between his death and ascension. Although the view that Jesus acquired a numerically distinct body at his resurrection may seem to receive some support from the Lucan account (24: 13–31), in which a risen Jesus walked with those who had known him without being recognized, this view seems wholly undercut by the claims that the resurrected body bore the wounds of the crucifixion and by the tradition of commentary on both the resurrection of Jesus and the general resurrection.

So a puzzling question presents itself to anyone who professes belief in the resurrection of Christ: exactly where was the body of Jesus during the supposed forty-day interval between his rising from the sepulcher and his ascension into Heaven witnessed by his disciples? Unsurprisingly, the question can quickly get even more puzzling, depending on one's further commitments, which may lead one to countenance even further

restrictions on an acceptable answer. For example, one might note that the strips of linen and the burial cloth that John 20: 3–9 describes as remaining on the floor of the tomb mean that the body had simply disappeared from its clothing as well as its tomb (as a way of arguing against the hypothesis that the body was stolen from its resting place by thieves, who presumably wouldn't have taken the time to disrobe it first). Or one might focus on a popular tradition found throughout Scripture and in The Apostles' Creed—that between his death and resurrection Jesus descended into Hell (interpreted as a genuine bodily change of location which permitted Jesus to preach the message of redemption to some of the departed, as opposed to an interpretation merely emphasizing his hellish agony and suffering on the cross). Or one might take the description of Luke 24: 31 at its word and maintain that the body of the risen Jesus could suddenly vanish from the sight of those seated at table with him. Or one might insist on the literalness of John 20: 19 (and again of John 20: 26) in which a risen Jesus abruptly appears in the midst of his disciples gathered together in a locked room without, the gospel writer intimates, entering through either a window or a door.

Understandably, to the extent that the gospel accounts of the resurrection are committed not only to the view that someone has risen from the dead, but also to the view that the risen man can apparently appear and disappear at will, they will have a tough time earning the respect of (or even a patient hearing from) those students of the modern worldview who have learned that medium-sized objects like human bodies simply don't behave like that. As before, though, the hypothesis of hyperspace can offer some protection from at least one form of criticism on this score.

To return one final time to the general theme of this chapter, then, let us acknowledge that a body moving ana or kata could leave its clothes or burial robes without taking them off, could vanish from a dinner table without a trace, and could appear in a locked room without passing through its windows, doors, or walls. In short, a body free to move in hyperspace could be positioned just inches away, yet remain undetectable for days on end, and could enter and leave our own three-space with exactly the ease and abruptness that is attributed to the risen Jesus.

A parting (tentative) comment: in the description of the ascension which opens the book of Acts (1: 1–11), the disciples who have just seen Jesus disappear for the last time are informed that "this same Jesus, who has been taken from you into heaven, will come back in the same way you have seen him go into heaven." Accordingly, one who is already committed to the relevant New Testament claims and who finds the discussion in this chapter promising, not only as a defensive maneuver to combat one popular style of criticism, but also as a candidate for the best explanation of a phenomenon he or she thinks requires explanation, should not be at all surprised if (like the next revolution in physics) the Second Coming turns out to take a path through higher-dimensional geometry.

NOTES

1. Of course, there are particularly aggressive Christians, too, who unreflectively and without a principled game plan cite biblical passages torn from their original context in opposition to this or that well-established scientific view. Such behavior has its own share of unsophisticated and unchallenging illustrations, as well.

2. Fortunately, nothing I say here will require verdicts on what is or is not central to Christianity for even on what the vexed term 'Christianity' means). One can pronounce on clear instances of being rich without first demarcating the line of separation between the rich and the poor. Similarly, one can recognize that the claims of the Virgin Birth and the resurrection of Christ are clear candidates for the kind of proposition I am here discussing, whereas the once common Christian presupposition of the geocentric theory of the heavens is not.

3. Or, once again, if there is, then it is grounded in moral rather than physical and metaphysical concerns.

4. For complete references and discussion of these and many more relevant texts, see Delumeau's *History of Paradise: The Garden of Eden in Myth and Tradition,* 1995, to which I am also indebted for the historical material in the following few paragraphs.

5. See especially Delumeau *ibid.*: ch. 9 for the history of debate on the timing of the events allegedly transpiring in the garden—down to the hour!

6. A quick note: I say 'the somewhat more plausible denial of evolutionary theory' not to suggest that I believe that theory to be false, but simply to register that I think it is grossly oversold. The case to be made not for the verdict that it is incorrect but instead for the verdict that it is much less defensible than is commonly reported is really quite impressive. . . .

7. For an inventory of and an introductory commentary on these sources, as well as for a taste of what they deliver, see Gustav Davidson's accessible and entertaining *A Dictionary of Angels* (New York: Free Press, 1971)—especially the introductory essay.

8. So why does Peter sink when he ventures out of the boat? It should be obvious that there is a variety of ways to respond (and that for present purposes it really doesn't matter which addition we tack on to the story). The only point being advanced here is that the perfectly reasonable thoughts backing the brief but apparently compelling objection reported above (e.g., that no man can stand unsupported on a surface of only water, that it is contrary to our understanding of the world that temporary bridges extending for miles can materialize and dematerialize without a trace, that the relative strengths of the fundamental forces don't go locally suspended from time to time, and so forth) need not be forfeited in order to provide a "just so" story that reconciles an allegedly offending report with the restrictions imposed by our modern worldview.

9. A quick acknowledgment: those who opt for the claim that Jesus (like other human persons) is identical to a material object have some explaining to do. One option is that being human is a phase sortal of certain persons who are embodied throughout their existence. Another option is that being material is not an essential property of those objects that exemplify it; in other words, one of the changes that certain things can survive is from material to non-material thing.

BIBLIOGRAPHY

Bynum, C. W. *The Resurrection of the Body in Western Christianity.* 200–1336. New York: Columbia University Press, 2005.

Rea, Michael. *A Materialist Metaphysics of the Human Person.* Chapter 7. Ithaca, NY: Cornell University Press, 2001.

PART SIX

Death and Immortality

Of all the many forms which natural religion has assumed none probably has exerted so deep and far-reaching an influence on human life as the belief in immortality and the worship of the dead; hence [a discussion] of this momentous creed and of the practical consequences which have been deduced from it can hardly fail to be at once instructive and impressive, whether we regard the record with complacency as a noble testimony to the aspiring genius of man, who claims to outlive the sun and the stars, or whether we view it with pity as a melancholy monument of fruitless labour and barren ingenuity expended in prying into that great mystery of which fools profess their knowledge and wise men confess their ignorance.

SIR JAMES FRAZIER, *The Belief in Immortality,* vol. 1 (London: Macmillan,1913), vii–viii.

IS THERE LIFE AFTER DEATH? Few questions have troubled humans as deeply as this one. Is this finite, short existence of three score and ten years all that we have? Or is there reason to hope for a blessed postmortem existence where love, justice, and peace, which we now experience in fragmented forms, will unfold in all their fullness and enable human existence to find fulfillment? Are we merely mortal or blessedly immortal?

Anthropological studies reveal a widespread and ancient sense of immortality. Prehistoric societies buried their dead with food so that the deceased would not be hungry in the next life. Most cultures and religions have some version of a belief in another life, whether it be in the form of a resurrected body, a transmigrated soul, reincarnation, or an ancestral spirit present with the tribe.

Let us begin by understanding what we mean by immortality. Being immortal is not simply a matter of living on through our works or in the memories of our loved ones. Rather, for our purposes, immortality involves freedom from death. To be immortal is to be the sort of being who will never undergo the permanent cessation of one's conscious existence.

For most people, death is the ultimate tragedy. It is the paramount evil, for it deprives us of all that we know and love on earth. Our fear of death is profound; we have a passionate longing to live again and to be with our loved ones. And yet there isn't a shred of direct empirical evidence that we shall live again. As far as we can tell scientifically, mental function is tied to brain function, so that when the latter comes permanently to an end, the former does as well. Some claim to have experienced the afterlife, but there are naturalistic explanations for such experiences and, in any case, their veridicality cannot be confirmed by empirical means.

Many have thought, however, that philosophical argument can shed light on the question of immortality. In the Western tradition three views have dominated, one denying life after death and two affirming it. The negative view, going back to the ancient Greek atomist philosophers Democritus and Leucippus, holds that we are identical with our bodies (including our brains), so that when the body dies, the self does as well. We may call this view materialist monism, because it does not allow for the possibility of a soul or spiritual self that can live without the body.

The positive views divide into dualist and monist theories of life after death. The dualist views separate the body from the soul or self of the agent and affirm that it is the soul or self that lives forever. This view was held by the pre-Socratic philosopher Pythagoras (570–500 BCE) and is developed by Plato (427–347 BCE). In modern philosophy it is represented by René Descartes (1596–1650). It is sometimes referred to as the Platonic-Cartesian view of immortality. These philosophers argue that we are essentially spiritual or mental beings and that our bodies are either unreal or not part of our essential selves. Death is merely the separation of our souls from our bodies, a sort of spiritual liberation.

Many in the dualist tradition maintain that the (typical) soul will be reincarnated several, perhaps many, times before attaining the final goal of permanent separation from the body. On this view—found in various strands of Pythagoreanism, Platonism, Buddhism, and Hinduism—embodiment is an undesirable state, and only those who lead the right sort of lifestyle have any hope of freeing themselves from the cycle of reincarnation. By way of contrast, Christian dualists deny reincarnation and maintain instead that the ultimate destination for the soul (after becoming disembodied at death) is to be re-embodied in one's *resurrected* earthly body. The difference between reincarnation and resurrection is just the difference between getting a brand new body (reincarnation) after death and getting one and the same body (resurrection). This is not to say, of course, that our bodies in the afterlife will have exactly the same properties—flaws, limitations, and so on—as our present earthly bodies. Indeed, according to the Christian tradition anyway, quite the opposite is the case: Our resurrected bodies will be greatly improved, or glorified. But the point is that the body you have in the afterlife will be the *same* body that you have now, despite its differences—much like your body after a successful diet or workout regimen is the same body you had before, albeit healthier, stronger, and in other respects better.

Although the Christian tradition has been predominantly dualistic, many Christians endorse a monistic view of immortality. This is the second of the two positive views on immortality just mentioned. On this view, either there is no soul or else the soul is not the sort of thing that can properly be said to "live" apart from the body. Either way, then, the afterlife can never be a disembodied life. Our hope for an afterlife is nothing other than a hope for our own resurrection—for the reconstitution or recreation or miraculous resuscitation of our present earthly bodies (albeit, again, in an improved or glorified form).

We begin this section with a selection from Plato defending the view that the soul can exist apart from the body. Although Plato has many arguments for this thesis, one of the most famous is found in the *Phaedo,* it is included in our first reading. One section is worth quoting in full:

> When the soul employs the body in any inquiry, and makes use of sight, or hearing, or any other sense—for inquiry with the body must signify inquiry with the senses—she is dragged away by the body to the things which are impermanent, changing, and the soul wanders about blindly, and becomes confused and dizzy, like a drunken man, from dealing with things that are changing.... [But] when the soul investigates any question by herself, she goes away to the pure and eternal, and immortal and unchangeable, to which she is intrinsically related, and so she comes to be ever with it, as soon as she is by herself, and can be so; and then she rests from her wandering and dwells with it unchangingly, for she is related to what is unchanging. And is not this state of the soul called wisdom?*

The argument may be reconstructed as follows:

1. If a person's soul while in the body is capable of any activity independently of the body, then it can perform that activity in separation from the body (i.e., after death, surviving death).
2. In pure or metaphysical thinking (i.e., in contemplating the forms and their interrelationships), a person's soul performs an activity independently of the body. No observation is necessary for this investigation.
3. Therefore, a person's soul can engage in pure or metaphysical thinking in separation from the body. That is, it can and must survive death.

This is a positive argument for the existence of the soul. Unfortunately, the second premise is dubious, for it could be the case that the mind's activity is dependent on the brain. And it is precisely this latter claim that is defended by Bertrand Russell in the second reading in this section. According to Russell, there is no reason at all to believe in the immortality of the soul because all of the best empirical evidence points to the conclusion that a person's mental life comes to an end with the death of her brain.

In our third reading, John Hick rejects the Platonic notion of an immortal and separable soul and urges instead a view according to which life after death requires the resurrection of the body, where resurrection is conceived as "God's re-creation or reconstitution of the human psychophysical individual." He briefly considers the question of what it would take to re-create a human body—that is, the question of what criteria have to be satisfied for a new body created at "resurrection time" to be the *same* body as the one that died—and then moves on to a discussion of what evidence we might have for believing in such an afterlife.

In our fourth reading, Jeffrey Olen devotes considerably more attention to questions about criteria of identity. He examines two views on the matter: the "memory criterion" and the "bodily criterion." According to the memory criterion, person A is the same person as person B if and only if A and B have the right sort of overlap in their memories and the right sort of continuity between their memories and other psychological states. For example, if B exists later than A, then B should remember a lot of what A remembers; furthermore, B should remember at least some of what A

Phaedo, 79 c–d, trans. Louis Pojman.

takes to be "present experience." There should also be some continuity among their goals, beliefs, desires, and other mental states. (This isn't to deny that goals, beliefs, and desires change over time. But the idea is that if B exists, say, a mere ten seconds later than A, and if B has beliefs, desires, goals, and memories virtually *none* of which overlap with A's, then B just isn't the same person as A.) Olen favors the psychological continuity criterion, and he argues furthermore in favor of the possibility of life after death. On his view, the mind is like computer software: Just as the same software can be transferred to different hardware, so too a mind can be transferred to a different brain (or other supporting medium). But to say that the mind can be transferred to a different medium is just to say that the mind can *change bodies*, and if it can change bodies, he contends, then the mind can survive the death of the body.

Finally, we close this section with an essay on the Hindu view of life, death, and reincarnation by Prasannatma Das.

IV.1   Immortality of the Soul

PLATO

Plato (c. 427–347 BCE) lived in Athens, was a student of Socrates, and is almost universally recognized as one of the most important philosophers who ever lived. Indeed, it has been remarked that the entire history of Western philosophy is but a footnote to Plato. The excerpts that comprise the following selection concern Plato's views about the soul. According to Plato, human beings are composed of two substances: body and soul. Of these, the true self is the soul, which lives on after the death of the body. All of Plato's writings are in the form of dialogues. In the first dialogue (from *Alcibiades I*) Socrates argues with Alcibiades about the true self. The second dialogue (from the *Phaedo*) takes place in prison, where Socrates awaits his execution. He is offered a way of escape but rejects it, arguing that it would be immoral to flee such a fate at this time and that he is certain of a better life after death.

FROM ALCIBIADES I

Soc. And is self-knowledge an easy thing, and was he to be lightly esteemed who inscribed the text on the temple at Delphi? Or is self-knowledge a difficult thing, which few are able to attain?

Al. At times, I fancy, Socrates, that anybody can know himself; at other times, the task appears to be very difficult.

Soc. But whether easy or difficult, Alcibiades, still there is no other way; knowing what we are, we shall know how to take care of ourselves, and if we are ignorant we shall not know.

Al. That is true.

Soc. Well, then, let us see in what way the self-existent can be discovered by us; that will give us a chance to discover our own existence, which without that we can never know.

Al. You say truly.

Soc. Come, now, I beseech you, tell me with whom you are conversing?—with whom but with me?

Reprinted from *Alcibiades I* and the *Phaedo*, translated by William Jowett (New York: Charles Scribner's Sons, 1889).

Al. Yes.

Soc. As I am with you?

Al. Yes.

Soc. That is to say, I, Socrates, am talking?

Al. Yes.

Soc. And I in talking use words?

Al. Certainly.

Soc. And talking and using words are, as you would say, the same?

Al. Very true.

Soc. And the user is not the same as the thing which he uses?

Al. What do you mean?

Soc. I will explain: the shoemaker, for example, uses a square tool, and a circular tool, and other tools for cutting?

Al. Yes.

Soc. But the tool is not the same as the cutter and user of the tool?

Al. Of course not.

Soc. And in the same way the instrument of the harper is to be distinguished from the harper himself?

Al. He is.

Soc. Now the question which I asked was whether you conceive the user to be always different from that which he uses?

Al. I do.

Soc. Then what shall we say of the shoemaker? Does he cut with his tools only or with his hands?

Al. With his hands as well.

Soc. He uses his hands too?

Al. Yes.

Soc. And does he use his eyes in cutting leather?

Al. He does.

Soc. And we admit that the user is not the same with the things which he uses?

Al. Yes.

Soc. Then the shoemaker and the harper are to be distinguished from the hands and feet which they use?

Al. That is clear.

Soc. And does not a man use the whole body?

Al. Certainly.

Soc. And that which uses is different from that which is used?

Al. True.

Soc. Then a man is not the same as his own body?

Al. That is the inference.

Soc. What is he, then?

Al. I cannot say.

Soc. Nay, you can say that he is the user of the body.

Al. Yes.

Soc. And the user of the body is the soul?

Al. Yes, the soul.

Soc. And the soul rules?

Al. Yes.

Soc. Let me make an assertion which will, I think, be universally admitted.

Al. What is that?

Soc. That man is one of three things.

Al. What are they?

Soc. Soul, body, or the union of the two.

Al. Certainly.

Soc. But did we not say that the actual ruling principle of the body is man?

Al. Yes, we did.

Soc. And does the body rule over itself?

Al. Certainly not.

Soc. It is subject, as we were saying?

Al. Yes.

Soc. Then that is not what we are seeking?

Al. It would seem not.

Soc. But may we say that the union of the two rules over the body, and consequently that this is man?

Al. Very likely.

Soc. The most unlikely of all things: for if one of the members is subject, the two united cannot possibly rule.

Al. True.

Soc. But since neither the body, nor the union of the two, is man, either man has no real existence, or the soul is man?

Al. Just so.

Soc. Would you have a more precise proof that the soul is man?

Al. No; I think that the proof is sufficient.

Soc. If the proof, although not quite precise, is fair, that is enough for us; more precise proof will be supplied when we have discovered that which we were led to omit, from a fear that the inquiry would be too much protracted.

Al. What was that?

Soc. What I meant, when I said that absolute existence must be first considered; but now, instead of absolute existence, we have been considering the nature of individual existence, and that may be sufficient; for surely there is nothing belonging to us which has more absolute existence than the soul?

Al. There is nothing.

Soc. Then we may truly conceive that you and I are conversing with one another, soul to soul?

Al. Very true.

Soc. And that is just what I was saying—that I, Socrates, am not arguing or talking with the face of Alcibiades, but with the real Alcibiades; and that is with his soul.

Al. True . . . .

FROM THE PHAEDO

Socrates: What again shall we say of the actual acquirement of knowledge?—is the body, if invited to share in the inquiry, a hinderer or a helper? I mean to say, have sight and hearing any truth in them? Are they not, as the poets are always telling us, inaccurate witnesses? and yet, if even they are inaccurate and indistinct, what is to be said of the other senses?—for you will allow that they are the best of them?

Certainly, he replied.

Then when does the soul attain truth?—for in attempting to consider anything in company with the body she is obviously deceived.

Yes, that is true.

Then must not existence be revealed to her in thought, if at all?

Yes.

And thought is best when the mind is gathered into herself and none of these things trouble her—neither sounds nor sights nor pain nor any pleasure,—when she has as little as possible to do with the body, and has no bodily sense or feeling, but is aspiring after being?

That is true.

And in this the philosopher dishonors the body; his soul runs away from the body and desires to be alone and by herself?

That is true.

Well, but there is another thing, Simmias: Is there or is there not an absolute justice?

Assuredly there is.

And an absolute beauty and absolute good?

Of course.

But did you ever behold any of them with your eyes?

Certainly not.

Or did you ever reach them with any other bodily sense? (and I speak not of these alone, but of absolute greatness, and health, and strength, and of the essence or true nature of everything). Has the reality of them ever been perceived by you through the bodily organs? or rather, is not the nearest approach to the knowledge of their several natures made by him who so orders his intellectual vision as to have the most exact conception of the essence of that which he considers?

Certainly.

And he attains to the knowledge of them in their highest purity who goes to each of them with the mind alone, not allowing when in the act of thought the intrusion or introduction of sight or any other sense in the company of reason, but with the very light of the mind in her clearness penetrates into the very light of truth in each; he has got rid, as far as he can, of eyes and ears and of the whole body, which he conceives of only as a disturbing element, hindering the soul from the acquisition of knowledge when in company with her—is not this the sort of man who, if ever man did, is likely to attain the knowledge of existence?

There is admirable truth in that, Socrates, replied Simmias.

And when they consider all this, must not true philosophers make a reflection, of which they will speak to one another in such words as these: We have found, they will say, a path of speculation which seems to bring us and the argument to the conclusion, that while we are in the body, and while the soul is mingled with this mass of evil our desire will not be satisfied, and our desire is of the truth. For the body is a source of endless trouble to us by reason of the mere requirement of food; and also is liable to diseases which overtake and impede us in the search after truth: and by filling us so full of loves, and lusts, and fears, and fancies, and idols, and every sort of folly, prevents our ever having, as people say, so much as a thought. From whence come wars, and fightings, and factions? whence but from the body and the lusts of the body? For wars are occasioned by the love of money, and money has to be acquired for the sake and in the service of the body; and in consequence of all these things the time which ought to be given to philosophy is lost. Moreover, if there is time and an inclination toward philosophy, yet the body introduces a turmoil and confusion and fear into the course of speculation, and hinders us from seeing the truth; and all experience shows that if we would have pure knowledge of anything we must be quit of the body, and the soul in herself must behold all things in themselves: then I suppose that we shall attain that which we desire, and of which we say that we are lovers, and that is wisdom; not while we live, but after death, as the argument shows; for if while in company with the body, the soul cannot have pure knowledge, one of two things seems to follow—either knowledge is not to be attained at all, or, if at all, after death. For then, and not till then, the soul will be in herself alone and without the body. In this present life, I reckon that we make the nearest approach to knowledge when we have the least possible concern or interest in the body, and are not saturated with the bodily nature, but remain pure until the hour when God himself is pleased to release us. And then the foolishness of the body will be cleared away and we shall be pure and hold converse with other pure souls, and know of ourselves the clear light everywhere; and this is surely the light of truth. For no impure thing is allowed to approach the pure. These are the sort of words, Simmias, which the true lovers of wisdom cannot help saying to one another, and thinking. You will agree with me in that?

Certainly, Socrates.

But if this is true, O my friend, then there is great hope that, going whither I go, I shall there be satisfied with that which has been the chief concern of you and me in our past lives. And now that the hour of departure is appointed to me, this is the hope with which I depart, and not I only, but every man who believes that he has his mind purified.

Certainly, replied Simmias.

And what is purification but the separation of the soul from the body, as I was saying before; the habit of the soul gathering and collecting herself into herself, out of all the courses of the body; the dwelling in her own place alone, as in another life, so also in this, as far as she can; the release of the soul from the chains of the body?

Very true, he said.

And what is that which is termed death, but this very separation and release of the soul from the body?

To be sure, he said.

And the true philosophers, and they only, study and are eager to release the soul. Is not the separation and release of the soul from the body their especial study?

That is true.

And as I was saying at first, there would be a ridiculous contradiction in men studying to live as nearly as they can in a state of death, and yet repining when death comes.

Certainly.

Then Simmias, as the true philosophers are ever studying death, to them, of all men, death is the least terrible. Look at the matter in this way: how inconsistent of them to have been always enemies of the body, and wanting to have the soul alone, and when this is granted to them, to be trembling and repining; instead of rejoicing at their departing to that place where, when they arrive, they hope to gain that which in life they loved (and this was wisdom), and at the same time to be rid of the company of their enemy. Many a man has been willing to go to the world below in the hope of seeing there an earthly love, or wife, or son, and conversing with them. And will he who is a true lover of wisdom, and is persuaded in like manner that only in the world below he can worthily enjoy her, still repine at death? Will he not depart with joy? Surely, he will, my friend, if he be a true philosopher. For he will have a firm conviction that there only, and nowhere else, he can find wisdom in her purity. And if this be true, he would be very absurd, as I was saying, if he were to fear death.

....

Socrates: And were we not saying long ago that the soul when using the body as an instrument of perception, that is to say, when using the sense of sight or hearing or some other sense (for the meaning of perceiving through the body is perceiving through the senses),— were we not saying that the soul too is then dragged by the body into the region of the changeable, and wanders and is confused; the world spins round her, and she is like a drunkard when under their influence?

Very true.

But when returning into herself she reflects; then she passes into the realm of purity, and eternity, and immortality, and unchangeableness, which are her kindred, and with them she ever lives, when she is by herself and is not let or hindered; then she ceases from her erring ways, and being in communion with the unchanging is unchanging. And this state of the soul is called wisdom?

That is well and truly said, Socrates, he replied.

And to which class is the soul more nearly alike and akin, as far as may be inferred from this argument, as well as from the preceding one?

I think, Socrates, that, in the opinion of every one who follows the argument, the soul will be infinitely more like the unchangeable,—even the most stupid person will not deny that.

And the body is more like the changing?

Yes.

Yet once more consider the matter in this light: When the soul and the body are united, then nature orders the soul to rule and govern, and the body to obey and serve. Now which of these two functions is akin to the divine? and which to the mortal? Does not the divine appear to you to be that which naturally orders and rules, and the mortal that which is subject and servant?

True.

And which does the soul resemble?

The soul resembles the divine, and the body the mortal,—there can be no doubt of that, Socrates.

IV.2　The Finality of Death

BERTRAND RUSSELL

Bertrand Russell (1872–1970), once a student and tutor at Cambridge University, was one of the most significant philosophers and social critics of the twentieth century. In this short essay, Russell outlines some of the major objections to the idea of life after death. He argues that it is not reasonable to believe that our personality and memories will survive the destruction of our bodies. He claims that the inclination to believe in immortality comes form emotional factors, notably the fear of death.

Before we can profitably discuss whether we shall continue to exist after death, it is well to be clear as to the sense in which a man is the same person as he was yesterday. Philosophers used to think that there were definite substances, the soul and the body, that each lasted on from day to day, that a soul, once created, continued to exist throughout all future time, whereas a body ceased temporarily from death till the resurrection of the body.

The part of this doctrine which concerns the present life is pretty certainly false. The matter of the body is continually changing by processes of nutriment and wastage. Even if it were not, atoms in physics are no longer supposed to have continuous existence; there is no sense in saying: this is the same atom as the one that existed a few minutes ago. The continuity of a human body is a matter of appearance and behavior, not of substance.

The same thing applies to the mind. We think and feel and act, but there is not, in addition to thoughts and feelings and actions, a bare entity, the mind or the soul, which does or suffers these occurrences. The mental continuity of a person is a continuity of habit and memory: there was yesterday one person whose feelings I can remember, and that person I regard as myself of yesterday; but, in fact, myself of yesterday was only certain mental occurrences which are now remembered and are regarded as part of the person who now recollects them. All that constitutes a person is a series of experiences connected by memory and by certain similarities of the sort we call habit.

If, therefore, we are to believe that a person survives death, we must believe that the memories and habits which constitute the person will continue to be exhibited in a new set of occurrences.

No one can prove that this will not happen. But it is easy to see that it is very unlikely. Our memories and habits are bound up with the structure of the brain, in much the same way in which a river is connected with the riverbed. The water in the river is always changing, but it keeps to the same course because previous rains have worn a channel. In like manner, previous events have worn a channel in the brain, and our thoughts flow along this channel. This is the cause of memory and mental habits. But the brain, as a structure, is dissolved at death, and memory therefore may be expected to be also dissolved. There is no more reason to think otherwise than to expect a river to persist in its old course after an earthquake has raised a mountain where a valley used to be.

All memory, and therefore (one may say) all minds, depend upon a property which is very noticeable in certain kinds of material structures but exists little if at all in other kinds. This is the property of forming habits as a result of frequent similar occurrences. For example: a bright light makes the pupils of the eyes contract; and if you repeatedly flash a light in a man's eyes and beat a gong at the same time, the gong alone will, in the end, cause his pupils to contract. This is a fact about the brain and nervous system— that is to say, about a certain material structure. It will be found that exactly similar facts explain our response to language and our use of it, our memories and the emotions they arouse, our moral or immoral habits of behavior, and indeed everything that constitutes our mental personality, except the part determined by heredity. The part determined by heredity is handed on to our posterity but cannot, in the individual, survive the disintegration of the body. Thus both the hereditary and the acquired parts of a personality are, so far as our experience goes, bound up with the characteristics of certain bodily structures. We all know that memory may be obliterated by an injury to the brain, that a virtuous person may be rendered vicious by encephalitis lethargica, and, that a clever child can be turned into an idiot by lack of iodine. In view of such familiar facts, it seems scarcely probable that the mind survives the total destruction of brain structure which occurs at death.

It is not rational arguments but emotions that cause belief in a future life.

The most important of these emotions is fear of death, which is instinctive and biologically useful. If we genuinely and wholeheartedly believed in the future life, we should cease completely to fear death. The effects would be curious, and probably such as most of us would deplore. But our human and subhuman ancestors have fought and exterminated their enemies throughout many geological ages and have profited by courage; it is therefore an advantage to the victors in the struggle for life to be able, on occasion, to overcome the natural fear of death. Among animals and savages, instinctive pugnacity suffices for this purpose; but at a certain stage of development, as the Mohammedans first proved, belief in Paradise has considerable military value as reinforcing natural pugnacity. We should therefore admit that militarists are wise in encouraging the belief in immortality, always supposing that this belief does not become so profound as to produce indifference to the affairs of the world.

Another emotion which encourages the belief in survival is admiration of the excellence of man. As the Bishop of Birmingham says, "His mind is a far finer instrument than anything that had appeared earlier—he knows right and wrong. He can build Westminster Abbey. He can make an airplane. He can calculate the distance of the sun . . . . Shall, then, man at death perish utterly? Does that incomparable instrument, his mind, vanish when life ceases?"

The Bishop proceeds to argue that "the universe has been shaped and is governed by an intelligent purpose," and that it would have been unintelligent, having made man, to let him perish.

To this argument there are many answers. In the first place, it has been found, in the scientific investigation of nature, that the intrusion of moral or aesthetic values has always been an obstacle to discovery. It used to be thought that the heavenly bodies must move in circles because the circle is the most perfect curve, that species must be immutable because God would only create what was perfect and what therefore stood in no need of improvement, that it was useless to combat epidemics except by repentance because they were sent as a punishment for sin, and so on. It has been found, however, that, so far as we can discover, nature is indifferent to our values and can only be understood by ignoring our notions of good and bad. The Universe may have a purpose, but nothing that we know suggests that, if so, this purpose has any similarity to ours.

Nor is there in this anything surprising. Dr. Barnes tells us that man "knows right and wrong." But, in fact, as anthropology shows, men's views of right and wrong have varied to such an extent that no single item has been permanent. We cannot say, therefore, that man knows right and wrong, but only that some men do. Which men? Nietzsche argued in favor of an ethic profoundly different from Christ's, and some powerful governments have accepted his teaching. If knowledge of right and wrong is to be an argument for immortality, we must first settle whether to believe Christ or Nietzsche, and then argue that Christians are immortal, but Hitler and Mussolini are not, or vice versa. The decision will obviously be made on the battlefield, not in the study. Those who have the best poison gas will have the ethic of the future and will therefore be the immortal ones.

Our feelings and beliefs on the subject of good and evil are, like everything else about us, natural facts, developed in the struggle for existence and not having any divine or supernatural origin. In one of Aesop's fables, a lion is shown pictures of huntsmen catching lions and remarks that, if he had painted them, they would have shown lions catching huntsmen. Man, says Dr. Barnes, is a fine fellow because he can make airplanes. A little while ago there was a popular song about the cleverness of flies in walking upside down on the ceiling, with the chorus: "Could Lloyd George do it? Could Mr. Baldwin do it? Could Ramsay Mac do it? Why, no." On this basis a very telling argument could be constructed by a theologically-minded fly, which no doubt the other flies would find most convincing.

Moreover, it is only when we think abstractly that we have such a high opinion of man. Of men in the concrete, most of us think the vast majority very bad. Civilized states spend more than half their revenue on killing each other's citizens. Consider the long history of the activities inspired by moral fervor: human sacrifices, persecutions of heretics, witch-hunts, pogroms leading up to wholesale extermination by poison gases, which one at least of Dr. Barnes's episcopal colleagues must be supposed to favor, since he holds pacifism to be un-Christian. Are these abominations, and the ethical doctrines by which they are prompted, really evidence of an intelligent Creator? And can we really wish that the men who practiced them should live forever? The world in which we live can be understood as a result of muddle and accident; but if it is the outcome of deliberate purpose, the purpose must have been that of a fiend. For my part, I find accident a less painful and more plausible hypothesis.

IV.3   Immortality and Resurrection

JOHN HICK

A short biographical sketch of John Hick precedes selection III.4. In the present article, Hick examines the Platonic notion of the immortality of the soul and argues that it is filled with problems. In its place he argues for the New Testament view of the recreation of the psycho-physical person, a holistic person who is body–soul in one. He then offers a thought experiment involving "John Smith" reappearances to show that re-creation is conceivable and worthy of rational belief. In the last part of this essay, Hick considers whether parapsychology can provide evidence for our survival of death.

THE IMMORTALITY OF THE SOUL

Some kind of distinction between physical body and immaterial or semimaterial soul seems to be as old as human culture; the existence of such a distinction has been indicated by the manner of burial of the earliest human skeletons yet discovered. Anthropologists offer various conjectures about the origin of the distinction: perhaps it was first suggested by memories of dead persons; by dreams of them; by the sight of reflections of oneself in water and on other bright surfaces; or by meditation upon the significance of religious rites which grew up spontaneously in face of the fact of death.

It was Plato (428/7–348/7 B.C.), the philosopher who has most deeply and lastingly influenced Western culture, who systematically developed the body-mind dichotomy and first attempted to prove the immortality of the soul.[1]

Plato argues that although the body belongs to the sensible world,[2] and shares its changing and impermanent nature, the intellect is related to the unchanging realities of which we are aware when we think not of particular good things but of Goodness itself, not of specific just acts but of justice itself, and of the other "universals" or eternal ideas in virtue of which physical things and events have their own specific characteristics. Being related to this higher and abiding realm, rather than to the evanescent world of sense, reason or the soul is immortal. Hence, one who devotes his life to the contemplation of eternal realities rather than to the gratification of the fleeting desires of the body will find at death that whereas his body turns to dust, his soul gravitates to the realm of the unchanging, there to live forever. Plato painted an awe-inspiring picture, of haunting beauty and persuasiveness, which has moved and elevated the minds of men in many different centuries and lands. Nevertheless, it is not today (as it was during the first centuries of the Christian era) the common philosophy of the West; and a demonstration of immortality which presupposes Plato's metaphysical system cannot claim to constitute a proof for the twentieth-century disbeliever.

Plato used the further argument that the only things that can suffer destruction are those that are composite, since to destroy something means to disintegrate it into its constituent parts. All material bodies are composite; the soul, however, is simple and therefore imperishable. This argument was adopted by Aquinas and has become standard in Roman Catholic theology, as in the following passage from the modern Catholic philosopher, Jacques Maritain:

> A spiritual soul cannot be corrupted, since it possesses no matter; it cannot be disintegrated since it has no substantial parts; it cannot lose its individual

John H. Hick, *Philosophy of Religion*, 3d ed., copyright 1983, pp. 122–32. Reprinted by permission of Prentice-Hall, Inc., Englewood Cliffs, N.J. Footnotes edited.

unity, since it is self-subsisting, nor its internal energy, since it contains within itself all the sources of its energies. The human soul cannot die. Once it exists, it cannot disappear; it will necessarily exist for ever, endure without end. Thus, philosophic reason, put to work by a great metaphysician like Thomas Aquinas, is able to prove the immortality of the human soul in a demonstrative manner.[3]

This type of reasoning has been criticized on several grounds. Kant pointed out that although it is true that a simple substance cannot disintegrate, consciousness may nevertheless cease to exist through the diminution of its intensity to zero.[4] Modern psychology has also questioned the basic premise that the mind is a simple entity. It seems instead to be a structure of only relative unity, normally fairly stable and tightly integrated but capable under stress of various degrees of division and dissolution. This comment from psychology makes it clear that the assumption that the soul is a simple substance is not an empirical observation but a metaphysical theory. As such, it cannot provide the basis for a general proof of immortality.

The body–soul distinction, first formulated as a philosophical doctrine in ancient Greece, was baptized into Christianity, ran through the medieval period, and entered the modern world with the public status of a self-evident truth when it was redefined in the seventeenth century by Descartes. Since World War II, however, the Cartesian mind–matter dualism, having been taken for granted for many centuries, has been strongly criticized by philosophers of the contemporary analytical school.[5] It is argued that the words that describe mental characteristics and operations—such as "intelligent," "thoughtful," "carefree," "happy," "calculating" and the like—apply in practice to types of human behaviour and to behavioral dispositions. They refer to the empirical individual, the observable human being who is born and grows and acts and feels and dies, and not to the shadowy proceedings of a mysterious "ghost in the machine." Man is thus very much what he appears to be—a creature of flesh and blood, who behaves and is capable of behaving in a characteristic range of ways—rather than a nonphysical soul incomprehensibly interacting with a physical body.

As a result of this development much mid-twentieth-century philosophy has come to see man in the way he is seen in the biblical writings, not as an eternal soul temporarily attached to a mortal body, but as a form of finite, mortal, psychophysical life. Thus, the Old Testament scholar, J. Pedersen, says of the Hebrews that for them "...the body is the soul in its outward form."[6] This way of thinking has led to quite a different conception of death from that found in Plato and the neo-Platonic strand in European thought.

THE RE-CREATION OF THE PSYCHOPHYSICAL PERSON

Only toward the end of the Old Testament period did after-life beliefs come to have any real importance in Judaism. Previously, Hebrew religious insight had focused so fully upon God's covenant with the nation, as an organism that continued through the centuries while successive generations lived and died, that the thought of a divine purpose for the individual, a purpose that transcended this present life, developed only when the breakdown of the nation as a political entity threw into prominence the individual and the problem of his personal destiny.

When a positive conviction arose of God's purpose holding the individual in being beyond the crisis of death, this conviction took the non-Platonic form of belief in the resurrection of the body. By the turn of the eras, this had become an article of faith for one Jewish sect, the Pharisees, although it was still rejected as an innovation by the more conservative Sadducees.

The religious difference between the Platonic belief in the immortality of the soul, and the Judaic-Christian belief in the resurrection of the body is that the latter postulates a special divine act of re-creation. This produces a sense of utter dependence upon God in the hour of death, a feeling that is in accordance with the biblical understanding of man as having been formed out of "the dust of the earth,"[7] a product (as we say today) of the slow evolution of life from its lowly beginnings in the primeval slime. Hence, in the Jewish and Christian conception, death is something real and fearful. It is not thought to be like walking from one room to another, or taking off an old coat and putting on a new one. It means sheer unqualified extinction—passing out from the lighted circle of life into "death's dateless night." Only through the sovereign creative love of God can there be a new existence beyond the grave.

What does "the resurrection of the dead" mean? Saint Paul's discussion provides the basic Christian answer to this question.[8] His conception of the general resurrection (distinguished from the unique resurrection of Jesus) has nothing to do with the resuscitation of corpses in a cemetery. It concerns God's re-creation or reconstitution of the human psychophysical individual, not as the organism that has died but as a *soma pneumatikon*, a "spiritual body," inhabiting a spiritual world as the physical body inhabits our present physical world.

A major problem confronting any such doctrine is that of providing criteria of personal identity to link the earthly life and the resurrection life. Paul does not specifically consider this question, but one may, perhaps, develop his thought along lines such as the following.[9]

Suppose, first, that someone—John Smith—living in the USA were suddenly and inexplicably to disappear from before the eyes of his friends, and that at the same moment an exact replica of him were inexplicably to appear in India. The person who appears in India is exactly similar in both physical and mental characteristics to the person who disappeared in America. There is continuity of memory, complete similarity of bodily features including fingerprints, hair and eye coloration, and stomach contents, and also of beliefs, habits, emotions, and mental dispositions. Further, the "John Smith" replica thinks of himself as being the John Smith who disappeared in the USA. After all possible tests have been made and have proved positive, the factors leading his friends to accept "John Smith" as John Smith would surely prevail and would cause them to overlook even his mysterious transference from one continent to another, rather than treat "John Smith," with all John Smith's memories and other characteristics, as someone other than John Smith.

Suppose, second, that our John Smith, instead of inexplicably disappearing, dies, but that at the moment of his death a "John Smith" replica, again complete with memories and all other characteristics, appears in India. Even with the corpse on our hands we would, I think, still have to accept this "John Smith" as the John Smith who died. We would have to say that he had been miraculously re-created in another place.

Now suppose, third, that on John Smith's death the "John Smith" replica appears, not in India, but as a resurrection replica in a different world altogether, a resurrection world inhabited only by resurrected persons. This world occupies its own space distinct from that with which we are now familiar. That is to say, an object in the resurrection world is not situated at any distance or in any direction from the objects in our present world, although each object in either world is spatially related to every other object in the same world.

This supposition provides a model by which one may conceive of the divine re-creation of the embodied human personality. In this model, the element of the strange and the mysterious has been reduced to a minimum by following the view of some of the early Church Fathers that the resurrection body has the same shape as the physical body,[10] and ignoring Paul's own hint that it may be as unlike the physical body as a full grain of wheat differs from the wheat seed.[11]

What is the basis for this Judaic-Christian belief in the divine recreation or reconstitution of the human personality after death? There is, of course, an argument from authority, in that life after death is taught throughout the New Testament (although very rarely in the Old Testament). But, more basically, belief in the resurrection arises as a corollary of faith in the sovereign purpose of God, which is not restricted by death and which holds man in being beyond his natural mortality. In the words of Martin Luther, "Anyone with whom God speaks, whether in wrath or in mercy, the same is certainly immortal. The Person of God who speaks, and the Word, show that we are creatures with whom God wills to speak, right into eternity, and in an immortal manner."[12] In a similar vein it is argued that if it be God's plan to create finite persons to exist in fellowship with himself, then it contradicts both his own intention and his love for the creatures made in his image if he allows men to pass out of existence when his purpose for them remains largely unfulfilled.

It is this promised fulfillment of God's purpose for man, in which the full possibilities of human nature will be realized, that constitutes the "heaven" symbolized in the New Testament as a joyous banquet in which all and sundry rejoice together. As we saw when discussing the problem of evil, no theodicy can succeed without drawing into itself this eschatological[13] faith in an eternal, and therefore infinite, good which thus outweighs all the pains and sorrows that have been endured on the way to it.

Balancing the idea of heaven in Christian tradition is the idea of *hell*. This, too, is relevant to the problem of theodicy. For just as the reconciling of God's goodness and power with the fact of evil requires that out of the travail of history there shall come in the end an eternal good for man, so likewise it would seem to preclude man's eternal misery. The only kind of evil that is finally incompatible with God's unlimited power and love would be utterly pointless and wasted suffering, pain which is never redeemed and worked into the fulfilling of God's good purpose. Unending torment would constitute precisely such suffering; for being eternal, it could never lead to a good end beyond itself. Thus, hell as conceived by its enthusiasts, such as Augustine or Calvin, is a major part of the problem of evil! If hell is construed as eternal torment, the theological motive behind the idea is directly at variance with the urge to seek a theodicy. However, it is by no means clear that the doctrine of eternal punishment can claim a secure New Testament basis.[14] If, on the other hand, "hell" means a continuation of the purgatorial suffering often experienced in this life, and leading eventually to the high good of heaven, it no longer stands in conflict with the needs of theodicy. Again, the idea of hell may be deliteralized and valued as a *mythos,* as a powerful and pregnant symbol of the grave responsibility inherent in man's freedom in relation to his Maker.

DOES PARAPSYCHOLOGY HELP?

The spiritualist movement claims that life after death has been proved by well-attested cases of communication between the living and the "dead." During the closing quarter of the nineteenth century and the decades of the present century this claim has been made the subject of careful and prolonged study by a number of responsible and competent persons.[15] This work, which may be approximately dated from the founding in London of the Society for Psychical Research in 1882, is known either by the name adopted by that society or in the United States by the name parapsychology.

Approaching the subject from the standpoint of our interest in this chapter, we may initially divide the phenomena studied by the parapsychologist into two groups. There are those phenomena that involve no reference to the idea of a life after death, chief among these being psychokinesis and extrasensory perception (ESP) in its various forms (such as telepathy, clairvoyance, and precognition). And there are those phenomena that raise the question of personal survival after death, such as the apparitions and other sensory manifestations of dead persons and the "spirit messages" received through mediums. This division is, however, only of preliminary use, for ESP has emerged as a clue to the understanding of much that occurs in the second group. We shall begin with a brief outline of the reasons that have induced the majority of workers in this field to be willing to postulate so strange an occurrence as telepathy.

Telepathy is a name for the mysterious fact that sometimes a thought in the mind of one person apparently causes a similar thought to occur to someone else when there are no normal means of communication between them, and under circumstances such that mere coincidence seems to be excluded.

For example, one person may draw a series of pictures or diagrams on paper and somehow transmit an impression of these to someone else in another room who then draws recognizable reproductions of them. This might well be a coincidence in the case of a single successful reproduction: but can a series consist entirely of coincidences?

Experiments have been devised to measure the probability of chance coincidence in supposed cases of telepathy. In the simplest of these, cards printed in turn with five different symbols are used. A pack of fifty, consisting of ten bearing each symbol, is then thoroughly shuffled, and the sender concentrates on the cards one at a time while the receiver (who of course can see neither sender nor cards) tries to write down the correct order of symbols. This procedure is repeated, with constant reshuffling, hundreds or thousands of times. Since there are only five different symbols, a random guess would stand one chance in five of being correct. Consequently, on the assumption that only "chance" is operating, the receiver should be right in about 20 percent of his tries, and wrong in about 80 per cent; and the longer the series, the closer should be the approach to this proportion. However, good telepathic subjects are right in a far larger number of cases than can be reconciled with random guessing. The deviation from chance expectation can be converted mathematically into "odds against chance" (increasing as the proportion of hits is maintained over a longer and longer series of tries). In this way, odds of over a million to one have been recorded. J. B. Rhine (Duke University) has reported results showing "antichance" values ranging from seven (which equals odds against chance of 100,000 to one) to eighty-two (which converts the odds against chance to billions).[16] S. G. Soal (London University) has reported positive results for precognitive telepathy with odds against chance of $10^{35} \times 5$, or of billions to one.[17] Other researchers have also recorded confirming results.[18] In the light of these reports, it is difficult to deny that some positive factor, and not merely "chance," is operating. "Telepathy" is simply a name for this unknown positive factor.

How does telepathy operate? Only negative conclusions seem to be justified to date. It can, for example, be said with reasonable certainty that telepathy does not consist in any kind of physical radiation, analogous to radio waves. For, first, telepathy is not delayed or weakened in proportion to distance, as are all known forms of radiation: and, second, there is no organ in the brain or elsewhere that can plausibly be regarded as its sending or receiving center. Telepathy appears to be a purely mental occurrence.

It is not, however, a matter of transferring or transporting a thought out of one mind into another—if, indeed, such an idea makes sense at all. The telepathized thought does not leave the sender's consciousness in order to enter that of the receiver. What happens would be better described by saying that the sender's thought gives rise to a mental "echo" in the mind of the receiver. This "echo" occurs at the unconscious level, and consequently the version of it that rises into the receiver's consciousness may be only fragmentary and may be distorted or symbolized in various ways, as in dreams.

According to one theory that has been tentatively suggested to explain telepathy, our minds are separate and mutually insulated only at the conscious (and preconscious) level. But at the deepest level of the unconscious, we are constantly influencing one another, and it is at this level that telepathy takes place.[19]

How is a telepathized thought directed to one particular receiver among so many? Apparently the thoughts are directed by some link of emotion or common interest. For example, two friends are sometimes telepathically aware of any grave crisis or shock experienced by the other, even though they are at opposite ends of the earth.

We shall turn now to the other branch of parapsychology, which has more obvious bearing upon our subject. The *Proceedings of the Society for Psychical Research* contains a large number of carefully recorded and satisfactorily attested cases of the appearance of the figure of someone who has recently died to living people (in rare instances to more than one at a time) who were, in many cases, at a distance and unaware of the death. The S.P.R. reports also establish beyond reasonable doubt that the minds that operate in the mediumistic trance, purporting to be spirits of the departed, sometimes give personal information the medium could not have acquired by normal means and at times even give information, later verified, which had not been known to any living person.

On the other hand, physical happenings, such as the "materializations" of spirit forms in a visible and tangible form, are much more doubtful. But even if we discount the entire range of physical phenomena, it remains true that the best cases of trance utterance are impressive and puzzling, and taken at face value are indicative of survival and communication after death. If, through a medium, one talks with an intelligence that gives a coherent impression of being an intimately known friend who has died and establishes identity by a wealth of private information and indefinable personal characteristics—as has occasionally happened—then we cannot dismiss without careful trial the theory that what is taking place is the return of a consciousness from the spirit world.

However, the advance of knowledge in the other branch of parapsychology, centering upon the study of extrasensory perception, has thrown unexpected light upon this apparent commerce with the departed. For it suggests that unconscious telepathic contact between the medium and his or her client is an important and possibly a sufficient explanatory factor. This was vividly illustrated by the experience of two women who decided to test the spirits by taking into their minds, over a period of weeks, the personality and atmosphere of an entirely imaginary character in an unpublished novel written by one of the women. After thus filling their minds with the characteristics of this fictitious person, they went to a reputable medium, who proceeded to describe accurately their imaginary friend as a visitant from beyond the grave and to deliver appropriate messages from him.

An even more striking case is that of the "direct voice" medium (i.e., a medium in whose seances the voice of the communicating "spirit" is heard apparently speaking out of the air) who produced the spirit of one "Gordon Davis" who spoke in his own recognizable voice, displayed considerable knowledge about Gordon Davis, and remembered his death. This was extremely impressive until it was discovered that Gordon Davis was still alive; he was, of all ghostly occupations, a real-estate agent, and had been trying to sell a house at the time when the seance took place![20]

Such cases suggest that genuine mediums are simply persons of exceptional telepathic sensitiveness who unconsciously derive the "spirits" from their clients' minds.

In connection with "ghosts," in the sense of apparitions of the dead, it has been established that there can be "meaningful hallucinations," the source of which is almost certainly telepathic. To quote a classic and somewhat dramatic example: a woman sitting by a lake sees the figure of a man running toward the lake and throwing himself in. A few days later a man commits suicide by throwing himself into this same lake. Presumably, the explanation of the vision is that the man's thought while he was contemplating suicide had been telepathically projected onto the scene via the woman's mind.

In many of the cases recorded there is delayed action. The telepathically projected thought lingers in the recipient's unconscious mind until a suitable state of inattention to the outside world enables it to appear to his conscious mind in a dramatized form—for example, by a hallucinatory voice or vision—by means of the same mechanism that operates in dreams.

If phantoms of the living can be created by previously experienced thoughts and emotions of the person whom they represent, the parallel possibility arises that phantoms of the dead are caused by thoughts and emotions that were experienced by the person represented when he was alive. In other words, ghosts may be "psychic footprints," a kind of mental trace left behind by the dead, but not involving the presence or even the continued existence of those whom they represent.

These considerations tend away from the hopeful view that parapsychology will open a window onto another world. However, it is too early for a final verdict; and in the meantime one should be careful not to confuse absence of knowledge with knowledge of absence.

NOTES

1. *Phaedo.*
2. The world known to us through our physical senses.
3. Jacques Maritain, *The Range of Reason* (London: Geoffrey Bles Ltd. and New York: Charles Scribner's Sons, 1953), p. 60.
4. Kant, *Critique of Pure Reason, Transcendental Dialectic,* "Refutation of Mendelessohn's Proof of the Permanence of the Soul."
5. Gilbert Ryle's *The Concept of Mind* (London: Hutchinson & Co., Ltd., 1949) is a classic statement of this critique.
6. *Israel* (London: Oxford Univ. Press, 1926), 1, 170.
7. Genesis 2:7; Psalm 103:14.
8. I Corinthians 15.
9. The following paragraphs are adapted, with permission, from a section of my article, "Theology and Verification," published in *Theology Today* (April, 1960) and reprinted in *The Existence of God* (New York: The Macmillan Company, 1964).
10. Irenaeus, *Against Heresies,* Book II, Chap. 34, para. 1.
11. 1 Corinthians 15:37.
12. Quoted by Emil Brunner, *Dogmatics,* II, 69.
13. From the Greek *eschaton,* end.
14. The Greek word *aionios* is used in the New Testament and is usually translated as "eternal" or "everlasting." It can bear either this meaning or the more limited meaning of "for the aeon, or age."
15. The list of presidents of the Society for Psychical Research includes the philosophers Henri Bergson, William James, Hans Driesch, Henry Sidgwick, F. C. S. Schiller, C. D. Broad, and H. H. Price; the psychologists William McDougall, Gardner Murphy, Franklin Prince, and R. H. Thouless; the physicists Sir William Crookes, Sir Oliver Lodge, Sir William Barrett, and Lord Rayleigh; and the classicist Gilbert Murray.
16. J. B. Rhine, *Extrasensory Perception* (Boston: Society for Psychical Research, 1935), Table XLIII, p. 162. See also Rhine, *New Frontiers of the Mind* (New York: Farrar and Rinehart, Inc.1937), pp. 69f.
17. S. G. Soal, *Proceedings of the Society for Psychical Research,* XLVI, 152–98 and XLVII, 21–150. See also S. G. Soal's *The Experimental Situation in Psychical Research* (London: The Society for Psychical Research, 1947).
18. For surveys of the experimental work, see Whately Carrington, *Telepathy* (London: Methuen & Co. Ltd., 1945); G. N. M. Tyrrell, *The Personality of Man* (London: Penguin Books Ltd., 1946); S. G. Soal and F. Bateman, *Modern Experiments in Telepathy* (London: Faber & Faber Ltd. and New Haven, Conn.: Yale University Press, 1954); and for important Russian work, L. L. Vasiliev, *Experiments in Mental Suggestion,* 1962 (Church Crookham: Institute for the Study of Mental Images, 1963—English translation).
19. Whately Carrington, *Telepathy* (London: Methuen & Co. Ltd., 1945), Chaps. 6–8.
20. S. G. Soal, "A Report of Some Communications Received through Mrs. Blanche Cooper," Sec. 4, *Proceedings of the Society for Psychical Research,* XXXV, 560–89.

IV.4   Personal Identity and Life After Death

JEFFREY OLEN

Jeffrey Olen (1946–   ) is a writer-philosopher who for many years taught philosophy at the University of Wisconsin at Stevens Point. In this essay he discusses the criteria of personal identity in order to determine what would have to survive our death if we were to be

From *Persons and Their World: An Introduction to Philosophy,* by Jeffrey Olen. Copyright © 1983 by Random House, Inc. Reprinted by permission of the publisher.

able to say that it is truly we who survive. Through some intriguing thought experiments, Olen builds a case for the possibility of survival. Olen has a functionalist view of person-hood, believing that "the human brain is analogous to a computer." On this view, a given brain state is also a given mental state because it performs the appropriate function in the appropriate "program." Olen argues that just as different computers can run the same program, so too different brains (or other media) can "run" the same mind. So we can change bodies and therefore survive the death of our own body just as long as our personalities and memories are preserved intact.

It is Sunday night. After a long night of hard drinking, John Badger puts on his pajamas, lowers the heat in his Wisconsin home to fifty-five degrees and climbs into bed beneath two heavy blankets. Meanwhile, in Florida, Joe Everglade kisses his wife goodnight and goes to sleep.

The next morning, two very confused men wake up. One wakes up in Wisconsin, wondering where he is and why he is wearing pajamas, lying under two heavy blankets, yet shivering from the cold. He looks out the window and sees nothing but pine trees and snow. The room is totally unfamiliar. Where is his wife? How did he get to this cold, strange place? Why does he have such a terrible hangover? He tries to spring out of bed with his usual verve but feels an unaccustomed aching in his joints. Arthritis? He wanders unsurely through the house until he finds the bathroom. What he sees in the mirror causes him to spin around in sudden fear. But there is nobody behind him. Then the fear intensifies as he realizes that it was his reflection that had stared back at him. But it was the reflection of a man thirty years older than himself, with coarser features and a weather-beaten face.

In Florida, a man awakens with a young woman's arm around him. When she too awakens, she snuggles against him and wishes him good morning. "Who are you?" he asks. "What am I doing in your bed?" She just laughs, then tells him that he will have to hurry if he is going to get in his ten miles of jogging. From the bathroom she asks him about his coming day. None of the names or places she mentions connect with anything he can remember. He climbs out of bed, marveling at the ease with which he does so, and looks

first out the window and then into the mirror over the dresser. The sun and swimming pool confound him. The handsome young man's reflection terrifies him.

Then the phone rings. The woman answers it. It is the man from Wisconsin. "What happened last night, Mary? How did I get here? How did I get to look this way?"

"Who is this?" she asks.

"Don't you recognize my voice, Mary?" But he knew that the voice was not his own. "It's Joe."

"Joe who?"

"Your husband."

She hangs up, believing it to be a crank call. When she returns to the bedroom, the man in her husband's robe asks how he got there from Wisconsin, and why he looks as he does.

PERSONAL IDENTITY

What happened in the above story? Who woke up in Joe Everglade's bed? Who woke up in John Badger's? Which one is Mary's husband? Has Badger awakened with Everglade's memories and Everglade with Badger's? Or have Badger and Everglade somehow switched bodies? How are we to decide? What considerations are relevant?

To ask such questions is to raise the problem of *personal identity*. It is to ask what makes a person the same person he was the day before. It is to ask how we determine that we are dealing with the same person that we have dealt with in the past. It is to ask what constitutes personal identity over time. It is also to ask what we mean by the same person. And to answer this question, we must ask what we mean by the word "person."

Persons

In the previous chapter, we asked what a human being is. We asked what human beings are made of, what the nature of the human mind is, and whether human beings are part of nature or distinct from it.

To ask what a *person* is, however, is to ask a different question. Although we often use the terms "person" and "human being" interchangeably, they do not mean the same thing. If we do use them interchangeably, it is only because all the persons we know of are human beings, and because, as far as we know, whenever we are confronted with the same human being we are confronted with the same person.

But the notion of a human being is a *biological* notion. To identify something as a human being is to identify it as a member of *Homo sapiens*, a particular species of animal. It is a type of organism defined by certain physical characteristics.

The notion of a person, on the other hand, is not a biological one. Suppose, for instance, that we find life on another planet, and that this life is remarkably like our own. The creatures we discover communicate through a language as rich as our own, act according to moral principles, have a legal system, and engage in science and art. Suppose also that despite these cultural similarities, this form of life is biologically different from human life. In that case, these creatures would be persons, but not humans. Think, for example, of the alien in *E.T.* Since he is biologically different from us, he is not human. He is, however, a person.

What, then, is a person? Although philosophers disagree on this point, the following features are relatively noncontroversial.

First, a person is an intelligent, rational creature. Second, it is a creature capable of a peculiar sort of consciousness—self-consciousness. Third, it not only has beliefs, desires, and so forth, but it has beliefs about its beliefs, desires, and so forth. Fourth, it is a creature to which we ascribe moral responsibility. Persons are responsible for their actions in a way that other things are not. They are subject to moral praise and moral blame. Fifth, a person is a creature that we treat in certain ways. To treat something as a person is to treat it as a member of our own moral community. It is to grant it certain rights, both moral and legal. Sixth, a person is a creature capable of reciprocity. It is capable of treating us as members of the same moral community. Finally, a person is capable of verbal communication. It can communicate by means of a *language*, not just by barks, howls, and tail-wagging.

Since, as far as we know, only human beings meet the above conditions, only human beings are considered to be persons. But once we recognize that to be a person is not precisely the same thing that it is to be a human being, we also recognize that other creatures, such as the alien in *E.T.*, is also a person. We also recognize that perhaps not all human beings are persons—human fetuses, for example, as some have argued. Certainly, in the American South before the end of the Civil War, slaves were not considered to be persons. We might also mention a remark of D'Artagnan, in Richard Lester's film version of *The Three Musketeers*. Posing as a French nobleman, he attempted to cross the English Channel with a companion. When a French official remarked that his pass was only for one person, D'Artagnan replied that he was only one person—his companion was a servant.

Moreover, once we recognize the distinction between human beings and persons, certain questions arise. Can one human being embody more than one person, either at the same time or successive times? In the example we introduced at the beginning of this chapter, has Badger's body become Everglade's and Everglade's Badger's? Can the person survive the death of the human being? Is there personal survival after the death of the body?

Concerning identity through time in general, two issues must be distinguished. First, we want to know how we can *tell* that something is the same thing we encountered previously. That is, we want to know what the *criteria* are for establishing identity through time. Second, we want to know what *makes* something the same thing it was previously. That is, we want to know what *constitutes* identity through time.

Although these issues are related, they are not the same, as the following example illustrates.

We can *tell* that someone has a case of the flu by checking for certain symptoms, such as fever, lack of energy, and sore muscles. But having these symptoms does not *constitute* having a case of the flu. It is the presence of a flu virus—not the symptoms—that makes an illness a case of the flu.

We commonly use two criteria for establishing personal identity. The first is the *bodily criterion*, the second the *memory criterion*. How do we apply them?

We apply the bodily criterion in two ways. First, we go by physical resemblance. If I meet someone on the street who looks, walks, and sounds just like Mary, I assume that it is Mary. Since the body I see resembles Mary's body exactly, I assume that the person I see is Mary. But that method can sometimes fail us, as in the case of identical twins. In such cases, we can apply the bodily criterion in another way. If I can discover that there is a continuous line from one place and time to another that connects Mary's body to the body I now see, I can assume that I now see Mary. Suppose, for example, that Mary and I went to the beach together, and have been together all afternoon. In that case, I can say that the person I am now with is the person I began the day with.

There are, however, times when the bodily criterion is not available. If Mary and Jane are identical twins, and I run across one of them on the street, I may have to ask who it is. That is, I may have to rely on Mary's memory of who she is. And, if I want to make sure that I am not being fooled, I may ask a few questions. If Mary remembers things that I believe only Mary can remember, and if she remembers them as happening to *her*, and not to somebody else, then I can safely say that it really is Mary.

Generally, the bodily criterion and the memory criterion do not conflict, so we use whichever is more convenient. But what happens if they do conflict? That is what happened in our imagined story. According to the bodily criterion, each person awoke in his own bed, but with the memories of someone else. According to the memory criterion, each person awoke in the other's bed with the body of someone else. Which criterion should we take as decisive? Which is fundamental, the memory criterion or the bodily criterion?

The Constitution of Personal Identity

To ask the above questions is to ask what *constitutes* personal identity. What is it that makes me the same person I was yesterday? What makes the author of this book the same person as the baby born to Sam and Belle Olen in 1946? Answers to these questions will allow us to say which criterion is fundamental.

Perhaps the most widely discussed answer to our question comes from John Locke (1632–1704), whose discussion of the topic set the stage for all future discussions. According to Locke, the bodily criterion cannot be fundamental. Since the concept of a person is most importantly the concept of a conscious being who can be held morally and legally responsible for past actions, it is *continuity of consciousness* that constitutes personal identity. The bodily criterion is fundamental for establishing sameness of *animal*, but not sameness of *person*.

Suppose, for instance, that John Badger had been a professional thief. If the person who awoke in Badger's bed could never remember any of Badger's life as his own, but had only Everglade's memories and personality traits, while the man who awoke in Everglade's bed remembered all of Badger's crimes as his own, would we be justified in jailing the man who awoke in Badger's bed while letting the man who awoke in Everglade's go free? Locke would say no. The person who awoke in Badger's bed was not Badger.

If we agree that it is sameness of consciousness that constitutes personal identity, we must then ask what constitutes sameness of consciousness. Some philosophers have felt that it is sameness of *mind*, where the mind is thought of as a continuing nonphysical substance. Although Locke did not deny that minds are nonphysical, he did not believe that sameness of nonphysical substance is the same thing as sameness of consciousness. If we can conceive of persons switching *physical* bodies, we can also conceive of persons switching *non*physical ones.

Then what does Locke take to be crucial for personal identity? *Memory.* It is my memory of the events of Jeffrey Olen's life as happening to me that makes me the person those events happened to. It is my memory of his experiences as *mine* that makes them mine.

Although Locke's answer seems at first glance a reasonable one, many philosophers have considered it inadequate. One reason for rejecting Locke's answer is that we don't remember everything that happened to us. If I don't remember anything that happened to me during a certain period, does that mean that whoever existed "in" my body then was not me? Hardly.

Another reason for rejecting Locke's answer is that memory is not always accurate. We often sincerely claim to remember things that never happened. There is a difference, then, between *genuine* memory and *apparent* memory. What marks this difference is the *truth* of the memory claim. If what I claim to remember is not true, it cannot be a case of genuine memory.

But that means that memory cannot constitute personal identity. If I claim to remember certain experiences as being my experiences, that does not make them mine, because my claim may be a case of apparent memory. If it is a case of genuine memory, that is because it is true that the remembered experiences are mine. But the memory does not *make* them mine. Rather, the fact that they are mine makes it a case of genuine memory. So Locke has the situation backward. But if memory does not constitute personal identity, what does?

Some philosophers have claimed that, regardless of Locke's views, it *must* be sameness of mind, where the mind is thought of as a continuing nonphysical entity. This entity can be thought of as the self. It is what makes us who we are. As long as the same self continues to exist, the same person continues to exist. The major problem with this answer is that it assumes the truth of mind-body dualism, a position we found good reason to reject in the previous chapter. But apart from that, there is another problem.

In one of the most famous passages in the history of philosophy, David Hume (1711–1776) argued that there is no such self—for reasons that have nothing to do with the rejection of dualism. No matter how hard we try, Hume said, we cannot discover such a self. Turning inward and examining our own consciousness, we find only individual experiences—thoughts, recollections, images, and the like. Try as we might, we cannot find a continuing self. In that case, we are justified in believing only that there are *experiences*—not that there is a continuing *experiencer*. Put another way, we have no reason to believe that there is anything persisting through time that underlies or unifies these experiences. There are just the experiences themselves.

But if we accept this view, and still require a continuing nonphysical entity for personal identity, we are forced to the conclusion that there is no such thing as personal identity. We are left, that is, with the position that the idea of a person existing through time is a mere fiction, however useful in daily life. And that is the position that Hume took. Instead of persons, he said, there are merely "bundles of ideas."

Thus, the view that personal identity requires sameness of mind can easily lead to the view that there is no personal identity. Since this conclusion seems manifestly false, we shall have to look elsewhere? But where?

The Primacy of the Bodily Criterion

If neither memory nor sameness of mind constitutes personal identity, perhaps we should accept the view that sameness of *body* does. Perhaps it is really the bodily criterion that is fundamental.

If we reflect on the problem faced by Locke's theory because of the distinction between genuine and apparent memory, it is tempting to accept the primacy of the bodily criterion. Once again, a sincere memory claim may be either genuine memory or apparent memory. How can we tell whether the claim that a previous experience was mine is genuine memory? By determining whether I was in the right place in the right time to have it. And how can we determine that? By the bodily criterion. If my *body* was there, then I was there. But that means that the memory criterion must rest on the bodily criterion. Also, accepting the primacy of the bodily criterion get us around Hume's problem. The self that persists through and has the experiences I call mine is my physical body.

This answer also has the advantage of being in keeping with materialism, a view accepted in the previous chapter. If human beings are purely physical, then persons must also be purely physical, whatever differences there may be between the notion of a person and the notion of a human being. But if persons are purely physical, what makes me the same person I was yesterday is no different in kind from what makes my typewriter the same typewriter it was yesterday. In both cases, we are dealing with a physical object existing through time. In the latter case, as long as we have the same physical materials (allowing for change of ribbon, change of keys, and the like) arranged in the same way, we have the same typewriter. So it is with persons. As long as we have the same physical materials (allowing for such changes as the replacement of cells) arranged in the same way, we have the same person.

Although this answer is a tempting one, it is not entirely satisfactory. Suppose that we could manage a brain transplant from one body to another. If we switched two brains, so that all the memories and personality traits of the persons involved were also switched, wouldn't we conclude that the persons, as well as their brains, had switched bodies? When such operations are performed in science-fiction stories, they are described this way.

But this possibility does not defeat the view that the bodily criterion is fundamental. It just forces us to hold that the bodily criterion must be applied to the brain, rather than the entire body. Personal identity then becomes a matter of brain identity. Same brain, same person. Unfortunately, even with this change, our answer does not seem satisfactory. Locke still seems somehow right. Let us see why.

Badger and Everglade Reconsidered

Returning to our tale of Badger and Everglade, we find that some troubling questions remain. If Mrs. Everglade continues to live with the man who awoke in her bed, might she not be committing adultery? Shouldn't she take in the man who awoke in Badger's bed? And, once again assuming that Badger was a professional thief, would justice really be served by jailing the man who awoke in his bed? However we answer these questions, one thing is certain—the two men would always feel that they had switched bodies. So, probably, would the people who knew them.

Furthermore, whenever we read science-fiction stories describing such matters, we invariably accept them as stories of switched bodies. But if we accept the bodily criterion as fundamental, we are accepting the impossible, and the two men in our story, Mrs. Everglade, and their friends are mistaken in their beliefs. How, then, are we to answer our questions?

If we are unsure, it is because such questions become very tricky at this point. Their trickiness seems to rest on two points. First, cases like the Badger-Everglade case do not happen in this world. Although we are prepared to accept them in science-fiction tales, we are totally unprepared to deal with them in real life.

Second, and this is a related point, we need some way of *explaining* such extraordinary occurrences. Unless we know how the memories of Badger and Everglade came to be reversed, we will be unable to decide the answers to our questions. In the movies, it is assumed that some nonphysical substance travels from one body to another, or that there has been a brain transplant of some sort. On these assumptions, we are of course willing to describe what happens as a change of body. This description seems to follow naturally from such explanations.

What explains what happened to Badger and Everglade? We can rule out change of nonphysical substance, because of what was said in the previous chapter and earlier in this chapter. If we explain what happened as the product of a brain switch, then the bodily criterion applied to the brain allows us to say that Badger and Everglade did awaken in each other's bed, and that Mrs. Everglade would be committing adultery should she live with the man who awoke in her bed.

Are there any other possible explanations? One that comes readily to mind is hypnotism. Suppose, then, that someone had hypnotized Badger and Everglade into believing that each was the other person. In that case, we should not say that there had been a body switch. Badger and Everglade awoke in their own beds, and a wave of the hypnotist's hand could demonstrate that to everyone concerned. Their memory claims are not genuine memories, but apparent ones.

But suppose it was not a case of hypnotism? What then? At this point, many people are stumped. What else could it be? The strong temptation is to say nothing. Without a brain transplant or hypnotism or something of the sort, the case is impossible.

Suppose that we accept this conclusion. If we do, we may say the following: The memory criterion and the bodily criterion cannot really conflict. If the memories are genuine, and not apparent, then whenever I remember certain experiences as being mine, it is possible to establish that the same brain is involved in the original experiences and the memory of them. Consequently, the memory criterion and the bodily criterion are equally fundamental. The memory criterion is fundamental in the sense that consciousness determines what part of the body is central to personal identity. Because sameness of consciousness requires sameness of brain, we ultimately must apply the bodily criterion to the brain. But the bodily criterion is also fundamental, because we assume that some physical object—the brain—must remain the same if the person is to remain the same.

Multiple Personality

In recent years there have been two well-known books, both made into films, each about a woman having several radically distinct personalities—*The Three Faces of Eve* and *Sybil*. Based on actual cases, the books give detailed and fascinating accounts of the lives of the two women.

Each personality had its own memories, its own values, its own behaviour patterns, even its own name. At any given time, Eve or Sybil would assume one of these personalities. Whatever happened to her during that time would be remembered as happening only to that personality. When Eve or Sybil assumed another personality, she would either claim not to know of these experiences or claim that they had happened to someone else. The other personalities were thought of and spoken of in the third person.

Unlike science fiction and fantasy cases, the multiple-personality phenomenon is something that happens in the real world. What are we to say about it? On the one hand, we are tempted to say that each woman embodied several persons. Very often their psychiatrists spoke as though that were true. On the other hand, there is an equally strong temptation to say that each woman embodied only one person, somehow split into different personalities. Thus, we sometimes call such cases instances of *split* personality, rather than of *multiple* personality.

The first temptation is due to the fact that each woman seems to embody several distinct streams of consciousness. That is, we are led to view each woman as consisting of several persons by the *memory criterion*. The second temptation is due to the fact that each woman has only one body. That is, we are led to view each woman as one person by the *bodily criterion*. Which criterion should we accept? If there is one body but several streams of consciousness, how many persons are there? When discussing the Badger-Everglade case, we said that our answer must depend on our explanation of what happened. I think that the same thing holds for the Eve and Sybil cases.

How are such cases explained? At present, they are generally given psychoanalytic explanations. A typical psychoanalytic explanation might go like this. All of us have various aspects to our personalities. Sometimes we are forced to repress some of these aspects for one reason or another. Perhaps one of them arouses deep feelings of guilt in us; perhaps we feel we must repress it to win the love of our parents. If the repressed aspect is strong enough, and if we are unwilling to recognize it as being ours, it can cause an inner conflict resulting in a case of split or multiple personality.

This type of explanation seems to require that there is one person managing the various aspects of his or her personality. It makes the phenomenon of multiple personality seem like a strategy unconsciously adopted by one person to resolve inner conflict. Thus, if we accept this type of explanation, it seems that we should accept the view that the phenomenon involves one badly fractured person, rather than several persons "in" one body. So when dealing with Eve and Sybil, we should rely on the bodily criterion, not the memory criterion.

The Memory Criterion Revisited

Although the answer given above is a tidy one, it may still seem unsatisfactory. Perhaps it is a cheap trick just to dismiss the Badger-Everglade case as mere fantasy and then ignore it. After all, if we can meaningfully describe such cases in books and films, don't we have to pay some attention to them? As long as we can imagine situations in which two persons can switch bodies without a brain transplant, don't we need a theory of personal identity to cover them?

Philosophers are divided on this point. Some think that a theory of personal identity has to account only for what can happen in this world, while others think it must account for whatever can happen in any conceivable world. Then again, some do not believe that there is any conceivable world in which two persons could change bodies without a brain switch, while there are others who are not sure that such things are impossible in the actual world.

Without trying to decide the matter, I can make the following suggestion for those who demand a theory of personal identity that does not rely on the assumption that genuine memory is tied to a particular brain.

In the previous chapter, I concluded that functionalism is the theory of mind most likely to be true. To have a mind, I said, is to embody a psychology. I also said that we don't merely move our bodies, but write poetry, caress the cheek of someone we love, and perform all sorts of human actions. I might have expressed this point by saying that we are not just human beings, but persons as well. What makes a human being a person? We are persons because we embody a psychology.

If that is true, then it may also be true that we are the persons we are because of the psychologies we embody. If it is a psychology that makes a human being a person, then it is a particular psychology that makes a particular human being a particular person. Sameness of psychology constitutes sameness of person. In that case, we can agree with this much of Locke's theory—it is continuity of consciousness that constitutes personal identity. But what is continuity of consciousness, if not memory?

An answer to this question is provided by the contemporary British philosopher Anthony Quinton. At any moment, we can isolate a number of mental states belonging to the same momentary consciousness. Right now, for instance, I am simultaneously aware of the sound and sight and feel of my typewriter, plus the feel and taste of my pipe, plus a variety of other things. Such *momentary* consciousnesses belong to a continuous series. Each one is linked to the one before it and the one following it by certain similarities and recollections. This series is my own *continuity* of consciousness, my own *stream* of consciousness. It is this stream of consciousness that makes me the same person I was yesterday.

If we accept Quinton's theory, we can then say that the memory criterion, not the bodily criterion, is fundamental. We can also say that, even if in this world continuity of consciousness requires sameness of brain, we can conceive of worlds in which it does not. To show this, let us offer another possible explanation of the Badger-Everglade situation.

Suppose a mad computer scientist has discovered a way to reprogram human beings. Suppose that he has found a way to make us the embodiment of any psychology he likes. Suppose further that he decided to experiment on Badger and Everglade, giving Badger Everglade's psychology and Everglade Badger's and that is why the events of our story occurred. With this explanation and the considerations of the previous paragraphs, we can conclude that Badger and Everglade did change bodies. By performing his experiment, the mad scientist has made it possible for a continuing stream of consciousness to pass from one body to another. He has, in effect, performed a body transplant. . . .

Should we accept Quinton's theory? There seems to be no good reason not to. In fact, there are at least two good reasons for accepting it. First, it seems consistent with a functionalist theory of the mind. Second, it allows us to make sense of science fiction stories while we continue to believe that in the real world to be the same person we were yesterday is to have the same brain.

LIFE AFTER DEATH

Is it possible for the person to survive the death of the body? Is there a sense in which we can continue to live after our bodies have died? Can there be a personal life after death?

According to one popular conception of life after death, at the death of the body the soul leaves the body and travels to a realm known as heaven. Of course, this story must be taken as metaphorical. Does the soul literally leave the body? How? Out of the mouth? Ears? And how does it get to heaven? By turning left at Mars? Moreover, if the soul remains disembodied, how can it perceive anything? What does it use as sense organs? And if all souls remain disembodied, how can one soul recognize another? What is there to recognize?

As these questions might suggest, much of this popular story trades on a confusion. The soul is thought of as a translucent physical substance much like Casper the ghost, through which other objects can pass as they do through air or water. But if the soul is *really* nonphysical, it can be nothing like that.

If this story is not to be taken literally, is there some version of it that we can admit as a possibility? Is there also the possibility of personal survival through reincarnation as it is often understood—the re-embodiment of the person without memory of the former embodiment?

Materialism and the Disembodied Soul

So far, we have considered both the mind and the body as they relate to personal identity. Have we neglected the soul? It may seem that we have, but philosophers who discuss the mind-body question and personal identity generally use the terms "mind" and "soul" interchangeably. Is the practice legitimate, or is it a confusion?

The practice seems to be thoroughly legitimate. If the soul is thought to be the crucial element of the person, it is difficult to see how it could be anything but the mind. If it is our character traits, personality, thoughts, likes and dislikes, memories, and continuity of experience that make us the persons we are, then they must belong to the soul. If they are taken to be

crucial for one's personal identity, then it seems impossible to separate them from one's soul.

Moreover, people who accept some version of the popular conception of life after death noted above believe in certain continuities between earthly experiences and heavenly ones. In heaven, it is believed, we remember our earthly lives, we recognize friends and relatives, our personalities are like our earthly personalities, and we are judged by God for our actions on earth. But if we believe any of this, we must also believe that the soul cannot be separated from the mind.

If that is the case, it is difficult to accept the continued existence of a disembodied soul. Once we accept some form of materialism, we seem compelled to believe that the soul must be embodied. Does that rule out the possibility of any version of the popular story being true?

Some philosophers think that it does. Suppose, for instance, that the mind-brain identity theory is true. In that case, when the brain dies, so does the mind. Since the mind is the repository of memory and personality traits, it is identical with the soul. So when the brain dies, so does the soul.

This is a powerful argument, and it has convinced a number of people. On the other hand, it has also kept a number of people from accepting materialism of any sort. If it is felt that materialism and life after death are incompatible, and if one is firmly committed to the belief in life after death, then it is natural for one to reject materialism.

Is there a way of reconciling materialism and life after death? I think so.

Although it seems necessary that persons must be embodied, it does not seem necessary that the same person must be embodied by the same body. In our discussion of personal identity, we allowed that Badger and Everglade might have changed bodies, depending on our explanation of the story. Let us try a similar story.

Mary Brown is old and sick. She knows she will die within a couple of weeks. One morning she does die. At the same time, in some other world, a woman wakes up believing herself to be Mary. She looks around to find herself in a totally unfamiliar place. Someone is sitting next to her. This other woman looks exactly like Mary's mother, who died years earlier, and believes herself to be Mary's mother. Certainly, she knows everything about Mary that Mary's mother would know.

Before the woman believing herself to be Mary can speak, she notices some surprising things about herself. She no longer feels old or sick. Her pains are gone, and her mind is as sharp as ever. When she asks where she is, she is told heaven. She is also told that her husband, father, and numerous old friends are waiting to see her. All of them are indistinguishable from the persons they claim to be. Meanwhile, back on earth, Mary Brown is pronounced dead. Is this woman in "heaven" really Mary Brown? How could we possibly explain the phenomenon?

Suppose we put the story in a religious context. Earlier, we saw that one possible explanation of the Badger-Everglade case is that some mad computer scientist had reprogrammed the two so that each embodied the psychology of the other. Suppose we replace the mad scientist with God, and say that God had kept a body in heaven for the purpose of embodying Mary's psychology when she died, and that the person believing herself to be Mary is the new embodiment of Mary's psychology. Would this count as a genuine case of life after death?

If we accept the Badger-Everglade story, appropriately explained, as a case of two persons switching bodies, there seems no reason to deny that Mary has continued to live "in" another body. But even if we are unsure of the Badger-Everglade case, we can approach Mary Brown's this way. What is it that we want to survive after death? Isn't it our memories, our consciousness of self, our personalities, our relations with others? What does it matter whether there is some nonphysical substance that survives? If that substance has no memories of a prior life, does not recognize the soul of others who were important in that earlier life, what comfort could such a continuing existence bring? In what sense would it be the survival of the *person*? How would it be significantly different from the return of the lifeless body to the soil?

If we assume that our story is a genuine case of personal survival of the death of the body, we may wonder about another point. Is it compatible with Christian belief? According to John Hick, a contemporary British philosopher who imagined a similar story, the answer is yes. In I Corinthians 15, Paul writes of the resurrection of the body—not of the physical body, but of some spiritual body. Although one can think of this spiritual body as a translucent ghost-like body that leaves the physical body at death, Hick offers another interpretation.

The human being, Hick says, becomes extinct at death. It is only through God's intervention that the spiritual body comes into existence. By the resurrection of this spiritual body, we are to understand a *recreation* or *reconstitution* of the person's body in heaven. But that is precisely what happened in our story.

Thus, a materialist view of the nature of human beings is not incompatible with the Christian view of life after death. Nor, for that matter, is it incompatible with the belief that the spiritual body is nonphysical. If we can make sense of the claim that there might be such things as nonphysical bodies, then there is no reason why a nonphysical body could not embody a psychology. Remember—according to functionalism, an abstract description such as a psychology is independent of any physical description. Just as we can play chess using almost anything as chess pieces, so can a psychology be embodied by almost anything, assuming that it is complex enough. So if there can be nonphysical bodies, there can be nonphysical persons. Of course, nothing said so far assures us that the Christian story—or any other story of life after death—is true. That is another matter. . . .

Reincarnation

Much of what has been said so far does, however, rule out the possibility of reincarnation as commonly understood. If human beings are purely physical, then there is no nonphysical substance that is the person that can be reincarnated in another earthly body. Moreover, even if there were such a substance, it is difficult to see how its continued existence in another body could count as the reincarnation of a particular person, *if* there is no other continuity between the old life and the new one. Once again, personal survival requires some continuity of consciousness. It is not sameness of *stuff* that constitutes personal identity, but sameness of consciousness. This requirement is often overlooked by believers in reincarnation.

But suppose that there is some continuity of consciousness in reincarnation. Suppose that memories and the rest do continue in the next incarnation, but that they are not easily accessible. Suppose, that is, that the slate is not wiped completely clean, but that what is written on it is hard to recover. In that case, the passage of the soul into a new incarnation would count as personal survival *if* there were such a soul to begin with.

Assuming, again, that there is not, what can we say about the possibility of reincarnation? To conceive of such a possibility, we must conceive of some very complicated reprogramming by God or some mad scientist or whatever. I shall leave it to you to come up with such a story, but I shall say this much. There does not seem to be any good reason to think that any such story is remotely plausible, least of all true.

The Final Word?

In this chapter we looked at two closely related questions: What constitutes personal identity? And is it possible for a person to survive the death of her own body?

The answer to the second question depended on the first. If we had concluded that the basis of personal identity is sameness of body, then we would have been forced to conclude that life after death is impossible. And there did seem to be good reason to come to these conclusions. How, we asked, could we assure that any memory claim is a case of genuine memory? Our answer was this. In the cases likely to confront us in our daily lives, we must establish some physical continuity between the person who had the original experience and the person who claims to remember it.

But the problem with this answer is that it is too limited. Because we can imagine cases like the Everglade-Badger example, and because our science-fiction tales and religious traditions offer stories of personal continuity without bodily continuity, we can say the following. Regardless of what happens in our daily lives, our concept of a person is a concept of something that does not seem tied to a particular body. Rather, our concept of a person seems to be tied to a particular stream of consciousness. If there is one continuing stream of consciousness over time, then there is one continuing person. Our question, then, was whether we can give a coherent account of continuity of consciousness from one body to another.

The answer was yes. Using the computer analogy of the functionalist, we can explain such continuity in terms of programming. If it is possible to "program" another brain to have the same psychology as the brain I now have, then it is possible for me to change bodies. And if it is possible for me to change bodies, then it is also possible for me to survive the death of my body.

IV.5   A Hindu Theory of Life, Death, and Reincarnation

PRASANNATMA DAS

When he wrote this article, Prasannatma Das was a young Hindu philosopher studying at the Krishna Temple in Vrindavan, India. In this essay he describes the basic Hindu view of karma—the doctrine that says the way we live in this life will determine our initial state in

This essay was commissioned for the first edition of *Life & Death*, ed. Louis Pojman (Jones & Bartlett, 1993) and is reprinted here by permission of the author. All references are to the *Bhagavad Gita*, translated by A. C. Bhaktivedanta Swami Prabbupada (Los Angeles: The Bhaktivedanta Book Trust, 1983).

the next life—and reincarnation—the notion that the same person lives in a different body in future lives based on the idea of karma. Prasannatma Das appeals to the *Bhagavad Gita*, the most sacred of Hindu scriptures, for his exposition. Lord Krishna, the main speaker in that work, is viewed by Hindus as an avatar (manifestation) of God. You should be aware that, as with most major religions, there are many versions of Hinduism. This is one important Hindu version of the meaning of life and death, but not the only one. The term *cosmogonal* in the quotation from Thoreau refers to the origin of the world.

A HINDU VIEW OF LIFE AND DEATH

In a previous age, there lived a wise king named Yudhisthira. Having been banished by an evil cousin, he and his four brothers were wandering in a forest. One day the youngest brother went to get water from a nearby lake. When, after a time, he did not come back, the next brother went. He did not come back either. Twice more this happened until finally Yudhisthira himself went. He came to the lake and was about to drink from it when suddenly a voice boomed forth, "Do not drink this water. I am the owner of this lake, and if you drink this water, you shall die like your brothers have before you!" Yudhisthira then saw the lifeless bodies of his brothers lying nearby. The voice continued. "You may drink of this water only on the condition that you answer my questions. If you answer them correctly, you and your brothers shall live. If you fail, then you too shall die."

The voice then presented a series of questions to the king, all of which he answered perfectly. One of these questions was, "Of all the amazing things in this world, what is the most amazing?" The king replied, "The most amazing thing is that although everyone sees his parents dying, and everything around him dying, still we live as though we will live forever. This is truly amazing."

It is indeed amazing that even in the face of inevitable death, few perceive the urgency of our predicament; however, in every culture and tradition there have been those thoughtful souls who have done so. Within the Hindu tradition many such seekers have found the teachings of Lord Krishna as presented in the *Bhagavad Gita* to be a source of knowledge and inspiration. Appearing as an episode in the great epic of ancient India,

the *Mahabharata*, the *Bhagavad Gita* is one of the most profound theological dialogues known to man. Henry David Thoreau once said, "In the morning I bathe my intellect in the stupendous and cosmogonal philosophy of the *Bhagavad Gita*, in comparison with which our modern world and its literature seem puny and trivial."

The first message of Lord Krishna's teaching in the *Bhagavad Gita* is that we are not these bodies. The body is constantly changing; we once had the body of a small baby, then that of a child, of an adult, of an old person, and eventually the body will return to the dust from whence it came. Yet when we look in the mirror we think that this body is what we are.

But what are we really? Krishna explains that we are the eternal soul within the body and what we call death is merely the soul leaving one body and going elsewhere:

> Never was there a time when I did not exist, nor you, nor all these kings; nor in the future shall any of these cease to be.

> As the embodied soul continuously passes, in this body, from boyhood to youth to old age, the soul similarly passes into another body at the time of death. A sober person is not bewildered by such a change.

> For the soul there is neither birth nor death at any time. He has not come into being, does not come into being, and will not come into being. He is unborn, eternal, ever-existing, and primeval. He is not slain when the body is slain.

> As a person puts on new garments, giving up old and useless ones, the soul similarly accepts new material bodies, giving up old and useless ones. (2.12–13, 20, 22)

Krishna is explaining that we are not these bodies; we are the soul inside. I am not a twenty-year-old college student about to fail his philosophy course, but rather I am an eternal spirit-soul who, out of ignorance of his true nature, now identifies himself with the temporary forms of this world. When I enter a new body, I remain the same person.

For example, imagine a candle over which a series of filters are placed; the light appears to be changing according to the color of the filter obscuring it—blue, green, etc. But the original source of the light, the flame, is not changing, only the covering is. In the same way, the soul does not change, only the covering, the body, changes.

Sometimes at night we look up at the sky and see that the clouds are luminous. From the glowing of the clouds we can understand that because the moon is behind them, the clouds themselves appear to be luminous. Similarly when examining this body we can infer the existence of the soul by its symptom consciousness, which pervades the body and gives it the appearance of being alive.

Another basic teaching of the *Bhagavad Gita* is the law of karma, which states that for every action there is a corresponding reaction, or "whatever goes around, comes around." Our situation in this life was caused by the activities and desires of our previous lives. Similarly our future existence—our body, education, amount of wealth, happiness and distress, etc., will be determined by how we live now. If we harm others then we must suffer in return, and if we do good then we correspondingly enjoy. Moreover, we are given a body which suits our consciousness. If, like an animal, a human spends his life eating, sleeping, mating, and defending, ignoring his higher capacities, then he may be placed into the body of an animal. At the time of death the consciousness we have cultivated during our life will carry us, the soul, to our next body. "Whatever state of being one remembers when he quits his body, that state he will attain without fail." (8.6)

The goal is not to come back to this world at all but to attain the supreme destination:

From the highest planet in the material world down to the lowest, all are places of misery wherein repeated birth and death take place. But one who attains to My abode...never takes birth again. (8.16)

Death is perceived according to the quality of one's existence. The ignorant see death as something to be feared. They have material desires, and death will defeat them. Those who are seeking wisdom understand death as an impetus to live correctly, as a time when their knowledge will be put to test. The most amazing thing in this world is that although everyone knows they are going to die, they still act as though they will live forever. Imagine a person who has received an eviction notice—he must vacate his apartment in two weeks. If he promptly prepared for this, and found another place to go, he would not be in anxiety. Unfortunately, even though our eviction notice was given at the time of birth, very few take heed.

Krishna states:

What is night for all living beings is the time of awakening for the self-controlled, and the time of awakening for all beings is the night for the introspective sage. (2.69)

There are different types of activities which have different values. There are pious activities which lead to taking birth in a situation of relative enjoyment, there are impious activities which lead to suffering and ignorance, and there are spiritual activities which lead one to God. Such spiritual activities are called *yoga*. (*Yoga* does not mean Indian gymnastics but actually refers to the process of reuniting one's self with God.)

This yoga, or real religious life, is not just a passive activity, but is an active cultivation. If a farmer wants to harvest crops, he must begin working early in the season; plowing the fields, planting seeds, watering, weeding, etc. The fruits of his labor will manifest themselves at harvest time. Similarly, one who desires to attain to perfection must engage in a cultivation of the soul which will yield the harvest of spiritual perfection. When death comes, he will taste the fruit of his endeavor.

In this world there is nothing so sublime and pure as transcendental knowledge. Such knowledge is the mature fruit of all mysticism. One who has become accomplished in the practice of devotional service enjoys this knowledge within himself in due course of time. "That is the way of the spiritual and godly life, after attaining which a person is not bewildered. If one is in this situation even at the hour of death, one can enter into the kingdom of God." (4.38; 2.72)

Death will come. No situation in this world is permanent. All changes. Whether a table, a car, a human body, a civilization, or a mountain, everything comes into being, remains for some time, and then finally dwindles and disappears. What of this world can survive the passage of time? As Krishna says, "One who has been born is sure to die." (2.27) Of this there is no doubt.

Yet many people do not see the urgency of our situation. "Yes, I know one day I shall have to die; but for now let me eat, drink, have fun, and get a big bank balance," they think. Dedicated to the pursuit of the temporary phenomena of this world, living a life of vanity, they die like ignorant animals without higher knowledge. They and their fantasies are put to ruin. Their valuable human form of life with its great potential of knowledge and self-realization is wasted.

On the other hand, a thoughtful person understands the reality of this world, and, like a student who knows he must pass a test before he can graduate, prepares himself. This process of preparation begins with inquiry. Who am I? When this body is finished, what happens to me? Why do I exist? How can I be happy? By nature the eternal soul is full of happiness and knowledge. But now that eternal, blissful, fully cognizant being is something like a fish out of water. The lost creature will not be happy until it is placed back into the water. Giving the fish a new car or expensive jewelry will not rectify its problem; it will not become happy in this way. So too, no degree of rearranging this material world will solve our problems; we will not be satisfied until we are back in the spiritual world. Thus a wise person is not interested in attaining any of the tempting but temporary offerings of this world, knowing that they have a beginning and an end. As the

founder of Christianity pointed out, "Seek ye first the kingdom of God, and all these things will be added unto you" (Luke 12.31). Therefore, "The yogis, abandoning attachment, act...only for the sake of purification." (5.11). [Yogis are holy men. Ed.]

The sage is not interested in attaining temporary things like fame, adoration or distinction.

> An intelligent person does not take part in the sources of misery, which are done to contact with the material senses...such pleasures have a beginning and an end, and so the wise man does not delight in them. (5.22)

He does not mind leaving this world because he is not attached to it. Rather he is interested in things with real value. Krishna lists some qualities which a thoughtful person might cultivate:

> Humility; pridelessness; non-violence; tolerance; simplicity approaching a bona fide spiritual master; cleanliness; steadiness; self-control; the perception of the evil of birth, death, old age, and disease; detachment; freedom from entanglement with children, wife, home and the rest; even-mindedness amid pleasant and unpleasant events; constant and unalloyed devotion to Me; aspiring to live in a solitary place; detachment from the general mass of people; accepting the importance of self-realization; and philosophical search for the Absolute Truth....(13.8–12)

A yogi has no desire to fulfill in this world. Thus he is not attached to it. Thus he does not mind leaving it. Thus he has no fear of death.

Since he has no personal desire in this world and has faith in God, he welcomes death in the same way that the kitten welcomes the jaws of the mother cat, whereas they are feared by the mouse. Krishna states:

> To those who are constantly devoted to serving Me with love, I give the understanding by which they can come back to Me.
>
> To show them special mercy, I, dwelling in their hearts, destroy with the shining lamp of knowledge the darkness born of ignorance. (10.10–11)

For those of us who are not enlightened beings, the fact that we must die can serve as an impetus to reach that higher transcendental state; what have we to lose? If we are wrong in our hopes, and death does indeed end all, then have we lost anything by our effort? And if our hopes are correct, then certainly we have all to gain.

A faithful man who is dedicated to transcendental knowledge and who subdues his senses is eligible to achieve such knowledge, and having achieved it he quickly attains the supreme spiritual peace.

When one is enlightened with the knowledge by which [ignorance] is destroyed, then his knowledge reveals everything, as the sun lights up everything in the daytime. (4.39, 5.16)

Faith and Reason

ONE OF THE MOST IMPORTANT and widely discussed issues in the philosophy of religion is the relationship of faith to reason. Is religious belief rational? And if so, is that because we have something like evidence or proof for the religious claims that we believe? Or might our religious beliefs be rendered rational in some other way?

In this section, we focus on two key issues in the debate over faith and reason. The first question, which is taken up by the essays in Part A, is the question whether it is appropriate to hold religious beliefs, or to engage in religious practices, simply because we find it in our best interests to do so. According to Blaise Pascal, even if we don't yet have *evidence* for believing in God, we do have strong pragmatic, or practical, reason to believe in God. Though this by itself doesn't necessarily render belief in God rational, Pascal does think it gives us good reason to live as if there is a God and to try to cultivate belief in God. But is he right? Many are inclined to think that cultivating a belief simply because it is in our best interests to hold it is positively irrational. Indeed, some would say it is morally repugnant. Cultivating beliefs on important matters for reasons of self-interest rather than as a result of hard-nosed objective inquiry might seem grossly irresponsible, and when acting on those beliefs has serious consequences for others (as is often the case with religious belief) such irresponsibility might also seem terribly immoral. Just imagine how you would feel if you discovered that many of your surgeon's beliefs about surgery were cultivated not as a result of reading medical journals but rather because he discovered that he'd feel better if he thought that it was sensible to follow this or that surgical procedure.

The second question is the question of how, if at all, religious belief might come to be rationally justified. Many suppose that in order for religious belief to be rational, we would need to have *propositional evidence*—roughly speaking, evidence of the sort that can, in principle, be expressed in sentences. Suppose you have the experience of seeming to see a boat on a lake, and suppose that, on the basis of this experience, you form the belief that there is a boat on a lake in front of you. In this case, you have no propositional evidence for your belief. Your only evidence is experiential. You haven't inferred your belief from anything else you believe; you have simply formed it on the basis of an experience. But, of course, we don't at all think that *this* fact renders your belief unjustified. In fact, we think that most of our perceptual beliefs are prime examples of justified belief. Might the same be the case for religious belief? Might religious belief be rationally grounded in experience? If not, then what would it take for religious belief to be justified? These and related questions are taken up in Part B of this section.

VII.A   PRAGMATIC JUSTIFICATION OF RELIGIOUS BELIEF

THIS SECTION CONTAINS readings that deal with the practical reasonableness of religious belief. Even if we cannot find good evidence for religious beliefs, would it perhaps be in our interest to get ourselves to believe in these propositions anyway? And would such believing be morally permissible? In the first reading, "The Wager," the renowned French physicist and mathematician Blaise Pascal (1623–1662) argues that if we do a cost–benefit analysis of the matter, we find that it is eminently reasonable to take steps to put ourselves in a position to believe that God exists—and this regardless of whether we have good evidence for that belief.

The argument goes something like this: Regarding the proposition 'God exists,' reason is neutral. It can neither prove nor disprove the proposition. But we must wager. That is, we must live as if God exists or as if he does not exist— where living as if God exists involves acting as if theistic doctrines (and, for Pascal, specifically Christian doctrines) are true. Living as if God exists doesn't guarantee that belief will follow; but, on Pascal's view, it makes belief more likely. And since the benefits associated with belief promise to be infinite (and the loss equally infinite if we bet against God's existence and turn out to be wrong), we might set forth the possibilities shown in Table 7.1. There is some sacrifice of earthly pleasures involved in betting on God. But the fact is, no matter how enormous the *finite* gain associated with betting against God's existence, the mere possibility of *infinite* gain associated with betting in favor of God's existence will always make the latter preferable to the former. In short, we have a clear self-interested reason for betting on God.

Pascal is commonly understood as suggesting that we ought to *believe* in God (as opposed to simply living as if God exists in the hope or expectation that evidentially grounded belief will follow) because it is in our interests to do so. In the second reading, "The Ethics of Belief," the British philosopher W. K. Clifford (1845–1879) assembles reason's roadblocks to such pragmatic justifications for religious belief. Clifford argues that there is an ethics to belief that makes it immoral to believe

TABLE 7.1

	God exists	God does not exist
Bet that God exists	A. Infinite gain with minimal finite loss	B. Overall finite loss in terms of sacrifice of earthly goods
Bet that God doesn't exist	C. Infinite loss with finite gain	D. Overall finite gain

something without sufficient evidence. Pragmatic justifications are not justifications at all but counterfeits of genuine justifications, which must always be based on evidence.

Clifford illustrates his thesis with the example of a shipowner who sends an emigrant ship to sea. He knows that the ship is old and not well built but fails to have the ship inspected. Dismissing from his mind all doubts about the vessel's seaworthiness, the owner trusts in Providence to care for his ship. He acquires a sincere and comfortable conviction in this way and collects his insurance money without a trace of guilt after the ship sinks and all the passengers drown. Clifford comments that although the shipowner sincerely believed that all was well with the ship, his sincerity in no way exculpates him because "he had no right to believe on such evidence as was before him." One has an obligation to get oneself in a position in which one will believe propositions only on sufficient evidence.

Some may object that the shipowner simply had an obligation to *act* in a certain way (viz., inspect the ship), not to *believe* in a certain way. Granted, the shipowner does have an obligation to inspect the ship; but the objection overlooks the function of believing in guiding action. "No man holding a strong belief on one side of a question, or even wishing to hold a belief on one side, can investigate it with such fairness and completeness as if he were really in doubt and unbiased; so that the existence of a belief not founded on fair inquiry unfits a man for the performance of this necessary duty." The general conclusion is that it is always wrong for anyone to believe anything on insufficient evidence.

The classic response to Clifford's ethics of belief is William James's "The Will to Believe" (1896), the last reading in this section. James argues that life would be greatly impoverished if we confined our beliefs to such a Scrooge-like epistemology as Clifford proposes. In everyday life, where the evidence for important propositions is often unclear, we must live by faith or cease to act at all. Although we may not make leaps of faith just anywhere, sometimes practical considerations force us to make decisions about propositions that do not have their truth value written on their faces.

In "The Sentiment of Rationality" (1879) James defines 'faith' as follows: "a belief in something concerning which doubt is still theoretically possible: and as the test of belief is willingness to act, one may say that faith is the readiness to act in a cause the prosperous issue of which is not certified to us in advance." In "The Will to Believe" he argues on behalf of the rationality of believing, even with insufficient evidence, certain kinds of hypotheses—namely, those where the choice between the hypothesis and its denial is *live, momentous,* and *unavoidable.* For, he argues, to withhold belief on such momentous matters until sufficient evidence is forthcoming may, in the end, be too costly.

There is a good illustration of this notion of faith in "The Sentiment of Rationality." A mountain climber in the Alps finds himself in a position from which he can escape only by means of an enormous leap. If he tries to calculate the evidence, believing only on sufficient evidence, he will be paralyzed by emotions of fear and mistrust and hence will be lost. Without evidence that he is capable of performing this feat successfully, the climber would be better off getting himself to believe that he can and will make the leap. "In this case . . . the part of wisdom clearly is to believe what one desires; for the belief is one of the indispensable preliminary conditions of the realization of its object. *There are then cases where faith creates its own verification.*"

James claims that religion may be such an optional hypothesis for many people, and in this case one has the right to believe the better story rather than the worse. To do so, one must will to believe what the evidence alone is inadequate to support.

There are two questions, one descriptive and the other normative, that you should keep in mind when you are reading these essays. The first is whether it is possible to believe propositions at will. In what sense can we get ourselves to believe propositions that the evidence doesn't force upon us. Surely we can't believe that the world is flat or that two plus two equals five simply by willing to do so, but which propositions (if any) are subject to volitional influences? Is it, then, psychologically impossible to believe something simply because it is in our interests to do so? Does it involve self-deception? If we know that the primary cause for our belief in a religious proposition is our desire to believe, can we rationally continue to believe that proposition?

The second question involves the ethics of belief, stressed by Clifford. Supposing that we can get ourselves to believe or disbelieve propositions for self-interested reasons, is this morally permissible? What are the arguments for and against integrity of belief? Note too that Pascal, unlike James, does not seem to suppose that we have *direct* voluntary control over our beliefs. Pascal's advice, again, is to *cultivate* belief—to *act* as if you believe (e.g., by going to church, participating in Mass, taking holy water, etc.) in the hope and expectation that belief will naturally follow. James, on the other hand, seems to be defending the rationality of acquiring beliefs simply by fiat of the will.

VII.A.1   The Wager

BLAISE PASCAL

Blaise Pascal was a renowned French physicist and mathematician. In 1654, at the age of 31, Pascal had an intense religious experience that completely changed his life. After this experience, he devoted himself to prayer and the study of Scripture, abandoned his mathematical and scientific endeavors, and set himself to the task of writing a defense of the Christian faith. The book was never finished, but the present selection is taken from Pascal's notes, compiled under the title *Pensees*. Here he argues that if we do a cost-benefit analysis of the matter, we find that it is eminently reasonable to take steps to get ourselves to believe that God exists regardless of whether we now have good evidence for that belief.

Infinite—nothing.—Our soul is cast into a body, where it finds number, time, dimension. Thereupon it reasons, and calls this nature, necessity, and can believe nothing else.

Unity joined to infinity adds nothing to it, no more than one foot to an infinite measure. The finite is annihilated in the presence of the infinite, and becomes a pure nothing. So our spirit before God, so our justice before divine justice. There is not so great disproportion between our justice and that of God, as between unity and infinity.

The justice of God must be vast like His compassion. Now, justice to the outcast is less vast, and ought less to offend our feelings than mercy towards the elect.

Reprinted from Blaise Pascal, *Thoughts*, translated by W. F. Trotter (New York: Collier & Son, 1910).

We know that there is an infinite, and are ignorant of its nature. As we know it to be false that numbers are finite, it is therefore true that there is an infinity in number. But we do not know what it is. It is false that it is even, it is false that it is odd; for the addition of a unit can make no change in its nature. Yet it is a number, and every number is odd or even (this is certainly true of every finite number). So we may well know that there is a God without knowing what He is. Is there not one substantial truth, seeing there are so many things which are not the truth itself?

We know then the existence and nature of the finite, because we also are finite and have extension. We know the existence of the infinite, and are ignorant of its nature, because it has extension like us, but not limits like us. But we know neither the existence nor the nature of God, because He has neither extension nor limits.

But by faith we know His existence; in glory we shall know His nature. Now, I have already shown that we may well know the existence of a thing, without knowing its nature.

Let us now speak according to natural lights.

If there is a God, He is infinitely incomprehensible, since, having neither parts nor limits, He has no affinity to us. We are then incapable of knowing either what He is or if He is. This being so, who will dare to undertake the decision of the question? Not we, who have no affinity to Him.

Who then will blame Christians for not being able to give a reason for their belief, since they profess a religion for which they cannot give a reason? They declare, in expounding it to the world, that it is a foolishness, *stultitiam;* and then you complain that they do not prove it! If they proved it, they would not keep their words; it is in lacking proofs, that they are not lacking in sense. "Yes, but although this excuses those who offer it as such, and takes away from them the blame of putting it forward without reason, it does not excuse those who receive it." Let us then examine this point, and say, "God is, or He is not." But to which side shall we incline? Reason can decide nothing here. There is an infinite chasm which separates us. A game is being played at the extremity of this infinite distance where heads or tails will turn up. What will you wager? According

to reason, you can do neither the one thing nor the other; according to reason, you can defend neither of the propositions.

Do not then reprove for error those who have made a choice; for you know nothing about it. "No, but I blame them for having made, not this choice, but a choice; for again both he who chooses heads and he who chooses tails are equally at fault, they are both in the wrong. The true course is not to wager at all."

—Yes; but you must wager. It is not optional. You are embarked. Which will you choose then; let us see. Since you must choose, let us see which interests you least. You have two things to lose, the true and the good; and two things to stake, your reason and your will, your knowledge and your happiness; and your nature has two things to shun, error and misery. Your reason is no more shocked in choosing one rather than the other, since you must of necessity choose. This is one point settled. But your happiness? Let us weigh the gain and the loss in wagering that God is. Let us estimate these two chances. If you gain, you gain all; if you lose, you lose nothing. Wager them without hesitation that He is.—"That is very fine. Yes, I must wager; but I may perhaps wager too much."—Let us see.

Since there is an equal risk of gain and of loss, if you had only to gain two lives, instead of one, you might still wager. But if there were three lives to gain, you would have to play (since you are under the necessity of playing), and you would be imprudent, when you are forced to play, not to chance your life to gain three at a game where there is an equal risk of loss and gain. But there is an eternity of life and happiness. And this being so, if there were an infinity of chances, of which one only would be for you, you would still be right in wagering one to win two, and you would act stupidly, being obliged to play, by refusing to stake one life against three at a game in which out of an infinity of an infinitely happy life to gain. But there is here an infinity of an infinitely happy life to gain, a chance of gain against a finite number of chances of loss, and what you stake is finite. It is all divided; wherever the infinite is and there is not an infinity of chances of loss against that of gain, there is no time to hesitate, you must give all. And thus, when one is forced to play, he must renounce reason to preserve his life, rather than risk it for infinite gain, as likely to happen as the loss of nothingness.

For it is no use to say it is uncertain if we will gain, and it is certain that we risk, and that the infinite distance between the *certainty* of what is staked and the *uncertainty* of what will be gained, equals the finite good which is certainly staked against the uncertain infinite. It is not so, as every player stakes a certainty to gain an uncertainty, and yet he stakes a finite certainty to gain a finite uncertainty, without transgressing against reason. There is not an infinite distance between the certainty staked and the uncertainty of the gain; that is untrue. In truth, there is an infinity between the certainty of gain and the certainty of loss. But the uncertainty of the gain is proportioned to the certainty of the stake according to the proportion of the chances of gain and loss. Hence it comes that, if there are as many risks on one side as on the other, the course is to play even; and then the certainty of the stake is equal to the uncertainty of the gain, so far is it from the fact that there is an infinite distance between them. And so our proposition is of infinite force, when there is the finite to stake in a game where there are equal risks of gain and loss, and the infinite to gain. This is demonstrable; and if men are capable of any truths, this is one.

VII.A.2   The Ethics of Belief

W. K. CLIFFORD

W. K. Clifford (1845–1879) was a British philosopher and mathematician. The selection that follows is perhaps his best known and most widely discussed philosophical essay. Clifford argues that there is an ethics to belief that makes it always wrong for anyone to believe anything on insufficient evidence. Pragmatic justifications are not justifications at all but counterfeits of genuine justifications, which must always be based on evidence.

A shipowner was about to send to sea an emigrant ship. He knew that she was old, and not over-well built at the first; that she had seen many seas and climes, and often had needed repairs. Doubts had been suggested to him that possibly she was not seaworthy. These doubts preyed upon his mind and made him unhappy; he thought that perhaps he ought to have her thoroughly overhauled and refitted, even though this should put him to great expense. Before the ship sailed, however, he succeeded in overcoming these melancholy reflections. He said to himself that she had gone safely through so many voyages and weathered so many storms that it was idle to suppose she would not come safely home from this trip also. He would put his trust in Providence, which could hardly fail to protect all these unhappy families that were leaving their fatherland to seek for better times elsewhere. He would dismiss from his mind all ungenerous suspicions about the honesty of builders and contractors. In such ways he acquired a sincere and comfortable conviction that his vessel was thoroughly safe and seaworthy; he watched her departure with a light heart, and benevolent wishes for the success of the exiles in their strange new home that was to be; and he got his insurance money when she went down in midocean and told no tales.

What shall we say of him? Surely this, that he was verily guilty of the death of those men. It is admitted that he did sincerely believe in the soundness of his ship; but the sincerity of his

Reprinted from W. K. Clifford, *Lectures and Essays* (London: Macmillan, 1879).

conviction can in no wise to help him, because he had no right to believe on such evidence as was before him. He had acquired his belief not by honestly earning it in patient investigation, but by stifling his doubts. And although in the end he may have felt so sure about it that he could not think otherwise, yet inasmuch as he had knowingly and willingly worked himself into that frame of mind, he must be held responsible for it.

Let us alter the case a little, and suppose that the ship was not unsound after all; that she made her voyage safely, and many others after it. Will that diminish the guilt of her owner? Not one jot. When an action is once done, it is right or wrong forever; no accidental failure of its good or evil fruits can possibly alter that. The man would not have been innocent, he would only have been not found out. The question of right or wrong has to do with the origin of his belief, not the matter of it; not what it was, but how he got it; not whether it turned out to be true or false, but whether he had a right to believe on such evidence as was before him.

There was once an island in which some of the inhabitants professed a religion teaching neither the doctrine of original sin nor that of eternal punishment. A suspicion got abroad that the professors of this religion had made use of unfair means to get their doctrines taught to children. They were accused of wresting the laws of their country in such a way as to remove children from the care of their natural and legal guardians; and even of stealing them away and keeping them concealed from their friends and relations. A certain number of men formed themselves into a society for the purpose of agitating the public about this matter. They published grave accusations against individual citizens of the highest position and character, and did all in their power to injure those citizens in the exercise of their professions. So great was the noise they made, that a Commission was appointed to investigate the facts; but after the Commission had carefully inquired into all the evidence that could be got, it appeared that the accused were innocent. Not only had they been accused on insufficient evidence, but the evidence of their innocence was such as the agitators might easily have obtained, if they had attempted a fair inquiry. After these disclosures the inhabitants of that country looked upon the members of the agitating society, not only as persons whose judgment was to be distrusted, but also as no longer to be counted honorable men. For although they had sincerely and conscientiously believed in the charges they had made, yet they had no right to believe on such evidence as was before them. Their sincere convictions, instead of being honestly earned by patient inquiring, were stolen by listening to the voice of prejudice and passion.

Let us vary this case also, and suppose, other things remaining as before, that a still more accurate investigation proved the accused to have been really guilty. Would this make any difference in the guilt of the accusers? Clearly not; the question is not whether their belief was true or false, but whether they entertained it on wrong grounds. They would no doubt say, "Now you see that we were right after all; next time perhaps you will believe us." And they might be believed, but they would not thereby become honorable men. They would not be innocent, they would only be not found out. Every one of them, if he chose to examine himself *in foro conscientiae*, would know that he had acquired and nourished a belief, when he had no right to believe on such evidence as was before him; and therein he would know that he had done a wrong thing.

It may be said, however, that in both of these supposed cases it is not the belief which is judged to be wrong, but the action following upon it. The shipowner might say, "I am perfectly certain that my ship is sound, but still I feel it my duty to have her examined, before trusting the lives of so many people to her." And it might be said to the agitator, "However convinced you were of the justice of your cause and the truth of your convictions, you ought not to have made a public attack upon any man's character until you had examined the evidence on both sides with the utmost patience and care."

In the first place, let us admit that, so far as it goes, this view of the case is right and necessary; right, because even when a man's belief is so fixed that he cannot think otherwise, he still has a choice in regard to the action suggested by it, and so cannot escape the duty of investigating on the ground of the strength of his convictions; and necessary, because those who are not yet capable of controlling their feelings and thoughts must have a plain rule dealing with overt acts.

But this being premised as necessary, it becomes clear that it is not sufficient, and that our previous judgment is required to supplement it. For it is not possible so to sever the belief from the action it suggests as to condemn the one without condemning the other. No man holding a strong belief on one side of a question, or even wishing to hold a belief on one side, can investigate it with such fairness and completeness as if he were really in doubt and unbiased; so that the existence of a belief not founded on fair inquiry unfits a man for the performance of this necessary duty.

Nor is that truly a belief at all which has not some influence upon the actions of him who holds it. He who truly believes that which prompts him to an action has looked upon the action to lust after it, he has committed it already in his heart. If a belief is not realized immediately in open deeds, it is stored up for the guidance of the future. It goes to make a part of that aggregate of beliefs which is the link between sensation and action at every moment of all our lives, and which is so organized and compacted together that no part of it can be isolated from the rest, but every new addition modifies the structure of the whole. No real belief, however trifling and fragmentary it may seem, is ever truly insignificant; it prepares us to receive more of its like, confirms those which resembled it before, and weakens others; and so gradually it lays a stealthy train in our inmost thoughts, which may some day explode into overt action, and leave its stamp upon our character forever.

And no one man's belief is in any case a private matter which concerns himself alone. Our lives are guided by that general conception of the course of things which has been created by society for social purposes. Our words, our phrases, our forms and processes and modes of thought are common property, fashioned and perfected from age to age; an heirloom which every succeeding generation inherits as a precious deposit and a sacred trust to be handed on to the next one, not unchanged but enlarged and purified, with some clear marks of its proper handiwork. Into this, for good or ill, is woven every belief of every man who has speech of his fellows. An awful privilege, and an awful responsibility, that we should help to create the world in which posterity will live.

In the two supposed cases which have been considered, it has been judged wrong to believe on insufficient evidence, or to nourish belief by suppressing doubts and avoiding investigation. The reason of this judgment is not far to seek: it is that in both these cases the belief held by one man was of great importance to other men. But for as much as no belief held by one man, however seemingly trivial the belief, and however obscure the believer, is ever actually insignificant or without its effect on the fate of mankind, we have no choice but to extend our judgment to all cases of belief whatever. Belief, that sacred faculty which prompts the decisions of our will, and knits into harmonious working all the compacted energies of our being, is ours not for ourselves, but for humanity. It is rightly used on truths which have been established by long experience and waiting toil, and which have stood in the fierce light of free and fearless questioning. Then it helps to bind men together, and to strengthen and direct their common action. It is desecrated when given to unproved and unquestioned statements, for the solace and private pleasure of the believer; to add a tinsel splendor to the plain straight road of our life and display a bright mirage beyond it; or even to drown the common sorrows of our kind by a self-deception which allows them not only to cast down, but also to degrade us. Whoso would deserve well of his fellows in this matter will guard the purity of his belief with a very fanaticism of jealous care, lest at any time it should rest on an unworthy object, and catch a stain which can never be wiped away.

It is not only the leader of men, statesman, philosopher or poet, that owes this bounden duty to mankind. Every rustic who delivers in the village alehouse his slow, infrequent sentences, may help to kill or keep alive the fatal superstitions which clog his race. Every hard-worked wife of an artisan may transmit to her children beliefs which shall knit society together, or rend it in pieces. No simplicity of mind, no obscurity of station, can escape the universal duty of questioning all that we believe.

It is true that this duty is a hard one, and the doubt which comes out of it is often a very bitter thing. It leaves us bare and powerless where we thought that we were safe and strong. To know all about anything is to know how to deal with it under all circumstances. We feel much happier and more secure when we think we know precisely what to do, no matter what happens, than when we have lost our way and do not know where to turn. And if we have supposed ourselves to know all about anything, and to be capable of doing what is fit in regard to it, we naturally do not like to find that we are really ignorant and powerless, that we have to begin again at the beginning, and try to learn what the thing is and how it is to be dealt with—if indeed anything can be learned about it. It is the sense of power attached to a sense of knowledge that makes men desirous of believing, and afraid of doubting.

This sense of power is the highest and best of pleasures when the belief on which it is founded is a true belief, and has been fairly earned by investigation. For then we may justly feel that it is common property, and holds good for others as well as for ourselves. Then we may be glad, not that I have learned secrets by which I am safer and stronger, but that we men have got mastery over more of the world; and we shall be strong, not for ourselves, but in the name of Man and in his strength. But if the belief has been accepted on insufficient evidence, the pleasure is a stolen one. Not only does it deceive ourselves by giving us a sense of power which we do not really possess, but it is sinful, because it is stolen in defiance of our duty to mankind. That duty is to guard ourselves from such beliefs as from a pestilence, which may shortly master our own body and then spread to the rest of the town. What would be thought of one who, for the sake of a sweet fruit, should deliberately run the risk of bringing a plague upon his family and his neighbors?

And, as in other such cases, it is not the risk only which has to be considered; for a bad action is always bad at the time when it is done, no matter what happens afterwards. Every time we let ourselves believe for unworthy reasons, we weaken our powers of self-control, of doubting, of judicially and fairly weighing evidence. We all suffer severely enough from the maintenance and support of false beliefs and the fatally wrong actions which they lead to, and the evil born when one such belief is entertained is great and wide. But a greater and wider evil arises when the credulous character is maintained and supported, when a habit of believing for unworthy reasons is fostered and made permanent. If I steal money from any person, there may be no harm done by the mere transfer of possession; he may not feel the loss, or it may prevent him from using the money badly. But I cannot help doing this great wrong towards Man, that I make myself dishonest. What hurts society is not that it should lose its property, but that it should become a den of thieves; for then it must cease to be society. This is why we ought not to do evil that good may come; for at any rate this great evil has come, that we have done evil and are made wicked thereby. In like manner, if I let myself believe anything on insufficient evidence, there may be no great harm done by the mere belief; it may be true after all, or I may never have occasion to exhibit it in outward acts. But I cannot help doing this great wrong toward Man, that I make myself credulous. The danger to society is not merely that it should believe wrong things, though that is great enough; but that it should become credulous, and lose the habit of testing things and inquiring into them; for then it must sink back into savagery.

The harm which is done by credulity in a man is not confined to the fostering of a credulous character in others, and consequent support of false beliefs. Habitual want of care about what I believe leads to habitual want of care in others about the truth of what is told to me. Men speak the truth to one another when each reveres the truth in his own mind and in the other's mind; but how shall my friend revere the truth in my mind when I myself am careless about it, when I believe things because I want to believe them, and because they are comforting and pleasant? Will he not learn to cry, "Peace," to me, when there is no peace? By such a course I shall surround myself with a thick atmosphere of false-hood and fraud, and in that must live. It may matter little to me, in my closed castle of sweet illusions and darling lies; but it matters much to Man that I have made my neighbors ready to deceive. The credulous man is father to the liar and the cheat; he lives in the bosom of this his family, and it is no marvel if he should become even as they are. So closely are our duties knit together, that whoso shall keep the whole law, and yet offend in one point, he is guilty of all.

To sum up: it is wrong always, everywhere and for anyone, to believe anything upon insufficient evidence.

If a man, holding a belief which he was taught in childhood or persuaded of afterwards, keeps down and pushes away any doubts which arise about it in his mind, purposely avoids the reading of books and the company of men that call in question or discuss it, and regards as impious those questions which cannot easily be asked without disturbing it—the life of that man is one long sin against mankind.

If this judgment seems harsh when applied to those simple souls who have never known better, who have been brought up from the cradle with a horror of doubt, and taught that their eternal welfare depends on what they believe, then it leads to the very serious question, Who hath made Israel to sin? . . .

Inquiry into the evidence of a doctrine is not to be made once for all, and then taken as finally settled. It is never lawful to stifle a doubt; for either it can be honestly answered by means of the inquiry already made, or else it proves that the inquiry was not complete.

"But," says one, "I am a busy man; I have no time for the long course of study which would be necessary to make me in any degree a competent judge of certain questions, or even able to understand the nature of the arguments." Then he should have no time to believe. . . .

VII.A.3   The Will to Believe

WILLIAM JAMES

William James (1842–1910) was a philosopher and psychologist, the elder brother of novelist Henry James, and one of the central figures in the American pragmatist school of philosophy. Among his more important works are *The Varieties of Religious Experience* (1902), *Pragmatism* (1907), and *The Meaning of Truth* (1909). In the present essay James argues, against W. K. Clifford, that sometimes practical considerations force us to make decisions on propositions for which we do not yet and, indeed, may never have sufficient evidence.

I

Let us give the name of hypothesis to anything that may be proposed to our belief; and just as the electricians speak of live and dead wires, let us speak of any hypothesis as either *live* or *dead*. A live hypothesis is one which appeals as a real possibility to him to whom it is proposed. If I ask you to believe in the Mahdi, the notion makes no electric connection with your nature—it refuses to scintillate with any credibility at all. As an hypothesis it is completely dead. To an Arab, however (even if he be not one of the Mahdi's followers), the hypothesis is among the mind's possibilities: It is alive. This shows that deadness and liveness in an hypothesis are not

---

Reprinted from William James, *The Will to Believe* (New York: Longmans Green & Co., 1897).

intrinsic properties, but relations to the individual thinker. They are measured by his willingness to act. The maximum of liveness in an hypothesis means willingness to act irrevocably. Practically, that means belief; but there is some believing tendency wherever there is willingness to act at all.

Next, let us call the decision between two hypotheses an option. Options may be of several kinds. They may be first, *living* or *dead;* secondly, *forced* or *avoidable;* thirdly, *momentous* or *trivial;* and for our purposes we may call an option a *genuine* option when it is of a forced, living, and momentous kind.

1. A living option is one in which both hypotheses are live ones. If I say to you: "Be a theosophist or be a Mohammedan," it is probably a dead option, because for you neither hypothesis is likely to be alive. But if I say: "Be an agnostic or be a Christian," it is otherwise: trained as you are, each hypothesis makes some appeal, however small, to your belief.

2. Next, if I say to you: "Choose between going out with your umbrella or without it," I do not offer you a genuine option, for it is not forced. You can easily avoid it by not going out at all. Similarly, if I say, "Either love me or hate me," "Either call my theory true or call it false," your option is avoidable. You may remain indifferent to me, neither loving nor hating, and you may decline to offer any judgment as to my theory. But if I say, "Either accept this truth or go without it," I put on you a forced option, for there is no standing place outside of the alternative. Every dilemma based on a complete logical disjunction, with no possibility of not choosing, is an option of this forced kind.

3. Finally, if I were Dr. Nansen and proposed to you to join my North Pole expedition, your option would be momentous; for this would probably be your similar opportunity, and your choice now would either exclude you from the North Pole sort of immortality altogether or put at least the chance of it into your hands. He who refuses to embrace a unique opportunity loses the prize as surely as if he tried and failed. Per contra, the option is trivial when the opportunity is not unique, when the stake is insignificant, or when the decision is reversible if it later proves unwise. Such trivial options abound in the scientific life. A chemist finds an hypothesis live enough to spend a year in its verification: he believes in it to that extent. But if his experiments prove inconclusive either way, he is quit for his loss of time, no vital harm being done.

It will facilitate our discussion if we keep all these distinctions well in mind.

II

The next matter to consider is the actual psychology of human opinion. When we look at certain facts, it seems as if our passional and volitional nature lay at the root of all our convictions. When we look at others, it seems as if they could do nothing when the intellect had once said its say. Let us take the latter facts up first.

Does it not seem preposterous on the very face of it to talk of our opinions being modifiable at will? Can our will either help or hinder our intellect in its perceptions of truth? Can we, by just willing it, believe that Abraham Lincoln's existence is a myth, and that the portraits of him in *McClure's Magazine* are all of some one else? Can we, by any effort of our will, or by any strength of wish that it were true, believe ourselves well and about when we are roaring with rheumatism in bed, or feel certain that the sum of the two one-dollar bills in our pocket must be a hundred dollars? We can say any of these things, but we are absolutely impotent to believe them; and of just such things is the whole fabric of the truths that we do believe in made up— matters of fact, immediate or remote, as Hume said, and relations between ideas, which are either there or not there for us if we see them so, and which if not there cannot be put there by any action of our own.

In Pascal's *Thoughts* there is a celebrated passage known in literature as Pascal's Wager. In it he tries to force us into Christianity by reasoning as if our concern with truth resembled our concern with the stakes in a game of chance. Translated freely his words are these: You must either believe or not believe that God is—which will you do? Your human reason cannot say. A game is going on between you and the nature of things which at the day of judgment will bring out either heads or tails. Weigh what your gains and your losses would be if you should stake all you have on heads, or God's existence: if you win in such case you gain eternal beatitude; if you lose, you lose nothing at all. If there were an infinity of chances and only one for God in this wager, still you ought to stake your all on God; for though you surely risk a finite loss by this procedure, any finite loss is reasonable, even a certain one is reasonable, if there is but the possibility of infinite gain. Go then, and take holy water, and have masses said: belief will come and stupefy your scruples. . . . Why should you not? At bottom, what have you to lose?

You probably feel that when religious faith expresses itself thus, in the language of the gaming-table, it is put to its last trumps. Surely Pascal's own personal belief in masses and holy water had far other springs; and this celebrated page of his is but an argument for others, a last desperate snatch at a weapon against the hardness of the unbelieving heart. We feel that a faith in masses and holy water adopted wilfully after such a mechanical calculation would lack the inner soul of faith's reality; and if we were ourselves in the place of the Deity, we should probably take particular pleasure in cutting off believers of this pattern from their infinite reward. It is evident that unless there be some preexisting tendency to believe in masses and holy water, the option offered to the will by Pascal is not a living option. Certainly no Turk ever took to masses and holy water on its account and even to us Protestants these means of salvation seem such foregone impossibilities that Pascal's logic, invoked for them specifically, leaves us unmoved. As well might the Mahdi write to us saying, "I am the Expected One whom God has created in his effulgence. You shall be infinitely happy if you confess me; otherwise you shall be cut off from the light of the sun. Weigh, then, your infinite gain if I am genuine against your finite sacrifice if I am not!" His logic would be that of Pascal; but he would vainly use it on us, for the

hypothesis he offers us is dead. No tendency to act on it exists in us to any degree.

The talk of believing by our volition seems, then from one point of view, simply silly. From another point of view it is worse than silly, it is vile. When one turns to the magnificent edifice of the physical sciences, and sees how it was reared; what thousands of disinterested moral lives of men lie buried in its mere foundations; what patience and postponement, what choking down of preference, what submission to the icy laws of outer fact are wrought into its very stones and mortar; how absolutely impersonal it stands in its vast augustness—then how besotted and contemptible seems every little sentimentalist who comes blowing his voluntary smoke-wreaths, and pretending to decide things from out of his private dream! Can we wonder if those bred in the rugged and manly school of science should feel like spewing such subjectivism out of their mouths? The whole system of loyalties which grow up in the schools of science go dead against its toleration; so that it is only natural that those who have caught the scientific fever should pass over to the opposite extreme, and write sometimes as if the incorruptibly truthful intellect ought positively to prefer bitterness and unacceptableness to the heart in its cup.

> *It fortifies my soul to know*
> *That though I perish, truth is so*

sings Clough, while Huxley exclaims: "My only consolation lies in the reflection that, however bad our posterity may become, so far as they hold by the plain rule of not pretending to believe what they have no reason to believe, because it may be to their advantage so to pretend [the word 'pretend' is surely here redundant], they will not have reached the lowest depths of immorality." And that delicious *enfant terrible* Clifford writes: "Belief is desecrated when given to unproved and unquestioned statements for the solace and private pleasure of the believer. . . . Whoso would deserve well of his fellows in this matter will guard the purity of his belief with a very fanaticism of jealous care, lest at any time it should rest on an unworthy object, and catch a stain which can never be wiped away. . . . If

[a] belief has been accepted on insufficient evidence [even though the belief be true, as Clifford on the same page explains] the pleasure is a stolen one....It is sinful because it is stolen in defiance of our duty to mankind. That duty is to guard ourselves from such beliefs as from a pestilence which may shortly master our own body and then spread to the rest of the town....It is wrong always, everywhere, and for every one, to believe anything upon insufficient evidence."

III

All this strikes one as healthy, even when expressed, as by Clifford, with somewhat too much of robustious pathos in the voice. Free will and simple wishing do seem, in the matter of our credences, to be only fifth wheels to the coach. Yet if any one should thereupon assume that intellectual insight is what remains after wish and will and sentimental preference have taken wing, or that pure reason is what then settles our opinions, he would fly quite as directly in the teeth of the facts.

It is only our already dead hypotheses that our willing nature is unable to bring to life again. But what has made them dead for us is for the most part a previous action of our willing nature of an antagonistic kind. When I say "willing nature," I do not mean only such deliberate volitions as may have set up habits of belief that we cannot now escape from—I mean all such factors of belief as fear and hope, prejudice and passion, imitation and partisanship, the circumpressure of our caste and set. As a matter of fact we find ourselves believing, we hardly know how or why. Mr. Balfour gives the name of "authority" to all those influences, born of the intellectual climate, that make hypotheses possible or impossible for us, alive or dead. Here in this room, we all of us believe in molecules and the conservation of energy, in democracy and necessary progress, in Protestant Christianity and the duty of fighting for "the doctrine of the immortal Monroe," all for no reasons worthy of the name. We see into these matters with no more inner clearness, and probably with much less, than any disbeliever in them might possess. His unconventionality

would probably have some grounds to show for its conclusions; but for us, not insight, but the *prestige* of the opinions, is what makes the spark shoot from them and light up our sleeping magazines of faith. Our reason is quite satisfied, in nine hundred and ninety-nine cases out of every thousand of us, if it can find a few arguments that will do to recite in case our credulity is criticized by some one else. Our faith is faith in some one else's faith, and in the greatest matters this is the most the case. Our belief in truth itself, for instance, that there is a truth, and that our minds and it are made for each other,—what is it but a passionate affirmation of desire, in which our social system backs us up? We want to have a truth; we want to believe that our experiments and studies and discussions must put us in a continually better and better position towards it; and on this line we agree to fight out our thinking lives. But if a pyrrhonistic sceptic asks *us how we know* all this, can our logic find a reply? No! certainly it cannot. It is just one volition against another,—we willing to go in for life upon a trust or assumption which he, for his part, does not care to make.

As a rule we disbelieve all facts and theories for which we have no use. Clifford's cosmic emotions find no use for Christian feelings. Huxley belabors the bishops because there is no use for sacerdotalism in his scheme of life. Newman, on the contrary, goes over to Romanism, and finds all sorts of reasons good for staying there, because a priestly system is for him an organic need and delight. Why do so few 'scientists' even look at the evidence for telepathy, so called? Because they think, as a leading biologist, now dead, once said to me, that even if such a thing were true, scientists ought to band together to keep it suppressed and concealed. It would undo the uniformity of Nature and all sorts of other things without which scientists cannot carry on their pursuits. But if this very man had been shown something which as a scientist he might *do* with telepathy, he might not only have examined the evidence, but even have found it good enough.

This very law which the logicians would impose upon us—if I may give the name of logicians to those who would rule out our willing nature here—is based on nothing but their own natural wish to exclude all elements for which they, in their professional quality of logicians, can find no use.

Evidently, then, our non-intellectual nature does influence our convictions. There are passional tendencies and volitions which run before and others which come after belief, and it is only the latter that are too late for the fair; and they are not too late when the previous passional work has been already in their own direction. Pascal's argument, instead of being powerless, then seems a regular clincher, and is the last stroke needed to make our faith in masses and holy water complete. The state of things is evidently far from simple; and pure insight and logic, whatever they might do ideally, are not the only things that really do produce our creeds.

IV

Our next duty, having recognized this mixed up state of affairs, is to ask whether it be simply reprehensible and pathological, or whether, on the contrary, we must treat it as a normal element in making up our minds. The thesis I defend is, briefly stated, this: *Our passional nature not only lawfully may, but must, decide an option between propositions, whenever it is a genuine option that cannot by its nature be decided on intellectual grounds; for to say, under such circumstances, "Do not decide, but leave the question open," is itself a passional decision—just like deciding yes or no—and is attended with the same risk of losing the truth....*

VII

One more point, small but important, and our preliminaries are done. There are two ways of looking at our duty in the matter of opinion—ways entirely different, and yet ways about whose difference the theory of knowledge seems hitherto to have shown very little concern. *We must know the truth; and we must avoid error*—these are our first and great commandments as would-be knowers; but they are not two ways of stating an identical commandment, they are two separable laws. Although it may indeed happen that when we believe the truth A, we escape as an incidental consequence from believing the falsehood B, it hardly ever happens that by merely disbelieving B we necessarily believe A. We may in escaping B fall into believing other falsehoods, C or D, just as bad as B; or we may escape B by not believing anything at all, not even A.

Believe truth! Shun error!—these, we see, are two materially different laws; and by choosing between them we may end by coloring differently our whole intellectual life. We may regard the chase for truth as paramount, and the avoidance of error as secondary; or we may, on the other hand, treat the avoidance of error as more imperative, and let truth take its chance. Clifford, in the instructive passage which I have quoted, exhorts us to the latter course. Believe nothing, he tells us, keep your mind in suspense forever, rather than by closing it on insufficient evidence incur the awful risk of believing lies. You, on the other hand, may think that the risk of being in error is a very small matter when compared with the blessings of real knowledge, and be ready to be duped many times in your investigation rather than postpone indefinitely the chance of guessing true. I myself find it impossible to go with Clifford. We must remember that these feelings of our duty about either truth or error are in any case only expressions of our passional life. Biologically considered, our minds are as ready to grind out falsehood as veracity, and he who says, "Better go without belief forever than believe a lie!" merely shows his own preponderant private horror of becoming a dupe. He may be critical of many of his desires and fears, but this fear he slavishly obeys. He cannot imagine any one questioning its binding force. For my own part, I have also a horror of being duped; but I can believe that worse things than being duped may happen to a man in this world; so Clifford's exhortation has to my ears a thoroughly fantastic sound. It is like a general informing his soldiers that it is better to keep out of battle forever than to risk a single wound. Not so are victories either over enemies or over nature gained. Our errors are surely not such awfully solemn things. In a world where we are so certain to incur them in spite of all our caution, a certain lightness of heart seems healthier than this excessive nervousness on their behalf. At any rate, it seems the fittest thing for the empiricist philosopher.

VIII

And now, after all this introduction, let us go straight at our question. I have said, and now repeat it, that not only as a matter of fact do we find our passional nature influencing us in our opinions, but that there are some options between opinions in which this influence must be regarded both as an inevitable and as a lawful determinant of our choice.

I fear here that some of you my hearers will begin to scent danger, and lend an inhospitable ear. Two first steps of passion you have indeed had to admit as necessary—we must think so as to avoid dupery, and we must think so as to gain truth; but the surest path to those ideal consummations, you will probably consider, is from now onwards to take no further passional step.

Well, of course, I agree as far as the facts will allow. Wherever the option between losing truth and gaining it is not momentous, we can throw the chance of *gaining truth* away, and at any rate save ourselves from any chance of *believing falsehood,* by not making up our minds at all till objective evidence has come. In scientific questions, this is almost always the case; and even in human affairs in general, the need of acting is seldom so urgent that a false belief to act on is better than no belief at all. Law courts, indeed, have to decide on the best evidence attainable for the moment, because a judge's duty is to make law as well as to ascertain it, and (as a learned judge once said to me) few cases are worth spending much time over: the great thing is to have them decided on *any* acceptable principle, and got out of the way. But in our dealings with objective nature we obviously are recorders, not makers, of the truth; and decisions for the mere sake of deciding promptly and getting on to the next business would be wholly out of place. Throughout the breadth of physical nature facts are what

they are quite independently of us, and seldom is there any such hurry about them that the risks of being duped by believing a premature theory need be faced. The questions here are always trivial options, the hypotheses are hardly living (at any rate not living for us spectators), the choice between believing truth or falsehood is seldom forced. The attitude of sceptical balance is therefore the absolutely wise one if we would escape mistakes. What difference, indeed, does it make to most of us whether we have or have not a theory of the Röntgen rays, whether we believe or not in mind-stuff, or have a conviction about the causality of conscious states? It makes no difference. Such options are not forced on us. On every account it is better not to make them, but still keep weighing reasons *pro et contra* with an indifferent hand.

I speak, of course, here of the purely judging mind. For purposes of discovery such indifference is to be less highly recommended, and science would be far less advanced than she is if the passionate desires of individuals to get their own faiths confirmed had been kept out of the game. See for example the sagacity which Spencer and Weismann now display. On the other hand, if you want an absolute duffer in an investigation, you must, after all, take the man who has no interest whatever in its results: he is the warranted incapable, the positive fool. The most useful investigator, because the most sensitive observer, is always he whose eager interest in one side of the question is balanced by an equally keen nervousness lest he become deceived.[1] Science has organized this nervousness into a regular *technique,* her so-called method of verification; and she has fallen so deeply in love with the method that one may even say she has ceased to care for truth by itself at all. It is only truth as technically verified that interests her. The truth of truths might come in merely affirmative form, and she would decline to touch it. Such truth as that, she might repeat with Clifford, would be stolen in defiance of her duty to mankind. Human passions, however, are stronger than technical rules. *"Le coeur a ses raisons,"* as Pascal says, *"que la raison ne connait pas"*;[2] and however indifferent to all but the bare rules of the game the umpire, the abstract intellect, may be, the concrete players who furnish him the materials to judge of are usually, each one of them, in love with some pet "live hypothesis" of his own. Let us agree, however, that wherever there is no forced option, the dispassionately judicial intellect with no pet hypothesis, saving us, as it does, from dupery at any rate, ought to be our ideal.

The question next arises: Are there not somewhere forced options in our speculative questions, and can we (as men who may be interested at least as much in positively gaining truth as in merely escaping dupery) always wait with impunity till the coercive evidence shall have arrived? It seems *a priori* improbable that the truth should be so nicely adjusted to our needs and powers as that. In the great boarding-house of nature, the cakes and the butter and the syrup seldom come out so even and leave the plates so clean. Indeed, we should view them with scientific suspicion if they did.

IX

Moral questions immediately present themselves as questions whose solution cannot wait for sensible proof. A moral question is a question not of what sensibly exists, but of what is good, or would be good if it did exist. Science can tell us what exists; but to compare the *worths,* both of what exists and of what does not exist, we must consult not science, but what Pascal calls our heart. . . .

Turn now from these wide questions of good to a certain class of questions of fact, questions concerning personal relations, states of mind between one man and another. *Do you like me or not?*—for example. Whether you do or not depends, in countless instances, on whether I meet you halfway, am willing to assume that you must like me, and show you trust and expectation. The previous faith on my part in your liking's existence is in such cases what makes your liking come. But if I stand aloof, and refuse to budge an inch until I have objective evidence, until you shall have done something apt, as the absolutists say, *ad extorquendum assensum meum,* ten to one your liking never comes.

How many women's hearts are vanquished by the mere sanguine insistence of some man that they *must* love him! He will not consent to the hypothesis that they cannot. The desire for a certain kind of truth here brings about that special truth's existence; and so it is in innumerable cases of other sorts. . . . *And where faith in a fact can help create the fact,* that would be an insane logic which should say that faith running ahead of scientific evidence is the "lowest kind of immorality" into which a thinking being can fall. Yet such is the logic by which our scientific absolutists pretend to regulate our lives!

X

In truths dependent on our personal action, then faith based on desire is certainly a lawful and possibly an indispensable thing.

But now, it will be said, these are all childish human cases, and have nothing to do with great cosmical matters, like the question of religious faith. Let us then pass on to that. Religions differ so much in their accidents that in discussing the religious question we must make it very generic and broad. What then do we now mean by the religious hypothesis? Science says things are; morality says some things are better than other things; and religion says essentially two things.

First, she says that the best things are the more eternal things, the overlapping things, the things in the universe that throw the last stone, so to speak and say the final word. "Perfection is eternal"—this phrase of Charles Secrétan seems a good way of putting this first affirmation of religion, an affirmation which obviously cannot yet be verified scientifically at all.

The second affirmation of religion is that we are better off even now if we believe her first affirmation to be true.

Now, let us consider what the logical elements of this situation are *in case the religious hypothesis in both its branches be really true.* (Of course, we must admit that possibility at the outset. If we are to discuss the question at all, it must involve a living option. If for any of you religion be a hypothesis that cannot, by any living possibility, be true, then you need go no farther.

I speak to the "saving remnant" alone.) So proceeding, we see, first, that religion offers itself as a *momentous* option. We are supposed to gain, even now, by our belief, and to lose by our non-belief, a certain vital good. Secondly religion is a *forced* option, so far as that good goes. We cannot escape the issue by remaining sceptical and waiting for more light, because, although we do avoid error in that way *if religion be untrue,* we lose the good, *if it be true,* just as certainly as if we positively chose to disbelieve. It is as if a man should hesitate indefinitely to ask a certain woman to marry him because he was not perfectly sure that she would prove an angel after he brought her home. Would he not cut himself off from that particular angel-possibility as decisively as if he went and married some one else? Scepticism, then, is not avoidance of option; it is option of a certain particular kind of risk. *Better risk loss of truth than chance of error*—that is your faith-vetoer's exact position. He is actively playing his stake as much as the believer is; he is backing the field against the religious hypothesis, just as the believer is backing the religious hypothesis against the field. To preach scepticism to us as a duty until "sufficient evidence" for religion to be found, is tantamount therefore to telling us, when in presence of the religious hypothesis, that to yield to our fear of its being error is wiser and better than to yield to our hope that it may be true. It is not intellect against all passions, then; it is only intellect with one passion laying down its law. And by what, forsooth, is the supreme wisdom of this passion warranted? Dupery for dupery, what proof is there that dupery through hope is so much worse than dupery through fear? I, for one, can see no proof; and I simply refuse obedience to the scientist's command to imitate his kind of option, in a case where my own stake is important enough to give me the right to choose my own form of risk. If religion be true and the evidence for it be still insufficient, I do not wish, by putting your extinguisher upon my nature (which feels to me as if it had after all some business in this matter), to forfeit my sole chance in life of getting upon the winning side—that chance depending, of course, on my willingness to run the risk of acting as if my passional need of taking the world religiously might be prophetic and right.

All this is on the supposition that it really may be prophetic and right, and that, even to us who are discussing the matter, religion is a live hypothesis which may be true. Now, to most of us religion comes in a still further way that makes a veto on our active faith even more illogical. The more perfect and more eternal aspect of the universe is represented in our religions as having personal form. The universe is no longer a mere *It* to us, but a *Thou,* if we are religious; and any relation that may be possible from person to person might be possible here. For instance, although in one sense we are passive portions of the universe, in another we show a curious autonomy, as if we were small active centers on our own account. We feel, too, as if the appeal of religion to us were made to our own active goodwill, as if evidence might be forever withheld from us unless we met the hypothesis halfway to take a trivial illusion; just as a man who in a company of gentlemen made no advances, asked a warrant for every concession, and believed no one's word without proof, would cut himself off by such churlishness from all the social rewards that a more trusting spirit would earn—so here, one who should shut himself up in snarling logicality and try to make the gods extort his recognition willy-nilly, or not get it at all, might cut himself off forever from his only opportunity of making the gods' acquaintance. This feeling, forced on us we know not whence that by obstinately believing that there are gods (although not to do so would be so easy both for our logic and our life) we are doing the universe the deepest service we can, seems part of the living essence of the religious hypothesis. If the hypothesis were true in all its parts, including this one, then pure intellectualism, with its veto on our making willing advances, would be an absurdity; and some participation of our sympathetic nature would be logically required. I therefore, for one, cannot see my way to accepting the agnostic rules for truth-seeking, or wilfully agree to keep my willing nature out of the game. I cannot do so for this plain reason, that *a rule of thinking which would absolutely prevent me from acknowledging certain kinds of truth if those kinds of truth were really there, would be an irrational rule.* That for me is the long and short of the formal logic of the situation, no matter what the kinds of truth might materially be.

I confess I do not see how this logic can be escaped. But sad experience makes me fear that some of you may still shrink from radically saying with me, *in abstracto,* that we have the right to believe at our own risk any hypothesis that is live enough to tempt our will. I suspect, however, that if this is so, it is because you have got away from the abstract logical point of view altogether, and are thinking (perhaps without realizing it) of some particular religious hypothesis which for you is dead. The freedom to "believe what we will" you apply to the case of some patent superstition; and the faith you think of is the faith defined by the schoolboy when he said, "Faith is when you believe something that you know ain't true." I can only repeat that this is misapprehension. *In concreto,* the freedom to believe can only cover living options which the intellect of the individual cannot by itself resolve; and living options never seem absurdities to him who has them to consider. When I look at the religious question as it really puts itself to concrete men, and when I think of all the possibilities which both practically and theoretically it involves, then this command that we shall put a stopper on our heart, instincts, and courage, and *wait*— acting of course meanwhile more or less as if religion were not true[3]—till doomsday, or till such time as our intellect and senses working together may have raked in evidence enough—this command, I say, seems to me the queerest idol ever manufactured in the philosophic cave. Were we scholastic absolutists, there might be more excuse. If we had an infallible intellect with its objective certitudes, we might feel ourselves disloyal to such a perfect organ or knowledge in not trusting to it exclusively, in not waiting for its releasing word. But if we are empiricists, if we believe that no bell in us tolls to let us know for certain when truth is in our grasp, then it seems a piece of idle fantasticality to preach so solemnly our duty of waiting for the bell. Indeed we may wait if we will—I hope you do not think

that I am denying that—but if we do so, we do so at our peril as much as if we believed. In either case we act, taking our life in our hands. No one of us ought to issue vetoes to the other, nor should we bandy words of abuse. We ought, on the contrary, delicately and profoundly to respect one another's mental freedom: then only shall we bring about the intellectual republic; then only shall we have that spirit of inner tolerance without which all our outer tolerance is soulless, and which is empiricism's glory; then only shall we live and let live, in speculative as well as in practical things.

I began by a reference to Fitz-James Stephen; let me end by a quotation from him. "What do you think of yourself? What do you think of the world? . . . These are questions with which all must deal as it seems good to them. They are riddles of the Sphinx, and in someway or other we must deal with them. . . . In all important transactions of life we have to take a leap in the dark. . . . If we decide to leave the riddles unanswered, that is a choice; if we waver in our answer, that, too, is a choice: but whatever choice we make, we make it at our peril. If a man chooses to turn his back altogether on God and the future no one can prevent him; no one can show beyond reasonable doubt that he is mistaken. If a man thinks otherwise and acts as he thinks, I do not see that any one can prove that he is mistaken. Each must act as he thinks best; and if he is wrong, so much the worse for him. We stand on a mountain pass in the midst of whirling snow and blinding mist, through which we get glimpses now and then of paths which may be deceptive. If we stand still we shall be frozen to death. If we take the wrong road we shall be dashed to pieces. We do not certainly know whether there is any right one. What must we do? 'Be strong and of a good courage.' Act for the best, hope for the best, and take what comes. . . . If death ends all, we cannot meet death better."

NOTES

1. Compare Wilfrid Ward's Essay "The Wish to Believe," in his *Witnesses to the Unseen* (Macmillan & Co., 1893).

2. "The heart has its reasons which reason does not know."

3. Since belief is measured by action, he who forbids us to believe religion to be true, necessarily also forbids us to act as we should if we did believe it to be true. The whole defence of religious faith hinges upon action. If the action required or inspired by the religious hypothesis is in no way different from that dictated by the naturalistic hypothesis, then religious faith is a pure superfluity, better pruned away, and controversy about its legitimacy is a piece of idle trifling, unworthy of serious minds. I myself believe, of course, that the religious hypothesis gives to the world an expression which specifically determines our reactions, and makes them in a large part unlike what they might be on a purely naturalistic scheme of belief.

VII.B   RATIONALITY AND JUSTIFIED RELIGIOUS BELIEF

IN THIS SECTION we are concerned with the contemporary discussion of the relationship of reason to religious belief. In the theoretical or epistemological sense (over against the pragmatic sense) of rationality, is it rational to believe religious propositions? Specifically, is it rational to believe that God exists? These readings offer various interpretations of the notion of rationality and show how they apply to theistic belief.

In the first reading, "Rational Theistic Belief without Proof," John Hick discusses the relevancy of the proofs or arguments for theistic beliefs that we studied in Part One. He argues that the proofs are largely irrelevant to religion. They are neither sufficient nor necessary for the religious life. Not only do the so-called proofs for the existence of God fail to accomplish what they set out to do, but even if they did demonstrate what they purported to demonstrate, this would at best only force our notional assent. They would not bring about the deep devotion and sense of worship necessary for a full religious life. Furthermore, they are not necessary, because believers have something *better*—an intense, coercive, indubitable experience, which convinces them of the reality of the being in question.

Hick develops a notion of religious experience as analogous to our experience of an external world. Neither the existence of an external world nor the existence of an external religious reality can be proven, but belief in each is a natural response to our experience. The main difference between the two kinds of experiences is that virtually everyone has external-world experiences, but only a relatively small minority of humankind have noticeable religious experiences. Should this undermine the argument from religious experience? Not necessarily, for it may be the case that the few have access to a higher reality. They cannot easily be dismissed as insane or simply hallucinating, for the "general intelligence and exceptionally high moral quality of the great religious figures clashes with any analysis of their experience in terms of abnormal psychology."

At the end of his article Hick applies his thesis about the sense of the presence of God to the problem of the plurality of religions. He suggests that there is a convergence of religious experience, indicating the existence of a common higher reality.

In our next reading, Alvin Plantinga argues that the evidentialist objections to theism (such as those put forth by W. K. Clifford in reading VII.A.2) fail because evidentialists have yet to establish a criterion for justification that excludes belief in God while at the same time counting as justified all of the clear cases of justified belief.

According to Plantinga, evidentialists embrace foundationalism—the view that all justified beliefs are properly basic or ultimately based on properly basic beliefs. A belief is basic if it is held without being based on, or inferred from, other beliefs, and it is properly basic if it is *justified* without being based on other beliefs. The beliefs that a juror forms about a defendant's guilt or innocence are likely neither basic nor properly basic. The juror will likely decide the defendant's guilt or innocence on the basis of other things that she believes (e.g., beliefs about what testimony was offered; beliefs about what's physically possible and impossible; etc.). And if the juror were simply to believe that the defendant is guilty without basing that belief on any evidence, the juror's belief would be irrational. Such beliefs, even if they are in fact held in the basic way, are not *properly* basic. On the other hand, perceptual beliefs—beliefs like 'There is a tree in front of me'—are typically regarded as being based on perceptual experience rather than on other beliefs. Thus, they are typically held in the basic way, and many of us think they are *properly* held in that way. You are rational, or justified, in believing that there is a tree in front of you if (other things being equal) you have tree-like experiences. So perceptual beliefs are examples of properly basic beliefs.

Moreover, Plantinga construes evidentialists as accepting *classical foundationalism.* According to classical foundationalism,

> A proposition *p* is properly basic for a person *S* if and only if *p* is either self-evident to *S* or incorrigible for *S* or evident to the senses for *S.*

Self-evident propositions are those that a person just sees as true immediately, such as that one plus two equals three or that a contradiction cannot be true. Incorrigible propositions are propositions about which one cannot be mistaken. Familiar examples include such beliefs as 'I am thinking' or 'I am in pain.' It is hard to see how one could believe that one is thinking, or believe that one is in pain, without its being true that one is thinking or in pain. Aquinas and John Locke add a third type of proposition, that which is evident to the senses, such as 'I see a tree.' The goal of the classical foundationalist is to protect our belief systems from error by allowing only solid or absolutely certain beliefs to make up the foundation of our belief systems. Plantinga shows that there are many beliefs that we seem to be justified in holding that do not fit into any of these three categories, such as memory beliefs (e.g., 'I ate breakfast this morning'), belief in an external world, and belief in other minds. These beliefs are not dependent on other beliefs, yet neither are they self-evident, incorrigible, or evident to the senses.

Plantinga then shows that the Protestant Reformers saw belief in God as properly basic. He invites us to consider this as a legitimate option and examines possible objections to it. His claim is that belief in God is properly basic and that none of the objections that he considers is successful.

In our third reading Michael Martin analyzes foundationalism in general as well as Plantinga's attempt to place belief in God in the foundations of a noetic structure. He argues that Plantinga's arguments against classical foundationalism are weak, and that his defense of the proper basicality of religious belief generalizes so that the tenets of virtually any belief system could as easily be characterized as properly basic.

In the final reading, "Faith, Hope, and Doubt," Louis Pojman examines the relationship between belief and faith and argues that religious faith can exist and flourish in the absence of belief. One may not be able to believe in God because of an insufficiency of evidence, but one may still live committed to a theistic world-view, in hope. Pojman argues that this is an authentic religious position, too often neglected in the literature.

VII.B.1   Rational Theistic Belief without Proof

JOHN HICK

A short biographical sketch of John Hick precedes selection III.4. In the present article, Hick argues that the so-called proofs for the existence of God are largely irrelevant for religion. Religious belief, he argues, can be rationally grounded in religious experience.

(A) THE RELIGIOUS REJECTION OF THE THEISTIC ARGUMENTS

We have seen that the major theistic arguments are all open to serious philosophical objections. Indeed we have in each case concluded, in agreement with the majority of contemporary philosophers, that these arguments fail to do what they profess to do. Neither those which undertake strictly to demonstrate the existence of an absolute Being, nor those which profess to show divine existence to be probable, are able to fulfil their promise. We have seen that it is impossible to demonstrate the reality of God by *a priori* reasoning, since such reasoning is confined to the realm of concepts; impossible to demonstrate it by *a posteriori* reasoning, since this would have to include a premise begging the very question at issue; and impossible to establish it as in a greater or lesser degree probable, since the notion of probability lacks any clear meaning in this context. A philosopher unacquainted with modern developments in theology might well assume that theologians would, *ex officio*, be supporters of the theistic proofs and would regard as a fatal blow this conclusion that there can be neither a strict demonstration of God's existence nor a valid probability argument for it. In fact however such an assumption would be true only of certain theological schools. It is true of the more traditional Roman Catholic theology, of sections of conservative Protestantism, and of most of those Protestant apologists who continue to work within the tradition of nineteenth-century idealism. It has never been true, on the other hand, of Jewish religious thought; and it is not true of that central stream of contemporary Protestant theology which has been influenced by the 'neo-orthodox' movement, the revival of Reformation studies and the 'existentialism' of Kierkegaard and his successors; or of the most significant contemporary Roman Catholic thinkers, who are on this issue (as on so many others) in advance of the official teaching of the magisterium. Accordingly we have now to take note of this theological rejection of the theistic proofs, ranging from a complete lack of concern for them to a positive repudiation of them as being religiously irrelevant or even harmful. There are several different considerations to be evaluated.

Reprinted from John Hick, *Arguments for the Existence of God* (Macmillan, London and Basingstoke, 1971) by permission of the publisher. Footnotes edited.

1. It has often been pointed out that for the man of faith, as he is depicted in the Bible, no theistic proofs are necessary. Philosophers in the rationalist tradition, holding that to know means to be able to prove, have been shocked to find that in the Bible, which is supposed to be the basis of Western religion, no attempt whatever is made to demonstrate the existence of God. Instead of professing to establish the divine reality by philosophical reasoning the Bible throughout takes this for granted. Indeed to the biblical writers it would have seemed absurd to try to establish by logical argumentation that God exists. For they were convinced that they were already having to do with him and he with them in all the affairs of their lives. They did not think of God as an inferred entity but as an experienced reality. Many of the biblical writers were (sometimes, though doubtless not all times) as vividly conscious of being in God's presence as they were of living in a material world. It is impossible to read their pages without realising that to them God was not a proposition completing a syllogism, or an idea adopted by the mind, but the supreme experiential reality. It would be as sensible for a husband to desire a philosophical proof of the existence of the wife and family who contribute so much of the meaning and value of his life as for the man of faith to seek for a proof of the existence of the God within whose purpose he believes that he lives and moves and has his being.

As Cook Wilson wrote:

> If we think of the existence of our friends; it is the 'direct knowledge' which we want: merely inferential knowledge seems a poor affair. To most men it would be as surprising as unwelcome to hear it could not be directly known whether there were such existences as their friends, and that it was only a matter of (probable) empirical argument and inference from facts which are directly known. And even if we convince ourselves on reflection that this is really the case, our actions prove that we have a confidence in the existence of our friends which can't be derived from an empirical argument (which can never be certain) for a man will risk his life for his friend. We don't want merely inferred friends. Could we possibly be satisfied with an inferred God?

In other words the man of faith has no need of theistic proofs; for he has something which for him is much better. However it does not follow from this that there may not be others who do need a theistic proof, nor does it follow that there are in fact no such proofs. All that has been said about the irrelevance of proofs to the life of faith may well be true, and yet it might still be the case that there are valid arguments capable of establishing the existence of God to those who stand outside the life of faith.

2. It has also often been pointed out that the God whose existence each of the traditional theistic proofs professes to establish is only an abstraction from and a pale shadow of the living God who is the putative object of biblical faith. A First Cause of the Universe might or might not be a deity to whom an unqualified devotion, love and trust would be appropriate; Aquinas's *Et hoc omnes intelligunt Deum* ('and this all understand to be God') is not the last step in a logical argument but merely an exercise of the custom of overlooking a gap in the argument at this point. A Necessary Being, and indeed a being who is metaphysically absolute in every respect—omnipotent, omniscient, eternal, uncreated—might be morally good or evil. As H. D. Aitken has remarked, 'Logically, there is no reason why an almighty and omniscient being might not be a perfect stinker.' A divine Designer of the world whose nature is read off from the appearances of nature might, as Hume showed, be finite or infinite, perfect or imperfect, omniscient or fallible, and might indeed be not one being but a veritable pantheon. It is only by going beyond what is proved, or claimed to have been proved, and identifying the First Cause, Necessary Being, or Mind behind Nature with the God of biblical faith that these proofs could ever properly impel to worship. By themselves and without supplementation of content and infusion of emotional life from religious traditions and experiences transcending the proofs themselves they would never lead to the life of faith.

The ontological argument on the other hand is in this respect in a different category. If it succeeds it establishes the reality of a being so perfect in every way that no more perfect can be conceived. Clearly if such a being is not worthy of worship none ever could be. It would therefore seem that, unlike the other proofs, the ontological argument, if it were logically sound, would present the relatively few persons who are capable of appreciating such abstract reasoning with a rational ground for worship. On the other hand, however, whilst this is the argument that would accomplish most if it succeeded it is also the argument which is most absolutely incapable of succeeding; for it is, as we have seen, inextricably involved in the fallacy of professing to deduce existence from a concept.

3. It is argued by some religious writers that a logical demonstration of the existence of God would be a form of coercion and would as such be incompatible with God's evident intention to treat his human creatures as free and responsible persons. A great deal of twentieth-century theology emphasises that God as the infinite personal reality, having made man as person in his own image, always treats men as persons, respecting their relative freedom and autonomy. He does not override the human mind by revealing himself in overwhelming majesty and power, but always approaches us in ways that leave room for an uncompelled response of human faith. Even God's own entry into our earthly history, it is said, was in an 'incognito' that could be penetrated only by the eyes of faith. As Pascal put it, 'willing to appear openly to those who seek him with all their heart and to be hidden from those who flee from him with all their heart, he so regulates the knowledge of himself that he has given indications of himself which are visible to those who seek him and not to those who do not seek him. There is enough light for those to see who only desire to see, and enough obscurity for those who have a contrary disposition.' God's self-revealing actions are accordingly always so mediated through the events of our temporal experience that men only become aware of the divine presence by interpreting and responding to these events in the way which we call religious faith. For if God were to disclose himself to us in the coercive manner in which our physical environment obtrudes itself we should be dwarfed to nothingness by

the infinite power thus irresistibly breaking open the privacy of our souls. Further, we should be spiritually blinded by God's perfect holiness and paralysed by his infinite energy; 'for human kind cannot bear very much reality.' Such a direct, unmediated confrontation breaking in upon us and shattering the frail autonomy of our finite nature would leave no ground for a free human response of trust, self-commitment and obedience. There could be no call for a man to venture upon a dawning consciousness of God's reality and thus to receive this consciousness as an authentic part of his own personal existence precisely because it has not been injected into him or clamped upon him by magisterial exercise of divine omnipotence.

The basic principle invoked here is that for the sake of creating a personal relationship of love and trust with his human creatures God does not force an awareness of himself upon them. And (according to the view which we are considering) it is only a further application of the same principle to add that a logically compelling demonstration of God's existence would likewise frustrate this purpose. For men—or at least those of them who are capable of following the proof—could then be forced to know that God is real. Thus Alasdair MacIntyre, when a Christian apologist, wrote: 'For if we could produce logically cogent arguments we should produce the kind of certitude that leaves no room for decision; where proof is in place, decision is not. We do not decide to accept Euclid's conclusions; we merely look to the rigour of his arguments. If the existence of God were demonstrable we should be as bereft of the possibility of making a free decision to love God as we should be if every utterance of doubt or unbelief was answered by thunderbolts from heaven.' This is the 'religious coercion' objection to the theistic proofs.

To what extent is it a sound objection? We may accept the theological doctrine that for God to force men to know him by the coercion of logic would be incompatible with his purpose of winning the voluntary response and worship of free moral beings. But the question still remains whether the theistic proofs could ever do this. Could a verbal proof of divine existence compel a consciousness of God comparable in coerciveness with a direct manifestation of his divine majesty and power? Could anyone be moved and shaken in their whole being by the demonstration of a proposition, as men have been by a numinous experience of overpowering impressiveness? Would the things that have just been said about an overwhelming display of divine glory really apply to verbal demonstrations—that infinite power would be irresistibly breaking in upon the privacy of our souls and that we should be blinded by God's perfect holiness and paralysed by his infinite energy? Indeed could a form of words, culminating in the proposition that 'God exists,' ever have power by itself to produce more than what Newman calls a notional assent in our minds?

It is of course true that the effect of purely rational considerations such as those which are brought to bear in the theistic proofs are much greater in some minds than in others. The more rational the mind the more considerable is the effect to be expected. In many persons—indeed taking mankind as a whole, in the great majority—the effect of a theistic proof, even when no logical flaw is found in it, would be virtually nil! But in more sophisticated minds the effect must be greater, and it is at least theoretically possible that there are minds so rational that purely logical considerations can move them as effectively as the evidence of their senses. It is therefore conceivable that someone who is initially agnostic might be presented with a philosophical proof of divine existence—say the ontological argument, with its definition of God as that than which no more perfect can be conceived—and might as a result be led to worship the being whose reality has thus been demonstrated to him. This seems to be possible; but I believe that even in such a case there must, in addition to an intelligent appreciation of the argument, be a distinctively religious response to the idea of God which the argument presents. Some propensity to respond to unlimited perfection as holy and as rightly claiming a response of unqualified worship and devotion must operate, over and above the purely intellectual capacity for logical calculation. For we can conceive of a purely or merely logical mind, a kind of human calculating machine, which is at the same time devoid of the capacity for numinous feeling and worshipping response. Such a being might infer that God exists but be no more existentially interested in this conclusion than many people are in, say, the fact that the Shasta Dam is 602 feet high. It therefore seems that when the acceptance of a theistic proof leads to worship, a religious reaction occurs which turns what would otherwise be a purely abstract conclusion into an immensely significant and moving fact. In Newman's terminology, when a notional assent to the proposition that God exists becomes a real assent, equivalent to an actual living belief and faith in God, there has been a free human response to an idea which could instead have been rejected by being held at the notional level. In other words, a verbal proof of God's existence cannot by itself break down our human freedom; it can only lead to a notional assent which has little or no positive religious value or substance.

I conclude, then, that the theological objections to the theistic proofs are considerably less strong than the philosophical ones; and that theologians who reject natural theology would therefore do well to do so primarily on philosophical rather than on theological grounds. These philosophical reasons are, as we have seen, very strong; and we therefore now have to consider whether, in the absence of any theistic proofs, it can nevertheless be rational to believe in the existence of God.

(B) CAN THERE BE RATIONAL THEISTIC BELIEF WITHOUT PROOFS?

During the period dominated by the traditional theistic arguments the existence of God was often treated by philosophers as something to be discovered through reasoning. It was seen as the conclusion of an inference; and the question of the rationality of the belief was equated with that of the soundness of the inference. But from a religious point of view, as we have already seen, there has always been something very odd about this approach. The situation which it envisages is that of people standing outside the realm of faith, for whom the apologist is trying to build a bridge of rational inference to carry them over the frontier into that realm. But of course this is not the way in which religious faith has originally or typically or normally come about. When the cosmological, ontological, teleological and moral arguments were developed, theistic belief was already a functioning part of an immemorially established and developing form of human life. The claims of religion are claims made by individuals and communities on the basis of their experience—and experience which is none the less their own for occurring within an inherited framework of ideas. We are not dealing with a merely conceivable metaphysical hypothesis which someone has speculatively invented but which hardly anyone seriously believes. We are concerned, rather, with convictions born out of experience and reflection and living within actual communities of faith and practice. Historically, then, the philosophical proofs of God have normally entered in to support and confirm but not to create belief. Accordingly the proper philosophical approach would seem to be a probing of the actual foundations and structure of a living and operative belief rather than of theoretical and nonoperative arguments subsequently formulated for holding those beliefs. The question is not whether it is possible to prove, starting from zero, that God exists; the question is whether the religious man, given the distinctively religious form of human existence in which he participates, is properly entitled as a rational person to believe what he does believe?

At this point we must consider what we mean by a rational belief. If by a belief we mean a proposition believed, then what we are to be concerned with here are not rational beliefs but rational believings. Propositions can be well-formed or ill-formed, and they can be true or false, but they cannot be rational or irrational. It is *people* who are rational or irrational, and derivatively their states and their actions, including their acts and states of believing. Further, apart from the believing of analytic propositions, which are true by definition and are therefore

rationally believed by anyone who understands them, the rationality of acts (or states) of believing has to be assessed separately in each case. For it is a function of the relation between the proposition believed and the evidence on the basis of which the believer believes it. It might conceivably be rational for Mr. X to believe p but not rational for Mr. Y to believe $p,$ because in relation to the data available to Mr. X p is worthy of belief but not in relation to the data available to Mr. $Y.$ Thus the question of the rationality of belief in the reality of God is the question of the rationality of a particular person's believing given the data that he is using; or that of the believing of a class of people who share the same body of data. Or putting the same point the other way round, any assessing of the belief-worthiness of the proposition that God exists must be an assessing of it in relation to particular ranges of data.

Now there is one area of data or evidence which is normally available to those who believe in God, and that provides a very important part of the ground of their believing, but which is normally not available to and therefore not taken into account by those who do not so believe; and this is religious experience. It seems that the religious man is in part basing his believing upon certain data of religious experience which the non-religious man is not using because he does not have them. Thus our question resolves itself into one about the theist's right, given his distinctively religious experience, to be certain that God exists. It is the question of the rationality or irrationality, the well-groundedness or ill-groundedness, of the religious man's claim to know God. The theist cannot hope to prove that God exists; but despite this it may nevertheless be possible for him to show it to be wholly reasonable for him to believe that God exists.

What is at issue here is not whether it is rational for someone else, who does not participate in the distinctively religious mode of experience, to believe in God on the basis of the religious man's reports. I am not proposing any kind of 'argument from religious experience' by which God is inferred as the cause of the special experiences described by mystics and other religious persons.

It is not the non-religious man's theoretical use of someone else's reported religious experience that is to be considered, but the religious man's own practical use of it. The question is whether he is acting rationally in trusting his own experience and in proceeding to live on the basis of it.

In order to investigate this question we must consider what counts as rational belief in an analogous case. The analogy that I propose is that between the religious person's claim to be conscious of God and any man's claim to be conscious of the physical world as an environment, existing independently of himself, of which he must take account.

In each instance a realm of putatively cognitive experience is taken to be veridical and is acted upon as such, even though its veridical character cannot be logically demonstrated. So far as sense experience is concerned this has emerged both from the failure of Descartes' attempt to provide a theoretical guarantee that our senses relate us to a real material environment, and from the success of Hume's attempt to show that our normal non-solipsist belief in an objective world of enduring objects around us in space is neither a product of, nor justifiable by, philosophical reasoning but is what has been called in some expositions of Hume's thought (though the term does not seem to have been used by Hume himself) a natural belief. It is a belief which naturally and indeed inevitably arises in the normal human mind in response to normal human perceptual experience. It is a belief on the basis of which we live and the rejection of which, in favour of a serious adoption of the solipsist alternative, would so disorient our relationship to other persons within a common material environment that we should be accounted insane. Our insanity would consist in the fact that we should no longer regard other people as independent centres of consciousness, with their own purposes and wills, with whom interpersonal relationships are possible. We should instead be living in a one-person world.

It is thus a basic truth in, or a presupposition of, our language that it is rational or sane to believe in the reality of the external world that we inhabit in common with other people, and irrational or insane not to do so.

What are the features of our sense experience in virtue of which we all take this view? They would seem to be twofold: the givenness or the involuntary character of this form of cognitive experience, and the fact that we can and do act successfully in terms of our belief in an external world. That is to say, being built and circumstanced as we are we cannot help initially believing as we do, and our belief is not contradicted, but on the contrary continuously confirmed, by our continuing experience. These characteristics jointly constitute a sufficient reason to trust and live on the basis of our perceptual experience in the absence of any positive reason to distrust it; and our inability to exclude the theoretical possibility of our experience as a whole being purely subjective does not constitute such a reason. This seems to be the principle on which, implicitly, we proceed. And it is, by definition, rational to proceed in this way. That is to say, this is the way in which all human beings do proceed and have proceeded, apart from a very small minority who have for that very reason been labelled by the majority as insane. This habitual acceptance of our perceptual experience is thus, we may say, part of our operative concept of human rationality.

We can therefore now ask whether a like principle may be invoked on behalf of a parallel response to religious experience. 'Religious experience' is of course a highly elastic concept. Let us restrict attention, for our present purpose, to the theistic 'sense of the presence of God,' the putative awareness of a transcendent divine Mind within whose field of consciousness we exist and with whom therefore we stand in a relationship of mutual awareness. This sense of 'living in the divine presence' does not take the form of a direct vision of God, but of experiencing events in history and in our own personal life as the medium of God's dealings with us. Thus religious differs from non-religious experience, not as the awareness of a different world, but as a different way of experiencing the same world. Events which can be experienced as having a purely natural significance are experienced by the religious mind as having also and at the same time religious significance and as mediating the presence and activity of God.

It is possible to study this type of religious experience either in its strongest instances, in the primary and seminal religious figures, or in its much weaker instances in ordinary adherents of the traditions originated by the great exemplars of faith. Since we are interested in the question of the claims which religious experience justifies it is appropriate to look at that experience in its strongest and purest forms. A description of this will accordingly apply only very partially to the ordinary rank-and-file believer either of today or in the past.

If then we consider the sense of living in the divine presence as this was expressed by, for example, Jesus of Nazareth, or by St. Paul, St. Francis, St. Anselm or the great prophets of the Old Testament, we find that their 'awareness of God' was so vivid that he was as indubitable a factor in their experience as was their physical environment. They could no more help believing in the reality of God than in the reality of the material world and of their human neighbours. Many of the pages of the Bible resound with the sense of God's presence as a building might reverberate from the tread of some gigantic being walking through it. God was known to the prophets and apostles as a dynamic will interacting with their own wills; a sheerly given personal reality, as inescapably to be reckoned with as destructive storm and life-giving sunshine, the fixed contours of the land, or the hatred of their enemies and the friendship of their neighbours.

Our question concerns, then, one whose 'experience of God' has this compelling quality, so that he is no more inclined to doubt its veridical character than to doubt the evidence of his senses. Is it rational for him to take the former, as it is certainly rational for him to take the latter, as reliably cognitive of an aspect of his total environment and thus as knowledge in terms of which to act? Are the two features noted above in our sense experience—its givenness, or involuntary character, and the fact that we can successfully act in terms of it—also found here? It seems that they are. The sense of the presence of God reported by the great religious figures has a similar involuntary and compelling quality; and as they proceed to live on the basis of it they are

sustained and confirmed by their further experiences in the conviction that they are living in relation, not to illusion, but to reality. It therefore seems prima facie, that the religious man is entitled to trust his religious experience and to proceed to conduct his life in terms of it.

The analogy operating within this argument is between our normal acceptance of our sense experiences as perception of an objective external world, and a corresponding acceptance of the religious experience of 'living in God's presence' as the awareness of a divine reality external to our own minds. In each case there is a solipsist alternative in which one can affirm *solus ipse* to the exclusion of the transcendent—in the one case denying a physical environment transcending our own private consciousness and in the other case denying a divine Mind transcending our own private consciousness. It should be noted that this analogy is not grounded in the perception of particular material objects and does not turn upon the contrast between veridical and illusory sense perceptions, but is grounded in our awareness of an objective external world as such and turns upon the contrast between this and a theoretically possible solipsist interpretation of the same stream of conscious experience.

(C) RELIGIOUS AND PERCEPTUAL BELIEF

Having thus set forth the analogy fairly boldly and starkly I now want to qualify it by exploring various differences between religious and sensory experience. The resulting picture will be more complex than the first rough outline presented so far; and yet its force as supporting the rationality of theistic faith will not, I think, in the end have been undermined.

The most obvious difference is that everyone has and cannot help having sense experiences, whereas not everyone has religious experiences, at any rate of the very vivid and distinct kind to which we have been referring. As bodily beings existing in a material environment, we cannot help interacting consciously with that environment. That is to say, we cannot help 'having' a stream of sense experiences; and we cannot help accepting this as the perception of a material world around us in space. When we open our eyes in daylight we cannot but receive the visual experiences that come to us; and likewise with the other senses. And the world which we thus perceive is not plastic to our wishes but presents itself to us as it is, whether we like it or not. Needless to say, our senses do not coerce us in any sense of the word 'coerce' that implies unwillingness on our part, as when a policeman coerces an unwilling suspect to accompany him to the police station. Sense experience is coercive in the sense that we cannot when sane believe that our material environment is not broadly as we perceive it to be, and that if we did momentarily persuade ourselves that what we experience is not there we should quickly be penalised by the environment and indeed, if we persisted, destroyed by it.

In contrast to this we are not obliged to interact consciously with a spiritual environment. Indeed it is a commonplace of much contemporary theology that God does not force an awareness of himself upon mankind but leaves us free to know him by an uncompelled response of faith. And yet once a man has allowed himself freely to become conscious of God—it is important to note—that experience is, at its top levels of intensity, coercive. It creates the situation of the person who *cannot help* believing in the reality of God. The apostle, prophet or saint may be so vividly aware of God that he can no more doubt the veracity of his religious awareness than of his sense experience. During the periods when he is living consciously in the presence of God, when God is to him the divine Thou, the question whether God exists simply does not arise. Our cognitive freedom in relation to God is not to be found at this point but at the prior stage of our coming to be aware of him. The individual's own free receptivity and responsiveness plays an essential part in his dawning consciousness of God; but once he *has* become conscious of God that consciousness can possess a coercive and indubitable quality.

It is a consequence of this situation that whereas everyone perceives and cannot help perceiving the physical world, by no means everyone experiences the presence of God. Indeed only rather few people experience religiously in the vivid and coercive way reported by the great biblical figures. And this fact immediately suggests a sceptical question. Since those who enjoy a compelling religious experience form such a small minority of mankind, ought we not to suspect that they are suffering from a delusion comparable with that of the paranoiac who hears threatening voices from the walls or the alcoholic who sees green snakes?

This is of course a possible judgment to make. But this judgment should not be made *a priori*, in the absence of specific grounds such as we have in the other cases mentioned. And it would in fact be difficult to point to adequate evidence to support this hypothesis. On the contrary the general intelligence and exceptionally high moral quality of the great religious figures clashes with any analysis of their experience in terms of abnormal psychology. Such analyses are not indicated, as is the parallel view of paranoiacs and alcoholics, by evidence of general disorientation to reality or of incapacity to live a productive and satisfying life. On the contrary, Jesus of Nazareth, for example, has been regarded by hundreds of millions of people as the fulfilment of the ideal possibilities of human nature. A more reasonable negative position would therefore seem to be the agnostic one that whilst it is proper for the religious man himself, given his distinctive mode of experience, to believe firmly in the reality of God, one does not oneself share that experience and therefore has no ground upon which to hold that belief. Theism is then not positively denied, but is on the other hand consciously and deliberately not affirmed. This agnostic position must be accepted by the theist as a proper one. For if it is reasonable for one man, on the basis of his distinctively religious experience, to affirm the reality of God it must also be reasonable for another man, in the absence of any such experience, not to affirm the reality of God.

The next question that must be raised is the closely connected one of the relation between rational belief and truth. I suggested earlier that, strictly, one should speak of rational believings rather than of rational beliefs. But nevertheless it is sometimes convenient to use the latter phrase, which we may then understand as follows. By a rational belief we shall mean a belief which it is rational for the one who holds it to hold, given the data available to him. Clearly such beliefs are not necessarily or always true. It is sometimes rational for an individual to have, on the basis of incomplete data, a belief which is in fact false. For example, it was once rational for people to believe that the sun revolves round the earth; for it was apparently perceived to do so, and the additional theoretical and observational data were not yet available from which it has since been inferred that it is the earth which revolves round the sun. If, then, a belief may be rational and yet false, may not the religious man's belief be of this kind? May it not be that when the data of religious experience are supplemented in the believer's mind by further data provided by the sciences of psychology or sociology, it ceases to be rational for him to believe in God? Might it not then be rational for him instead to believe that his 'experience of the presence of God' is to be understood as an effect of a buried infancy memory of his father as a benevolent higher power; or of the pressure upon him of the human social organism of which he is a cell; or in accordance with some other naturalistic theory of the nature of religion?

Certainly this is possible. Indeed we must say, more generally, that all our beliefs, other than our acceptance of logically self-certifying propositions, are in principle open to revision or retraction in the light of new data. It is always conceivable that something which it is now rational for us to believe, it may one day not be rational for us to believe. But the difference which this general principle properly makes to our present believing varies from a maximum in relation to beliefs involving a considerable theoretical element, such as the higher-level hypotheses of the sciences, to a minimum in relation to perceptual beliefs, such as the belief that I now see a sheet of paper before me. And I have argued that so far as the great primary religious figures are concerned, belief in the reality of God is closer to the latter in that it is analogous to belief in the reality of the perceived material world. It is not an explanatory hypothesis, logically comparable with those developed in the sciences, but a perceptual belief. God was not, for Amos or Jeremiah or Jesus of Nazareth, an inferred entity but an experienced personal presence. If this is so, it is appropriate that the religious man's belief in the reality of God should be no more provisional than his belief in the reality of the physical world. The situation is in each case that given the experience which he has and which is part of him, he cannot help accepting as 'there' such aspects of his environment as he experiences. He cannot help believing either in the reality of the material world which he is conscious of inhabiting, or of the personal divine presence which is overwhelmingly evident to him and to which his mode of living is a free response. And I have been suggesting that it is as reasonable for him to hold and to act upon the one belief as the other.

VII.B.2   Religious Belief without Evidence

ALVIN PLANTINGA

Alvin Plantinga's biographical sketch precedes selection III.7. In the present article, Plantinga argues that it is rational to believe in God in spite of the lack of propositional evidence for such belief. He argues that evidentialists are plausibly understood as accepting a version of classical foundationalism, according to which (a) every justified belief is either properly basic

This article consists of selections from *Rationality and Religious Belief*, edited by C. F. Delaney, copyright © 1979, and *Faith and Rationality*, edited by Alvin Plantinga and Nicholas Wolterstorff, copyright © 1983, by permission of the publisher, the University of Notre Dame Press, and the author. Footnotes deleted.

(i.e., justified without being based on other beliefs), or ultimately based on properly basic beliefs, and (b) a belief is properly basic if, and only if, it is either self-evident, incorrigible (so that one can't be mistaken about its truth), or evident to the senses. Plantinga then shows that there are many beliefs that seem clearly justified but that do not fit the classical foundationalist's criterion for justified belief. He notes that the Protestant Reformers saw belief in God as properly basic, and invites us to consider this view as a legitimate alternative to the classical foundationlist's position.

What I mean to discuss, in this paper, is the question, Is belief in God rational? That is to say, I wish to discuss the question "Is it rational, or reasonable, or rationally acceptable, to believe in God?" I mean to discuss this question, not answer it. My initial aim is not to argue that religious belief is rational (although I think it is) but to try to understand this question.

The first thing to note is that I have stated the question misleadingly. What I really want to discuss is whether it is rational to believe that God exists—that there is such a person as God. Of course there is an important difference between believing that God exists and believing *in* God. To believe that God exists is just to accept a certain proposition—the proposition that there really is such a person as God—as true. According to the book of James (2:19) the devils believe this proposition, and they tremble. To believe *in* God, however, is to trust him, to commit your life to him, to make his purposes your own. The devils do not do that. So there is a difference between believing in God and believing that he exists; for purposes of economy, however, I shall use the phrase 'belief in God' as a synonym for 'belief that God exists.'

Our question, therefore, is whether belief in God is rational. This question is widely asked and widely answered. Many philosophers—most prominently, those in the great tradition of natural theology—have argued that belief in God *is* rational; they have typically done so by providing what they took to be *demonstrations* or *proofs* of God's existence. Many others have argued that belief in God is *ir*rational. If we call those of the first group 'natural theologians,' perhaps we should call those of the second 'natural atheologians.' (That would at any rate be kinder than calling them 'unnatural theologians.') J. L. Mackie,

for example, opens his statement of the problem of evil as follows: "I think, however, that a more telling criticism can be made by way of the traditional problem of evil. Here it can be shown, not merely that religious beliefs lack rational support, but that they are positively irrational. . . ." And a very large number of philosophers take it that a central question—perhaps *the* central question—of philosophy of religion is the question whether religious belief in general and belief in God in particular is rationally acceptable.

Now an apparently straightforward and promising way to approach this question would be to take a definition of rationality and see whether belief in God conforms to it. The chief difficulty with this appealing course, however, is that no such definition of rationality seems to be available. If there were such a definition, it would set out some conditions for a belief's being rationally acceptable—conditions that are severally necessary and jointly sufficient. That is, each of the conditions would have to be met by a belief that is rationally acceptable; and if a belief met all the conditions, then it would follow that it is rationally acceptable. But it is monumentally difficult to find any non-trivial necessary conditions at all. Surely, for example, we cannot insist that S's belief that p is rational only if it is *true*. For consider Newton's belief that if x, y and z are moving colinearly, then the motion of z with respect to x is the sum of the motions of y with respect to x and z with respect to y. No doubt Newton was rational in accepting this belief; yet it was false, at least if contemporary physicists are to be trusted. And if they aren't—that is, if they are wrong in contradicting Newton—then they exemplify what I'm speaking of; they rationally believe a proposition which, as it turns out, is false.

Nor can we say that a belief is rationally acceptable only if it is possibly true, not necessarily false in the broadly logical sense. For example, I might do the sum of $735 + 421 + 9,216$ several times and get the same answer: $10,362$. I am then rational in believing that $735 + 421 + 9,216 = 10,362$, even though the fact is I've made the same error each time—failed to carry a '1' from the first column—and thus believe what is necessarily false. Or I might be a mathematical neophyte who hears from his teacher that every continuous function is differentiable. I need not be irrational in believing this, despite the fact that it is necessarily false. Examples of this sort can be multiplied.

So this question presents something of an initial enigma in that it is by no means easy to say what it is for a belief to be rational. And the fact is those philosophers who ask this question about belief in God do not typically try to answer it by giving necessary and sufficient conditions for rational belief. Instead, they typically ask whether the believer has *evidence* or *sufficient evidence* for his belief; or they may try to argue that in fact there is sufficient evidence for the proposition that there is *no* God; but in any case they try to answer this question by finding evidence for or against theistic belief. Philosophers who think there are sound arguments for the existence of God—the natural theologians—claim there is good evidence *for* this proposition; philosophers who believe that there are sound arguments for the non-existence of God naturally claim that there is evidence *against* this proposition. But they concur in holding that belief in God is rational only if there is, on balance, a preponderance of evidence for it—or less radically, only if there is not, on balance, a preponderance of evidence against it.

The nineteenth-century philosopher W. K. Clifford provides a splendid if somewhat strident example of the view that the believer in God must have evidence if he is not to be irrational. Here he does not discriminate against religious belief; he apparently holds that a belief of any sort at all is rationally acceptable only if there is sufficient evidence for it. And he goes on to insist that it is wicked, immoral, monstrous, and perhaps even impolite to accept a belief for which one does not have sufficient evidence:

> Whoso would deserve well of his fellows in this matter will guard the purity of his belief with a very fanaticism of jealous care, lest at any time it should rest on an unworthy object, and catch a stain which can never be wiped away.

He adds that if a

> belief has been accepted on insufficient evidence, the pleasure is a stolen one. Not only does it deceive ourselves by giving us a sense of power which we do not really possess, but it is sinful, because it is stolen in defiance of our duty to mankind. That duty is to guard ourselves from such beliefs as from a pestilence which may shortly master our body and spread to the rest of the town.

And finally:

> To sum up: it is wrong always, everywhere, and for anyone to believe anything upon insufficient evidence.

(It is not hard to detect, in these quotations, the "tone of robustious pathos" with which William James credits him.) Clifford finds it utterly obvious, furthermore, that those who believe in God do indeed so believe on insufficient evidence and thus deserve the above abuse. A believer in God is, on his view, at best a harmless pest and at worst a menace to society; in either case he should be discouraged.

Now there are some initial problems with Clifford's claim. For example, he doesn't tell us how *much* evidence is sufficient. More important, the notion of evidence is about as difficult as that of rationality: What is evidence? How do you know when you have some? How do you know when you have sufficient or enough? Suppose, furthermore, that a person thinks he has sufficient evidence for a proposition p when in fact he does not—would he then be irrational in believing p? Presumably a person can have sufficient evidence for what is false—else either Newton did not have sufficient evidence for his physical beliefs or contemporary physicists don't have enough for *theirs*. Suppose, then, that a person has sufficient evidence for the false proposition that he has sufficient evidence for p. Is he then irrational in believing *p*? Presumably not; but if not, having sufficient evidence is not, contrary to Clifford's claim, a necessary condition for believing *p* rationally.

But suppose we temporarily concede that these initial difficulties can be resolved and take a deeper look at Clifford's position. What is essential to it is the claim that we must evaluate the rationality of belief in God by examining its relation to *other* propositions. We are directed to estimate its rationality by determining whether we have evidence for it—whether we know, or at any rate rationality believe, some other propositions which stand in the appropriate relation to the proposition in question. And belief in God is rational, or reasonable, or rationally acceptable, on this view, only if there are other propositions with respect to which it is thus evident.

According to the Cliffordian position, then, there is a set of propositions *E* such that my belief in God is rational if and only if it is evident with respect to *E*—if and only if *E* constitutes, on balance, evidence for it. But what propositions are to be found in *E*? Do we know that belief in God is not itself in *E*? If it is, of course, then it is certainly evident with respect to *E*. How does a proposition get into *E* anyway? How do we decide which propositions are the ones such that my belief in God is rational if and only if it is evident with respect to them? Should we say that *E* contains the propositions that I *know*? But then, for our question to be interesting, we should first have to argue or agree that I don't know that God exists—that I only *believe* it, whether rationally or irrationally. This position is widely taken for granted, and indeed taken for granted by theists as well as others. But why should the latter concede that he doesn't know that God exists—that at best he rationally believes it? The Bible regularly speaks of *knowledge* in this context—not just rational or well-founded belief. Of course it is true that the believer has *faith*—faith in God, faith in what He reveals, faith that God exists—but this by no means settles the issue. The question is whether he doesn't also *know* that God exists. Indeed, according to the Heidelberg Catechism, knowledge is an essential element of faith, so that one has true faith that p only if he knows that *p*:

> True faith is not only a certain (i.e., sure) knowledge whereby I hold for truth all that God has revealed in His word, but also a deep-rooted assurance created in me by the Holy Spirit through the gospel that not only others but I too have had my sins forgiven, have been made forever right with God and have been granted salvation. (Q 21)

So from this point of view a man has true faith that *p* only if he knows that *p* and also meets a certain further condition: roughly (where *p* is a universal proposition) that of accepting the universal instantiation of *p* with respect to himself. Now of course the theist may be unwilling to concede that he does not have true faith that God exists; accordingly he may be unwilling to concede—initially, at any rate—that he does not know, but only believes that God exists....

[After a discussion of other attacks on theism from an evidentialist perspective, Plantinga turns to the foundationalist theory of knowledge, beginning with the classical version of that doctrine, held by Aquinas, Descartes, Locke, Clifford, and many others. Ed. note.]

[Both] Aquinas and the evidentialist objector [to theism] concur in holding that belief in God is rationally acceptable only if there is evidence for it—if, that is, it is probable with respect to some body of propositions that constitutes the evidence. And here we can get a better understanding of Aquinas and the evidentialist objector if we see them as accepting some version of *classical foundationalism*. This is a picture or total way of looking at faith, knowledge, justified belief, rationality, and allied topics. This picture has been enormously popular in Western thought; and despite a substantial opposing groundswell, I think it remains the dominant way of thinking about these topics. According to the foundationalist some propositions are properly basic and some are not; those that are not are rationally accepted only on the basis of *evidence*, where the evidence must trace back, ultimately, to what *is* properly basic. The existence of God, furthermore, is not among the propositions that are properly basic; hence a person is rational in accepting theistic belief only if he has evidence for it. The vast majority of those in the western world who have thought about our topic have accepted some form of classical foundationalism. The evidentialist objection to belief in God, furthermore, is obviously rooted in this way of looking at things. So suppose we try to achieve a deeper understanding of it.

Earlier I said the first thing to see about the evidentialist objection is that it is a *normative* contention or claim. The same thing must be said about foundationalism; this thesis is a normative thesis, a thesis about how a system of beliefs *ought* to be structured, a thesis about the properties of a correct, or acceptable, or rightly structured system of beliefs. According to the foundationalist there are norms, or duties, or obligations with respect to belief just as there are with respect to actions. To conform to these duties and obligations is to be rational; to fail to measure up to them is to be irrational. To be rational, then, is to exercise one's epistemic powers *properly*—to exercise them in such a way as to go contrary to none of the norms for such exercise....

I think we can understand foundationalism more fully if we introduce the idea of a *noetic structure*. A person's noetic structure is the set of propositions he believes, together with certain epistemic relations that hold among him and these propositions. As we have seen, some of my beliefs may be based upon others; it may be that there are a pair of propositions A and B such that I believe B, and believe A *on the basis of B.* An account of a person's noetic structure, then, would specify which of his beliefs are basic and which nonbasic. Of course it is abstractly possible that *none* of his beliefs is basic; perhaps he holds just three beliefs, *A, B,* and *C,* and believes each of them on the basis of the other two. We might think this improper or irrational, but that is not to say it could not be done. And it is also possible that *all* of his beliefs are basic; perhaps he believes a lot of propositions but does not believe any of them on the basis of any others. In the typical case however, a noetic structure will include both basic and nonbasic beliefs. It may be useful to give some examples of beliefs that are often basic for a person. Suppose I seem to see a tree; I have that characteristic sort of experience that goes with perceiving a tree. I may then believe the proposition that I see a tree. It is *possible* that I believe that proposition *on the basis of* the proposition that I seem to see a tree; in the typical case, however, I will not believe the former on the basis of the latter because in the typical case I will not believe the latter at all. I will not be paying any attention to my experience but will be concentrating on the tree. Of course I *can* turn my attention to my experience, notice how things look to me, and acquire the belief that I seem to see something that looks like *that;* and if you challenge my claim that I see a tree, perhaps I *will* thus turn my attention to my experience. But in the typical case I will not believe that I see a tree on the basis of a proposition about my experience; for I believe A on the basis of B only if I believe B, and in the typical case where I perceive a tree I do not believe (or entertain) any propositions about my experience. Typically I take such a proposition as basic. Similarly, I believe I had breakfast this morning; this too is basic for me. I do not believe this proposition on the basis of some proposition about my experience—for example, that I seem to remember having had breakfast. In the typical case I will not have even considered *that* question—the question whether I *seem* to remember having had breakfast; instead I simply believe that I had breakfast; I take it as a basic.

Second, an account of a noetic structure will include what we might call an index of *degree* of belief. I hold some of my beliefs much more firmly than others. I believe both that $2 + 1 = 3$ and that London, England, is north of Saskatoon, Saskatchewan; but I believe the former more resolutely than the latter. Some beliefs I hold with maximum firmness; others I do in fact accept, but in a much more tentative way....

Third, a somewhat vaguer notion: an account of S's noetic structure would include something like an index of *depth of ingression*. Some of my beliefs are, we might say, on the periphery of my noetic structure. I accept them, and may even accept them firmly, but I could give them up without much change elsewhere in my noetic structure. I believe there are some large boulders on the top of the Grand Teton. If I come to give up this belief (say by climbing it and not finding any), that change need not have extensive reverberations throughout the rest of my noetic structure; it could be accommodated with minimal alteration elsewhere. So its depth of ingression into my noetic structure is not great. On the other hand, if I were to come to believe that there simply is no such thing as the Grand Teton, or no mountains at all, or no such thing as the state of Wyoming, that would have much greater reverberations. And suppose I were to come to think there had not been much of a past (that the world was created just five minutes ago, complete with all its apparent memories and traces of the past) or that there were not any other persons: these changes would have even greater reverberations; these beliefs of mine have great depth of ingression into my noetic structure....

Now foundationalism is best construed, I think, as a thesis about *rational* noetic structures. A noetic structure is rational if it could be the noetic structure of a person who was completely rational. To be completely rational, as I am here using the term, is not to believe only what is true, or to believe all the logical consequences of what one believes, or to believe all necessary truths with equal firmness, or to be uninfluenced by emotion in forming belief; it is, instead, to do the right thing with respect to one's believings. It is to violate no epistemic duties. From this point of view, a rational person is one whose believings meet the appropriate standards; to criticize a person as irrational is to criticize her for failing to fulfill these duties or responsibilities, for failing to conform to the relevant norms or standards. To draw the ethical analogy, the irrational is the impermissible; the rational is the permissible....

A rational noetic structure, then, is one that could be the noetic structure of a wholly rational person; and foundationalism, as I say, is a thesis about such noetic structures. We may think of the foundationalist as beginning with the observation that some of our beliefs are based upon others. According to the foundationalist a rational noetic structure will *have a foundation*—a set of beliefs not accepted on the basis of others; in a rational noetic structure some beliefs will be basic. Nonbasic beliefs, of course, will be accepted on the basis of other beliefs, which may be accepted on the basis of still other beliefs, and so on until the foundations are reached. In a rational noetic structure, therefore, every nonbasic belief is ultimately accepted on the basis of basic beliefs....

According to the foundationalist, therefore, every rational noetic structure has a foundation, and all nonbasic beliefs are ultimately accepted on the basis of beliefs in the foundations. But a belief cannot properly be accepted on the basis of just *any* other belief; in a rational noetic structure, A will be accepted on the basis of B only if B *supports* A or is a member of a set of beliefs that together support A. It is not clear just what this relation—call it the "supports" relation—is; and different foundationalists propose different candidates. Presumably, however, it lies in the neighborhood of *evidence*; if A supports B, then A is evidence for B, or makes B evident; or perhaps B is likely or probable with respect to B. This relation admits of degrees. My belief that Feike can swim is supported by my knowledge that nine out of ten Frisians can swim and Feike is a Frisian; it is supported more strongly by my knowledge that the evening paper contains a picture of Feike triumphantly finishing first in the fifteen-hundred meter freestyle in the 1980 summer Olympics. And the foundationalist holds, sensibly enough, that in a rational noetic structure the strength of a nonbasic belief will depend upon the degree of support from foundational beliefs....

By way of summary, then, let us say that according to foundationalism: (1) in a rational noetic structure the believed-on-the-basis-of relation is asymmetric and irreflexive, (2) a rational noetic structure has a foundation, and (3) in a rational noetic structure nonbasic belief is proportional in strength to support from the foundations.

CONDITIONS OF PROPER BASICALITY

Next we note a further and fundamental feature of classic varieties of foundationalism: they all lay down certain conditions of proper basicality. From the foundationalist point of view not just any kind of belief can be found in the foundations of a rational noetic structure; a belief to be properly basic (that is, basic in a rational noetic structure) must meet certain conditions. It must be capable of functioning foundationally, capable of bearing its share of the weight of the whole noetic structure. Thus Thomas Aquinas, as we have seen, holds that a proposition is properly basic for a person only if it is self-evident to him or "evident to the senses."

Suppose we take a brief look at self-evidence. Under what conditions does a proposition have it? What kinds of propositions are self-evident? Examples would include very simple arithmetical truths such as

(1) $2 + 1 = 3$;

simple truths of logic such as

(2) No man is both married and unmarried;

perhaps the generalizations of simple truths of logic, such as

(3) For any proposition p the conjunction of p with its denial is false;

and certain propositions expressing identity and diversity; for example,

(4) Redness is distinct from greenness,
(5) The property of being prime is distinct from the property of being composite,

and

(6) The proposition all men are mortal is distinct from the proposition all mortals are men.

....

Still other candidates—candidates which may be less than entirely uncontroversial—come from many other areas; for example,

(7) If p is necessarily true and p entails q, then q is necessarily true,
(8) If e_1 occurs before e_2 and e_2 occurs before e_3, then e_1 occurs before e_3,

and

(9) It is wrong to cause unnecessary (and unwanted) pain just for the fun of it.

What is it that characterizes these propositions? According to the tradition the outstanding characteristic of a self-evident proposition is that one simply sees it to be true upon grasping or understanding it. Understanding a self-evident proposition is sufficient for apprehending its truth. Of course this notion must be relativized to *persons;* what is self-evident to you might not be to me. Very simple arithmetical truths will be self-evident to nearly all of us, but a truth like $17 + 18 = 35$ may be self-evident only to some. And of course a proposition is self-evident to a person only if he does in fact grasp it, so a proposition will not be self-evident to those who do not apprehend the concepts it involves. As Aquinas says, some propositions are self-evident only to the learned; his example is the truth that immaterial substances do not occupy space. Among those propositions whose concepts not everyone grasps, some are such that anyone who *did* grasp them would see their truth; for example,

(10) A model of a first-order theory T assigns truth to the axioms of T.

Others—$17 + 13 = 30$, for example—may be such that some but not all of those who apprehend them also see that they are true.

But how shall we understand this "seeing that they are true"? Those who speak of self-evidence explicitly turn to this visual metaphor and expressly explain self-evidence by reference to vision. There are two important aspects to the metaphor and two corresponding components to the idea of self-evidence. First, there is the *epistemic* component: a proposition p is self-evident to a person S only if S has *immediate* knowledge of p—that is, knows p, and does not know p on the basis of his knowledge of other propositions. Consider a simple arithmetic truth such as $2 + 1 = 3$ and compare it with one like $24 \times 24 = 576$. I know each of these propositions, and I know the second but not the first on the basis of computation, which is a kind of inference. So I have immediate knowledge of the first but not the second.

But there is also a phenomenological component. Consider again our two propositions; the first but not the second has about it a kind of luminous aura or glow when you bring it to mind or consider it. Locke speaks, in this connection, of an "evident luster"; a self-evident proposition, he says, displays a kind of "clarity and brightness to the attentive mind." Descartes speaks instead of "clarity and distinctness"; each, I think, is referring to the same phenomenological feature. And this feature is connected with another: upon understanding a proposition of this sort one feels a strong inclination to accept it; this luminous obviousness seems to compel or at least impel assent. Aquinas and Locke, indeed, held that a person, or at any rate a normal, well-formed human being, finds it impossible to withhold assent when considering a self-evident proposition. The phenomenological component of the idea of self-evidence, then, seems to have a double aspect: there is the luminous aura that $2 + 1 = 3$ displays, and there is also an experienced tendency to accept or believe it. Perhaps, indeed, the luminous aura *just is* the experienced impulsion toward acceptance; perhaps these are the very same thing. In that case the phenomenological component would not have the double aspect I suggested it did have; in either case, however, we must recognize this phenomenological aspect of self-evidence.

Aquinas therefore holds that self-evident propositions are properly basic. I think he means to add that propositions "evident to the senses" are also properly basic. By this latter term I think he means to refer to *perceptual* propositions—propositions whose truth or falsehood we can determine by looking or employing some other sense. He has in mind, I think, such propositions as

(11) There is a tree before me,
(12) I am wearing shoes,

and

(13) That tree's leaves are yellow.

So Aquinas holds that a proposition is properly basic if and only if it is either self-evident or evident to the senses. Other foundationalists have insisted that propositions basic in a rational noetic structure must be certain in some important sense. Thus it is plausible to see Descartes

as holding that the foundations of a rational noetic structure include, not such propositions as (11)–(13), but more cautious claims—claims about one's own mental life; for example,

(14) It seems to me that I see a tree,
(15) I seem to see something green,

or, as Professor Chisholm puts it,

(16) I am appeared greenly to.

Propositions of this latter sort seem to enjoy a kind of immunity from error not enjoyed by those of the former. I could be mistaken in thinking I see a pink rat; perhaps I am hallucinating or the victim of an illusion. But it is at the least very much harder to see that I could be mistaken in believing that I *seem* to see a pink rat, in believing that I am appeared pinkly (or pink ratly) to. Suppose we say that a proposition with respect to which I enjoy this sort of immunity from error is incorrigible for me; then perhaps Descartes means to hold that a proposition is properly basic for S only if it is either self-evident or incorrigible for S.

By way of explicit definition:

(17) p is incorrigible for S if and only if (a) it is not possible that S believes p and p be false, and (b) it is not possible that S believe $\sim p$ and p be true.

....

Here we have a further characteristic of foundationalism: the claim that not just any proposition is properly basic. Ancient and medieval foundationalists tended to hold that a proposition is properly basic for a person only if it is either self-evident or evident to the senses: modern foundationalists—Descartes, Locke, Leibniz, and the like—tended to hold that a proposition is properly basic for S only if either self-evident or incorrigible for S. Of course this is a historical generalization and is thus perilous; but perhaps it is worth the risk. And now let us say that a *classical foundationalist* is any one who is either an ancient and medieval or a modern foundationalist.

The Collapse of Foundationalism

Now suppose we return to the main question: Why should not belief in God be among the foundations of my noetic structure? The answer, on the part of the classical foundationalist, was that even if this belief is *true*, it does not have the characterstics a proposition must have to deserve a place in the foundations. There is no room in the foundations for a proposition that can be rationally accepted only on the basis of other propositions. The only properly basic propositions are those that are self-evident or incorrigible or evident to the senses. Since the proposition that God exists is none of the above, it is not properly basic for anyone; that is, no well-formed, rational noetic structure contains this proposition in its foundations. But now we must take a closer look at this fundamental principle of classical foundationalism:

(18) A proposition *p* is properly basic for a person *S* if and only if *p* is either self-evident to *S* or incorrigible for *S* or evident to the senses for *S*.

(18) contains two claims: first, a proposition is properly basic *if* it is self-evident, incorrigible, or evident to the senses, and, second, a proposition is properly basic *only if* it meets this condition. The first seems true enough; suppose we concede it. But what is to be said for the second? Is there any reason to accept it? Why does the foundationalist accept it? Why does he think the theist ought to?

We should note first that if this thesis, and the correlative foundationalist thesis that a proposition is rationally acceptable only if it follows from or is probable with respect to what is properly basic—if these claims are true, then enormous quantities of what we all in fact believe are irrational. One crucial lesson to be learned from the development of modern philosophy—Descartes through Hume, roughly—is just this: relative to propositions that are self-evident and incorrigible, most of the beliefs that form the stock in trade of ordinary everyday life are not probable—at any rate there is no reason to think they are probable. Consider all those propositions that entail, say, that there

are enduring physical objects, or that there are persons distinct from myself, or that the world has existed for more than five minutes: none of these propositions, I think, is more probable than not with respect to what is self-evident or incorrigible for me; at any rate no one has given good reason to think any of them is. And now suppose we add to the foundations propositions that are evident to the senses, thereby moving from modern to ancient and medieval foundationalism. Then propositions entailing the existence of material objects will of course be probable with respect to the foundations, because included therein. But the same cannot be said either for propositions about the past or for propositions entailing the existence of persons distinct from myself; as before, these will not be probable with respect to what is properly basic.

And does not this show that the thesis in question is false? The contention is that

(19) *A* is properly basic for me only if *A* is self-evident or incorrigible or evident to the senses for me.

But many propositions that do not meet these conditions *are* properly basic for me. I believe, for example, that I had lunch this noon. I do not believe this proposition on the basis of other propositions; I take it as basic; it is in the foundations of my noetic structure. Furthermore, I am entirely rational in so taking it, even though this proposition is neither self-evident nor evident to the senses nor incorrigible for me. Of course this may not convince the foundationalist; he may think that in fact I do *not* take that proposition as basic, or perhaps he will bite the bullet and maintain that if I really *do* take it as basic, then the fact is I *am*, so far forth, irrational.

Perhaps the following will be more convincing. According to the classical foundationalist (call him *F*) a person *S* is rational in accepting (19) only if either (19) is properly basic (self-evident or incorrigible or evident to the senses) for him, or he believes (19) on the basis of propositions that are properly basic for him and support (19). Now presumably if *F* knows of some support for (19) from propositions that are self-evident or evident to the senses or incorrigible, he will be able to provide a good argument—deductive, inductive, probabilistic or whatever—whose premises are self-evident or evident to the senses or incorrigible and whose conclusion is (19). So far as I know, no foundationalist has provided such an argument. It therefore appears that the foundationalist does not know of any support for (19) from propositions that are (on his account) properly basic. So if he is to be rational in accepting (19), he must (on his own account) accept it as basic. But according to (19) itself, (19) is properly basic for *F* only if (19) is self-evident or incorrigible or evident to the senses for him. Clearly (19) meets none of these conditions. Hence it is not properly basic for *F*. But then *F* is self-referentially inconsistent in accepting (19); he accepts (19) as basic, despite the fact that (19) does not meet the condition for proper basicality that (19) itself lays down.

Furthermore, (19) is either false or such that in accepting it the foundationalist is violating his epistemic responsibilities. For *F* does not know of any argument or evidence for (19). Hence if it is true, he will be violating his epistemic responsibilities in accepting it. So (19) is either false or such that *F* cannot rationally accept it. Still further, if the theist were to accept (19) at the foundationalist's urging but without argument, he would be adding to his noetic structure a proposition that is either false or such that in accepting it he violates his noetic responsibilities. But if there is such a thing as the ethics of belief, surely it will proscribe believing a proposition one knows to be either false or such that one ought not to believe it. Accordingly, I ought not to accept (19) in the absence of argument from premises that meet the condition it lays down. The same goes for the foundationalist: if he cannot find such an argument for (19), he ought to give it up. Furthermore, he ought not to urge and I ought not to accept any objection to theistic belief that crucially depends upon a proposition that is true only if I ought not to believe it. . . .

Now we could canvass revisions of (19), and later I shall look into the proper procedure for discovering and justifying such criteria for proper basicality. It is evident, however, that classical foundationalism is bankrupt, and insofar as the evidentialist objection is rooted in classical foundationalism, it is poorly rooted indeed.

Of course the evidentialist objection *need* not presuppose classical foundationalism; someone who accepted quite a different version of foundationalism could no doubt urge this objection. But in order to evaluate it, we should have to see what criterion of proper basicality was being invoked. In the absence of such specification the objection remains at best a promissory note. So far as the present discussion goes, then, the next move is up to the evidentialist objector. He must specify a criterion for proper basicality that is free from self-referential difficulties, rules out belief in God as properly basic, and is such that there is some reason to think it is true. . . .

THE REFORMED OBJECTION TO NATURAL THEOLOGY

Suppose we think of natural theology as the attempt to prove or demonstrate the existence of God. This enterprise has a long and impressive history—a history stretching back to the dawn of Christendom and boasting among its adherents many of the truly great thinkers of the Western world. One thinks, for example, of Anselm, Aquinas, Scotus, and Ockham, of Descartes, Spinoza, and Leibniz. Recently—since the time of Kant, perhaps—the tradition of natural theology has not been as overwhelming as it once was; yet it continues to have able defenders both within and without officially Catholic philosophy.

Many Christians, however, have been less than totally impressed. In particular Reformed or Calvinist theologians have for the most part taken a dim view of this enterprise. A few Reformed thinkers—B. B. Warfield, for example—endorse the theistic proofs, but for the most part the Reformed attitude has ranged from tepid endorsement, through indifference, to suspicion, hostility, and outright accusations of blasphemy. And this stance is initially puzzling. It looks a little like the attitude some Christians adopt toward faith healing: it can't be done, but even if it could it shouldn't be. What exactly, or even approximately, do these sons and daughters of the Reformation have against proving the existence of God? What *could* they have against it? What could be less objectionable to any but the most obdurate atheist?

The Objection Initially Stated

By way of answering this question, I want to consider three representative Reformed thinkers. Let us begin with the nineteenth-century Dutch theologian Herman Bavinck:

> A distinct natural theology, obtained apart from any revelation, merely through observation and study of the universe in which man lives, does not exist. . . .
>
> Scripture urges us to behold heaven and earth, birds and ants, flowers and lilies, in order that we may see and recognize God in them. "Lift up your eyes on high, and see who hath created these." Is. 40:26. Scripture does not reason in the abstract. It does not make God the conclusion of a syllogism, leaving it to us whether we think the argument holds or not. But it speaks with authority. Both theologically and religiously it proceeds from God as the starting point.
>
> We receive the impression that belief in the existence of God is based entirely upon these proofs. But indeed that would be "a wretched faith, which, before it invokes God, must first prove his existence." The contrary, however, is the truth. There is not a single object the existence of which we hesitate to accept until definite proofs are furnished. Of the existence of self, of the world round about us, of logical and moral laws, etc., we are so deeply convinced because of the indelible impressions which all these things make upon our consciousness that we need no arguments or demonstration. Spontaneously, altogether involuntarily: without any constraint or coercion, we accept that existence. Now the same is true in regard to the existence of God. The so-called proofs are by no means the final grounds of our most certain conviction that God exists. This certainty is established only by faith; that is, by the spontaneous testimony which forces itself upon us from every side.

According to Bavinck, then, belief in the existence of God is not based upon proofs or arguments. By "argument" here I think he means arguments in the style of natural theology—the sort given by Aquinas and Scotus and later by Descartes, Leibniz, Clarke, and others. And what he means to say, I think, is that Christians do not *need* such arguments. Do not need them for what?

Here I think Bavinck means to hold two things. First, arguments or proofs are not, in general, the source of the believer's confidence in God. Typically the believer does not believe in God on the basis of arguments; nor does he believe such truths as that God has created the world on the basis of arguments. Second, argument is not needed for *rational justification;* the believer is entirely within his epistemic right in believing, for example, that God has created the world, even if he has no argument at all for that conclusion. The believer does not need natural theology in order to achieve rationality or epistemic propriety in believing; his belief in God can be perfectly rational even if he knows of no cogent argument, deductive or inductive, for the existence of God—indeed, even if there is no such argument.

Bavinck has three further points. First he means to add, I think, that we cannot come to knowledge of God on the basis of argument; the arguments of natural theology just do not work. (And he follows this passage with a more or less traditional attempt to refute the theistic proofs, including an endorsement of some of Kant's fashionable confusions about the ontological argument.) Second, Scripture "proceeds from God as the starting point," and so should the believer. There is nothing by way of proofs or arguments for God's existence in the Bible; that is simply presupposed. The same should be true of the Christian believer then; he should *start* from belief in God rather than from the premises of some argument whose conclusion is that God exists. What is it that makes those premises a better starting point anyway? And third, Bavinck points out that belief in God relevantly resembles belief in the existence of the self and of the external world—and, we might add, belief in other minds and the past. In none of these areas do we typically *have* proof or arguments, or *need* proofs or arguments.

Suppose we turn next to John Calvin, who is as good a Calvinist as any. According to Calvin

God has implanted in us all an innate tendency, or *nisus,* or disposition to believe in him:

> 'There is within the human mind, and indeed by natural instinct, an awareness of divinity.' This we take to be beyond controversy. To prevent anyone from taking refuge in the pretense of ignorance, God himself has implanted in all men a certain understanding of his divine majesty. Ever renewing its memory, he repeatedly sheds fresh drops. Since, therefore, men one and all perceive that there is a God and that he is their Maker, they are condemned by their own testimony because they have failed to honor him and to consecrate their lives to his will. If ignorance of God is to be looked for anywhere, surely one is most likely to find an example of it among the more backward folk and those more remote from civilization. Yet there is, as the eminent pagan says, no nation so barbarous, no people so savage, that they have not a deep-seated conviction that there is a God. So deeply does the common conception occupy the minds of all, so tenaciously does it inhere in the hearts of all! Therefore, since from the beginning of the world there has been no region, no city, in short, no household, that could do without religion, there lies in this a tacit confession of a sense of deity inscribed in the hearts of all.
>
> Indeed, the perversity of the impious, who though they struggle furiously are unable to extricate themselves from the fear of God, is abundant testimony that this conviction, namely, that *there is some God,* is naturally inborn in all, and is fixed deep within, as it were in the very marrow.... From this we conclude *that it is not a doctrine that must first be learned in school,* but one of which each of us is master from his mother's womb and which nature itself permits no one to forget.

Calvin's claim, then, is that God has created us in such a way that we have a strong tendency or inclination toward belief in him. This tendency has been in part overlaid or suppressed by sin. Were it not for the existence of sin in the world, human beings would believe in God to the same degree and with the same natural spontaneity that we believe in the existence of other persons, an external world, or the past. This is the natural human condition; it is because of our presently unnatural sinful condition that many of us find belief in God difficult or absurd. The fact is, Calvin thinks, one who does not believe in God is in an epistemically substandard position—rather like a man who does not believe that his wife exists, or thinks she is like a cleverly constructed robot and has no thoughts, feelings, or consciousness.

Although this disposition to believe in God is partially suppressed, it is nonetheless universally present. And it is triggered or actuated by a widely realized condition:

> Lest anyone, then, be excluded from access to happiness, he not only sowed in men's minds that seed of religion of which we have spoken, but revealed himself and daily discloses himself in the whole workmanship of the universe. As a consequence, men cannot open their eyes without being compelled to see him.

Like Kant, Calvin is especially impressed in this connection, by the marvelous compages of the starry heavens above:

> Even the common folk and the most untutored, who have been taught only by the aid of the eyes, cannot be unaware of the excellence of divine art, for it reveals itself in this innumerable and yet distinct and well-ordered variety of the heavenly host.

And Calvin's claim is that one who accedes to this tendency and in these circumstances accepts the belief that God has created the world—perhaps upon beholding the starry heavens, or the splendid majesty of the mountains, or the intricate, articulate beauty of a tiny flower—is entirely within his epistemic rights in so doing. It is not that such a person is justified or rational in so believing by virtue of having an implicit argument—some version of the teleological argument, say. No; he does not need any argument for justification or rationality. His belief need not be based on any other propositions at all; under these conditions he is perfectly rational in accepting belief in God in the utter absence of any argument, deductive or inductive. Indeed, a person in these conditions, says Calvin, *knows* that God exists.

Elsewhere Calvin speaks of "arguments from reason" or rational arguments:

The prophets and apostles do not boast either of their keenness or of anything that obtains credit for them as they speak; nor do they dwell upon rational proofs. Rather, they bring forward God's holy name, that by it the whole world may be brought into obedience to him. Now we ought to see how apparent it is not only by plausible opinion but by clear truth that they do not call upon God's name heedlessly or falsely. If we desire to provide in the best way for our consciences—that they may not be perpetually beset by the instability of doubt or vacillation, and that they may not also boggle at the smallest quibbles—we ought to seek our conviction in a higher place than human reasons, judgments, or conjectures, that is, in the secret testimony of the Spirit. (book 1, chapter 7, p. 78)

Here the subject for discussion is not belief in the existence of God, but belief that God is the author of the Scriptures; I think it is clear, however, that Calvin would say the same thing about belief in God's existence. The Christian does not *need* natural theology, either as the source of his confidence or to justify his belief. Furthermore, the Christian *ought* not to believe on the basis of argument; if he does, his faith is likely to be "unstable and wavering," the "subject of perpetual doubt." If my belief in God is based on argument, then if I am to be properly rational, epistemically responsible, I shall have to keep checking the philosophical journals to see whether, say, Antony Flew has finally come up with a good objection to my favorite argument. This could be bothersome and time-consuming; and what do I do if someone does find a flaw in my argument? Stop going to church? From Calvin's point of view believing in the existence of God on the basis of rational argument is like believing in the existence of your spouse on the basis of the analogical argument for other minds—whimsical at best and unlikely to delight the person concerned. . . .

Karl Barth joins Calvin and Bavinck in holding that the believer in God is entirely within his epistemic rights in believing as he does even if he does not know of any good theistic argument. They all hold that belief in God is *properly basic*—that is, such that it is rational to accept it

without accepting it on the basis of any other proposition or beliefs at all. In fact, they think the Christian ought not to accept belief in God on the basis of argument; to do so is to run the risk of a faith that is unstable and wavering, subject to all the wayward whim and fancy of the latest academic fashion. What the Reformers held was that a believer is entirely rational, entirely within his epistemic rights, in *starting with* belief in God, in accepting it as basic, and in taking it as premise for argument to other conclusions.

In rejecting natural theology, therefore, these Reformed thinkers mean to say first of all that the propriety or rightness of belief in God in no way depends upon the success or availability of the sort of theistic arguments that form the natural theologian's stock in trade. I think this is their central claim here, and their central insight. As these Reformed thinkers see things, one who takes belief in God as basic is not thereby violating any epistemic duties or revealing a defect in his noetic structure; quite the reverse. The correct or proper way to believe in God, they thought, was not on the basis of arguments from natural theology or anywhere else; the correct way is to take belief in God as basic.

I spoke earlier of classical foundationalism, a view that incorporates the following three theses:

(1) In every rational noetic structure there is a set of beliefs taken as basic—that is, not accepted on the basis of any other beliefs,

(2) In a rational noetic structure nonbasic belief is proportional to support from the foundations,

and

(3) In a rational noetic structure basic beliefs will be self-evident or incorrigible or evident to the senses.

Now I think these three Reformed thinkers should be understood as rejecting classical foundationalism. They may have been inclined to accept (1); they show no objection to (2); but they were utterly at odds with the idea that the foundations of a rational noetic structure can at most include propositions that are self-evident or evident to the senses or incorrigible. In particular, they were prepared to insist that a rational noetic structure can include belief in God as basic. As Bavinck put it, "Scripture . . . does not make God the conclusion of a syllogism, leaving it to us whether we think the argument holds or not. But it speaks with authority. Both theologically and religiously it proceeds from God as the starting point." And of course Bavinck means to say that we must emulate Scripture here.

In the passages I quoted earlier, Calvin claims the believer does not need argument—does not need it, among other things, for epistemic respectability. We may understand him as holding, I think, that a rational noetic structure may very well contain belief in God among its foundations. Indeed, he means to go further, and in two separate directions. In the first place he thinks a Christian *ought* not believe in God on the basis of other propositions; a proper and well-formed Christian noetic structure will *in fact* have belief in God among its foundations. And in the second place Calvin claims that one who takes belief in God as basic can *know* that God exists. Calvin holds that one can *rationally accept* belief in God as basic; he also claims that one can *know* that God exists even if he has no argument, even if he does not believe on the basis of other propositions. A foundationalist is likely to hold that some properly basic beliefs are such that anyone who accepts them *knows* them. More exactly, he is likely to hold that among the beliefs properly basic for a person S, some are such that if S accepts them, S knows them. He could go on to say that *other* properly basic beliefs cannot be known if taken as basic, but only rationally believed; and he might think of the existence of God as a case in point. Calvin will have none of this; as he sees it, one needs no arguments to know that God exists. . . .

IS BELIEF IN GOD PROPERLY BASIC?

The Great Pumpkin Objection

It is tempting to raise the following sort of question. If belief in God is properly basic, why cannot *just any* belief be properly basic? Could we not say the same for any bizarre

aberration we can think of? What about voodoo or astrology? What about the belief that the Great Pumpkin returns every Halloween? Could I properly take *that* as a basic? Suppose I believe that if I flap my arms with sufficient vigor, I can take off and fly about the room; could I defend myself against the charge of irrationality by claiming this belief is basic? If we say that belief in God is properly basic, will we not be committed to holding that just anything, or nearly anything, can properly be taken as basic, thus throwing wide the gates to irrationalism and superstition?

Certainly not. According to the Reformed epistemologist certain beliefs are properly basic in certain circumstances; those same beliefs may *not* be properly basic in other circumstances. Consider the belief that I see a tree: this belief is properly basic in circumstances that are hard to describe in detail, but include my being appeared to in a certain characteristic way; that same belief is not properly basic in circumstances including, say, my knowledge that I am sitting in the living room listening to music with my eyes closed. What the Reformed epistemologist holds is that there are widely realized circumstances in which belief in God is properly basic; but why should that be thought to commit him to the idea that just about *any* belief is properly basic in any circumstances, or even to the vastly weaker claim that for any belief there are circumstances in which it is properly basic? Is it just that he rejects the criteria for proper basicality purveyed by classical foundationalism? But why should *that* be thought to commit him to such tolerance of irrationality? Consider an analogy. In the palmy days of positivism the positivists went about confidently wielding their verifiability criterion and declaring meaningless much that was clearly meaningful. Now suppose someone rejected a formulation of that criterion—the one to be found in the second edition of A. J. Ayer's *Language, Truth and Logic*, for example. Would that mean she was committed to holding that

(1) T'was brillig; and the slithy toves did gyre and gymble in the wabe,

contrary to appearances, makes good sense? Of course not. But then the same goes for the Reformed epistemologist: the fact that he rejects the criterion of proper basicality purveyed by classical foundationalism does not mean that he is committed to supposing just anything is properly basic.

But what then is the problem? Is it that the Reformed epistemologist not only rejects those criteria for proper basicality but seems in no hurry to produce what he takes to be a better substitute? If he has no such criterion, how can he fairly reject belief in the Great Pumpkin as properly basic?

This objection betrays an important misconception. How do we rightly arrive at or develop criteria for meaningfulness, or justified belief, or proper basicality? Where do they come from? Must one have such a criterion before one can sensibly make any judgments—positive or negative—about proper basicality? Surely not. Suppose I do not know of a satisfactory substitute for the criteria proposed by classical foundationalism; I am nevertheless entirely within my epistemic rights in holding that certain propositions in certain conditions are not properly basic.

Some propositions seem self-evident when in fact they are not; that is the lesson of some of the Russell paradoxes. Nevertheless it would be irrational to take as basic the denial of a proposition that seems self-evident to you. Similarly, suppose it seems to you that you see a tree; you would then be irrational in taking as basic the proposition that you do not see a tree or that there are no trees; in the same way, even if I do not know of some illuminating criterion of meaning, I can quite properly declare (1) (above) meaningless.

And this raises an important question—one Roderick Chisholm has taught us to ask. What is the status of criteria for knowledge, or proper basicality, or justified belief? Typically these are universal statements. The modern foundationalist's criterion for proper basicality, for example, is doubly universal:

(2) For any proposition A and person S, A is properly basic for S if and only if A is incorrigible for S or self-evident to S.

But how could one know a thing like that? What are its credentials? Clearly enough, (2) is not self-evident or just obviously true. But if it is not, how does one arrive at it? What sorts of arguments would be appropriate? Of course a foundationalist might find (2) so appealing he simply takes it to be true, neither offering argument for it nor accepting it on the basis of other things he believes. If he does so, however, his noetic structure will be self-referentially incoherent. (2) itself is neither self-evident nor incorrigible; hence if he accepts (2) as basic, the modern foundationalist violates in accepting it the condition of proper basicality he himself lays down. On the other hand, perhaps the foundationalist will try to produce some argument for it from premises that are self-evident or incorrigible: it is exceeding hard to see, however, what such an argument might be like. And until he has produced such arguments, what shall the rest of us do—we who do not find (2) at all obvious or compelling? How could he use (2) to show us that belief in God, for example, is not properly basic? Why should we believe (2) or pay it any attention?

The fact is, I think, that neither (2) nor any other revealing necessary and sufficient condition for proper basicality follows from clearly self-evident premises by clearly acceptable arguments. And hence the proper way to arrive at such a criterion is, broadly speaking, *inductive*. We must assemble examples of beliefs and conditions such that the former are obviously properly basic in the latter, and examples of beliefs and conditions such that the former are obviously not properly basic in the latter. We must then frame hypotheses as to the necessary and sufficient conditions of proper basicality and test these hypotheses by reference to those examples. Under the right conditions, for example, it is clearly rational to believe that you see a human person before you: a being who has thoughts and feelings, who knows and believes things, who makes decisions and acts. It is clear, furthermore, that you are under no obligation to reason to this belief from others you hold; under those conditions that belief is properly basic for you. But then (2) must be mistaken; the belief in question, under those circumstances, is properly basic, though neither self-evident nor incorrigible for you. Similarly, you may seem to remember that you had breakfast this morning, and perhaps you know of no reason to suppose your memory is playing you tricks. If so, you are entirely justified in taking that belief as basic. Of course it is not properly basic on the criteria offered by classical foundationalists, but that fact counts not against you but against those criteria....

Accordingly, criteria for proper basicality must be reached from below rather than above; they should not be presented *ex cathedra* but argued to and tested by a relevant set of examples. But there is no reason to assume, in advance, that everyone will agree on the examples. The Christian will of course suppose that belief in God is entirely proper and rational; if he does not accept this belief on the basis of other propositions, he will conclude that it is basic for him and quite properly so. Followers of Bertrand Russell and Madelyn Murray O'Hare may disagree; but how is that relevant? Must my criteria, or those of the Christian community, conform to their examples? Surely not. The Christian community is responsible to *its* set of examples, not to theirs....

So, the Reformed epistemologist can properly hold that belief in the Great Pumpkin is not properly basic, even though he holds that belief in God is properly basic and even if he has no full-fledged criterion of proper basicality. Of course he is committed to supposing that there is a relevant *difference* between belief in God and belief in the Great Pumpkin if he holds that the former but not the latter is properly basic. But this should prove no great embarrassment; there are plenty of candidates. These candidates are to be found in the neighborhood of the conditions that justify and ground belief in God—conditions I shall discuss in the next section. Thus, for example, the Reformed epistemologist may concur with Calvin in holding that God has implanted in us a natural tendency to see his hand in the world around us; the same cannot be said for the Great Pumpkin, there being no Great Pumpkin and no natural tendency to accept beliefs about the Great Pumpkin.

VII.B.3 A Critique of Plantinga's Religious Epistemology

MICHAEL MARTIN

Michael Martin (1932–   ) is professor emeritus of philosophy at Boston University and the author of numerous works both popular and academic in the fields of philosophy of science and philosophy of religion. In this essay, taken from his *Atheism: A Philosophical Justification* (1990), Martin argues that Plantinga's defense of the proper basicality of belief in God fails, that his arguments against classical foundationalism are weak, that his logic leads to an extreme relativism, and that his foundationalism has serious problems.

RELIGIOUS BELIEFS AND BASIC BELIEFS

One recent attempt to justify religious beliefs argues that some religious beliefs—for example,

the belief that God exists—should be considered as basic beliefs that form the foundations of all other beliefs. The best-known advocate of this position is Alvin Plantinga, whose theory is based on a critique of classical foundationalism.

Foundationalism

Foundationalism was once a widely accepted view in epistemology; and although it has undergone modifications, it still has many advocates. The motivation for the view seems compelling. If we try to justify all our beliefs in terms of other beliefs, the justification generates an infinite regress or vicious circularity. Therefore, there must be some beliefs that do not need to be justified by other beliefs. Because they form the foundation of all knowledge, these are called basic beliefs, and the statements expressing them are called basic statements.

Foundationalism is usually considered a normative theory. It sets standards of what are properly basic beliefs and standards of how nonbasic beliefs are to be related to basic ones. Not every belief could be basic and not every relation could link nonbasic beliefs to basic ones. According to the classical normative account of foundationalism, if one believes that a self-evident statement P is true because of the statement's self-evidence, then P is a properly basic one. According to this view, if a statement is self-evident, no conscious inference or calculation is required to determine its truth; one can merely look at it and know immediately that it is true. For example, certain simple and true statements of mathematics $(2 + 2 = 4)$ and logic (either p or $\sim$p) are self-evidently true to almost everyone, while some more complex statements of mathematics and logic are self-evidently true only to some. Consequently, statements such as $2 + 2 = 4$ are considered basic statements for almost everyone while the more complex statements are basic only to some.

In addition to self-evident statements, classical foundationalists held that beliefs based on direct perception are properly basic and the statements expressing such beliefs—sometimes called statements that are evident to the senses—were considered basic statements. Some foundationalists included, in the class of statements that are evident to the senses, ones about observed physical objects (There is a blue bird in the tree). However, in modern times it has been more common for foundationalists to restrict statements that are evident to the senses to ones about immediate sense impressions (I seem to see a blue bird in the tree, or I am being appeared to bluely, or perhaps, Here now blue sense datum). According to the classical foundationalist account, statements that are evident to the senses are incorrigible; that is, one cannot believe such statements and be mistaken.

Denying that any statement is incorrigible, many contemporary epistemologists, although sympathetic with the foundationalist program, have maintained that statements that are evident to the senses are either initially credible or self-warranted. Moreover, some contemporary foundationalists have argued that memory statements, such as "I remember having breakfast ten minutes ago" should be included in the class of properly basic statements. Classical foundationalism also maintained that nonbasic beliefs had to be justified in terms of basic beliefs. Thus in order for a person P's nonbasic statement NS_1 (Other people have minds) to be justified, it would either have to follow logically from P's set of basic statements BS_1 & BS_2 & ... BS_n or be probable relative to that set of statements. However, those contemporary foundationalists who maintain that properly basic statements are only initially credible allow that it is possible that a person P's basic statements BS_1 could be shown to be false if it conflicted with many of the well-supported nonbasic statements NS_1 & NS_2 & ... NS_n of P. In addition, some have argued that deductive and inductive principles of inference must be supplemented with other principles of derivation. Consequently, a person P's nonbasic statement NS_1 is justified only if it follows from P's set of basic statements or is probable relative to this set or is justified relative to this set by means of certain special epistemic principles.

Plantinga's Critique of Foundationalism

Plantinga characterizes foundationalism as follows:

> Ancient and medieval foundationalists tended to hold that a proposition is properly basic for a person only if it is either self-evident or evident to the senses: modern foundationalists—Descartes, Locke, Leibniz, and the like—tended to hold that a proposition is properly basic for S only if

either self-evident or incorrigible for S. Let us now say that a *classical foundationalist* is any one who is either an ancient and medieval or a modern foundationalist.

He defines properly basic statements in terms of this understanding of foundationalism. Consider:

(1) A proposition p is properly basic for a person S if and only if p is self-evident to S, or incorrigible, or evident to the senses.

Plantinga gives two basic arguments against foundationalism so understood. (a) He maintains that many of the statements we know to be true cannot be justified in foundationalist terms. These statements are not properly basic according to the definition given above, nor can they be justified by either deductive or inductive inference from properly basic statements. As examples of such statements Plantinga cites "Other people have minds" and "The world existed five minutes ago." To be sure, he says, such statements are basic for most people in a descriptive sense. According to classical foundationalists, however, they should not be, since they are not self-evident, not incorrigible, and not evident to the senses. According to Plantinga, examples such as these show that there is something very wrong with classical foundationalism.

(b) Plantinga argues also that foundationalists are unable to justify (1) in their own terms; that is, they have not shown that (1) follows from properly basic statements or is probable relative to these. Moreover, (1) is not itself self-evident or incorrigible or evident to the senses. Consequently, he argues, a foundationalist who accepts (1) is being "self-referentially inconsistent"; such a person accepts a statement that does not meet the person's own conditions for being properly basic. Thus he concludes that classical foundationalism is "bankrupt."

Belief in God as Properly Basic

Following a long line of reformed thinkers—that is, thinkers influenced by the doctrines of John Calvin, Plantinga contends that traditional arguments for the existence of God are not needed for rational belief. He cites with approval Calvin's claim that God created humans in such a way that they have a strong tendency to believe in God. According to Plantinga, Calvin maintained:

> Were it not for the existence of sin in the world, human beings would believe in God to the same degree and with the same natural spontaneity that we believe in the existence of other persons, an external world, or the past. This is the natural human condition; it is because of our presently unnatural sinful condition that many of us find belief in God difficult or absurd. The fact is, Calvin thinks, one who does not believe in God is in an epistemically substandard position—rather like a man who does not believe that his wife exists, or thinks she is like a cleverly constructed robot and has no thoughts, feelings, or consciousness.

Although this natural tendency to believe in God may be partially suppressed, Plantinga argues, it is triggered by "a widely realizable condition." For example, it may be triggered "in beholding the starry heavens, or the splendid majesty of the mountains, or the intricate, articulate beauty of a tiny flower." This natural tendency to accept God in these circumstances is perfectly rational. No argument for God is needed. Plantinga maintains that the best interpretation of Calvin's views, as well as those of the reformed thinkers he cites, is that they rejected classical foundationalism and maintained that belief in God can itself be a properly basic belief.

Surprisingly, Plantinga insists that although belief in God and belief about God's attributes and actions are properly basic, for reformed epistemologists this does not mean that there are no justifying circumstances or that they are without grounds. The circumstances that trigger the natural tendency to believe in God and to believe certain things about God provide the justifying circumstances for belief. So although beliefs about God are properly basic, they are not groundless.

How can we understand this? Plantinga draws an analogy between basic statements of religion and basic statements of perceptual belief and memory. A perceptual belief, he says, is taken as properly basic only under certain circumstances. For example, if I know that I am wearing rose-tinted glasses, then I am not justified in saying that the statement "I see a rose-colored wall before me" is properly basic; and if I know that my memory is unreliable, I am not justified in saying that the statement "I remember that I had breakfast" is properly basic. Although Plantinga admits that these conditions may be hard to specify, he maintains that their presence is necessary in order to claim that a perceptual or memory statement is basic. Similarly, he maintains that not every statement about God that is not based on argument or evidence should be considered properly basic. A statement is properly basic only in the right circumstances. What circumstances are right? Plantinga gives no general account, but in addition to the triggering condition mentioned above, the right conditions include reading the Bible, having done something wrong, and being in grave danger. Thus if one is reading the Bible and believes that God is speaking to one, then the belief is properly basic.

Furthermore, Plantinga insists that although reformed epistemologists allow belief in God as a properly basic belief, this does not mean they must allow that anything at all can be a basic belief. To be sure, he admits that he and other reformed epistemologists have not supplied us with any criterion of what is properly basic. He argues, however, that this is not necessary. One can know that some beliefs in some circumstances are not properly basic without having an explicitly formulated criterion of basicness. Thus Plantinga says that reformed epistemologists can correctly maintain that belief in voodoo or astrology or the Great Pumpkin is not a basic belief.

How is one to arrive at a criterion for being properly basic? According to Plantinga the route is "broadly speaking, *inductive*." He adds, "We must assemble examples of beliefs and conditions such that the former are obviously properly basic in the latter. . . . We must frame hypotheses as to the necessary and sufficient conditions of proper basicality and test these hypotheses by reference to these examples."

He argues that, using this procedure,

> the Christian will of course suppose that belief in God is entirely proper and rational; if he does

not accept this belief on the basis of other propositions, he will conclude that it is basic for him and quite properly so. Followers of Russell and Madelyn Murray O'Hair [sic] may disagree; but how is that relevant? Must my criteria, or those of the Christian community, conform to their examples? Surely not. The Christian community is responsible to its set of examples, not to theirs.

Evaluation of Plantinga's Critique of Foundationalism

Recall that Plantinga argues that classical foundationalists are being self-referentially inconsistent. But as James Tomberlin has pointed out, since what is self-evident is relative to persons, a classical foundationalist (CF) could argue that (1) is self-evident and that if Plantinga were sufficiently attentive, the truth of (1) would become clear to him. Tomberlin argues that this response is similar to Calvin's view that in beholding the starry heavens, the properly attuned theist senses the existence of God. As Tomberlin puts it: "If the theist may be so attuned, why can't the classical foundationalist enjoy a similar relation to (1)? No, I do not think that Plantinga has precluded CF's rejoinder; and consequently he has not proved that (1) fails to be self-evident to the classical foundationalist."

However, even if Plantinga can show that (1) is not self-evident for classical foundationalists, he has not shown that (1) could not be deductively or inductively inferred from statements that are self-evident or incorrigible or evident to the senses. As Philip Quinn has argued, the classical foundationalist can use the broadly inductive procedures suggested by Plantinga to arrive at (1). Since the community of classical foundationalists is responsible for its own set of examples of properly basic beliefs and the conditions that justify them, it would not be surprising that the hypothesis they came up with in order to account for their examples would be (1).

Furthermore, even if Plantinga has refuted classical foundationalism, this would hardly dispose of foundationalism. Contemporary foundationalism has seriously modified the classical theory, and it is not at all clear that in the light of these modifications, Plantinga's critique could be sustained. Recall that one of his criticisms was that a statement such as "The world existed five minutes ago" could not be justified on classical foundationalist grounds. Since contemporary foundationalists include memory statements in the class of basic statements, there would not seem to be any particular problem in justifying such a statement, for "I remember having my breakfast ten minutes ago" can be a properly basic statement. Furthermore, if basic statements only have to be initially credible and not self-evident or incorrigible or evident to the senses, the criticism of self-referential inconsistency is much easier to meet. It is not at all implausible to suppose that a criterion of basicality in term of initial credibility is itself either initially credible or based on statements that are.

Plantinga is aware that there is more to foundationalism than the classical formulation of it. He says:

> Of course the evidentialist objection *need not* presuppose classical foundationalism; someone who accepted a different version of foundationalism could no doubt urge this objection. But in order to evaluate it, we should have to see what criterion of properly basic was being invoked. In the absence of such specification the objection remains at best a promissory note. So far as the present discussion goes, then, the next move is up to the evidentialist objector.

Many contemporary foundationalist theories have been constructed on nonclassical lines. Indeed, it may be safe to say that few contemporary foundationalists accept the classical view or even take it seriously. Moreover, these contemporary versions are hardly promissory notes, as Plantinga must be aware. Indeed, his refutation of classical foundationalism has just about as much relevance for contemporary foundationalism as a refutation of the emotive theory in ethics has for contemporary ethical noncognitivism. The next move, therefore, does not seem to be up to contemporary foundationalists. Plantinga must go on to show that his critique has relevance to the contemporary foundationalist program and that, given the best contemporary formulations of foundationalism, beliefs about God can be basic statements. This he has yet to do.

The Trouble with Reformed Foundationalism

What can one say about Plantinga's ingenious attempt to save theism from the charge of irrationality by making beliefs about God basic?

(1) Plantinga's claim that his proposal would not allow just any belief to become a basic belief is misleading. It is true that it would not allow just any belief to become a basic belief *from the point of view of reformed epistemologists*. However it would seem to allow any belief at all to become basic from the point of view of some community. Although reformed epistemologists would not have to accept voodoo beliefs as rational, voodoo followers would be able to claim that insofar as they are basic in the voodoo community they are rational and, moreover, that reformed thought was irrational in this community. Indeed, Plantinga's proposal would generate many different communities that could *legitimately* claim that their basic beliefs are rational and that these beliefs conflict with basic beliefs of other communities. Among the communities generated might be devil worshipers, flat earthers, and believers in fairies just so long as belief in the devil, the flatness of the earth, and fairies was basic in the respective communities.

(2) On this view the rationality of any belief is absurdly easy to obtain. The cherished belief that is held without reason by any group could be considered properly basic by the group's members. There would be no way to make a critical evaluation of any beliefs so considered. The community's most cherished beliefs and the conditions that, according to the community, correctly trigger such beliefs would be accepted uncritically by the members of the community as just so many more examples of basic beliefs and justifying conditions. The more philosophical members of the community could go on to propose hypotheses as to the necessary and sufficient conditions for inclusion in this set. Perhaps, using this inductive procedure, a criterion could be formulated. However, what examples the hypotheses must account for would be decided by the community. As Plantinga says, each community would be responsible only to its own set of examples in formulating a

criterion, and each would decide what is to be included in this set.

(3) Plantinga seems to suppose that there is a consensus in the Christian community about what beliefs are basic and what conditions justify these beliefs. But this is not so. Some Christians believe in God on the basis of the traditional arguments or on the basis of religious experiences; their belief in God is not basic. There would, then, certainly be no agreement in the Christian community over whether belief in God is basic or nonbasic. More important, there would be no agreement on whether doctrinal beliefs concerning the authority of the pope, the makeup of the Trinity, the nature of Christ, the means of salvation, and so on were true, let alone basic. Some Christian sects would hold certain doctrinal beliefs to be basic and rational; others would hold the same beliefs to be irrational and, indeed, the gravest of heresies. Moreover, there would be no agreement over the conditions for basic belief. Some Christians might believe that a belief is properly basic when it is triggered by listening to the pope. Others would violently disagree. Even where there was agreement over the right conditions, these would seem to justify conflicting basic beliefs and, consequently, conflicting religious sects founded on them. For example, a woman named Jones, the founder of sect S_1, might read the Bible and be impressed that God is speaking to her and telling her that p, a man named Smith, the founder of sect S_2, might read the Bible and be impressed that God is speaking to him and telling him that $\sim$p. So Jones's belief that p and Smith's belief that $\sim$p would both be properly basic. One might wonder how this differs from the doctrinal disputes that have gone on for centuries among Christian sects and persist to this day. The difference is that on Plantinga's proposal each sect could *justifiably* claim that its belief, for which there might be no evidence or argument, was completely rational.

(4) So long as belief that there is no God was basic for them, atheists could also justify the claim that belief in God is irrational relative to their basic beliefs and the conditions that trigger them without critically evaluating any of the usual reasons for believing in God. Just as theistic

belief might be triggered by viewing the starry heavens above and reading the Bible, so atheistic beliefs might be triggered by viewing the massacre of innocent children below and reading the writings of Robert Ingersoll. Theists may disagree, but is that relevant? To paraphrase Plantinga: Must atheists' criteria conform to the Christian communities' criteria? Surely not. The atheistic community is responsible to *its* set of examples, not to theirs.

(5) There may not at present be any clear criterion for what can be a basic belief, but belief in God seems peculiarly inappropriate for inclusion in the class since there are clear disanalogies between it and the basic beliefs allowable by classical foundationalism. For example, in his critique of classical foundationalism, Plantinga has suggested that belief in other minds and the external world should be considered basic. There are many plausible alternatives to belief in an all-good, all-powerful, all-knowing God, but there are few, if any, plausible alternatives to belief in other minds and the external world. Moreover, even if one disagrees with these arguments that seem to provide evidence against the existence of God, surely one must attempt to meet them. Although there are many skeptical arguments against belief in other minds and the external world, there are in contrast no seriously accepted arguments purporting to show that there are no other minds or no external world. In this world, atheism and agnosticism are live options for many intelligent people; solipsism is an option only for the mentally ill.

(6) As we have seen, Plantinga, following Calvin, says that some conditions that trigger belief in God or particular beliefs about God also justify these beliefs and that, although these beliefs concerning God are basic, they are not groundless. Although Plantinga gave no general account of what these justifying conditions are, he presented some examples of what he meant and likened these justifying conditions to those of properly basic perceptual and memory statements. The problem here is the weakness of the analogy. As Plantinga points out, before we take a perceptual or memory belief as properly basic we must have evidence that our perception or

memory is not faulty. Part of the justification for believing that our perception or memory is not faulty is that in general it agrees with the perception or memory of our epistemological peers—that is, our equals in intelligence, perspicacity, honesty, thoroughness, and other relevant epistemic virtues, as well as with our other experiences. For example, unless my perceptions generally agreed with other perceivers with normal eyesight in normal circumstances and with my nonvisual experience—for example, that I feel something solid when I reach out—there would be no justification for supposing that my belief that I see a rose-colored wall in front of me is properly basic. Plantinga admits that if I know my memory is unreliable, my belief that I had breakfast should not be taken as properly basic. However, one knows that one's memory is reliable by determining whether it coheres with the memory reports of other people whose memory is normal and with one's other experiences.

As we have already seen, lack of agreement is commonplace in religious contexts. Different beliefs are triggered in different people when they behold the starry heavens or when they read the Bible. Beholding the starry heavens can trigger a pantheistic belief or a purely aesthetic response without any religious component. Sometimes no particular response or belief at all is triggered. From what we know about the variations of religious belief, it is likely that people would not have theistic beliefs when they beheld the starry heavens if they had been raised in non-theistic environments. Similarly, a variety of beliefs and responses are triggered when the Bible is read. Some people are puzzled and confused by the contradictions, others become skeptical of the biblical stories, others believe that God is speaking to them and has appointed them as his spokesperson, others believe God is speaking to them but has appointed no one as his spokesperson. In short, there is no consensus in the Christian community, let alone among Bible readers generally. So unlike perception and memory, there are no grounds for claiming that a belief in God is properly basic since the conditions that trigger it yield widespread disagreement among epistemological peers.

(7) Part of the trouble with Plantinga's account of basic belief is the assumption he makes concerning what it means to say that a person accepts one proposition on the basis of accepting another. According to Michael Levine, Plantinga understands the relation in this way:

(A) For any person S, and distinct propositions p and q, S believes q on the basis of p only if S entertains p, S accepts p, S infers q from p, and S accepts q.

Contemporary foundationalists do not accept (A) as a correct account of the relation of accepting one proposition on the basis of another. The following seems more in accord with contemporary understanding:

(B) For any person S and distinct propositions p and q, if S believes q, and S *would* cite p if queried under optimal conditions about his reasons for believing in q, then S believes q on the basis of P.

On (B) it seems unlikely that any nonepistemologically deficient person—for example, a normal adult—would be unable to cite any reason for believing in God if this person did believe in God. Consequently, Plantinga's claim that "the mature theist does not typically accept belief in God ... as a conclusion from other things that he believes" is irrelevant if his claim is understood in terms of (A) and probably false if understood in terms of (B).

(8) Finally, to consider belief in God as a basic belief seems completely out of keeping with the spirit and intention of foundationalism. Whatever else it was and whatever its problems, foundationalism was an attempt to provide critical tools for objectively appraising knowledge claims and provide a nonrelativistic basis for knowledge. Plantinga's foundationalism is radically relativistic and puts any belief beyond rational appraisal once it is declared basic.

The Trouble with Foundationalism

So far in my critique of Plantinga's attempt to incorporate beliefs in or about God into the set of properly basic beliefs that form the foundation of knowledge, I have uncritically accepted the idea that the structure of knowledge must have a foundation in terms of basic beliefs. But as Laurence Bonjour has recently shown, there is a serious problem with any foundationalist account of knowledge.

According to all foundationalist accounts, basic statements are justified noninferentially. For example, contemporary foundationalists who hold a moderate position maintain that properly basic statements, although not incorrigible or self-evident, are highly justified without inductive or deductive support. But it may be asked, where does this justification come from? As Bonjour argues, a basic constraint on any standards or justification for empirical knowledge is that there is a good reason for thinking that those standards lead to truth. So if basic beliefs are to provide a foundation for knowledge for the moderate foundationalist, then whatever the criterion for being properly basic, it must provide a good reason for supposing that basic beliefs are true. Further, such a criterion must provide grounds for the person who holds a basic belief to suppose that it is true. Thus moderate foundationalism must hold that for any person P, basic belief B, and criterion of being properly basic f, in order for P to be justified in holding properly basic belief B, P must be justified in believing the premises of the following justifying argument:

(1) B has feature ϕ.
(2) Beliefs having feature ϕ are likely to be true.

---

(3) Therefore, B is highly likely to be true.

Although, as Bonjour argues, it might be possible that one of the two premises in the above argument could be known to be true on an *a priori* basis, it does not seem possible that both premises could be known *a priori*. Once this is granted, it follows that B is not basic after all, since B's justification would depend on some other empirical belief. But if B is properly basic, its justification cannot depend on any other empirical belief. Bonjour goes on to meet objections to his argument showing that a coherent account of the structure of empirical knowledge can be developed to overcome this problem of foundationalism and that the objections usually raised against the coherence theory can be answered. Surely any defender of foundationalism must meet Bonjour's challenge.

As we have seen, when Plantinga proposes that belief about God can be considered properly basic, he admits that he did not have any criterion for being properly basic. But Bonjour's argument tends to show that whatever criterion Plantinga might offer, there will be a problem for reformed foundationalism. If Bonjour is correct, whatever this criterion is, it will have to provide a good reason for supposing that properly basic beliefs are true, and this will involve knowledge of further empirical beliefs. In order to defend his position, Plantinga must refute Bonjour's argument.

CONCLUSION

In Chapter 1 it was argued that there was a strong presumption that belief in God should be based on epistemic reasons. Some theists disagree, maintaining that religious belief is basic or should be based on faith. The conclusion here is that this argument fails. Although not all theories of faith have been examined here, the ones that were are representative enough to give us confidence that all such arguments will fail.

In a way Aquinas seems to agree with our position. He maintains that belief in the existence of God should be based on epistemic reasons; and, as we shall see in Chapter 14, he believed the arguments he produced provided such reasons. However, he believed that certain Christian dogmas were not provable by means of argument and must be based on faith. But even here he thought that one could have good epistemic reason to believe that these dogmas were revealed by God. He was wrong, however, to suppose that they were. Kierkegaard's view that faith in God should be based on absurdities and improbabilities was rejected, since the arguments he used to support this view were unsound and, in any case, his view led to fanaticism. Wittgensteinian fideism was also rejected, since it led to absurdities and presupposed an indefensible view of meaning and language.

Plantinga's reformed foundationalism has some interesting similarities to the doctrine that belief in God should be based on faith, but should not be identified with it. To be sure, his view is similar to that of Aquinas, who maintains that particular Christian doctrines, although not themselves based on reason, are rational. The basic difference between the Aquinas and Plantinga positions is that Aquinas attempts to provide epistemic reasons that would persuade all rational beings to accept certain propositions as revealed truths. Plantinga provides no such reason other than the argument that belief in God is basic and some such beliefs, including belief in God, are completely rational. Thus Plantinga's views differ markedly from those of Kierkegaard, who forsook any appeal to rationality in justifying religious belief. Plantinga's views also differ in important respects from Wittgensteinian fideism. While Wittgensteinian fideism appeals to ordinary religious practice and language to justify belief in God, Plantinga appeals to theoretical considerations from epistemology. Nevertheless, Plantinga's reformed foundationalism should be rejected since his arguments against classical foundationalism are weak, the logic of his position leads to a radical and absurd relativism, and foundationalism in general has serious problems.

VII.B.4   Faith, Hope, and Doubt

LOUIS P. POJMAN

Brief biographical remarks about Louis Pojman precede selection II.5. In the present selection, Pojman examines the relationship between belief and faith and argues that belief is not necessary for religious faith. One may not be able to believe in God because of an insufficiency of evidence, but one may still live in hope, committed to a theistic worldview.

Many religious people have a problem because they doubt various credal statements contained in their religions. Propositional beliefs are often looked upon as necessary, though not sufficient, conditions for salvation. This doubt causes great anxiety and raises the question of the importance of belief in religion and in life in general. It is a question that has been neglected in the philosophy of religion and theology. In this paper I shall explore the question of the importance of belief as a religious attitude and suggest that there is at least one other attitude which may be adequate for religious faith, even in the absence of belief—that attitude being hope. I shall develop a concept of *faith as hope* as an alternative to the usual notion that makes a propositional belief that God exists a necessary condition for faith, as Plantinga implies in the following quotation. For simplicity's sake I shall concentrate on the most important proposition in Western religious creeds, which states that God exists (defined broadly as a benevolent, supreme Being, who is responsible for the creation of the universe), but the analysis could be applied *mutatis mutandis* to many other important propositions in religion (e.g., the Incarnation and the doctrine of the Trinity).

> It is worth noting, by way of conclusion, that the mature believer, the mature theist, does not typically accept belief in God tentatively, or hypothetically, or until something better comes along. Nor, I think, does he accept it as a conclusion from other things he believes; he accepts it as basic, as a part of the foundations of his noetic structure. The mature theist commits himself to belief in God: this means that he accepts belief in God as basic (Alvin Plantinga, "Is Belief in God Rational?").

Entombed in a secure prison, thinking our situation quite hopeless, we may find unutterable joy in the information that there is, after all, the slimmest possibility of escape. Hope provides comfort, and hope does not always require probability. But we must believe that what we hope for is at least possible (Gretchen Weirob in John Perry's *A Dialogue on Personal Identity and Immortality*).

INTRODUCTION

Traditionally, orthodox Christianity has claimed (1) that faith in God and Christ entails belief that God exists and that Christ is God incarnate and (2) that without faith we are damned to eternal hell. Thus doubt is an unacceptable propositional attitude. I argue that this thesis is misguided. One may doubt—that is, lack propositional belief—and yet have faith in God and Christ.

Let me preface my remarks with a confession. I am a religious doubter. Doubt has haunted my life as long as I can remember. My mother was a devout Roman Catholic and my father an equally convinced rationalistic atheist. From an early age metaphysical tension produced in me a sense of wonder about religion. In the process of seeking a solution to this conflict, at the age of seven I became a Protestant. But doubts continued to haunt me. I recall coming home from my high school biology class, where we had studied naturalistic evolution, and weeping over the Bible, trying to reconcile evolution with the creation account in Genesis 1 through 3. Finally, when I was about 15, I went to a minister and confessed my doubts about God and Christianity. He listened carefully and said the situation was grave indeed. My eternal soul was at stake. Thus I must will myself to believe the message of Christianity. He quoted Romans 14:23: "He that doubteth is damned . . . for whatsoever is not of faith is sin." I was thrown into paroxysms of despair, for the attempt to get myself to believe that God exists or that Christ is perfect God and perfect man failed. Yet, I wanted to believe with all my heart, and some days I would find myself believing—only to wake up the next day with doubts. Hence, this preoccupation with faith and doubt. Hence, this paper.

I. IS BELIEF A NECESSARY CONDITION FOR SALVATION?

According to traditional Christianity, belief is a necessary condition for salvation. Paul says in Romans 10:10, "If you confess with your lips that Jesus is Lord and believe in your heart that God raised him from the dead, you will be saved." In Hebrews 11 we are told that he who would please God must believe that He exists and is a rewarder of them that seek Him. The Athanasian Creed, an official doctrine of orthodox Christianity, states that salvation requires that one believe not only that God exists but also that God is triune and that Christ is perfect God and perfect man.[1] Most theologians and philosophers hold, at the least, that Christian faith requires propositional belief.[2] You can be judged and condemned according to your beliefs. As Romans 14:23 states, "He that doubteth is damned."

The basic argument goes like this:

1. Faith in God through Christ is a necessary and sufficient condition for eternal salvation.
2. Belief that God exists is a necessary condition for faith.
3. Therefore belief is a necessary condition for salvation.
4. Therefore, doubt—the absence of belief—is an unacceptable attitude for salvation. No doubter will be saved.

Let us begin with some definitions:

1. **Belief**—an involuntary assenting of the mind to a proposition (a "yessing" to a proposition), a feeling of conviction about *p*—a *nonvolitional event*.

Consider the following belief line, defined in terms of subjective probability, the degree to which I think the proposition is probable. Let "*S*" stand for the believer or *subject,* "*B*" for *believe,* and "*p*" for the *proposition* in question. Then we can roughly locate our beliefs on the Belief Line. Greater than 0.5 equals various degrees of positive belief that *p*. Less than 0.5 equals various degrees of unbelief (or belief that the complement, "not-p" is true). 0.5 equals agnosticism or suspension of judgment.

Belief Line

$$0 \text{ ——————————} 0.5 \text{ ——————————} 1$$

SB not-p Not-SBp & Not-SB not-p SBp

2. **Acceptance**—deciding to include p in the set of propositions that you are willing to act on in certain contexts—a *volitional act*.

For example, in a *legal* context—say a jury, where there is insufficient evidence to convict an accused criminal—I may believe the subject is guilty but accept the proposition that he is not because the high standards of criminal justice have not been met; or in a *scientific* context—say, in testing the hypothesis that a formula will lead to the development of cold fusion—I may not believe the hypothesis I am testing is true but accept it for purposes of the experiment). Acceptance is different from belief in that we have some direct control over our acceptances, whereas we don't over our beliefs. We may or may not believe our acceptances and we may or may not accept our beliefs.

3. **Faith**—a commitment to something X (e.g., a person, hypothesis, religion, or worldview).

Faith is a *deep* kind of acceptance. An acceptance can be tentative. For example, when I make a marriage vow, I will to be faithful until death to my beloved, whether or not I believe that I will succeed. If my marriage vow were merely an acceptance, I suppose, it would be "I promise to be faithful to you for at least three years or until I lose interest in you." Faith involves commitment to its object. Under normal circumstances, it involves trusting and obeying the object of faith or doing what has the best chance of bringing its goals to fulfillment. It is a *volitional act*.

We may note at this point that the New Testament word *pistis* can be translated as either belief or faith. The distinction is discernible only by the context.

II. PHENOMENOLOGY OF BELIEF

First we must understand what is involved in direct volitionalism (the act of acquiring a belief directly by willing to have it). The following features seem to be necessary and jointly sufficient conditions for a minimally interesting thesis of volitionalism:

1. The acquisition is a basic act. That is, some of our beliefs are obtained by acts of will directly upon being willed. Believing itself need not be an action. It may be dispositional. The volitionalist need not assert that all belief acquisitions occur via the fiat of the will, only that some of them do.

2. The acquisition must be done in full consciousness of what one is doing. The paradigm cases of acts of will are those in which the agent deliberates over two courses of action and decides on one of them. However, acts of will may take place with greater or lesser awareness. Here our notion of will is ambiguous between two meanings: "desiring" and "deciding." Sometimes by "act of will" we mean simply a desire that manifests itself in action, such as my being hungry and finding myself going to the refrigerator or tired and finding myself heading for bed. We are not always aware of our desires or intentions. There is a difference between this type of willing and the sort where we are fully aware of a decision to perform an act. If we obtain beliefs via the will in the weaker sense of desiring, of which we are only dimly aware, how can we ever be sure that it was really an act of will that caused the belief directly rather than the will simply being an accompaniment of the belief? That is, there is a difference between willing to believe and believing willingly. The latter case is not an instance of acquiring a belief by fiat of the will; only the former is. In order for the volitionalist to make his case, he must assert that the acts of will that produce beliefs are decisions of which he is fully aware.

3. The belief must be acquired independently of evidential considerations. That is, the evidence is not what is decisive in forming the belief. Perhaps the belief may be influenced by evidence (testimony, memory, inductive experience, and the like), so that the leap of faith cannot occur

at just any time over any proposition, but only over propositions that have some evidence in their favor, though still inadequately supported by that evidence. They have an initial subjective probability of—or just under—0.5. According to Descartes, we ought to withhold belief in such situations where the evidence is exactly equal, whereas with Kierkegaard religious and existential considerations may justify leaps of believing even when the evidence is weighted against the proposition in question. William James prescribes such leaps only when the option is forced, living, and momentous. It may not be possible to volit* in the way Kierkegaard prescribes without a miracle of grace, as he suggests, but the volitionalist would have to assert that volitional belief goes beyond all evidence at one's disposal and hence the believer must acquire the belief through an act of choice that goes beyond evidential considerations. It is as though we place our volitional finger on the mental scales of evidence assessment, tipping the scale one way or the other.

In sum, then, a volit must be an act of will whereby I acquire a belief directly upon willing to have the belief, and it is an act made in full consciousness and independently of evidential considerations. The act of acquiring a belief may itself not be a belief but a way of moving from mere entertainment of a proposition to the disposition of having the belief. There is much to be said in favor of volitionalism. It seems to extend the scope of human freedom to an important domain, and it seems to fit our experience of believing where we are conscious of having made a choice. The teacher who sees that the evidence against a pupil's honesty is great and yet decides to trust him, believing that somehow he is innocent in spite of the evidence, and the theist who believes in God in spite of insufficient evidence, seem to be everyday examples confirming our inclination toward a volitional account of belief formation. We suspect, at times, that many of our beliefs, while not formed through *fully conscious* volits, have been formed through *half-aware* desires, for on introspection we note that past beliefs have been acquired in ways that could not have taken the evidence seriously into consideration. Volitionalism seems a good explanatory theory to account for a great deal of our cognitive experience.

Nonetheless, there are considerations which may make us question whether, upon reflection, volitionalism is the correct account of our situation. I will argue that choosing is not the natural way in which we acquire beliefs, and that whereas it may not be logically *im*possible that some people volit, it seems psychologically odd and even conceptually incoherent.

1. Beliefs-Are-Not-Chosen Argument against Volitionalism

Beliefs are not chosen but occur involuntarily as responses to states of affairs in the world. Beliefs are, to use Frank Ramsey's metaphor, mappings in the mind by which we steer our lives. As such, the states of affairs that beliefs represent exist independently of the mind; they exist independently of whether we want them to exist. Insofar as beliefs presume to represent the way the world is, and hence serve as effective guides to action, the will seems superfluous. Believing seems more like seeing than looking, falling than jumping, catching a cold than catching a ball, getting drunk than taking a drink, blushing than smiling, getting a headache than giving one to someone else. Indeed, this involuntary, passive aspect seems true on introspection of most propositional attitudes: anger, envy, fearing, suspecting, and doubting—although not necessarily of imagining or entertaining a proposition, where an active element may often be present.

When a person acquires a belief, the world forces itself upon him. Consider perceptual beliefs. If I am in a normal physiological condition and open my eyes, I cannot help but see certain things—for example, this piece of white

---

*Volit: (v.) to acquire a belief by choosing to have it or (n.) a belief acquired by exercising one's will.
Voliting: obtaining beliefs by choosing to have them.

paper in front of me. It seems intuitively obvious that I don't have to choose to have a belief that I see this piece of white paper before I believe I see it. Here "seeing is believing." This is not to deny a certain active element in perception. I can explore my environment—focus on certain features and turn from others. I can direct my perceptual mechanism, but once I do this the perceptions I obtain come of themselves whether or not I will to have them. I may even have an aversion to white paper and not want to have such a perception, but I cannot help having it. Likewise, if I am in a normal physiological state and someone nearby turns on loud music, I hear it. I cannot help believing that I hear it. Belief is forced on me.[3]

2. Logic-of-Belief Argument against Volitionalism

The notion of volitional believing involves a conceptual confusion; it is broadly speaking a logical mistake. There is something incoherent in stating that one can obtain or sustain a belief in full consciousness *simply* by a basic act of the will—that is, purposefully disregarding the evidence connection. This strategy does not altogether rule out the possibility of voliting when one is less than fully conscious (although one is not truly voliting if one is not fully conscious), but it asserts that when full consciousness enters, the "belief" will wither from one's noetic structure. One cannot believe in full consciousness "that *p* and I believe that *p* for other than truth considerations." If you understand that to believe that *p* is to believe that *p* is true and that *wishing never makes it so,* then there is simply no epistemic reason for believing *p*. Suppose I say that I believe I have $1,000,000 in my checking account, and suppose that when you point out to me that there is no reason to believe this, I respond, "I know that there is not the slightest reason to suppose that there is $1,000,000 in my checking account, but I believe it anyway, simply because I want to." If you were convinced that I was not joking, you would probably conclude that I was insane or didn't know what I was talking about.

If I said that I somehow find myself believing that I have $1,000,000 but don't know why, you might suppose that there is a memory trace of my having deposited $1,000,000 into my account or evidence to that effect in the guise of an intuition that caused my belief. But if I denied that and said—"No, I don't have any memory trace of depositing of $1,000,000 in my account; in fact, I'm sure that I never deposited $1,000,000 in the account; I just find it good to believe that it's there, so I have chosen to believe it,"—you would be stumped.

The point is that because beliefs are just about the way the world is and are made true (or false) depending on the way the world is, it is a confusion to believe that any given belief is true simply on the basis of being its being willed. As soon as the believer—assuming that he understands these basic concepts—discovers the basis of his belief as being caused by the will alone, he must drop the belief. In this regard, saying "I believe that *p*, but I believe it only because I want to believe it," has the same incoherence attached to it as G. E. Moore's paradoxical, "I believe *p* but it is false that *p*." Structurally, neither is a strictly logical contradiction, but both show an incoherence that might be broadly called contradictory.

If this reasoning is sound, then we cannot be judged for our beliefs because beliefs are not actions. That is, if *ought* implies *can*, and we cannot acquire beliefs directly by choosing them, we cannot be judged according to our beliefs. Of course, we can be judged by our actions and by how well we have investigated the evidence and paid attention to the arguments on the various sides of the issue. That leads to the matter of the ethics of belief.

III. THE ETHICS OF BELIEF

Of course we can obtain beliefs indirectly by willing to have them. I can desire to believe that I am innocent of an unjust act against my neighbor—say directing my drain pipes to drain onto his property. I can bring to mind all the nasty things my neighbor may have done and use autosuggestion to convince myself that I am justified in redirecting may drain pipes toward his property, thus bringing about the desired belief. This manipulation of the mind is immoral. At the least, there is a strong case against indirect volitionalism.

W. K. Clifford has given a classic absolutist injunction against voliting: "It is wrong always, everywhere and for anyone to believe anything on insufficient evidence." This may have the sound of too "robustious pathos in the voice" as James notes, but it may sound hyperbolic only because we have not taken truth seriously enough. Nevertheless, I defend the principle of an ethic of belief only as a *prima facie* moral principle—one which can be overridden by other moral principles—but which has strong presumptive force.[4]

Why do we want true justified beliefs—beliefs based on the best evidence available?

We want true justified beliefs because beliefs make up our road map of life; they guide our desires. If I believe that I can fly and jump out of the top of the Empire State Building to take a short cut to Columbia University, I'm likely to be disappointed. If I want to live a long life and believe that living on alcohol and poison ivy will enable me to do so, I will not attain my desire.

The importance of having well-justified beliefs is connected with truth-seeking in general. We believe that these two concepts are closely related, so the best way to assure ourselves of having true beliefs is to seek to develop one's belief-forming mechanisms in such ways as to become good judges of various types of evidence, attaining the best possible justification of our beliefs. The value of having the best possible justified beliefs can be defended on both deontological grounds with regard to the individual and on teleological or utilitarian grounds with regard to society as a whole. The deontological argument is connected with our notion of autonomy. To be an autonomous person is to have at one's disposal a high degree of warranted beliefs upon which to base one's actions. There is a tendency to lower one's freedom of choice as one lowers the repertoire of well-justified beliefs regarding a plan of action, and because it is a generally accepted moral principle that it is wrong to lessen one's autonomy or personhood, it is wrong to lessen the degree of justification of one's beliefs on important matters. Hence, there is a general presumption against beliefs by *willing* to have them. Cognitive voliting is a sort of lying or cheating in that it enjoins believing against what has the best guarantee of being the truth. When a friend or doctor lies to a terminally ill patient about her condition, the patient is deprived of the best evidence available for making decisions about her limited future. She is being treated less than fully autonomously. Whereas a form of paternalism may sometimes be justified, there is always a presumption against it and in favor of truth-telling. We even say that the patient has a *right* to know what the evidence points to. Cognitive voliting is a sort of lying to oneself, which, as such, decreases one's own freedom and personhood. It is a type of doxastic suicide that may be justified only in extreme circumstances. If there is something intrinsically wrong about lying (making it *prima facie* wrong), then there is something intrinsically wrong with cognitive voliting, either directly or indirectly. Whether it be Pascal, William James, John Henry Newman, or Søren Kierkegaard, all prescriptive volitionalists (consciously or not) seem to undervalue the principle of truthfulness and its relationship to personal autonomy.

The utilitarian, or teleological, argument against cognitive voliting is fairly straightforward. General truthfulness is a *desideratum* without which society cannot function. Without it language itself would not be possible because it depends on faithful use of words and sentences to stand for appropriately similar objects and states of affairs. Communication depends on a general adherence to accurate reporting. More specifically, it is very important that a society have true beliefs with regard to important issues so that actions that are based on beliefs have a firm basis.

The doctor who cheated her way through medical school and who, as a consequence, lacks appropriate beliefs about certain symptoms may endanger a patient's health. A politician who fails to take into consideration the amount of pollutants being discharged into the air or water by large corporations that support his candidacy may endanger the health and even the lives of his constituents. Even the passer-by who gives wrong information to a stranger who asks for directions may seriously inconvenience the stranger. Here Clifford's point about believing against the evidence is well taken, despite its all-too-robustious tone: the shipowner who failed to make necessary repairs on his vessel and "chose" to believe that the ship was seaworthy is guilty of the deaths of the passengers. "He had no right to believe on such evidence as was before him." It is because beliefs are action-guiding maps by which we steer and, as such, tend to cause actions, that society has a keen interest in our having the best justified beliefs possible regarding important matters.

Some people object to my model of the verific person, the truth-seeker, as being neutral on the matter of religion. They point out that the issue is too important to permit neutrality as an appropriate attitude. Let me clear this up by making a distinction between *neutrality* and *impartiality*. The verific person is not neutral but impartial. For a proper model of the verific person—one seeking to proportion his or her beliefs to the strength of the evidence—consider the referee in an Army vs. Notre Dame football game. The veterans of foreign wars and Army alumni will tend to be biased toward Army, considering close calls against "their" team by the referee as clear instances of poor officiating—even of injustice. Roman Catholics throughout the nation will tend to be biased toward Notre Dame, seeing close calls against "their" team by the referee as clear instances of poor officiating—even of injustice. The neutral person is the atheist pacifist in the crowd—the one who doesn't care who wins the game. But the impartial person is the referee who, knowing that his wife has just bet their family fortune on the underdog, Notre Dame, still manages to call a fair game. He is able to separate his concerns about his financial security from his ability to discern the right calls in appropriate situations. The verific person is one who can be trusted to reach sound judgments where others are driven by bias, prejudice, and self-interest.

If we have a moral duty not to volit but to seek the truth impartially and passionately, then we ought not to obtain religious beliefs by willing to have them; instead we should follow the best evidence we can get.

IV. HOPE AS THE PROPER RELIGIOUS PROPOSITIONAL ATTITUDE FOR DOUBTERS

For those who find it impossible to believe directly that God exists and who follow an ethic of belief acquisition (voliting), hope may be a sufficient substitute for belief. I can hope that God exists without believing that He does.

Let us first analyze the concept of hope in order to determine whether it is a viable option. Consider some examples of hope.

1. Ryan hopes that he will get an A in his philosophy course.
2. Mary hopes that Tom will marry her.
3. Susan hopes that Happy Dancer will win the Kentucky Derby next week.
4. Steve hopes that the Cubs won their game yesterday.
5. Although Bill desires a cigarette, he hopes he will not give into his desire.
6. Christy hopes her saying "no" to Ron's proposal of marriage is the right decision.

If we look closely at these examples of hoping, we can pick out salient features of the concept. First of all, hope involves *belief in the possibility* that a state of affairs obtains or can obtain. We cannot hope for what we believe to be impossible. If Ryan hopes to get an A in philosophy, he must believe that it is possible to do so, and if Mary hopes that Tom will marry her, she must deem it possible. The *Oxford English Dictionary* defines *hope* as an "expectation of something desired," but this seems too strong. Expectation implies belief that something will occur, whereas we may hope even when we do not expect the object to obtain, as when Mary hopes that Tom will marry her or when Steve hopes the languishing Cubs won their game against the awesome Atlanta Braves. Susan may hope that Happy Dancer will win the race even though she doesn't expect that to happen. Thus belief that the object of desire will obtain does not seem necessary for hope. It is enough that the hoper believe that the proposition in question is possible, though not necessarily probable (it has a subjective probability of greater than 0 but not necessarily greater than 0.5).

Second, hope precludes certainty. Mary is not certain that Tom will marry her, and Susan is not certain that Happy Dancer will win the race. There must be an apparent possibility that the state of affairs will not obtain. We would think it odd to say, "Steve knows that the Cubs won the game yesterday, for he was there, but he still hopes that the Cubs won the game." As Paul wrote in Romans 8:24, "For hope that is seen is not hope: for what a man sees, why does he yet hope for?" Hope entails uncertainty, a subjective probability index of greater than 0 but less than 1.

Third, hope entails desire (or a pro-attitude) for the state of affairs in question to obtain or for the proposition to be true. In all of the preceding examples a propositional content can be seen as the object of desire. The states of affairs envisaged evoke a pro-attitude. The subject wants some proposition p to be true. It matters not whether the state of affairs is past (case 4) or present (cases 5 and 6) or future (cases 1 through 3), although it generally turns out, because of the role hope plays in goal orientation, that the state of affairs will be a future situation.

Fourth, the desire involved in hoping must be motivational— greater than mere *wishing*. I may wish to live forever, but if I don't think it is sufficiently probable or possible, it will not serve as a spring for action. I can wish, but not hope, for what I believe to be impossible—as when I wish I were twenty-years-old again. If I hope for some state of affairs to occur, under appropriate circumstances I will do what I can to bring it about—as Ryan will study hard to earn his A in philosophy. Bill's hope that he will not give in to his first-order desire for a cigarette will lead him to strive to reject the weed now being offered to him.

In this regard, hoping involves a willingness to run some risk because of the positive valuation of the object in question. Consider case 3 (Susan hopes Happy Dancer will win the Kentucky Derby). For this to be the case, Susan must be disposed to act in some way as to manifest trust in Happy Dancer. She may bet on the horse without believing he will win the race, and the degree to which she hopes Happy Dancer will win the race may be reflected in how much she is willing to bet.

Fifth, hoping—unlike believing—is typically under our direct control. I may decide to hope that the Cubs will win, but it doesn't make sense to decide to believe that they will win. I hear that my enemy is suffering and find myself hoping that he will suffer great harm. Then I reflect that this *schadenfreude* is a loathsome attitude and decide to change it (to hoping he will suffer only as he deserves!). I may or may not be able to give up a hope, but, unlike a belief, normally I am able to alter the degree to which I hope for something. I may find that I am hoping too strongly that I will get an A—I notice that I am preoccupied with it to the point of distraction—and decide to invest less hope in that goal. It seems that the degree of hope has something to do with cost–benefit analysis about the pay-off involved in obtaining a goal. The greater the combination of the (perceived) probability of p obtaining and the value to me of its obtaining, the more likely I am to hope for p. So reflection on the cost–benefits of p will affect hope. Still, I can exercise some voluntary control over my hopes in a way that I can't over beliefs.

Sixth, hoping—like wanting—is evaluative in a way that believing is not. We may have morally unacceptable hopes, but not morally unacceptable beliefs. Consider the difference between:

i. "I believe that we are heading toward World War III in which nuclear weapons will destroy the world."

and

ii. "I hope that we are heading toward World War III in which nuclear weapons will destroy the world."

Beliefs may be formed through a culpable lack of attention and thus have a moral dimension, but a belief itself cannot be judged moral or immoral. This is applicable to beliefs about racial or gender differences. Sometimes being a "racist" or a "sexist" is defined by holding that people of different races or genders have different native cognitive abilities. The inference is then made that because racism and sexism are immoral, anyone holding these beliefs is immoral. Such beliefs may be false, but unless the believer has obtained the belief through immoral activities, there is nothing immoral in having such beliefs, as such. So either racism and sexism should be defined differently (as immoral actions) or the charge of immorality should be dropped (if it is simply the cognitive feature that is in question).

Finally, we must make a distinction between ordinary hope (such as hoping you will receive a high grade) and deep hope. Consider Susan's situation as she hopes that Happy Dancer will win. She may believe that horse has only a 1-in-10 chance of winning the Kentucky Derby, but she may judge this to be significantly better than the official odds of 100-to-1 against him. Suppose that she has only $10 but wants desperately to enter a professional program that costs $1,000. She has no hope of getting the money elsewhere, and if she bets on Happy Dancer and wins, she will get the required amount. Because she believes that the real odds are better than the official odds and that winning will enable her to get into the professional program, she bets her $10 on the horse. She commits herself to Happy Dancer although she never *believes* that he will win. We might call such cases where one is disposed to risk something significant on the possibility of the proposition's being true *deep* or *profound* hope. When the risk involves something of enormous value, we might call it *desperate* hope.

We conclude, then, that *hoping is distinguished from believing* in that it may involve a strong volitional or affective aspect in a way that believing does not and that, as such, it is subject to moral assessment in a way that believing is not. Hoping is desiderative, but it is more inclined to action than mere wishing. Hope may be ordinary or profound.

Let us apply this distinction to religious faith. Can hope serve as a *type of faith* in a religion like Christianity without the belief that the object of faith exists? Let me tell a story to help focus our discussion.

Suppose that when Moses decides to launch a pre-emptive strike against the Amalekites in obedience to the command of Yahweh (in the book of Exodus in the Hebrew Bible), his brother Aaron doubts whether such a pre-emptive strike is morally right, let alone the command of God. Aaron is inclined to make a treaty with the neighboring tribe. He doubts whether Yahweh has revealed such a command to Moses, doubts whether God appeared to Moses in the burning bush, and wonders whether Moses is hallucinating. When Moses points out that God annihilated the Egyptian pharaoh's army, Aaron is inclined to see that deed as merely the army's getting caught in a flash flood. When Moses offers the fact that a cloud pillar leads them by day and that a pillar of fire leads them by night, Aaron entertains the supposition that the clouds are natural phenomena and the appearance of "fire" is simply the effect of the rays of the setting sun on the distant sands. Aaron is agnostic about both the existence of Yahweh and His "revelation" to Moses. Although he cannot bring himself to overcome his doubts, he opts for the better story. He decides to accept the proposition that Yahweh exists and has revealed himself to Moses, and so he lives according to this hypothesis as an experimental faith. He assists Moses in every way in carrying out the campaign. He proclaims the need for his people to fight against the enemy, helps hold up Moses's arms during the battle, and urges the warriors on to victory in the name of God.

True, Aaron may not act out of spontaneous abandon as Moses does. On the other hand, his scrupulous doubt may help him to notice problems and evidence that might otherwise be neglected and to which the true believer may be impervious. This awareness may signal danger that may be avoided, thus saving the tribe from disaster. Doubt may have as many virtues as belief, although they may be different.

Moses is the true believer, whereas Aaron—the doubter—lives in hope, *profound* hope. He believes that it would be a good thing if Moses's convictions are true and that it is possible that they are true, and so he decides to throw in his lot with his brother, living as if God exists and has revealed his plans to Moses.

The point may be put more simply. Suppose you are fleeing a murderous gang of desperados—perhaps members of the Mafia—who are bent on your annihilation. You come to the edge of a cliff that overlooks a yawning gorge. You find a rope spanning the gorge—tied to a tree on the cliff on the opposite side—and a man who announces that he is a tight-rope walker and can carry you over the gorge on the rope. He doesn't look as if he can do it, so you wonder whether he is insane or simply overconfident. He takes a few steps on the rope to assure you that he can balance himself. You agree that it's possible that he can navigate the rope across the gorge, but you have grave doubts about whether he can carry you. But your options are limited. Soon your pursuers will be upon you. You must decide. Whereas you still don't believe that the "tight-rope walker" can save you, you decide to trust him. You place your faith in his ability, climb on his back, close your eyes (so as not to look down into the yawning gorge), and do your best to relax and obey his commands in adjusting your body as he steps onto the rope. You have a profound, even *desperate,* hope that he will be successful.

This is how I see religious hope functioning in the midst of doubt. The verific person recognizes the tragedy of existence, that unless there is a God and life after death, the meaning of life is less than glorious, but if there is a God and life after death, the meaning of that life is glorious. There is just enough evidence to whet his or her appetite, to inspire hope, a decision to live according to theism or Christianity as an experimental hypothesis, but not enough evidence to cause belief. So keeping his or her mind open, the hoper opts for the better story, gets on the back of what may be the Divine Tight-Rope Walker, and commits to the pilgrimage. Perhaps the analogy is imperfect, for it may be possible to get off the tight-rope walker's back in actual existence and to get back to the cliff. Perhaps the Mafia men make a wrong turn or take their time searching for you. Still, the alternative to the tight-rope walker is not exactly welcoming: death and the extinction of all life in a solar system that will one day be extinguished. We may still learn to enjoy the fruits of finite love and resign ourselves to a final, cold fate. As Russell wrote:

> Brief and powerless is man's life; on him and all his race the slow, sure doom falls pitiless and dark. Blind to good and evil, reckless of destruction, omnipotent matter rolls on its relentless way; for man, condemned today to lose his dearest, tomorrow himself to pass through the gate of darkness, it remains only to cherish, ere yet the blow fall, the lofty thoughts that ennoble his little day; disdaining the coward terrors of the slave of Fate, to worship at the shrine that his own hands have built; undismayed by the empire of chance, to preserve a mind free from the wanton tyranny that rules his outward life; proudly defiant of the irresistible forces that tolerate, for a moment, his knowledge and his condemnation, to sustain alone, a weary but unyielding Atlas, the world that his own ideals have fashioned despite the trampling march of unconscious power.[5]

But if there is some evidence for something better, something eternal, someone benevolent who rules the universe and will redeem the world from evil and despair, isn't it worth betting on that worldview? Shouldn't we, at least, consider getting on the back of the tight-rope walker and letting him carry us across the gorge?

CONCLUSION

1. What's so great about belief? Note that the Epistle of James tells us that belief is insufficient for salvation, for "the devils believe and also tremble" (James 2:19). Note too that the verse quoted by the minister to me as a 15-year-old (Romans 14:23) was taken out of context. The passage reads: "For meat destroy not the work of God. All things are pure; but it is evil for that man who eateth with offense. It is good neither to eat flesh, nor to drink wine, nor any thing whereby thy brother stumbleth, or is offended, or is made weak. Hast thou faith? Have it to thyself before God. Happy is he that condemneth not himself in that thing which he alloweth. And he that doubteth is damned if he eats,

because he eateth not of faith, for whatsoever is not of faith is sin." The passage is not about one's eternal salvation but about eating meat previously offered to idols. Paul is saying, "Let your conscience be your guide here. If your conscience condemns you—if you have doubts about this act— then refrain!"

2. Can we be judged (condemned) for our beliefs? No, not for our beliefs, as such, for they are not things we choose, so we're not (directly) responsible for them; we can be judged only according to what we have responsibly done (ought implies can).

a. We can be judged only for things over which we have control.
b. We only have control over our actions.
c. Beliefs are not actions.
d. Therefore we cannot be judged for our beliefs, but only for our actions.

Although we have some *indirect* control over acquiring beliefs, we ought not violate the ethics of belief and force ourselves to believe more than the evidence warrants.

3. We can be judged by how faithful we have been to the light we have, to how well we have lived, including how well we have impartially sought the truth. We may adopt theism and/or Christianity as experimental faith, living by hope in God, yet keeping our minds open to new evidence that may confirm or disconfirm our decision.

If this argument is sound, the people who truly have faith in God are those who live with moral integrity within their lights—some unbelievers will be in heaven and some religious, true believers, who never doubted, will be absent. My supposition is that they will be in purgatory. What is purgatory? It is a large philosophy department where people who compromised the truth and the good will be taught to think critically and morally, according to the ethics of belief. The faculty, God's servants in truth-seeking, will be David Hume, John Stuart Mill, Voltaire, Immanuel Kant, and Bertrand Russell.

NOTES

1. Whoever desires to be saved must above all things hold the Catholic faith. Unless a man keeps it in its entirety, inviolate, he will assuredly perish eternally. Now this is the Catholic faith, that we worship one God in Trinity and Trinity in unity without either confusing the persons or dividing the substance.... So he who desires to be saved should think thus of the Trinity.

   It is necessary, however, to eternal salvation that he should also faithfully believe in the Incarnation of our Lord Jesus Christ. Now the right faith is that we should believe and confess that our Lord Jesus Christ, the Son of God, is equally both God and man.

   This is the Catholic faith. Unless a man believes it faithfully and steadfastly, he will not be able to be saved. (Athanasian Creed).

2. Most theologians and Christian philosophers hold that belief is a necessary condition for faith. For example, Alvin Plantinga writes, "The mature theist does not typically accept belief in God tentatively or hypothetically or until something better comes along. Nor, I think, does he accept it as a conclusion from other things he believes; he accepts it as basic, as a part of the foundations of his noetic structure. The mature theist commits himself to belief in God: this means that he accepts belief in God as basic." ("Is Belief in God Rational" in *Rationality and Religious Belief*, ed. C. F. Delaney, Notre Dame University Press, 1979, p. 27). See Reading VII.B.2 in this book.

3. Much more needs to be said than can be said here. I have developed a fuller argument against direct volitionalism in my book *What Can We Know?* (Wadsworth Publishing Co., 2001).

4. Many philosophers have criticized Clifford's advice as being self-referentially incoherent. It doesn't have sufficient evidence for itself. But, suitably modified, I think this problem can be overcome. We can give reasons why we ought generally to try to believe according to the evidence, and if these reasons are sound, then we do have sufficient evidence for accepting the principle. See W. K. Clifford, Reading VII.B.2 in this book.

5. Bertrand Russell, "A Free Man's Worship," reading X.3 in this book.

Science, Religion, and Evolution

WHAT IS THE RELATIONSHIP between science and religion? Many think that the relationship is one of conflict: Scientific theories, and the modern scientific worldview, contradict the claims of religion, and so religious believers ought to approach science with a wary and skeptical eye. Others, however, think that the relationship must necessarily be one of concord. All truth is God's truth, some are inclined to say; thus, to the extent that science is (as it seems to be) a way of discovering the truth about the world, it cannot possibly come into conflict with religious truth (whatever the religious truth might happen to be).

The tension (or alleged tension) between science and religion is interesting and important for at least three interconnected reasons. First, scientific and religious beliefs both make a big difference in how we live our lives and in how we interact with others. Medical disasters, environmental disasters, mechanical disasters, new vaccines, better telecommunication equipment, and so on are all caused at least in part by people's beliefs in the domain covered by science. And people have been persecuted, tortured, and killed as a result of people's religious beliefs. They have also benefited from mind-boggling generosity or been subjected to unimaginable cruelty as a result of such beliefs; and, according to many religious believers, one's very eternal destiny depends critically on one's own personal religious beliefs. Second, the methods of science have established an impressive and publicly measurable track record of success as a way of investigating their domain. No method of forming religious belief can make the same claim. Third, taken as a whole, the fields of theology and religion are a lot like philosophy: a mess of disagreement on matters big and small, with arguments typically founded on little more than what seems "obviously to be true" or on what seems to have been "revealed by God (or the gods)." So it is deeply worrisome when science and religion appear to conflict because that seems to suggest that a lot of people (either religious believers of a particular sort or else the scientific establishment) are forming and propagating false beliefs on topics that matter quite a lot. Consider, in this vein, W. K. Clifford's attitude (expressed in essay VII.A.2) toward people like the negligent shipowner, who quite literally put the lives of others in jeopardy because of their sloppy belief-forming habits.

Neither religion nor science is to be treated lightly, and any apparent conflict between them is rightly very disturbing.

For this reason, questions about the relationship between science and religion are receiving a lot of attention in the scientific, philosophical, and theological literature and also in the popular media. Although many questions in this general area deserve our consideration, in the present section we shall focus on just two. (a) What is the nature of the relationship between science and religion? Are they disparate disciplines, irremediably in conflict, or somehow partners in a common quest? (b) Is it the case that, as those in the so-called "Intelligent Design Movement" allege, good science in fact points toward the existence of God or some other sort of intelligent designer? These questions are taken up, respectively, in each of the two sections that follow.

VIII.A   WAYS OF RELATING SCIENCE AND RELIGION

In his 1989–1990 Gifford Lectures, Ian Barbour proposed what has become a widely influential taxonomy of the ways in which science and religion might be thought to relate to one another:

1. *Conflict:* Science and religion investigate common questions, but their theories contradict one another and so compete with one another for our acceptance.
2. *Independence:* Science and religion are separate disciplines addressing distinct, nonoverlapping subjects.
3. *Dialogue:* Science and religion share some common methods and presuppositions, and can fruitfully employ one another's concepts in developing their respective theories.
4. *Integration:* Science and religion are partners in a common quest for a comprehensive understanding of the world, and the theories and results of science can be brought to bear in fruitful ways on the development of theories in theology, and vice versa.

There has been much discussion about whether this fourfold classification is adequate to capture all of the different ways in which science might be thought to relate to religion. (Some have proposed eight- or ninefold classification schemes.) For our purposes, however, it is perhaps more useful to collapse Barbour's taxonomy into just two options: independence and overlap. Some people think that science and religion investigate a common subject matter. Those who do will see at least the possibility for conflict, but they might also hope for a more fruitful sort of interaction—what Barbour might call dialogue or integration. Others think that science and religion investigate wholly different questions. On this view, any apparent conflict is simply the result of misunderstanding the nature and limits of science, the nature and bounds of religion, or both.

We begin with a selection in which Richard Dawkins forcefully articulates an antireligious version of the idea that science and religion overlap in their subject matter but are irremediably in conflict with one another. On Dawkins's view, both science and religion aim at telling us true stories about things like the origin of life, but one of the main differences is that science pursues this aim in a rational and objective way whereas religion does not. The main vice of religion, Dawkins says, is *faith,* and this, he thinks, is a vice that science wholly avoids. Thus, when the theories of science and religion conflict—as they inevitably do—the scientific theories are always to be preferred precisely because they, unlike religious theories, are grounded in evidence rather than faith. There are a lot of questions that one might want to raise about Dawkins's essay, but two rather important ones seem to be these: (a) Is it really true that there is no faith at all involved in believing a scientific theory? and (b) Why is "rational moral *philosophy*" (which Dawkins recommends at the end of his essay as a better alternative to religion) any better off evidentially speaking than religion?

Whereas Dawkins regards religion ultimately as a virulent influence in the world—he characterizes it as a "brain virus"—Stephen Jay Gould regards it as valuable and important as long as it stays within the bounds of its proper *magisterium* (teaching authority). In our second reading in this section, Gould articulates his view that science and religion constitute nonoverlapping realms of teaching authority. Broadly speaking, the proper domain of science is matters of fact, the proper domain of religion is matters of value, and as long as each confines its claims to subjects falling within its proper domain, both will make valuable contributions to human life and human understanding, and there will not even be the appearance of conflict between the two.

Gould, an important and influential paleontologist, speaks as a representative of the magisterium of science, and he cites Pope John Paul II as a representative of the magisterium of religion who shares his view that science and religion do not overlap. However, we have included as our third reading in this section excerpts from two essays by Pope John Paul II that together seem to provide an excellent contrast both to Dawkins's suggestion that conflict is inevitable (religion being, by and large, just bad science) and to Gould's suggestion that the two modes of inquiry concern themselves with wholly nonoverlapping domains. In the first essay, "Lessons from the Galileo Case," John Paul II urges the view that there can be no *true conflict* between science and religion because both are simply different branches of inquiry cooperating in the task of discovering the total truth about the world. To whatever extent there seems to be conflict, then, either science has erred in its reflections upon the relevant empirical data or else religion has gone astray in its understanding of the meaning of divine revelation. However, we can and sometimes do find points of apparent conflict. Thus, for example, in his "Message on Evolution to the Pontifical Academy of Sciences," he notes that certain ways of developing evolutionary theory will contradict Catholic doctrines about the soul and about original sin. In those cases, he argues, Catholic doctrine is to be preferred. But here too caution on both sides is required: The church should look carefully to see whether its understanding of divine revelation has been articulated in the most perspicuous manner or whether the apparent conflict might be avoided by a clearer statement of the relevant doctrines. And one must also be careful to distinguish between those aspects of scientific theory that are virtually undeniable in light of the empirical data and those that, in one way or another, represent rationally contestable extrapolations from the data.

VIII.A.1 Science Versus Religion

RICHARD DAWKINS

Richard Dawkins (1941–   ) is professor of biology at Oxford University and the author of several important books, including *The Selfish Gene* (1976), *The Blind Watchmaker* (1986), and *The God Delusion* (2006). He argues that science is a far more defensible process than religion for securing truth. We begin with two short excerpts from *The Blind Watchmaker* and then move on to his general lecture.

All appearances to the contrary, the only watchmaker in nature is the blind forces of physics, albeit deployed in a very special way. A true watchmaker has foresight; he designs his cogs and springs, and plans their interconnections, with a future in his mind's eye. Natural selection, the blind, unconscious automatic processes that Darwin discovered, and which we now know is the explanation for the existence and apparently purposeful form of all life, has no purpose in mind. It has no mind and no mind's eye. It does not plan for the future. It has no vision, or foresight, no sight at all. If it can be said to play the role of watchmaker in nature, it is the blind watchmaker.

DAWKINS, *The Blind Watchmaker*, Norton, 1986, p. 5

Although atheism might have been logically tenable before Darwin, Darwin made it possible to be an intellectually fulfilled atheist.

op. cit., pp. 6–7

IS SCIENCE A RELIGION?

It is fashionable to wax apocalyptic about the threat to humanity posed by the AIDS virus, "mad cow" disease, and many others, but I think a case can be made that *faith* is one of the world's great evils, comparable to the smallpox virus but harder to eradicate.

Faith, being belief that isn't based on evidence, is the principle vice of any religion. And who,

looking at Northern Ireland or the Middle East, can be confident that the brain virus of faith is not exceedingly dangerous? One of the stories told to young Muslim suicide bombers is that martyrdom is the quickest way to heaven—and not just heaven but a special part of heaven where they will receive their special reward of 72 virgin brides. It occurs to me that our best hope may be to provide a kind of "spiritual arms control": send in specially trained theologians to deescalate the going rate in virgins.

Given the dangers of faith—and considering the accomplishments of reason and observation in the activity called science—I find it ironic that, whenever I lecture publicly, there always seems to be someone who comes forward and says, "Of course, your science is just a religion like ours. Fundamentally, science just comes down to faith, doesn't it?"

Well, science is not religion and it doesn't just come down to faith. Although it has many of religion's virtues, it has none of its vices. Science is based upon verifiable evidence. Religious faith not only lacks evidence, its independence from evidence is its pride and joy, shouted from the rooftops. Why else would Christians wax critical of doubting Thomas? The other apostles are held up to us as exemplars of virtue because faith was enough for them. Doubting Thomas, on the other hand, required evidence. Perhaps he should be the patron saint of scientists.

Transcript of a speech delivered to the American Humanist Association, accepting the award of 1996 Humanist of the Year.

One reason I receive the comment about science being a religion is because I believe in the fact of evolution. I even believe in it with passionate conviction. To some, this may superficially look like faith. But the evidence that makes me believe in evolution is not only overwhelmingly strong; it is freely available to anyone who takes the trouble to read up on it. Anyone can study the same evidence that I have and presumably come to the same conclusion. But if you have a belief that is based solely on faith, I can't examine your reasons. You can retreat behind the private wall of faith where I can't reach you.

Now in practice, of course, individual scientists do sometimes slip back into the vice of faith, and a few may believe so single-mindedly in a favorite theory that they occasionally falsify evidence. However, the fact that this sometimes happens doesn't alter the principle that, when they do so, they do it with shame and not with pride. The method of science is so designed that it usually finds them out in the end.

Science is actually one of the most moral, one of the most honest disciplines around—because science would completely collapse if it weren't for a scrupulous adherence to honesty in the reporting of evidence. (As James Randi has pointed out, this is one reason why scientists are so often fooled by paranormal tricksters and why the debunking role is better played by professional conjurors; scientists just don't anticipate deliberate dishonesty as well.) There are other professions (no need to mention lawyers specifically) in which falsifying evidence or at least twisting it is precisely what people are paid for and get brownie points for doing.

Science, then, is free of the main vice of religion, which is faith. But, as I pointed out, science does have some of religion's virtues. Religion may aspire to provide its followers with various benefits—among them explanation, consolation, and uplift. Science, too, has something to offer in these areas.

Humans have a great hunger for explanation. It may be one of the main reasons why humanity so universally has religion, since religions do aspire to provide explanations. We come to our individual consciousness in a mysterious universe and long to understand it. Most religions offer a cosmology and a biology, a theory of life, a theory of origins, and reasons for existence. In doing so, they demonstrate that religion is, in a sense, science; it's just bad science. Don't fall for the argument that religion and science operate on separate dimensions and are concerned with quite separate sorts of questions. Religions have historically always attempted to answer the questions that properly belong to science. Thus religions should not be allowed now to retreat from the ground upon which they have traditionally attempted to fight. They do offer both a cosmology and a biology; however, in both cases it is false.

Consolation is harder for science to provide. Unlike religion, science cannot offer the bereaved a glorious reunion with their loved ones in the hereafter. Those wronged on this earth cannot, on a scientific view, anticipate a sweet comeuppance for their tormentors in a life to come. It could be argued that, if the idea of an afterlife is an illusion (as I believe it is), the consolation it offers is hollow. But that's not necessarily so; a false belief can be just as comforting as a true one, provided the believer never discovers its falsity. But if consolation comes that cheap, science can weigh in with other cheap palliatives, such as pain-killing drugs, whose comfort may or may not be illusory, but they do work.

Uplift, however, is where science really comes into its own. All the great religions have a place for awe, for ecstatic transport at the wonder and beauty of creation. And it's exactly this feeling of spine-shivering, breath-catching awe—almost worship—this flooding of the chest with ecstatic wonder, that modern science can provide. And it does so beyond the wildest dreams of saints and mystics. The fact that the supernatural has no place in our explanations, in our understanding of so much about the universe and life, doesn't diminish the awe. Quite the contrary. The merest glance through a microscope at the brain of an ant or through a telescope at a long-ago galaxy of a billion worlds is enough to render poky and parochial the very psalms of praise.

Now, as I say, when it is put to me that science or some particular part of science, like evolutionary theory, is just a religion like any other, I usually deny it with indignation. But I've begun to wonder whether perhaps that's the wrong tactic. Perhaps the right tactic is to accept the charge gratefully and demand equal time for science in religious education classes. And the more I think about it, the more I realize that an excellent case could be made for this. So I want to talk a little bit about religious education and the place that science might play in it.

I do feel very strongly about the way children are brought up. I'm not entirely familiar with the way things are in the United States, and what I say may have more relevance to the United Kingdom, where there is state-obliged, legally enforced religious instruction for all children. That's unconstitutional in the United States, but I presume that children are nevertheless given religious instruction in whatever particular religion their parents deem suitable.

Which brings me to my point about mental child abuse. In a 1995 issue of the *Independent,* one of London's leading newspapers, there was a photograph of a rather sweet and touching scene. It was Christmas time, and the picture showed three children dressed up as the three wise men for a nativity play. The accompanying story described one child as a Muslim, one as a Hindu, and one as a Christian. The supposedly sweet and touching point of the story was that they were all taking part in this nativity play.

What is not sweet and touching is that these children were all four years old. How can you possibly describe a child of four as a Muslim or a Christian or a Hindu or a Jew? Would you talk about a four-year-old economic monetarist? Would you talk about a four-year-old neo-isolationist or a four-year-old liberal Republican? There are opinions about the cosmos and the world that children, once grown, will presumably be in a position to evaluate for themselves. Religion is the one field in our culture about which it is absolutely accepted, without question—without even noticing how bizarre it is—that parents have a total and absolute say in what their children are going to be,

how their children are going to be raised, what opinions their children are going to have about the cosmos, about life, about existence. Do you see what I mean about mental child abuse?

Looking now at the various things that religious education might be expected to accomplish, one of its aims could be to encourage children to reflect upon the deep questions of existence, to invite them to rise above the humdrum preoccupations of ordinary life and think sub *specie aleternitatis.*

Science can offer a vision of life and the universe which, as I've already remarked, for humbling poetic inspiration far outclasses any of the mutually contradictory faiths and disappointingly recent traditions of the world's religions.

For example, how could any child in a religious education class fail to be inspired if we could get across to them some inkling of the age of the universe? Suppose that, at the moment of Christ's death, the news of it had started traveling at the maximum possible speed around the universe outwards from the earth? How far would the terrible tidings have traveled by now? Following the theory of special relativity, the answer is that the news could not, under any circumstances whatever, have reached more than one-fiftieth of the way across one galaxy—not one-thousandth of the way to our nearest neighboring galaxy in the 100-million-galaxy strong universe. The universe at large couldn't possibly be anything other than indifferent to Christ, his birth, his passion, and his death. Even such momentous news as the origin of life on Earth could have traveled only across our little local cluster of galaxies. Yet so ancient was that event on our earthly time-scale that, if you span its age with your open arms, the whole of human history, the whole of human culture, would fall in the dust from your fingertip at a single stroke of a nail file.

The argument from design, an important part of the history of religion, wouldn't be ignored in my religious education classes, needless to say. The children would look at the spellbinding wonders of the living kingdoms and would consider Darwinism alongside the creationist alternatives and make up their own minds. I think the children would have no difficulty in making up their minds the right way if presented with the evidence. What worries me is not the question of equal time but that, as far as I can see, children in the United Kingdom and the United States are essentially given *no* time with evolution yet are taught creationism (whether at school, in church, or at home).

It would also be interesting to teach more than one theory of creation. The dominant one in this culture happens to be the Jewish creation myth, which is taken over from the Babylonian creation myth. There are, of course, lots and lots of others, and perhaps they should all be given equal time (except that wouldn't leave much time for studying anything else). I understand that there are Hindus who believe that the world was created in a cosmic butter churn and Nigerian peoples who believe that the world was created by God from the excrement of ants. Surely these stories have as much right to equal time as the Judeo-Christian myth of Adam and Eve.

So much for Genesis; now let's move on to the prophets. Halley's Comet will return without fail in the year 2062. Biblical or Delphic prophecies don't begin to aspire to such accuracy; astrologers and Nostradamians dare not commit themselves to factual prognostications but, rather, disguise their charlatanry in a smokescreen of vagueness. When comets have appeared in the past, they've often been taken as portents of disaster. Astrology has played an important part in various religious traditions, including Hinduism. The three wise men I mentioned earlier were said to have been led to the cradle of Jesus by a star. We might ask the children by what physical route do they imagine the alleged stellar influence on human affairs could travel.

Incidentally, there was a shocking program on the BBC radio around Christmas 1995 featuring an astronomer, a bishop, and a journalist who were sent off on an assignment to retrace the steps of the three wise men. Well, you could understand the participation of the bishop and the journalist (who happened to be a religious writer), but the astronomer was a supposedly respectable astronomy writer,

and yet she went along with this! All along the route, she talked about the portents of when Saturn and Jupiter were in the ascendant up Uranus or whatever it was. She doesn't actually believe in astrology, but one of the problems is that our culture has been taught to become tolerant of it, even vaguely amused by it—so much so that even scientific people who don't believe in astrology sort of think it's a bit of harmless fun. I take astrology very seriously indeed: I think it's deeply pernicious because it undermines rationality, and I should like to see campaigns against it.

When the religious education class turns to ethics, I don't think science actually has a lot to say, and I would replace it with rational moral philosophy. Do the children think there are absolute standards of right and wrong? And if so, where do they come from? Can you make up good working principles of right and wrong, like "do as you would be done by" and "the greatest good for the greatest number" (whatever that is supposed to mean)? It's a rewarding question, whatever your personal morality, to ask as an evolutionist where morals come from; by what route has the human brain gained its tendency to have ethics and morals, a feeling of right and wrong?

Should we value human life above all other life? Is there a rigid wall to be built around the species *Homo sapiens, or* should we talk about whether there are other species which are entitled to our humanistic sympathies? Should we, for example, follow the right-to-life lobby, which is wholly preoccupied with *human* life, and value the life of a human fetus with the faculties of a worm over the life of a thinking and feeling chimpanzee? What is the basis of this fence we erect around *Homo sapiens*—even around a small piece of fetal tissue? (Not a very sound evolutionary idea when you think about it.) When, in our evolutionary descent from our common ancestor with chimpanzees, did the fence suddenly rear itself up?

Well, moving on, then, from morals to last things, to eschatology, we know from the second law of thermodynamics that all complexity, all life, all laughter, all sorrow, is hell-bent on leveling itself out into cold nothingness in the end. They—and we—can never be more than temporary, local buckings of the great universal slide into the abyss of uniformity.

We know that the universe is expanding and will probably expand forever, although it's possible it may contract again. We know that, whatever happens to the universe, the sun will engulf the earth in about 60 million centuries from now.

Time itself began at a certain moment, and time may end at a certain moment—or it may not. Time may come locally to an end in miniature crunches called black holes. The laws of the universe seem to be true all over the universe. Why is this? Might the laws change in these crunches? To be really speculative, time could begin again with new laws of physics, new physical constants. And it has even been suggested that there could be many universes, each one isolated so completely that, for it, the others don't exist. Then again, there might be a Darwinian selection among universes.

So science could give a good account of itself in religious education. But it wouldn't be enough. I believe that some familiarity with the King James versions of the Bible is important for anyone wanting to understand the allusions that appear in English literature. Together with Book of Common Prayer, the Bible gets 58 pages in the *Oxford Dictionary of Quotations*. Only Shakespeare has more. I do think that not having any kind of biblical education is unfortunate if children want to read English literature and understand the provenance of phrases like "through a glass darkly," " all flesh is as grass," "the race is not to the swift," "crying in the wilderness," "reaping the whirlwind," "amid the alien corn," "Eyeless in Gaza," "Job's comforters," and "the widow's mite."

I want to return now to the charge that science is just a faith. The more extreme version of this charge—and one that I often encounter as both a scientist and a rationalist—is an accusation of zealotry and bigotry in scientists themselves as great as that found in religious people. Sometimes there may be a little bit of justice in this accusation; but as zealous bigots, we scientists are mere amateurs at the game. We're content to *argue* with those who disagree with us. We don't kill them.

But I would want to deny even the lesser charge of purely verbal zealotry. There is a very, very important difference between feeling strongly, even passionately, about something because we have thought about and examined the evidence for it on the one hand, and feeling strongly about something because it has been internally revealed to us, or internally revealed to somebody else in history and subsequently hallowed by tradition. There's all the difference in the world between a belief that one is prepared to defend by quoting evidence and logic and a belief that is supported by nothing more than tradition, authority, or revelation.

VIII.A.2   Nonoverlapping Magisteria

STEPHEN JAY GOULD

Stephen Jay Gould (1941–2002) was a leading figure in paleontology, evolutionary biology, and the history of science, and was the author of several important books, both popular and scholarly, on these subjects. He taught at Harvard University and also worked at the

Originally published in *Natural History* (1997, March). Reprinted with permission from the author and *Natural History*. © 1997 The American Museum of Natural History.

American Museum of Natural History. In this essay, he argues that science and religion constitute *nonoverlapping magisteria*—separate domains of teaching authority that are concerned with wholly different subjects of inquiry.

Incongruous places often inspire anomalous stories. In early 1984, I spent several nights at the Vatican housed in a hotel built for itinerant priests. While pondering over such puzzling issues as the intended function of the bidets in each bathroom, and hungering for something other than plum jam on my breakfast rolls (why did the basket only contain hundreds of identical plum packets and not a one of, say, strawberry?), I encountered yet another among the innumerable issues of contrasting cultures that can make life so interesting. Our crowd (present in Rome for a meeting on nuclear winter sponsored by the Pontifical Academy of Sciences) shared the hotel with a group of French and Italian Jesuit priests who were also professional scientists.

At lunch, the priests called me over to their table to pose a problem that had been troubling them. What, they wanted to know, was going on in America with all this talk about "scientific creationism"? One asked me: "Is evolution really in some kind of trouble; and if so, what could such trouble be? I have always been taught that no doctrinal conflict exists between evolution and Catholic faith, and the evidence for evolution seems both entirely satisfactory and utterly overwhelming. Have I missed something?"

A lively pastiche of French, Italian, and English conversation then ensued for half an hour or so, but the priests all seemed reassured by my general answer: Evolution has encountered no intellectual trouble; no new arguments have been offered. Creationism is a homegrown phenomenon of American sociocultural history—a splinter movement (unfortunately rather more of a beam these days) of Protestant fundamentalists who believe that every word of the Bible must be literally true, whatever such a claim might mean. We all left satisfied, but I certainly felt bemused by the anomaly of my role as a Jewish agnostic, trying to reassure a group of Catholic priests that evolution remained both true and entirely consistent with religious belief.

Another story in the same mold: I am often asked whether I ever encounter creationism as a live issue among my Harvard undergraduate students. I reply that only once, in nearly thirty years of teaching, did I experience such an incident. A very sincere and serious freshman student came to my office hours with the following question that had clearly been troubling him deeply: "I am a devout Christian and have never had any reason to doubt evolution, an idea that seems both exciting and particularly well documented. But my roommate, a proselytizing Evangelical, has been insisting with enormous vigor that I cannot be both a real Christian and an evolutionist. So tell me, can a person believe both in God and evolution?" Again, I gulped hard, did my intellectual duty, and reassured him that evolution was both true and entirely compatible with Christian belief—a position I hold sincerely, but still an odd situation for a Jewish agnostic.

These two stories illustrate a cardinal point, frequently unrecognized but absolutely central to any understanding of the status and impact of the politically potent, fundamentalist doctrine known by its self-proclaimed oxymoron as "scientific creationism"—the claim that the Bible is literally true, that all organisms were created during six days of twenty-four hours, that the earth is only a few thousand years old, and that evolution must therefore be false. Creationism does not pit science against religion (as my opening stories indicate), for no such conflict exists. Creationism does not raise any unsettled intellectual issues about the nature of biology or the history of life. Creationism is a local and parochial movement, powerful only in the United States among Western nations, and prevalent only among the few sectors of American Protestantism that choose to read the Bible as an inerrant document, literally true in every jot and tittle.

I do not doubt that one could find an occasional nun who would prefer to teach creationism in her parochial school biology class, or an occasional orthodox rabbi who does the same in his yeshiva, but creationism based on biblical literalism makes little sense in either Catholicism or Judaism, for neither religion maintains any extensive tradition for reading the Bible as literal truth rather than illuminating literature, based partly on metaphor and allegory (essential components of all good writing) and demanding interpretation for proper understanding. Most Protestant groups, of course, take the same position—the fundamentalist fringe notwithstanding.

The position that I have just outlined by personal stories and general statements represents the standard attitude of all major Western religions (and of Western science) today. (I cannot, through ignorance, speak of Eastern religions, although I suspect that the same position would prevail in most cases.) The lack of conflict between science and religion arises from a lack of overlap between their respective domains of professional expertise—science in the empirical constitution of the universe, and religion in the search for proper ethical values and the spiritual meaning of our lives. The attainment of wisdom in a full life requires extensive attention to both domains—for a great book tells us that the truth can make us free and that we will live in optimal harmony with our fellows when we learn to do justly, love mercy, and walk humbly.

In the context of this standard position, I was enormously puzzled by a statement issued by Pope John Paul II on October 22, 1996, to the Pontifical Academy of Sciences, the same body that had sponsored my earlier trip to the Vatican. In this document, entitled "Truth Cannot Contradict Truth," the pope defended both the evidence for evolution and the consistency of the theory with Catholic religious doctrine. Newspapers throughout the world responded with front-page headlines, as in the *New York Times* for October 25: "Pope Bolsters Church's Support for Scientific View of Evolution."

Now I know about "slow news days," and I do admit that nothing else was strongly competing for headlines at that particular moment. (The *Times* could muster nothing more exciting for a lead story than Ross Perot's refusal to take Bob Dole's advice and quit the presidential race.) Still, I couldn't help feeling immensely puzzled by all the attention paid to the pope's statement (while being wryly pleased, of course, for we need all the good press we can get, especially from respected outside sources). The Catholic Church had never opposed evolution and had no reason to do so. Why had the pope issued such a statement at all? And why had the press responded with an orgy of worldwide, front-page coverage?

I could only conclude at first, and wrongly as I soon learned, that journalists throughout the world must deeply misunderstand the relationship between science and religion, and must therefore be elevating a minor papal comment to unwarranted notice. Perhaps most people really do think that a war exists between science and religion, and that (to cite a particularly newsworthy case) evolution must be intrinsically opposed to Christianity. In such a context, a papal admission of evolution's legitimate status might be regarded as major news indeed—a sort of modern equivalent for a story that never happened, but would have made the biggest journalistic splash of 1640: Pope Urban VIII releases his most famous prisoner from house arrest and humbly apologizes, "Sorry, Signor Galileo...the sun, er, is central."

But I then discovered that the prominent coverage of papal satisfaction with evolution had not been an error of non-Catholic Anglophone journalists. The Vatican itself had issued the statement as a major news release. And Italian newspapers had featured, if anything, even bigger headlines and longer stories. The conservative *Il Giornale*, for example, shouted from its masthead: "Pope Says We May Descend from Monkeys."

Clearly, I was out to lunch. Something novel or surprising must lurk within the papal statement, but what could it be?—especially given the accuracy of my primary impression (as I later verified) that the Catholic Church values scientific study, views science as no threat to religion in general or Catholic doctrine in particular, and has long accepted both the legitimacy of evolution as a field of study and the potential harmony of evolutionary conclusions with Catholic faith.

As a former constituent of Tip O'Neill's, I certainly know that "all politics is local"—and that the Vatican undoubtedly has its own internal reasons, quite opaque to me, for announcing papal support of evolution in a major statement. Still, I knew that I was missing some important key, and I felt frustrated. I then remembered the primary rule of intellectual life: when puzzled, it never hurts to read the primary documents—a rather simple and self-evident principle that has, nonetheless, completely disappeared from large sectors of the American experience.

I knew that Pope Pius XII (not one of my favorite figures in twentieth-century history, to say the least) had made the primary statement in a 1950 encyclical entitled *Humani Generis*. I knew the main thrust of his message: Catholics could believe whatever science determined about the evolution of the human body, so long as they accepted that, at some time of his choosing, God had infused the soul into such a creature. I also knew that I had no problem with this statement, for whatever my private beliefs about souls, science cannot touch such a subject and therefore cannot be threatened by any theological position on such a legitimately and intrinsically religious issue. Pope Pius XII, in other words, had properly acknowledged and respected the separate domains of science and theology. Thus, I found myself in total agreement with *Humani Generis*—but I had never read the document in full (not much of an impediment to stating an opinion these days).

I quickly got the relevant writings from, of all places, the Internet. (The pope is prominently on-line, but a Luddite like me is not. So I got a computer-literate associate to dredge up the documents. I do love the fracture of stereotypes implied by finding religion so hep and a scientist so square.) Having now read in full both Pope Pius's *Humani Generis* of 1950 and Pope John Paul's proclamation of October 1996, I finally understand why the recent statement seems so new, revealing, and worthy of all those headlines.

And the message could not be more welcome for evolutionists and friends of both science and religion.

The text of *Humani Generis* focuses on the magisterium (or teaching authority) of the Church—a word derived not from any concept of majesty or awe but from the different notion of teaching, for *magister* is Latin for "teacher." We may, I think, adopt this word and concept to express the central point of this essay and the principled resolution of supposed "conflict" or "warfare" between science and religion. No such conflict should exist because each subject has a legitimate magisterium, or domain of teaching authority—and these magisteria do not overlap (the principle that I would like to designate as NOMA, or "nonoverlapping magisteria"). The net of science covers the empirical universe: what is it made of (fact) and why does it work this way (theory). The net of religion extends over questions of moral meaning and value. These two magisteria do not overlap, nor do they encompass all inquiry (consider, for starters, the magisterium of art and the meaning of beauty). To cite the arch clichés, we get the age of rocks, and religion retains the rock of ages; we study how the heavens go, and they determine how to go to heaven.

This resolution might remain all neat and clean if the nonoverlapping magisteria (NOMA) of science and religion were separated by an extensive no man's land. But, in fact, the two magisteria bump right up against each other, interdigitating in wondrously complex ways along their joint border. Many of our deepest questions call upon aspects of both for different parts of a full answer—and the sorting of legitimate domains can become quite complex and difficult. To cite just two broad questions involving both evolutionary facts and moral arguments: Since evolution made us the only earthly creatures with advanced consciousness, what responsibilities are so entailed for our relations with other species? What do our genealogical ties with other organisms imply about the meaning of human life?

Pius XII's *Humani Generis* is a highly traditionalist document by a deeply conservative man forced to face all the "isms" and cynicisms that rode the wake of World War II and informed the struggle to rebuild human decency from the ashes of the Holocaust. The encyclical, subtitled "Concerning some false opinions which threaten to undermine the foundations of Catholic doctrine," begins with a statement of embattlement:

> Disagreement and error among men on moral and religious matters have always been a cause of profound sorrow to all good men, but above all to the true and loyal sons of the Church, especially today, when we see the principles of Christian culture being attacked on all sides.

Pius lashes out, in turn, at various external enemies of the Church: pantheism, existentialism, dialectical materialism, historicism, and of course and preeminently, communism. He then notes with sadness that some well-meaning folks within the Church have fallen into a dangerous relativism—"a theological pacifism and egalitarianism, in which all points of view become equally valid"—in order to include people of wavering faith who yearn for the embrace of Christian religion but do not wish to accept the particularly Catholic magisterium.

What is this world coming to when these noxious novelties can so discombobulate a revealed and established order? Speaking as a conservative's conservative, Pius laments:

> Novelties of this kind have already borne their deadly fruit in almost all branches of theology.... Some question whether angels are personal beings, and whether matter and spirit differ essentially.... Some even say that the doctrine of Transubstantiation, based on an antiquated philosophic notion of substance, should be so modified that the Real Presence of Christ in the Holy Eucharist be reduced to a kind of symbolism.

Pius first mentions evolution to decry a misuse by overextension often promulgated by zealous supporters of the anathematized "isms":

> Some imprudently and indiscreetly hold that evolution...explains the origin of all things.... Communists gladly subscribe to this opinion so that, when the souls of men have been deprived of every idea of a personal God,

they may the more efficaciously defend and propagate their dialectical materialism.

Pius's major statement on evolution occurs near the end of the encyclical in paragraphs 35 through 37. He accepts the standard model of NOMA and begins by acknowledging that evolution lies in a difficult area where the domains press hard against each other. "It remains for US now to speak about those questions which, although they pertain to the positive sciences, are nevertheless more or less connected with the truths of the Christian faith."[1]

Pius then writes the well-known words that permit Catholics to entertain the evolution of the human body (a factual issue under the magisterium of science), so long as they accept the divine Creation and infusion of the soul (a theological notion under the magisterium of religion).

> The Teaching Authority of the Church does not forbid that, in conformity with the present state of human sciences and sacred theology, research and discussions, on the part of men experienced in both fields, take place with regard to the doctrine of evolution, in as far as it inquires into the origin of the human body as coming from pre-existent and living matter—for the Catholic faith obliges us to hold that souls are immediately created by God.

I had, up to here, found nothing surprising in *Humani Generis,* and nothing to relieve my puzzlement about the novelty of Pope John Paul's recent statement. But I read further and realized that Pope Pius had said more about evolution, something I had never seen quoted, and that made John Paul's statement most interesting indeed. In short, Pius forcefully proclaimed that while evolution may be legitimate in principle, the theory, in fact, had not been proven and might well be entirely wrong. One gets the strong impression, moreover, that Pius was rooting pretty hard for a verdict of falsity.

Continuing directly from the last quotation, Pius advises us about the proper study of evolution:

> However, this must be done in such a way that the reasons for both opinions, that is, those

favorable and those unfavorable to evolution, be weighed and judged with the necessary seriousness, moderation and measure....Some, however, rashly transgress this liberty of discussion, when they act as if the origin of the human body from pre-existing and living matter were already completely certain and proved by the facts which have been discovered up to now and by reasoning on those facts, and as if there were nothing in the sources of divine revelation which demands the greatest moderation and caution in this question.

To summarize, Pius generally accepts the NOMA principle of nonoverlapping magisteria in permitting Catholics to entertain the hypothesis of evolution for the human body so long as they accept the divine infusion of the soul. But he then offers some (holy) fatherly advice to scientists about the status of evolution as a scientific concept: the idea is not yet proven, and you all need to be especially cautious because evolution raises many troubling issues right on the border of my magisterium. One may read this second theme in two different ways: either as a gratuitous incursion into a different magisterium or as a helpful perspective from an intelligent and concerned outsider. As a man of good will, and in the interest of conciliation, I am happy to embrace the latter reading.

In any case, this rarely quoted second claim (that evolution remains both unproven and a bit dangerous)—and not the familiar first argument for the NOMA principle (that Catholics may accept the evolution of the body so long as they embrace the creation of the soul)—defines the novelty and the interest of John Paul's recent statement.

John Paul begins by summarizing Pius's older encyclical of 1950, and particularly by reaffirming the NOMA principle—nothing new here, and no cause for extended publicity:

> In his encyclical "Humani Generis" (1950), my predecessor Pius XII had already stated that there was no opposition between evolution and the doctrine of the faith about man and his vocation.

To emphasize the power of NOMA, John Paul poses a potential problem and a sound resolution:

How can we reconcile science's claim for physical continuity in human evolution with Catholicism's insistence that the soul must enter at a moment of divine infusion:

> With man, then, we find ourselves in the presence of an ontological difference, an ontological leap, one could say. However, does not the posing of such ontological discontinuity run counter to that physical continuity which seems to be the main thread of research into evolution in the field of physics and chemistry? Consideration of the method used in the various branches of knowledge makes it possible to reconcile two points of view which would seem irreconcilable. The sciences of observation describe and measure the multiple manifestations of life with increasing precision and correlate them with the time line. The moment of transition to the spiritual cannot be the object of this kind of observation.

The novelty and news value of John Paul's statement lies, rather, in his profound revision of Pius's second and rarely quoted claim that evolution, while conceivable in principle and reconcilable with religion, can cite little persuasive evidence, and may well be false. John Paul states—and I can only say amen, and thanks for noticing—that the half century between Pius's surveying the ruins of World War II and his own pontificate heralding the dawn of a new millennium has witnessed such a growth of data, and such a refinement of theory, that evolution can no longer be doubted by people of good will:

> Pius XII added...that this opinion [evolution] should not be adopted as though it were a certain, proven doctrine....Today, almost half a century after the publication of the encyclical, new knowledge has led to the recognition of more than one hypothesis in the theory of evolution. It is indeed remarkable that this theory has been progressively accepted by researchers, following a series of discoveries in various fields of knowledge. The convergence, neither sought nor fabricated, of the results of work that was conducted independently is in itself a significant argument in favor of the theory.

In conclusion, Pius had grudgingly admitted evolution as a legitimate hypothesis that he regarded as only tentatively supported and potentially (as I suspect he hoped) untrue. John Paul, nearly fifty years later, reaffirms the legitimacy of evolution under the NOMA principle—no news here—but then adds that additional data and theory have placed the factuality of evolution beyond reasonable doubt. Sincere Christians must now accept evolution not merely as a plausible possibility but also as an effectively proven fact. In other words, official Catholic opinion on evolution has moved from "say it ain't so, but we can deal with it if we have to" (Pius's grudging view of 1950) to John Paul's entirely welcoming "it has been proven true; we always celebrate nature's factuality, and we look forward to interesting discussions of theological implications." I happily endorse this turn of events as gospel—literally *good news.* I may represent the magisterium of science, but I welcome the support of a primary leader from the other major magisterium of our complex lives. And I recall the wisdom of King Solomon: "As cold waters to a thirsty soul, so is good news from a far country" (Prov. 25:25).

Just as religion must bear the cross of its hard-liners, I have some scientific colleagues, including a few prominent enough to wield influence by their writings, who view this rapprochement of the separate magisteria with dismay. To colleagues like me—agnostic scientists who welcome and celebrate the rapprochement, especially the pope's latest statement—they say: "C'mon, be honest; you know that religion is addlepated, superstitious, old-fashioned b.s.; you're only making those welcoming noises because religion is so powerful, and we need to be diplomatic in order to assure public support and funding for science." I do not think that this attitude is common among scientists, but such a position fills me with dismay—and I therefore end this essay with a personal statement about religion, as a testimony to what I regard as a virtual consensus among thoughtful scientists (who support the NOMA principle as firmly as the pope does).

I am not, personally, a believer or a religious man in any sense of institutional commitment or practice. But I have enormous respect for religion, and the subject has always fascinated me, beyond almost all others (with a few exceptions, like evolution, paleontology, and baseball). Much of this fascination lies in the historical paradox that throughout. Western history organized religion has fostered both the most unspeakable horrors and the most heart-rending examples of human goodness in the face of personal danger. (The evil, I believe, lies in the occasional confluence of religion with secular power. The Catholic Church has sponsored its share of horrors, from Inquisitions to liquidations—but only because this institution held such secular power during so much of Western history. When my folks held similar power more briefly in Old Testament times, they committed just as many atrocities with many of the same rationales.)

I believe, with all my heart, in a respectful, even loving concordat between our magisteria—the NOMA solution. NOMA represents a principled position on moral and intellectual grounds, not a mere diplomatic stance. NOMA also cuts both ways. If religion can no longer dictate the nature of factual conclusions properly under the magisterium of science, then scientists cannot claim higher insight into moral truth from any superior knowledge of the world's empirical constitution. This mutual humility has important practical consequences in a world of such diverse passions.

Religion is too important to too many people for any dismissal or denigration of the comfort still sought by many folks from theology. I may, for example, privately suspect that papal insistence on divine infusion of the soul represents a sop to our fears, a device for maintaining a belief in human superiority within an evolutionary world offering no privileged position to any creature. But I also know that souls represent a subject outside the magisterium of science. My world cannot prove or disprove such a notion, and the concept of souls cannot threaten or impact my domain. Moreover, while I cannot personally accept the Catholic view of souls, I surely honor the metaphorical value of such a concept both for grounding moral discussion and for expressing what we most value about human potentiality: our decency, care, and all the ethical and intellectual struggles that the evolution of consciousness imposed upon us.

As a moral position (and therefore not as a deduction from my knowledge of nature's factuality), I prefer the "cold bath" theory that nature can be truly "cruel" and "indifferent"—in the utterly inappropriate terms of our ethical discourse—because nature was not constructed as our eventual abode, didn't know we were coming (we are, after all, interlopers of the latest geological microsecond), and doesn't give a damn about us (speaking metaphorically). I regard such a position as liberating, not depressing, because we then become free to conduct moral discourse—and nothing could be more important—in our own terms, spared from the delusion that we might read moral truth passively from nature's factuality.

But I recognize that such a position frightens many people, and that a more spiritual view of nature retains broad appeal (acknowledging the factuality of evolution and other phenomena, but still seeking some intrinsic meaning in human terms, and from the magisterium of religion). I do appreciate, for example, the struggles of a man who wrote to the *New York Times* on November 3, 1996, to state both his pain and his endorsement of John Paul's statement:

> Pope John Paul II's acceptance of evolution touches the doubt in my heart. The problem of pain and suffering in a world created by a God who is all love and light is hard enough to bear, even if one is a creationist. But at least a creationist can say that the original creation, coming from the hand of God was good, harmonious, innocent and gentle. What can one say about evolution, even a spiritual theory of evolution? Pain and suffering, mindless cruelty and terror are its means of creation. Evolution's engine is the grinding of predatory teeth upon the screaming, living flesh and bones of prey. . . . If evolution be true, my faith has rougher seas to sail.

I don't agree with this man, but we could have a wonderful argument. I would push the "cold bath" theory; he would (presumably) advocate the theme of inherent spiritual meaning in nature, however opaque the signal. But we would both be enlightened and filled with better understanding of these deep and ultimately unanswerable issues. Here, I believe, lies the greatest strength and necessity of NOMA, the nonoverlapping magisteria of science and religion. NOMA permits—indeed enjoins—the prospect of respectful discourse, of constant input from both magisteria toward the common goal of wisdom. If human beings are anything special, we are the creatures that must ponder and talk. Pope John Paul II would surely point out to me that his magisterium has always recognized this distinction, for *in principio erat verbum*—"In the beginning was the Word."

Postscript

Carl Sagan organized and attended the Vatican meeting that introduces this essay; he also shared my concern for fruitful cooperation between the different but vital realms of science and religion. Carl was also one of my dearest friends. I learned of his untimely death on the same day that I read the proofs for this essay. I could only recall Nehru's observations on Gandhi's death—that the light had gone out, and darkness reigned everywhere. But I then contemplated what Carl had done in his short sixty-two years and remembered John Dryden's ode for Henry Purcell, a great musician who died even younger: "He long ere this had tuned the jarring spheres, and left no bell below."

The days I spent with Carl in Rome were the best of our friendship. We delighted in walking around the Eternal City, feasting on its history and architecture—and its food! Carl took special delight in the anonymity that he still enjoyed in a nation that had not yet aired Cosmos, the greatest media work in popular science of all time.

I dedicate this essay to his memory. Carl also shared my personal suspicion about the nonexistence of souls—but I cannot think of a better reason for hoping we are wrong than the prospect of spending eternity roaming the cosmos in friendship and conversation with this wonderful soul.

NOTE

1. Interestingly, the main thrust of these paragraphs does not address evolution in general but lies in refuting a doctrine that Pius calls "polygenism," or the notion of human ancestry from multiple parents—for he regards such an idea as incompatible with the doctrine of original sin, "which proceeds from a sin actually committed by an individual Adam and which, through generation, is passed on to all and is in everyone as his own." In this one instance, Pius may be transgressing the NOMA principle—but I cannot judge, for I do not understand the details of Catholic theology and therefore do not know how symbolically such a statement may be read. If Pius is arguing that we cannot entertain a theory about derivation of all modern humans from an ancestral population rather than through an ancestral individual (a potential fact) because such an idea would question the doctrine or original sin (a theological construct), then I would declare him out of line for letting the magisterium of religion dictate a conclusion within the magisterium of science.

VIII.A.3   Faith and Science: Lessons from the Galileo Case and Message on Evolution

POPE JOHN PAUL II

Pope John Paul II, originally Karol Józef Wojtyla (1920–2005), served as Pope of the Roman Catholic Church from 1978 until his death in 2005. The present selection consists of two of his more important addresses on the relationship between faith and science: *Lessons from the Galileo Case* (1992) and *Message on Evolution to the Pontifical Academy of Sciences* (1996). In these essays, he argues that although there can be no true conflict between religion and science, apparent conflicts sometimes do arise. When that happens, we must take care to be sure that divine revelation has been properly interpreted and understood, but we must also distinguish between those aspects of scientific theory that report the observed data and those that, in one way or another, go beyond the data.

FAITH CAN NEVER CONFLICT WITH REASON

[. . .]

5. A twofold question is at the heart of the debate of which Galileo was the centre. The first is of the epistemological order and concerns biblical hermeneutics. In this regard, two points must again be raised. In the first place, like most of his adversaries, Galileo made no distinction between the scientific approach to natural phenomena and a reflection on nature, of the philosophical order, which that approach generally calls for. That is why he rejected the suggestion made to him to present the Copernican system as a hypothesis, inasmuch as it had not been confirmed by irrefutable proof. Such therefore, was an exigency

of the experimental method of which he was the inspired founder.

Secondly, the geocentric representation of the world was commonly admitted in the culture of the time as fully agreeing with the teaching of the Bible of which certain expressions, taken literally seemed to affirm geocentrism. The problem posed by theologians of that age was, therefore, that of the compatibility between heliocentrism and Scripture.

Thus the new science, with its methods and the freedom of research which they implied, obliged theologians to examine their own criteria of scriptural interpretation. Most of them did not know how to do so.

Paradoxically, Galileo, a sincere believer, showed himself to be more perceptive in this regard than the theologians who opposed him. "If Scripture cannot err," he wrote to Benedetto Castelli, "certain of its interpreters and commentators can and do so in many ways."[1] We also know of his letter to Christine de Lorraine (1615) which is like a short treatise on biblical hermeneutics.[2]

6. From this we can now draw our first conclusion. The birth of a new way of approaching the study of natural phenomena demands a clarification on the part of all disciplines of knowledge. It obliges them to define more clearly their own field, their approach, their methods, as well as the precise import of their conclusions. In other words, this new way requires each discipline to become more rigorously aware of its own nature.

The upset caused by the Copernican system thus demanded epistemological reflection on the biblical sciences, an effort which later would produce abundant fruit in modern exegetical works and which has found sanction and a new stimulus in the Dogmatic Constitution *Dei Verbum* of the Second Vatican Council.

7. The crisis that I have just recalled is not the only factor to have had repercussions on biblical interpretation. Here we are concerned with the second aspect of the problem, its pastoral dimension.

By virtue of her own mission, the Church has the duty to be attentive to the pastoral consequences of her teaching. Before all else, let it be clear that this teaching must correspond to the truth. But it is a question of knowing how to judge a new scientific datum when it seems to contradict the truths of faith. The pastoral judgement which the Copernican theory required was difficult to make, in so far as geocentrism seemed to be a part of scriptural teaching itself. It would have been necessary all at once to overcome habits of thought and to devise a way of teaching capable of enlightening the people of God. Let us say, in a general way, that the pastor ought to show a genuine boldness, avoiding the double trap of a hesitant attitude and of hasty judgement, both of which can cause considerable harm.

8. Another crisis, similar to the one we are speaking of, can be mentioned here. In the last century and at the beginning of our own, advances in the historical sciences made it possible to acquire a new understanding of the Bible and of the biblical world. The rationalist context in which these data were most often presented seemed to make them dangerous to the Christian faith. Certain people, in their concern to defend the faith, thought it necessary to reject firmly-based historical conclusions. That was a hasty and unhappy decision. The work of a pioneer like Fr. Lagrange was able to make the necessary discernment on the basis of dependable criteria.

It is necessary to repeat here what I said above. It is a duty for theologians to keep themselves regularly informed of scientific advances in order to examine if such be necessary, whether or not there are reasons for taking them into account in their reflection or for introducing changes in their teaching.

9. If contemporary culture is marked by a tendency to scientism, the cultural horizon of Galileo's age was uniform and carried the imprint of a particular philosophical formation. The unitary character of culture, which in itself is positive and desirable even in our own day, was one of the reasons for Galileo's condemnation. The majority of theologians did not recognize the formal distinction between Sacred Scripture and its interpretation, and this led them unduly to transpose into the realm of

the doctrine of the faith a question which in fact pertained to scientific investigation.

In fact, as Cardinal Poupard has recalled, Robert Bellarmine, who had seen what was truly at stake in the debate personally felt that, in the face of possible scientific proofs that the earth orbited round the sun, one should "interpret with great circumspection" every biblical passage which seems to affirm that the earth is immobile and "say that we do not understand, rather than affirm that what has been demonstrated is false."[3] Before Bellarmine, this same wisdom and same respect for the divine Word guided St Augustine when he wrote: "If it happens that the authority of Sacred Scripture is set in opposition to clear and certain reasoning, this must mean that the person who interprets Scripture does not understand it correctly. It is not the meaning of Scripture which is opposed to the truth but the meaning which he has wanted to give to it. That which is opposed to Scripture is not what is in Scripture but what he has placed there himself, believing that this is what Scripture meant."[4] A century ago, Pope Leo XIII echoed this advice in his Encyclical *Providentissimus Deus:* "Truth cannot contradict truth and we may be sure that some mistake has been made either in the interpretation of the sacred words, or in the polemical discussion itself."[5]

Cardinal Poupard has also reminded us that the sentence of 1633 was not irreformable, and that the debate which had not ceased to evolve thereafter, was closed in 1820 with the imprimatur given to the work of Canon Settele.[6]

10. From the beginning of the Age of Enlightenment down to our own day, the Galileo case has been a sort of "myth," in which the image fabricated out of the events was quite far removed from reality. In this perspective, the Galileo case was the symbol of the Church's supposed rejection of scientific progress, or of "dogmatic" obscurantism opposed to the free search for truth. This myth has played a considerable cultural role. It has helped to anchor a number of scientists of good faith in the idea that there was an incompatibility between the spirit of science and its

rules of research on the one hand and the Christian faith on the other. A tragic mutual incomprehension has been interpreted as the reflection of a fundamental opposition between science and faith. The clarifications furnished by recent historical studies enable us to state that this sad misunderstanding now belongs to the past.

11. From the Galileo affair we can learn a lesson which remains valid in relation to similar situations which occur today and which may occur in the future.

In Galileo's time, to depict the world as lacking an absolute physical reference point was, so to speak, inconceivable. And since the cosmos, as it was then known, was contained within the solar system alone, this reference point could only be situated in the earth or in the sun. Today, after Einstein and within the perspective of contemporary cosmology neither of these two reference points has the importance they once had. This observation, it goes without saying, is not directed against the validity of Galileo's position in the debate; it is only meant to show that often, beyond two partial and contrasting perceptions, there exists a wider perception which includes them and goes beyond both of them.

12. Another lesson which we can draw is that the different branches of knowledge call for different methods. Thanks to his intuition as a brilliant physicist and by relying on different arguments, Galileo, who practically invented the experimental method, understood why only the sun could function as the centre of the world, as it was then known, that is to say, as a planetary system. The error of the theologians of the time, when they maintained the centrality of the earth, was to think that our understanding of the physical world's structure was, in some way, imposed by the literal sense of Sacred Scripture. Let us recall the celebrated saying attributed to Baronius "Spiritui Sancto mentem fuisse nos docere quomodo ad coelum eatur, non quomodo coelum gradiatur." In fact, the Bible does not concern itself with the details of the physical world, the understanding of which is the competence of human experience and reasoning. There exist two realms of

knowledge, one which has its source in Revelation and one which reason can discover by its own power. To the latter belong especially the experimental sciences and philosophy. The distinction between the two realms of knowledge ought not to be understood as opposition. The two realms are not altogether foreign to each other, they have points of contact. The methodologies proper to each make it possible to bring out different aspects of reality....

MAGISTERIUM IS CONCERNED WITH QUESTION OF EVOLUTION FOR IT INVOLVES CONCEPTION OF MAN

Science at the Dawn of the Third Millenium

[...]

3. Before offering a few more specific reflections on the theme of the origin of life and evolution, I would remind you that the magisterium of the Church has already made some pronouncements on these matters, within her own proper sphere of competence. I will cite two such interventions here.

In his encyclical *Humani Generis* (1950), my predecessor Pius XII has already affirmed that there is no conflict between evolution and the doctrine of the faith regarding man and his vocation, provided that we do not lose sight of certain fixed points.

For my part, when I received the participants in the plenary assembly of your Academy on October 31, 1992, I used the occasion—and the example of Galileo—to draw attention to the necessity of using a rigorous hermeneutical approach in seeking a concrete interpretation of the inspired texts. It is important to set proper limits to the understanding of Scripture, excluding any unseasonable interpretations which would make it mean something which it is not intended to mean. In order to mark out the limits of their own proper fields, theologians and those working on the exegesis of the Scripture need to be well informed regarding the results of the latest scientific research.

Evolution and the Church's Magisterium

4. Taking into account the scientific research of the era, and also the proper requirements of theology, the encyclical *Humani Generis* treated the doctrine of "evolutionism" as a serious hypothesis, worthy of investigation and serious study, alongside the opposite hypothesis. Pius XII added two methodological conditions for this study: one could not adopt this opinion as if it were a certain and demonstrable doctrine, and one could not totally set aside the teaching Revelation on the relevant questions. He also set out the conditions on which this opinion would be compatible with the Christian faith—a point to which I shall return.

Today, more than a half-century after the appearance of that encyclical, some new findings lead us toward the recognition of evolution as more than an hypothesis. In fact it is remarkable that this theory has had progressively greater influence on the spirit of researchers, following a series of discoveries in different scholarly disciplines. The convergence in the results of these independent studies—which was neither planned nor sought—constitutes in itself a significant argument in favor of the theory.

What is the significance of a theory such as this one? To open this question is to enter into the field of epistemology. A theory is a meta-scientific elaboration, which is distinct from, but in harmony with, the results of observation. With the help of such a theory a group of data and independent facts can be related to one another and interpreted in one comprehensive explanation. The theory proves its validity by the measure to which it can be verified. It is constantly being tested against the facts; when it can no longer explain these facts, it shows its limits and its lack of usefulness, and it must be revised.

Moreover, the elaboration of a theory such as that of evolution, while obedient to the need for consistency with the observed data, must also involve importing some ideas from the philosophy of nature.

And to tell the truth, rather than speaking about the theory of evolution, it is more accurate to speak of the theories of evolution. The use of the plural is required here—in part because of the diversity of explanations regarding the mechanism of evolution, and in part because of the diversity of philosophies involved. There are materialist and reductionist theories, as well as spiritualist theories. Here the final judgment is within the competence of philosophy and, beyond that, of theology.

5. The magisterium of the Church takes a direct interest in the question of evolution, because it touches on the conception of man, whom Revelation tells us is created in the image and likeness of God. The conciliar constitution *Gaudium et Spes* has given us a magnificent exposition of this doctrine, which is one of the essential elements of Christian thought. The Council recalled that "man is the only creature on earth that God wanted for its own sake." In other words, the human person cannot be subordinated as a means to an end, or as an instrument of either the species or the society; he has a value of his own. He is a person. By this intelligence and his will, he is capable of entering into relationship, of communion, of solidarity, of the gift of himself to others like himself. St. Thomas observed that man's resemblance to God resides especially in his speculative intellect, because his relationship with the object of his knowledge is like God's relationship with his creation. (*Summa Theologica* I-II, q 3, a 5, ad 1) But even beyond that, man is called to enter into a loving relationship with God himself, a relationship which will find its full expression at the end of time, in eternity. Within the mystery of the risen Christ the full grandeur of this vocation is revealed to us. (*Gaudium et Spes,* 22) It is by virtue of his eternal soul that the whole person, including his body, possesses such great dignity. Pius XII underlined the essential point: if the origin of the human body comes through living matter which existed previously, the spiritual soul is created directly by God ("animas enim a Deo immediate creari catholica fides non retimere iubet"). (*Humani Generis*)

As a result, the theories of evolution which, because of the philosophies which inspire them, regard the spirit either as emerging from the forces of living matter, or as a simple epiphenomenon of that matter, are incompatible with the truth about man. They are therefore unable to serve as the basis for the dignity of the human person.

6. With man, we find ourselves facing a different ontological order—an ontological leap, we could say. But in posing such a great ontological discontinuity, are we not breaking up the physical continuity which seems to be the main line of research about evolution in the fields of physics and chemistry? An appreciation for the different methods used in different fields of scholarship allows us to bring together two points of view which at first might seem irreconcilable. The sciences of observation describe and measure, with ever greater precision, the many manifestations of life, and write them down along the time-line. The moment of passage into the spiritual realm is not something that can be observed in this way—although we can nevertheless discern, through experimental research, a series of very valuable signs of what is specifically human life. But the experience of metaphysical knowledge, of self-consciousness and self-awareness, of moral conscience, of liberty, or of aesthetic and religious experience—these must be analyzed through philosophical reflection, while theology seeks to clarify the ultimate meaning of the Creator's designs. . . .

NOTES

1. Letter of 21 November 1613, in *Edizione nazionale delle Opere de Galileo Galilei*, dir. A. Favaro, edition of 1968, vol. V. p. 282.
2. Letter to Christine de Lorraine, 1615, in *Edizione nazionale delle Opere de Galileo Galilei,* dir. A Favaro, edition of 1968, vol. V, pp. 307–348.
3. Letter to Fr A. Foscarini, 12 April 1615, cf. *Edizione nazionale delle Opere de Galileo Galilei*, dir. A. Favaro, edition of 1968, vol. XII, p. 172.
4. Saint Augustine, *Espitula* 143, n. 7 PL 33, col. 588.
5. Leonis XIII Pont. Max. Acta, vol. XIII (1894), p. 361. Cf. Pontificia Academia Scientiarum Copernico, Galilei e la Chiesa. Fine della controversia (1820). Gli atti del Sant'Ufficio, a cura di W. Brandmuller e E. J. Griepl, Firenze, Olschki, 1992.

VIII.B   EVOLUTION, NATURALISM, AND INTELLIGENT DESIGN

In Part One of this book, we looked at William Paley's argument from design, an argument that reasons to the existence of a designer from the fact that some things in the world *appear* to be products of design. Organisms, for example, are complex, and their parts are functionally organized, just like the parts of machines. So, Paley argued, just like machines, organisms must be the products of design. As we noted, however, Darwinian evolutionary theory throws a wrench into this argument. For evolutionary theory tells a story according to which, given world enough and time, complex objects with functionally organized parts can come into existence as a result of purely natural processes, wholly apart from the activity of any sort of designer.

There have been, broadly speaking, two main lines of response to the Darwinian objection to Paley's argument. One response has been to try to debunk evolutionary theory altogether. The chief proponents of this response have been the so-called "creation-scientists"—writers such as Henry Morris, Duane Gish, Jonathan Sarfati, Ken Ham, and others associated with both the Institute for Creation Research and Answers in Genesis. On their view, evolutionary theory is fatally flawed, the product of bad science. Moreover, good science actually supports rather than contradicts a fairly literal reading of the creation story found in *Genesis*, the first book of the Hebrew and Christian scriptures. Nevertheless, although it is hard to deny the *possibility* that science might move beyond evolutionary theory—just as science has moved beyond other highly successful paradigms—the arguments of the creation-scientists have been largely unsuccessful and, indeed, rarely taken seriously in the academy.[1]

The other response, represented in various ways by the readings that follow, has been to shift the focus of attention onto other alleged empirical evidence of design in the universe. As just noted, Paley's argument from design cited biological complexity and functional organization as the evidence from which we infer the existence of a designer. His argument was vulnerable to attack by Darwinians precisely because Darwinian evolutionary theory purports to explain Paley's evidence without appealing to a designer. But proponents of the *fine-tuning* argument from design (see selection I.C.4), as well as leading figures in the Intelligent Design movement, insist that there is other evidence of design that isn't adequately explained either by Darwinian evolutionary theory or by any other extant scientific theory. Moreover, Alvin Plantinga and others have argued that, contrary to common opinion, there is in fact a sort of interesting tension between evolutionary theory and *atheism*. If this argument is sound, then, oddly enough, evolutionary theory itself may point in the direction of a designer.

The fine-tuning argument is, at present, the most widely discussed and respected of the alleged empirical arguments for the existence of a designer. Since that argument has already been discussed in Part I of this book, however, we omit it from this section. Thus, the first four readings focus on some of the most important arguments arising out of the Intelligent Design movement, and the final two readings address Alvin Plantinga's widely discussed argument for the conclusion that, far from undermining belief in God, evolutionary theory actually undermines certain brands of atheism.

We begin in this section with an article by William Dembski outlining the central ideas of his work on the detection of design. On Dembski's view, design is an empirically detectable property, and so there is no in-principle obstacle to detecting a cosmic designer by way of scientific investigation.

That design is empirically detectable is undeniable. Plagiarism, for example, is a common intellectual crime on college campuses, and it is typically fairly easy to detect. But, of course, the empirical detection of plagiarism is, in large part, the empirical detection of design. For constructing a case in support of the conclusion that Student X plagiarized her paper will involve, among other things, constructing a case for the conclusion that X's paper resembles some source material S *by design* rather than by chance. Note too that the case for the conclusion that X plagiarized her paper will appeal (as in the fine-tuning argument) to the fact that it is vastly *improbable* that X's paper match the source S by chance, but that the odds of a match are not all that slim on the design hypothesis. The match therefore constitutes evidence of design.

But now an important question arises: We don't *always* infer design from improbability. You take a trip to Spain, for example. While you are walking through the streets of Madrid, you bump into an old friend—one you haven't seen or heard from in years and who happens (like you) to be in Spain only for the weekend. What are the odds of this happening? Very slim indeed. But, of course, you won't feel forced to conclude that your meeting was arranged by an intelligent designer. Likewise, lottery winners don't feel forced to conclude that they won only because the lottery was rigged in their favor. The improbable happens all the time, and we quite often think that it is perfectly rational to chalk such events up to chance. Why not, then, in the case of apparent plagiarism? Is it just that the odds of X's paper matching the source are much slimmer than the odds of your bumping into an old friend while wandering about in Spain? Or is there some other difference?

This is precisely the question that Dembski aims to address in our first reading. On his view, the improbable outcomes that warrant design inferences are just those that are *specified*. Very roughly, a specified complex (improbable) event is one that conforms to an independently established pattern. Had someone predicted that you would bump into your friend in Spain, that event would have conformed to an independent "specification." One would then rightly suspect design of some sort. (How else could a prediction like that be made?) Likewise, the match between X's paper and the source S seems to be an instance of specified complexity: The event (the material on the paper) matches an independently specified "pattern" (the source, S); and the precise arrangement of words and so on that constitutes the event is very improbable.

On Dembski's view, the sort of fine-tuning discussed by Robin Collins (selection I.C.4) is also an instance of specified complexity warranting a design inference. So too is the property of *irreducible complexity* discussed in our second reading by Michael Behe. According to Behe, some, but not all, biological structures have the property of being such that (a) they are composed of interacting parts, (b) they have some particular function, and (c) the removal of any part would render the structure nonfunctional. Having these three features is what it is for something to be irreducibly complex. And, on Behe's view, the interesting thing about irreducibly complex structures is that they cannot be produced by the sorts of *gradual* processes posited by Darwinian evolutionary theory. Or, at any rate, it is vastly improbable that they be produced by such processes. Thus, he thinks, the existence of such structures constitutes a decisive objection against Darwinian evolutionary theory. Unlike the scientific creationists, Behe doesn't argue that science points toward a literal reading of *Genesis*, nor does he seem to think that science points toward a paradigm radically different from evolutionary theory. Rather, his conclusion seems to be more modest: Purely naturalistic, or Darwinian, versions of evolutionary theory cannot account for irreducibly complex structures. Thus, at the very least, whatever else one says about evolutionary theory, room must somehow be made for the activity of a designer to account for the existence of such structures.

The arguments of Behe and Dembski have received a great deal of attention, both in the popular media and in the scholarly literature. The two readings that follow theirs represent some of the better, more persuasive criticisms of their work. Against Behe, Philip Kitcher argues (among other things) that Behe's argument rests on the presupposition that precursors to irreducibly complex structures would have to look the way the structure itself would look if you simply subtracted one of its parts. But, Kitcher argues, there's no reason to think that Darwinian evolutionary theory is committed to that presupposition. Thus, he writes:

> What Darwinism is committed to (at most) is the idea that modifications of DNA sequence (insertions, deletions, base changes, translocations) could yield a sequence of organisms culminating in a bacterium with a flagellum [one of Behe's examples of an irreducibly complex structure], with selective advantages for the later member of each adjacent pair. To work out what the members of this sequence of organisms might have been like, our ideas should be educated by the details of how the flagellum is actually assembled and the loci in the bacterial genome that are involved. Until we know these things, it's quite likely that any efforts to describe precursors or intermediates will be whistling in the dark. Behe's examples cunningly exploit our ability to give a molecular analysis of the end product and our ignorance of the molecular details of how it is produced.[2]

Against Dembski, Michael Murray argues that Dembski's criteria for detecting design are fatally flawed. Furthermore, he argues that contrary to what Dembski and other leading figures in the intelligent Design Movement claim, there is good reason to doubt that Intelligent Design Theory represents anything like a viable scientific research program.

Finally, in the last two readings of this section, we turn to a different sort of argument—Alvin Plantinga's argument for the conclusion that if we think that our cognitive faculties are reliable, then we ought not to accept both evolutionary theory and naturalism (which he characterizes as the view that there is no God or any other supernatural entity). Here is a highly simplified version of the argument:

1. If there is no God, Darwinian evolutionary theory is probably correct.
2. Darwinian evolutionary theory says that . . .
   a. . . . our minds came into existence as a result of chance processes
   b. . . . our minds are the way they are because they produce *behavior* that contributes to survival
3. But: You don't need *true beliefs* to survive.
4. And: The odds of creatures with minds that can form true beliefs (about anything) coming into existence as a result of chance processes are astronomically small.
5. So: Belief in Darwinian evolutionary theory gives us good reason to think that it's unlikely that our minds are able to produce true beliefs.

6. So: A naturalist—someone who believes that there is no God or any other sort of supernatural entity—has good reason to doubt everything she believes (including naturalism and the Darwinian theory of evolution).

7. It is irrational to believe something you have good reason to doubt.

8. So: It is irrational to accept naturalism.

If Plantinga is right, then, surprisingly, those who take themselves to be rationally committed to some form of evolutionary theory ought to *reject* naturalism and embrace some theistic version of evolutionary theory.

In our sixth and final reading in this section, Michael Bergmann raises objections against Plantinga's evolutionary argument against naturalism.

NOTES

1. Interested readers might want to look at Jonathan Sarfati's *Refuting Evolution* (2000) for an up-to-date and, in some respects, improved summary and defense of the main arguments of the creation-scientists, and at Philip Kitcher's *Abusing Science: The Case against Creationism* (1982) for a thorough and trenchant critique of their views.

2. Philip Kitcher, *Abusing Science: The Case against Creationism* (1992).

VIII.B.1   Signs of Intelligence: A Primer on the Detection of Intelligent Design

WILLIAM DEMBSKI

William Dembski (1960–   ) is research professor of philosophy at Southwestern Baptist Theological Seminary. He holds doctoral degrees in mathematics and philosophy and a master's degree in theology. His works include *The Design Inference* (1988), *No Free Lunch* (2001), and *The Design Revolution* (2004), and he is one of the leading figures in the Intelligent Design movement. In this essay, Dembski lays out the central tenets of his views about how to detect intelligent design.

Intelligent design examines the distinction between three modes of explanation: necessity, chance, and design. In our workaday lives we find it important to distinguish between these modes of explanation. Did she fall or was she pushed? And if she fell, was it simply bad luck or was her fall unavoidable? More generally, given an event, object, or structure, we want to know:

1. Did it have to happen?
2. Did it happen by accident?
3. Did an intelligent agent cause it to happen?

Given an event to be explained, the first thing to determine is whether it had to happen. If so, the event is necessary. By "necessary" I don't just mean logically necessary, as in true across all possible worlds, but I also include physical necessity, as in a law-like relation between antecedent circumstances and consequent events. Not all events are necessary.

Events that happen but do not have to happen are said to be contingent. In our everyday lives we distinguish two types of contingency:

From William Dembski and James Kushiner (eds.), *Signs of Intelligence: Understanding Intelligent Design* (Grand Rapids, MI: Brazos Press, 2001). © 2001 by The Fellowship of St. James. Used with permission. Notes deleted.

one blind, the other directed. A blind contingency lacks a superintending intelligence and is usually characterized by probabilities. Blind contingency is another name for chance. A directed contingency, on the other hand, is the result of a superintending intelligence. Directed contingency is another name for design.

AN ANCIENT QUESTION

This characterization of necessity, chance, and design is pretheoretical and therefore inadequate for building a precise scientific theory of design. We therefore need to inquire whether there is a principled way to distinguish these modes of explanation. Philosophers and scientists have disagreed not only about how to distinguish these modes of explanation, but also about their very legitimacy. The Epicureans, for instance, gave pride of place to chance. The Stoics, on the other hand, emphasized necessity and design, but rejected chance. In the Middle Ages, Moses Maimonides contended with the Islamic interpreters of Aristotle who viewed the heavens as, in Maimonides's words, "the necessary result of natural laws." Where the Islamic philosophers saw necessity, Maimonides saw design.

In arguing for design in his *Guide for the Perplexed*, Maimonides looked to the irregular distribution of stars in the heavens. For him that irregularity demonstrated contingency. But was that contingency the result of chance of design? Neither Maimonides nor the Islamic interpreters of Aristotle had any use for Epicurus and his views on chance. For them chance could never be fundamental but was at best a placeholder for ignorance. Thus for Maimonides and his Islamic colleagues, the question was whether a principled distinction could be drawn between necessity and design. Maimonides, arguing from observed contingency in nature, said yes. The Islamic philosophers, intent on keeping Aristotle pure of theology, said no.

A MODERN DEMISE

Modern science has also struggled with how to distinguish between necessity, chance, and design. Newtonian mechanics, construed as a set of deterministic physical laws, seemed only to permit necessity. Nonetheless, in the General Scholium to his *Principia*, Newton claimed that the stability of the planetary system depended not only on the regular action of the universal law of gravitation, but also on the precise initial positioning of the planets and comets in relation to the sun. As he explained: "Though these bodies may, indeed, persevere in their orbits by the mere laws of gravity, yet they could by no means have at first derived the regular position of the orbits themselves from those laws. . . . [Thus] this most beautiful system of the sun, planets, and comets, could only proceed from the counsel and dominion of an intelligent and powerful being." Like Maimonides, Newton saw both necessity and design as legitimate explanations, but gave short shrift to chance.

Newton published his *Principia* in the seventeenth century. By the nineteenth century, necessity was still in, chance was still out, but design had lost much of its appeal. When asked by Napoleon where God fit into his equations of celestial mechanics, astronomer and mathematician Laplace famously replied, "Sire, I have no need of that hypothesis." In place of a designing intelligence that precisely positioned the heavenly bodies, Laplace proposed his nebular hypothesis, which accounted for the origin of the solar system strictly as the result of natural gravitational forces.

Since Laplace's day, science has largely dispensed with design. Certainly Darwin played a crucial role here by eliminating design from biology. Yet at the same time science was dispensing with design, it was also dispensing with Laplace's vision of a deterministic universe (recall Laplace's famous demon who could predict the future and retrodict the past with perfect precision provided that present positions and momenta of particles were fully known). With the rise of statistical mechanics and then quantum mechanics, the role of chance in physics came to be regarded as ineliminable. Consequently, a deterministic, necessitarian universe has given way to a stochastic universe in which chance and necessity are both regarded as fundamental modes of scientific explanation, neither being reducible to the other. To sum up, contemporary science allows a principled distinction between necessity and chance, but repudiates design.

BACON AND ARISTOTLE

But was science right to repudiate design? My aim in *The Design Inference* is to rehabilitate design. I argue that design is a legitimate and fundamental mode of scientific explanation on a par with chance and necessity. Since my aim is to rehabilitate design, it will help to review why design was removed from science in the first place. Design, in the form of Aristotle's formal and final causes, after all, had once occupied a perfectly legitimate role within natural philosophy, or what we now call science. With the rise of modern science, however, these causes fell into disrepute.

We can see how this happened by considering Francis Bacon. Bacon, a contemporary of Galileo and Kepler, though himself not a scientist, was a terrific propagandist for science. Bacon was concerned about the proper conduct of science and provided detailed canons for experimental observation, the recording of data, and drawing inferences from data. What interests us here, however, is what he did with Aristotle's four causes. For Aristotle, to understand any phenomenon properly, one had to understand its four causes, namely its material, efficient, formal, and final cause.

Two points about Aristotle's causes are relevant to this discussion. First, Aristotle gave equal weight to all four causes and would have regarded any inquiry that omitted one of his causes as fundamentally deficient. Second, Bacon adamantly opposed the inclusion of formal and final causes within science (see his *Advancement of Learning*). For Bacon, formal and final causes belonged to metaphysics and not to science. Science, according to Bacon, needed to limit itself to material and efficient causes, thereby freeing science from the sterility that inevitably results when science and metaphysics are conflated. This was Bacon's line, and he argued it forcefully.

We see Bacon's line championed in our own day. For instance, in his book *Chance and Necessity*, biologist and Nobel laureate Jacques Monod argued that chance and necessity alone suffice to account for every aspect of the universe. Now whatever else we might want to say about chance and necessity, they provide at best a reductive account of Aristotle's formal causes and leave no room for Aristotle's final causes. Indeed, Monod explicitly denies any place for purpose within science.

Now I don't want to give the impression that I'm advocating a return to Aristotle's theory of causation. There are problems with Aristotle's theory, and it needed to be replaced. My concern, however, is with what replaced it. By limiting scientific inquiry to material and efficient causes, which are of course, perfectly compatible with chance and necessity, Bacon championed a view of science that could only end up excluding design.

THE DESIGN INSTINCT

But suppose we lay aside *a priori* prohibitions against design. In that case, what is wrong with explaining something as designed by an intelligent agent? Certainly there are many everyday occurrences that we explain by appealing to design. Moreover, in our daily lives it is absolutely crucial to distinguish accident from design. We demand answers to such questions as: Did she fall or was she pushed? Did someone die accidentally or commit suicide? Was this song conceived independently or was it plagiarized? Did someone just get lucky on the stock market or was there insider trading?

Not only do we demand answers to such questions, but entire industries are also devoted to drawing the distinction between accident and design. Here we can include forensic science, intellectual property law, insurance claims investigation, cryptography, and random number generation—to name but a few. Science itself needs to draw this distinction to keep itself honest. As a January 1998 issue of *Science* made clear, plagiarism and data falsification are far more common in science than we would like to admit. What keeps these abuses in check is our ability to detect them.

If design is so readily detectable outside of science, and if its detectability is one of the key factors keeping scientists honest, why should design be barred from the actual content of science? There's a worry here. The worry is that when we leave the constricted domain of human artifacts and enter the unbounded domain of scientific inquiry, the distinction between design and nondesign cannot be reliably drawn. Consider, for instance, the following remark by Darwin in the concluding chapter of his *Origin of Species:*

> Several eminent naturalists have of late published their belief that a multitude of reputed species in each genus are not real species; but that other species are real, that is, have been independently created....Nevertheless they do not pretend that they can define, or even conjecture, which are the created forms of life, and which are those produced by secondary laws. They admit variation as a *vera causa* in one case, they arbitrarily reject it in another, without assigning any distinction in the two cases.

It's this worry of falsely attributing something to design (here construed as creation) only to have it overturned later, that has prevented design from entering science proper.

This worry, though perhaps understandable in the past, can no longer be justified. There does in fact exist a rigorous criterion for discriminating intelligently from unintelligently caused objects. Many special sciences already use this criterion, though in a pretheoretic form (e.g., forensic science, artificial intelligence, cryptography, archeology, and the search for extraterrestrial intelligence). In *The Design Inference* I identify and make precise this criterion. I call it the *complexity-specification criterion.* When intelligent agents act, they leave behind a characteristic trademark or signature—what I call *specified complexity.* The complexity-specification criterion detects design by identifying this trademark of designed objects.

THE COMPLEXITY-SPECIFICATION CRITERION

A detailed explanation and justification of the complexity-specification criterion is technical and can be found in *The Design Inference.* Nevertheless, the basic idea is straightforward and easily illustrated. Consider how the radio astronomers in the movie *Contact* detected an extraterrestrial intelligence. This movie, based on a novel by Carl Sagan, was an enjoyable piece of propaganda for the SETI research program—the Search for

Extraterrestrial Intelligence. To make the movie interesting, the SETI researchers in *Contact* actually did find an extraterrestrial intelligence (the nonfictional SETI program has yet to be so lucky).

How, then, did the SETI researchers in *Contact* convince themselves that they had found an extraterrestrial intelligence? To increase their chances of finding an extraterrestrial intelligence, SETI researchers monitor millions of radio signals from outer space. Many natural objects in space produce radio waves (e.g., pulsars). Looking for signs of design among all these naturally produced radio signals is like looking for a needle in a haystack. To sift through the haystack, SETI researchers run the signals they monitor through computers programmed with pattern-matchers. So long as a signal doesn't match one of the preset patterns, it will pass through the pattern-matching sieve (and that even if it has an intelligent source). If, on the other hand, it does match one of these patterns, then, depending on the pattern matched, the SETI researchers may have cause for celebration.

The SETI researchers in *Contact* did find a signal worthy of celebration, namely the following:

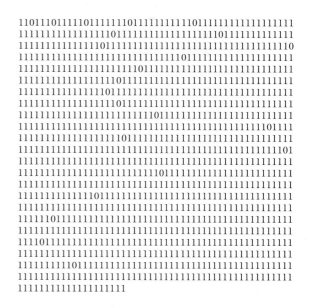

The SETI researchers in *Contact* received this signal as a sequence of 1,126 beats and pauses, where 1s correspond to beats and 0s to pauses. This sequence represents the prime numbers from 2 to 101, where a given prime number is

represented by the corresponding number of beats (i.e., 1s), and the individual prime numbers are separated by pauses (i.e., 0s). The SETI researchers in *Contact* took this signal as decisive confirmation of an extraterrestrial intelligence.

What is it about this signal that implicates design? Whenever we infer design, we must establish three things: *contingency, complexity,* and *specification*. Contingency ensures that the object in question is not the result of an automatic and therefore unintelligent process that had no choice in its production. Complexity ensures that the object is not so simple that it can readily be explained by chance. Finally, specification ensures that the object exhibits the type of pattern characteristic of intelligence. Let us examine these three requirements more closely.

Contingency

In practice, to establish the contingency of an object, event, or structure, one must establish that it is compatible with the regularities involved in its production, but that these regularities also permit any number of alternatives to it. Typically these regularities are conceived as natural laws or algorithms. By being compatible with but not required by the regularities involved in its production, an object, event, or structure becomes irreducible to any underlying physical necessity. Michael Polanyi and Timothy Lenoir have both described this method of establishing contingency.

The method applies quite generally: the position of Scrabble pieces on a Scrabble board is irreducible to the natural laws governing the motion of Scrabble pieces; the configuration of ink on a sheet of paper is irreducible to the physics and chemistry of paper and ink; the sequencing of DNA bases is irreducible to the bonding affinities between the bases; and so on. In the case at hand, the sequence of 0s and 1s to form a sequence of prime numbers is irreducible to the laws of physics that govern the transmission of radio signals. We therefore regard the sequence as contingent.

Complexity

To see next why complexity is crucial for inferring design, consider the following sequence of bits:

110111011111

These are the first twelve bits in the previous sequence representing the prime numbers 2, 3, and 5 respectively. Now it is a sure bet that no SETI researcher, if confronted with this twelve-bit sequence, is going to contact the science editor at the *New York Times*, hold a press conference, and announce that an extraterrestrial intelligence has been discovered. No headline is going to read, "Aliens Master First Three Prime Numbers!"

The problem is that this sequence is much too short (and thus too simple) to establish that an extraterrestrial intelligence with knowledge of prime numbers produced it. A randomly beating radio source might by chance just happen to produce this sequence. A sequence of 1,126 bits representing the prime numbers from 2 to 101; however, is a different story. Here the sequence is sufficiently long (and therefore sufficiently complex) to allow that an extraterrestrial intelligence could have produced it.

Complexity as I am describing it here is a form of probability. (Later in this essay I will require a more general conception of complexity to unpack the logic of design inferences. But for now complexity as a form of probability is all we need.) To see the connection between complexity and probability, consider a combination lock. The more possible combinations of the lock, the more complex the mechanism, and, correspondingly, the more improbable that the mechanism can be opened by chance. Complexity and probability therefore vary inversely: the greater the complexity, the smaller the probability. Thus to determine whether something is sufficiently complex to warrant a design inference is to determine whether it has sufficiently complex to warrant a design inference is to determine whether it has sufficiently small probability.

Even so, complexity (or improbability) isn't enough to eliminate chance and establish design. If I flip a coin one thousand times, I'll participate in a highly complex (i.e., highly improbable) event. Indeed, the sequence I end up flipping will be one in a trillion trillion trillion..., where the ellipsis indicates twenty-two more "trillions." This sequence of coin tosses won't, however, trigger a design inference. Though complex, this sequence won't exhibit a suitable pattern. Contrast this with the previous sequence representing the prime numbers from 2 to 101. Not only is this sequence complex, but it also embodies a suitable pattern. The SETI researcher who in the movie *Contact* discovered this sequence put it this way: "This isn't noise; this has structure."

Specification

What is a *suitable* pattern for inferring design? Not just any pattern will do. Some patterns can legitimately be employed to infer design whereas others cannot. The intuition underlying the distinction between patterns that alternately succeed or fail to implicate design is, however, easily motivated. Consider the case of an archer. Suppose an archer stands fifty meters from a large wall with bow and arrow in hand. The wall is sufficiently large that the archer cannot help but hit it. Now suppose each time the archer shoots an arrow at the wall, the archer paints a target around the arrow so that the arrow sits squarely in the bull's-eye. What can be concluded from this scenario? Absolutely nothing about the archer's ability as an archer. Yes, a pattern is being matched, but it is a pattern fixed only after the arrow has been shot. The pattern is thus purely *ad hoc*.

But suppose instead the archer paints a fixed target on the wall and then shoots at it. Suppose the archer shoots a hundred arrows, and each time hits a perfect bull's-eye. What can be concluded from this second scenario? Confronted with this second scenario we are obligated to infer that here is a world-class archer, one whose shots cannot legitimately be referred to luck, but rather must be referred to the archer's skill and mastery. Skill and mastery are of course instances of design.

The archer example introduces three elements that are essential for inferring design:

1. A reference class of possible events (here the arrow hitting the wall at some unspecified place);
2. A pattern that restricts the reference class of possible events (here a target on the wall); and
3. The precise event that has occurred (here the arrow hitting the wall at some precise location).

In a design inference, the reference class, the pattern, and the event are linked, with the pattern mediating between event and reference class, and

helping to decide whether the event is due to chance or design. Note that in determining whether an event is sufficiently improbable or complex to implicate design, the relevant improbability is not that of the precise event that occurred, but that of the target/pattern. Indeed, the bigger the target, the easier it is to hit it by chance and thus apart from design.

The type of pattern in which an archer fixes a target first and then shoots at it is common to statistics, where it is known as setting a *rejection region* prior to an experiment. In statistics, if the outcome of an experiment falls within a rejection region, the chance hypothesis supposedly responsible for the outcome is rejected. The reason for setting a rejection region prior to an experiment is to forestall what statisticians call "data snooping" or "cherry picking." Just about any data set will contain strange and improbable patterns if we look hard enough. By forcing experimenters to set their rejection regions prior to an experiment, the statistician protects the experiment from spurious patterns that could just as well result from chance.

Now a little reflection makes clear that a pattern need not be given prior to an event to eliminate chance and implicate design. Consider the following cipher text:

nfuijolt ju jt mjlf b xfbtfm

Initially this looks like a random sequence of letters and spaces—you lack any pattern for rejecting chance and inferring design.

But suppose that someone comes along and tells you to treat this sequence as a Caesar cipher, moving each letter one notch down the alphabet. Now the sequence reads,

methinks it is like a weasel

Even though the pattern (in this case, the decrypted text) is given after the fact, it still is the right sort of pattern for eliminating chance and inferring design. In contrast to statistics, which always identifies its patterns before an experiment is performed, cryptanalysis must discover its patterns after the fact. In both instances, however, the patterns are suitable for inferring design.

Patterns thus divide into two types: those that in the presence of complexity warrant a design inference and those that, despite the presence of complexity, do not warrant a design inference. The first type of pattern I call a *specification,* the second a *fabrication.* Specifications are the non-*ad hoc* patterns that can legitimately be used to eliminate chance and warrant a design inference. In contrast, fabrications are the *ad hoc* patterns that cannot legitimately be used to warrant a design inference.

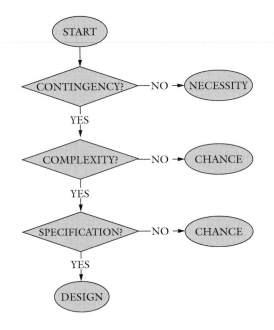

To sum up, the complexity-specification criterion detects design by establishing three things: contingency, complexity, and specification. When called to explain an event, object, or structure, we have to decide: Are we going to attribute it to *necessity, chance,* or *design?* According to the complexity-specification criterion, to answer this question is to answer three simpler questions: Is it contingent? Is it complex? Is it specified? Consequently, the complexity-specification criterion can be represented as a flowchart with three decision nodes. I call this flowchart the Explanatory Filter.

INDEPENDENT PATTERNS ARE DETACHABLE

For a pattern to count as a specification, the important thing is not when it was identified, but whether in a certain well-defined sense it is *independent* of the event it describes. Drawing a target around an arrow already embedded in a wall is not independent of the arrow's trajectory. Consequently, such a target/pattern cannot be used to attribute the arrow's trajectory to design. Patterns that are specifications cannot simply be read off the events whose design is in question. Rather, to count as specifications, patterns must be suitably independent of events. I refer to this relation of independence as *detachability,* and say that a pattern is detachable only if it satisfies that relation.

Detachability can be understood as asking this question: Given an event (whose design is in question) and a pattern describing it, would we be able to construct that pattern if we had no knowledge of which event occurred? Assume an event has occurred. A pattern describing the event is given. The event is one from a range of possible events. If all we knew was the range of possible events without any specifics about which event actually occurred, could we still construct the pattern describing the event? If so, the pattern is detachable from the event.

A TRICK WITH COINS

To see what's at stake, consider the following example. (It was this example that finally clarified for me what transforms a pattern *simpliciter* into a pattern *qua* specification.) The following event E to all appearances was obtained by flipping a fair coin one hundred times:

```
THTTTHHTHHTTTTTHTHTTHHHTTHTHHHTH
HTTTTTTTHTTHTTTHHTHTTTHTHTHTHHTTHH
HTTTHTTHHTHTHTHHHHTTHHTHHHHTHHH
HTT                                      E
```

Is E the product of chance or not? A standard trick of statistics professors with an introductory statistics class is to divide the class in two and have students in one half of the class each flip a coin one hundred times and write down the sequence of heads and tails on a slip of paper; students in the other half each generate with their minds a "random-looking" string that mimics the tossing of a coin one hundred times and also write down the sequence of heads and tails on a slip of paper. When the students then hand in their slips of paper, it is the professor's job to sort the papers into two piles, those generated by flipping a fair coin, and those concocted in the students' heads. To the amazement of the students, the statistics professor is typically able to sort the papers with 100 percent accuracy.

There's no mystery here. The statistics professor simply looks for a repetition of six or seven heads or tails in a row to distinguish the truly random from the pseudo-random sequences. In a hundred coin flips, one is quite likely to see such a repetition. On the other hand, people concocting pseudo-random sequences with their minds tend to alternate between heads and tails too frequently. Whereas with a truly random sequence of coin tosses there is a 50 percent chance that one toss will differ from the next, as a matter of human psychology people expect that one toss will differ from the next around 70 percent of the time.

How, then, will our statistics professor fare when confronted with E? Will she attribute E to chance or to the musings of someone trying to mimic chance? According to the professor's crude randomness checker, E would be assigned to the pile of sequences presumed to be truly random, for E contains a repetition of seven tails in a row. Everything that at first blush would lead us to regard E as truly random checks out. There are exactly fifty alternations between heads and tails (as opposed to the seventy that would be expected from human beings trying to mimic chance). What's more, the relative frequencies of heads and tails check out: there were forty-nine heads and fifty-one tails. Thus it's not as though the coin supposedly responsible for generating E was heavily biased in favor of one side versus the other.

BUT IS IT REALLY CHANCE?

Suppose, however, that our statistics professor suspects she is not up against a neophyte statistics student, but instead a fellow statistician who is trying to put one over on her. To help organize her problem, study it more carefully, and enter it into a computer, she will find it convenient to let strings of 0s and 1s represent the outcomes

of coin flips, with 1 corresponding to heads and 0 to tails. In that case the following pattern D will correspond to the event E:

```
0100011011000001010011100101110111000000010010
0011010001010110011110001001101010111100110111
10111100
```

Now, the mere fact that the event E conforms to the pattern D is no reason to think that E did not occur by chance. As things stand, the pattern D has simply been read off the event E.

But D need not have been read off of E. Indeed, D could have been constructed without recourse to E. To see this, let us rewrite D as follows:

$$
\begin{array}{l}
0 \\
1 \\
00 \\
01 \\
10 \\
11 \\
000 \\
001 \\
010 \\
011 \\
100 \\
101 \\
110 \\
111 \\
0000 \\
0001 \\
0010 \\
0011 \\
0100 \\
0101 \\
0110 \\
0111 \\
1000 \\
1001 \\
1010 \\
1011 \\
1100 \\
1101 \\
1110 \\
1111 \\
00 \qquad \text{D}
\end{array}
$$

By viewing D this way, anyone with the least exposure to binary arithmetic immediately recognizes that D was constructed simply by writing binary numbers in ascending order, starting with the one-digit binary numbers (i.e., 0 and 1), proceeding then to the two-digit binary numbers (i.e., 00, 01, 10, and 11), and continuing on until one hundred digits were recorded. It's therefore intuitively clear that D does not describe a truly random event (i.e., an event gotten by tossing a fair coin), but rather a pseudo-random event, concocted by doing a little binary arithmetic.

SIDE INFORMATION DOES THE TRICK

Although it's now intuitively clear why chance cannot properly explain E, we need to consider more closely why this mode of explanation fails here. We started with a putative chance event E, supposedly the result of flipping a fair coin one hundred times. Since heads and tails each have probability ½, and since this probability gets multiplied for each flip of the coin, it follows that the probability of E is 2^{-100}, or approximately 10^{-30}.

In addition, we constructed a pattern D to which E conforms. Initially D proved insufficient to eliminate chance as the explanation of E since in its construction D was simply read off E. Rather, to eliminate chance we also had to recognize that D could have been constructed quite easily by performing some simple arithmetic operations with binary numbers. Thus to eliminate chance we needed to employ additional *side information,* which in this case consisted of our knowledge of binary arithmetic. This side information detached the pattern D from the event E and thereby rendered D a specification.

For side information to detach a pattern from an event, it must satisfy two conditions, *conditional independence* and *tractability*. First, the side information must be conditionally independent of the event E. Conditional independence, a well-defined notion from probability theory, means that the probability of E doesn't change once the side information is taken into account. Conditional independence is the standard probabilistic way of unpacking epistemic independence. Two things are epistemically independent if knowledge about one thing (in this case the side information) does not affect knowledge

about the other (in this case the occurrence of E). This is certainly the case here since our knowledge of binary arithmetic does not affect the probabilities we assign to coin tosses.

The second condition, the tractability condition, requires that the side information enable us to construct the pattern D to which E conforms. This is evidently the case here as well, since our knowledge of binary arithmetic enables us to arrange binary numbers in ascending order, and thereby construct the pattern D.

But what exactly is this ability to construct a pattern on the basis of side information? Perhaps the most slippery words in philosophy are "can," "able," and "enable." Fortunately, just as there is a precise theory for characterizing the epistemic independence between an event and side information—namely, probability theory—so too there is a precise theory for characterizing the ability to construct a pattern on the basis of side information—namely, complexity theory.

COMPLEXITY THEORY

Complexity theory, conceived now quite generally and not merely as a form of probability, assesses the difficulty of tasks given the resources available for accomplishing those tasks. If I may generalize computational complexity theory, it ranks tasks according to difficulty and then determines which tasks are sufficiently manageable to be doable or tractable. For instance, given current technology we find sending a person to the moon tractable, but sending a person to the nearest galaxy intractable.

In the tractability condition, the task to be accomplished is the construction of a pattern, and the resources for accomplishing that task are side information. Thus, for the tractability condition to be satisfied, side information must provide the resources necessary for constructing the pattern in question. All of this admits a precise complexity-theoretic formulation and makes definite what I called "the ability to construct a pattern on the basis of side information."

Taken jointly, the tractability and conditional independence conditions mean that side information enables us to construct the pattern to which an event conforms, yet without recourse to the actual event. This is the crucial insight. Because the side information is conditionally and therefore epistemically independent of the event, any pattern constructed from this side information is obtained without recourse to the event. In this way any pattern that is constructed from such side information avoids the charge of being *ad hoc*. These, then, are the detachable patterns. These are the specifications.

A MATTER OF CHOICE

The complexity-specification criterion is exactly the right instrument for detecting design. To see why, we need to understand what makes intelligent agents detectable in the first place. The principal characteristic of intelligent agency is choice. Even the etymology of the word "intelligent" makes this clear. "Intelligent" derives from two Latin words, the preposition *inter,* meaning between, and the verb *lego,* meaning to choose or select. Thus, according to its etymology, intelligence consists in *choosing between* For an intelligent agent to act is therefore to choose from a range of competing possibilities.

This is true not just of humans, but of animals as well as of extraterrestrial intelligences. A rat navigating a maze must choose whether to go right or left at various points in the maze. When SETI researchers attempt to discover intelligence in the extraterrestrial radio transmissions they are monitoring, they assume an extraterrestrial intelligence could have chosen any number of possible radio transmissions, and then attempt to match the transmissions they observe with certain patterns as opposed to others. Whenever a human being utters meaningful speech, a choice is made from a range of possible sound combinations that might have been uttered. Intelligent agency always entails discrimination, choosing certain things, ruling out others.

RECOGNIZING INTELLIGENCE

Given this characterization of intelligent agency, the crucial question is how to recognize it. Intelligent agents act by making a choice. How, then, do we recognize that an intelligent agent has made a choice? A bottle of ink spills accidentally onto a sheet of paper; someone takes a fountain pen and writes a message on a sheet of paper. In both instances ink is applied to paper. In both instances one among an almost infinite set of possibilities is realized. In both instances a contingency is actualized and others are ruled out. Yet in one instance we ascribe agency, in the other chance.

What is the relevant difference? Not only do we need to observe that a contingency was actualized, but we need also to be able to specify that contingency. The contingency must conform to an independently given pattern, and we must be able independently to construct that pattern. A random inkblot is unspecified; a message written with ink on paper is specified. The exact message recorded may not be specified, but orthographic, syntactic, and semantic constraints will nonetheless specify it.

Actualizing one among several competing possibilities, ruling out the rest, and specifying the one that was actualized encapsulates how we recognize intelligent agency, or equivalently, how we detect design. Experimental psychologists who study animal learning and behavior have known this all along. To learn a task an animal must acquire the ability to actualize behaviors suitable for the task as well as the ability to rule out behaviors unsuitable for the task. Moreover, for a psychologist to recognize that an animal has learned a task, it is necessary not only to observe the animal making the appropriate discrimination, but also to specify the discrimination.

RATS AND MAZES

Thus, to recognize whether a rat has successfully learned how to traverse a maze, a psychologist must first specify which sequence of right and left turns conducts the rat out of the maze. No doubt, a rat randomly wandering a maze also discriminates a sequence of right and left turns. But by randomly wandering the maze, the rat gives no indication that it can discriminate the appropriate sequence of right and left turns for exiting the maze. Consequently, the psychologist studying the rat will have no reason to think the rat has learned how to traverse the maze.

Only if the rat executes the sequence of right and left turns specified by the psychologist will the psychologist recognize that the rat has learned how to traverse the maze. Now it is precisely the learned behaviors we regard as intelligent in animals. Hence it is no surprise that the same scheme for recognizing animal learning recurs for recognizing intelligent agency generally, to wit: actualizing one among several competing possibilities, ruling out the others, and specifying the one actualized.

Note that complexity is implicit here as well. To see this, consider again a rat traversing a maze, but now take a very simple maze in which two right turns conduct the rat out of the maze. How will a psychologist studying the rat determine whether it has learned to exit the maze? Just putting the rat in the maze will not be enough. Because the maze is so simple, the rat by chance could just happen to take two right turns and thereby exit the maze. The psychologist will therefore be uncertain whether the rat actually learned to exit this maze or just got lucky.

But contrast this with a complicated maze in which a rat must take just the right sequence of left and right turns to exit the maze. Suppose the rat must take one hundred appropriate right and left turns, and that any mistake will prevent the rat from exiting the maze. A psychologist who sees the rat take no erroneous turns and quickly exit the maze will be convinced that the rat has indeed learned how to exit the maze, and that it was not dumb luck.

This general scheme for recognizing intelligent agency is but a thinly disguised form of the complexity-specification criterion. In general, to recognize intelligent agency we must observe an actualization of one among several competing possibilities, note which possibilities were ruled out, and then be able to specify the possibility that was actualized. What's more, the competing possibilities that were ruled out must be live possibilities, and sufficiently numerous so that specifying the possibility that was actualized cannot be attributed to chance. In terms of complexity, this is just another way of saying that the range of possibilities is complex. In terms of probability, this is just another way of saying that the possibility that was actualized has small probability.

All the elements in this general scheme for recognizing intelligent agency (i.e., actualizing, ruling out, and specifying) find their counterpart in the complexity-specification criterion. It follows that this criterion formalizes what we have been doing right along when we recognize intelligent agency. The complexity-specification criterion pinpoints how we detect design.

DESIGN, METAPHYSICS, AND BEYOND

Where is this work on design heading? Specified complexity, that key trademark of design, is, as it turns out, a form of information (though one considerably richer than Claude Shannon's purely statistical form of it). Although called by different names and developed with different degrees of rigor, specified complexity is starting to have an effect on the special sciences.

For instance, specified complexity is what Michael Behe has uncovered with his irreducibly complex biochemical machines, what Manfred Eigen regards as the great mystery of life's origin, what for cosmologists underlies the fine-tuning of the universe, what David Chalmers hopes will ground a comprehensive theory of human consciousness, what enables Maxwell's demon to outsmart a thermodynamic system tending toward thermal equilibrium, and what within the Kolmogorov-Chaitin theory of algorithmic information identifies the highly compressible, nonrandom strings of digits. How complex specified information gets from an organism's environment into an organism's genome was one of the key questions at the October 1999 Santa Fe Institute symposium, "Complexity, Information & Design: A Critical Appraisal."

Shannon's purely statistical theory of information is giving way to a richer theory of complex specified information whose possibilities are only now coming to light. A natural sequel to *The Design Inference* is therefore to develop a general theory of complex specified information.

Yet despite its far-reaching implications for science. I regard the ultimate significance of this work on design to lie in metaphysics. In my view, design died not at the hands of nineteenth-century evolutionary biology, but at the hands of the mechanical philosophy two centuries earlier—and that despite the popularity of British natural theology at the time. Though the originators of the mechanical philosophy were typically theists, the design they retained was at best an uneasy rider on top of a mechanistic view of nature. Design is neither use nor ornament within a strictly mechanistic world of particles or other mindless entities organized by equally mindless principles of association, even if these be natural laws ordained by God.

The primary challenge, once the broader implications of design for science have been worked out, is therefore to develop a relational ontology in which the problem of being resolves thus: to be is to be in communion, and to be in communion is to transmit and receive information. Such an ontology will not only safeguard science and leave adequate breathing space for design, but will also make sense of the world as sacrament.

The world is a mirror representing the divine life. The mechanical philosophy was ever blind to this fact. Intelligent design, on the other hand, readily embraces the sacramental nature of physical reality. Indeed, intelligent design is just the Logos theology of John's Gospel restated in the idiom of information theory.

VIII.B.2   Molecular Machines: Experimental Support for the Design Inference

MICHAEL BEHE

Michael Behe (1952–   ) is professor of biochemistry at Lehigh University. He is one of the leading figures in the Intelligent Design movement and is the author of *Darwin's Black Box* (1996). In this article, Behe presents the core idea of Darwin's Black Box: the claim that irreducible complexity, an empirically detectable property of some but not all biological structures, could not have been produced by the sorts of gradual processes posited by Darwinian evolutionary theory.

DARWINISM'S PROSPERITY

Within a short time after Charles Darwin published *The Origin of Species* the explanatory power of the theory of evolution was recognized by the great majority of biologists. The hypothesis readily resolved the problems of homologous resemblance, rudimentary organs, species abundance, extinction, and biogeography. The rival theory of the time, which posited creation of species by a supernatural being, appeared to most reasonable minds to be much less plausible, since it would have a putative Creator attending to details that seemed to be beneath His dignity.

As time went on the theory of evolution obliterated the rival theory of creation, and virtually all working scientists studied the biological world from a Darwinian perspective. Most educated people now lived in a world where the wonder and diversity of the biological kingdom were produced by the simple, elegant principle of natural selection.

However, in science a successful theory is not necessarily a correct theory. In the course of history there have also been other theories which achieved the triumph that Darwinism achieved, which brought many experimental and observational facts into a coherent framework, and which appealed to people's intuitions about how the world should work. Those theories also promised to explain much of the universe with a few simple principles. But, by and large, those other theories are now dead.

Originally published in *Cosmic Pursuit* (1998, vol. 1 no. 2 pp. 27–35); copyright by Michael J. Behe. Reprinted by permission.

A good example of this is the replacement of Newton's mechanical view of the universe by Einstein's relativistic universe. Although Newton's model accounted for the results of many experiments in his time, it failed to explain aspects of gravitation. Einstein solved that problem and others by completely rethinking the structure of the universe.

Similarly, Darwin's theory of evolution prospered by explaining much of the data of his time and the first half of the 20th century, but my article will show that Darwinism has been unable to account for phenomena uncovered by the efforts of modern biochemistry during the second half of this century. I will do this by emphasizing the fact that life at its most fundamental level is irreducibly complex and that such complexity is incompatible with undirected evolution.

A SERIES OF EYES

How do we see?

In the 19th century the anatomy of the eye was known in great detail and the sophisticated mechanisms it employs to deliver an accurate picture of the outside world astounded everyone who was familiar with them. Scientists of the 19th century correctly observed that if a person were so unfortunate as to be missing one of the eye's many integrated features, such as the lens, or iris, or ocular muscles, the inevitable result would be a severe loss of vision or outright blindness. Thus it was concluded that the eye could only function if it were nearly intact.

As Charles Darwin was considering possible objections to his theory of evolution by natural selection in *The Origin of Species* he discussed the problem of the eye in a section of the book appropriately entitled "Organs of extreme perfection and complication." He realized that if in one generation an organ of the complexity of the eye suddenly appeared, the event would be tantamount to a miracle. Somehow, for Darwinian evolution to be believable, the difficulty that the public had in envisioning the gradual formation of complex organs had to be removed.

Darwin succeeded brilliantly, not by actually describing a real pathway that evolution might have used in constructing the eye, but rather by pointing to a variety of animals that were known to have eyes of various constructions, ranging from a simple light sensitive spot to the complex vertebrate camera eye, and suggesting that the evolution of the human eye might have involved similar organs as intermediates.

But the question remains, how do we see? Although Darwin was able to persuade much of the world that a modern eye could be produced gradually from a much simpler structure, he did not even attempt to explain how the simple light sensitive spot that was his starting point actually worked. When discussing the eye Darwin dismissed the question of its ultimate mechanism by stating: "How a nerve comes to be sensitive to light hardly concerns us more than how life itself originated."

He had an excellent reason for declining to answer the question: 19th century science had not progressed to the point where the matter could even be approached. The question of how the eye works—that is, what happens when a photon of light first impinges on the retina—simply could not be answered at that time. As a matter of fact, no question about the underlying mechanism of life could be answered at that time. How do animal muscles cause movement? How does photosynthesis work? How is energy extracted from food? How does the body fight infection? All such questions were unanswerable.

THE CALVIN AND HOBBES APPROACH

Now, it appears to be a characteristic of the human mind that when it lacks understanding of a process, then it seems easy to imagine simple steps leading from nonfunction to function. A happy example of this is seen in the popular comic strip *Calvin and Hobbes*. Little boy Calvin is always having adventures in the company of his tiger Hobbes by jumping in a box and traveling back in time, or grabbing a toy ray gun and "transmogrifying" himself into various animal shapes, or again using a box as a duplicator and making copies of himself to deal with worldly powers such as his mom and his teachers. A small child such as Calvin finds it easy to imagine that a box just might be able to fly like an airplane (or something), because Calvin doesn't know how airplanes work.

A good example from the biological world of complex changes appearing to be simple is the belief in spontaneous generation. One of the chief proponents of the theory of spontaneous generation during the middle of the 19th century was Ernst Haeckel, a great admirer of Darwin and an eager popularizer of Darwin's theory. From the limited view of cells that 19th century microscopes provided, Haeckel believed that a cell was a "simple little lump of albuminous combination of carbon," not much different from a piece of microscopic Jell-O®. Thus it seemed to Haeckel that such simple life could easily be produced from inanimate material.

In 1859, the year of the publication of *The Origin of Species,* an exploratory vessel, the H.M.S. Cyclops, dredged up some curious-looking mud from the sea bottom. Eventually Haeckel came to observe the mud and thought that it closely resembled some cells he had seen under a microscope. Excitedly he brought this to the attention of no less a personage than Thomas Henry Huxley, Darwin's great friend and defender, who observed the mud for himself. Huxley, too, became convinced that it was Urschleim (that is, protoplasm), the progenitor of life itself, and Huxley named the mud *Bathybius haeckelii* after the eminent proponent of abiogenesis.

The mud failed to grow. In later years, with the development of new biochemical techniques and improved microscopes, the complexity of the cell was revealed. The "simple lumps" were shown to contain thousands of different types of organic molecules, proteins, and nucleic acids, many discrete subcellular structures, specialized compartments for specialized processes, and an extremely complicated architecture. Looking back from the perspective of our time, the episode of *Bathybius haeckelii* seems silly or downright embarrassing, but it shouldn't. Haeckel and Huxley were behaving naturally, like Calvin: since they were unaware of the complexity of cells, they found it easy to believe that cells could originate from simple mud.

Throughout history there have been many other examples, similar to that of Haeckel, Huxley, and the cell, where a key piece of a particular scientific puzzle was beyond the understanding of the age. In science there is even a whimsical term for a machine or structure or process that does something, but the actual mechanism by which it accomplishes its task is unknown: it is called a "black box." In Darwin's time all of biology was a black box: not only the cell, or the eye, or digestion, or immunity, but every biological structure and function because, ultimately, no one could explain how biological processes occurred.

Biology has progressed tremendously due to the model that Darwin put forth. But the black boxes Darwin accepted are now being opened, and our view of the world is again being shaken.

Take our modern understanding of proteins, for example.

PROTEINS

In order to understand the molecular basis of life it is necessary to understand how things called "proteins" work. Proteins are the machinery of living tissue that build the structures and carry out the chemical reactions necessary for life. For example, the first of many steps necessary for the conversion of sugar to biologically-usable forms of energy is carried out by a protein called hexokinase. Skin is made in large measure of a protein called collagen. When light impinges on your retina it interacts first with a protein called rhodopsin. A typical cell contains thousands and thousands of different types of proteins to perform the many tasks necessary for life, much like a carpenter's workshop might contain many different kinds of tools for various carpentry tasks.

What do these versatile tools look like? The basic structure of proteins is quite simple: they are formed by hooking together in a chain discrete subunits called amino acids. Although the protein chain can consist of anywhere from about 50 to about 1,000 amino acid links, each position can only contain one of 20 different amino acids. In this they are much like words: words can come in various lengths but they are made up from a discrete set of 26 letters.

Now, a protein in a cell does not float around like a floppy chain; rather, it folds up into a very precise structure which can be quite different for different types of proteins. Two different amino acid sequences—two different proteins—can be folded to structures as specific and different from each other as a three-eighths inch wrench and a jigsaw. And like the household tools, if the shape of the proteins is significantly warped then they fail to do their jobs.

THE EYESIGHT OF MAN

In general, biological processes on the molecular level are performed by networks of proteins, each member of which carries out a particular task in a chain.

Let us return to the question, how do we see? Although to Darwin the primary event of vision was a black box, through the efforts of many biochemists an answer to the question of sight is at hand. The answer involves a long chain of steps that begin when light strikes the retina and a photon is absorbed by an organic molecule called 11-cis-retinal, causing it to rearrange itself within picoseconds. This causes a corresponding change to the protein, rhodopsin, which is tightly bound to it, so that it can react with another protein called transducin, which in turn causes a molecule called GDP to be exchanged with a molecule called GTP.

To make a long story short, this exchange begins a long series of further bindings between still more specialized molecular machinery, and scientists now understand a great deal about the system of gateways, pumps, ion channels, critical concentrations, and attenuated signals that result in a current to finally be transmitted down the optic nerve to the brain, interpreted as vision. Biochemists also understand the many chemical reactions involved in restoring all these changed or depleted parts to make a new cycle possible.

TO EXPLAIN LIFE

Although space doesn't permit me to give the details of the biochemistry of vision here, I have given the steps in my talks. Biochemists know what it means to "explain" vision. They know the level of explanation that biological science eventually must aim for. In order to say that some function is understood, every relevant step in the process must be elucidated. The relevant steps in biological processes occur ultimately at the molecular level, so a satisfactory explanation of a biological phenomenon such as sight, or digestion, or immunity, must include a molecular explanation.

It is no longer sufficient, now that the black box of vision has been opened, for an "evolutionary explanation" of that power to invoke only the anatomical structures of whole eyes, as Darwin did in the 19th century and as most popularizers of evolution continue to do today. Anatomy is, quite simply, irrelevant. So is the fossil record. It does not matter whether or not the fossil record is consistent with evolutionary theory, any more than it mattered in physics that Newton's theory was consistent with everyday experience. The fossil record has nothing to tell us about, say, whether or how the interactions of 11-cis-retinal with rhodopsin, transducin, and phosphodiesterase could have developed, step by step.

"How a nerve comes to be sensitive to light hardly concerns us more than how life itself originated," said Darwin in the 19th century. But both phenomena have attracted the interest of modern biochemistry in the past few decades. The story of the slow paralysis of research on life's origin is quite interesting, but space precludes its retelling here. Suffice it to say that at present the field of origin-of-life studies has dissolved into a cacophony of conflicting models, each unconvincing, seriously incomplete, and incompatible with competing models. In private even most evolutionary biologists will admit that science has no explanation for the beginning of life.

The same problems which beset origin-of-life research also bedevil efforts to show how virtually any complex biochemical system came about. Biochemistry has revealed a molecular world which stoutly resists explanation by the same theory that has long been applied at the level of the whole organism. Neither of Darwin's black boxes—the origin of life or the origin of vision (or other complex biochemical systems)—has been accounted for by his theory.

IRREDUCIBLE COMPLEXITY

In *The Origin of Species* Darwin stated:

> If it could be demonstrated that any complex organ existed which could not possibly have been formed by numerous, successive, slight modifications, my theory would absolutely break down.

A system which meets Darwin's criterion is one which exhibits irreducible complexity. By irreducible complexity I mean a single system which is composed of several interacting parts that contribute to the basic function, and where the removal of any one of the parts causes the system to effectively cease functioning. An irreducibly complex system cannot be produced directly by slight, successive modification of a precursor system, since any precursor to an irreducibly complex system is by definition nonfunctional.

Since natural selection requires a function to select, an irreducibly complex biological system, if there is such a thing, would have to arise as an integrated unit for natural selection to have anything to act on. It is almost universally conceded that such a sudden event would be irreconcilable with the gradualism Darwin envisioned. At this point, however, "irreducibly complex" is just a term, whose power resides mostly in its definition. We must now ask if any real thing is in fact irreducibly complex, and, if so, then are any irreducibly complex things also biological systems?

Consider the humble mousetrap (Figure). The mousetraps that my family uses in our home to deal with unwelcome rodents consist of a number of parts. There are: 1) a flat wooden platform to act as a base; 2) a metal hammer, which does the actual job of crushing the little mouse; 3) a wire spring with extended ends to press against the platform and the hammer when the trap is charged; 4) a sensitive catch which releases when slight pressure is applied; and 5) a metal bar which holds the hammer back when the trap is charged and connects to the catch. There are also assorted staples and screws to hold the system together.

If any one of the components of the mousetrap (the base, hammer, spring, catch, or holding bar) is removed, then the trap does not function. In other words, the simple little mousetrap has no

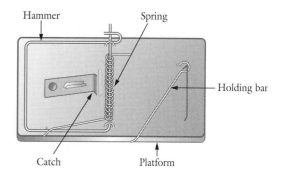

FIGURE 1 A household mousetrap. The working parts of the trap are labeled. If any of the parts is missing, the trap does not function.

ability to trap a mouse until several separate parts are all assembled.

Because the mousetrap is necessarily composed of several parts, it is irreducibly complex. Thus, irreducibly complex systems exist.

MOLECULAR MACHINES

Now, are any biochemical systems irreducibly complex? Yes, it turns out that many are.

Earlier we discussed proteins. In many biological structures proteins are simply components of larger molecular machines. Like the picture tube, wires, metal bolts and screws that comprise a television set, many proteins are part of structures that only function when virtually all of the components have been assembled.

A good example of this is a cilium. Cilia are hairlike organelles on the surfaces of many animal and lower plant cells that serve to move fluid over the cell's surface or to "row" single cells through a fluid. In humans, for example, epithelial cells lining the respiratory tract each have about 200 cilia that beat in synchrony to sweep mucus towards the throat for elimination.

A cilium consists of a membrane-coated bundle of fibers called an axoneme. An axoneme contains a ring of 9 double microtubules surrounding two central single microtubules. Each outer doublet consists of a ring of 13 filaments (subfiber A) fused to an assembly of 10 filaments (subfiber B). The filaments of the microtubules are composed of two proteins called alpha and beta tubulin. The 11 microtubules

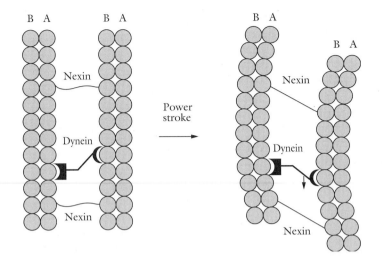

FIGURE 2 Schematic drawing of part of a cilium. The power stroke of the motor protein dynein, attached to one microtublule, against subfiber B of a neighboring microtubule causes the fibers to slide past each other. The flexible linker protein, nexin, converts the sliding motion to a bending motion.

forming an axoneme are held together by three types of connectors: subfibers A are joined to the central microtubules by radial spokes; adjacent outer doublets are joined by linkers that consist of a highly elastic protein called nexin; and the central microtubules are joined by a connecting bridge. Finally, every subfiber A bears two arms, an inner arm and an outer arm, both containing the protein dynein.

But how does a cilium work? Experiments have indicated that ciliary motion results from the chemically-powered "walking" of the dynein arms on one microtubule up the neighboring subfiber B of a second microtubule so that the two microtubules slide past each other (Figure 2). However, the protein cross-links between microtubules in an intact cilium prevent neighboring microtubules from sliding past each other by more than a short distance. These cross-links, therefore, convert the dynein-induced sliding motion to a bending motion of the entire axoneme.

Now, let us sit back, review the workings of the cilium, and consider what it implies. Cilia are composed of at least a half dozen proteins: alpha-tubulin, beta-tubulin, dynein, nexin, spoke protein, and a central bridge protein. These combine to perform one task, ciliary

motion, and all of these proteins must be present for the cilium to function. If the tubulins are absent, then there are no filaments to slide; if the dynein is missing, then the cilium remains rigid and motionless; if nexin or the other connecting proteins are missing, then the axoneme falls apart when the filaments slide.

What we see in the cilium, then, is not just profound complexity, but it is also irreducible complexity on the molecular scale. Recall that by "irreducible complexity" we mean an apparatus that requires several distinct components for the whole to work. My mousetrap must have a base, hammer, spring, catch, and holding bar, all working together, in order to function. Similarly, the cilium, as it is constituted, must have the sliding filaments, connecting proteins, and motor proteins for function to occur. In the absence of any one of those components, the apparatus is useless.

The components of cilia are single molecules. This means that there are no more black boxes to invoke; the complexity of the cilium is final, fundamental. And just as scientists, when they began to learn the complexities of the cell, realized how silly it was to think that life arose spontaneously in a single step or a

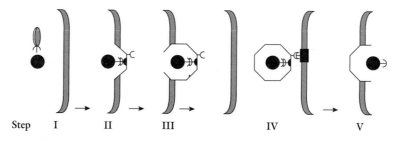

FIGURE 3 Transport of a protein from the ER to the lysosome. Step I: A specific enzyme (gray oval) places a marker on the protein (black sphere). This takes place within the ER, which is delimited by a barrier membrane (cross-hatched bar with ends curving to the left). Step II: The marker is specifically recognized by a receptor protein and the clathrin vesicle (hexagonal shape) begins to form. Step III: The clathrin vesicle is completed and buds off from the ER membrane. Step IV: The clathrin vesicle crosses the cytoplasm and attaches through another specific marker to a receptor protein (dark gray box) on the lysosomal membrane and releases its cargo.

few steps from ocean mud, so too we now realize that the complex cilium can not be reached in a single step or a few steps.

But since the complexity of the cilium is irreducible, then it can not have functional precursors. Since the irreducibly complex cilium can not have functional precursors it can not be produced by natural selection, which requires a continuum of function to work. Natural selection is powerless when there is no function to select. We can go further and say that, if the cilium can not be produced by natural selection, then the cilium was designed.

A NON-MECHANICAL EXAMPLE

A non-mechanical example of irreducible complexity can be seen in the system that targets proteins for delivery to subcellular compartments. In order to find their way to the compartments where they are needed to perform specialized tasks, certain proteins contain a special amino acid sequence near the beginning called a "signal sequence."

As the proteins are being synthesized by ribosomes, a complex molecular assemblage called the signal recognition particle or SRP, binds to the signal sequence. This causes synthesis of the protein to halt temporarily. During the pause in protein synthesis the SRP is bound by the transmembrane SRP receptor, which causes protein synthesis to resume and which allows passage of the protein into the interior of the endoplasmic reticulum (ER). As the protein passes into the ER the signal sequence is cut off.

For many proteins the ER is just a way station on their travels to their final destinations (Figure 3). Proteins which will end up in a lysosome are enzymatically "tagged" with a carbohydrate residue called mannose-6-phosphate while still in the ER. An area of the ER membrane then begins to concentrate several proteins; one protein, clathrin, forms a sort of geodesic dome called a coated vesicle which buds off from the ER. In the dome there is also a receptor protein which binds to both the clathrin and to the mannose-6-phosphate group of the protein which is being transported. The coated vesicle then leaves the ER, travels through the cytoplasm, and binds to the lysosome through another specific receptor protein. Finally, in a maneuver involving several more proteins, the vesicle fuses with the lysosome and the protein arrives at its destination.

During its travels our protein interacted with dozens of macromolecules to achieve one purpose: its arrival in the lysosome. Virtually all components of the transport system are necessary for the system to operate, and therefore the system is irreducible. And since all of the components of the system are comprised of single or several molecules, there are no black boxes to invoke. The consequences of even a single gap in the transport chain can be seen in the hereditary defect known as I-cell disease. It results from a deficiency of the enzyme that places the mannose-6-phosphate on proteins to be targeted to the lysosomes. I-cell disease is characterized by progressive retardation, skeletal deformities, and early death.

THE STUDY OF "MOLECULAR EVOLUTION"

Other examples of irreducible complexity abound, including aspects of protein transport, blood clotting, closed circular DNA, electron transport, the bacterial flagellum, telomeres, photosynthesis, transcription regulation, and much more. Examples of irreducible complexity can be found on virtually every page of a biochemistry textbook. But if these things cannot be explained by Darwinian evolution, how has the scientific community regarded these phenomena of the past forty years.?

A good place to look for an answer to that question is in the *Journal of Molecular Evolution*. *JME* is a journal that was begun specifically to deal with the topic of how evolution occurs on the molecular level. It has high scientific standards, and is edited by prominent figures in the field. In a recent issue of *JME* there were published eleven articles; of these, all eleven were concerned simply with the analysis of protein or DNA sequences. None of the papers discussed detailed models for intermediates in the development of complex biomolecular structures.

In the past ten years *JME* has published 886 papers. Of these, 95 discussed the chemical synthesis of molecules thought to be necessary for the origin of life, 44 proposed mathematical models to improve sequence analysis, 20 concerned the evolutionary implications of current structures and 719 were analyses of protein or polynucleotide sequences. However, there weren't any papers discussing detailed models for intermediates in the development of complex biomolecular structures. This is not a peculiarity of *JME*. No papers are to be found that discuss detailed models for intermediates in the development of

complex biomolecular structures in the *Proceedings of the National Academy of Science, Nature, Science,* the *Journal of Molecular Biology* or, to my knowledge, any journal whatsoever.

Sequence comparisons overwhelmingly dominate the literature of molecular evolution. But sequence comparisons simply can't account for the development of complex biochemical systems any more than Darwin's comparison of simple and complex eyes told him how vision worked. Thus in this area science is mute.

DETECTION OF DESIGN

What's going on? Imagine a room in which a body lies crushed, flat as a pancake. A dozen detectives crawl around, examining the floor with magnifying glasses for any clue to the identity of the perpetrator. In the middle of the room next to the body stands a large, gray elephant. The detectives carefully avoid bumping into the pachyderm's legs as they crawl, and never even glance at it. Over time the detectives get frustrated with their lack of progress but resolutely press on, looking even more closely at the floor. You see, textbooks say detectives must "get their man," so they never consider elephants.

There is an elephant in the roomful of scientists who are trying to explain the development of life. The elephant is labeled "intelligent design." To a person who does not feel obliged to restrict his search to unintelligent causes, the straightforward conclusion is that many biochemical systems were designed. They were designed *not* by the laws of nature, not by chance and necessity. Rather, they were *planned*. The designer knew what the systems would look like when they were completed; the designer took steps to bring the systems about. Life on earth at its most fundamental level, in its most critical components, is the product of intelligent activity.

The conclusion of intelligent design flows naturally from the data itself—not from sacred books or sectarian beliefs. Inferring that biochemical systems were designed by an intelligent agent is a humdrum process that requires no new principles of logic or science. It comes simply from the hard work that biochemistry has done over the past forty years, combined with consideration of the way in which we reach conclusions of design every day.

What is "design"? Design is simply the *purposeful arrangement of parts*. The scientific question is how we detect design. This can be done in various ways, but design can most easily be inferred for mechanical objects.

Systems made entirely from natural components can also evince design. For example, suppose you are walking with a friend in the woods. All of a sudden your friend is pulled high in the air and left dangling by his foot from a vine attached to a tree branch.

After cutting him down you reconstruct the trap. You see that the vine was wrapped around the tree branch, and the end pulled tightly down to the ground. It was securely anchored to the ground by a forked branch. The branch was attached to another vine—hidden by leaves—so that, when the trigger-vine was disturbed, it would pull down the forked stick, releasing the spring-vine. The end of the vine formed a loop with a slipknot to grab an appendage and snap it up into the air. Even though the trap was made completely of natural materials you would quickly conclude that it was the product of intelligent design.

Intelligent design is a good explanation for a number of biochemical systems, but I should insert a word of caution. Intelligent design theory has to be seen in context: it does not try to explain everything. We live in a complex world where lots of different things can happen. When deciding how various rocks came to be shaped the way they are a geologist might consider a whole range of factors: rain, wind, the movement of glaciers, the activity of moss and lichens, volcanic action, nuclear explosions, asteroid impact, or the hand of a sculptor. The shape of one rock might have been determined primarily by one mechanism, the shape of another rock by another mechanism.

Similarly, evolutionary biologists have recognized that a number of factors might have affected the development of life: common descent, natural selection, migration, population size, founder effects (effects that may be due to the limited number of organisms that begin a new species), genetic drift (spread of "neutral," nonselective mutations), gene flow (the incorporation of genes into a population from a separate population), linkage (occurrence of two genes on the same chromosome), and much more. The fact that some biochemical systems were designed by an intelligent agent does not mean that any of the other factors are not operative, common, or important.

CONCLUSION

It is often said that science must avoid any conclusions which smack of the supernatural. But this seems to me to be both bad logic and bad science. Science is not a game in which arbitrary rules are used to decide what explanations are to be permitted. Rather, it is an effort to make true statements about physical reality. It was only about sixty years ago that the expansion of the universe was first observed. This fact immediately suggested a singular event—that at some time in the distant past the universe began expanding from an extremely small size.

To many people this inference was loaded with overtones of a supernatural event—the creation, the beginning of the universe. The prominent physicist A. S. Eddington probably spoke for many physicists in voicing his disgust with such a notion:

> Philosophically, the notion of an abrupt beginning to the present order of Nature is repugnant to me, as I think it must be to most; and even those who would welcome a proof of the intervention of a Creator will probably consider that a single winding-up at some remote epoch is not really the kind of relation between God and his world that brings satisfaction to the mind.

Nonetheless, the big bang hypothesis was embraced by physics and over the years has proven to be a very fruitful paradigm. The point here is that physics followed the data where it seemed to lead, even though some thought the model gave aid and comfort to religion. In the present day, as biochemistry multiplies examples of fantastically complex molecular systems, systems which discourage even an attempt to explain how they may have arisen, we should take a lesson from physics. The conclusion of design flows naturally from the data; we should not shrink from it; we should embrace it and build on it.

In concluding, it is important to realize that we are not inferring design from what we do not know, but from what we do know. We are not inferring design to account for a black box, but to account for an open box. A man from a primitive culture who sees an automobile might guess that it was powered by the wind or by an antelope hidden under the car, but when he opens up the hood and sees the engine he immediately realizes that it was designed. In the same way biochemistry has opened up the cell to examine what makes it run and we see that it, too, was designed.

It was a shock to the people of the 19th century when they discovered, from observations science had made, that many features of the biological world could be ascribed to the elegant principle of natural selection. It is a shock to us in the twentieth century to discover, from observations science has made, that the fundamental mechanisms of life cannot be ascribed to natural selection, and therefore were designed. But we must deal with our shock as best we can and go on. The theory of undirected evolution is already dead, but the work of science continues.

VIII.B.3 Born-Again Creationism

PHILIP KITCHER

Philip Kitcher (1947–   ) is professor of philosophy at Columbia University and is one of the leading figures in the philosophy of science. He is the author of *The Advancement of Science* (1993) and *Abusing Science: The Case Against Creationism* (1982). The selection here is an excerpt from his essay, "Born-Again Creationism," in which he responds to several recent attacks on Darwinian evolutionary theory, including Michael Behe's. Among other things, Kitcher contends that Behe's argument illegitimately exploits our ignorance of how genetic changes might influence the overall structure and appearance of an organism. In short, Behe claims that certain evolutionary transitions are highly probable or impossible when in fact, according to Kitcher, there is simply no basis for such claims.

1. THE CREATIONIST REFORMATION

In the beginning, creationists believed that the world was young. But creation "science" was without form and void. A deluge of objections drowned the idea that major kinds of plants and animals had been fashioned a few thousand years ago and been hardly modified since. Then the spirit of piety brooded on the waters and brought forth something new. "Let there be design!" exclaimed the reformers—and lo! there was born-again creationism.

Out in Santee, California, about twenty miles from where I used to live, the old movement, dedicated to the possibility of interpreting *Genesis* literally, continues to ply its wares. Its spokesmen still peddle the familiar fallacies, their misunderstandings of the second law of thermodynamics, their curious views about radiometric dating with apparently revolutionary implications for microphysics, the plundering of debates in evolutionary theory for lines that can be usefully separated from their context, and so forth. But the most prominent creationists on the current intellectual scene are a new species, much smoother and more savvy. Not for them the commitment to a literal interpretation of *Genesis* with all the attendant difficulties. Some of them even veer close to accepting the so-called fact of evolution, the claim, adopted by most scientists within a dozen years of the publication of Darwin's *Origin,* that living

From Robert T. Pennock (ed.), *Intelligent Design Creationism and Its Critics* (Cambridge, MA: MIT Press, 2001.) © 2001 by Massachusetts Institute of Technology. Used with permission.

things are related and that the history of life has been a process of descent with modification. The sticking point for the born-again creationists, as it was for many late-nineteenth-century thinkers, is the mechanism of evolutionary change. They want to argue that natural selection is inadequate, indeed that no natural process could have produced the diversity of organisms, and thus that there must be some designing agent, who didn't just start the process but who has intervened throughout the history of life.

From the viewpoint of religious fundamentalists the creationist Reformation is something of a cop-out. Yet for many believers, the new movement delivers everything they want—particularly the vision of a personal God who supervises the history of life and nudges it to fulfill His purposes—and even militant evangelicals may come to appreciate the virtues of discretion. Moreover the high priests of the Reformation are clad in academic respectability, Professors of Law at University of California-Berkeley and of Biochemistry at Lehigh, and two of the movement's main cheerleaders are highly respected philosophers who teach at Notre Dame. Creationism is no longer hick, but *chic*.

2. WHY LITERALISM FAILED

In understanding the motivations for, and the shortcomings of, born-again creationism, it's helpful to begin by seeing why the movement had to retreat. The early days of the old-style "creation-science" campaign were highly successful. Duane Gish, debating champion for the original movement, crafted a brilliant strategy. He threw together a smorgasbord of apparent problems for evolutionary biology, displayed them very quickly before his audiences, and challenged his opponents to respond. At first, the biologists who debated him laboriously offered details to show that one or two of the problems Gish had raised could be solved, but then their time would run out and the audience would leave thinking that most of the objections were unanswerable. In the middle 1980s, however, two important changes took place: first, defenders of evolutionary theory began to take the same care in formulating answers as Gish had given to posing the problems, and there were

quick, and elegant, ways of responding to the commonly reiterated challenges; second, and more important, debaters began to fight back, asking how the observable features of the distribution and characteristics of plants and organisms, both those alive and those fossilized, could be rendered compatible with a literal interpretation of *Genesis*.

Suppose that the earth really was created about ten thousand years ago, with the major kinds fashioned then, and diversifying only a little since. How are we to account for the distributions of isotopes in the earth's crust? How are we to explain the regular, worldwide, ordering of the fossils? The only creationist response to the latter question has been to invoke the Noachian deluge: the order is as it is because of the relative positions of the organisms at the time the flood struck. Take this suggestion seriously, and you face some obvious puzzles: sharks and dolphins are found at the same depths, but, of course, the sharks occur much, much lower in the fossil record; pine trees, fir trees, and deciduous trees are mixed in forests around the globe, and yet the deciduous trees are latecomers in the worldwide fossil record. Maybe we should suppose that the oaks and beeches saw the waters rising and outran their evergreen rivals?

Far from being a solution to creationism's problems, the Flood is a real disaster. Consider biogeography. The ark lands on Ararat, say eight thousand years ágo, and out pop the animals (let's be kind and forget the plants). We now have eight thousand years for the marsupials to find their way to Australia, crossing several large bodies of water in the process. Perhaps you can imagine a few energetic kangaroos making it—but the wombats? Moreover, creationists think that while the animals were sorting themselves out, there was diversification of species within the "basic kinds"; jackals, coyotes, foxes, and dogs descend, so the story goes, from a common "dog kind." Now despite all the sarcasm that they have lavished on orthodox evolutionary theory's allegedly high rates of speciation, a simple calculation shows that the rates of speciation "creation-science" would require to manage the supposed amount of species diversification are truly breathtaking, orders of magnitude greater than any that have been dreamed of in evolutionary theory. Finally, to touch on just one more problem, creationists have to account for the survival of thousands of parasites that are specific to our species. During the days on the ark, these would have had to be carried by less than ten people. One can only speculate about the degree of ill-health that Noah and his crew must have suffered.

A major difficulty for old-style creationism has always been the fact that very similar anatomical structures are co-opted to different ends in species whose ways of life diverge radically. Moles, bats, whales, and dogs have forelimbs based on the same bone architecture that has to be adapted to their methods of locomotion. Not only is it highly implausible that the common blueprint reflects an especially bright idea from a designer who saw the best ways to fashion a burrowing tool, a wing, a flipper, and a leg, but the obvious explanation is that shared bone structure reflects shared ancestry. That explanation has only been deepened as studies of chromosome banding patterns have related common patterns among species evolutionists take to be related, as comparisons of proteins have exposed common sequences of amino acids, and, most recently, as genomic sequencing has shown the affinities in the ordering of bases in the DNA of organisms. Two points are especially noteworthy. First, like the anatomical residues of previously functional structures (such as the rudimentary pelvis found in whales), parts of our junk DNA have an uncanny resemblance to truncated, or mutilated, versions of genes found in other mammals, other vertebrates, or other animals. Second, the genetic kinship even among distantly related organisms is so great that a human sequence was identified as implicated in colon cancer by recognizing its similarity to a gene coding for a DNA repair enzyme in yeast. The evidence for common ancestry is so overwhelming that even the born-again creationist, Michael Behe is moved to admit that it is "fairly convincing" and that he has "no particular reason to doubt it" (DBB [*Darwin's Black Box*] 5).[1] (Notice that Behe doesn't quite commit himself here—in fact, to use an example from Richard Dawkins that Behe, and others, have discussed, there's an obvious line to describe Behe's phraseology: METHINKS IS A WEASEL.)

Imagine creationists becoming aware, at some level, of this little piece of history, and retreating to the bunker in which they plot strategy. What would they come up with? First, the familiar idea that the best defense is a good offense: they need to return to the tried-and-true, give-'em-hell, Duane Gish fire and brimstone attack on evolutionary theory. Second, they need to expose less to counterattack, and that means giving up on the disastrous "creation model" with all the absurdities that *Genesis*-as-literal-truth brings in its train; better to make biology safe for the central tenets of religion by talking about a design model so softly focused that nobody can raise nasty questions about parasites on the ark or the wombats' dash for the Antipodes. Third, they should do something to mute the evolutionists' most successful arguments, those that draw on the vast number of cross-species comparisons at all levels to establish common descent; this last is a matter of some delicacy, since too blatant a commitment to descent with modification might seem incompatible with creative design. So the best tactic here is a carefully choreographed waltz—advance a little toward accepting the "fact of evolution" here, back away there; as we shall see, some protagonists have an exquisite mastery of the steps.

Surprise, surprise. Born-again creationism has arrived at just this strategy. I'm going to look at the two most influential versions.

3. THE HEDGEHOG AND THE FOX

Isaiah Berlin's famous division that contrasts hedgehogs (people with one big idea) and foxes (people with lots of little ideas) applies not only to thinkers but to creationists as well. The two most prominent figures on the neo-creo scene are Michael Behe (a hedgehog) and Phillip Johnson (a fox), both of whom receive plaudits from such distinguished philosophers as Alvin Plantinga and Peter van Inwagen. (Since Plantinga and van Inwagen have displayed considerable skill in articulating and analyzing philosophical arguments, the only charitable interpretation of their fulsome blurbs is that a combination of *Schwärmerei* for creationist doctrine and profound ignorance of relevant bits of biology has induced them to put their brains in cold storage.) Johnson, a lawyer by training, is a far more subtle rhetorician than Gish, and he moves from topic to topic smoothly, discreetly making up the rules of evidence to suit his case as he goes. Many of his attack strategies refine those of country-bumpkin creationism, although, like the White Knight in Alice, he has a few masterpieces of his own invention.*

Behe, by contrast, mounts his case for born-again creationism by taking one large problem, and posing it again and again. The problem isn't particularly new: it's the old issue of "complex organs" that Darwin tried to confront in the *Origin*. Behe gives it a new twist by drawing on his background as a biochemist, and describing the minute details of mechanisms in organisms so as to make it seem impossible that they could ever have emerged from a stepwise natural process.

4. BEHE'S BIG IDEA

Here's the general form of the problem. Given our increased knowledge of the molecular structures in cells and the chemical reactions that go on within and among cells, it's possible to describe structures and processes in exceptionally fine detail. Many structures have large numbers of constituent molecules and the precise details of their fit together are essential for them to fulfill their functions. Similarly, many biochemical pathways require numerous enzymes to interact with one another, in appropriate relative concentrations, so that some important process can occur. Faced with either of these situations, you can pose an obvious question: how could organisms with the pertinent structures or processes have evolved from organisms that lacked them? That question is an explicit invitation to describe an ancestral sequence of organisms that culminated in one with the structures or processes at the end, where each change in the sequence is supposed to carry some selective advantage. If you now pose the question many times over, canvass various possibilities, and conclude that not only has no evolutionist proposed any satisfactory sequences, but that there are systematic reasons

for thinking that the structure or process could not have been built up gradually, you have an attack strategy that appears very convincing.

That, in outline, is Behe's big idea. Here's a typical passage, summarizing his quite lucid and accessible description of the structures of cilia and flagella:

> . . . as biochemists have begun to examine apparently simple structures like cilia and flagella, they have discovered staggering complexity, with dozens or even hundreds of precisely tailored parts. It is very likely that many of the parts we have not considered here are required for any cilium to function in a cell. As the number of required parts increases, the difficulty of gradually putting the system together skyrockets, and the likelihood of indirect scenarios plummets. Darwin looks more and more forlorn. (DBB 73)

This sounds like a completely recalcitrant problem for evolutionists, but it's worth asking just why precisely Darwin should look more and more forlorn.

Notice first that lots of sciences face all sorts of unresolved questions. To take an example close to hand, Behe's own discussions of cilia frankly acknowledge that there's a lot still to learn about molecular structure and its contributions to function. So the fact that evolutionary biologists haven't yet come up with a sequence of organisms culminating in bacteria with flagella or cilia might be regarded as signaling a need for further research on the important open problem of how such bacteria evolved. Not so! declares Behe. We have here "irreducible complexity," and it's just impossible to imagine a sequence of organisms adding component molecules to build the structures up gradually.

What does this mean? Is Behe supposing that his examples point to failure of natural selection as a mechanism for evolution? If so, then perhaps he believes that there was a sequence of organisms that ended up with a bacterium with a flagellum (say), but that the intermediates in this sequence added molecules to no immediate purpose, presumably being at selective disadvantage because of this. (Maybe the Good Lord tempers the

---

*Editor's note: Discussion of Johnson's work has been omitted from this selection.

wind to the shorn bacterium.) Or does he just dispense with intermediates entirely, thinking that the Creator simply introduced all the right molecules *de novo*? In that case, despite his claims, he really does doubt common descent. Behe's actual position is impossible to discern because he has learned Duane Gish's lesson (Always attack! Never explain!). I'll return at the very end to the cloudiness of Behe's account of the history of life.

Clearly, Behe thinks that Darwinian evolutionary theory requires some sequence of precursors for bacteria with flagella and that no appropriate sequence could exist. But why does he believe this? Here's a simple-minded version of the argument. Assume that the flagellum needs 137 proteins. Then Darwinians are required to produce a sequence of 138 organisms, the first having none of the proteins and each one having one more protein than its predecessor. Now, we're supposed to be moved by the plight of organisms numbers 2 to 137, each of which contains proteins that can't serve any function, and is therefore, presumably, a target of selection. Only number 1, the ancestor, and number 138, in which all the protein constituents come together to form the flagellum, have just what it takes to function. The intermediates would wither in the struggle for existence. Hence evolution under natural selection couldn't have brought the bacterium from there to here.[2]

But this story is just plain silly, and Darwinians ought to disavow any commitment to it. After all, it's a common theme of evolutionary biology that constituents of a cell, a tissue, or an organism, are put to new uses because of some modification of the genotype. So maybe the immediate precursor of the proud possessor of the flagellum is a bacterium in which all the protein constituents were already present, but in which some other feature of the cell chemistry interferes with the reaction that builds the flagellum. A genetic change removes the interference (maybe a protein assumes a slightly different configuration, binding to something that would have bound to one of the constituents of the flagellum, preventing the assembly). "But, Professor Kitcher [creos always try to be polite], do you have any evidence for this scenario?" Of course not. That is to shift the question. We were offered a proof of the impossibility of a particular sequence, and when one tries to show that the proof is invalid by inventing possible instances, it's not pertinent to ask for reasons to think that those instances exist. If they genuinely reveal that what was was declared to be impossible isn't, then we no longer have a claim that the Darwinian sequence couldn't have occurred, but simply an open problem of the kind that spurs scientists in any field to engage in research.

Behe has made it look as though there's something more here by inviting us to think about the sequence of precursors in a very particular way. He doesn't actually say that proteins have to be added one at a time—he surely knows very well that that would provoke the reaction I've offered—but his defense of the idea that there just couldn't be a sequence of organisms leading up to bacteria with flagella insinuates, again and again, that the problem is that the alleged intermediates would have to have lots of the components lying around like so many monkey-wrenches in the intracellular works. This strategy is hardly unprecedented. Country-bumpkin creos offered a cruder version when they dictated to evolutionists what fossil intermediates would have to be like the transitional forms on the way to birds would have to have had half-scales and half-feathers, halfway wings—or so we are told.[3] Behe has made up his own ideas about what transitional organisms must have been like, and then argued that such organisms couldn't have existed.

In fact, we don't need to compare my guesswork with his. What Darwinism is committed to (at most) is the idea that modifications of DNA sequence (insertions, deletions, base changes, translocations) could yield a sequence of organisms culminating in a bacterium with a flagellum, with selective advantages for the later member of each adjacent pair. To work out what the members of this sequence of organisms might have been like, our ideas should be educated by the details of how the flagellum is actually assembled and the loci in the bacterial genome that are involved. Until we know these things, it's quite likely that any efforts to describe precursors or intermediates will be whistling in the dark. Behe's examples cunningly exploit our ability to give a molecular analysis of the end product and our ignorance of the molecular details of how it is produced.

Throughout his book, Behe repeats the same story. He describes, often charmingly, the complexities of molecular structures and processes. There would be nothing to complain of if he stopped here and said: "Here are some interesting problems for molecularly minded evolutionists to work on, and, in a few decades time, perhaps, in light of increased knowledge of how development works at the molecular level, we may be able to see what the precursors were like." But he doesn't. He tries to argue that the precursors and intermediates required by Darwinian evolutionary theory couldn't have existed. This strategy has to fail because Behe himself is just as ignorant about the molecular basis of development as his Darwinian opponents. Hence he hasn't a clue what kinds of precursors and intermediates the Darwinian account is actually committed to—so it's impossible to demonstrate that the commitment can't be honored. However, again and again, Behe disguises his ignorance by suggesting to the reader that the Darwinian story must take a very particular form—that it has to consist in something like the simple addition of components, for example—and on that basis he can manufacture the illusion of giving an impossibility proof.

Although this is the main rhetorical trick of the book, there are some important subsidiary bits of legerdemain. Like pre-Reformation creationists, Behe loves to flash probability calculations, offering spurious precision to his criticisms. Here's his attack on a scenario for the evolution of a blood-clotting mechanism, tentatively proposed by Russell Doolittle:

> . . . let's do our own quick calculation. Consider that animals with blood-clotting cascades have roughly 10,000 genes, each of which is divided into an average of three pieces. This gives a total of about 30,000 gene pieces. TPA [Tissue Plasminogen Activator] has four different types of domains. By "variously shuffling," the odds of getting those four domains together is 30,000 to the fourth power, which is approximately one-tenth to the eighteenth power. Now, if the Irish Sweepstakes had odds of winning of one-tenth to the eighteenth power, and if a million people played the lottery each year, it would take an average of about a thousand billion years before *anyone* (not just a particular person) won the lottery. . . . Doolittle apparently needs to

shuffle and deal himself a number of perfect bridge hands to win the game. (DBB 94)

This sounds quite powerful, and Behe drives home the point by noting that Doolittle provides no quantitative estimates, adding that "without numbers, there is no science" (DBB 95)—presumably to emphasize that born-again creationists are better scientists than the distinguished figures they attack. But consider a humdrum phenomenon suggested by Behe's analogy to bridge. Imagine that you take a standard deck of cards and deal yourself thirteen. What's the probability that you got exactly those cards in exactly that order? The answer is 1 in 4×10^{21}. Suppose you repeat this process ten times. You'll now have received ten standard bridge hands, ten sets of thirteen cards, each one delivered in a particular order. The chance of getting just those cards in just that order is 1 in $4^{10} \times 10^{210}$. This is approximately 1 in 10^{222}. Notice that the denominator is far larger than that of Behe's trifling 10^{18}. So it must be *really* improbable that you (or anyone else) would ever receive just those cards in just that order in the entire history of the universe. But, whatever the cards were, you did.

What my analogy shows is that, if you describe events that actually occur from a particular perspective, you can make them look improbable. Thus, given a description of the steps in Doolittle's scenario for the evolution of TPA, the fact that you can make the probability look small doesn't mean that that isn't (or couldn't) have been the way things happened. One possibility is that the evolution of blood-clotting was genuinely improbable. But there are others.

Return to your experiment with the deck of cards. Let's suppose that all the hands you were dealt were pretty mundane—fairly evenly distributed among the suits, with a scattering of high cards in each. If you calculated the probability of receiving ten mundane hands in succession, it would of course be much higher than the priority of being dealt those very particular mundane hands with the cards arriving in just that sequence (although it wouldn't be as large as you might expect). There might be an analogue for blood-clotting, depending on how many candidates there are among the

3,000 "gene pieces" to which Behe alludes that would yield a protein product able to play the necessary role. Suppose that there are a hundred acceptable candidates for each position. That means that the chance of success on any particular draw is $(1/30)^4$, which is about 1 in 2.5 million. Now, if there were 10,000 tries per year, it would take, on average, two or three centuries to arrive at the right combination, a flicker of an instant in evolutionary time.

Of course, neither Behe nor I knows how tolerant the blood-clotting system is, how many different molecular ways it allows to get the job done. Thus we can't say if the right way to look at the problem is to think of the situation as the analogue to being dealt a very particular sequence of cards in a very particular order, or whether the right comparison is with cases in which a more general type of sequence occurs. But these two suggestions don't exhaust the relevant cases.

Suppose you knew the exact order of cards in the deck prior to each deal. Then the probability that the particular sequence would occur would be extremely high (barring fumbling or sleight of hand, the probability would be 1). The sequence only *looks* improbable because we don't know the order. Perhaps that's true for the Doolittle shuffling process as well. Given the initial distribution of pieces of DNA, plus the details of the biochemical milieu, principles of chemical recombination might actually make it very probable that the cascade Doolittle hypothesizes would ensue. Once again, nobody knows whether this is so. Behe simply assumes that it isn't.

Let me sum up. There are two questions to pose: What is the probability that the Doolittle sequence would occur? What is the significance of a low value for that probability? The answer to the first question is that we haven't a clue: it might be close to 1, it might be small but significant enough to make it likely that the sequence would occur in a flicker of evolutionary time, or it might be truly tiny (as Behe suggests). The answer to the second question is that genuinely improbable things sometimes happen, and one shouldn't confuse improbability with impossibility. Once these points are recognized, it's clear

that, for all its rhetorical force, Behe's appeal to numbers smacks more of numerology than of science. As with his main line of argument, it turns out to be an attempt to parlay ignorance of molecular details into an impossibility proof.

I postpone until the very end another fundamental difficulty with Behe's argument for design, to wit his fuzzy faith that appeal to a creator will make all these "difficulties" evaporate. As we shall see, both he and Johnson try to hide any positive views. With good reason....

6. WHERE'S THE BEEF?

I come at last to the most basic difficulty with the neo-creo attack, its dim suggestions that the scientific world needs a shot of supernaturalism. The born-again creationists tread different paths to a common destination. Whether hedgehogs or foxes, they conclude that evolutionary theory is beset by problems...and they portray the establishment as dogmatic in its insistence on excluding creative design: given that the going story of life and its history is such a shambles, why are these evolutionists so obstinate in thinking that some "purely naturalistic process" produced people? When this conclusion is made explicit, there's a natural question to pose to the neo-creos. How exactly is the appeal to creative design supposed to help?

I've been contending throughout that the charges of "insoluble problems" are wildly overblown. But let's play along for a bit. Consider the difficulties that Behe...cites and suppose that they really do need to be addressed. Why should we think that invoking creative design with all its theological resonances, is just the ticket for solving them?

Behe...[doesn't]...say. [He has] learned from the failures of pre-Reformation creationism, and they know much, much better than to put their literalist cards out on the table. Fine. But we ought to be a little curious about what sort of magic a creative design model might be able to work.

Let's ... concede to [Behe] that we haven't a clue about how you can produce the bacterial flagellum or the clotting cascade in small steps. We might think we'd get some clues once developmental molecular genetics has developed a bit, but maybe Behe has a plausible proposal that will save us the wait and the trouble. What could it be? Well, it has to involve creative design, so we can assume that the unbridgeable gaps between the bacteria sans flagella and their fully equipped successors are transcended through the activities of some Creator or "creative force." Continuing to be generous, let's give Behe the personalized version.

So what does the Creator do? Option 1: He (we'll throw in patriarchy as well) arranges the selection regime for the hapless intermediates, directs the mutations, and so forth; so, in accord with a doctrine Behe has "no particular reason to doubt," organisms are linked by descent, and the Creator's work is devoted to making sure that just the right mutations arise in the right order and that the organisms on the way to the complex final state are protected against the consequences of having lots of useless spare parts that will be assembled at some final stage. Option 2: the Creator dispenses with a lot of the intermediate steps by cunningly arranging for lots of mutations to happen at once; if 183 new proteins are needed for the new structure, then zap! He strikes the appropriate loci with his magical mutating finger; or maybe He does it in two goes of 92 and 91 (with a protective environmental regime for the halfway stages); or in three interventions of 61 mutations a trick.... Here, again, organisms are related by descent with modification, although the "descent" and the "modifications" are a bit abnormal. Option 3: the Creator gives up on mutation and selection entirely, simply creating a bunch of organisms with the right molecular stuff *de novo;* of course, if Behe thinks that this is the way things worked, then He really does have doubts about descent with modification.

The first point to note is that there's absolutely no evidence in favor of any of these options—they are the kinds of things to which one would be driven only if one thought that Behe's Big Problem was so intractable that there was no alternative. But matters are actually much worse than that, as one can see by posing questions about the Creator's psychology. Why should anyone think that the kind of Creator for whom Behe and Johnson both want to make room would undertake any of

these projects? In Option 1, we envisage a Creator with the power to direct mutations and contrive protective environments who prefers simulating natural selection with gerrymandered selection pressures to directing all the needed mutations at once. In Option 2, we envisage a Creator who has the power to create organisms, but who prefers to simulate descent by the magic of mass mutation rather than simply producing the kinds of organisms He wants (either successively or simultaneously). In Option 3, we envisage a Creator who creates all the kinds of organisms He wants, as He wants them, but equips them with the genomic junk found in organisms He's created earlier. I am no engineer, but these visions inspire me to echo Alfonso X on the complexities of the Ptolemaic account of the solar system—had the Creator consulted me at the Creation, I think I could have given Him useful advice.

Perhaps I am being unfair. Maybe the project of design looks ludicrous because I have selected the wrong options for Creative intervention. Behe could easily answer my concerns by coming up with an alternative, one that would explain how creative design has figured in the history of life on our planet and how that creative design is part of a project worthy of his favorite Creator. I'm inclined to think that he won't do that, that the silence in neo-creo positive proposals will continue to be deafening. After all, positive doctrines and explanations have always been creationism's Achilles Heel.

Notice that the line of argument in which I'm now engaged isn't a defense of evolutionary theory. For the sake of argument, I've conceded that evolutionary theory faces deep and intractable problems, although I've spent most of my time arguing that that's totally false. To show that the problems alleged to face evolutionary theory can't be solved by appealing to creative design isn't to rehabilitate the theory, for one doesn't always have to adopt the better of two alternatives. But in demonstrating that evolutionary theory is clearly superior to the imaginable members of the creationist family I ought to sap the motivation of those who are drawn to creationism. Attacking evolutionary theory was supposed to make room for God, but, as we've seen, there's not much hope for an active role for the Deity in any successor to evolutionary theory. . . .

NOTES

I am extremely grateful to Dan Dennett and Ed Curley for sharing with me their unpublished discussions of the creationist writers I discuss here. I have also learned much from an illuminating essay by Niall Shanks and Karl Joplin, "Redundant Complexity: A Critical Analysis of Intelligent Design in Biochemistry," *Philosophy of Science*. 66, 1999, 268–282. Finally, I'd like to thank Robert Pennock for his editorial encouragement and for the insights

of his own excellent treatment of the neo-creos in *Tower of Babel.*

1. I'll be quoting extensively from two creationist works, Michael Behe, *Darwin's Black Box: The Biochemical Challenge to Evolution*, New York: The Free Press, 1996 (cited as DBB) and Phillip Johnson, *Darwin on Trial*, Washington D.C.: Regnery Gateway, 1993 (cited as DOT).
2. I borrow this pithy formulation from Dan Dennett.
3. For further discussion of this issue, see my *Abusing Science: The Case against Creationism*, Cambridge MA.: MIT Press, p. 117.

VIII.B.4   Natural Providence (Or Design Trouble)

MICHAEL J. MURRAY

Michael Murray (1963–   ) is professor of philosophy at Franklin and Marshall College and works primarily in the fields of philosophy of religion and history of modern philosophy. In this article he raises objections against William Dembski's theory about how to detect intelligent design. He also argues, against Dembski, that even if the existence of a designer were empirically detectable, this fact should not have any impact on the actual practice of natural science.

Recent work in Intelligent Design Theory (IDT) reopens a number of questions concerning the nature of God's providence over creation. Friends of IDT claim that their "explanatory filter" allows us to detect design empirically and that this provides a way to make appeal to supernatural design in properly scientific explanations while at the same time undercutting methodological naturalism. I argue here that the explanatory filter is fatally flawed, and that detection of design would not undercut methodological naturalism in any case. Friends of IDT fail to see this because they adopt a Newtonian conception of natural providence, while failing to consider a preferable Leibnizian conception.

I. INTRODUCTION

The history of discussions concerning divine providence contains two distinct strands. The first strand concerns God's providence over those features of his creation that directly concern human beings. Discussions concerning foreknowledge and freedom, freedom and predestination, soteriological election, etc. fall under this strand. In the sixteenth century, and for the latter portion of the twentieth century, this is the strand that has been most pronounced in Christian philosophical discussions of providence. However, while traditional theistic religions hold that God exercises providential control over human affairs, they also hold that God's providential activity has a wider scope, extending to the workings of all of nature. The Christian

From *Faith and Philosophy*, Vol. 20, No. 3, July 2003. Copyright © 2003 The Society of Christian Philosophers. Used with permission.

faith specifically holds that God's intentions and handiwork are not merely evident in those features of creation that centrally concern human beings, but throughout the whole of creation. This second strand held sway in discussions of providence in the late seventeenth and early eighteenth centuries, most notably in the disputes between Leibniz and the Newtonians. Recently, interest in questions regarding natural providence has resurfaced, and this resurgence is due in large part to the work in Intelligent Design Theory.

Intelligent Design theorists contend that the deliverances of natural science show us that much of the natural world can only be explained by appeal to intelligent design, and that this means that natural science must be willing to accommodate appeals to design. This position is distinctively Newtonian and, I think, mistaken. In this paper I want to show how one can happily admit evidence of design in nature, while rejecting the claim that this has any implications for the practice of natural science at all. Rather, friends of Intelligent Design should favor a Leibnizian model in which design is perfectly compatible with thoroughgoing nomic regularity in nature, and thus with a form of methodological naturalism in scientific practice.

II. INTELLIGENT DESIGN THEORY

In the last five years or so, advocates of so-called Intelligent Design Theory, or IDT, have argued that Christians need to take their beliefs about natural providence more seriously, and that when they do, this will have an impact on how they think about the workings of nature itself. Christians believe, they argue, that God is not one to create the universe and then leave it to its own devices. Christian commitments concerning miracles and prayer are sufficient to demonstrate that. Since God is intimately connected with his creation, Christians are thereby committed to thinking that certain states of the natural world are brought about directly by the divine hand. Any such events, of course, are going to be ones which cannot be truthfully accounted for by appeal merely to natural entities and their native powers. All attempts to explain such immediately divinely caused states of affairs by appeal only to natural entities and their native powers will thereby end up either in frustration or error.

Friends of IDT are, however, quick to point out that contemporary natural science is firmly committed to a policy of methodological naturalism in science. Thus, in cases where God's activity has in fact played a role in causing states of nature, the contemporary scientist will, they claim, necessarily land in frustration and error. Christian scientists who are willing to countenance the hand of design in natural explanations will not be at such a disadvantage. For these scientists' awareness of divine activity in the world leaves them open to the possibility that states of nature might not be explicable by reference to natural entities and their native powers. And if there are reliable empirical means for discerning when states of nature cannot be naturally explained, the Christian scientist will have a distinct advantage here. She will be able to defend an empirically grounded, scientific explanation for the phenomenon in question that does not end in frustration or error.

IDT theorists thus commend such a program to the scientific community generally, and to the Christian scientific community specifically. To that end, they have offered intriguing arguments for the claim that design can be discerned by empirical means and that in some cases, scientific explanations that invoke design are vastly preferable to the best explanations available under methodological naturalism.

However, and perhaps not surprisingly, IDT is not a monolith. A closer look at the work of IDT advocates reveals that they do not all understand IDT or its implications in the same way. The somewhat more than casual observer comes away with the impression that some claim a greater reach for IDT than others. In particular, defenders of the view claim that IDT demonstrates one of the following increasingly bold claims:

1) Intelligent design in the natural world, if it exists, is empirically detectable.
2) The natural world exhibits empirically detectable intelligent design.
3) The natural world exhibits empirically detectable intelligent design that can only be accounted for by direct intervention of a designing agent.

4) The natural world exhibits empirically detectable intelligent design that can only be accounted for by direct intervention of a designing agent and this requires that science reject methodological naturalism.

Christian philosophers should and do exhibit a good deal of sympathy with the motivation and substance of IDT. Christian natural scientists, however, seem to exhibit a great deal of reticence about IDT and its purported relevance for scientific practice.

In what follows I will examine three of the four claims above and consider whether or not IDT advocates have given us good reasons to adopt them. Although I will ignore (2) here, I will argue that their work has given us good reason to adopt (1), but not (3) and (4). Instead, I will argue that even though IDT advocates have given us reason to think that design is detectable in nature, there are no possible empirical grounds that could lead us to endorse (3). Since, by their lights, endorsing (3) provides us with the only reason for seeking to dump methodological naturalism, we thus also have reason for rejecting both conjuncts of (4).

III. THE "EXPLANATORY FILTER"

William Dembski has undoubtedly done more than any other friend of IDT to make the case for the empirical detectability of intelligent design. It will be important to lay out Dembski's view here in brief. According to Dembski, there are only three general explanatory paradigms available when we aim to explain the existence of an object, event, or state of affairs: law, chance, or design.[1] Dembski characterizes the three explanatory paradigms as follows:

> To attribute an event to law is to say that the event will almost always happen given certain antecedent circumstances. To attribute an event to chance is to say that its occurrence is characterized by some (perhaps not fully specified) probability distribution according to which the event might equally well not have happened. To attribute an event to design is to say that it cannot plausibly be referred to either law or chance.[2]

In some cases, Dembski says that we attribute an event to law when we regard the event as necessary

or, more cautiously, as the "almost inevitable outcome of prior circumstances in conjunction with the laws of nature." The point here is straightforward enough. If one were to stumble across an ornate naturally occurring scolecite crystal, one might think that they had stumbled upon a masterful work of art. Consultation with a local geochemist, however, would reveal that scolecite is the crystalline form of hydrated calcium aluminum silicate, and that such crystals form due to the fact that the lattice structure in the crystal represents the minimal energy state for hydrated calcium aluminum silicate in solid form. While it might look like such a remarkable structure requires intelligent intervention, its occurrence is almost inevitable given certain conditions and the laws governing crystal formation.

What about an event which is not explained as the almost inevitable outcome of prior circumstances in conjunction with natural laws? Such might be the case for a) events which result from probabilistic laws (where the occurrence of the event in question is improbable), or b) events for which there is no underlying law-like regularity which governs the occurrence of such events. In these cases, Dembski claims we must first ask whether or not the event is complex. If not, then it is reasonable to conclude that the event is the result of chance.

To illustrate, Dembski asks us to consider a scene from the film *Contact* in which researchers searching for extraterrestrial life receive a signal consisting of pulses and pauses. Interpreting pulses as 1's and pauses as 0's, the fictional researchers find that an extra-galactic signal they received represents the prime numbers from 2 to 101 in base 2. In the film, this gives the researchers a strong motive for believing that intelligent design was responsible for the signal. Yet, as Dembski points out, if the researchers had received a series of pulses and pauses yielding the sequence 11011101111 no one would have thought this result worthy of an inference to design, even though this constitutes the first 5 prime numbers in base 2. The reason this shorter sequence is more reasonably attributed to chance than design is the *lack of sufficient complexity*. The string is too short to conclude with any confidence that it results from anything other than chance.

In cases where events are a) complex and b) not explicable as the inevitable outcome of conditions and laws, the appropriate explanatory inference depends on the *sort of complexity* involved. If I, in a moment of bad gamesmanship, throw a Scrabble game out of the window, the resulting arrangement of tiles on the ground outside will be complex and not explicable as the inevitable outcome of natural laws. However, no one could reasonably conclude that that arrangement of tiles was the result of intelligent design. Though an intelligent agent threw the game pieces, the arrangement might have just as easily resulted from the game box being blown off the windowsill as from being thrown.

However, if you were to pass by my window and find the very same Scrabble pieces arranged in such a way as to spell out the sentence "WELCOME TO PENNSYLVANIA" you would be quite confident that this arrangement was the result of design. Though the arrangement of thrown pieces and carefully placed pieces both exhibit a high degree of complexity, the latter instances an outcome that we would regard as *favored* in some sense, whereas the former would not. Dembski labels such favored outcomes "specified complexity." Thus, in cases of complex, non-nomically inevitable events, unspecified complexity is best explained by chance, whereas specified complexity is explained by design.

Dembski claims that his "explanatory filter" is nothing but an explicit and carefully formulated explanation of the sorts of ordinary reasoning processes we employ when explaining events generally. If we stumble across a large, perfectly pyramidal shaped structure in the Central American jungle (i.e., a pyramid), we are able to infer reasonably that the structure was intelligently designed since we can reasonably infer that such structures do not arise from inevitable nomic processes, and they exhibit a high degree of "specified complexity."

In what follows I will raise two difficulties for the explanatory filter. The first concerns the detection of the specification of complexity which licenses the design inference. The second concerns the claim that events explained as the result of inevitable nomic regularities should not be regarded as designed. I will address the former in section IV briefly, and the latter in sections V through VIII in some detail.

IV. SPECIFIED COMPLEXITY?

When we are trying to determine if a complex event exhibits specification, it is the *pattern* exhibited by the event that is the focus of attention. Dembski claims that a complex event exhibits specified complexity when the pattern the event displays is *detachable*. For the sake of clarity, note that it is the *pattern the event exemplifies* rather than *the event itself* which is detachable. Roughly, a pattern is detachable if we can construct the pattern independent of our knowledge of the event which instances the pattern. In other words, if the pattern instanced in the event is one we can derive only after becoming acquainted with the outcomes, the pattern is not detachable.

Dembski illustrates this with a case in which an election official was convicted of tampering when it was discovered that in 40 out of 41 cases, he gave Democrats the privileged top spot on the ballot. Given our knowledge of how elections work and the aims of a corrupt Democratic official, we can, without knowing any actual outcomes, know what a "cheating pattern" looks like. It looks like Democrats getting top billing every time (or nearly every time). If that pattern is a pattern we can "come up with" without consulting any actual ballots we would have a *detachable pattern*.

More specifically, a pattern is detachable if we can "come up with it" via *side information* which exhibits *conditional independence* and *tractability*. In the election case, our side information consists of information about what a pattern of cheating by a corrupt election official would look like. Such side information is *conditionally independent* when we have access to it in a way that is independent of our knowledge of the actual election outcomes. The side information is *tractable* when we are able, using that independent information, to construct the pattern which the event displays. As we saw, the side information in the election case is tractable as well since we can construct "election ballot cheating patterns" from our knowledge of how cheating would be accomplished.

Thus we have a recipe for discerning specified complexity. If the pattern displayed by the complex event in question is detachable (i.e., can be derived from side information that is both conditionally independent and tractable), then the event exhibits specified complexity and is designed (unless explained by "law").

The trouble with Dembski's account however is that too many, perhaps all, patterns end up exhibiting specified complexity. The reason for this is that if we help ourselves to the right side information, we can generate a host of detachable patterns that should be regarded as the result of chance. In the election case, we can specify all patterns of outcomes (Democrats on top 41 times, 40 times, 39 times, in all of their permutations) by simply using an algorithm which delivers every possible outcome of ballot placement. That is, if my side information is an algorithm which will spit out a list of all possible placements of Democrats and Republicans on the ballot, then we will be able to specify *any pattern* by using side information (the algorithm) that is truly *conditionally independent* and *tractable*.[3]

What we need here, no doubt, is a restriction on side information so that we can correspondingly restrict the range of patterns that will count as "specified." But how should we do that? The only way, it appears, is to have in mind in advance what sorts of outcomes are privileged, and then consider cases in which side information would yield these privileged outcomes. Thus, in the case of the Scrabble tiles above, if the pattern of tiles is one that spells out a coherent sentence in the English language, it counts as specified. So, side information concerning the formation of coherent English sentences should be permitted.

Unfortunately, this sort of exercise is futile. We were looking for a way of objectively determining which events exhibit patterns of specified complexity. But on the "restricted side information" strategy, this is silly. To restrict side information we must already *know* how to pick out specified complexity in the first place. Thus, rather than the explanatory filter helping us to figure out when there is specified complexity and thus design, the filters success requires that we *already* be capable of picking out design independently.

How then should we (or rather, how *do* we) detect design among the occurrences of improbable outcomes? I am not sure. But I, like friends of IDT, am confident we can do it. Perhaps we should take a cue from the old fashioned design arguments which said that "specified outcomes" are ones that exhibit patterns that intelligent beings often purpose to bring about in the world. So, when events exemplify patterns which are useful or aesthetically pleasing, we can regard them as likely to have resulted from design rather than chance.

Peter van Inwagen has offered a principle in another context which we might be able to employ here as well. In considering patterns of fine-tuning in the cosmos, van Inwagen proposes that we might be able to distinguish improbable but unspecified outcomes from equally improbable but specified outcomes by using the following principle, slightly modified here:

> Suppose that there is a certain non-nomically determined fact that has no known explanation; suppose that one can think of a possible explanation of that fact, an explanation that (if only it were true) is a very good explanation; then it is wrong to say that that event stands in no more need of an explanation than an otherwise similar event for which no such explanation is available.[4]

On this principle, we look at events which exhibit patterns not explained by law and see if a plausible alternative (read "design") explanation can be given. If so, we should regard the event as likely designed. If not, we should regard it as a result of chance. Thus, if we see Democrats receiving top billing in 40 out of 41 elections, and we notice that the election official is biased towards Democratic candidates, we have a pattern that admits of an explanation which, if true, is a very good one (cheating). But when the pattern is Democrats on top 21 times, Republicans 20 times, no such corresponding good explanation can be found, and the pattern can, and should, be taken as random.

The upshot of this first criticism of Dembski is that the explanatory filter as described is flawed, but not fatally so. We can still see a way of distinguishing chance and design, though the method of doing so is far less rule governed and objective than perhaps the friends of IDT would wish for.

V. NOMIC REGULARITY AND THE DEFEAT OF DESIGN

I turn now to a second problem for Dembski's explanatory filter. The above criticism focuses on the way in which Dembski distinguishes explanations via chance and design. This criticism concerns the distinction of explanations via law and design. In describing Dembski's explanatory filter we have seen that the first node in the decision tree requires us to determine if the event is the (nearly) inevitable outcome of nomic regularities. If so, the explanation is law, not chance or design. If we can discern some law-like way that an event, even a complex specified event, comes about, this defeats the design explanation. Michael Behe, in his book *Darwin's Black Box,* makes this claim repeatedly in referring to the "irreducibly complex" biochemical processes and structures he treats. He writes:

> How do we confidently detect design? For discrete physical systems–if there is not a separate route to their production, design is evident when a number of separate, interacting components are ordered in such a way as to accomplish a function beyond the individual components.[5]

And later,

> We must also consider the laws of nature. The laws of nature can organize matter . . . . The most relevant laws are those of biological reproduction, mutation, and natural selection. If a biological structure can be explained in terms of natural laws, then we cannot conclude that it was designed.[6]

Thus, for Behe, success at explaining an event via nomic regularities trumps design explanations.

However, this seems to entail a claim that many IDT advocates deny, sometimes strenuously, namely, that appeal to intelligent design requires appeal to supernatural intervention in the course of nature. One cannot have it both ways. If my success at explaining an event's occurrence through law-like processes undercuts a design explanation, then the presence of design

requires that some events be caused in a non-nomically regular way, i.e., miraculously. This is simple modus tollens.[7]

Behe is not alone in such claims. Here, for example, is Phillip Johnson:

> If God had created a lifeless world, even with oceans rich in amino acids and other organic molecules, and thereafter had left matter alone, life would not have come into existence. If God had done nothing but create a world of bacteria and protozoa, it would still be a world of bacteria and protozoa. Whatever may have been the case in the remote past, the chemicals we see today have no observable tendency or ability to form complex plants and animals. Persons who believe that chemicals unassisted by intelligence can combine to create life, or that bacteria can evolve by natural processes into complex animals, are making an a priori assumption that nature has the resources to do its own creating. I call such persons metaphysical naturalists.[8]

Although Johnson is not as explicit here, the point is the same. Natural entities, operating via their natural powers, are incapable of explaining the existence of the complex biological entities we find. Thus, explanation of such entities must require reference to supernatural intervention into the course of nature.

Above I noted, however, that many friends of IDT deny that design has any such implications. Dembski, to cite one example, insists that even though we might be able to assert confidently that a designer is required to explain an event, this has no direct implications for the *way* in which the designer brought the event about. Dembski claims the question of whether an intelligent cause was involved, the *detectability question,* is independent of the question of how such a designer acted, the *modality question.*

> The point I want to stress, however, is that the detectability and modality questions are largely independent, with the . . . answer to one question not necessarily affecting the correct answer to the other.[9]

And yet, in the same work, Dembski indicates that a *sine qua non* of IDT is that it appeals to divine interventions. In the following passage,

Dembski is explaining the difference between IDT and naturalistic evolution, claiming, it appears, that the course of nature will have gaps in the former but not the latter:

> The first thing to notice is that naturalistic evolution and intelligent design both make definite assertions of fact. To see this, consider your own personal genealogy. Here you are. You had parents. They in turn had parents. They too had parents. And so on. If we run the video camera back in time, generation upon generation, what do we see? Do we see a continuous chain of natural causes which go from apes to small furry mammals to reptiles to slugs and slime molds to blue-green algae and finally all the way back to prebiotic soup, with no event in the chain ever signaling the activity of an intelligent cause? Or as we trace back the genealogy, do we find events that clearly signal the activity of an intelligent cause? There exist reliable criteria for inferring the activity of intelligent causes. Does the natural history display clear marks of intelligence and thereby warrant a design inference, or does it not? To answer this question one way is to embrace intelligent design; to answer it the other way is to embrace naturalistic evolution.[10]

Perhaps one might think that these remarks don't force Dembski to hold that IDT requires divine intervention in the processes of nature. After all, he merely says that if IDT is correct, some event in the chain will "signal" the activity of a designer. Perhaps this just means that such activity is detectable, leaving the modality question still wide open. Yet a few pages earlier Dembski is clear that the earmarks of design in question cannot be seen if the natural causal nexus is uninterrupted. As a result, he claims, so-called theistic evolution and atheistic evolution are identical in scientific content.

Thus, it seems that IDT advocates might consistently hold that the answer to the detectability question leaves the modality question open. But the Explanatory Filter contradicts this, by holding that if the modality question yields a nomically regular answer, the detectability question must be answered in the negative. And this implies that if design is detectable, there must have been intervention. We now turn to see why this claim is deeply problematic.

VI. INTERVENTION AND DECK-STACKING

Imagine that I invite you and two other friends to my home for a friendly game of high stakes poker. In order to insure the integrity of the game, I propose that we play each hand with a freshly opened deck of preshuffled cards. After five hands of five-card stud you grow suspicious. The reason: I have won every pot with a hand of four aces.

Convinced that I am cheating, you set out to figure out how I have done it. You look up my sleeve, my pant leg, under my hat, all to no avail. It becomes clear to you that I did not break the rules by unfairly adding cards to, or removing cards from, my hand during the game. All attempts to discover signs of intervention during the course of the game come up empty. What should you conclude? Perhaps one might conclude that no rules of poker playing were violated during the course of the game and *thus* that there was no cheating after all. No contravention of the rules during the game, no cheating.

One of the other losers is, however, not convinced by such reasoning. While it might be true that there was no cheating by *intervention,* there are other ways to manipulate the game to get the favored outcome. How? The answer is, of course, easily discovered in the neatly stacked pile of "new pre-shuffled" decks at the edge of the table. Upon examining the first, we notice that among the cards at the top of the deck, every fourth one is an ace. The jig is up! All I had to do is control certain initial conditions, i.e., who dealt the hands, and I would be a guaranteed winner.

Here we have a case in which the earmarks of intelligent intervention are clear. It is reasonable for us to expect that no one would, just by chance, win five rounds of poker with hands of four aces. But there are two very different ways in which intelligent agency might have secured the result, by *intervention* and by *deck-stacking*.

Notice two important implications of the distinction that I will return to later. First, the inference that we make that cheating occurred here (call it "the cheating inference") was made in

[a] way that was *indifferent* to our knowledge of how it was pulled off. It might be the case that someone looking at the game that we played would plainly see that no rules of poker playing were violated. The game was utterly "nomically regular." Nonetheless, the cheating inference would not be undercut.

The relevance of this observation should be obvious. As we saw earlier, IDT advocates, most notably Behe and Johnson, argue that design inferences are defeated if the processes that lead to the designed outcome are nomically regular. This is a mistake. Even if the designed outcomes can be explained by appeal to the regular operations of the laws of nature, inferences to design can still be warranted.

The second implication, the flip-side of the first perhaps, is that if all we had access to was the outcomes of the poker games, there would be no way in principle to discern whether or not the cheating occurred via deck-stacking or intervention. So, if we imagine that after each hand, the players laid out their sets of five cards on a separate table, and one had access only to those final results, we could tell that the one player had cheated, but would have nothing to offer about whether deck-stacking or intervention explained it.

This second implication is important because it helps us think through the relevance of design for the philosophy of science generally. As we have seen, friends of IDT offer arguments along the lines of the following:

1) If design inferences concerning natural phenomena are warranted, then intelligent agency has played a role in bringing about some natural phenomena.
2) If intelligent agency has played a role in bringing about some natural phenomena, then purely naturalistic science will fail to explain truly such phenomena.
3) If purely naturalistic science will fail to explain truly such phenomena, then any methodologically naturalistic science will necessarily ultimately lead to errant explanations.
4) Any methodology that necessarily ultimately leads to errant explanations should be abandoned.

5) Thus, if design inferences are warranted, methodological naturalism should be abandoned.

Although the argument might look plausible on first glance, there is something deeply mistaken about it. And the cheating analogy makes clear that the trouble is premise 2. To see this we must consider first what the analogue for methodological naturalism would be in the cheating case. The answer can only be that it is an attempt to explain the outcomes of poker games by appeal to the rules of poker play. Call this "methodological rule-following." Can we explain the outcomes of the game described earlier by adopting methodological rule-following? In one sense we can. That is, if the role of the explainer here is simply to explain what rules brought us from the starting point of the game (cracking open the deck) to the (apparently designed) outcome, the answer is yes. Knowing the rules of poker would be sufficient to explain the outcomes in that sense. In another sense, of course, the explanation will be incomplete, since we have not explained every feature of the outcome about which we are curious, specifically, those features that tipped us off to the presence of cheating.

This leads us directly to the question of what it is exactly that scientific inquiry is supposed to be doing. We will turn to this question below. For the moment I want us to take note of this point, namely, that the success of "law" explanations has nothing to do with cheating inferences or design inferences. This means, of course, that Dembski's explanatory filter requires further adjusting. As we will see, however, the required adjustment will force friends of IDT to abandon intelligent design as a paradigm of natural science inconsistent with methodological naturalism.

VII. DESIGN AND NATURAL SCIENCE

Critics of IDT have frequently replied that methodological naturalism either cannot or should not be abandoned in science. But why should there be such insistence on maintaining methodological naturalism? Assume, for a moment, that God did miraculously intervene in the course of nature to bring about the origin of life, or the origin of the first instances of distinct biological kinds, or the origin of (some or all) human beings? If the scientist were by fiat to be blocked from countenancing such causes, then scientific attempts to understand these phenomena would be doomed to frustration or falsity. How absurd for the Christian, if he or she is convinced, perhaps by the contents of revelation, that God did act in just such a fashion, to reject the true explanation. How, on the naturalistic view, should the Christian scientist proceed when trying to explain scientifically the origins of natural kinds? Should she offer the best naturalistic explanation available, knowing all along that while the explanation is the best *scientific* one, it is nonetheless ultimately false? Why not rather drop such artificial, partisan barriers, and attempt to give the *right explanation* rather than the best "merely scientific" explanation or the best "merely theological" explanation?

One common reply to this question is simply that such explanations transcend the bounds of science properly construed. I think many Christian philosophers bristle at the suggestion that appeals to divine intervention rule out an explanation as "genuinely scientific." That strikes too close to the little tolerated view that bringing God into, for example, philosophy makes one's work not "genuinely philosophical." Why not rather say, as we do in philosophy, and as friends of IDT do concerning science, that we should lift such *ad hoc* restrictions, and let the chips fall where they may? If the best explanation for a philosophical problem requires appeal to the supernatural, so be it; and likewise in the case of science. This is just what IDT advocates are stumping for.

So perhaps disciplinary territorialism should not rule out Intelligent Design as a genuinely scientific explanation. But we are not out of the woods yet. For even though countenancing design as an explanation might in principle count as genuine science, it cannot if the design hypothesis is not empirically distinguishable from explanations which appeal only to the natural powers of natural substances. If such empirical distinguishability is not possible, then there is no scientifically respectable way, by IDT's own

lights, to defend intelligent design as an explanation distinct from law and chance.

But why think that IDT advocates are stuck with this problem, a problem we might call the *empirical vacuity* problem? The answer, once again, can be found in the poker case above. If,

a) one acknowledges that designed outcomes might in principle be explained either via deck-stacking or intervention and,
b) we have no access to the actual sequence of events that led to the obtaining of the apparently designed outcome,[11] then,
c) there are no empirical grounds for favoring explanations via law *over* explanation via design.

The point becomes clear when we consider cases in which friends of IDT think design is empirically detectable. The two most commonly discussed cases are those concerning so-called cosmological fine-tuning and concerning irreducible biological complexity. For reasons that will become clear shortly, I will focus on just the latter here. The details of the argument concerning irreducible complexity are widely known and I won't repeat them here. Irreducible biological complexity is a notion introduced by Michael Behe in his widely cited work *Darwin's Black Box*. In the book, Behe gives numerous examples of microbiological structures and of biochemical processes which are a) complex, b) such that the function they perform for the organism is essential for the organism's survival, and c) such that were the structure or process to lack some of the parts it has, it would be unable to perform its essential function, rendering it, from the organism's standpoint, totally non-functional—perhaps even maladaptive.

Since structures or processes which contain only proper subsets of the parts of the fully functional structure or process are non-functional, standard Darwinian models cannot explain these complex structures or processes. Standard Darwinism requires that such complex structures arise by gradual accretion of parts, accompanied by gradual improvement in adaptiveness. Thus, these irreducibly complex structures must have come into existence some other way. Given the complexity of the structures and processes in question, and the fact that the whole organism in which the structure or process is instantiated requires that structure or process to exist, it is incredible, claims Behe, that the process comes into existence by any other means than design.

Behe's argument has generated a good deal of controversy. Most of that controversy has been with advocates of some variant of Darwinism arguing that purely natural processes *can* account for such structures after all (either because such complex structures can arise all at once, or because precursors to the complex structure are not non-functional in the way Behe contends). Consider, however, a different worry about Behe's argument. Earlier I noted that Behe asserts that if some nomically regular process were discovered which explains the origins of the irreducibly complex structures, this would provide a defeater for design. The cheating example made clear that this was a mistake. Since we do not have access to the actual sequence of events which generated the irreducibly complex outcome, we cannot tell whether or not the process came about via intervention or deck-stacking. Undoubtedly it would take a good deal of up front design work to insure that nomically regular processes would generate the irreducibly complex outcomes Behe points to. But God is smart, omniscient in fact, and would no doubt be able to figure out how to secure such results through deck-stacking.[12]

And so we are compelled to admit that events which display the earmarks of design leave us in the dark about whether or not the chain of events leading up to designed event came about by intervention or purely nomically regular processes. The friend of IDT is, at this juncture, likely to reply that far from a surprise, this result is just what IDT has claimed all along. After all, doesn't Dembski himself distinguish between detectability and modality? No doubt he does. But this reply misses the thrust of the argument. The claim here is that designed events can be caused by either intervention or deck-stacking-plus-nomic-regularity (or something more complex if indeterminacy is relevant; see note 12 for more on this). If all we have access to is apparently designed outcomes, we cannot distinguish between those that result via "law" (deck-stacking) and those that result from "design" (intervention). Thus, we cannot engage in the

project suggested by IDT advocates after all, namely, setting aside methodological naturalism and letting the explanatory chips fall where they may. The explanatory chips can't discriminate between these competitors.

VIII. OBJECTION AND REPLY

Before proceeding further, let me pause to respond to a worry that may arise at this point in the dialectic. The friend of IDT may, at this point, object as follows: "Let's say that one does accept (a) and (b) above. You have claimed that in such a case one cannot empirically distinguish between cases in which an apparently designed event results from intervention and from nomically regular processes. Surely this is false. For if that were so, it would mean that we could not decide whether or not the pyramids in the jungle are caused by law or intervention. But this is surely wrong. We are quite confident that pyramids result from design and not mere nomic regularity. And this shows that we have the ability to distinguish law from design after all."

The imaginary critic is correct, except concerning what he takes the objection to imply. Of course we can see that the pyramids are designed. What I have claimed here is that we must admit that the design either arose via intervention or deck-stacking. That is, either intelligent beings intervened in the course of nature to secure the designed outcome, or someone set up the universe from the beginning so that this otherwise unexpected arrangement of matter would arise through nomically regular processes. We favor intervention in *this* case (i.e., the pyramid case) because we see that the outcomes (pyramids) serve the sorts of aims that intelligent *human creatures* typically have. Thus we have good reason to suspect that human creatures, and not mere nomically regular processes, caused them. But if someone could show us a time lapse video of universal history in which pyramids come to be via a nomically regular process, we should still conclude that this is a case of design, but of the deck-stacking sort.

So, a good reason (but not the commonly professed reason) why such explanations should not be favored in science is because there are no empirical grounds for favoring them over their methodologically natural competitors. Of course, if God were to privilege us with a revelation which filled us in on all of the occasions in which he directly intervened in natural affairs to bring about events that could not have occurred given the natural powers of natural entities alone, then the theist would be required to say that any explanation of the event (or its causal consequences) is incomplete without reference to divine causal activity. But absent this, IDT in its boldest form (the form described as (4) in section II) stalls.

IX. LESS BOLD VERSIONS OF IDT

In the remainder of this paper I want to consider two fall-back positions that friends of IDT might defend. Each provides a way of maintaining the integrity of design in science without falling into the greedier version with its errant methodological implications. What if, in light of the above, friends of IDT contend that we should scrap the explanatory filter, recognizing that law does not defeat design in explanation after all, but still admit that, whether the designed event comes to be by deck-stacking or intervention, a *complete* explanation will need to make reference to the activity of designer. And if scientists are honest seekers of complete explanations of natural phenomena, they are still going to be obliged to take Intelligent Design seriously in their final rendering.

There is a sense in which this fall back is clearly on target. Regardless of how the cheating occurred, intelligent agency is required in the complete explanation. Still, we can fairly ask at this juncture whether or not scientists are or should be concerned with complete explanations as described here. The answer is no. The reason for this is that when a deck-stacking explanation is sufficient (and one always would be in these cases)[13] scientists, theists or not, will be able to explain how the events came to be simply by appeal to the existence and activity of some set of theoretically postulated natural substances and their powers. To use Dembski's analogy, if we were to watch the time lapse video of universal history, nomic regularity would be preserved at each instant. As a result, it would be best for us to see the deliverances of IDT as helpful natural theology, but useless science. Irreducible complexity or fine tuning might provide us with evidence of intelligent design, and thus with arguments for the existence of God. But they do not provide us with scientific explanations that compete with methodologically natural ones. As a result, the first fall back position will not take us where the friends of IDT want to go (though it might still be able to deliver some important and interesting results in natural theology nonetheless).

Perhaps the friends of IDT might avail themselves of one last ditch. Dembski and others have argued that the value of IDT lies not merely in the fact that it is better able than methodological naturalism to explain, say, irreducible biological complexity, but that the IDT hypothesis is, in the sense employed by Kuhn, fertile or fecund. Thus, even if we were to drop the explanatory filter and the claim that complete scientific explanations must make appeal to design, we might still hold that belief in design might provide a useful background assumption when we are theorizing. Far from being a science-stopper, as God-of-the-gaps science is often claimed to be, IDT promotes fertile scientific theorizing. Thus, our belief that nature is designed might lead us to see the world in ways we otherwise would not.

It is hard to know what to make of this suggestion *a priori*. Leibniz, no friend of divine intervention in proper science, argued that scientific speculation that proceeds on the assumption of design was likely to be fertile in this way, though ultimate scientific explanations would not, he arued, make reference to facts about design. His favorite example concerned Snell's Law, the law describing the behavior of refracting light (and electromagnetic radiation generally). Leibniz claimed that Snell was led to his formulation of the law because it represents light as travelling by the path of least resistance. This makes sense from the design perspective and so provided a good place to start experimenting concerning the behavior of refracting light.[14]

Friends of IDT have suggested some concrete ways in which the fertility of IDT might be manifest in contemporary science. Two recurring examples are: a) it might lead us to think that "junk" DNA has some important function after all and b) it might similarly lead us to look for the function of so called vestigial organs."[15]

While it might be the case that approaching natural science in this way will sometimes yield fruit, the likelihood of red herrings runs equally strong. The reason for this is that IDT will provide a fertile theoretical backdrop in a certain domain only if (a) we can be fairly confident of what the designer's intentions are in that domain, and (b) we are sure that the specific matter under investigation is relevant to those intentions. With respect to the first, we can imagine how far astray we might be led in the search for the function of vestigial organs if one of God's chief aims in constructing organ systems was aesthetic. Attempts to look for the functional utility provided by such organs would lead either to frustration or falsity. With respect to the second, consider the handle end of a plastic fork. Often, such forks will have a sharp burr at the end which is a result of the manufacturing process. The fork could have been produced in a way so that this was absent. But all things considered, the manufacturer found it better suited to its aims to bring it about through a process that left this burr. These burrs have no purpose and serve no function. They are byproducts of a contingent process of manufacture. And there is no reason to think that similar byproducts would be absent even from intelligently designed nature. Perhaps hairy armpits are an example. The point however is straightforward. Even Christians who claim to have a good bit of special revelation concerning God's purposes for the natural world have precious little of value when it comes to help with fertile scientific theorizing.[16]

Some have argued that there is something suspect about framing a view of providence in the way that the deck-stacker does, and that this should lead the Christian to favor interventionism. A deck-stacking God is the God of deism. Christians, on the other hand, see a God whose direct handiwork is evidenced repeatedly in the pages of Scripture and in the metaphysical speculations of philosophers. Plantinga claims:

> First and most important, according to serious theism, God is constantly, immediately intimately and directly active in his creation: he constantly upholds it in existence and providentially governs it. He is immediately and directly active in everything from the Big Bang to the sparrow's fall. Literally nothing happens without his upholding hand. Second, natural laws are not in any way independent of God, and are perhaps best thought of as regularities in the ways in which he treats the stuff he has made, or perhaps as counterfactuals of divine freedom. (Hence there is nothing in the least untoward in the thought that on some occasions God might do something in a way different from his usual way—e.g., raise someone from the dead or change water into wine.)....God is already and always intimately acting in nature, which depends from moment to moment for its existence upon immediate divine activity....[17]

Likewise, Paul Helm argues in *The Providence of God* that deistic views of God as deck-stacker are inconsistent with Christian commitments to divine miraculous intervention and to the power of petitionary prayer. Helm describes the view as one according to which:

> [God], in creating the universe, creates it in such a way that he does not *need* to exercise a superintending care of it. This is the deistic view.[18]

Concerning petitionary prayer, Helm contends:

> According to the Christian faith, God answers petitionary prayer. That is, certain things happen in the universe because people ask God that they happen, and God is pleased to do what they ask. Had they not asked, the event in question would not have occurred; or at least, had they not asked, there is no reason to think that the event would have occurred. A deist, however, (at least if he is consistent) will find no place for petitionary prayer.[19]

Other Christians have argued, on the contrary, that there is something unworthy of a theism which countenances a God who once creates the natural order and yet leaves it without the resources to bring about the desired results. The most vocal advocate of this line in the contemporary arena is Howard Van Till who argues:

> I believe that the universe in its present form is to be seen as a potentiality of the creation that has been actualized by the exercise of its God-given creaturely capabilities. For this to be possible, however, the creation's formational economy must be astoundingly robust and gapless—lacking none of the resources

or capabilities necessary to make possible the sort of continuous actualization of new structures and life forms as now envisioned by the natural sciences. The optimally-equipped character of the universe's formational economy is, I believe, a vivid manifestation of the fact that it is the product, not of mere accident or happenstance, as the worldview of naturalism would have it, but of *intention*. In other words, the universe bears the marks of being the *product of thoughtful conceptualization for the accomplishment of some purpose.*[20]

Similar sentiments were staked out and defended with perhaps even more gusto in the past. Leibniz was aware of the fact that in the 1706 version of Query 31 of the *Optiks* Newton endorsed the claim that God on occasion directly intervenes to maintain nature's integrity. In particular, Newton claims that this was necessary to prevent the planets from falling in on each other. Leibniz, near the end of his life, seeks to provoke one prominent Newtonian spokesperson, Samuel Clarke, on the matter. In the third paragraph of his opening letter to Clarke, Leibniz acerbically remarks:

> Sir Isaac Newton, and his followers, also have a very odd opinion concerning the work of God. According to their doctrine, God Almighty wants to wind up his watch from time to time: otherwise it would cease to move. He had not, it seems, sufficient foresight to make it a perpetual motion. Nay, the machine of God's making, is so imperfect, according to these gentlemen; that he is obliged to clean it now and then by an extraordinary concourse and even to mend it, as a clockmaker mends his work; who must consequently be so much the more unskillful a workman, as he is more often obliged to mend his work and set it right. According to my opinion, the same force and vigor remains always in the world, and only passes from one part of matter to another, agreeably to the laws of nature, and the beautiful pre-established order. And I hold, that when God works miracles, he does not do it in order to supply the wants of nature, but those of grace. Whoever thinks otherwise must needs have a very mean notion of the wisdom and power of God.[21]

If one favors the sentiments expressed by Plantinga and Helm above, one might be inclined to break the empirical deadlock between deck-stacking and intervention in favor of intervention. If one were

to favor van Till and Leibniz, one would likely be inclined in the opposite direction. In the end, however, the philosophical grounds for deciding this dispute may turn out to be no more useful than the empirical evidence (i.e., not at all).

I am not sure how to defend the claim that the considerations appealed to by Leibniz are more persuasive than those appealed to by Plantinga. Nonetheless, I am inclined toward the deck-stacking model, and it is a model which according to Helm, faces a pair of serious objections from miracles and petitionary prayer. Can the deck-stacker successfully respond to these?

One might think that the challenge concerning miracles is rather easily met. In order to meet it one would first have to conceive of miracles in a way different than perhaps most Christians have, i.e., as violations of laws of nature. I think there are decisive independent reasons for jettisoning this conception of miracles, making any proposed reconception easier to swallow.[22] On this alternative view, miracles would have to consist of arrangements of matter that were intentionally brought about by God via deck-stacking and nomic regularity, which arrangements would have been exceedingly improbable without God having stacked the deck in precisely the way that he did. Thus, though we all know it would be exceedingly improbable, it could be the case that all of the water molecules in the Red Sea at the time of the Israelite crossing were such that their velocity and direction caused the parting of the Sea for just the amount of time needed for the Israelites to cross. Similar accounts can be given for miracles ranging from Elisha's floating axe head to Christ's resurrection. Still, it is an open question whether or not all miracles could be accounted for via deck-stacking.[23]

Initially, it is hard to see how petitionary prayer raises any more trouble for the deck-stacker than it does for the advocate of complete foreknowledge or robust providence over human affairs generally. In any of these cases, if God has middle knowledge, and thus knows what will in fact be prayed for in advance, God can determine that an event, X, will occur in a world at least in part because someone prayed for X to occur.

It should be noted as well that Plantinga's arguments do not pack any punch against the sort of deck-stacking view of natural providence I am defending here. Deck-stackers can heartily support divine conservation and the possibility for divine intervention into the order or nature if needed.

But do the arguments of Van Till and Leibniz have any force for friends of deck-stacking? I think they do. For those who are not advocates of divine openness, it is hard to see what motives God might have for electing to create the world and then later supplement his work, a la Newton and Clarke, to bring about all of the aims he has for it. No doubt, universe creation and providential superintending of universes are tricky businesses, and perhaps no set of natural entities and powers could, through deck-stacking, bring off everything God intended for his creation to accomplish. But we cannot with any confidence at all proclaim that God couldn't bring about, say, all the arrangements of created things we now see about us through deck-stacking. Opponents of deck-stacking will be happy to point out that we can't proclaim with any confidence that he *could* do it either.

And this brings us back to one of the central questions of the paper: Does any of this have any practical implications for the practice of science? At best I think the implication is this. If we cannot establish a preference for intervention over deck-stacking by empirical means (and we can't) or philosophical arguments (perhaps we can't) we should simply appeal to induction. God usually works by law-like means, so we should infer that probably he does the same here and that if he did not, our ability to know that would be outstripped. Perhaps this just adds up to sound intellectual humility. To me, it sounds like methodological naturalism.[24]

NOTES

1. See William A. Dembski, *Mere Creation* (Downers Grove, IL: InterVarsity Press, 1998:): 98–104. Also see William A. Dembski, *The Design Inference* (New York: Cambridge University Press, 1998) 36–47, and William A. Dembski, *Intelligent Design* (Downers Grove, IL: InterVarsity Press, 1999): 133–134. For simplicity's sake I will refer only to "events" in what follows though the explanatory filter is meant to apply to objects, events, and states of affairs.

2. See Dembski, *Mere Creation*, 98.

3. I should note here that Robin Collins has independently hit upon a similar criticism of Dembski. However, he proposes a resolution that is distinct form the one I propose here. See Robin Collins, "An Evaluation of William A. Dembski's *The Design Inference*," in *Christian Scholar's Review*, vol. XXX., no. 3 (Spring 2001).

4. See Peter van Inwagen, *Metaphysics* (Boulder, CO: Westview Press, 1993): 135.

5. See Michael J. Behe, *Darwin's Black Box: The Biochemical Challenge to Evolution* (New York: Free Press, 1996): 194.

6. *Ibid.,* 203.

7. With one modification. The modus tollens only tells us that designed events are ones that are not explicable in terms of nomic regularities. No doubt, this is a necessary condition of the miraculous as normally understood, but not a sufficient condition. For sufficiency, one would have to include the claim that the event had a divine cause. But one would think that this is had for free on IDT.

8. See Howard J. Van Till, and Phillip E. Johnson, "God and Evolution: An Exchange," *First Things* (June/July 1993): 38.

9. See Dembski's *intelligent Design*, 240.

10. *Ibid.,* 116.

11. It must be added "and we cannot with reasonable certainty re-create the very sequence of events that led to the designed outcome."

12. One might think that in a Newtonian world such deck-stacking might be a possibility, but that in a physical world shot through with quantum indeterminacy, deck-stacking cannot be guaranteed to yield any old physically possible arrangement without intervention along the way. This may be right, and whether or not it is depends on whether or not God has middle knowledge with respect to subjunctive conditionals concerning causally indeterministic natural events. Perhaps those who balk at middle knowledge generally might find little comfort here. Even if we reject middle knowledge, however, it is still *possible*, perhaps even *likely*, that God could stack the universal deck in a way that would bring about the instances of design we see without any intervention. For example, if God could not know the outcomes of indeterministic physical processes, God might still set in motion a number of chains of events which are such that each carries some (perhaps high) probability of yielding the outcome he desires (organic life perhaps). In this way, God might be able to bring about the outcome by

deck-stacking without middle knowledge, though such outcomes could not be *guaranteed*.

What if it were to happen that God could not, given indeterminacy, secure even a high likelihood of the desired outcome? Even if such were the case, God could form an intention to intervene only if the all chains of events set in motion seem to be turning into dead ends. Thus, he might do everything possible via deck-stacking to set in motion chains of events that will lead to organic life, and only intervene if necessary. If that is how things are (or were) in the actual world, it might be the case that God actually intervened to bring about irreducibly complex results, but it might not as well. Available evidence would not settle the matter. The same sort of modal ignorance that leaves us in the dark concerning the actualizability of a world with free creatures who never sin, leaves us in the dark about the actualizability of a world where deck-stacking yields irreducible complexity.

13. That may strike the reader as puzzling. But given what has gone before it should not be. Perhaps one might think that in some cases, no explanation in terms of the natural powers of natural substances is possible. But what would make such an explanation impossible? Sometimes, critics of methodological naturalism claim that the impossibility is really just a very high improbability. For irreducibly complex structures to have arise by law would have required a chance arrangement of matter in the primordial soup/clay/what have you that strains credibility. But credibility is strained here only if we think that deck-stacking was not involved. Perhaps there are some cases where the claim is not that naturalistic explanations are improbable, but that they are downright impossible. One might think such cases can be found in miraculous events. Water cannot turn to wine given the natural powers of natural substances. That, an objector might hold, is surely impossible, not just improbable. It might be the case that some miracles do present us with cases where the explanation requires intervention. Two things should be said in response. First, none of the cases presented by IDT advocates are anything like water-to-wine miracles. They are, rather, cases of credibility-straining-improbabilities. Second, as I will discuss in the text below when treating miracles directly, the claim that miracles of the water-to-wine sort require direct intervention is not irresistible. As we will see, Christian thinkers such as Leibniz have cogently defended the possibility of a no-intervention world, even in the face of such miracles.

14. See G. W. Leibniz, *Discourse on Metaphysics* ¶22 found in *Philosophical Essays*, eds. Roger Ariew, and Daniel Garber (Indianapolis, IN: Hackett Publishing Company, 1989): 55.

15. See Dembski's *Intelligent Design*, 150.

16. I say this with apologies to those who favor a literal six 24 hour day reading of the Genesis 1-3. Perhaps in such a case we would have some evidence that would be fruitful for theorizing. But even in that case, it is not evidence that assists us by putting us in touch with the aims of a designer. The fruitfulness in this case is simply due to the fact that we are made aware of facts about universal origins that might otherwise not be empirically accessible.

17. See Alvin Plantinga, "Methodological Naturalism?", in *Facets of Faith and Science*, ed. J. van der Meer (Lanham, MA: University Press of America, 1996).

18. See Paul Helm, *The Providence of God* (Downers Grove, IL: InterVarsity Press, 1994): 75–76.

19. *Ibid.*, 77–78.

20. See Howard J. Van Till, "The Creation: Intelligently Designed or Optimally Equipped?" *Theology Today* 55, no. 3 (1998): 362.

21. See *The Leibniz-Clarke Correspondence*, ed. H. G. Alexander (Manchester: Manchester University Press, 1956): 11–12, ¶4.

22. The case I have in mind is made by Jan Cover in "Miracles and the Christian Faith" in *Reason for the Hope Within*, ed. Michael Murray (Grand Rapids: Eerdmans Publishing Company, 1999): 345–374. Though I commend the account Cover gives, I will not be adopting the same conception he adopts in this essay. Cover characterizes miracles as events that exceed the power of the natural substances involved in the event. Even this will be too strong for the deck-stacker.

23. Perhaps not all miracles could be accounted for in this way. Miracles in which, say, water is turned to wine do not seem to involve anything that deck-stacking could account for. Perhaps instantaneous rearrangements of quarks could transmute hydrogen and oxygen molecules into the complex aromatic hydrocarbons that would be needed in fine wine. If anyone can be a proficient alchemist, no doubt God can. I leave it to the physicists to determine the plausibility of potentially accounting for all Biblical miracles in this fashion. Note, however, that the physicist alone might not be up to the task. It could be the case, for all our feeble powers can discern, that certain natural substances have natural powers that are only actualized under extremely rare

circumstances. Thus perhaps under just the right conditions (conditions that might include an incarnate man in Palestine uttering certain words), water molecules or their parts can actualize powers to transmute into wine. In principle the effects of such powers should be reproducible. Whether they are in fact depends on how finely tuned the conditions must be to actualize the power.

24. Thanks to Glenn Ross, Bill Hasker, Timothy O'Connor, Del Ratzsch, Gary Mar, Philip Clayton, Robin Collins, and two anonymous referees for this journal for helpful comments on earlier drafts of this paper.

VIII.B.5   An Evolutionary Argument against Naturalism

ALVIN PLANTINGA

Brief biographical remarks about Alvin Plantinga appear before selection III.7. In this article, Alvin Plantinga analyzes David Hume's epistemic skepticism, according to which we lack knowledge altogether, opposes it to Thomas Reid's Christian commonsense philosophy, and applies the results to naturalism (the view that there is no God or any other supernatural entity). He argues that naturalism is essentially Humean, so that anyone who adopts it has no knowledge at all, let alone knowledge of naturalism. Naturalism is self-undermining. If it is true, we are not justified in believing it, for Darwinian evolutionary theory (to which naturalists are presently committed) offers convincing reason to doubt that our cognitive faculties are successfully aimed at truth.

... Now turn to the question whether our cognitive faculties are reliable and do, in fact, produce for the most part true belief. Given Hume's complete agnosticism about the origins of his cognitive faculties, something like his deeply agnostic attitude to that question is no more than sensible. For suppose Hume asks himself how likely it is that our cognitive faculties are reliable, given his views (or rather lack of views) about the origin and provenance of ourselves and those faculties. What is the probability that our faculties produce the considerable preponderance of true belief over false required by reliability, given his views of their origin and purpose (if any)? I should think he would have to say that this probability is either low or inscrutable—impossible to determine. From his point of view, there are innumerable scenarios, innumerable ways in which we and our cognitive faculties could have come into being: perhaps we have been created by God,

but perhaps we and the world are the result of some kind of vegetative principle, or a result of copulation on the part of animals we have no knowledge of, or the result of Russell's accidental collocation of atoms, or of. . . . On many of these scenarios, our cognitive faculties wouldn't be reliable (although they might contribute to fitness or survival); perhaps on others they would be reliable; on balance, one just wouldn't know what to think about this probability.

We can see this more fully as follows. Let R be the proposition that our cognitive faculties are reliable: now what is the likelihood of R? As Reid points out, we all instinctively believe or assume that our cognitive faculties are indeed reliable; but what is the probability of that assumption, given the relevant facts? Well, what are the relevant facts? First, they would be facts about those faculties: the probability of R given (relative to) the population of China would not be

Reprinted from *Warranted Christian Belief* (Oxford University Press, 2000) by permission. Footnotes deleted.

relevant. And presumably the relevant facts would be facts about how these faculties originated; whether they were designed; if so, by whom and with what end in view; what constraints governed their development; and what their purpose and function is, if, indeed, they have a purpose and function. Were they, as Reid thought, created in us by a being who intends that they function reliably to give us knowledge about our environment, ourselves, and God himself—all the knowledge needed for us to attain shalom, to be the sort of beings God intended us to be? On that scenario, the purpose of our cognitive faculties would be (in part, at least) to supply us with true beliefs on those topics, and (given that they are functioning properly) there would be a high probability of their doing just that.

Did they, by contrast, arise by way of some chance mechanism, something like the mindless swerve of atoms in the Democritian void? What is the likelihood, on *that* possibility, that our cognitive faculties are reliable? Well, you might think it pretty low. More likely, you may think that you simply can't say what that probability is: perhaps it is high (though presumably not very high), perhaps it is low; you simply can't tell. There will be many more such scenarios, says Hume, some involving vegetative origin, some copulative origin, some still other kinds of origin; with respect to them, too, the probability that our cognitive faculties are reliable is simply inscrutable. So first, Hume thinks his grasp of the whole set of relevant scenarios is at best infirm; second, with respect to many of these scenarios, those possible origins, the probability of R is inscrutable; and finally, the probability with respect to any of these scenarios that it is in fact the truth of the matter is also, as far as Hume is concerned, quite inscrutable.

But that means that the probability of R, given Hume's agnosticism, is also inscrutable for Hume. Let F be the relevant facts about their origin, purpose, and provenance: my claim is that, for Hume, P(R/F) (the probability of R on F) is inscrutable. He simply doesn't know what it is and has no opinion about its value, although presumably it wouldn't be very high. Another way to put it: the probability of R, given Hume's agnosticism, is inscrutable.

And that gives Hume a reason to be agnostic with respect to R as well; it gives him a reason to doubt that R is, in fact, true. For our cognitive faculties, our belief-producing mechanisms, are a bit like measuring instruments (more exactly, measuring instruments under an interpretation). Our faculties produce beliefs; for each belief, there is the content of that belief, the proposition believed, a proposition that is true if and only if the belief is true. Now a state of a measuring instrument (relative to a scheme of interpretation) can also be said (in an analogically extended sense) to have content. For definiteness, consider a thermometer and suppose its pointer is resting on the number 70. Given the natural scheme of interpretation, this state can be said to have the content that the ambient temperature is 70°F. And of course a thermometer is *reliable* only if the propositions it delivers in this way are for the most part true, or nearly true.

Imagine, then, that you embark on a voyage of space exploration and land on a planet revolving about a distant sun. This planet has a favorable atmosphere, but you know little more about it. You crack the hatch, step out, and immediately find something that looks a lot like a radio; it periodically emits strings of sounds that, oddly enough, form sentences in English. The sentences emitted by this instrument express propositions only about topics of which you have no knowledge: what the weather is like in Beijing at the moment, whether Caesar had eggs on toast on the morning he crossed the Rubicon, whether the first human being to cross the Bering Strait and set foot on North America was left-handed, and the like. A bit unduly impressed with your find, you initially form the opinion that this quasi radio speaks the truth: that is, the propositions expressed (in English) by those sentences are true. But then you recall that you have no idea at all as to what the purpose of this apparent instrument is, whether it *has* a purpose, or how it came to be. You see that the probability of its being reliable, given what you know about it, is for you inscrutable. Then (in the absence of investigation) you have a *defeater* for your initial belief that the thing does, in fact, speak the truth, a reason to reject that belief, a reason to give it up, to be agnostic with respect to it.

Relative to your beliefs about the origin, purpose, and provenance of this apparent instrument, the probability that it is a reliable source of information is low or (more likely) inscrutable. And that gives you a defeater for your original and hasty belief that the thing really does speak the truth. If you don't have or get further information about its reliability, the reasonable course is agnosticism about that proposition.

The same goes, I think, in the case of Humean views (or nonviews) about our origins and the origin and purpose, if any, of our cognitive faculties. Suppose I join Hume in that agnosticism. Then P(R/F) is for me inscrutable (as for Hume); I have no idea what the probability of my faculties being reliable is, given the relevant facts about their origin and purpose. But then I have a defeater for my original belief or assumption that my faculties are in fact reliable. If I have or can get no further information about their reliability, the reasonable course for me is agnosticism with respect to R, giving it up, failing to believe it. It isn't that rationality requires that I believe its *denial*, but it does require that I not believe *it*.

Suppose, therefore, that I *am* agnostic with respect to R: I believe neither it nor its denial. And now consider any belief *B* I have: that belief, of course, will be a deliverance of my cognitive faculties. However, I don't believe that my cognitive faculties are reliable—not because I've never thought about the question, but because I *have* thought about it and seen that P(R/F) is inscrutable for me. Well, what does rationality require with respect to this belief *B*? The clear answer seems to be that I have a defeater for this belief too, a reason to withhold it, to be agnostic with respect to it. Perhaps it isn't possible, given my nature, that I *be* agnostic with respect to it, at least much of the time; as Hume says, nature may not permit this. Still, this agnosticism is what reason requires, just as Hume suggests (though for different reasons). And we can take one further step with Hume. Because *B* is just *any* belief I hold—because I have a defeater for just any belief I hold—I also have a defeater for my belief that I *have* a defeater for *B*. This universal, all-purpose defeater provided by my agnosticism is also a defeater for *itself*, a self-defeating defeater. And hence this complex, confusing, multilayered,

reflexive skepticism Hume describes, a skepticism in which I am skeptical of my beliefs and also of my doubts, and of the beliefs that lead to those doubts, and of my doubts with respect to those doubts, and the beliefs leading to *them*. Thus the true skeptic will be skeptical all the way down; he "will be diffident of his philosophical doubts, as well as his philosophical conviction."

Here we can imagine the following response: "Hey, hang on a minute! You said Hume and any similarly situated agnostic has a defeater for R, a belief to which he is inclined by nature—and you added that the rational course for them therefore is to give up belief in R—*provided they have no other information* about the reliability of their faculties. But what about that strong natural inclination to believe that our faculties are in fact reliable? Doesn't *that* count as 'other information'?" According to Reid (who might object to being pressed into service in defense of Hume), this belief in the reliability of our faculties is a *first principle*:

> Another first principle is—*That the natural faculties, by which we distinguish truth from error, are not fallacious....*

He goes on:

> If any truth can be said to be prior to all others in the order of nature, this seems to have the best claim; because, in every instance of assent, whether upon intuitive, demonstrative, or probable evidence, the truth of our faculties is taken for granted....

Surely there is truth here: this conviction is one normal human beings ordinarily have, and, as Reid gleefully points outs, even skeptics also seem to assume, in the course of ordinary daily living, to be sure, but most poignantly when proposing their skeptical arguments, that their faculties are functioning reliably. Very few skeptics, in offering their skeptical arguments, preface the argument by saying something like, "Well, here is an argument for general skepticism with respect to our cognitive faculties; of course I realize that the premises of this argument are themselves produced by cognitive faculties whose reliability the conclusion impugns, and of whose truth I am therefore extremely doubtful."

But our question is whether this belief can sensibly be pressed into service as information that can defeat the defeater provided for R by Hume's agnosticism about the origin and provenance of ourselves and our faculties. As Reid clearly sees, it cannot. If the general reliability of our cognitive faculties is under question, we can't hope to answer the question whether they *are* reliable by pointing out that these faculties themselves deliver the belief that they are, in fact, reliable. "If a man's honesty were called into question," says Reid, "it would be ridiculous to refer it to the man's own word, whether he be honest or not." . . . Concede that it is part of our nature to assume R; concede further that it is part of our nature to take R in the *basic* way, so that this conviction is not given or achieved by argument and evidence but comes with our mother's milk; concede still further, if you like, that this belief is produced by our cognitive faculties functioning properly. None of this, clearly enough, can serve to defeat the defeater for R provided by Hume's agnosticism. That is because any doubt about our cognitive faculties generally is a doubt about the specific faculty that produces this conviction; therefore we can't allay such a doubt by appealing to the deliverances of that faculty.

2. NATURALISM AND LACK OF KNOWLEDGE

Agnosticism with respect to our origins is one way to reject the theistic belief that we human beings have been created in the image of God: as we have seen, agnosticism with respect to origins destroys knowledge. There is another way to reject the belief in question: by accepting a belief incompatible with it, for example, philosophical or metaphysical naturalism. As Bas van Fraassen notes, it isn't easy to say precisely what naturalism *is;* for present purposes, suppose we take it to be the view that there is no such person as God, nor anyone or anything at all like him (it isn't that you believe, for example, that there are one or more finite gods). Paradigm cases of naturalism would be the views of Daniel Dennett in *Darwin's Dangerous Idea* or Bertrand Russell in "A Free Man's Worship": you think that "man is the product of causes which had no prevision of

the end they were achieving, that his origin, his growth, his hopes and fears, his loves and his beliefs, are but the outcome of accidental collocations of atoms." (Perhaps you even go so far as to add, with Richard Dawkins, that the very idea that there is such a person as God is really a kind of cognitive virus, an epistemic sickness or disease, distorting the cognitive stance of what would otherwise be reasonable and rational human beings.) Unlike Hume, therefore, you are not agnostic as to whether there is such a person as God or any being at all like him; you think there is not.

There is likely to be a further difference between you and Hume. Having rejected theism, Hume had no comparable story to put in its place: he was left with no idea as to how humanity arose, under what conditions our cognitive faculties came to be, and so on. The contemporary naturalist, however, is in a different condition; for naturalism now sports a shared myth or story about ourselves and our origins, a set of shared beliefs about who we are, where we come from, and how we got here. The story is familiar; I shall be brief. We human beings have arrived on the scene after millions, indeed, billions of years of organic evolution. In the beginning, there was just inorganic matter; somehow, and by way of processes of which we currently have no grasp, life, despite its enormous and daunting complexity at even the simplest level, arose from nonliving matter, and arose just by way of the regularities studied in physics and chemistry. Once life arose, random genetic mutation and natural selection, those great twin engines of evolution, swung into action. These genetic mutations are multiply random: they weren't intended by anyone, of course, but also were not directed by any sort of natural teleology and do not arise at the behest of the design plan of the organism. They are "not in a response to the needs of the organism" (Ernst Mayr); they just unaccountably appear. Occasionally, some of them yield an adaptive advantage; their possessors come to predominate in the population, and they are passed on to the next and subsequent generations. In this way, all the enormous variety of flora and fauna we behold came into being.

Including ourselves and our cognitive systems. These systems and the underlying mechanisms have also been selected for, directly or indirectly, in the course of evolution. Consider, for example, the mammalian brain in all its enormous complexity. It could have been directly selected for in the following sense: at each stage in its development, the new stage (by virtue of the structures and behaviors it helped bestow) contributed to fitness and conferred an evolutionary advantage, giving its possessors a better chance of surviving and reproducing. Alternatively, at certain stages new structures (or new modifications of old structures) arose, not because they were themselves selected for, but because they were genetically associated with something else that *was* selected for (pliotropy). Either way these structures were not selected for their penchant for producing true beliefs in us; instead, they conferred an adaptive advantage or were genetically associated with something that conferred such an advantage. And the ultimate purpose or function, if any, of these belief producing mechanisms will not be the production of true beliefs, but *survival*—of the gene, genotype, individual, species, whatever.

If you are a naturalist and also believe these things, then you are what I shall call an *ordinary* naturalist. In chapter 12 of *Warrant and Proper Function* (WPF), I argued that an ordinary naturalist is like Hume in that she has a defeater for any belief she holds—including, ironically enough, ordinary naturalism itself, so that ordinary naturalism is self-defeating. I shall not repeat that argument; instead, I will take this opportunity to make some corrections, simplifications, and additions....

In essence, the main argument is for the conclusions that P(R/N&E&C) (which I'll abbreviate as P(R/N)...) is either low or inscrutable; in either case, so I argued, one who accepts N (and also grasps the argument for a low or inscrutable value of P(R/N)) has a *defeater* for R. This induces a defeater, for him, for any belief produced by his cognitive faculties, including N itself; hence, ordinary naturalism is self-defeating. Now I argued that P(R/N) is low or inscrutable by noting first that natural selection isn't interested in *true belief* but in *adaptive behavior* (taken broadly), so that everything turns on the relation between belief and behavior. I then presented five mutually exclusive and jointly

exhaustive possibilities for the relation between belief and behavior, arguing with respect to each possibility P_i that $P(R/N\&P_i)$ is low or inscrutable, yielding the result that P(R/N) is low or inscrutable.

Here we can simplify by dropping two of the five possibilities, leaving just epiphenomenalism, semantic epiphenomenalism (perhaps 'content epiphenomenalism' would be a more felicitous name), and the common sense ('folk psychological') view of the causal relation between belief and behavior. The first possibility (call it 'P_1') is epiphenomenalism, the proposition that belief (conscious belief) isn't involved in the causal chain leading to behavior at all. This view was named and suggested by T. H. Huxley ("Darwin's bulldog"). Although epiphenomenalism runs counter to our common-sense ways of thinking, it is nonetheless widely popular among those enthusiastic about the "scientific" study of human beings. According to *Time*, a few years ago the eminent biologist J. M. Smith "wrote that he had never understood why organisms have feelings. After all, orthodox biologists believe that behavior, however complex, is governed entirely by biochemistry and that the attendant sensations—fear, pain, wonder, love—are just shadows cast by that biochemistry, not themselves vital to the organism's behavior."

And the same can be said for conscious belief. if "behavior, however complex, is governed entirely by biochemistry," there seems to be no room for conscious belief to become involved in the causal story, no way in which conscious belief can get its hand in; it will be causally inert. Furthermore, if this possibility were, in fact, actual, then evolution would not have been able to mold and shape our beliefs, or belief-producing structures, weeding out falsehood and encouraging truth; for then our beliefs would be, so to speak, *invisible* to evolution. Which beliefs (if any) an organism had, under this scenario, would be merely accidental as far as evolution is concerned. It wouldn't make any difference to behavior or fitness what beliefs our cognitive mechanisms had produced, because (under this scenario) those beliefs play no role in the production or explanation of behavior. What then is the probability of R on this scenario? That is, what is

$P(R/N\&P_1)$? What reliability requires, of course, is that a large preponderance of our beliefs be true. Now most large sets of propositions do not meet that condition; but one large set of beliefs—at any rate, of beliefs we human beings are capable of having—would seem to be about as likely as any other on this scenario. Hence we couldn't claim with a straight face that there is a high probability, on this scenario, that most of our beliefs are true. Perhaps the verdict is that this probability is relatively low; just for definiteness, let's say it's in the neighborhood of .3 or so. Alternatively, we might think that the right attitude here is that we simply can't make a sensible estimate of this probability, so that $P(R/N\&P_1)$ is inscrutable.

The second possibility as to the relation between belief and behavior (call it P_2) is semantic epiphenomenalism. From a naturalistic point of view, the natural thing to think is that human beings are material objects. Well, suppose that's what they are: then what sort of thing will a belief—perhaps the belief that Cartesian dualism is false—*be*? Presumably it will be a long-standing neural or neuronal event of some kind. This neural event will have *electrochemical* properties: the number of neurons involved; the way in which the neurons involved are connected with each other, with other neuronal events, with muscles, with sense organs, and so on; the average rate and intensity of neuronal firing in various parts of this event and the ways in which this changes over time and with respect to input from other areas. (Call these the 'syntax' of the belief.) Of course it is easy to see how *these* properties of this neuronal event should have causal influence on behavior. A given belief is neurally connected both with other beliefs and with muscles; we can see how electrical impulses coming from the belief can negotiate the usual neuronal channels and ultimately cause muscular contraction.

Now if this belief is really a *belief*, then it will also have *other* properties, properties in addition to its syntax or neurophysiological properties. In particular, it will have *content*; it will be the belief that *p*, for some proposition *p*—in this case, the proposition *Cartesian dualism is false*. But how does the *content* of this neuronal event—that *proposition*—get involved in the

causal chain leading to behavior? Under this scenario, it will be difficult or impossible to see how a belief can have causal influence on our behavior or action *by virtue of its content*. Suppose the belief had had the same electrochemical properties but some entirely different content, perhaps the proposition *Cartesian dualism is true*; would that have made any difference to its role in the causation of behavior? It is certainly hard to see how: there would have been the same electrical impulses traveling down the same channels, issuing in the same muscular contractions. The neurophysiological properties seem to have swept the field when it comes to the causation of behavior; there seems to be no way in which content can get its foot in the door. Of course, it is the *content* of my beliefs, not their electrochemical properties, that is the subject of truth and falsehood: a belief is true just if the proposition that constitutes its content is true. As in the epiphenomenalist scenario, therefore, the content of belief would be invisible to evolution. Accordingly, the fact that we have survived and evolved, that our cognitive equipment was good enough to enable our ancestors to survive and reproduce—that fact would tell us nothing at all about the *truth* of our beliefs or the reliability of our cognitive faculties. It would tell something about the *neurophysiological* properties of our beliefs; it would tell us that, by virtue of these properties, those beliefs have played a role in the production of adaptive behavior. But it would tell us nothing about the *contents* of these beliefs, and hence nothing about their truth or falsehood. On this scenario as on the last, therefore, we couldn't sensibly claim a high probability for R. As with the last scenario, the best we could say, I think, is that this probability is either low or inscrutable; $P(R/N\&P_2)$ is low or inscrutable, just as is $P(R/N\&P_1)$.

Finally, what is the probability of R, given $N\&P_3$, the commonsense (folk psychological) view as to the causal relation between behavior and belief? According to folk psychology, belief serves as a (partial) *cause* and thus *explanation* of behavior—and this explicitly holds for the content of belief. I want a beer and believe there is one in the fridge; that belief, we ordinarily think, partly explains those movements of that large lumpy object that is my body as it heaves itself out of the armchair, moves over to the fridge, opens it, and extracts the beer.

Can we mount an argument from the evolutionary origins of the processes, whatever they are, that produce these beliefs to the reliability of those processes? Could we argue, for example, that these beliefs of ours are connected with behavior in such a way that false belief would produce maladaptive behavior, behavior which would tend to reduce the probability of the believers' surviving and reproducing? No. False belief doesn't by any means guarantee maladaptive action. Perhaps a primitive tribe thinks that everything is really alive, or is a witch or a demon of some sort; and perhaps all or nearly all of their beliefs are of the form *this witch is F* or *that demon is G: this witch is good to eat,* or *that demon is likely to eat me if I give it a chance.* If they ascribe the right properties to the right witches, their beliefs could be adaptive while nonetheless (assuming that in fact there aren't any witches) false. Also, of course, there is the fact that behavior, if it is partly produced by belief, is also partly produced by desire: it is belief and desire, along with other things, that together produce behavior. But then clearly there could be many different systems of belief and desire that yield the same bit of adaptive behavior, and in many of those systems the belief components are largely false; there are many possible belief—desire systems that yield the whole course of my behavior, where in each system most of the beliefs are false. The fact that my behavior (or that of my ancestors) has been adaptive, therefore, is at best a third-rate reason for thinking my beliefs mostly true and my cognitive faculties reliable—and that is true even given the commonsense view of the relation of belief to behavior. So we can't sensibly argue from the fact that our behavior (or that of our ancestors) has been adaptive, to the conclusion that our beliefs are mostly true and our cognitive faculties reliable. It isn't easy to estimate $P(R/N\&P_3)$; if it isn't inscrutable, perhaps it is moderately high. To concede as much as possible to the opposition, let's say that this probability is either inscrutable or in the neighborhood of .9.

Note that epiphenomenalism simpliciter and semantic epiphenomenalism unite in declaring or implying that the content of belief lacks causal efficacy with respect to behavior; the content of belief does not get involved in the causal chain leading to behavior. So perhaps we can reduce these two possibilities to one: the possibility that the content of belief has no causal efficacy. Call this possibility -C. What we have so far seen is that the probability of R on N&-C is low or inscrutable and that the probability of R on N&C is also inscrutable or at best moderate. Now what we are looking for is P(R/N). Because C and -C are jointly exhaustive and mutually exclusive, the calculus of probabilities tells us that

$$P(R/N) = P(R/N\&C) \times P(C/N) + P(R/N\& - C) \times P(-C/N),$$

that is, the probability of R on N is the weighted average of the probabilities of R on N&C and N&-C—weighted by the probabilities of C and -C on N.

We have already noted that the left-hand term of the first of the two products on the right side of the equality is either moderately high or inscrutable; the second is either low or inscrutable. What remains is to evaluate the weights, the right-hand terms of the two products. So what is the probability of -C, given ordinary naturalism: what is the probability that one or the other of the two epiphenomenalistic scenarios is true? Note that according to Robert Cummins, semantic epiphenomenalism is in fact the received view as to the relation between belief and behavior. That is because it is extremely hard to envisage a way, given materialism, in which the content of a belief *could* get causally involved in behavior. If a belief just is a neural structure of some kind—a structure that somehow possesses content—then it is exceedingly hard to see how content can get involved in the causal chain leading to behavior: had a given such structure had a different content, its causal contribution to behavior, one thinks, would be the same. By contrast, if a belief is not a material structure at all but a nonphysical bit of consciousness, it is hard to see that there is any room for it in the causal chain leading to behavior; what causes the muscular contractions involved in behavior will be states of the nervous system, with no point at which this nonphysical bit of consciousness makes a causal contribution. So it is exceedingly hard to see, given N, how the content of a belief can have causal efficacy.

It is exceedingly hard to see, that is, how epiphenomenalism—semantic or simpliciter—can be avoided, given N. (There have been some valiant efforts, but things don't look hopeful.) So it looks as if P(-C/N) will have to be estimated as relatively high; let's say (for definiteness) .7, in which case P(C/N) will be .3. Of course we could easily be wrong—we don't really have a solid way of telling—so perhaps the conservative position here is that this probability, too, is inscrutable: one simply can't tell what it is. Given current knowledge, therefore, P(-C/N) is either high or inscrutable. And if P(-C/N) is inscrutable, then the same goes, naturally enough, for P(C/N). What does that mean for the sum of these two products, i.e., P(R/N)?

Well, we really have several possibilities. Suppose we think first about the matter from the point of view of someone who doesn't find any of the probabilities involved inscrutable. Then P(C/N) will be in the neighborhood of .3, P(-C/N) in the neighborhood of .7, and P(R/N&-C) perhaps in the neighborhood of .2. This leaves P(R/N&C), the probability that R is true, given ordinary naturalism together with the commonsense or folk-theoretical view as to the relation between belief and behavior. Given that this probability is not inscrutable, let's say that it is in the neighborhood of .9. And given these estimates, P(R/N) will be in the neighborhood of .4. Suppose, however, we think the probabilities involved are inscrutable: then we will have to say the same for P(R/N). Therefore, P(R/N) is either relatively low—less than .5, at any rate—or inscrutable.

In either case, however, doesn't the ordinary naturalist—at any rate, one who sees that P(R/N) is low or inscrutable—have a defeater for R, and for the proposition that his own cognitive faculties are reliable? I say he does. To see how, we must note some analogies with clear cases. First, there are the analogies I mentioned in WPF . . . ; here are a couple more. Return . . . to that voyage of space exploration and the radio-like device that emitted sounds that constitute English sentences, sentences that express propositions of whose truth

value you are ignorant. At first, you were inclined to believe these propositions, if only because of shock and astonishment. After a bit of cool reflection, however, you realize that you know nothing at all about the purpose, if any, of this instrument, or who or what constructed it. The probability that this device is reliable, given what you know about it, is low or inscrutable; and this gives you a defeater for your initial belief that the instrument indeed speaks the truth. Consider another analogy. You start thinking seriously about the possibility that you are a brain in a vat, being subjected to experiment by Alpha Centaurian cognitive scientists in such a way that your cognitive faculties are not, in fact, reliable. For one reason or another, you come to think this probability is greater than .5; then you have a defeater for your belief that your cognitive faculties are reliable. Suppose instead that you think this is a genuine possibility, but you can't make any estimate at all of its likelihood, so that you can't make any estimate at all of the probability that your faculties are reliable: as far as you can tell, the probability could be anywhere between 0 and 1. Then too you have a defeater for your natural belief that your cognitive faculties are reliable.

The same goes for the naturalist who realizes that P(R/N) is low or inscrutable. With respect to those factors crucially important for coming to a sensible view of the reliability of his belief-producing mechanisms—how they were formed and what their purpose is, if any—he must concede that the probability that those faculties are reliable is at best inscrutable. Unless he has some other information, the right attitude would be to withhold R. But then something like Hume's attitude toward my beliefs would be the appropriate one. I recognize that I can't help forming most of the beliefs I do form; for example, it isn't within my power, just now, to withhold the belief that there are trees and grass outside my window. However, because I now do not believe that my cognitive faculties are reliable (I withhold that proposition), I also realize that these beliefs produced by my cognitive faculties are no more likely to be true than false: I therefore assume a certain skeptical distance with respect to them. And, because my doubts about my beliefs themselves depend on my beliefs, I also assume a certain skeptical distance with respect to these doubts, and with respect to the beliefs prompting those doubts, and with respect to the beliefs prompting the doubts about those doubts.... The ordinary naturalist, therefore, should join Hume in this same skeptical, ironic attitude toward his beliefs. This holds, of course, for N itself; for this reason, we might say that N is self-defeating, in that if it is accepted in the ordinary way, it provides a defeater for itself, a defeater that can't be defeated....

By way of conclusion: the noetic effects of sin don't necessarily include failure to know anything; Calvin (if that is what, in fact, he thought) goes too far. Still, something in the same general neighborhood is true. If I reject theism in favor of ordinary naturalism, and also see that P(R/N) is low or inscrutable, then I will have a defeater for any belief I hold. If so, I will not, if forming beliefs rationally, hold any belief firmly enough to constitute knowledge. The same goes if I am merely agnostic as between theism and ordinary naturalism. And the same goes if I am agnostic about my origin and the origin of my cognitive faculties. So rejection of theistic belief doesn't automatically produce skepticism: many who don't believe in God know much. But that is only because they don't accurately think through the consequences of this rejection. Once they do, they will lose their knowledge; here, therefore, is another of those cases where, by learning more, one comes to know less....

VIII.B.6   Commonsense Naturalism

MICHAEL BERGMANN

Michael Bergmann (1964–   ) is professor of philosophy at Purdue University and works primarily in the fields of epistemology and philosophy of religion. In the article from which the present selection has been excerpted, Bergmann draws on the work of Thomas Reid to provide a response on behalf of the naturalist to Alvin Plantinga's evolutionary argument against naturalism.

I. INTRODUCTION

Metaphysical naturalism is, roughly speaking, the view that there are no supernatural beings—no such beings as, for example, God or angels or ghosts.[1] Thomas Reid was a theist and, therefore, not a naturalist. Consequently, one wouldn't expect to find in Reid's writings an argument in support of naturalism. But one *can* find in Reid the resources for a defense of naturalism against

a certain sort of objection to it. In this chapter I will propose a Reid-inspired commonsense response to Alvin Plantinga's evolutionary argument against naturalism. It is a response whose relevance extends far beyond Plantinga's argument. For it also serves as a preliminary defense and illustration of some of the main elements in a commonsense response to skepticism.

Plantinga has recently argued (in *Warrant and Proper Function*, chapter 12, and in "Naturalism

From James Beilby (ed.), *Naturalism Defeated? Essays on Plantinga's Evolutionary Argument against Naturalism*. Ithaca: Cornell University Press. Used with permission. Notes renumbered.

Thanks to Jan Cover, Keith Lehrer, Trenton Merricks, Michael Rea, William Rowe, Dale Tuggy, and especially Thomas Crisp and Alvin Plantinga for comments on earlier drafts. An earlier version of this chapter was read at the Twentieth World Congress in Philosophy in Boston. My thanks to the audience members as well as my fellow presenters, Richard Otte and William Ramsey, for helpful advice. Finally, I would like to acknowledge the support of the Purdue Research Foundation for a Summer Faculty Grant that enabled me to work on this project.

Defeated")[2] that naturalism is self-defeating. He asks us to imagine a race of creatures about whom we know nothing except that they form and change beliefs and that they came into existence via the mechanisms of evolution. Then he asks us to consider the probability that the cognitive faculties of these creatures are reliable—more specifically, he asks us to consider the probability that their cognitive faculties are reliable given naturalism and evolution. We can express this probability as P(R/N&E) where 'R' is the claim that the cognitive faculties in question are reliable, 'N' is the claim that naturalism is true, and 'E' is the claim that these faculties came into existence by way of the mechanisms of evolution. Plantinga thinks P(R/N&E) is low or inscrutable because evolutionary processes aim at adaptive behavior and having reliable faculties doesn't seem particularly probable with respect to adaptive behavior. This is so, he thinks, when P(R/N&E) is specified to the hypothetical creatures mentioned. But he also thinks P(R/N&E) is low or inscrutable when we specify it to ourselves—there being no relevant difference between ourselves and the creatures in his example.

That's the first stage of Plantinga's argument. In the second stage he points out that the fact that P(R/N&E) is low or inscrutable constitutes a *defeater* for R for anyone who endorses N&E. Then he says that if you're a naturalist, the sensible thing for you to believe is that evolution is true (you have no recourse to divine creation). So the naturalist should believe N&E. But then, once apprised of Plantinga's argument, the naturalist will have a defeater for R. And a defeater for R is a defeater for every one of a person's beliefs—including belief in N. This, says Plantinga, makes naturalism self-defeating. (Notice that Plantinga's argument can be construed as an argument—starting from naturalistic premises—for global skepticism. This is why my Reidian response to it can be used as an example of how to respond to more typical skeptical challenges.)

For the purposes of this chapter, I will grant to Plantinga the conclusion of the first stage of his argument—that P(R/N&E) is low or inscrutable when specified to us. My contention is simply that this does not necessarily constitute a defeater for R (for the supporter of N&E). In order to defend this view I will first explain, in the next section, a response Plantinga gives to the probabilistic argument from evil. Then, in sections 3 and 4, I will present a view of Reid's that makes possible a *Reidian* response to Plantinga's evolutionary argument against naturalism that parallels *Plantinga's* response to the probabilistic argument from evil.[3] In section...8 I will develop Reid's commonsense response in the context of considering a variety of objections to it. I will conclude in section 9 by connecting that response as well as my defense and development of it with the more general issue of skepticism.

I should note at the outset that my Reidian response isn't merely an ad hominem attack on Plantinga. True, Plantinga endorses a Reidian epistemology, so a Reidian response patterned after a response Plantinga himself gives in another setting will, if successful, create a special problem for him. But the Reidian response I offer relies on elements of Reid's epistemology that have a much wider appeal than does Plantinga's own epistemology. It depends on the Reidian views that (i) a belief can be *noninferentially* justified or warranted—that is, justified or warranted even if formed on the basis of an experience rather than on the basis of another belief [4]—and that (ii) among our noninferentially justified beliefs are a good number of our commonsense beliefs. The sort of foundationalism inherent in (i) is not the least bit unusual among contemporary epistemologists. And the commonsensism endorsed in (ii) is thoroughly intertwined with the particularist approach to philosophical analysis that is commonly employed in contemporary metaphysics, ethics, and epistemology.[5] So although the response I propose will be of no use to those who reject (i) and (ii), its benefits are by no means limited to those who accept Plantinga's epistemology.

One more preliminary remark. Some will wonder if my use of Reid (a theist) in defense of naturalism is something of which Reid himself would approve. To soften up such readers, I will include a quotation from Reid in which he suggests that one needn't be a theist to believe with justification in the reliability of one's senses:

> Shall we say, then, that this belief [in the reliability of our senses] is the inspiration of the Almighty? I think this may be said in a good sense; for I take it

to be the immediate effect of our constitution, which is the work of the Almighty. But, if inspiration be understood to imply a persuasion of its coming from God, our belief of the objects of sense is not inspiration; for a man would believe his senses though he had no notion of a Deity. He who is persuaded that he is the workmanship of God, and that it is a part of his constitution to believe his senses, may think that a good reason to confirm his belief. But he had the belief before he could give this or any other reason for it.[6]

I'm sure that Reid would say that similar remarks apply to the naturalist's belief in R.

II. PLANTINGA ON THE ARGUMENT FROM EVIL

Plantinga has a lot to say about the probabilistic argument from evil.[7] I don't propose to discuss all of it here. But one thing he says is of particular interest for our purposes. Suppose that $P(G/HE)$ is low (where G is the claim that God exists and HE is the claim that there are horrendous evils). What follows concerning the rationality or reasonableness or warrant for the belief that G? Not much, says Plantinga. For someone who believes that $P(G/HE)$ is low might also believe some other proposition Q and recognize that $P(G/HE\&Q)$ is high. If so, the fact that she also believes that $P(G/HE)$ is low won't make it unreasonable for her to believe G. But, says Plantinga, suppose we grant to the atheist objector that $P(G/k)$ is low (where k is the *total* relevant propositional evidence at one's disposal). What follows then concerning the rationality of holding G? Again not much, says Plantinga.

Here's an example he uses to explain why.[8] Suppose that a letter has gone missing, that you have an obvious motive for stealing it, and that both circumstantial evidence and eyewitnesses place you at the scene of the crime with ample opportunity to steal the letter. You claim to have been out alone for a walk in the woods at the time the letter was stolen (call this claim 'W').

But because of the strength of the case against you (and the fact that you have done things of this sort in the past), others are extremely doubtful of W. They sensibly conclude that $P(W/k)$—where k is their total propositional evidence—is quite

low. However, you clearly remember being out in the woods for a walk earlier in the day at the time the letter was stolen. This memory involves a belief ground that is *nonpropositional*; it involves a *seeming* of some sort that results in your taking a particular memory belief to be obviously correct under the circumstances (the phenomenology of these belief grounds is familiar enough but it is very difficult to describe). You, unlike those who think you are guilty, have the experiential evidence of *its seeming to you like you were out for a walk earlier in the day* and that very evidence grounds the belief that you did not steal the letter.[9]

So you know you didn't steal the letter and you know this on the basis of *non*propositional evidence. Nevertheless, your total relevant *propositional* evidence is more or less the same as that of those who think you are guilty.[10] You too agree that $P(W/k)$ is low. Yet this doesn't in the least suggest that you are irrational to believe W; for you clearly remember being out in the woods at the time in question. The point is that a proposition's being improbable on everything else you know or believe doesn't make belief in it irrational. And this is so even if these other things you believe are clearly *relevant* bits of evidence. For you may have in addition to all the *propositional* evidence at your disposal certain *non*propositional evidence. And this nonpropositional evidence may be strong enough to make it completely reasonable for you to hold the belief in question even while recognizing that the belief is improbable on your total relevant *propositional* evidence. Furthermore, given that this total relevant propositional evidence is all your accusers have to go on, you can also concede that your accusers are completely reasonable in thinking you are guilty. They are in this unfortunate situation because they lack an important bit of (nonpropositional) evidence that only you have.

Plantinga applies these considerations to the theist confronted with the probabilistic argument from evil in the following way. A person might have sufficiently strong nonpropositional evidence for G by way of what John Calvin calls 'the *sensus divinitatis.*' This faculty triggers belief in God (or beliefs about God) in response to certain experiences and circumstances. We observe the beauty and majesty of a starry night, are overwhelmed with a sense of awe, and find ourselves thinking *God has created this universe;* we recognize that we have done something that is wrong, feel guilty before God, and find ourselves thinking *God disapproves of this;* when life is sweet and satisfying we are overcome with a sense of gratitude and believe *God is to be thanked and praised.* In each case, we have a belief about God formed not on the basis of other beliefs but on the basis of experiences.[11] In cases where this evidence is sufficiently strong, one can come to rationally believe in God's existence despite recognizing that P(G/k) is low. The nonpropositional evidence makes rational a belief that is improbable with respect to one's total relevant propositional evidence.

In evaluating Plantinga's response to the argument from evil, one might wonder whether there *is* any such nonpropositional evidence for theism and, if so, how strong it is. But the main point I want to draw attention to is that the belief that P(G/k) is low does not in itself constitute a defeater for G (for the person whose total relevant propositional evidence is k). In addition, it must be the case that the person in question has no sufficiently strong *non*propositional evidence for G.

III. REID ON KNOWING R

Reid (or Reid as I understand him) says that we know R not by basing that belief on other beliefs but instead in the basic way. According to Reid, R is a first principle: "Another first principle is, that the natural faculties, by which we distinguish truth from error, are not fallacious."[12] And first principles, says Reid, are properly believed *noninferentially.*[13] We obtain this noninferential knowledge of first principles—which he also calls 'principles of common sense,' 'self-evident truths,' and 'intuitive judgments'—by employing that branch of our faculty of reason he calls 'common sense.'[14] The idea isn't that we have a faculty for knowing in the basic way things like "You shouldn't try to drive downtown in a hurry during rush hour." Common wisdom of this latter sort is cultural and learned and will vary across times and places. Reid is talking about something else. He's speaking

of a faculty whereby we form beliefs naturally held by sane humans in normal circumstances—noninferential beliefs that are not the result of education but of our constitution (though they are certainly acquired sometime after birth).[15] Reid thinks that by means of this faculty we know both contingent and necessary truths.[16] What he thinks of as knowledge via common sense of necessary truths is what we would call 'a priori knowledge.' Examples he gives of necessary truths known via common sense are the axioms of logic and mathematics.[17] Examples he gives (in addition to R) of contingent truths known noninferentially via common sense are beliefs such as "The thoughts of which I am conscious are *my* thoughts," "Other humans have minds," and "I have some degree of control over my actions."[18]

So Reid thinks we know R and other first principles (both contingent and necessary) in the basic way by means of common sense. Now, just as there is a mechanism by which we form sense perceptual beliefs in the basic way, so also there is a mechanism of sorts for forming our commonsense beliefs. Sense perception seems to work as follows: we experience sensations (visual, tactile, etc.) and on the basis of them form beliefs in the existence of external objects having certain qualities. The ground of our sense perceptual beliefs is our sense experience, not other beliefs. It is because they aren't based on other beliefs that they are called basic or noninferential. Now consider what Reid says about how commonsense beliefs in first principles are formed:

> We may observe, that opinions which contradict first principles are distinguished from other errors by this; that they are not only false, but absurd: and, to discountenance absurdity, nature has given us a particular emotion, to wit, that of ridicule, which seems intended for this very purpose of putting out of countenance what is absurd, either in opinion or practice.[19]

The idea is that when we entertain the contrary of a first principle, we experience the emotion of ridicule. On the basis of this experience, we dismiss as absurd the contrary of the first principle and believe the first principle. In other words, we consider the contrary of a first principle and have an experience that prompts this sort of belief: "That's absolutely nuts! It's ridiculous!" It thereby also prompts belief in the first principle itself, though, as Reid notes, we rarely attend to beliefs in first principles.[20] Just as in the case of sense perception, the ground of the first principle belief is an experience not a belief.

IV. A REIDIAN RESPONSE TO PLANTINGA

It should now be pretty obvious how a Reidian could respond to Plantinga's evolutionary argument against naturalism. She could combine *Plantinga's* method of responding to the probabilistic argument from evil with *Reid's* account of how we can know R in the basic way. For the sake of argument, we've conceded to Plantinga that P(R/N&E) is low or inscrutable. He says this is a defeater for R. But the commonsense naturalist can respond as follows: "Even if a naturalist believed that P(R/N&E) is low or inscrutable, this needn't give her a defeater for R. For she could have *non*propositional evidence for R that is sufficiently strong to make belief in R rational, reasonable, and warranted—even for someone whose total relevant *propositional* evidence, k, was such that P(R/k) is low or inscrutable. The nonpropositional evidence she has could be of the sort Reid describes."

To clarify this Reidian response, let me briefly consider two objections to it that are based on misunderstanding. The first has to do with the parallel between ourselves and the hypothetical creatures mentioned in stage one of Plantinga's evolutionary argument. It seems that the conjunction of the belief that N&E and the belief that P(R/N&E) is low or inscrutable *does*—when specified to these hypothetical creatures—constitute a defeater for our belief that *their* cognitive faculties are reliable. But then why should the same beliefs specified to ourselves not constitute a defeater for R specified to us? There is no relevant difference between the two cases since the facts concerning our origins are the same.

But there is a relevant difference. It may be true that if P(R/N&E) is assigned a low value when specified to the hypothetical creatures then it should also be assigned a low value when specified to us. But it's *not* true that if belief in that low probability claim results in a defeater in the case of the hypothetical creatures it also results in a defeater in our own case. First let's be clear about what exactly gets defeated in the case of the hypothetical creatures. It is *our* belief that *their* faculties are reliable. But notice that, in thinking about these hypothetical creatures, all we have to go on is *propositional* evidence; we have no *non*propositional evidence for R specified to them (recall how little we know about them). That's why it is plausible to think that the belief that N&E along with the belief that P(R/N&E) is low or inscrutable (where both beliefs are specified to these hypothetical creatures) constitutes a defeater for our belief that *their* faculties our reliable. But of course things are different with our belief in the reliability of *our own* cognitive faculties. In our own case, we have *non*propositional evidence *in addition to* the sort of propositional evidence we have in the case of the hypothetical creatures. That's why the belief that P(R/N&E) is low or inscrutable along with the belief that N&E (where both beliefs are specified to us) does not constitute a defeater for our belief that our own faculties are reliable.[21]

A second objection is that the Reidian response implies that R is beyond defeat. But R *could* be defeated. Suppose someone became convinced that she was the victim of a Cartesian demon. This would give her a defeater for R.

That seems right. But nothing I've said conflicts with it. Consider again the example of your being falsely accused of stealing a letter when you clearly remember your innocence. The circumstantial (propositional) evidence fails to defeat your memory belief. But that doesn't mean that your memory belief is beyond defeat. You could become convinced that the memory in question was planted in you artificially by someone intending to deceive you. This would create a defeater for it. Or consider theism and horrendous evil. You might believe G in the basic way and thereby have a lot of warrant for it. If so, then the fact that you also think P(G/HE) is low does not defeat your belief that G. But you could become convinced that your belief in G is the product of a Freudian sort of wish fulfillment—a way of forming beliefs that you take to be unreliable. Then you would have a defeater for your theistic belief.[22] In the same way, belief in the Cartesian demon might be a defeater for R even though belief in N&E together with belief in the low probability of R on N&E is not. Notice that the presence of these defeaters (the Freudian defeater for G or the Cartesian defeater for R) is compatible with the existence of nonpropositional evidence for G or for R. It's not that this nonpropositional evidence has no effect; rather, it's that its effect has been defeated by the stronger contrary effect of the defeater in question.[23]

VIII. BUT IS REID'S ACCOUNT TRUE?

. . . But how does this help the naturalist if Reid's account isn't true or even plausible? In order for my commonsense response to Plantinga to be useful, we need some reason to take Reid's account seriously. I don't have the space here to launch into a full-fledged defense of Reid's account of commonsense knowledge. However, I would at least like to say *something* in support of Reid's view and to explain some of the considerations that attract me to it.

But first, let's make the task more manageable. There is no need to defend all of Reid's views on common sense. One certainly doesn't need to agree with Reid about which propositions are first principles. For the purposes of this chapter, what matters is that we justifiably believe R via common sense. Nor does one need to hold Reid's views on the details of how one comes to believe in first principles like R— details such as whether we have a faculty of common sense or whether there is an emotion of ridicule. What matters for my Reidian response to Plantinga is that *we believe R noninferentially on the basis of some sort of nonpropositional evidence and thereby have a lot of justification or warrant for it.* Our question, then, is whether this last (italicized) suggestion can be taken seriously.

As a matter of fact, it *is* taken seriously. I've mentioned above that the particularist approach to epistemology is currently quite popular among analytic philosophers. Those who employ it rely heavily on the noninferential knowledge they have of Moorean truths—truths such as that we aren't being deceived by a Cartesian demon about the external world or about the past and that we aren't brains in vats. According to the particularist methodology, accounts of justification according to which it turns out that we aren't justified in believing such Moorean truths are, thereby, disqualified. The question of *how* it is that such epistemologists know these Moorean truths isn't very often addressed. But it seems that any answer given will be something along the lines suggested by Reid's account sketched above in section 3. At the very least, it will involve justified or warranted noninferential belief in R.

Furthermore, a defense of Reid's account could be developed along the following lines. First one could point out that sense perceptual beliefs based on sense experiences can be justified despite the fact that we lack compelling noncircular inductive or deductive arguments from the existence of such experiences to the truth of the beliefs they ground.[24] Then one could point out that a priori knowledge also involves belief processes in which a belief is based on a certain sort of seeming—a seeming which is an experience of some sort.[25] In this case too it looks like there is no deductive or inductive argument from the existence of such an experiential ground to the truth of the a priori belief based on it. But this doesn't cast doubt on the justification of our a priori beliefs any more than a similar concern casts doubt on the justification of our sense perceptual beliefs. In each case (sense perceptual and a priori) the belief is noninferentially justified as a result of its being based on the experiential ground in question.

Once one has shown that the above suggestions are plausible one could then argue that commonsense belief in contingent truths is very much like a priori belief insofar as they each have the same sort of experiential ground (i.e., a certain sort of seeming). Because it is plausible to take seriously both the existence of justified a priori beliefs as well as the account of them as experience based, it is also plausible to take seriously both the existence of justified commonsense beliefs in contingent truths as well as an account of them as experience based. Our starting point is the fact that we *do* seem to have justified noninferential beliefs of each kind despite the fact that in each case the belief in question is based on a ground from whose existence we can't deductively or inductively infer the truth of the belief it grounds. And my suggestion is that since many philosophers are inclined to express very little resistance to an account of justified sense perceptual belief according to which the justifying grounds don't entail the truth of the belief, there should also be very little resistance to similar accounts of justified a priori or commonsense belief—especially when such accounts fit so nicely with our introspective understanding of what is going on in typical cases of what seem like justified a priori or commonsense beliefs.

The above remarks are meant to gesture in the direction of a defense of that part of Reid's account that is employed in my response to Plantinga. They are *not* intended to put to rest all doubts those who resist Reid's account might have. To do that one would have to defend the existence of a priori belief as well as the account of it as experience based. And one would also need to consider whether the differences between commonsense belief and a priori belief prevent us from moving from a favorable evaluation of our account of justified a priori belief to a favorable evaluation of a similar account of commonsense belief. For example, one might think (though I don't) that although we *can* have noninferential knowledge of propositions that are general and necessary as well as of propositions that are particular and contingent, we *can't* have noninferential knowledge of propositions that are general and contingent. If this were true, it would suggest that a priori knowledge (which is typically of truths that are general and necessary) is acceptable in a way that commonsense knowledge (which at least sometimes is supposedly of general and contingent truths like R) is not. But dealing with these sorts of concerns is a project for another occasion. Here I merely hope to have shown that a plausible defense of the required elements of Reid's account of commonsense knowledge is by no means out of the question. . . .

NOTES

1. This is how Alvin Plantinga characterizes the view he attacks in his evolutionary argument against naturalism ("Naturalism Defeated," unpublished). See also Plantinga, "Respondeo," in *Warrant in Contemporary Epistemology: Essays in Honor of Plantinga's Theory of Knowledge*, ed. Jonathan Kvanvig (Lanham, Md.: Rowman and Littlefield, 1996), 350–352. Since the naturalism under discussion in this paper is the sort—whatever it is—that Plantinga is attacking, it would be best to begin with his understanding of it. Another similar characterization of metaphysical naturalism is Michael Devitt's. He says that it amounts to physicalism—the view that all entities are physical entities ("Naturalism and the A Priori," *Philosophical Studies* 92 [1998]: 46). If I were trying to give a precise account of metaphysical naturalism, much more would have to be said. But this will do for our purposes. See the essays in *Midwest Studies in Philosophy,* vol. 19, *Philosophical Naturalism,* ed. Peter French, Theodore Uehling, and Howard Wettstein (Notre Dame: University of Notre Dame Press, 1994), and in *Naturalism: A Critical Appraisal,* ed. Steven Wagner and Richard Warner (Notre Dame: University of Notre Dame Press, 1993), for various attempts to clarify what naturalism is, as well as the essays in *Objections to Physicalism,* ed. Howard Robinson (New York: Clarendon Press, 1993), for discussions of what physicalism is. See also section 7 of this chapter [omitted here], where I discuss varieties of naturalism other than the sort roughly defined here. For a defense of the view that naturalism isn't a thesis at all but rather a research program (more specifically, a plan to conduct inquiry using only the methods of the natural sciences), see Michael Rea, *World without Design: The Ontological Consequences of Naturalism* (Oxford: Clarendon Press, 2002).

2. *Warrant and Proper Function* (New York: Oxford University Press, 1993), hereafter *WPF;* and "Naturalism Defeated."

3. Keith Lehrer's response to Plantinga's evolutionary argument against naturalism is superficially similar to my own. In giving his response to that argument he too draws upon Plantinga's response to the problem of evil (see Lehrer, "Proper Function versus Systematic Coherence," *Warrant in Contemporary Epistemology: Essays in Honor of Plantinga's Theory of Knowledge,* ed. Jonathan Kvanvig [Lanham, Md.: Rowman and Littlefield, 1996]) and upon Reid (see Keith Lehrer and

Bradley Warner, "Reid, God and Epistemology," *American Catholic Philosophical Quarterly* 74 [2000]: 357–372). But the use Lehrer makes of Reid and of Plantinga's response to the problem of evil is quite unlike the use I make of them. So our responses to Plantinga's evolutionary argument against naturalism are, in the end, very different (which is what one might expect given that I'm an externalist foundationlist and that Lehrer is at least very sympathetic to an internalist sort of coherentism).

4. In saying that (i) is a Reidian view, I'm assuming that he is a foundationalist. Lehrer challenges that assumption. In support of a coherentist reading, Lehrer points out passages in Reid which could be taken as saying that the justification of each of our beliefs depends on a further belief about the trustworthiness of that original belief's source. See Lehrer, "Chisholm, Reid and the Problem of the Epistemic Surd," *Philosophical Studies* 60 (1990): 42–43. This isn't the place to defend the view that Reid is a foundationalist. So I'll just say that I read those passages in Reid as saying that we *can* be justified in the further belief that our belief sources are trustworthy, not that we *must* be in order for our beliefs produced by those sources to be justified.

5. See Roderick Chisholm. "The Problem of the Criterion," in *The Foundations of Knowing* (Minneapolis: University of Minnesota Press, 1982), 61–75, for an account of this particularist approach.

6. Thomas Reid, *Essays on the Intellectual Powers* (Cambridge: MIT Press, 1969), 294–295; hereafter Reid, *Essays*. See also Reid, *Inquiries and Essays*, ed. Ronald Beanblossom and Keith Lehrer (Indianapolis: Hackett Publishing, 1983), 203; hereafter Reid, *Inquiries*, Reid's *Essays* is complete but his *Inquiries* (which isn't complete) is more readily available. I will give references to both where possible.

7. See Plantinga, "The Probabilistic Argument from Evil," *Philosophical Studies* 35 (1979): 1–53; "Epistemic Probability and Evil," *Archivo di filosofia* 56 (1988); "On Being Evidentially Challenged," in *The Evidential Argument from Evil*, ed. Daniel Howard-Snyder (Bloomington: Indiana University Press, 1996), 244–261; and "Degenerate Evidence and Rowe's New Evidential Argument from Evil," *Noûs* 32 (1998): 531–544.

8. Plantinga, "Epistemic Probability and Evil," in *The Evidential Argument from Evil*, ed. Daniel Howard-Snyder (Bloomington: Indiana University Press, 1996), 88–89.

9. When I describe the experience as one of its *seeming to you that you were out for a walk in the woods earlier in the day*, I don't mean to suggest that the experience has a propositional content. I'm just saying that the experience in question is a seeming that inclines you to believe that you were out for a walk in the woods earlier in the day.

10. We have to imagine the case so that you have all the propositional evidence your accusers have and that additionally all you have is the memory experience and the belief that W. In particular, you don't have any beliefs about your memory experience or about how trustworthy it is, etc. Your belief that W is based solely on the memory experience in question and nothing other than the belief that W is based on that memory experience. One might think that, upon being accused and thinking carefully about your memory experience, you will form additional beliefs on the basis of it. But we can stipulate that we are focusing on the time before you are accused—the point at which you first learn of all the evidence that exists against you.

11. Plantinga, "Reason and Belief in God," in *Faith and Rationality,* ed. Alvin Plantinga and Nicholas Wolterstorff (Notre Dame: University of Notre Dame Press, 1983), 80–81.

12. Reid, *Essays*, 630; Reid, *Inquiries*, 275.

13. Reid, *Essays*, 593.

14. Ibid., 567. The other branch of reason enables us "to draw conclusions that are not self-evident from those that are."

15. See ibid., essay 6, chap. 4, "Of First Principles in General," parts of which are included in Reid, *Inquiries*.

16. Reid, *Essays*, 614–615.

17. Ibid., 644; Reid, *Inquiries*, 284–285.

18. Reid, *Essays*, 611–643.

19. Ibid., 606; Reid, *Inquiries*, 259.

20. Reid, *Essays*, 632–633; Reid, *Inquiries*, 277.

21. Thus Plantinga is right when he says in *WPF*, 229, that the person considering R specified to the hypothetical creatures has no source of information about R other than the propositional evidence mentioned. But when he considers (223–234) what other sources of information we might have for R specified to *us*, he considers only other *propositional* evidence for R. And he considers it only as a candidate for being a defeater of a defeater for R instead of thinking of the other source of information about R as

something that prevents us from having a defeater for R in the first place. He fails to acknowledge that we have nonpropositional evidence for R specified to us and that this is a relevant difference between the two cases; it's a difference that results in our having a defeater in the one case and not in the other.

22. Notice that the mere *existence* of the Freudian explanation is not in itself a defeater for G, just as the mere existence of the Cartesian demon hypothesis is not in itself a defeater for R. It must also be the case that the alternative hypothesis in question is reasonable and/or believed.

23. Those sane humans for whom R is defeated (assuming there are such) are not counterexamples to my earlier suggestion that the outputs of R are beliefs naturally held by *all* sane humans in normal circumstances. For in order to be defeated, these beliefs had to first be held. And, in fact, they *are* held in normal circumstances; it is only in *abnormal* circumstances that someone comes to later believe she is the victim of a Cartesian demon.

24. See William Alston, *The Reliability of Sense Perception* (Ithaca, N.Y.: Cornell University Press, 1993) for an extended critique of various attempts to show that there is some such connection between sense experiences and the beliefs they ground.

25. See Plantinga, *WPF*, chap. 6. Because the experiential ground of a priori beliefs is nonempirical the beliefs are still properly called 'a priori' rather than 'posterior.'

Religious Pluralism

IS THERE ONLY ONE WAY to God? If God exists, why hasn't he revealed himself in all times and places to all nations and people? Or has he done so, but through different faiths, through different symbols, and different interpretations of himself? Are all religions simply different paths to the same ultimate reality?

In the last twenty years or so, the question of religious pluralism has become a burning issue among theologians and philosophers of religion. On the one side are the *pluralists,* those who hold that all religions, or at least all major religions, are different paths to the same God, or ultimate reality. On the other side are the *exclusivists,* who argue that there is only one way to God. Pluralist philosophers like John Hick (see our first reading in this section) believe that the major religions—Judaism, Christianity, Hinduism, Buddhism, and Islam—are different paths to the same ultimate reality. The Buddhist parable of the six blind men is sometimes used to illustrate this point:

> Once upon a time a group of religious seekers from different traditions came together and began to discuss the nature of God. Offering quite different answers, they began quarreling among themselves as to who was right and who wrong. Finally, when no hope for a reconciliation was in sight, they called in the Buddha and asked him to tell them who was right. The Buddha proceeded to tell the following story.
>
> There was once a king who asked his servants to bring him all the blind people in a town and an elephant. Six blind men and an elephant were soon set before him. The king instructed the blind men to feel the animal and describe the elephant. "An elephant is like a large waterpot," said the first who touched the elephant's head. "Your Majesty, he's wrong," said the second, as he touched an ear. "An elephant is like a fan." "No," insisted a third, "an elephant is like a snake," as he held his trunk. "On the contrary, you're all mistaken," said a fourth, as he held the tusks, "An elephant is like two prongs of a plow." The fifth man demurred and said, "It is quite clear that an elephant is like a pillar," as he grasped the animal's rear leg. "You're all mistaken," insisted the sixth. "An elephant is a long snake," and he held up the tail. Then they all began to shout at each other about their convictions of the nature of an elephant.
>
> After telling the story the Buddha commented, "How can you be so sure of what you cannot see. We are all like blind people in this world. We cannot see God. Each of you may be partly right, yet none completely so."

The religious pluralist calls on us to give up our claims to exclusivity and accept the thesis that many paths lead to God and to salvation or liberation. As Lord Krishna says in the *Bhagavad Gita,* "In whatever way men approach me, I am gracious to them; men everywhere follow my path."

On the other side of the debate are exclusivists. They believe that only one way leads to God or salvation. Whereas Hinduism, reflected in the words of Lord Krishna (above), has tended to be pluralistic, Christianity and Islam have tended to exclusivity. In the Gospel of John, Jesus says, "I am the way, the truth, and the life, no man cometh to the Father but by me." And Peter says in the Book of Acts, "Neither is there salvation in any other; for there is none other name under heaven given among men, whereby we must be saved." The inspiration of the missionary movement within Christianity and Islam has been to bring salvation to those who would otherwise be lost.

Christians and Muslims have historically rejected pluralism. If Christ or Mohammed is the unique way to God, the other creeds must be erroneous since they deny these claims. Since Muslims and Christians believe that they have good reasons for their beliefs, why should they give them up? Why should they give up their claims to exclusivity?

One consideration given by the pluralists is that it is an empirical fact that people generally adhere to the religion of their geographical location, of their native culture. Thus, Indians are likely to be Hindus, Tibetans Buddhists, Israelis Jews, Arabs Muslims, and Europeans and Americans Christians. If we recognize the accidentality of our religious preference, shouldn't we give up the claim to exclusivity?

The exclusivist responds that one may give up a claim to *certainty* as he or she recognizes that other traditions have different beliefs. But if on reexamination of one's position, one still finds oneself adhering to one's position, then the person might be perfectly reasonable in continuing to think that her religion offers the only path to God or salvation. The fact that one's religious beliefs are partly a result of where one lives doesn't by itself show that exclusivist claims are false. At best, the exclusivist will say, it shows that sociological factors have some role to play in determining how easy it is for one to happen upon the truth.

In our readings, John Hick defends the pluralist position and Alvin Plantinga defends religious exclusivity. He argues that religious exclusivity is not (or need not be) morally or epistemically improper and that a certain exclusivity is present no matter what we believe. That is, suppose the pluralist believes that all the major religions are equally good paths to God. In that case, the pluralist is an *exclusivist* with regard to that belief. Believing anything implies that those who believe the contrary of what you believe are wrong. So we are all inevitably exclusivist in one way or another.

David Basinger, in the third reading, attempts to reconcile Hick's religious pluralism with Plantinga's exclusivism. Basinger argues that, properly understood, the two positions are compatible, both offering valid insights on the diversity of religious phenomena.

In our fourth reading the Dalai Lama reflects on the Buddhist perspective on world religions, indicating some areas of unity within diversity. And, in our final reading, Joseph Runzo identifies six different responses to the relationship between one's own religion and other religions. He defends religious relativism, which holds that first order truth-claims about reality are relative to the worldview of a particular culture.

IX.1   Religious Pluralism and Ultimate Reality

JOHN HICK

Biographical remarks about John Hick precede selection III.4. In this essay from his path-breaking work, *God and the Universe of Faiths* (1973), Hick sets forth the thesis that God historically revealed himself (or itself) through various individuals in various situations where geographic isolation prevented a common revelation to all humanity. Each major religion has a different interpretation of the same ultimate reality, to the same salvation. Now the time has come to engage in interreligious dialogue so that we may discover our common bonds and realize that other religious people participate in ultimate reality as validly as we do within our religion, "for all these exist in time, as ways through time to eternity."

Let me begin by proposing a working definition of religion as an understanding of the universe, together with an appropriate way of living within it, which involves reference beyond the natural world to God or gods or to the Absolute or to a transcendent order or process. Such a definition includes such theistic faiths as Judaism, Christianity, Islam, Sikhism; the theistic Hinduism of the Bhagavad Gītā; the semi-theistic faith of Mahayana Buddhism and the non-theistic faiths of Theravada Buddhism and non-theistic Hinduism. It does not however include purely naturalistic systems of belief, such as communism and humanism, immensely important though these are today as alternatives to religious life.

When we look back into the past we find that religion has been a virtually universal dimension of human life—so much so that man has been defined as the religious animal. For he has displayed an innate tendency to experience his environment as being religiously as well as naturally significant, and to feel required to live in it as such. To quote the anthropologist, Raymond Firth, "religion is universal in human societies." "In every human community on earth today," says Wilfred Cantwell Smith, "there exists something that we, as sophisticated observers, may term religion, or a religion. And we are able to

see it in each case as the latest development in a continuous tradition that goes back, we can now affirm, for at least one hundred thousand years." In the life of primitive man this religious tendency is expressed in a belief in sacred objects endowed with *mana*, and in a multitude of natural and ancestral spirits needing to be carefully propitiated. The divine was here crudely apprehended as a plurality of quasianimal forces which could to some extent be controlled by ritualistic and magical procedures. This represents the simplest beginning of man's awareness of the transcendent in the infancy of the human race—an infancy which is also to some extent still available for study in the life of primitive tribes today.

The development of religion and religions begins to emerge into the light of recorded history as the third millennium B.C. moves towards the period around 2000 B.C. There are two main regions of the earth in which civilisation seems first to have arisen and in which religions first took a shape that is at least dimly discernible to us as we peer back through the mists of time—these being Mesopotamia in the Near East and the Indus valley of northern India. In Mesopotamia men lived in nomadic shepherd tribes, each worshipping its own god. Then the tribes gradually coalesced into nation states, the former tribal gods becoming ranked in hierarchies (some however being lost by amalgamation in the process) dominated by great national deities such as Marduk of Babylon, the Sumerian Ishtar, Amon of Thebes, Jahweh of Israel, the Greek Zeus, and so on. Further east in the Indus valley there was likewise a wealth of gods and goddesses, though apparently not so much tribal or national in character as expressive of the basic forces of nature, above all fertility. The many deities of the Near East and of India expressed man's awareness of the divine at the dawn of documentary history, some four thousand years ago. It is perhaps worth stressing that the picture was by no means a wholly pleasant one. The tribal and national gods were often martial and cruel, sometimes requiring human sacrifices. And although rather little is known about the very early, pre-Aryan Indian deities, it is certain that later Indian deities have vividly symbolised the cruel and destructive as well as the beneficent aspects of nature.

These early developments in the two cradles of civilisation, Mesopotamia and the Indus valley, can be described as the growth of natural religion, prior to any special intrusions of divine revelation or illumination. Primitive spirit-worship expressed man's fears of unknown forces; his reverence for nature deities expressed his sense of dependence upon realities greater than himself; and his tribal gods expressed the unity and continuity of his group over against other groups. One can in fact discern all sorts of causal connections between the forms which early religion took and the material circumstances of man's life, indicating the large part played by the human element within the history of religion. For example, Trevor Ling points out that life in ancient India (apart from the Punjab immediately prior to the Aryan invasions) was agricultural and was organised in small village units; and suggests that "among agricultural peoples, aware of the fertile earth which brings forth from itself and nourishes its progeny upon its broad bosom, it is the mother-principle which seems important." Accordingly God the Mother, and a variety of more specialised female deities, have always held a prominent place in Indian religious thought and mythology. This contrasts with the characteristically male expression of deity in the Semitic religions, which had their origins among nomadic, pastoral, herd-keeping peoples in the Near East. The divine was known to the desert-dwelling herdsmen who founded the Israelite tradition as God the King and Father; and this conception has continued both in later Judaism and in Christianity, and was renewed out of the desert experience of Mohammed in the Islamic religion. Such regional variations in our human ways of conceiving the divine have persisted through time into the developed world faiths that we know today. The typical western conception of God is still predominantly in terms of the male principle of power and authority; and in the typical Indian conceptions of deity the female principle still plays a distinctly larger part than in the west.

Here then was the natural condition of man's religious life: religion without revelation. But sometime around 800 B.C. there began what has been called the golden age of religious creativity. This consisted in a remarkable series of revelatory experiences occurring during the next five hundred or so years in different parts of the world, experiences which deepened and purified men's conception of the ultimate, and which religious faith can only attribute to the pressure of the divine Spirit upon the human spirit. First came the early Jewish prophets, Amos, Hosea and first Isaiah, declaring that they had heard the Word of the Lord claiming their obedience and demanding a new level of righteousness and justice in the life of Israel. Then in Persia the great prophet Zoroaster appeared; China produced Lao-tzu and then Confucius; in India the Upanishads were written, and Gotama the Buddha lived, and Mahavira, the founder of the Jain religion and, probably about the end of this period, the writing of the Bhagavad Gītā, and Greece produced Pythagoras and then, ending this golden age, Socrates and Plato. Then after the gap of some three hundred years came Jesus of Nazareth and the emergence of Christianity; and after another gap the prophet Mohammed and the rise of Islam.

The suggestion that we must consider is that these were all moments of divine revelation. But let us ask, in order to test this thought, whether we should not expect God to make his revelation in a single mighty act, rather than to produce a number of different, and therefore presumably partial, revelations at different times and places? I think that in seeing the answer to this question we receive an important clue to the place of the religions of the world in the divine purpose. For when we remember the facts of history and geography we realise that in the period we are speaking of, between two and three thousand years ago, it was not possible for God to reveal himself through any human mediation to all mankind. A world-wide revelation might be possible today, thanks to the inventions of printing, and even more of radio, TV and communication satellites. But in the technology of the ancient world this was not possible. Although on a time scale of centuries and millennia there has been a slow diffusion and interaction of cultures, particularly within the vast Euro-Asian land mass, yet the more striking fact for our present purpose is the fragmented character of the ancient world. Communications between the different groups of humanity was then so limited and slow that for all practical purposes men inhabited different worlds. For the most part people in Europe, in India, in Arabia, in Africa, in China were unaware of the others' existence. And as the world was fragmented, so was its religious life. If there was to be a revelation of the divine reality to mankind it had to be a pluriform revelation, a series of revealing experiences occurring independently within the different streams of human history. And since religion and culture were one, the great creative moments of revelation and illumination have influenced the development of the various cultures, giving them the coherence and impetus to expand into larger units, thus creating the vast, many-sided historical entities which we call the world religions.

Each of these religio-cultural complexes has expanded until it touched the boundaries of another such complex spreading out from another centre. Thus each major occasion of divine revelation has slowly transformed the primitive and national religions within the sphere of its influence into what we now know as the world faiths. The early Dravidian and Aryan polytheisms of India were drawn through the religious experience and thought of the Brahmins into what the

west calls Hinduism. The national and mystery cults of the Mediterranean world and then of northern Europe were drawn by influences stemming from the life and teaching of Christ into what has become Christianity. The early polytheism of the Arab peoples has been transformed under the influence of Mohammed and his message into Islam. Great areas of Southeast Asia, of China, Tibet and Japan were drawn into the spreading Buddhist movement. None of these expansions from different centres of revelation has of course been simple and uncontested, and a number of alternatives which proved less durable have perished or been absorbed in the process—for example, Mithraism has disappeared altogether; and Zoroastrianism, whilst it greatly influenced the development of the Judaic-Christian tradition, and has to that extent been absorbed, only survives directly today on a small scale in Parseeism.

Seen in this historical context these movements of faith—the Judaic-Christian, the Buddhist, the Hindu, the Muslim—are not essentially rivals. They began at different times and in different places, and each expanded outwards into the surrounding world of primitive natural religion until most of the world was drawn up into one or other of the great revealed faiths. And once this global pattern had become established it has ever since remained fairly stable. It is true that the process of establishment involved conflict in the case of Islam's entry into India and the virtual expulsion of Buddhism from India in the medieval period, and in the case of Islam's advance into Europe and then its retreat at the end of the medieval period. But since the frontiers of the different world faiths became more or less fixed there has been little penetration of one faith into societies moulded by another. The most successful missionary efforts of the great faiths continue to this day to be "downwards" into the remaining world of relatively primitive religions rather than "sideways" into territories dominated by another world faith. For example, as between Christianity and Islam there has been little more than rather rare individual conversions; but both faiths have successful missions in Africa. Again, the Christian population of the Indian subcontinent, after more than two centuries of missionary effort, is only about 2.7 per cent; but on the other hand the Christian missions in the South Pacific are fairly successful. Thus the general picture, so far as the great world religions is concerned, is that each has gone through an early period of geographical expansion, converting a region of the world from its more primitive religious state, and has thereafter continued in a comparatively settled condition within more of less stable boundaries.

Now it is of course possible to see this entire development from the primitive forms of religion up to and including the great world faiths as the history of man's most persistent illusion, growing from crude fantasies into sophisticated metaphysical speculations. But from the standpoint of religious faith the only reasonable hypothesis is that this historical picture represents a movement of divine self-revelation to mankind. This hypothesis offers a general answer to the question of the relation between the different world religions and of the truths which they embody. It suggests to us that the same divine reality has always been self-revealingly active towards mankind, and that the differences of human response are related to different human circumstances. These circumstances—ethnic, geographical, climatic, economic, sociological, historical—have produced the existing differentiations of human culture, and within each main cultural region the response to the divine has taken its own characteristic forms. In each case the post-primitive response has been initiated by some spiritually outstanding individual or succession of individuals, developing in the course of time into one of the great religio-cultural phenomena which we call the world religions. Thus Islam embodies the main response of the Arabic peoples to the divine reality; Hinduism, the main (though not the only) response of the peoples of India; Buddhism, the main response of the peoples of South-east Asia and parts of northern Asia; Christianity, the main response of the European peoples, both within Europe itself and in their emigrations to the Americas and Australasia.

Thus it is, I think, intelligible historically why the revelation of the divine reality to man, and the disclosure of the divine will for human life, had to occur separately within the different streams of human life. We can see how these revelations took different forms related to the different mentalities of the peoples to whom they came and developed within these different cultures into the vast and many-sided historical phenomena of the world religions.

But let us now ask whether this is intelligible theologically. What about the conflicting truth claims of the different faiths? Is the divine nature personal or non-personal; does deity become incarnate in the world; are human beings born again and again on earth; is the Bible, or the Koran, or the Bhagavad Gītā the Word of God? If what Christianity says in answer to these questions is true, must not what Hinduism says be to a large extent false? If what Buddhism says is true, must not what Islam says be largely false?

Let us begin with the recognition, which is made in all the main religious traditions, that the ultimate divine reality is infinite and as such transcends the grasp of the human mind. God, to use our Christian term, is infinite. He is not a thing, a part of the universe, existing alongside other things; nor is he a being falling under a certain kind. And therefore he cannot be defined or encompassed by human thought. We cannot draw boundaries around his nature and say that he is this and no more. If we could fully define God, describing his inner being and his outer limits, this would not be God. The God whom our minds can penetrate and whom our thoughts can circumnavigate is merely a finite and partial image of God.

From this it follows that the different encounters with the transcendent within the different religious traditions may all be encounters with the one infinite reality; though with partially different and overlapping aspects of that reality. This is a very familiar thought in Indian religious literature. We read, for example, in the ancient Rig-Vedas, dating back to perhaps as much as a thousand years before Christ:

> *They call it Indra, Mitra, Varuna, and Agni*
> *And also heavenly, beautiful Garutman:*
> *The real is one, though sages name it*
> *variously.*

We might translate this thought into the terms of the faiths represented today in Britain:

*They call it Jahweh, Allah, Krishna, Param
 Atma,
And also holy, blessed Trinity:
The real is one, though sages name it
 differently.*

And in the Bhagavad Gītā the Lord Krishna, the personal God of love, says, "However men approach me, even so do I accept them: for, on all sides, whatever path they may choose is mine."

Again, there is the parable of the blind men and the elephant, said to have been told by the Buddha. An elephant was brought to a group of blind men who had never encountered such an animal before. One felt a leg and reported that an elephant is a great living pillar. Another felt the trunk and reported that an elephant is a great snake. Another felt the tusk and reported than an elephant is like a sharp ploughshare. And so on. And then they all quarrelled together, each claiming that his own account was the truth and therefore all the others false. In fact of course they were all true, but each referring only to one aspect of the total reality and all expressed in very imperfect analogies.

Now the possibility, indeed the probability, that we have seriously to consider is that many different accounts of the divine reality may be true, though all expressed in imperfect human analogies, but that none is "the truth, the whole truth, and nothing but the truth." May it not be that the different concepts of God, as Jahweh, Allah, Krishna, Param Atma, Holy Trinity, and so on: and likewise the different concepts of the hidden structure of reality, as the eternal emanation of Brahman or as an immense cosmic process culminating in Nirvana, are all images of the divine, each expressing some aspect or range of aspects and yet none by itself fully and exhaustively corresponding to the infinite nature of the ultimate reality?

Two immediate qualifications however to this hypothesis. First, the idea that we are considering is not that any and every conception of God or of the transcendent is valid, still less all equally valid; but that every conception of the divine which has come out of a great revelatory religious experience and has been tested though a long tradition of worship, and has sustained human faith over centuries of time and in millions of lives, is likely to represent a genuine encounter with the divine reality. And second, the parable of the blind men and the elephant is of course only a parable and like most parables it is designed to make one point and must not be pressed as an analogy at other points. The suggestion is not that the different encounters with the divine which lie at the basis of the great religious traditions are responses to different *parts* of the divine. They are rather encounters from different historical and cultural standpoints with the same infinite divine reality and as such they lead to differently focused awareness of the reality. The indications of this are most evident in worship and prayer. What is said about God in the theological treatises of the different faiths is indeed often widely different. But it is in prayer that a belief in God comes alive and does its main work. And when we turn from abstract theology to the living stuff of worship we meet again and again the overlap and confluence of faiths.

Here, for example, is a Muslim prayer at the feast of Ramadan:

Praise be to God, Lord of creation, Source of all livelihood, who orders the morning, Lord of majesty and honour, of grace and beneficence. He who is so far that he may not be seen and so near that he witnesses the secret things. Blessed be he and for ever exalted.

And here is a Sikh creed used at the morning prayer:

> *There is but one God. He is all that is.*
> *He is the Creator of all things and He is*
> *all pervasive.*
> *He is without fear and without enmity.*
> *He is timeless, unborn and self-existent. He*
> *is the Enlightener*
> *And can be realised by grace of Himself alone.*
> *He was in the beginning; He was in all*
> *ages.*
> *The True One is, was, O Nanak, and shall*
> *for ever be.*

And here again is a verse from the Koran:

To God belongs the praise. Lord of the heavens and Lord of the earth, the Lord of all being. His is the dominion in the heavens and in the earth: he is the Almighty, the All-wise.

Turning now to the Hindu idea of the many incarnations of God, here is a verse from the Rāmāyana:

Seers and sages, saints and hermits, fix on Him
their reverent gaze,
And in faint and trembling accents, holy
scripture hymns His praise.
He the omnipresent spirit, lord of heaven and
earth and hell,
To redeem His people, freely has vouchsafed
with men to dwell.

And from the rich literature of devotional song here is a Bhakti hymn of the Vaishnavite branch of Hinduism:

Now all my days with joy I'll fill, full to the
brim
With all my heart to Vitthal cling, and only
Him.
He will sweep utterly away all dole and care;
And all in sunder shall I rend illusion's snare.
O altogether dear is He, and He alone,
For all my burden He will take to be His own.
Lo, all the sorrow of the world will straight way
cease,
And all unending now shall be the reign of
peace.

And a Muslim mystical verse:

Love came a guest
Within my breast,
My soul was spread,
Love banqueted.

And finally another Hindu (Vaishnavite) devotional hymn:

O save me, save me, Mightiest, Save me and set
me free.
O let the love that fills my breast Cling to thee
lovingly.
Grant me to taste how sweet thou art; Grant
me but this, I pray.
And never shall my love depart Or turn from
thee away.
Then I thy name shall magnify And tell thy
praise abroad,

For very love and gladness I Shall dance before
my God.

Such prayers and hymns as these must express, surely, diverse encounters with the same divine reality. These encounters have taken place within different human cultures by people of different ways of thought and feeling, with different histories and different frameworks of philosophical thought, and have developed into different systems of theology embodied in different religious structures and organisations. These resulting large-scale religio-cultural phenomena are what we call the religions of the world. But must there not lie behind them the same infinite divine reality, and may not our divisions into Christian, Hindu, Muslim, Jew, and soon, and all that goes with them, accordingly represent secondary, human, historical developments?

There is a further problem, however, which now arises. I have been speaking so far of the ultimate reality in a variety of terms—the Father, Son and Spirit of Christianity, the Jahweh of Judaism, the Allah of Islam, and so on—but always thus far in theistic terms, as a personal God under one name or another. But what of the non-theistic religions? What of the non-theistic Hinduism according to which the ultimate reality, Brahman, is not He but It; and what about Buddhism, which in one form is agnostic concerning the existence of God even though in another form it has come to worship the Buddha himself? Can these non-theistic faiths be seen as encounters with the same divine reality that is encountered in theistic religion?

Speaking very tentatively, I think it is possible that the sense of the divine as non-personal may indeed reflect an aspect of the same infinite reality that is encountered as personal in theistic religious experience. The question can be pursued both as a matter of pure theology and in relation to religious experience. Theologically, the Hindu distinction between Nirguna Brahman and Saguna Brahman is important and should be adopted into western religious thought. Detaching the distinction, then from its Hindu context we may say that Nirguna God is the eternal self-existent divine reality, beyond the scope of all human categories, including personality; and

Saguna God is God in relation to his creation and with the attributes which express this relationship, such as personality, omnipotence, goodness, love and omniscience. Thus the one ultimate reality is both Nirguna and non-personal, and Saguna and personal, in a duality which is in principle acceptable to human understanding. When we turn to men's religious awareness of God we are speaking of Saguna God, God in relation to man. And here the larger traditions of both east and west report a dual experience of the divine as personal and as other than personal. It will be a sufficient reminder of the strand of personal relationship with the divine in Hinduism to mention Iswaru, the personal God who represents the Absolute as known and worshipped by finite persons. It should also be remembered that the characterisation of Brahman as *satcitananda,* absolute being, consciousness and bliss, is not far from the conception of infinitely transcendent personal life. Thus there is both the thought and the experience of the personal divine within Hinduism. But there is likewise the thought and the experience of God as other than personal within Christianity. Rudolph Otto describes this strand in the mysticism of Meister Eckhart. He says:

> The divine, which on the one hand is conceived in symbols taken from the social sphere, as Lord, King, Father, Judge—a person in relation to persons—is on the other hand denoted in dynamic symbols as the power of life, as light and life, as spirit ebbing and flowing, as truth, knowledge, essential justice and holiness, a glowing fire that penetrates and pervades. It is characterized as the principle of a renewed, supernatural Life, mediating and giving itself, breaking forth in the living man as his nova vita, as the content of his life and being. What is here insisted upon is not so much an immanent God, as an "experienced" God, known as an inward principle of the power of new being and life. Eckhart knows this *deuteros theos* besides the personal God . . .

Let me now try to draw the threads together and to project them into the future. I have been suggesting that Christianity is a way of salvation which, beginning some two thousand years ago, has become the principal way of salvation in three continents. The other great faiths are likewise of salvation, providing the principal path to the divine reality for other large sections of humanity. I have also suggested that the idea that Jesus proclaimed himself as God incarnate, and as the sole point of saving contact between God and man, is without adequate historical foundation and represents a doctrine developed by the church. We should therefore not infer, from the christian experience of redemption through Christ, that salvation cannot be experienced in any other way. The alternative possibility is that the ultimate divine reality—in our christian terms, God—has always been pressing in upon the human spirit, but in ways which leave men free to open or close themselves to the divine presence. Human life has developed along characteristically different lines in the main areas of civilisation, and these differences have naturally entered into the ways in which men have apprehended and responded to God. For the great religious figures through whose experience divine revelation has come have each been conditioned by a particular history and culture. One can hardly imagine Gotama the Buddha except in the setting of the India of his time, or Jesus the Christ except against the background of Old Testament Judaism, or Mohammed except in the setting of Arabia. And human history and culture have likewise shaped the development of the webs of religious creeds, practices and organisations which we know as the great world faiths.

It is thus possible to consider the hypothesis that they are all, at their experiential roots, in contact with the same ultimate reality, but that their differing experiences of that reality, interacting over the centuries with the different thought-forms of different cultures, have led to increasing differentiation and contrasting elaboration—so that Hinduism, for example, is a very different phenomenon from Christianity, and very different ways of conceiving and experiencing the divine occur within them.

However, now that the religious traditions are consciously interacting with each other in the "one world" of today, in mutual observation and dialogue, it is possible that their future developments may be on gradually converging courses. For during the next few centuries they will no doubt continue to change, and it may be that they will grow closer together, and even that one day such names as "Christianity," "Buddhism," "Islam," "Hinduism," will no longer describe the then current configurations of men's religious experience and belief. I am not here thinking of the extinction of human religiousness in a universal wave of secularisation. This is of course a possible future; and indeed many think it the most likely future to come about. But if man is an indelibly religious animal he will always, even in his secular cultures, experience a sense of the transcendent by which he will be both troubled and uplifted. The future I am thinking of is accordingly one in which what we now call the different religions will constitute the past history of different emphases and variations within a global religious life. I do not mean that all men everywhere will be overtly religious, any more than they are today. I mean rather that the discoveries now taking place by men of different faiths of central common ground, hitherto largely concealed by the variety of cultural forms in which it was expressed, may eventually render obsolete the sense of belonging to rival ideological communities. Not that all religious men will think alike, or worship in the same way or experience the divine identically. On the contrary, so long as there is a rich variety of human cultures—and let us hope there will always be this—we should expect there to be correspondingly different forms of religious cult, ritual and organisation, conceptualised in different theological doctrines. And so long as there is a wide spectrum of human psychological types—and again let us hope that there will always be this—we should expect there to be correspondingly different

emphases between, for example, the sense of the divine as just and as merciful, between *karma* and *bhakti*; or between worship as formal and communal and worship as free and personal. Thus we may expect the different world faiths to continue as religio-cultural phenomena, though phenomena which are increasingly influencing one another's development. The relation between them will then perhaps be somewhat like that now obtaining between the different denominations of Christianity in Europe or the United States. That is to say, there will in most countries be a dominant religious tradition, with other traditions present in varying strengths, but with considerable awareness on all hands of what they have in common; with some degree of osmosis of membership through their institutional walls; with a large degree of practical cooperation; and even conceivably with some interchange of ministry.

Beyond this the ultimate unity of faiths will be an eschatological unity in which each is both fulfilled and transcended—fulfilled in so far as it is true, transcended in so far as it is less than the whole truth. And indeed even such fulfilling must be a transcending; for the function of a religion is to bring us to a right relationship with the ultimate divine reality, to awareness of our true nature and our place in the Whole, into the presence of God. In the eternal life there is no longer any place for religions; the pilgrim has no need of a way after he has finally arrived. In St. John's vision of the heavenly city at the end of our christian scriptures it is said that there is no temple—no christian church or chapel, no jewish synagogue, no hindu or buddhist temple, no muslim mosque, no sikh gurdwara. . . . For all these exist in time, as ways through time to eternity.

IX.2   A Defense of Religious Exclusivism

ALVIN PLANTINGA

Biographical remarks about Alvin Plantinga appear before selection III.7. In this selection, Plantinga argues for three theses: (1) The religious exclusivist is not necessarily guilty of any

This essay appeared in print for the first time in an earlier edition of this text. Reprinted by permission of Alvin Plantinga. Endnotes edited.

moral wrongdoing; (2) the religious exclusivist is not necessarily guilty of any epistemic fault; (3) some exclusivism in our beliefs is inevitable. If a person truly believes his or her creed, it may be wrong to expect him or her to treat all religions as equally good ways to God, or even as ways to God *simpliciter*. Nevertheless, Plantinga agrees that the knowledge of other religions is something to be sought, and that this may lessen our assurance in our own belief.

When I was a graduate student at Yale, the philosophy department prided itself on diversity, and it was indeed diverse. There were idealists, pragmatists, phenomenologists, existentialists, Whiteheadians, historians of philosophy, a token positivist, and what could only be described as observers of the passing intellectual scene. In some ways, this was indeed something to take pride in; a student could behold and encounter real, live representatives of many of the main traditions in philosophy. However, it also had an unintended and unhappy side effect. If anyone raised a philosophical question inside, but particularly outside, of class, the typical response would be to catalog some of the various different answers the world has seen: There is the Aristotelian answer, the existentialist answer, the Cartesian answer, Heidegger's answer, perhaps the Buddhist answer, and so on. But the question "What is the truth about this matter?" was often greeted with disdain as unduly naive. There are all these different answers, all endorsed by people of great intellectual power and great dedication to philosophy; for every argument *for* one of these positions, there is another *against* it; would it not be excessively naive, or perhaps arbitrary, to suppose that one of these is in fact true, the others being false? Or, if even there really is a truth of the matter, so that one of them is true and conflicting ones false, wouldn't it be merely arbitrary, in the face of this embarrassment of riches, to *endorse* one of them as the truth, consigning the others to falsehood? How could you possibly know which was true?

A similar attitude is sometimes urged with respect to the impressive variety of religions the world displays. There are theistic religions but also at least some nontheistic religions (or perhaps nontheistic strands) among the enormous variety of religions going under the names Hinduism and Buddhism; among the theistic religions, there are strands of Hinduism and Buddhism and American Indian religion as well as Islam, Judaism, and Christianity; and all differ significantly from each other. Isn't it somehow arbitrary, or irrational, or unjustified, or unwarranted, or even oppressive and imperialistic to endorse one of these as opposed to all the others? According to Jean Bodin, "each is refuted by all";[1] must we not agree? It is in this neighborhood that the so-called problem of pluralism arises. Of course, many concerns and problems can come under this rubric; the specific problem I mean to discuss can be thought of as follows. To put it in an internal and personal way, I find myself with religious beliefs, and religious beliefs that I realize aren't shared by nearly everyone else. For example, I believe both

(1) The world was created by God, an almighty, all-knowing, and perfectly good personal being (one that holds beliefs; has aims, plans, and intentions; and can act to accomplish these aims).

(2) Human beings require salvation, and God has provided a unique way of salvation through the incarnation, life, sacrificial death, and resurrection of his divine son.

Now there are many who do not believe these things. First, there are those who agree with me on (1) but not (2): They are non-Christian theistic religions. Second, there are those who don't accept either (1) or (2) but nonetheless do believe that there is something beyond the natural world, a something such that human well-being and salvation depend upon standing in a right relation to it. Third, in the West and since the Enlightenment, anyway, there are people—*naturalists,* we may call them—who don't believe any of these three things. And my problem is this: When I become really aware of these other ways of looking at the world, these other ways of responding religiously to the world, what must or should I do? What is the right sort of attitude to take? What sort of impact should this awareness have on the beliefs I hold and the strength with which I hold them? My question is this: How should I think about the great religious diversity the world in fact displays? Can I sensibly remain an adherent of just one of these religions, rejecting the others? And here I am thinking specifically of *beliefs.* Of course, there is a great deal more to any religion or religious practice than just belief, and I don't for a moment mean to deny it. But belief is a crucially important part of most religions; it is a crucially important part of *my* religion; and the question I mean to ask here is, What does the awareness of religious diversity mean or should mean for my religious beliefs?

Some speak here of a *new* awareness of religious diversity and speak of this new awareness as constituting (for us in the West) a crisis, a revolution, an intellectual development of the same magnitude as the Copernican revolution of the sixteenth century and the alleged discovery of evolution and our animal origins in the nineteenth.[2] No doubt there is at least some truth to this. Of course, the fact is all along many Western Christians and Jews have known that there are other religions and that not nearly everyone shares *their* religion. The ancient Israelites—some of the prophets, say—were clearly aware of Canaanite religion; and the apostle Paul said that he preached "Christ crucified, a stumbling block to Jews and folly to the Greeks" (1 Corinthians 1:23). Other early Christians, the Christian martyrs, say, must have suspected that not everyone believed as they did; and the church fathers, in offering defenses of Christianity, were certainly apprised of this fact. Thomas Aquinas, again, was clearly aware of those to whom he addressed the *Summa Contra Gentiles;* and the fact that there are non-Christian religions would have come as no surprise to the Jesuit missionaries of the sixteenth and seventeenth centuries or to the Methodist missionaries of the nineteenth. To come to more recent times, when I was a child, *The Banner,* the official publication of my church, contained a small column for children; it was written by "Uncle Dick" who exhorted us to save our nickels and send them to our Indian cousins at the Navaho mission in New Mexico. Both we and our elders knew that the Navahos had or had had a religion

different from Christianity, and part of the point of sending the nickels was to try to rectify that situation.

Still, in recent years, probably more of us Christian Westerners have become aware of the world's religious diversity; we have probably learned more about people of other religious persuasions, and we have come to see that they display what looks like real piety, devoutness, and spirituality. What is new, perhaps, is a more widespread sympathy for other religions, a tendency to see them as more valuable, as containing more by way of truth, and a new feeling of solidarity with their practitioners.

Now there are several possible reactions to awareness of religious diversity. One is to continue to believe—what you have all along believed; you learn about this diversity but continue to believe that is, take to be true—such propositions as (1) and (2) above, consequently taking to be false any beliefs, religious or otherwise, that are incompatible with (1) and (2). Following current practice, I will call this *exclusivism;* the exclusivist holds that the tenets or some of the tenets of *one* religion—Christianity, let's say—are in fact true; he adds, naturally enough, that any propositions, including other religious beliefs, that are incompatible with those tenets are false. And there is a fairly widespread apprehension that there is something seriously wrong with exclusivism. It is irrational, or egotistical and unjustified,[3] or intellectually arrogant,[4] or elitist,[5] or a manifestation of harmful pride,[6] or even oppressive and imperialistic.[7] The claim is that exclusivism as such is or involves a vice of some sort: It is wrong or deplorable. It is this claim I want to examine. I propose to argue that exclusivism need not involve either epistemic or moral failure and that, furthermore, something like it is wholly unavoidable, given our human condition.

These objections, of course, are not to the *truth* of (1) or (2) or any other proposition someone might accept in this exclusivist way (although objections of that sort are also put forward); they are instead directed to the *propriety or rightness* of exclusivism. There are initially two different kinds of indictments of exclusivism: broadly moral, or ethical, indictments and other broadly intellectual, or epistemic, indictments. These overlap in interesting ways as we will see below. But initially, anyway, we can take some of the complaints about exclusivism as *intellectual* criticisms: It is *irrational* or *unjustified* to think in an exclusivistic way. The other large body of complaint is moral: There is something *morally* suspect about exclusivism—it is arbitrary, or intellectually arrogant, or imperialistic. As Joseph Runzo suggests, exclusivism is "neither tolerable nor any longer intellectually honest in the context of our contemporary knowledge of other faiths."[8] I want to consider both kinds of claims or criticisms; I propose to argue that the exclusivist as such is not necessarily guilty of any of these charges.

MORAL OBJECTIONS TO EXCLUSIVISM

I turn to the moral complaints: that the exclusivist is intellectually arrogant, or egotistical or self-servingly arbitrary, or dishonest, or imperialistic, or oppressive. But first, I provide three qualifications. An exclusivist, like anyone else, will probably be guilty of some or of all of these things to at least some degree, perhaps particularly the first two. The question, however, is whether she is guilty of these things just by virtue of being an exclusivist. Second, I will use the term *exclusivism* in such a way that you don't count as an exclusivist unless you are rather fully aware of other faiths, have had their existence and their claims called to your attention with some force and perhaps fairly frequently, and have to some degree reflected on the problem of pluralism, asking yourself such questions as whether it is or could be really true that the Lord has revealed Himself and His programs to us Christians, say, in a way in which He hasn't revealed Himself to those of other faiths. Thus, my grandmother, for example, would not have counted as an exclusivist. She had, of course, *heard* of the heathen, as she called them, but the idea that perhaps Christians could learn from them, and learn from them with respect to religious matters, had not so much as entered her head; and the fact that it *hadn't* entered her head, I take it, was not a matter of moral dereliction on her part. This same would go for a Buddhist or Hindu peasant. These people are not, I think, properly charged with arrogance or other moral flaws in believing as they do.

Third, suppose I am an exclusivist with respect to (1), for example, but nonculpably believe, like Aquinas, say, that I have a knock-down, drag-out argument, a demonstration or conclusive proof of the proposition that there is such a person as God; and suppose I think further (and nonculpably) that if those who don't believe (1) were to be apprised of this argument (and had the ability and training necessary to grasp it and were to think about the argument fairly and reflectively), *they* too would come to believe (1)? Then I could hardly be charged with these moral faults. My condition would be like that of Gödel, let's say, upon having recognized that he had a proof for the incompleteness of arithmetic. True, many of his colleagues and peers didn't believe that arithmetic was incomplete, and some believed that it was complete; but presumably Gödel wasn't arbitrary or egotistical in believing that arithmetic is in fact incomplete. Furthermore, he would not have been at fault had he nonculpably but *mistakenly* believed that he had found such a proof. Accordingly, I will use the term *exclusivist* in such a way that you don't count as an exclusivist if you nonculpably think you know of a demonstration or conclusive argument for the beliefs with respect to which you are an exclusivist, or even if you nonculpably think you know of an argument that would convince all or most intelligent and honest people of the truth of that proposition. So an exclusivist, as I use the term, not only believes something like (1) or (2) and thinks false any proposition incompatible with it; she also meets a further condition C that is hard to state precisely and in detail (and in fact any attempt to do so would involve a long and presently irrelevant discussion of *ceteris paribus* clauses). Suffice it to say that C includes (a) being rather fully aware of other religions, (b) knowing that there is much that at the least looks like genuine piety and devoutness in them, and (c) believing that you know of no arguments that would necessarily convince all or most honest and intelligent dissenters.

Given these qualifications then, why should we think that an exclusivist is properly charged with these moral faults? I will deal first and most briefly with charges of oppression and imperialism: I think we must say that they are on the face of it wholly implausible. I daresay there are some among you who reject some of the things I believe; I do not believe that you are thereby oppressing me, even if you do not believe you have an argument that would convince me. It is conceivable that exclusivism might in some way *contribute* to oppression, but it isn't in itself oppressive.

The more important moral charge is that there is a sort of self-serving arbitrariness, an arrogance or egotism, in accepting such propositions as (1) or (2) under condition *C;* exclusivism is guilty of some serious moral fault or flaw. According to Wilfred Cantwell Smith, "... except at the cost of insensitivity or delinquency, it is morally not possible actually to go out into the world and say to devout, intelligent, fellow human beings: '...we believe that we know God and we are right; you believe that you know God, and you are totally wrong.'"[9]

So what can the exclusivist have to say for himself? Well, it must be conceded immediately that if he believes (1) or (2), then he must also believe that those who believe something incompatible with them are mistaken and believe what is false. That's no more than simple logic. Furthermore, he must also believe that those who do not believe as he does—those who believe neither (1) nor (2), whether or not they believe their negations—*fail* to believe something that is deep and important and that he *does* believe. He must therefore see himself as *privileged* with respect to those others—those others of both kinds. There is something of great value, he must think, that *he* has and *they* lack. They are ignorant of something—something of great importance—of which he has knowledge. But does this make him properly subject to the above censure?

I think the answer must be no. Or if the answer is yes, then I think we have here a genuine moral dilemma; for in our earthly life here below, as my Sunday School teacher used to say, there is no real alternative; there is no reflective attitude that is not open to the same strictures. These charges of arrogance are a philosophical tar baby: Get close enough to them to use them against the exclusivist and you are likely to find them stuck fast to yourself. How so? Well, as an exclusivist, I realize that I can't convince others that they should believe as I do, but I nonetheless continue to believe as I do. The charge is that I am, as a result, arrogant or egotistical, arbitrarily preferring my way of doing things to other ways.[10] But what are my alternatives with respect to a proposition like (1)? There seem to be three choices. I can continue to hold it; I can withhold it, in Roderick Chisholm's sense, believing neither it nor its denial, and I can accept its denial. Consider the third way, a way taken by those pluralists who, like John Hick, hold that such propositions as (1) and (2) and their colleagues from other faiths are literally false, although in some way still valid responses to the Real. This seems to me to be no advance at all with respect to the arrogance or egotism problem; this is not a way out. For if I do this, I will then be in the very same condition as I am now: I will believe many propositions others don't believe and will be in condition *C* with respect to those propositions. For I will then believe the denials of (1) and (2) (as well as the denials of many other propositions explicitly accepted by those of other faiths). Many others, of course, do not believe the denials of (1) and (2) and in fact believe (1) and (2). Further, I will not know of any arguments that can be counted on to persuade those who do believe (1) or (2) (or propositions accepted by the adherents of other religions). I am therefore in the condition of believing propositions that many others do not believe and furthermore am in condition *C*. If, in the case of those who believe (1) and (2), that is sufficient for intellectual arrogance or egotism, the same goes for those who believe their denials.

So consider the second option: I can instead *withhold* the proposition in question. I can say to myself: "The right course here, given that I can't or couldn't convince these others of what I believe, is to believe neither these propositions nor their denials." The pluralist objector to exclusivism can say that the right course, under condition *C,* is to abstain from believing the offending proposition and also abstain from believing its denial; call him, therefore, "the abstemious pluralist." But does he thus really avoid the condition that, on the part of the exclusivist, leads to the charges of egotism and arrogance in this way?

Think, for a moment, about disagreement. Disagreement, fundamentally, is a matter of adopting conflicting propositional attitudes with respect to a given proposition. In the simplest and most familiar case, I disagree with you if there is some proposition p such that I believe p and you believe $-p$. But that's just the simplest case; there are also others. The one that is presently of interest is this: I believe p and you withhold it, fail to believe it. Call the first kind of disagreement "contradicting"; call the second "dissenting."

My claim is that if contradicting others (under the condition C spelled out above) is arrogant and egotistical, so is dissenting (under that same condition). Suppose you believe some proposition p but I don't; perhaps you believe that it is wrong to discriminate against people simply on the grounds of race, but I, recognizing that there are many people who disagree with you, do not believe this proposition. I don't disbelieve it either, of course, but in the circumstances I think the right thing to do is to abstain from belief. Then am I not implicitly condemning your attitude, your *believing* the proposition, as somehow improper—naive, perhaps, or unjustified, or in some other way less than optimal? I am implicitly saying that my attitude is the superior one; I think my course of action here is the right one and yours somehow wrong, inadequate, improper, in the circumstances at best second-rate. Of course, I realize that there is no question, here, of *showing* you that your attitude is wrong or improper or naive; so am I not guilty of intellectual arrogance? Of a sort of egotism, thinking I know better than you, arrogating to myself a privileged status with respect to you? The problem for the exclusivist was that she was obliged to think she possessed a truth missed by many others; the problem for the abstemious pluralist is that he is obliged to think that he possesses a virtue others don't or acts rightly where others don't. If, in condition C, one is arrogant by way of believing a proposition others don't, isn't one equally, under those reflective conditions, arrogant by way of withholding a proposition others don't?

Perhaps you will respond by saying that the abstemious pluralist gets into trouble, falls into arrogance, by way of implicitly saying or believing that his way of proceeding is better or wiser than other ways pursued by other people; and perhaps he can escape by abstaining from *that* view as well. Can't he escape the problem by refraining from believing that racial bigotry is wrong and also refraining from holding the view that it is *better*, under the conditions that obtain, to withhold that proposition than to assert and believe it? Well, yes he can; then he has no *reason* for his abstention; he doesn't believe that abstention is better or more appropriate; he simply does abstain. Does this get him off the egotistical hook? Perhaps. But then he can't, in consistency, also hold that there is something wrong with *not* abstaining, with coming right out and *believing* that bigotry is wrong; he loses his objection to the exclusivist. Accordingly, this way out is not available for the abstemious pluralist who accuses the exclusivist of arrogance and egotism.

Indeed, I think we can show that the abstemious pluralist who brings charges of intellectual arrogance against exclusivism is hoist with his own petard, holds a position that in a certain way is self-referentially inconsistent in the circumstances. For he believes

(3) If S knows that others don't believe p and that he is in condition C with respect to p, then S should not believe p.

This or something like it is the ground of the charges he brings against the exclusivist. But the abstemious pluralist realizes that many do not accept (3); and I suppose he also realizes that it is unlikely that he can find arguments for (3) that will convince them; hence, he knows that condition obtains. Given his acceptance of (3), therefore, the right course for him is to abstain from believing (3). Under the conditions that do in fact obtain—namely, his knowledge that others don't accept it and that condition C obtains—he can't properly accept it.

I am therefore inclined to think that one can't, in the circumstances, properly hold (3) or any other proposition that will do the job. One can't find here some principle on the basis of which to hold that the exclusivist is doing the wrong thing, suffers from some moral fault—that is, one can't find such a principle that doesn't, as we might put it, fall victim to itself.

So the abstemious pluralist is hoist with his own petard; but even apart from this dialectical argument (which in any event some will think unduly cute), aren't the charges unconvincing and implausible? I must concede that there are a variety of ways in which I can be and have been intellectually arrogant and egotistic; I have certainly fallen into this vice in the past and no doubt am not free of it now. But am I really arrogant and egotistic just by virtue of believing what I know others don't believe, where I can't show them that I am right? Suppose I think the matter over, consider the objections as carefully as I can, realize that I am finite and furthermore a sinner, certainly no better than those with whom I disagree; but suppose it still seems clear to me that the proposition in question is true. Can I really be behaving immorally in continuing to believe it? I am dead sure that it is wrong to try to advance my career by telling lies about my colleagues; I realize there are those who disagree; I also realize that in all likelihood there is no way I can find to show them that they are wrong; nonetheless I think they are wrong. If I think this after careful reflection, if I consider the claims of those who disagree as sympathetically as I can, if I try my level best to ascertain the truth here, and it *still* seems to me sleazy, wrong, and despicable to lie about my colleagues to advance my career, could I really be doing what is immoral by continuing to believe as before? I can't see how. If, after careful reflection and thought, you find yourself convinced that the right propositional attitude to take to (1) and (2) in the face of the facts of religious pluralism is abstention from belief, how could you properly be taxed with egotism, either for so believing or for so abstaining? Even if you knew others did not agree with you?

EPISTEMIC OBJECTIONS TO EXCLUSIVISM

I turn now to *epistemic* objections to exclusivism. There are many different specifically epistemic virtues and a corresponding plethora of epistemic vices. The ones with which the exclusivist is most frequently charged, however, are *irrationality* and *lack of justification* in holding his exclusivist beliefs. The claim is that as an exclusivist he holds unjustified beliefs and/or irrational beliefs. Better, *he* is unjustified or irrational in holding these beliefs. I will therefore consider those two claims, and I will argue that the exclusivist views need not be either unjustified or irrational. I will then turn to the question whether his beliefs could have *warrant*—that property, whatever precisely it is, that distinguishes knowledge from mere true belief—and whether they could have enough warrant for knowledge.

JUSTIFICATION

The pluralist objector sometimes claims that to hold exclusivist views, in condition *C,* is *unjustified*—*epistemically* unjustified. Is this true? And what does he mean when he makes this claim? As even a brief glance at the contemporary epistemological literature will show, justification is a protean and multifarious notion. There are, I think, substantially two possibilities as to what he means. The central core of the notion, its beating heart, the paradigmatic center to which most of the myriad contemporary variations are related by way of analogical extension and family resemblance, is the notion of *being within one's intellectual rights,* having violated no intellectual or cognitive duties or obligations in the formation and sustenance of the belief in question. This is the palimpsest, going back to Rene Descartes and especially John Locke, that underlies the multitudinous battery of contemporary inscriptions. There is no space to argue that point here; but chances are, when the pluralist objector to exclusivism claims that the latter is unjustified, it is some notion lying in this neighborhood that he has in mind. (Here we should note the very close connection between the moral objections to exclusivism and the objection that exclusivism is epistemically unjustified.)

The duties involved, naturally enough, would be specifically *epistemic* duties: perhaps a duty to proportion degree of belief to (propositional) evidence from what is *certain,* that is, self-evident or incorrigible, as with Locke, or perhaps to try one's best to get into and stay in the right relation to the truth, as with Chisholm, the leading contemporary champion of the justificationist tradition with respect to knowledge. But at present there is widespread (and as I see it, correct) agreement that there is no duty of the Lockean kind. Perhaps there is one of the Chisholmian kind; but isn't the exclusivist conforming to that duty if, after the sort of careful, indeed prayerful consideration I mentioned in the response to the moral objection, it still seems to him strongly that (1), say, is true and he accordingly still believes it? It is therefore very hard to see that the exclusivist is necessarily unjustified in this way.

The second possibility for understanding the charge—the charge that exclusivism is epistemically unjustified—has to do with the oft-repeated claim that exclusivism is intellectually *arbitrary*. Perhaps the idea is that there is an intellectual duty to treat similar cases similarly; the exclusivist violates this duty by arbitrarily choosing to believe (for the moment going along with the fiction that we *choose* beliefs of this sort) (1) and (2) in the face of the plurality of conflicting religious beliefs the world presents. But suppose there is such a duty. Clearly you do not violate it if you nonculpably think the beliefs in question are not on a par. And as an exclusivist, I *do* think (nonculpably, I hope) that they are not on a par: I think (1) and (2) *true* and those incompatible with either of them *false*.

The rejoinder, of course, will be that it is not alethic parity (their having the same truth value) that is at issue: it is *epistemic* parity that counts. What kind of epistemic parity? What would be relevant, here, I should think, would be *internal* or internalist epistemic parity: parity with respect to what is internally available to the believer. What is internally available to the believer includes, for example, detectable relationships between the belief in question and other beliefs you hold; so internal parity would include parity of propositional evidence. What is internally available to the believer also includes the *phenomenology* that goes with the beliefs in question: the *sensuous* phenomenology but also the nonsensuous phenomenology involved, for example, in the belief's just having the feel of being *right*. But once more, then, (1) and (2) are not on an internal par, for the exclusivist, with beliefs that are incompatible with them. (1) and (2), after

all, seem to me to be true; they have for me the phenomenology that accompanies that seeming. The same cannot be said for propositions incompatible with them. If, furthermore, John Calvin is right in thinking that there is such a thing as the *Sensus Divinitatis* and the Internal Testimony of the Holy Spirit, then perhaps (1) and (2) are produced in me by those belief-producing processes and have for me the phenomenology that goes with them; the same is not true for propositions incompatible with them.

But then the next rejoinder: Isn't it probably true that those who reject (1) and (2) in favor of other beliefs have propositional evidence for their beliefs that is on a par with mine for my beliefs? And isn't it also probably true that the same or similar phenomenology accompanies their beliefs as accompanies mine? So that those beliefs really are epistemically and internally on a par with (1) and (2), and the exclusivist is still treating like cases differently? I don't think so; I think there really are arguments available for (1), at least, that are not available for its competitors. And as for similar phenomenology, this is not easy to say; it is not easy to look into the breast of another; the secrets of the human heart are hard to fathom; it is hard indeed to discover this sort of thing even with respect to someone you know really well. I am prepared, however, to stipulate both sorts of parity. Let's agree for purposes of argument that these beliefs are on an epistemic par in the sense that those of a different religious tradition have the same sort of internally available markers—evidence, phenomenology and the like—for their beliefs as I have for (1) and (2). What follows?

Return to the case of moral belief. King David took Bathsheba, made her pregnant, and then, after the failure of various stratagems to get her husband Uriah to think the baby was his, arranged for him to be killed. The prophet Nathan came to David and told him a story about a rich man and a poor man. The rich man had many flocks and herds; the poor man had only a single ewe lamb, which grew up with his children, "ate at his table, drank from his cup, lay in his bosom, and was like a daughter to him." The rich man had unexpected guests. Rather than slaughter one of his own sheep, he took the poor man's single ewe lamb, slaughtered it, and served it to his guests. David exploded in anger: "The man who did this deserves to die!" Then, in one of the most riveting passages in all the Bible, Nathan turns to David and declares, "You are that man!" And then David sees what he has done.

My interest here is in David's reaction to the story. I agree with David: Such injustice is utterly and despicably wrong; there are really no words for it. I believe that such an action is wrong, and I believe that the proposition that it *isn't* wrong—either because really *nothing* is wrong, or because even if some things are wrong, *this* isn't—is false. As a matter of fact, there isn't a lot I believe more strongly. I recognize, however, that there are those who disagree with me; and once more, I doubt that I could find an argument to show them that I am right and they wrong. Further, for all I know, their conflicting beliefs have for them the same internally available epistemic markers, the same phenomenology, as mine have for me. Am I then being arbitrary, treating similar cases differently in continuing to hold, as I do, that in fact that kind of behavior *is* dreadfully wrong? I don't think so. Am I wrong in thinking racial bigotry despicable, even though I know that there are others who disagree, and even if I think they have the same internal markers for their beliefs as I have for mine? I don't think so. I believe in serious actualism, the view that no objects have properties in worlds in which they do not exist, not even nonexistence. Others do not believe this, and perhaps the internal markers of their dissenting views have for them the same quality as my views have for me. Am I being arbitrary in continuing to think as I do? I can't see how.

And the reason here is this: in each of these cases, the believer in question doesn't really think the beliefs in question *are* on a relevant epistemic par. She may agree that she and those who dissent are equally convinced of the truth of their belief and even that they are internally on a par, that the internally available markers are similar, or relevantly similar. But she must still think that there is an important epistemic difference, she thinks that somehow the other person has *made a mistake,* or *has a blind spot,* or hasn't been wholly attentive, or hasn't received some grace she has, or is in some way epistemically

less fortunate. And, of course, the pluralist critic is in no better case. He thinks the thing to do when there is internal epistemic parity is to withhold judgment; he knows that there are others who don't think so, and for all he knows that belief has internal parity with his; if he continues in that belief, therefore, he will be in the same condition as the exclusivist; and if he doesn't continue in this belief, he no longer has an objection to the exclusivist.

But couldn't I be wrong? Of course I could! But I don't avoid that risk by withholding all religious (or philosophical or moral) beliefs; I can go wrong that way as well as any other, treating all religions, or all philosophical thoughts, or all moral views as on a par. Again, there is no safe haven here, no way to avoid risk. In particular, you won't reach a safe haven by trying to take the same attitude toward all the historically available patterns of belief and withholding; for in so doing, you adopt a particular pattern of belief and withholding, one incompatible with some adopted by others. "You pays your money and you takes your choice," realizing that you, like anyone else, can be desperately wrong. But what else can you do? You don't really have an alternative. And how can you do better than believe and withhold according to what, after serious and responsible consideration, seems to you to be the right pattern of belief and withholding?

Irrationality

I therefore can't see how it can be sensibly maintained that the exclusivist is unjustified in his exclusivist views; but perhaps, as is sometimes claimed, he or his view is *irrational.* Irrationality, however, is many things to many people; so there is a prior question: What is it to be irrational? More exactly, precisely what quality is it that the objector is attributing to the exclusivist (in condition C) when the former says the latter's exclusivist beliefs are irrational? Since the charge is never developed at all fully, it isn't easy to say. So suppose we simply consider the main varieties of irrationality (or, if you prefer, the main senses of "irrational") and ask whether any of them attach to the exclusivist just by virtue of being an exclusivist. I believe there are substantially five varieties of rationality, five distinct but analogically connected senses of the term *rational;* fortunately not all of them require detailed consideration.

Aristotelian Rationality

This is the sense in which man is a rational animal, one that has *ratio,* one that can look before and after, can hold beliefs, make inferences and is capable of knowledge. This is perhaps the basic sense, the one of which the others are analogical extensions. It is also, presumably irrelevant in the present context; at any rate I hope the objector does not mean to hold that an exclusivist will by that token no longer be a rational animal.

The Deliverances of Reason

To be rational in the Aristotelian sense is to possess reason: the power or thinking, believing, inferring, reasoning, knowing. Aristotelian rationality is thus *generic.* But there is an important more specific sense lurking in the neighborhood; this is the sense that goes with reason taken more narrowly, as the source of a priori knowledge and belief. An important use of *rational* analogically connected with the first has to do with reason taken in this more narrow way. It is by reason thus construed that we know *self-evident* beliefs—beliefs so obvious that you can't so much as grasp them without seeing that they couldn't be false. These will be among the *deliverances of reason.* Of course there are other beliefs—$38 \times 39 = 1482$, for example—that are not self-evident but are a consequence of self-evident beliefs by way of arguments that are self-evidently valid; these too are among the deliverances of reason. So say that the deliverances of reason is the set of those propositions that are self-evident for us human beings, closed under self-evident consequence. This yields another sense of rationality: a belief is *rational* if it is among the deliverances of reason and *irrational* if it is contrary to the deliverances of reason. (A belief can therefore be neither rational nor irrational, in this sense.) This sense of *rational* is an analogical extension of the fundamental sense, but it is itself extended by analogy to still other senses. Thus, we can broaden the category of reason to include memory, experience, induction,

probability, and whatever else goes into science; this is the sense of the term when reason is sometimes contrasted with faith. And we can also soften the requirement for self-evidence, recognizing both that self-evidence or a priori warrant is a matter of degree and that there are many propositions that have a priori warrant, but are not such that no one who understands them can fail to believe them.[11]

Is the exclusivist irrational in *these* senses? I think not; at any rate, the question whether he is isn't the question at issue. His exclusivist beliefs are irrational in these senses only if there is a good argument from the deliverances of reason (taken broadly) to the denials of what he believes. I do not believe that there are any such arguments. Presumably, the same goes for the pluralist objector: at any rate, his objection is not that (1) and (2) are demonstrably false or even that there are good arguments against them from the deliverances of reason; his objection is instead that there is something wrong or subpar with believing them in condition C. This sense too, then, is irrelevant to our present concerns.

The Deontological Sense

This sense of the term has to do with intellectual *requirement,* or *duty,* or *obligation;* a person's belief is irrational in this sense if in forming or holding it she violates such a duty. This is the sense of *irrational* in which according to many contemporary evidentialist objectors to theistic belief, those who believe in God without propositional evidence are irrational. Irrationality in this sense is a matter of failing to conform to intellectual or epistemic duties; the analogical connection with the first, Aristotelian sense is that these duties are thought to be among the deliverances of reason (and hence among the deliverances of the power by virtue of which human beings are rational in the Aristotelian sense). But we have already considered whether the exclusivist is flouting duties; we need say no more about the matter here. As we say, the exclusivist is not necessarily irrational in this sense either.

Zweckrationalität

A common and very important notion of rationality is *means-end rationality*—what our continental cousins, following Max Weber, sometimes call *Zweckrationalität,* the sort of rationality displayed by your actions if they are well calculated to achieve your goals. (Again, the analogical connection with the first sense is clear: The calculation in question requires the power by virtue of which we are rational in Aristotle's sense.) Clearly, there is a whole constellation of notions lurking in the nearby bushes: What would *in fact* contribute to your goals? What you *take* it would contribute to your goals? What you *would* take it would contribute to your goals if you were sufficiently acute, or knew enough, or weren't distracted by lust, greed, pride, ambition, and the like? What you would take it would contribute to your goals if you weren't thus distracted and were also to reflect sufficiently? and so on. This notion of rationality has assumed enormous importance in the last 150 years or so. (Among its laurels, for example, is the complete domination of the development of the discipline of economics.) Rationality thus construed is a matter of knowing how to get what you want; it is the cunning of reason. Is the exclusivist properly charged with irrationality in this sense? Does his believing in the way he does interfere with his attaining some of his goals, or is it a markedly inferior way of attaining those goals?

An initial *caveat*: It isn't clear that this notion of rationality applies to belief at all. It isn't clear that in *believing* something, I am acting to achieve some goal. If believing is an action at all, it is very far from being the paradigmatic kind of action taken to achieve some end; we don't have a choice as to whether to have beliefs, and we don't have a lot of choice with respect to which beliefs we have. But suppose we set this *caveat* aside and stipulate for purposes of argument that we have sufficient control over our beliefs for them to qualify as actions. Would the exclusivist's beliefs then be irrational in this sense? Well, that depends upon what his goals are; if among his goals for religious belief is, for example, not believing anything not believed by someone else, then indeed it would be. But, of course, he needn't have that goal. If I do have an end or goal in holding such beliefs as (1) and (2), it would presumably be that of believing the truth on this exceedingly important matter or perhaps that of trying to get in touch as adequately as possible with God, or more broadly with the deepest reality. And if (1) and (2) are *true,* believing them will be a way of doing exactly that. It is only if they are *not* true, then, that believing them could sensibly be thought to be irrational in this means-ends sense. Because the objector does not propose to take as a premise the proposition that (1) and (2) are false—he holds only that there is some flaw involved in *believing* them—this also is presumably not what he means.

Rationality as Sanity and Proper Function

One in the grip of pathological confusion, or flight of ideas, or certain kinds of agnosia, or the manic phase of manic-depressive psychosis will often be said to be irrational; the episode may pass, after which he has regained rationality. Here *rationality* means absence of dysfunction, disorder, impairment, or pathology with respect to rational faculties. So this variety of rationality is again analogically related to Aristotelian rationality; a person is rational in this sense when no malfunction obstructs her use of the faculties by virtue of the possession of which she is rational in the Aristotelian sense. Rationality as sanity does not require possession of particularly exalted rational faculties; it requires only normality (in the nonstatistical sense) or health, or proper function. This use of the term, naturally enough, is prominent in psychiatric discussions—Oliver Sacks's male patient who mistook his wife for a hat, for example, was thus irrational. This fifth and final sense of rationality is itself a family of analogically related senses. The fundamental sense here is that of sanity and proper function, but there are other closely related senses. Thus, we may say that a belief (in certain circumstances) is irrational, not because no sane person would hold it, but because no person who was sane and had also undergone a certain course of education would hold it or because no person who was sane and furthermore was as intelligent as we and our friends would hold it; alternatively and more briefly, the idea is not merely that no one who was functioning properly in those circumstances would hold it, but rather no one who was functioning *optimally,* as well or nearly as well as human beings ordinarily do (leaving aside the occasional great genius) would hold it. And this sense of rationality leads directly to the notion of *warrant;* I turn now to that notion; in treating it, we will also treat *ambulando*—this fifth kind of irrationality.

Warrant

So we come to the third version of the epistemic objection: that at any rate the exclusivist doesn't have warrant, or anyway *much* warrant (enough warrant for knowledge) for his exclusivistic views. Many pluralists—for example, Hick, Runzo, and Cantwell Smith—unite in declaring that, at any rate, the exclusivist certainly can't *know* that his exclusivistic views are true. But is this really true? I will argue briefly that it is not. At any rate, from the perspective of each of the major contemporary accounts of knowledge, it may very well be that the exclusivist knows (1) or (2) or both. First, consider the two main internalistic accounts of knowledge: the justified true belief accounts and the coherentist accounts. As I have already argued, it seems clear that a theist, a believer in (1) could certainly be *justified* (in the primary sense) in believing as she does: she could be flouting no intellectual or cognitive duties or obligations. But then on the most straightforward justified true belief account of knowledge, she can also *know* that it is true—if, that is, it *can* be true. More exactly, what must be possible is that both the exclusivist is justified in believing (1) and/or (2) and they be true. Presumably, the pluralist does not mean to dispute this possibility.

For concreteness, consider the account of justification given by the classical foundationalist Chisholm. On this view, a belief has warrant for me to the extent that accepting it is apt for the fulfillment of my epistemic duty, which (roughly speaking) is that of trying to get and remain in the right relation to the truth. But if after the most careful, thorough, open, and prayerful consideration, it still seems to me—perhaps more strongly than ever—that (1) and (2) are true, then clearly accepting them has great aptness for the fulfillment of that duty.

A similarly brief argument can be given with respect to *coherentism,* the view that what constitutes warrant is coherence with some body of belief. We must distinguish two varieties of coherentism. On the one hand, it might be held that what is required is coherence with some or all of the other beliefs I actually hold; on the other, that what is required is coherence with my *verific* noetic structure (Keith Lehrer's term): the set of beliefs that remains when all the false ones are deleted or replaced by their contradictories. But surely a coherent set of beliefs could include both (1) and (2) together with the beliefs involved in being in condition C, what would be required, perhaps, would be that the set of beliefs contain some explanation of why it is that others do not believe as I do. And if (1) and (2) are true, then surely (and a fortiori) there can be coherent verific noetic structures that include them. Hence, neither of these versions of coherentism rule out the possibility that the exclusivist in condition C could know (1) and/or (2).

And now consider the main externalist accounts. The most popular externalist account at present would be one or another version of *reliabilism.* And there is an oft-repeated pluralistic argument that seems to be designed to appeal to reliabilist intuitions. The conclusion of this argument is not always clear, but here is its premise, in Hick's words:

> For it is evident that in some ninety-nine percent of cases the religion which an individual professes and to which he or she adheres depends upon the accidents of birth. Someone born to Buddhist parents in Thailand is very likely to be a Buddhist, someone born to Muslim parents in Saudi Arabia to be a Muslim, someone born to Christian parents in Mexico to be a Christian, and so on.

As a matter of sociological fact, this may be right. Furthermore, it can certainly produce a sense of intellectual vertigo. But what is one to do with this fact, if fact it is, and what follows from it? Does it follow, for example, that I ought not to accept the religious views that I have been brought up to accept, or the ones that I find myself inclined to accept, or the ones that seem to me to be true? Or that the belief producing processes that have produced those beliefs in me are unreliable? Surely not. Furthermore, self-referential problems once more loom; this argument is another philosophical tar baby.

For suppose we concede that if I had been born of Muslim parents in Morocco rather than Christian parents in Michigan, my beliefs would have been quite different. (For one thing, I probably wouldn't believe that I was born in Michigan.) The same goes for the pluralist. Pluralism isn't and hasn't been widely popular in the world at large; if the pluralist had been born in Madagascar, or medieval France, he probably wouldn't have been a pluralist. Does it follow that he shouldn't be a pluralist or that his pluralist beliefs are produced in him by an unreliable belief producing process? I doubt it. Suppose I hold the following, or something similar:

(4) If S's religious or philosophical beliefs are such that if S had been born elsewhere and else when, she wouldn't have held them, then those beliefs are produced by unreliable belief producing mechanisms and hence have no warrant.

Once more I will be hoist with my own petard. For in all probability, someone born in Mexico to Christian parents wouldn't believe (4) itself. No matter what philosophical and religious beliefs we hold and withhold (so it seems), there are places and times such that if we have been born there and then, then we would not have displayed the pattern of holding and withholding of religious and philosophical beliefs we *do* display. As I said, this can indeed be vertiginous; but what can we make of it? What can we infer from it about what has warrant and how we should conduct our intellectual lives? That's not easy to say. Can we infer *anything at all* about what has warrant or how we should conduct our intellectual lives? Not obviously.

To return to reliabilism then: For simplicity, let's take the version of reliabilism according to which S knows p if the belief that p is produced in S by a reliable belief producing mechanism or process. I don't have the space here to go into this matter in sufficient detail, but it seems pretty clear that if (1) and (2) are true, then it *could* be that the beliefs that (1) and (2) be produced in me by a reliable belief-producing process. For either we are thinking of *concrete* belief producing processes, like your memory or John's powers of a priori reasoning (tokens as opposed to types),

or else we are thinking of types of belief producing processes (type reliabilism). The problem with the latter is that there are an enormous number of *different* types of belief producing processes for any given belief, some of which are reliable and some of which are not; the problem (and a horrifying problem it is) is to say which of these is the type the reliability of which determines whether the belief in question has warrant. So the first (token reliabilism) is a better way of stating reliabilism. But then clearly enough if (1) or (2) are true, they could be produced in me by a reliable belief-producing process. Calvin's *Sensus Divinitatis*, for example, could be working in the exclusivist in such a way as to reliably produce the belief that (1) is true; Calvin's Internal Testimony of the Holy Spirit could do the same for (2). If (1) and (2) are true, therefore, then from a reliabilist perspective there is no reason whatever to think that the exclusivist might not know that they are true.

There is another brand of externalism which seems to me to be closer to the truth than reliabilism call it (*faute de mieux*) "proper functionalism." This view can be stated to a first approximation as follows: S knows p if (1) the belief that p is produced in S by cognitive faculties that are functioning properly (working as they ought to work, suffering from no dysfunction), (2) the cognitive environment in which p is produced is appropriate for those faculties, (3) the purpose of the module of the epistemic faculties producing the belief in question is to produce true beliefs (alternatively, the module of the design plan governing the production of p is aimed at the production of true beliefs), and (4) the objective probability of a belief's being true, given that it is produced under those conditions, is high. All of this needs explanation, of course; for present purposes, perhaps, we can collapse the account into the first condition. But then clearly it could be, if (1) and (2) are true, that they are produced in me by cognitive faculties functioning properly under condition C. For suppose (1) is true. Then it is surely possible that God has created us human beings with something like Calvin's *Sensus Divinitatis*, a belief producing process that in a wide variety of circumstances functions properly to produce

(1) or some very similar belief. Furthermore it is also possible that in response to the human condition of sin and misery, God has provided for us human beings a means of salvation, which he has revealed in the Bible. Still further, perhaps he has arranged for us to come to believe what he means to teach there by way of the operation of something like the Internal Testimony of the Holy Spirit of which Calvin speaks. So on this view, too, if (1) and (2) are true, it is certainly possible that the exclusivist know that they are. We can be sure that the exclusivist's views are irrational in this sense, then, only if they are false; but the pluralist objector does not mean to claim that they are false; this version of the objection, therefore, also fails. The exclusivist isn't necessarily irrational, and indeed might *know* that (1) and (2) are true, if indeed they *are* true.

All this seems right. But don't the realities of religious pluralism count for anything at all? Is there nothing at all to the claims of the pluralists? Could that really be right? Of course not. For many or most exclusivists, I think, an awareness of the enormous variety of human religious response functions as a *defeater* for such beliefs as (1) and (2)—an *undercutting defeater,* as opposed to a rebutting defeater. It calls into question, to some degree or other, the sources of one's belief in (1) or (2). It doesn't or needn't do so by way of an *argument;* and indeed there isn't a very powerful argument from the proposition that many apparently devout people around the world dissent from (1) and (2) to the conclusion that (1) and (2) are false. Instead, it works more directly; it directly reduces the level of confidence or degree of belief in the proposition in question. From a Christian perspective, this situation of religious pluralism and our awareness of it is itself a manifestation of our miserable human condition; and it may deprive us of some of the comfort and peace the Lord has promised his followers. It can also deprive the exclusivist of the *knowledge* that (1) and (2) *are* true, if even they are true and he *believes* that they are. Because degree of warrant depends in part on degree of belief, it is possible, though not necessary, that knowledge of the facts of religious pluralism should reduce an exclusivist's degree of belief and hence of warrant for (1) and (2) in such a

way as to deprive him of knowledge of (1) and (2). He might be such that if he *hadn't* known the facts of pluralism, then he would have known (1) and (2), but now that he *does* know those facts, he doesn't know (1) and (2). In this way, he may come to know less by knowing more.

Things *could* go this way with the exclusivist. On the other hand, they *needn't* go this way. Consider once more the moral parallel. Perhaps you have always believed it deeply wrong for a counselor to use his position of trust to seduce a client. Perhaps you discover that others disagree; they think it more like a minor peccadillo, like running a red light when there's no traffic; and you realize that possibly these people have the same internal markers for their beliefs that you have for yours. You think the matter over more fully, imaginatively recreate and rehearse such situations, become more aware of just what is involved in such a situation (the breach of trust, the breaking of implied promises, the injustice and unfairness, the nasty irony of a situation in which someone comes to a counselor seeking help but receives only hurt), and come to believe even more fully that such an action is wrong—and indeed to have more warrant for that belief. But something similar can happen in the case of religious beliefs. A fresh or heightened awareness of the facts of religious pluralism could bring about a reappraisal of one's religious life, a reawakening, a new or renewed and deepened grasp and apprehension of (1) and (2). From Calvin's perspective, it could serve as an occasion for a renewed and more powerful working of the belief-producing processes by which we come to apprehend (1) and (2). In that way, knowledge of the facts of pluralism could initially serve as a defeater, but in the long run have precisely the opposite effect.

NOTES

1. *Colloquium Heptaplomeres de Rerum Sublimium Arcanis Abditis,* written by 1593 but first published in 1857. English translation by Marion Kuntz (Princeton, N.J.: Princeton Univ. Press, 1975), p. 256.

2. Joseph Runzo: "Today, the impressive piety and evident rationality of the belief systems of other religious traditions, inescapably confronts Christians

with a crisis and a potential revolution." "God, Commitment, and Other Faiths: Pluralism vs. Relativism," *Faith and Philosophy* 5, no. 4 (October 1988): 343f. (Reading IX.5 in this book.)

3. Gary Gutting: "Applying these considerations to religious belief, we seem led to the conclusion that, because believers have many epistemic peers who do not share their belief in God..., they have no right to maintain their belief without a justification. If they do so, they are guilty of epistemological egoism." *Religious Belief and Religious Skepticism* (Notre Dame, Ind.: Univ. of Notre Dame Press, 1982), p. 90 (but see the following pages for an important qualification).

4. Wilfred Cantwell Smith: "Here my submission is that on this front the traditional doctrinal position of the Church has in fact militated against its traditional moral position, and has in fact encouraged Christians to approach other men immorally. Christ has taught us humility, but we have approached them with arrogance.... This charge of arrogance is a serious one." *Religious Diversity* (New York: Harper & Row, 1976), p. 13.

5. Runzo: "Ethically, Religious Exclusivism has the morally repugnant result of making those who have privileged knowledge, or who are intellectually astute, a religious elite, while penalizing those who happen to have no access to the putatively correct religious view, or who are incapable of advanced understanding." Op. cit., p. 348.

6. John Hick: "But natural pride, despite its positive contribution to human life, becomes harmful when it is elevated to the level of dogma and is built into the belief system of a religious community. This happens when its sense of its own validity and worth is expressed in doctrines implying an exclusive or a decisively superior access to the truth or the power to save." "Religious Pluralism and Absolute Claims," *Religious Pluralism* (Notre Dame, Ind.: Univ. of Notre Dame Press, 1984), p. 197.

7. John Cobb: "I agree with the liberal theists that even in Pannenberg's case, the quest for an absolute as a basis for understanding reflects the long tradition of Christian imperialism and triumphalism rather than the pluralistic spirit." "The Meaning of Pluralism or Christian Self-Understanding," *Religious Pluralism*, ed. Leroy Rouner (Notre Dame, Ind.: Univ. of Notre Dame Press, 1984), p. 171.

8. "God, Commitment, and Other Faiths: Pluralism vs. Relativism" *Faith and Philosophy* 5, no. 4 (October 1988):357.

9. Smith, op. cit., p. 14.

10. John Hick: "...the only reason for treating one's tradition differently from others is the very human but not very cogent reason that it is one's own!" *An Interpretation of Religion*, loc. cit.

11. *An Interpretation of Religion* (New Haven, Conn.: Yale Univ. Press, 1989), p. 2.

IX.3 Hick's Religious Pluralism and "Reformed Epistemology"—A Middle Ground

DAVID BASINGER

David Basinger is professor of philosophy at Roberts Wesleyan College in Rochester, New York, and is the author of several works in the philosophy of religion. His goal in this article is to analyze comparatively the influential argument for religious pluralism offered by John Hick and the argument for religious exclusivism (sectarianism) that can be generated by proponents of what has come to be labeled 'Reformed epistemology.' He argues that while Hick and the Reformed exclusivist appear to be giving us incompatible responses to the same question about the true nature of 'religious' reality, they are actually responding to related but distinct questions, each of which must be considered by those desiring to give a religious explanation for the phenomenon of religious diversity. Moreover, he concludes that the insights of neither ought to be emphasized at the expense of the other.

Reprinted from *Faith and Philosophy* Vol. 5:4, October 1988 by permission. Endnotes deleted.

No one denies that the basic tenets of many religious perspectives are, if taken literally, quite incompatible. The salvific claims of some forms of Judeo-Christian thought, for example, condemn the proponents of all other perspectives to hell, while the incompatible salvific claims of some forms of Islamic thought do the same.

Such incompatibility is normally explained in one of three basic ways. The nontheist argues that all religious claims are false, the product perhaps of wish fulfillment. The religious pluralist argues that the basic claims of at least all of the major world religions are more or less accurate descriptions of the same reality. Finally, the religious exclusivist argues that the tenets of only one religion (or some limited number of religions) are to any significant degree accurate descriptions of reality.

The purpose of this discussion is to analyze comparatively the influential argument for religious pluralism offered by John Hick and the argument for religious exclusivism which can be (and perhaps has been) generated by proponents of what has come to be labeled 'Reformed Epistemology.' I shall argue that while Hick and the Reformed epistemologist appear to be giving us incompatible responses to the same question about the true nature of 'religious' reality, they are actually responding to related, but distinct questions, each of which must be considered by those desiring to give a religious explanation for the phenomenon of religious diversity. Moreover, I shall conclude that the insights offered by both Hick and the Reformed epistemologist are of value and, accordingly, that those of neither ought to be emphasized at the expense of the other.

JOHN HICK'S THEOLOGICAL PLURALISM

Hick's contention is not that different religions make no conflicting truth claims. In fact, he believes that "the differences of belief between (and within) the traditions are legion," and has often in great detail discussed them. His basic claim, rather, is that such differences are best seen as "different ways of conceiving and experiencing the one ultimate divine Reality."

However, if the various religions are really "responses to a single ultimate transcendent Reality," how then do we account for such significant differences? The best explanation, we are told, is the assumption that "the limitless divine reality has been thought and experienced by different human mentalities forming and formed by different intellectual frameworks and devotional techniques." Or, as Hick has stated the point elsewhere, the best explanation is the assumption that the correspondingly different ways of responding to divine reality "owe their differences to the modes of thinking, perceiving and feeling which have developed within the different patterns of human existence embodied in the various cultures of the earth." Each "constitutes a valid context of salvation/liberation; but none constitutes the one and only such context."

But why accept such a pluralistic explanation? Why not hold, rather, that there is no higher Reality beyond us and thus that all religious claims are false—i.e., why not opt for naturalism? Or why not adopt the exclusivistic contention that the religious claims of only one perspective are true?

Hick does not reject naturalism because he sees it to be an untenable position. It is certainly *possible,* he tells us, that the "entire realm of [religious] experience is delusory or hallucinatory, simply a human projection, and not in any way or degree a result of the presence of a greater divine reality." In fact, since the "universe of which we are part is religiously ambiguous," it is not even *unreasonable* or *implausible* "to interpret any aspect of it, including our religious experience, in non-religious as well as religious ways."

However, he is quick to add, "it is perfectly reasonable and sane for us to trust our experience"—including our religious experience—"as generally cognitive of reality except when we have some reason to doubt it." Moreover, "the mere theoretical possibility that any or all [religious experience] may be illusory does not count as a reason to doubt it." Nor is religious experience overturned by the fact that the great religious figures of the past, including Jesus, held a number of beliefs which we today reject as arising from the now outmoded science of their day, or by the fact that some people find "it impossible to accept that the profound dimension of pain and suffering is the measure of the cost of creation through creaturely freedom."

He acknowledges that those who have "no positive ground for religious belief within their own experience" often do see such factors as "insuperable barriers" to religious belief. But given the ambiguous nature of the evidence, he argues, it cannot be demonstrated that all rational people must see it this way. That is, belief in a supernatural realm can't be shown to be any less plausible than disbelief. Accordingly, he concludes, "those who actually participate in this field of religious experience are fully entitled, as sane and rational persons, to take the risk of trusting their own experience together with that of their tradition, and of proceeding to live and to believe on the basis of it, rather than taking the alternative risk of distrusting it and so—for the time being at least—turning their backs on God."

But why choose pluralism as the best religious hypothesis? Why does Hick believe we ought not be exclusivists? It is not because he sees exclusivism as incoherent. It is certainly possible, he grants, that "one particular 'Ptolemaic' religious vision does correspond uniquely with how things are." Nor does Hick claim to have some privileged "cosmic vantage point from which [he can] observe both the divine reality in itself and the different partial human awarenesses of that reality." But when we individually consider the evidence in the case, he argues, the result is less ambiguous. When "we start from the phenomenological fact of the various forms of religious experience, and we seek an hypothesis which will make sense of this realm of phenomena" from a religious point of view, "the theory that most naturally suggests itself postulates a divine Reality which is itself limitless, exceeding the scope of human conceptuality and language, but which is humanly thought and experienced in various conditioned and limited ways."

What is this evidence which makes the pluralistic hypothesis so "considerably more probable" than exclusivism? For one thing, Hick informs us, a credible religious hypothesis must account for the fact, "evident to ordinary people (even though not always taken into account by theologians) that in the great majority of cases—say 98 to 99 percent—the religion in which a person believes and to which he adheres depends upon where he was born." Moreover, a credible hypothesis must account for the fact that within all of the major religious traditions, "basically the same salvific process is taking place, namely the transformation of human existence from self-centeredness to Reality-centeredness." And while pluralism "illuminates" these otherwise baffling facts, the strict exclusivist's view "has come to seem increasingly implausible and unrealistic."

But even more importantly, he maintains, a credible religious hypothesis must account for the fact, of which "we have become irreversibly aware in the present century, as the result of anthropological, sociological and psychological studies and the work of philosophy of language, that there is no one universal and invariable" pattern for interpreting human experience, but rather a range of significantly different patterns or conceptual schemes "which have developed within the major cultural streams." And when considered in light of this, Hick concludes, a "pluralistic theory becomes inevitable."

THE REFORMED OBJECTION

There are two basic ways in which Hick's pluralistic position can be critiqued. One "appropriate critical response," according to Hick himself, "would be to offer a better [religious] hypothesis." That is, one way to challenge Hick is to claim that the evidence he cites is better explained by some form of exclusivism.

But there is another, potentially more powerful type of objection, one which finds its roots in the currently popular 'Reformed Epistemology' being championed by philosophers such as Alvin Plantinga. I will first briefly outline Plantinga's latest version of this epistemological approach and then discuss its impact on Hick's position.

According to Plantinga, it has been widely held since the Enlightenment that if theistic beliefs—e.g., religious hypotheses—are to be considered rational, they must be based on propositional evidence. It is not enough for the theist just to refute objections to any such belief. The theist "must also have something like an argument for the belief, or some positive reason to think that the belief is true." But this is incorrect, Plantinga maintains. There are beliefs which acquire their warrant propositionally—i.e., have warrant conferred on them by an evidential line of reasoning from other beliefs. And for such beliefs, it may well be true that proponents need something like an argument for their veridicality.

However, there are also, he tells us, *basic* beliefs which are not based on propositional evidence and, thus, do not require propositional warrant. In fact, *if* such beliefs can be affirmed "without either violating an epistemic duty or displaying some kind of noetic defect," they can be considered *properly* basic. And, according to Plantinga, many theistic beliefs can be properly basic: "Under widely realized conditions it is perfectly rational, reasonable, intellectually respectable and acceptable to believe [certain theistic tenets] without believing [them] on the basis of [propositional] evidence."

But what are such conditions? Under what conditions can a belief have positive epistemic status if it is not conferred by other propositions whose epistemic status is not in question? The answer, Plantinga informs us, lies in an analysis of belief formation.

[We have] cognitive faculties designed to enable us to achieve true beliefs with respect to a wide variety of propositions—propositions about our immediate environment, about our interior lives, about the thoughts and experiences of other persons, about our universe at large, about right and wrong, about the whole realm of *abstracta*—numbers, properties, propositions, states of affairs, possible worlds and their like, about modality—what is necessary and possible—and about [ourselves]. These faculties work in such a way that under the appropriate circumstances we form the appropriate belief. More exactly, the appropriate belief is *formed in us;* in the typical case we do not *decide* to hold or form the belief in question, but simply find ourselves with it. Upon considering an instance of *modus ponens,* I find myself believing its corresponding conditional; upon being appeared to in the familiar way, I find myself holding the belief that there is a large tree before me; upon being asked what I had for breakfast, I reflect for a moment and find myself with the belief that what I had was eggs on toast. In these and other cases I do not *decide* what to believe; I don't total up the evidence

(I'm being appeared to redly; on most occasions when thus appeared to I am in the presence of something red, so most probably in this case I am) and make a decision as to what seems best supported; I simply find myself believing.

And from a theistic point of view, Plantinga continues, the same is true in the religious realm. Just as it is true that when our senses or memory are functioning properly, "appropriate belief is formed in us," so it is that God has created us with faculties which will, "when they are working the way they were designed to work by the being who designed and created us and them," produce true theistic beliefs. Moreover, if these faculties are functioning properly, a basic belief thus formed has "positive epistemic status to the degree [the individual in question finds herself] inclined to accept it."

What, though, of the alleged counter-evidence to such theistic beliefs? What, for example, of all the arguments the conclusion of which is that God does not exist? Can they all be dismissed as irrelevant? Not immediately, answers Plantinga. We must seriously consider potential defeaters of our basic beliefs. With respect to the belief that God exists, for example, we must seriously consider the claim that religious belief is mere wish fulfillment and the claim that God's existence is incompatible with (or at least improbable given) the amount of evil in the world.

But to undercut such defeaters, he continues, we need not engage in positive apologetics: produce propositional evidence for our beliefs. We need only engage in negative apologetics: refute such arguments. Moreover, it is Plantinga's conviction that such defeaters do normally exist. "The non-propositional warrant enjoyed by [a person's] belief in God, for example, [seems] itself sufficient to turn back the challenge offered by some alleged defeaters"—e.g., the claim that theistic belief is mere wish fulfillment. And other defeaters such as the "problem of evil," he tells us, can be undercut by identifying validity or soundness problems or even by appealing to the fact that "experts think it unsound or that the experts are evenly divided as to its soundness."

Do Plantinga or other proponents of this Reformed epistemology maintain that their exclusivistic religious hypotheses are properly basic and can thus be 'defended' in the manner just outlined? I am not *certain* that they do. However, when Plantinga, for example, claims that "God exists" is for most adult theists properly basic, he appears to have in mind a classical Christian conception of the divine—i.e., a being who is the triune, omnipotent, omniscient, perfectly good, *ex nihilo* creator of the universe. In fact, given his recent claim that "the internal testimony of the Holy Spirit...is a source of reliable and perfectly acceptable beliefs about what is communicated [by God] in Scripture," and the manner in which most who make such a claim view the truth claims of the other world religions, it would appear that Plantinga's 'basic' conception of God is quite exclusive.

However, even if no Reformed epistemologist actually does affirm an exclusivistic hypothesis she claims is properly basic, it is obvious that the Reformed analysis of belief justification can be used to critique Hick's line of reasoning. Hick claims that an objective inductive assessment of the relevant evidence makes his pluralistic thesis a more plausible religious explanation than any of the competing exclusivistic hypotheses. But a Reformed exclusivist could easily argue that this approach to the issue is misguided. My affirmation of an exclusivistic Christian perspective, such an argument might begin, is not evidential in nature. It is, rather, simply a belief I have found formed in me, much like the belief that I am seeing a tree in front of me or the belief that killing innocent children is wrong.

Now, of course, I must seriously consider the allegedly formidable defeaters with which pluralists such as Hick have presented me. I must consider the fact, for example, that the exclusive beliefs simply formed in most people are not similar to mine, but rather tend to mirror those beliefs found in the cultures in which such people have been raised. But I do not agree with Hick that this fact is best explained by a pluralistic hypothesis. I attribute this phenomenon to other factors such as the epistemic blindness with which most of humanity has been plagued since the fall.

Moreover, to defend my position—to maintain justifiably (rationally) that I am right and Hick is wrong—I need not, as Hick seems to suggest, produce objective 'proof' that his hypothesis is weaker than mine. That is, I need not produce 'evidence' that would lead most rational people to agree with me. That would be to involve myself in Classical Foundationalism, which is increasingly being recognized as a bankrupt epistemological methodology. All I need do is undercut Hick's defeaters—i.e., show that his challenge does not require me to abandon my exclusivity thesis. And this I can easily do. For Hick has not demonstrated that my thesis is self-contradictory. And it is extremely doubtful that there exists any other non-question-begging criterion for plausibility by which he could even attempt to demonstrate that my thesis is less plausible (less probable) than his.

Hick, of course, believes firmly that his hypothesis makes the most sense. But why should this bother me? By his own admission, many individuals firmly believe that, given the amount of seemingly gratuitous evil in the world, God's nonexistence is by far most plausible. Yet this does not keep him from affirming theism. He simply reserves the right to see things differently and continues to believe. And there is no reason why I cannot do the same.

Moreover, even if what others believed were relevant, by Hick's own admission, the majority of theists doubt that his thesis is true. Or, at the very least, I could rightly maintain that "the experts are evenly divided as to its soundness." Thus, given the criteria for defeater assessment which we Reformed exclusivists affirm, Hick's defeaters are clearly undercut. And, accordingly, I remain perfectly justified in continuing to hold that my exclusivity thesis is correct and, therefore, that all incompatible competing hypotheses are false.

A MIDDLE GROUND

It is tempting to see Hick and the Reformed exclusivist as espousing incompatible approaches to the question of religious diversity. If Hick is correct—if the issue is primarily evidential in nature—then the Reformed exclusivist is misguided and vice versa. But this, I believe, is an inaccurate assessment of the situation. There are two equally important, but distinct, questions which arise in this context, and Hick and the

Reformed exclusivist, it seems to me, each *primarily* address only one.

The Reformed exclusivist is primarily interested in the following question:

Q1. Under what conditions is an individual within her epistemic rights (is she rational) in affirming one of the many mutually exclusive religious diversity hypotheses?

In response, as we have seen, the Reformed exclusivist argues (or at least could argue) that a person need not grant that her religious hypothesis (belief) requires propositional (evidential) warrant. She is within her epistemic rights in maintaining that it is a *basic* belief. And if she does so, then to preserve rationality, she is not required to 'prove' in some objective manner that her hypothesis is most plausible. She is fulfilling all epistemic requirements solely by defending her hypothesis against claims that it is less plausible than competitors.

It seems to me that the Reformed exclusivist is basically right on this point. I do believe, for reasons mentioned later in this essay, that attempts by any knowledgeable exclusivist to define her hypothesis will ultimately require her to enter the realm of positive apologetics—i.e., will require her to engage in a comparative analysis of her exclusivistic beliefs. But I wholeheartedly agree with the Reformed exclusivist's contention that to preserve rationality, she need not actually demonstrate that her hypothesis is most plausible. She need ultimately only defend herself against the claim that a thoughtful assessment of the matter makes the affirmation of some incompatible perspective—i.e., pluralism or some incompatible exclusivistic perspective—the only rational option. And this, I believe, she can clearly do.

What this means, of course, is that if Hick is actually arguing that pluralism is the only rational option, then I think he is wrong. And his claim that pluralism "is considerably more probable" than exclusivism does, it must be granted, make it appear as if he believes pluralism to be the only hypothesis a knowledgeable theist can justifiably affirm.

But Hick never actually calls his opponents irrational in this context. That is, while Hick clearly believes that sincere, knowledgeable exclusivists are *wrong,* he has never to my knowledge claimed that they are guilty of violating the basic epistemic rules governing rational belief. Accordingly, it seems best to assume that Q1—a concern with what can be rationally affirmed—is not Hick's primary interest in this context.

But what then is it with which Hick is concerned? As we have seen, Q1 is defensive in nature. It asks for identification of conditions under which we can justifiably continue to affirm a belief we *already* hold. But *why* hold the specific religious beliefs we desire to defend? Why, specifically, choose to defend religious pluralism rather than exclusivism or vice versa? Or, to state this question of 'belief origin' more formally:

Q2. Given that an individual can be within her epistemic rights (can be rational) in affirming either exclusivism or pluralism, upon what basis should her actual choice be made?

This is the type of question in which I believe Hick is primarily interested.

Now, it might be tempting for a Reformed exclusivist to contend that she is exempt from the consideration of Q2. As I see it, she might begin, this question is based on the assumption that individuals consciously choose their religious belief systems. But the exclusivistic hypothesis which I affirm was not the result of a conscious attempt to choose the most plausible option. I have simply discovered this exclusivistic hypothesis formed in me in much the same fashion I find my visual and moral beliefs just formed in me. And thus Hick's question is simply irrelevant to my position.

But such a response will not do. There is no reason to deny that Reformed exclusivists do have, let's say, a Calvinistic religious hypothesis just formed in them. However, although almost everyone in every culture does in the appropriate context have similar 'tree-beliefs' just formed in them, there is no such unanimity within the religious realm. As Hick rightly points out, the religious belief that the overwhelming majority of people in any given culture find just formed in them is the dominant hypothesis of that culture or subculture. Moreover, the dominant religious hypotheses in most of these cultures are exclusivistic—i.e., incompatible with one another.

Accordingly, it seems to me that Hick can rightly be interpreted as offering the following challenge to the knowledgeable Reformed exclusivist (the exclusivist aware of pervasive religious diversity): I will grant that your exclusivistic beliefs were not originally the product of conscious deliberation. But given that most sincere theists initially go through a type of religious belief-forming process similar to yours and yet usually find formed in themselves the dominant exclusivistic hypotheses of their own culture, upon what basis can you justifiably continue to claim that the hypothesis you affirm has some special status just because you found it formed in you? Or, to state the question somewhat differently, Hick's analysis of religious diversity challenges knowledgeable Reformed exclusivists to ask themselves why they now believe that their religious belief-forming mechanisms are functioning properly while the analogous mechanisms in all others are faulty.

Some Reformed exclusivists, as we have seen, have a ready response. Because of 'the fall,' they maintain, most individuals suffer from religious epistemic blindness—i.e., do not possess properly functioning religious belief-forming mechanisms. Only our mechanisms are trustworthy. However, every exclusivistic religious tradition can—and many do—make such claims. Hence, an analogous Hickian question again faces knowledgeable Reformed exclusivists: Why do you believe that only those religious belief-forming mechanisms which produce exclusivistic beliefs compatible with yours do not suffer from epistemic blindness?

Reformed exclusivists cannot at this point argue that they have found this belief just formed in them for it is *now* the reliability of the belief-forming mechanism, itself, which is being questioned. Nor, since they are anti-foundationalists, can Reformed exclusivists argue that the evidence demonstrates conclusively that their religious position is correct. So upon what then can they base their crucial belief that their belief-forming mechanisms *alone* produce true beliefs?

They must, it seems to me, ultimately fall back on the contention that their belief-forming mechanisms can alone be trusted because that set of beliefs thus generated appears to them to form the most plausible religious explanatory hypothesis available. But to respond in this fashion brings them into basic methodological agreement with Hick's position on Q2. That is, it appears that knowledgeable Reformed exclusivists must ultimately maintain with Hick that when attempting to discover which of the many self-consistent hypotheses that *can* rationally be affirmed is the one that *ought* to be affirmed, a person must finally decide which hypothesis she believes best explains the phenomena. Or, to state this important point differently yet, what Hick's analysis of religious diversity demonstrates, I believe, is that even for those knowledgeable Reformed exclusivists who claim to find their religious perspectives just formed in them, a conscious choice among competing religious hypotheses is ultimately called for.

This is not to say, it must again be emphasized, that such Reformed exclusivists must attempt to 'prove' their choice is best. But, given the culturally relative nature of religious belief-forming mechanisms, a simple appeal to such a mechanism seems inadequate as a basis for such exclusivists to continue to affirm their perspective. It seems rather that knowledgeable exclusivists must ultimately make a conscious decision whether to retain the religious hypothesis that has been formed in them or choose another. And it further appears that they should feel some prima facie obligation to consider the available options—consciously consider the nature of the various religious hypotheses formed in people—before doing so.

Now, of course, to agree that such a comparative analysis should be undertaken is not to say that Hick's pluralistic hypothesis, is, in fact, the most plausible alternative. I agree with the Reformed exclusivist that 'plausibility' is a very subjective concept. Thus, I doubt that the serious consideration of the competing explanatory hypotheses for religious phenomena, even by knowledgeable open-minded individuals, will produce consensus.

However, I do not see this as in any sense diminishing the importance of engaging in the type of comparative analysis suggested. For even if such comparative assessment will not lead to consensus, it will produce two significant benefits. First, only by such assessment, I feel, can a person acquire 'ownership' of her religious hypothesis. That is, only by such an assessment can she insure herself that her belief is not solely the product of environmental conditioning. Second, such an assessment should lead all concerned to be more tolerant of those with whom they ultimately disagree. And in an age where radical religious exclusivism again threatens world peace, I believe such tolerance to be of inestimable value.

This does not mean, let me again emphasize in closing, that the consideration of Q1—the consideration of the conditions under which a religious hypothesis can be rationally affirmed—is unimportant or even less important than the consideration of Q2. It is crucial that we recognize who must actually shoulder the 'burden of proof' in this context. And we need to thank Reformed exclusivists for helping us think more clearly about this matter. But I fear that a preoccupation with Q1 can keep us from seeing the importance of Q2—the consideration of the basis upon which we choose the hypothesis to be defended—and the comparative assessments of hypotheses to which such consideration leads us. And we need to thank pluralists such as Hick for drawing our attention to this fact.

IX.4   Buddhism, Christianity, and the Prospects for World Religion

DALAI LAMA

Dalai Lama, originally Tenzin Gyatso (1935–   ), the spiritual and temporal head of Tibet, was born in China. In 1937 he was designated the fourteenth Dalai Lama, but his right to rule was delayed until 1950. An ardent advocate of nonviolent liberation, he was awarded the Nobel Prize for Peace in 1989. In this selection he responds to questions from Jose Ignacio Cabezon on the possibility of a religious integration of Buddhism and Christianity. The Dalai Lama (referred to as 'His Holiness') doesn't think such an integration is possible, for there are unique features in these religions that cannot be compromised without loss of identity. But he argues that all the major religions have much in common. They aim at the same goal of permanent happiness, and all encourage moral integrity. These common concerns should enable people of all faiths to find common ground in building a better world of peace and justice.

Question: Do you see any possibility of an integration of Christianity and Buddhism in the West? An overall religion for Western society?

His Holiness: It depends upon what you mean by integration. If you mean by this the possibility of the integration of Buddhism and Christianity within a society, where they co-exist side by side, then I would answer affirmatively. If, however, your view of integration envisions all of society following some sort of composite religion which is neither pure Buddhism nor pure Christianity, then I would have to consider this form of integration implausible.

It is, of course, quite possible for a country to be predominantly Christian, and yet that some of the people of that country choose to follow Buddhism. I think it is quite possible that a person who is basically a Christian, who accepts the idea of a God, who believes in God, could at the same time incorporate certain Buddhist ideas and techniques into his/her practice. The teachings of love, compassion, and kindness are

Reprinted from *The Bodhgaya Interviews,* ed. Jose Ignacio Cabezon (Snow Lion Publications, 1988) by permission.

present in Christianity and also in Buddhism. Particularly in the Bodhisattva vehicle there are many techniques which focus on developing compassion, kindness, etc. These are things which can be practiced at the same time by Christians and by Buddhists. While remaining committed to Christianity it is quite conceivable that a person may choose to undergo training in meditation, concentration, and onepointedness of mind, that, while remaining a Christian, one may choose to practice Buddhist ideas. This is another possible and very viable kind of integration.

Question: Is there any conflict between the Buddhist teachings and the idea of a creator God who exists independently from us?

His Holiness: If we view the world's religions from the widest possible viewpoint, and examine their ultimate goal, we find that all of the major world religions, whether Christianity or Islam, Hinduism or Buddhism, are directed to the achievement of permanent human happiness. They are all directed toward that goal. All religions emphasize the fact that the true follower must be honest and gentle, in other words, that a truly religious person must always strive to be a better human being. To this end, the different world's religions teach different doctrines which will help transform the person. In this regard, all religions are the same, there is no conflict. This is something we must emphasize. We must consider the question of religious diversity from *this* viewpoint. And when we do, we find no conflict.

Now from the philosophical point of view, the theory that God is the creator, is almighty and permanent, is in contradiction to the Buddhist teachings. From this point of view there is disagreement. For Buddhists, the universe has no first cause and hence no creator, nor can there be such a thing as a permanent, primordially pure being. So, of course, doctrinally, there is conflict. The views are opposite to one another. But if we consider the purpose of these different philosophies, then we see that they are the same. This is my belief

Different kinds of food have different tastes: one may be very hot, one may be very sour, and one very sweet. They are opposite tastes, they conflict. But whether a dish is concocted to taste sweet, sour or hot, it is nonetheless made in this

way so as to taste good. Some people prefer very spicy hot foods with a lot of chili peppers. Many Indians and Tibetans have a liking for such dishes. Others are very fond of bland tasting foods. It is a wonderful thing to have variety. It is an expression of individuality; it is a personal thing.

Likewise, the variety of the different world religious philosophies is a very useful and beautiful thing. For certain people, the idea of God as creator and of everything depending on his will is beneficial and soothing, and so for that person such a doctrine is worthwhile. For someone else, the idea that there is no creator, that ultimately, one is oneself the creator—in that everything depends upon oneself—is more appropriate. For certain people, it may be a more effective method of spiritual growth, it may be more beneficial. For such persons, this idea is better and for the other type of person, the other idea is more suitable. You see, there is no conflict, no problem. This is my belief.

Now conflicting doctrines are something which is not unknown even within Buddhism itself. The Mādhyamikas and Cittamtrins, two Buddhist philosophical subschools, accept the theory of emptiness. The Vaibhṣikas and Sautrāntikas, two others, accept another theory, the theory of selflessness, which, strictly speaking, is not the same as the doctrine of emptiness as posited by the two higher schools. So there exists this difference, some schools accepting the emptiness of phenomena and others not. There also exists a difference as regards the way in which the two upper schools explain the doctrine of emptiness. For the Cittamtrinsamtrins, emptiness is set forth in terms of the non-duality of subject and object. The Mādhyamikas, however, repudiate the notion that emptiness is tantamount to idealism, the claim that everything is of the nature of mind. So you see, even within Buddhism, the Mādhyamikas and Cittamtrins schools are in conflict. The Mādhyamikas are again divided into Prāsaṅgikas and Svātantrikas, and between these two sub-schools there is also conflict. The latter accept that things exist by virtue of an inherent characteristic, while the former do not.

So you see, conflict in the philosophical field is nothing to be surprised at. It exists within Buddhism itself. . . .

Question: I would like to know the role that consciousness plays in the process of reincarnation.

His Holiness: In general, there are different levels of consciousness. The more rough or gross levels of consciousness are very heavily dependent upon the physical or material sphere. Since one's own physical aggregate (the body) changes from birth to birth, so too do these gross levels of consciousness. The more subtle the level of consciousness, however, the more independent of the physical sphere and hence the more likely that it will remain from one life to the next. But in general, whether more subtle or more gross, all levels of consciousness are of the same nature.

Question: It is generally said that teachers of other religions, no matter how great, cannot attain liberation without turning to the Buddhist path. Now suppose there is a great teacher, say he is a Śaivite, and suppose he upholds very strict discipline and is totally dedicated to other people all of the time, always giving of himself. Is this person, simply because he follows Śiva, incapable of attaining liberation, and if so, what can be done to help him?

His Holiness: During the Buddha's own time, there were many non-Buddhist teachers whom the Buddha could not help, for whom he could do nothing. So he just let them be.

The Buddha Śkyamuni was an extraordinary being, he was the manifestation *(nirmnakya),* the physical appearance, of an already enlightened being. But while some people recognized him as a Buddha, others regarded him as a black magician with strange and evil powers. So, you see, even the Buddha Śkyamuni himself was not accepted as an enlightened being by all of his contemporaries. Different human beings have different mental predispositions, and there are cases when even the Buddha himself could not do much to overcome these—there was a limit.

Now today, the followers of Śiva have their own religious practices and they reap some benefit from engaging in their own forms of worship. Through this, their life will gradually change. Now my own position on this question is that Śivaji's followers should practice according to their own beliefs and traditions, Christians must genuinely and sincerely follow what they believe, and so forth. That is sufficient.

Question: But they will not attain liberation!

His Holiness: We Buddhists ourselves will not be liberated at once. In our own case, it will take time. Gradually we will be able to reach *mokṣa* or *nirvna,* but the majority of Buddhists will not achieve this within their own lifetimes. So there's no hurry. If Buddhists themselves have to wait, perhaps many lifetimes, for their goal, why should we expect that it be different for non-Buddhists? So, you see, nothing much can be done.

Suppose, for example, you try to convert someone from another religion to the Buddhist religion, and you argue with them trying to convince them of the inferiority of their position. And suppose you do not succeed, suppose they do not become Buddhist. On the one hand, you have failed in your task, and on the other hand, you may have weakened the trust they have in their own religion, so that they may come to doubt their own faith. What have you accomplished by all this? It is of no use. When we come into contact with the followers of different religions, we should not argue. Instead, we should advise them to follow their own beliefs as sincerely and as truthfully as possible. For if they do so, they will no doubt reap certain benefit. Of this there is no doubt. Even in the immediate future they will be able to achieve more happiness and more satisfaction. Do you agree?

This is the way I usually act in such matters, it is my belief. When I meet the followers of different religions, I always praise them, for it is enough, it is sufficient, that they are following the moral teachings that are emphasized in every religion. It is enough, as I mentioned earlier, that they are trying to become better human beings. This in itself is very good and worthy of praise.

Question: But is it only the Buddha who can be the ultimate source of refuge?

His Holiness: Here, you see, it is necessary to examine what is meant by liberation or salvation. Liberation in which "a mind that understands the sphere of reality annihilates all defilements in the sphere of reality" is a state that only Buddhists can accomplish. This kind of *mokṣa* or *nirvna* is only explained in the Buddhist scriptures, and is achieved only through Buddhist practice.

According to certain religions, however, salvation is a place, a beautiful paradise, like a peaceful valley. To attain such a state as this, to achieve such a state of *mokṣa*, does not require the practice of emptiness, the understanding of reality. In Buddhism itself, we believe that through the accumulation of merit one can obtain rebirth in heavenly paradises like Tuṣita....

Question: Could you please give us some brief advice which we can take with us into our daily lives?

His Holiness: I don't know, I don't really have that much to say—I'll simply say this. We are all human beings, and from this point of view we are the same. We all want happiness, and we do not want suffering. If we consider this point, we will find that there are no differences between people of different faiths, races, color or cultures. We all have this common wish for happiness.

Actually, we Buddhists are supposed to save all sentient beings, but practically speaking, this may be too broad a notion for most people. In any case, we must at least think in terms of helping all human beings. This is very important. Even if we cannot think in terms of sentient beings inhabiting different worlds, we should nonetheless think in terms of the human beings on our own planet. To do this is to take a practical approach to the problem. It is necessary to help others, not only in our prayers, but in our daily lives. If we find we cannot help another, the least we can do is to desist from harming them. We must not cheat others or lie to them. We must be honest human beings, sincere human beings.

On a very practical level, such attitudes are things which we need. Whether one is a believer, a religious person, or not, is another matter. Simply as an inhabitant of the world, as a member of the human family, we need this this kind of attitude. It is through such an attitude that real and lasting world peace and harmony can be achieved. Through harmony, friendship, and respecting one another, we can solve many problems. Through such means, it is possible to overcome problems in the right way, without difficulties.

This is what I believe, and wherever I go, whether it be to a communist country like the Soviet Union or Mongolia, or to a capitalist and democratic country like the United States and the countries of Western Europe, I express this same message. This is my advice, my suggestion. It is what I feel. I myself practice this as much as I can. If you find you agree with me, and you find some value in what I have said, then it has been worthwhile.

You see, sometimes religious persons, people who are genuinely engaged in the practice of religion, withdraw from the sphere of human activity. In my opinion, this is not good. It is not right. But I should qualify this. In certain cases, when a person genuinely wishes to engage in intensive meditation, for example when someone wishes to attain *śamatha*, then it is alright to seek isolation for certain limited periods of time. But such cases are by far the exception, and the vast majority of us must work out a genuine religious practice within the context of human society.

In Buddhism, both learning and practice are extremely important and they must go hand in hand. Without knowledge, just to rely on faith, faith and more faith is good but not sufficient. So the intellectual part must definitely be present. At the same time, strictly intellectual development without faith and practice, is also of no use. It is necessary to combine knowledge born from study with sincere practice in our daily lives. These two must go together....

Question: The Christian notion of God is that He is omniscient, all-compassionate, all-powerful, and the creator. The Buddhist notion of Buddha is the same, except that He is not the Creator. To what extent does the Buddha exist apart from our minds, as the Christians believe their God to?

His Holiness: There are two ways of interpreting this question. The general question is whether the Buddha is a separate thing from mind. Now in one sense, this could be asking whether or not the Buddha is a phenomenon imputed or labelled by mind, and of course all phenomena in this sense must be said to be labelled by name and conceptual thought. The Buddha is not a separate phenomenon from mind because our minds impute or label Him by means of words and conceptual thought.

In another sense, the question could be asking about the relationship of buddhahood to our own minds, and in this sense we must say that buddhahood, or the state of a buddha, is the object to be attained by us. Buddhahood is the resultant object of refuge. Our minds are related to buddhahood (they are not separate from buddhahood) in the sense that this is something that we will gradually attain by the systematic purification of our minds. Hence, by purifying our minds step by step, we will eventually attain the state of buddhahood. And that buddha which we will eventually become is of the same continuity as ourselves. But that buddha which we will become is different, for example, from Śkyamuni Buddha. They are two distinct persons. We cannot attain Śkyamuni Buddha's enlightenment, because that is His own individual thing.

If instead the question is referring to whether or not our minds are separate from the state of buddhahood, and if we take Buddhahood to refer to the essential purity of the mind, then of course this is something which we possess even now. Even today, our minds have the nature of essential purity. This is something called the "buddha nature." The very nature of the mind, the mere quality of knowledge and clarity without being affected by conceptual thoughts, that too we may call "buddha nature." To be exact, it is the innermost clear light mind which is called the "buddha nature."

Question: When creating merit, one must acknowledge that Christians create merit as well as Buddhists, so that the whole source of merit cannot reside solely in the object, i.e., Buddha or God, to which one is making offerings. This leads me to think that the source of merit is in our own minds. Could you please comment on this?

His Holiness: The main thing is motivation, but probably there is some difference in regard to the object to which one makes offering and so forth. The pure motivation must, however, be based on reasoning, that is, it must be verified by valid cognition; it must be unmistaken. But no doubt that the main point is the motivation.

For example, when we generate great compassion we take as our object sentient beings. But it is not due to anything on the side of sentient beings, on the part of sentient beings, that great compassion is special. It is not due to any blessing from sentient beings that great compassion is special. Nonetheless, when we meditate

in this way on great compassion and we generate it from our hearts, we know that there is a tremendous amount of benefit that results from this. This is not, however, due to anything from the side of sentient beings, from the object of the great compassion. It is simply by thinking of the kindness of sentient beings and so forth that we generate great compassion and that benefit comes, but not due to the blessing of (or anything inherent in) sentient beings themselves. So strictly from the point of view of motivation, from one's own motivation, a great amount of benefit can result, isn't it so?

Likewise, when we take the Buddha as our object, if our motivation is that of great faith, of very strong faith, and we make offerings and so forth, then again, great benefit can result from this. Although a suitable object is necessary, that is, an object which, for example, has limitless good qualities, nonetheless the principal thing is our motivation, i.e., the strong faith. Still there is probably some difference as regards the kind of object to which one is making these offerings.

From one point of view, were sentient beings not to exist, then we could not take them as our object, and great compassion could not arise. So from this perspective, the object is, once again, very important. If suffering sentient beings did not exist, compassion could never arise. So from that point of view, the object, sentient beings, is a special one....

Question: To what do you attribute the growing fascination in the West, especially in America, with Eastern religions. I include many, many cults and practices which are becoming extremely strong in America. To what do you attribute, in this particular age, the reasons for this fascination, and would you encourage people who are dissatisfied with their own Western way of life, having been brought up in the Mosaic religions (Christianity, Judaism and Islam), dissatisfied with their lack of spiritual refreshment, would you encourage them to search further in their own religions or to look into Buddhism as an alternative?

His Holiness: That's a tricky question. Of course, from the Buddhist viewpoint, we are all human beings and we all have every right to investigate either one's own religion or another religion. This is our right. I think that on the whole a comparative study of different religious traditions is useful.

I generally believe that every major religion has the potential for giving any human being good advice; there is no question that this is so. But we must always keep in mind that different individuals have different mental predispositions. This means that for some individuals one religious system or philosophy will be more suitable than another. The only way one can come to a proper conclusion as to what is most suitable for *oneself is* through comparative study. Hence, we look and study, and we find a teaching that is most suitable to our own taste. This, you see, is my feeling.

I cannot advise everyone to practice Buddhism. That I cannot do. Certainly, for some people the Buddhist religion or ideology is most suitable, most effective. But that does not mean it is suitable for *all.*

IX.5　God, Commitment, and Other Faiths: Pluralism Versus Relativism

JOSEPH RUNZO

Joseph Runzo is professor of philosophy at Chapman University in Orange, California, and the author of several works in the philosophy of religion. He has written the following abstract of his article.

This paper addresses the challenge of the problem of religious pluralism: How can we remain fully committed to our most basic truth-claims about God and yet take full account of the claims of other world religious traditions? Six possible responses to this problem are delineated and assessed. Among the possible responses, certain strengths are identified in inclusivism, although they are rejected. Focusing then on religious pluralism and religious relativism, these two views are extensively compared and contrasted. Finally, Christian relativism is defended on the grounds that it best incorporates the strengths, without the salient weaknesses, of other possible responses to the conflicting truth-claims of the world religions.

How should Christians respond responsibly to the conflicting claims of other faiths? More pointedly, should Christians abjure traditional claims to the one truth and the one way to salvation? As even Descartes (rather quaintly) observes in his *Discourse on Method,*

> . . . I further recognised in the course of my travels that all those whose sentiments are very contrary to ours are yet not necessarily barbarians or savages, but may be possessed of reason in as great or even a greater degree than ourselves. I also considered how very different the self-same man, identical in mind and spirit, may become, according as he is brought up from childhood amongst the French or Germans, or has passed his whole life amongst Chinese or cannibals.

Religious beliefs, like many philosophical orientations, seem largely an accident of birth. If you are born in India, you are likely to be a Hindu; if born in France, you are likely to be a Christian. Moreover, on their own grounds, Buddhists and Muslims and adherents of other great

Crises in religion historically precipitate revolutions in religious thought. Today, the impressive piety and evident rationality of the belief systems of *other* religious traditions, inescapably confronts Christians with a crisis—and a potential revolution.

Reprinted from *Faith and Philosophy* Vol. 5:4, October 1988 by permission. Endnotes deleted.

religious faiths, seem rationally justified in their beliefs. This raises the *problem of religious pluralism*: the mutually conflicting systems of truth-claims of the world's religions, if taken separately, appear rationally justified—but are they *correct*? Is only one system of religious truth-claims correct, is more than one system correct, or are all religious systems mistaken?

Descartes, concluding from the diversity of opinion which he observed that "it is much more custom and example that persuade us than any certain knowledge," attempts to arrive at a method for attaining certainty, despite the fact that "there is nothing imaginable so strange or so little credible that it has not been maintained by one philosopher or other." Likewise, is there one correct religious system, and can we know what it is? Or is the search for universal or certain truth in religious matters as overambitious as Descartes was philosophically overly ambitious?

A major problem with the desire for a comforting certainty in religious matters is identified in Tillich's observation that the church has become all too insular: "theologians have become careless in safeguarding their idea of a personal God from slipping into 'henotheistic' mythology (the belief in *one* god who, however, remains particular and bound to a particular group)." But if henotheism poses a danger on one side, a too ready acceptance of pluralism in religion poses a danger on the other side. For an uncritical pluralism undermines the strength of commitment of faith. How then can we both remain fully committed to our most basic truth-claims about God, and at the same time take full account of religious pluralism? Christians today must be responsive to other faiths, but responsive *within* the Christian vision expressed in the Vatican II Declaration *Nostra Aetate*: "... all peoples comprise a single community, and have a single origin ... God ... One also is their final goal: God."

After explaining why the problem of religious pluralism is a problem of conflicting truth-claims, I will set out six possible responses, religious and nonreligious, to the conflicting *truth*-claims of the world's religions. Then I will assess each response in turn from an external, religious (but not necessarily Christian) point of view, ultimately focusing on the Pluralist and Relativist responses. I will end by defending the Relativist response from an internal, Christian perspective, and explain how it incorporates strengths, without some of the salient weaknesses, of other possible responses to the conflicting truth-claims of the world religions.

I

In the *Dynamics of Faith*, Tillich suggests that "The conflict between religions is not a conflict between forms of belief, but it is a conflict between expressions of our ultimate concern.... All decisions of faith are existential, not thoeretical, decisions." It *would* be a gross distortion of faith to reduce it to merely theoretical concerns or to questions of belief. But in avoiding this intellectualist distortion of faith Tillich is mistaken to suggest that the conflict between religions is not a conflict between truth claims. True, a religious way of life importantly involves such elements as ritual and symbols, and a moral ordering of one's life. But our beliefs, or more comprehensively, our worldviews—i.e., the total cognitive web of our interrelated concepts, beliefs, and processes of rational thought—determine the very nature of our ultimate concern. For all experience, understanding, and praxis—whether it concerns the mundane or the *mysterium tremendum*—is structured by our worldviews. Consequently, conflicts between religious traditions fundamentally stem from conflicts of belief, conflicts over specific claims about how meaning and value are to be achieved, and what is the desired telos for humankind.

In assessing the conflict of truth-claims among world religions it must be kept in mind that a religion is not itself true or false any more than any other human institution such as art, government, or law, is in and of itself true or false. A total institution—aesthetic, political, legal, or religious—is only more or less expedient, only more or less effective in meeting its intended goals. What is true or false, and what is most fundamentally in conflict between such systems, are the underlying, specific truth-claims within the systems. Now, in the conflict of religious truth-claims, all of the world's major religions agree that the divine, or the Absolute, or the Real, is

One, transcends the natural order, and is ultimately inexpressible. As *Ecclesiastes* puts it, God "has put eternity into man's mind, yet so that he cannot find out what God has done from the beginning to the end." (Eccles. 3:11, RSV) But though they have this general point of agreement, and though each religious tradition includes truth claims and even scriptural material which is expendable, there is a fundamental or "vital core" of beliefs in each religion which is definitive of that very tradition. And it is particular elements of this "vital core" of beliefs that are incompatible among world religions.

For instance, there is no intractable conflict between claims in the Muslim tradition that Mahdis will periodically appear to revive faith in God, and orthodox Christian claims that Jesus represents the final prophetic revelation of God. For Christians could come to accept, and Sunnis could come to reject, further prophetic revelations from God *via* Mahdis, without impugning the respective orthodox status of Jesus or Mohammed. But traditionally it *is* essential to monotheistic traditions, like Christianity, Islam, Judaism and Ramanujan Hinduism, that the correct human perception of the divine is the perception of a personal deity. In contrast, on a Hinayana (Theravada) Buddhist view, God does not exist, and in much of the Hindu tradition, the notion of a personal deity is talk about an illusory state of affairs bound to this life. Or, to take another trenchant conflict among religious truth-claims, consider some of the diverse notions of the relation of humanity to Ultimate Reality. In Hinayana Buddhism there is no real question of one's relation to ultimate reality, for the goal of liberation is the complete extinction of the ego; in Islam the basic human relation to God is one of slave to master; in orthodox Judaism the central relation is one of a servant to his or her God.

Thus, because they make essentially different truth-claims, different religious traditions are structured by *essentially* different worldviews, offering *essentially* different paths to what is perceived as Ultimate Reality. Since a person's worldview, then, is inherently constitutive of their religious way of life, the question is whether the differences in *truth-claims* among the world religions, and the consequent differences in the (putative) paths to Ultimate Reality, are significant or ultimately irrelevant.

We can also see that the conflict among the world religions is fundamentally a conflict of *truth-claims* if we consider the meaning of "faith" and of "religion." Faith is the more encompassing notion. Faith can be either religious or non-religious: we speak of faith in the progress of science or in the inevitableness of dialectical materialism, as much as of Christian or Muslim faith. Therefore, I will use the term "faith" to refer to a person's fundamental commitment to any worldview, a commitment which is a total dispositional state of the person involving affective, conative, and cognitive elements.

Religion, on the other hand, involves a particular form of faith, focused within a specific religious tradition. To distinguish religious from non-religious faith, I will define a religion or religious tradition as a set of symbols and rituals, myths and stories, concepts and truth-claims, which a community believes gives ultimate meaning to life, *via* its connection to a transcendent God or Ultimate Reality *beyond* the natural order. Thus religion is a *human* construct (or institution) which fundamentally involves beliefs at two levels: (I) it involves the meta-belief that the religion in question does indeed refer to a transcendent reality which gives meaning to life, and (II) it involves specific beliefs—including vital core beliefs—about the nature of that ultimate reality and the way in which it gives meaning to life. The first sort of belief, (I), is shared by the world religions. The second sort of belief, (II), is the point of conflict among the world religions.

II

There are six possible responses, religious and nonreligious, to the conflicting truth-claims of vital core beliefs among the world religions:

1. *Atheism:* all religions are mistaken.
2. *Religious Exclusivism:* only one world religion is correct, and all others are mistaken.
3. *Religious Inclusivism:* only one world religion is fully correct, but other world religions participate in or partially reveal some of the truth of the one correct religion.

4. *Religious Subjectivism:* each world religion is correct, and each is correct insofar as it is best for the individual who adheres to it.

5. *Religious Pluralism:* ultimately all world religions are correct, each offering a different, salvific path and partial perspective *vis-a-vis* the one Ultimate Reality.

6. *Religious Relativism:* at least one, and probably more than one, world religion is correct, and the correctness of a religion is relative to the worldview(s) of its community of adherents.

One obvious response to the conflicting truth-claims of the world's religions is the Atheist response, (1). Is it not most plausible, given the enormity of the conflict among truth-claims, that all religious traditions are simply false in different ways, rather than that one is correct, or that several are correct in different ways? In the absence of a generally acceptable deductive proof or inductive proof with a high probability, for the existence of God or the Absolute, there is no incontrovertible reply to this query. Indeed, there are important sociological and psychological arguments, like those of Feuerbach and Freud, which lend support to the Atheist response.

At stake here is the basic religious presupposition that only reference to a transcendent divine or ultimate reality gives ultimate meaning to human life. This meta-belief (I) is supported in the various religious traditions by appeals to religious experience, purported transformations of people's lives, the claimed necessity of a "leap of faith," and so on. These are internal considerations which will not, of course, prove that the Atheist response (1) must be mistaken. But in this discussion we can set aside the Atheist response if we take the basic religious meta-belief (I) as a presupposition.

Turning to the second response, Exclusivism in its strongest form is exemplified by the traditional Roman Catholic dogma, *Extra ecclesiam nulla salus.* Exclusivism is the view that salvation can only be found either (as in the dogma just cited) inside a particular *institutional* structure, or on the basis of a specified tradition of religious beliefs, symbols, and rituals—e.g., as Karl Barth says of Christianity, "the Christian religion is

true, because it has pleased God, who alone can be the judge in this matter, to affirm it to be the true religion." But such unqualified Exclusivism seems untenable in the face of the problem of religious pluralism. In Ernst Troeltsch's words, regarding Christianity,

> a study of the non-Christian religions convinced me more and more that their naive claims to absolute validity are also genuinely such. I found Buddhism and Brahminism especially to be really humane and spiritual religions, capable of appealing in precisely the same way to the inner certitude and devotion of their followers as Christianity, . . .

Principal considerations against Exclusivism within any religious tradition include the following: Historically, it is largely a matter of geographical accident whether one grows up as a Hindu or Buddhist, Christian or Muslim, etc. Theologically, a strict reading of Exclusivism condemns the vast majority of humanity to perdition, which certainly appears contrary to the notion of a loving God, as well as seeming to contradict the idea of an Absolute which is the telos of all humankind. Ethically, Religious Exclusivism has the morally repugnant result of making those who have privileged knowledge, or who are intellectually astute, a religious elite, while penalizing those who happen to have no access to the putatively correct religious views, or who are incapable of advanced understanding. Sociologically, Exclusivism is a concomitant of sectarianism, serving as a rationale for enforcing discipline and communal cohesion. Epistemologically, one could not *know* with certainty that there is only one correct set of religious truth-claims or only one institutional structure providing a path to salvation—a consideration exacerbated by the fact that all religions at some point make Exclusivist claims. And religiously, Exclusivism is highly presumptuous, ignoring the fact that religious truth-claims are human constructs, human attempts to know Ultimate Reality, subject to the limitations and fallibility of the human mind.

It is of course possible that the Exclusivism of some particular religious tradition is correct. But given these weighty considerations against Exclusivism, we must turn to responses (3)–(6), responses that hold that in some form each of the great world religions is at least in part correctly directed toward the divine or Absolute. The problem is how to avoid the serious moral, theological, empirical, and epistemological deficiencies of Exclusivism without dissipating the very cohesiveness and vitality of one's own religious tradition which Exclusivism properly seeks to protect.

III

A natural alternative to take to meet these concerns is Inclusivism. This has become an especially prominent view in Roman Catholic theology since Vatican II. Religious Inclusivists jointly hold two theses: That other religions convey part of the truth about Ultimate Reality and the relation of humanity to Ultimate Reality, but that only one's own tradition most fully provides an understanding of Ultimate Reality, and most adequately provides a path to salvation. Thus, *Nostra Aetate* states both that "The Catholic Church rejects nothing which is true and holy in [other] religions," and that the cross of Christ "is the sign of God's all-embracing love" and "the fountain from which every grace flows."

From these foundations, Christian Inclusivism has been developed in considerable detail by Karl Rahner, who suggests that those in the non-Christian traditions can be "anonymous" Christians. Since, Rahner suggests, " we have to keep in mind...the necessity of Christian faith *and* the universal salvific will of God's love and omnipotence,"

> we can only reconcile them by saying that somehow all men must be capable of being members of the Church; and this capacity must not be understood merely in the sense of an abstract and purely logical possibility, but as a real and historically concrete one.

In the same vein, R. C. Zaehner offers an historical argument for Inclusivism:

> The drive towards the integration of...the personal and the collective, has been characteristic of the most original thinkers in [all religions] during the first two-thirds of the twentieth century.... This unity in diversity is the birthright of the Catholic Church...all the other religions, in their historical development, grow into 'other Catholic Churches'

> ...[For while one God] is the inspiration of all religions and peculiar to none...The only religion that has from the beginning been both communal and individual is Christianity.

Inclusivism is typically based on the notion that one's own religion most fully possesses a particular element which is most essential to religion. Zaehner looks to the integration of the personal and collective; Kant holds that true religiosity is identical to the moral life; Schleiermacher proposes that underlying genuine religion is "the feeling of absolute dependence"; Rudolph Otto emphasizes a numinous sense of the holy, a sense of the *mysterium tremendum; Nostra Aetate* declares that "from ancient times down to the present, there has existed among diverse peoples a certain perception of that hidden power which hovers over the course of things and over the events of human life"; and John Baillie suggests that all humans have a knowledge of God through a felt presence of the divine such that all people "already believe in him."

That other religious traditions, in accordance with the religious meta-belief (I), might provide some apprehension of Ultimate Reality, is not at issue here. Rather, Inclusivism supposes that a *particular* sort of apprehension and understanding of Ultimate Reality is elemental to all religion. However, in the first place we could not *know* that all humans have the same sort of elemental apprehension of Ultimate Reality. Second, the empirical evidence supports precisely the opposite supposition. Even in the broadest terms, the notion of an elemental apprehension of Ultimate Reality is understood in personal terms in the monotheistic traditions, while it is *non-personal* in Confucianism and in Hindu and Buddhist traditions. And third, each religion tends to see itself as the culmination of *the* elemental apprehension of Ultimate Reality: "other religions can have their own fulfillment theology. Sri Aurobindo sees the world religious process converging on Mother India rather than the Cosmic Christ, and Sir Muhammad Iqbal sees it converging upon a kind of ideal Islam."

So when Rahner, for example, says that the Christian has, "other things being equal, a still greater chance of salvation than someone who is merely an anonymous Christian," this can only be a statement of faith, not one of certain knowledge. Yet the strength of Inclusivism is this unequivocal faith—*within* an acceptance of other traditions—that one's own religion is salvific. Inclusivism expresses an appropriate religious disposition. But Inclusivism ultimately fails as a warranted epistemological thesis. This failure leads us to the pluralistic types of responses to the problem of religious pluralism.

IV

Subjectivism, Pluralism, and Relativism are all pluralistic responses to the conflicting truth-claims of world religions. All three views share a basic *idealist epistemology*: i.e., they share the basic assumption that the world we experience and understand is not the world independent of our perceiving but a world at least in part structured by our minds. Thus these pluralistic views share the epistemic view expressed in the Kantian dictum that "[sensible] intuitions without concepts are blind," a view sometimes expressed in the contemporary notion that all experiencing is experiencing-*as*. But further, they share the assumption that there is more than one set of human concepts—more than one worldview—which is valid for understanding the world. Thus they share the sort of *pluralist* epistemology expressed by William James in *The Varieties of Religious Experience*: "why in the name of common sense need we assume that only one...system of ideas can be true? The obvious outcome of our total experience is that the world can be handled according to many systems of ideas,..." The three pluralistic religious responses all hold that one's perception of religious truth is in some sense relative to one's worldview. Typically this view is supported on the grounds of the ineluctable enculturation or the historicity of all thought and experience, or, as in the Whorf hypothesis, by suggesting a necessary connection between language, which varies from community to community, and truth, which consequently varies.

The most radical of the pluralistic responses to the conflicting truth-claims of the world religions is Subjectivism, where religious truth and salvation

are literally as varied as individuals are diverse. As a general view in epistemology, subjectivism is a form of relativism about truth. It is the extreme epistemological position that truth is relative to each individual's idiosyncratic worldview. Thus, on a Religious Subjectivist's view, religion is a radically private affair, often understood as purely a matter of one's individual relation to the divine or Absolute. But subjectivism, and therefore Religious Subjectivism, is conceptually incoherent. Truth bearers are statements or propositions. Statements or propositions are comprised of concepts. And precisely what Wittgenstein's "private-language" argument demonstrates is that concepts are social constructions and cannot be purely private, individual understandings. Thus, since statements and propositions are comprised of concepts, and concepts are social constructs, truth cannot be idiosyncratically individualistic. Religious Subjectivism, then, must be rejected.

The two remaining pluralistic views, Religious Pluralism and Religious Relativism, are often conflated. John Hick offers a concise description of Pluralism as the view that "There is not merely one way but a plurality of ways of salvation or liberation...taking place in different ways within the contexts of all the great religious traditions." Pluralism holds that there is only one Ultimate Reality, but that Ultimate Reality is properly, though only partially, understood in different ways. Following a metaphor which Hick employs, just as the historian does not have direct access to figures of history, and consequently different historians develop different perspectives on historical figures like Genghis Khan or Sun Yat-Sen because of historians' different methods of inquiry, cultural backgrounds, etc., so too, different religious traditions or different theologies, not having direct access to the divine, offer different encultured "images" of the one Ultimate Reality. On the Pluralist account, there is no ultimate conflict between these different perspectives, since there still remains one set of truths, even if those truths are imperfectly and only partially understood within each perspective. Religious Pluralism, then, focuses on the viability of different religious *perspectives* on Ultimate Reality.

Religious Relativism, in contrast, is directly a thesis about differences of religious *truth-claims*.

The Religious Relativist minimally holds the general epistemic view, which I shall designate as "conceptual relativism," that first-order truth-claims about reality—e.g., that persons or that subatomic particles or that God exists—are relative to the worldview of a particular society. More precisely, a conceptual relativist definitively holds that, corresponding to differences of worldview, there are mutually incompatible, yet individually adequate, sets of conceptual-schema-relative truths. Thus for the Religious Relativist, unlike the Pluralist, truth itself is relative and plural.

However, Religious Pluralism and Religious Relativism do share two underlying Kantian theses. They share the Kantian metaphysical division (though the Kantian terminology may not be employed) between noumena and phenomena, distinguishing between God in Himself or the Absolute in itself, and God or the Absolute as humanly experienced. And as we have seen, they share the Kantian epistemic notion that all experience, and so all religious experience, is structured by the (culturally and historically conditioned) worldview of the percipient. Thus, Religious Pluralism and Religious Relativism hold that differences of religious perception cannot just be treated as a matter of some people simply being wrong about the nature of the divine Reality, but rather that such differences of perception are inherent to religious perception and conception. Given these points of fundamental agreement, which position, Pluralism or Relativism, better accounts for the conflicting truth-claims of the world religions?

V

An important exponent of Religious Pluralism is Wilfred Cantwell Smith. Cantwell Smith argues that the notions of "religion" and of "a religion" are obsolete. He holds that only God and humanity are "givens"—global universals—and that the centrality given to religion is misguided and the conception of a religion as a belief system mistaken. Rather than starting from a particular religious tradition and then considering God and humanity, one should start from God and humanity and consider particular religious traditions from this global perspective. Smith reaches the Pluralist conclusion that the one truth about the religious life of humankind is conveyed in the various Buddhist, Christian, Islamic, and so on, forms.

Quite correctly, I think, Smith is attempting to circumvent the obstacles which *religion often* places between humans and their response to the divine. But there are several problems with his approach. First, he suggests replacing the worldview(s) of particular religious traditions with another worldview on which it is presupposed that God and humanity are givens in the experience of all humans. This is neither a neutral worldview, nor one which will be shared by all religious persons. Many adherents of particular religious worldviews would reject the generalized approach to the divine Cantwell Smith proposes as so amorphous that it fails to capture *their* religious beliefs. Second, Smith's position rests on the dubious thesis, which we have already addressed, that there is a universal, innate experience or conception of the divine. Smith himself effectively argues against *Christian* Exclusivism by asking: "how could one possibly know?" that only the Christian faith is correct. But the same argument is equally applicable to Smith's own position: how could one possibly *know* that there is a global, innate apprehension or "givenness" of God and humanity? If anything, the evidence most strongly supports the conclusion that all humankind does not share the same innate concept or primal experience of Ultimate Reality, much less of the nature of God, or even of humanity, *per se*.

John Hick has developed another, rather impressive and comprehensive, Pluralist approach, in part by following out a key aspect of Cantwell Smith's work, viz. the rejection of the idea that a religion is fundamentally a set of beliefs. Proposing instead that religion definitively concerns "the transformation of human existence from self-centeredness to Reality-centeredness," Hick essentially argues that the apparently conflicting truth-claims of the world's religions are, in the final analysis, irrelevant, and that the world religions can be reconciled, and the integrity of each preserved, through this more fundamental shared goal of moving from self- to Reality-centeredness.

Hick explicitly employs the two Kantian theses underlying both Pluralism and Relativism.

He employs the Kantian thesis that all experience is structured by the mind by suggesting that specific forms of religious awareness "are formed by the presence of the divine Reality, . . . coming to consciousness in terms of the different sets of religious concepts and structures of religious meaning that operate within the different religious traditions," i.e., as divine *personae* (e.g., Yahweh, Allah, etc.) for theists and *as* divine *impersonae* (e.g., Brahman, the Dharma, the Tao, etc.) for non-theists. Regarding the phenomenal/noumenal distinction, he supports the distinction between personal and non-personal divine phenomena and the Eternal noumenon, on the basis of what he takes to be strong inductive evidence from religious experience. And indeed we do find consistent differentiation in the world religions between Ultimate Reality as we experience it and as it is in itself. There is the Hindu distinction between *saguna* Brahman and *nirguna* Brahman; the Jewish Cabalistic distinction between the God of the Bible and En Soph; and in the Christian tradition, Eckhart's distinction between God *qua* Trinity and the Godhead itself, and more recently, Tillich's notion of "the God above the God of theism," and so on.

Hick does allow for the logical possibility that only one religion might be correct, but he thinks that the overwhelming facts of religious diversity make Religious Pluralism the most plausible response to the conflicting truth-claims of world religions. A comprehensive Religious Pluralism like Hick's fully confronts the diversity of religious truth-claims. As such, it is an admirable and helpful response to the challenge which these conflicting claims presents. But even so, Religious Pluralism has significant shortcomings.

VI

Religious Pluralism fails to adequately account for the necessary, central role of cognition in religious faith. Hick suggests that differences of belief among the world religions are of great philosophical importance as elements within our respective theories about the universe; but they are not of great religious, i.e. soteriological, importance. For different groups can hold incompatible sets of theories all of which constitute intellectual frameworks within which the process of salvation/liberation can proceed.

Of course, even incompatible theories can serve as guides to the same religious goal. But from this it neither follows that systems of belief and theory are irrelevant to guiding one to that goal, nor that it is unimportant which particular belief system one holds for reaching that end. Rather, the cognitive content of religious faith is essential for providing a coherent and sufficiently comprehensive view of reality as a basis for purposive action and an effective, directive guide to "salvation/liberation." Further, the *specific* cognitive content of one's faith is of paramount importance since it is precisely what delimits one's specific path to salvation/liberation. And the specific path to salvation/liberation is not just a means to an end but is itself an integral part of the goal of salvation/liberation. This is expressed in the New Testament in the idea that the Kingdom of God is not future but begins in the lives of those who enter the new covenant now: "asked by the Pharisees when the kingdom was coming, he [Jesus] answered them, 'The kingdom of God is not coming with signs to be observed; . . . the kingdom of God is in the midst of you.'" (Luke 17:20–21, RSV) Consequently, since the specific path to salvation/liberation is itself part of that very salvation/liberation, a specific religious worldview is importantly constitutive of what makes a way of life a (particular) *religious* way of life.

Indeed, it would seem that specific religious cognitive content is essential to making it meaningful even to be committed at all to a religious way of life. True, de-emphasizing specific doctrines—such as the idea that the Christ-event is the definitive self-revelation of the divine—makes it easier to reconcile apparently conflicting religious truth claims, especially the notion of a personal God with the notion of a non-personal Absolute. But the more such specific doctrines are set aside, the more questionable it becomes whether a *religious,* as opposed to a non-religious, commitment is what gives life ultimate significance. Insofar as the specificity of religious doctrines is de-emphasized, the basic religious meta-belief (I) that religion does indeed refer to a transcendent Reality which gives meaning to life becomes less plausible. The plausibility of (I) rests in large part on the evidence of religious experience. But as any hypothesis about the nature of reality is made more indefinite, the available inductive evidence to support that hypothesis is not increased, as for example Hick's defense of Religious Pluralism seems to suggest, but decreased. For evidence for an indefinite hypothesis is correspondingly indefinite or ambiguous.

Another difficulty with Religious Pluralism is this. Exactly what a recognition of pluralism in general seems to acknowledge is that humans, and human conceptions, fundamentally differ. But then, to the extent that the differences of human conception embedded in the world religions are regarded as inconsequential, the dignity of the individual and the value of each distinct community of faith is lessened.

To see how this applies to Christianity, consider Maurice Wiles' observation that, "there are two fundamental characteristics of the conception of God . . . it must be a profoundly personal concept, . . . And secondly it is God in relation to us with which we have to do." The Christian understanding that the universe is under the providence of a God who has revealed Himself as a personal being—One who understands and loves humanity—is and must be a conception of God as He manifests Himself to us. Yet this conception of an essentially *personal* God is not incidental but central to both corporate and individual Christian faith. Hick attempts to account for this by suggesting that among the world religions the Real is experienced as *either* personal or non-personal. While this Religious Pluralist view properly acknowledges that theistic understanding is an understanding of Ultimate Reality not *an sich* but *as* it confronts us in history, it obviates the significance of the Christian understanding of a personal God as *somehow* correctly revealing the nature of Ultimate Reality in itself. A personal reality might have non-personal aspects, but it could not be identical to something which is non-personal. Hence, this Pluralist account entails that the monotheist's experience of a *personal* divine reality *cannot,* to that extent, correctly represent the nature of the Real in itself.

Finally, Religious Pluralism is deficient insofar as it unintentionally undermines the sense of the reality of God. It is part of the fundamental meta-belief (I) of religion that the God or the Absolute of which humans speak is real and not a metaphysical illusion or psychological delusion. But if the God of which monotheists speak is only an "image," only a perspective on an unknowable, noumenal reality, then the God of history will not be a real God. I will address this last point more fully below.

These deficiencies must be met if a pluralistic resolution to the conflicting truth-claims of the world religions is to be successful. Yet despite these shortcomings, Religious Pluralism has an obvious strength which must be retained for any successful pluralistic resolution. Religious Pluralism offers a reconciliation of the disparate world religious traditions which avoids the theologically unacceptable and epistemically unsupportable religious imperialism which we find in Exclusivism, and even in Inclusivism.

VII

If, then, we reject the religious imperialism of the Exclusivist and Inclusivist views that one's own tradition must be either the sole or at least the fullest arbiter of truth about the divine, we have two choices about how to deal with the irreducible plurality of religious conception and experience. We can either take the approach of Pluralism, treat the incompatible beliefs among differing religious worldviews as ultimately inessential, and conclude that the great world religions simply offer different perspectives on Ultimate Reality. Or we can accept the doctrines which adherents of different world religions so ardently profess and passionately follow as *essential* to their faith. I have suggested that the former approach runs the danger of undermining the basic religious meta-belief (I), and reducing the substance of religious worldviews to vacuity, obviating just those differences in the path to salvation/liberation which give significance to each individual religious tradition. If I am right about this, we are led to conclude that different religions have different constitutive sets of truth-claims, and that while these sets of core truth-claims are mutually incompatible—each set of truth-claims is probably adequate in itself.

This is the Religious Relativist response to the problem of religious pluralism. Granted, the different religious worldviews among the world's great religious traditions are complementary insofar as they have a commonality in the religious experiences and perceptions of humankind. But different religious worldviews are, ultimately, irreducibly plural, with features that are incompatible if not contradictory *vis-a-vis* other religious worldviews. Further, corresponding to each distinct religious worldview, there is a different set of possible religious *experiences*. For what can be experienced depends on what *can* be real or unreal, and what can be real—i.e., what is possible—is determined by the percipient's worldview. This means that each distinct religious worldview delineates a distinct possible divine reality—though just to the extent that religious worldviews "overlap," characteristics of these distinct possible divine realities will overlap.

For instance, monotheistic truth-claims will be most directly about God as humans experience Him, for they are most directly above divine reality *relative to* a particular theistic worldview. But then each theology, as a product of human constructive reasoning, will delimit only one *possible* divine reality. There will be other *contrasting*—though not totally mutually exclusive—valid theologies, held by other sincere women and men of faith, delimiting other possible divine phenomenal realities.

Importantly, on this Religious Relativist account, "The" God of history, delimited by the strictures of a particular theology is *not,* if He exists, somehow unreal *vis-a-vis* the noumenal. God *qua* noumenal lies "behind," so to speak, the possible plurality of real phenomenal divine realities, delimited by different monotheistic worldviews. But noumenal and phenomenal reality are two different categories of reality. And just as there is nothing unreal about nuclear weapons or pains or piano concertos because they are part of phenomenal reality, "The" God of history, "The" God one confronts, is not less real, if He exists, just because He is not in the category of the noumenal. What could be *more* real than that which we do experience? And to try to transcend our experience for something putatively "untainted" by human thought is not only the worst sort of degenerate Platonism, it is to turn away from the means we *do* have in experience for understanding the divine and our own humanity in relation to the divine.

Among the possible responses to the problem of religious pluralism, this Religious Relativist account of a possible plurality of phenomenal divine realities seems to offer the best explanation of the differing experiences and incompatible conceptions of the great religious traditions. The Atheist response to the problem of religious pluralism is ruled out if we presuppose the religious metabelief (I). Religious Exclusivism is neither tolerable nor any longer intellectually honest in the context of our contemporary knowledge of other faiths. Religious Subjectivism is conceptually incoherent. Religious Inclusivism does not go far enough toward solving the problem of religious pluralism. And Religious Pluralism has serious deficiencies which Religious Relativism avoids.

First, Religious Relativism reasserts the central role which cognition has in a religious life. The path to salvation is itself part of the salvific process. And one's religious worldview, as a guide for attitudes and actions, is inseparable from the path. Moreover, if all experience is conceptualized, then one will quite literally not be able to have any experience of the divine without a worldview which, e.g., enables one to experience the world as under the providence of God, or as an environment for working out one's *Karma*, etc. But then, as Religious Relativism asserts, *specific* truth-claims are essential to a religious tradition and way of life, and the conflict among the claims of the world religions cannot be resolved by de-emphasizing those conflicting claims.

Second, it follows from this that Religious Relativism treats adherents of each religious tradition with fullest dignity. Regarding Christianity, we could say, as the Pluralist must, that the doctrine of the Incarnation cannot be taken literally and cannot mean for *any* Christian that Jesus uniquely manifests the presence of God. Or, we can allow that on some worldviews this would be a perfectly rational view, delineating a world where Jesus *is* the definitive self-manifestation of God. Ironically, we fall back into a certain measure of the old absolutism that undergirds Exclusivism if we take the inflexible, even though Pluralist, first course. In contrast, Relativism not only allows with Pluralism that the world's great religions could have the same telos, it allows for the likelihood that more than one of the conflicting sets of *specific* truth-claims, which adherents of the differing world religions themselves regard as vital to their faith, is correct.

Third, that it is essential for the direct object of theological conception to be a *real* God seems to leave a Pluralist view like Hick's caught between two problematic options. As in his earlier work, the God of theology can be characterized as an "image" of God. But then the God of theology does not have the ontological status of an existent entity with causal properties in the phenomenal world. This will unintentionally reduce the sense of the reality of God, for what theology would then be most directly referring to would not be *God,* but a human *idea* of the noumenal. So to speak about *God,* would be to speak about something noumenal about which we can only know that we do not know its true character. In contrast, on Religious Relativism the God of theology can be a *real* God, not just a conception of or perspective on the divine. God *qua* phenomenal is not just, in Tillich's phrase, "a symbol for God."

On the other hand, the Pluralist might hold, as Hick does in his more recent work, that the divine phenomena just *are* the divine noumenon as experienced by humans via their particular religio-cultural perspectives. While this does indicate a more substantive ontological status for divine personae and impersonae, it threatens to collapse the phenomena/noumena distinction and runs counter to the basic idealist epistemology which underlies both Pluralism and Relativism. First, this suggests that the divine noumenon is itself experienced. One can postulate an unexperienced divine noumenon, and one can talk about divine phenomena which are (putatively) experienced. But this cannot amount to talk about the same thing—even if in different ways—for that would effectively be to eliminate the divine noumenon. And given an idealist epistemology, one cannot claim that the divine noumenon is experienced insofar as it appears to us in various ways, *even though* we cannot characterize the noumenal. For the conceptualization of all experience implies that what we experience can, in principle, be characterized.

Second, that a particular divine phenomenon somehow manifests the divine noumenon is a matter of faith. And while it could be a matter of reasonable faith for an individual to claim that the divine phenomenon which they experience somehow manifests Ultimate Reality in itself, it would not make sense to say that it was a matter of one's *faith* that the various divine phenomena, which adherents of all the great world religions feel that they experience, all *do* manifest Ultimate Reality. Rather this would amount to a hypothesis or theory about the world religions. And I do not see how we could know that this hypothesis is true; how could we know that the divine phenomena of all the great world religions *are* (or most probably are) the divine noumenon as experienced by humans? One's faith warrants one's own religious commitment; it cannot warrant the mutually conflicting commitments of others.

In contrast, on a Religious Relativist account, what is putatively experienced is not the noumenal Ultimate Reality, but e.g., the *real* God of history. Now, I do think that it is a mistake to suppose that one can *know* that specific claims which we make about phenomenal divine reality are also true of the divine noumenon, since this would obviate the very point of the noumena/phenomena distinction. But I think it is perfectly sensible to make the bare claim that there is a noumenal—*whatever* its character—which, so to speak, "lies behind" the phenomenal reality which we experience. Presumably there is no one-to-one correspondence between phenomena and noumena and hence no *direct* check from our successes and failures to the nature of the noumenal. But the greater the correspondence between our conception of the phenomenal and the character of the noumenal (whatever it is), the more our purposive activity, carried out within phenomenal reality as we understand it, will be successful and the closer—in principle—our understanding of the phenomenal will correspond to the noumenal. For the monotheist it is a matter of faith that, in this manner, one's *own* experience of the presence of "The" God of history does increase, on the whole, one's understanding of God in Himself.

VIII

One obvious point of resistance to this Religious Relativist account is the notion that there may be more than one phenomenal reality, and more than one phenomenal divine reality. But this notion initially seems strange only because we are used to thinking in terms of that one possible world which we regard as *the* (unique) actual world. Commonly, we treat any other conception of the actual world as simply false or mistaken. But if one accepts the idea that phenomenal reality is relative to a worldview, and that therefore there is a plurality of actual worlds corresponding to the plurality of distinct worldviews, that does not undermine or alter what we call the actual world—i.e., the world delimited by our schemas.

Recognizing that others might be responding to a different phenomenal God is like recognizing that others might rationally claim to discern a cyclical recurrence of events in history where you discern none. One can accept that there *could* be states of affairs which others but not you experience, without thereby committing yourself to the existence of any *particular* such state of affairs. To have faith in only one real (phenomenal) God is to say that for *oneself* there is only one real God who lives and moves and has His being; for others there may be other real entities which are "The" God of *their* history. But just as any actual event or state of affairs is by definition an event or state of affairs in your actual world, any actual event which you acknowledge as an act of God is an act of the real God who confronts you within (your) history....

X

While the Pluralist attempts to solve the problem of religious pluralism by setting aside conflicting truth claims and emphasizing a universality and unity to all religions, the Religious Relativist can resolve the problem of religious pluralism by accepting these conflicting truth-claims as an appropriate manifestation of divine/human interaction. In the spirit of the Leibnizian notion that not just the quantity of good, but the variety of good things makes this "the best of all possible worlds"—the world that a good God would create—we *should expect* correct religious beliefs and veridical religious experiences to be as richly varied as human needs and human individuality. Contrary to the Pluralist conception, an ultimate uniformity of the central elements of all religious traditions is not an ultimate value. Where Pluralism tends to homogenize religion, if one believes that God indeed has providence over the world, then precisely what the evidence of the world we find ourselves in indicates is that a diversity of religious truth-claims is intrinsically valuable, and divinely valued. Rather than a problem to be solved, the conflicting truth-claims of the great religious traditions, and even conflicting systems *within* traditions, can be accepted as a profound indication of God's manifest love and delight in the diverse worlds of His creatures.

That our religious beliefs have a correlation to the transcendent divine reality is a matter of faith. Since our perception and understanding are ineluctably limited to our worldview, even if what we believe is true about God *qua* phenomenal turns out to be true also of God *qua* noumenal, we could never *know* that that was so. We cannot *know* that we possess the requisite conceptual resources to apply to God in Himself, or *know* that we have formed ideas which are true of God *qua* noumenal, or *know* that our ideas do properly refer to the noumenal God. But just because we cannot know these things to be true *vis-a-vis* the noumenal God, this clearly does not entail that they are not the case. I do not see how it could be shown that it is *impossible* that our concepts or beliefs do in fact correctly refer to the noumenal. Quite the contrary, it is a matter of reasonable faith that Christian religious experience and theological conception *do* provide the basis for proper reference and proper talk about God in Himself. Yet to acknowledge that we cannot transcend our worldviews, and that they in turn are inescapably structured by our limiting socio-historical perspective, is to recognize the fundamental fallibility and finitude of even our noblest conceptions and highest values. There is thus a religiously appropriate humbleness which Religious Relativism brings to our claims to religious truth.

Faced with the inescapable challenge of the claims of other faiths, it may now be time for

Christians to move toward a Christian Relativism. A Christian Relativism would combine the strengths of Exclusivism and Inclusivism, and of Pluralism, without their respective disadvantages. A Christian Relativism would enable us to say, on the one hand, that salvation through Christ is definitive, without committing us, on the other hand, to the unsupportable view that salvation is exclusively Christian. A Christian Relativism would sustain Christian commitment and support Christian claims to truth, without claiming to be the only truth.

PART TEN

Religion and Ethics

IN EXAMINING THE RELATIONSHIP of religion to ethics, the central problem that one confronts is the question of whether and to what extent moral standards depend upon God or upon religion. Is morality autonomous, so that even God is subject to the moral order? Or are the facts about goodness and morality somehow dependent upon the will of God?

This problem dates back at least to Plato. As Socrates asks in our first reading, taken from the *Euthyphro,* "Do the gods love holiness because it is holy, or is it holy because the gods love it?" According to one theory, called the divine command theory, ethical principles are simply the commands of God. They derive their validity from God's commanding them. Without God, there would be no universally valid morality. As Dostoevsky wrote in *The Brothers Karamazov,* "If God doesn't exist, everything is permissible." Many interpret the writings of Nietzsche as representing such a nihilistic ethics. The opposing viewpoint is that ethical values are autonomous and that even God must keep the moral law, which exists independently of him. God, of course, *knows* what is right—better than we do. But God commands what he does because it is good, not the other way around.

The motivation for the divine command theory is to preserve or do justice both to the sovereignty of God and to his aseity (i.e., his absolute independence). God is thought to be somehow less sovereign or more dependent if he is not the source of all goodness and morality. If the moral law is independent of God's will, then there is something external to God that constrains his actions (he must, after all, be good) and over which he has no control. Furthermore, it seems that, in this case, the goodness of God depends on the nature of the moral law; and so God is not completely independent of everything. For this reason, then, those who prefer full-strength conceptions of divine sovereignty and aseity will be attracted to a divine command theory.

The central problem for the divine command theory, however, is that it seems to imply that what is in fact morally wrong (indeed, morally heinous) might have turned out to be good, and even morally required. For if morality depends on God's commands, then if God had commanded cruelty, cruelty would not only have been morally permitted, it would have been morally obligatory. Of course, one might be tempted to insist that God *couldn't* command such things because God is necessarily such as to love and command just those things that he in fact loves and commands—the things that are, in fact, good. But one might think that this reply is unhelpful, for even if God *can't* command what is in fact cruel, it still seems as if the divine command theorist is committed to saying that if God *had* (impossibly) commanded cruelty, then cruelty would have been a good things to do. And that conclusion seems mistaken. So at first glance anyway, it appears rather difficult to escape this particular problem.

Our first reading in this section—a selection from Plato's *Euthyphro*—raises the question of whether standards of goodness depend on God or vice versa. Our second reading, Robert M. Adams's "A Modified Divine Command Theory of Ethical Wrongness," seeks to articulate a version of the divine command theory that avoids the conclusion that if God were to command cruelty for its own sake then we would be obliged to obey. At the heart of his view is the idea that moral language would simply break down in the unthinkable case of God commanding the performance of what we take to be morally reprehensible actions.

In the third reading, Bertrand Russell articulates his vision of a godless world in which there is, nevertheless, real good and evil. Russell's picture, then, is of a world in which morality is independent of religion and ethics. In our fourth and final reading, however, George Mavrodes takes issue with Russell's picture. He argues that Russell's wholly secular ethic suffers from a serious inadequacy: It cannot satisfactorily answer the question, "Why should I be moral all of the time?" For, on its account, the common goods at which morality aims are often just those goods that we sacrifice in carrying out our moral obligations.

X.1   Morality and Religion

PLATO

A short biographical sketch of Plato precedes selection VI.1. In the present selection, Plato portrays his mentor, Socrates, engaged in a dialogue with the self-righteously religious Euthyphro, who is going to court to report his father for having killed a slave. In the course of the discussion Socrates raises what is known as the question of the divine command theory of ethics: Is the good good because God loves it, or does God love the good because it is good?

Socrates. But shall we . . . say that whatever all the gods hate is unholy, and whatever they all love is holy: while whatever some of them love, and others hate, is either both or neither? Do you wish us now to define holiness and unholiness in this manner?

Euthyphro. Why not, Socrates?

Socr. There is no reason why I should not, Euthyphro. It is for you to consider whether that definition will help you to instruct me as you promised.

Euth. Well, I should say that holiness is what all the gods love, and that unholiness is what they all hate.

Socr. Are we to examine this definition, Euthyphro, and see if it is a good one? Or are we to be content to accept the bare assertions of other men, or of ourselves, without asking any questions? Or must we examine the assertions?

Euth. We must examine them. But for my part I think that the definition is right this time.

Reprinted from the *Euthyphro,* translated by William Jowett (New York: Charles Scribner's Sons, 1889).

Socr. We shall know that better in a little while, my good friend. Now consider this question. Do the gods love holiness because it is holy, or is it holy because they love it?

Euth. I do not understand you, Socrates.

Socr. I will try to explain myself: we speak of a thing being carried and carrying, and being led and leading, and being seen and seeing; and you understand that all such expressions mean different things, and what the difference is.

Euth. Yes, I think I understand.

Socr. And we talk of a thing being loved, and, which is different, of a thing loving?

Euth. Of course.

Socr. Now tell me: is a thing which is being carried in a state of being carried, because it is carried, or for some other reason?

Euth. No, because it is carried.

Socr. And a thing is in a state of being led, because it is led, and of being seen, because it is seen?

Euth. Certainly.

Socr. Then a thing is not seen because it is in a state of being seen; it is in a state of being seen because it is seen; and a thing is not led because it is in a state of being led; it is in a state of being led because it is led: and a thing is not carried because it is in a state of being carried; it is in a state of being carried because it is carried. Is my meaning clear now, Euthyphro? I mean this: if anything becomes, or is affected, it does not become because it is in a state of becoming; it is in a state of becoming because it becomes; and it is not affected because it is in a state of being affected; it is in a state of being affected because it is affected. Do you not agree?

Euth. I do.

Socr. Is not that which is being loved in a state, either of becoming, or of being affected in some way by something?

Euth. Certainly.

Socr. Then the same is true here as in the former cases. A thing is not loved by those who love it because it is in a state of being loved. It is in a state of being loved because they love it.

Euth. Necessarily.

Socr. Well, then, Euthyphro, what do we say about holiness? Is it not loved by all the gods, according to your definition?

Euth. Yes.

Socr. Because it is holy, or for some other reason?

Euth. No, because it is holy.

Socr. Then it is loved by the gods because it is holy; it is not holy because it is loved by them?

Euth. It seems so.

Socr. But then what is pleasing to the gods is pleasing to them, and is in a state of being loved by them, because they love it?

Euth. Of course.

Socr. Then holiness is not what is pleasing to the gods, and what is pleasing to the gods is not holy, as you say, Euthyphro. They are different things.

Euth. And why, Socrates?

Socr. Because we are agreed that the gods love holiness because it is holy; and that it is not holy because they love it. Is not this so?

Euth. Yes.

Socr. And that what is pleasing to the gods because they love it, is pleasing to them by reason of this same love; and that they do not love it because it is pleasing to them.

Euth. True.

Socr. Then, my dear Euthyphro, holiness, and what is pleasing to the gods, are different things. If the gods had loved holiness because it is holy, they would also have loved what is pleasing to them because it is pleasing to them; but if what is pleasing to them had been pleasing to them because they loved it, then holiness too would have been holiness, because they loved it. But now you see that they are opposite things, and wholly different from each other. For the one is of a sort to be loved because it is loved: while the other is loved, because it is of a sort to be loved. My question, Euthyphro, was, What is holiness? But it turns out that you have not explained to me the essence of holiness; you have been content to mention an attribute which belongs to it, namely, that all the gods love it. You have not yet told me what is its essence. Do not, if you please, keep from me what holiness is; begin again and tell me that. Never mind whether the gods love it, or whether it has other attributes: we shall not differ on that point. Do your best to make it clear to me what is holiness and what is unholiness.

X.2   A Modified Divine Command Theory of Ethical Wrongness

ROBERT M. ADAMS

Robert Adams (1937–   ) was, until his retirement, professor of philosophy at Yale University, and he is a leading figure in the diverse fields of metaphysics, ethics, philosophy of religion, and history of modern philosophy. In this essay, Adams seeks to articulate a modified version of the divine command theory—a view according to which we would not be obligated to behave in a cruel way if, unthinkably, God were to command cruelty. At the heart of his view is the idea that moral language would simply break down in the case where God commands cruelty or other acts that we regard as morally evil.

I

It is widely held that all those theories are indefensible which attempt to explain in terms of the will or commands of God what it is for an act to be ethically right or wrong. In this paper I shall state such a theory, which I believe to be defensible; and I shall try to defend it against what seem to me to be the most important and interesting objections to it. I call my theory a *modified* divine command theory because in it I renounce certain claims that are commonly made in divine command analyses of ethical terms. (I should add that it is *my* theory only in that I shall state it, and that I believe it is defensible—not that I am sure it is correct.) I present it as a theory of ethical *wrongness* partly for convenience. It could also be presented as a theory of the nature of ethical obligatoriness or of ethical permittedness. Indeed, I will have occasion to make some remarks about the concept of ethical permittedness. But as we shall see (in section IV) I am not prepared to claim that the theory can be extended to all ethical terms; and it is therefore important that it not be presented as a theory about ethical terms in general.

It will be helpful to begin with the statement of a simple, *unmodified* divine command theory

of ethical wrongness. This is the theory that ethical wrongness *consists in* being contrary to God's commands, or that the word 'wrong' in ethical contexts *means* 'contrary to God's commands.' It implies that the following two statement forms are logically equivalent.

(1) It is wrong (for A) to do X.
(2) It is contrary to God's commands (for A)
      to do X.

Of course that is not all that the theory implies. It also implies that (2) is conceptually prior to (1), so that the meaning of (1) is to be explained in terms of (2), and not the other way around. It might prove fairly difficult to state or explain in what that conceptual priority consists, but I shall not go into that here. I do not wish ultimately to defend the theory in its unmodified form, and I think I have stated it fully enough for my present purposes.

I have stated it as a theory about the meaning of the word 'wrong' in ethical contexts. The most obvious objection to the theory is that the word 'wrong' is used in ethical contexts by many people who cannot mean by it what the theory says they must mean, since they do not believe that there exists a God. This objection seems to me sufficient to refute the theory if it is presented as an analysis of

From *Religion and Morality: A Collection of Essays,* Gene H. Outka, ed., Anchor Press, 1973. Reprinted with permission.

I am indebted to many who have read, or heard, and discussed versions of this essay, and particularly to Richard Brandt, William Frankena, John Reeder, and Stephen Stich, for helpful criticisms.

what *everybody* means by 'wrong' in ethical contexts. The theory cannot reasonably be offered except as a theory about what the word 'wrong' means as used by *some but not all* people in ethical contexts. Let us say that the theory offers an analysis of the meaning of 'wrong' in Judeo-Christian religious ethical discourse. This restriction of scope will apply to my modified divine command theory too. This restriction obviously gives rise to a possible objection. Isn't it more plausible to suppose that Judeo-Christian believers use 'wrong' with the same meaning as other people do? This problem will be discussed in section VI.

In section II, I will discuss what seems to me the most important objection to the unmodified divine command theory, and suggest how the theory can be modified to meet it. Section III will be devoted to a brief but fairly comprehensive account of the use of 'wrong' in Judeo-Christian ethical discourse, from the point of view of the modified divine command theory. The theory will be further elaborated in dealing with objections in sections IV to VI. In a seventh and final section, I will note some problems arising from unresolved issues in the general theory of analysis and meaning, and briefly discuss their bearing on the modified divine command theory.

II

The following seems to me to be the gravest objection to the divine command theory of ethical wrongness, in the form in which I have stated it. Suppose God should command me to make it my chief end in life to inflict suffering on other human beings, for no other reason than that he commanded it. (For convenience I shall abbreviate this hypothesis to 'Suppose God should command cruelty for its own sake.') Will it seriously be claimed that in that case it would be wrong for me not to practice cruelty for its own sake? I see three possible answers to this question.

(1) It might be claimed that it is logically impossible for God to command cruelty for its own sake. In that case, of course, we need not worry about whether it would be wrong to disobey if he did command it. It is senseless to agonize about what one should do in a logically impossible situation. This solution to the problem seems

unlikely to be available to the divine command theorist, however. For why would he hold that it is logically impossible for God to command cruelty for its own sake? Some theologians (for instance, Thomas Aquinas) have believed (a) that what is right and wrong is independent of God's will, *and* (b) that God always does right by the necessity of his nature. Such theologians, if they believe that it would be wrong for God to command cruelty for its own sake, have reason to believe that it is logically impossible for him to do so. But the divine command theorist, who does not agree that what is right and wrong is independent of God's will, does not seem to have such a reason to deny that it is logically possible for God to command cruelty for its own sake.

(2) Let us assume that it is logically possible for God to command cruelty for its own sake. In that case the divine command theory seems to imply that it would be wrong not to practice cruelty for its own sake. There have been at least a few adherents of divine command ethics who have been prepared to accept this consequence. William Ockham held that those acts which we call "theft," "adultery," and "hatred of God" would be meritorious if God had commanded them.[1] He would surely have said the same about what I have been calling the practice of "cruelty for its own sake."

This position is one which I suspect most of us are likely to find somewhat shocking, even repulsive. We should therefore be particularly careful not to misunderstand it. We need not imagine that Ockham disciplined himself to be ready to practice cruelty for its own sake if God should command it. It was doubtless an article of faith for him that God is unalterably opposed to any such practice. The mere logical possibility that theft, adultery, and cruelty might have been commanded by God (and therefore meritorious) doubtless did not represent in Ockham's view any real possibility.

(3) Nonetheless, the view that if God commanded cruelty for its own sake it would be wrong not to practice it seems unacceptable to me; and I think many, perhaps most, other Jewish and Christian believers would find it unacceptable too. I must make clear the sense in which I find it unsatisfactory. It is not that I find an internal inconsistency in it. And I would not deny that it may reflect, accurately enough, the way in which

some believers use the word 'wrong.' I might as well frankly avow that I am looking for a divine command theory which at least might possibly be a correct account of how *I* use the word 'wrong.' I do not use the word 'wrong' in such a way that I would say that it would be wrong not to practice cruelty if God commanded it, and I am sure that many other believers agree with me on this point.

But now have I not rejected the divine command theory? I have assumed that it would be logically possible for God to command cruelty for its own sake. And I have rejected the view that if God commanded cruelty for its own sake, it would be wrong not to obey. It seems to follow that I am committed to the view that in certain logically possible circumstances it would not be wrong to disobey God. This position seems to be inconsistent with the theory that 'wrong' means 'contrary to God's commands.'

I want to argue, however, that it is still open to me to accept a modified form of the divine command theory of ethical wrongness. According to the modified divine command theory, when I say, 'It is wrong to do X,' (at least part of) what I *mean* is that it is contrary to God's commands to do X. 'It is wrong to do X' *implies* 'It is contrary to God's commands to do X.' But 'It is contrary to God's commands to do X' implies 'It is wrong to do X' only if certain conditions are assumed—namely, only if it is assumed that God has the character which I believe him to have, of loving his human creatures. If God were really to command us to make cruelty our goal, then he would not have that character of loving us, and I would not say it would be wrong to disobey him.

But do I say that it would be wrong to obey him in such a case? This is the point at which I am in danger of abandoning the divine command theory completely. I do abandon it completely if I say both of the following things.

(A) It would be wrong to obey God if he commanded cruelty for its own sake.
(B) In (A), 'wrong' is used in what is for me its normal ethical sense.

If I assert both (A) and (B), it is clear that I cannot consistently maintain that 'wrong' in its normal ethical sense for me means or implies 'contrary to God's commands.'

But from the fact that I deny that it would be wrong to disobey God if He commanded cruelty for its own sake, it does not follow that I must accept (A) and (B). Of course someone might claim that obedience and disobedience would both be ethically permitted in such a case; but that is not the view that I am suggesting. If I adopt the modified divine command theory as an analysis of my present concept of ethical wrongness (and if I adopt a similar analysis of my concept of ethical permittedness), I will not hold either that it would be wrong to disobey, or that it would be ethically permitted to disobey, or that it would be wrong to obey, or that it would be ethically permitted to obey, if God commanded cruelty for its own sake. For I will say that my concept of ethical wrongness (and my concept of ethical permittedness) would "break down" if I really believed that God commanded cruelty for its own sake. Or to put the matter somewhat more prosaically, I will say that my concepts of ethical wrongness and permittedness could not serve the functions they now serve, because using those concepts I could not call any action ethically wrong or ethically permitted, if I believed that God's will was so unloving. This position can be explained or developed in either of two ways, each of which has its advantages.

I could say that by 'X is ethically wrong' I mean 'X is contrary to the commands of a *loving* God' (i.e., 'There is a *loving* God and X is contrary to his commands') and by 'X is ethically permitted' I mean 'X is in accord with the commands of a *loving* God' (i.e., 'There is a *loving* God and X is not contrary to his commands'). On this analysis we can reason as follows. If there is only one God and he commands cruelty for its own sake, then presumably there is not a *loving* God. If there is not a loving God then neither 'X is ethically wrong' nor 'X is ethically permitted' is true of any X. Using my present concepts of ethical wrongness and permittedness, therefore, I could not (consistently) call any action ethically wrong or permitted if I believed that God commanded cruelty for its own sake. This way of developing the modified divine command theory is the simpler and neater of the two, and that might reasonably lead one to choose it for the construction of a theological ethical theory. On the other hand, I think it is also simpler and neater than ordinary religious ethical discourse, in which (for example) it may be felt that the statement that a certain act is wrong is *about* the will or commands of God in a way in which it is not about his love.

In this essay I shall prefer a second, rather similar, but somewhat untidier, understanding of the modified divine command theory, because I think it may lead us into some insights about the complexities of actual religious ethical discourse. According to this second version of the theory, the statement that something is ethically wrong (or permitted) says something about the will or commands of God, but not about his love. Every such statement, however, *presupposes* that certain conditions for the applicability of the believer's concepts of ethical right and wrong are satisfied. Among these conditions is that God does not command cruelty for its own sake—or, more generally, that God loves his human creatures. It need not be assumed that God's love is the only such condition.

The modified divine command theorist can say that the possibility of God commanding cruelty for its own sake is not provided for in the Judeo-Christian religious ethical system as he understands it. The possibility is not provided for, in the sense that the concepts of right and wrong have not been developed in such a way that actions could be correctly said to be right or wrong if God were believed to command cruelty for its own sake. The modified divine command theorist agrees that it is logically possible[2] that God should command cruelty for its own sake; but he holds that it is unthinkable that God should do so. To have *faith* in God is not just to believe that he exists, but also to trust his love for mankind. The believer's concepts of ethical wrongness and permittedness are developed within the framework of his (or the religious community's) religious life, and therefore within the framework of the assumption that God loves us. The concept of the will or commands of God has a certain function in the believer's life, and the use of the words 'right' (in the sense of 'ethically permitted') and 'wrong' is tied to that function of that concept. But one of the reasons why the concept of the will of God can function as it does is that the love which God is believed to have toward men

arouses in the believer certain attitudes of love toward God and devotion to his will. If the believer thinks about the unthinkable but logically possible situation in which God commands cruelty for its own sake, he finds that in relation to that kind of command of God he cannot take up the same attitude, and that the concept of the will or commands of God could not then have the same function in his life. For this reason he will not say that it would be wrong to disobey God, or right to obey him, in that situation. At the same time he will not say that it would be wrong to obey God in that situation, because he is accustomed to use the word 'wrong' to say that something is contrary to the will of God, and it does not seem to him to be the right word to use to express his own personal revulsion toward an act against which there would be no divine authority. Similarly, he will not say that it would be "right" in the sense of 'ethically permitted,' to disobey God's command of cruelty; for that does not seem to him to be the right way to express his own personal attitude toward an act which would not be in accord with a divine authority. In this way the believer's concepts of ethical rightness and wrongness would break down in the situation in which he believed that God commanded cruelty for its own sake; that is, they would not function as they now do, because he would not be prepared to use them to say that any action was right or wrong.

III

It is clear that according to this modified divine command theory, the meaning of the word 'wrong' in Judeo-Christian ethical discourse must be understood in terms of a complex of relations which believers' use of the word has, not only to their beliefs about God's commands, but also to their attitudes toward certain types of action. I think it will help us to understand the theory better if we can give a brief but fairly comprehensive description of the most important features of the Judeo-Christian ethical use of 'wrong,' from the point of view of the modified divine command theory. That is what I shall try to do in this section.

(1) 'Wrong' and 'contrary to God's commands' at least contextually imply each other in Judeo-Christian ethical discourse. 'It is wrong to

do X' will be assented to by the sincere Jewish or Christian believer if and only if he assents to 'It is contrary to God's commands to do X.' This is a fact sufficiently well known that the known believer who says the one commits himself publicly to the other.

Indeed 'wrong' and such expressions as 'against the will of God' seem to be used interchangeably in religious ethical discourse. If a believer asks his pastor, "Do you think it's always against the will of God to use contraceptives?" and the pastor replies, "I don't see anything wrong with the use of contraceptives in many cases," the pastor has answered the same question the inquirer asked.

(2) In ethical contexts, the statement that a certain action is wrong normally expresses certain volitional and emotional attitudes toward that action. In particular it normally expresses an intention, or at least an inclination, not to perform the action, and/or dispositions to feel guilty if one has performed it, to discourage others from performing it, and to react with anger, sorrow, or diminished respect toward others if they have performed it. I think this is true of Judeo-Christian ethical discourse as well as of other ethical discourse.

The interchangeability of 'wrong' and 'against' the will of God' applies in full force here. It seems to make no difference to the expressive function of an ethical statement in a Judeo-Christian context which of these expressions is used. So far as I can see, the feelings and dispositions normally expressed by 'It is wrong to commit suicide' in a Judeo-Christian context are exactly the same as those normally expressed by 'It is against God's will to commit suicide,' or by 'Suicide is a violation of the commandments of God.'

I am speaking of attitudes *normally* expressed by statements that it is wrong to do a certain thing, or that it would be against God's will or commands to do that thing. I am not claiming that such attitudes are *always* expressed by statements of those sorts. Neither am I now suggesting any analysis of the *meaning* of the statements in terms of the attitudes they normally express. The relation between the meaning of the statements and the attitudes expressed is a matter about which I shall have somewhat more to say, later

in this section and in section VI. At this point I am simply observing that in fact statements of the forms 'It is wrong to do X,' 'It is against God's will to do X,' 'X is a violation of the commandments of God,' normally do express certain attitudes, and that in Judeo-Christian ethical discourse they all typically express the same attitudes.

Of course these attitudes can be specified only within certain very wide limits of normality. The experience of guilt, for instance, or the feelings that one has about conduct of others of which one disapproves, vary greatly from one individual to another, and in the same individual from one occasion to another.

(3) In a Judeo-Christian context, moreover, the attitudes expressed by a statement that something is wrong are normally quite strongly affected and colored by specifically religious feelings and interests. They are apt to be motivated in various degrees by, and mixed in various proportions with, love, devotion, and loyalty toward God, and/or fear of God. Ethical wrongdoing is seen and experienced as *sin,* as rupture of personal or communal relationship with God. The normal feelings and experience of guilt for Judeo-Christian believers surely cannot be separated from beliefs, and ritual and devotional practices, having to do with God's judgment and forgiveness.

In all sin there is offense against a person (God), even when there is no offense against any other human person—for instance, if I have a vice which harms me but does not importantly harm any other human being. Therefore in the Judeo-Christian tradition reactions which are appropriate when one has offended another person are felt to be appropriate reactions to any ethical fault, regardless of whether another human being has been offended. I think this affects rather importantly the emotional connections of the word 'wrong' in Judeo-Christian discourse.

(4) When a Judeo-Christian believer is trying to decide, in an ethical way, whether it would be wrong for him to do a certain thing, he typically thinks of himself as trying to determine whether it would be against God's will for him to do it. His deliberations may turn on the interpretation of certain religiously authoritative texts. They may be partly carried out in the form of prayer. It is quite possible, however, that his deliberations

will take forms more familiar to the nonbeliever. Possibly his theology will encourage him to give some weight to his own intuitions and feelings about the matter, and those of other people. Such encouragement might be provided, for instance, by a doctrine of the leading of the Holy Spirit. Probably the believer will accept certain very general ethical principles as expressing commandments of God, and most of these may be principles which many nonbelievers would also accept (for instance, that it is always, or with very few exceptions, wrong to kill another human being). The believer's deliberation might consist entirely of reasoning from such general principles. But he would still regard it as an attempt to discover God's will on the matter.

(5) Typically, the Judeo-Christian believer is a nonnaturalist objectivist about ethical wrongness. When he says that something is (ethically) wrong, he means to be stating what he believes to be a fact of a certain sort—what I shall call a "nonnatural objective fact." Such a fact is objective in the sense that whether it obtains or not does not depend on whether any human being thinks it does. It is harder to give a satisfactory explanation of what I mean by 'nonnatural' here. Let us say that a nonnatural fact is one which does not consist simply in any fact or complex of facts which can be stated entirely in the languages of physics, chemistry, biology, and human psychology. That way of putting it obviously raises questions which it leaves unanswered, but I hope it may be clear enough for present purposes.

That ethical facts are objective and nonnatural has been believed by many people, including some famous philosophers—for instance, Plato and G. E. Moore. The term 'nonnaturalism' is sometimes used rather narrowly, to refer to a position held by Moore, and positions closely resembling it. Clearly, I am using 'nonnaturalist' in a broader sense here.

Given that the facts of wrongness asserted in Judeo-Christian ethics are nonnatural in the sense explained above, and that they accordingly do not consist entirely in facts of physics, chemistry, biology, and human psychology, the question arises, in what they do consist. According to the divine command theory (even the modified divine command theory), insofar as they are nonnatural and objective, they consist in facts about the will or commands of God. I think this is really the central point in a divine command theory of ethical wrongness. This is the point at which the divine command theory is distinguished from alternative theological theories of ethical wrongness, such as the theory that facts of ethical rightness and wrongness are objective, nonnatural facts about ideas or essences subsisting eternally in God's understanding, not subject to his will but guiding it.

The divine command account of the nonnatural fact-stating function of Judeo-Christian ethical discourse has at least one advantage over its competitors. It is clear, I think, that in stating that X is wrong a believer normally commits himself to the view that X is contrary to the will or commands of God. And the fact (if it is a fact) that X is contrary to the will or commands of God is surely a nonnatural objective fact. But it is not nearly so clear that in saying that X is wrong, the believer normally commits himself to belief in any *other* nonnatural objective fact. (The preceding sentence presupposes the rejection of the Moorean view that the fact that X is wrong[3] is an objective nonnatural fact which cannot and should not be analyzed in terms of other facts, natural or nonnatural.)

(6) The modified divine command theorist cannot consistently claim that 'wrong' and 'contrary to God's commands' have exactly the same meaning for him. For he admits that there is a logically possible situation which he would describe by saying, 'God commands cruelty for its own sake,' but not by saying, 'It would be wrong not to practice cruelty for its own sake.' If there were not at least some little difference between the meanings with which he actually, normally uses the expressions 'wrong' and 'contrary to God's commands,' there would be no reason for them to differ in their applicability or inapplicability to the far-out unthinkable case. We may now be in a position to improve somewhat our understanding of what the modified divine command theorist can suppose that difference in meaning to be, and of why he supposes that the believer is unwilling to say that disobedience to a divine command of cruelty for its own sake would be wrong.

We have seen that the expressions 'It is wrong' and 'It is contrary to God's commands' or 'It is against the will of God' have virtually the same uses in religious ethical discourse, and the same functions in the religious ethical life. No doubt they differ slightly in the situations in which they are most likely to be used and the emotional overtones they are most apt to carry. But in all situations experienced or expected by the believer as a believer they at least contextually imply each other, and normally express the same or extremely similar emotional and volitional attitudes.

There is also a difference in meaning, however: a difference which is normally of no practical importance. All three of the following are aspects of the normal use of 'It is wrong' in the life and conversation of believers. (a) It is used to state what are believed to be facts about the will or commands of God. (b) It is used in formulating decisions and arguments about what to do (i.e., not just in deciding what one *ought* to do, but in deciding *what to do*). (c) It expresses certain emotional and volitional attitudes toward the action under discussion. 'It is wrong' is commonly used to do all three of those things at once.

The same is true of 'It is contrary to God's commands' and 'It is against the will of God.' They are commonly used by believers to do the same three things, and to do them at once. But because of their grammatical form and their formal relationships with other straightforwardly descriptive expressions about God, they are taken to be, first and last, descriptive expressions about God and his relation to whatever actions are under discussion. They can therefore be used to state what are supposed to be facts about God, even when one's emotional and decision-making attitude toward those supposed facts is quite contrary to the attitudes normally expressed by the words 'against the will of God.'

In the case of 'It is wrong,' however, it is not clear that one of its functions, or one of the aspects of its normal use, is to be preferred in case of conflict with the others. I am not willing to say, 'It would be wrong not to do X,' when both my own attitude and the attitude of most other people toward the doing of X under the indicated circumstances is one of unqualified revulsion. On the other hand, neither am I willing to say, 'It would be wrong to do X,' when I would merely be expressing my own personal revulsion (and perhaps

that of other people as well) but nothing that I could regard as clothed in the majesty of a divine authority. The believer's concept of ethical wrongness therefore breaks down if one tries to apply it to the unthinkable case in which God commands cruelty for its own sake.

None of this seems to me inconsistent with the claim that part of what the believer normally means in saying 'X is wrong' is that X is contrary to God's will or commands.

IV

The modified divine command theory clearly conceives of believers as valuing some things independently of their relation to God's commands. If the believer will not say that it would be wrong not to practice cruelty for its own sake if God commanded it, that is because he values kindness, and has a revulsion for cruelty, in a way that is at least to some extent independent of his belief that God commands kindness and forbids cruelty. This point may be made the basis of both philosophical and theological objections to the modified divine command theory, but I think the objections can be answered.

The philosophical objection is, roughly, that if there are some things I value independently of their relation to God's commands, then my value concepts cannot rightly be analyzed in terms of God's commands. According to the modified divine command theory, the acceptability of divine command ethics depends in part on the believer's independent positive valuation of the sorts of things that God is believed to command. But then, the philosophical critic objects, the believer must have a prior, nontheological conception of ethical right and wrong, in terms of which he judges God's commandments to be acceptable—and to admit that the believer has a prior, nontheological conception of ethical right and wrong is to abandon the divine command theory.

The weakness of this philosophical objection is that it fails to note the distinctions that can be drawn among various value concepts. From the fact that the believer values some things independently of his beliefs about God's commands, the objector concludes, illegitimately, that the believer must have a conception of ethical right and wrong that is independent of his beliefs about God's commands. This inference is illegitimate because there can be valuations which do not imply or presuppose a judgment of ethical right or wrong. For instance, I may simply like something, or want something, or feel a revulsion at something.

What the modified divine command theorist will hold, then, is that the believer values some things independently of their relation to God's commands, but that these valuations are not judgments of ethical right and wrong and do not of themselves imply judgments of ethical right and wrong. He will maintain, on the other hand, that such independent valuations are involved in, or even necessary for, judgments of ethical right and wrong which also involve beliefs about God's will or commands. The adherent of a divine command ethics will normally be able to give reasons for his adherence. Such reasons might include: "Because I am grateful to God for his love"; "Because I find it the most satisfying form of ethical life"; "Because there's got to be an objective moral law if life isn't to fall to pieces, and I can't understand what it would be if not the will of God."[4] As we have already noted, the modified divine command theorist also has reasons why he would not accept a divine command ethics in certain logically possible situations which he believes not to be actual. All of these reasons seem to me to involve valuations that are independent of divine command ethics. The person who has such reasons wants certain things—happiness, certain satisfactions—for himself and others; he hates cruelty and loves kindness; he has perhaps a certain unique and "numinous" awe of God. And these are not attitudes which he has simply because of his beliefs about God's commands.[5] They are not attitudes, however, which presuppose judgments of moral right and wrong.

It is sometimes objected to divine command theories of moral obligation, or of ethical rightness and wrongness, that one must have some reason for obeying God's commands or for adopting a divine command ethics, and that therefore a nontheological concept of moral obligation or of ethical rightness and wrongness must be presupposed, in order that one may judge that one ought to obey God's commands.[6] This objection is groundless. For one can certainly have reasons for doing something which do not involve believing one morally ought to do it or believing it would be ethically wrong not to do it.

I grant that in giving reasons for his attitudes toward God's commands the believer will probably use or presuppose concepts which, in the context, it is reasonable to count as nontheological value concepts (e.g., concepts of satisfactoriness and repulsiveness). Perhaps some of them might count as moral concepts. But all that the defender of a divine command theory of ethical wrongness has to maintain is that the concept of ethical wrongness which occurs in the ethical thought and discourse of believers is not one of the concepts which are used or presupposed in this way. Divine command theorists, including the modified divine command theorist, need not maintain that *all* value concepts, or even all moral concepts, must be understood in terms of God's commands.

In fact some well-known philosophers have held forms of divine command theory which quite explicitly presuppose some nontheological value concepts. Locke, for instance, says in his *Essay.*

> Good and evil . . . are nothing but pleasure or pain, or that which occasions or procures pleasure or pain to us. *Moral good and evil,* then, is only the conformity or disagreement of our voluntary actions to some law, whereby good or evil is drawn on us from the will and power of the law-maker . . . (*Essay,* II, xxviii, 5)[7]

Locke goes on to distinguish three laws, or types of law, by reference to which actions are commonly judged as to moral good and evil: "(1) The *divine* law. (2) The *civil* law. (3) The law of *opinion* or *reputation,* if I may so call it" (*Essay,* II, xxviii, 7). Of these three Locke says that the third is "the common *measure of virtue and vice*" (*Essay,* II, xxviii, 11). In Locke's opinion the terms 'virtue' and 'vice' are particularly closely attached to the praise and blame of society. But the terms 'duty' and 'sin' are connected with the commandments of God. About the divine law Locke says,

> This is the only true touchstone of *moral rectitude;* and by comparing them to this law, it is that men judge of the most considerable *moral good* or *evil* of their actions: that is, whether, as *duties or sins,* they are like to procure them happiness or misery from the hands of the ALMIGHTY (*Essay,* II, xxviii, 8).

The structure of Locke's analysis is clear enough. By 'good' and 'evil' we *mean* (nontheologically enough) pleasurable and painful. By 'morally good' and 'morally evil' we *mean* that the actions so described agree or disagree with some law under which the agent stands to be rewarded or punished. By 'duty' and 'sin,' which denote the most important sort of moral good and evil, we *mean* (theologically now) actions which are apt to cause the agent good or evil (in the nontheological sense) because they agree or disagree with the law of God. I take it that the divine command theory advocated by Peter Geach,[8] and hinted at by G.E.M. Anscombe,[9] is similar in structure, though not in all details, to Locke's.

The modified divine command theory that I have in mind does not rely as heavily as Locke's theory does on God's power to reward and punish, nor do I wish to assume Locke's analysis of 'good' and 'evil.' The point I want to make by discussing Locke here is just that there are many different value concepts and it is clearly possible to give one or more of them a theological analysis while giving others a nontheological analysis. And I do assume that the modified divine command theorist will give a nontheological analysis of some value concepts although he gives a theological analysis of the concept of ethical wrongness. For instance, he may give a nontheological analysis, perhaps a naturalistic one or a non-cognitivist one, of the meaning of 'satisfactory' and 'repulsive,' as he uses them in some contexts. He may even regard as *moral* concepts some value concepts of which he gives a nontheological analysis.

For it is not essential to a divine command theory of ethical wrongness to maintain that all valuing, or all value concepts, or even all moral concepts, depend on beliefs about God's commands. What is essential to such a theory is to maintain that when a believer says something is (ethically) *wrong*, at least part of what he means is that the action in question is contrary to God's will or commands. Another way of putting the matter is this. What depends on beliefs about God and his will is not all of the religious person's value concepts, nor in general his ability to value things, but only his ability to appraise actions (and possible actions) in terms of their relation to a superhuman, nonnaturally objective, law.

Indeed, it is obvious that Judeo-Christian ethics presupposes concepts that have at least ethical overtones and that are not essentially theological but have their background in human social relations and political institutions—such as the concepts of promise, kindness, law, and command. What the specifically theological doctrines introduce into Judeo-Christian ethics, according to the divine command theory, is the belief in a law that is superior to all human laws.

This version of the divine command theory may seem *theologically* objectionable to some believers. One of the reasons, surely, why divine command theories of ethics have appealed to some theologians is that such theories seem especially congruous with the religious demand that God be the object of our highest allegiance. If our supreme commitment in life is to doing what is right just because it is right, and if what is right is right just because God wills or commands it, then surely our highest allegiance is to God. But the modified divine command theory seems not to have this advantage. For the modified divine command theorist is forced to admit, as we have seen, that he has reason for his adherence to a divine command ethics, and that his having these reasons implies that there are some things which he values independently of his beliefs about God's commands. It is therefore not correct to say of him that he is committed to doing the will of God *just* because it is the will of God; he is committed to doing it partly because of other things which he values independently. Indeed it appears that there are certain logically possible situations in which his present attitudes would not commit him to obey God's commands (for instance, if God commanded cruelty for its own sake). This may even suggest that he values some things, not just independently of God's commands, but more than God's commands.

We have here a real problem in religious ethical motivation. The Judeo-Christian believer is supposed to make God the supreme focus of his loyalties; that is clear. One possible interpretation of this fact is the following. Obedience to whatever God may command is (or at least ought to be) the one thing that the believer values for its own sake and more than anything and everything else. Anything else that he values, he values (or ought to) only to a lesser degree and as a means to obedience to God. This conception of religious ethical motivation is obviously favorable to an *un*modified divine command theory of ethical wrongness.

But I think it is not a realistic conception. Loyalty to God, for instance, is very often explained, by believers themselves, as motivated by gratitude for benefits conferred. And I think it is clear in most cases that the gratitude presupposes that the benefits are valued, at least to some extent, independently of loyalty to God. Similarly, I do not think that most devout Judeo-Christian believers would say that it would be wrong to disobey God if he commanded cruelty for its own sake. And if I am right about that I think it shows that their positive valuation of (emotional/volitional pro-attitude toward) doing *whatever* God may command is not clearly greater than their independent negative valuation of cruelty.

In analyzing ethical motivation in general, as well as Judeo-Christian ethical motivation in particular, it is probably a mistake to suppose that there is (or can be expected to be) one only thing that is valued supremely and for its own sake, with nothing else being valued independently of it. The motivation for a person's ethical orientation in life is normally much more complex than that, and involves a plurality of emotional and volitional attitudes of different sorts which are at least partly independent of each other. At any rate, I think the modified divine command theorist is bound to say that that is true of his ethical motivation.

In what sense, then, can the modified divine command theorist maintain that God is the supreme focus of his loyalties? I suggest the following interpretation of the single-hearted loyalty to God which is demanded in Judeo-Christian religion. In this interpretation the crucial idea is *not* that some one thing is valued for its own sake and more than anything else, and nothing else valued independently of it. It is freely admitted that the religious person will have a plurality of motives for his ethical position, and that these will be at least partly independent of each other. It is admitted further that a desire to obey the commands of God (*whatever* they may be) may not be the strongest of these motives. What will be claimed is that certain beliefs about God enable the believer to integrate or focus his motives in a loyalty to God and

his commands. Some of these beliefs are about what God commands or wills (contingently: that is, although he could logically have commanded or willed something else instead).

Some of the motives in question might be called egoistic; they include desires for satisfactions for oneself—which God is believed to have given or to be going to give. Other motives may be desires for satisfaction for other people—these may be called altruistic. Still other motives might not be desires for anyone's satisfaction, but might be valuations of certain kinds of action for their own sakes—these might be called idealistic. I do not think my argument depends heavily on this particular classification, but it seems plausible that all of these types, and perhaps others as well, might be distinguished among the motives for a religious person's ethical position. Obviously such motives might pull one in different directions, conflicting with one another. But in Judeo-Christian ethics beliefs about what God does in fact will (although he could have willed otherwise) are supposed to enable one to *fuse* these motives, so to speak, into one's devotion to God and his will, so that they all pull together. Doubtless the believer will still have some motives which conflict with his loyalty to God. But the religious ideal is that these should all be merely momentary desires and impulses, and kept under control. They ought not to be allowed to influence voluntary action. The deeper, more stable, and controlling desires, intentions, and psychic energies are supposed to be fused in devotion to God. As I interpret it, however, it need not be inconsistent with the Judeo-Christian ethical and religious ideal that this fusion of motives, this integration of moral energies, depends on belief in certain propositions which are taken to be contingent truths about God.

Lest it be thought that I am proposing unprecedented theological positions, or simply altering Judeo-Christian religious beliefs to suit my theories, I will call to my aid on this point a theologian known for his insistence on the sovereignty of God. Karl Barth seems to me to hold a divine command theory of ethics. But when he raises the question of why we should obey God, he rejects with scorn the suggestion that God's *power* provides the basis for his claim on us. "By deciding for God [man] has definitely decided not to be obedient to power as power."[10] God's claim on us is based rather on his grace. "God calls us and orders us and claims us by being gracious to us in Jesus Christ."[11] I do not mean to suggest that Barth would agree with everything I have said about motivation, or that he offers a lucid account of a divine command theory. But he does agree with the position I have proposed on this point, that the believer's loyalty is not to be construed as a loyalty to God *as* all-powerful, nor to God *whatever* he might conceivably have willed. It is a loyalty to God *as* having a certain attitude toward us, a certain will for us, which God was free not to have, but to which, in Barth's view, he has committed himself irrevocably in Jesus Christ. The believer's devotion is not to merely possible commands of God as such, but to God's actual (and gracious) will.

V

The ascription of moral qualities to God is commonly thought to cause problems for divine command theories of ethics. It is doubted that God, as an agent, can properly be called 'good' in the moral sense if he is not subject to a moral law that is not of his own making. For if he is morally good, mustn't he do what is right *because* it is right? And how can he do that, if what's right is right because he wills it? Or it may be charged that divine command theories trivialize the claim that God is good. If 'X is (morally) good' means roughly 'X does what God wills,' then 'God is (morally) good' means only that God does what he wills—which is surely much less than people are normally taken to mean when they say that God is (morally) good. In this section I will suggest an answer to these objections.

Surely no analysis of Judeo-Christian ethical discourse can be regarded as adequate which does not provide for a sense in which the believer can seriously assert that God is good. Indeed an adequate analysis should provide a plausible account of what believers do in fact mean when they say, 'God is good.' I believe that a divine command theory of ethical (rightness and) wrongness can include such an account. I will try to indicate its chief features.

(1) In saying 'God is good' one is normally expressing a favorable emotional attitude toward God. I shall not try to determine whether or not this is part of the meaning of 'God is good'; but it is normally, perhaps almost always, at least one of the things one is doing if one says that God is good. If we were to try to be more precise about the type of favorable emotional attitude normally expressed by 'God is good,' I suspect we would find that the attitude expressed is most commonly one of *gratitude*.

(2) This leads to a second point, which is that when God is called 'good' it is very often meant that he is *good to us,* or *good to* the speaker. 'Good' is sometimes virtually a synonym for 'kind.' And for the modified divine command theorist it is not a trivial truth that God is kind. In saying that God is good in the sense of 'kind,' one presupposes, of course, that there are some things which the beneficiaries of God's goodness value. We need not discuss here whether the beneficiaries must value them independently of their beliefs about God's will. For the modified divine command theorist does admit that there are some things which believers value independently of their beliefs about God's commands. Nothing that the modified divine command theorist says about the meaning of ('right' and) 'wrong' implies that it is a trivial truth that God bestows on his creatures things that they value.

(3) I would not suggest that the descriptive force of 'good' as applied to God is exhausted by the notion of kindness. 'God is good' must be taken in many contexts as ascribing to God, rather generally, qualities of character which the believing speaker regards as virtues in human beings. Among such qualities might be faithfulness, ethical consistency, a forgiving disposition, and, in general, various aspects of love, as well as kindness. Not that there is some definite list of qualities, the ascription of which to God is clearly implied by the claim that God is good. But saying that God is good normally commits one to the position that God has some important set of qualities which one regards as virtues in human beings.

(4) It will not be thought that God has *all* the qualities which are virtues in human beings. Some such qualities are logically inapplicable to a being such as God is supposed to be. For example,

aside from certain complications arising from the doctrine of the incarnation, it would be logically inappropriate to speak of God as controlling his sexual desires. (He doesn't have any.) And given some widely held conceptions of God and his relation to the world, it would hardly make sense to speak of him as *courageous*. For if he is impassible and has predetermined absolutely everything that happens, he has no risks to face and cannot endure (because he cannot suffer) pain or displeasure.[12]

Believers in God's goodness also typically think he lacks some human virtues which would *not* be logically inapplicable to a being like him. A virtuous man, for instance, does not intentionally cause the death of other human beings, except under exceptional circumstances. But God has intentionally brought it about that all men die. There are agonizing forms of the problem of evil; but I think that for most Judeo-Christian believers (especially those who believe in life after death), this is not one of them. They believe that God's making men mortal and his commanding them not to kill each other, fit together in a larger pattern of harmonious purposes. How then can one distinguish between human virtues which God must have if he is good and human virtues which God may lack and still be good? This is an interesting and important question, but I will not attempt here to formulate a precise or adequate criterion for making the distinction. I fear it would require a lengthy digression from the issues with which we are principally concerned.

(5) If we accept a divine command theory of ethical rightness and wrongness, I think we shall have to say that *dutifulness* is a human virtue which, like sexual chastity, is logically inapplicable to God. God cannot either do or fail to do his duty, since he does not have a duty—at least not in the most important sense in which human beings have a duty. For he is not subject to a moral law not of his own making. Dutifulness is one virtuous disposition which men can have that God cannot have. But there are other virtuous dispositions which God can have as well as men. Love, for instance. It hardly makes sense to say that God does what he does *because* it is right. But it does not follow that God cannot have any reason for doing what he does. It does not even follow that he

cannot have reasons of a type on which it would be morally virtuous for a man to act. For example, he might do something because he knew it would make his creatures happier.

(6) The modified divine command theorist must deny that in calling God 'good' one presupposes a standard of moral rightness and wrongness superior to the will of God, by reference to which it is determined whether God's character is virtuous or not. And I think he can consistently deny that. He can say that morally virtuous and vicious qualities of character are those which agree and conflict, respectively, with God's commands, and that it is their agreement or disagreement with God's commands that makes them virtuous or vicious. But the believer normally thinks he has at least a general idea of what qualities of character are in fact virtuous and vicious (approved and disapproved by God). Having such an idea, he can apply the word 'good' descriptively to God, meaning that (with some exceptions, as I have noted) God has the qualities which the believer regards as virtues, such as faithfulness and kindness.

I will sum up by contrasting what the believer can mean when he says, 'Moses is good,' with what he can mean when he says, 'God is good,' according to the modified divine command theory. When the believer says, 'Moses is good,' (a) he normally is expressing a favorable emotional attitude toward Moses (normally, though perhaps not always—sometimes a person's moral goodness displeases us). (b) He normally implies that Moses possesses a large proportion of those qualities of character which are recognized in the religious-ethical community as virtues, and few if any of those which are regarded as vices. (c) He normally implies that the qualities of Moses' character on the basis of which he describes Moses as good are qualities approved by God.

When the believer says, 'God is good,' (a) he normally is expressing a favorable emotional attitude toward God, and I think exceptions on this point would be rarer than in the case of statements that a man is good. (b) He normally is ascribing to God certain qualities of character. He may mean primarily that God is kind or benevolent, that he is *good* to human beings or certain ones of them. Or he may mean that

God possesses (with some exceptions) those qualities of character which are regarded as virtues in the religious-ethical community. (c) Whereas in saying, 'Moses is good,' the believer was stating or implying that the qualities of character which he was ascribing to Moses conform to a standard of ethical rightness which is independent of the will of Moses, he is not stating or implying that the qualities of character which he ascribes to God conform to a standard of ethical rightness which is independent of the will of God.

VI

As I noted at the outset, the divine command theory of ethical wrongness, even in its modified form, has the consequence that believers and nonbelievers use the word 'wrong' with different meanings in ethical contexts, since it will hardly be thought that nonbelievers mean by 'wrong' what the theory says believers mean by it. This consequence gives rise to an objection. For the phenomena of common moral discourse between believers and nonbelievers suggest that they mean the same thing by 'wrong' in ethical contexts. In the present section I shall try to explain how the modified divine command theorist can account for the facts of common ethical discourse.

I will first indicate what I think the troublesome facts are. Judeo-Christian believers enter into ethical discussions with people whose religious or antireligious beliefs they do not know. It seems to be possible to conduct quite a lot of ethical discourse, with apparent understanding, without knowing one's partner's views on religious issues. Believers also discuss ethical questions with persons who are known to them to be nonbelievers. They agree with such persons, disagree with them, and try to persuade them, about what acts are morally wrong. (Or at least it is normally *said,* by the participants and others, that they agree and disagree about such issues.) Believers ascribe, to people who are known not to believe in God, beliefs that certain acts are morally wrong. Yet surely believers do not suppose that nonbelievers, in calling acts wrong, mean that they are contrary to the will or commandments of God. Under

these circumstances how can the believer really mean 'contrary to the will or commandments of God' when he says 'wrong'? If he agrees and disagrees with nonbelievers about what is wrong, if he ascribes to them beliefs that certain acts are wrong, must he not be using 'wrong' in a nontheological sense?

What I shall argue is that in some ordinary (and I fear imprecise) sense of 'mean,' what believers and nonbelievers mean by 'wrong' in ethical contexts may well be partly the same and partly different. There are agreements between believers and nonbelievers which make common moral discourse between them possible. But these agreements do not show that the two groups mean exactly the same thing by 'wrong.' They do not show that 'contrary to God's will or commands' is not part of what believers mean by 'wrong.'

Let us consider first the agreements which make possible common moral discourse between believers and nonbelievers.

(1) One important agreement, which is so obvious as to be easily overlooked, is that they use many of the same ethical terms—'wrong,' 'right,' 'ought,' 'duty,' and others. And they may utter many of the same ethical sentences, such as 'Racial discrimination is morally wrong.' In determining what people believe we rely very heavily on what they say (when they seem to be speaking sincerely)—and that means, in large part, on the words that they use and the sentences they utter. If I know that somebody says, with apparent sincerity, 'Racial discrimination is morally wrong,' I will normally ascribe to him the belief that racial discrimination is morally wrong, even if I also know that he does not mean *exactly* the same thing as I do by 'racial discrimination' or 'morally wrong.' Of course if I know he means something *completely* different, I would not ascribe the belief to him without explicit qualification.

I would not claim that believers and nonbelievers use *all* the same ethical terms. 'Sin,' 'law of God,' and 'Christian,' for instance, occur as ethical terms in the discourse of many believers, but would be much less likely to occur in the same way in nonbelievers' discourse.

(2) The shared ethical terms have the same basic grammatical status for believers as for

nonbelievers, and at least many of the same logical connections with other expressions. Everyone agrees, for instance, in treating 'wrong' as an adjective and 'Racial discrimination is morally wrong' as a declarative sentence. '(All) racial discrimination is morally wrong' would be treated by all parties as expressing an A-type (universal affirmative) proposition, from which consequences can be drawn by syllogistic reasoning or the predicate calculus. All agree that if X is morally wrong, then it isn't morally right and refraining from X is morally obligatory. Such grammatical and formal agreements are important to common moral discourse.

(3) There is a great deal of agreement, among believers and nonbelievers, as to what types of action they call 'wrong' in an ethical sense and I think that that agreement is one of the things that make common moral discourse possible.[13] It is certainly not complete agreement. Obviously there is a lot of ethical disagreement in the world. Much of it cuts right across religious lines, but not all of it does. There are things which are typically called 'wrong' by members of some religious groups, and not by others. Nonetheless there are types of action which everyone or almost everyone would call morally wrong, such as torturing someone to death because he accidentally broke a small window in your house. Moreover any two people (including any one believer and one nonbeliever) are likely to find some actions they both call wrong that not everyone does. I imagine that most ethical discussion takes place among people whose area of agreement in what they call wrong is relatively large.

There is probably much less agreement about the most basic issues in moral theory than there is about many ethical issues of less generality. There is much more unanimity in what people (sincerely) say in answer to such questions as 'Was what Hitler did to the Jews wrong'? or 'Is it normally wrong to disobey the laws of one's country'? than in what they (sincerely) say in answer to such questions as 'Is it always right to do the act which will have the best results'? or 'Is pleasure the only thing that is good for its own sake'? The issue between adherents and nonadherents of divine command ethics is typical of basic issues in ethical and metaethical theory in this respect.

(4) The emotional and volitional attitudes normally expressed by the statement that something is 'wrong' are similar in believers and nonbelievers. They are not exactly the same; the attitudes typically expressed by the believer's statement that something is 'wrong' are importantly related to his religious practice and beliefs about God, and this doubtless makes them different in some ways from the attitudes expressed by nonbelievers uttering the same sentence. But the attitudes are certainly similar, and that is important for the possibility of common moral discourse.

(5) Perhaps even more important is the related fact that the social functions of a statement that something is (morally) 'wrong' are similar for believers and nonbelievers. To say that something someone else is known to have done is 'wrong' is commonly to attack him. If you say that something you are known to have done is 'wrong,' you abandon certain types of defense. To say that a public policy is 'wrong' is normally to register oneself as opposed to it, and is sometimes a signal that one is willing to be supportive of common action to change it. These social functions of moral discourse are extremely important. It is perhaps not surprising that we are inclined to say that two people agree with each other when they both utter the same sentence and thereby indicate their readiness to take the same side in a conflict.

Let us sum up these observations about the conditions which make common moral discourse between believers and nonbelievers possible. (1) They use many of the same ethical terms, such as 'wrong.' (2) They treat those terms as having the same basic grammatical and logical status, and many of the same logical connections with other expressions. (3) They agree to a large extent about what types of action are to be called 'wrong.' To call an action 'wrong' is, among other things, to classify it with certain other actions, and there is considerable agreement between believers and nonbelievers as to what actions those are. (4) The emotional and volitional attitudes which believers and nonbelievers normally express in saying that something is 'wrong' are similar, and (5) saying that something is 'wrong' has much the same social functions for believers and nonbelievers.

So far as I can see, none of this is inconsistent with the modified divine command theory of ethical wrongness. According to that theory there are several things which are true of the believer's use of 'wrong' which cannot plausibly be supposed to be true of the nonbeliever's. In saying 'X is wrong,' the believer commits himself (subjectively, at least, and publicly if he is known to be a believer) to the claim that X is contrary to God's will or commandments. The believer will not say that anything would be wrong, under any possible circumstances, if it were not contrary to God's will or commandments. In many contexts he uses the term 'wrong' interchangeably with 'against the will of God' or 'against the commandments of God.' The heart of the modified divine command theory, I have suggested, is the claim that when the believer says, 'X is wrong,' one thing he means to be doing is stating a nonnatural objective fact about X, and the nonnatural objective fact he means to be stating is that X is contrary to the will or commandments of God. This claim may be true even though the uses of 'wrong' by believers and nonbelievers are similar in all five of the ways pointed out above.

Suppose these contentions of the modified divine command theory are correct. (I think they are very plausible as claims about the ethical discourse of at least some religious believers.) In that case believers and nonbelievers surely do not mean exactly the same thing by 'X is wrong' in ethical contexts. But neither is it plausible to suppose that they mean entirely different things, given the phenomena of common moral discourse. We must suppose, then, that their meaning is partly the same and partly different. 'Contrary to God's will or commands' must be taken as expressing only part of the meaning with which the believer uses 'wrong.' Some of the similarities between believers' and nonbelievers' use of 'wrong' must also be taken as expressing parts of the meaning with which the believer uses 'wrong.' This view of the matter agrees with the account of the modified divine command theory in section III, where I pointed out that the modified divine command theorist cannot mean exactly the same thing by 'wrong' that he means by 'contrary to God's commands.'

We have here a situation which commonly arises when some people hold, and others do not hold, a given theory about the nature of something which everyone talks about. The chemist, who believes that water is a compound of hydrogen and oxygen, and the man who knows nothing of chemistry, surely do not use the word 'water' in entirely different senses, but neither is it very plausible to suppose that they use it with exactly the same meaning. I am inclined to say that in some fairly ordinary sense of 'mean,' a phenomenalist, and a philosopher who holds some conflicting theory about what it is for a physical object to exist, do not mean exactly the same thing by 'There is a bottle of milk in the refrigerator.' But they certainly do not mean entirely different things, and they can agree that there is a bottle of milk in the refrigerator.

VII

These remarks bring us face to face with some important issues in the general theory of analysis and meaning. What are the criteria for determining whether two utterers of the same expression mean exactly the same thing by it, or something partly different, or something entirely different? What is the relation between philosophical analyses, and philosophical theories about the natures of things, on the one hand, and the meanings of terms in ordinary discourse on the other hand? I have permitted myself the liberty of speaking as if these issues did not exist. But their existence is notorious, and I certainly cannot resolve them in this essay. Indeed, I do not have resolutions to offer.

In view of these uncertainties in the theory of meaning, it is worth noting that much of what the modified divine command theorist wants to say can be said without making claims about the *meaning* of ethical terms. He wants to say, for instance, that believers' claims that certain acts are wrong normally express certain attitudes toward those acts, whether or not that is part of their meaning; that an act is wrong if and only if it is contrary to God's will or commands (assuming God loves us); that nonetheless, if God commanded cruelty for its own sake, neither obedience nor disobedience would be ethically wrong or ethically permitted; that if an act is contrary to God's will or commands that is a nonnatural objective fact about it; and that that is the only nonnatural objective fact which obtains if and only if the act is wrong. These are among the most important claims of the modified divine command theory—perhaps they include the very most important. But in the form in which I have just stated them, they are not claims about the *meaning* of ethical terms.

I do not mean to reject the claims about the meanings of terms in religious ethical discourse which I have included in the modified divine command theory. In the absence of general solutions to general problems in the theory of meaning, we may perhaps say what seems to us intuitively plausible in particular cases. That is presumably what the modified divine command theorist is doing when he claims that 'contrary to the will or commands of God' is part of the meaning of '(ethically) wrong' for many Judeo-Christian believers. And I think it is fair to say that if we have found unresolved problems about meaning in the modified divine command theory, they are problems much more about what we mean in general by 'meaning' than about what Judeo-Christian believers mean by 'wrong.'

NOTES

1. Guillelmus de Occam, *Super 4 libros sententiarum,* bk. II, qu. 19, O, in vol. IV of his *Opera plurima* (Lyon, 1494–6; réimpression en fac-similé, Farnborough, Hants., England: Gregg Press, 1962). I am not claiming that Ockham held a divine command theory of exactly the same sort that I have been discussing.

2. Perhaps he will even think it is causally possible, but I do not regard any view on that issue as an integral part of the theory. The question whether it is causally possible for God to act 'out of character' is a difficult one, which we need not go into here.

3. Moore took goodness and badness as primitive, rather than rightness and wrongness; but that need not concern us here.

4. The mention of moral law in the last of these reasons may presuppose the ability to *mention* concepts of moral right and wrong, which may or may not be theological and which may or may not be concepts one uses oneself to make judgments of right and wrong. So far as I can see, it does not *presuppose* the *use* of such concepts to make judgments of right and wrong, or one's adoption of them for such use, which is the crucial point here.

5. The independence ascribed to these attitudes is not a *genetic* independence. It may be that the person would not have come to have some of them had it not been for his religious beliefs. The point is that he has come to hold them in such a way that his holding them does not now depend entirely on his beliefs about God's commands.

6. I take A. C. Ewing to be offering an objection of this type on p. 112 of his book *Ethics* (London: English Univs. Press, 1953).

7. I quote from John Yolton's edition of *An Essay Concerning Human Understanding,* 2 vols. (London and New York: Everyman's Library, 1967).

8. In *God and the Soul* (London: Routledge, 1969), ch. 9.

9. In "Modern Moral Philosophy," *Philosophy,* 33 (1958), pp. 1–19.

10. Karl Barth, *Church Dogmatics,* vol. II, pt. 2, trans. G. W. Bromiley and others (Edinburgh: T. & T. Clark, 1957), p. 553.

11. Ibid., p. 560.

12. The argument here is similar to one which is used for another purpose by Ninian Smart in "Omnipotence, Evil, and Superman," *Philosophy,* 36 (1961), reprinted in Nelson Pike, ed., *God and Evil* (Englewood Cliffs, N.J.: Prentice-Hall, 1964), pp. 103–12.

    I do not mean to endorse the doctrines of divine impassibility and theological determinism.

13. Cf. Ludwig Wittgenstein, *Philosophical Investigations,* 2d ed. (Oxford: Blackwell, 1958), pt. 1, sec. 242: "If language is to be a means of communication there must be agreement not only in definitions but also (queer as this may sound) in judgments." In contemporary society I think it may well be the case that because there is not agreement in ethical definitions, common ethical discourse requires a measure of agreement in ethical judgments. (I do not mean to comment here more broadly on the truth or falsity of Wittgenstein's statement as a statement about the conditions of linguistic communication in general.)

X.3   A Free Man's Worship

BERTRAND RUSSELL

Biographical remarks about Bertrand Russell precede selection VI.2. In this essay written in 1903, Russell disagrees with Kant on the need for religion as the culmination of ethics. We can be both moral and happy without God. The world is absurd, a godless tragedy in which "Nature, omnipotent but blind, in the revolutions of her secular hurryings through the abysses of space, has brought forth at last a child, subject still to her power, but gifted with sight, with knowledge of good and evil, with the capacity of judging all the works of his unthinking Mother." It is this conscious power of moral evaluation that makes the child superior to his omnipotent Mother. He has the capacity to reason, to evaluate, to create, and to live committed to ideals. So in spite of suffering; despair, and death, human beings are free and life may be meaningful.

To Dr. Faustus in his study Mephistopheles told the history of the Creation, saying:

"The endless praises of the choirs of angels had begun to grow wearisome; for, after all, did he not deserve their praise? Had he not given them endless joy? Would it not be more amusing to obtain undeserved praise, to be worshipped by beings whom he tortured? He smiled inwardly, and resolved that the great drama should be performed.

'For countless ages the hot nebula whirled aimlessly through space. At length it began to take shape, the central mass threw off planets, the planets cooled, boiling seas and burning mountains heaved and tossed, from black masses of cloud hot sheets of rain deluged the barely solid crust. And now the first germ of life grew in the depths of the ocean, and developed rapidly in the fructifying warmth into vast forest trees, huge ferns springing from the damp mould, sea monsters breeding, fighting, devouring, and passing away. And from the monsters, as the play unfolded itself, Man was born, with the power of thought, the knowledge of good and evil, and the cruel thirst for worship. And Man saw that all is passing in this mad, monstrous world, that all is struggling to snatch, at any cost, a few brief moments of life before Death's inexorable decree. And Man said: "There is a hidden purpose, could we but fathom it, and the

purpose is good; for we must reverence something, and in the visible world there is nothing worthy of reverence." And Man stood aside from the struggle, resolving that God intended harmony to come out of chaos by human efforts. And when he followed the instincts which God had transmitted to him from his ancestry of beasts of prey, he called it Sin, and asked God to forgive him. But he doubted whether he could be justly forgiven, until he invented a divine Plan by which God's wrath was to have been appeased. And seeing the present was bad, he made it yet worse, that thereby the future might be better. And he gave God thanks for the strength that enabled him to forgo even the joys that were possible. And God smiled; and when he saw that Man had become perfect in renunciation and worship, he sent another sun through the sky, which crashed into Man's sun; and all returned gain to nebula.

"Yes," he murmured, "it was a good play; I will have it performed again."

Such, in outline, but even more purposeless, more void of meaning, is the world which Science presents for our belief Amid such a world, if anywhere, our ideals henceforward must find a home. That Man is the product of causes which had no prevision of the end they were achieving; that his origin, his growth, his hopes and fears,

---

his loves and his beliefs, are but the outcome of accidental collocations of atoms; that no fire, no heroism, no intensity of thought and feeling, can preserve an individual life beyond the grave; that all the labours of the ages, all the devotion, all the inspiration, all the noonday brightness of human genius, are destined to extinction in the vast death of the solar system, and that the whole temple of Man's achievement must inevitably be buried beneath the debris of a universe in ruins—all these things, if not quite beyond dispute, are yet so nearly certain, that no philosophy which rejects them can hope to stand. Only within the scaffolding of these truths, only on the firm foundation of unyielding despair, can the soul's habitation henceforth be safely built.

How, in such an alien and inhuman world, can so powerless a creature as Man preserve his aspirations untarnished? A strange mystery it is that Nature, omnipotent but blind, in the revolutions of her secular hurryings through the abysses of space, has brought forth at last a child, subject still to her power, but gifted with sight, with knowledge of good and evil, with the capacity of judging all the works of his unthinking Mother. In spite of Death, the mark and seal of the parental control, Man is yet free, during his brief years, to examine, to criticize, to know, and in imagination to create. To him alone, in the world with which he is acquainted, this freedom belongs; and in this lies his superiority to the resistless forces that control his outward life.

The savage, like ourselves, feels the oppression of his impotence before the powers of Nature; but having in himself nothing that he respects more than Power, he is willing to prostrate himself before his gods, without inquiring whether they are worthy of his worship. Pathetic and very terrible is the long history of cruelty and torture, of degradation and human sacrifice, endured in the hope of placating the jealous gods: surely, the trembling believer thinks, when what is most precious has been freely given, their lust for blood must be appeased, and more will not be required. The religion of Moloch—as such creeds may be generically called—is in essence the cringing submission of the slave, who dare not, even in his heart, allow the thought that his master deserves no adulation. Since the independence of ideals is not yet

acknowledged, Power may be freely worshipped, and receive an unlimited respect, despite its wanton infliction of pain.

But gradually, as morality grows bolder, the claim of the ideal world begins to be felt; and worship, if it is not to cease, must be given to gods of another kind than those created by the savage. Some, though they feel the demands of the ideal, will still consciously reject them, still urging that naked Power is worthy of worship. Such is the attitude inculcated in God's answer to Job out of the whirlwind: the divine power and knowledge are paraded, but of the divine goodness there is no hint. Such also is the attitude of those who, in our own day, base their morality upon the struggle for survival, maintaining that the survivors are necessarily the fittest. But others, not content with an answer so repugnant to the moral sense, will adopt the position which we have become accustomed to regard as specially religious, maintaining that, in some hidden manner, the world of fact is really harmonious with the world of ideals. Thus Man creates God, all-powerful and all-good, the mystic unity of what is and what should be.

But the world of fact, after all, is not good; and, in submitting our judgement to it, there is an element of slavishness from which our thoughts must be purged. For in all things it is well to exalt the dignity of Man, by freeing him as far as possible from the tyranny of non-human Power. When we have realized that Power is largely bad, that Man, with his knowledge of good and evil, is but a helpless atom in a world which has no such knowledge, the choice is again presented to us: Shall we worship Force, or shall we worship Goodness? Shall our God exist and be evil, or shall he be recognized as the creation of our own conscience?

The answer to this question is very momentous, and affects profoundly our whole morality. The worship of Force, to which Carlyle and Nietzsche and the creed of Militarism have accustomed us, is the result of failure to maintain our own ideals against a hostile universe: it is itself a prostrate submission to evil, a sacrifice of our best to Moloch. If strength indeed is to be respected, let us respect rather the strength of those who refuse that false 'recognition of facts' which fails to recognize that facts are often bad. Let us admit that, in the world we know, there are many things that would be better otherwise, and that the ideals to which we do and must adhere are not realized in the realm of matter. Let us preserve our respect for truth, for beauty, for the ideal of perfection which life does not permit us to attain, though none of these things meet with the approval of the unconscious universe. If Power is bad, as it seems to be, let us reject it from our hearts. In this lies Man's true freedom: in determination to worship only the God created by our own love of the good, to respect only the heaven which inspires the insight of our best moments. In action, in desire, we must submit perpetually to the tyranny of outside forces; but in thought, in aspiration, we are free, free from our fellow men, free from the petty planet on which our bodies impotently crawl, free even, while we live, from the tyranny of death. Let us learn, then, that energy of faith which enables us to live constantly in the vision of the good; and let us descend, in action, into the world of fact, with that vision always before us.

When first the opposition of fact and ideal grows fully visible, a spirit of fiery revolt, of fierce hatred of the gods, seems necessary to the assertion of freedom. To defy with Promethean constancy a hostile universe, to keep its evil always in view, always actively hated, to refuse no pain that the malice of Power can invent, appears to be the duty of all who will not bow before the inevitable. But indignation is still a bondage, for it compels our thoughts to be occupied with an evil world; and in the fierceness of desire from which rebellion springs there is a kind of self-assertion which it is necessary for the wise to overcome. Indignation is a submission of our thoughts, but not of our desires; the Stoic freedom in which wisdom consists is found in the submission of our desires, but not of our thoughts. From the submission of our desires springs the virtue of resignation; from the freedom of our thoughts springs the whole world of art and philosophy, and the vision of beauty by which, at last, we half reconquer the reluctant world. But the vision of beauty is possible only to unfettered contemplation, to thoughts not weighted by the load of eager wishes; and thus Freedom comes only to those who no longer ask of life that it shall yield them any of those personal goods that are subject to the mutations of Time.

Although the necessity of renunciation is evidence of the existence of evil, yet Christianity, in preaching it, has shown a wisdom exceeding that of the Promethean philosophy of rebellion. It must be admitted that, of the things we desire, some, though they prove impossible, are yet real goods; others, however, as ardently longed for, do not form part of a fully purified ideal. The belief that what must be renounced is bad, though sometimes false, is far less often false than untamed passion supposes; and the creed of religion, by providing a reason for proving that it is never false, has been the means of purifying our hopes by the discovery of many austere truths.

But there is in resignation a further good element: even real goods, when they are unattainable, ought not to be fretfully desired. To every man comes, sooner or later, the great renunciation. For the young, there is nothing unattainable; a good thing desired with the whole force of a passionate will, and yet impossible, is to them not credible. Yet, by death, by illness, by poverty, or by the voice of duty, we must learn, each one of us, that the world was not made for us, and that, however beautiful may be the things we crave, Fate may nevertheless forbid them. It is the part of courage, when misfortune comes, to bear without repining the ruin of our hopes, to turn away our thoughts from vain regrets. This degree of submission to Power is not only just and right: it is the very gate of wisdom.

But passive renunciation is not the whole of wisdom; for not by renunciation alone can we build a temple for the worship of our own ideals. Haunting foreshadowings of the temple appear in the realm of imagination, in music, in architecture, in the untroubled kingdom of reason, and in the golden sunset magic of lyrics, where beauty shines and glows, remote from the touch of sorrow, remote from the fear of change, remote from the failures and disenchantments of the world of fact. In the contemplation of these things the vision of heaven will shape itself in our hearts, giving at once a touchstone to judge the world about us, and an inspiration by which to fashion to our needs whatever is not incapable of serving as a stone in the sacred temple.

Except for those rare spirits that are born without sin, there is a cavern of darkness to be traversed before that temple can be entered. The gate of the cavern is despair, and its floor is paved with the gravestones of abandoned hopes. There Self must die; there the eagerness, the greed of untamed desire must be slain, for only so can the soul be free from the empire of Fate. But out of the cavern, the Gate of Renunciation leads again to the daylight of wisdom, by whose radiance a new insight, a new joy, a new tenderness, shine forth to gladden the pilgrim's heart.

When, without the bitterness of impotent rebellion, we have learnt both to resign ourselves to the outward rule of Fate and to recognize that the non-human world is unworthy of our worship, it becomes possible at last so to transform and refashion the unconscious universe, so to transmute it in the crucible of imagination, that a new image of shining gold replaces the old idol of clay. In all the multiform facts of the world—in the visual shapes of trees and mountains and clouds, in the events of the life of Man, even in the very omnipotence of Death—the insight of creative idealism can find the reflection of a beauty which its own thoughts first made. In this way mind asserts its subtle mastery over the thoughtless forces of Nature. The more evil the material with which it deals, the more thwarting to untrained desire, the greater is its achievement in inducing the reluctant rock to yield up its hidden treasures, the prouder its victory in compelling the opposing forces to swell the pageant of its triumph. Of all the arts, Tragedy is the proudest, the most triumphant; for it builds its shining citadel in the very centre of the enemy's country, on the very summit of his highest mountain; from its impregnable watchtowers, his camps and arsenals, his columns and forts, are all revealed; within its walls the free life continues, while the legions of Death and Pain and Despair, and all the servile captains of tyrant Fate, afford the burghers of that dauntless city new spectacles of beauty. Happy those sacred ramparts, thrice happy the dwellers on that all-seeing eminence. Honour to those brave warriors who, through countless ages of warfare, have preserved for us the priceless heritage of liberty, and have kept undefiled by sacrilegious invaders the home of the unsubdued.

But the beauty of Tragedy does but make visible a quality which, in more or less obvious shapes, is present always and everywhere in life. In the

spectacle of Death, in the endurance of intolerable pain, and in the irrevocableness of a vanished past, there is a sacredness, an overpowering awe, a feeling of the vastness, the depth, the inexhaustible mystery of existence, in which, as by some strange marriage of pain, the sufferer is bound to the world by bonds of sorrow. In these moments of insight, we lose all eagerness of temporary desire, all struggling and striving for petty ends, all care for the little trivial things that, to a superficial view, make up the common life of day by day; we see, surrounding the narrow raft illumined by the flickering light of human comradeship, the dark ocean on whose rolling waves we toss for a brief hour; from the great night without, a chill blast breaks in upon our refuge; all the loneliness of humanity amid hostile forces is concentrated upon the individual soul, which must struggle alone, with what of courage it can command, against the whole weight of a universe that cares nothing for its hopes and fears. Victory, in this struggle with the powers of darkness, is the true baptism into the glorious company of heroes, the true initiation into the overmastering beauty of human existence. From that awful encounter of the soul with the outer world, renunciation, wisdom, and charity are born; and with their birth a new life begins. To take into the inmost shrine of the soul the irresistible forces whose puppets we seem to be—Death and change, the irrevocableness of the past, and the powerlessness of Man before the blind hurry of the universe from vanity to vanity—to feel these things and know them is to conquer them.

This is the reason why the Past has such magical power. The beauty of its motionless and silent pictures is like the enchanted purity of late autumn, when the leaves, though one breath would make them fall, still glow against the sky in golden glory. The Past does not change or strive; like Duncan, after life's fitful fever it sleeps well; what was eager and grasping, what was petty and transitory, has faded away; the things that were beautiful and eternal shine out of it like stars in the night. Its beauty, to a soul not worthy of it, is unendurable; but to a soul which has conquered Fate it is the key of religion.

The life of Man, viewed outwardly, is but a small thing in comparison with the forces of

Nature. The slave is doomed to worship Time and Fate and Death, because they are greater than anything he finds in himself, and because all his thoughts are of things which they devour. But, great as they are, to think of them greatly, to feel their passionless splendour, is greater still. And such thought makes us free men; we no longer bow before the inevitable in Oriental subjection, but we absorb it, and make it a part of ourselves. To abandon the struggle for private happiness, to expel all eagerness of temporary desire, to burn with passion for eternal things—this is emancipation, and this is the free man's worship. And this liberation is effected by a contemplation of Fate; for Fate itself is subdued by the mind which leaves nothing to be purged by the purifying fire of Time.

United with his fellow men by the strongest of all ties, the tie of a common doom, the free man finds that a new vision is with him always, shedding over every daily task the light of love. The life of Man is a long march through the night, surrounded by invisible foes, tortured by weariness and pain, towards a goal that few can hope to reach, and where none may tarry long. One by one, as they march, our comrades vanish from our sight, seized by the silent orders of omnipotent Death. Very brief is the time in which we can help them, in which their happiness or misery is decided. Be it ours to shed sunshine on their path, to lighten their sorrows by the balm of sympathy, to give them the pure joy of a never-tiring affection, to strengthen failing courage, to instil faith in hours of despair. Let us not weigh in grudging scales their merits and demerits, but let us think only of their need—of the sorrows, the difficulties, perhaps the blindnesses, that make the misery of their lives; let us remember that they are fellow-sufferers in the same darkness, actors in the same tragedy with ourselves. And so, when their day is over, when their good and their evil have become eternal by the immortality of the past, be it ours to feel that, where they suffered, where they failed, no deed of ours was the cause; but wherever a spark of the divine fire kindled in their hearts, we were ready with encouragement, with sympathy, with brave words in which high courage glowed.

Brief and powerless is Man's life; on him and all his race the slow, sure doom falls pitiless and dark. Blind to good and evil, reckless of destruction, omnipotent matter rolls on its relentless way; for Man, condemned today to lose his dearest, tomorrow himself to pass through the gate of darkness, it remains only to cherish, ere yet the blow fall, the lofty thoughts that ennoble his little day; disdaining the coward terrors of the salve of Fate, to worship at the shrine that his own hands have built; undismayed by the empire of chance, to preserve a mind free from the wanton tyranny that rules his outward life; proudly defiant of the irresistible forces that tolerate, for a moment, his knowledge and his condemnation, to sustain alone, a weary but unyielding Atlas, the world that his own ideals have fashioned despite the trampling march of unconscious power.

X.4 Religion and the Queerness of Morality

GEORGE MAVRODES

George Mavrodes is professor emeritus of philosophy at the University of Michigan and is one of the leading figures in contemporary philosophy of religion. His works include *Belief in God: A Study in the Epistemology of Religion (1970)* and *Revelation in Religious Belief* (1988). In this essay, Mavrodes opposes Bertrand Russell's secular view of ethics and explores the suggestion that morality somehow depends on religion.

Reprinted from George I. Mavrodes, "Religion and the Queerness of Morality," in *Rationality, Religious Belief and Moral Commitment: Essays in the Philosophy of Religion,* edited by Robert Audi and William J. Wainwright.

Many arguments for the existence of God may be construed as claiming that there is some feature of the world that would somehow make no sense unless there was something else that had a stronger version of that feature or some analogue of it. So, for example, the cosmological line of argument may be thought of as centering upon the claim that the way in which the world exists (called "contingent" existence) would be incomprehensible unless there were something else—that is, God—that had a stronger grip upon existence (that is, "necessary" existence).

Now, a number of thinkers have held a view something like this with respect to morality. They have claimed that in some important way morality is dependent upon religion—dependent, that is, in such a way that if religion were to fail, morality would fail also. And they have held that the dependence was more than psychological, that is, if religion were to fail, it would somehow be *proper* (perhaps logically or perhaps in some other way) for morality to fail also. One way of expressing this theme is by Dostoevsky's "if there is no God, then everything is permitted," a sentiment that in this century has been prominently echoed by Sartre. But perhaps the most substantial philosophical thinker of the modern period to espouse this view, though in a rather idiosyncratic way, was Immanuel Kant, who held that the existence of God was a necessary postulate of 'practical' (that is, moral) reason.

On the other hand, it has recently been popular for moral philosophers to deny this theme and to maintain that the dependence of morality on religion is, at best, merely psychological. Were religion to fail, so they apparently hold, this would grant no sanction for the failure of morality. For morality stands on its own feet, whatever those feet may turn out to be.

Now, the suggestion that morality somehow depends on religion is rather attractive to me. It is this suggestion that I wish to explore in this paper, even though it seems unusually difficult to formulate clearly the features of this suggestion that make it attractive. I will begin by mentioning briefly some aspects that I will not discuss.

First, beyond this paragraph I will not discuss the claim that morality cannot survive psychologically without the support of religious belief. At least in the short run, this proposal seems to me false. For there certainly seem to be people who reject religious belief, at least in the ordinary sense, but who apparently have a concern with morality and who try to live a moral life. Whether the proposal may have more force if it is understood in a broader way, as applying to whole cultures, epochs, and so forth, I do not know.

Second, I will not discuss the attempt to define some or all moral terms by the use of religious terms, or vice versa. But this should not be taken as implying any judgment about this project.

Third, beyond this paragraph I shall not discuss the suggestion that moral statements may be entailed by religious statements and so may be "justified" by religious doctrines or beliefs. It is popular now to hold that no such alleged entailment can be valid. But the reason usually cited for this view is the more general doctrine that moral statements cannot be validly deduced from nonmoral statements, a doctrine usually traced to Hume. Now, to my mind the most important problem raised by this general doctrine is that of finding some interpretation of it that is both significant and not plainly false. If it is taken to mean merely that there is some set of statements that entails no moral statement, then it strikes me as probably true, but trivial. At any rate, we should then need another reason to suppose that religious statements fall in this category. If, on the other hand, it is taken to mean that one can divide the domain of statements into two classes, the moral and the nonmoral, and that none of the latter entail any of the former, then it is false. I, at any rate, do not know a version of this doctrine that seems relevant to the religious case and that has any reasonable likelihood of being true. But I am not concerned on this occasion with the possibly useful project of deducing morality from religion, and so I will not pursue it further. My interest is closer to a move in the other direction, that of deducing religion from morality. (I am not quite satisfied with this way of putting it and will try to explain this dissatisfaction later on.)

For the remainder of this discussion, then, my project is as follows. I will outline one rather common nonreligious view of the world, calling attention to what I take to be its most relevant features. Then I shall try to portray some sense of the odd status that morality would have in a world of that sort. I shall be hoping, of course, that you will notice that this odd status is not the one that you recognize morality to have in the actual world. But it will perhaps be obvious that the "worldview" amendments required would move substantially toward a religious position.

First, then, the nonreligious view. I take a short and powerful statement of it from a 1903 essay by Bertrand Russell, "A Free Man's Worship."

> That man is the product of causes which had no prevision of the end they were achieving; that his origin, his growth, his hopes and fears, his loves and his beliefs are but the outcome of accidental collocations of atoms; that no fire, no heroism, no intensity of thought and feeling, can preserve an individual life beyond the grave; that all the labors of the ages, all the devotion, all the inspiration, all the noonday brightness of human genius, are destined to extinction in the vast death of the solar system, and that the whole temple of man's achievement must inevitably be buried beneath the debris of a universe in ruins—all these things, if not quite beyond dispute, are yet so nearly certain that no philosophy which rejects them can hope to stand. Only within the scaffolding of these truths, only on the firm foundation of unyielding despair, can the soul's habitation henceforth be safely built.[1]

For convenience, I will call a world that satisfies the description given here a "Russellian world." But we are primarily interested in what the status of morality would be in the actual world if that world should turn out to be Russellian. I shall therefore sometimes augment the description of a Russellian world with obvious features of the actual world.

What are the most relevant features of a Russellian world? The following strike me as especially important: (1) Such phenomena as minds, mental activities, consciousness, and so forth are the products of entities and causes that give no indication of being mental themselves. In Russell's words, the causes are "accidental collocations of atoms" with "no prevision of the end they were achieving." Though not stated explicitly by Russell, we might add the doctrine, a commonplace in modern science, that mental phenomena—and indeed life itself—are comparative latecomers in the long

history of the earth. (2) Human life is bounded by physical death and each individual comes to a permanent end at his physical death. We might add to this the observation that the span of human life is comparatively short, enough so that in some cases we can, with fair confidence, predict the major consequences of certain actions insofar as they will affect a given individual throughout his whole remaining life. (3) Not only each individual but also the human race as a species is doomed to extinction "beneath the debris of a universe in ruins."

So much, then, for the main features of a Russellian world. Because the notion of benefits and goods plays an important part in the remainder of my discussion, I want to introduce one further technical expression—"Russellian benefit." A Russellian benefit is one that could accrue to a person in a Russellian world. A contented old age would be, I suppose, a Russellian benefit, as would a thrill of sexual pleasure or a good reputation. Going to heaven when one dies, though a benefit, is not a Russellian benefit. Russellian benefits are only the benefits possible in a Russellian world. But one can have Russellian benefits even if the world is not Russellian. In such a case there might, however, also be other benefits, such as going to heaven.

Could the actual world be Russellian? Well, I take it to be an important feature of the actual world that human beings exist in it and that in it their actions fall, at least sometimes, within the sphere of morality—that is, they have moral obligations to act (or to refrain from acting) in certain ways. And if they do not act in those ways, then they are properly subject to a special and peculiar sort of adverse judgment (unless it happens that there are special circumstances that serve to excuse their failure to fulfill the obligations). People who do not fulfill their obligations are not merely stupid or weak or unlucky; they are morally reprehensible.

Now, I do not have much to say in an illuminating manner about the notion of moral obligation, but I could perhaps make a few preliminary observations about how I understand this notion. First, I take it that morality includes, or results in, judgments of the form "*N* ought to do (or to avoid doing)_____" or "it is *N's* duty to do (or to avoid doing)_____." That is, morality ascribes to particular people an obligation to do a certain thing on a certain occasion. No doubt morality includes other things as well—general moral rules, for example. I shall, however, focus on judgments of the sort just mentioned, and when I speak without further qualification of someone's having an obligation I intend it to be understood in terms of such a judgment.

Second, many authors distinguish prima facie obligations from obligations "all things considered." Probably this is a useful distinction. For the most part, however, I intend to ignore prima facie obligations and to focus upon our obligations all things considered, what we might call our "final obligations." These are the obligations that a particular person has in some concrete circumstance at a particular place and time, when all the aspects of the situation have been taken into account. It identifies the action that, if not done, will properly subject the person to the special adverse judgment.

Finally, it is, I think, a striking feature of moral obligations that a person's being unwilling to fulfill the obligation is irrelevant to having the obligation and is also irrelevant to the adverse judgment in case the obligation is not fulfilled. Perhaps even more important is the fact that, at least for some obligations, it is also irrelevant in both these ways for one to point out that he does not see how fulfilling the obligations can do him any good. In fact, unless we are greatly mistaken about our obligations, it seems clear that in a Russellian world there are an appreciable number of cases in which fulfilling an obligation would result in a loss of good to ourselves. On the most prosaic level, this must be true of some cases of repaying a debt, keeping a promise, refraining from stealing, and so on. And it must also be true of those rarer but more striking cases of obligation to risk death or serious injury in the performance of a duty. People have, of course, differed as to what is good for humans. But so far as I can see, the point I have been making will hold for any candidate that is plausible in a Russellian world. Pleasure, happiness, esteem, contentment, self-realization, knowledge—all of these can suffer from the fulfillment of a moral obligation.

It is not, however, a *necessary* truth that some of our obligations are such that their fulfillment

will yield no net benefit, within Russellian limits, to their fulfiller. It is not contradictory to maintain that, for every obligation that I have, a corresponding benefit awaits me within the confines of this world and this life. While such a contention would not be contradictory, however, it would nevertheless be false. I discuss below one version of this contention. At present it must suffice to say that a person who accepts this claim will probably find the remainder of what I have to say correspondingly less plausible.

Well, where are we now? I claim that in the actual world we have some obligations that, when we fulfill them, will confer on us no net Russellian benefit—in fact, they will result in a Russellian loss. If the world is Russellian, then Russellian benefits and losses are the only benefits and losses, and also then we have moral obligations whose fulfillment will result in a net loss of good to the one who fulfills them. I suggest, however, that it would be very strange to have such obligations—strange not simply in the sense of being unexpected or surprising but in some deeper way. I do not suggest that it is strange in the sense of having a straightforward logical defect, of being self-contradictory to claim that we have such obligations. Perhaps the best thing to say is that were it a fact that we had such obligations, then the world that included such a fact would be absurd—we would be living in a crazy world.

Now, whatever success I may have in this paper will in large part be a function of my success (or lack thereof) in getting across a sense of that absurdity, that queerness. On some accounts of morality, in a Russellian world there would not be the strangeness that I allege. Perhaps, then, I can convey some of that strangeness by mentioning those views of morality that would eliminate it. In fact, I believe that a good bit of their appeal is just the fact that they do get rid of this queerness.

First, I suspect that morality will not be queer in the way I suggest, even in a Russellian world, if judgments about obligations are properly to be analyzed in terms of the speaker rather than in terms of the subject of the judgment. And I more than suspect that this will be the case if such judgments are analyzed in terms of the speaker's attitude or feeling toward some action, and/or his attempt or inclination to incite a similar attitude in someone else. It may be, of course, that there is something odd about the supposition that human beings, consciousness, and so forth, could arise at all in a Russellian world. A person who was impressed by that oddity might he attracted toward some "teleological" line of reasoning in the direction of a more religious view. But I think that this oddity is not the one I am touching on here. Once given the existence of human beings with capabilities for feelings and attitudes, there does not seem to be anything further that is queer in the supposition that a speaker might have an attitude toward some action, might express that attitude, and might attempt (or succeed) in inciting someone else to have a similar attitude. Anyone, therefore, who can be satisfied with such an analysis will probably not be troubled by the queerness that I allege.

Second, for similar reasons, this queerness will also be dissipated by any account that understands judgments about obligations purely in terms of the feelings, attitudes, and so forth of the subject of the judgment. For, given again that there are human beings with consciousness, it does not seem to be any additional oddity that the subject of a moral judgment might have feelings or attitudes about an actual or prospective action of his own. The assumption that morality is to be understood in this way takes many forms. In a closely related area, for example, it appears as the assumption—so common now that it can pass almost unnoticed—that guilt could not be anything other than guilt *feelings,* and that the "problem" of guilt is just the problem generated by such feelings.

In connection with our topic here, however, we might look at the way in which this sort of analysis enters into one plausible-sounding explanation of morality in a Russellian world, an explanation that has a scientific flavor. The existence of morality in a Russellian world, it may be said, is not at all absurd because its existence there can be given a perfectly straightforward explanation: morality has a survival value for a species such as ours because it makes possible continued cooperation and things of that sort. So it is no more absurd that people have moral obligations than it is absurd that they have opposable thumbs.

I think that this line of explanation will work only if one analyzes obligations into feelings, or beliefs. I think it is plausible (though I am not sure it is correct) to suppose that everyone's having feelings of moral obligation might have survival value for a species such as Man, given of course that these feelings were attached to patterns of action that contributed to such survival. And if that is so, then it is not implausible to suppose that there may be a survival value for the species even in a moral feeling that leads to the death of the individual who has it. So far so good. But this observation, even if true, is not relevant to the queerness with which I am here concerned. For I have not suggested that the existence of moral feelings would be absurd in a Russellian world; it is rather the existence of moral *obligations* that is absurd, and I think it important to make the distinction. It is quite possible, it seems to me, for one to feel (or to believe) that he has a certain obligation without actually having it, and also vice versa. Now, beliefs and feelings will presumably have some effect upon actions, and this effect may possibly contribute to the survival of the species. But, so far as I can see, the addition of actual moral obligations to these moral beliefs and feelings will make no further contribution to action nor will the actual obligations have an effect upon action in the absence of the corresponding feelings and beliefs. So it seems that neither with nor without the appropriate feelings will moral obligations contribute to the survival of the species. Consequently, an "evolutionary" approach such as this cannot serve to explain the existence of moral obligations, unless one rejects my distinction and equates the obligations with the feelings.

And finally, I think that morality will not be queer in the way I allege, or at least it will not be as queer as I think, if it should be the case that every obligation yields a Russellian benefit to the one who fulfills it. Given the caveat expressed earlier, one can perhaps make some sense out of the notion of a Russellian good or benefit for a sentient organism in a Russellian world. And one could, I suppose, without further queerness imagine that such an organism might aim toward achieving such goods. And we could further suppose that there were certain actions—those that were "obligations"—that would, in contrast with other actions, actually yield such benefits to the organism that performed them. And finally, it might not be too implausible to claim that an organism that failed to perform such an action was defective in some way and that some adverse judgment was appropriate.

Morality, however, seems to require us to hold that certain organisms (namely, human beings) have in addition to their ordinary properties and relations another special relation to certain actions. This relation is that of being "obligated" to perform those actions. And some of those actions are pretty clearly such that they will yield only Russellian losses to the one who performs them. Nevertheless, we are supposed to hold that a person who does not perform an action to which he is thus related is defective in some serious and important way and an adverse judgment is appropriate against him. And that certainly does seem odd.

The recognition of this oddity—or perhaps better, this absurdity—is not simply a resolution to concern ourselves only with what "pays." Here the position of Kant is especially suggestive. He held that a truly moral action is undertaken purely out of respect for the moral law and with no concern at all for reward. There seems to be no room at all here for any worry about what will "pay." But he also held that the moral enterprise needs, in a deep and radical way, the postulate of a God who can, and will, make happiness correspond to virtue. This postulate is "necessary" for practical reason. Perhaps we could put this Kantian demand in the language I have been using here, saying that the moral enterprise would make no sense in a world in which that correspondence ultimately failed.

I suspect that what we have in Kant is the recognition that there cannot be, in any "reasonable" way, a moral demand upon me, unless reality itself is committed to morality in some deep way. It makes sense only if there is a moral demand on the world too and only if reality will in the end satisfy that demand. This theme of the deep grounding of morality is one to which I return briefly near the end of this paper.

The oddity we have been considering is, I suspect, the most important root of the celebrated and somewhat confused question, "Why should I be moral?" Characteristically, I think, the person who asks that question is asking to have the queerness of that situation illuminated. From time to time there are philosophers who make an attempt to argue—perhaps only a half-hearted attempt—that being moral really is in one's interest after all. Kurt Baier, it seems to me, proposes a reply of this sort. He says:

> Moralities are systems of principles whose acceptance by everyone as overruling the dictates of self-interest is in the interest of everyone alike though following the rules of a morality is not of course identical with following self-interest. . . .
>
> The answer to our question "Why should we be moral?" is therefore as follows. We should be moral because being moral is following rules designed to overrule self-interest whenever it is in the interest of everyone alike that everyone should set aside his interest.[2]

As I say, this seems to be an argument to the effect that it really is in everyone's interest to be moral. I suppose that Baier is here probably talking about Russellian interests. At least, we must interpret him in that way if his argument is to be applicable in this context, and I will proceed on that assumption. But how exactly is the argument to be made out?

It appears here to begin with a premise something like

(A) It is in everyone's best interest (including mine, presumably) for everyone (including me) to be moral.

This premise itself appears to be supported earlier by reference to Hobbes. As I understand it, the idea is that without morality people will live in a "state of nature," and life will be nasty, brutish, and short. Well, perhaps so. At any rate, let us accept (A) for the moment. From (A) we can derive

(B) It is in my best interest for everyone (including me) to be moral.

And from (B) perhaps one derives

(C) It is in my best interest for me to be moral.

And (C) may be taken to answer the question, "Why should I be moral?" Furthermore, if (C) is true, then moral obligation will at least not have the sort of queerness that I have been alleging.

Unfortunately, however, the argument outlined above is invalid. The derivation of (B) from (A) may be all right, but the derivation of (C) from (B) is invalid. What does follow from (B) is

(C′) It is in my best interest for me to be *moral if everyone else is moral.*

The argument thus serves to show that it is in a given person's interest to be moral only on the assumption that everyone else in the world is moral. It might, of course, be difficult to find someone ready to make that assumption.

There is, however, something more of interest in this argument. I said that the derivation of (B) from (A) may be all right. But in fact is it? If it is not all right, then this argument would fail even if everyone else in the world were moral. Now (A) can be interpreted as referring to "everyone's best interest" ("the interest of everyone alike," in Baier's own words) either collectively or distributively; that is, it may be taken as referring to the best interest of the whole group considered as a single unit, or as referring to the best interest of each individual in the group. But if (A) is interpreted in the collective sense, then (B) does not follow from it. It may not be in *my* best interest for everyone to act morally, even if it is in the best interest of the group as a whole, for the interest of the group as a whole may be advanced by the sacrificing of my interest. On this interpretation of (A), then, the argument will not answer the question "Why should I be moral?" even on the supposition that everyone else is moral.

If (A) is interpreted in the distributive sense, on the other hand, then (B) does follow from it, and the foregoing objection is not applicable. But another objection arises. Though (A) in the collective sense has some plausibility, it is hard to imagine that it is true in the distributive sense. Hobbes may have been right in supposing that life in the state of nature would be short, etc. But some lives are short anyway. In fact, some lives are short just because the demands of morality are observed. Such a life is not bound to have been shorter in the state of nature. Nor is it bound to have been less happy, less pleasurable, and so forth. In fact, does it not seem obvious that *my* best Russellian interest will be further advanced in a situation in which everyone else

acts morally but I act immorally (in selected cases) than it will be in case everyone, including me, acts morally? It certainly seems so. It can, of course, be observed that if I act immorally then so will other people, perhaps reducing my benefits. In the present state of the world that is certainly true. But in the present state of the world it is also true, as I observed earlier, that many other people will act immorally *anyway,* regardless of what I do.

A more realistic approach is taken by Richard Brandt.[3] He asks, "is it *reasonable* for me to do my duty if it conflicts seriously with my personal welfare?" After distinguishing several possible senses of this question, he chooses a single one to discuss further, presumably a sense that he thinks important. As reformulated, the question is now: "Given that doing *x* is my duty and that doing some conflicting act *y* will maximize my personal welfare, will the performance of *x* instead of *y* satisfy my reflective preferences better?" And the conclusion to which he comes is that "the correct answer may vary from one person to another. It depends on what kind of person one is, what one cares about." And within Russellian limits Brandt must surely be right in this. But he goes on to say, "It is, of course, no defense of one's failure to do one's duty, before others or society, to say that doing so is not 'reasonable' for one in this sense." And this is just to bring the queer element back in. It is to suppose that besides "the kind of person" I am and my particular pattern of "cares" and interests there is something else, my duty, which may go against these and in any case properly overrides them. And one feels that there must be some sense of "reasonable" in which one can ask whether a world in which that is true is a reasonable world, whether such a world makes any sense.

This completes my survey of some ethical or metaethical views that would eliminate or minimize this sort of queerness of morality. I turn now to another sort of view, stronger I think than any of these others, which accepts that queerness but goes no further. And one who holds this view will also hold, I think, that the question "Why should I be moral?" must be rejected in one way or another. A person who holds this view will say that it is simply a fact that we have the moral obligations that we do have, and that is all there is to it. If they sometimes result in a loss of good, then that too is just a fact. These may be puzzling or surprising facts, but there are lots of puzzling and surprising things about the world. In a Russellian world, morality will be, I suppose, an "emergent" phenomenon; it will be a feature of certain effects though it is not a feature of their causes. But the wetness of water is an emergent feature, too. It is not a property of either hydrogen or oxygen. And there is really nothing more to be said; somewhere we must come to an end of reasons and explanations. We have our duties. We can fulfill them and be moral, or we can ignore them and be immoral. If all that is crazy and absurd—well, so be it. Who are we to say that the world is not crazy and absurd?

Such a view was once suggested by William Alston in a criticism of Hasting Rashdall's moral argument for God's existence. Alston attributed to Rashdall the view that "God is required as a locus for the moral law." But Alston then went on to ask, "Why could it not just be an ultimate fact about the universe that kindness is good and cruelty bad? This seems to have been Plato's view." And if we rephrase Alston's query slightly to refer to obligations, we might be tempted to say, "Why not indeed?"

I say that this is perhaps the strongest reply against me. Since it involves no argument, there is no argument to be refuted. And I have already said that, so far as I can see, its central contention is not self-contradictory. Nor do I think of any other useful argument to the effect that the world is not absurd and crazy in this way. The reference to Plato, however, might be worth following for a moment. Perhaps Plato did think that goodness, or some such thing related to morality, was an ultimate fact about the world. But a Platonic world is not very close to a Russellian world. Plato was not a Christian, of course, but his worldview has very often been taken to be congenial (especially congenial compared to some other philosophical views) to a religious understanding of the world. He would not have been satisfied, I think, with Russell's "accidental collocations of atoms," nor would he have taken the force of the grave to be "so nearly

certain." The idea of the Good seems to play a metaphysical role in his thought. It is somehow fundamental to what is as well as to what ought to be, much more fundamental to reality than are the atoms. A Platonic man, therefore, who sets himself to live in accordance with the Good aligns himself with what is deepest and most basic in existence. Or to put it another way, we might say that whatever values a Platonic world imposes on a man are values to which the Platonic world itself is committed, through and through.

Not so, of course, for a Russellian world. Values and obligations cannot be deep in such a world. They have a grip only upon surface phenomena, probably only upon man. What is deep in a Russellian world must be such things as matter and energy, or perhaps natural law, chance, or chaos. If it really were a fact that one had obligations in a Russellian world, then something would be laid upon man that might cost a man everything but that went no further than man. And that difference from a Platonic world seems to make all the difference.

This discussion suggests, I think, that there are two related ways in which morality is queer in a Russellian world. Or maybe they are better construed as two aspects of the queerness we have been exploring. In most of the preceding discussion I have been focusing on the strangeness of an overriding demand that does not seem to conduce to the good of the person on whom it is laid. (In fact, it does not even promise his good.) Here, however, we focus on the fact that this demand—radical enough in the human life on which it is laid—is *superficial* in a Russellian world. Something that reaches close to the heart of my own life, perhaps even demanding the sacrifice of that life, is not deep at all in the world in which (on a Russellian view) that life is lived. And that, too, seems absurd.

This brings to an end the major part of my discussion. If I have been successful at all you will have shared with me to some extent in the sense of the queerness of morality, its absurdity in a Russellian world. If you also share the conviction that it cannot in the end be absurd in that way, then perhaps you will also be attracted to some religious view of the world. Perhaps you also will say that morality must have some deeper grip upon the world than a Russellian view allows. And, consequently, things like mind and purpose must also be deeper in the real world than they would be in a Russellian world. They must be more original, more controlling. The accidental collocation of atoms cannot be either primeval or final, nor can the grave be an end. But or course that would be only a beginning, a sketch waiting to be filled in.

We cannot here do much to fill it in further. But I should like to close with a final, and rather tentative suggestion, as to a direction in which one might move in thinking about the place of morality in the world. It is suggested to me by certain elements in my own religion, Christianity.

I come more and more to think that morality, while a fact, is a twisted and distorted fact. Or perhaps better, that it is a barely recognizable version of another fact, a version adapted to a twisted and distorted world. It is something like, I suppose, the way in which the pine that grows at timberline, wind blasted and twisted low against the rock, is a version of the tall and symmetrical tree that grows lower on the slopes. I think it may be that the related notions of sacrifice and gift represent (or come close to representing) the fact, that is, the pattern of life, whose distorted version we know here as morality. Imagine a situation, an "economy" if you will, in which no one ever buys or trades for or seizes any good thing. But whatever good he enjoys is either one which he himself has created or else one which he receives as a free and unconditional gift. And as soon as he has tasted it and seen that it is good he stands ready to give it away in his turn as soon as the opportunity arises. In such a place, if one were to speak either of his rights or his duties, his remark might be met with puzzled laughter as his hearers struggled to recall an ancient world in which those terms referred to something important.

We have, of course, even now some occasions that tend in this direction. Within some families perhaps, or even in a regiment in desperate battle, people may for a time pass largely beyond morality and live lives of gift and sacrifice. On those occasions nothing would he lost if the moral concepts and the moral language were to disappear. But it is probably not possible that such situations and occasions should be more than rare exceptions in the daily life of the present world. Christianity, however, which tells us that the present world is "fallen" and hence leads us to expect a distortion in its important features, also tells us that one day the redemption of the world will be complete and that then all things shall be made new. And it seems to me to suggest an "economy" more akin to that of gift and sacrifice than to that of rights and duties. If something like that should be true, then perhaps morality, like the Marxist state, is destined to wither away (unless perchance it should happen to survive in hell).

Christianity, then, I think is related to the queerness or morality in one way and perhaps in two. In the first instance, it provides a view of the world in which morality is not an absurdity. It gives morality a deeper place in the world than does a Russellian view and thus permits it to "make sense." But in the second instance, it perhaps suggests that morality is not the deepest thing, that it is provisional and transitory, that it is due to serve its use and then to pass away in favor of something richer and deeper. Perhaps we can say that it begins by inverting the quotation with which I began and by telling us that, since God exists, not everything is permitted; but it may also go on to tell us that, since God exists, in the end there shall be no occasion for any prohibition.

NOTES

1. Bertrand Russell, *Mysticism and Logic* (New York: Barnes & Noble, 1917), pp. 47–48.
2. Kurt Baier, *The Moral Point of View* (Ithaca: Cornell University Press, 1958), p. 314.
3. Richard Brandt, *Ethical Theory* (Englewood Cliffs, N.J.: Prentice Hall, 1959), pp. 375–78.

General

Craig, William Lane, and J. P. Moreland. *Philosophical Foundations for a Christian Worldview*. Downers Grove, IL: InterVarsity Press, 2003.

Davies, Brian. *Philosophy of Religion: A Guide and Anthology*. New York: Oxford University Press, 2000. Especially good on the traditional arguments for the existence of God.

Flint, Thomas, and Michael Rea. *The Oxford Handbook of Philosophical Theology*. Oxford, Eng.: Oxford University Press, 2008.

Harrison, Jonathan. *God, Freedom and Immortality*. Aldershot, Eng.: Ashgate Publishing Co., 1999. Perhaps the most comprehensive critical analysis of philosophy of religion to appear in many years.

Hick, John. *Arguments for the Existence of God*. London: Macmillan, 1971. A clearly written, insightful examination of the central arguments.

Mackie, J. L. *The Miracle of Theism*. Oxford, Eng.: Oxford University Press, 1982. A lively discussion of the proofs for the existence of God and other issues by one of the ablest atheist philosophers of our time.

Martin, Michael. *Atheism*. Philadelphia: Temple University Press, 1990. The most comprehensive attack on theism in the English language. Clearly set forth.

Murray, Michael. *Reason for the Hope Within*. Grand Rapids, MI: Eerdmans, 1998.

Murray, Michael, and Michael Rea. *Introduction to Philosophy of Religion*. Cambridge, Eng.: Cambridge University Press, 2008.

Peterson, Michael, William Hasker, Bruce Reichenbach, and David Basinger. *Reason and Religious Belief*. New York: Oxford University Press, 1991. A clearly written, helpful book from a theist point of view.

Pojman, Louis. *Philosophy of Religion*. New York: McGraw-Hill, 2000.

Rowe, William. *Philosophy of Religion: An Introduction*. Belmont, CA: Wadsworth, 1978. A readable, reliable introductory work by a first-rate scholar.

Swinburne, Richard. *The Existence of God*, 2nd edition. Oxford, Eng.: Oxford University Press, 2004. Perhaps the most sustained and cogent defense of theism in the literature.

Tomberlin, James, ed. *Philosophical Perspectives, 5. Philosophy or Religion 1991*. Atascadero, CA: Ridgeview, 1991. Contains important, recent articles on several issues in philosophy of religion.

Wainwright, William J. *Philosophy of Religion*. Belmont, CA: Wadsworth, 1998. A careful, well-argued text from a theistic perspective.

———. *The Oxford Handbook of Philosophy of Religion*. Oxford, Eng.: Oxford University Press, 2005.

Bibliography for Part I

The Ontological Argument

Barnes, Jonathan. *The Ontological Argument*. London: Macmillan, 1972. A good general discussion of the argument.

Hartshorne, Charles. *The Logic of Perfection*. LaSalle, IL: Open Court, 1962.

———. *Anselm's Discovery*. LaSalle, IL: Open Court, 1965.

Oppy, Graham. *Ontological Arguments and Belief in God*. New York: Cambridge University Press, 1995.

Plantinga, Alvin, ed. *The Ontological Argument from St. Anselm to Contemporary Philosophers*. Garden City, NY: Doubleday, 1965.

The Cosmological Argument

Craig, William. *The Cosmological Argument from Plato to Leibniz*. New York: Barnes & Noble, 1980. A good survey of the history of the argument.

———. *The Kalām Cosmological Argument*. New York: Harper & Row, 1980.

Gale, Richard. *On the Nature and Existence of God*. Cambridge, Eng.: Cambridge University Press, 1992. Chapter 7 is an excellent discussion of the argument.

Moreland, J. P., and Kai Nielsen, eds. *Does God Exist?: The Great Debate*. Nashville: Thomas Nelson, 1990.

Rowe, William. *The Cosmological Argument*. Princeton, NJ: Princeton University Press, 1971. A thorough and penetrating study.

Taylor, Richard. *Metaphysics*. Englewood Cliffs, NJ: Prentice Hall, 1983.

The Teleological Argument

Manson, Neil. *God and Design*. New York: Routledge, 2003.

McPherson, Thomas. *The Argument from Design*. London: Macmillan, 1972. A good introduction to the various forms of the argument.

Salmon, Wesley. "Religion and Science. A New Look at Hume's Dialogue." *Philosophical Studies* 33 (1978):145.

Swinburne, Richard. "The Argument from Design." *Philosophy* 43 (1968):199–212. A detailed response to Hume.

———. "The Argument from Design—A Defence." *Religious Studies* 8 (1972):193–205.

Tennant, R. R. *Philosophical Theology*. Cambridge, Eng.: Cambridge University Press, 1928–30. A classic post-Humean version of the teleological argument.

Bibliography for Part II

Alston, William. *Perceiving God*. Ithaca, NY: Cornell University Press, 1991. An important recent work on the epistemology of religious experience.

Freud, Sigmund. *The Future of an Illusion*. New York: Norton, 1961. Contains his famous theory that religion is the outgrowth of the projection of the father image.

Gale, Richard. "Mysticism and Philosophy." *Journal of Philosophy* 57 (1960). A clear analysis and cogent critique of some key concepts and arguments related to mystical experience. (Republished in *Contemporary Philosophy of Religion*, ed. Steven M. Cahn and David Shatz. Oxford, Eng.: Oxford University Press, 1982.)

———. *On the Nature and Existence of God*. Cambridge, MA: Cambridge University Press, 1991. Chapter 8 contains a penetrating critique.

Gutting, Gary. *Religious Belief and Religious Skepticism*. Notre Dame, IN: University of Notre Dame Press, 1982.

James, William. *Varieties of Religious Experience*. New York: Modern Library, 1902. This marvelous treatise is the definitive work on the subject.

Martin, C. B. "A Religious Way of Knowing." *Mind* 61 (1952). A watershed article. (Reprinted and expanded in his book *Religious Belief*. Chap. 5. Ithaca, NY: Cornell University Press, 1959.)

Mavrodes, George. *Belief in God*. New York: Random House, 1970. Chap. 3.

Otto, Rudolf. *The Idea of the Holy*, trans. J. W. Harvey. Oxford, Eng.: Oxford University Press, 1923. A classic study of religious experience.

Rowe, William. *Philosophy of Religion*. Belmont, CA: Wadsworth, 1978. A valuable commentary on some of the major work in the field.

Stace, Walter T. *Time and Eternity*. Princeton, NJ: Princeton University Press, 1952.

———. ed. The *Teaching of the Mystics*. New York: New American Library, 1960.

Wainwright, William. "Mysticism and Sense Perception." *Religious Studies* 9 (1973). Perhaps the best modern analysis of mysticism.

———. *Mysticism*. Madison: University of Wisconsin Press, 1981. A comprehensive and sympathetic study of mysticism.

Bibliography for Part III

Adams, Marilyn McCord, and Robert Merrihew Adams, eds. *The Problem of Evil*. Oxford, Eng.: Oxford University Press, 1990. The best collection of contemporary articles on the subject, containing essays by J. L. Mackie, Nelson Pike, Alvin Plantinga, William Rowe, Robert M. Adams, John Hick, and others.

Draper, Paul. "Pain and Pleasure: An Evidential Problem for Theists," *Noûs* 23 (1989). An intricate and well-crafted challenge to theists.

Gale, Richard. *On the Nature and Existence of God*. Cambridge, Eng.: Cambridge University Press, 1991. Contains a careful analysis of the problem of evil and the free will defense.

Hick, John. *Evil and the God of Love*. London: Macmillan, 1966. A classic defense of theodicy.

Howard-Snyder, Daniel, ed. *The Evidential Argument from Evil*. Bloomington, IN: Indiana University Press, 1996.

Lewis, C. S. *The Problem of Pain*. London: Geoffrey Bles, 1940. Clearly and cogently written.

Mackie, J. L. "Evil and Omnipotence." *Mind* 64 (1955):200–12. One of the earlier contemporary attacks on the existence of God from the argument from evil, used in many anthologies.

———. *The Miracle of Theism*. Oxford, Eng.: Oxford University Press, 1982. Chap. 9. An insightful and well-argued chapter from an atheist's point of view.

McCloskey, H. J. "God and Evil." *The Philosophical Quarterly* 10 (1960):97–114. A sharp attack on theism, arguing that given the problem of evil, theism is indefensible.

Peterson, Michael, ed. *The Problem of Evil*. Notre Dame, IN: University of Notre Dame Press, 1992.

Pike, Nelson. "Human on Evil." *The Philosophical Review* 72 (1963):180–97. A trenchant criticism of Hume's position.

Plantinga, Alvin. *The Nature of Necessity*. Oxford, Eng.: Clarendon Press, 1974. Chap. 9. An excellent article developing in detail a version of the free will defense. In this version all evil is reduced to moral evil, with the devil being held accountable for natural evil. (A more accessible version of this argument is found in Plantinga's work *God, Freedom and Evil*. New York: Harper & Row, 1974.)

Schlesinger, George N. "Suffering and Evil." In *Contemporary Philosophy of Religion*, edited by Steven M. Cahn and David Schatz. Oxford, Eng.: Oxford University Press, 1982. Schlesinger argues that when a complaint applies to every situation, it applies to none. Hence, because one could always complain that God could have created a better world, one cannot complain that this one could be better.

———. "Natural Evil." *American Philosophical Quarterly* 15 (1978):295–301. A detailed response to the charge that natural evil undermines theism.

Wainwright, William J. "God and the Necessity of Physical Evils." *Sophia* 11 (1972):16–19.

Wykstra, Stephen J. "The Humean Obstacle to Evidential Arguments from Suffering: On Avoiding the Evils of 'Appearance.'" *International Journal of Philosophy of Religion* 16 (1984).

Bibliography for Part IV

Davis, Stephen T. *Logic and The Nature of God*. Grand Rapids, MI: Eerdmans, 1983. A very perceptive and lucid analysis of the attributes of God.

Geach, Peter. *Providence and Evil*. Cambridge, MA: Cambridge University Press, 1977. An important work on the attributes of God.

Fischer, John Martin, ed. *God, Foreknowledge, and Freedom*. Palo Alto, CA: Stanford University Press, 1989. An important collection of essays.

Hartshorne, Charles. *The Divine Reality*. New Haven, CT: Yale University Press, 1948. A very good exposition of the process theological view of God and his attributes.

Kenny, Anthony, ed. *Aquinas: A Collection of Critical Essays*. New York: Doubleday, 1969. In this good collection, Kenny's own essay on divine foreknowledge and human freedom stands out.

Kretzmann, Norman. "Ominiscience and Immutability." *Journal of Philosophy* 63 (1966):409–21. A cogent article on the incoherence of the notion of immutability.

Pike, Nelson. *God and Time*. Ithaca, NY: Cornell University Press, 1970. A seminal work that has rightly played a central role in the debate on God's eternity.

Stump, Eleonore, and Norman Kretzmann. "Eternity." *Journal of Philosophy* 78 (August 1981): 429–58. A sophisticated defense of the traditional view of God's timeless eternity.

Swinburne, Richard. *The Coherence of Theism*, Revised Edition. Oxford, Eng.: Oxford University Press, 1993. A highly original work on the attributes of God, cogently argued.

Urban, Linwood, and Douglas Walton, eds. *The Power of God*. Oxford, Eng.: Oxford University Press, 1978. The best available collection of articles on divine omnipotence.

Wierenga, Edward R. *The Nature of God: An Inquiry into Divine Attributes*. Ithaca, NY: Cornell University Press, 1989. A careful analysis of the attributes of God, cogently and insightfully argued.

Wolterstorff, Nicholas. "God Everlasting." In *God and the Good*, edited by C. Orlebeke and L. Smedes. Grand Rapids, MI: Eerdmans, 1975. Possibly the best defense of the thesis that God's eternity is temporal rather than timeless.

Bibliography for Part V

Broad, C. D. "Hume's Theory of the Credibility of Miracles." *Proceedings of the Aristotelian Society* 17 (1916–17). An insightful critique of Hume.

Flew, Antony. "Miracles." In *Encyclopedia of Philosophy*, edited by Paul Edwards. New York: Macmillan, 1966. A good survey of the problem, containing a Humean version of the attack on miracles.

Geisler, Norman L. *Miracles and Modern Thought*. Grand Rapids, MI: Zondervan, 1982. A clearly written apology for an evangelical position that comes to terms with major philosophical opponents. Valuable for its terse analyses, although it tend to oversimplify the opposition.

Holland, R. F. "The Miraculous." *American Philosophical Quarterly* 2 (1965):43–51.

Lewis, C. S. *Miracles*. New York: Macmillan, 1947. A cogently and clearly argued defense of miracles.

Nowell-Smith, Patrick. "Miracles." In *New Essays in Philosophical Theology,* edited by Antony Flew and Alasdair Macintyre. London: Macmillan, 1955. Attacks the concept of miracles as unscientific and, as such, incoherent.

Rowe, William. *Philosophy of Religion*. Belmont, CA: Wadsworth, 1978. Chap. 9. A lucid introductory discussion of the overall problem.

Smart, Ninian. *Philosophers and Religious Truth*. London: SCM, 1964. Chap. 2. A defense of miracles against the charge that they are unscientific.

Swinburne, Richard. *The Concept of Miracle*. London: Macmillan, 1970. A development of the ideas contained in his articles in Part V of this volume.

Bibliography for Part VI

Ducasse, Curt John. *A Critical Examination of the Belief in Life After Death*. Springfield, IL: Thomas, 1961. One of the most comprehensive defenses of the Platonic–Cartesian view of immortality.

Edwards, Paul, ed. *Immortality*. New York: Macmillan, 1992. The best collection of articles available. Edward's own introductory article is valuable.

Geach, Peter. *God and the Soul*. London: Routledge & Kegan Paul, 1969. An examination of the concept of the soul.

Flew, Antony. "Immortality." In *Encyclopedia of Philosophy,* edited by Paul Edwards. New York: Free Press, 1965. A helpful survey of the history of the notion of immortality and the arguments connected with it.

Johnson, Raynor. *The Imprisoned Splendor*. London: Hodder and Stoughton, 1953. A defense of reincarnation.

Lamont, Corliss. *The Illusion of Immortality*. New York: Philosophical Library, 1965. A strong attack on several arguments for immortality.

Moody, Raymond. *Life After Life*. New York: Bantam Books, 1976. A fascinating, though controversial, account of near-death experiences.

Penelhum, Terrence. *Survival and Disembodied Existence*. London: Routledge & Kegan Paul, 1970. A fine-tuned examination of the key concepts and arguments associated with both the Platonic and the reconstitution views of survival.

Perry, John. *Personal Identity and Immortality*. Indianapolis: Hackett, 1979. An excellent dialogue on the subject.

Purtill, Richard. *Thinking About Religion*. Englewood Cliffs, NJ: Prentice Hall, 1978. Chaps. 9 and 10. A fascinating defense of the Christian notion of life after death.

Quinton, Anthony. "The Soul." *Journal of Philosophy* 59 (1962):393–409. A good survey and analysis of concepts and arguments associated with the notion of the soul.

van Inwagen, Peter. "The Possibility of Resurrection," *International Journal for Philosophy of Religion* 9 (1978):114–121.

Bibliography for Part VII

Davis, Stephen. *Faith, Skepticism and Evidence*. Lewisburg, PA: Bucknell University Press, 1978. Examines the concepts discussed in this section.

Delaney, C. F., ed. *Rationality and Religious Belief*. Notre Dame, IN: University of Notre Dame Press, 1978.

Jordan, Jeff, ed. *Gambling on God: Essays on Pascal's Wager*. Lanham, MD: Rowman & Littlefield, 1994.

Mackie, J. L. *The Miracle of Theism: Arguments for and Against the Existence of God*. Oxford, Eng.: Clarendon Press, 1982. Probably the best defense of atheism in recent years, taking into consideration every major argument in the field.

Mavrodes, George. *Belief in God*. New York: Random House, 1970. A clear presentation of religious epistemology.

Mitchell, Basil. *The Justification of Religious Belief*. London: Macmillan, 1973. A good discussion of the cumulative case for theism.

Plantinga, Alvin, and Nicholas Wolterstorff, eds. *Faith and Rationality*. Notre Dame, IN: University of Notre Dame Press, 1983. A valuable collection from a Reformed Christian perspective.

Pojman, Loius. *Religious Belief and the Will*. London: Routledge & Kegan Paul, 1986. Contains a history of the subjects faith and reason.

Swinburne, Richard. *Faith and Reason*. Oxford, Eng: Clarendon Press, 1981. One of the best studies of the subject in recent years.

Bibliography for Part VIII

Barbour, Ian. *Religion and Science*. San Francisco, CA: Harper San Francisco, 1997.

———. *When Science Meets Religion*. San Francisco, CA: Harper San Francisco, 2000.

Behe, Michael. *Darwin's Black Box.* New York, NY: Free Press, 1999.

Bielby, James, ed. *Naturalism Defeated?* Ithaca, NY: Cornell University Press, 2002.

Dawkins, Richard. *The Blind Watchmaker.* New York: NY: W. W. Norton, 1986.

Dembski, William. *The Design Inference.* New York: Cambridge University Press, 1991.

———. *No Free Lunch.* Lanham, MD: Rowman & Littlefield, 2001.

———. *The Design Revolution.* Downers Grove, IL: InterVarsity Press, 2004.

Dembski, William, and James Kushiner. *Signs of Intelligence.* Grand Rapids, MI: Brazos Press, 2001.

Forrest, Barbara, and Paul Gross. *Creationism's Trojan Horse: The Wedge of Intelligent Design.* Oxford, Eng.: Oxford University Press, 2004.

Gilkey, Langdon. "Darwin and Christian Thought" in the *Christian Century*, 1960.

Gould, Stephen Jay. *Rocks of Ages: Science and Religion in the Fullness of Life.* New York, NY: Ballantine Books, 1999.

Kitcher, Philip. *Abusing Science: The Case Against Creationism.* Cambridge, MA: MIT Press, 1982.

Miller, James B. *An Evolving Dialogue: Theological and Scientific Perspectives on Evolution.* Trinity Press International, 2001.

Murphy, Nancy. *Theology in the Age of Scientific Reasoning.* Ithaca, NY: Cornell University Press, 1990.

Pennock, Robert. *Intelligent Design Creationism and its Critics.* New York: MIT Press, 2001.

Plantinga, Alvin. *Warrant and Proper Function.* Oxford University Press, 1993.

———. *Warranted Christian Belief.* Oxford University Press, 2000.

Polkinghorne, John. *Belief in God in an Age of Science.* New Haven, CT: Yale University Press, 1998.

Bibliography for Part IX

Dean, Thomas, ed. *Religious Pluralism and Truth: Essays on Cross-Cultural Philosophy of Religion.* SUNY Press, 1995.

Heim, S. Mark. *Salvations: Truth and Difference in Religion.* Maryknoll, NY: Orbis, 1993.

Hick, John. *God and the Universe of Faiths.* London: Macmillan, 1973.

———. *An Interpretation of Religion: Human Responses to the Transcendent.* New Haven, CT: Yale University Press, 1989.

———. Advisory ed. *Religious Pluralism.* A special issue of *Faith and Philosophy* 5, no. 4 (October 1988). Contains important essays by John Hick, Joseph Runzo, William Alston, and others.

Hick, John, and Paul Knitter, eds. *The Myth of Christian Uniqueness: Towards a Pluralistic Theology of Religions.* Maryknoll, NY: Orbis, 1987.

Ogden, Schubert. *Is There Only One True Religion or Are There Many?* Dallas, TX: SMU Press, 1992.

———. *Doing Theology Today.* Valley Forge, PA: Trinity Press, 1996.

Smith, Wilfred Cantwell. *Towards a World Theology.* Philadelphia: Westminster, 1981. An important work in religious pluralism.

Yandell, Keith. "Religious Experience and Rational Appraisal." *Religious Studies* 8 (June 1974). Seeks a middle ground between pluralism and exclusivism.

Bibliography for Part X

Hare, John E. *The Moral Gap.* New York NY: Oxford University Press, 1996.

Helm, Paul, ed. *The Divine Command Theory of Ethics.* Oxford, Eng.: Oxford University Press, 1979. This work contains a good selection of material on the subject.

Kierkegaard, Søren. *Fear and Trembling*, translated by Howard V. Hong and Edna H. Hong. Princeton, NJ: Princeton University Press, 1983. A classic work on the relation of religion to morality.

Nielson, Kai. *Ethics Without God.* London: Pemberton Books, 1973. A clearly written description of humanistic ethics.

Outka, Gene, and J. P. Reeder, eds. *Religion and Morality: A Collection of Essays.* New York: Anchor Books, 1973. A good collection of essays.

Pojman, Louis. "Ethics: Religious and Secular." *The Modern Schoolman*, Vol. 70, Nov. 1992, pp. 1–30.

Quinn, Philip. *Divine Commands and Moral Requirements.* Oxford, Eng.: Clarendon Press, 1978. An incisive treatise on the subject.